COLLINS
ATLAS
OF THE
WORLD

Collins Atlas of the World

Collins
An Imprint of HarperCollins*Publishers*
77-85 Fulham Palace Road, Hammersmith, London W6 8JB

First published 1996, reprinted with revisions 1997

Maps © HarperCollins*Publishers*

The contents of this edition of Collins Atlas of the World
are believed correct at the time of printing. Nevertheless
the publisher can accept no responsibility for errors or
omissions, changes in the detail given or for any expense
or loss thereby caused.

Printed in Italy

ISBN 0 00 448562 9

Globe images : data © 1995 The Living Earth, Inc.
Cover photograph: Zefa Pictures

LH9749 Imp 002

COLLINS
ATLAS
OF THE WORLD

HarperCollinsPublishers

CONTENTS

GLOBAL VIEW *2–3*

COUNTRIES *4–5*

NATIONAL STATISTICS 6

INTERNATIONAL ORGANIZATIONS *7*

CITY PLANS *8–9*

SCANDINAVIA and the
BALTIC STATES 1:4M *10–11*

West RUSSIAN
FEDERATION 1:6M *12–13*

MOSCOW REGION 1:3M *14*

UKRAINE and MOLDOVA 1:3M *15*

UNITED KINGDOM and
REPUBLIC OF IRELAND 1:3M *16–17*

NETHERLANDS,
GERMANY, POLAND,
CZECH REPUBLIC,
SLOVAKIA
and HUNGARY
1:3M *18–19*

FRANCE and SWITZERLAND
1:3M *20–21*

MEDITERRANEAN LANDS
1:9M *22–23*

SPAIN and PORTUGAL 1:3M *24–25*

ITALY, AUSTRIA, SLOVENIA,
CROATIA and
BOSNIA-HERZEGOVINA
1:3M *26–27*

ROMANIA, BULGARIA,
YUGOSLAVIA, ALBANIA
and GREECE
1:3M *28–29*

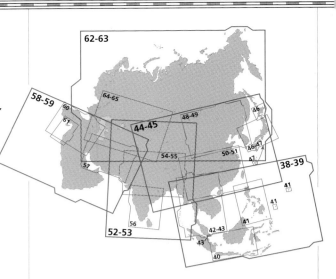

North CHINA, North KOREA
and South KOREA
1:6M *48–49*

South CHINA 1:6M *50–51*

South ASIA 1:12M *52–53*

PAKISTAN, North INDIA
and BANGLADESH
1:6M *54–55*

South INDIA
and SRI LANKA 1:6M *56*

AFGHANISTAN, IRAN
and THE GULF 1:6.6M *57*

THE MIDDLE EAST 1:10.8M *58–59*

TURKEY, IRAQ, SYRIA,
JORDAN and
TRANSCAUCASIAN REPUBLICS
1:6.6M *60*

LEBANON, ISRAEL
and Lower EGYPT 1:3.3M *61*

RUSSIAN FEDERATION 1:18M *62–63*
Central ASIA 1:7.5M *64–65*

THE WORLD

MAPS *6–24*

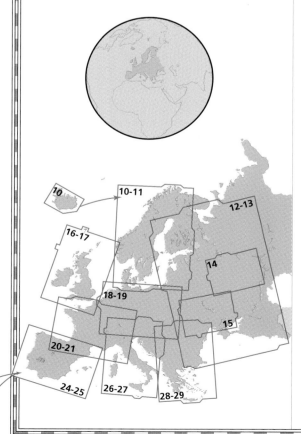

GEOGRAPHICAL
COMPARISONS *6–7*

CLIMATE *8–9*

CLIMATE GRAPHS *10–11*

VEGETATION *12–13*

EARTHQUAKES
and VOLCANOES *14–15*

ENERGY *16–17*

POPULATION *18–19*

CITIES *20–21*

COUNTRIES *22–23*

TIME ZONES *24*

SYMBOLS *1*

EUROPE

MAPS *2–29*

ASIA

MAPS *30–65*

GLOBAL VIEW *30–31*

COUNTRIES *32–33*

NATIONAL STATISTICS *34*

INTERNATIONAL
ORGANIZATIONS *35*

CITY PLANS *36–37*

Southeast ASIA 1:12.9M *38–39*

Central INDONESIA 1:6M *40*

PHILIPPINES 1:6M *41*

MYANMAR, THAILAND,
VIETNAM, LAOS, CAMBODIA and
MALAYSIA 1:6M *42–43*

East ASIA 1:12.6M *44–45*

JAPAN 1:3.3M *46–47*

AFRICA

MAPS *66 – 83*

GLOBAL VIEW *66–67*

COUNTRIES:INTERNATIONAL
ORGANIZATIONS *68–69*

NATIONAL STATISTICS *70*

CITY PLANS *71*

Northeast AFRICA 1:7.5M *72–73*

Northwest AFRICA 1:7.5M *74–75*

West AFRICA 1:7.5M *76–77*

West Central AFRICA 1:7.5M *78–79*

East Central AFRICA 1:7.5M *80–81*

South AFRICA 1:7.5M *82–83*

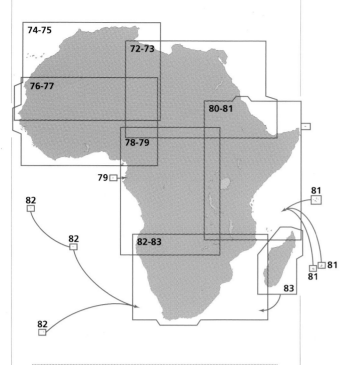

NORTH AMERICA
MAPS *102 –133*

GLOBAL VIEW *102–103*

COUNTRIES *104*

NATIONAL STATISTICS:
INTERNATIONAL
ORGANIZATIONS *105*

CITY PLANS *106–107*

CANADA 1:15M *108–109*

West CANADA 1:6M *110–111*

Central and East CANADA
1:6M *112–113*

South Central CANADA
1:3M *114–115*

UNITED STATES OF AMERICA
1:10M *116–117*

East
UNITED STATES OF AMERICA
1:6M *118–119*

Northeast
UNITED STATES OF AMERICA
1:3M *120–121*

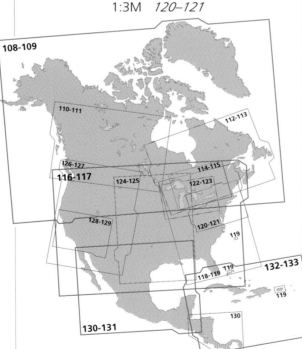

THE GREAT LAKES 1:3M *122–123*

Central
UNITED STATES OF AMERICA
1:6M *124–125*

West
UNITED STATES OF AMERICA
1:6M *126–127*

Southwest
UNITED STATES OF AMERICA
1:3M *128–129*

MEXICO and CENTRAL
AMERICA 1:6.6M *130–131*

CARIBBEAN 1:6.6M *132–133*

SOUTH AMERICA
MAPS *134 – 147*

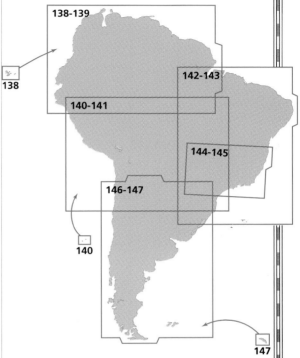

GLOBAL VIEW *134–135*

COUNTRIES:
INTERNATIONAL
ORGANIZATIONS *136*

NATIONAL STATISTICS:
CITY PLANS *137*

North
SOUTH AMERICA 1:7.5M *138–139*

Central
SOUTH AMERICA 1:7.5M *140–141*

East
SOUTH AMERICA 1:7.5M *142–143*

Southeast
BRAZIL 1:3.75M *144–145*

South
SOUTH AMERICA 1:7.5M *146–147*

OCEANS & POLAR
MAPS *148 –152*

ATLANTIC OCEAN 1:48M *148*

INDIAN OCEAN 1:48M *149*

PACIFIC OCEAN 1:48M *150–151*

ANTARCTICA 1:24M *152*

INDEX
PAGES *153–199*

OCEANIA
MAPS *84 –101*

GLOBAL VIEW *84–85*

COUNTRIES *86–87*

NATIONAL STATISTICS:
INTERNATIONAL
ORGANIZATIONS *88*

CITY PLANS *89*

SOUTH PACIFIC *90–91*

NEW ZEALAND 1:3M *92–93*

AUSTRALIA 1:11M *94–95*

Southeast AUSTRALIA 1:6M *96–97*

Northeast AUSTRALIA 1:6M *98–99*

West AUSTRALIA 1:6M *100–101*

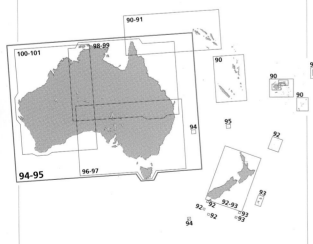

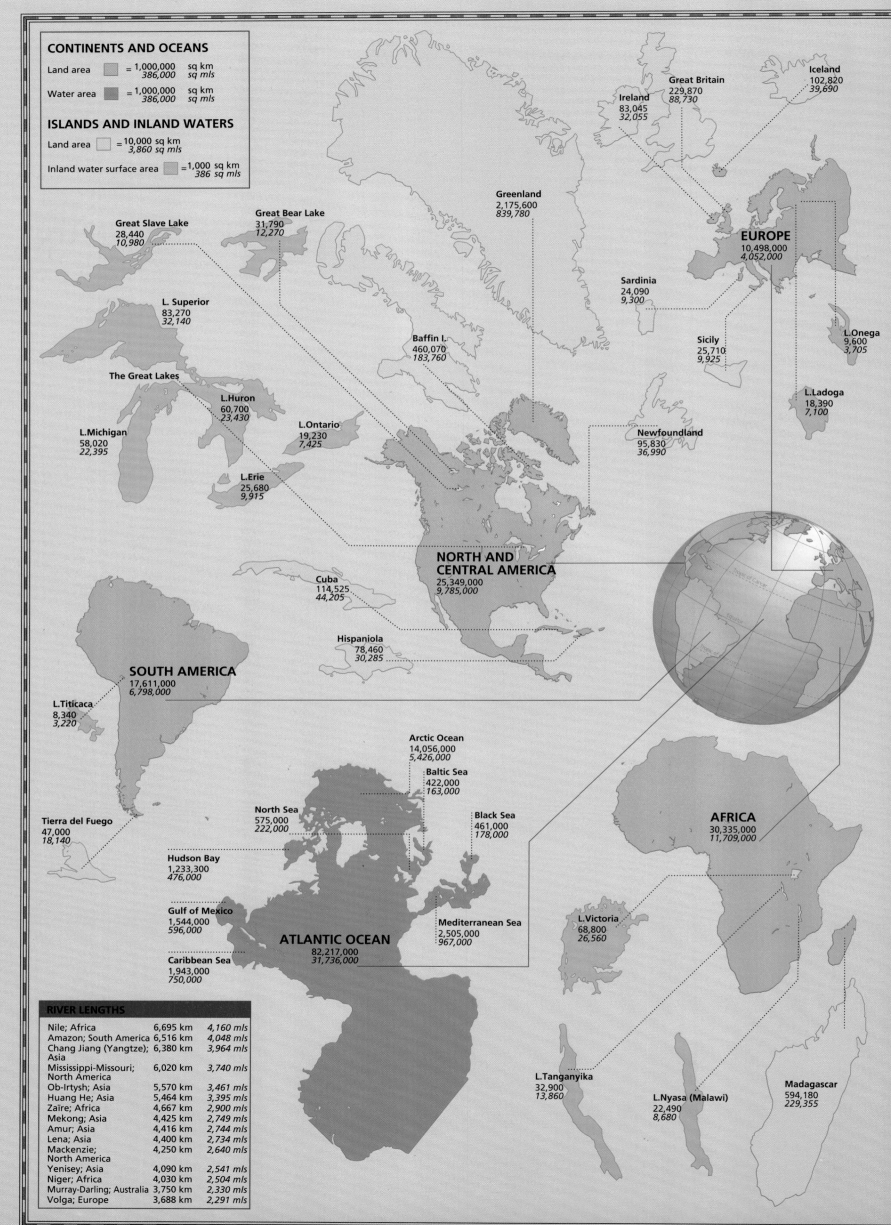

CONTINENTS AND OCEANS

Land area ▭ = 1,000,000 sq km
386,000 sq mls

Water area ▭ = 1,000,000 sq km
386,000 sq mls

ISLANDS AND INLAND WATERS

Land area ▭ = 10,000 sq km
3,860 sq mls

Inland water surface area ▭ = 1,000 sq km
386 sq mls

Great Slave Lake
28,440
10,980

Great Bear Lake
31,790
12,270

Greenland
2,175,600
839,780

Ireland
83,045
32,055

Great Britain
229,870
88,730

Iceland
102,820
39,690

EUROPE
10,498,000
4,052,000

Sardinia
24,090
9,300

L.Superior
83,270
32,140

Baffin I.
460,070
183,760

Sicily
25,710
9,925

L.Onega
9,600
3,705

The Great Lakes

L.Huron
60,700
23,430

L.Ontario
19,230
7,425

L.Ladoga
18,390
7,100

L.Michigan
58,020
22,395

Newfoundland
95,830
36,990

L.Erie
25,680
9,915

**NORTH AND
CENTRAL AMERICA**
25,349,000
9,785,000

Cuba
114,525
44,205

Hispaniola
78,460
30,285

SOUTH AMERICA
17,611,000
6,798,000

L.Titicaca
8,340
3,220

Arctic Ocean
14,056,000
5,426,000

Baltic Sea
422,000
163,000

Black Sea
461,000
178,000

AFRICA
30,335,000
11,709,000

North Sea
575,000
222,000

Tierra del Fuego
47,000
18,140

Hudson Bay
1,233,300
476,000

Gulf of Mexico
1,544,000
596,000

ATLANTIC OCEAN
82,217,000
31,736,000

Mediterranean Sea
2,505,000
967,000

L.Victoria
68,800
26,560

Caribbean Sea
1,943,000
750,000

L.Tanganyika
32,900
13,860

L.Nyasa (Malawi)
22,490
8,680

Madagascar
594,180
229,355

RIVER LENGTHS

Nile; Africa	6,695 km	*4,160 mls*
Amazon; South America	6,516 km	*4,048 mls*
Chang Jiang (Yangtze); Asia	6,380 km	*3,964 mls*
Mississippi-Missouri; North America	6,020 km	*3,740 mls*
Ob-Irtysh; Asia	5,570 km	*3,461 mls*
Huang He; Asia	5,464 km	*3,395 mls*
Zaïre; Africa	4,667 km	*2,900 mls*
Mekong; Asia	4,425 km	*2,749 mls*
Amur; Asia	4,416 km	*2,744 mls*
Lena; Asia	4,400 km	*2,734 mls*
Mackenzie; North America	4,250 km	*2,640 mls*
Yenisey; Asia	4,090 km	*2,541 mls*
Niger; Africa	4,030 km	*2,504 mls*
Murray-Darling; Australia	3,750 km	*2,330 mls*
Volga; Europe	3,688 km	*2,291 mls*

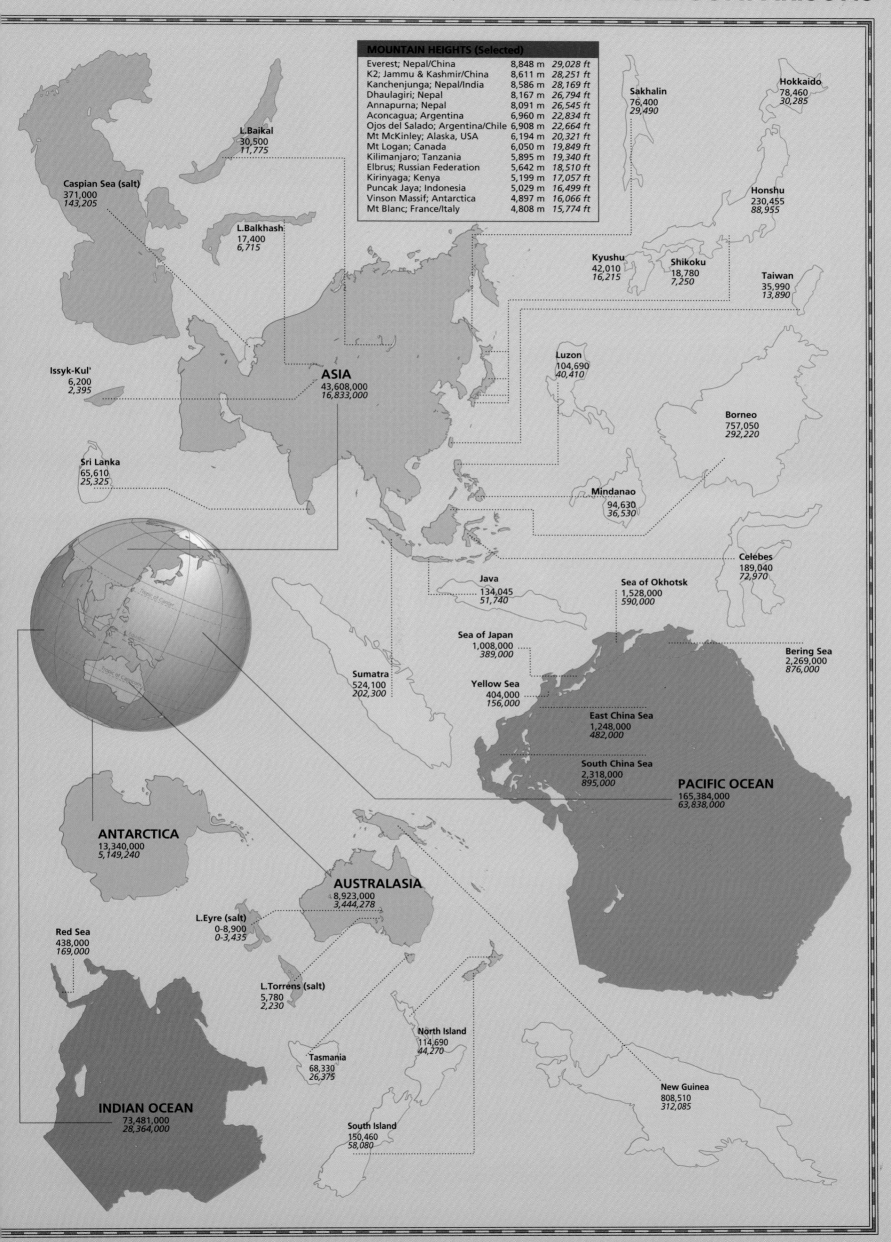

MOUNTAIN HEIGHTS (Selected)

Everest; Nepal/China	8,848 m	29,028 ft
K2; Jammu & Kashmir/China	8,611 m	28,251 ft
Kanchenjunga; Nepal/India	8,586 m	28,169 ft
Dhaulagiri; Nepal	8,167 m	26,794 ft
Annapurna; Nepal	8,091 m	26,545 ft
Aconcagua; Argentina	6,960 m	22,834 ft
Ojos del Salado; Argentina/Chile	6,908 m	22,664 ft
Mt McKinley; Alaska, USA	6,194 m	20,321 ft
Mt Logan; Canada	6,050 m	19,849 ft
Kilimanjaro; Tanzania	5,895 m	19,340 ft
Elbrus; Russian Federation	5,642 m	18,510 ft
Kirinyaga; Kenya	5,199 m	17,057 ft
Puncak Jaya; Indonesia	5,029 m	16,499 ft
Vinson Massif; Antarctica	4,897 m	16,066 ft
Mt Blanc; France/Italy	4,808 m	15,774 ft

L.Baikal
30,500
11,775

Caspian Sea (salt)
371,000
143,205

L.Balkhash
17,400
6,715

Sakhalin
76,400
29,490

Hokkaido
78,460
30,285

Honshu
230,455
88,955

Kyushu
42,010
16,215

Shikoku
18,780
7,250

Taiwan
35,990
13,890

Issyk-Kul'
6,200
2,395

ASIA
43,608,000
16,833,000

Luzon
104,690
40,410

Borneo
757,050
292,220

Sri Lanka
65,610
25,325

Mindanao
94,630
36,530

Celebes
189,040
72,970

Java
134,045
51,740

Sea of Okhotsk
1,528,000
590,000

Bering Sea
2,269,000
876,000

Sea of Japan
1,008,000
389,000

Sumatra
524,100
202,300

Yellow Sea
404,000
156,000

East China Sea
1,248,000
482,000

South China Sea
2,318,000
895,000

PACIFIC OCEAN
165,384,000
63,838,000

ANTARCTICA
13,340,000
5,149,240

AUSTRALASIA
8,923,000
3,444,278

L.Eyre (salt)
0-8,900
0-3,435

Red Sea
438,000
169,000

L.Torrens (salt)
5,780
2,230

North Island
114,690
44,270

Tasmania
68,330
26,375

New Guinea
808,510
312,085

INDIAN OCEAN
73,481,000
28,364,000

South Island
150,460
58,080

Arctic Circle

Tropic of Cancer

Equator

Tropic of Capricorn

CLIMATIC REGIONS

1	Ice cap
2	Tundra climate, warmest month below 10°C
3	Sub-arctic, rainy climate with severe cold winters and less than 4 months over 10°C
4	Continental climate, rainy with warmest month below 22°c
5	Continental climate, rainy with warmest month above 20°C
6	Temperate, rainy climate with mild winter, coolest month above 0°C
7	Wet subtropical, coolest month above 0°C, warmest month above 22°C
8	Mediterranean, rainy with mild wet winter, dry summer
9	Semi-arid, dry climate
10	Desert climate
11	Rainy tropical climate, constantly wet throughout the year
12	Rainy tropical climate, constantly wet throughout the year

Equatorial Scale 1:66 000 000

OCEAN CURRENTS

Arctic Circle

Alaska
Californian
Gulf Stream
North Atlantic Drift
Canaries
Oya Shio
Kamchatka
Kuro Shio

Tropic of Cancer

North Equatorial
North Equatorial
SW Monsoon
North Equatorial

Equatorial Counter
Equatorial Counter
Equatorial Counter

Equator

South Equatorial
South Equatorial
South Equatorial
South Equatorial

Peru (Humbolt)
Brazil
Benguela
Agulhas
East Australia Coast

Falkland

West Wind Drift
West Wind Drift

Tropic of Capricorn

Antarctic Circle

Ocean Currents

Cold Ocean Currents →
Warm Ocean Currents →
Seasonal Ocean Currents →

Robinson Projection

© HarperCollins Publishers

TROPICAL STORMS

Tropical Storm Tracks
(winds over 62km per hour)

→ Cyclone track

→ Typhoon track
(China Sea and adjoining area)

→ Willy-willies
(Australian tropical storm)

→ Hurricanes

Source area for tropical storms

Area of regular tornado activity

• Major tropical storms

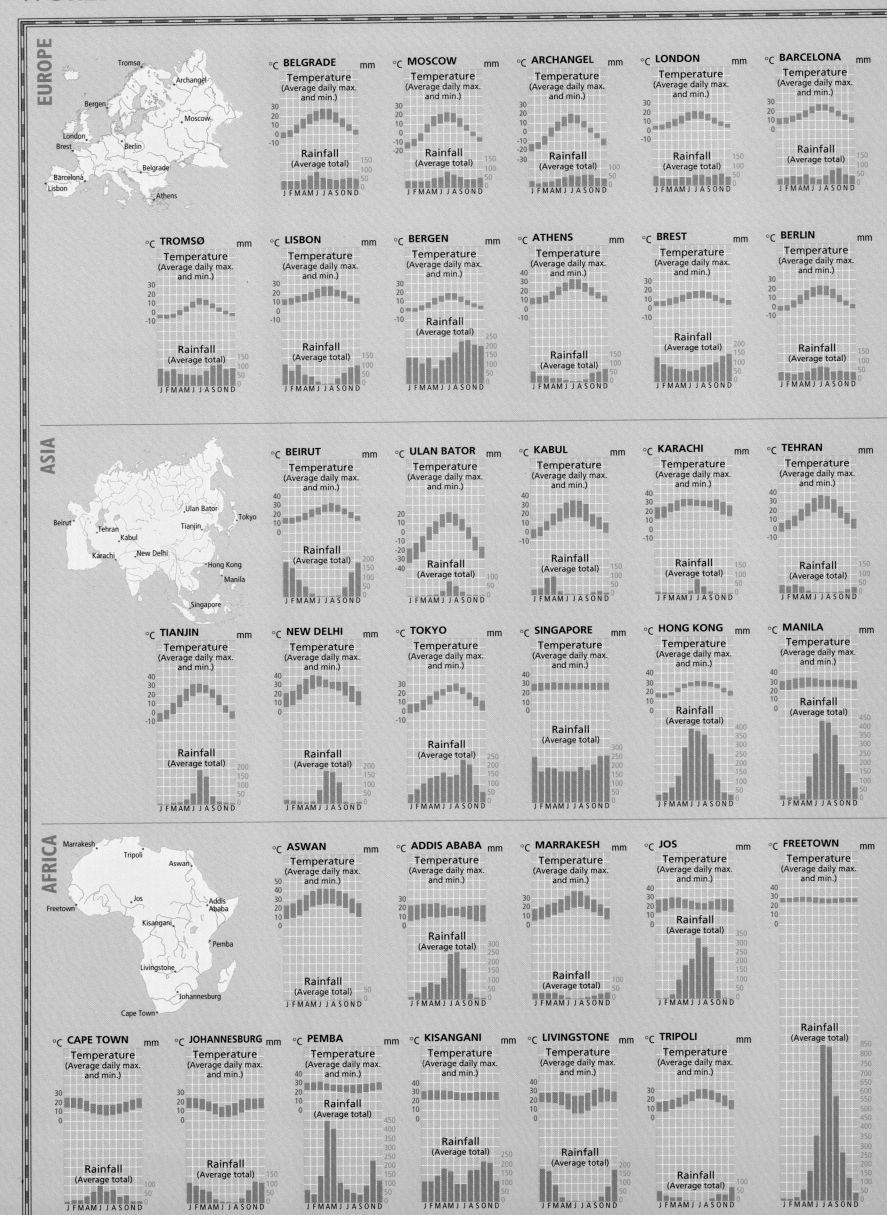

EUROPE

BELGRADE
Temperature (Average daily max. and min.)
Rainfall (Average total)

MOSCOW
Temperature (Average daily max. and min.)
Rainfall (Average total)

ARCHANGEL
Temperature (Average daily max. and min.)
Rainfall (Average total)

LONDON
Temperature (Average daily max. and min.)
Rainfall (Average total)

BARCELONA
Temperature (Average daily max. and min.)
Rainfall (Average total)

TROMSØ
Temperature (Average daily max. and min.)
Rainfall (Average total)

LISBON
Temperature (Average daily max. and min.)
Rainfall (Average total)

BERGEN
Temperature (Average daily max. and min.)
Rainfall (Average total)

ATHENS
Temperature (Average daily max. and min.)
Rainfall (Average total)

BREST
Temperature (Average daily max. and min.)
Rainfall (Average total)

BERLIN
Temperature (Average daily max. and min.)
Rainfall (Average total)

ASIA

BEIRUT
Temperature (Average daily max. and min.)
Rainfall (Average total)

ULAN BATOR
Temperature (Average daily max. and min.)
Rainfall (Average total)

KABUL
Temperature (Average daily max. and min.)
Rainfall (Average total)

KARACHI
Temperature (Average daily max. and min.)
Rainfall (Average total)

TEHRAN
Temperature (Average daily max. and min.)
Rainfall (Average total)

TIANJIN
Temperature (Average daily max. and min.)
Rainfall (Average total)

NEW DELHI
Temperature (Average daily max. and min.)
Rainfall (Average total)

TOKYO
Temperature (Average daily max. and min.)
Rainfall (Average total)

SINGAPORE
Temperature (Average daily max. and min.)
Rainfall (Average total)

HONG KONG
Temperature (Average daily max. and min.)
Rainfall (Average total)

MANILA
Temperature (Average daily max. and min.)
Rainfall (Average total)

AFRICA

ASWAN
Temperature (Average daily max. and min.)
Rainfall (Average total)

ADDIS ABABA
Temperature (Average daily max. and min.)
Rainfall (Average total)

MARRAKESH
Temperature (Average daily max. and min.)
Rainfall (Average total)

JOS
Temperature (Average daily max. and min.)
Rainfall (Average total)

FREETOWN
Temperature (Average daily max. and min.)
Rainfall (Average total)

CAPE TOWN
Temperature (Average daily max. and min.)
Rainfall (Average total)

JOHANNESBURG
Temperature (Average daily max. and min.)
Rainfall (Average total)

PEMBA
Temperature (Average daily max. and min.)
Rainfall (Average total)

KISANGANI
Temperature (Average daily max. and min.)
Rainfall (Average total)

LIVINGSTONE
Temperature (Average daily max. and min.)
Rainfall (Average total)

TRIPOLI
Temperature (Average daily max. and min.)
Rainfall (Average total)

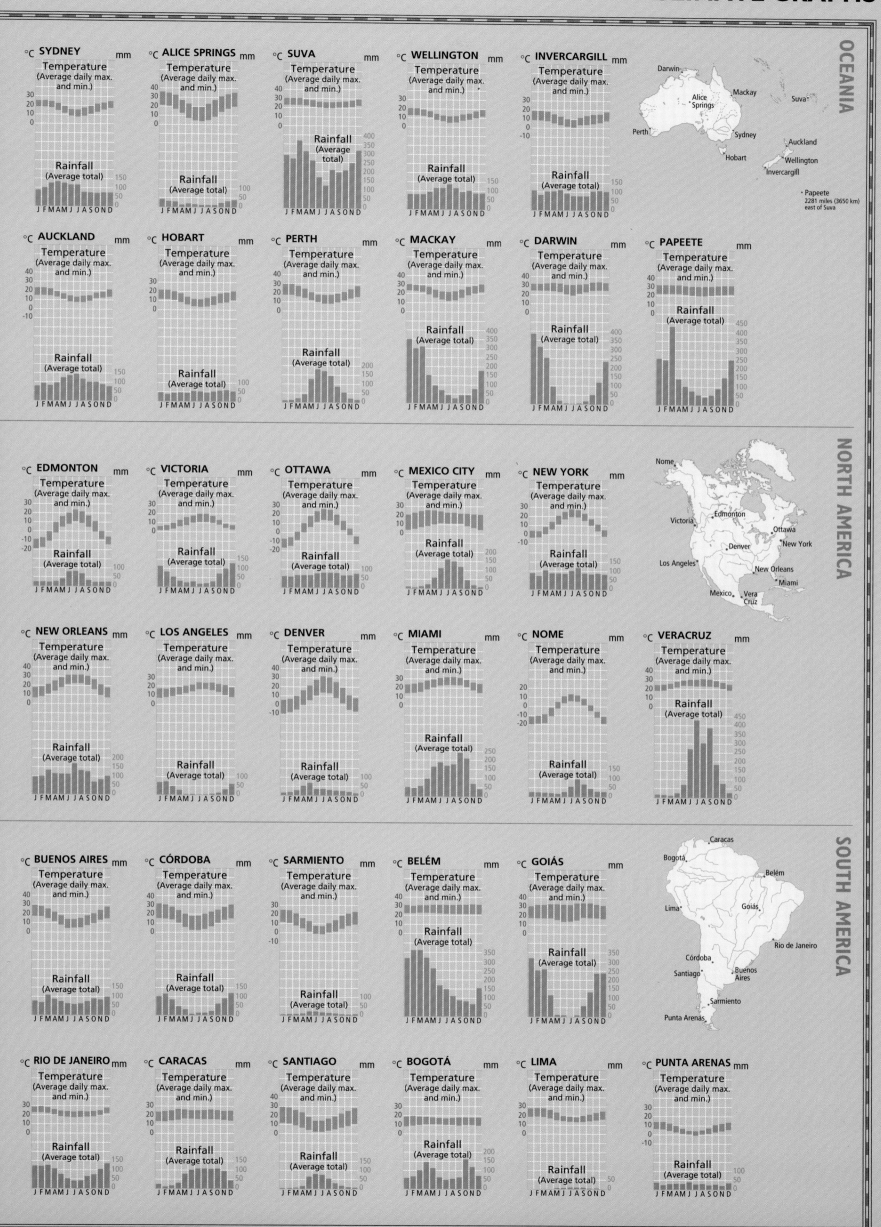

OCEANIA

NORTH AMERICA

SOUTH AMERICA

Equatorial Scale 1:66 000 000

Ice cap and ice shelf

Mountain vegetation
Stunted vegetation growth found on mountains of mid- and high altitudes and at very high altitudes in tropical latitudes. Absence of trees apart from low growing forms of birch and willow. Mosses and lichens are abundant.

Tundra
Region of restricted plant growth confined mostly between latitudes north of 60° N and south of the polar ice cap. Vegetation is characterised by mosses, lichens, rushes, grasses and flowering herbs.

Boreal forest (Taiga)
Continuous zone in northern hemisphere found between latitudes 50° N and 70° N. Characteristic form of vegetation is the coniferous tree with the dominant species being pine, larch, spruce and fir.

Conifer forest
Different formations of coniferous forest to that of the boreal forest, found in western North America, southeastern USA and southern Brazil. Pine, spruce and larch are dominant.

Mixed forest, mid-latitudes
Transition zone in north-central Europe, east-central North America and eastern Asia with a mixture of areas of broadleaf trees and areas of conifer trees in almost equal numbers.

Broadleaf forest
Deciduous forest found mainly in the mid-latitudes of the northern hemisphere. Before 1500 a wide variety of species existed eg. oak, ash, beech, elm, maple, hickory, alder, and birch, but due to exploitation little original forest remains.

Mediterranean scrub
Areas of shrub dominated vegetation located in the Mediterranean basin and similar bio-climatic regions in coastal parts of California, Chile, South Africa and southern Australia. A variety of aromatic herbaceous plants grow beneath low shrub thickets, pines, oaks or gorse.

Prairie
Areas of grassland where long grasses are dominant, found in central North America, the Veld of eastern South Africa and the Pampas of Argentina. Sward grasses and bunch grasses grow up to 1 metre high.

Robinson Projection

© HarperCollinsPublishers

Steppe
Areas of grassland where short grasses are dominant, traditionally the wild grasslands of Euroasia but also found extensively in central North America, central and southern Africa and Australia. Drought resistant grasses grow with colourful flowering herbs.

Savannah
Grassland found in the tropics to the north and south of the tropical rain forests of South America and Africa and around the desert fringes of Australia. Grasses are interspersed with scattered thorn bushes or deciduous trees such as acacia in Africa and eucalypts in Australia.

Tropical rain forest (Selva)
Dense forest located in tropical areas of high rainfall and continuous high temperature, particularly Central America, northern South America, west-central Africa and southeast Asia. Up to three tree layers grow above a variable shrub layer.

Monsoon forest
Deciduous forest mostly occuring in eastern India, parts of Southeast Asia and northern and northeastern Australia, growing in association with the monsoon climate.

Dry tropical forest
Semi-deciduous forest growing in semi-desert areas of South America and the Indian sub-continent where rainfall is usually less than 250mm per annum. Thorny scrub and low to medium sized trees with thick bark and deep roots characterise the vegetation.

Sub-tropical forest
Hardleaf evergreen forests growing between the latitudes of 15° to 40° north and south of the equator in China, Japan, Australia, New Zealand and South Africa.

Dry tropical scrub and thorn forest
Low-growing widely spaced shrubs, bushes and succulents are characteristic of this vegetation growing in extensive areas of Central and South America, Africa, the Indian sub-continent and Australia.

Desert vegetation
Limited vegetation growth in the harsh, dry conditions of desert areas. Xerophytic shrubs, grasses and cacti adapt themselves by relying on the chance occurence of rain, storing water when it is available in short bursts and limiting water loss.

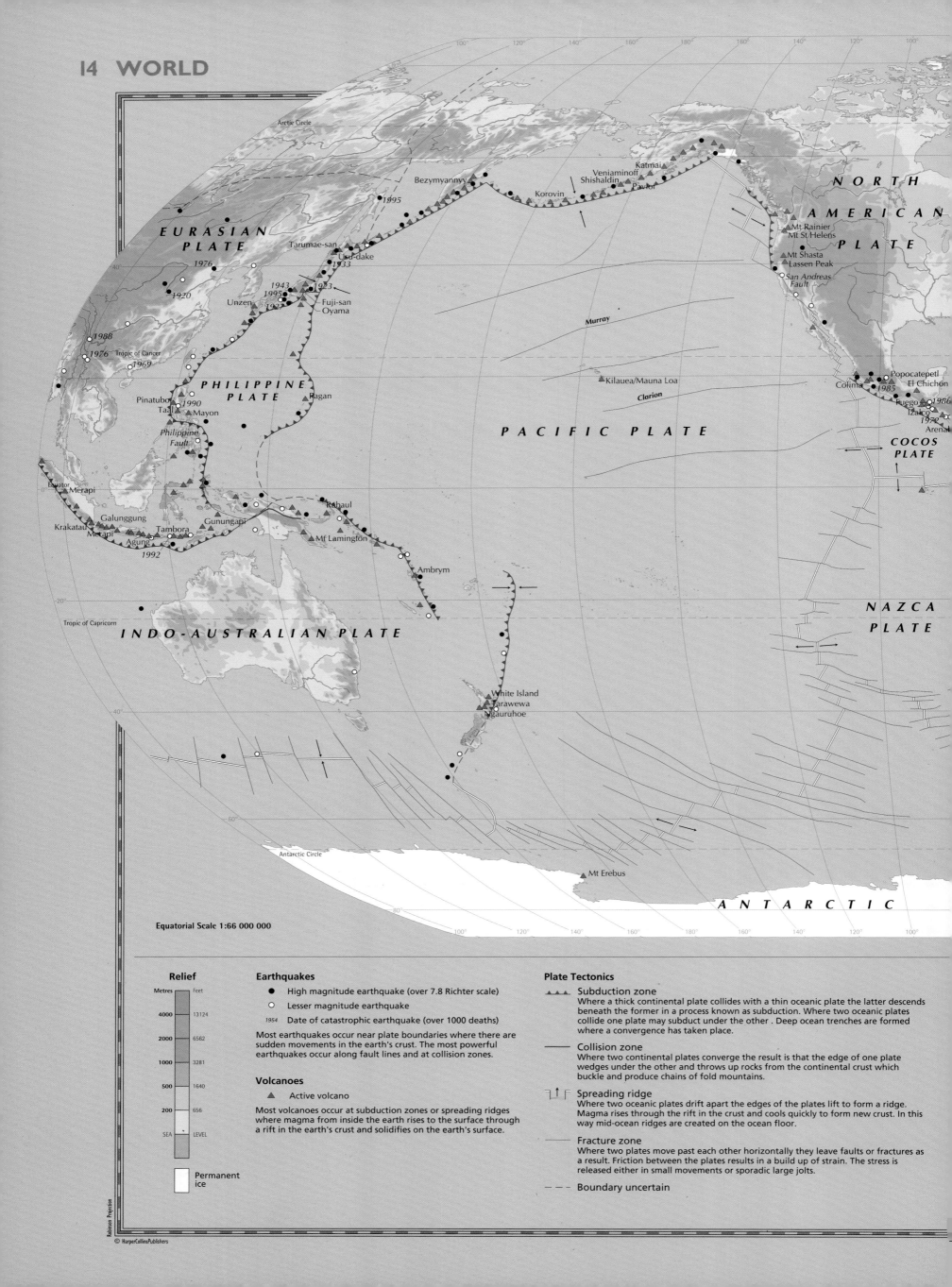

NORTH AMERICAN PLATE

EURASIAN PLATE

Arctic Circle

Bezymyannyy
1995

Korovin
Veniaminoff
Shishaldin
Pavlof
Katmai

Tarumae-san
Usu-dake
1933

1976

1920

1943
1995
1923
1927
Unzen
Fuji-san
Oyama

Mt Rainier
Mt St Helens
Mt Shasta
Lassen Peak
San Andreas Fault

1988

1976 Tropic of Cancer
1969

Murray

PHILIPPINE PLATE

Pagan

Pinatubo
1990
Taal
Mayon

Philippine Fault

Kilauea/Mauna Loa

Clarion

PACIFIC PLATE

Popocatepetl
Colima
El Chichon
1985
Fuego
Izalco
1986
1979

COCOS PLATE

Arenal

Equator
Merapi

Krakatau
Galunggung
Metapi
Agung
Tambora
Gunungapi
Mt Lamington

Rabaul

1992

INDO-AUSTRALIAN PLATE

Ambrym

NAZCA PLATE

Tropic of Capricorn

White Island
Tarawewa
Ngauruhoe

Antarctic Circle

Mt Erebus

ANTARCTIC

Equatorial Scale 1:66 000 000

Robinson Projection

© HarperCollinsPublishers

Earthquakes

● High magnitude earthquake (over 7.8 Richter scale)

○ Lesser magnitude earthquake

1954 Date of catastrophic earthquake (over 1000 deaths)

Most earthquakes occur near plate boundaries where there are sudden movements in the earth's crust. The most powerful earthquakes occur along fault lines and at collision zones.

Volcanoes

▲ Active volcano

Most volcanoes occur at subduction zones or spreading ridges where magma from inside the earth rises to the surface through a rift in the earth's crust and solidifies on the earth's surface.

Plate Tectonics

▲▲▲ Subduction zone

Where a thick continental plate collides with a thin oceanic plate the latter descends beneath the former in a process known as subduction. Where two oceanic plates collide one plate may subduct under the other . Deep ocean trenches are formed where a convergence has taken place.

——— Collision zone

Where two continental plates converge the result is that the edge of one plate wedges under the other and throws up rocks from the continental crust which buckle and produce chains of fold mountains.

Spreading ridge

Where two oceanic plates drift apart the edges of the plates lift to form a ridge. Magma rises through the rift in the crust and cools quickly to form new crust. In this way mid-ocean ridges are created on the ocean floor.

——— Fracture zone

Where two plates move past each other horizontally they leave faults or fractures as a result. Friction between the plates results in a build up of strain. The stress is released either in small movements or sporadic large jolts.

– – – Boundary uncertain

EURASIAN PLATE

Beerenberg
Hekla
Surtsey

Gibbs

1976 *1940* *1977*
1915 *1980* *1963*
Vesuvius
1908 Etna *1970* *1976* *1988*
1980 *1975* *1983*
1954 *1966* *1990* *1974*
1962 *1968* *1978* *1905*
1960 *1972* *1981*
1935 *1991* *1988*
Tropic of Cancer
1993
1967

Oceanographer

Pico de Teide

ARABIAN PLATE

Owen

CARIBBEAN PLATE

Soufrière
Mt Pelée
Poás
Irazú
Nevado del Ruiz
1967
Galeras
1987
Cotopaxi
Sangay

SOUTH AMERICAN PLATE

1946

El Misti

1982

AFRICAN PLATE

Lake Nyos
Mt Cameroon

Romanche Chain

Ascension

Nyiragongo
Ol Doinyo Lengai
Kilimanjaro
African Rift System

SOMALI PLATE

Equator

Karthala

Mauritius

INDO-AUSTRALIAN PLATE

Piton de la Fournaise

Tropic of Capricorn

Challenger
1944
Tupungato
Azul
El Llaima
1960 Villarrica

Tristan da Cunha

Agulhas

Falkland

Big Ben

Deception I

Arctic Circle

PLATE

Antarctic Circle

Plate Tectonics

NORTH AMERICA
EURASIA
SOUTH AMERICA
AFRICA
ANTARCTICA
AUSTRALIA

50 MILLION YEARS AGO

LAURASIA
GONDWANALAND

100 MILLION YEARS AGO

LAURASIA
GONDWANALAND

150 MILLION YEARS AGO

PANGAEA
TETHYS

200 MILLION YEARS AGO

ENERGY PRODUCTION | ENERGY RESOURCES

ENERGY RESOURCES

- Oil
- Gas
- Coal
- Lignite
- Uranium
- Hydro
- Oil pipeline
- Gas pipeline
- Gas pipeline under construction

ENERGY PRODUCTION

OIL PRODUCTION
1995

Percentage of world production

- Middle East
- North America
- former Soviet Union
- Asia and Australasia
- Africa
- Europe
- South and Central America

Robinson Projection

© HarperCollins Publishers

Equatorial Scale 1:66 000 000

Energy production in kilogram equivalents of all types of energy produced per capita, per year, by country.

kg per capita

- 25000 - 105000
- 2500 - 24999
- 2000 - 2499
- 1454 - 1999
- World average
- 1000 - 1454
- 100 - 999
- 0 - 99
- No data available

Energy consumption in kilogram equivalents
of all types of energy used per capita,
per year, by country.

kg per capita

25000 - 50000

10000 - 24999

5000 - 9999

1400 - 4999
World
average
1000 - 1400

500 - 999

0 - 499

No data
available

OIL CONSUMPTION

1995

ENERGY CONSUMPTION

Percentage of world consumption

Africa

Middle East

South and Central America

former Soviet Union

Europe

Asia and Australasia

North America

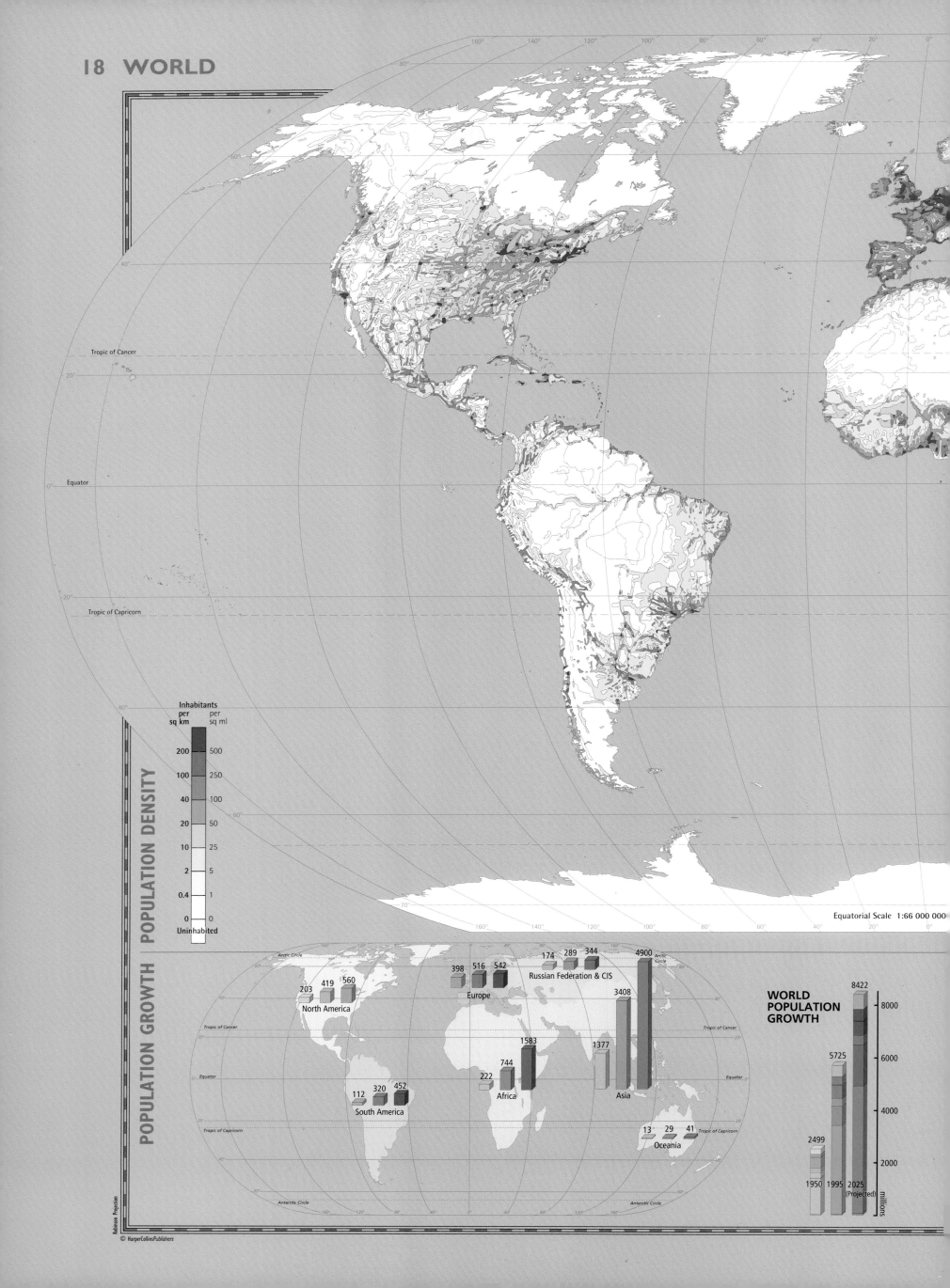

POPULATION DENSITY

Inhabitants

per sq km	per sq ml
200	500
100	250
40	100
20	50
10	25
2	5
0.4	1
0	0

Uninhabited

Equatorial Scale 1:66 000 000

POPULATION GROWTH

North America: 203, 419, 560

Europe: 398, 516, 542

Russian Federation & CIS: 174, 289, 344

South America: 112, 320, 452

Africa: 222, 744, 1583

Asia: 1377, 3408, 4900

Oceania: 13, 29, 41

WORLD POPULATION GROWTH

1950	1995	2025 (Projected)
2499	5725	8422

millions: 8000, 6000, 4000, 2000

Robinson Projection

© HarperCollins Publishers

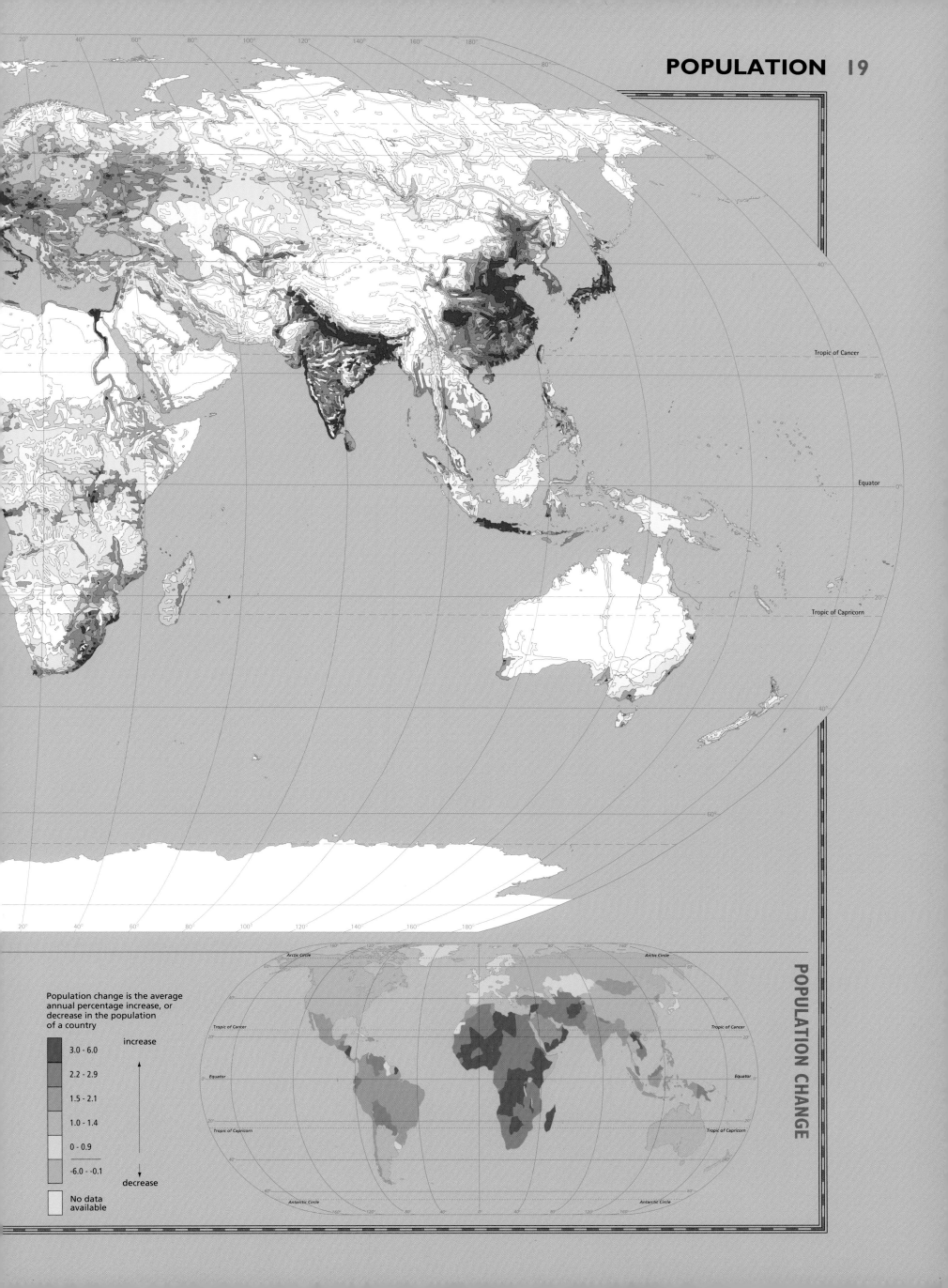

Population change is the average annual percentage increase, or decrease in the population of a country

increase

3.0 - 6.0

2.2 - 2.9

1.5 - 2.1

1.0 - 1.4

0 - 0.9

-6.0 - -0.1

decrease

No data available

Arctic Circle

Tropic of Cancer

Equator

Tropic of Capricorn

Antarctic Circle

Tropic of Cancer

Equator

Tropic of Capricorn

Tropic of Cancer

Equator

Tropic of Capricorn

GROWTH IN CITY POPULATIONS

Urban (city) population as a percentage of the total population.

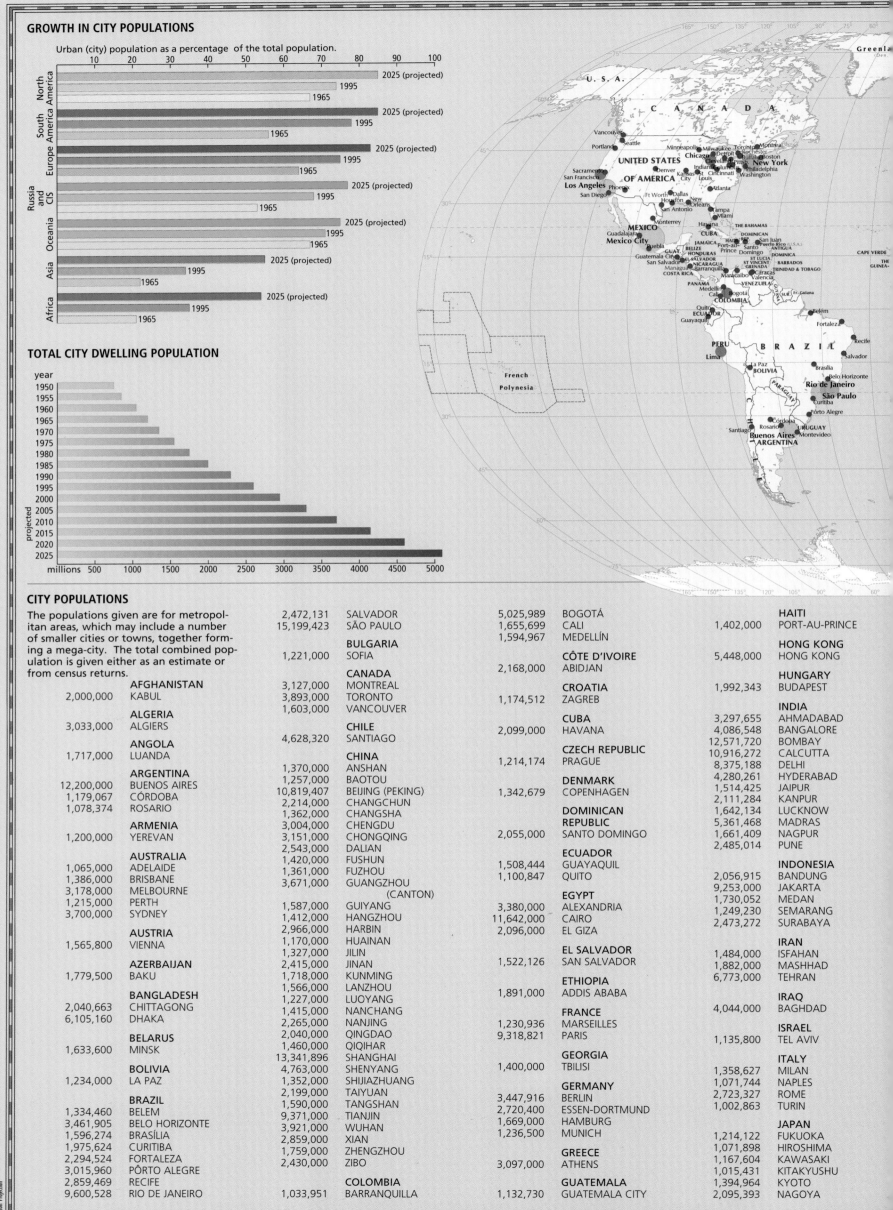

Region		% urban
North America	2025 (projected)	
	1995	
	1965	
South America	2025 (projected)	
	1995	
	1965	
Europe	2025 (projected)	
	1995	
	1965	
Russia and CIS	2025 (projected)	
	1995	
	1965	
Oceania	2025 (projected)	
	1995	
	1965	
Asia	2025 (projected)	
	1995	
	1965	
Africa	2025 (projected)	
	1995	
	1965	

TOTAL CITY DWELLING POPULATION

year: 1950, 1955, 1960, 1965, 1970, 1975, 1980, 1985, 1990, 1995, 2000, 2005, 2010, 2015, 2020, 2025 (projected)

millions: 500 1000 1500 2000 2500 3000 3500 4000 4500 5000

Robinson Projection

© HarperCollinsPublishers

CITY POPULATIONS

The populations given are for metropolitan areas, which may include a number of smaller cities or towns, together forming a mega-city. The total combined population is given either as an estimate or from census returns.

Population	City
	AFGHANISTAN
2,000,000	KABUL
	ALGERIA
3,033,000	ALGIERS
	ANGOLA
1,717,000	LUANDA
	ARGENTINA
12,200,000	BUENOS AIRES
1,179,067	CÓRDOBA
1,078,374	ROSARIO
	ARMENIA
1,200,000	YEREVAN
	AUSTRALIA
1,065,000	ADELAIDE
1,386,000	BRISBANE
3,178,000	MELBOURNE
1,215,000	PERTH
3,700,000	SYDNEY
	AUSTRIA
1,565,800	VIENNA
	AZERBAIJAN
1,779,500	BAKU
	BANGLADESH
2,040,663	CHITTAGONG
6,105,160	DHAKA
	BELARUS
1,633,600	MINSK
	BOLIVIA
1,234,000	LA PAZ
	BRAZIL
1,334,460	BELEM
3,461,905	BELO HORIZONTE
1,596,274	BRASÍLIA
1,975,624	CURITIBA
2,294,524	FORTALEZA
3,015,960	PÔRTO ALEGRE
2,859,469	RECIFE
9,600,528	RIO DE JANEIRO

Population	City
2,472,131	SALVADOR
15,199,423	SÃO PAULO
	BULGARIA
1,221,000	SOFIA
	CANADA
3,127,000	MONTREAL
3,893,000	TORONTO
1,603,000	VANCOUVER
	CHILE
4,628,320	SANTIAGO
	CHINA
1,370,000	ANSHAN
1,257,000	BAOTOU
10,819,407	BEIJING (PEKING)
2,214,000	CHANGCHUN
1,362,000	CHANGSHA
3,004,000	CHENGDU
3,151,000	CHONGQING
2,543,000	DALIAN
1,420,000	FUSHUN
1,361,000	FUZHOU
3,671,000	GUANGZHOU (CANTON)
1,587,000	GUIYANG
1,412,000	HANGZHOU
2,966,000	HARBIN
1,170,000	HUAINAN
1,327,000	JILIN
2,415,000	JINAN
1,718,000	KUNMING
1,566,000	LANZHOU
1,227,000	LUOYANG
1,415,000	NANCHANG
2,265,000	NANJING
2,040,000	QINGDAO
1,460,000	QIQIHAR
13,341,896	SHANGHAI
4,763,000	SHENYANG
1,352,000	SHIJIAZHUANG
2,199,000	TAIYUAN
1,590,000	TANGSHAN
9,371,000	TIANJIN
3,921,000	WUHAN
2,859,000	XIAN
1,759,000	ZHENGZHOU
2,430,000	ZIBO
	COLOMBIA
1,033,951	BARRANQUILLA

Population	City
5,025,989	BOGOTÁ
1,655,699	CALI
1,594,967	MEDELLÍN
	CÔTE D'IVOIRE
2,168,000	ABIDJAN
	CROATIA
1,174,512	ZAGREB
	CUBA
2,099,000	HAVANA
	CZECH REPUBLIC
1,214,174	PRAGUE
	DENMARK
1,342,679	COPENHAGEN
	DOMINICAN REPUBLIC
2,055,000	SANTO DOMINGO
	ECUADOR
1,508,444	GUAYAQUIL
1,100,847	QUITO
	EGYPT
3,380,000	ALEXANDRIA
11,642,000	CAIRO
2,096,000	EL GIZA
	EL SALVADOR
1,522,126	SAN SALVADOR
	ETHIOPIA
1,891,000	ADDIS ABABA
	FRANCE
1,230,936	MARSEILLES
9,318,821	PARIS
	GEORGIA
1,400,000	TBILISI
	GERMANY
3,447,916	BERLIN
2,720,400	ESSEN-DORTMUND
1,669,000	HAMBURG
1,236,500	MUNICH
	GREECE
3,097,000	ATHENS
	GUATEMALA
1,132,730	GUATEMALA CITY

Population	City
	HAITI
1,402,000	PORT-AU-PRINCE
	HONG KONG
5,448,000	HONG KONG
	HUNGARY
1,992,343	BUDAPEST
	INDIA
3,297,655	AHMADABAD
4,086,548	BANGALORE
12,571,720	BOMBAY
10,916,272	CALCUTTA
8,375,188	DELHI
4,280,261	HYDERABAD
1,514,425	JAIPUR
2,111,284	KANPUR
1,642,134	LUCKNOW
5,361,468	MADRAS
1,661,409	NAGPUR
2,485,014	PUNE
	INDONESIA
2,056,915	BANDUNG
9,253,000	JAKARTA
1,730,052	MEDAN
1,249,230	SEMARANG
2,473,272	SURABAYA
	IRAN
1,484,000	ISFAHAN
1,882,000	MASHHAD
6,773,000	TEHRAN
	IRAQ
4,044,000	BAGHDAD
	ISRAEL
1,135,800	TEL AVIV
	ITALY
1,358,627	MILAN
1,071,744	NAPLES
2,723,327	ROME
1,002,863	TURIN
	JAPAN
1,214,122	FUKUOKA
1,071,898	HIROSHIMA
1,167,604	KAWASAKI
1,015,431	KITAKYUSHU
1,394,964	KYOTO
2,095,393	NAGOYA

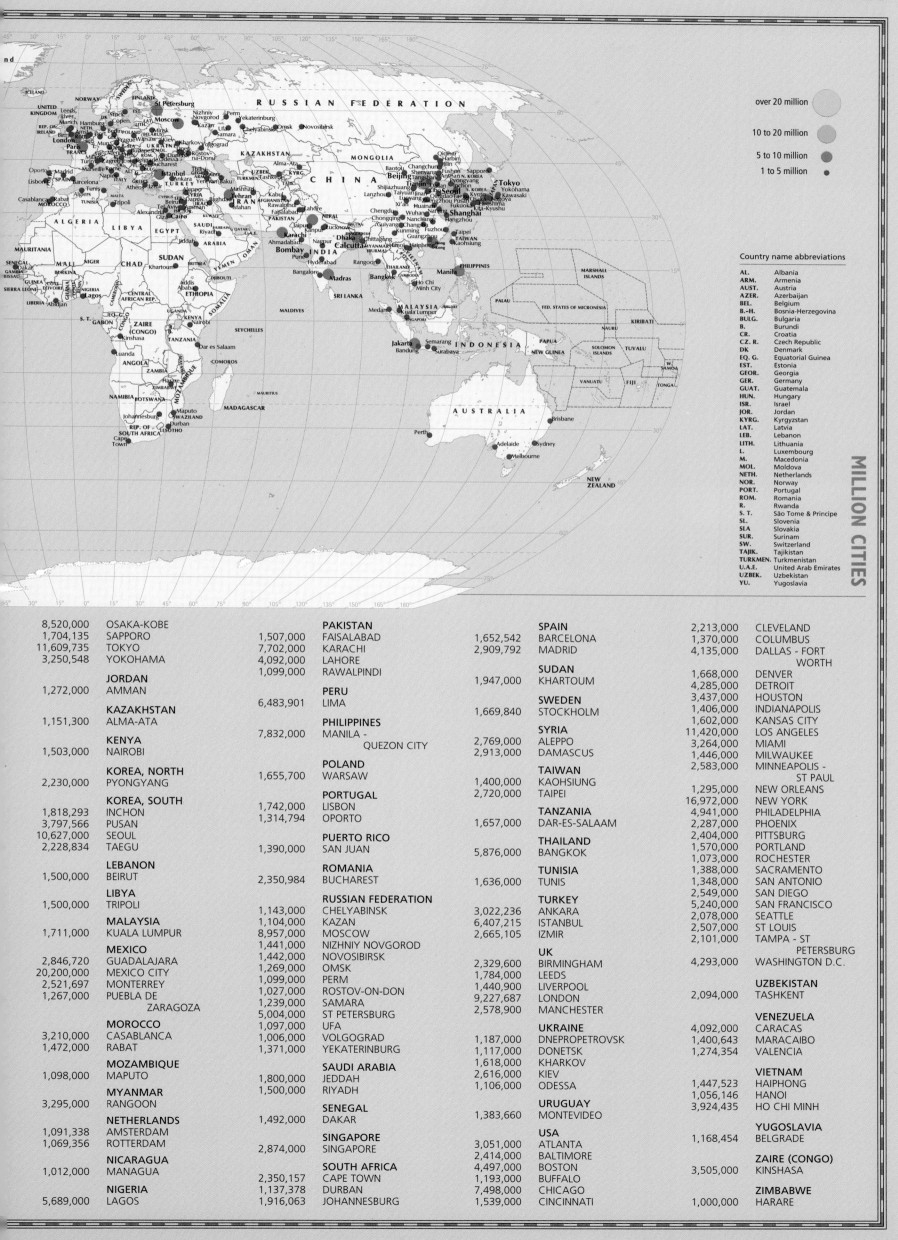

over 20 million
10 to 20 million
5 to 10 million
1 to 5 million

Country name abbreviations

AL.	Albania
ARM.	Armenia
AUST.	Austria
AZER.	Azerbaijan
BEL.	Belgium
B.-H.	Bosnia-Herzegovina
BULG.	Bulgaria
B.	Burundi
CR.	Croatia
CZ. R.	Czech Republic
DK	Denmark
EQ. G.	Equatorial Guinea
EST.	Estonia
GEOR.	Georgia
GER.	Germany
GUAT.	Guatemala
HUN.	Hungary
ISR.	Israel
JOR.	Jordan
KYRG.	Kyrgyzstan
LAT.	Latvia
LEB.	Lebanon
LITH.	Lithuania
L.	Luxembourg
M.	Macedonia
MOL.	Moldova
NETH.	Netherlands
NOR.	Norway
PORT.	Portugal
ROM.	Romania
R.	Rwanda
S. T.	São Tome & Principe
SL.	Slovenia
SLA	Slovakia
SUR.	Surinam
SW.	Switzerland
TAJIK.	Tajikistan
TURKMEN.	Turkmenistan
U.A.E.	United Arab Emirates
UZBEK.	Uzbekistan
YU.	Yugoslavia

MILLION CITIES

8,520,000 OSAKA-KOBE
1,704,135 SAPPORO
11,609,735 TOKYO
3,250,548 YOKOHAMA

JORDAN
1,272,000 AMMAN

KAZAKHSTAN
1,151,300 ALMA-ATA

KENYA
1,503,000 NAIROBI

KOREA, NORTH
2,230,000 PYONGYANG

KOREA, SOUTH
1,818,293 INCHON
3,797,566 PUSAN
10,627,000 SEOUL
2,228,834 TAEGU

LEBANON
1,500,000 BEIRUT

LIBYA
1,500,000 TRIPOLI

MALAYSIA
1,711,000 KUALA LUMPUR

MEXICO
2,846,720 GUADALAJARA
20,200,000 MEXICO CITY
2,521,697 MONTERREY
1,267,000 PUEBLA DE ZARAGOZA

MOROCCO
3,210,000 CASABLANCA
1,472,000 RABAT

MOZAMBIQUE
1,098,000 MAPUTO

MYANMAR
3,295,000 RANGOON

NETHERLANDS
1,091,338 AMSTERDAM
1,069,356 ROTTERDAM

NICARAGUA
1,012,000 MANAGUA

NIGERIA
5,689,000 LAGOS

PAKISTAN
1,507,000 FAISALABAD
7,702,000 KARACHI
4,092,000 LAHORE
1,099,000 RAWALPINDI

PERU
6,483,901 LIMA

PHILIPPINES
7,832,000 MANILA - QUEZON CITY

POLAND
1,655,700 WARSAW

PORTUGAL
1,742,000 LISBON
1,314,794 OPORTO

PUERTO RICO
1,390,000 SAN JUAN

ROMANIA
2,350,984 BUCHAREST

RUSSIAN FEDERATION
1,143,000 CHELYABINSK
1,104,000 KAZAN
8,957,000 MOSCOW
1,441,000 NIZHNIY NOVGOROD
1,442,000 NOVOSIBIRSK
1,269,000 OMSK
1,099,000 PERM
1,027,000 ROSTOV-ON-DON
1,239,000 SAMARA
5,004,000 ST PETERSBURG
1,097,000 UFA
1,006,000 VOLGOGRAD
1,371,000 YEKATERINBURG

SAUDI ARABIA
1,800,000 JEDDAH
1,500,000 RIYADH

SENEGAL
1,492,000 DAKAR

SINGAPORE
2,874,000 SINGAPORE

SOUTH AFRICA
2,350,157 CAPE TOWN
1,137,378 DURBAN
1,916,063 JOHANNESBURG

SPAIN
1,652,542 BARCELONA
2,909,792 MADRID

SUDAN
1,947,000 KHARTOUM

SWEDEN
1,669,840 STOCKHOLM

SYRIA
2,769,000 ALEPPO
2,913,000 DAMASCUS

TAIWAN
1,400,000 KAOHSIUNG
2,720,000 TAIPEI

TANZANIA
1,657,000 DAR-ES-SALAAM

THAILAND
5,876,000 BANGKOK

TUNISIA
1,636,000 TUNIS

TURKEY
3,022,236 ANKARA
6,407,215 ISTANBUL
2,665,105 IZMIR

UK
2,329,600 BIRMINGHAM
1,784,000 LEEDS
1,440,900 LIVERPOOL
9,227,687 LONDON
2,578,900 MANCHESTER

UKRAINE
1,187,000 DNEPROPETROVSK
1,117,000 DONETSK
1,618,000 KHARKOV
2,616,000 KIEV
1,106,000 ODESSA

URUGUAY
1,383,660 MONTEVIDEO

USA
3,051,000 ATLANTA
2,414,000 BALTIMORE
4,497,000 BOSTON
1,193,000 BUFFALO
7,498,000 CHICAGO
1,539,000 CINCINNATI
2,213,000 CLEVELAND
1,370,000 COLUMBUS
4,135,000 DALLAS - FORT WORTH
1,668,000 DENVER
4,285,000 DETROIT
3,437,000 HOUSTON
1,406,000 INDIANAPOLIS
1,602,000 KANSAS CITY
11,420,000 LOS ANGELES
3,264,000 MIAMI
1,446,000 MILWAUKEE
2,583,000 MINNEAPOLIS - ST PAUL
1,295,000 NEW ORLEANS
16,972,000 NEW YORK
4,941,000 PHILADELPHIA
2,287,000 PHOENIX
2,404,000 PITTSBURG
1,570,000 PORTLAND
1,073,000 ROCHESTER
1,388,000 SACRAMENTO
1,348,000 SAN ANTONIO
2,549,000 SAN DIEGO
5,240,000 SAN FRANCISCO
2,078,000 SEATTLE
2,507,000 ST LOUIS
2,101,000 TAMPA - ST PETERSBURG
4,293,000 WASHINGTON D.C.

UZBEKISTAN
2,094,000 TASHKENT

VENEZUELA
4,092,000 CARACAS
1,400,643 MARACAIBO
1,274,354 VALENCIA

VIETNAM
1,447,523 HAIPHONG
1,056,146 HANOI
3,924,435 HO CHI MINH

YUGOSLAVIA
1,168,454 BELGRADE

ZAIRE (CONGO)
3,505,000 KINSHASA

ZIMBABWE
1,000,000 HARARE

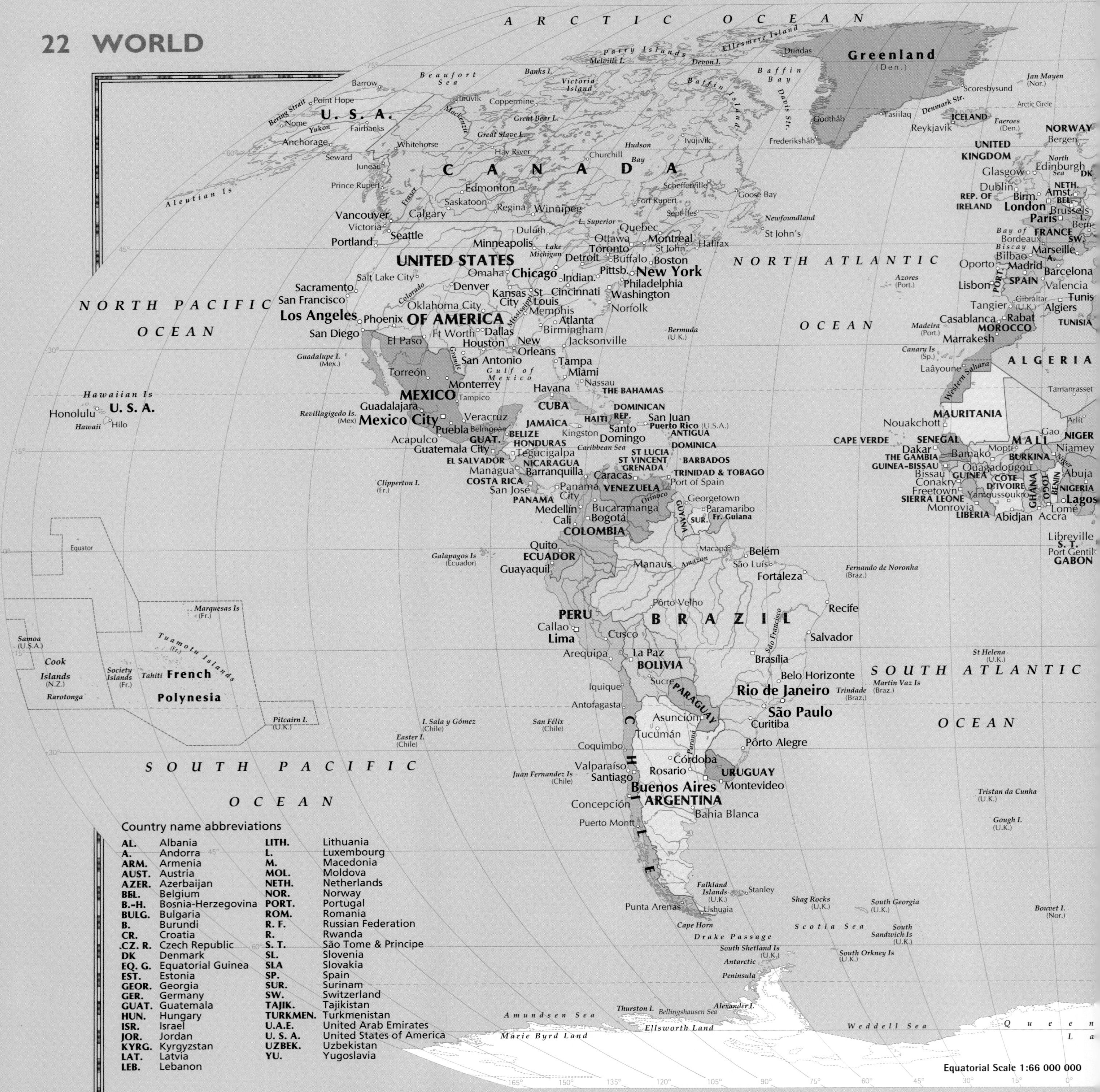

ARCTIC OCEAN

Greenland (Den.)

Map labels (North America / Arctic):

Parry Islands · Ellesmere Island · Dundas · Devon I. · Baffin Island · Baffin Bay · Davis Str. · Melville I. · Banks I. · Victoria Island · Beaufort Sea · Coppermine · Inuvik · Barrow · Point Hope · Nome · Anchorage · Yukon · Fairbanks · Seward · Juneau · Whitehorse · Prince Rupert · Great Bear L. · Great Slave L. · Hay River · Mackenzie · Fort Rupert · Schefferville · Goose Bay · Ivujivik · Frederikshåb · Godthåb · Tasiilaq · Scoresbysund · Jan Mayen (Nor.) · Arctic Circle

U.S.A. · CANADA

Aleutian Is · Vancouver · Victoria · Portland · Seattle · Calgary · Edmonton · Saskatoon · Regina · Winnipeg · Churchill · Hudson Bay · L. Superior · Duluth · Ottawa · Quebec · Montreal · Sept-Iles · Newfoundland · St John's · Halifax · St John · Toronto · Buffalo · Boston · New York · Detroit · Pittsb. · Philadelphia · Washington · Norfolk

UNITED STATES OF AMERICA

Minneapolis · Lake Michigan · Chicago · Indian. · Cincinnati · Sacramento · San Francisco · Salt Lake City · Denver · Omaha · Kansas City · St Louis · Memphis · Los Angeles · Phoenix · Colorado · Oklahoma City · Fort Worth · Dallas · Birmingham · Atlanta · San Diego · El Paso · Houston · San Antonio · New Orleans · Jacksonville · Tampa · Miami · Rio Grande · Gulf of Mexico · Bermuda (U.K.)

MEXICO

Guadalupe I. (Mex.) · Torreón · Monterrey · Tampico · Havana · THE BAHAMAS · Nassau · Revillagigedo Is. (Mex.) · Guadalajara · Mexico City · Puebla · Veracruz · Acapulco · CUBA · DOMINICAN REP. · HAITI · JAMAICA · Kingston · Santo Domingo · San Juan · Puerto Rico (U.S.A.) · ANTIGUA · DOMINICA · Belmopan · BELIZE · GUAT. · Guatemala City · HONDURAS · Tegucigalpa · EL SALVADOR · NICARAGUA · Managua · COSTA RICA · San José · Caribbean Sea · ST LUCIA · ST VINCENT · GRENADA · BARBADOS · TRINIDAD & TOBAGO · Port of Spain · PANAMA · Panama City · Barranquilla · Caracas · VENEZUELA

South America:

Clipperton I. (Fr.) · Medellín · Cali · Bucaramanga · Bogotá · COLOMBIA · Georgetown · Paramaribo · GUYANA · SUR. · Fr. Guiana · Quito · ECUADOR · Guayaquil · Galapagos Is (Ecuador) · Equator · Manaus · Macapá · Belém · São Luís · Fortaleza · Fernando de Noronha (Braz.) · PERU · Callao · Lima · Cusco · Porto Velho · B R A Z I L · Amazon · São Francisco · Recife · Salvador · Arequipa · La Paz · BOLIVIA · Sucre · Brasília · Belo Horizonte · SOUTH ATLANTIC OCEAN · St Helena (U.K.) · Iquique · PARAGUAY · Rio de Janeiro · Trindade (Braz.) · Martin Vaz Is (Braz.) · Antofagasta · Asunción · São Paulo · Curitiba · Pôrto Alegre · Tucumán · Coquimbo · CHILE · Córdoba · URUGUAY · Valparaíso · Rosario · Santiago · Montevideo · Buenos Aires · ARGENTINA · Concepción · Bahía Blanca · Puerto Montt · Falkland Islands (U.K.) · Stanley · Shag Rocks (U.K.) · South Georgia (U.K.) · Tristan da Cunha (U.K.) · Gough I. (U.K.) · Punta Arenas · Ushuaia · Cape Horn · Drake Passage · South Shetland Is (U.K.) · South Orkney Is (U.K.) · Scotia Sea · South Sandwich Is (U.K.) · Bouvet I. (Nor.)

Pacific:

NORTH PACIFIC OCEAN · Hawaiian Is U.S.A. · Honolulu · Hawaii · Hilo · Samoa (U.S.A.) · Cook Islands (N.Z.) · Rarotonga · Society Islands (Fr.) · Tahiti · French Polynesia · Marquesas Is (Fr.) · Tuamotu Islands (Fr.) · Pitcairn I. (U.K.) · Easter I. (Chile) · I. Sala y Gómez (Chile) · San Félix (Chile) · San Félix (Chile) · Juan Fernandez Is (Chile) · SOUTH PACIFIC OCEAN

Europe / Atlantic:

ICELAND · Reykjavik · Faeroes (Den.) · Denmark Str. · NORWAY · Bergen · UNITED KINGDOM · Glasgow · Edinburgh · DK · Dublin · REP. OF IRELAND · London · NETH. · Amst. · BEL. · Brussels · Birm. · Paris · FRANCE · SW. · Bern · A. · Marseille · Bordeaux · Bilbao · Oporto · PORT. · Lisbon · Madrid · SPAIN · Barcelona · Valencia · Gibraltar · Tunis · Algiers · TUNISIA · Bay of Biscay · Azores (Port.) · Madeira (Port.) · Canary Is (Sp.) · Casablanca · Rabat · MOROCCO · Marrakesh · Laâyoune · Western Sahara · ALGERIA · Tamanrasset · Tangier · NORTH ATLANTIC OCEAN

Africa:

MAURITANIA · Nouakchott · CAPE VERDE · SENEGAL · Dakar · THE GAMBIA · GUINEA-BISSAU · Bissau · Conakry · GUINEA · SIERRA LEONE · Freetown · Monrovia · LIBERIA · MALI · Bamako · Mopti · BURKINA · Ouagadougou · Arlit · NIGER · Niamey · Gao · Yamoussoukro · CÔTE D'IVOIRE · GHANA · Accra · Abidjan · TOGO · BENIN · Lomé · NIGERIA · Abuja · Lagos · Libreville · GABON · Port Gentil · S.T. · Arlit

---

Country name abbreviations

AL.	Albania	LITH.	Lithuania
A.	Andorra	L.	Luxembourg
ARM.	Armenia	M.	Macedonia
AUST.	Austria	MOL.	Moldova
AZER.	Azerbaijan	NETH.	Netherlands
BEL.	Belgium	NOR.	Norway
B.-H.	Bosnia-Herzegovina	PORT.	Portugal
BULG.	Bulgaria	ROM.	Romania
B.	Burundi	R.F.	Russian Federation
CR.	Croatia	R.	Rwanda
CZ. R.	Czech Republic	S.T.	São Tome & Principe
DK	Denmark	SL.	Slovenia
EQ. G.	Equatorial Guinea	SLA	Slovakia
EST.	Estonia	SP.	Spain
GEOR.	Georgia	SUR.	Surinam
GER.	Germany	SW.	Switzerland
GUAT.	Guatemala	TAJIK.	Tajikistan
HUN.	Hungary	TURKMEN.	Turkmenistan
ISR.	Israel	U.A.E.	United Arab Emirates
JOR.	Jordan	U.S.A.	United States of America
KYRG.	Kyrgyzstan	UZBEK.	Uzbekistan
LAT.	Latvia	YU.	Yugoslavia
LEB.	Lebanon		

Equatorial Scale 1:66 000 000

Robinson Projection

© HarperCollinsPublishers

LANGUAGES

Arctic Circle · Samoyede · Tungusi · Kirghiz · Mongol · Turkoman · Turki · Tropic of Cancer · Arabic · Tuareg · Hausa · Kru · Nilotic · Somali · Swahili · Malay · Javanese · Equator · Tropic of Capricorn · Antarctic Circle

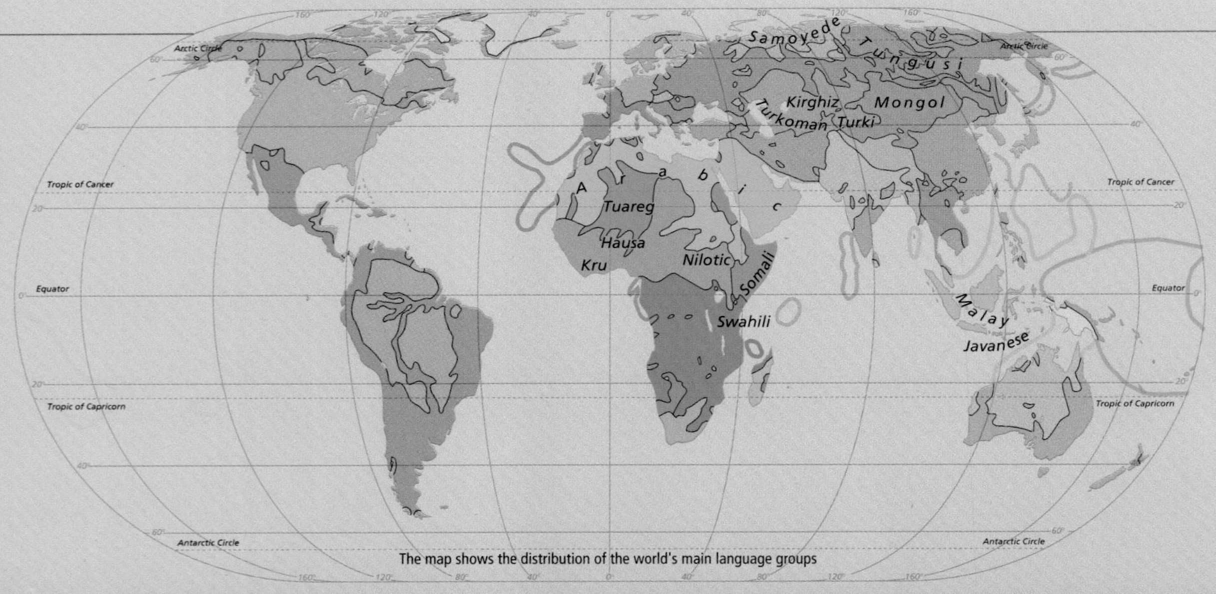

The map shows the distribution of the world's main language groups

Indo-European	Ural-Altaic
Germanic	Semitic — Uralian Group
Romance	Hamitic — Altaic Group
Slavic	Sudanese — Korean Japanese
Irano Armenian	Bantu
Indo-Aryan	

Sino-Tibetan
Tibeto Burman
Bushman Hottentot — Sinitic
Austronesian — Tai
Melanesian — Amerindian
Papuan Australian
Polynesian — Other Groups or isolated Languages

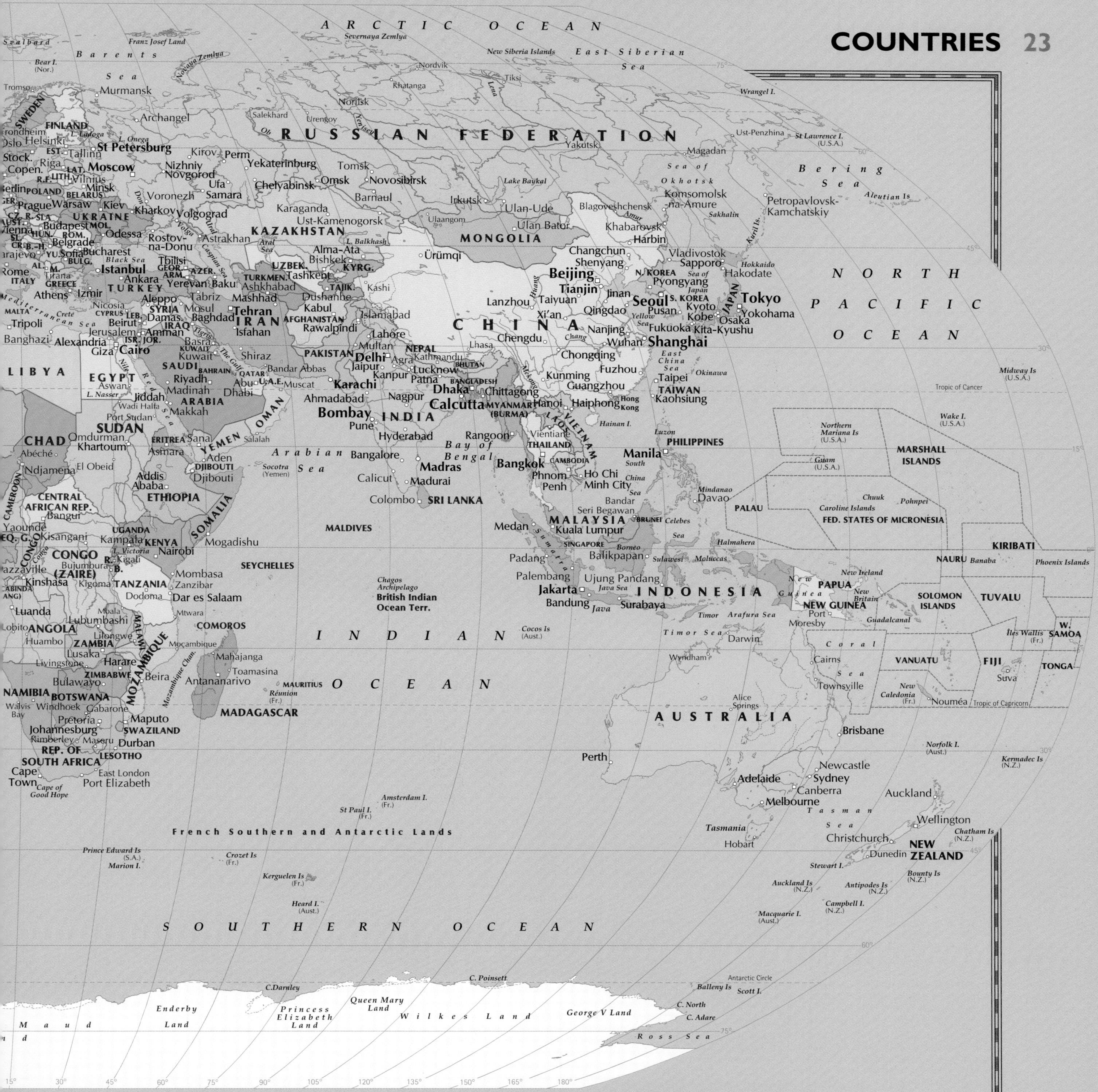

RELIGIONS

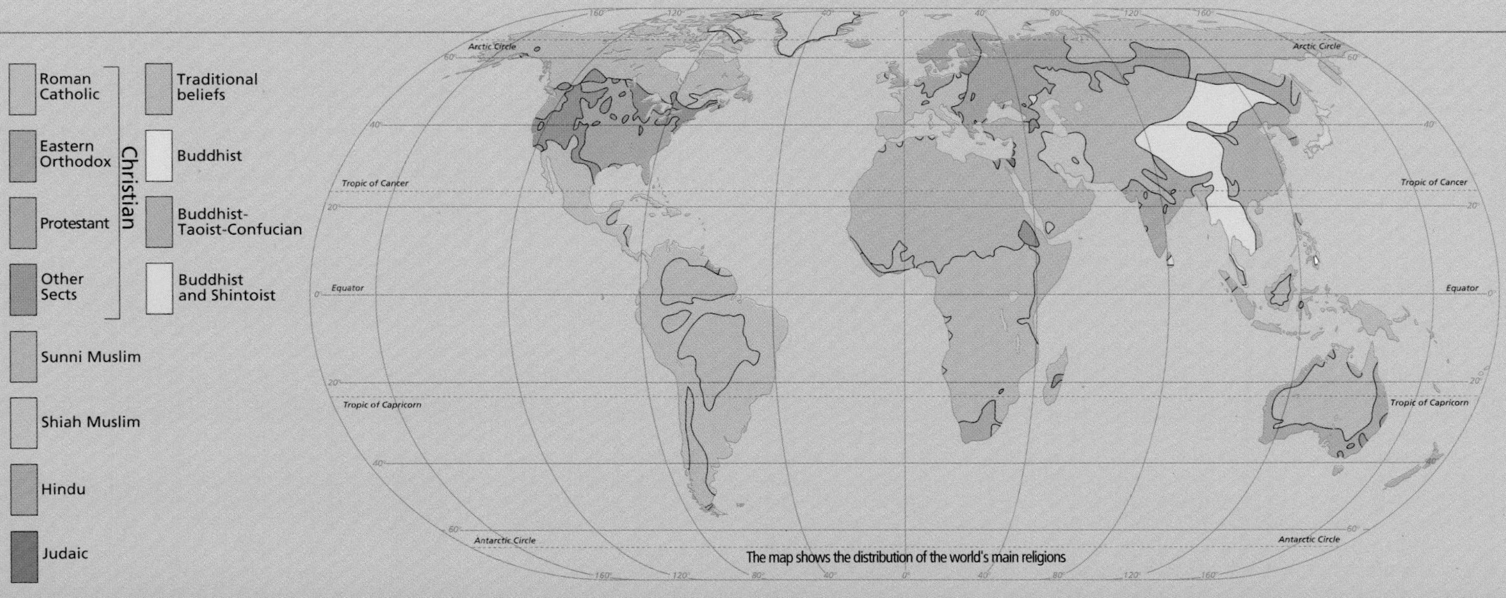

Christian
- Roman Catholic
- Eastern Orthodox
- Protestant
- Other Sects

- Sunni Muslim
- Shiah Muslim
- Hindu
- Judaic
- Traditional beliefs
- Buddhist
- Buddhist-Taoist-Confucian
- Buddhist and Shintoist

The map shows the distribution of the world's main religions

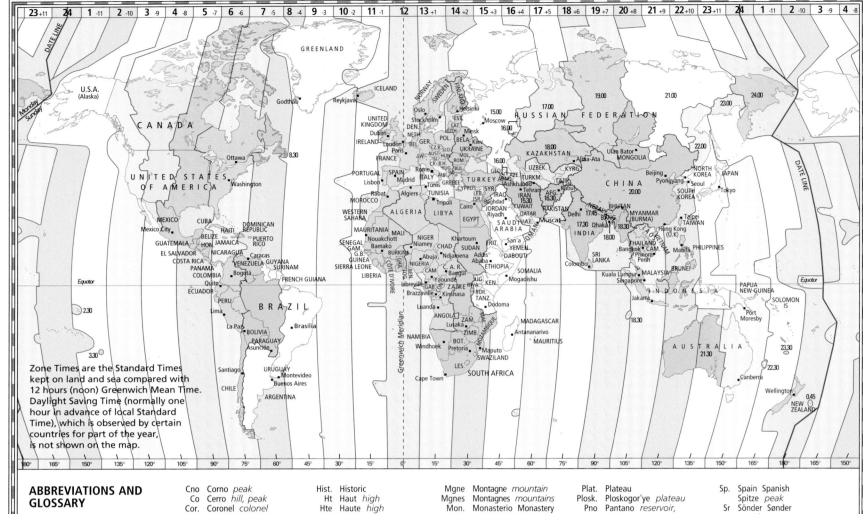

Zone Times are the Standard Times kept on land and sea compared with 12 hours (noon) Greenwich Mean Time. Daylight Saving Time (normally one hour in advance of local Standard Time), which is observed by certain countries for part of the year, is not shown on the map.

ABBREVIATIONS AND GLOSSARY

A. Alp Alpen Alpi *alp*
Alt *upper*
Abbe Abbaye *abbey*
Afr. Africa African
Ag. Agia Agioi Agion
Agios *saint*
Aig. Aiguille *peak*
Akr. Ákra Akrotírion
Akrotirion
cape, point
Anch. Anchorage
Appno Appennino *mountains*
Aqued. Aqueduct
Ar. Arroyo *water course*
Arch. Archipel
Archipelago
Archipiélago
archipelago
Arr. Arrecife *reef*
Ay. Áyioi Áyion Áyios
saint

B. Baai Bahía Baía
Baie Baja Bay
Bucht Bukhta
Bukt *bay*
Bad *spa*
Ban *village*
Bir *well*
Bayou *inlet*
Bc Banc (sand) bank
Bca Boca *mouth*
Bg Berg *mountain*
Bge Barrage
Bge. Barragem *reservoir*
Bgt Bight Bugt *bay*
Bi Bani Beni *tribe*
(sons of)
Bj Burj *hills*
Bk Bank
Bn Basin
Bol. Bol'shoy Bol'shoye
Bol'shaya Bol'shiye *big*
Bos. Bosanski *town*
Br. Bredning *bay*
Brüke *bridge*
Burun Burnu *point,
cape*
Bt Bukit *bay*
Bü. Büyük *big*

C. Cabo Cap *cape,
headland*
Cape
Col *high pass*
Ç. Çay *river*
Cabo Cabeço *summit*
Cach. Cachoeira Cachoeiro
waterfall
Can. Canal Canale *canal,
channel*
Cañon Canyon *canyon*
Cat. Cataract
Catena *mountains*
Cd Ciudad *town city*
Ch. Chaung *stream*
Chott *salt lake, marsh*
Chan. Channel
Che Chaîne *mountain
chain*
Cma Cima *summit*

Cno Corno *peak*
Co Cerro *hill, peak*
Cor. Coronel *colonel*
Cord. Cordillera *mountain
chain*
Cr. Creek
Cuch. Cuchilla *chain of
mountains*
Czo Cozzo *mountain*

D. Da *big, river*
Dag Dagh Dağı
mountain
Dağlan *mountains*
Danau *lake*
Darreh *valley*
Daryácheh *lake*
Diavlos *hill*
-d. -dake *peak*
Dj. Djebel *mountain*
Dr Doctor
Dz. Dzong *castle, fort*

Eil. Eiland *island*
Eilanden *islands*
Emb. Embalse *reservoir*
Equat. Equatorial
Escarp. Escarpment
Est. Estuary
Etg Etang *lake, lagoon*

F. Firth
Fj. Fjell *mountain*
Fjord Fjördur *fjord*
Fk Fork
Fl. Fleuve *river*
Fte Fonte *well*

G. Gebel *mountain*
Göl Gölö Göl *lake*
G. Golfe Golfo Gulf
gulf, bay
Góra *mountain*
Guba *bay*
Gunung *mountain*
-g. -gawa *river*
Gd Grand *big*
Gde Grande *big*
Geb. Gebergte *mountain
range*
Gebirge *mountains*
Gen. General
Gez. Gezira *island*
Ghub. Ghubbat *bay*
Gl. Glacier
Gob. Gobernador *governor*
Grp Group
Gr. Graben *trench, ditch*
Gross Grosse
Grande *big*
Gt Great Groot Groote
big
Gy Góry Gory *mountains*

H. Hawr *lake*
Hill
Hoch *high*
Hora *mountain*
Hory *mountains*
Halv. Halvøy *peninsula*
Harb. Harbour
Hd Head
Hg. Hegység *mountains*
Hgts Heights

Hist. Historic
Ht Haut *high*
Hte Haute *high*

I. Île Ilha Insel Isla
Island Isle
island, isle
Isola Isole *island*
im imeni *in the name of*
In. Inder Indre Inner
Inre *inner*
Inlet *inlet*
Inf. Inferior Infrieure *lower*
Is Islas Îles Ilhas
Islands Isles
islands, isles
Isr. Israel
Isth. Isthmus

J. Jabal Jebel *mountain*
Jibāl *mountains*
Jrvi Jaure Jezero
Jezioro *lake*
Jökull *glacier*

K. Kaap Kap Kapp *cape*
Kaikyō *strait*
Kato Káto *lower*
Kiang *river or stream*
Ko *island, lake, inlet*
Koh Küh Kühha
island
Kolpos *gulf*
Kopf *hill*
Kuala *estuary*
Kyst *coast*
Kan. Kanal Kanaal *canal*
Kep. Kepulauan
archipelago, islands
Kg Kampong *village*
Kompong *landing
place*
Kong *king*
Kh. Khawr *inlet*
Khirbet *ruins*
Khr Khrebet *mountain
range*
Kl. Klein Kleine *small*
Kör. Körfez Körfezi *bay,
gulf*
K. Küçük *small*

L. Lac Lago Lake
Liman Limni *lake*
Liçen Loch Lough
lake, loch
Lam *stream*
Lag. Lagoon Laguna
Lagôa *lagoon*
Ldg Landing
Lit. Little

M. Mae *river*
Me *great, chief,
mother*
Meer *lake, sea*
Muang *kingdom,
province, town*
Muong *town*
Mys *cape*
Mf Massif *mountains,
upland*
Mgna Montagna *mountain*

Mgne Montagne *mountain*
Mgnes Montagnes *mountains*
Mon. Monasterio Monastery
monastery
Monument *monument*
Mt Mont Mount
mountain
Mt. Mountain
Mte Monte *mountain*
Mtes Montes *mountains*
Mti Monti Munţi
mountains
Mtii Munţii *mountains*
Mtn Mountain
Mth Mouth
Mths Mouths
Mts Monts Mountains

N. Nam *south(ern),
river*
Neu Ny *new*
Nevado *peak*
Nudo *mountain*
Noord Nord Nörre
Nørre *north*
Nos *spit, point*
Nac. Nacional *national*
Nat. National
Nic. Nicaragua
Nizh. Nizhneye Nizhniy
Nizhnyaya *lower*
Nizm. Nizmennost' *lowland*
N.O. Noord Oost Nord Ost
northeast
Nov. Novyy Novaya
Noviye
Novoye *new*
Nr Nether
Nva Nueva *new*

O. Oost Ost *east*
Ostrov *island*
Ø Østre *east*
Ob. Ober *upper, higher*
Oc. Ocean
Ode Oude *old*
Ogl. Oglat *well*
Or. Óri Óros Ori
mountains
Oros *mountain*
Orm. Ormos *bay*
O-va Ostrova *islands*
Ot Olet *mountain*
Öv. Över Over *upper*
Oz. Ozero *lake*
Ozera *lakes*

P. Pass
Pic Pico Piz *peak,
summit*
Pulau *island*
Pou *mountain*
P.P. Pulau-pulau *islands*
Pass. Passage
Peg. Pegunungan
mountain range
Pen. Peninsula Penisola
peninsula
Per. Pereval *pass*
Phn. Phnom *hill, mountain*
Pgio Poggio *hill*
Pl. Planina Planinski
mountain(s)
Pla Playa *beach*

Plat. Plateau
Plosk. Ploskogor'ye *plateau*
Pno Pantano *reservoir,
swamp*
Por. Porog *rapids*
P-ov Poluostrov *peninsula*
Pr. Proliv *strait*
Przylądek *cape*
Pres. Presidente *president*
Presqu. Presqu'île *peninsula*
Prom. Promontory
Prov. Province Provincial
Psa Presa *dam*
Pso Passo *dam*
Pt Point
Pont *bridge*
Petit *small*
Pta Ponta Punta *cape,
point*
Puerta *narrow pass*
Pte Pointe *cape, point*
Ponte Puente *bridge*
Pto Porto Puerto *harbour,
port*
Pzo Pizzo *mountain*
peak, mountain

Q Qala *castle, fort*

R. Reshteh *mountain
range*
Rūd *river*
Ra. Range
Rca Rocca *rock, fortress*
Reg. Region
Rep. Republic
Res. Reserve
Reservoir
Resp. Respublika *republic*
Rf Reef
Rge Ridge
Riba Ribeira *coast, bottom
of the river valley*
Rte Route

S. Salar Salina *salt pan*
San São *saint*
See *lake*
Seto *strait, channel*
Sjö *lake*
Sör Süd Sud Syd *south*
sur *on*
Sa Serra Sierra
mountain range
Sab. Sabkhat *salt flat*
Sc. Scoglio *rock, reef*
Sd Sound Sund *sound*
Seb. Sebjet Sebkhat Sebkra
salt flat
Serr. Serranía *mountain
range*
Sev. Severnaya Severnyy
north(ern)
Sh. Shā'ib *watercourse*
Shaṭṭ *river (-mouth)*
Shima *island*
Shankou *pass*
Si Sidi *lord, master*
Sk. Shuiku *reservoir*
Skt Sankt *saint*
Smt Seamount
Snra Senhora *Mrs, lady*
Snro Senhoro *Mr, gentle-
man*

Sp. Spain Spanish
Spitze *peak*
Sr Sönder Sønder
southern
Sr. Sredniy Srednyaya
middle
St Saint Sint
Staryy *old*
St. Stor Store *big*
Stung *river*
Sta Santa *saint*
Ste Sainte *saint*
Store *big*
Sto Santo *saint*
Str. Strait Stretta *strait*
Sv. Sväty Sveti *holy,
saint*

T. Tal *valley*
Tall Tell *hill*
Tepe Tepesi *hill, peak*
Terr. Territory
Tg Tanjung Tanjong
cape, point
Tk Teluk *bay*
Tmt Tablemount
Tr. Trench Trough
Tre Torre *tower, fortress*
Tte Teniente *lieutenant*

Ug Ujung *point, cape*
Unt. Unter *lower*
Upr Upper

V. Val Valle Valley *valley*
Väster Vest Vester
west(ern)
Vatn *lake*
Ville *town*
Vorder *near*
Va Vila *small town*
Vol. Volcán Volcan
Volcano *volcano*
Vdkhr. Vodokhranilishche
reservoir
Vdskh. Vodoskhovshche
Vodaskhovishcha
reservoir
Vel. Velikiy Velikaya
Velikiye *big*
Verkh. Verkhniy Verkhneye
Verkhne *upper*
Verkhnyaya *upper*
Vost. Vostochnyy *eastern*
Vozv. Vozvyshennost'
hills, upland

W. Wadi *watercourse*
Wald *forest*
Wan *bay*
Water *water*
Wr Wester

-y -yama *mountain*
Yt. Ytre Ytter Ytri *outer*
Yuzh. Yuzhnaya Yuzhno
Yuzhnyy *southern*

Zal. Zaliv *bay*
Zap. Zapadnyy Zapadnaya
Zapadno Zapadnoye
western
Zem. Zemlya *land*

RELIEF

METRES		FEET
6000		19686
5000		16409
4000		13124
3000		9843
2000		6562
1000		3281
500		1640
200		656
SEA		LEVEL
200		656
2000		6562
4000		13124
6000		19686

Contour intervals used in layer colouring in the insets

METRES		FEET
4000		13124
3000		9843
2000		6562
1500		4921
1000		3281
500		1640
200		656
100		328
SEA		LEVEL
100		328
200		656
1000		3281
3000		9843

213 △ Summit
height in metres

PHYSICAL FEATURES

- Freshwater lake
- Seasonal freshwater lake
- Saltwater lake *or* Lagoon
- Seasonal saltwater lake
- Dry salt lake *or* Salt pan
- Marsh
- River
- Waterfall
- Dam *or* Barrage
- Seasonal river or Wadi
- Canal
- Flood dyke
- Reef
- ▲ Volcano
- Lava field
- Sandy desert
- Rocky desert
- Oasis
- Escarpment
- Mountain pass
- Ice cap *or* Glacier

COMMUNICATIONS

- Motorway
- Motorway tunnel

Motorways are classified separately at scales greater than 1:4 million, at smaller scales motorways are classified with main roads.

- Main road
- Main road *under construction*
- Main road tunnel
- Other road
- Other road *under construction*
- Other road tunnel
- Track
- Car ferry
- Main railway
- Main railway *under construction*
- Main railway tunnel
- Other railway
- Other railway *under construction*
- Other railway tunnel
- Train ferry
- ⊕ Main airport
- ✦ Other airport

BOUNDARIES

Reference maps

- International
- International *through water*
- International *disputed*
- Ceasefire line
- main administrative (U.K.)
- main administrative (U.K.) *through water*
- main administrative
- main administrative *through water*

Continent maps

- International
- International *disputed*
- Ceasefire line
- main administrative

OTHER FEATURES

- National park
- Reserve
- Ancient wall
- ∴ Historic *or* Tourist site

SETTLEMENTS

POPULATION	NATIONAL CAPITAL	ADMINISTRATIVE CAPITAL	CITY OR TOWN
Over 5 million	▣ **Beijing**	◉ **Tianjin**	◉ **New York**
1 to 5 million	▣ **Soul**	◉ **Lagos**	◉ **Barranquilla**
500000 to 1 million	▣ **Bangui**	◎ **Douala**	◎ **Memphis**
100000 to 500000	□ Wellington	○ Mansa	○ Mara
50000 to 100000	□ Port of Spain	○ Lubango	○ Arecibo
10000 to 50000	▫ Malabo	○ Chinhoyi	○ El Tigre
Less than 10000	▫ Roseau	○ Áti	○ Soledad

Urban area

STYLES OF LETTERING

Country name	**FRANCE**	**BARBADOS**		
Main administrative name	PORTO			
Area name	*ARTOIS*			
Physical feature	**ISLAND**	**LAKE**	**MOUNTAIN**	**RIVER**
	Gran Canaria	*LAKE ERIE*	*SOUTHERN ALPS*	*Zambezi*

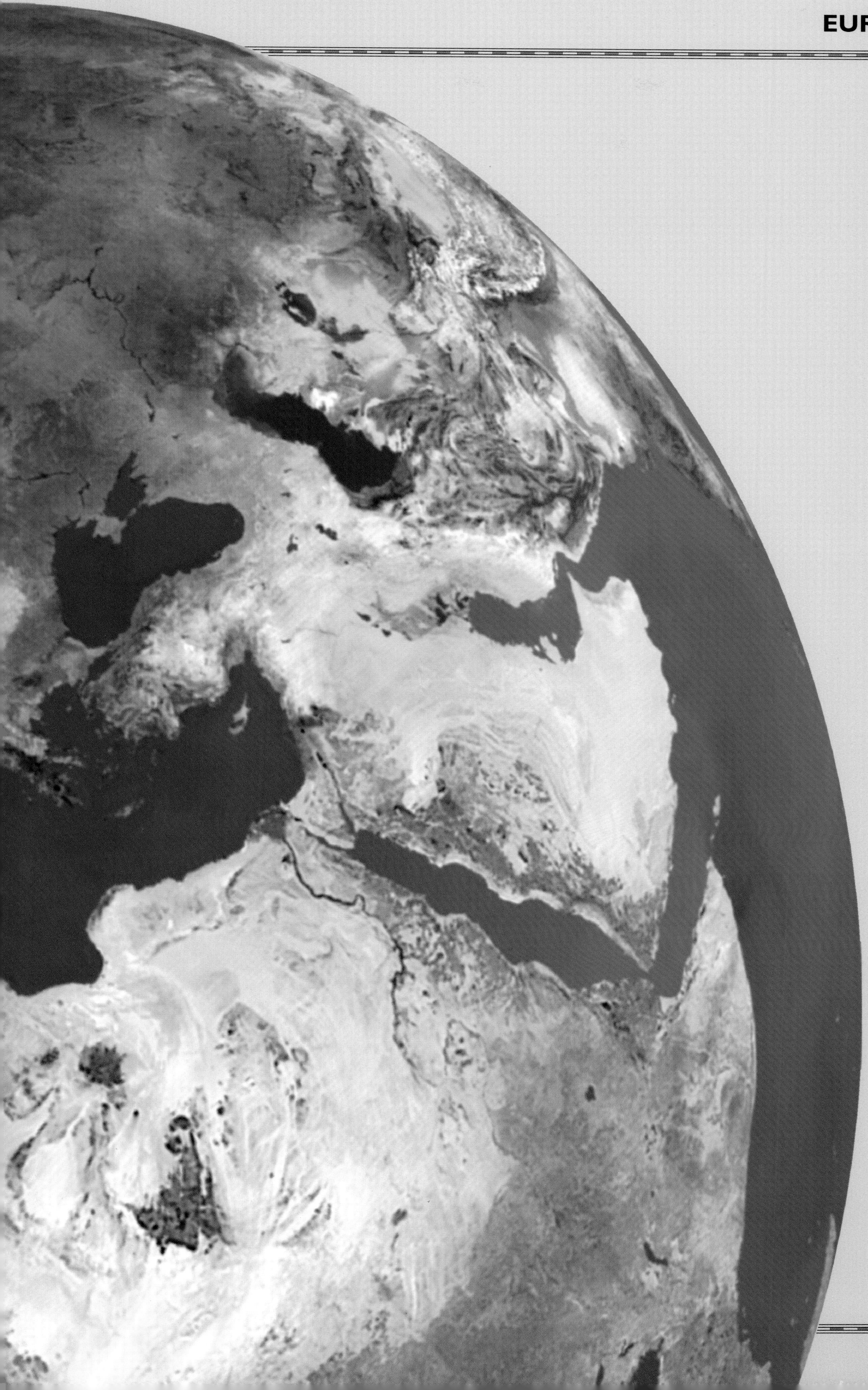

1:15 500 000

COUNTRY	AREA		POPULATION		Form of Government	Capital City	MAIN LANGUAGES	MAIN RELIGIONS	CURRENCY
	sqml	sqkm	total	density per sqml sqkm					
ALBANIA	11 100	28 748	3 414 000	308 119	republic	Tirana	Albanian (Gheg, Tosk dialects), Greek,	Muslim, Greek Orthodox, Roman Catholic	Lek
ANDORRA	180	465	65 000	362 140	principality	Andorra la Vella	Catalan, Spanish, French	Roman Catholic	French franc, Spanish peseta
AUSTRIA	32 377	83 855	8 031 000	248 96	republic	Vienna	German, Serbo-Croat,	Roman Catholic, Protestant	Schilling
AZORES	868	2 247	237 800	274 106	Portuguese territory	Ponta Delgada	Turkish Portuguese	Roman Catholic, Protestant	Port. escudo
BELARUS	80 155	207 600	10 355 000	129 50	republic	Minsk	Belorussian, Russian, Ukrainian	Belorussian Orthodox, Roman Catholic	Rouble
BELGIUM	11 784	30 520	10 080 000	855 330	monarchy	Brussels	Dutch (Flemish), French, German (all official), Italian	Roman Catholic, Protestant	Franc
BOSNIA-HERZEGOVINA	19 741	51 130	4 459 000	226 87	republic	Sarajevo	Serbo-Croat	Sunni Muslim, Serbian Orthodox, Roman Catholic, Protestant	Dinar
BULGARIA	42 855	110 994	8 443 000	197 76	republic	Sofia	Bulgarian, Turkish, Romany, Macedonian	Bulgarian Orthodox, Sunni Muslim	Lev
CHANNEL ISLANDS	75	195	147 000	1952 754	UK territory	St Helier, St Peter Port	English, French	Protestant, Roman Catholic	Pound
CROATIA	21 829	56 538	4 777 000	219 84	republic	Zagreb	Serbo-Croat	Roman Catholic, Orthodox, Sunni Muslim	Kuna
CZECH REPUBLIC	30 450	78 864	10 336 000	339 131	republic	Prague	Czech, Moravian, Slovak	Roman Catholic, Protestant	Koruna
DENMARK	16 631	43 075	5 205 000	313 121	monarchy	Copenhagen	Danish	Protestant, Roman Catholic	Krone
ESTONIA	17 452	45 200	1 499 000	86 33	republic	Tallinn	Estonian, Russian	Protestant, Russian Orthodox	Kroon
FAROE ISLANDS	540	1 399	47 000	87 34	Danish territory	Tórshavn	Danish, Faeroese	Protestant	Danish krone
FINLAND	130 559	338 145	5 088 000	39 15	republic	Helsinki	Finnish, Swedish	Protestant, Finnish (Greek) Orthodox	Markka
FRANCE	210 026	543 965	57 903 000	276 106	republic	Paris	French, French dialects, Arabic, German (Alsatian), Breton	Roman Catholic, Protestant, Sunni Muslim	Franc
GERMANY	138 174	357 868	81 410 000	589 227	republic	Berlin	German, Turkish	Protestant, Roman Catholic, Sunni Muslim	Mark
GIBRALTAR	3	7	28 000	11157 4308	UK territory	Gibraltar	English, Spanish	Roman Catholic, Protestant, Sunni Muslim	Pound
GREECE	50 949	131 957	10 426 000	205 79	republic	Athens	Greek, Macedonian	Greek Orthodox, Sunni Muslim	Drachma
HUNGARY	35 919	93 030	10 261 000	286 110	republic	Budapest	Hungarian, Romany, German, Slovak	Roman Catholic, Protestant	Forint
ICELAND	39 699	102 820	266 000	7 3	republic	Reykjavik	Icelandic	Protestant, Roman Catholic	Króna
ISLE OF MAN	221	572	73 000	331 128	UK territory	Douglas	English	Protestant, Roman Catholic	Pound
ITALY	116 311	301 245	57 193 000	492 190	republic	Rome	Italian, Italian dialects	Roman Catholic	Lira
LATVIA	24 595	63 700	2 548 000	104 40	republic	Riga	Latvian, Russian	Protestant, Roman Catholic, Russian Orthodox	Lat
LIECHTENSTEIN	62	160	31 000	502 194	monarchy	Vaduz	German	Roman Catholic, Protestant	Swiss franc
LITHUANIA	25 174	65 200	3 721 000	148 57	republic	Vilnius	Lithuanian, Russian, Polish	Roman Catholic, Protestant, Russian Orthodox	Litas
LUXEMBOURG	998	2 586	404 000	405 156	monarchy	Luxembourg	Letzeburgish (Luxembourgian), German, French, Portuguese	Roman Catholic, Protestant	Franc
MACEDONIA, Former Yugoslavian Republic of	9 928	25 713	2 142 000	216 83	republic	Skopje	Macedonian, Albanian, Serbo-Croat, Turkish, Romany	Macedonian Orthodox, Sunni Muslim, Roman Catholic	Denar
MADEIRA	307	794	253 000	825 319	Port territory	Funchal	Portuguese	Roman Catholic, Protestant	Port. escudo
MALTA	122	316	368 000	3016 1165	republic	Valletta	Maltese, English	Roman Catholic	Lira
MOLDOVA	13 012	33 700	4 350 000	334 129	republic	Chişinău	Romanian, Russian, Ukrainian, Gagauz	Moldovan Orthodox, Russian Orthodox	Leu
MONACO	1	2	31 000	41174 15897	monarchy	Monaco	French, Monegasque, Italian	Roman Catholic	French franc
NETHERLANDS	16 033	41 526	15 380 000	959 370	monarchy	Amsterdam	Dutch, Frisian, Turkish, Indonesian languages	Roman Catholic, Protestant, Sunni Muslim	Guilder
NORWAY	125 050	323 878	4 325 000	35 13	monarchy	Oslo	Norwegian	Protestant, Roman Catholic	Krone
POLAND	120 728	312 683	38 544 000	319 123	republic	Warsaw	Polish, German	Roman Catholic, Polish Orthodox	Złoty
PORTUGAL	34 340	88 940	9 902 000	288 111	republic	Lisbon	Portuguese	Roman Catholic, Protestant	Escudo
REPUBLIC OF IRELAND	27 136	70 282	3 571 000	132 51	republic	Dublin	English, Irish	Roman Catholic, Protestant	Punt
ROMANIA	91 699	237 500	22 731 000	248 96	republic	Bucharest	Romanian, Hungarian	Romanian Orthodox, Roman Catholic, Protestant	Leu
RUSSIAN FEDERATION	6 592 849	17 075 400	148 673 000	23 9	republic	Moscow	Russian, Tatar, Ukrainian, many local languages	Russian Orthodox, Sunni, Muslim, other Christian, Jewish	Rouble
RUSSIAN FEDERATION IN EUROPE	1 527 343	3 955 800	106 918 000	70 27					
SAN MARINO	24	61	25 000	1061 410	republic	San Marino	Italian	Roman Catholic	Ital. lira
SLOVAKIA	18 933	49 035	5 347 000	282 109	republic	Bratislava	Slovak, Hungarian, Czech	Roman Catholic, Protestant, Orthodox	Koruna
SLOVENIA	7 819	20 251	1 989 000	254 98	republic	Ljubljana	Slovene, Serbo-Croat	Roman Catholic, Protestant	Tólar
SPAIN	194 897	504 782	39 143 000	201 78	monarchy	Madrid	Spanish, Catalan, Galician, Basque	Roman Catholic	Peseta
SWEDEN	173 732	449 964	8 781 000	51 20	monarchy	Stockholm	Swedish	Protestant, Roman Catholic	Krona
SWITZERLAND	15 943	41 293	6 995 000	439 169	federation	Bern	German, French, Italian, Romansch	Roman Catholic, Protestant	Franc
UNITED KINGDOM	94 241	244 082	58 395 000	620 239	monarchy	London	English, South Indian languages, Chinese, Welsh, Gaelic	Protestant, Roman Catholic, Muslim, Sikh, Hindu, Jewish	Pound
UKRAINE	233 090	603 700	51 910 000	223 86	republic	Kiev	Ukrainian, Russian, regional languages	Ukrainian Orthodox, Roman Catholic	Karbovanets
VATICAN CITY		0.44	1 000	5886 2273	ecclesiastical state		Italian	Roman Catholic	Ital. lira
YUGOSLAVIA	39 449	102 173	10 516 000	267 103	republic	Belgrade	Serbo-Croat, Albanian,	Serbian Orthodox, Montenegrin	Dinar

Greenland
(Den.)

Greenland Sea

Spitsbergen

Svalbard (Nor.)

B A R E N T S *Kara Sea*

S E A

Novaya Zemlya

Denmark Strait

Jan Mayen (Nor.)

Gulf of Ob

Reykjavik **ICELAND**

Lappland

White Sea

NETHERLANDS

LUXEMBOURG

LIECHENSTEIN

BELGIUM

NORWEGIAN SEA

NORWAY

SWEDEN

FINLAND

Lake Onega

R U S S I A N

F E D E R A T I O N

Faeroes (Den.) *Törshavn*

Lake Ladoga

UNITED KINGDOM

Shetland

Oslo▪

Helsinki▪

Stockholm▪

Tallinn

Gulf of Finland

Rybinsk Res.

Moscow▪

Orkney

N O R T H

Skagerrak

Kattegat

DENMARK

Vättern

ESTONIA

Lake Peipus

Gulf of Bothnia

Baltic Sea

Riga▪

LATVIA

KAZAKHSTAN

REP. OF IRELAND

I. of Man

Dublin▪

S E A

Copenhagen▪

Gotland

Öland

LITHUANIA

RUS. FED.

Vilnius▪

Minsk▪

London▪

NETHERLANDS

Amsterdam▪

The Hague▪

Berlin▪

BELARUS

English Channel

Brussels▪

GERMANY

Bonn▪

POLAND

Warsaw▪

Channel Is

BELGIUM

LUXEMBOURG

Luxembourg▪

Prague▪

Paris▪

CZECH REP.

UKRAINE

Kiev▪

Bay of Biscay

FRANCE

Vienna▪

Carpathian Mts.

SLOVAKIA

Bratislava▪

LIECHTEN-STEIN

AUSTRIA

MOLDOVA

Pyrenees

SWITZERLAND

Bern▪

HUNGARY

Budapest▪

Chisinau▪

A L P S

Ljubljana▪

ROMANIA

Sea of Azov

SLOVENIA

Zagreb▪

Crimea

Caucasus

MONACO

CROATIA

SAN MARINO

BOSNIA-HERZ.

Belgrade▪

Bucharest▪

Black Sea

GEORGIA

PORTUGAL

Andorra ANDORRA

Sarajevo▪

YUGO-SLAVIA

AZERBAIJAN

ARMENIA

▪Lisbon

ITALY

Adriatic Sea

BULGARIA

AZER.

Madrid▪

Corsica

Rome▪

Sofia▪

S P A I N

Balearic Islands

Menorca

Ibiza *Mallorca*

Sardinia

Skopje▪

Tirana▪

MACEDONIA

Istanbul▪

Sea of Marmara

Ankara▪

Str. of Gibraltar

M E D

ALBANIA

Aegean Sea

T U R K E Y

Corfu

GREECE

Sicily

Ionian Sea

Athens▪

Caspian Sea

Valletta▪

MALTA

Crete

Rhodes **CYPRUS** Nicosia▪

R A N E A N S E A

■ EUROPEAN FREE TRADE ASSOCIATION (EFTA)

Founded in 1960 by the Stockholm Convention, the original members were Austria, Denmark, Norway, Portugal, Sweden, Switzerland and the United Kingdom. Denmark and the United Kingdom left in 1972 to join the EU, as did Portugal in 1985. The original objectives were to eliminate tariffs and other trade restrictions between members, and to create a free-trade area throughout Western Europe. The formation of the EEA virtually achieves this.

Headquarters : Geneva, Switzerland

EUROPEAN ECONOMIC AREA (EEA)

On 1 January 1994 the EU nations and the EFTA nations (except Liechtenstein, who later joined in April 1995), formed the European Economic Area, the World's largest multi-lateral trading area.

■ EUROPEAN UNION (EU)

Originally the European Economic Community, founded by the Treaty of Rome in 1957, which was signed by Belgium, France, West Germany, Italy, Luxembourg and the Netherlands. Denmark, the Republic of Ireland and the United Kingdom joined in 1973; Greece joined in 1981 and Spain and Portugal in 1986; the former East Germany became a part of the EU following the reunification of Germany in October 1990. The objectives, under the Treaty of Rome, are to lay the foundations of an ever closer union among the peoples of Europe, and to ensure economic and social progress.

Headquarters : Brussels, Belgium

■ COMMONWEALTH OF INDEPENDENT STATES (CIS)

Established by the Minsk Agreement signed by Belarus, the Russian Federation and Ukraine on 8 December 1991 following the collapse of the U.S.S.R. The Alma-Ata Declaration was signed on 21 December 1991 by these countries and Armenia, Kazakhstan, Kyrgyzstan, Moldova, Tajikistan, Turkmenistan and Uzbekistan; Azerbaijan also signed the declaration but did not formally join until September 1993; Georgia was admitted in December 1993.

Headquarters : Minsk, Belarus

see map above

BELARUS

UKRAINE

MOLDOVA

GEORGIA

AZERBAIJAN

ARMENIA

RUSSIAN FEDERATION

KAZAKHSTAN

UZBEKISTAN

KYRGYZSTAN

TAJIKISTAN

TURKMENISTAN

■ ORGANIZATION FOR ECONOMIC CO-OPERATION AND DEVELOPMENT (OECD)

Established in 1961 as the successor to the Organization for European Economic Co-operation (OEEC) which was set up in 1948 to administer the Marshall Plan for the post-World War II reconstruction of Europe, the OECD's objective is to promote economic and social welfare throughout the OECD area. It does this by assisting member governments in the formulation and co-ordination of policies to meet this objective; it also aims to stimulate and harmonise members' efforts in favour of developing countries.

Headquarters : Paris, France

CANADA

U.S.A.

MEXICO

ICELAND

IRELAND

PORTUGAL

SPAIN

NORWAY

U.K.

FRANCE

NETH.

BELG.

LUX.

SWITZ.

ITALY

GREECE

FINLAND

SWEDEN

DENMARK

GERMANY

AUSTRIA

TURKEY

JAPAN

AUSTRALIA

NEW ZEALAND

© HarperCollinsPublishers

KEY TO MAPS

- Built-up areas
- Park or open space
- Open water
- Important building
- Cemetery
- Lake
- River or canal
- Main road
- Road
- Other road
- Railway
- Airport

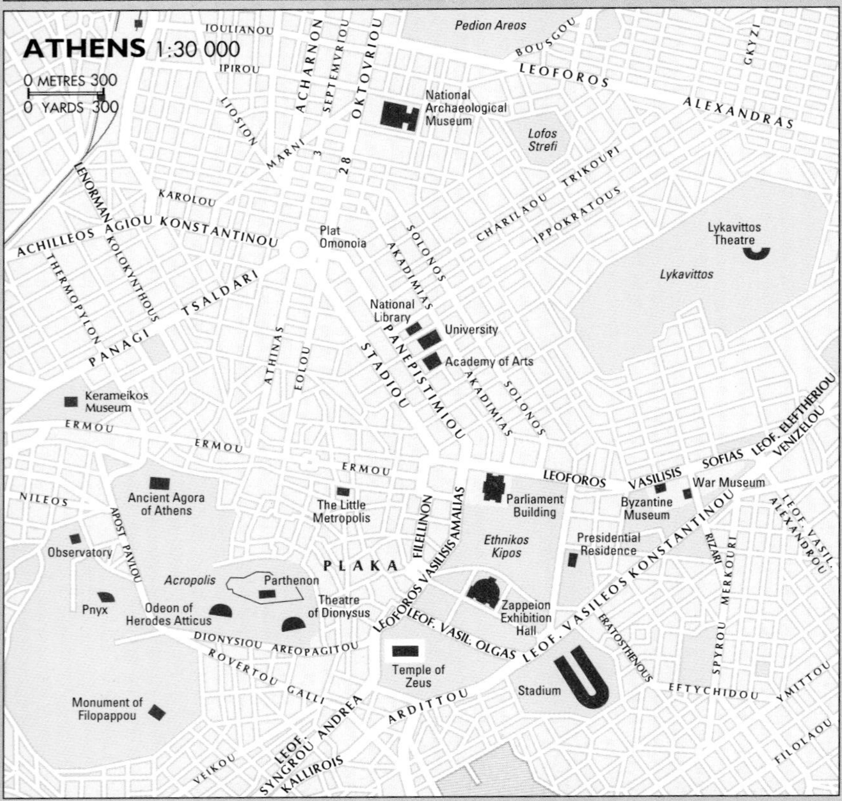

Map locator labels: St Petersburg, Moscow, London, Amsterdam, Berlin, Brussels, Paris, Vienna, Madrid, Rome, Athens

AMSTERDAM 1:25 000

0 METRES 250
0 YARDS 250

Het IJ, IJhaven, Openhaven, PRINS HENDRIKKADE, DE RUIJTERKADE, PIET HIENKADE, Dijksgracht, Oosterdok, Centraal Station, Museum Amstelkring, PRINS HENDRIKKADE, Ned. Scheepvaartmuseum, Entrepotdok, Nieuwe Vaart, Artis, PLANTAGE MIDDENLAAN, Hortus Botanicus, Mozes-en Aaronkerk, Heren, VALKENBURGERSTRAAT, Rembrandthuis, Stadhuis en Muziektheater, Amstel, Nieuwe, MACERE BRUG, Amstelstraat, Nieuwe Keizers, SARPHATIKADE, Prinsengr, KOKTERKADE, SARPHATISTRAAT, MAURITSKADE, WIBAUTSTRAAT, OOST, WESPERZIDE, Singelgracht, STADHOUDERSKADE, WETERINGSCHANS, WETERINGSCHANS, OUD ZUID, MUSEUM STRAAT, Rijksmuseum, Van Gogh Museum, JAN LUIJKENSTRAAT, STADHOUDERSKADE, Vondelpark, MARNIXSTRAAT, Singel, Heregracht, Keizersgracht, Prinsengracht, LEIDSESTRAAT, Bijbels Museum, Madame Tussaud, Allard Pierson Museum, Amsterdams Historisch Museum, Koninklijk Paleis, Nationaal Monument, ROKIN, KALVERSTRAAT, NIEUWEZIJDS VOORBURGWAL, DAMRAK, CENTRUM, Nieuwe Kerk, Oude Kerk, Waaggebouw, Koninklijk Paleis, RAADHUISSTRAAT, Westerkerk, Anne Frankhuis, ROZEN GRACHT, Haarlem gracht, Eilandsgracht, Oudeschans, Rotes, Nieuwe Keizers

ATHENS 1:30 000

0 METRES 300
0 YARDS 300

TOULIOU, ACHARNON, SEPTEMVRIOU, OKTOVRIOU, Pedion Areos, BOUSGOU, GYZI, IPIROU, LEOFOROS, ALEXANDRAS, National Archaeological Museum, KAROLOU, MARNI, Lofos Strefi, Lykavittos Theatre, LIOSION, CHARILAOU TRIKOUPI, IPPOKRATOUS, Lykavittos, ACHILLEOS, AGIOU KONSTANTINOU, SOLONOS, AKADIMIAS, Plat Omonola, National Library, University, Academy of Arts, THERMOPYLON, PANAGI TSALDARI, ATHINAS, STADIOU, PANEPISTIMIOU, SOLONOS, AKADIMIAS, ERMOU, Kerameikos Museum, ERMOU, ERMOU, VASILISSIS SOFIAS, VENIZELOU, War Museum, Byzantine Museum, Parliament Building, Presidential Residence, Ancient Agora of Athens, The Little Metropolis, Ethnikos Kipos, NILEOS, APOST PAVLOU, Observatory, Acropolis, Parthenon, Pnyx, Odeon of Herodes Atticus, Theatre of Dionysus, Zappeion Exhibition Hall, Temple of Zeus, Stadium, Monument of Filopappou, DIONYSIOU AREOPAGITOU, ROVERTOU GALLI, VEIROU, LEOF SYNGROU ANDREA, KALLIROIS, ARDITTOU, TILOLAOU, EFTYCHIDOU, YMITTOU, PLAKA, LEOFOROS, VASILISSIS, AMALIAS, FILELLINON, LEOF VASIL OLGAS, LEOT VASILEOS KONSTANTINOU, ERATOSTHENOUS, SPYROU MERKOURI, LEOT VASIL, ALEXANDROU

BERLIN 1:65 000

0 METRES 650
0 YARDS 650

Schiffahrtskanal, SELLER STRASSE, CHAUSSEESTRASSE, Museum für Naturk. und Zoologischer, MOABIT, ALT-MOABIT, Spree, Lehrter Bahnhof, INVALIDENSTRASSE, Museuminsel, Humboldt Universität, Staats- bibliothek, Rotes Rathaus, BEUSSELSTRASSE, Kongress-halle, Reichstag, Akademie der Künste, Schloss Bellevue, Brandenburg Tor, UNTER DEN LINDEN, Staats Oper, St Hedwigs Kathedrale, Nikolaikirche, OTTO-SUHR-ALLEE, STRASSE DES 17 JUNI, Siegessäule, TIERGARTEN, Technische Universität, Schiller Theater, Hochschule f. Musik, Philharmonie, Neue Nationalgalerie, Staatsbibliothek, Anhalter Bahnhof, BISMARCKSTRASSE, CHARLOTTENBURG, KANTSTRASSE, Zoologischer Garten, Aquarium, Europa Center, Landwehrkanal, Berlin Museum, KURFÜRSTENDAMM, LIETZENBURGER, STRASSE, KLEIST-STRASSE, POTSDAMER STRASSE, BÜLOWSTRASSE, HALLESCHES UFER, GITSCHINER STRASSE, WILMERSDORF, Bundeshaus, Amerika Gedenk Bibliothek, HOHENZOLLERNDAMM, YORCKSTRASSE, GNEISENAUSTRASSE, KREUZBERG, BUNDESALLEE, SCHÖNEBERG, HAUPTSTRASSE, Rathaus Schöneberg, TEMPELHOF, BAB RING BERLIN (WEST), Schöneberg Sporthalle, Zentralflughafen Tempelhof

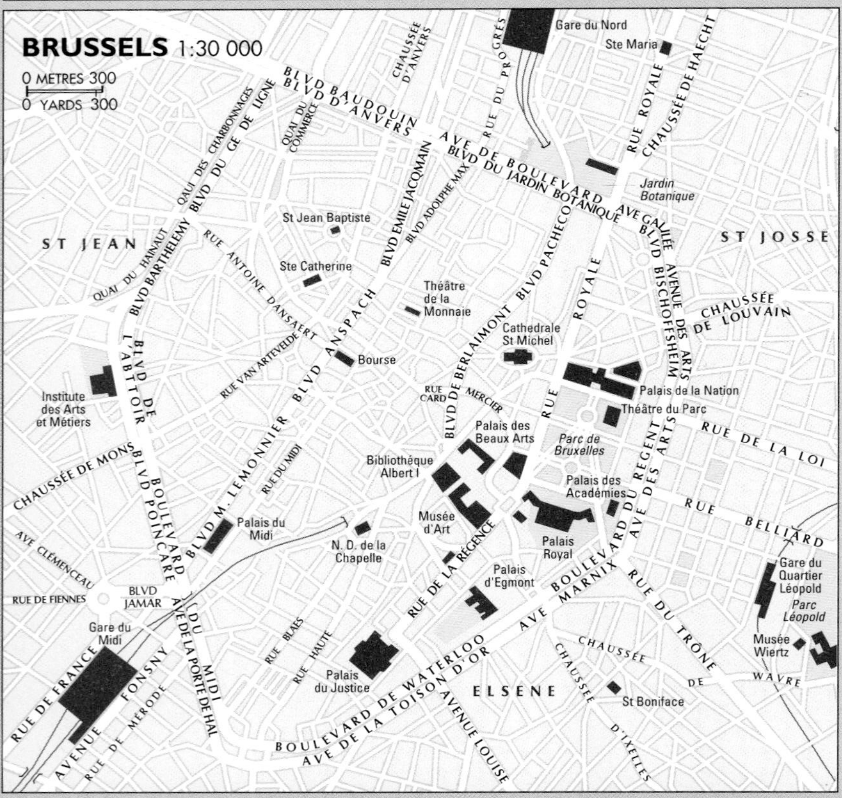

BRUSSELS 1:30 000

0 METRES 300
0 YARDS 300

Gare du Nord, Ste Marie, CHAUSSÉE D'ANVERS, BLVD BAUDOUIN, BLVD ANVERS, RUE ROYALE, CHAUSSÉE DE HAECHT, QUAI DU COMMERCE, AVE DU BOULEVARD, AVE DU JARDIN BOTANIQUE, Jardin Botanique, ST JOSSE, BLVD EMILE JACQMAIN, BLVD ADOLPHE MAX, GALERIE DU PROGRÈS, AVENUE DES ARTS, CHAUSSÉE DE LOUVAIN, ST JEAN, St Jean Baptiste, Ste Catherine, RUE ANTOINE DANSAERT, Théâtre de la Monnaie, Bourse, Cathédrale St Michel, BLVD DE BERLAIMONT, BLVD PACHECO, RUE ROYALE, Théâtre du Parc, Palais de la Nation, QUAI DU HAINAUT, BLVD BARTHELEMY, Institute des Arts et Métiers, Palais des Beaux Arts, Parc de Bruxelles, Palais des Académies, RUE DE LA LOI, RUE BELLIARD, Bibliothèque Albert I, Musée d'Art, RUE DE LA RÉGENCE, Palais Royal, Parc de Léopold, RUE DE LA REGENCE, N. D. de la Chapelle, Palais d'Egmont, Musée Wiertz, BLVD DE L'ABATTOIR, Palais du Midi, BLVD M. LEMONNIER, BLVD POINCARÉ, CHAUSSÉE DE MONS, Palais du Justice, St Boniface, Gare du Quartier Léopold, AVE MARNIX, AVE DES ARTS, RUE DU TRÔNE, CHAUSSÉE DE WAVRE, ELSENE, BLVD JAMAR, Gare du Midi, RUE DE FIENNES, RUE DE FRANCE, AVE FONSNY, AVE DE LA PORTE HAL, BOULEVARD DE WATERLOO, AVE DE LA TOISON D'OR, AVENUE LOUISE, AVE CLÉMENCEAU, D'IXELLES

LONDON 1:100 000

0 METRES 1000
0 YARDS 1000

HIGHBURY, HAMPSTEAD, CAMDEN RD, KINGSLAND ROAD, KILBURN, ST JOHN'S WOOD, London Zoo, St Pancras Station, Kings Cross Station, SHOREDITCH, PRINCE ALBERT ROAD, Lord's Cricket Ground, Regent's Park, Euston Station, British Museum Library, Smithfield Market, Liverpool St Sta., HARROW ROAD, WESTWAY, Marylebone Station, HOLBORN, St. Paul's Cathedral, Fenchurch St Station, PADDINGTON, Paddington Station, A40(M), NOTTING HILL, BAYSWATER ROAD, Hyde Park, Charing Cross Sta., The Tower, Kensington Palace, Kensington Gardens, PICCADILLY, St. James's Palace, SOUTHWARK, London Bridge Sta., Holland Park, KENSINGTON, Albert Hall, Nat. History Mus., Victoria & Albert Mus., Green Park, Buckingham Palace, Westminster Abbey, Houses of Parliament, Waterloo Station, CROMWELL ROAD, Olympia, Victoria Station, Imperial War Museum, BERMONDSEY, OLD KENT RD, EARLS COURT, Earls Court Exhibition Centre, Tate Gallery, LAMBETH, CHELSEA, Chelsea Bridge, The Oval, Burgess Park, Football Stadium, KING'S ROAD, Battersea Park, CAMBERWELL, PECKHAM RD, Football Stadium, Putney Bridge, PARSONS GREEN, Thames, Clapham Junction, Clapham Common, CLAPHAM, BRIXTON, Ruskin Park, Peckham, BRIXTON ROAD

© HarperCollinsPublishers

MADRID 1:25 000

0 METRES 250
0 YARDS 250

Parque de la Montaña · Estación del Norte · CUESTA DE SAN VICENTE · Palacio Real · Campo del Moro · Nuestra Señora de la Almudena · PASEO DE LA VIRGEN DEL PUERTO · Teatro Real · Plaza Mayor · CALLE MAYOR · San Francisco el Grande · CALLE DE TOLEDO · RONDA DE SEGOVIA · PASEO IMPERIAL · PASEO DE LOS PONTONES · CALLE DE SEGOVIA · CENTRO · Palacio del Senado · Palacio de Buenavista · GRAN VIA · GRAN VIA · Congreso · Real Academia de Belles Artes · Circulo de Bellas Artes · CALLE DE ALCALA · Puerta de Alcalá · Palacio de Comunicaciones · Bolsa · Palacio de Villahermosa · Museo del Prado · Museo Municipal · Palacio de Justicia · Biblioteca Nacional · Museo Arqueológico National · PASEO DE RECOLETOS · PASEO DE LA CASTELLANA · CALLE GENOVA · San Isidro · CALLE DE LAS HUERTAS · CALLE DE LA MAGDALENA · CALLE DE ATOCHA · Centro de Arte Reina Sofía · RONDA DE ATOCHA · RONDA DE TOLEDO · PASEO DE SANTA MARIA DE LA CABEZA · Jardín Botánico · Estación Atocha · CALLE DE ARGUMOSA · CALLE DE MENDEZ ALVARO

MOSCOW 1:70 000

0 METRES 700
0 YARDS 700

Puppet Theatre · Yaroslavl' Station · Leningrad Station · Kazan' Station · Old Moscow Circus · Biological Museum · Zoo Park · Planetarium · Chekhov Museum · Museum of Revolution · Bol'shoy Theatre · Polytechnical Museum · Kursk Station · World Trade Centre · Krasnaya Presnya Park · Pushkin Museum · Historical Museum · G.U.M. · Lenin's Tomb · St Basil's Cath. · Red Square · Central Concert Hall · Library of Foreign Literature · Military Academy · Kiyev Station · Tolstoy Museum · Art Gallery · Novospasskiy Monastery · Novodevichiy Convent · Gor'kiy Park · Pavelets Station · Lenin Central Stadium · Donskoy Monastery

PARIS 1:100 000

0 METRES 1000
0 YARDS 1000

ASNIÈRES-S.-SEINE · CLICHY · ST OUEN · LA PLAINE-ST-DENIS · COURBEVOIE · BÉCON-LES-BRUYÈRES · LA DÉFENSE · LEVALLOIS-PERRET · VILLIERS · LE PARC · NEUILLY-S.-SEINE · MONTMARTRE · Sacré-Coeur · LA CHAPELLE · Gare du Nord · Gare de l'Est · BELLVILLE · Parc des Buttes Chaumont · LES BATIGNOLLES · Gare St-Lazare · Opéra · Arc de Triomphe · Place Charles de Gaulle · AVENUE DES CHAMPS-ELYSÉES · Grand Palais · Palais Royal · Louvre · Place de la Concorde · Centre Pompidou · Hôtel de Ville · Place de la République · Place de la Bastille · Bois de Boulogne · Hippodrome d'Auteuil · PASSY · Palais de Chaillot · Tour Eiffel · Musée d'Orsay · Ile de la Cité · Notre-Dame · RIVOLI · AUTEUIL · Invalides · Chambre des Députés · Panthéon · Jardin des Plantes · Gare de Lyon · Palais d'Austerlitz · Palais des Omnisports de Bercy · GRENELLE · Palais du Luxembourg · Gare Montparnasse · VAUGIRARD · Gare Place d'Italie · BOULOGNE-BILLANCOURT · Héliport · VANVES · MALAKOFF · Cité universitaire · Ile St-Germain · QUAI DE STALINGRAD · AVENUE DE VERDUN · BOULEVARD BRUNE · AVE D'ITALIE

ROME 1:40 000

0 METRES 400
0 YARDS 400

Stazione Roma-Viterbo · Villa Borghese · SOLARIO · CORSO D'ITALIA · Piazza del Popolo · Trinità dei Monti · XX SETTEMBRE · Museo Nazionale Romano · Museo Vaticani · Città del Vaticano · Castel Sant'Angelo · Palazzo Barberini · Terme di Diocleziano · Stazione Centrale · Basilica di San Pietro · Fontana di Trevi · Palazzo del Quirinale · VIA NAZIONALE · Santa Maria Maggiore · Piazza Navona · Pantheon · Vittoriano · VIA CAVOUR · Villa Abamelek · Palazzo Corsini · Teatro di Marcello · Foro Romano · Colosseo · Arco di Costantino · TRASTEVERE · Santa Maria in Trastevere · Mte Palatino · Circo Massimo · VIA LABICANA · Villa Sciarra · Parco di Porta Capena · Terme di Caracalla

St PETERSBURG 1:100 000

0 METRES 1000
0 YARDS 1000

PRIMORSKIY PROSPEKT · PROSPEKT MARSHALA ZHUKOVA · Yelagin Palace · Elagin Ostrov · Kamennyy Ostrov · Aptekarskiy Ostrov · Primorskij Park Pobedy · Kirov Stadium · Kirovskiye Ostrova · STOYKA · Botanical Museum · Petrovskiy Ostrov · Petrogradskiy Ostrov · Planetarium · SVERDLOVSKAYA NAB · Finland Station · Artillery Museum · Peter and Paul Fortress · Smol'nyy Monastery · Dekabristov Ostrov · ARSENAL'NAYA NAB · Smol'nyy Institute · Lenin Stadium · The Hermitage & Winter Palace · Summer Palace · Tauride Palace · Russian Museum · State University · Academy of Arts · Admiralty · Bronze Horseman · Kazan Cathedral · Gostinyy Dvor · Moscow Station · Vasil'yevskiy Ostrov · Smolenskoye Cemetery · St Isaac's Cathedral · Saltykov-Shchedrin Library · Marinskiy Theatre · St Nicolas Cathedral · Vitebsk Station · NEVSKIY PROSPEKT · Belyy Ostrov · Gutuevskij Ostrov · Kanonerskij Ostrov · Baltic Station · Warsaw Station · Narva Triumphal Arch · Moscow Triumphal Arch · Aleksandr Nevskiy Monastery · Volkovskoye Lyuteranskoye Cemetery · SMOLENSKOYE · VOLKOVO

VIENNA 1:25 000

0 METRES 250
0 YARDS 250

Votiv-Kirche · Börse · Börseplatz · Dianabad · UNIVERSITÄTSSTRASSE · Universität · Museum für Volkskunde · Schottenstift · Kirche Maria am Gestade · Ruprechts-Kirche · Urania · Schönborn-park · Landesgericht · Rathaus · Rathaus Park · Burgtheater · Kirche Am Hof · Uhrenmuseum · Kammeroper · MARIA-THERESIEN-STR · SCHOTTENRING · OBERE DONAU-STR. · FRANZ-JOSEFS-KAI · PRATERSTRASSE · Maria-Treu-Kloster · Theater in der Josefstadt · JOSEFSTADT · Palais Liechtenstein · Peters-Kirche · Stephans-Kirche · Erzbischöfliches Palais · Akademie der Wissenschaft · Dominikaner-Kirche · Museum für angewandte Kunst · JOSEFSTÄDTER STRASSE · STADIONGASSE · Parlament · Michaeler-platz · Michaeler-Kirche · Franziskaner-Kirche · Deutschordens-Kirche · Palais Auersperg · Volksgarten · Hofburg · Neue Burg · Burggarten · Malteser-Kirche · Anna-Kirche · Ursulinen-Kirche · St-Ulrichs-Kirche · NEUSTIFTGASSE · BURGGASSE · Justizpalast · Heldenplatz · Burgtor · Naturhist. Museum · Kunsthist. Museum · Staatsoper · OPERNRING · Kapuziner-Kirche · Stadtpark · Kursalon · Beethoven Denkmal · NEUBAU · Messepalast · Renaissance-Bühne · Stiftskirche · Akademie der bildenden Künste · KÄRNTNERRING · SCHUBERTRING · Musikverein · Konzerthaus · Am Modenapark · MARIAHILF · Maria-Hilf Kirche · Theater an der Wien · Karls-Kirche · KARLSPLATZ · Hist. Museum der Stadt Wien · Technische Universität · SCHWARZENBERGPLATZ · Schwarzenberggarten · NEULING-GASSE · Esterhazy-park · Alfred Grünwald Park · GUMPENDORFER STR · LINKE WIENZEILE · RECHTE WIENZEILE · LOTHRINGER STRASSE · PRINZ-EUGEN-STRASSE · WIEDEN · Palais Schwarzenberg · Unteres Belvedere · Oberes Belvedere · Theresianum · Botanischer Garten · Botanisches Institut · Bahnhof Wien-Mitte · AM HEUMARKT · Bahnhof Rennweg · MAYERHOF-GASSE

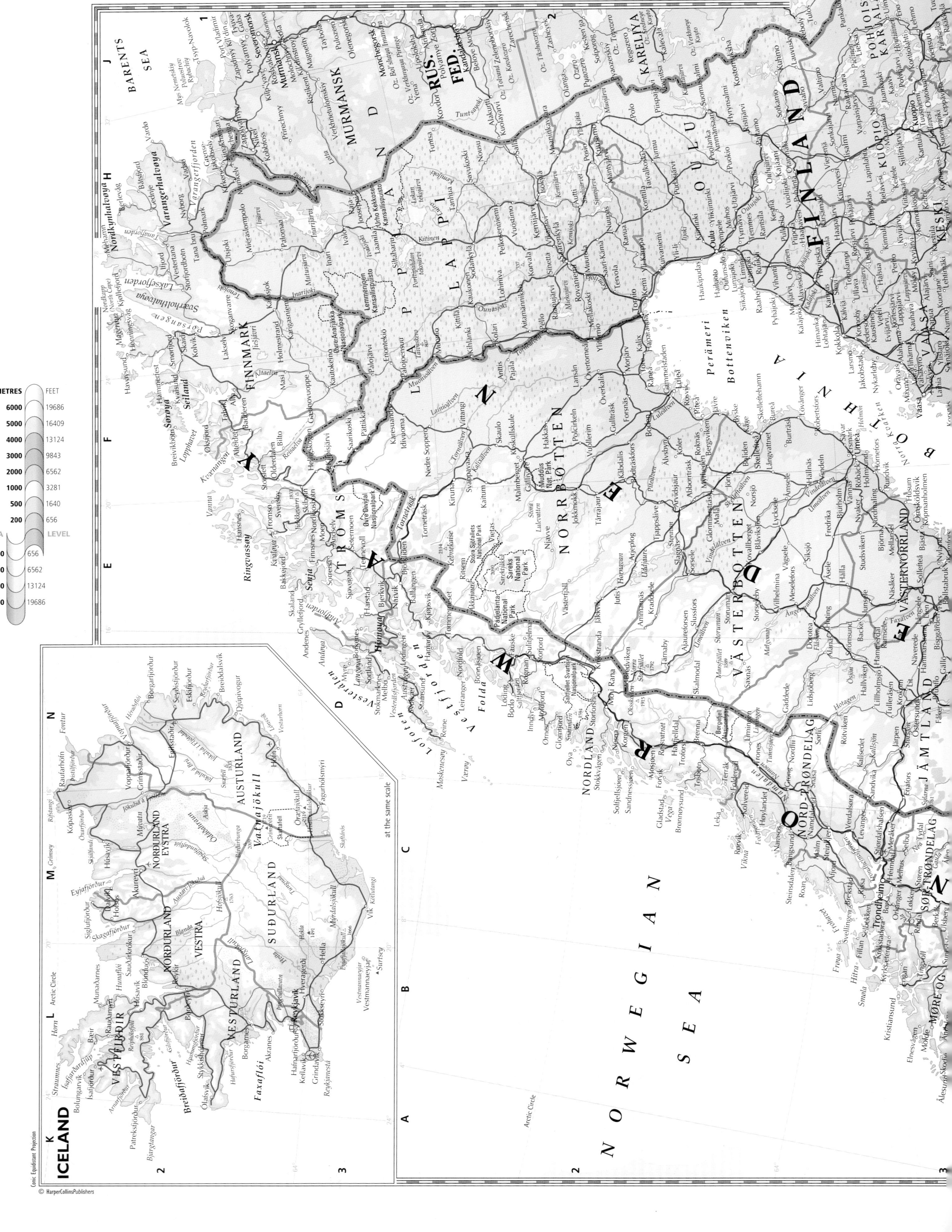

BARENTS SEA

RUS. FED.

MURMANSK

LAPLAND

FINNMARK

FINLAND

OULU

KARELIYA

KUOPIO

POHJOIS-KARJALA

KESKI

VARSINAIS-SUOMI

TROMS

NORRBOTTEN

VÄSTERBOTTEN

VÄSTERNORRLAND

NORDLAND

NORD-TRØNDELAG

SØR-TRØNDELAG

JÄMTLAND

MØRE OG

NORWEGIAN SEA

Arctic Circle

METRES FEET
6000 19686
5000 16409
4000 13124
3000 9843
2000 6562
1000 3281
500 1640
200 656
SEA LEVEL
200 656
2000 6562
4000 13124
6000 19686

ICELAND

VESTFIRÐIR

NORÐURLAND VESTRA

NORÐURLAND EYSTRA

AUSTURLAND

VESTURLAND

SUÐURLAND

Vatnajökull

Reykjavík

Conic Equidistant Projection

at the same scale

© HarperCollins Publishers

1:4 000 000

| 0 | 25 | 50 | 75 | 100 | 125 | 150 MILES |

| 0 | 50 | 100 | 150 | 200 | 250 KM |

1:6 000 000

0   40   80   120   160   200 MILES
0   40   80   120   160   200   240   280   320 KM

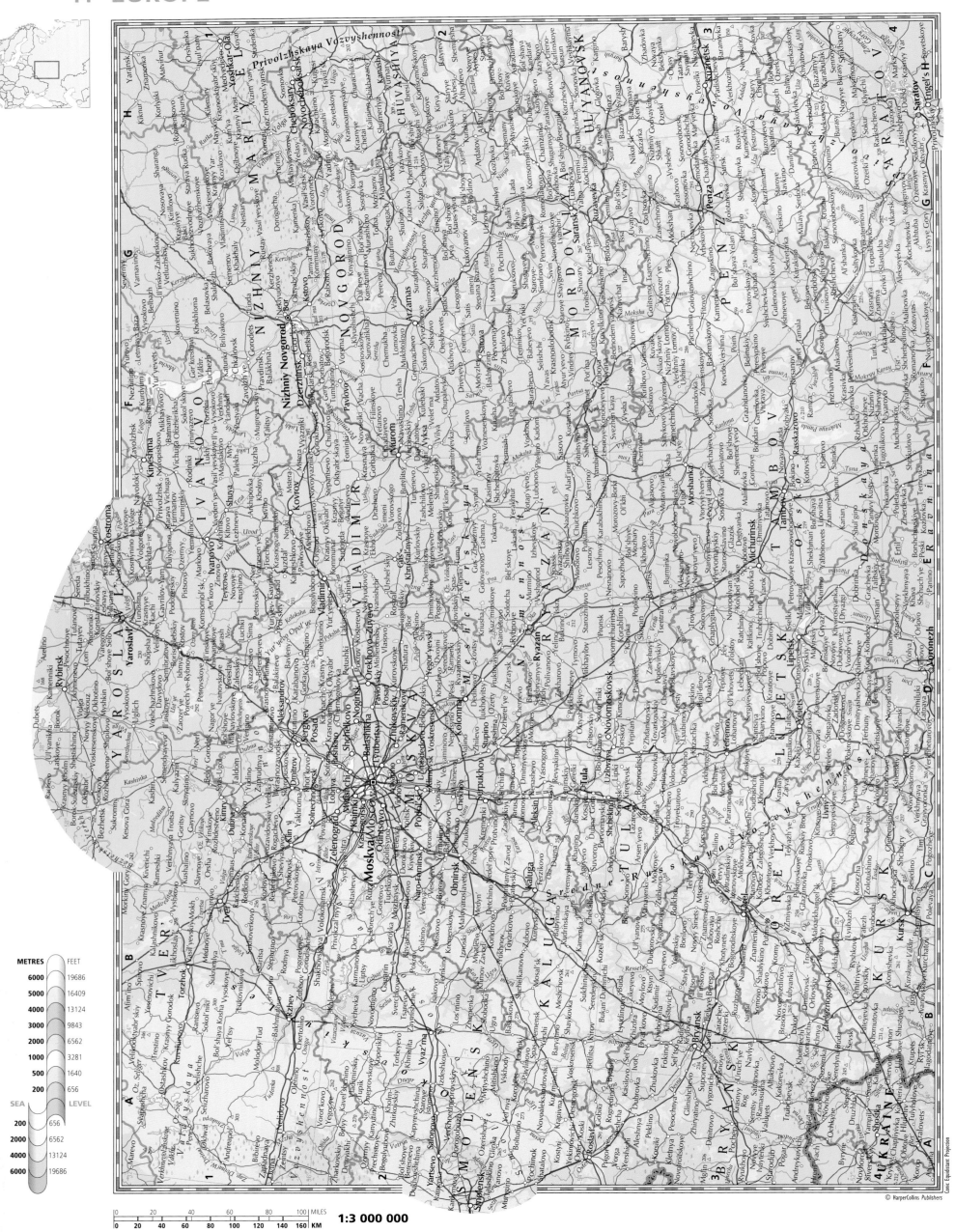

1:3 000 000

RUSSIAN FEDERATION

BELARUS

UKRAINE

MOLDOVA (MOLDAVIA)

ROMANIA

Black Sea

Sea of Azov

Regions / oblasts labelled: KURSK · BELGOROD · KHARKIV · DONETS'K · ZAPORIZHZHYA · SUMY · POLTAVA · DNIPROPETROVS'K · KHERSON · CHERNIHIV · KYIV · CHERKASY · KIROVOHRAD · MYKOLAYIV · ODESA · ZHYTOMYR · VINNYTSYA · BREST · HOMEL' · VOLYN' · RIVNE · L'VIV · TERNOPIL' · IVANO-FRANKIVS'K · KHMEL'NYTS'KYY · CHERNIVTSI · CARPATHIAN MTS

Major cities: Kharkiv · Donets'k · Mariupol' · Berdyans'k · Melitopol' · Zaporizhzhya · Dnipropetrovs'k · Kryvyy Rih · Kherson · Mykolayiv · Odesa · Kirovohrad · Cherkasy · Poltava · Sumy · Chernihiv · Kyiv (Kiev) · Zhytomyr · Vinnytsya · Rivne · Ternopil' · L'viv · Ivano-Frankivs'k · Chernivtsi · Chişinău · Tiraspol · Tighina (Bender) · Iaşi · Bacău

Conic Equidistant Projection

© HarperCollins Publishers

1:3 000 000

METRES		FEET
6000		19686
5000		16409
4000		13124
3000		9843
2000		6562
1000		3281
500		1640
200		656
SEA LEVEL		SEA LEVEL
200		656
2000		6562
4000		13124
6000		19686

MILES	0	20	40	60	80	100
KM	0	20 40 60 80 100 120 140 160				

NORWAY

SOGN OG FJORDANE
HORDALAND
Bergen
Oslo

Eidsen, Naustdal, Florø, Førde, Svelgen, Sandane, Stryn, Hornindal, Stadlandet, Ulstein, Måløy, Eikefjord, Stongfjorden, Askvoll, Hyllestad, Husøy, Sula, Hardbakke, Fedje, Radøy, Tjeldstø, Kleppestø, Flatøy, Fitjar, Store Sottra, Steinsland, Osøyro, Hufarøy, Bremnes, Langevåg, Ulsira, Åkrehamn, Skudeneshavn, Karmøy, Haugesund, Kopervik, Grindavik, Suldal, Sveio, Stord, Bømlo

FAEROES (FØROYAR)
(Denmark)

Eiði, Mikladalur, Klaksvik, Borðoy, Fuglafjørður, Viðareiði, Streymoy, Vestmanna, Eysturoy, Nólsoy, Tórshavn, Skopun, Vágar, Sørvágur, Sandoy, Hvalba, Tvøroyri, Suðuroy, Sumba, Skúvoy, Dímunarfjørður, Húsavik

NORTH SEA

ATLANTIC OCEAN

SCOTLAND

GRAMPIAN MOUNTAINS

Aberdeen, Dundee, Edinburgh, Glasgow, Paisley, Greenock, Falkirk, Dunfermline, Kirkcaldy, Leith, St Andrews, Arbroath, Montrose, Stonehaven, Inverbervie, Peterhead, Fraserburgh, Banff, Macduff, Elgin, Lossiemouth, Buckie, Keith, Huntly, Turriff, Inverurie, Stirling, Perth, Crieff, Callander, Dumbarton, Kilmarnock, Ayr, Largs, Rothesay, Dunoon

Inverness, Nairn, Forres, Grantown, Aviemore, Kingussie, Fort Augustus, Fort William, Mallaig, Kyle of Lochalsh, Broadford, Portree, Ullapool, Lochinver, Scourie, Durness, Cape Wrath, Tongue, Lairg, Bonar Bridge, Dornoch, Tain, Cromarty, Dingwall, Gairloch, Applecross, Stromeferry, Helmsdale, Brora, Golspie, Kinbrace, Thurso, Wick, Latheron, Lybster, John o' Groats, Dunnet Head, Duncansby Head

Grampian Mountains, Cairngorm Mts, Ben Nevis

Shetland Is
Herma Ness, Unst, Yell, Fetlar, Out Skerries, Whalsay, Isle of Noss, Bressay, Lerwick, Mainland, Scalloway, Sumburgh Head, Hillswick, Isbister, The Faither, Papa Stour, Fair Isle, Foula

Orkney Is
North Ronaldsay, Sanday, Stronsay, Auskerry, Westray, Papa Westray, Rousay, Shapinsay, Eday, Mainland, Kirkwall, Burwick, South Ronaldsay, St Margaret's Hope, Hoy, Stromness, Birsay, Pentland Firth

Outer Hebrides
Butt of Lewis, Stornoway, Lewis, Tarbert (An Tairbeart), Harris, Eilean Leòdhais, North Uist (Uibhist a Tuath), Benbecula (Beinn na Faoghla), South Uist (Uibhist a Deas), Barra, Eriskay, Flannan Is, St Kilda

Inner Hebrides
Skye, Raasay, Rum (Rùm), Eigg, Muck, Canna, Coll, Tiree, Mull, Tobermory, Iona, Colonsay, Jura, Islay, Gigha, Port Ellen, Port Askaig, Oban, Ardnamurchan, Point of Ardnamurchan

The Minch, Little Minch, Sea of the Hebrides

Loch Ness, Loch Lochy, Loch Linnhe, Loch Fyne, Loch Tay, Loch Rannoch, Loch Shin, Loch More, Loch Maree, Firth of Forth, Firth of Tay, Moray Firth, Dornoch Firth

Rona, Sula Sgeir, Sule Skerry, Sule Stack

Rockall

METRES	FEET
6000	19686
5000	16409
4000	13124
3000	9843
2000	6562
1000	3281
500	1640
200	656
SEA LEVEL	
200	656
2000	6562
4000	13124
6000	19686

at the same scale

Conic Equidistant Projection

© HarperCollins Publishers

1:3 000 000

|0 20 40 60 80 100 MILES|
|0 20 40 60 80 100 120 140 160 KM|

NETHERLANDS,

NORTH SEA

DENMARK

NETHERLANDS

BELGIUM

GERMANY

FRANCE

LUXEMBOURG

SWITZERLAND

ITALY

METRES		FEET
6000		19686
5000		16409
4000		13124
3000		9843
2000		6562
1000		3281
500		1640
200		656
SEA		LEVEL
200		656
2000		6562
4000		13124
6000		19686

Conic Equidistant Projection

© HarperCollinsPublishers

1:3 000 000

1:3 000 000

| 0 | 20 | 40 | 60 | 80 | 100 MILES |

| 0 | 20 | 40 | 60 | 80 | 100 | 120 | 140 | 160 KM |

Lambert Conformal Conic Projection

METRES | FEET
6000 | 19686
5000 | 16409
4000 | 13124
3000 | 9843
2000 | 6562
1000 | 3281
500 | 1640
200 | 656

SEA LEVEL

200 | 656
2000 | 6562
4000 | 13124
6000 | 19686

BAY OF BISCAY
(*MAR CANTÁBRICO*)

Costa Verde

A T L A N T I C

O C E A N

P O R T U G A L

S P A I N

METRES	FEET
6000	19686
5000	16409
4000	13124
3000	9843
2000	6562
1000	3281
500	1640
200	656
SEA	LEVEL
200	656
2000	6562
4000	13124
6000	19686

MADEIRA
(Portugal)

Ilha de Porto Santo
Porto Santo

Porto Moniz
Calheta
Ribeira Brava
Câmara de Lobos
Faial
Machico
Funchal

Ilha da Madeira

Ilhas Desertas
Deserta Grande
Bugio

at the same scale

Conic Equidistant Projection

© HarperCollinsPublishers

Costa de la Luz

GOLFO DE CÁDIZ

Costa del Sol

Strait of Gibraltar

MOROCCO

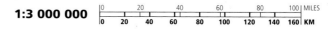

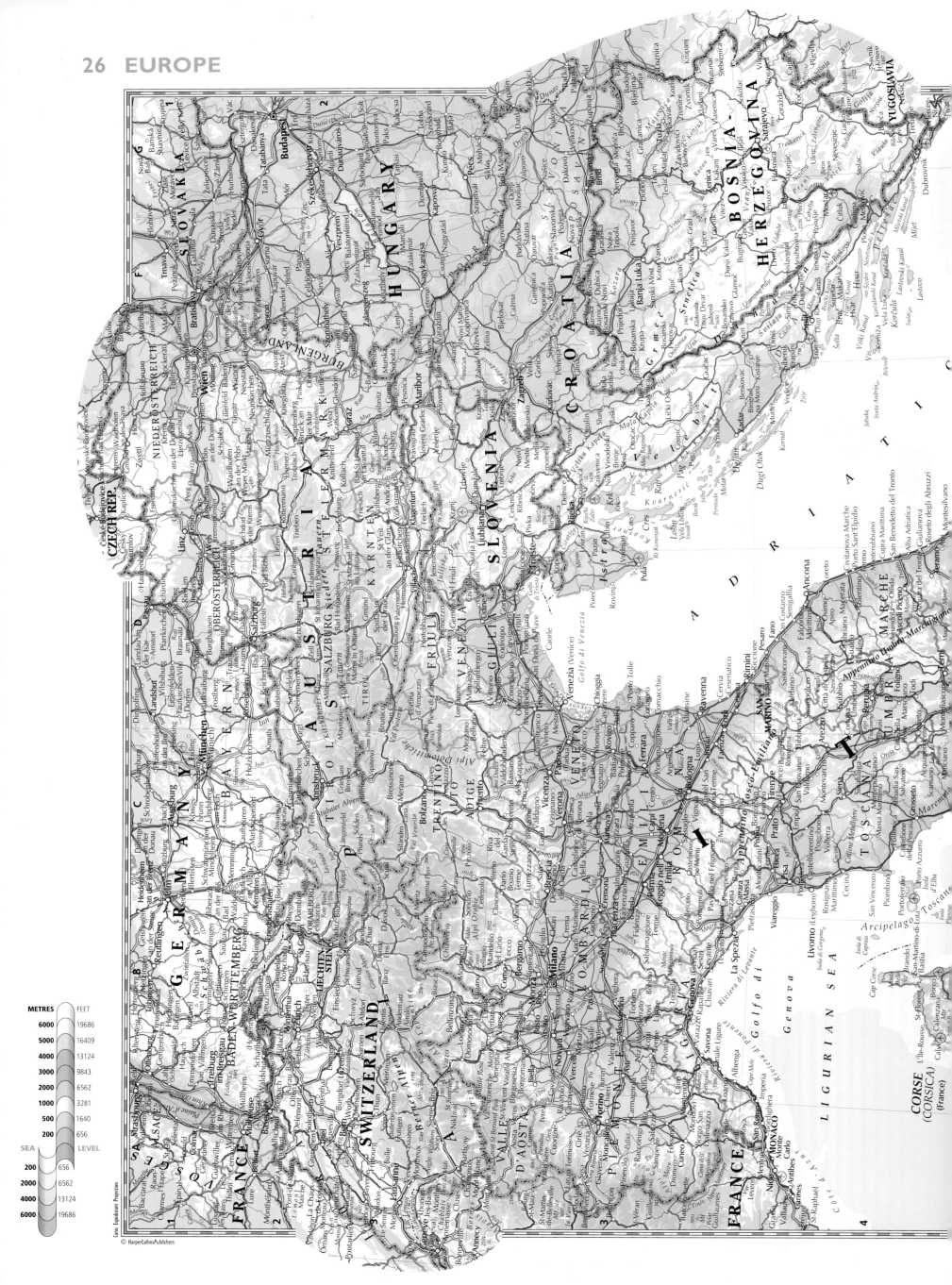

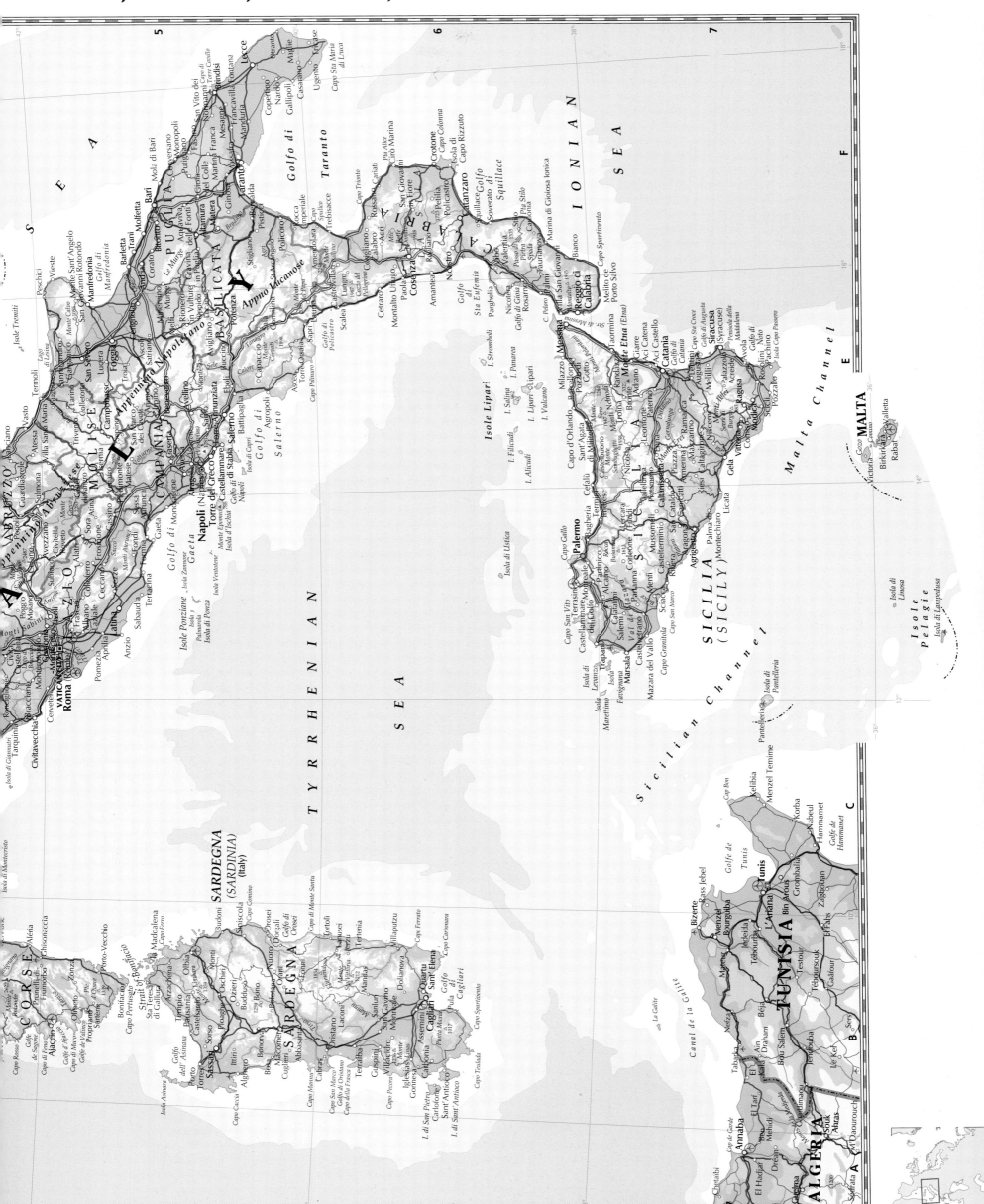

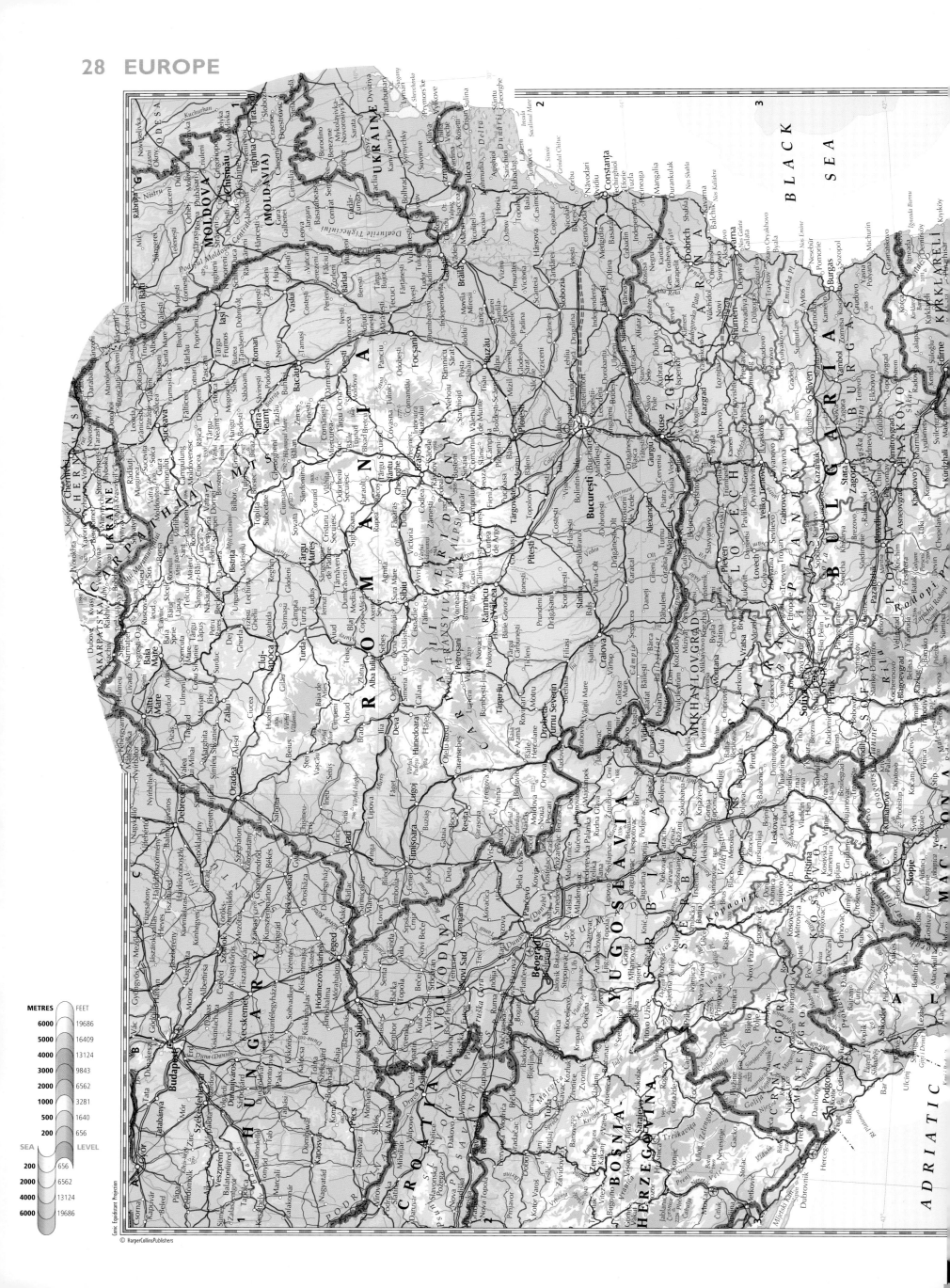

METRES | FEET
6000 | 19686
5000 | 16409
4000 | 13124
3000 | 9843
2000 | 6562
1000 | 3281
500 | 1640
200 | 656
SEA | LEVEL
200 | 656
2000 | 6562
4000 | 13124
6000 | 19686

Conic Equidistant Projection

© HarperCollinsPublishers

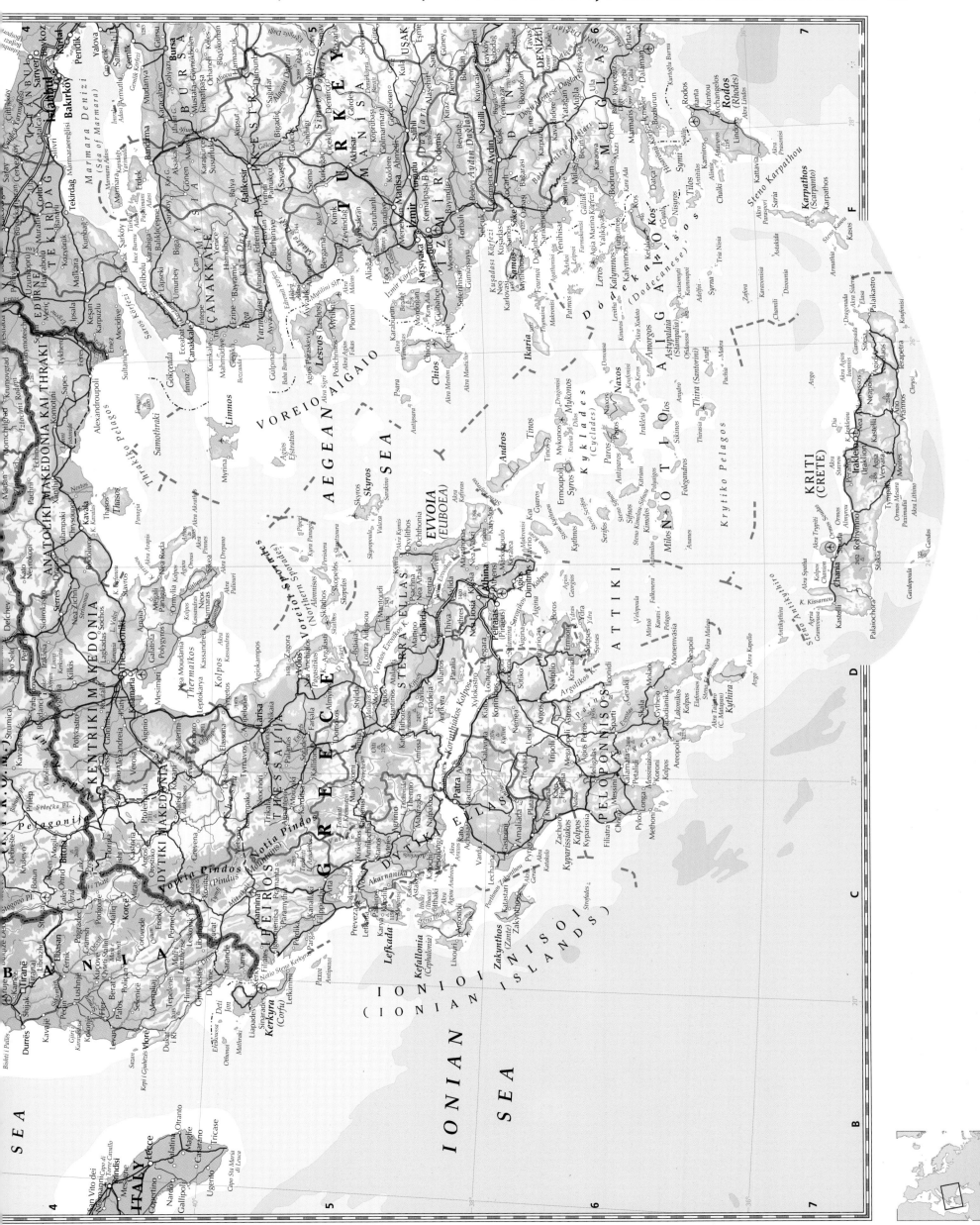

1:3 000 000

| | 0 | 20 | 40 | 60 | 80 | 100 | MILES |

| | 0 | 20 | 40 | 60 | 80 | 100 | 120 | 140 | 160 | KM |

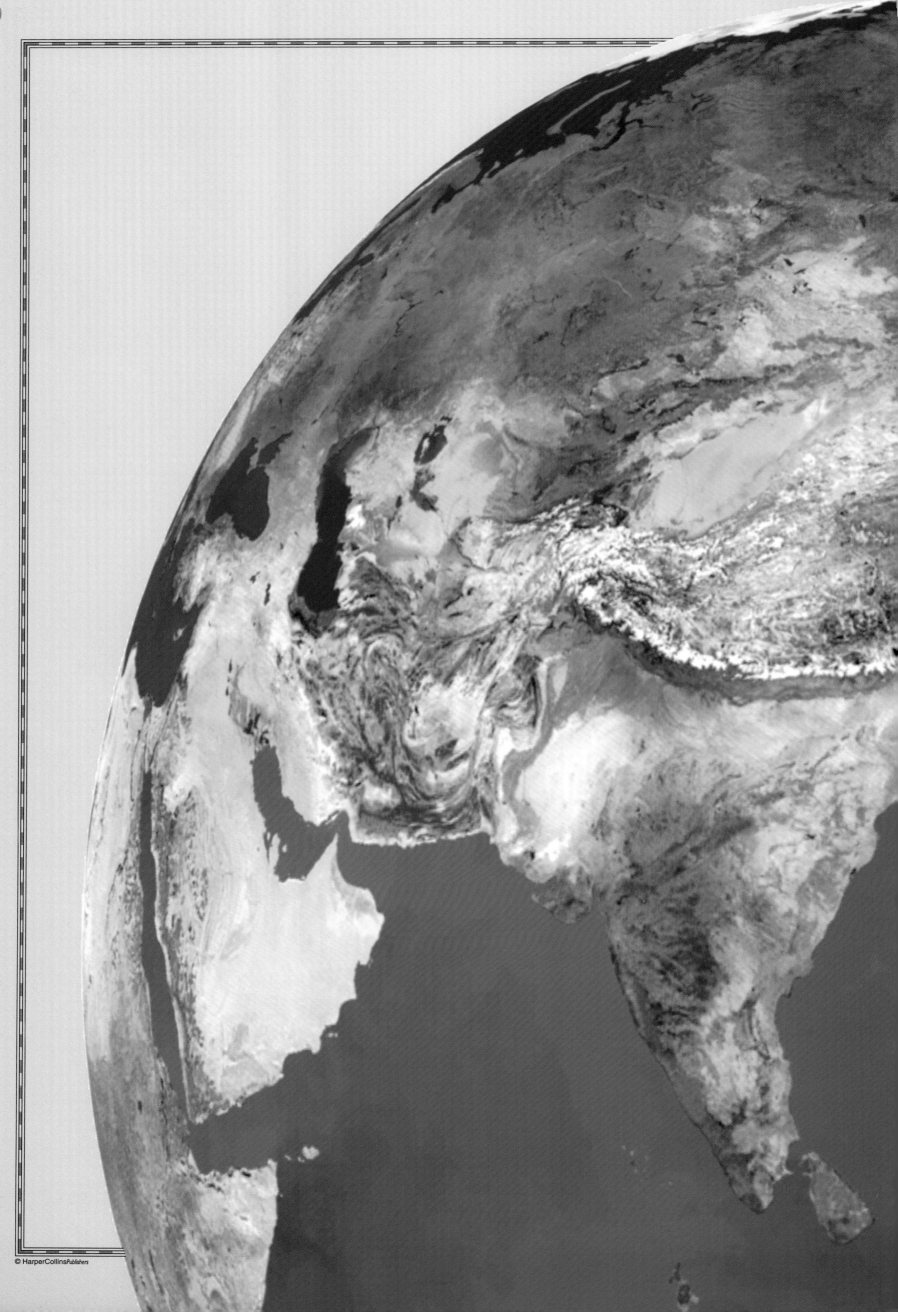

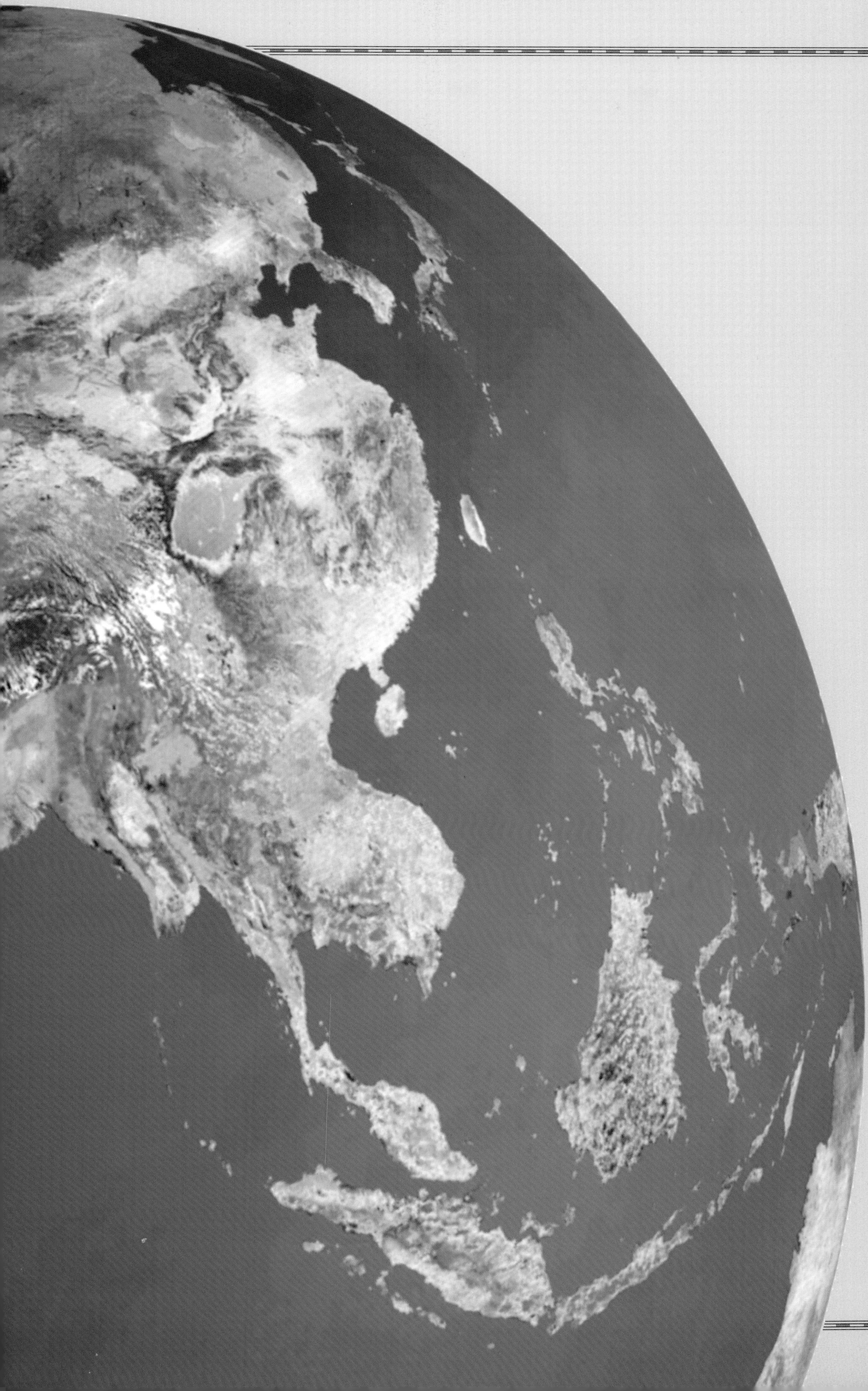

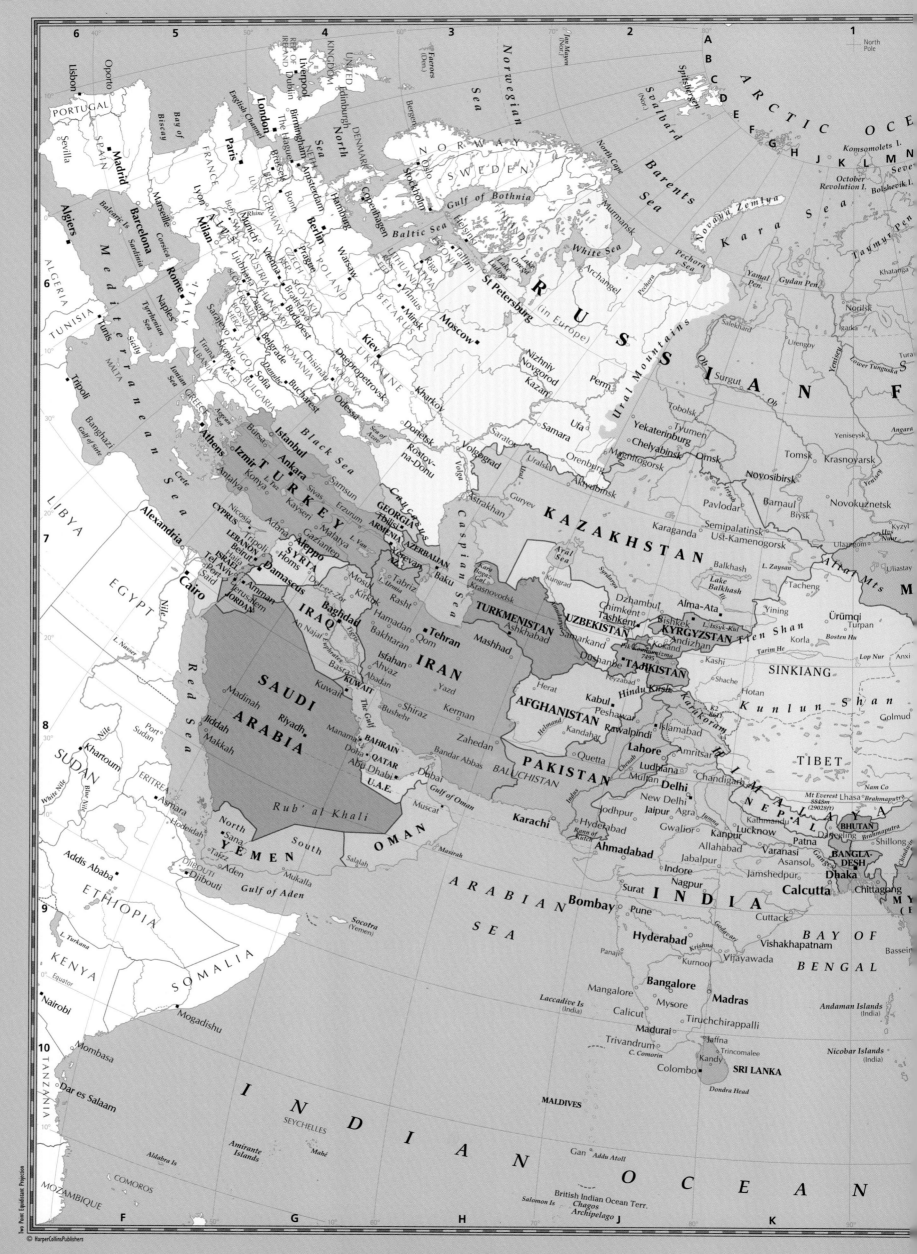

1:30 000 000

0	250	500	750	1000 MILES

| 0 | 250 | 500 | 750 | 1000 | 1250 | 1500 KM |

COUNTRY	AREA		POPULATION			Form of Government	Capital City	MAIN LANGUAGES	MAIN RELIGIONS	CURRENCY
	sq ml	sq km	total	density per sq ml	sq km					
AFGHANISTAN	251 825	652 225	18 879 000	75	29	republic	Kabul	Dari, Pushtu, Uzbek, Turkmen	Sunni & Shi'a Muslim	Afghani
ARMENIA	11 506	29 800	3 548 000	308	119	republic	Yerevan	Armenian, Azeri, Russian	Arm. Orthodox, RC, Muslim	Dram
AZERBAIJAN	33 436	86 600	7 472 000	223	86	republic	Baku	Azeri, Armenian, Russian, Lezgian	Shi'a & Sunni Muslim, Russ. and Arm. Orthodox	Manat
BAHRAIN	267	691	9 568 000	35863	13847	monarchy	Manama	Arabic, English	Shi'a & Sunni Muslim, Christian	Dinar
BANGLADESH	55 598	143 998	117 787 000	2119	818	republic	Dhaka	Bengali, Bihari, Hindi, English, local lang.	Muslim, Hindu, Buddhist, Christian	Taka
BHUTAN	18 000	46 620	1 614 000	90	35	monarchy	Thimphu	Dzongkha, Nepali, Assamese, English	Buddhist, Hindu, Muslim	Ngultrum
BRUNEI	2 226	5 765	280 000	126	49	monarchy	Bandar Seri Begawan	Malay, English, Chinese	Muslim, Buddhist, Christian	Dollar (ringgit)
CAMBODIA	69 884	181 000	9 568 000	137	53	monarchy	Phnom Penh	Khmer, Vietnamese	Buddhist, RC, Sunni Muslim	Riel
CHINA	3 691 484	9 560 900	1 208 842 000	327	126	republic	Beijing	Chinese, regional lang.	Confucian, Taoist, Buddhist, Muslim, RC	Yuan
CYPRUS	3 572	9 251	726 000	203	78	republic	Nicosia	Greek, Turkish, English	Greek Orthodox, Muslim	Pound
GEORGIA	26 911	69 700	5 450 000	203	78	republic	Tbilisi	Georgian, Russian, Armenian, Azeri, Ossetian, Abkhaz	Orthodox, Muslim	Lari
HONG KONG	415	1 075	6 061 000	14603	5638	UK territory from 1.7.97 Special Administrative Region of China		Chinese, English	Buddhist, Taoist, Protestant	Dollar
INDIA	1 269 219	3 287 263	918 570 000	724	279	republic	New Delhi	Hindi, English, regional lang.	Hindu, Muslim, Sikh, Christian, Buddhist, Jain	Rupee
INDONESIA	741 102	1 919 445	190 676 000	257	99	republic	Jakarta	Indonesian, local lang.	Muslim, Protestant, RC Hindu, Buddhist	Rupiah
IRAN	636 296	1 648 000	59 778 000	94	36	republic	Tehran	Farsi, Azeri, Kurdish, regional lang.	Shi'a & Sunni Muslim, Baha'i, Christian, Zoroastrian	Rial
IRAQ	169 235	438 317	19 925 000	118	45	republic	Baghdad	Arabic, Kurdish, Turkmen	Shi'a & Sunni Muslim, RC	Dinar
ISRAEL	8 019	20 770	5 399 000	673	260	republic	Jerusalem	Hebrew, Arabic, Yiddish, English	Jewish, Muslim, Christian, Druze	Shekel
JAPAN	145 841	377 727	124 961 000	857	331	monarchy	Tokyo	Japanese	Shintoist, Buddhist, Christian	Yen
JORDAN	34 443	89 206	5 198 000	151	58	monarchy	Amman	Arabic	Sunni & Shi'a Muslim, Christian	Dinar
KAZAKHSTAN	1 049 155	2 717 300	17 027 000	16	6	republic	Alma-Ata	Kazakh, Russian, German, Ukrainian, Uzbek, Tatar	Muslim, Russ. Orthodox, Protestant	Tanga
KUWAIT	6 880	17 818	1 620 000	235	91	monarchy	Kuwait	Arabic	Sunni & Shi'a Muslim, Christian, Hindu	Dinar
KYRGYZSTAN	76 641	198 500	4 473 000	58	23	republic	Bishkek	Kirghiz, Russian, Uzbek	Muslim, Russian Orthodox	Som
LAOS	91 429	236 800	4 742 000	52	20	republic	Vientiane	Lao, local languages	Buddhist, trad. beliefs, RC, Sunni Muslim	Kip
LEBANON	4 036	10 452	2 915 000	722	279	republic	Beirut	Arabic, French, Armenian	Shi'a & Sunni Muslim, Protestant, RC	Pound
MACAU	7	17	403 000	61398	23706	Portuguese terr.	Macau	Chinese, Portuguese	Buddhist, RC, Protestant	Pataca
MALAYSIA	128 559	332 965	20 097 000	156	60	federation	Kuala Lumpur	Malay, English, Chinese, Tamil, local lang.	Muslim, Buddhist, Hindu, Christian, trad. beliefs	Dollar (ringgit)
MALDIVES	115	298	246 000	2138	826	republic	Male	Divehi (Maldivian)	Sunni Muslim	Rufiyaa
MONGOLIA	604 250	1 565 000	2 363 000	4	2	republic	Ulan Bator	Khalka (Mongolian), Kazakh, local lang.	Buddhist, Muslim, trad. beliefs	Tugrik
MYANMAR	261 228	676 577	43 922 000	168	65	republic	Rangoon	Burmese, Shan, Karen, local lang.	Buddhist, Muslim, Protestant, RC	Kyat
NEPAL	56 827	147 181	21 360 000	376	145	monarchy	Kathmandu	Nepali, Maithili, Bhojpuri, English, local lang.	Hindu, Buddhist, Muslim	Rupee
NORTH KOREA	46 540	120 538	23 483 000	505	195	republic	Pyongyang	Korean	Trad. beliefs, Chondoist, Buddhist, Confucian, Taoist	Won
OMAN	105 000	271 950	2 096 000	20	8	monarchy	Muscat	Arabic, Baluchi, Farsi, Swahili, Indian lang.	Muslim,	Rial
PAKISTAN	310 403	803 940	126 467 000	407	157	republic	Islamabad	Urdu, Punjabi, Sindhi, Pushtu, English	Muslim, Christian, Hindu	Rupee
PALAU	192	497	17 000	89	34	republic	Koror	Palauan, English	RC, Protestant, trad.beliefs	US dollar
PHILIPPINES	115 831	300 000	68 624 000	592	229	republic	Manila	English, Filipino, Cebuano, local lang.	RC, Aglipayan, Muslim, Protestant	Peso
QATAR	4 416	11 437	593 000	134	52	monarchy	Doha	Arabic, Indian lang.	Muslim, Christian, Hindu	Riyal
RUSSIAN FEDERATION	6 592 849	17 075 400	148 673 000	23	9	republic	Moscow	Russian, Tatar, Ukrainian, local lang.	Russ. Orthodox, Muslim, other Christian, Jewish	Rouble
RUSSIAN FEDERATION (IN ASIA)	5 065 506	13 119 600	41 755 000	8	3					
SAUDI ARABIA	849 425	2 200 000	17 451 000	21	8	monarchy	Riyadh	Arabic	Sunni & Shi'a Muslim	Riyal
SINGAPORE	247	639	2 930 000	11876	4585	republic	Singapore	Chinese, English, Malay, Tamil	Buddhist, Taoist, Muslim, Christian, Hindu	Dollar
SOUTH KOREA	38 330	99 274	44 453 000	1160	448	republic	Seoul	Korean	Buddhist, Protestant, RC, Confucian, trad. beliefs	Won
SRI LANKA	25 332	65 610	17 865 000	705	272	republic	Colombo	Sinhalese, Tamil, English	Buddhist, Hindu, Muslim, RC	Rupee
SYRIA	71 498	185 180	13 844 000	194	75	republic	Damascus	Arabic, Kurdish, Armenian	Muslim, Christian	Pound
TAIWAN	13 969	36 179	21 074 000	1509	582	republic	Taipei	Chinese, local lang.	Buddhist, Taoist, Confucian, Christian	Dollar
TAJIKISTAN	55 251	143 100	5 933 000	107	41	republic	Dushanbe	Tajik, Uzbek, Russian	Muslim	Rouble
THAILAND	198 115	513 115	59 396 000	300	116	monarchy	Bangkok	Thai, Lao, Chinese, Malay, Mon-Khmer lang.	Buddhist, Muslim	Baht
TURKEY	300 948	779 452	60 576 000	201	78	republic	Ankara	Turkish, Kurdish	Sunni & Shi'a Muslim	Lira
TURKMENISTAN	188 456	488 100	4 010 000	21	8	republic	Ashkhabad	Turkmen, Russian	Muslim	Manat
UNITED ARAB EMIRATES	30 000	77 700	1 861 000	62	24	federation	Abu Dhabi	Arabic, English, Hindi, Urdu, Farsi	Sunni & Shi'a Muslim, Christian	Dirham
UZBEKISTAN	172 742	447 400	22 633 000	131	51	republic	Tashkent	Uzbek, Russian, Tajik, Kazakh	Muslim, Russ.Orthodox	Som
VIETNAM	127 246	329 565	72 510 000	570	220	republic	Hanoi	Vietnamese, Thai, Khmer, Chinese, local lang.	Buddhist, Taoist, RC, Cao Dai, Hoa Hao	Dong
YEMEN	203 850	527 968	12 672 000	62	24	republic	Sana	Arabic	Sunni & Shi'a Muslim	Dinar, rial

REP. OF IRELAND
UNITED KINGDOM
NORWAY
Norwegian Sea
ARCTIC OCEAN
East Siberian Sea
BERING SEA
Aleutian Islands

FRANCE
BEL.
LUX.
NETH.
DENMARK
SWEDEN
FINLAND
Barents Sea
Kara Sea
Laptev Sea

SW.
ITALY
CZECH REP.
AUSTRIA
GERMANY
POLAND
ESTONIA
LTH. LATVIA
CROATIA
SLOV.
BOSNIA-HERZ.
HUNGARY
SLOV.
BELARUS
Moscow
Ural Mountains
RUSSIAN FEDERATION
Sea of Okhotsk
NORTH PACIFIC OCEAN

YUGO.
ALBANIA
MACE.
ROMANIA
MOL.
UKRAINE
GREECE
Black Sea
BULGARIA

TURKEY
CYPRUS
Nicosia
LEBANON
Beirut
ISRAEL
JORDAN
Amman
GEORGIA
Tbilisi
ARMENIA
Yerevan
AZER.
Baku
SYRIA
Damascus
Baghdad
IRAQ
Tehran
KAZAKHSTAN
Caspian Sea
Ashkhabad
Tashkent
Bishkek
Alma-Ata
KYRGYZSTAN
Ulan Bator
MONGOLIA
Gobi Desert
Sea of Japan
NORTH KOREA
Pyongyang
Honshu
Tokyo
JAPAN
Seoul
SOUTH KOREA

EGYPT
SAUDI ARABIA
KUWAIT
Kuwait
Riyadh
BAHRAIN
Manama
QATAR
Doha
Abu Dhabi
U.A.E.
IRAN
UZBEKISTAN
TURKMENISTAN
Dushanbe
TAJIKISTAN
Kabul
AFGHANISTAN
Islamabad
PAKISTAN
HIMALAYA
CHINA
Beijing
East China Sea
Taipei
TAIWAN
Northern Mariana Is (U.S.A.)

Saná
Rub' al Khali
Muscat
OMAN
New Delhi
NEPAL
Kathmandu
BHUTAN
BANGLA-DESH
Dhaka
FED. STATES OF MICRONESIA

DJIBOUTI
YEMEN
ARABIAN SEA
INDIA
MYANMAR (BURMA)
LAOS
Hanoi
Manila
PHILIPPINES
PALAU

SOMALIA
Mogadishu
BAY OF BENGAL
Rangoon
Vientiane
THAILAND
Bangkok
CAMBODIA
Phnom Penh
VIETNAM
South China Sea

INDIAN OCEAN
SEYCHELLES
MALDIVES
Colombo
SRI LANKA
Gulf of Thailand
BRUNEI
Bandar Seri Begawan
PAPUA NEW GUINEA
Port Moresby
Arafura Sea

Kuala Lumpur
MALAYSIA
SINGAPORE
Sumatra
INDONESIA
Jakarta
AUSTRALIA

ASSOCIATION OF SOUTH EAST ASIAN NATIONS (ASEAN)

Established at a meeting in Bangkok in 1967, ASEAN replaced the Association of South East Asia (ASA) which had been established in 1961. The objectives of ASEAN are to promote economic, political and social co-operation. The founder members were Indonesia, Malysia, the Philippines, Singapore and Thailand; Brunei joined in 1984 and Vietnam in 1995. Cambodia, Laos and Myanmar have applied for membership.

Headquarters : Jakarta, Indonesia

BRUNEI
JORDAN
AZERBAIJAN
KUWAIT
BAHRAIN
GEORGIA
QATAR
DJIBOUTI
MOLDOVA
SYRIA
PALESTINE
LEBANON
ARMENIA

ASIA PACIFIC ECONOMIC CO-OPERATION FORUM (APEC)

see page 88 for information

COMMONWEALTH OF INDEPENDENT STATES

see page 7 for information

ORGANIZATION OF PETROLEUM EXPORTING COUNTRIES (OPEC)

Established in 1960 at a meeting in Baghdad, to co-ordinate the price and supply policies of oil-producing states, and to provide member countries with economic and technical aid. Member countries are Algeria, Ecuador, Gabon, Indonesia, Iran, Iraq, Kuwait, Libya, Nigeria, Qatar, Saudi Arabia, U.A.E. and Venezuela.

Headquarters : Vienna, Austria

ALGERIA
LIBYA
VENEZUELA
NIGERIA
ECUADOR
GABON
see map above for Asian members of OPEC

ARAB LEAGUE

The Arab League was founded in 1945 in Cairo, by Egypt, Syria, Iraq, Lebanon, Jordan, Saudi Arabia and Yemen. Egypt's membership was suspended in 1979 because of its peace treaty with Israel; Egypt was re-admitted in 1989.

The membership has now been extended to include Algeria, Bahrain, Djibouti, Kuwait, Libya, Mauritania, Morocco, Oman, Palestine, Qatar, Somalia, Sudan, Tunisia and U.A.E.

Headquarters : Cairo, Egypt

MOROCCO
TUNISIA
ALGERIA
LIBYA
MAURITANIA
SUDAN
SOMALIA
see map above for Asian members of the Arab League

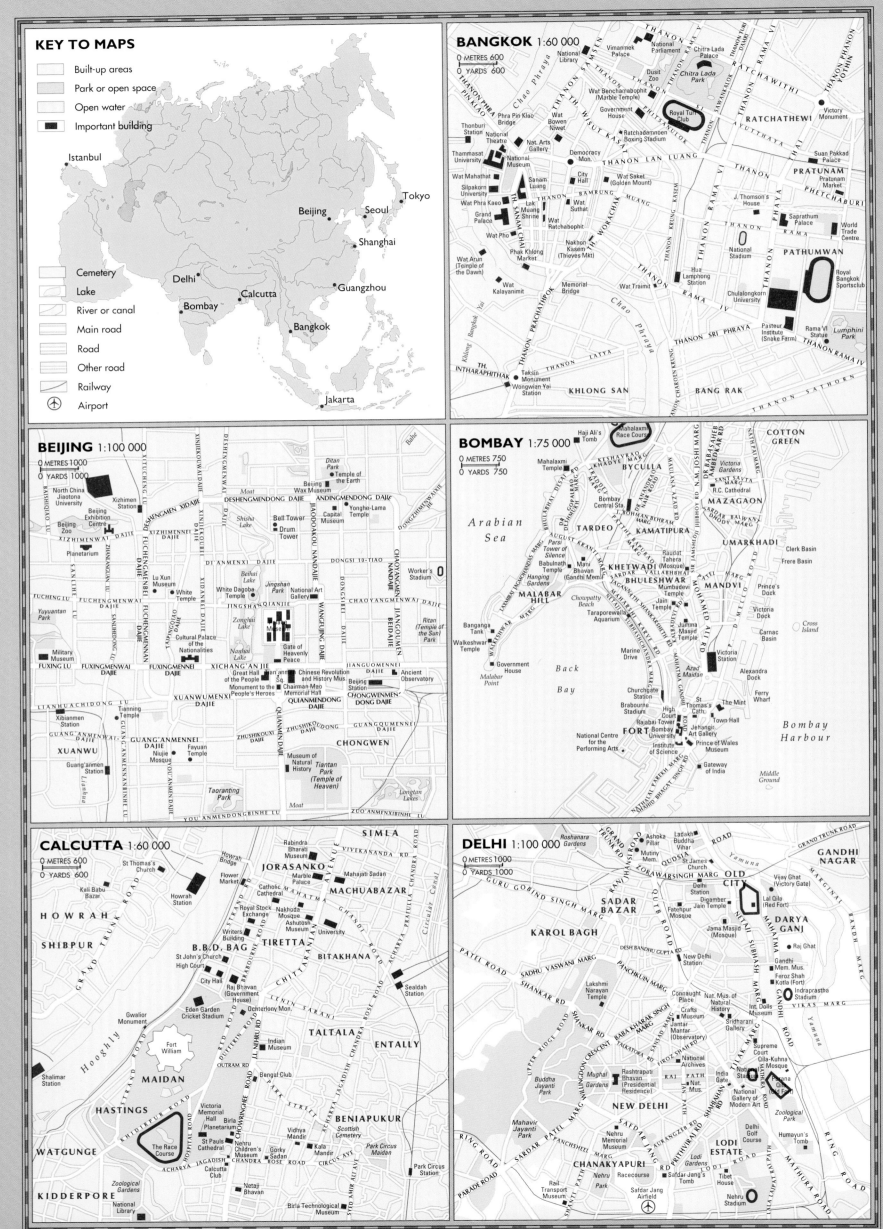

KEY TO MAPS

- Built-up areas
- Park or open space
- Open water
- Important building

Istanbul
Tokyo
Seoul
Beijing
Shanghai
Delhi
Calcutta
Guangzhou
Bombay
Bangkok
Jakarta

- Cemetery
- Lake
- River or canal
- Main road
- Road
- Other road
- Railway
- Airport

BANGKOK 1:60 000

0 METRES 600
0 YARDS 600

BEIJING 1:100 000

0 METRES 1000
0 YARDS 1000

BOMBAY 1:75 000

0 METRES 750
0 YARDS 750

Arabian Sea

Back Bay

Bombay Harbour

CALCUTTA 1:60 000

0 METRES 600
0 YARDS 600

DELHI 1:100 000

0 METRES 1000
0 YARDS 1000

© HarperCollinsPublishers

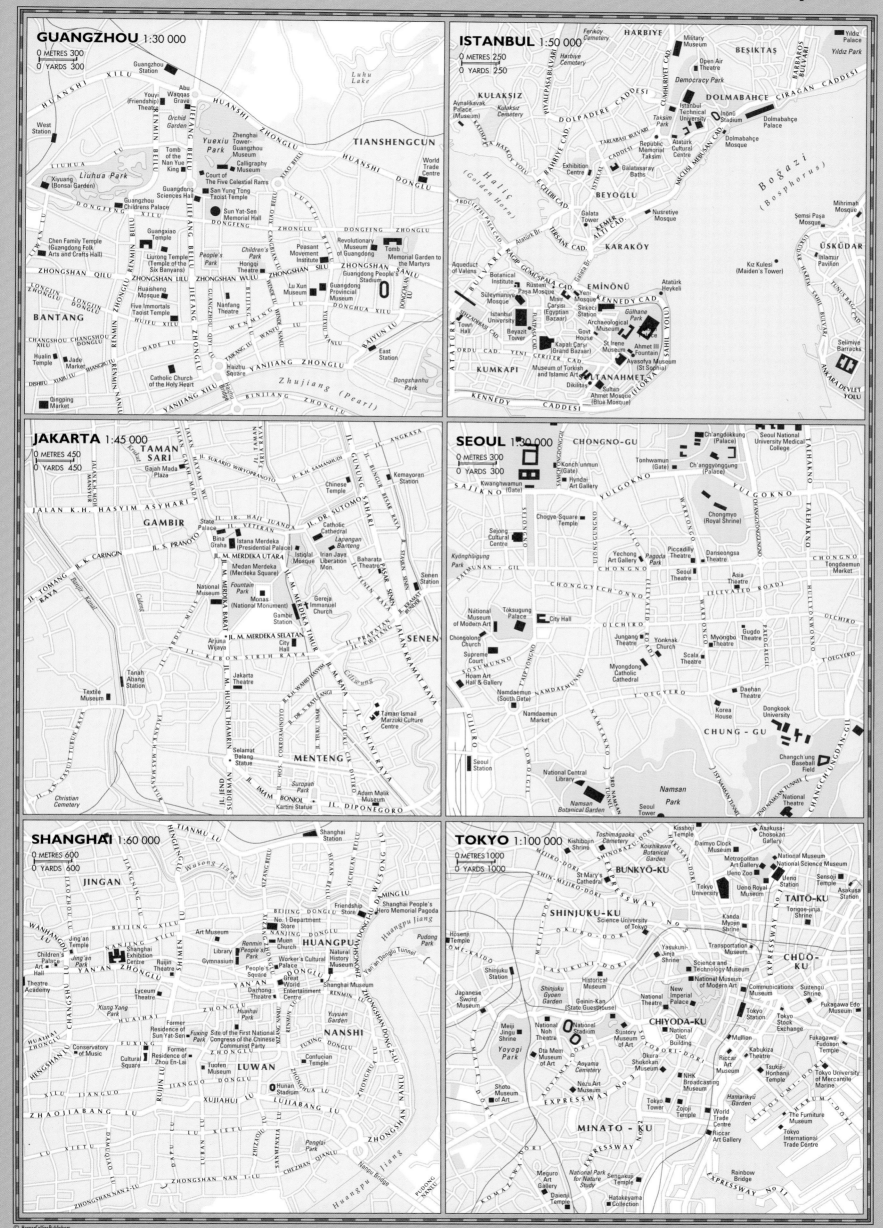

GUANGZHOU 1:30 000

0 METRES 300
0 YARDS 300

Guangzhou Station
Youyi (Friendship) Theatre
Abu Waqqas Grave
Orchid Garden
West Station
Tomb of the Nan Yue King
Yuexiu Park
Zhenghai Tower - Guangzhou Museum
Calligraphy Museum
Xiyuan (Bonsai Garden)
Liuhua Park
Court of The Five Celestial Rams
San Yung Tong Taoist Temple
Guangzhou Childrens Palace
Guangdong Sciences Hall
Sun Yat-Sen Memorial Hall
Guangxiao Temple
Chen Family Temple (Guangdong Folk Arts and Crafts Hall)
Liurong Temple (Temple of the Six Banyans)
Huaisheng Mosque
Peasant Movement Institute
Children's Park
Revolutionary Museum of Guangdong
Tomb
Memorial Garden to the Martyrs
Hongqi Theatre
People's Park
BANTANG
Five Immortals Taoist Temple
Guangdong Provincial Museum
Guangdong People's Stadium
Lu Xun Museum
Hualin Temple
Jade Market
East Station
Catholic Church of the Holy Heart
Qingping Market
Haizhu Square
Haizhu Bridge
Zhujiang (Pearl)
Dongshanhu Park
TIANSHENGCUN
World Trade Centre
Luhu Lake

ISTANBUL 1:50 000

0 METRES 250
0 YARDS 250

Ferikoy Cemetery
HARBIYE
Military Museum
Yıldız Park
Yıldız Museum
BEŞİKTAŞ
Open Air Theatre
Democracy Park
İstanbul Technical University
İnönü Stadium
DOLMABAHÇE
Dolmabahçe Palace
Dolmabahçe Mosque
ÇIRAGAN CADDESİ
KULAKSIZ
Aynalıkavak Palace (Museum)
Kulaksız Cemetery
Taksim Park
Atatürk Cultural Centre
Republic Memorial Taksim
Exhibition Centre
Galatasaray Baths
BEYOĞLU
Nusretiye Mosque
Galata Tower
KARAKÖY
ÜSKÜDAR
Şemsi Paşa Mosque
Mihrimah Mosque
İhlamur Pavilion
Halis (Golden Horn)
Aqueduct of Valens
Botanical Institute
Rüstem Paşa Mosque
Süleymaniye Mosque
Yeni Mosque
EMİNÖNÜ
Mısır Çarşısı (Egyptian Bazaar)
Sirkeci Station
Atatürk Heykeli
Gülhane Park
Kız Kulesi (Maiden's Tower)
İstanbul University
Town Hall
Beyazıt Tower
Govt House
Archaeological Museum
Ahmet III Fountain
KUMKAPI
Ordu Cad
Yeni
Kapalı Çarşı (Grand Bazaar)
St Irene Museum
Ayasofya Museum (St Sophia)
SULTANAHMET
Museum of Turkish and Islamic Arts
Dikilitaş
Sultan Ahmet Mosque (Blue Mosque)
KENNEDY CADDESİ
Selimiye Barracks
Ankara Devlet Yolu
Boğazı (Bosphorus)

JAKARTA 1:45 000

0 METRES 450
0 YARDS 450

TAMAN SARI
Gajah Mada Plaza
Chinese Temple
Kemayoran Station
State Palace
Bina Graha
GAMBIR
Catholic Cathedral
Istana Merdeka (Presidential Palace)
Lapangan Banteng
Istiqlal Mosque
Irian Jaya Liberation Mon.
Medan Merdeka (Merdeka Square)
National Museum
Fountain Park
Monas (National Monument)
Gambir Station
Gereja Immanuel Church
Senen Station
Arjuna Wijaya
City Hall
SENEN
Jakarta Theatre
Tanah Abang Station
Textile Museum
Taman Ismail Marzuki Culture Centre
MENTENG
Selamat Datang Statue
Suropati Park
Christian Cemetery
Kartini Statue
Adam Malik Museum

SEOUL 1:30 000

0 METRES 300
0 YARDS 300

CHONGNO-GU
Ch'angdokkung (Palace)
Seoul National University Medical College
Tonhwamun (Gate)
Ch'anggyonggung (Palace)
Konch'unmun (Gate)
Hyundai Art Gallery
Kwanghwamun (Gate)
Chongmyo (Royal Shrine)
Chogye-Square Temple
Sejong Cultural Centre
Kyŏnghŭigung Park
Yechong Art Gallery
Pagoda Park
Piccadilly Theatre
Danseongsa Theatre
CHONGNO
Seoul Theatre
Asia Theatre
Tongdaemun Market
National Museum of Modern Art
Toksugung Palace
City Hall
Jungang Theatre
Yŏnknak Church
Gugdo Theatre
Myŏngbo Theatre
Scala Theatre
Chongdong Church
Supreme Court
Hoam Art Hall & Gallery
Myongdong Catholic Cathedral
Namdaemun (South Gate)
Daehan Theatre
Namdaemun Market
Korea House
Dongkook University
CHUNG-GU
Changch'ung Baseball Field
Seoul Station
National Central Library
Namsan Botanical Garden
Seoul Tower
Namsan Park
National Theatre

SHANGHAI 1:60 000

0 METRES 600
0 YARDS 600

Shanghai Station
JINGAN
Art Museum
No. 1 Department Store
Friendship Store
Shanghai People's Hero Memorial Pagoda
Jing'an Temple
Children's Palace Art Hall
Shanghai Exhibition Centre
Library
Renmin People's Park
Muen Church
HUANGPU
Natural History Museum
Pudong Park
Theatre Academy
Gymnasium
Lyceum Theatre
Ruijin Theatre
People's Square
Worker's Cultural Palace
Dazhong Theatre
Great World Entertainment Centre
Shanghai Museum
Xiang Yang Park
Huaihai Park
Conservatory of Music
Former Residence of Sun Yat-Sen
Fuxing Park
Site of the First National Congress of the Chinese Communist Party
NANSHI
Former Residence of Zhou En-Lai
Cultural Square
Tuofen Museum
Confucian Temple
LUWAN
Yuyuan Garden
Hunan Stadium
Penglai Park

TOKYO 1:100 000

0 METRES 1000
0 YARDS 1000

Kisshoji Temple
Asakusa-Choosokan Gallery
Toshimagaoka Cemetery
Kishibojin Shrine
Koishikawa Botanical Garden
Daimyo Clock Museum
Metropolitan Art Gallery
National Museum
National Science Museum
BUNKYO-KU
Tokyo University
Ueno Zoo
Ueno Station
Sensoji Temple
Ueno Royal Museum
Asakusa Station
TAITO-KU
St Mary's Cathedral
Torigoe-jinja Shrine
Hosenji Temple
Science University of Tokyo
SHINJUKU-KU
Kanda Myojin Shrine
Yasukuni-Jinja Shrine
Transportation Museum
CHUO-KU
Shinjuku Station
Science and Technology Museum
National Theatre
National Museum of Modern Art
Japanese Sword Museum
Shinjuku Gyoen Garden
Geinin-Kan (State Guesthouse)
New Imperial Palace
Communications Museum
Suitengu Shrine
Meiji Jingu Shrine
National Noh Theatre
National Stadium
CHIYODA-KU
National Museum of Art
National Diet Building
Tokyo Station
Tokyo Stock Exchange
Fukagawa Edo Museum
Yoyogi Park
Ota Mem Museum of Art
Suntory Museum of Art
Mullion
Riccar Art Museum
Kabukiza Theatre
Tsukiji-Honhanji Temple
Fukagawa-Fudoson Temple
Aoyama Cemetery
Nezu Art Museum
NHK Broadcasting Centre
Shukokan Museum
Tokyo University of Mercantile Marine
Shoto Museum of Art
Tokyo Tower
Zojoji Temple
World Trade Centre
Riccar Art Gallery
Hamarikyu Garden
The Furniture Museum
Tokyo International Trade Centre
MINATO-KU
Meguro Art Gallery
National Park for Nature Study
Sengakuji Temple
Daienji Temple
Hatakeyama Collection
Rainbow Bridge
EXPRESSWAY NO 11

© HarperCollins Publishers

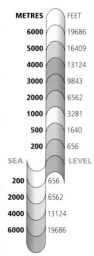

© HarperCollinsPublishers

1:12 900 000

0	100	200	300	400	500 MILES

| 0 | 100 | 200 | 300 | 400 | 500 | 600 | 700 | 800 KM |

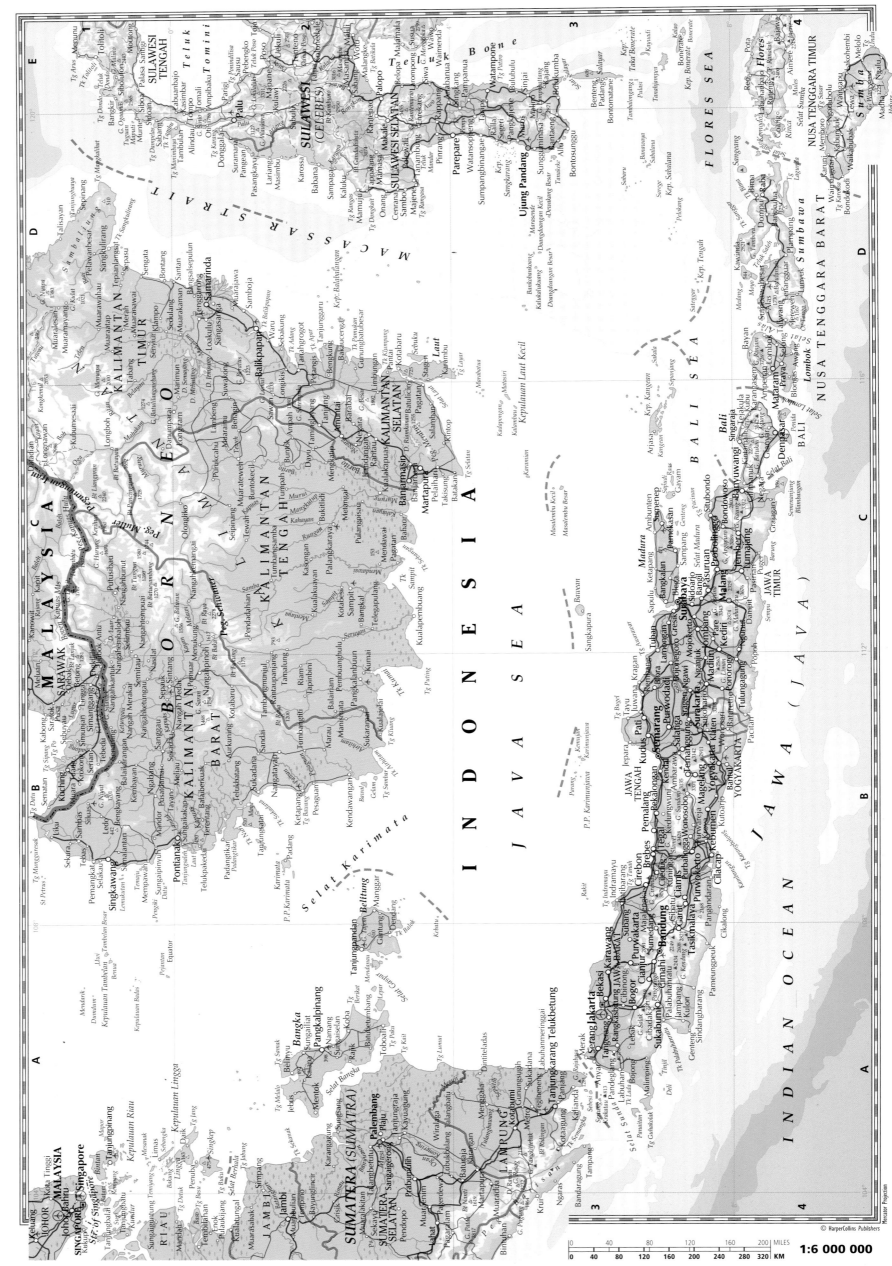

PALAU
1:1.5M

GUAM
(U.S.A.)
1:1.5M

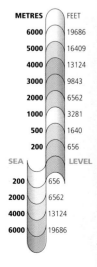

PHILIPPINE SEA

SOUTH CHINA SEA

LUZON

MINDORO

PANAY

NEGROS

SAMAR

LEYTE

CEBU

BOHOL

PALAWAN

MINDANAO

SULU SEA

CELEBES SEA

Moro Gulf

Bohol Sea

Visayan Sea

Sibuyan Sea

Sulu Archipelago

Calamian Group

MALAYSIA

SABAH

INDONESIA

Manila
Quezon City
Davao
Cagayan de Oro
Zamboanga
General Santos
Cebu
Baguio

METRES	FEET
6000	19686
5000	16409
4000	13124
3000	9843
2000	6562
1000	3281
500	1640
200	656
SEA	LEVEL
200	656
2000	6562
4000	13124
6000	19686

1:6 000 000

0 40 80 120 160 200 MILES
0 40 80 120 160 200 240 280 320 KM

© HarperCollinsPublishers

Mercator Projection

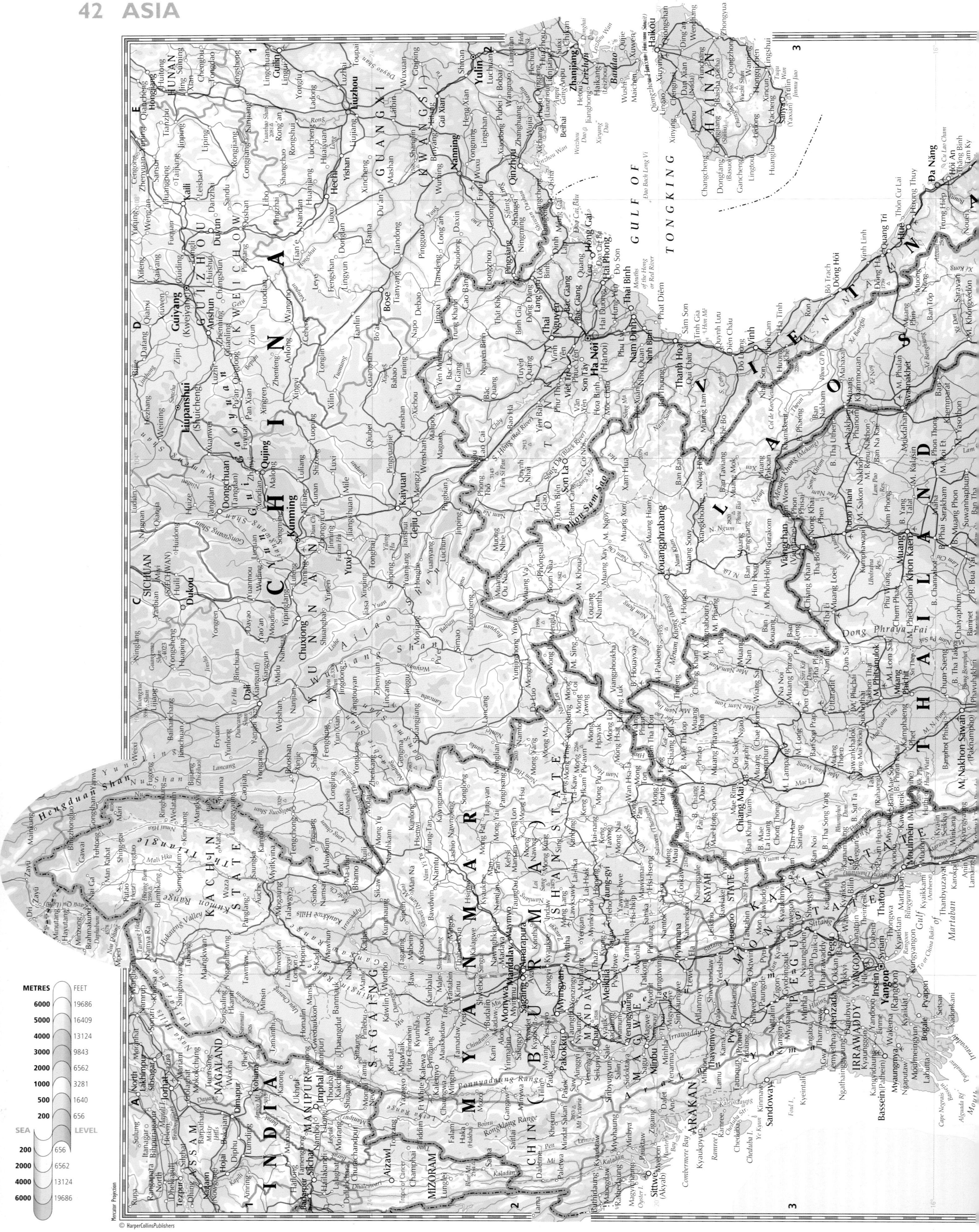

METRES | FEET
6000 | 19686
5000 | 16409
4000 | 13124
3000 | 9843
2000 | 6562
1000 | 3281
500 | 1640
200 | 656

SEA | LEVEL

200 | 656
2000 | 6562
4000 | 13124
6000 | 19686

Mercator Projection

© HarperCollinsPublishers

CHINA

HUNAN

GUIZHOU (KWEICHOW)

GUANGXI (KWANGSI)

HAINAN

GULF OF TONGKING

YUNNAN

SICHUAN (SZECHWAN)

MYANMAR (BURMA)

KACHIN STATE

SAGAING

SHAN STATE

KAYAH STATE

KAREN STATE

MON STATE

PEGU

IRRAWADDY

ARAKAN

CHIN (Tiang)

MIZORAM

MANIPUR

NAGALAND

ASSAM

INDIA

LAOS

THAILAND

VIETNAM

Guiyang (Kweiyang)

Kunming

Nanning

Guilin

Liuzhou

Wuzhou

Haikou

Hanoi (Ha Nôi)

Hai Phong

Vientiane

Louangphrabang

Mandalay

Yangon (Rangoon)

Chiang Mai

SINGAPORE
1:375 000

1:6 000 000

MILES 0 40 80 120 160 200

KM 0 40 80 120 160 200 240 280 320

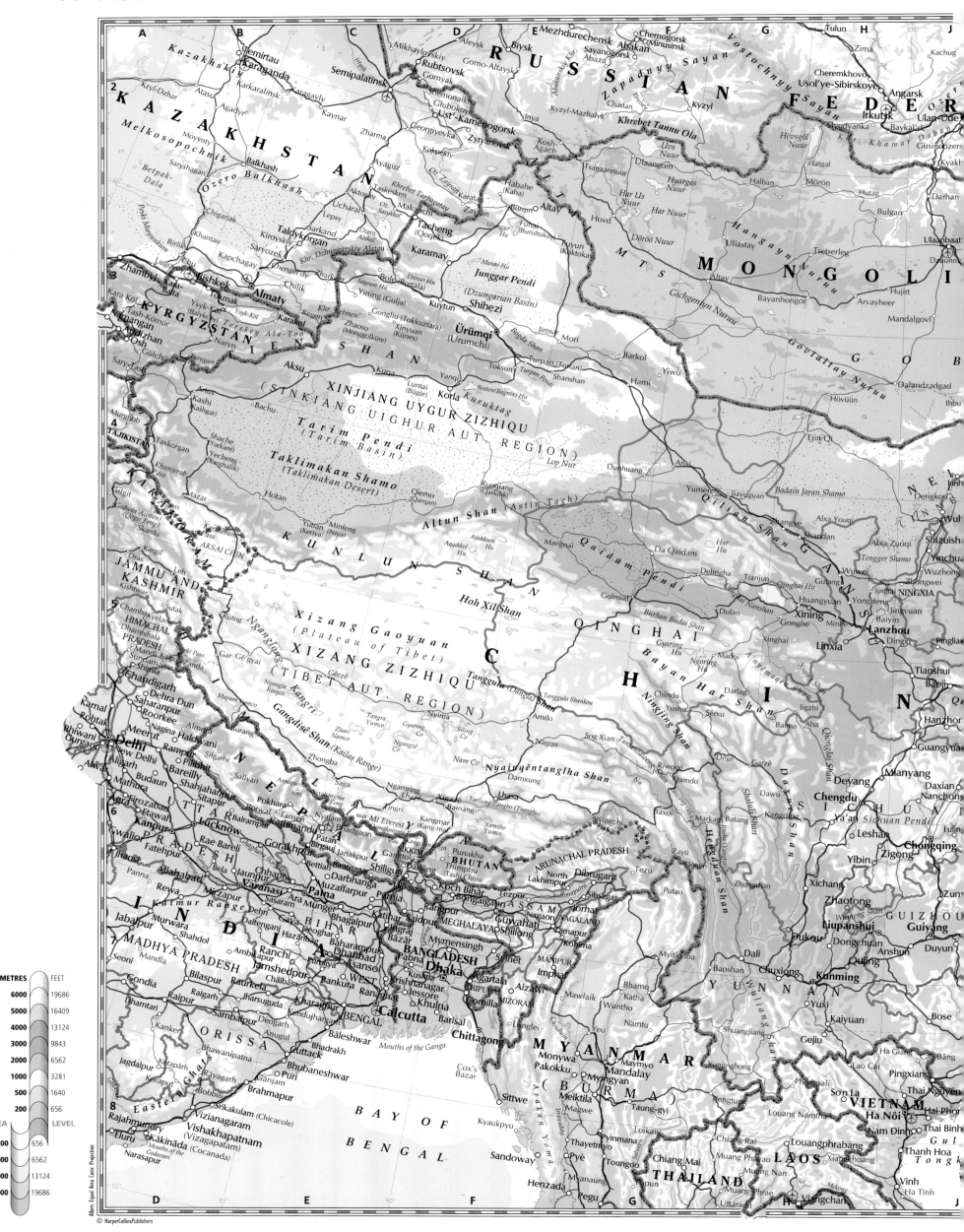

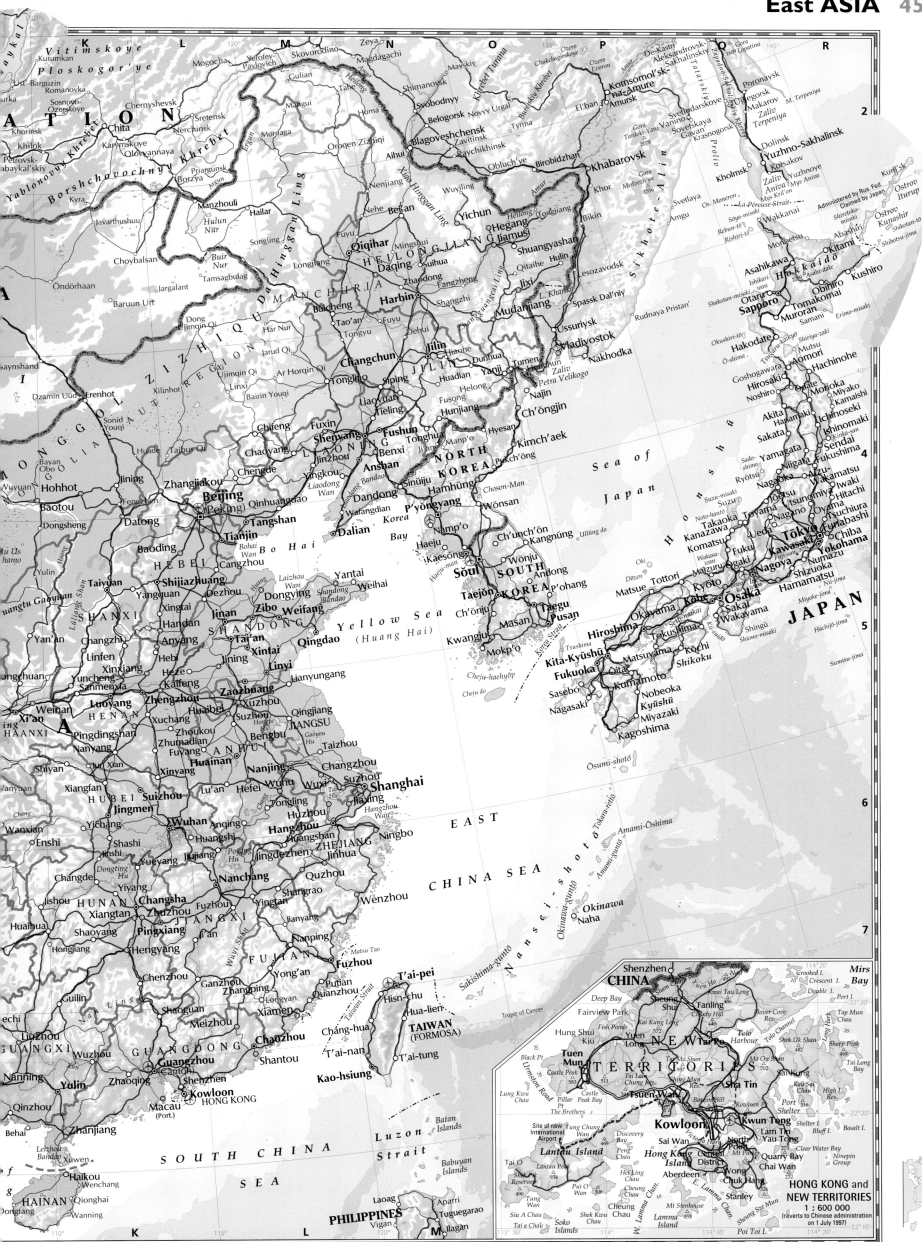

HONG KONG and
NEW TERRITORIES
1 : 600 000
(reverts to Chinese administration
on 1 July 1997)

1:12 600 000

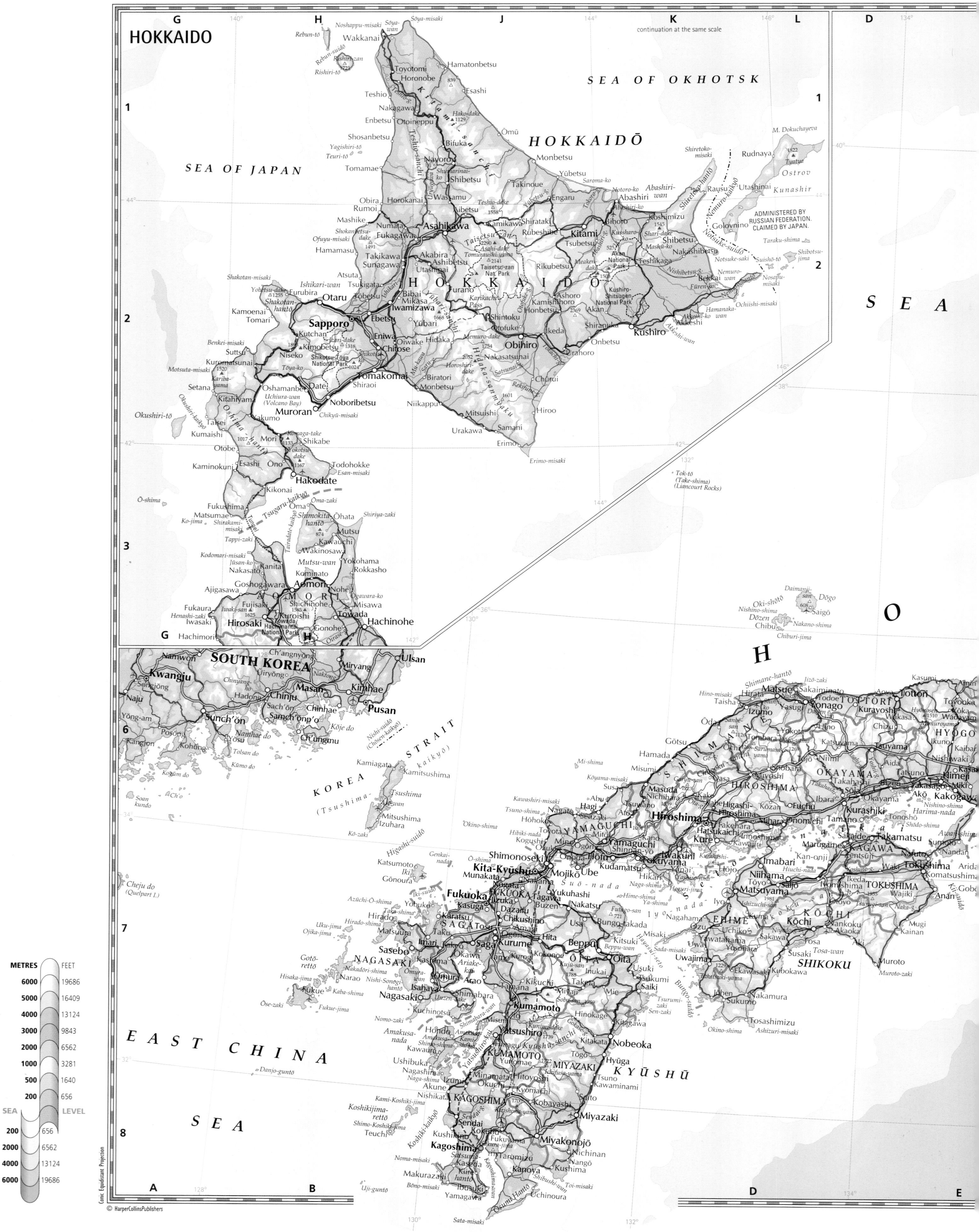

HOKKAIDO
continuation at the same scale
SEA OF OKHOTSK
SEA OF JAPAN
HOKKAIDŌ
ADMINISTERED BY RUSSIAN FEDERATION. CLAIMED BY JAPAN.
Kunashir Ostrov
Wakkanai
Sōya-misaki
Rebun-tō
Rishiri-tō
Toyotomi
Horonobe
Hamatonbetsu
Esashi
Teshio
Nakagawa
Enbetsu
Otoineppu
Bifuka
Ōmū
Monbetsu
Nayoro
Shibetsu
Yūbetsu
Abashiri
Rumoi
Asahikawa
Kitami
Bihoro
Shari
Shibetsu
Nakashibetsu
Nemuro
Takikawa
Sunagawa
Ashibetsu
Furano
Otaru
Sapporo
Ebetsu
Iwamizawa
Yūbari
Chitose
Tomakomai
Obihiro
Kushiro
Akkeshi
Date
Muroran
Noboribetsu
Hiroo
Samani
Erimo
Erimo-misaki
Hakodate
Esashi
Matsumae
Tsugaru-kaikyō
Mutsu
Mutsu-wan
Aomori
Hirosaki
Towada
Hachinohe
AOMORI
Tok-tō (Take-shima) (Liancourt Rocks)
SOUTH KOREA
Kwangju
Chinju
Masan
Pusan
Ulsan
Miryang
Kimhae
Sunch'ŏn
Yŏsu
KOREA STRAIT
Tsushima
Cheju do (Quelpart I.)
EAST CHINA SEA
Oki-shotō
Dōgo
Saigō
SEA OF JAPAN
SHIMANE
Matsue
Izumo
Yonago
TOTTORI
Tottori
Kurayoshi
HYOGO
Himeji
Kakogawa
OKAYAMA
Okayama
Kurashiki
HIROSHIMA
Hiroshima
Fukuyama
Onomichi
Kure
Masuda
Hamada
YAMAGUCHI
Yamaguchi
Hōfu
Tokuyama
Iwakuni
Ube
Shimonoseki
Kita-Kyūshū
Mojikō
Fukuoka
FUKUOKA
Kurume
Saga
SAGA
Sasebo
NAGASAKI
Nagasaki
Isahaya
Shimabara
Kumamoto
Yatsushiro
KUMAMOTO
Ōita
ŌITA
Beppu
Saiki
Nobeoka
MIYAZAKI
Miyazaki
Miyakonojō
KAGOSHIMA
Kagoshima
Sendai
Kanoya
KYŪSHŪ
Takamatsu
KAGAWA
Tokushima
TOKUSHIMA
Matsuyama
EHIME
Imabari
Niihama
Kōchi
KŌCHI
SHIKOKU
Uwajima
Muroto
Goto-rettō
Koshikijima-rettō
Satsuma-hantō
Ōsumi-hantō
Sata-misaki
Conic Equidistant Projection
METRES FEET
6000 19686
5000 16409
4000 13124
3000 9843
2000 6562
1000 3281
500 1640
200 656
SEA LEVEL
200 656
2000 6562
4000 13124
6000 19686

IWO JIMA (Japan) 1:300 000

OKINAWA (Japan) 1:1.2M

1:3 300 000

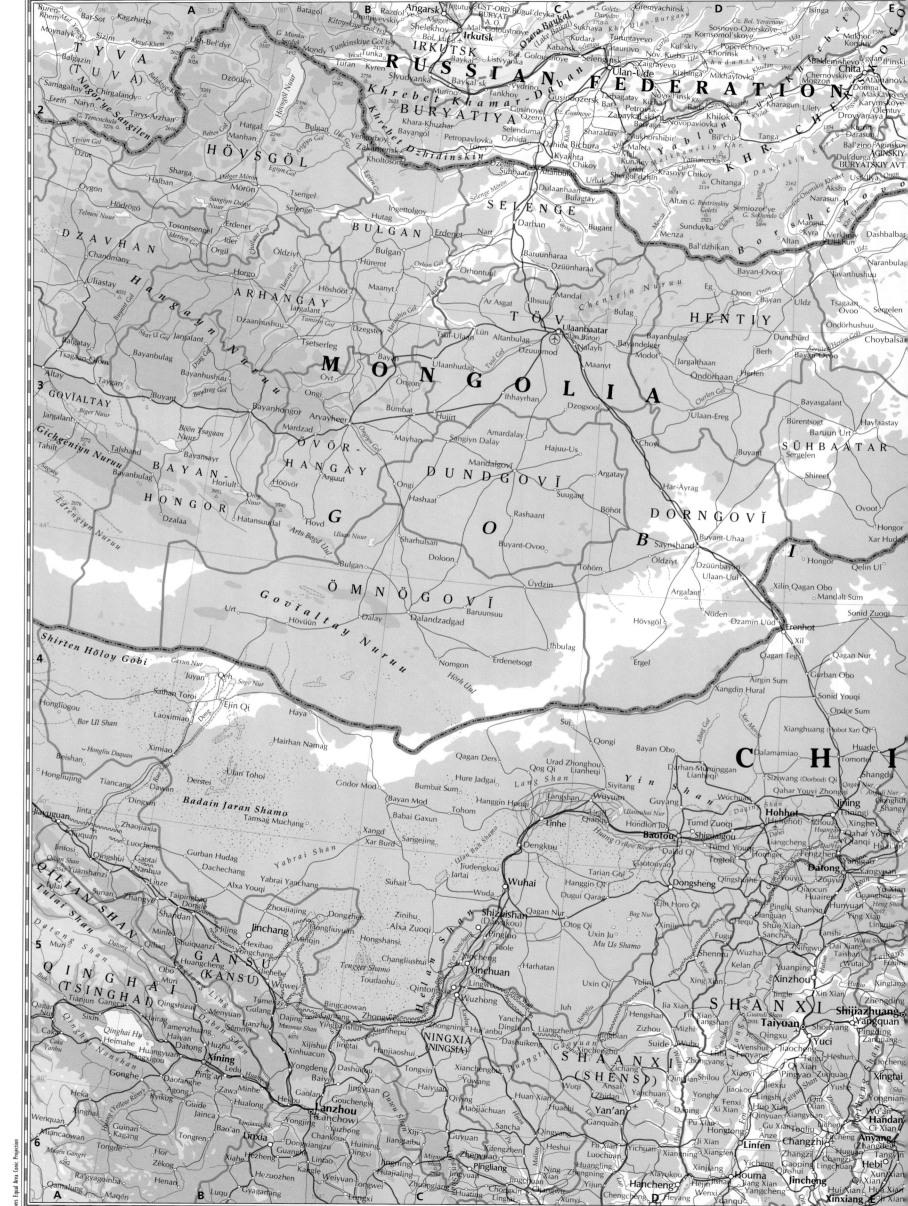

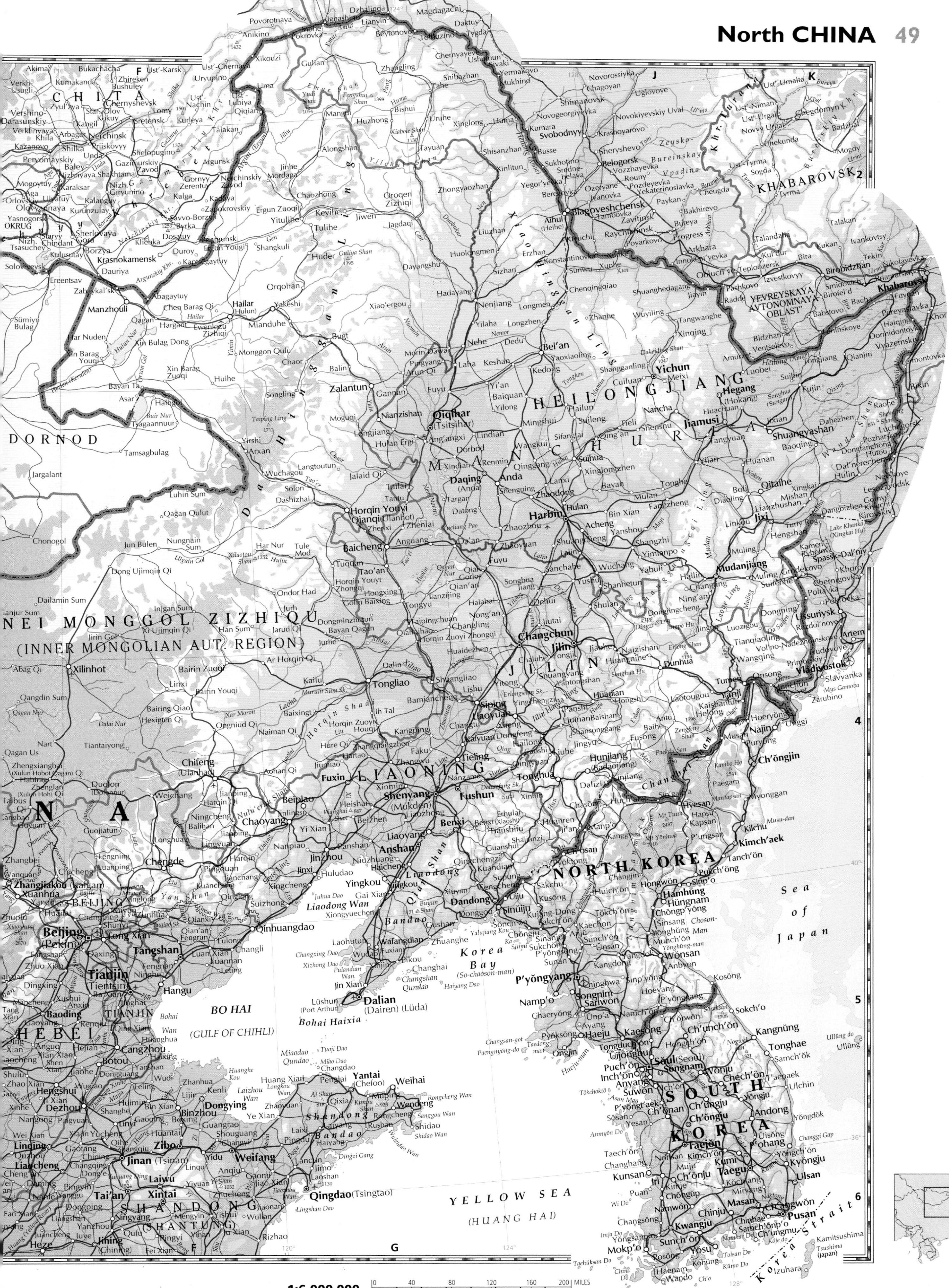

CHITA

KHABAROVSK

YEVREYSKAYA AVTONOMNAYA OBLAST'

DORNOD

NEI MONGGOL ZIZHIQU
(INNER MONGOLIAN AUT. REGION)

HEILONGJIANG

M A N C H U R I A

Qiqihar (Tsitsihar)

Daqing (Anda)

Harbin

Yichun

Hegang

Jiamusi

Shuangyashan

Mudanjiang

Jixi

CHINA

Chifeng (Ulanhao)

Tongliao

Changchun

JILIN

Jilin

Siping

Dunhua

Yanji

Shenyang (Mukden)

Fushun

Benxi

LIAONING

Anshan

Liaoyang

Jinzhou

Dandong

NORTH KOREA

Hamhŭng

Hŭngnam

Sinŭiju

Zhangjiakou (Kalgan)

BEIJING

Beijing (Peking)

Tangshan

Tianjin (Tientsin)

Qinhuangdao

Lüshun (Port Arthur)

Dalian (Dairen) (Lüda)

BO HAI
(GULF OF CHIHLI)

Korea Bay
(So-chaoson-man)

P'yŏngyang

Namp'o

Sŏul (Seoul)

Inch'ŏn

Sea of Japan

Wŏnsan

HEBEI

Baoding

Cangzhou

Yantai (Chefoo)

Weihai

Haeju

Kaesŏng

SOUTH KOREA

Jinan (Tsinan)

Zibo

Weifang

Taejŏn

Taegu

SHANDONG (SHANTUNG)

Qingdao (Tsingtao)

YELLOW SEA
(HUANG HAI)

Kwangju

Pusan

Korea Strait

1:6 000 000

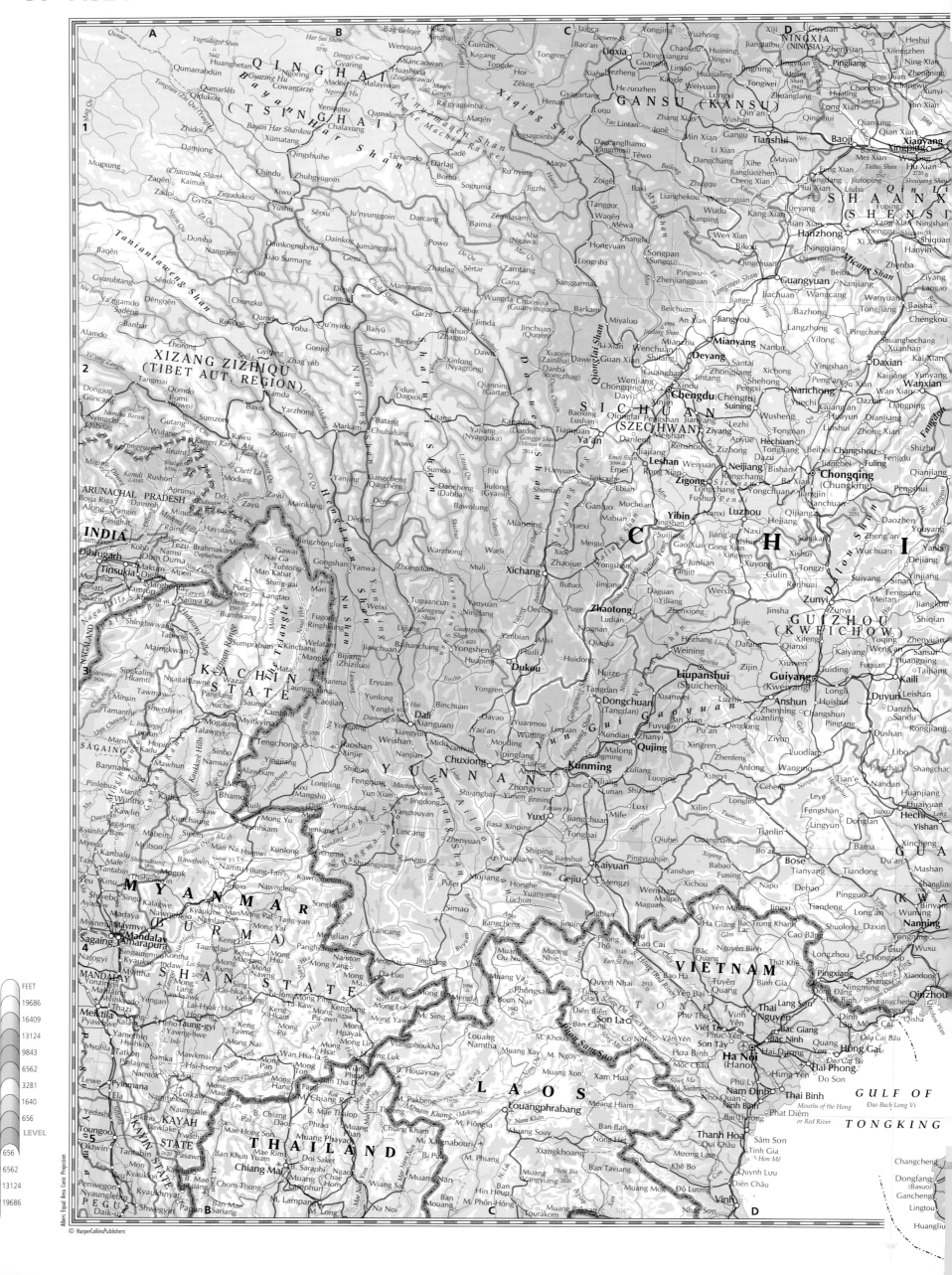

1:6 000 000

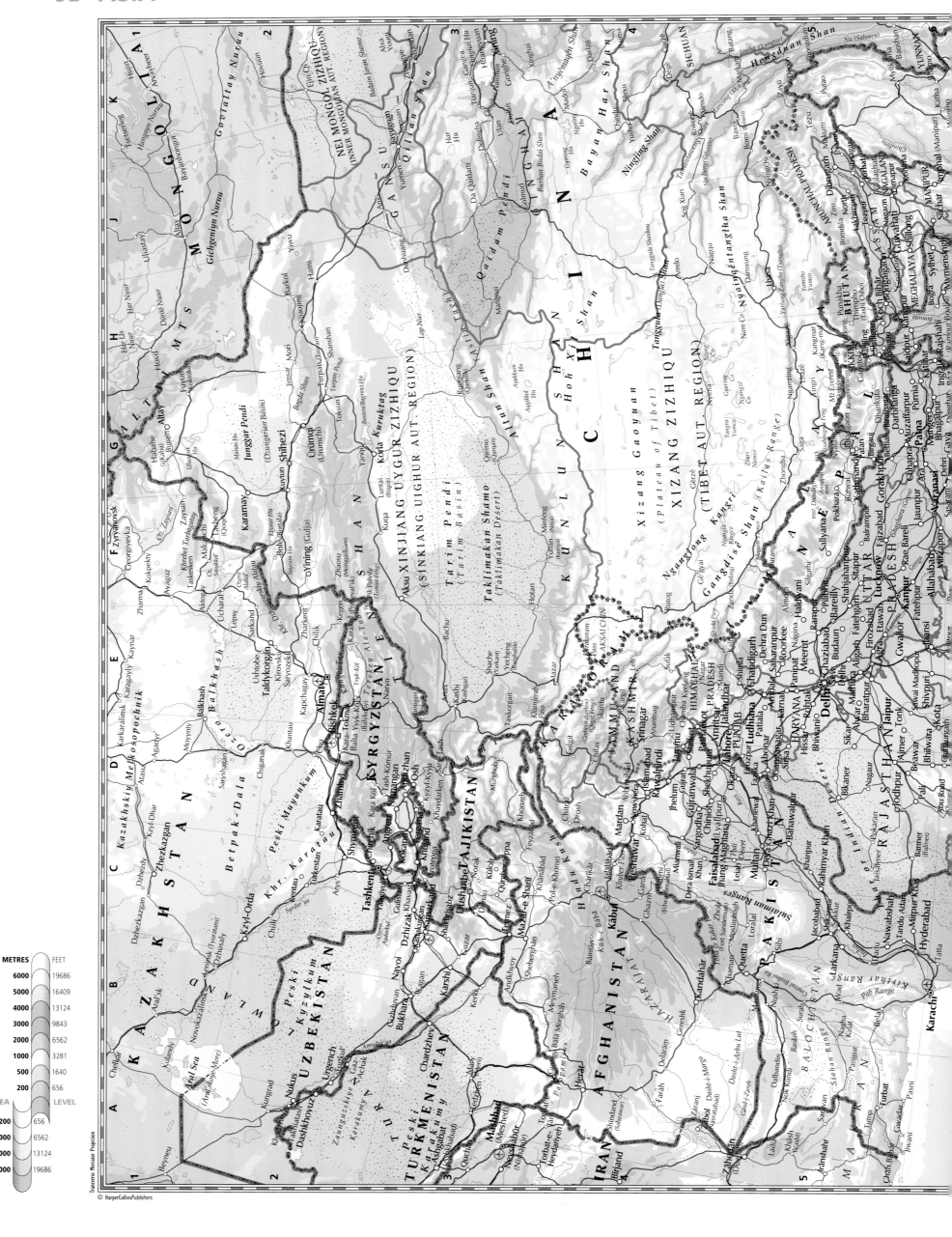

METRES	FEET
6000	19686
5000	16409
4000	13124
3000	9843
2000	6562
1000	3281
500	1640
200	656
SEA	LEVEL
200	656
2000	6562
4000	13124
6000	19686

Transverse Mercator Projection

© HarperCollinsPublishers

1:12 000 000

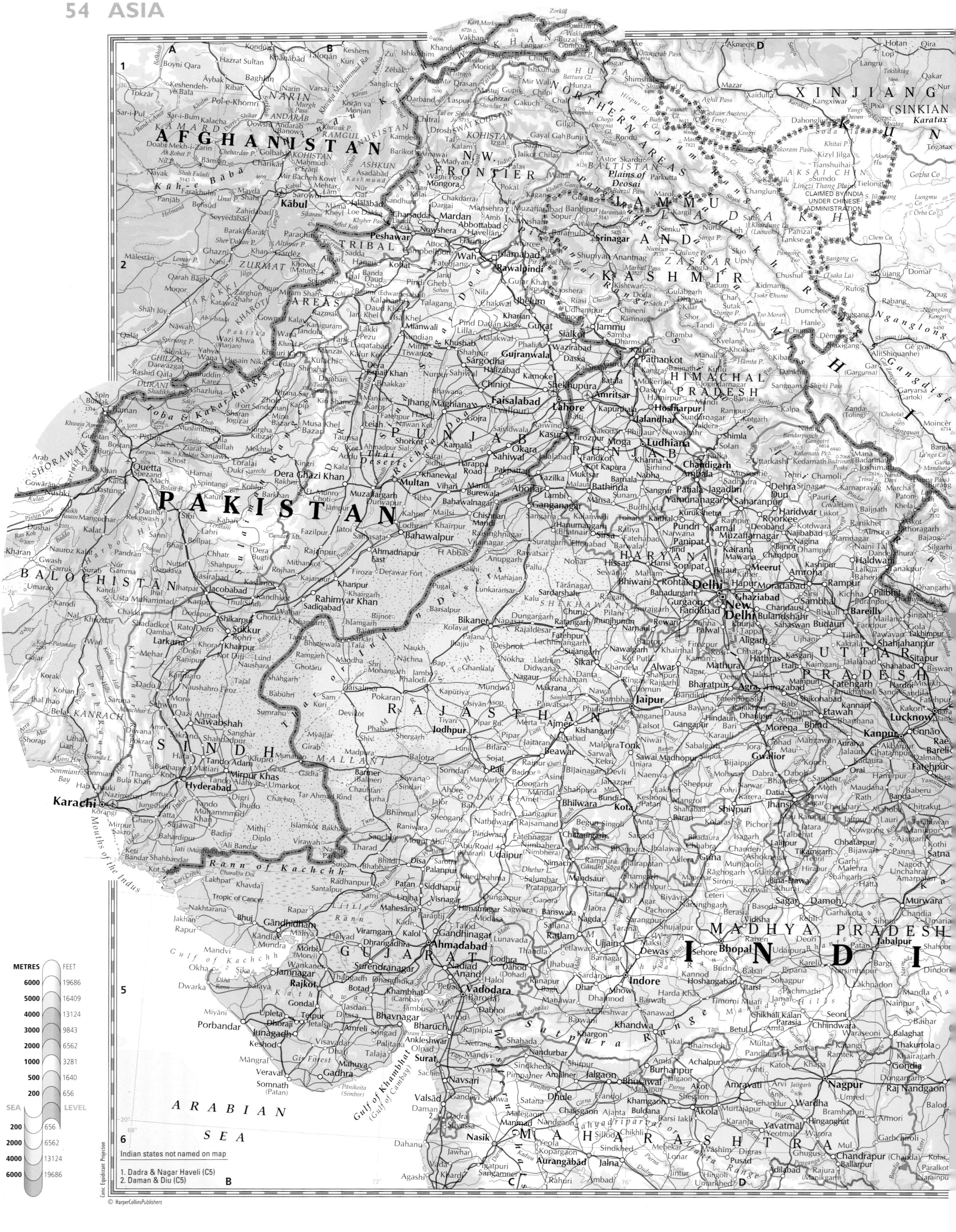

AFGHANISTAN

PAKISTAN

INDIA

XINJIANG (SINKIAN)

JAMMU AND KASHMIR

HIMACHAL PRADESH

PUNJAB

HARYANA

RAJASTHAN

UTTAR PRADESH

MADHYA PRADESH

GUJARAT

MAHARASHTRA

SINDH

BALOCHISTAN

N.W. FRONTIER

TRIBAL AREAS

NORTHERN AREAS

ARABIAN SEA

Tropic of Cancer

Mouths of the Indus

Gulf of Kachchh

Gulf of Khambhat (Gulf of Cambay)

Rann of Kachchh

Little Rann

THAR DESERT

ARAVALLI RANGE

Satpura Range

Aksai Chin — CLAIMED BY INDIA UNDER CHINESE ADMINISTRATION

Major cities: Kābul, Peshawar, Islamabad, Rawalpindi, Lahore, Faisalabad (Lyallpur), Multan, Quetta, Sukkur, Hyderabad, Karachi, Srinagar, Jammu, Amritsar, Ludhiana, Chandigarh, Shimla, Delhi, New Delhi, Ghaziabad, Meerut, Jaipur, Jodhpur, Ajmer, Kota, Udaipur, Gwalior, Jhansi, Kanpur, Lucknow, Bareilly, Ahmadābād, Vadodara (Baroda), Surat, Rajkot, Jamnagar, Bhopal, Indore, Ujjain, Jabalpur, Nagpur, Aurangabad, Nasik

METRES	FEET
6000	19686
5000	16409
4000	13124
3000	9843
2000	6562
1000	3281
500	1640
200	656
SEA	LEVEL
200	656
2000	6562
4000	13124
6000	19686

Indian states not named on map

1. Dadra & Nagar Haveli (C5)
2. Daman & Diu (C5)

CHINA

QINGHAI (TSINGHAI)

XIZANG GAOYUAN (PLATEAU OF TIBET)

KUN LUN SHAN

UYGUR ZIZHIQU (UIGHUR AUT. REGION)

XIZANG ZIZHIQU (TIBET AUT. REGION)

Hoh Xil Shan

Tanggula (Danglə) Shan

Nyainqêntanglha Shan

H I M A L A Y A

NEPAL

Kathmandu

Patan

Pokhara

SIKKIM

BHUTAN

Thimphu

Punakha

Gangtok

Darjiling

Shiliguri

ARUNACHAL PRADESH

ASSAM

Guwahati

NAGALAND

Kohima

MANIPUR

Imphal

MIZORAM

Aizawl

TRIPURA

Agartala

MEGHALAYA

Shillong

KHASI HILLS

GARO HILLS

KACHIN STATE

SAGAING

BANGLADESH

DHAKA

Dhaka

Rajshahi

Khulna

Barisal

CHITTAGONG

Chittagong

Comilla

Sylhet

Silchar

BIHAR

Patna

Gaya

Ranchi

Jamshedpur

WEST BENGAL

Calcutta

Haora

Kharagpur

Medinipur

Asansol

Durgapur

Dhanbad

Bokaro

CHOTA NAGPUR

ORISSA

Cuttack

Bhubaneswar

Sambalpur

Raurkela

Puri

Konārka (Black Pagoda)

Varanasi

Allahabad

Gorakhpur

Fyzabad

Mirzapur

MYANMAR (BURMA)

ARAKAN

Sittwe (Akyab)

Cox's Bazar

Mouths of the Ganga

BAY OF BENGAL

Brahmaputra

Yarlung Zangbo (Brahmaputra)

Lhasa

Xigazê

Gyangze (Gyantse)

Nagarze

Mt Everest (Qomolangma Feng) 8848

Naga Hills

1:6 000 000

| 0 | 40 | 80 | 120 | 160 | 200 MILES |

| 0 | 40 | 80 | 120 | 160 | 200 | 240 | 280 | 320 KM |

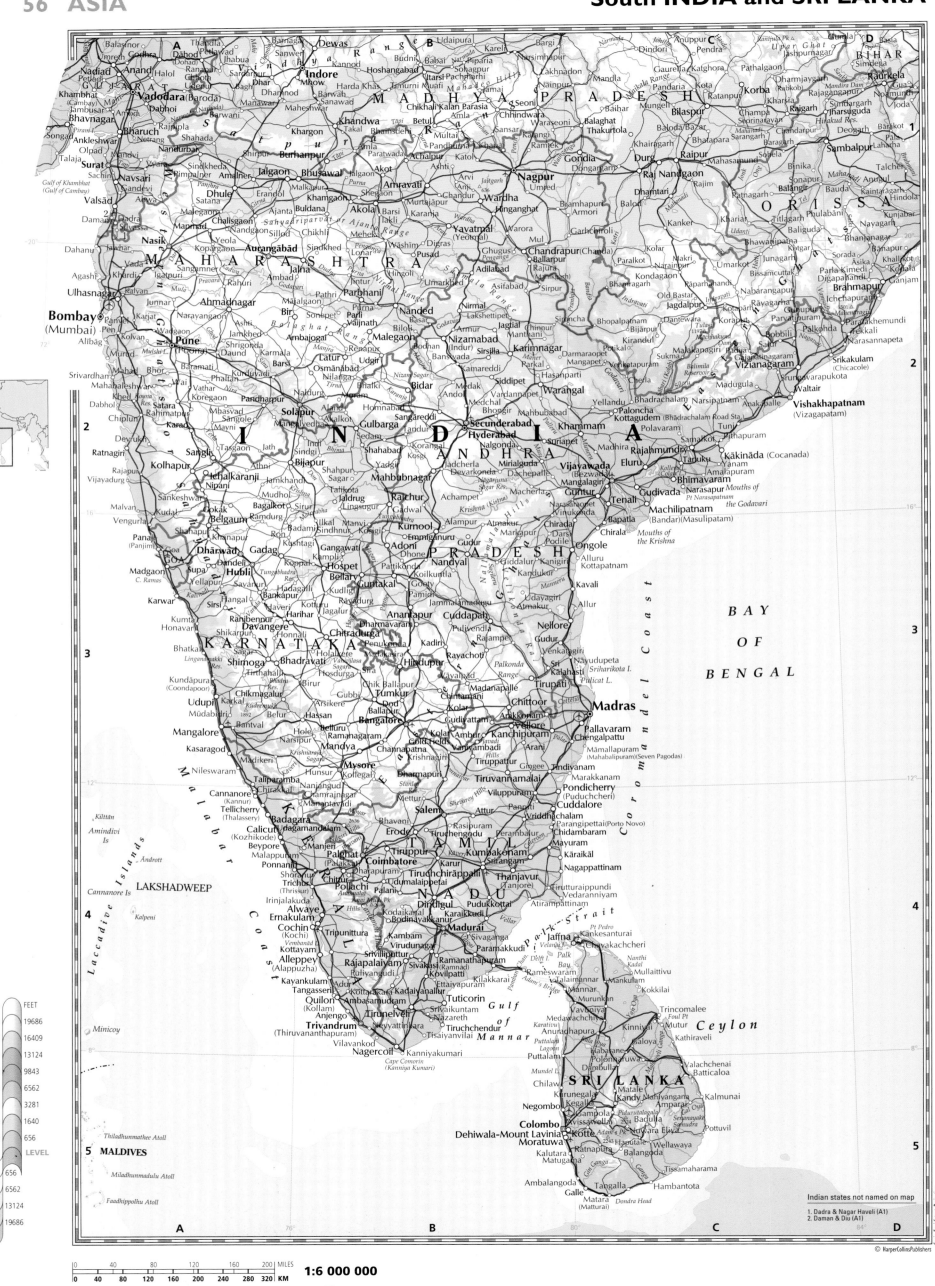

BAY

OF

BENGAL

Indian states not named on map

1. Dadra & Nagar Haveli (A1)
2. Daman & Diu (A1)

METRES / FEET

6000	19686
5000	16409
4000	13124
3000	9843
2000	6562
1000	3281
500	1640
200	656
SEA LEVEL	
200	656
2000	6562
4000	13124
6000	19686

1:6 000 000

Conic Equidistant Projection

© HarperCollins Publishers

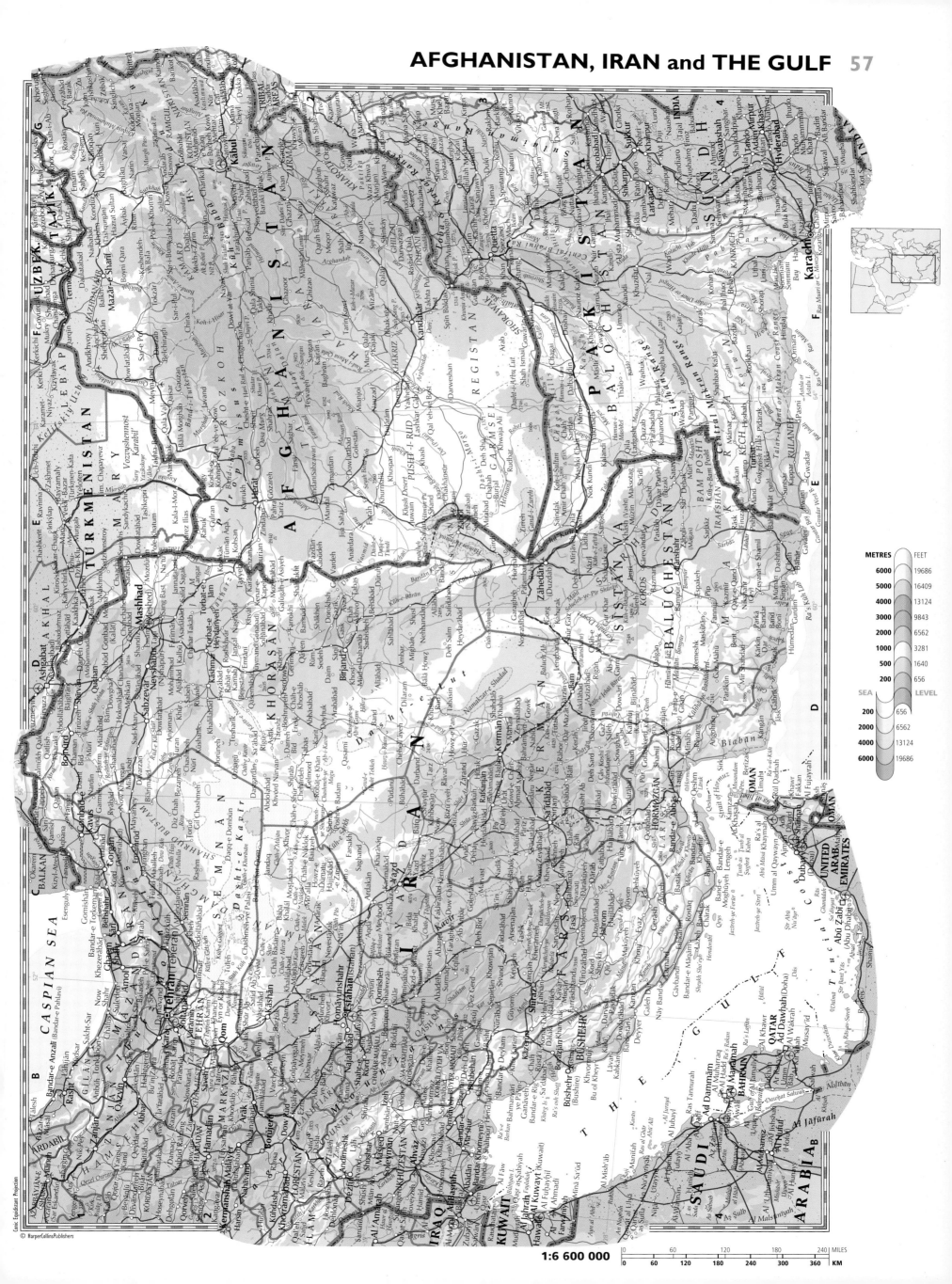

Conic Equidistant Projection

1:6 600 000

METRES		FEET
6000		19686
5000		16409
4000		13124
3000		9843
2000		6562
1000		3281
500		1640
200		656
SEA		LEVEL
200		656
2000		6562
4000		13124
6000		19686

0 60 120 180 240 MILES
0 60 120 180 240 300 360 KM

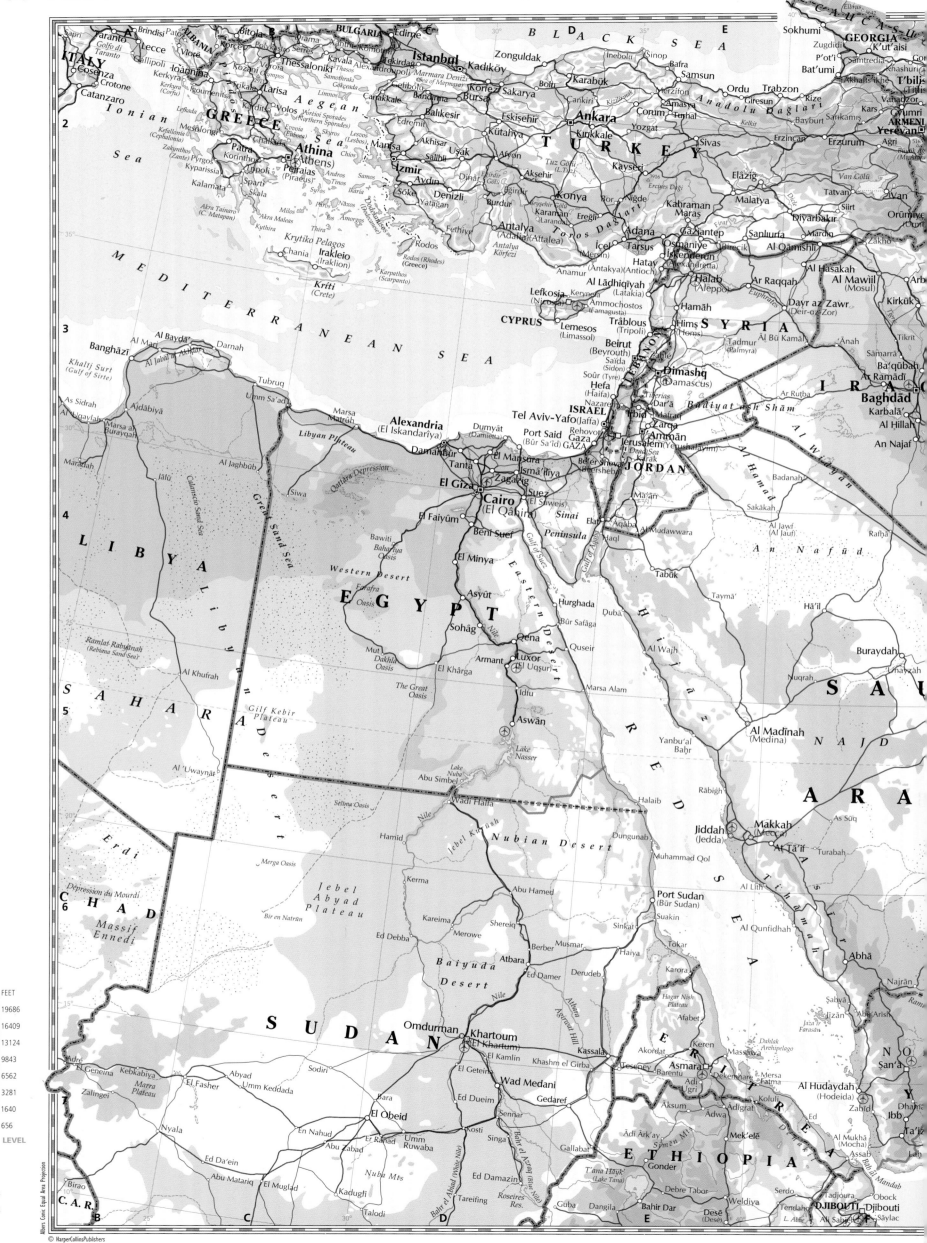

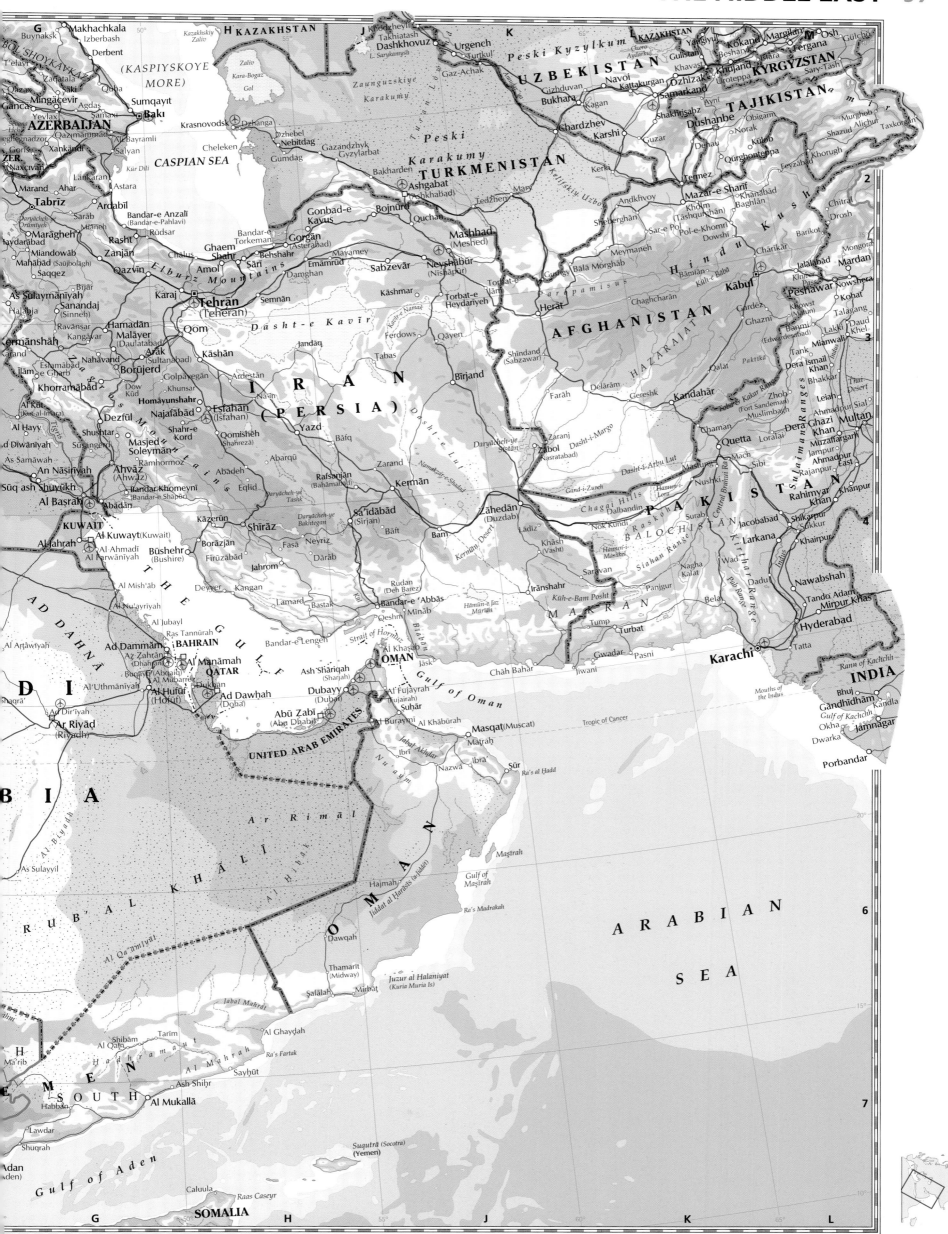

1:10 800 000

TURKEY, IRAQ, SYRIA, JORDAN and TRANSCAUCASIAN REPUBLICS

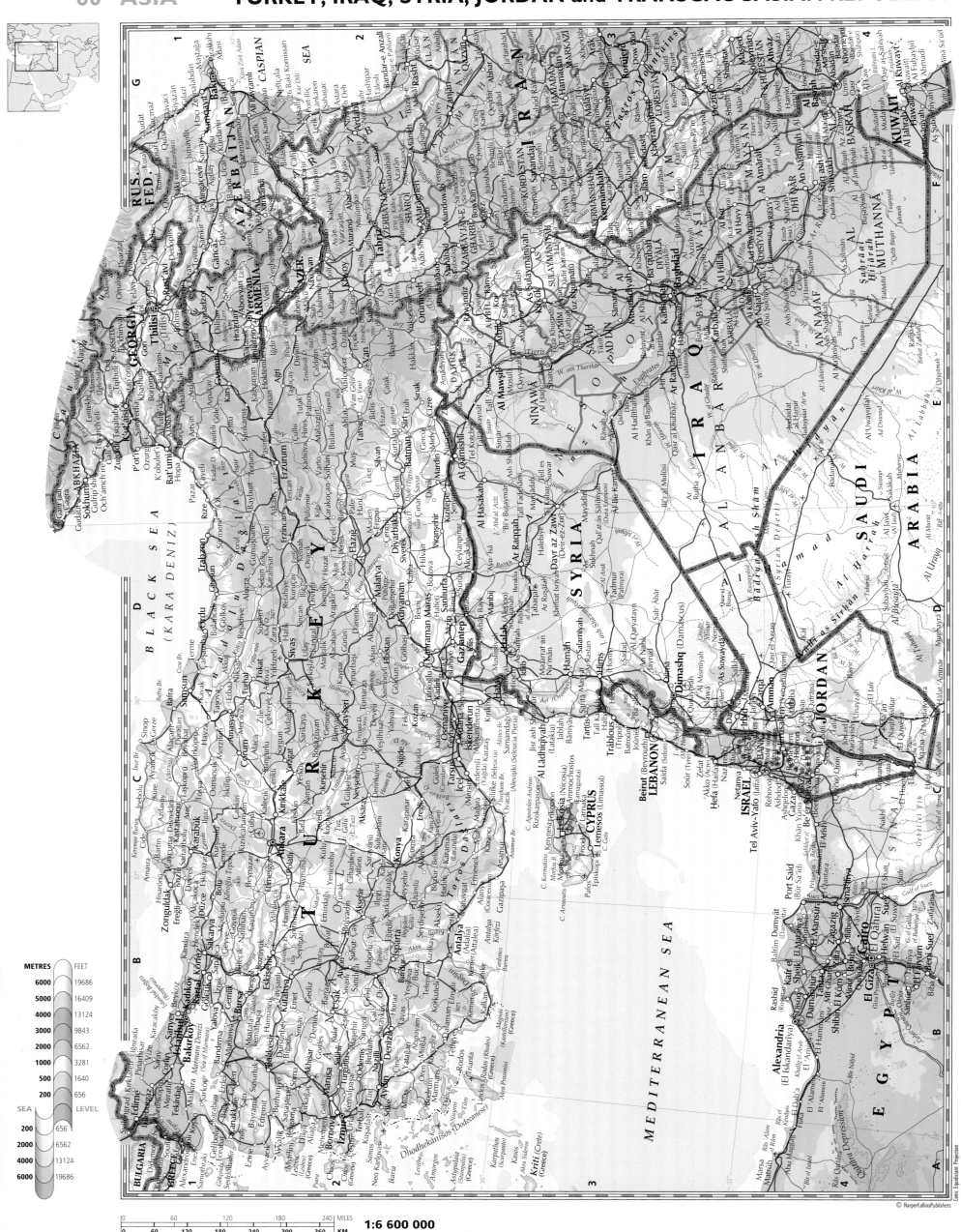

METRES / FEET

6000 / 19686
5000 / 16409
4000 / 13124
3000 / 9843
2000 / 6562
1000 / 3281
500 / 1640
200 / 656

SEA / LEVEL

200 / 656
2000 / 6562
4000 / 13124
6000 / 19686

1:6 600 000

© HarperCollinsPublishers

0   60   120   180   240 MILES
0   60   120   180   240   300   360 KM

Conic Equidistant Projection

1:3 300 000

METRES		FEET
6000		19686
5000		16409
4000		13124
3000		9843
2000		6562
1000		3281
500		1640
200		656
SEA		LEVEL
200		656
2000		6562
4000		13124
6000		19686

METRES FEET
6000 19686
5000 16409
4000 13124
3000 9843
2000 6562
1000 3281
500 1640
200 656
SEA LEVEL
200 656
2000 6562
4000 13124
6000 19686

Conic Equidistant Projection

© HarperCollinsPublishers

RUSSIAN FEDERATION

METRES / FEET

METRES	FEET
6000	19686
5000	16409
4000	13124
3000	9843
2000	6562
1000	3281
500	1640
200	656
SEA	LEVEL
200	656
2000	6562
4000	13124
6000	19686

Conic Equidistant Projection

© HarperCollinsPublishers

1:7 500 000

0	75	150	225	300	MILES
0	75	150	225	300	375	450	KM

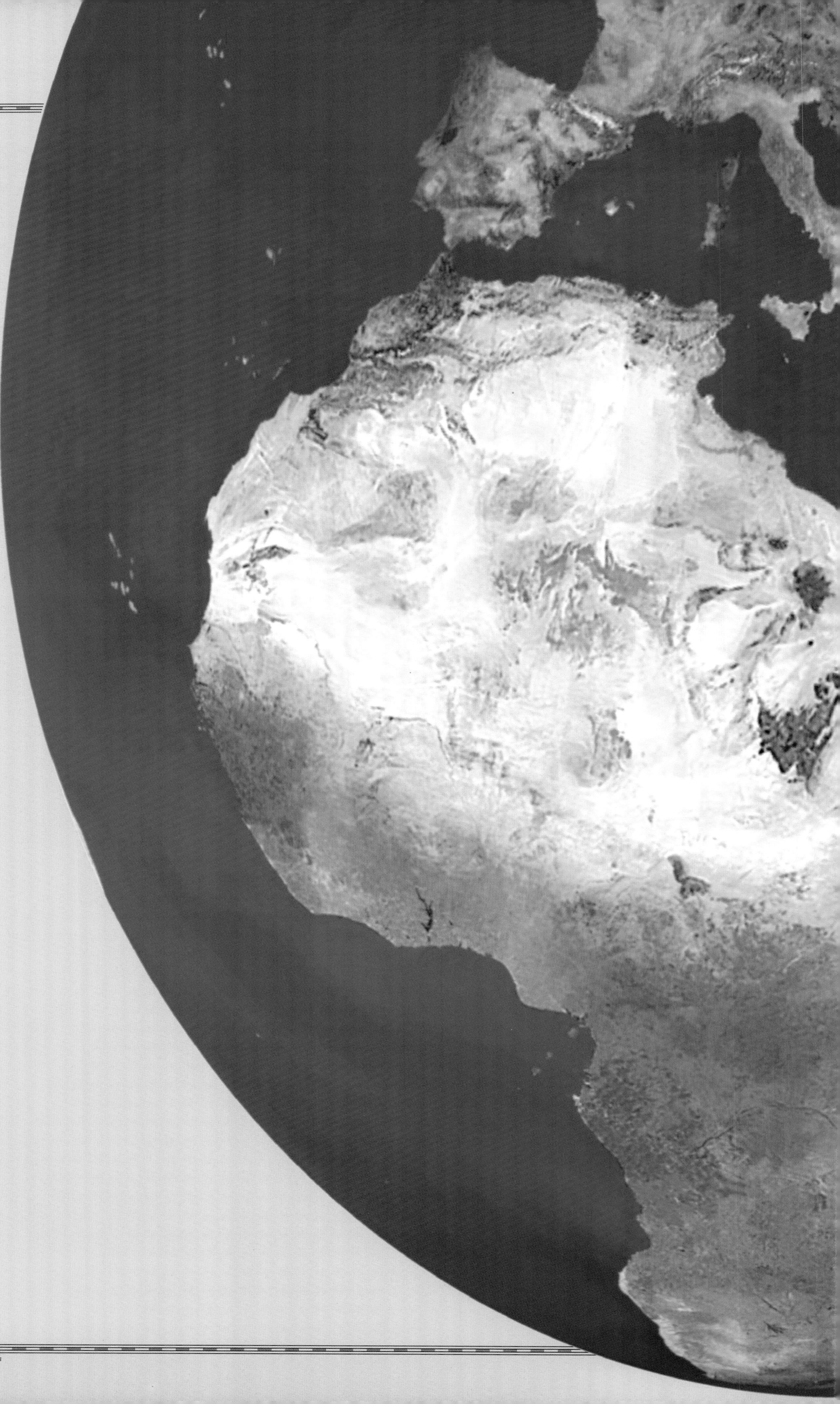

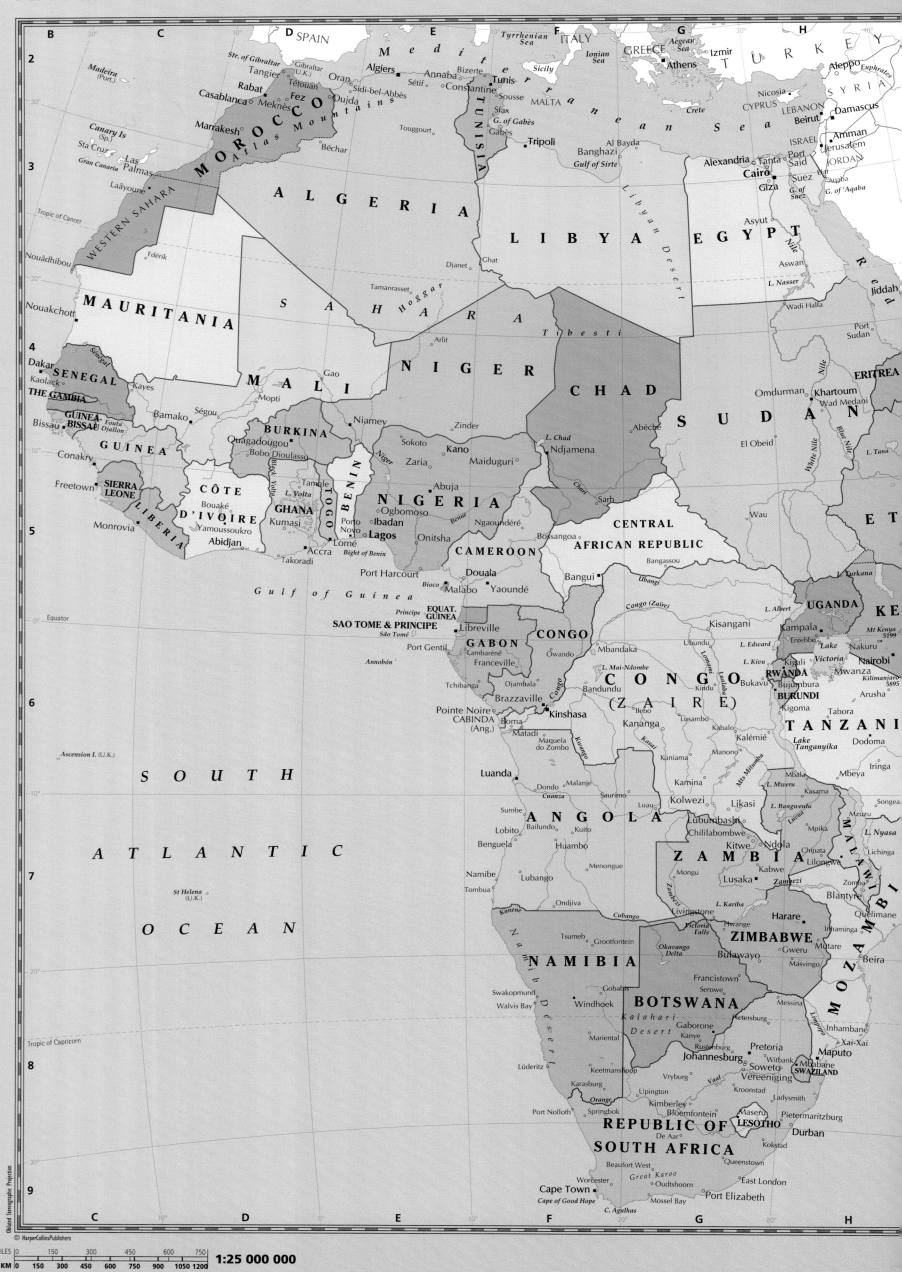

© HarperCollinsPublishers

Oxford Stereographic Projection

MILES 0   150   300   450   600   750

KM 0   150 300 450 600 750 900 1050 1200

1:25 000 000

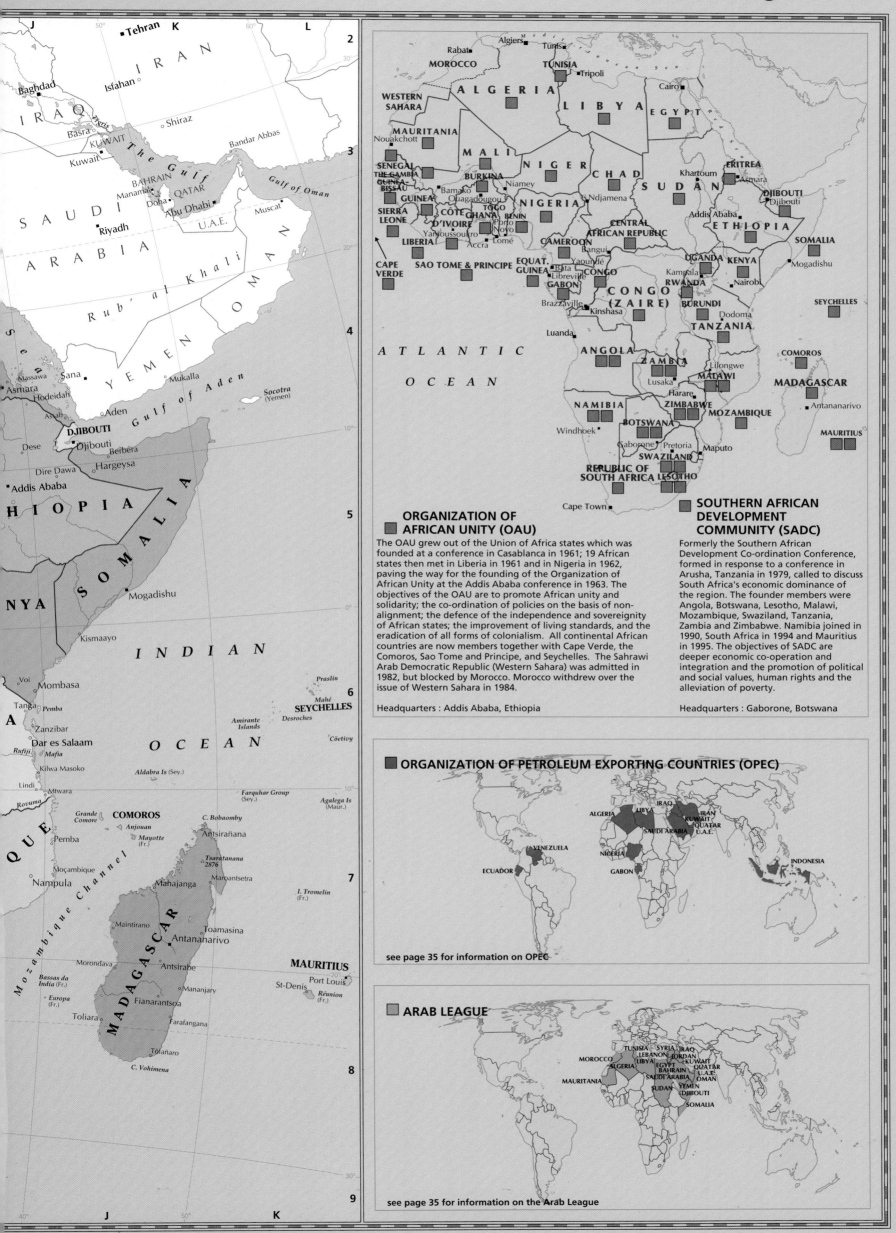

ORGANIZATION OF AFRICAN UNITY (OAU)

The OAU grew out of the Union of Africa states which was founded at a conference in Casablanca in 1961; 19 African states then met in Liberia in 1961 and in Nigeria in 1962, paving the way for the founding of the Organization of African Unity at the Addis Ababa conference in 1963. The objectives of the OAU are to promote African unity and solidarity; the co-ordination of policies on the basis of non-alignment; the defence of the independence and sovereignty of African states; the improvement of living standards, and the eradication of all forms of colonialism. All continental African countries are now members together with Cape Verde, the Comoros, Sao Tome and Principe, and Seychelles. The Sahrawi Arab Democratic Republic (Western Sahara) was admitted in 1982, but blocked by Morocco. Morocco withdrew over the issue of Western Sahara in 1984.

Headquarters : Addis Ababa, Ethiopia

SOUTHERN AFRICAN DEVELOPMENT COMMUNITY (SADC)

Formerly the Southern African Development Co-ordination Conference, formed in response to a conference in Arusha, Tanzania in 1979, called to discuss South Africa's economic dominance of the region. The founder members were Angola, Botswana, Lesotho, Malawi, Mozambique, Swaziland, Tanzania, Zambia and Zimbabwe. Namibia joined in 1990, South Africa in 1994 and Mauritius in 1995. The objectives of SADC are deeper economic co-operation and integration and the promotion of political and social values, human rights and the alleviation of poverty.

Headquarters : Gaborone, Botswana

ORGANIZATION OF PETROLEUM EXPORTING COUNTRIES (OPEC)

see page 35 for information on OPEC

ARAB LEAGUE

see page 35 for information on the Arab League

COUNTRY	AREA sq ml	AREA sq km	POPULATION total	density per sq ml	density per sq km	FORM OF GOVERNMENT	CAPITAL CITY	MAIN LANGUAGES	MAIN RELIGIONS	CURRENCY
ALGERIA	919 595	2 381 741	27 561 000	30	12	republic	Algiers	Arabic, French, Berber	Muslim, R.C.	Dinar
ANGOLA	481 354	1 246 700	10 674 000	22	9	republic	Luanda	Portuguese, local lang	R.C., Protestant, trad. beliefs	Kwanza
BENIN	43 483	112 620	5 387 000	124	48	republic	Porto Novo	French, Fon, Yoruba, Adja, local lang	Trad. beliefs, R.C., Muslim	CFA franc
BOTSWANA	224 468	581 370	1 443 000	6	2	republic	Gaborone	English (official), Setswana, Shona, local lang	Trad. beliefs, Protestant, R.C.	Pula
BURKINA	105 869	274 200	9 889 000	93	36	republic	Ouagadougou	French, More (Mossi), Fulani, local lang	Trad. beliefs, Muslim, R.C.	CFA franc
BURUNDI	10 747	27 835	6 134 000	571	220	republic	Bujumbura	Kirundi (Hutu, Tutsi), French	R.C., trad. beliefs, Protestant, Muslim	Franc
CAMEROON	183 569	475 442	12 871 000	70	27	republic	Yaoundé	French, English, Fang, Bamileke, local lang	Trad. beliefs, R.C., Muslim, Protestant	CFA franc
CAPE VERDE	1 557	4 033	381 000	245	94	republic	Praia	Portuguese, Portuguese Creole	R.C., Protestant, trad. beliefs	Escudo
C. A. R.	240 324	622 436	3 235 000	13	5	republic	Bangui	French, Sango, Banda, Baya, local lang	Protestant, R.C., trad. beliefs, Muslim	CFA franc
CHAD	495 755	1 284 000	6 214 000	13	5	republic	Ndjamena	Arabic, French, local lang	Muslim, trad. beliefs, R.C.	CFA franc
COMOROS	719	1 862	630 000	876	338	republic	Moroni	Comorian, French, Arabic	Muslim, R.C.	Franc
CONGO	132 047	342 000	2 516 000	19	7	republic	Brazzaville	French, Kongo, Monokutuba, local lang	R.C., Protestant, trad. beliefs, Muslim	CFA franc
CÔTE D'IVOIRE	124 504	322 463	13 695 000	110	42	republic	Yamoussoukro	French, Akan, Kru, Gur, local lang	Trad. beliefs, Muslim, R.C.	CFA franc
DJIBOUTI	8 958	23 200	566 000	63	24	republic	Djibouti	Somali, French, Arabic, Issa, Afar	Muslim, R.C.	Franc
EGYPT	386 199	1 000 250	57 851 000	150	58	republic	Cairo	Arabic, French	Muslim, Coptic Christian	Pound
EQUATORIAL GUINEA	10 831	28 051	389 000	36	14	republic	Malabo	Spanish, Fang	R.C., trad. beliefs	CFA franc
ERITREA	45 328	117 400	3 437 000	76	29	republic	Asmara	Tigrinya, Arabic, Tigre, English	Muslim, Coptic Christian	Ethiopian birr
ETHIOPIA	437 794	1 133 880	54 938 000	125	48	republic	Addis Ababa	Amharic, Oromo, local lang	Ethiopian Orthodox, Muslim, trad. beliefs	Birr
GABON	103 347	267 667	1 283 000	12	5	republic	Libreville	French, Fang, local lang	R.C., Protestant, trad. beliefs	CFA franc
GAMBIA	4 361	11 295	1 081 000	248	96	republic	Banjul	English, Malinke, Fulani, Wolof	Muslim, Protestant	Dalasi
GHANA	92 100	238 537	16 944 000	184	71	republic	Accra	English, Hausa, Akan, local lang	Protestant, R.C., Muslim, trad. beliefs	Cedi
GUINEA	94 926	245 857	6 501 000	68	26	republic	Conakry	French, Fulani, Malinke, local lang	Muslim, trad. beliefs, R.C.	Franc
GUINEA-BISSAU	13 948	36 125	1 050 000	75	29	republic	Bissau	Portuguese, Portuguese Creole, local lang	Trad. beliefs, Muslim, R.C.	Peso
KENYA	224 961	582 646	29 292 000	130	50	republic	Nairobi	Swahili, English, local lang	R.C., Protestant, trad. beliefs	Shilling
LESOTHO	11 720	30 355	1 996 000	170	66	monarchy	Maseru	Sesotho, English, Zulu	R.C., Protestant, trad. beliefs	Loti
LIBERIA	43 000	111 369	2 700 000	63	24	republic	Monrovia	English, Creole, local lang	Trad. beliefs, Muslim, Protestant, R.C.	Dollar
LIBYA	679 362	1 759 540	4 899 000	7	3	republic	Tripoli	Arabic, Berber	Muslim, R.C.	Dinar
MADAGASCAR	226 658	587 041	14 303 000	63	24	republic	Antananarivo	Malagasy, French	Trad. beliefs, R.C., Protestant, Muslim	Franc
MALAWI	45 747	118 484	9 461 000	207	80	republic	Lilongwe	English, Chichewa, Lomwe, local lang	Protestant, R.C., trad. beliefs, Muslim	Kwacha
MALI	478 821	1 240 140	10 462 000	22	8	republic	Bamako	French, Bambara, local lang	Muslim, trad. beliefs, R.C.	CFA franc
MAURITANIA	397 955	1 030 700	2 211 000	6	2	republic	Nouakchott	Arabic, French, local lang	Muslim	Ouguiya
MAURITIUS	788	2 040	1 113 000	1413	546	republic	Port Louis	English, French Creole, Hindi, Indian languages	Hindu, R.C., Muslim, Protestant	Rupee
MOROCCO	172 414	446 550	26 590 000	154	60	monarchy	Rabat	Arabic, Berber, French, Spanish	Muslim, R.C.	Dirham
MOZAMBIQUE	308 642	799 380	16 614 000	54	21	republic	Maputo	Portuguese, Makua, Tsonga, local lang	Trad. beliefs, R.C., Muslim	Metical
NAMIBIA	318 261	824 292	1 500 000	5	2	republic	Windhoek	English, Afrikaans, German, Ovambo, local lang	Protestant, R.C.	Dollar
NIGER	489 191	1 267 000	8 846 000	18	7	republic	Niamey	French, Hausa, Fulani, local lang	Muslim, trad. beliefs	CFA franc
NIGERIA	356 669	923 768	108 467 000	304	117	republic	Abuja	English, Creole, Hausa, Yoruba, Ibo, Fulani	Muslim, Protestant, R.C., trad. beliefs	Naira
RÉUNION	985	2 551	644 000	654	252	French territory	St-Denis	French, French Creole	R.C.	French franc
RWANDA	10 169	26 338	7 750 000	762	294	republic	Kigali	Kinyarwanda, French, English	R.C., trad. beliefs, Protestant, Muslim	Franc
SÃO TOMÉ AND PRÍNCIPE	372	964	125 000	336	130	republic	São Tomé	Portuguese, Portuguese Creole	R.C., Protestant	Dobra
SENEGAL	75 954	196 720	8 102 000	107	41	republic	Dakar	French, Wolof, Fulani, local lang	Muslim, R.C., trad. beliefs	CFA franc
SEYCHELLES	176	455	74 000	421	163	republic	Victoria	Seychellois, English	R.C., Protestant	Rupee
SIERRA LEONE	27 699	71 740	4 402 000	159	61	republic	Freetown	English, Creole, Mende, Temne, local lang	Trad. beliefs, Muslim, Protestant, R.C.	Leone
SOMALIA	246 201	637 657	9 077 000	37	14	republic	Mogadishu	Somali, Arabic	Muslim	Shilling
SOUTH AFRICA	470 689	1 219 080	40 436 000	86	33	republic	Pretoria/Cape Town	Afrikaans, English, local lang	Protestant, R.C., Muslim, Hindu	Rand
SUDAN	967 500	2 505 813	28 947 000	30	12	republic	Khartoum	Arabic, Dinka, Nubian, Beja, Nuer, local lang	Muslim, trad. beliefs, R.C., Protestant	Dinar
SWAZILAND	6 704	17 364	879 000	131	51	monarchy	Mbabane	Swazi, English	Protestant, R.C., trad. beliefs	Emalangeni
TANZANIA	364 900	945 087	28 846 000	79	31	republic	Dodoma	Swahili, English, Nyamwezi, local lang	R.C., Muslim, trad. beliefs, Protestant	Shilling
TOGO	21 925	56 785	3 928 000	179	69	republic	Lomé	French, Ewe, Kabre, local lang	Trad. beliefs, R.C., Muslim, Protestant	CFA franc
TUNISIA	63 379	164 150	8 814 000	139	54	republic	Tunis	Arabic, French	Muslim	Dinar
UGANDA	93 065	241 038	20 621 000	222	86	republic	Kampala	English, Swahili, Luganda, local lang	R.C., Protestant, Muslim, trad. beliefs	Shilling
ZAIRE (CONGO)	905 568	2 345 410	42 552 000	47	18	republic	Kinshasa	French, Lingala, Swahili, Kongo, local lang	R.C., Protestant, Muslim, trad. beliefs	Zaïre
ZAMBIA	290 586	752 614	9 196 000	32	12	republic	Lusaka	English, Bemba, Nyanja, Tonga, local lang	Protestant, R.C., trad. beliefs, Muslim	Kwacha
ZIMBABWE	150 873	390 759	11 150 000	74	29	republic	Harare	English, Shona, Ndebele	Protestant, R.C., trad. beliefs	Dollar

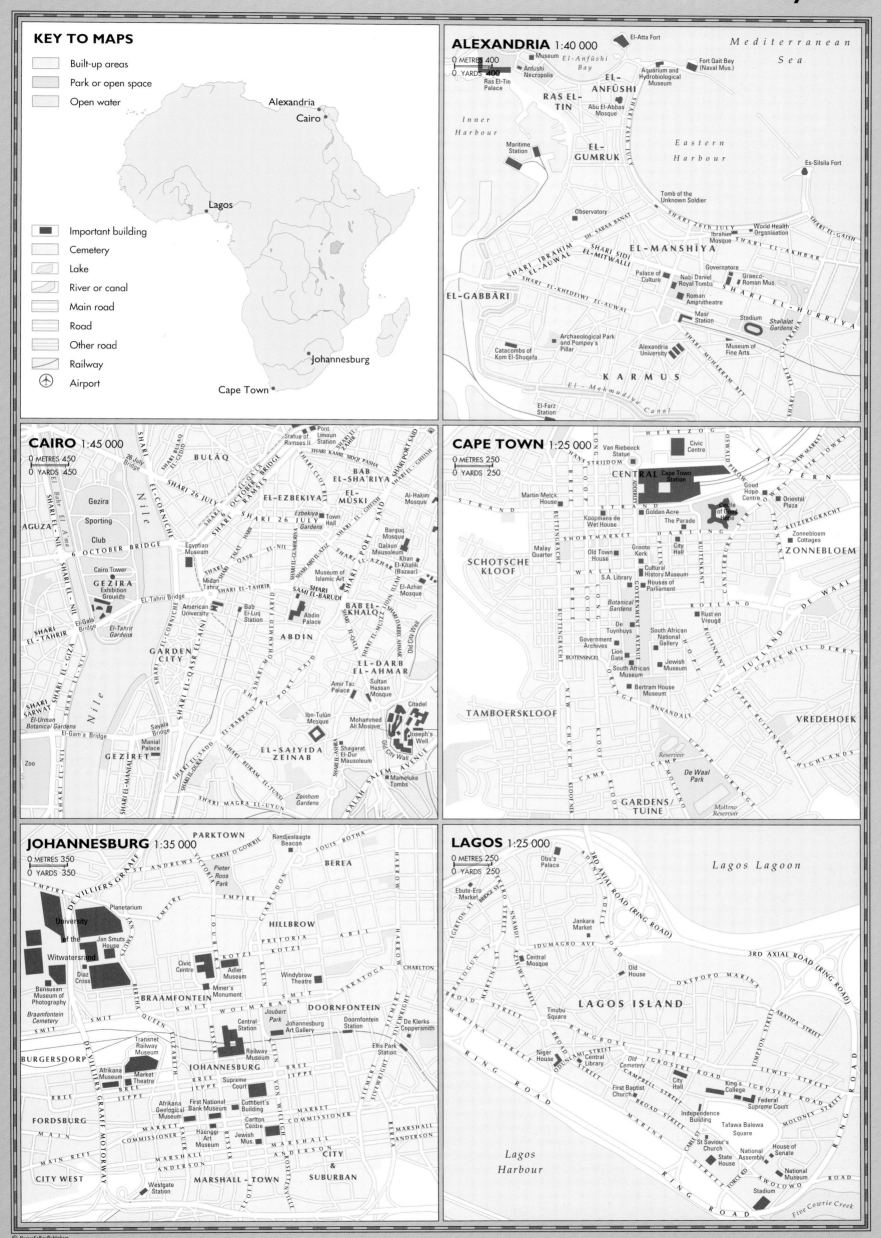

KEY TO MAPS

Built-up areas
Park or open space
Open water

Important building
Cemetery
Lake
River or canal
Main road
Road
Other road
Railway
Airport

ALEXANDRIA 1:40 000

CAIRO 1:45 000

CAPE TOWN 1:25 000

JOHANNESBURG 1:35 000

LAGOS 1:25 000

© HarperCollinsPublishers

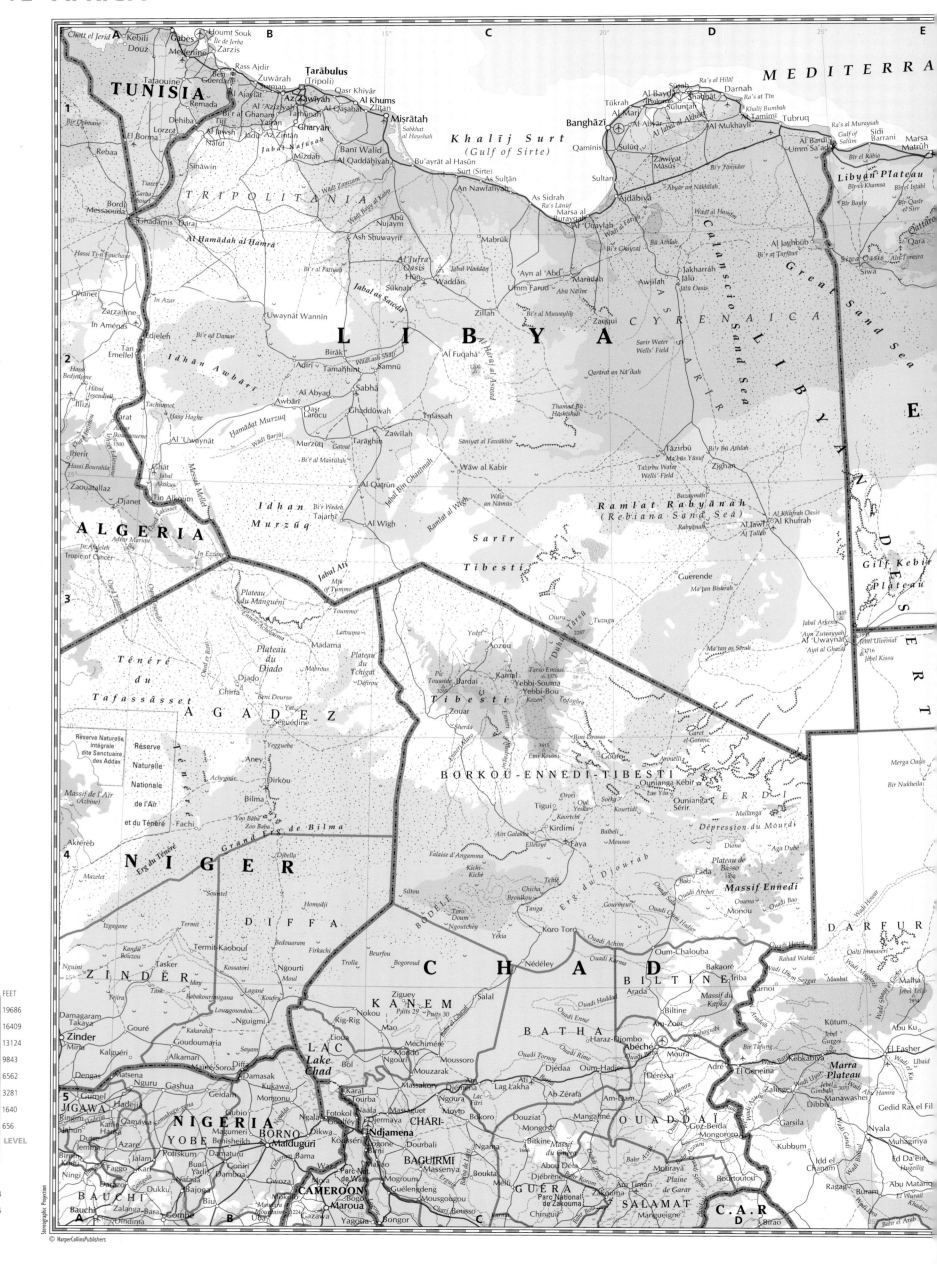

TUNISIA

LIBYA

ALGERIA

NIGER

CHAD

NIGERIA

CAMEROON

MEDITERRA

Khalīj Surt
(Gulf of Sirte)

TRIPOLITANIA

CYRENAICA

Great Sand Sea

LIBYAN DESERT

Ṭarābulus
(Tripoli)

Banghāzī

Tibesti

Tibesti

BORKOU-ENNEDI-TIBESTI

Massif Ennedi

DARFUR

ZINDER

DIFFA

KANEM

BILTINE

BATHA

Lake
Chad

LAC

BORNO

YOBE

JIGAWA

BAUCHI

CHARI-

BAGUIRMI

GUÉRA

OUADDAÏ

SALAMAT

C.A.R.

Ndjamena

Maiduguri

METRES	FEET
6000	19686
5000	16409
4000	13124
3000	9843
2000	6562
1000	3281
500	1640
200	656
SEA	**LEVEL**
200	656
2000	6562
4000	13124
6000	19686

Stereographic Projection

© HarperCollinsPublishers

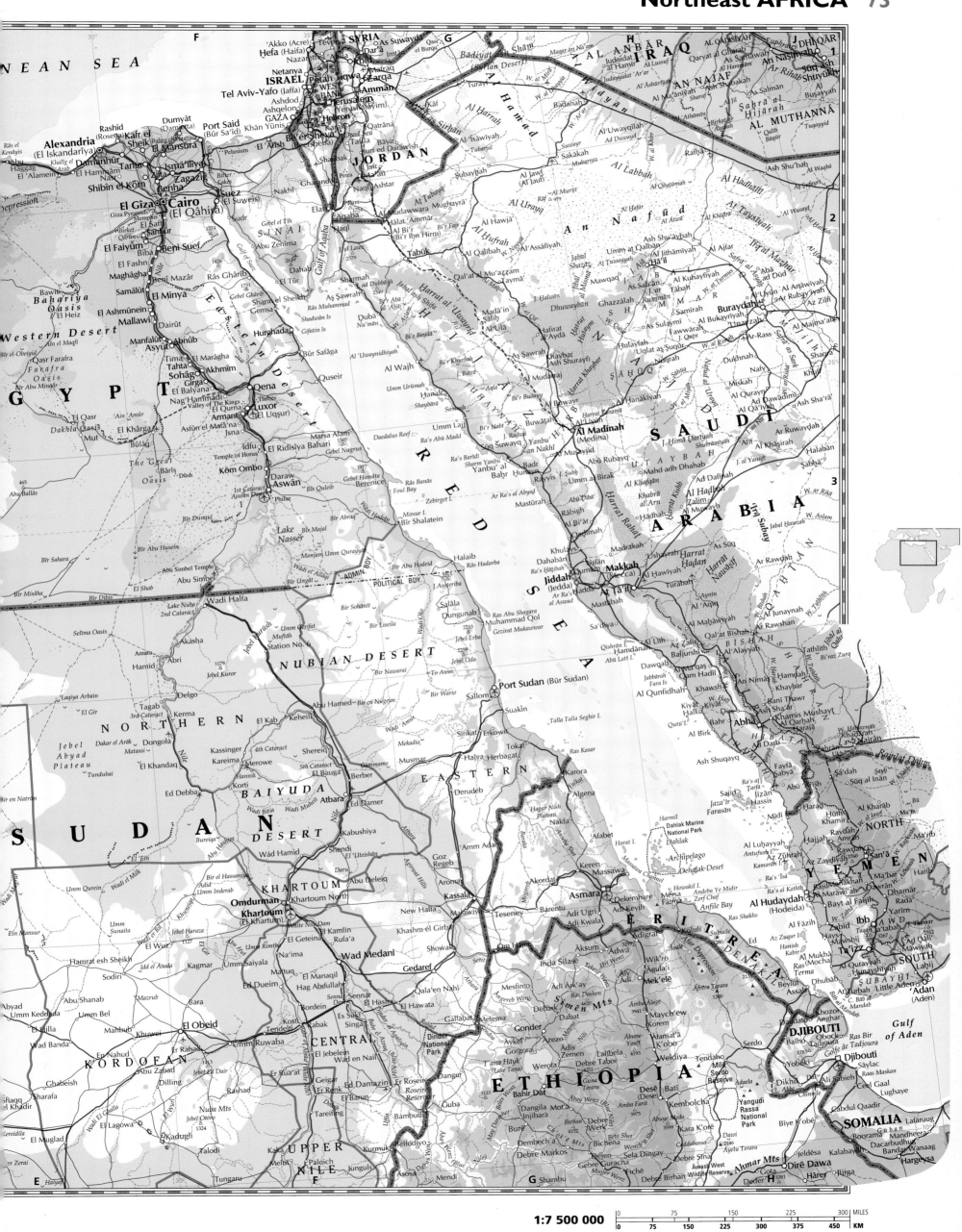

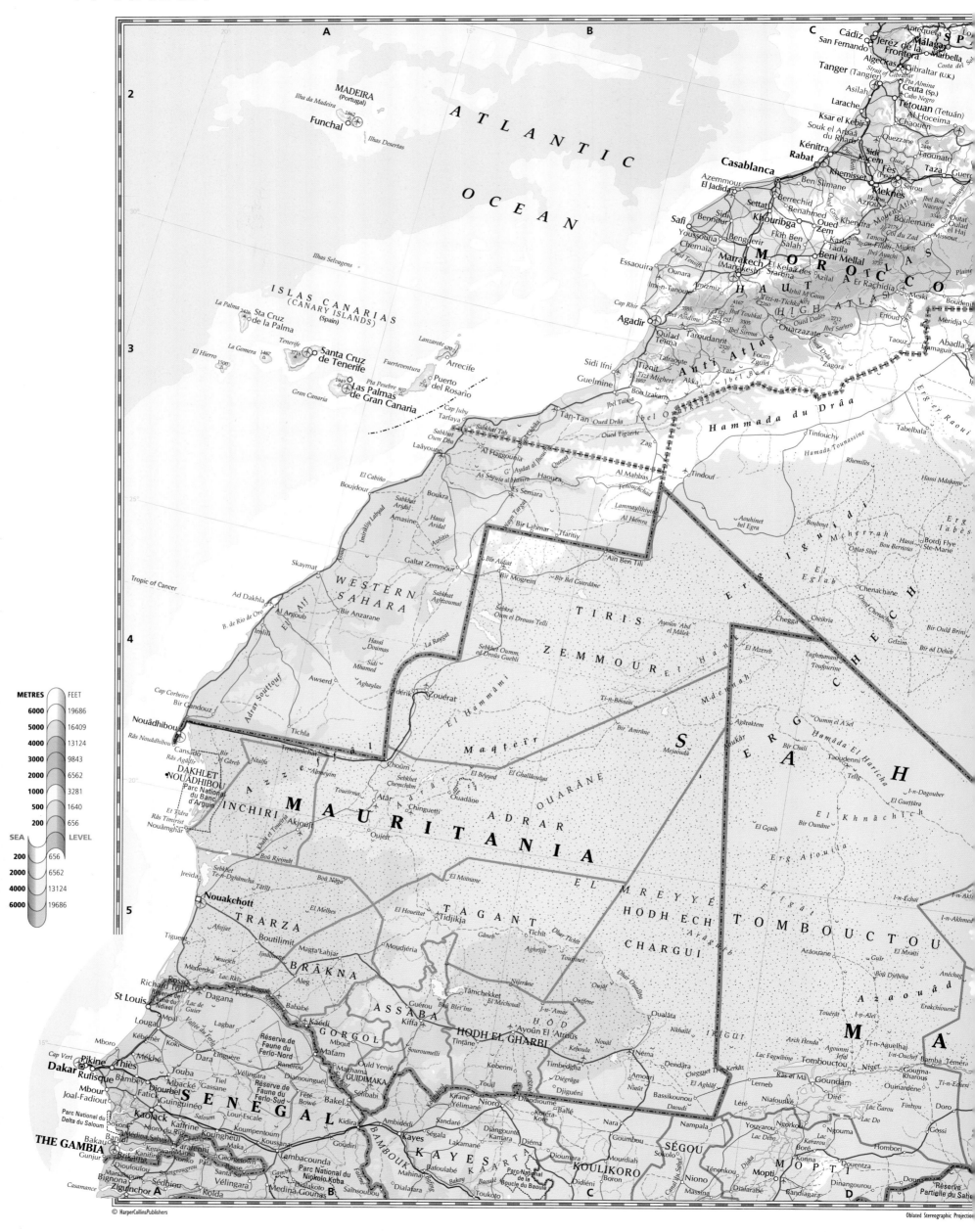

METRES / FEET

METRES	FEET
6000	19686
5000	16409
4000	13124
3000	9843
2000	6562
1000	3281
500	1640
200	656

SEA LEVEL

200	656
2000	6562
4000	13124
6000	19686

A T L A N T I C   O C E A N

MADEIRA (Portugal)
Funchal
Ilhas Desertas

Ilhas Selvagens

ISLAS CANARIAS (CANARY ISLANDS) (Spain)

MOROCCO

Casablanca
Rabat
Agadir

WESTERN SAHARA

Tropic of Cancer

Nouâdhibou

MAURITANIA

Nouakchott

SENEGAL

Dakar

THE GAMBIA

S A H A R A

TIRIS ZEMMOUR

ADRAR

TAGANT

BRÂKNA

GORGOL

ASSABA

HODH ECH CHARGUI

TOMBOUCTOU

HODH EL GHARBI

KAYES

KOULIKORO

SÉGOU

MOPTI

© HarperCollinsPublishers

Oblated Stereographic Projection

MEDITERRANEAN SEA

ITALY

MALTA
Valletta

TUNISIA

ALGERIA

LIBYA

TRIPOLITANIA

Khalīj Surt
(Gulf of Sirte)

Grand Erg Occidental

Grand Erg Oriental

Plateau du Tademaït
(Tademaït Plateau)

Plateau du Tinrhert

Idhan Awbari

Idhan Murzūq

SAHARA

Tanezrouft

H o g g a r

Tassili-n-Ajjer

Ténéré du Tafassâsset

Plateau du Manguéni

Plateau du Djado

Plateau du Tchigaï

Tibesti

AGADEZ

BORKOU-
ENNEDI-
TIBESTI

CHAD

MALI

NIGER

GAO

KIDAL

TAHOUA

ZINDER

DIFFA

KANEM

1:7 500 000

0   75   150   225   300 MILES

0 75 150 225 300 375 450 KM

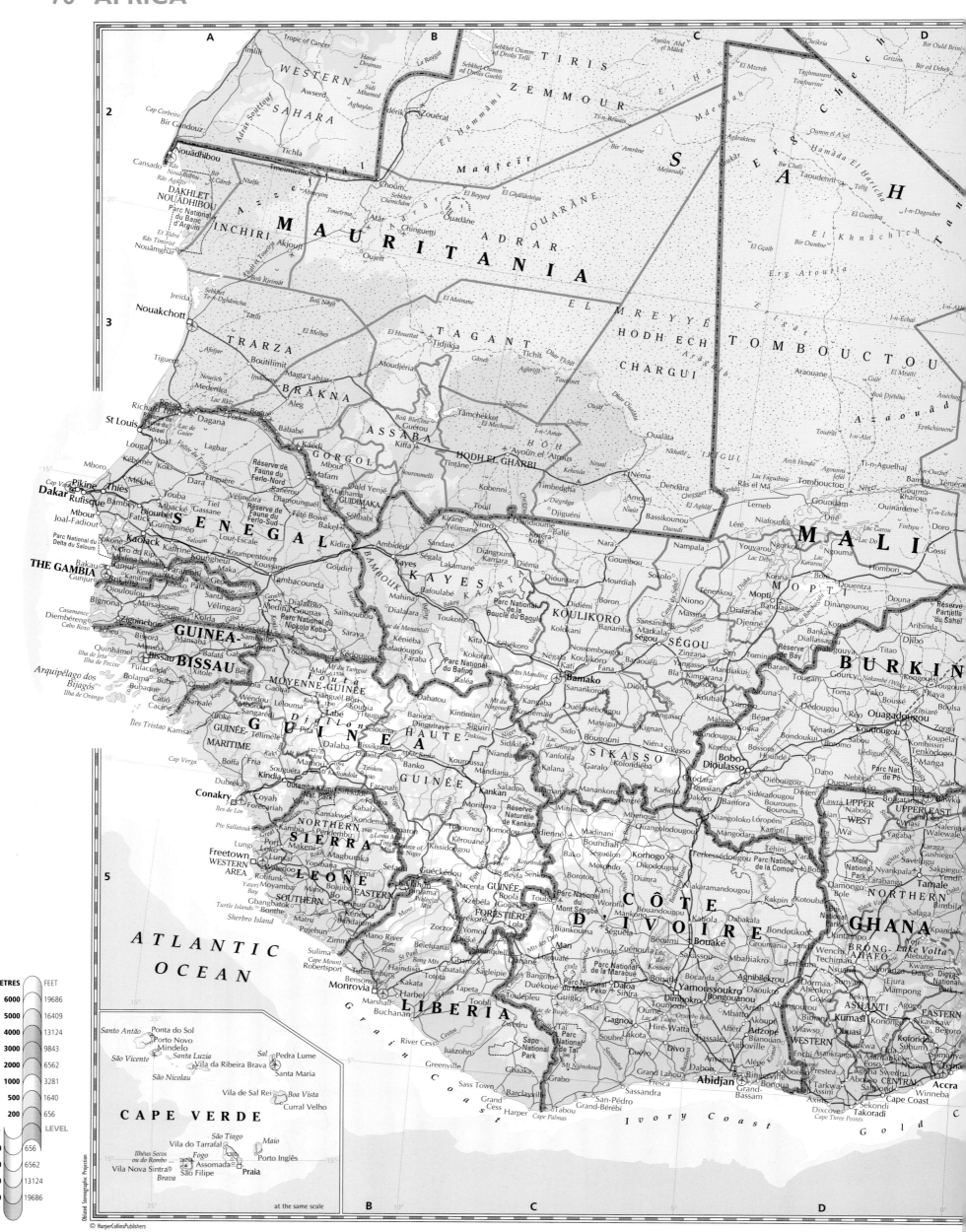

ATLANTIC
OCEAN

METRES   FEET
6000   19686
5000   16409
4000   13124
3000   9843
2000   6562
1000   3281
500   1640
200   656
SEA   LEVEL
200   656
2000   6562
4000   13124
6000   19686

Obland Stereographic Projection

© HarperCollins Publishers

CAPE VERDE

at the same scale

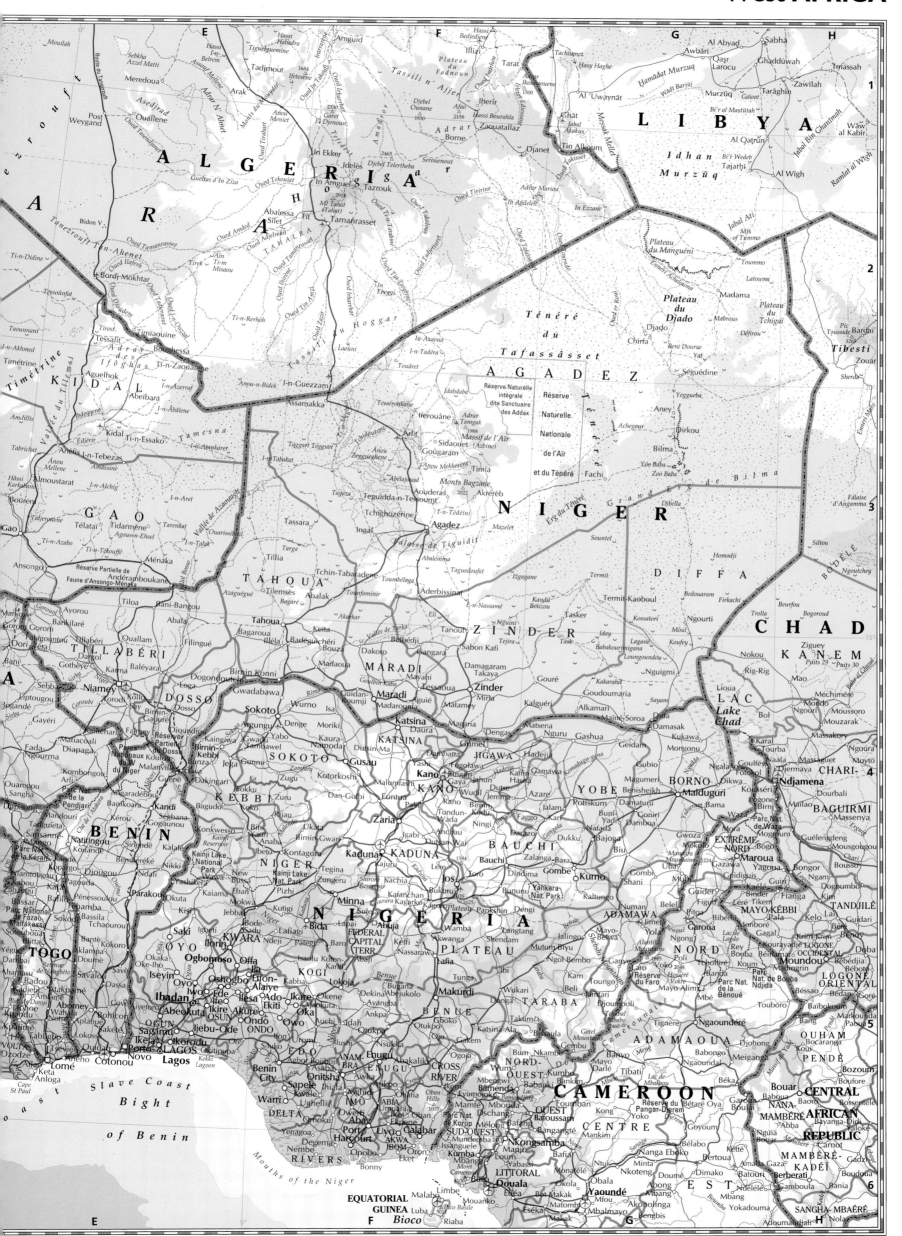

LIBYA

ALGERIA

NIGER

CHAD

NIGERIA

BENIN

TOGO

CAMEROON

CENTRAL
AFRICAN
REPUBLIC

EQUATORIAL
GUINEA

Slave Coast

Bight

of Benin

Mouths of the Niger

1:7 500 000

| 0 | 75 | 150 | 225 | 300 | MILES |

| 0 | 75 | 150 | 225 | 300 | 375 | 450 | KM |

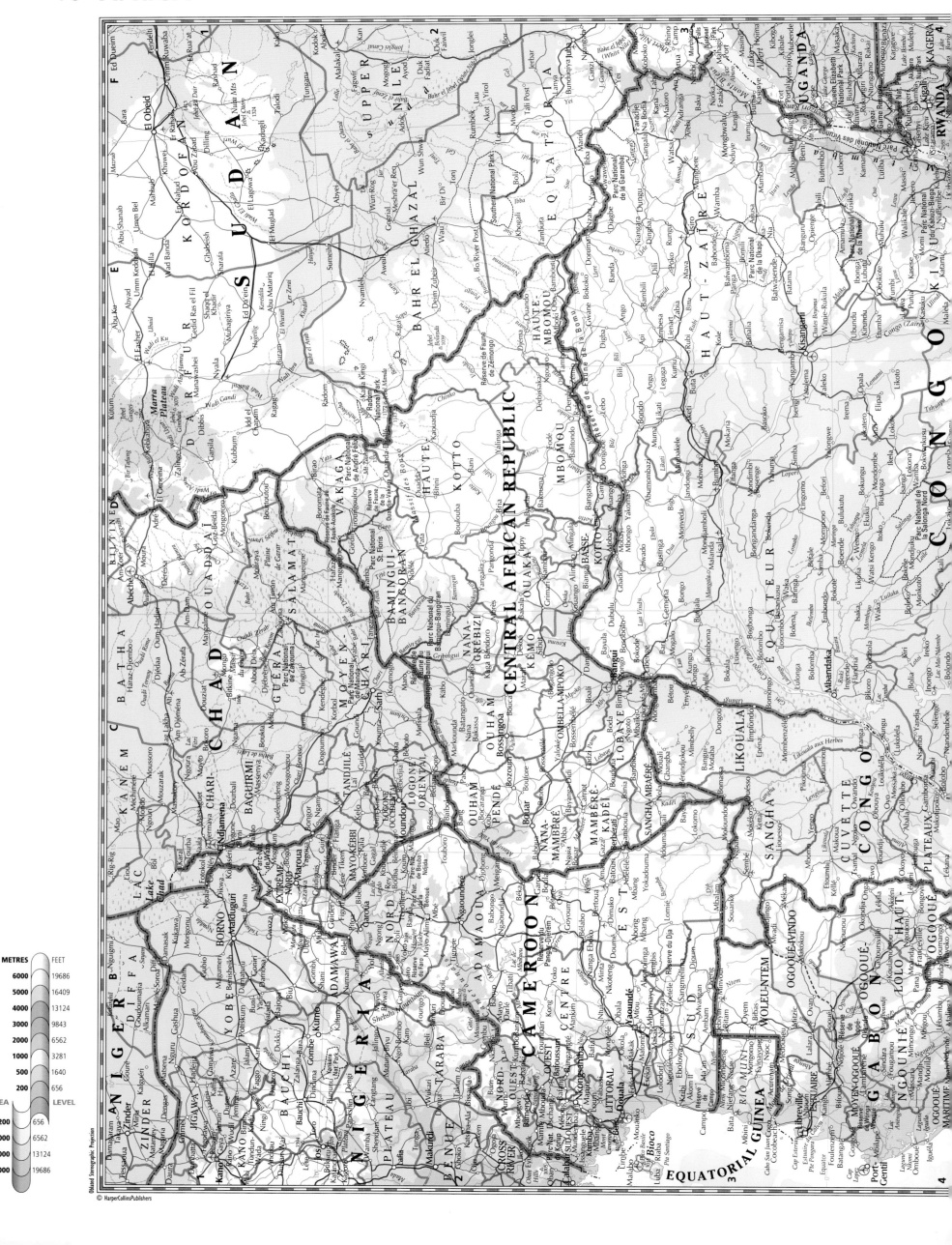

METRES | FEET
6000 | 19686
5000 | 16409
4000 | 13124
3000 | 9843
2000 | 6562
1000 | 3281
500 | 1640
200 | 656
SEA | LEVEL
200 | 656
2000 | 6562
4000 | 13124
6000 | 19686

Oblated Stereographic Projection

© HarperCollinsPublishers

ATLANTIC

OCEAN

1:7 500 000

| 0 | | 75 | | 150 | | 225 | | 300 MILES |

| 0 | 75 | 150 | 225 | 300 | 375 | 450 KM |

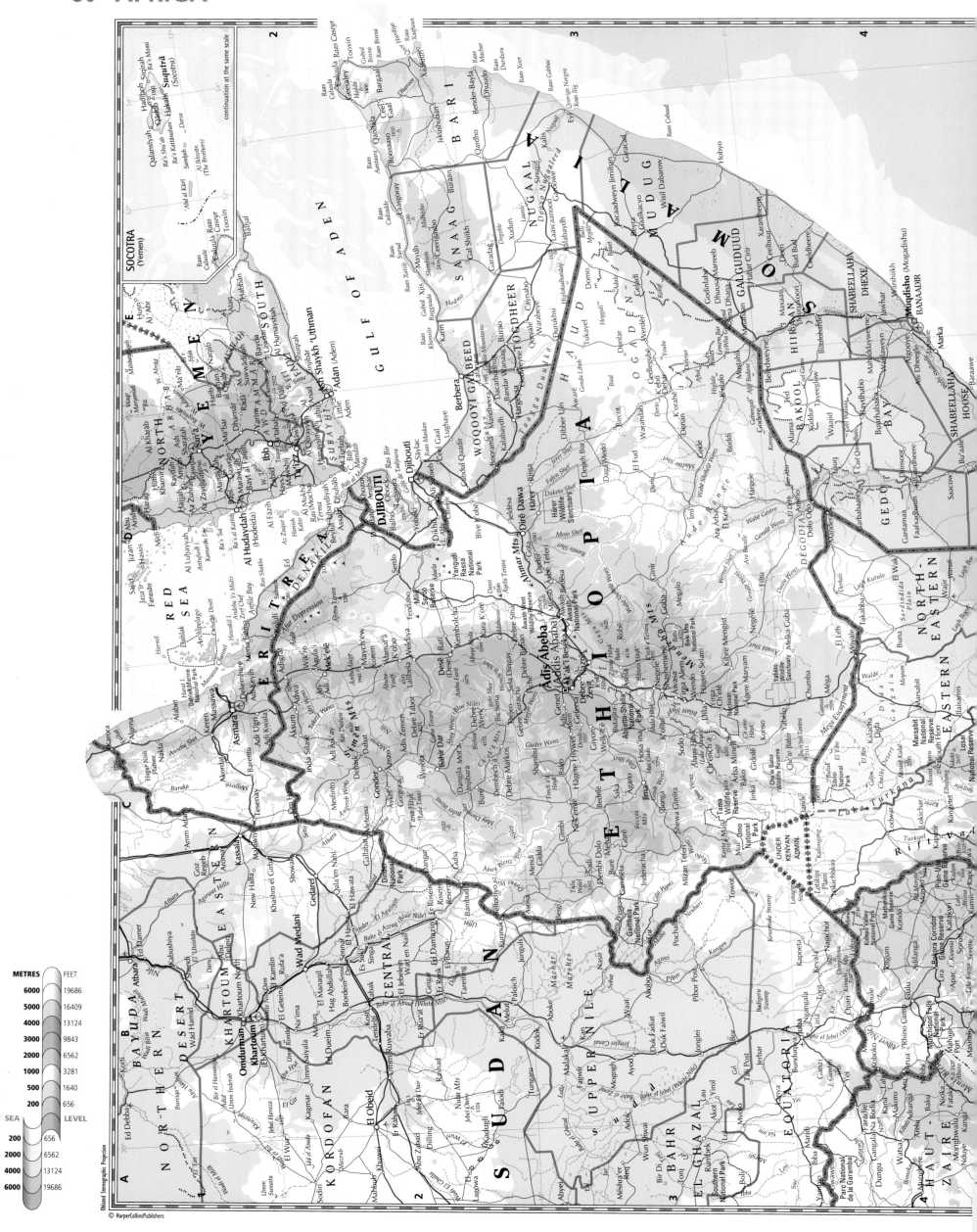

SEYCHELLES 1:3M

Equator

Bird I.
Denis I.
Aride I. Curieuse I. The Sisters
Booby I. Marie-Anne I.
Cousin Is. Felicité I.
Silhouette I. Praslin I. Corfu I. La Digue I.
North I. Mamelle I.
Frigate I.
Thérèse I. Victoria Reef I. L'Îlot
Trevor Pt Mahé
Anse Boileau Cascade
Takamaka Anse Royal

RODRIGUES I. (Mauritius) 1:1.5M

Port Mathurin
Île Coton
Pte la Fouce
Corfu I. Port South Coast
Topaz I.
Gombani

MAHÉ 1:1.5M

North Pt
St Anne I.
Victoria
Seychelles
Thérèse I. Anse
Anse Boileau Sancta Mariae
Takamaka Capucin

MAURITIUS 1:1.5M

Round I.
Flat I. Gabriel I.
Cannoniers Pt Grande Baie
C. Malheureux
Goodlands
Triolet Rivière du Rempart
Pamplemousses Poste de Flacq
Port Louis Beau Bassin Centre de Flacq
Rose Hill St Pierre Quatre Bornes
Médine Vacoas Phoenix Mt Blanche
Curepipe
Tamarin Vieux Grand Port
Plaine Mahébourg
Pt Sud St Pierre Union Vale
Chemin Grenier Bénares
Souillac
Ombre Surinam

RÉUNION (France) 1:1.5M

Au Vent
St-Denis
Ste-Marie
Ste-Suzanne
St-André Bras-Panon
St-Benoît
La Possession Salazie Ste-Rose
Le Port Ste-Anne
St-Paul St-Gilles La Plaine
Cilaos Le Tampon Ste-Philippe de la Table
Pte des Galets St-Louis Entre-Deux
B. de St-Leu Les Avirons
Étang-Salé Stella Matutina St-Joseph
St-Pierre
Petite-Île St-Pierre
Pte de Langevin
Sous le Vent

INDIAN OCEAN

COMOROS
Njazidja (Grande Comore)
Mitsamiouli
Mutsamudu Nzwani (Anjouan)
Moroni Fomboni Domoni
Mwali (Mohéli)

MAYOTTE (France)
Mamoudzou Dzaoudzi

Aldabra Is. (Seychelles)

SOMALIA / JUBBADA / HOOSE / DHEXE

KENYA
Mombasa
Nairobi
Malindi

TANZANIA
Dar es Salaam
Dodoma
Zanzibar I.
Pemba I.
Arusha
Mwanza
Tabora

UGANDA
Kampala

RWANDA
Kigali

BURUNDI
Bujumbura

CONGO (ZAIRE)

LAKE VICTORIA

ZAMBIA

MALAWI
Lilongwe
Lake Nyasa (L. Niassa) (L. Malawi)

MOZAMBIQUE
Pemba

ZIMBABWE

1:7 500 000

0   75   150   225   300 MILES
0   75 150 225 300 375 450 KM

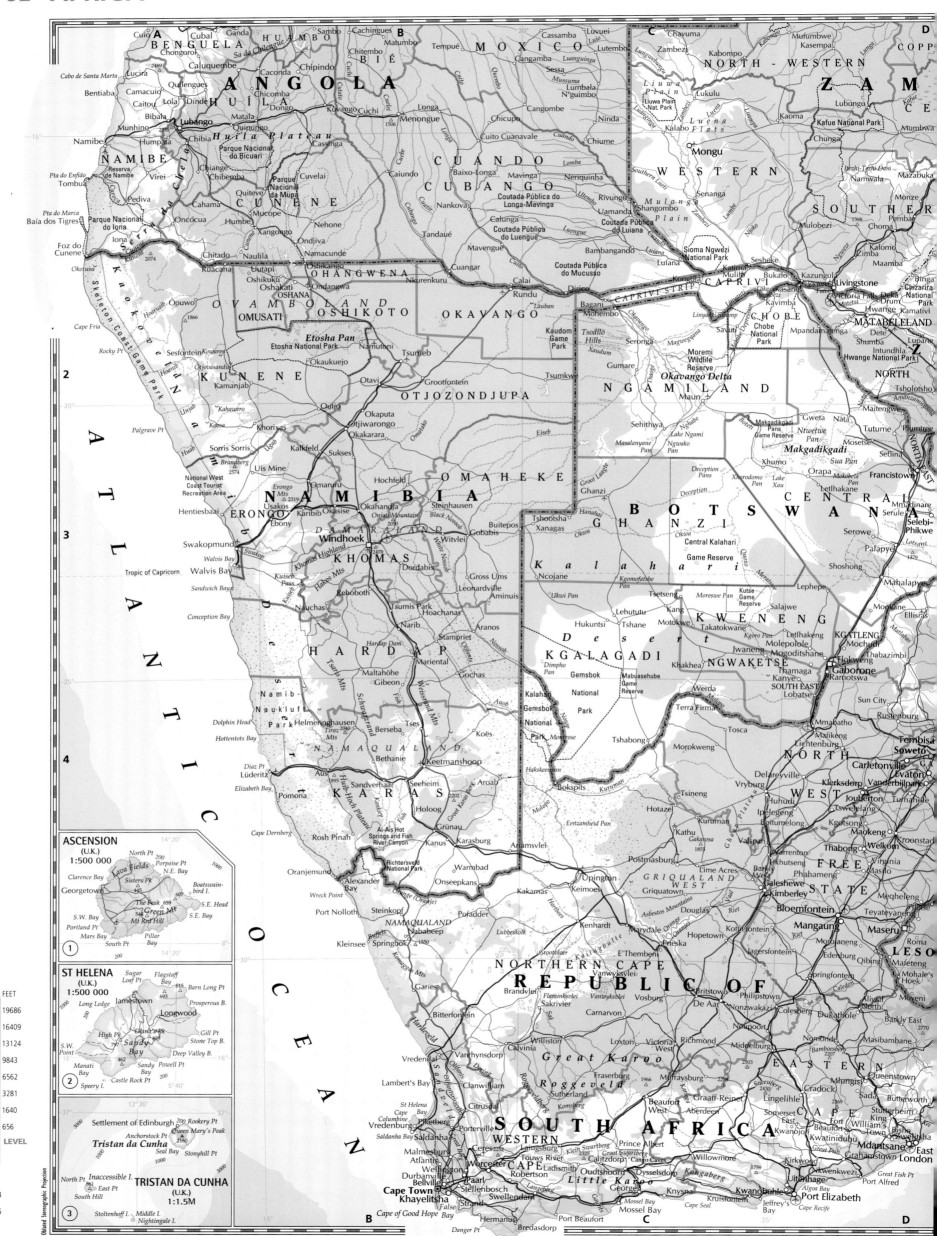

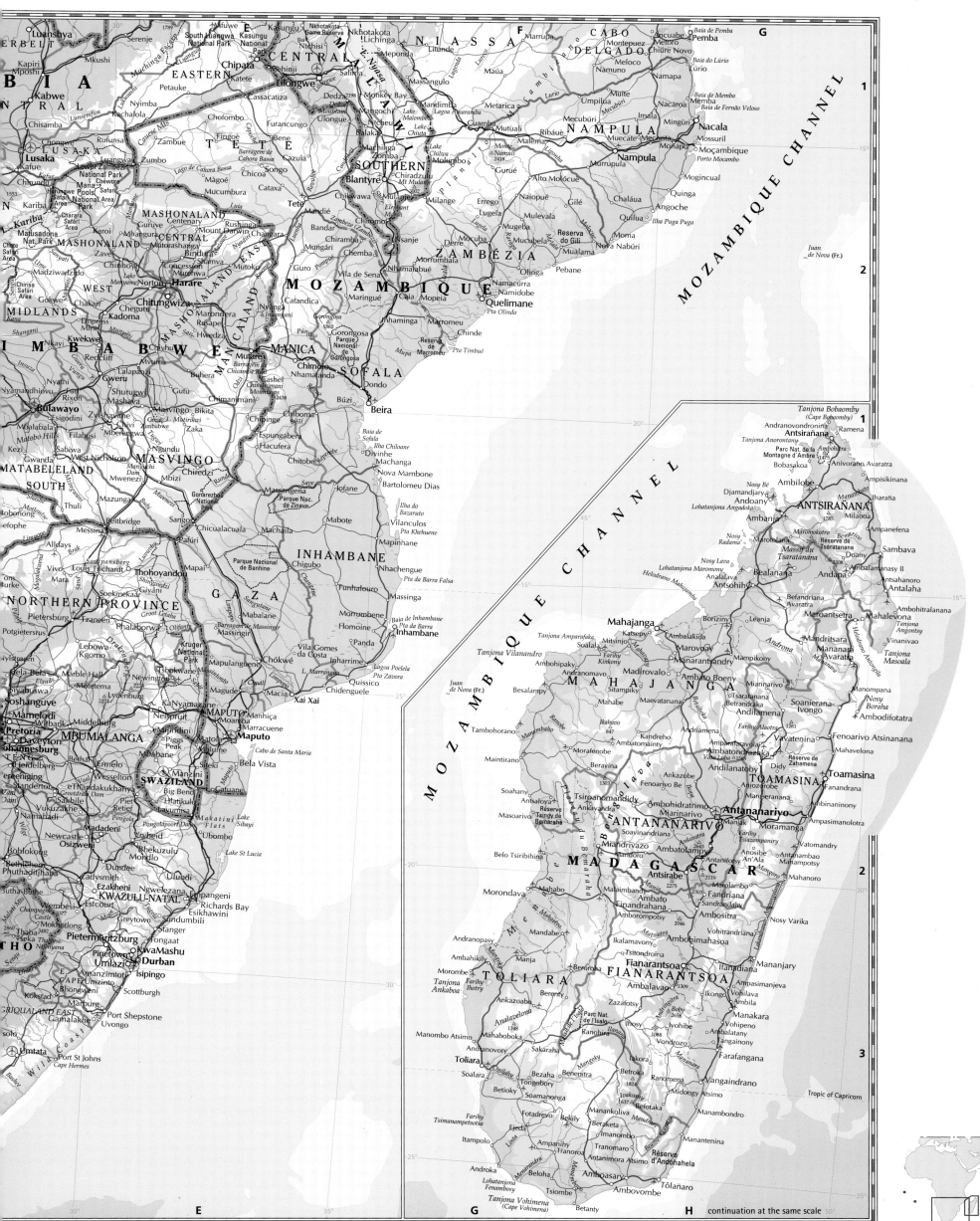

1 : 7 500 000

| 0 | 75 | 150 | 225 | 300 | MILES |

| 0 | 75 | 150 | 225 | 300 | 375 | 450 | KM |

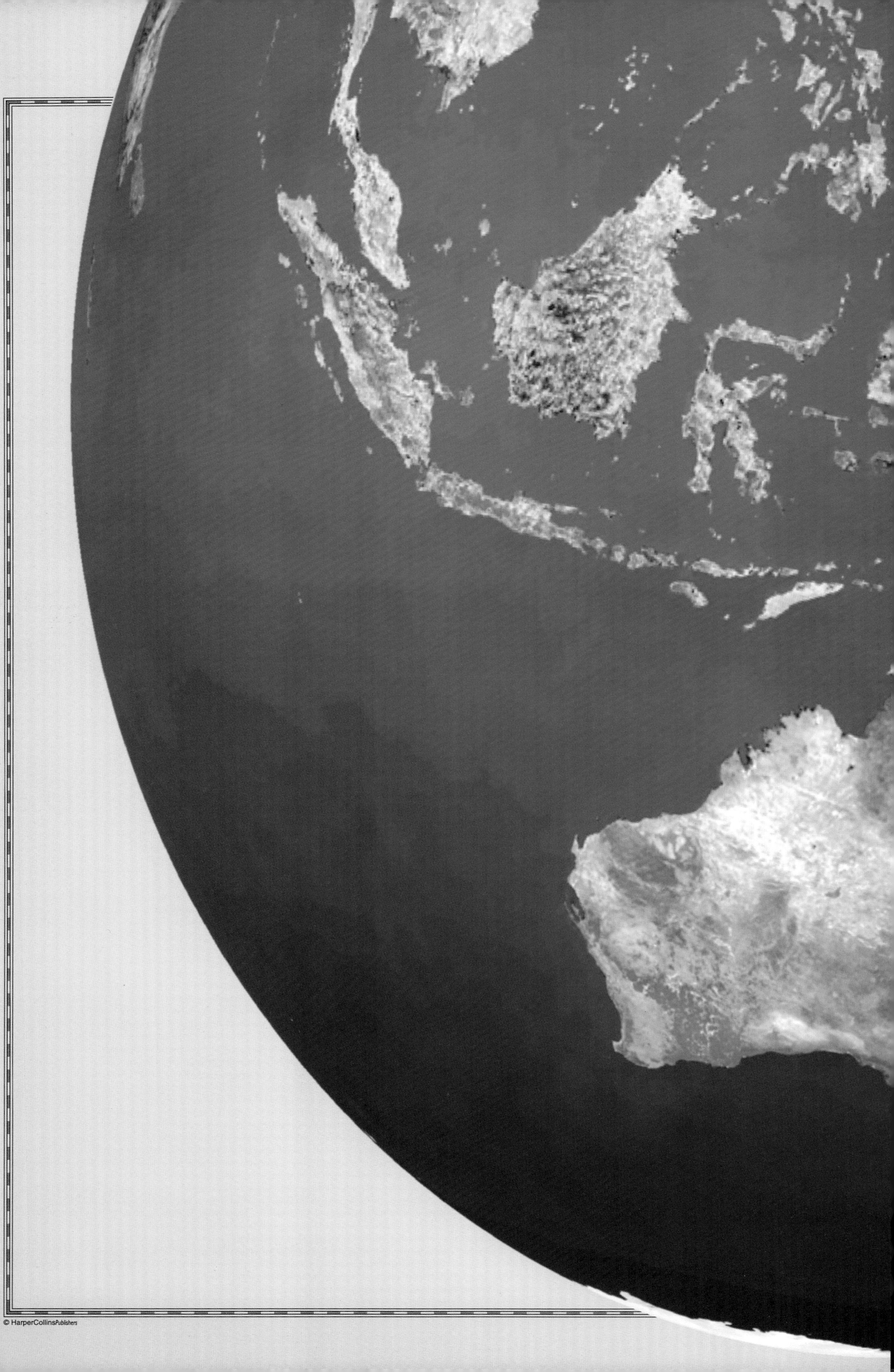

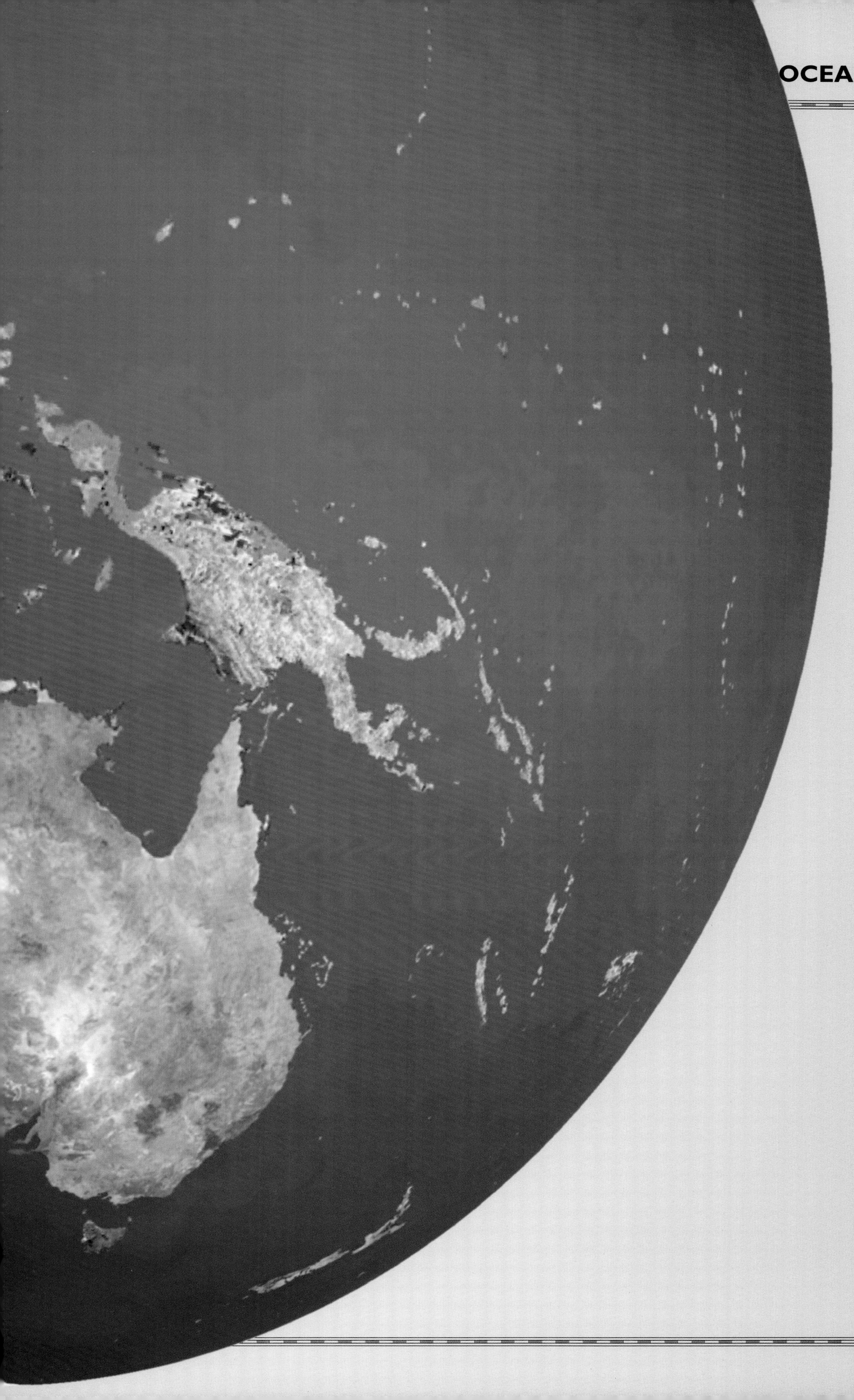

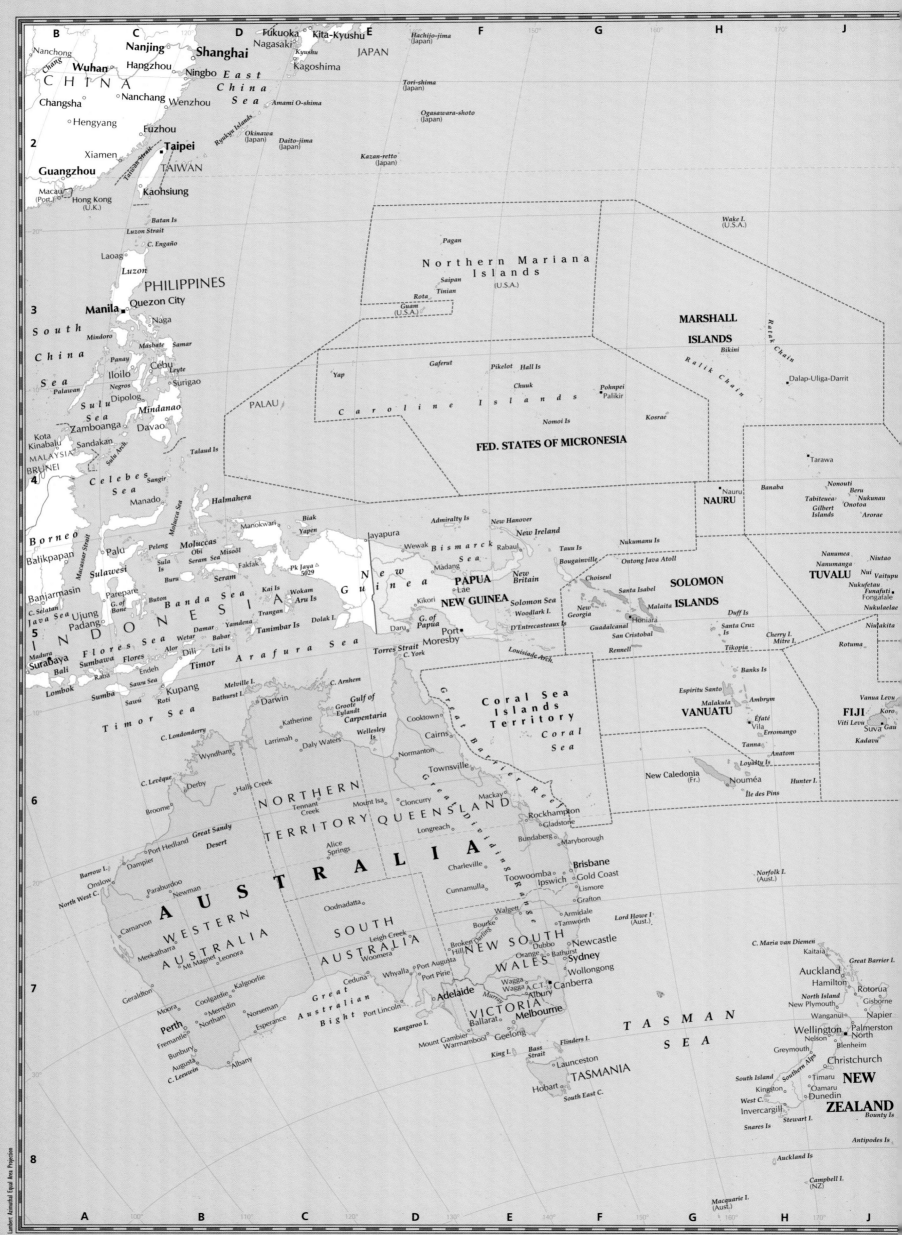

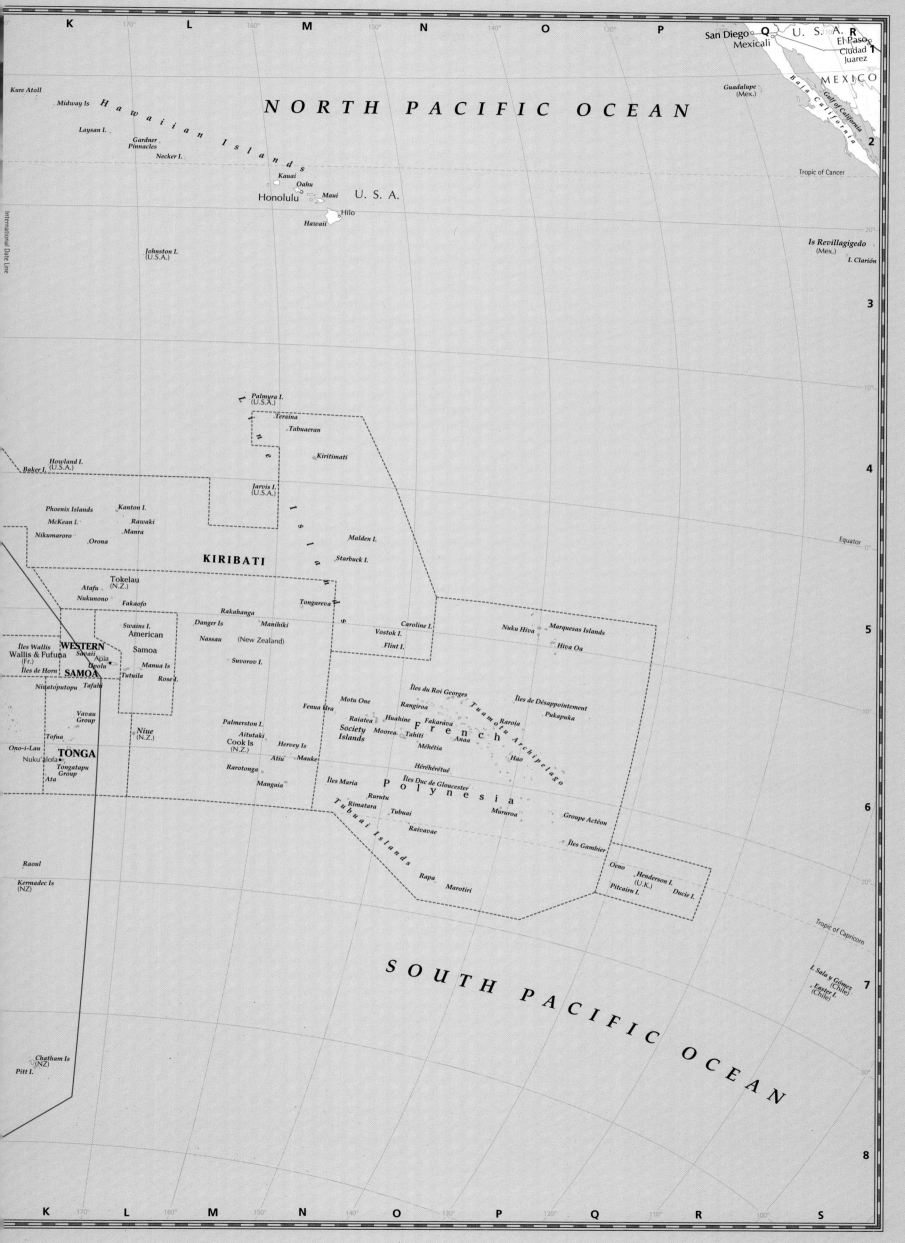

NORTH PACIFIC OCEAN

SOUTH PACIFIC OCEAN

1:30 000 000

Kure Atoll
Midway Is
Laysan I.
Gardner Pinnacles
Necker I.
Hawaiian Islands
Kauai
Oahu
Maui
Honolulu
Hilo
Hawaii
U.S.A.

Johnston I. (U.S.A.)

International Date Line

Palmyra I. (U.S.A.)
Teraina
Tabuaeran
Kiritimati
Line Islands

Howland I.
Baker I. (U.S.A.)
Jarvis I. (U.S.A.)
Phoenix Islands
McKean I.
Nikumaroro
Kanton I.
Rawaki
Orona
Manra
Malden I.
Starbuck I.
KIRIBATI

Atafu
Nukunono
Fakaofo
Tokelau (N.Z.)
Rakahanga
Tongareva
Swains I.
American Samoa
Danger Is
Nassau
Manihiki
(New Zealand)
Caroline I.
Vostok I.
Flint I.
Nuku Hiva
Marquesas Islands
Hiva Oa

Îles Wallis
Wallis & Futuna (Fr.)
Îles de Horn
WESTERN SAMOA
Savaii
Upolu
Apia
Manua Is
Tutuila
Rose I.
Suvorov I.

Niuatoputopu
Tafahi
Vavau Group
Tofua
Ono-i-Lau
Niue (N.Z.)
Palmerston I.
Aitutaki
Cook Is (N.Z.)
Atiu
Hervey Is
Mauke
Fenua Ura
Motu One
Raiatea
Huahine
Moorea
Tahiti
Mehetia
Rangiroa
Fakarava
Anaa
Îles du Roi Georges
Îles de Désappointement
Raroia
Pukapuka
Tuamotu Archipelago
French
Hao
TONGA
Nuku'alofa
Tongatapu Group
Ata
Rarotonga
Mangaia
Îles Maria
Rimatara
Raivavae
Rurutu
Tubuai
Tubuai Islands
Héréhérétué
Îles Duc de Gloucester
Polynesia
Mururoa
Groupe Actéon
Îles Gambier

Raoul
Kermadec Is (NZ)
Oeno
Henderson I. (U.K.)
Pitcairn I.
Ducie I.

Rapa
Marotiri

Chatham Is (NZ)
Pitt I.

San Diego
Mexicali
El Paso
Ciudad Juarez
U.S.A.
Guadalupe (Mex.)
MEXICO
Gulf of California
Baja California

Tropic of Cancer
Is Revillagigedo (Mex.)
I. Clarión
Equator
Tropic of Capricorn
I. Sala y Gómez (Chile)
Easter I. (Chile)

1000 MILES
1500 KM

National Statistics: International Organizations

COUNTRY	AREA sq ml	AREA sq km	POPULATION total	POPULATION density per sq ml	POPULATION density per sq km	Form of Government	Capital City	MAIN LANGUAGES	MAIN RELIGIONS	CURRENCY
AMERICAN SAMOA	76	197	55 000	723	279	US territory	Pago Pago	Samoan, English	Protestant, RC	US dollar
AUSTRALIA	2 966 153	7 682 300	17 838 000	6	2	federation	Canberra	English, Italian, Greek, Aboriginal languages	Protestant, RC, Orthodox, Aboriginal beliefs	Dollar
FIJI	7 077	18 330	784 000	111	43	republic	Suva	English, Fijian, Hindi	Protestant, Hindu, RC, Sunni Muslim	Dollar
FRENCH POLYNESIA	1 261	3 265	215 000	171	66	French territory	Papeete	French, Polynesian languages	Protestant, RC, Mormon	Pacific franc
GUAM	209	541	146 000	699	270	US territory	Agana	Chamorro, English, Tagalog	RC	US dollar
KIRIBATI	277	717	77 000	278	107	republic	Bairiki	I-Kiribati (Gilbertese), English	RC, Protestant, Baha'i, Mormon	Austr. dollar
MARSHALL ISLANDS	70	181	54 000	773	298	republic	Dalap-Uliga-Darrit	Marshallese, English	Protestant, RC	US dollar
FED. STATES OF MICRONESIA	271	701	104 000	384	148	republic	Palikir	English, Trukese, Pohnpeian, local languages	Protestant, RC	US dollar
NAURU	8	21	11 000	1357	524	republic	Yaren	Nauruan, Gilbertese, English	Protestant, RC	Austr. dollar
NEW CALEDONIA	7 358	19 058	184 000	25	10	French territory	Nouméa	French, local languages	RC, Protestant, Sunni Muslim	Pacific franc
NEW ZEALAND	104 454	270 534	3 493 000	33	13	monarchy	Wellington	English, Maori	Protestant, RC	Dollar
NIUE	100	258	2 000	20	8	NZ territory	Alofi	English, Polynesian (Niuean)	Protestant, Mormon, RC	NZ dollar
NORTH. MARIANA IS.	184	477	47 000	255	99	US territory	Saipan	English, Chamorro, Tagalog, local languages	RC, Protestant	US dollar
PAPUA NEW GUINEA	178 704	462 840	3 997 000	22	9	monarchy	Port Moresby	English, Tok Pisin, many local languages	Protestant, RC, traditional beliefs	Kina
SOLOMON ISLANDS	10 954	28 370	366 000	33	13	monarchy	Honiara	English, Pidgin, many local languages	Protestant, RC	Dollar
TOKELAU	4	10	2 000	518	200	NZ territory		English, Tokelauan	Protestant, RC	NZ dollar
TONGA	289	748	98 000	339	131	monarchy	Nuku'alofa	Tongan, English	Protestant, RC, Mormon	Pa'anga
TUVALU	10	25	9 000	932	360	monarchy	Fongafale	Tuvaluan, English (official)	Protestant	Dollar
VANUATU	4 707	12 190	165 000	35	14	republic	Port-Vila	English, Bislama, French	Protestant, RC, traditional beliefs	Vatu
WALLIS AND FUTUNA	106	274	14 000	132	51	French territory	Mata-Utu	French, Polynesian	RC	Pacific franc
WESTERN SAMOA	1 093	2 831	164 000	150	58	monarchy	Apia	Samoan, English	Protestant, RC, Mormon	Tala

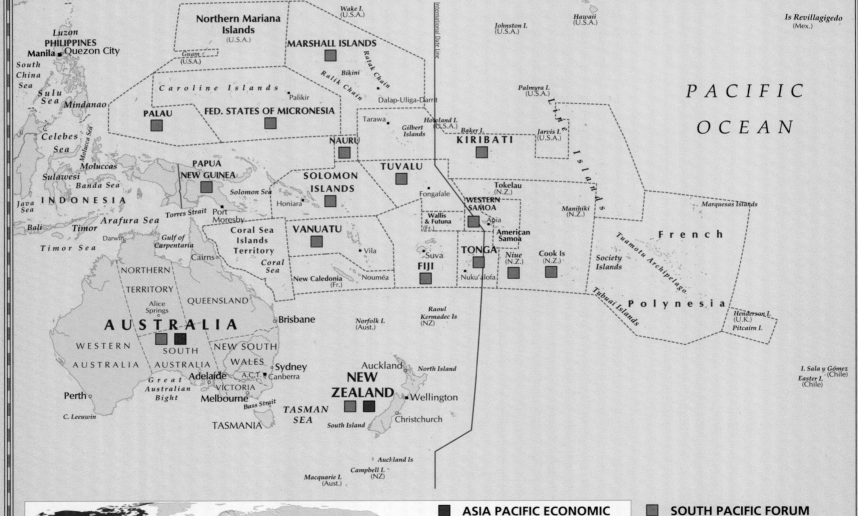

ASIA PACIFIC ECONOMIC CO-OPERATION FORUM (APEC)

Formed in 1989 to promote trade and economic co-operation, with the long term aim of the creation of a Pacific free trade area. The original members were Australia, Brunei, Canada, Indonesia, Japan, Malaysia, New Zealand, the Philippines, Singapore, South Korea, Thailand and U.S.A.. China, Hong Kong and Taiwan joined in 1991, Mexico and Papua New Guinea in 1993, and Chile in 1994.

Headquarters : Singapore

SOUTH PACIFIC FORUM

Originally established as a 'Trade Bureau' in 1972, it later became the South Pacific Bureau for Economic Co-operation (SPEC), before its current title was approved in 1988, and ratified in 1993. The objectives are to encourage and promote regional co-operation through trade and investment, and economic development including telecommunications and air transport. There are 16 members: Australia, the Cook Islands, Federated States of Micronesia, Fiji, Kiribati, Marshall Islands, Nauru, New Zealand, Niue, Palau, Papua New Guinea, Solomon Islands, Tonga, Tuvalu, Vanuatu and Western Samoa. In 1990 five of the smallest island states : Kiribati, the Cook Islands, Nauru, Niue and Tuvalu formed an economic sub-group to address their specific concerns.

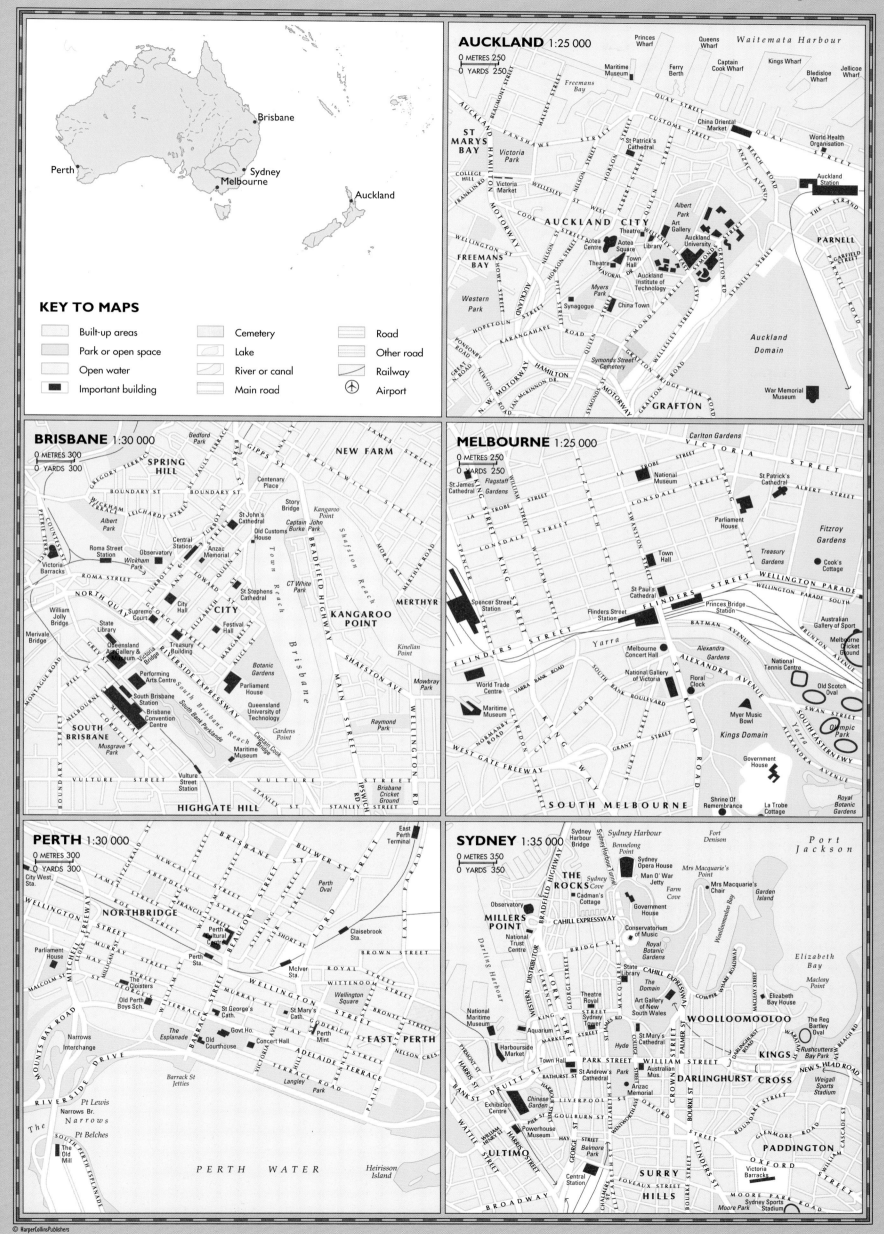

KEY TO MAPS

- Built-up areas
- Park or open space
- Open water
- Important building
- Cemetery
- Lake
- River or canal
- Main road
- Road
- Other road
- Railway
- Airport

AUCKLAND 1:25 000

0 METRES 250
0 YARDS 250

Waitemata Harbour
Princes Wharf · Queens Wharf · Kings Wharf · Bledisloe Wharf · Jellicoe Wharf
Captain Cook Wharf
Maritime Museum · Ferry Berth
China Oriental Market
World Health Organisation
QUAY STREET
CUSTOMS STREET
Freemans Bay
ST MARYS BAY
St Patrick's Cathedral
Auckland Station
THE STRAND
PARNELL
Garfield Street
Victoria Park
COLLEGE HILL
FRANKLIN ST
Victoria Market
WELLESLEY
Albert Park
Art Gallery
Auckland University
AUCKLAND CITY
Theatre
Aotea Centre
Aotea Square
Library
Town Hall
Theatre
MAYORAL DR
Auckland Institute of Technology
FREEMANS BAY
Western Park
Myers Park
Synagogue
China Town
Auckland Domain
HOPETOUN STREET
KARANGAHAPE ROAD
SYMONDS STREET
Symonds Street Cemetery
PONSONBY ROAD
GREAT N. RD
NEWTON RD
HAMILTON
N. W. MOTORWAY
N. W. ROAD
IAN McKINNON DR
SYMONDS ST MOTORWAY
GRAFTON BRIDGE
PARK ROAD
GRAFTON
War Memorial Museum

BRISBANE 1:30 000

0 METRES 300
0 YARDS 300

Bedford Park
SPRING HILL
GIPPS STREET
JAMES STREET
NEW FARM
BRUNSWICK STREET
Centenary Place
GREGORY TERRACE
BOUNDARY ST
BOUNDARY ST
WICKHAM TERRACE
LEICHHARDT STREET
Story Bridge
Kangaroo Point
Albert Park
St John's Cathedral
Old Customs House
Captain John Burke
COUNTESS ST
PETRIE TERRACE
Central Station
Observatory
Anzac Memorial
Roma Street Station
Wickham Park
CT White Park
Victoria Barracks
ROMA STREET
NORTH QUAY
City Hall
St Stephens Cathedral
CITY
KANGAROO POINT
MERTHYR
William Jolly Bridge
State Library
Supreme Court
Festival Hall
Treasury Building
SHAFSTON AVE
Merivale Bridge
Queensland Art Gallery & Museum
Performing Arts Centre
Botanic Gardens
Parliament House
Kinellan Point
MAIN STREET
Mowbray Park
South Brisbane Station
SOUTH BRISBANE
Brisbane Convention Centre
Queensland University of Technology
Gardens Point
Raymond Park
WELLINGTON
Musgrave Park
Captain Cook Bridge
Maritime Museum
VULTURE STREET
VULTURE STREET
Vulture Street Station
STANLEY ST
HIGHGATE HILL
STANLEY STREET
Brisbane Cricket Ground
IPSWICH RD

PERTH 1:30 000

0 METRES 300
0 YARDS 300

East Perth Terminal
BRISBANE STREET
BULWER STREET
LORD STREET
City West Sta.
NEWCASTLE STREET
ABERDEEN STREET
Perth Oval
NORTHBRIDGE
JAMES STREET
FITZGERALD STREET
FRANCIS STREET
Perth Cultural Centre
Claisebrook Sta.
WELLINGTON STREET
Perth Sta.
BROWN STREET
Parliament House
MURRAY STREET
The Cloisters
G.P.O.
St George's Cath.
McIver Sta.
Royal Street
WITTENOOM STREET
MITCHELL FREEWAY
MALCOLM STREET
HAY STREET
The Cloisters
Old Perth Boys Sch.
St Mary's Cath.
Govt. Ho.
Perth Mint
Wellington Square
GOODERICH STREET
BRONTE STREET
NELSON CRES
EAST PERTH
Narrows Interchange
The Esplanade
Old Courthouse
Concert Hall
ADELAIDE TERRACE
Langley Park
MOUNTS BAY ROAD
RIVERSIDE DRIVE
Barrack St Jetties
Pt Lewis
Narrows Br.
The Narrows
Pt Belches
The Old Mill
The Esplanade
PERTH WATER
Heirisson Island
SOUTH PERTH ESPLANADE

MELBOURNE 1:25 000

0 METRES 250
0 YARDS 250

Carlton Gardens
VICTORIA STREET
St Patrick's Cathedral
ALBERT STREET
National Museum
LA TROBE STREET
Flagstaff Gardens
St James Cathedral
SPRING STREET
LONSDALE STREET
Parliament House
Fitzroy Gardens
WILLIAM STREET
ELIZABETH STREET
SWANSTON STREET
KING STREET
Town Hall
Treasury Gardens
Cook's Cottage
SPENCER STREET
LONSDALE STREET
St Paul's Cathedral
WELLINGTON PARADE
WELLINGTON PARADE SOUTH
Spencer Street Station
Flinders Street Station
FLINDERS STREET
Princes Bridge Station
BATMAN AVENUE
BRUNTON AVENUE
Australian Gallery of Sport
Melbourne Cricket Ground
Yarra
Melbourne Concert Hall
Alexandra Gardens
ALEXANDRA AVENUE
National Tennis Centre
World Trade Centre
YARRA BANK ROAD
National Gallery of Victoria
Floral Clock
ST KILDA ROAD
SOUTH BANK BOULEVARD
Old Scotch Oval
SWAN STREET
Maritime Museum
Myer Music Bowl
SOUTHEASTERN FWY
Olympic Park
NORMANBY ROAD
CLARENDON STREET
CITY ROAD
Kings Domain
ALEXANDRA AVENUE
WEST GATE FREEWAY
KING WAY
STURT STREET
GRANT STREET
Government House
SOUTH MELBOURNE
Shrine Of Remembrance
La Trobe Cottage
Royal Botanic Gardens

SYDNEY 1:35 000

0 METRES 350
0 YARDS 350

Sydney Harbour Bridge
Sydney Harbour
Bennelong Point
Fort Denison
Port Jackson
Sydney Opera House
Sydney Cove
Man O' War Jetty
Mrs Macquarie's Point
THE ROCKS
Cadman's Cottage
Farm Cove
Mrs Macquarie's Chair
Garden Island
MILLERS POINT
Observatory
Government House
CAHILL EXPRESSWAY
National Trust Centre
Conservatorium of Music
Woolloomooloo Bay
BRIDGE ST
Royal Botanic Gardens
Elizabeth Bay
WESTERN DISTRIBUTOR
State Library
The Domain
Macleay Point
BRADFIELD HIGHWAY
Darling Harbour
Theatre Royal
CLARENCE STREET
YORK STREET
GEORGE STREET
Art Gallery of New South Wales
Elizabeth Bay House
National Maritime Museum
Aquarium
KING STREET
MARKET STREET
Hyde Park
ST JAMES ROAD
St Mary's Cathedral
WOOLLOOMOOLOO
COWPER WHARF ROADWAY
The Reg Bartley Oval
Rushcutters Bay Park
KINGS CROSS
Harbourside Market
Town Hall
PARK STREET
Australian Mus.
WILLIAM STREET
DARLINGHURST
NEW S. HEAD ROAD
Weigall Sports Stadium
PYRMONT ST
HARRIS ST
DRUITT ST
St Andrew's Cathedral
BATHURST ST
Anzac Memorial
CROWN ST
PALMER ST
BOURKE STREET
FLINDERS STREET
OXFORD STREET
PADDINGTON
WATTLE STREET
Chinese Garden
Exhibition Centre
LIVERPOOL STREET
GOULBURN STREET
CAMPBELL STREET
Powerhouse Museum
HAY STREET
Belmore Park
Central Station
SURRY HILLS
GEORGE STREET
ELIZABETH STREET
FOVEAUX STREET
Victoria Barracks
MOORE PARK ROAD
GLENMORE ROAD
Sydney Sports Ground
Moore Park
Sydney Sports Stadium
ULTIMO
BROADWAY

PACIFIC OCEAN

Admiralty Islands

Bismarck Archipelago

New Ireland

Bismarck Sea

NEW

P A P U A

New Britain

GUINEA

NEW GUINEA

Solomon Sea

Bougainville Island

SOLOMON ISLANDS

Gulf of Papua

Port Moresby

AUSTRALIA

C O R A L   S E A

PAPUA NEW GUINEA and SOLOMON ISLANDS
1:10M

VANUATU and NEW CALEDONIA
1:7.5M

Banks Islands

Espíritu Santo

V A N U A T U

Malakula

CORAL SEA

Erromango

Tanna

Is Loyauté (Loyalty Is) (France)

NEW CALEDONIA (NOUVELLE CALÉDONIE) (France)

Lifou

Maré

FIJI
1:6M

VAVA'U GROUP (Tonga)
1:1.5M

Uta Vava'u

TONGATAPU GROUP (Tonga)
1:1.5M

Tongatapu

'Eua

TONGA
1:5M

Vava'u Group

Ha'apai Group

Nomuka Group

Tongatapu Group

VANUA LEVU (Fiji)
1:2.5 M

Great Sea Reef

Ringgold Isles

Taveuni

Koro Sea

Koro

Vanua Levu

Viti Levu

Bligh Water

Koro Sea

Suva

VITI LEVU (Fiji)
1:2.5M

© HarperCollinsPublishers

Ogasawara-shoto
9156
Kazan-retto

Midway Is
Laysan I.
Gardner Pinnacles
Necker I.
Kauai
Oahu
Honolulu
Maui
Hilo (U.S.A.)
HAWAII

Tropic of Cancer

Tinian
Saipan
Rota
Guam (U.S.A.)
NORTHERN MARIANA ISLANDS (U.S.A.)
1564

Challenger Deep
11022

MARSHALL
ISLANDS

Wake I. (U.S.A.)
1823

Johnston I. (U.S.A.)

7022

Gaferut
Pikelot
Hall Is
Chuuk
Bikini
Ralik Chain
Ratak Chain

10°

Caroline Islands

Nomoi Is
Pohnpei
Kosrae

FED. STATES OF MICRONESIA

Palmyra I. (U.S.A.)
Teraina
Tabuaeran
Kiritimati (Christmas I.)

7208
6887

NAURU

Banaba
Tabiteuea
Beru
Nonouti
Nukunau
Onotoa
Arorae
Gilbert Islands

Howland I. (U.S.A.)
Baker I. (U.S.A.)

Equator

Jayapura
Wewak
Admiralty Is
New Hanover

Bismarck Sea
Rabaul
Madang
New Ireland
Tauu Is
Nukumanu Is

Phoenix Islands
McKean I.
Kanton I.
Rawaki
Nikumaroro
Orona
Manra

Jarvis I. (U.S.A.)

Malden I.

KIRIBATI

Starbuck I.

Nuku Hiva
Marquesas Islands
Hiva Oa

Mt Wilhelm
4508
PAPUA
NEW GUINEA
Lae
Kikori
Port Moresby
Daru

Bougainville
Choiseul
Santa Isabel
New Georgia
Woodlark I.
D'Entrecasteaux Is
Louisiade Arch.

Honiara
Guadalcanal
Malaita
San Cristobal
Rennell
SOLOMON ISLANDS

Santa Cruz Is
Duff Is
Tikopia

Rotuma

Nanumea
Nanumanga
Niutao
Nui
Vaitupu
Nukufetau
TUVALU

Atafu
Nukunono
Fakaofo
Tokelau

Swains I.

Danger Is
Manihiki
Rakahanga

Caroline I.
Vostok I.
Flint I.

Tongareva

FRENCH

Iles de Désappointement
King George Is
Rangiroa
Fakarava
Raroia
Pukapuka
Archipel des Tuamotu
Hao

C. York
Cape York Pen.
Gulf of Carpentaria
Cooktown
Cairns
Wellesley Is
Normanton

CORAL SEA IS TERR.

Coral Sea

Espiritu Santo
Malakula
Ambrym
Efaté
VANUATU
Erromango
Tanna
Anatom

New Caledonia
Nouméa
Iles des Pins
Loyalty Is
7633
Hunter I.

Banks Is
Iles Wallis (Fr.)
Hoorn Is (Fr.)

W. SAMOA
Savai'i
Upolu
American Samoa
Manu'a Is
Rose I.
Tutuila

Vanua Levu
FIJI
Viti Levu
Suva
Kadavu
Koro
Cau

Vava'u Group
Niuatoputapu
Tofua

Niue (N.Z.)

Palmerston I.
Fenua Ura
Raiatea
Huahine
Motu One
Arch. de la Société
Tahaa

POLYNESIA

Suvorov I.
Nassau

Aitutaki
Hervey Is
Cook Islands (N.Z.)
Rarotonga
Mangaia
Atiu
Mauke
Rurutu
Hérehérétué

Tubai
Raivavae
Iles Maria
Rimatara
Tubuai Islands

TONGA
Ata
Tongatapu Group

Horizon Depth
10882

Rapa
Marotiri

(France)

Tropic of Capricorn

Oeno (U.K.)
Henderson I. (U.K.)
Gambier Is
Mangareva
Pitcairn I. (U.K.)
Ducie I. (U.K.)
Groupe Actéon

Mururoa

AUSTRALIA
Roma
Toowoomba
Brisbane
Gold Coast
Cunnamulla
Bourke
Walgett
Grafton
Armidale
Taree
Tamworth
Dubbo
Orange
Newcastle
Sydney
Wollongong
Canberra
Mt Kosciusko
Albury
Melbourne
Geelong
Ballarat
Horsham

South Fiji Basin

Norfolk I. (Aust.)
Lord Howe I. (Aust.)
Raoul

SOUTH FIJI BASIN

10047

5420

SOUTH PACIFIC OCEAN

Adelaide
Mildura
Murray
Lachlan

TASMAN SEA

C. Maria van Diemen

Auckland
Hamilton
Rotorua
New Plymouth
Wanganui
Napier
Bay of Plenty
North Island
NEW
PALMERSTON NORTH
Wellington
ZEALAND

Launceston
Devonport
Tasmania
Hobart
South East C.

Nelson
Greymouth
Mt Cook
South Island
Kingston
West C.
Timaru
Southern Alps
Christchurch
Dunedin
Invercargill
Stewart I.
Chatham Is (N.Z.)
Pitt I.

Auckland Is (N.Z.)

6096

Campbell I. (N.Z.)

1:40M

Inset 9 / 10

Savai'i
Asau
Samalaeulu
Puapua
Salelologa
Apia
Taga
Malua
Upolu
Tutuila
Lalomanu
Pago Pago
Leone
Tula
Ofu
Olosega
Tau
Manua Is

WESTERN SAMOA
AMERICAN SAMOA (U.S.A.)

SAMOAN ISLANDS
1:6M

Archipel de la Société (Society Is)
Maupiti
Iles sous le Vent
Bora-Bora
Raiatea
Huahine
Moorea
Tahiti
Papeete

Ahé
Manihi
Takaroa
Takapoto
Rangiroa
Arutua
Apataki
Matalva
Iles Palliser
Kaukura
Toau
Fakarava
Makatea
Katiu
Makemo
Faaite
Tahanea
Iles Raeffsky
Hikueru
Anaa
Haraiki
Amanu
Marokau
Ravahere
Nengonengo
Manuhangi
Paraoa
Tepoto
Napuka
Iles de Désappointement
Takumé
Fangatau
Fakaina
Marutéa
Tauére
Hao
Nukutavake
Anuanu Raro

Archipel des Tuamotu (Tuamotu Is)

FRENCH POLYNESIA (France)
1:15M

Inset 11

Pte Aroa
Pte Hauru
Papetoai
Teavaro
Haapiti
Moorea
Pte Nuupere
Mahina
Papeari
Papenoo
Tiarei
Mahaena
Hitiaa
Papeete
Faaa
Afareaitu
Punaauia
Aorai
2241
Orohena
Tahiti
Paea
Maraa
Papara
Atimaono
Mataiea
Vairao
Teahupoo
Taravao
Tautira

TAHITI and MOOREA (French Polynesia)
1:1.5M

Inset 12

Savai'i
Puava
Safotu
Safotulafai
Samalaeulu
Matavanu Crater
Puapua
Tuasivi
Salelologa
Falealupo
Sataua
Asau
Satupaitea
Vailoa
Taga
Palauli
Mulifanua
Faleasiu
Leulumoega
Apia
Samatau
Mulivai
Lotofaga
Upolu

WESTERN SAMOA
1:2.5M

Inset 13

Tutuila
Pago Pago
Leone
Nuuuli
Vaitogi
Steps Pt
C. Matatula
Tula
Aunuu
Ofu
Olosega
Maia
Luma
Manua Is
Tau

AMERICAN SAMOA (U.S.A.)
1:2.5M

Inset 14

Young's Rock
Adamstown
Pt Christian
Bounty Bay
Adam's Rock
St Paul's Point
Tautama

PITCAIRN I. (U.K.)
1:200 000

Inset 15

Punta Salinas
Bahia Cumberland
San Juan Bautista
El Yunque
Santa Clara

ROBINSON CRUSOE, JUAN FERNANDEZ IS (Chile)
1:1.25M

See pp176-177 for location
See pp150-151 for location

Inset 16

Cabo Norte
Pta Rosalia
Terevaka
Bahia La Pérouse
Motu Tautara
Pudi
 Katiki
O'Higgins
Hanga Roa
Mataveri
Rano Kao
Vaihu
Pta Cuidado
Motu Iti
Motu Nui
Pta Baja
Cabo Sur
Roggeveen

EASTER I. (Chile)
1:750 000

KERMADEC IS
(New Zealand) 1:6M

Denham B. Herald Islets
Raoul I.

Macdonald Rock
Macauley I.
Curtis I.

Havre Rock
L'Esperance Rock

500
1000
2000

AUCKLAND IS
(New Zealand) 1:3M

Conic Equidistant Projection

Enderby I.
North West C. Port Ross
Ewing I.
Disappointment I. Norman Inlet
Cavern Pt
Bristow Pt
South West C. C. Bennett Mt Dick Carnley Harb.
Adams I.

CAMPBELL I.
(New Zealand) 1:1.2M

Bull Rock
North East Harb.
Courrejolles Pt North West B. Perseverance Harbour
North West B. Mt Eizard
Dent I. Mt Honey South East Harb.
Jacquemart I. Monument Harb.

SNARES IS
(New Zealand) 1:300 000

High I. North Promontory
North East Boat Harbour
Island North East Harbour
South Promontory
South East Harbour
Broughton I.

Vancouver
Rock
Western Chain

METRES FEET
6000 19686
5000 16409
4000 13124
3000 9843
2000 6562
1000 3281
500 1640
200 656
SEA LEVEL
200 656
2000 6562
4000 13124
6000 19686

NORTH ISLAND

NORTHLAND

AUCKLAND

WAIKATO

BAY OF PLENTY

GISBORNE

HAWKE'S BAY

TARANAKI

MANAWATU
WANGANUI

Cape Reinga
North Cape
Three Kings Is
Cape Maria van Diemen
Te Paki
Ninety Mile Beach
Ahipara
Kaitaia
Awanui
Mangonui
Doubtless Bay
Cape Karikari
Rangaunu Bay
Great Exhibition Bay
Ahipara Bay
Tauroa Pt
Herekino
Broadwood
Kohukohu
Rawene
Kaikohe
Okaihau
Kerikeri
Russell
Bay of Islands
Cape Brett
Whangaruru
Hokianga Harbour
Waimamaku
Donnelly's Crossing
Dargaville
Kaihu
Maungaturoto
Te Kopuru
Tangaihe
Paparoa
Kaipara Harbour
Maungatapere
Whangarei
Hikurangi
Poor Knights Is
Whangarei Harbour
Bream Head
Bream Bay
Bream Tail
Hen and Chickens Is
Waipu
Waiotira
Kaiwaka
Wellsford
Warkworth
Leigh
Cape Rodney
Little Barrier I.
Great Barrier Island
Port Fitzroy
Cradock Channel
Colville Channel
Cape Barrier
Coromandel
Coromandel Peninsula
Coromandel Range
Whitianga
Mercury Islands
The Aldermen Is
Mayor I.
Whangamata
Whangaparaoa
Orewa
AUCKLAND
Takapuna
Manukau
Manukau Harbour
Waiuku
Port Waikato
Pukekohe
Papakura
Firth of Thames
Thames
Paeroa
Waihi
Whitianga
Waihou
Te Aroha
Katikati
Tauranga
Mount Maunganui
Matakana Island
Te Puke
Maketu
Whakatane
Opotiki
BAY OF PLENTY
Bay of Plenty
White I.
Cape Runaway
Te Araroa
East Cape
Hicks Bay
Tikitiki
Ruatoria
Tokomaru Bay
Tolaga Bay
Gisborne
Poverty Bay
Young Nick's Head
Table Cape
Mahia Peninsula
Portland I.
Wairoa
Napier
Hastings
Havelock North
Cape Kidnappers
HAWKE BAY
Waipawa
Waipukurau
Porangahau
Cape Turnagain
Dannevirke
Woodville
Pahiatua
Eketahuna
Palmerston North
Feilding
Bulls
Foxton
Foxton Beach
Shannon
Levin
Otaki
Waikanae
Paraparaumu
Kapiti I.
Hamilton
Cambridge
Te Awamutu
Otorohanga
Te Kuiti
Raglan
Kawhia
Kawhia Harbour
Aotea Harbour
Ngaruawahia
Huntly
Glen Afton
Morrinsville
Matamata
Putaruru
Tokoroa
Mangakino
Taumarunui
Ongarue
Lake Taupo
Taupo
Turangi
Raetihi
Ohakune
Waiouru
National Park
Tongariro National Park
Mt Ruapehu
Mt Ngauruhoe
Mt Tongariro
Rotorua
Lake Rotorua
Murupara
Kawerau
Whakatane
Mt Tarawera
Lake Taupo
Rangitaiki
Wanganui
Marton
Taihape
Hunterville
Mangaweka
Waverley
Patea
Hawera
Manaia
Opunake
Pihama
Eltham
Stratford
Mt Egmont
Cape Egmont
Egmont National Park
New Plymouth
Waitara
Inglewood
Oakura
Mokau
Awakino
Urenui
Uruti
North Taranaki Bight
South Taranaki Bight
Waitotara

Cape Farewell
Farewell Spit
Collingwood
Golden Bay
Separation Pt
D'Urville I.
Stephens I.
Cape Stephens

T A S M A N   S E A

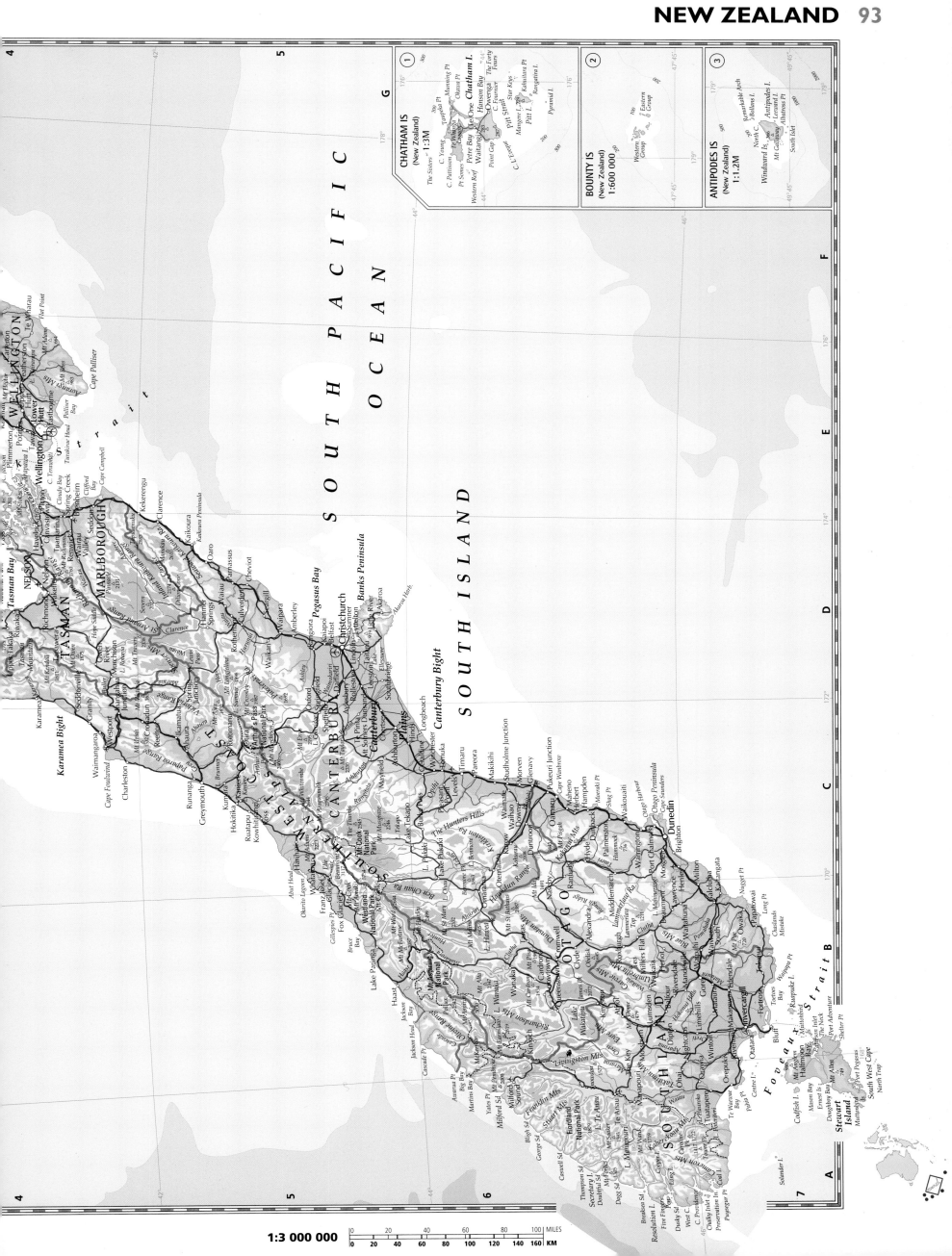

SOUTH PACIFIC OCEAN

SOUTH ISLAND

SOUTH OCEAN

CHATHAM IS
(New Zealand) 1:3M

BOUNTY IS
(New Zealand)
1:600 000

ANTIPODES IS
(New Zealand) 1:1.2M

1:3 000 000

| 0 | 20 | 40 | 60 | 80 | 100 | MILES |
| 0 | 20 | 40 | 60 | 80 | 100 | 120 | 140 | 160 | KM |

Sea
C. Wessel
Wessel Is
Elcho I.
Buckingham B.
Melville B.
Nhulunbuy
Anthem B.
C. Arnhem
Woodah I.
Alyangula
Groote
Eylandt
Bickerton I.
Maria I.
Limmen Bight
Sir Edward Pellew
Group
Vanderlin I.
Borroloola

Gulf of
Carpentaria

Barkly Tableland

Mornington I.
Wellesley Islands
Bentinck I.
Karumba
Burketown
Normanton
Camooweal
Kajabbi
Mount Isa
Cloncurry
Julia Creek
Richmond
Dajarra
Hughenden
Boulia
Winton

Gulf of Port Moresby
Papua
Torres Strait
Prince of Wales I.
Badu I.
Moa I.
Endeavour Str.
Bamaga
C. York
Cape
York
Peninsula
Weipa
Albatross Bay
C. Grenville
C. Direction
Coen
Princess
Charlotte Bay
C. Melville
Osprey
Reef
C. Flattery
Laura
Cooktown
Weary B.
Mossman
Cairns
Mareeba
Atherton
Ravenshoe
Innisfail
Tully
Ingham
Hinchinbrook I.
Magnetic I.
Townsville
Ayr
Bowen
Charters
Towers
Proserpine
Whitsunday I.
Mt Dalrymple
Mackay
Sarina

CORAL SEA

CORAL SEA ISLANDS
TERRITORY

Îles Chesterfield
(New Caledonia)

Solomon Sea

QUEENSLAND

GREAT BARRIER REEF

GREAT DIVIDING RANGE

Simpson
Desert

A
L
I
A

Birdsville
Windorah
Longreach
Barcaldine
Charleville
Quilpie

Clermont
Emerald
Blackwater
Springsure
Blackall
Yaraka
Buckland
Tableland

Rockhampton
Yeppoon
Keppel B.
Curtis I.
Gladstone

Tropic of Capricorn

TASMANIA

1:11 000 000

NORFOLK I.
(Australia)
1:900 000

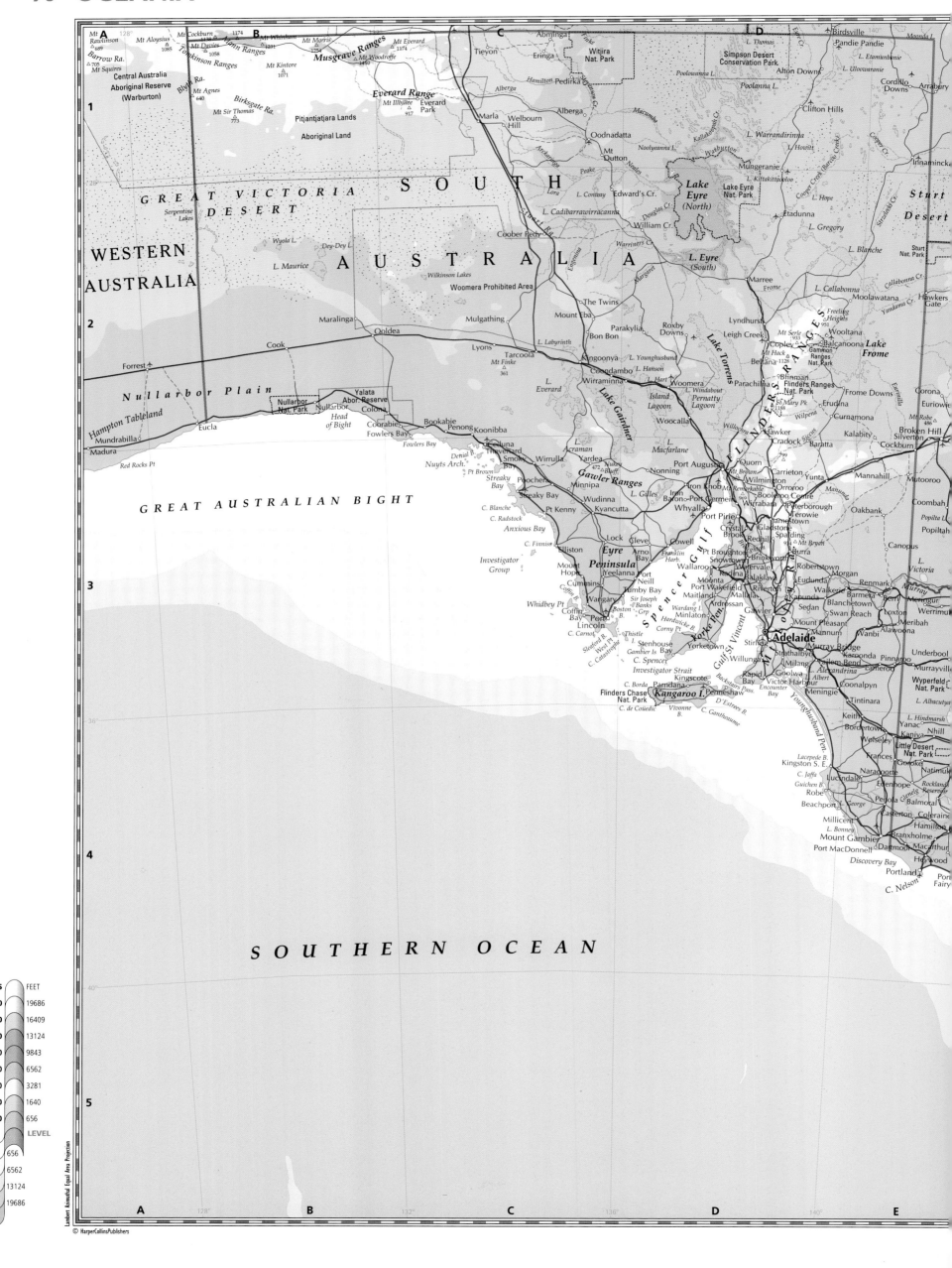

WESTERN AUSTRALIA

SOUTH AUSTRALIA

GREAT VICTORIA DESERT

Musgrave Ranges

Everard Range

Pitjantjatjara Lands

Aboriginal Land

Central Australia
Aboriginal Reserve
(Warburton)

Nullarbor Plain

Hampton Tableland

GREAT AUSTRALIAN BIGHT

Eyre Peninsula

Gawler Ranges

FLINDERS RANGES

Lake Eyre
(North)

Lake Eyre
(South)

Lake Torrens

Lake Gairdner

Simpson Desert
Conservation Park

Witjira Nat. Park

Sturt Desert

Spencer Gulf

Yorke Pen.

Gulf St. Vincent

Adelaide

Kangaroo I.

Flinders Chase
Nat. Park

SOUTHERN OCEAN

METRES		FEET
6000		19686
5000		16409
4000		13124
3000		9843
2000		6562
1000		3281
500		1640
200		656
SEA		LEVEL
200		656
2000		6562
4000		13124
6000		19686

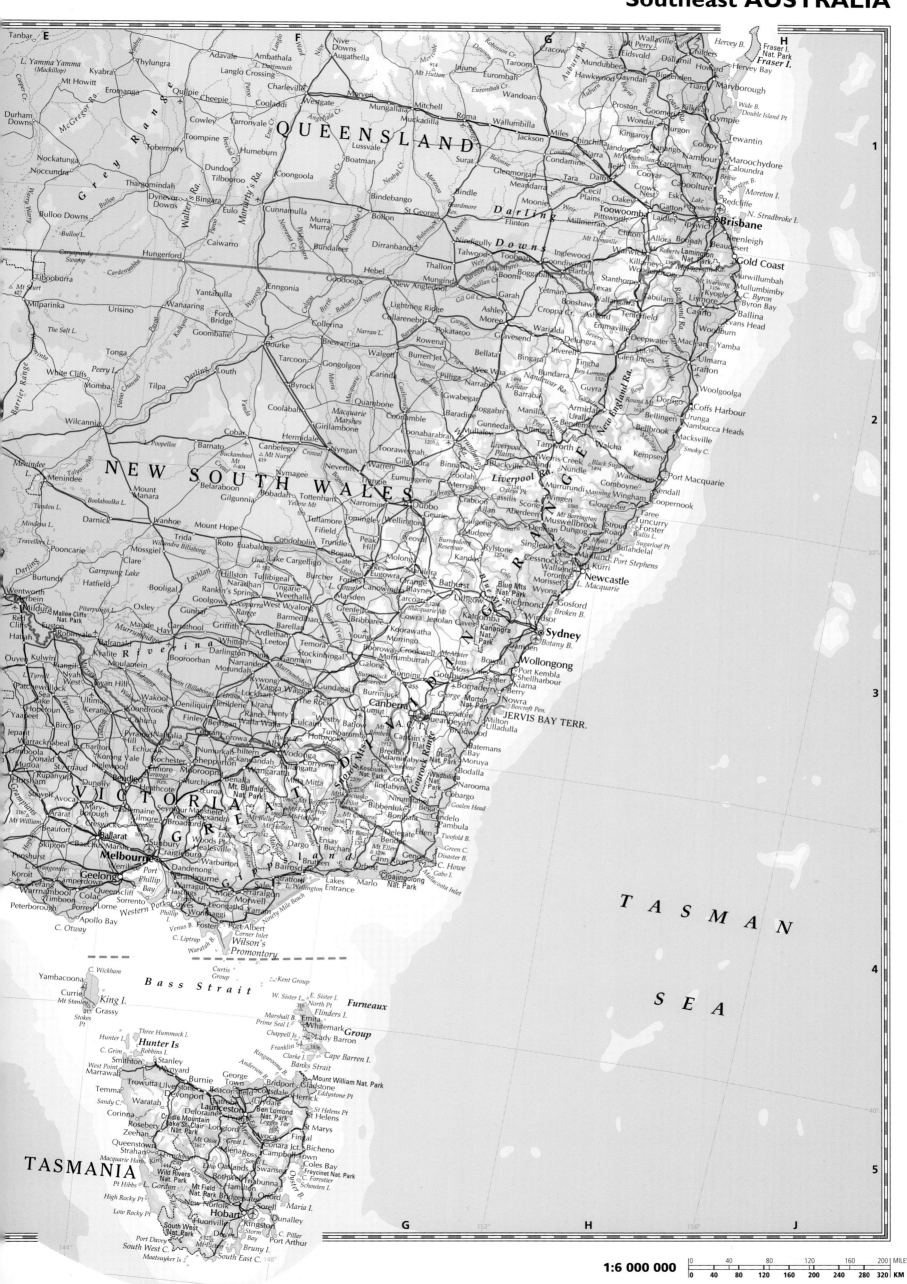

QUEENSLAND

NEW SOUTH WALES

VICTORIA

Brisbane

Gold Coast

Newcastle

Sydney

Wollongong

Canberra
A.C.T.

JERVIS BAY TERR.

Melbourne

Geelong

GREAT
DIVIDING
RANGE

Darling Downs

Riverina

Snowy Mts.

Gippsland

TASMAN

SEA

Bass Strait

Furneaux
Group

Hunter Is

TASMANIA

Hobart

1:6 000 000

0 40 80 120 160 200 MILES
0 40 80 120 160 200 240 280 320 KM

A 128°

1

TIMOR SEA

C. Van Diemen
Dundas Str.
Croker I.
McCluer I.
C. Wessel
Gurig Nat. Park
Grant I.
Wessel Is
Bathurst I.
Melville I. Abor. Land
Cobourg Pen.
Goulburn Is
Drysdale I.
The English Company's Is
Truant I.
Gordon B.
Bathurst I. Abor. Land
Melville I.
Junction B.
Boucaut B.
C. Stewart
Elcho I.
Mitchell Pt
C. Gambier
Van Diemen Gulf
Napier Broome B.
Melville B.
Nhulunbuy
C. Hotham
Clarence Str.
Field I.
Howard I.
C. Arnhem
Port Dagun
Beagle Gulf
Darwin
Oenpelli
Arnhem B.
Port Bradshaw

Pt Blaze
Peron Is.
Rum Jungle
Wagait Abor. Land
Woolwonga Abor. Land
Jabiru
Arnhem Land
C. Shield
Woodah I.
Anson Bay
Batchelor
Adelaide River
Kakadu National Park
Arnhem Land Aboriginal Land
C. Barrow
Alyangula
C. Scott
Burrundie
Mt Saunders 305
Arnhem Land
Bickerton I.
Groote Eylandt
Daly
Pine Creek
Katherine Gorge Nat. Park
Groote Eylandt Abor. Land
C. Beatrice

2

Joseph Bonaparte Gulf

Daly River Aboriginal Land
Katherine
Beswick Abor. Land
Numbulwar
Edward I.
Gulf of Carpentaria

Pearce Pt
Wingate Mts
Mataranka
Roper
Limmen Bight
Maria I.
Forrest River Abor. Res.
Fitzmaurice
Willeroo
Larrimah
Cox
West I.
Sir Edward Pellew Group
Vanderlin I.
Forrest
Legune
Timber Creek
Victoria River
Nutwood Downs
Port McArthur
Mornington I.
Wyndham
Kununurra
Victoria River Downs
Daly Waters
Borroloola
Gununa
Denham I.
Wellesley Is
C. Van Diemen
Bountiful I.

Durack Ra.
Carr Boyd Ra.
Gregory Nat. Park
Dunmarra
Manangoora
Robinson River
Calvert Hills
Bentinck I.
S. Wellesley Is
Lake Argyle
Waterloo
Victoria River Downs
Sturt Plain
Newcastle Waters
Westmoreland
Burketown
Mt Lush
Turkey Creek
Mt John
Stirling Cr.
Montejinnie
Beetaloo
Anthony Lagoon
Nicholson
Doomadgee Abor. Land
Inverleigh
Floraville
Kimberley Plateau
Bungle Bungle Nat. Park
Mt Misru
Kalkaringi
L. Woods
Eva Downs
Barkly Tableland
Doomadgee
Leichhardt Falls
Antrim Plateau
Inverway
Hooker Creek Abor. Reserve
Banka Banka
Brunette Downs
Lawn Hill
Gregory Downs
Talawanta

3

Halls Creek
Gordon Downs
Lajamanu
Rockhampton Downs
Mt Sylvester
Alexandria
Mt Drummond
Riversleigh
Lorraine
Kamileroi
McClintock Ra.
Denison Plains
Winnecke Cr.
NORTHERN
Frewena
Alroy Downs
Camooweal
Billiluna
TERRITORY
Mt Woodcock 373
Tennant Creek
Mt Samuel 436
Axon Downs
Soudan
Lake Julius
Kajabbi
Quamby

WESTERN
Gregory Lake
Balgo Mission
Balwina Abor. Reserve
Tanami
Central Desert
Tanami Desert
Aboriginal Land
Davenport Ra.
Kurundi
Austral Downs
Barkly Downs
Mingera Cr.
Ft Constantine
Cloncurry

AUSTRALIA
Stansmore Ra.
Warrabri Abor. Reserve
Hatches Creek
Lake Nash
Mount Isa
Malbon
L. White
L. Wills
Willowra Aboriginal Land Trust
Mt Strzelecki 636
Murray Downs
Elkedra
Elkedra
Woodroffe
Headingly
Urandangi
Duchess
Selwyn Range
L. Hazlett
Lander
Hanson
Dajarra

4

Central Australia Aboriginal Reserve
Lake Mackay
Aboriginal Land
Singleton 844
Barrow Creek
Ammaroo
Sandover
Mt Hogarth 339
Tobermory
Chatsworth
Lake Mackay
Mt Davenport 817
Yuendumu
Yuendumu Abor. Reserve
Reynolds Ra.
Central Mt Stuart 844
Ti Tree
Bundey
Ooratippra
Roxborough Downs
Herbert Downs
Boulia
Anga Ra.
Stuart Bluff Ra.
Central Mt Wedge
Mt Freeling 998
Hamilton
L. MacDonald
Ehrenberg Ra.
Mt Liebig 1524
Mt Edward 1416
Mt Hay 1249
Mt Laughlen 1167
Mt Riddock 1105
Mt Brassey 1128
Marshall
Marion Downs
Mt Leisler 901
Mt Lyell Brown 881
Mt Ziel 1510
Alice Springs
Ambalindum
Georgina
Springvale
Barons Ra.
Haasts Bluff
Haast Bluff
Macdonnell Ranges
Waterhouse Ra.
Hale
Sandringham
Bonython Ra.
George Gills Ra.
Hermannsburg
Palm Valley
James Ranges
Santa Teresa
Todd
Lake Philippi
Bedourie
L. Hopkins
L. Neale
Tempe Downs
Finke Gorge Nat. Park
Glengyle
Cluny
L. Machattie

Rawlinson Ra.
Lake Amadeus
Angas Downs
Palmer
Simpson Desert
L. Koolivoo
Monkira
Petermann Aboriginal Land
Yulara
Ayers Rock
Erldunda
Finke
L. Muncoonie
Bilpa Morea Claypan
Mooraberree
Mt Deering 1219
Petermann Ranges
Mt Olga 1069
Uluru (Ayers Rock) 1069
Uluru Nat. Park
Rumbalara
Andado
Durrie
Betoota
Mann Ranges
Kulgera
Goyder
Simpson Desert Nat. Park
Diamantina
Birdsville

5

Mt Rawlinson 1689
Mt Aloysius 1085
Mt Cockburn 1174
Mt Morris
Musgrave Ranges
Mt Everard
Abminga
Witjira Nat. Park
L. Thomas
Pandie Pandie
Barrow Ra.
Central Australia Aboriginal Reserve (Warburton)
Mt Davies 1058
Mt Whinham 1231
Mt Woodroffe 1440
Tieyon
Eringa
Simpson Desert Conservation Park
Alton Downs
L. Etamunbanie
Mt Squires 705
Tomkinson Ranges
Mt Kintore 1071
Poolowanna L.
Poolanna L.
L. Ulloowarangunna
Blyth Ra.
Mt Agnes 640
Birksgate Ra.
Pitjantjatjara Lands
Everard Range
Mt Illbillee 917
Everard Park
Alberga
Hamilton
Pedirka
Cordillo Downs
Arrabury
Mt Sir Thomas 773
Marla
Welbourn Hill
Alberga
Macumba
Clifton Hills
Aboriginal Land
Oodnadatta
Mt Dutton
L. Warrandirinna
L. Howitt
Innamincka

SOUTH
Woomera Prohibited Area
Serpentine Lakes
Mt Dutton
Peake
Neales
Lake Eyre (North)
Lake Eyre Nat. Park
Strzelecki Des.

6
GREAT VICTORIA DESERT
Wyola L.
Dey-Dey L.
L. Maurice
Coober Pedy
AUSTRALIA
Cadibarrawirracanna
Warriners Cr.
William Cr.
Cooper Creek
L. Gregory
L. Eyre (South)
L. Blanche

METRES | FEET
6000 | 19686
5000 | 16409
4000 | 13124
3000 | 9843
2000 | 6562
1000 | 3281
500 | 1640
200 | 656
SEA LEVEL
200 | 656
2000 | 6562
4000 | 13124
6000 | 19686

Lambert Azimuthal Equal Area Projection

© HarperCollinsPublishers

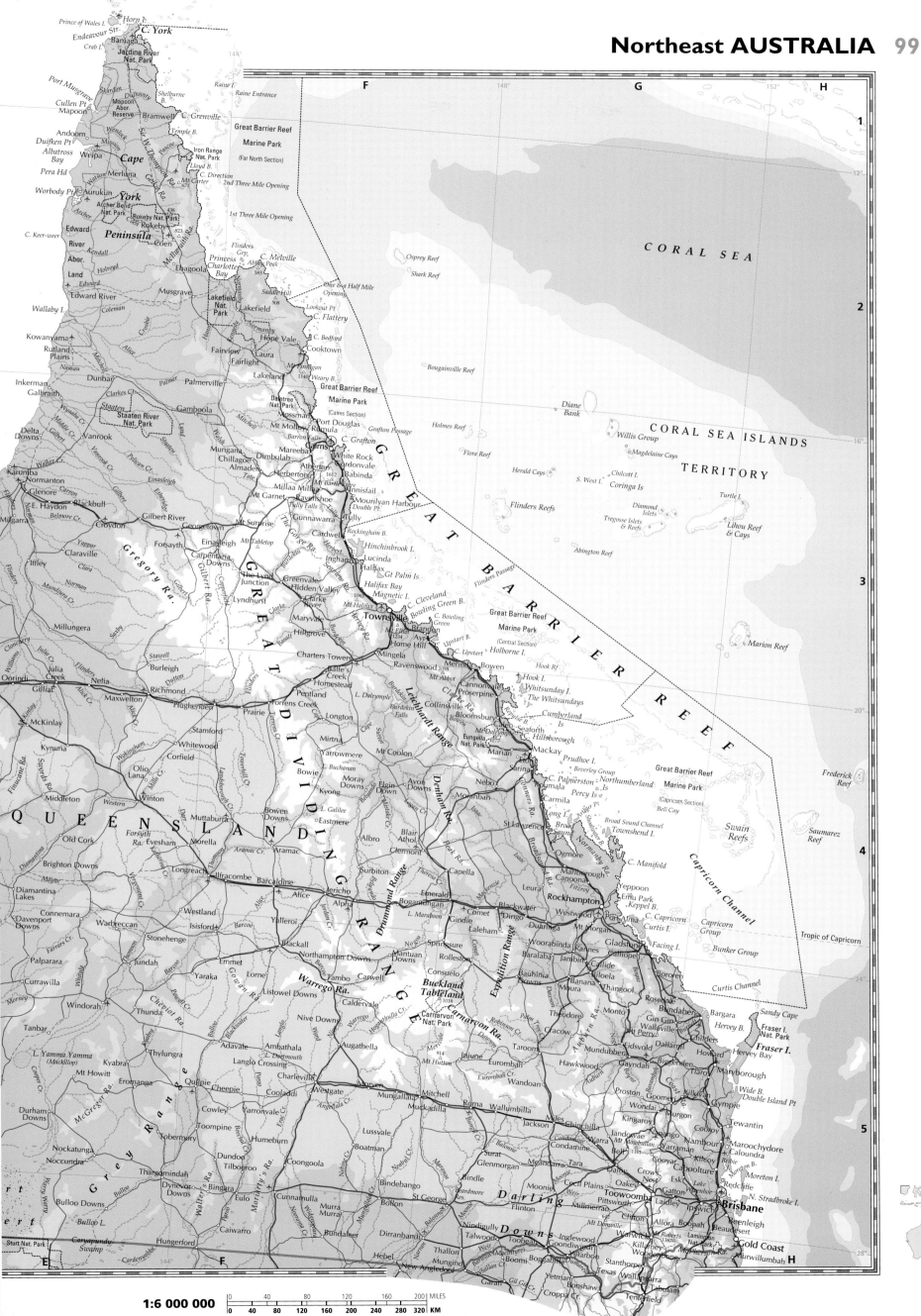

Northeast AUSTRALIA

99

CORAL SEA

CORAL SEA ISLANDS

TERRITORY

GREAT BARRIER REEF

QUEENSLAND

GREAT DIVIDING RANGE

Cape York Peninsula

Prince of Wales I.
Horn I.
C. York
Endeavour Str.
Banana
Jardine River Nat. Park
Crab I.
Port Musgrave
Skardon
Shelburne B.
Cullen Pt
Dulhunty
Mapoon Abor. Reserve
Bramwell
C. Grenville
Mapoon
Andoom
Weipa
Merluna
Iron Range Nat. Park
Lloyd B.
Duifken Pt
Albatross Bay
Mt Carter 671
C. Direction
Pera Hd
Worbody Pt
Aurukun
Watson
Cape
York
C. Keer-weer
Edward River
Archer Bend Nat. Park
Rokeby Nat. Park
Coen
Peninsula
C. Keer-weer
Kendall
Holroyd
Edward
Edward River Abor.
Land
Flinders Grp.
C. Melville
Wallaby I.
Coleman
Princess Charlotte Bay
Ebagoola
Abley Peak
Kowanyama
Musgrave
Lakefield Nat. Park
Lakefield
Saddle Hill
Rutland Plains
Nassau
One & Half Mile Opening
Lookout Pt
C. Flattery
Inkerman
Dunbar
Fairview
Hope Vale
C. Bedford
Galbraith
Fairlight
Cooktown
Laura
Mt Finnigan
Delta Downs
Staaten River Nat. Park
Lakeland
Weary B.
Karumba
Normanton
Gamboola
Daintree Nat. Park
Mossman
Normanby
Glenore
Blackbull
Gilbert River
Port Douglas
E. Haydon
Croydon
Georgetown
Mungana
Dimbulah
Rumula
Cairns
Milgarra
Forsayth
Chillagoe
Almaden
White Rock
Gordonvale
Babinda
Einasleigh
Herberton
Atherton
Innisfail
Mt Garnet
Millaa Millaa
Mourilyan Harbour
Ravenshoe
Double Pt
Mt Surprise
Gunnawarra
Tully
The Lynd Junction
Cardwell
Hinchinbrook I.
Lyndhurst
Greenvale
Ingham
Lucinda
Maryvale
Hidden Valley
Halifax
Gt Palm Is
Clarke River
Halifax Bay
Mt Halifax
Magnetic I.
Townsville
C. Cleveland
Bowling Green B.
Brandon
C. Bowling Green
Home Hill
Ayr
Charters Towers
Mingela
Merinda
Bowen
Ravenswood
C. Upstart
Holborne I.
Balfe's Creek
Mt Abbot
Homestead
Cannonvale
Proserpine
Whitsunday I.
Pentland
L. Dalrymple
Collinsville
The Whitsundays
Prairie
Bloomsbury
Cumberland Is
Hughenden
Bowie
Seaforth
Hillsborough
Mt Coolon
Eungella Nat. Park
Marian
Mackay
Moray Downs
Avon Downs
Nebo
Prudhoe I.
Elgin Downs
Moranbah
Kyong
Northumberland Is
Eastmere
St Lawrence
Carmila
Albro
Blair Athol
Clermont
Broad Sound Channel
Surbiton
Capella
Ogmore
C. Manifold
Emerald
Marlborough
Bogantungan
Blackwater
Rockhampton
Alpha
Comet
Dingo
Westwood
Port Alma
Jericho
Gindie
Duaringa
Mt Morgan
Barcaldine
Laleham
C. Capricorn
Springsure
Rolleston
Gladstone
Northampton Downs
Consuelo
Baralaba
Jambin
Carwell
Buckland Tableland
Bauhinia Downs
Biloela
Tambo
Carnarvon Nat. Park
Banana
Listowel Downs
Moura
Nive Downs
Theodore
Caldervale
Cracow
Tropic of Capricorn
Augathella
Mt Hutton
Taroom
Cracow
Eidsvold
Mundubbera
Charleville
Mitchell
Roma
Wandoan
Gayndah
Maryborough
Wallumbilla
Jackson
Chinchilla
Kingaroy
Gympie
Cooladdi
Muckadilla
Miles
Wondai
Cowley
Surat
Dalby
Nambour
Mungallala
Glenmorgan
Oakey
Toowoomba
Brisbane
Bollon
St George
Tara
Dalby
Ipswich
Dirranbandi
Moonie
Millmerran
Warwick
Gold Coast
Thallon
Goondiwindi
Stanthorpe
Texas
Tenterfield

CORAL SEA ISLANDS TERRITORY
Osprey Reef
Shark Reef
Bougainville Reef
Diane Bank
Willis Group
Flora Reef
Magdaline Cays
Herald Cays
S. West I.
Chilcott I.
Coringa Is
Flinders Reefs
Diamond Islets
Tregosse Islets & Reefs
Abington Reef
Lihou Reef & Cays
Turtle I.
Marion Reef
Frederick Reef
Saumarez Reef
Swain Reefs
Capricorn Channel
Bunker Group
Curtis Channel
Sandy Cape
Fraser I. Nat. Park
Fraser I.
Hervey Bay
Double Island Pt

Great Barrier Reef Marine Park (Far North Section)
Great Barrier Reef Marine Park (Cairns Section)
Great Barrier Reef Marine Park (Central Section)
Great Barrier Reef Marine Park (Capricorn Section)

1:6 000 000

0 40 80 120 160 200 MILES

0 40 80 120 160 200 240 280 320 KM

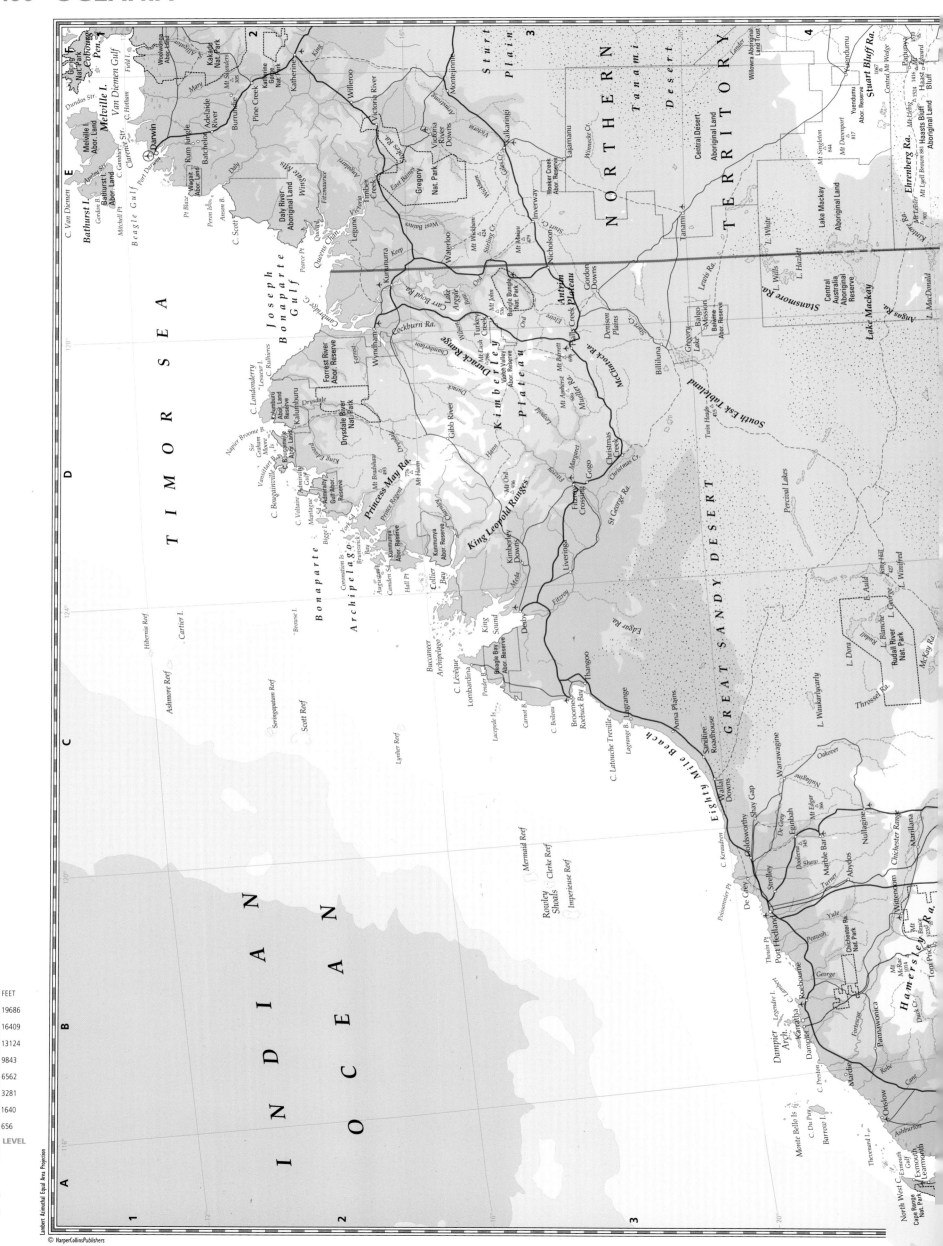

INDIAN OCEAN

TIMOR SEA

Joseph Bonaparte Gulf

NORTHERN TERRITORY

Sturt Plain

Tanami Desert

GREAT SANDY DESERT

Kimberley Plateau

King Leopold Ranges

Hamersley Ra.

Lambert Azimuthal Equal Area Projection

© HarperCollinsPublishers

METRES		FEET
6000		19686
5000		16409
4000		13124
3000		9843
2000		6562
1000		3281
500		1640
200		656
SEA		LEVEL
200		656
2000		6562
4000		13124
6000		19686

West AUSTRALIA 101

SOUTH

AUSTRALIA6

W E S T E R N

A U S T R A L I A

Gibson Desert

G R E A T   V I C T O R I A   D E S E R T

Nullarbor Plain

G R E A T   A U S T R A L I A N   B I G H T

Musgrave Ranges

Mann Ranges

Tomkinson Ranges

Petermann Ranges

Uluru Nat. Park

Lake Amadeus

Archipelago of the Recherche

Hamersley Ra. Nat. Park

Barlee Ra.

Kenneth Ra.

Robinson Ranges

Wallaby Range

Carnarvon Ra.

Rawlinson Ra.

Shark Bay

Lake MacLeod

Darling Range

Stirling Ra.

Perth

Fremantle

Rockingham

Mandurah

Bunbury

Busselton

Geraldton

Kalgoorlie

Coolgardie

Norseman

Esperance

Eucla

Cook

Forrest

Rawlinna

Balladonia

Madura

Nullarbor Nat. Park

Hampton Tableland

Mundrabilla

Woomera Prohibited Area

Maralinga

Yalata Abor. Reserve

Ooldea

Cocklebiddy

Tropic of Capricorn

1:6 000 000

0   40   80   120   160   200 MILES

0   40   80   120   160   200   240   280   320 KM

COUNTRY	AREA		POPULATION			Form of Government	Capital City	MAIN LANGUAGES	MAIN RELIGIONS	CURRENCY
	sqml	sqkm	total	density per sqml	sqkm					
ANGUILLA	60	155	8 000	134	52	UK territory	The Valley	English	Protestant, RC	E. Carib. dollar
ANTIGUA & BARBUDA	171	442	65 000	381	147	monarchy	St John's	English, Creole	Protestant, RC	E. Carib. dollar
THE BAHAMAS	5 382	13 939	272 000	51	20	monarchy	Nassau	English, Creole, French Creole	Protestant, RC	Dollar
BARBADOS	166	430	264 000	1590	614	monarchy	Bridgetown	English, Creole (Bajan)	Protestant, RC	Dollar
BELIZE	8 867	22 965	211 000	24	9	monarchy	Belmopan	English, Creole, Spanish, Mayan	RC, Protestant, Hindu	Dollar
BERMUDA	21	54	63 000	3022	1167	UK territory	Hamilton	English	Protestant, RC	Dollar
CANADA	3 849 674	9 970 610	29 251 000	8	3	federation	Ottawa	English, French, Amerindian languages, Inuktitut (Eskimo)	RC, Protestant, Greek Orthodox, Jewish	Dollar
CAYMAN ISLANDS	100	259	31 000	310	120	UK territory	George Town	English	Protestant, RC	Dollar
COSTA RICA	19 730	51 100	3 071 000	156	60	republic	San José	Spanish	RC, Protestant	Colón
CUBA	42 803	110 860	10 960 000	256	99	republic	Havana	Spanish	RC, Protestant	Peso
DOMINICA	290	750	71 000	245	95	republic	Roseau	English, French Creole	RC, Protestant	E. Carib. dollar,
DOMINICAN REPUBLIC	18 704	48 442	7 769 000	415	160	republic	Santo Domingo	Spanish, French Creole	RC, Protestant	Peso
EL SALVADOR	8 124	21 041	5 641 000	694	268	republic	San Salvador	Spanish	RC, Protestant	Colón
GREENLAND	840 004	2 175 600	55 000			Danish territory	Nuuk	Greenlandic, Danish	Protestant	Danish krone
GRENADA	146	378	92 000	630	243	monarchy	St George's	English, Creole	RC, Protestant	E. Carib. dollar
GUADELOUPE	687	1 780	421 000	613	237	French territory	Basse-Terre	French, French Creole	RC, Hindu	French franc
GUATEMALA	42 043	108 890	10 322 000	246	95	republic	Guatemala City	Spanish, Mayan languages	RC, Protestant	Quetzal
HAITI	10 714	27 750	7 041 000	657	254	republic	Port-au-Prince	French, French Creole	RC, Protestant, Voodoo	Gourde
HONDURAS	43 277	112 088	5 770 000	133	51	republic	Tegucigalpa	Spanish, Amerindian languages	RC, Protestant	Lempira
JAMAICA	4 244	10 991	2 429 000	572	221	monarchy	Kingston	English, Creole	Protestant, RC, Rastafarian	Dollar
MARTINIQUE	417	1 079	375 000	900	348	French territory	Fort-de-France	French, French Creole	RC, Protestant, Hindu, traditional beliefs	French franc
MEXICO	761 604	1 972 545	93 008 000	122	47	republic	Mexico City	Spanish, many Amerindian languages	RC, Protestant	Peso
MONTSERRAT	39	100	11 000	285	110	UK territory	Plymouth	English	Protestant, RC	E. Carib. dollar
NETH. ANTILLES (North)	26	68	35 240	1342	518	Neth. territory		Dutch, Papiamento, English	RC, Protestant	Guilder
NICARAGUA	50 193	130 000	4 401 000	88	34	republic	Managua	Spanish, Amerindian languages	RC, Protestant	Córdoba
PANAMA	29 762	77 082	2 583 000	87	34	republic	Panama City	Spanish, English Creole, Amerindian languages	RC, Protestant, Sunni Muslim, Baha'i	Balboa
PUERTO RICO	3 515	9 104	3 686 000	1049	405	US territory	San Juan	Spanish, English	RC, Protestant	US dollar
ST KITTS & NEVIS	101	261	41 000	407	157	monarchy	Basseterre	English, Creole	Protestant, RC	E. Carib. dollar
ST LUCIA	238	616	141 000	593	229	monarchy	Castries	English, French Creole	RC, Protestant	E. Carib. dollar
ST PIERRE & MIQUELON	93	242	6 000	64	25	French territory	St-Pierre	French	RC	French franc
ST VINCENT & THE GRENADINES	150	389	111 000	739	285	monarchy	Kingstown	English, Creole	Protestant, RC	E. Carib. dollar
TURKS & CAICOS IS.	166	430	14 000	84	33	UK territory	Grand Turk	English	Protestant	US dollar
USA	3 787 425	9 809 386	260 660 000	69	27	republic	Washington	English, Spanish, Amerindian languages	Protestant, RC, Sunni Muslim, Jewish, Mormon	Dollar
VIRGIN ISLANDS (UK)	59	153	18 000	305	118	UK territory	Road Town	English	Protestant, RC	US dollar
VIRGIN ISLANDS (USA)	136	352	104 000	765	295	US territory	Charlotte Amalie	English, Spanish	Protestant, RC	US dollar

OECD
see page 7 for information

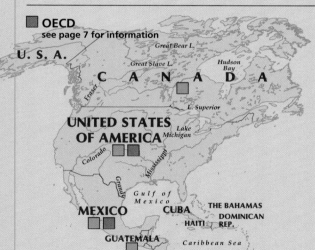

ORGANIZATION OF AMERICAN STATES (OAS)

The OAS claims to be the oldest regional organization in the world, tracing its origins back to the Congress of Panama in 1826. The Charter of the present OAS was signed in Bogota, Colombia in 1948 and came into force in 1951. There are 34 member states spread throughout North and South America. Cuba was suspended in 1962. Its objectives include the strengthening of peace and security, the promotion of democracy, the solution of political, juridical and economic problems and the promotion of economic, social and cultural development.

Headquarters : Washington, U.S.A.

CARIBBEAN COMMUNITY (CARICOM)

Following a series of initiatives in the 1960's to promote Caribbean regional co-operation CARICOM was established in 1973. The original members were Barbados, Guyana, Jamaica and Trinidad and Tobago; in May 1974, Belize, Dominica, Grenada, Montserrat, St Lucia and St Vincent joined followed by Antigua and St Kitts-Nevis in August 1974, the Bahamas in 1984 and Surinam in 1995. The objectives of CARICOM are to foster co-operation, co-ordinate foreign policy, and to formulate and carry out common policies on health, education and culture, communications and industrial relations.

Headquarters: Georgetown, Guyana

© HarperCollinsPublishers

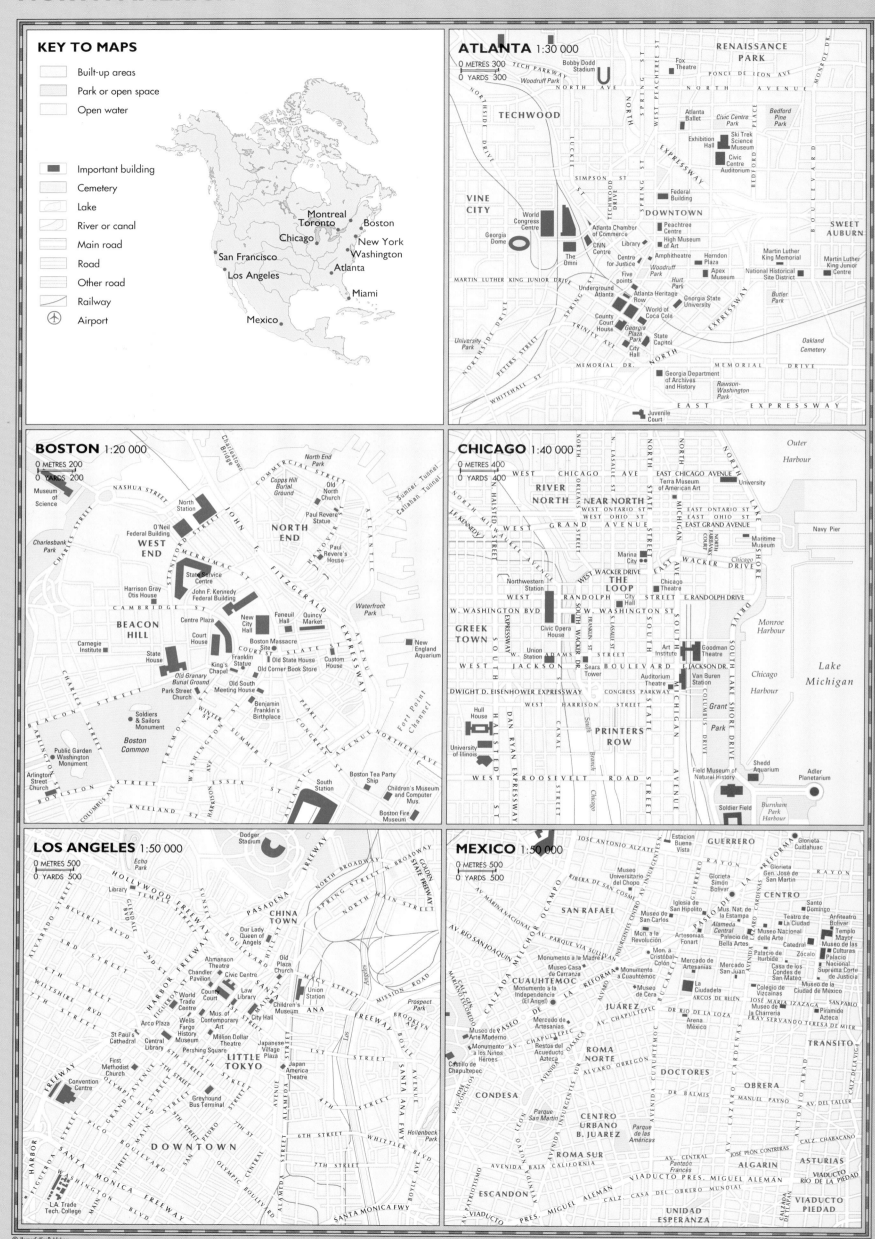

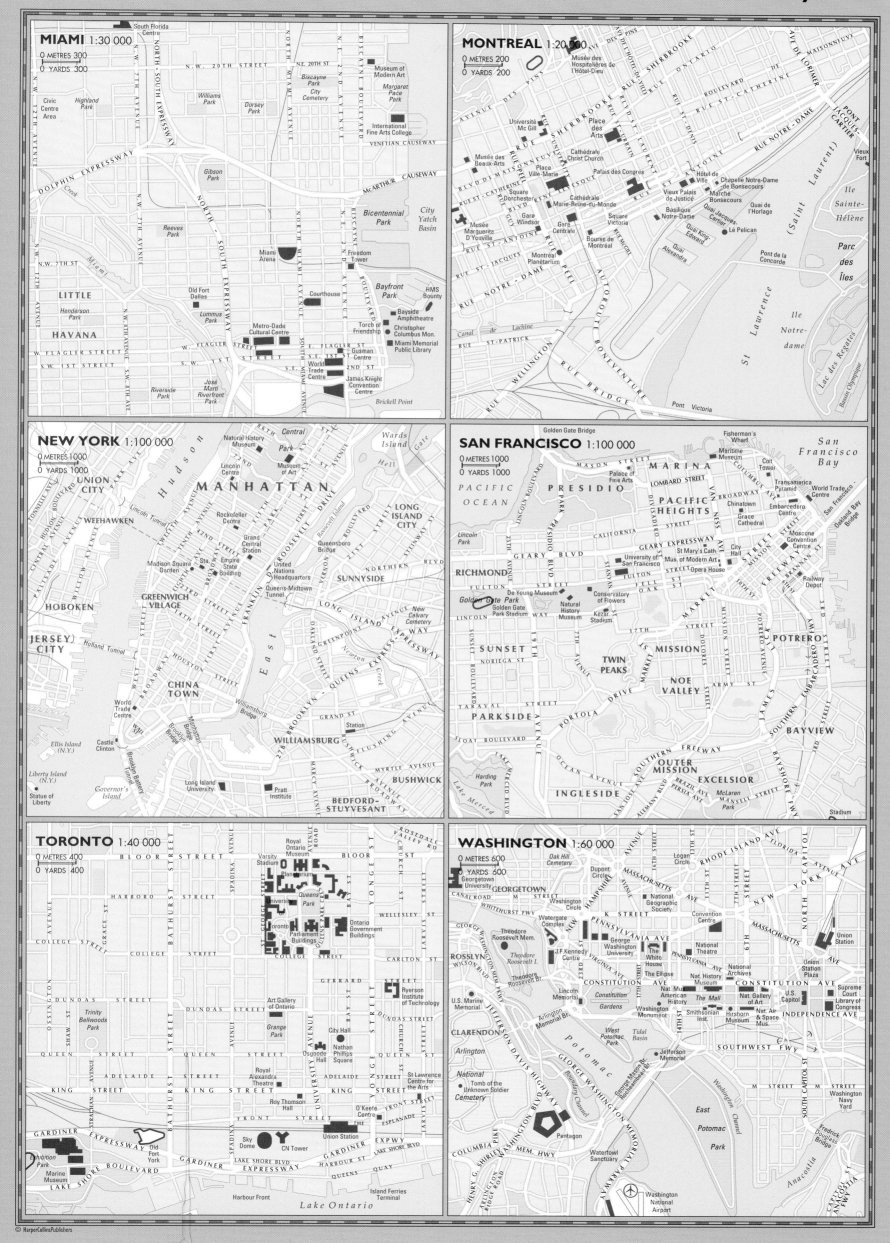

MIAMI 1:30 000

0 METRES 300
0 YARDS 300

MONTREAL 1:20 000

0 METRES 200
0 YARDS 200

NEW YORK 1:100 000

0 METRES 1000
0 YARDS 1000

SAN FRANCISCO 1:100 000

0 METRES 1000
0 YARDS 1000

TORONTO 1:40 000

0 METRES 400
0 YARDS 400

WASHINGTON 1:60 000

0 METRES 600
0 YARDS 600

© HarperCollinsPublishers

METRES | FEET
6000 | 19686
5000 | 16409
4000 | 13124
3000 | 9843
2000 | 6562
1000 | 3281
500 | 1640
200 | 656
SEA | LEVEL
200 | 656
2000 | 6562
4000 | 13124
6000 | 19686

Chamberlin Trimetric Projection

© HarperCollinsPublishers

1:13 000 000

MILES
0 100 200 300 400 500

KM
0 100 200 300 400 500 600 700 800

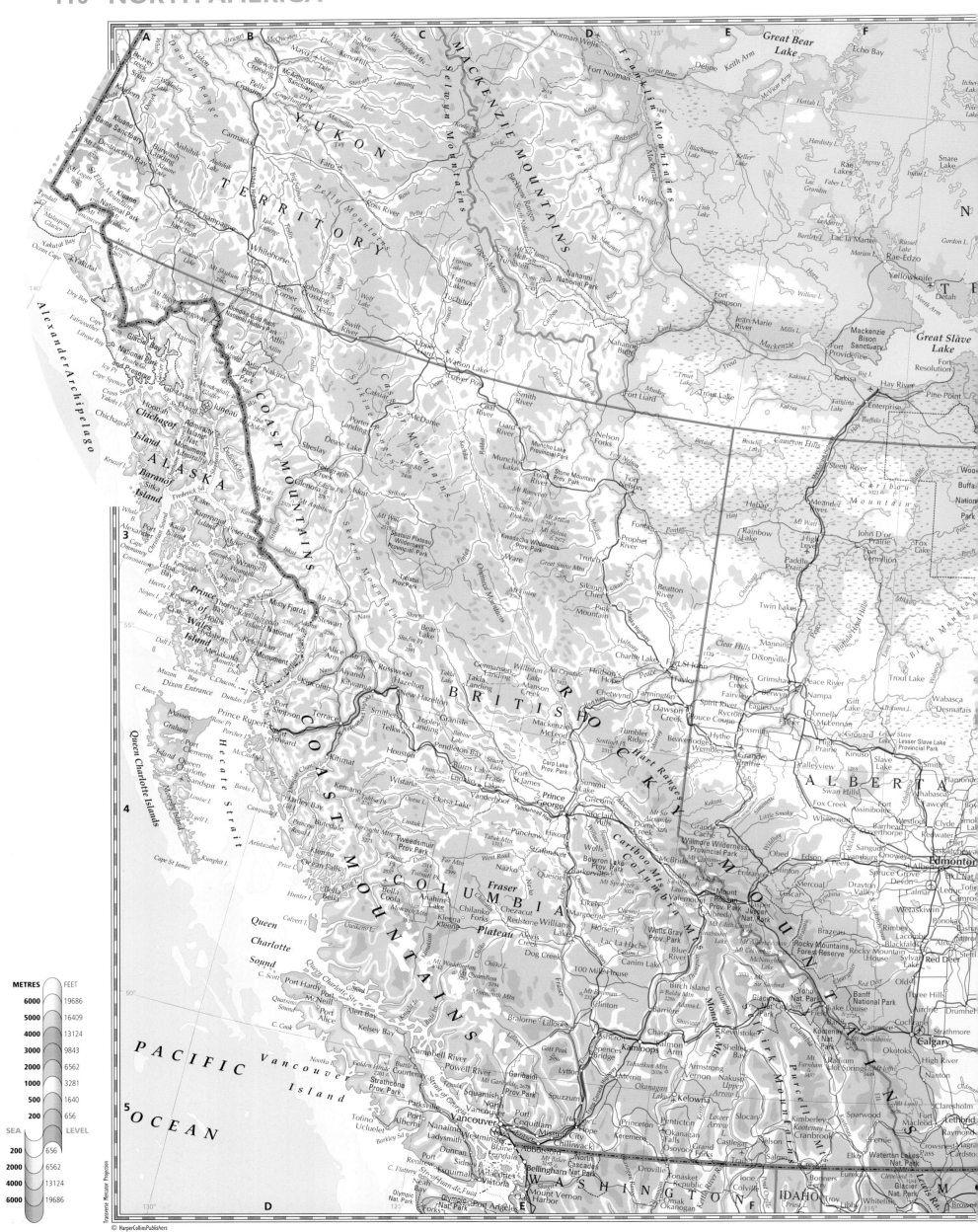

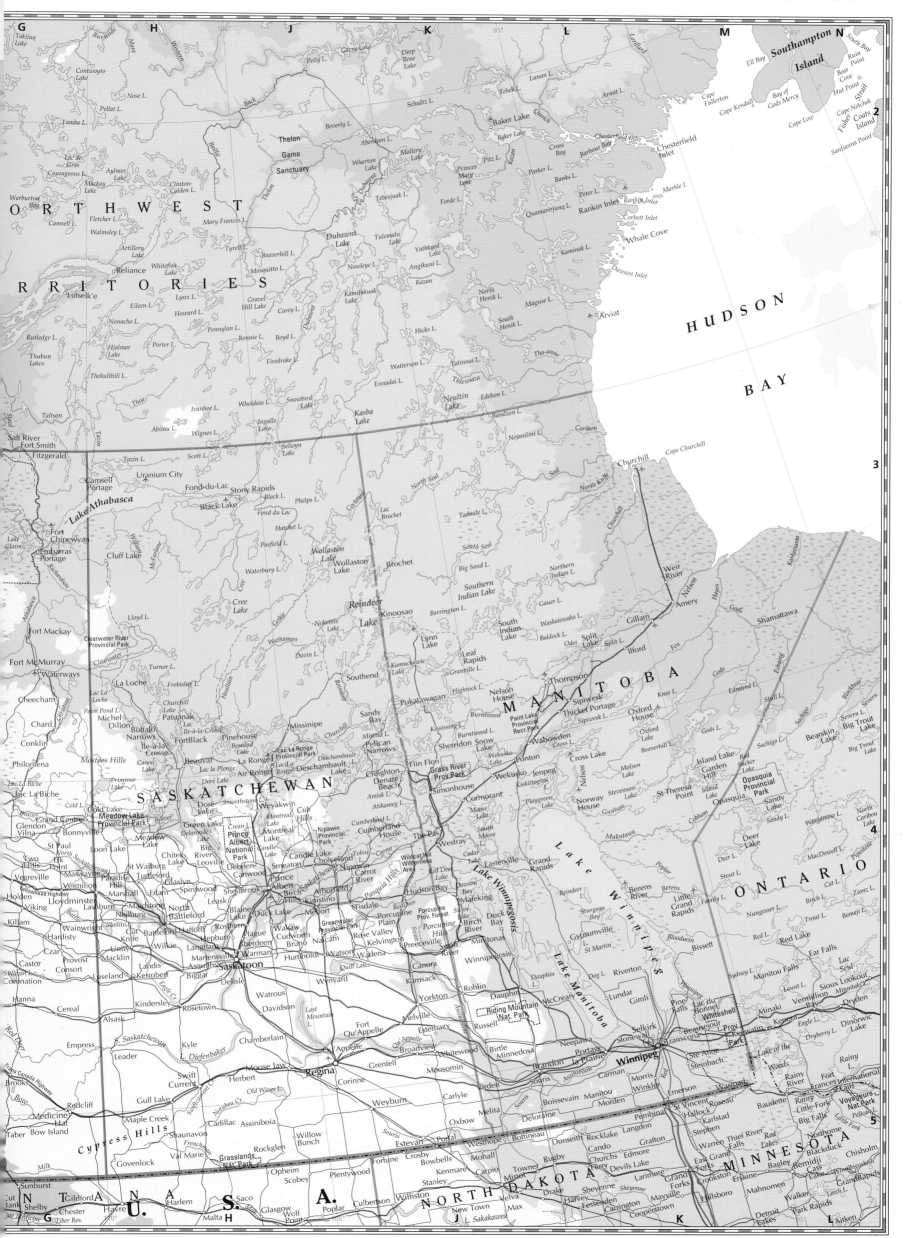

1:6 000 000

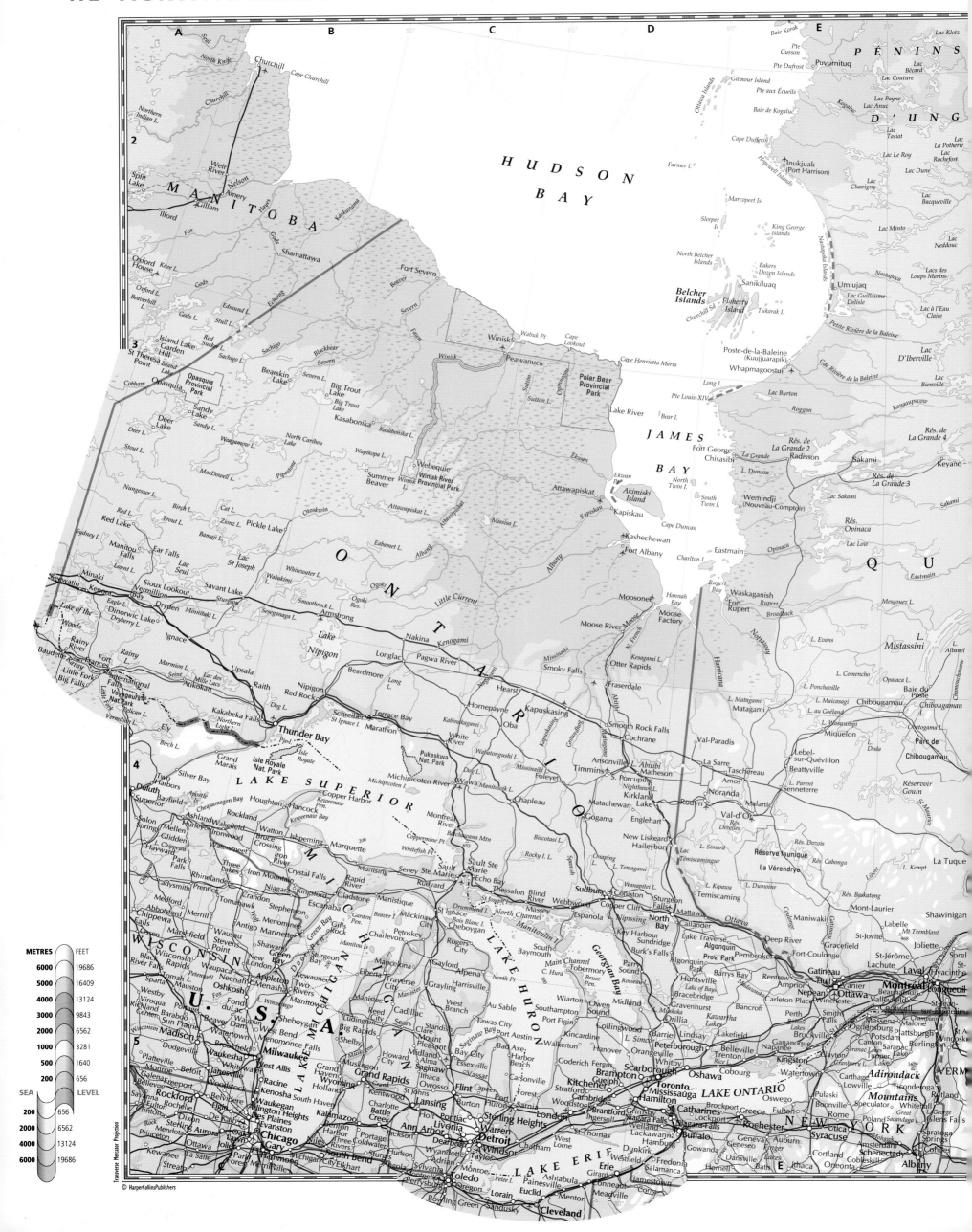

© HarperCollins Publishers

Transverse Mercator Projection

METRES	FEET
6000	19686
5000	16409
4000	13124
3000	9843
2000	6562
1000	3281
500	1640
200	656
SEA	LEVEL
200	656
2000	6562
4000	13124
6000	19686

ATLANTIC OCEAN

Labrador Sea

UNGAVA BAY

LABRADOR

NEWFOUNDLAND

QUÉBEC

Gulf of St Lawrence
(Golfe du St-Laurent)

NEW BRUNSWICK

NOVA SCOTIA

PRINCE EDWARD ISLAND

Cape Breton Island

MAINE

NEW HAMPSHIRE

St-Pierre-et-Miquelon (France)

Avalon Peninsula

Île d'Anticosti

Péninsule de Gaspé

Bay of Fundy

Cabot Strait

Strait of Belle Isle

Smallwood Res.

Réservoir Manicouagan

Happy Valley-Goose Bay

Goose Bay

Corner Brook

Gander

St John's

Halifax

Dartmouth

Truro

Sydney

Charlottetown

Summerside

Fredericton

Québec

Sept-Îles

Baie Comeau

Schefferville

Churchill Falls

Wabush

Labrador City

Fermont

Gagnon

Nain

Hebron

Hopedale

Makkovik

Cartwright

Rigolet

Portland

1:6 000 000

| 0 | 40 | 80 | 120 | 160 | 200 MILES |
| 0 | 40 | 80 | 120 | 160 | 200 | 240 | 280 | 320 KM |

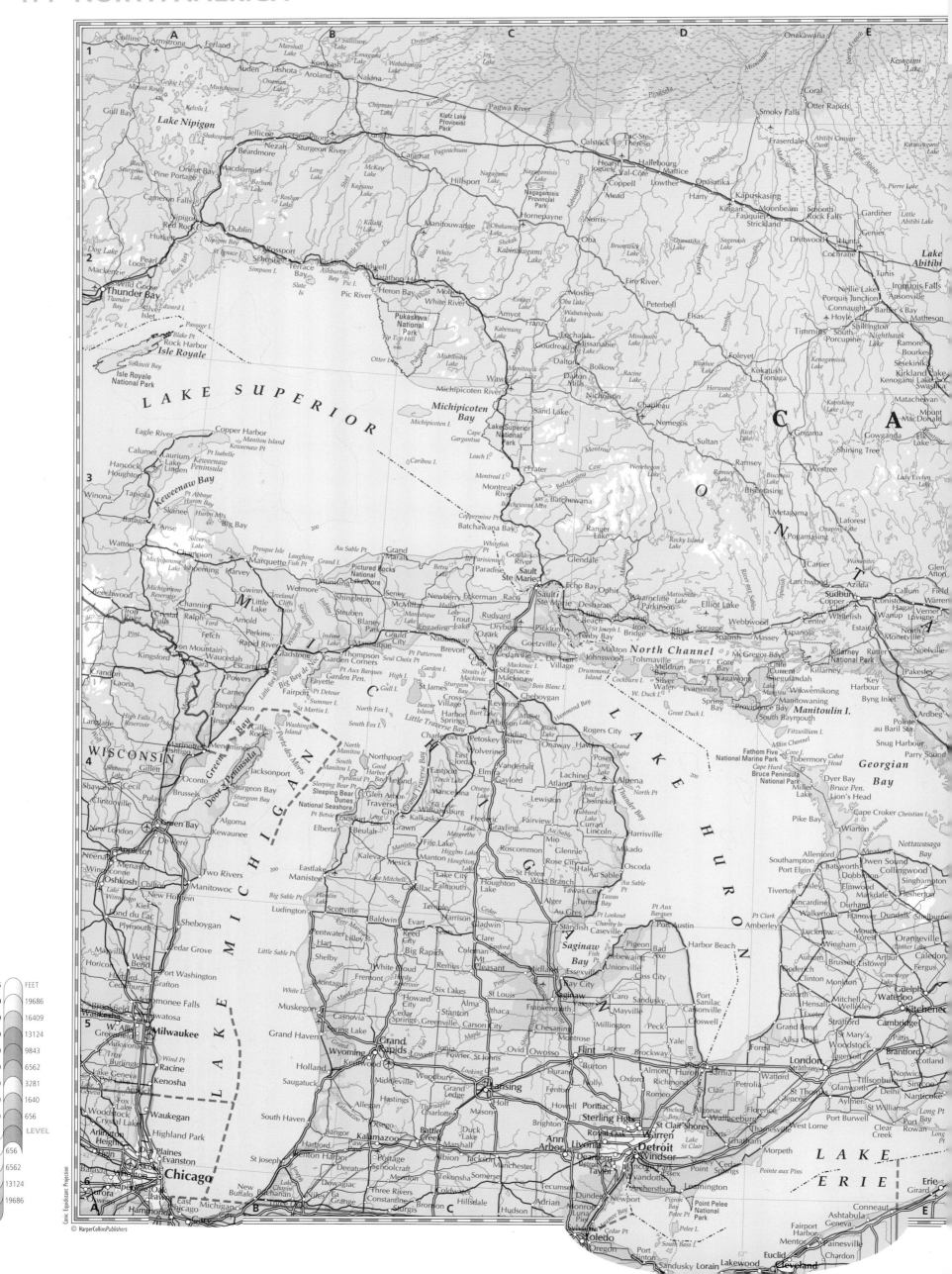

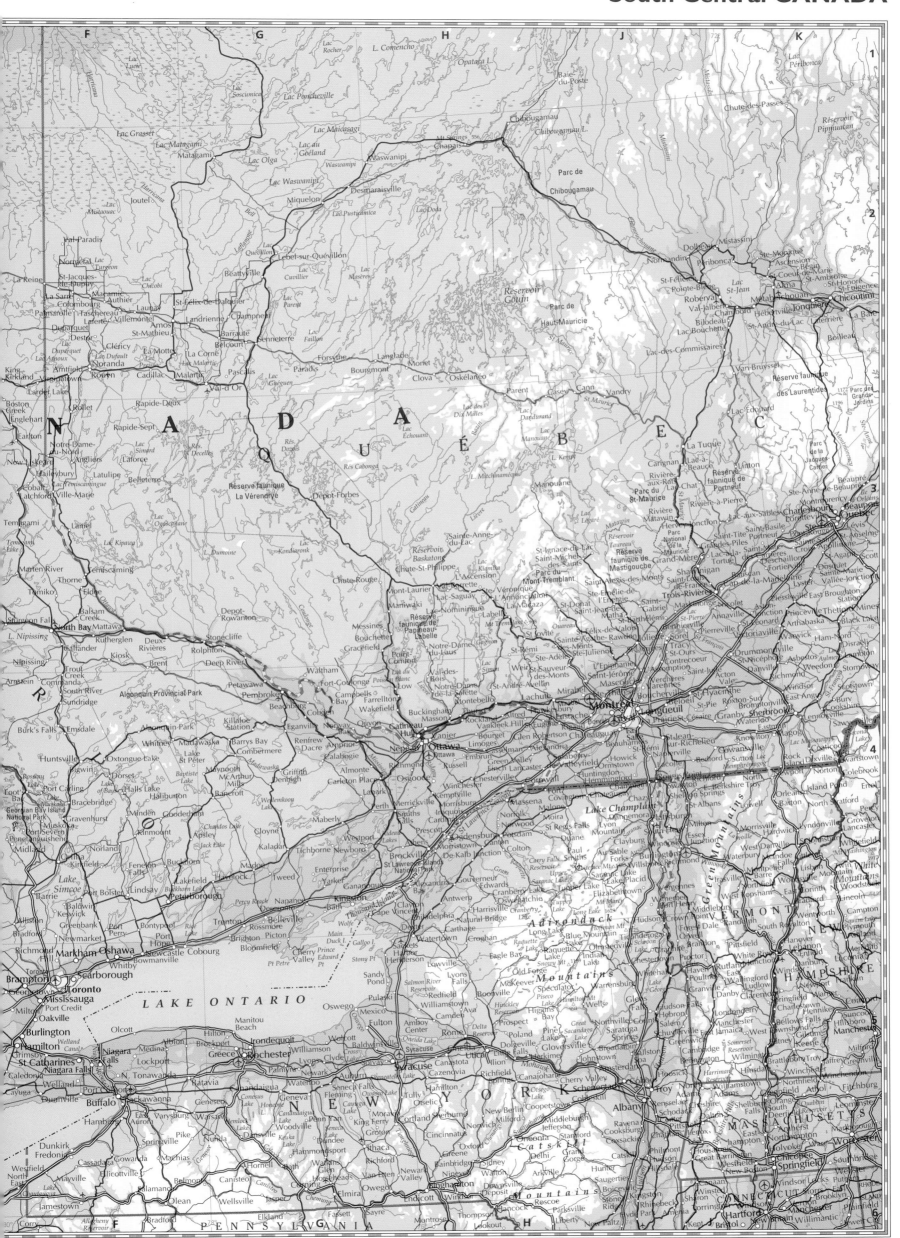

1:3 000 000

MILES
0 20 40 60 80 100

KM
0 20 40 60 80 100 120 140 160

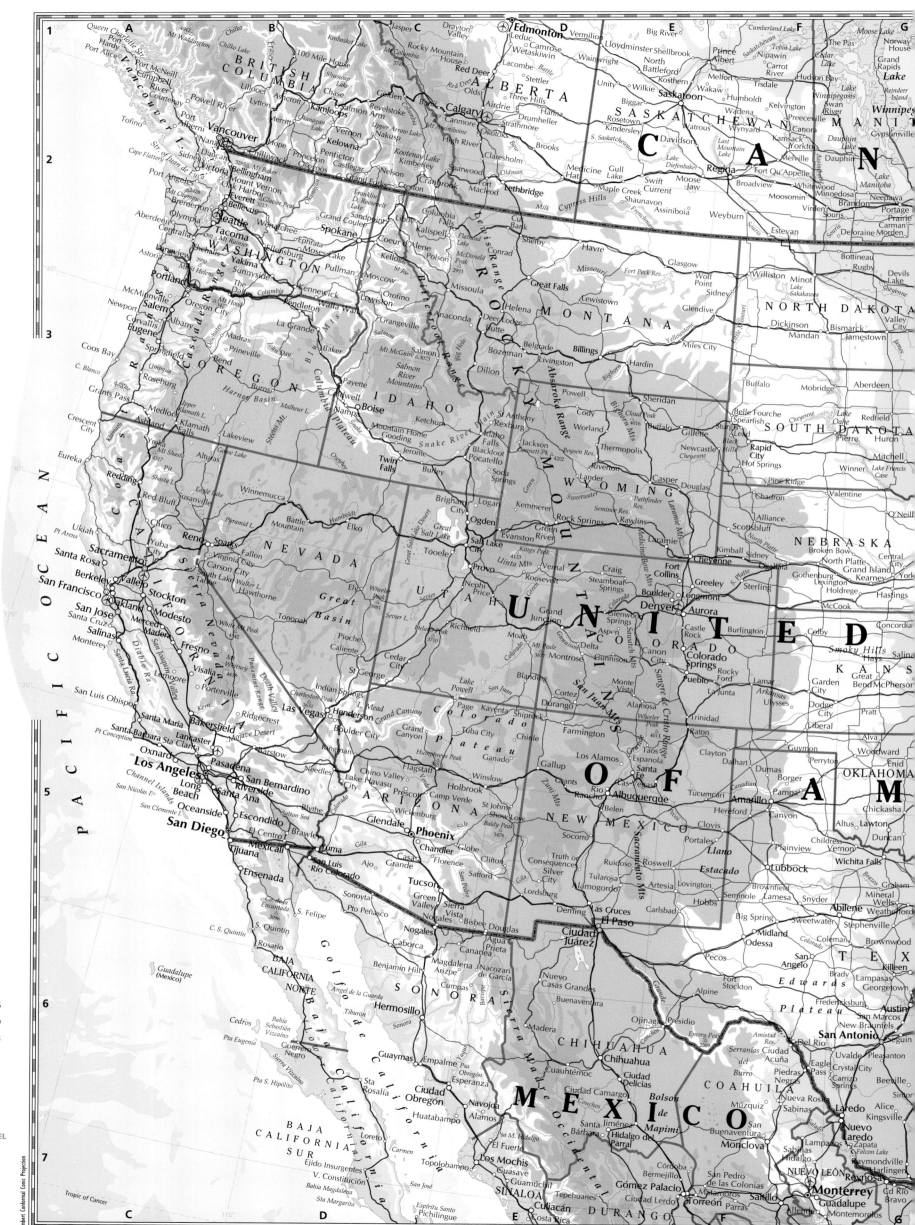

METRES | FEET
6000 | 19686
5000 | 16409
4000 | 13124
3000 | 9843
2000 | 6562
1000 | 3281
500 | 1640
200 | 656
SEA | LEVEL
200 | 656
2000 | 6562
4000 | 13124
6000 | 19686

Lambert Conformal Conic Projection

© HarperCollinsPublishers

ATLANTIC OCEAN

GULF OF MEXICO

THE BAHAMAS

QUÉBEC ONTARIO NEW BRUNSWICK NOVA SCOTIA MAINE VERMONT NEW HAMP. MASS. CONN.

LAKE SUPERIOR LAKE MICHIGAN LAKE HURON LAKE ERIE Lake Ontario

MINNESOTA WISCONSIN MICHIGAN IOWA ILLINOIS INDIANA OHIO PENNSYLVANIA NEW YORK NEW JERSEY

MISSOURI KENTUCKY WEST VIRGINIA VIRGINIA MARYLAND DELAWARE

ARKANSAS TENNESSEE NORTH CAROLINA SOUTH CAROLINA

LOUISIANA MISSISSIPPI ALABAMA GEORGIA

FLORIDA

STATES ERICA

Winnipeg Minneapolis St Paul Milwaukee Madison Chicago Detroit Cleveland Pittsburgh Philadelphia New York Boston Providence

Des Moines Omaha Lincoln Kansas City St Louis Indianapolis Columbus Cincinnati Washington D.C. Baltimore Richmond Norfolk

Wichita Tulsa Springfield Nashville Knoxville Charlotte Raleigh Greensboro Durham

Oklahoma City Little Rock Memphis Chattanooga Atlanta Columbia Charleston

Dallas Fort Worth Houston Shreveport Jackson Birmingham Montgomery Savannah

New Orleans Baton Rouge Mobile Pensacola Tallahassee Jacksonville

Tampa St Petersburg Orlando West Palm Beach Fort Lauderdale Hollywood Miami Key West

Corpus Christi Matamoros

Montreal Ottawa Toronto Québec Thunder Bay Duluth

1 : 10 000 000

0   100   200   300 MILES
0 100 200 300 400 500 KM

CANADA

QUÉBEC

ONTARIO

NEW BRUNSWICK

MAINE

VERMONT

NEW HAMPSHIRE

MASSACHUSETTS

CONNECTICUT

NEW YORK

PENNSYLVANIA

NEW JERSEY

DELAWARE

MARYLAND

WEST VIRGINIA

VIRGINIA

OHIO

INDIANA

KENTUCKY

MICHIGAN

WISCONSIN

ILLINOIS

IOWA

MISSOURI

MINNESOTA

ATLANTIC OCEAN

LAKE SUPERIOR

LAKE HURON

LAKE MICHIGAN

LAKE ONTARIO

LAKE ERIE

Georgian Bay

Chesapeake Bay

Long Island

St Lawrence

Major cities: Quebec, Montreal, Ottawa, Toronto, Hamilton, London, Detroit, Cleveland, Buffalo, Rochester, Syracuse, Albany, Boston, Providence, New York, Newark, Philadelphia, Baltimore, Washington D.C., Richmond, Pittsburgh, Columbus, Cincinnati, Indianapolis, Chicago, Milwaukee, Lansing, Toledo, Fort Wayne, Louisville, Frankfort, Springfield, Madison, Green Bay, Sudbury, Thunder Bay, Duluth, St Louis

METRES		FEET
6000		19686
5000		16409
4000		13124
3000		9843
2000		6562
1000		3281
500		1640
200		656
SEA		LEVEL
200		656
2000		6562
4000		13124
6000		19686

Lambert Conformal Conic Projection

© HarperCollinsPublishers

BERMUDA (United Kingdom) 1:500 000

NEW PROVIDENCE (The Bahamas) 1:600 000

PUERTO RICO and VIRGIN ISLANDS 1:3M

1:6 000 000

| | 40 | 80 | 120 | 160 | 200 | MILES |

| 0 | 40 | 80 | 120 | 160 | 200 | 240 | 280 | 320 | KM |

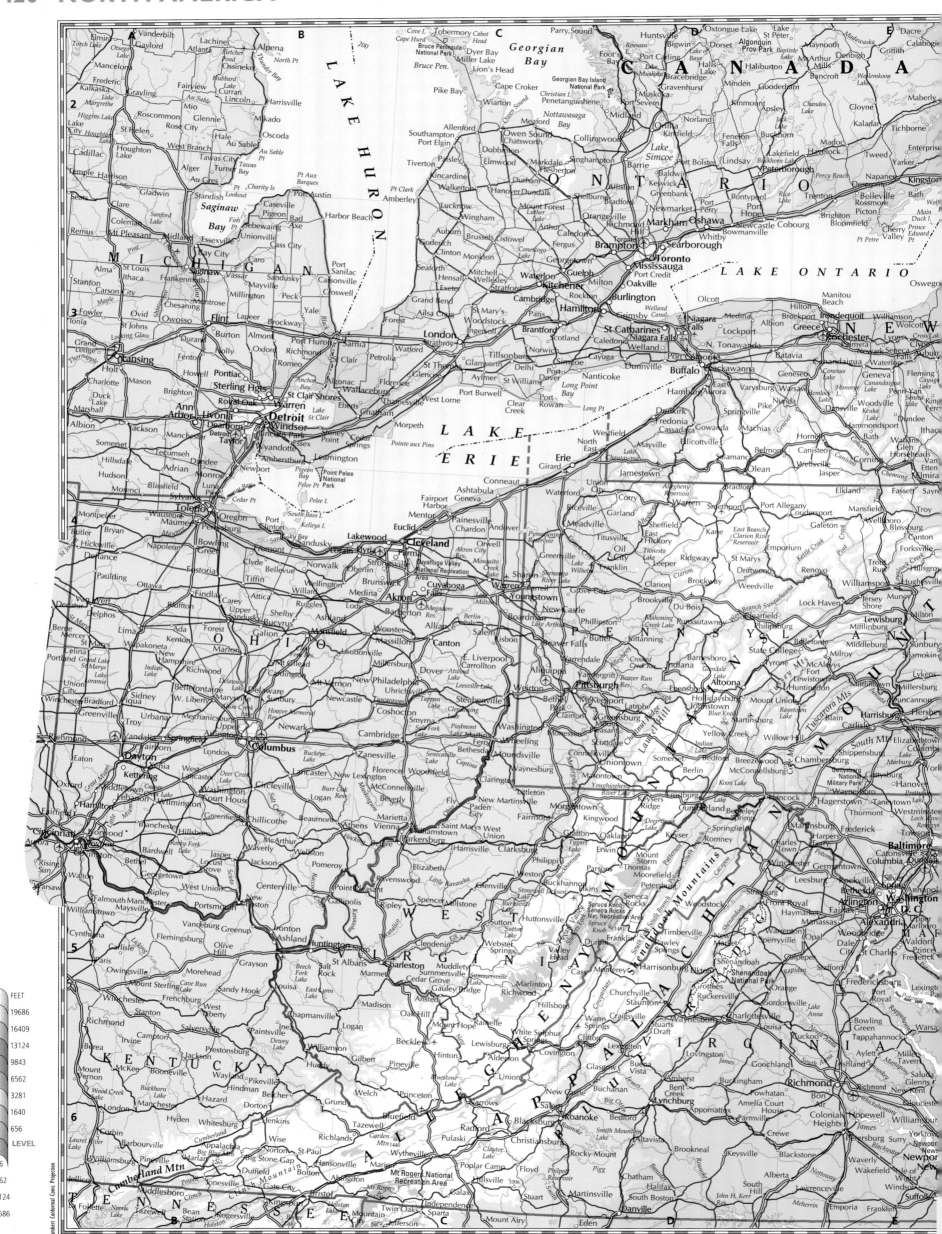

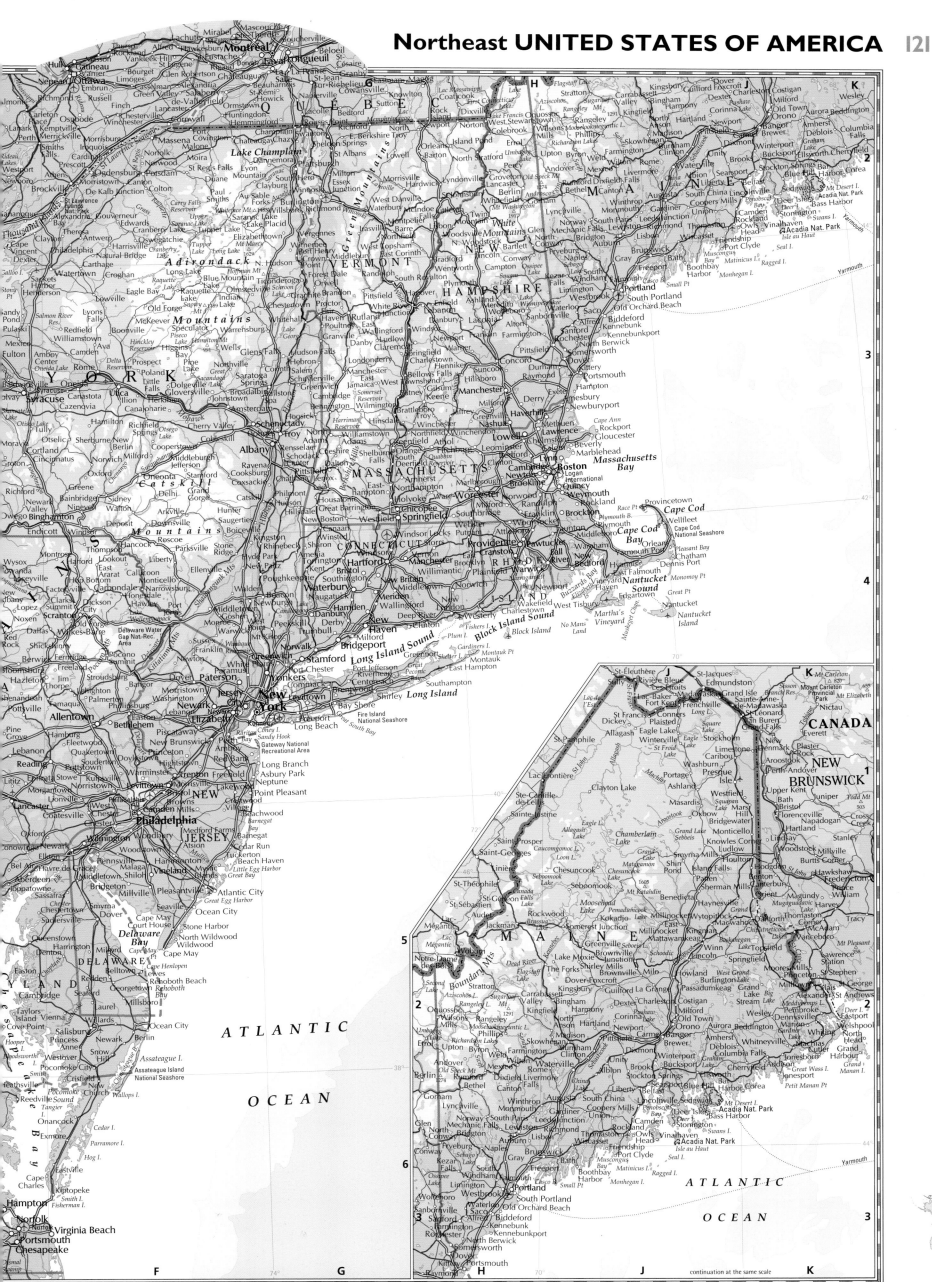

1:3 000 000

| 0 | 20 | 40 | 60 | 80 | 100 | MILES |

| 0 | 20 | 40 | 60 | 80 | 100 | 120 | 140 | 160 | KM |

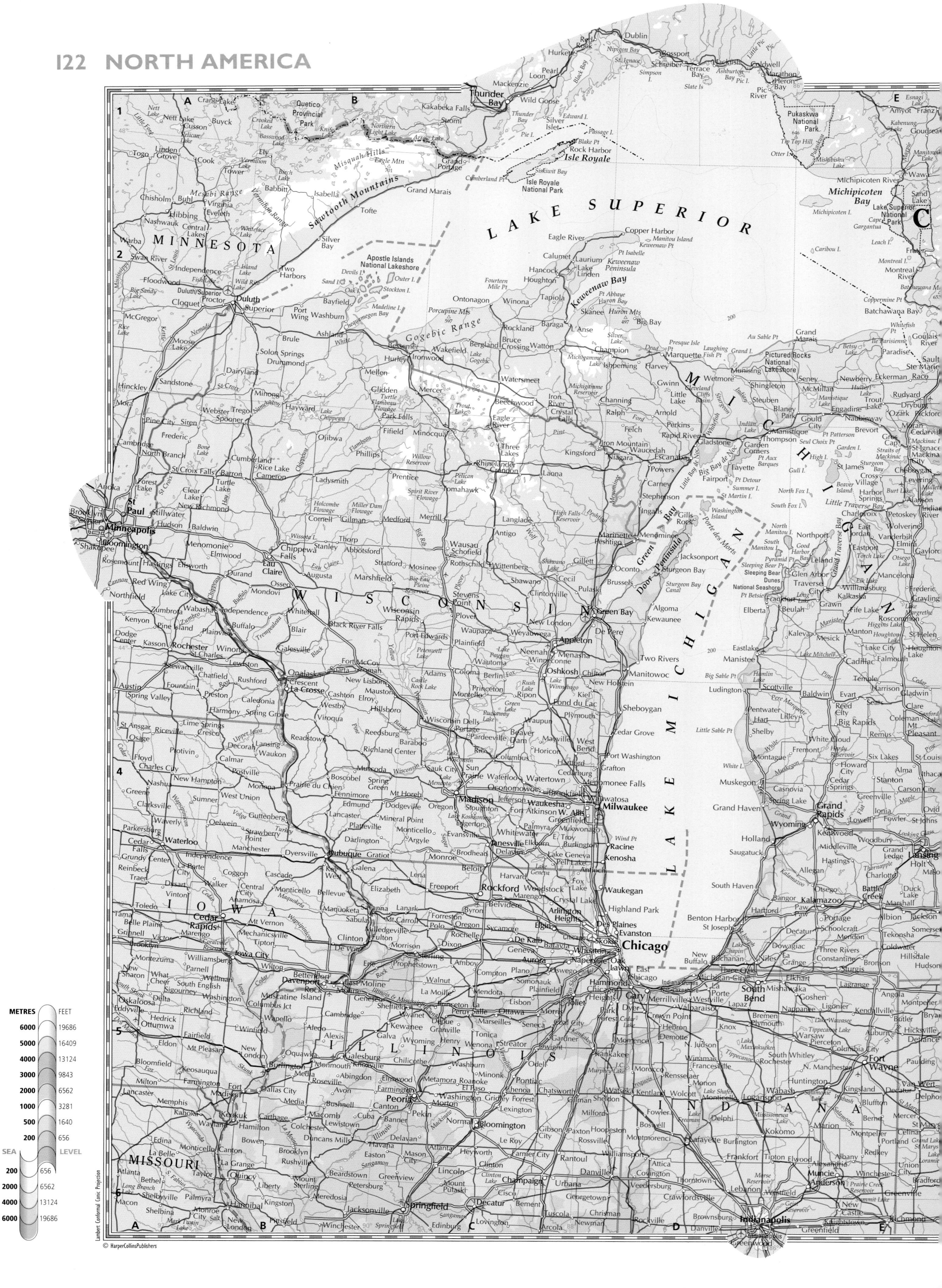
LAKE SUPERIOR
LAKE MICHIGAN
MINNESOTA
WISCONSIN
MICHIGAN
IOWA
ILLINOIS
INDIANA
MISSOURI
Thunder Bay
Isle Royale
Isle Royale National Park
Apostle Islands National Lakeshore
Pukaskwa National Park
Quetico Provincial Park
Pictured Rocks National Lakeshore
Sleeping Bear Dunes National Seashore
Keweenaw Peninsula
Keweenaw Bay
Green Bay
Door Peninsula
Michipicoten Bay
Sawtooth Mountains
Misquah Hills
Gogebic Range
Mesabi Range
Duluth
Superior
St Paul
Minneapolis
Bloomington
Rochester
Eau Claire
La Crosse
Wausau
Green Bay
Appleton
Oshkosh
Madison
Milwaukee
Racine
Kenosha
Dubuque
Cedar Rapids
Iowa City
Davenport
Waterloo
Rockford
Chicago
Joliet
Peoria
Bloomington
Champaign
Springfield
Decatur
Gary
Hammond
South Bend
Fort Wayne
Lafayette
Kokomo
Muncie
Anderson
Indianapolis
Kalamazoo
Grand Rapids
Lansing
Muskegon
Marquette
METRES
FEET
6000
19686
5000
16409
4000
13124
3000
9843
2000
6562
1000
3281
500
1640
200
656
SEA
LEVEL
200
656
2000
6562
4000
13124
6000
19686
Lambert Conformal Conic Projection
© HarperCollinsPublishers

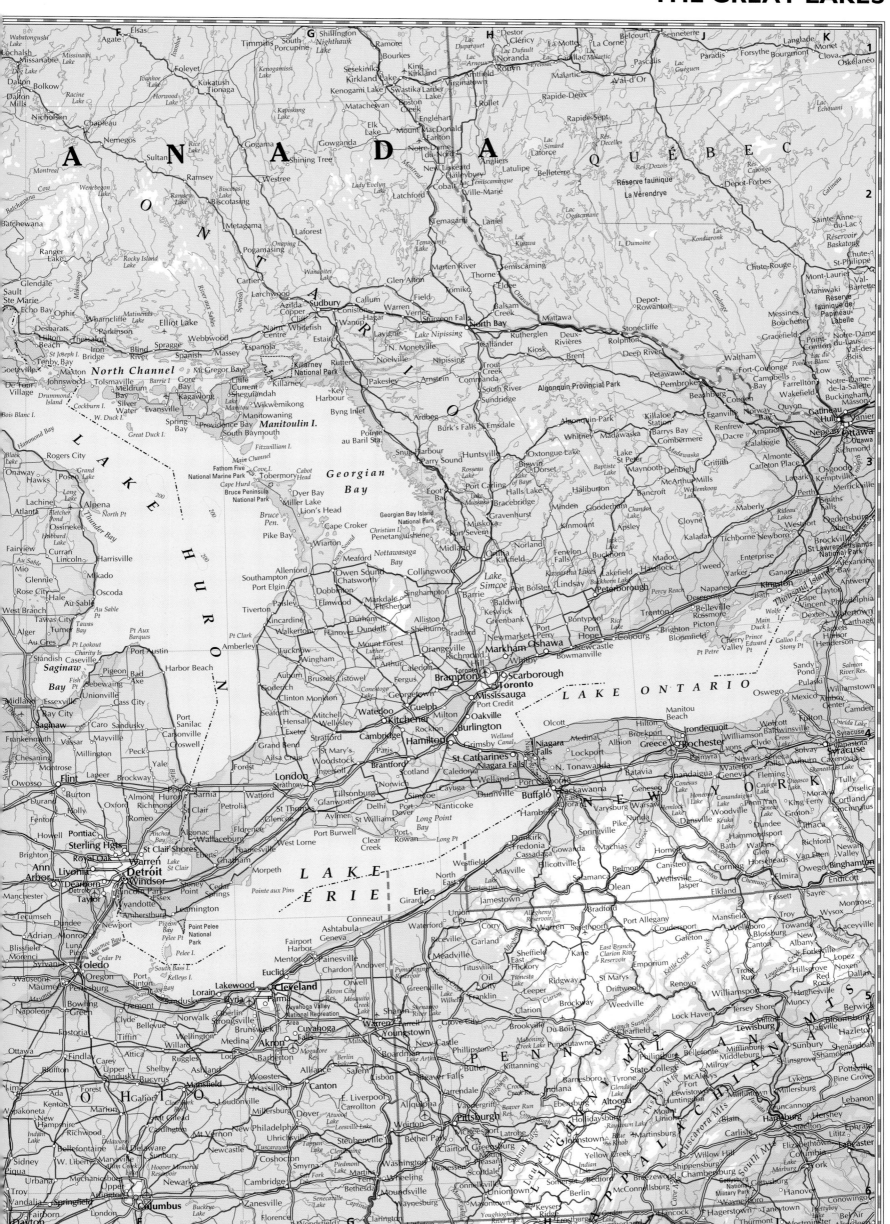

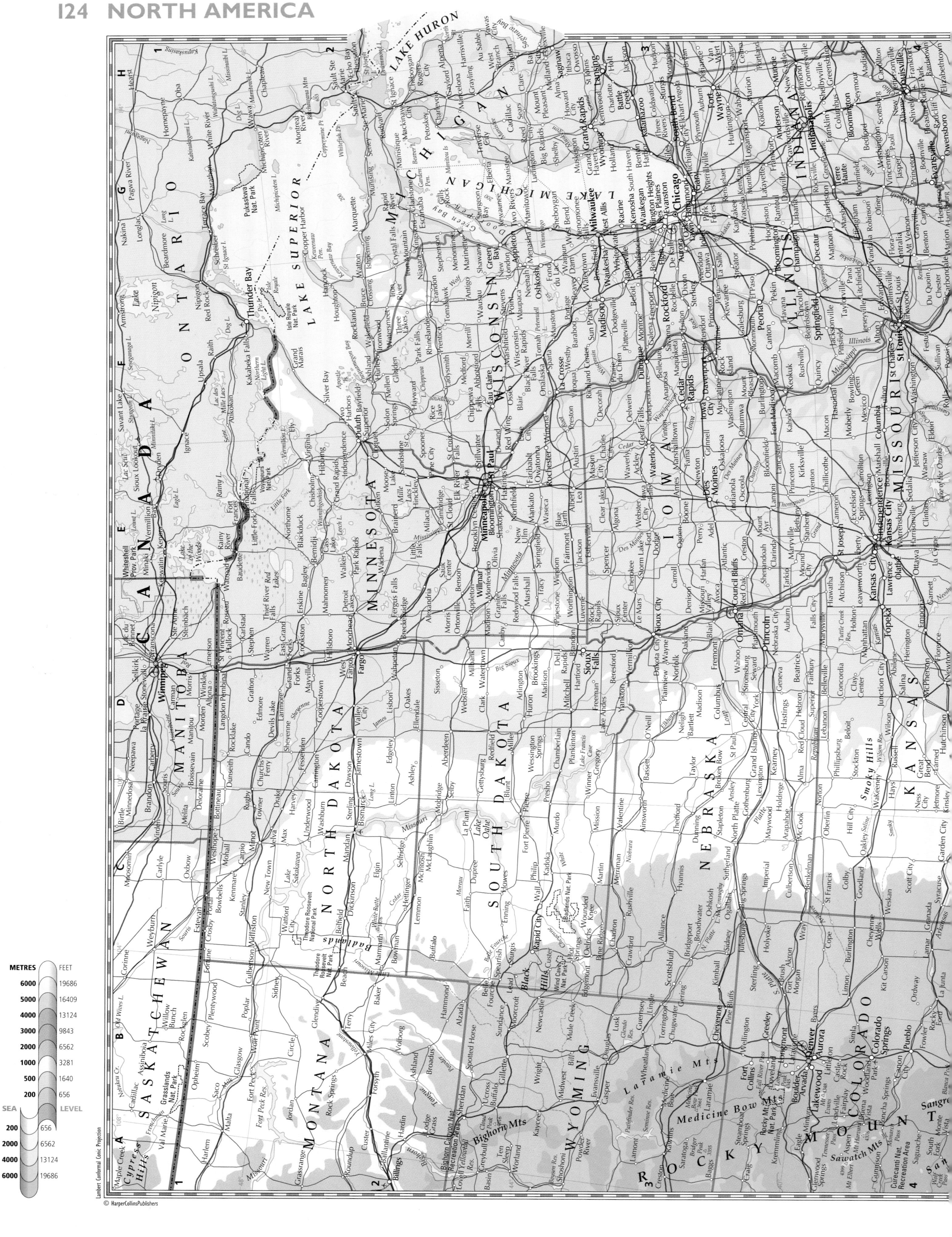

LAKE HURON

LAKE SUPERIOR

LAKE MICHIGAN

ONTARIO

CANADA

MANITOBA

SASKATCHEWAN

MINNESOTA

NORTH DAKOTA

SOUTH DAKOTA

NEBRASKA

KANSAS

IOWA

MISSOURI

ILLINOIS

INDIANA

WISCONSIN

MICHIGAN

MONTANA

WYOMING

COLORADO

ROCKY MOUNTAINS

Winnipeg · Thunder Bay · Duluth · Superior · Minneapolis · St Paul · Fargo · Bismarck · Sioux Falls · Sioux City · Des Moines · Omaha · Lincoln · Kansas City · St Louis · Chicago · Milwaukee · Madison · Green Bay · Grand Rapids · Indianapolis · Springfield · Denver · Colorado Springs · Pueblo · Rapid City · Billings

Black Hills · Bighorn Mts · Laramie Mts · Medicine Bow · Smoky Hills · Badlands · Cypress Hills

Missouri · Mississippi · Platte

METRES		FEET
6000		19686
5000		16409
4000		13124
3000		9843
2000		6562
1000		3281
500		1640
200		656
SEA		LEVEL
200		656
2000		6562
4000		13124
6000		19686

Lambert Conformal Conic Projection

© HarperCollins Publishers

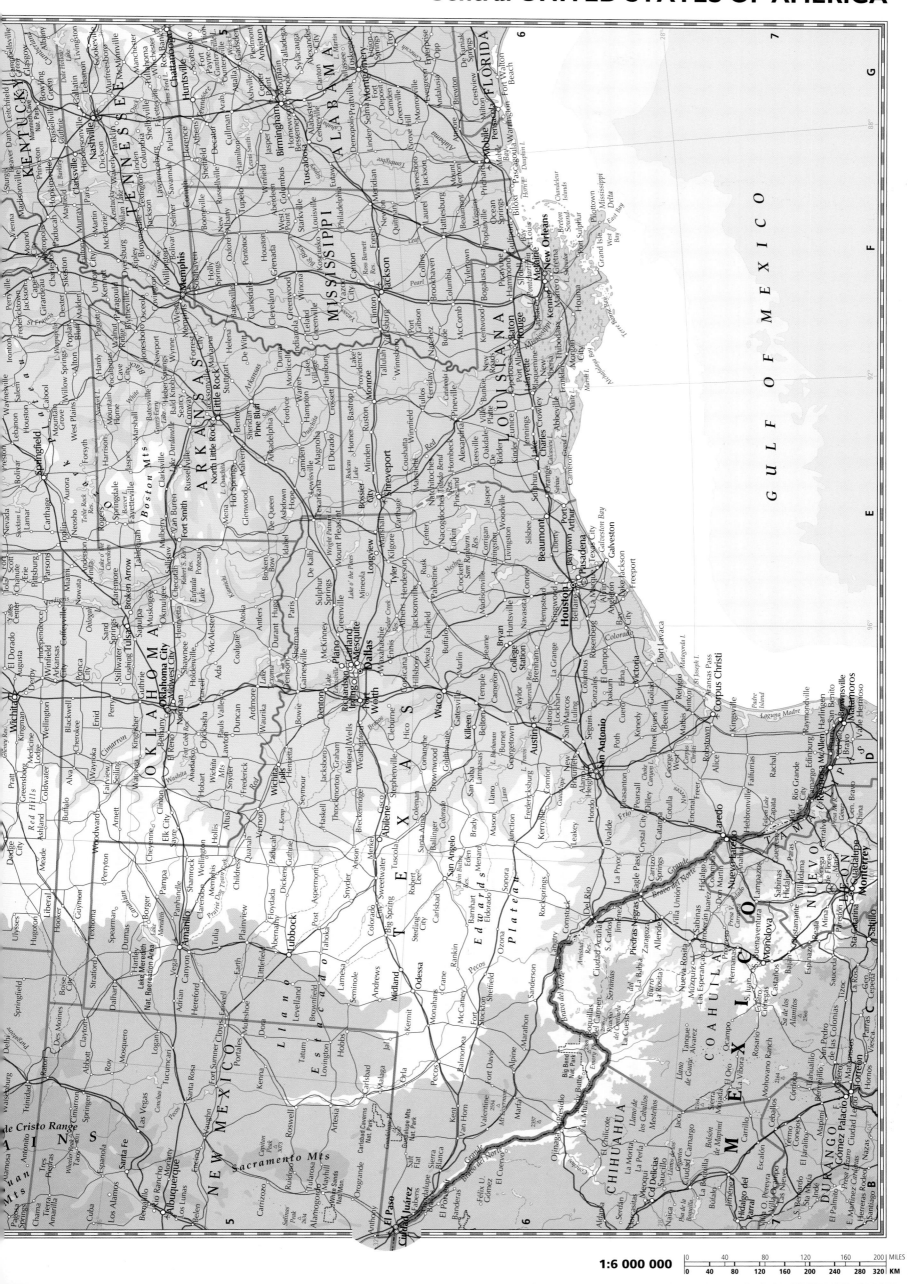

1:6 000 000

| 0 | 40 | 80 | 120 | 160 | 200 | MILES |

| 0 | 40 | 80 | 120 | 160 | 200 | 240 | 280 | 320 | KM |

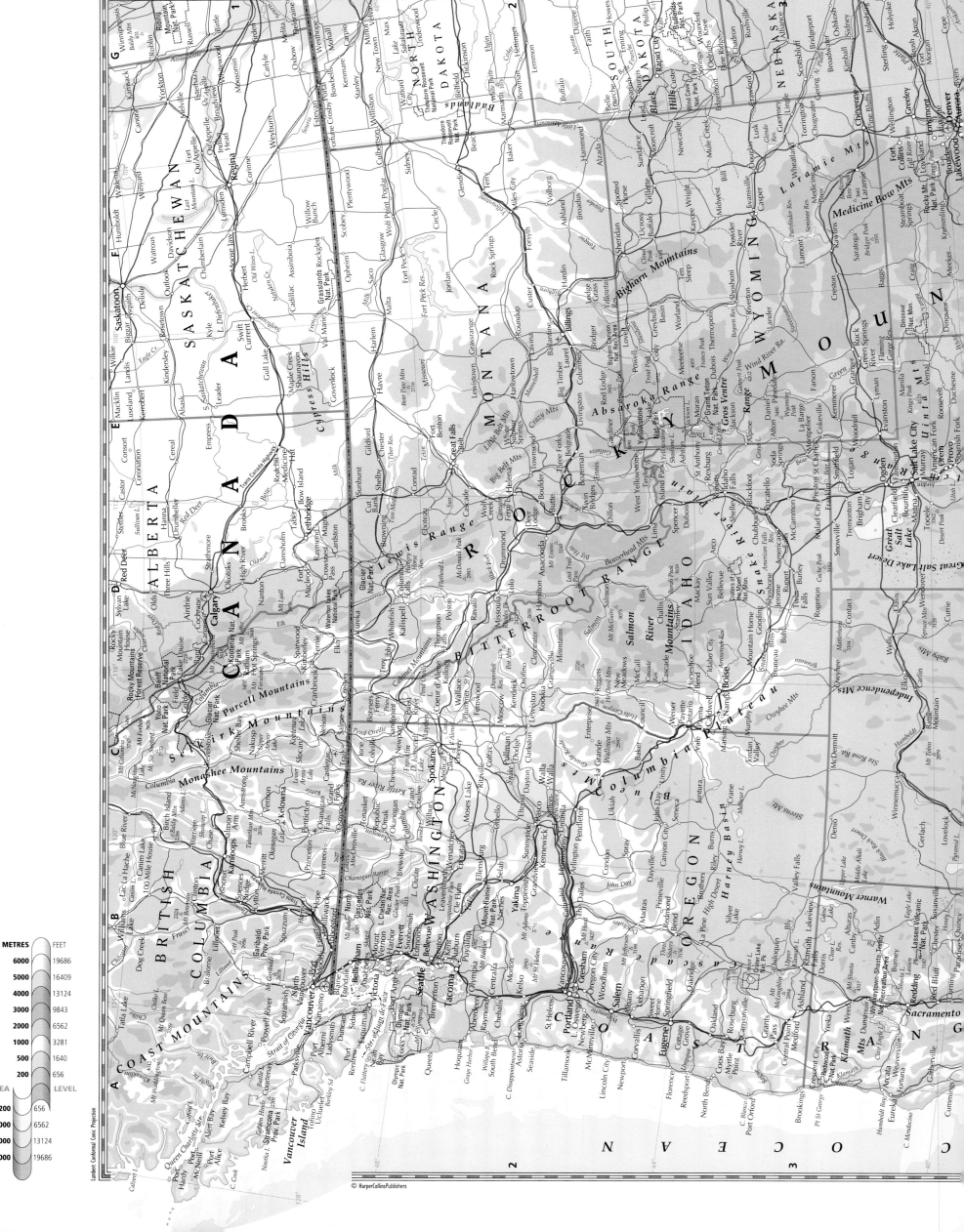

1:6 000 000

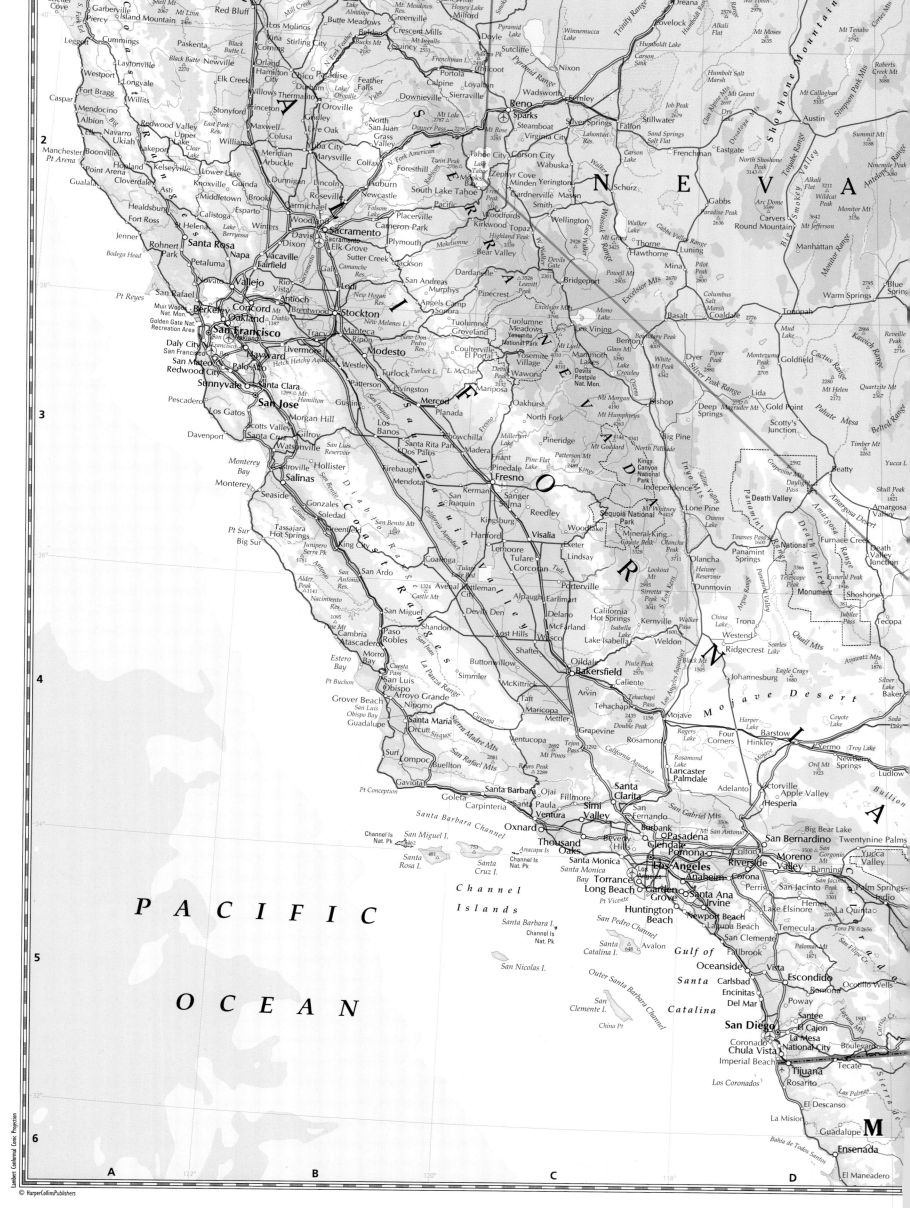

Lambert Conformal Conic Projection

METRES		FEET
6000		19686
5000		16409
4000		13124
3000		9843
2000		6562
1000		3281
500		1640
200		656
SEA		LEVEL
200		656
2000		6562
4000		13124
6000		19686

PACIFIC

OCEAN

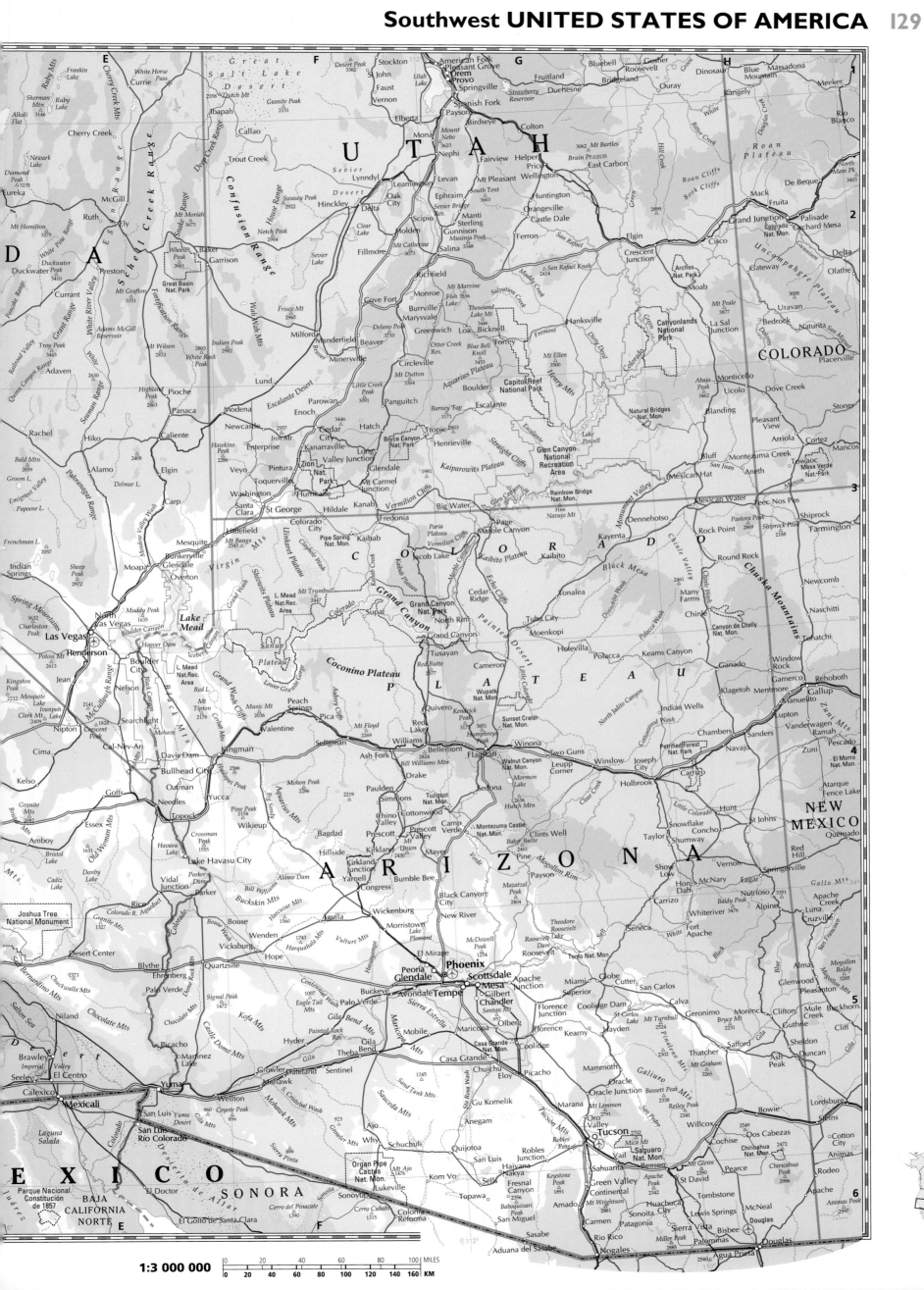

1:3 000 000

| 0 | 20 | 40 | 60 | 80 | 100 MILES |
| 0 | 20 | 40 | 60 | 80 | 100 | 120 | 140 | 160 KM |

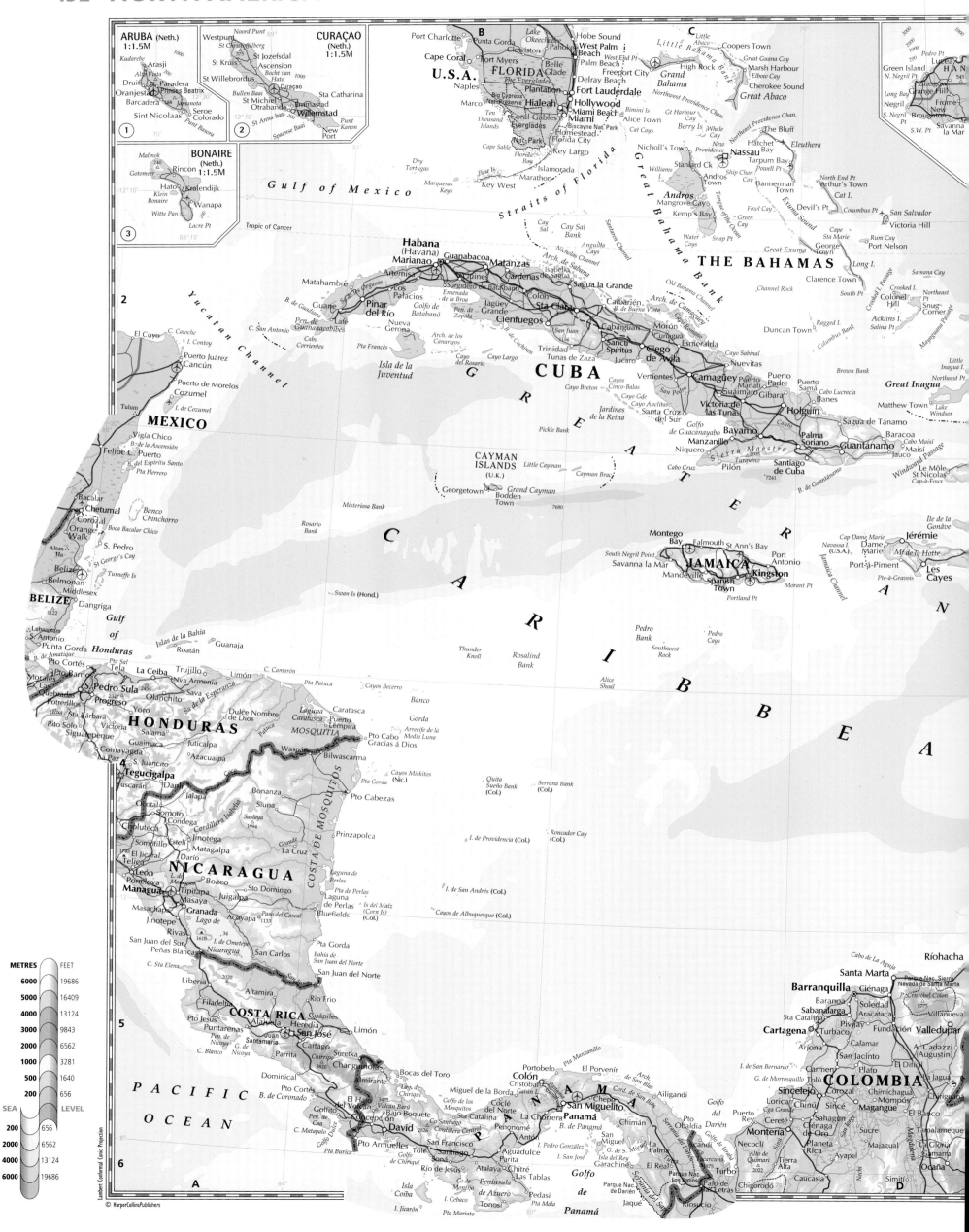

ARUBA (Neth.)
1:1.5M

Kudarebe
Arasji
Alto Vista
Paradera
Druif
Barcadera
Oranjestad
Prinses Beatrix
Jamanota 188
Sint Nicolaas
Seroe Colorado

CURAÇAO (Neth.)
1:1.5M

Westpunt
Noord Punt
St Christoffelberg 375
St Jozefsdal
Ascension
Bocht van Hato
Curaçao
St Kruis
St Willebrordus
Bullen Baai
St Michiel
Otrabanda
Willemstad
Sta Catharina

BONAIRE (Neth.)
1:1.5M

Malmok
Gotomeer
Rincon
Hato
Klein Bonaire
Kralendijk
Witte Pan
Wanapa
Lacre Pt

MEXICO

El Cuyo
C. Catoche
I. Contoy
Puerto Juárez
Cancún
Puerto de Morelos
Cozumel
I. de Cozumel
Tulum
Vigía Chico
B. de la Ascensión
Felipe C. Puerto
B. del Espíritu Santo
Pta Herrero
Bacalar
Chetumal
Corozal
Banco Chinchorro
Orange Walk
Boca Bacalar Chico
S. Pedro
BELIZE
St George's Cay
Belize
Turneffe Is
Belmopan
Middlesex
Dangriga

Yucatan Channel

Gulf of Mexico

Tropic of Cancer

Dry Tortugas
Marquesas Keys

U.S.A.

Port Charlotte
Punta Gorda
Cape Coral
Fort Myers
Naples
Marco
Ten Thousand Islands
Cape Sable
FLORIDA
Cleviston
Pahokee
Belle Glade
The Everglades
Big Cypress Nat. Preserve
Everglades Nat. Park
Marathon
Key West
Key Largo
Islamorada
Florida Bay
Cay Sal
Cay Sal Bank

Hobe Sound
West Palm Beach
Palm Beach
West End Pt
Freeport City
Grand Bahama
Delray Beach
Fort Lauderdale
Pompano Beach
Hollywood
Miami Beach
Miami
Coral Gables
Biscayne Nat. Park
Homestead
Florida City
Bimini Is
Alice Town
Cat Cays
Gun Cay
Nicholl's Town
Andros
Mangrove Cayo
Kemp's Bay

Little Abaco
Coopers Town
Great Guana Cay
Marsh Harbour
Elbow Cay
Cherokee Sound
High Rock
Great Abaco

Berry Is
New Providence
Nassau
Andros Town
Fresh Creek
Williams I.
Ship Chan. Cay
Fowl Cay

THE BAHAMAS

Northwest Providence Chan.
Northeast Providence Chan.
Whale Cay
Stafford Ck
Tarpum Bay
Powell Pt
Green Cay
Water Cay
Snap Pt
Great Exuma
George Town
Exuma Sound

Arthur's Town
Cat I.
Columbus Pt
San Salvador
Victoria Hill
Cape Sta Marie
Rum Cay
Port Nelson
Long I.
Clarence Town
Channel Rock
South Pt
Crooked I.
Crooked I. Passage
Colonel Hill
Snug Corner
Acklins I.
Salina Pt
Ragged I.
Duncan Town
Columbus Bank
Brown Bank
Samana Cay
Northeast Pt
Great Inagua
Matthew Town
Lake Windsor
Little Inagua I.
Northeast Pt

Habana (Havana)
Guanabacoa
Marianao
Matanzas
Matahambre
Cárdenas
Artemisa
Güines
Surgidero de Batabanó
Isabella de Sagua
Sagua la Grande
Pinar del Río
Los Palacios
Guane
Nueva Gerona
B. de Guanahacabibes
Pen. de Guanahacabibes
Cabo Corrientes
Pta Francés
Isla de la Juventud
Colón
Sta Clara
Jagüey Grande
Cienfuegos
Arch. de Sabana
Arch. de Camagüey
Old Bahama Channel
San Juan
Trinidad
Tunas de Zaza
Sancti Spíritus
Ciego de Ávila
Morón
Ciénaga
Esmeralda
Camagüey
Nuevitas
Cayo Sabinal
Puerto Padre
Victoria de las Tunas
Holguín
Cabo Lucrecia
Banes
Gibara
Bayamo
Manzanillo
Niquero
Palma Soriano
Baracoa
Cabo Maisí
Maisí
Guantánamo
Jauco
Pilón
Santiago de Cuba
B. de Guantánamo

CUBA

GREATER

Golfo de Guacanayabo
Jardines de la Reina
Santa Cruz del Sur
Pickle Bank
Cayo Breton
Cayo Anclitas
Cayo Gde
San Pedro
Cabo Cruz
Sierra Maestra

CAYMAN ISLANDS (U.K.)

Georgetown
Grand Cayman
Bodden Town
Little Cayman
Cayman Brac
Misteriosa Bank
Rosario Bank

Cap-à-Foux
Île de la Gonâve
Cap Dame Marie
Navassa I. (U.S.A.)
Jérémie
Dame Marie
Mt de la Hotte
Port-à-Piment
Les Cayes
Pte-à-Gravois

Montego Bay
Falmouth
St Ann's Bay
Port Antonio
South Negril Point
Savanna la Mar
JAMAICA
Mandeville
Spanish Town
Kingston
Portland Pt
Morant Pt
Jamaica Channel

C A R I B B E A N

Pedro Bank
Southwest Rock
Pedro Cays
Swan Is (Hond.)
Misteriosa
Thunder Knoll
Rosalind Bank
Alice Shoal

Gulf of Honduras
Islas de la Bahía
Guanaja
Roatán
Lubaantun
S. Antonio
Punta Gorda
B. de Amatique
Pto Cortés
Pto Barrios
Morales
Las Quebradas
S. Pedro Sula
Ulúa
Pito Solo
Sta Bárbara
Victoria
Siguatepeque
Comayagua
La Paz
Juancito
Tegucigalpa
Yuscarán
Danlí
Ocotal
Somoto
Choluteca
Somotillo
Estelí
El Jicaral
Telica
Darío
León
Poneloya
Managua
Masachapa
Masaya
Tipitapa
Granada
Jinotepe
Rivas
San Juan del Sur
Peñas Blancas
Liberia
Filadelfia
Santa Cruz
Tela
La Ceiba
Trujillo
Limón
C. Camarón
Sava
Olanchito
Yoro
Progreso
Potrerillos
Guaimaca
Salamá
Dulce Nombre de Dios
Juticalpa
Azacualpa
Jalapa
Bonanza
Siuna
Saslaya 1994
Condega
Jinotega
Matagalpa
Boaco
Juigalpa
Sto Domingo
La Cruz
Grande
Acoyapa
Lago de Nicaragua
I. de Ometepe
San Carlos
Pta Patuca
Pta Gorda
Puerto Lempira
Gracias á Dios
Pto Cabo
Arrecife de la Media Luna
Cayos Miskitos (Nic.)
Pta Gorda
Pto Cabezas
Prinzapolca
Costa de Mosquitos
Laguna de Perlas
Bluefields
Is del Maíz (Corn Is) (Col.)
Laguna de Perlas
Pta de Perlas
Banco Gorda
Cayos Becerro
Banco
Quita Sueño Bank (Col.)
Serrana Bank (Col.)
Roncador Cay (Col.)
I. de Providencia (Col.)
I. de San Andrés (Col.)
Cayos de Albuquerque (Col.)

HONDURAS

NICARAGUA

COSTA RICA

Alajuela
Heredia
San José
Puntarenas
Pen. de Nicoya
Santamaría
Parrita
Chirripó 3820
G. de Nicoya
Dominical
Pto Cortés
B. de Coronado
Pen. de Osa
Golfito
Pta Burica
Pto Armuelles
Golfo de Chiriquí
Isla Coiba

Cuápiles
Limón
Suretka
Changuinola
Bocas del Toro
Almirante
Lago Gatún
David
El Hato
Volcán Barú 3475
Concepción
San Francisco
Aguadulce
Soná
Santiago
Tolé
Río de Jesús
Atalaya
Chitré
Las Tablas
Pedasí
Pta Mala
Pta Mariato
I. Jicarón
Tonosí
Pen. de Azuero
I. Cebaco
I. Gobernadora
Golfo de Panamá

Portobelo
El Porvenír
Colón
Miguel de la Borda
Arch. de San Blas
Gatún L.
Panamá
La Chorrera
San Miguelito
Chepo
Chimán
San Miguel
I. del Rey
Garachiné
El Real
Jaqué

PANAMÁ

Golfo de los Mosquitos
Cord. Central
Ailigandi
Golfo del Darién
I. de San Bernardo
G. de Morrosquillo
Puerto Obaldía

Cabo de La Aguja
Santa Marta
Ríohacha
Barranquilla
Ciénaga
Parque Nac. Sierra Nevada de Santa Marta
Pico Cristóbal Colón 5775
Villanueva
Valledupar
Soledad
Baranoa
Sabanalarga
Aracataca
Fundación
Cartagena
Turbaco
Calamar
El Difícil
Arjona
San Jacinto
Carmen
Plato
Mompós
COLOMBIA
Sincelejo
Sincé
Magangué
Chinú
Planeta Rica
Montería
Cereté
Cerro de Quimarí 2022
Tierra Alta
Turbo
Caucasia
Ayapel
Majagual
Chigorodó

PACIFIC OCEAN

Golfo de Panamá

METRES / FEET
6000 / 19686
5000 / 16409
4000 / 13124
3000 / 9843
2000 / 6562
1000 / 3281
500 / 1640
200 / 656
SEA LEVEL
200 / 656
2000 / 6562
4000 / 13124
6000 / 19686

Lambert Conformal Conic Projection

© HarperCollins Publishers

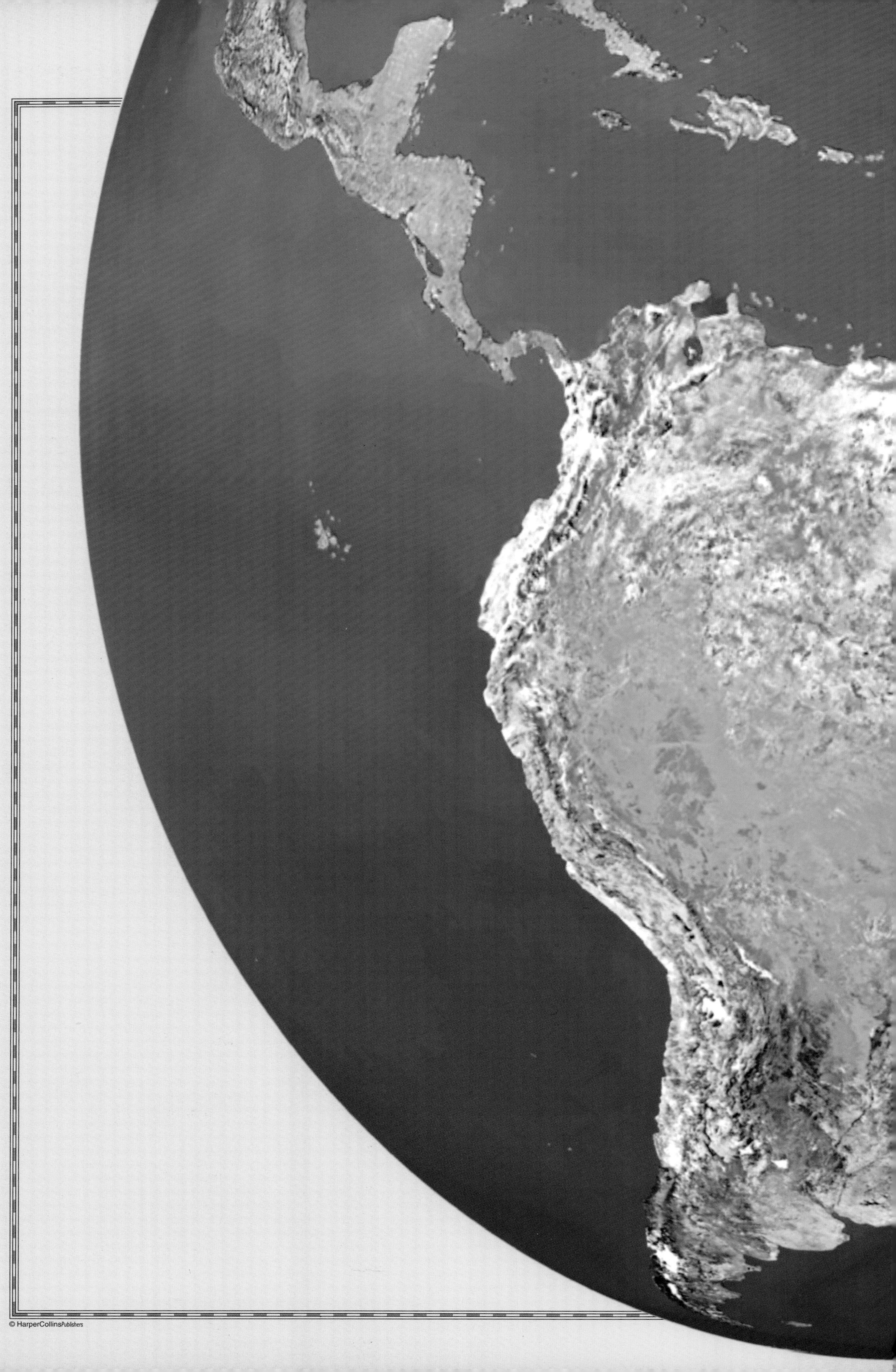

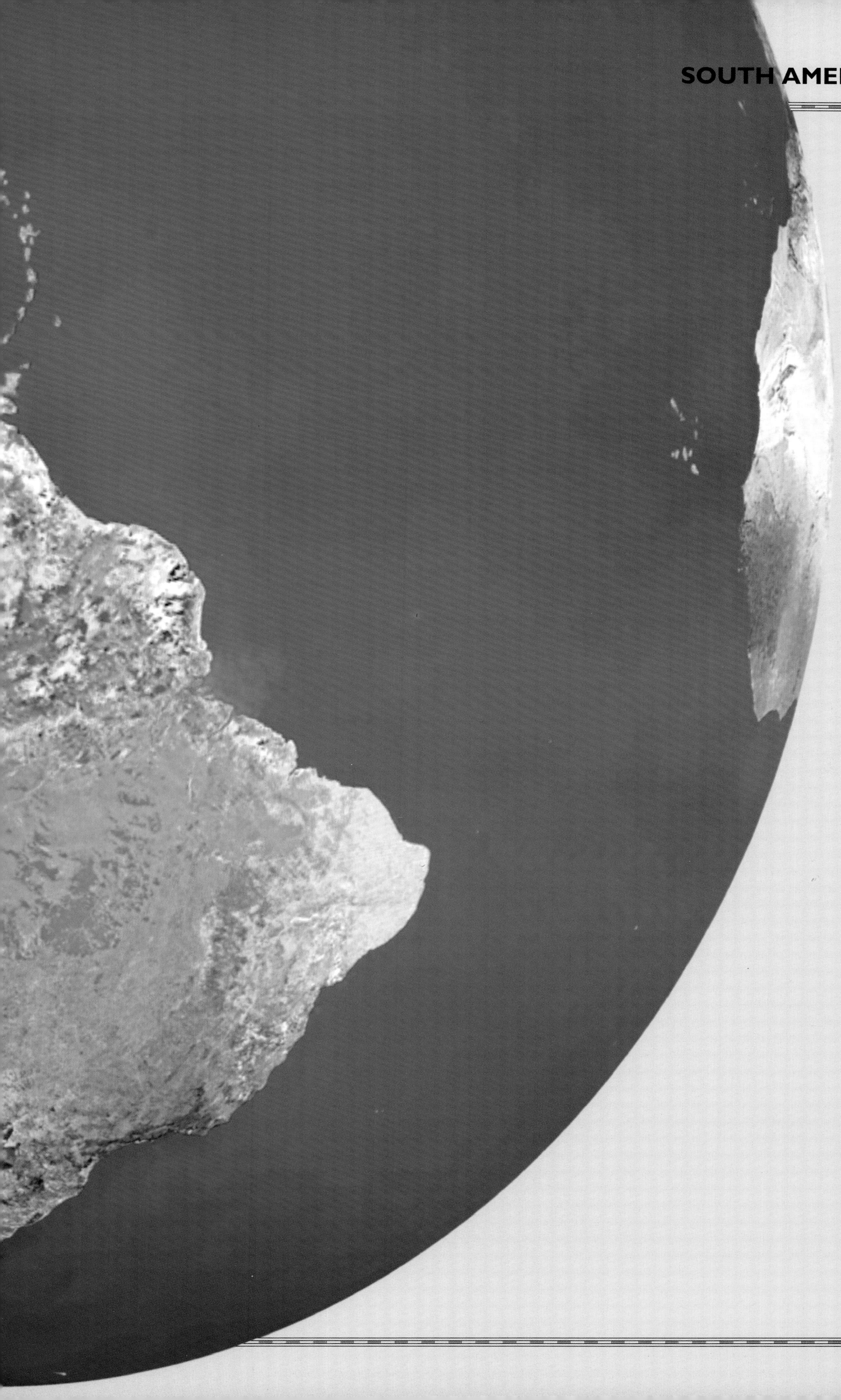

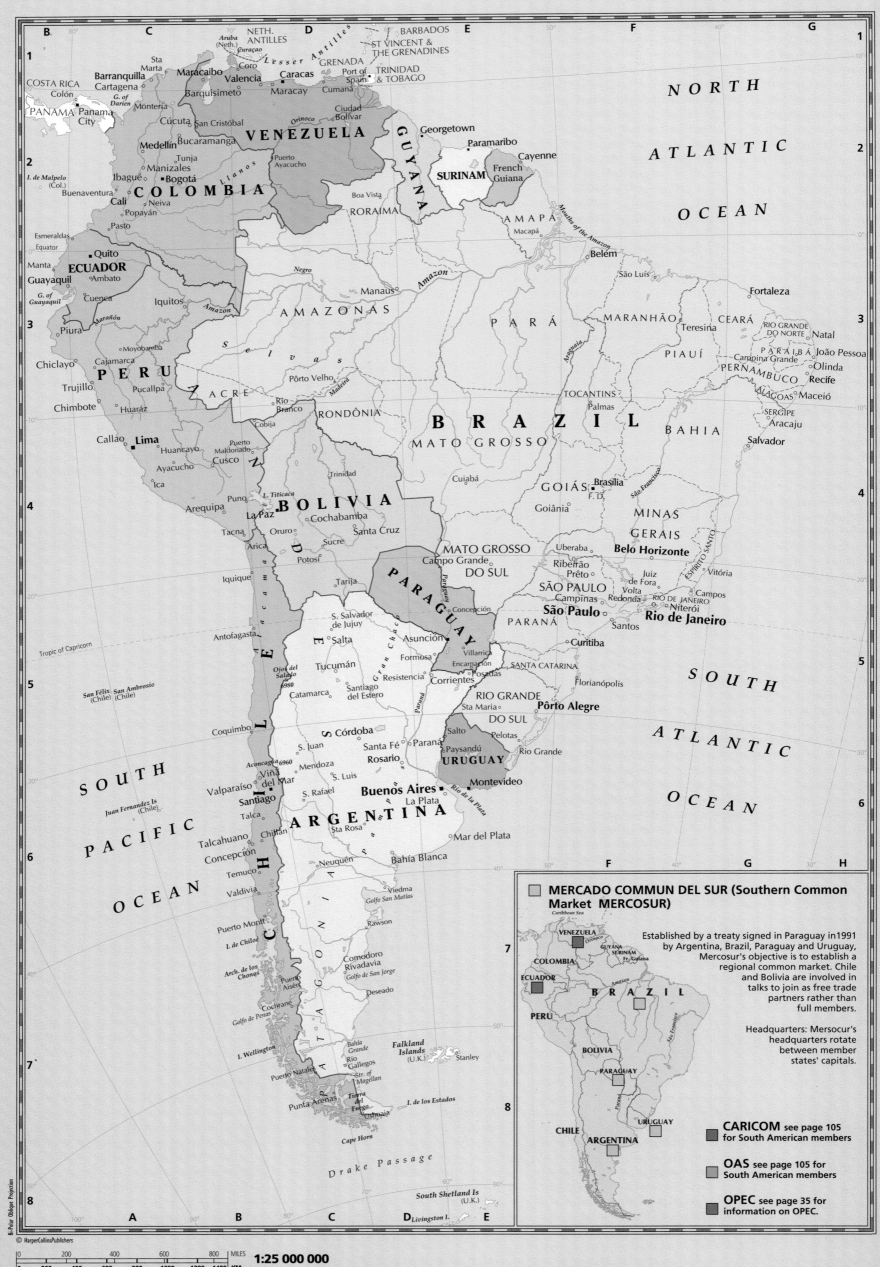

MERCADO COMMUN DEL SUR (Southern Common Market MERCOSUR)

Established by a treaty signed in Paraguay in 1991 by Argentina, Brazil, Paraguay and Uruguay, Mercosur's objective is to establish a regional common market. Chile and Bolivia are involved in talks to join as free trade partners rather than full members.

Headquarters: Mersocur's headquarters rotate between member states' capitals.

CARICOM see page 105 for South American members

OAS see page 105 for South American members

OPEC see page 35 for information on OPEC.

© HarperCollins Publishers

Bi-Polar Oblique Projection

1:25 000 000

0   200   400   600   800   MILES
0   200   400   600   800   1000   1200   1400   KM

COUNTRY	AREA		POPULATION		FORM OF GOVERNMENT	CAPITAL CITY	MAIN LANGUAGES	MAIN RELIGIONS	CURRENCY
	sq ml	sq km	total	density per sq ml sq km					
ARGENTINA	1 068 302	2 766 889	34 180 000	32 12	republic	Buenos Aires	Spanish, Italian, Amerindian languages	RC, Protestant, Jewish	Peso
ARUBA	75	193	69 000	926 358	Netherlands terr.	Oranjestad	Dutch , Papiamento, English	RC, Protestant	Florin
BOLIVIA	424 164	1 098 581	7 237 000	17 7	republic	La Paz	Spanish, Quechua, Aymara	RC, Protestant, Baha'i	Boliviano
BRAZIL	3 286 488	8 511 965	153 725 000	47 18	republic	Brasília	Portuguese, German, Japanese, Italian, Amerindian languages	RC, Spiritist, Protestant	Real
CHILE	292 258	756 945	13 994 000	48 18	republic	Santiago	Spanish, Amerindian languages	RC, Protestant	Peso
COLOMBIA	440 831	1 141 748	34 520 000	78 30	republic	Bogotá	Spanish, Amerindian languages	RC, Protestant	Peso
ECUADOR	105 037	272 045	11 221 000	107 41	republic	Quito	Spanish, Quechua, Amerind. lang.	RC, Protestant	Sucre
FALKLAND ISLANDS	4 699	12 170	2 000		UK territory	Stanley	English	Protestant, RC	Pound
FRENCH GUIANA	34 749	90 000	141 000	4 2	French territory	Cayenne	French, French Creole	RC, Protestant	French franc
GUYANA	83 000	214 969	825 000	10 4	republic	Georgetown	English, Creole, Hindi, Amerind. lang.	Protestant, Hindu, RC, Muslim	Dollar
NETH. ANTILLES (South)	283	732	158 206	560 216	Neth terr.	Willemstad	Dutch, Papiamento, English	RC, Protestant	Guilder
PARAGUAY	157 048	406 752	4 700 000	30 12	republic	Asunción	Spanish, Guaraní	RC, Protestant	Guaraní
PERU	496 225	1 285 216	23 088 000	47 18	republic	Lima	Spanish, Quechua, Aymara	RC, Protestant	Sol
SURINAM	63 251	163 820	418 000	7 3	republic	Paramaribo	Dutch, Surinamese, English, Hindi, Javanese	Hindu, RC, Protestant, Muslim	Guilder
TRINIDAD AND TOBAGO	1 981	5 130	1 250 000	631 244	republic	Port of Spain	English, Creole, Hindi	RC, Hindu, Protestant, Muslim	Dollar
URUGUAY	68 037	176 215	3 167 000	47 18	republic	Montevideo	Spanish	RC, Protestant, Jewish	Peso
VENEZUELA	352 144	912 050	21 177 000	60 23	republic	Caracas	Spanish, Amerindian languages	RC, Protestant	Bolívar

CITY PLANS

KEY TO MAPS

Built-up areas

Park or open space

Open water

Important building

Cemetery

Lake

River or canal

Main road

Road

Other road

Railway

Airport

BUENOS AIRES 1:100 000

RIO DE JANEIRO 1:100 000

SAO PAULO 1:50 000

© HarperCollinsPublishers

CARIBBEAN SEA

NETHERLANDS ANTILLES

VENEZUELA

COLOMBIA

ECUADOR

GALAPAGOS IS
(Ecuador)
at the same scale

PERU

PANAMA

Golfo de Panamá

Golfo de Guayaquil

METRES		FEET
6000		19686
5000		16409
4000		13124
3000		9843
2000		6562
1000		3281
500		1640
200		656
SEA		LEVEL
200		656
2000		6562
4000		13124
6000		19686

Lambert Azimuthal Equal Area Projection

© HarperCollinsPublishers

1:7 500 000

0 75 150 225 300 MILES
0 75 150 225 300 375 450 KM

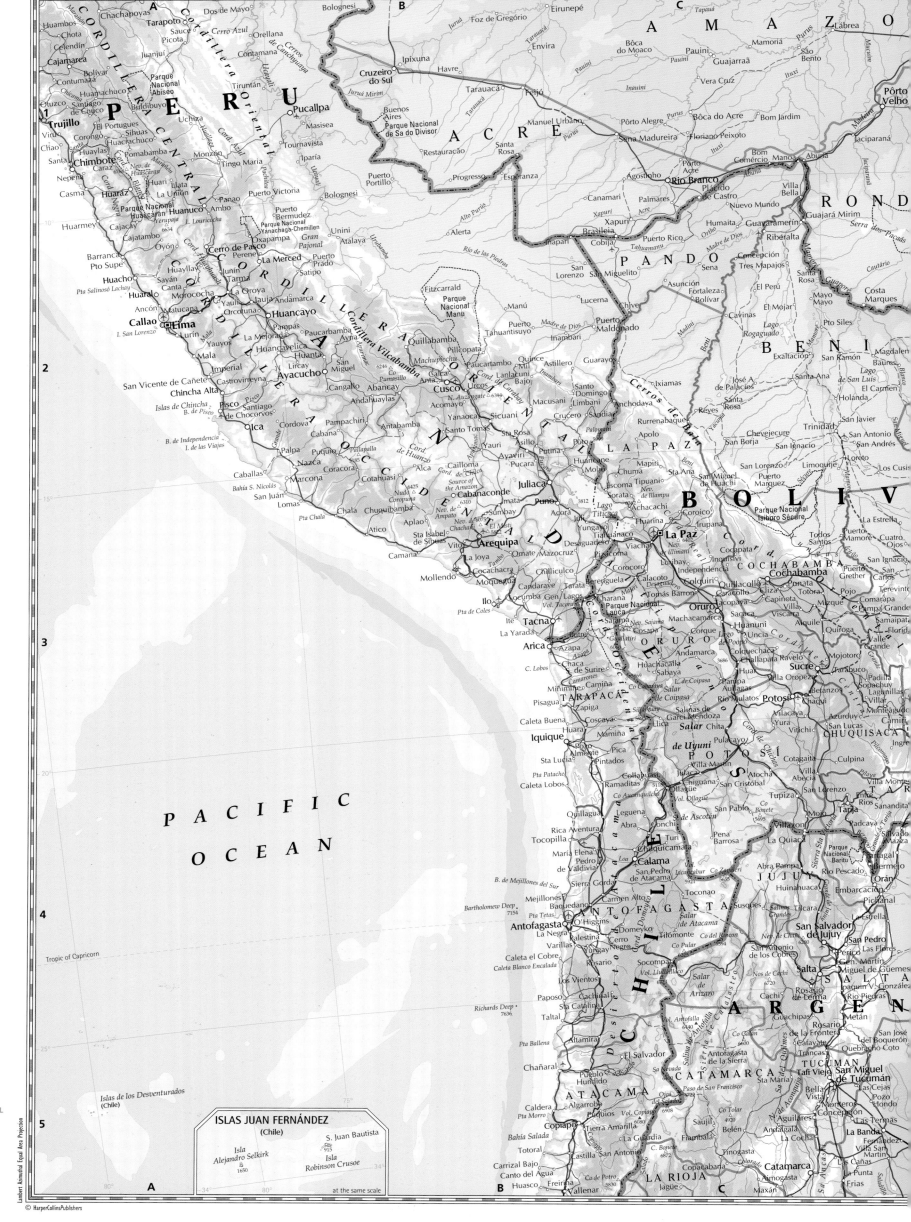

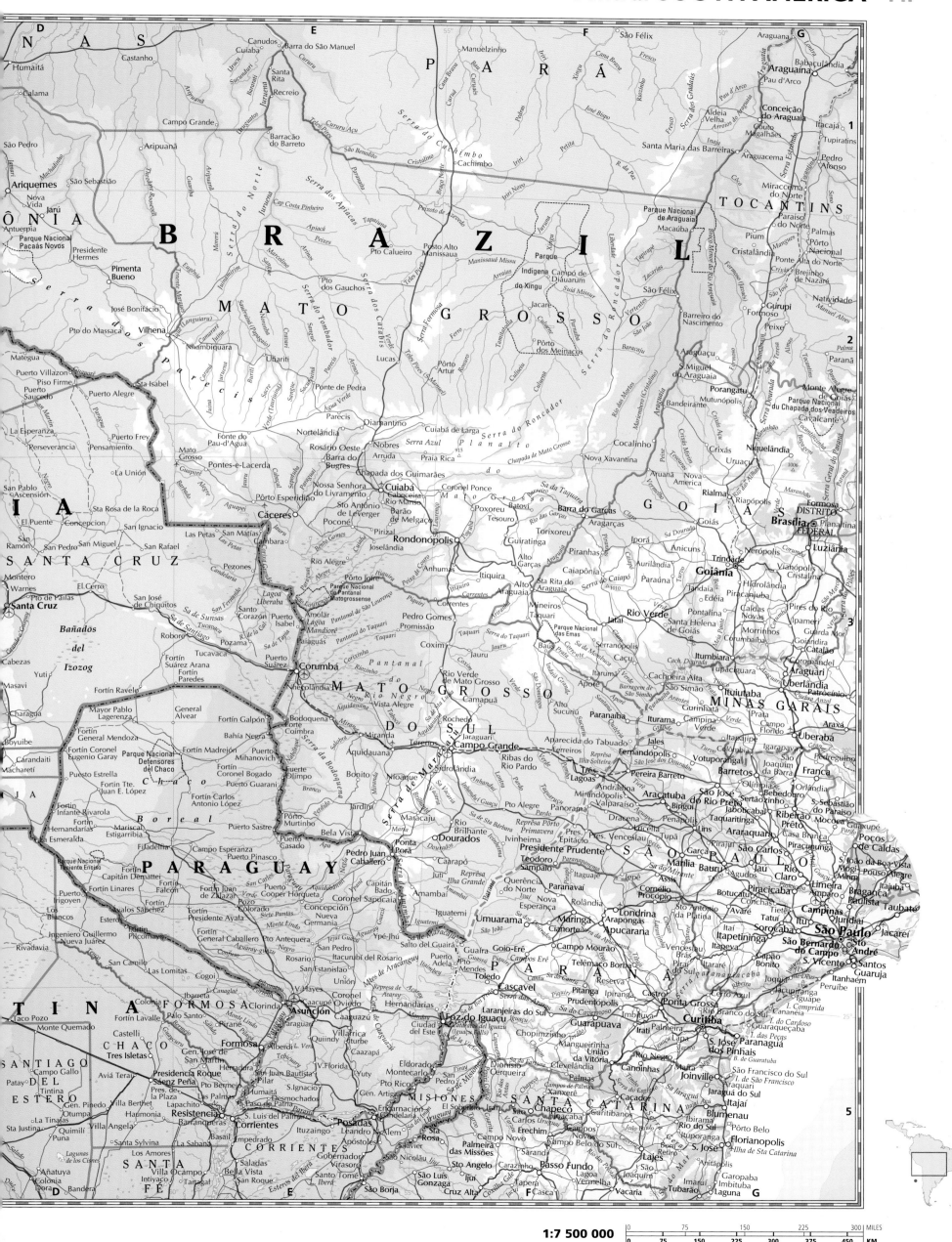

1:7 500 000

| 0 | 75 | 150 | 225 | 300 MILES |

| 0 | 75 | 150 | 225 | 300 | 375 | 450 KM |

METRES FEET
6000 19686
5000 16409
4000 13124
3000 9843
2000 6562
1000 3281
500 1640
200 656
SEA LEVEL
200 656
2000 6562
4000 13124
6000 19686

Lambert Azimuthal Equal Area Projection

© HarperCollins Publishers

States / Regions: RIO GRANDE DO NORTE, PARAÍBA, PERNAMBUCO, ALAGOAS, SERGIPE, BAHIA, PIAUÍ, MARANHÃO, PARÁ, TOCANTINS, MATO GROSSO, CHAPADA DIAMANTINA

Cities: Natal, João Pessoa, Recife, Olinda, Maceió, Aracaju, Salvador, Fortaleza, Teresina, São Luís, Belém, Macapá, Santarém, Altamira, Marabá, Tucuruí, Imperatriz, Caxias, Codó, Sobral, Mossoró, Campina Grande, Caruaru, Petrolina, Juazeiro, Feira de Santana, Araguaína, Barreiras

Equator

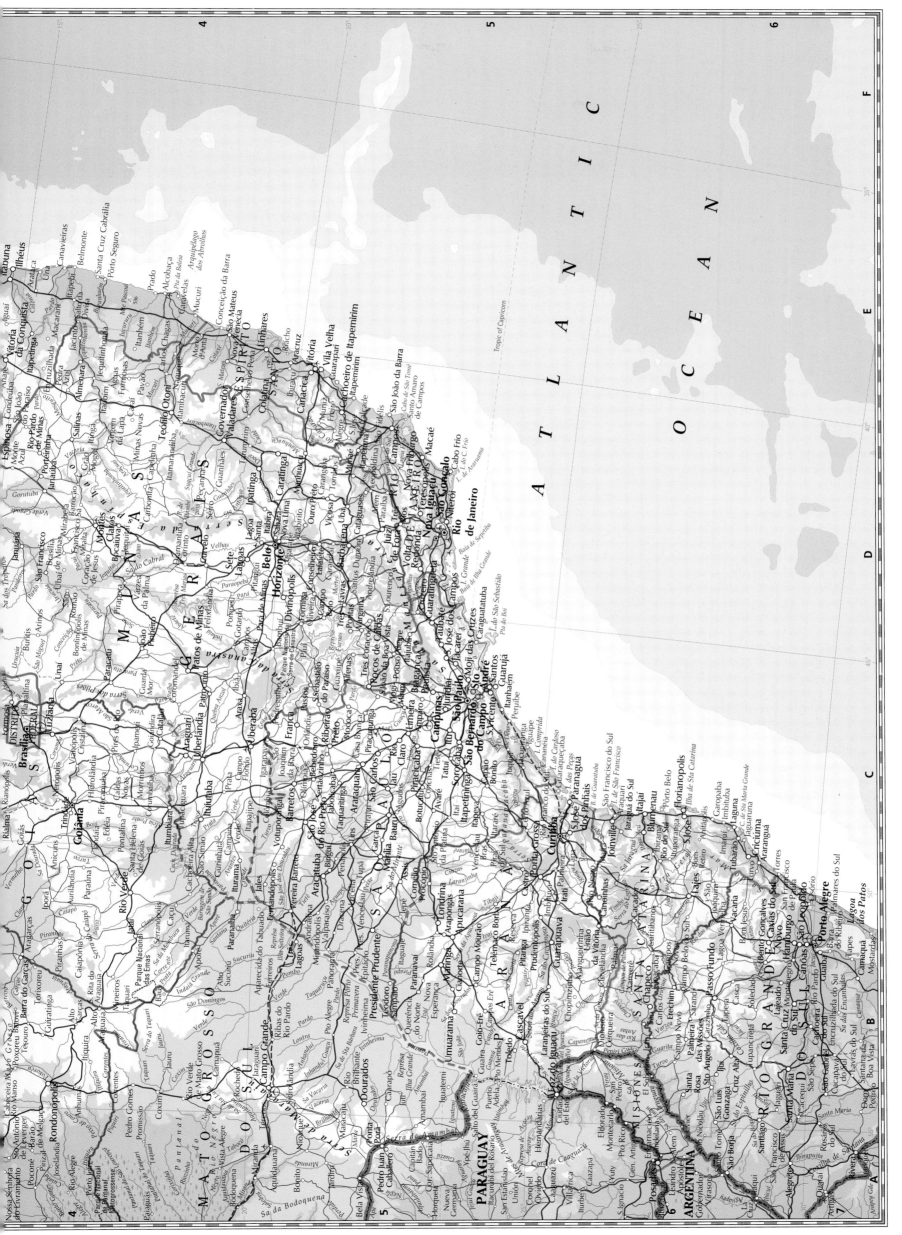

1:7 500 000

| 0 | 75 | | 150 | 225 | 300 | MILES |
| 0 | 75 | 150 | 225 | 300 | 375 | 450 | KM |

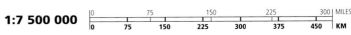

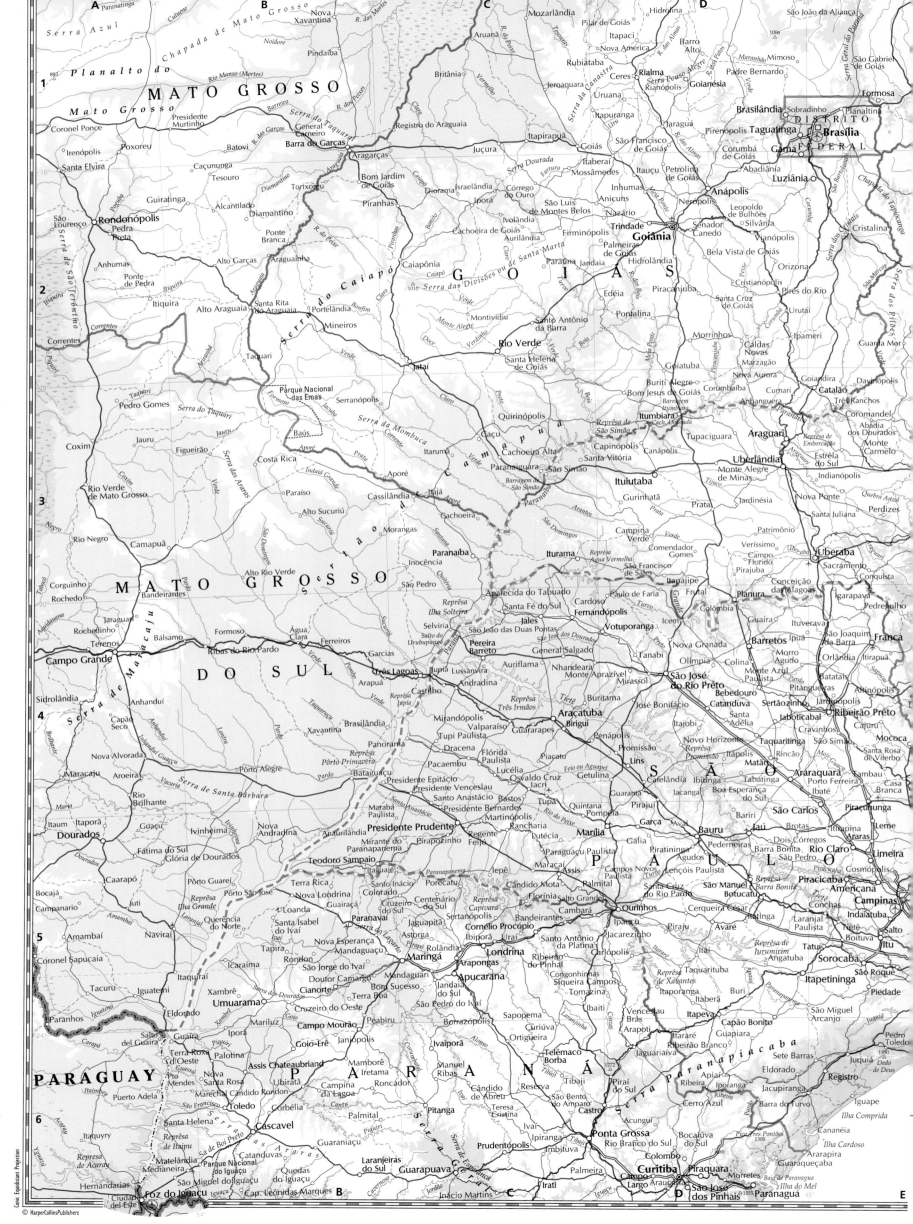

METRES / FEET
6000 / 19686
5000 / 16409
4000 / 13124
3000 / 9843
2000 / 6562
1000 / 3281
500 / 1640
200 / 656
SEA LEVEL
200 / 656
2000 / 6562
4000 / 13124
6000 / 19686

Conic Equidistant Projection

© HarperCollinsPublishers

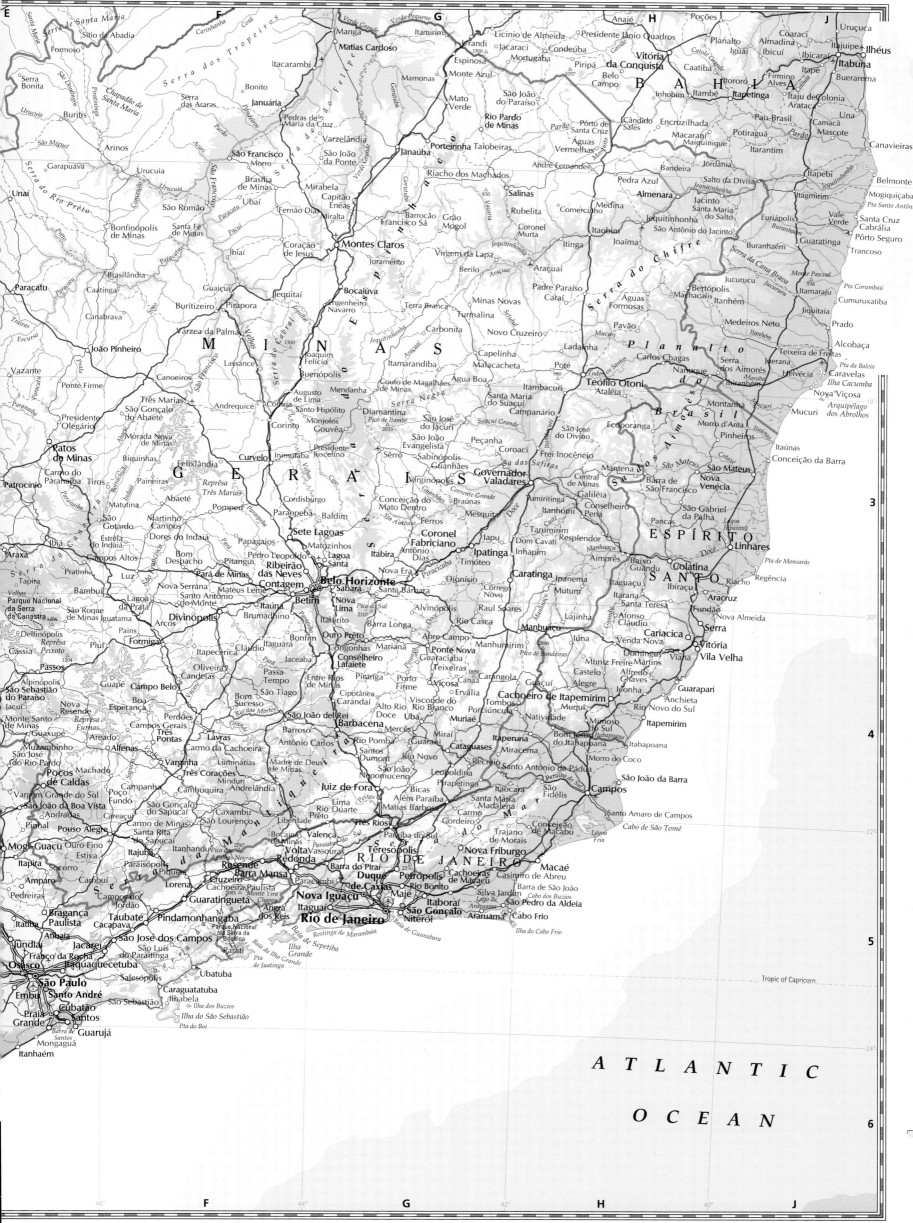

1:3 750 000

| 0 | 20 | 40 | 60 | 80 | 100 | 120 | MILES |
| 0 | 40 | 80 | 120 | 160 | 200 | KM |

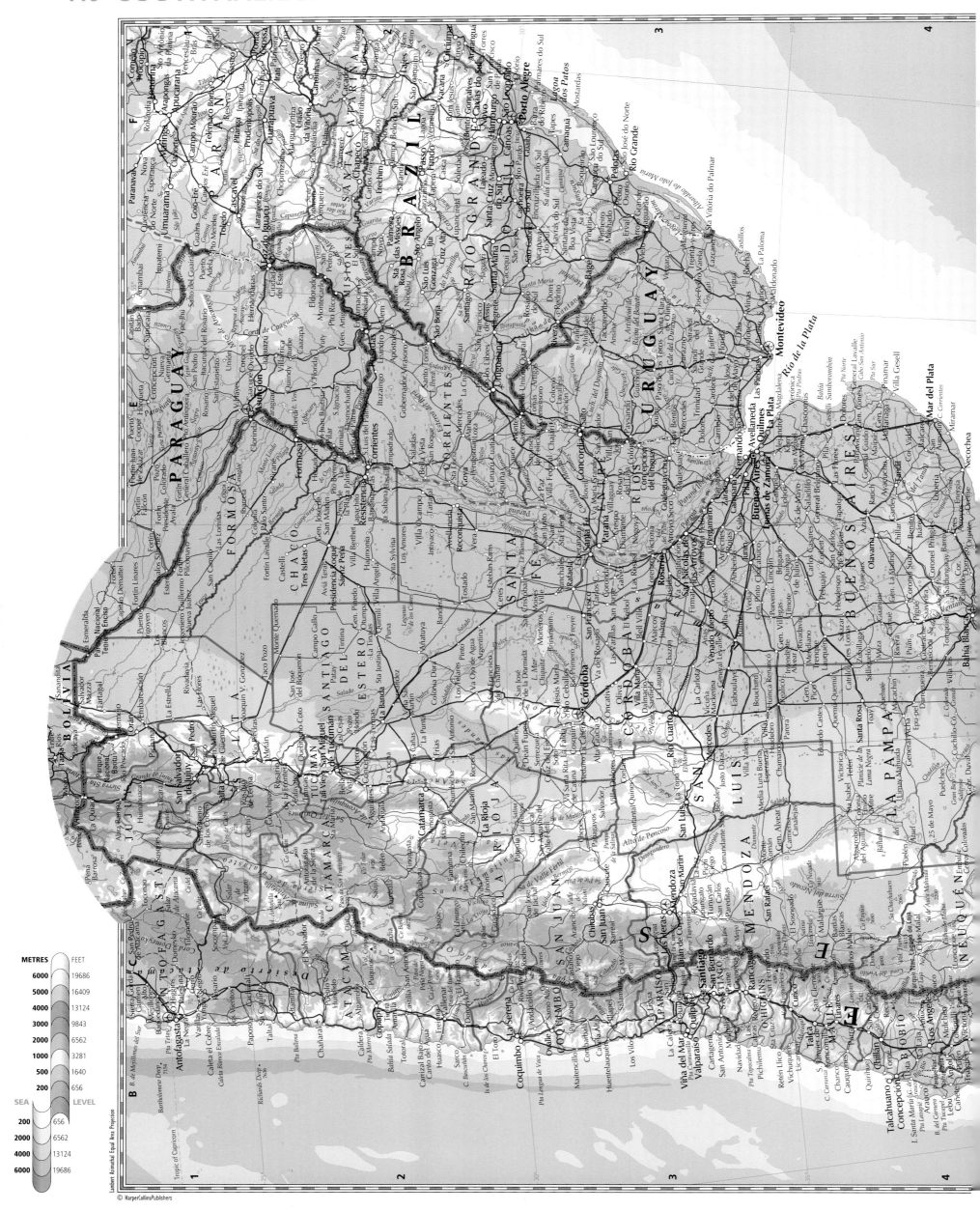

METRES | FEET
6000 | 19686
5000 | 16409
4000 | 13124
3000 | 9843
2000 | 6562
1000 | 3281
500 | 1640
200 | 656
SEA | LEVEL
200 | 656
2000 | 6562
4000 | 13124
6000 | 19686

Lambert Azimuthal Equal Area Projection

© HarperCollinsPublishers

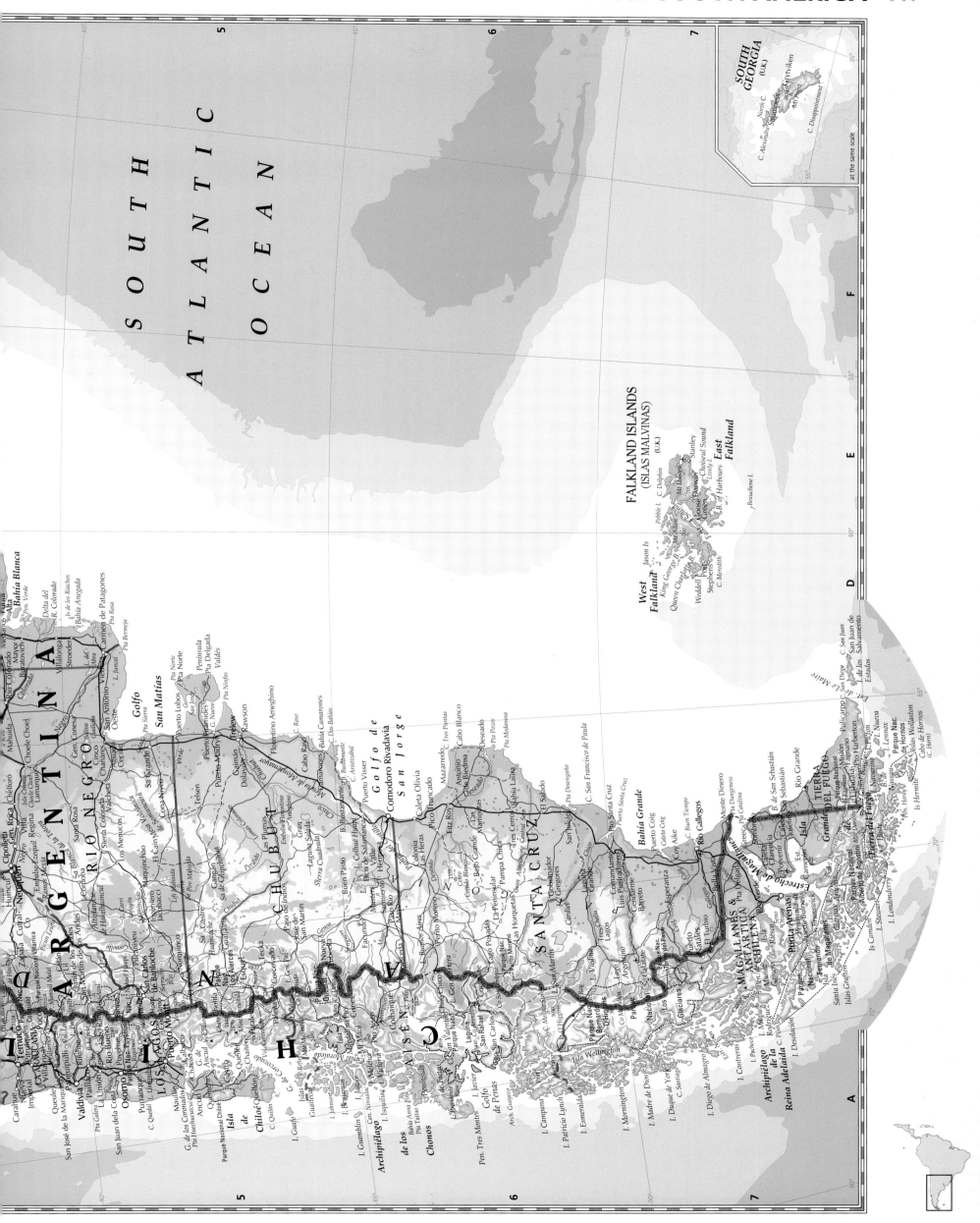

SOUTH ATLANTIC OCEAN

SOUTH GEORGIA (U.K.)

at the same scale

FALKLAND ISLANDS
(ISLAS MALVINAS) (U.K.)

West Falkland

East Falkland

Stanley

ARGENTINA

RÍO NEGRO

CHUBUT

SANTA CRUZ

MAGALLANES & ANTÁRTICA CHILENA

TIERRA DEL FUEGO

C H I L E

A I S É N

LOS LAGOS

Golfo San Matías

Golfo de San Jorge

Bahía Grande

Estrecho de Magallanes

Archipiélago de los Chonos

Archipiélago de la Reina Adelaida

1:7 500 000

| 0 | 75 | 150 | 225 | 300 | MILES |

| 0 | 75 | 150 | 225 | 300 | 375 | 450 | KM |

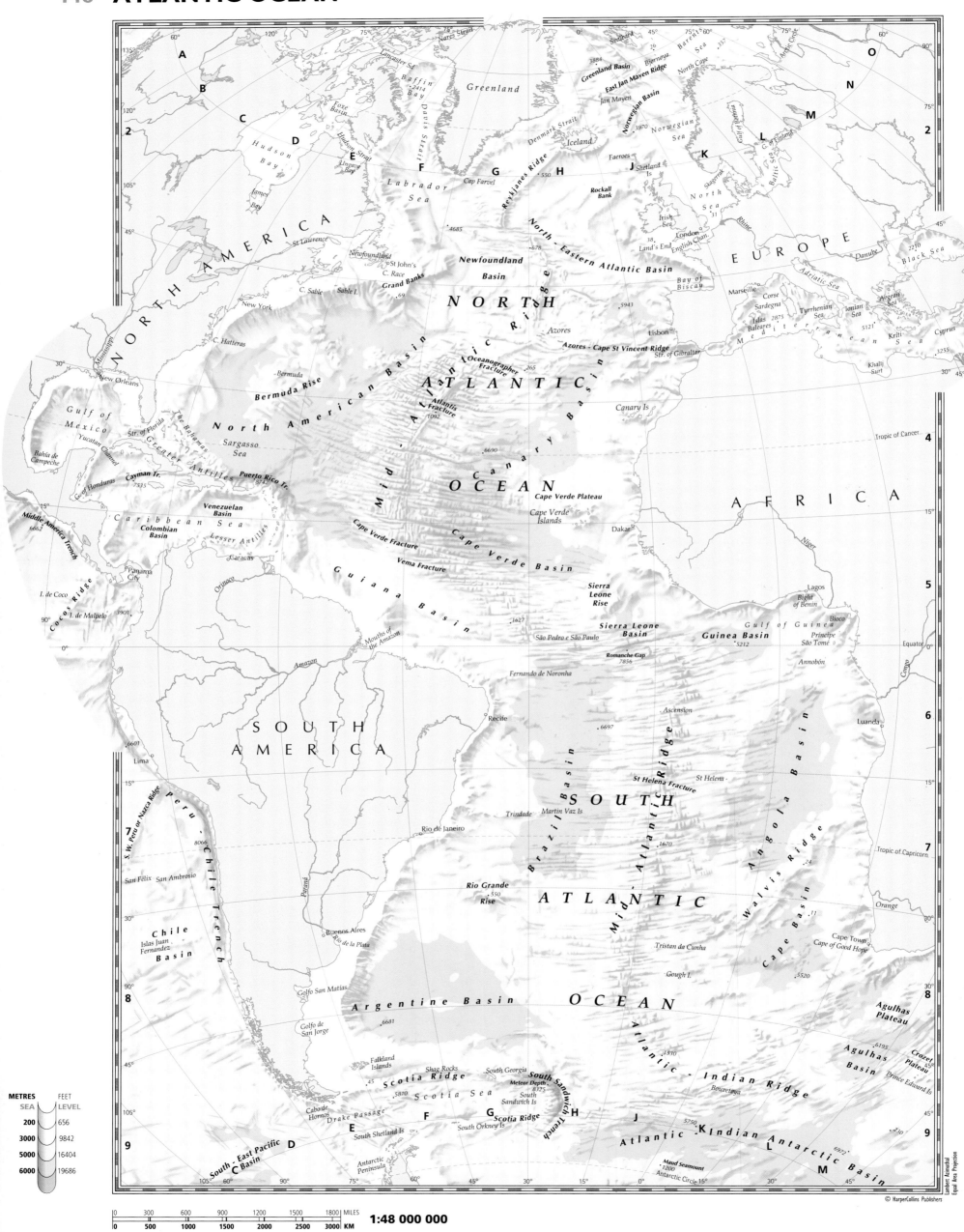

METRES
SEA

FEET
LEVEL

200	656
3000	9842
5000	16404
6000	19686

1:48 000 000

© HarperCollins Publishers

Lambert Azimuthal
Equal Area Projection

0   300   600   900   1200   1500   1800 MILES

0   500   1000   1500   2000   2500   3000 KM

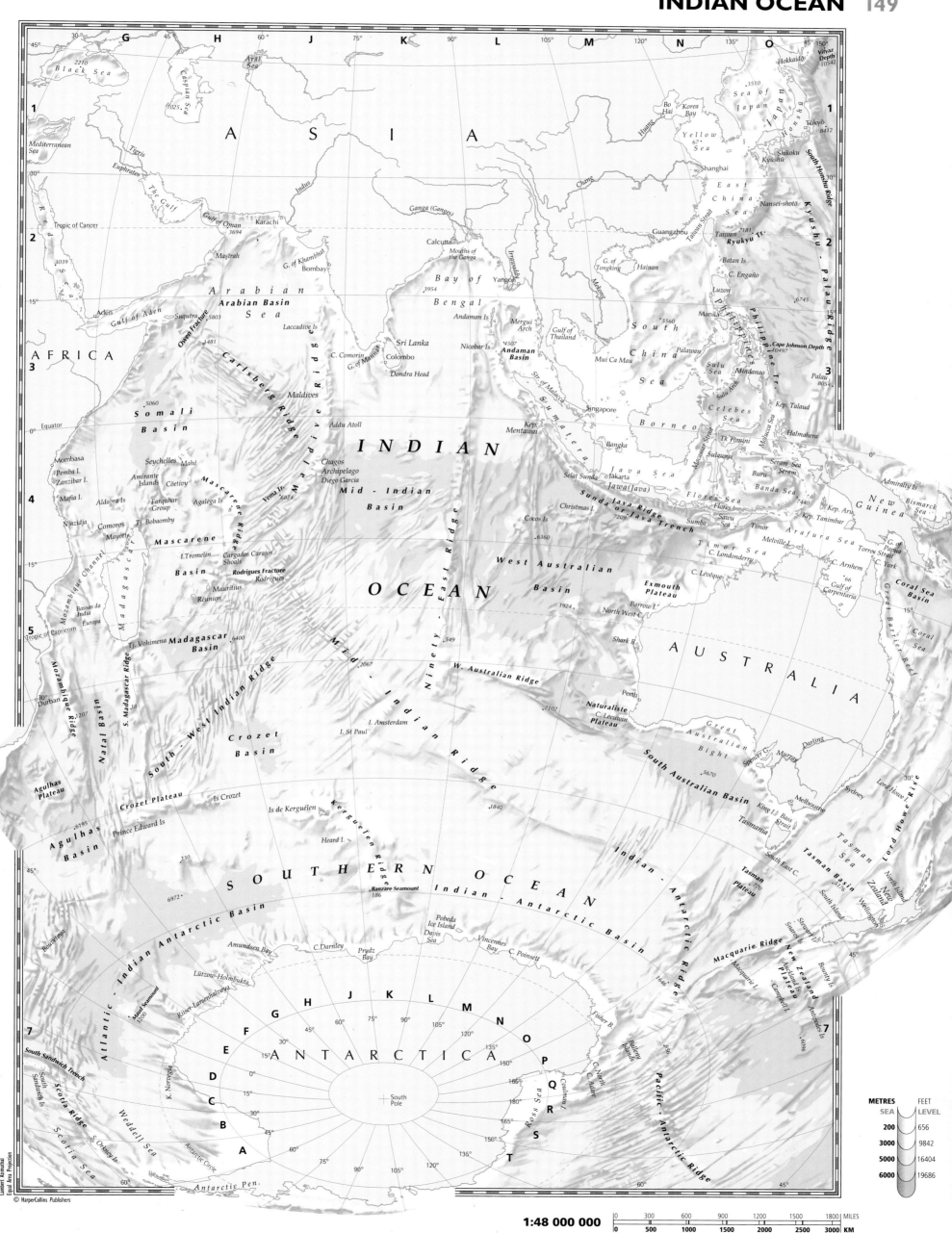

Lambert Azimuthal
Equal Area Projection

1:48 000 000

METRES	FEET
SEA	LEVEL
200	656
3000	9842
5000	16404
6000	19686

0	300	600	900	1200	1500	1800	MILES
0	500	1000	1500	2000	2500	3000	KM

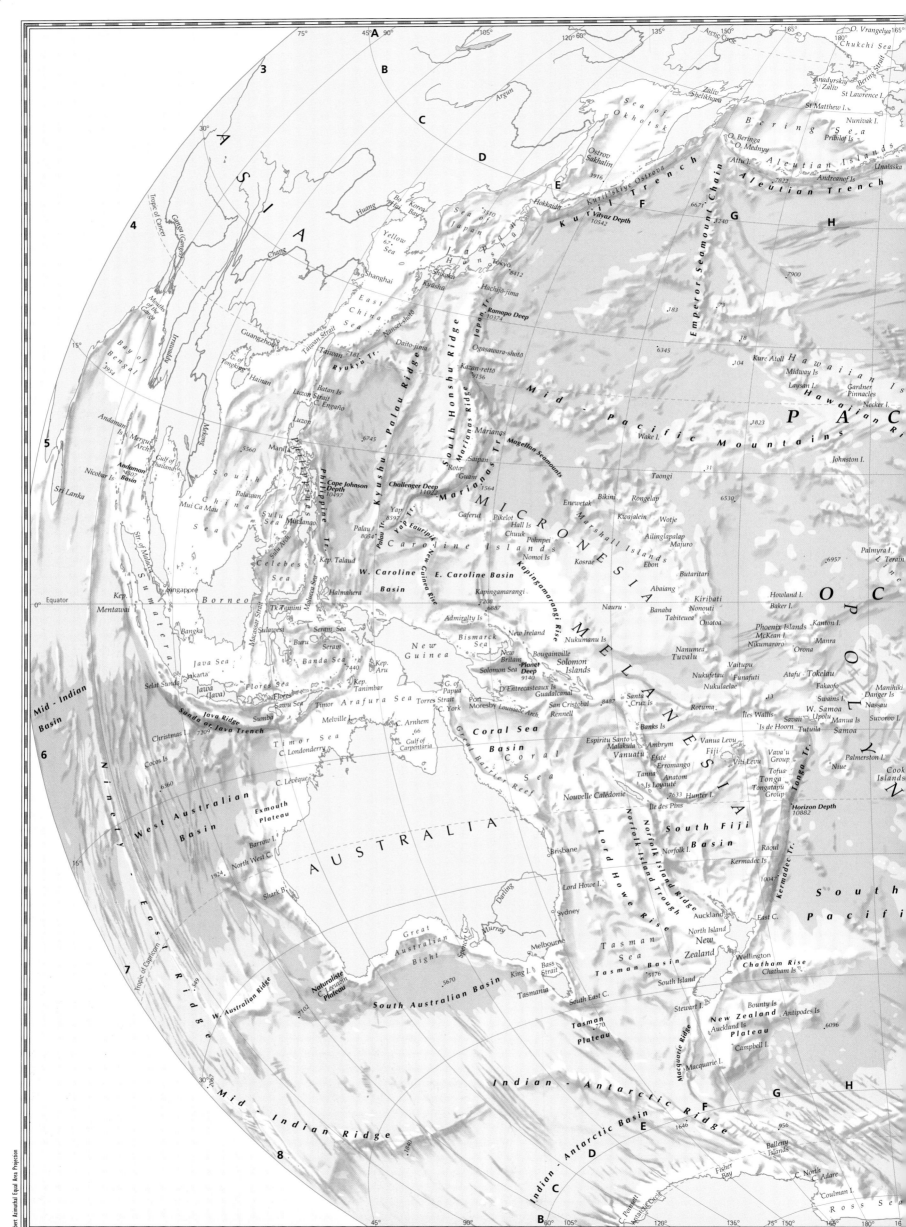

Lambert Azimuthal Equal Area Projection

METRES	FEET
SEA	LEVEL
200	656
3000	9842
5000	16404
6000	19686

Pt Barrow
Mackenzie
Gulf of Alaska
Kodiak I.
Alexander Archipelago
Queen Charlotte Islands
Vancouver Island
Vancouver
Columbia

NORTH AMERICA

Hudson Bay
James Bay
New York
C. Hatteras

Mid-Atlantic Ridge
North American Basin
Atlantis Fracture
Bermuda
Bermuda Rise

Mendocino Seascarp
C. Mendocino
2733
San Francisco
Erben Tablemount
412
Los Angeles
Murray Seascarp
.6217
Guadalupe
Golfo de California
Colorado
Grande
Missouri
Mississippi
New Orleans
Gulf of Mexico
Bahia de Campeche
Str. of Florida
The Bahamas
Greater Antilles
Yucatan Channel
Puerto Rico Tr.
Cayman Tr.
7535
G. of Honduras

IFIC
I s l a n d s
Kauai
Oahu
Maui
Hawaii
R i d g e
7022

Molokai Fracture Zone
Clarion Fracture Zone
Is Revillagigedo
I. Clarión
I. Socorro
G. de Tehuantepec
Tehuantepec Ridge
Middle America Trench
6662
Venezuelan Basin
Colombian Basin
Caribbean Sea
Lesser Antilles
Caracas
Cape Verde Fracture
Vema Fracture
Guiana Basin

E A N
Tabuaeran
Kiritimati
Jarvis I.
Malden I.
Starbuck I.
Tongareva
Caroline I.
Flint I.

Clipperton Fracture Zone
Clipperton I.
.20
.10
I. de Coco
Cocos Ridge
I. de Malpelo
3901.
Panama City
Islas Galápagos
Carnegie Ridge
G. de Guayaquil
Mouths of the Amazon
Amazon
0°

Nuku Hiva
Is Marquises
Hiva Oa
Is du Roi Georges
Is Tuamotu
Îles de Désappointement
Fenua Ura
Raiatea
Is de la Société
Tahiti
Raroia
Anaa
Hao
4385.
1929.
Lima
.3007
SOUTH AMERICA

Hervey Is
Rarotonga
Mangaia
Îles Maria
Héréhérétué
Tubuai
Mururoa
Îles Duc de Gloucester
Groupe Actéon
Is Gambier
Henderson I.
Pitcairn I.
Ducie I.
.5470
Peru Basin
S.W. Peru or Nazca Ridge

E S I A
West Basin
.5420
Raivavae
Is Tubuai
Rapa
3344.
East Pacific Rise
Easter Island Fracture Zone
Easter I.
I. Sala y Gómez
571.
San Félix
San Ambrosio
8066.
15°

Challenger Fracture Zone
Is Juan Fernández
Robinson Crusoe
.2743
Chile Basin
Santiago
Parraná
Río de Janeiro

Pacific-Antarctic Ridge
Eltanin Fracture Zone
East Pacific Ridge
Buenos Aires
Río de la Plata
30°

J K L M N O P
5230.
South-East Pacific Basin
Amundsen Sea
Peter I Oy
Golfo de San Jorge
Cabo de Hornos
Drake Passage
Scotia Sea
Scotia Ridge
Falkland Islands
Argentine Basin
.6651
Golfo San Matias

1:48 000 000

| 0 | 300 | 600 | 900 | 1200 | 1500 | 1800 | MILES |

| 0 | 500 | 1000 | 1500 | 2000 | 2500 | 3000 | KM |

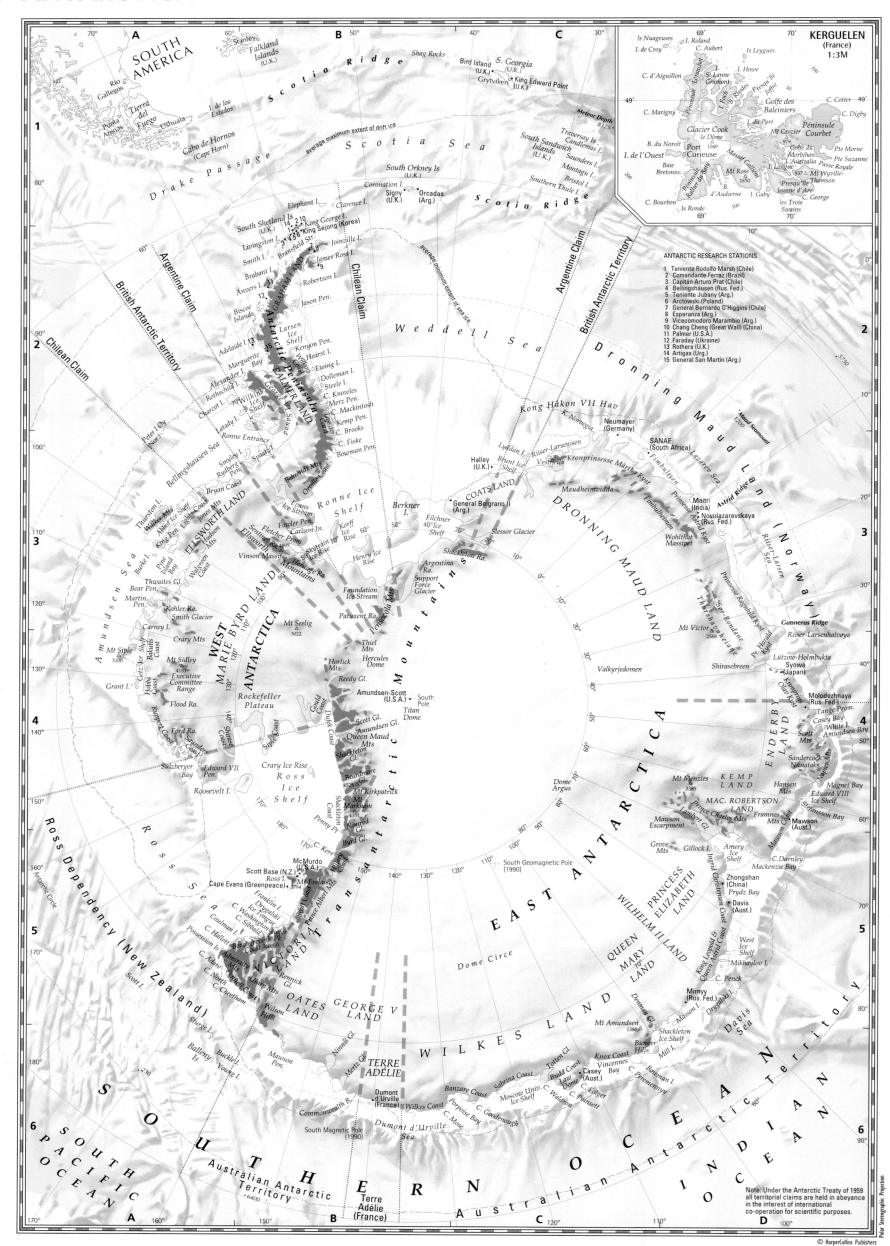

KERGUELEN
(France)
1:3M

ANTARCTIC RESEARCH STATIONS
1 Teniente Rodolfo Marsh (Chile)
2 Comandante Ferraz (Brazil)
3 Capitán Arturo Prat (Chile)
4 Bellingshausen (Rus. Fed.)
5 Teniente Jubany (Arg.)
6 Arctowski (Poland)
7 General Bernardo O'Higgins (Chile)
8 Esperanza (Arg.)
9 Vicecomodoro Marambio (Arg.)
10 Chang Cheng (Great Wall) (China)
11 Palmer (U.S.A.)
12 Faraday (Ukraine)
13 Rothera (U.K.)
14 Artigas (Ur.)
15 General San Martin (Arg.)

Note: Under the Antarctic Treaty of 1959 all territorial claims are held in abeyance in the interest of international co-operation for scientific purposes.

Polar Stereographic Projection

METRES / FEET
SEA / LEVEL
200 / 656
3000 / 9842
5000 / 16404
6000 / 19686

0 200 400 600 800 MILES
0 200 400 600 800 1000 1200 KM

1:24 000 000

© HarperCollins Publishers

THE INDEX INCLUDES the names on the maps in the ATLAS of the WORLD section. Names are indexed to the largest scale map on which they appear, and can be located using the grid reference letters and numbers around the map frame. Names on insets have a symbol: □, followed by the inset number. Although the maps have been revised to account for the change in name from Zaire to Congo and the reversion of Hong Kong to Chinese rule, this index reflects the prior situation.

Abbreviations used to describe features in the index are explained on the right. Abbreviations used in feature names on the maps and in the index, are explained on page 24. A glossary of alternative name forms is included on page 199.

A.C.T.	Australian Capital Territory	i., I.	island	r.	river
b.	bay	is, Is	islands	reg.	region
B.C.	British Columbia	l.	lake	Rep.	Republic
Bos.-Herz.	Bosnia-Herzegovina	lag.	lagoon	res.	reserve
c.	cape			resr	reservoir
chan.	channel	mt.	mountain	Rus. Fed.	Russian Federation
		mts	mountains		
div.	division	N.	North	S.	South
		nat. park.	national park	Str.	Strait
est.	estuary	N.W.T.	Northwest Territories		
				Terr.	Territory
g.	gulf	pen.	peninsula	U.A.E.	United Arab Emirates
gl.	glacier	plat.	plateau	U.K.	United Kingdom
		P.N.G.	Papua New Guinea	U.S.A.	United States of America
h.	hill, hills	pt	point	v.	valley

A

18 C3 Aachen Germany
18 E4 Aalen Germany
18 B3 Aalst Belgium
21 J3 Aarau Switz.
21 H3 Aarberg Switz.
18 B3 Aarschot Belgium
50 C1 Aba China
77 F5 Aba Nigeria
78 F3 Aba Zaire
73 H2 Abā ad Dūd Saudi Arabia
139 F5 Abacaxis r. Brazil
57 B3 Abādān Iran
57 C3 Abādeh Iran
144 E3 Abadia dos Dourados Brazil
144 D2 Abadiânia Brazil
74 D2 Abadla Algeria
145 F3 Abaeté Brazil
145 F3 Abaeté r. Brazil
142 C1 Abaetetuba Brazil
49 F2 Abagaytuy Rus. Fed.
24 B1 A Baiuca Spain
77 F5 Abaji Nigeria
127 E4 Abajo Pk summit U.S.A.
65 M2 Abakan Rus. Fed.
65 L2 Abakan r. Rus. Fed.
65 L2 Abakanskiy Khrebet mt. ra. Rus. Fed.
78 C4 Abala Congo
77 F4 Abala Niger
77 F3 Abalak Niger
75 F4 Abalessa Algeria
57 C3 Ab Anbār Iran
140 B2 Abanga r. Gabon
78 B3 Abanga r. Gabon
25 F3 Abanilla Spain
73 G2 Abarqū Iran
46 K1 Abashiri Japan
46 K2 Abashiri-gawa r. Japan
46 K2 Abashiri-ko l. Japan
46 K1 Abashiri-wan b. Japan
81 C5 Abasula waterhole Kenya
65 H1 Abatskiy Rus. Fed.
90 □11 Abau P.N.G.
65 H3 Abay Kazak.
65 M2 Abaza Rus. Fed.
78 C2 Abba C.A.R.
26 C4 Abbadia San Salvatore Italy
57 D2 Abbāsābād Iran
27 B5 Abbasanta Italy
122 C2 Abbaye, Pt pt U.S.A.
21 K2 Abbe, L. l. Ethiopia
18 A4 Abbeville France
125 E6 Abbeville U.S.A.
119 D5 Abbeville U.S.A.
99 F2 Abbey Peak h. Aust.
10 E2 Abborrträsk Sweden
152 A3 Abbot Ice Shelf ice Ant.
99 F4 Abbot Aust.
116 E5 Abbotsford Can.
122 B3 Abbotsford U.S.A.
127 H4 Abbott U.S.A.
60 D2 'Abd al 'Azīz, J. h. Syria
80 □1 'Abd al Kūrī i. Socotra Yemen
12 J4 Abdī Rus. Fed.
57 C2 Abdollāhābād Iran
57 C2 Abdollāhābād Iran
64 D2 Abdulino Rus. Fed.
72 D5 Abéché Chad
57 B3 Āb-e Garm Iran
77 E3 Abéla/Abala well Mali
77 F3 Abejukolo Nigeria
93 D4 Abel Tasman National Park nat. park N.Z.
76 D5 Abengourou Côte d'Ivoire
24 D3 Abenójar Spain
11 C5 Åbenrå Denmark
18 E4 Abensberg Germany
77 E5 Abeokuta Nigeria
17 E6 Aberaeron U.K.
17 F6 Aberdare U.K.
97 G3 Aberdeen Aust.
111 H4 Aberdeen Can.
45 Aberdeen Hong Kong
83 E6 Aberdeen R.S.A.
16 F3 Aberdeen U.K.
121 E5 Aberdeen U.S.A.
125 D5 Aberdeen U.S.A.
124 D2 Aberdeen U.S.A.
122 B2 Aberdeen U.S.A.
111 J2 Aberdeen Lake l. Can.
17 F6 Aberfeldy U.K.
16 E4 Abergavenny U.K.
125 C6 Abernathy U.S.A.
17 E5 Aberystwyth U.K.
73 H4 Abhā Saudi Arabia
57 B2 Abhar r. Iran
77 F5 Abia div. Nigeria
80 C3 Ābīata-Shalla National Park nat. park Ethiopia
57 D2 Ābīk Iran
57 A2 Ab-i-Kavir salt flat Iran
47 H6 Abiko Japan
16 E3 Abington U.K.
126 D4 Abilene U.S.A.
125 D5 Abilene U.S.A.
17 F6 Abingdon U.K.
122 B6 Abingdon U.S.A.
120 C6 Abingdon U.S.A.
99 G3 Abington Reef reef Coral Sea Islands Terr. Pac. Oc.
13 F6 Abinsk Rus. Fed.
57 F1 Ab-i-Rahuk Afghanistan
140 A1 Abiseo, Parque Nacional nat. park Peru
111 H2 Abitau Lake l. Can.
114 E2 Abitibi r. Can.
114 E2 Abitibi Canyon Dam dam Can.
114 E2 Abitibi, Lake l. Can.
57 C1 Abkhazia div. Georgia
96 C1 Abminga Aust.
76 D5 Abnûb Egypt
76 D5 Aboisso Côte d'Ivoire
77 E5 Abomey Benin
77 E4 Abong India
78 B3 Abong Mbang Cameroon

76 D5 Abooso Ghana
41 A4 Aborlan Phil.
72 C5 Abou Déïa Chad
60 F1 Abovyan Armenia
140 C4 Abra Chile
80 E1 Abrād, W. w Yemen
133 D2 Abraham's Bay The Bahamas
147 D5 Abra, L. del l. Arg.
146 C1 Abra Pampa Arg.
145 G4 Abre Campo Brazil
73 F3 'Abrī Sudan
145 J2 Abrolhos, Arquipélago dos is Brazil
28 D1 Abrud Romania
27 D4 Abruzzo div. Italy
126 E2 Absaroka Range mt. ra. U.S.A.
59 H1 Abşeron Yarımdası pen. Azerbaijan
46 C6 Abu Japan
61 D2 Abū aḍ Ḍuhūr Syria
57 B4 Abū 'Alī i. Saudi Arabia
57 C4 Abual Jirab i. U.A.E.
61 D5 Abū 'Amūd, W. w Jordan
73 H4 Abū 'Arīsh Saudi Arabia
61 C4 Abū Aweigila well Egypt
73 E3 Abū Ballūs h. Egypt
73 G3 Abu Deleiq Sudan
73 F4 Abu Durba Egypt
61 B5 Abū Durba Egypt
61 D3 Abū Hafrah, W. w Jordan
73 E1 Abū Haggag Egypt
60 C2 Abū Hallūfa, J. h. Jordan
73 F4 Abu Hamed Sudan
73 F4 Abū Hashim w Sudan
77 F5 Abuja Nigeria
61 A4 Abu Kebir Egypt
72 E5 Abu Ku Sudan
47 H5 Abukuma-gawa r. Japan
26 B2 Abula r. Italy
78 C2 Abumombazi Zaire
78 A4 Abuná r. Bolivia
140 C1 Abunã r. Bolivia
138 B2 Abunai Brazil
72 C2 Abū Nā'im well Libya
80 C2 Abuye Meda mt. Ethiopia
41 A4 Abuyog Phil.
73 G4 Abū Zabad Sudan
73 G2 Abū Zabī Iran
73 F2 Abū Zanīma Egypt
73 E3 Abyad Sudan
72 D1 Abyār an Nakhīlah well Libya
61 C5 Abyār Banī Murr well Saudi Arabia
100 B4 Abydos Aust.
72 E3 Abyei Sudan
72 D5 Bé Zérafa Chad
121 J2 Acadia Nat. Park nat. park U.S.A.
131 H5 Acambaro Mexico
131 H4 Acandí Colombia
131 G5 Acaponeta Mexico
131 H5 Acapulco Mexico
142 C1 Acará Brazil
142 D1 Acará Miri r. Brazil
142 D1 Acaraú Brazil
145 E3 Acaray, r. Paraguay
142 E2 Acari Brazil
145 F1 Acari r. Brazil
138 D1 Acarigua Venezuela
131 H5 Acatlán Mexico
131 H5 Acatzingo Mexico
131 H5 Acayucán Mexico
76 D5 Accra Ghana
140 C2 Achacachi Bolivia
138 D2 Achaguas Venezuela
54 C3 Achalpur India
21 G3 Achenpass pass Switz.
49 H1 Acheng China
54 E3 Achham div. Nepal
94 □4 Achilles Is is Lord Howe I. Pac. Oc.
110 C3 Achinsk Kazak.
16 E3 Achnasheen U.K.
16 E3 Achosnich U.K.
24 B1 A Coruña Spain
25 E4 Acquapendente Italy
26 D3 Acqui Terme Italy
96 C3 Acraman, L. salt flat Aust.
140 C3 Acre div. Brazil
27 F6 Acri Italy
74 A4 Acrioca r. mt. Western Sahara
19 J5 Acs Hungary
151 L7 Actéon, Groupe is Fr. Poly. Pac. Oc.
115 J4 Acton Vale Can.
142 E2 Açu Brazil
131 H5 Acula Mexico
125 C5 Adrian U.S.A.

47 □1 Ada Japan
120 B4 Ada U.S.A.
125 D5 Ada U.S.A.
28 C2 Ada Yugo.
41 □2 Adacao Guam Pac. Oc.
11 G4 Adaaduna Latvia
80 D2 Adaela well Ethiopia
24 D2 Adaja r. Spain
80 E3 Adale well Ethiopia
78 B2 Adamaoua div. Cameroon
77 G5 Adamawa div. Nigeria
97 G4 Adaminaby Aust.
147 E2 Adam, Mt h. Falkland Is.
76 D5 Adzopé Côte d'Ivoire
19 L3 Adamów Poland
13 H6 Adyk Rus. Fed.
29 E5 Aegean Sea sea Greece/Turkey
18 D2 Aerzen Germany
24 B1 A Estrada Spain
91 □11 Afaahiti Fr. Poly. Pac. Oc.
80 C1 Afabet Eritrea
80 D3 Afaf Badane well Ethiopia
29 G6 Afantou Greece
75 F3 Afao mt. Algeria
80 D2 Afar Depression depres- sion Eritrea/Ethiopia
91 □14 Afareaitu Fr. Poly. Pac. Oc.
76 D5 Afféri Côte d'Ivoire
139 F2 Affobakka Surinam
32 H6 Afghanistan country Asia
80 E4 Afgooye Somalia
79 □2 Afiamalu Western Samoa
73 H3 'Afīf Saudi Arabia
77 F5 Afikpo Nigeria
60 C2 Afin r. Turkey
60 C1 Afrin Syria
60 D2 Afşin Turkey
18 B2 Afsluitdijk dam Netherlands
80 D3 Aftol well Ethiopia
142 B1 Afuá Brazil
61 C3 'Afula Israel
60 B2 Afyon Turkey
77 F3 Agadez Niger
74 B2 Agadir Morocco
65 H3 Agadyr' Kazak.
131 H5 Agalteca Honduras
55 G5 Agartala India
18 D2 Agathenburg Germany
98 D2 Agaro Ethiopia
61 C3 Agora Israel
55 G5 Agartala India
92 E5 Agathonisi i. Greece
18 D2 Agde France
21 F5 Agen France
80 D2 Agen France
29 E4 Aghios Dimitrios Attiki Greece
29 E5 Aghios Georgios i. Greece
29 D6 Agios Konstantinos Stereo Ellas Greece
29 F7 Agios Nikolaos Kriti Greece
29 F5 Agios Paraskevi Greece
29 D7 Agios Vasileios Greece
75 F3 Agirwat Hills h. Sudan
28 F1 Agnita Romania
75 D5 Agok India
47 G4 Agano r. Japan
55 H4 Agartala India

130 E5 Aguas Japan
138 C3 Agua de Dios Colombia
119 □3 Aguadilla Puerto Rico
147 C5 Aguado Cecilio Arg.
130 K7 Aguaduce Panama
141 E3 Aguapeí r. Brazil
146 E2 Aguapey r. Arg.
130 C2 Agua Prieta Mexico
141 E4 Aguaray-guazu r. Paraguay
24 B2 A Guardia Spain
138 D2 Aguaro-Guariquito, Parque Nacional nat. park Venezuela
130 E4 Aguascalientes Mexico
145 H2 Águas Formosas Brazil
145 H1 Águas Vermelhas Brazil
24 D1 Águeda r. Spain
145 D5 Agudos Brazil
24 B2 Águeda Portugal
77 F3 Aguelhok Mali
75 F4 Aguemour reg. Algeria
77 F4 Aguié Niger
129 F5 Aguila U.S.A.
24 D1 Aguilar de Campóo Spain
146 C2 Aguilares Arg.
25 F4 Águilas Spain
41 B4 Aguisan Phil.
119 □3 Aguijereada, Pta pt Puerto Rico
80 C2 Agula'i Ethiopia
149 F7 Agulhas Bank Indian Ocean
82 C5 Agulhas, Cape c. R.S.A.
145 H5 Agulhas Negras, Pico das mt. Brazil
149 F6 Agulhas Plateau Indian Ocean
40 C2 Agung, G. vol Indon.
41 B4 Agusan r. Phil.
13 D7 Ağva Turkey
80 B3 Agwei r. Sudan
131 F5 Agwi Mexico
54 D2 Aḥaggar mts Algeria
75 E4 Ahaggar, Tassili oua-n- Ahaggar mts Algeria
92 E1 Ahipara Bay b. N.Z.
91 □11 Ahitenoa N.Z.
55 H4 Ajka Hungary
60 E2 Ahlat Turkey
18 C3 Ahlen Germany
54 C4 Ahmadabad India
57 B3 Ahmadi Iran
54 B3 Ahmadnagar India
54 B4 Ahmadpur East Pakistan
54 B3 Ahmadpur Sial Pakistan
80 C2 Ahmar Mountains mt. ra. Ethiopia
80 B3 Ak'ak'i Beseka Ethiopia
29 F5 Ahmeti Turkey
72 B3 Ahnet, reg. Algeria
55 G4 Ahoskie India
80 E2 Ahrweiler Germany
11 G3 Ähtäri Finland
81 B5 Ahvaz Iran
56 B4 Ahvenanmaa i. Finland
92 D2 Ahuriri r. N.Z.
82 B4 Ai-Ais Hot Springs and Fish River Canyon res. Namibia
72 D5 Aibag Gol r. China
46 J2 Aibetsu Japan
60 E2 Aibonito Puerto Rico
92 B6 Ahuriri r. N.Z.
81 F2 Aid U.S.A.
127 □1 Aiea U.S.A.
75 E4 Aïn Ben Tili Mauritania
24 C1 Aigina r. Spain
29 D6 Aigina Greece
21 K4 Aigle Switz.
146 F3 Aigúá Uruguay
29 D4 Aigion Greece
92 B6 Aigina i. Greece
21 G5 Aigurande France
18 C3 Aïn Defla Algeria
60 B3 Aiken U.S.A.

109 J1 Air Force I. i. Can.
48 D4 Airgin Sum China
40 B2 Airhitam r. Indon.
40 B2 Airhitam, Tk b. Indon.
77 F3 Aïr, Massif de l' mts Niger
21 J3 Airolo Switz.
111 H3 Air Ronge Can.
20 D3 Airvault France
147 B6 Aisén div. Chile
147 B6 Aisén, Pto Chile
49 G5 Ai Shan h. China
110 B2 Aishihik Can.
110 B2 Aishihik Lake l. Can.
29 E7 Akra Agios Ioannis pt Greece
29 E7 Akra Agiou Andreou pt Greece
90 □1 Aitape P.N.G.
124 E2 Aitkin U.S.A.
87 L6 Aitutaki i. Cook Islands Pac. Oc.
28 D2 Aiud Romania
21 F4 Aix r. France
21 G5 Aix-en-Provence France
21 G4 Aix, J. mt. Turkey
20 E4 Aix-en-Provence France
21 G4 Aix-les-Bains France
54 D2 Āīj 'Ādī Ethiopia
110 D3 Aiyansh Can.
55 F5 Aiyar Res. India
54 E4 Aiyetoro Nigeria
55 G5 Aizawl India
55 G4 Aizkraukle Latvia
47 G5 Aizu-wakamatsu Japan
21 J6 Ajaccio France
21 J6 Ajaccio, Golfe d' b. France
54 E4 Ajaigarh India
13 D7 Ajã, I. mts Saudi Arabia
131 F5 Ajalpán Mexico
65 M2 Alash, Plato plat. Rus. Fed.
131 H5 Ajmer India
94 □1 Akabira Japan
75 E4 Akabli Algeria
54 D5 Akalkot India
47 G4 Akan National Park nat. park Japan
80 C1 Akanthou Cyprus
64 E4 Akaoka Japan
47 F4 Akabira Japan
13 D7 Akçakoca Turkey
29 F5 Akçay r. Turkey
60 B2 Akçakale Turkey
60 C2 Akçakoyunlu Turkey
60 D1 Akdağ mt. Turkey
29 G6 Akdağ mt. Turkey
13 D8 Akdağmadeni Turkey
11 F4 Åland i. Finland
80 E2 Akdhnour India
46 A1 Akeshi Japan
80 C2 Ak'ordat Eritrea

80 B3 Akobo Sudan
54 D5 Akola India
78 B3 Akom II Cameroon
78 B3 Akonolinga Cameroon
80 C1 Akordat Eritrea
60 C2 Akören Turkey
54 D5 Akot India
80 B3 Akot Sudan
21 H3 Akoupé Côte d'Ivoire
113 G1 Akpatok Island i. Can.
65 L3 Akpinar Turkey
25 J4 Akqi China
29 E5 Akra Agios Fokas pt Greece
29 E7 Akra Agios Ioannis pt Greece
29 E7 Akra Agiou Andreou pt Greece
29 E4 Akra Akrathos pt Greece
29 E4 Akra Arapis pt Greece
29 C5 Akra Araxos pt Greece
29 E4 Akrid, Jabal al mt. ra. Syria
29 D5 Akra Drepano pt Greece
29 C5 Akra Geraki pt Greece
11 F3 Åland is Finland
21 H3 Aland r. France
11 E3 Åland div. Sweden
57 C3 Ālandūr Iran
57 C2 Āland r. Iran
140 B3 Alca Peru
24 B3 Alcácer do Sal Portugal
24 C3 Alcáçovas Portugal
43 C7 Alang Besar i. Indon.
122 A3 Alantika Mountains mt. ra. Cameroon/Nigeria
24 E2 Alcalá de Henares Spain
24 D4 Alcalá de los Gazules Spain
24 D4 Alcalá la Real Spain
27 D7 Alcamo Italy
24 C3 Alcanar Spain
24 C2 Alcañices Spain
24 F2 Alcaniz Spain
142 C1 Alcântara Brazil
24 C3 Alcântara II, Embalse de resr Spain
142 B2 Alcantilado Brazil
25 E3 Alcaraz Spain
24 E3 Alcaraz, Sierra de mt. ra. Spain
24 D4 Alcaudete Spain
24 E3 Alcázar de San Juan Spain
13 F5 Alchevs'k Ukraine
24 C3 Alcoba Spain
145 J2 Alcobaça Brazil
24 C3 Alconchel Spain
24 E3 Alcoy Spain
25 F3 Alcúdia Spain
119 □3 Aldabra Islands is Seychelles
130 D2 Aldama Chihuahua Mexico
131 F4 Aldama Tamaulipas Mexico
65 O3 Aldan r. Rus. Fed.
65 O4 Aldan r. Rus. Fed.
145 H5 Aldeia Velha Brazil
142 E2 Aldeia Velha Brazil
17 H5 Aldeburgh U.K.
18 B3 Aldenhoven Germany
17 H7 Alderney i. Channel Is.
17 G6 Aldershot U.K.
128 A2 Alder Peak summit U.S.A.
120 C6 Alderson Can.
14 D2 Aledo U.S.A.
122 B5 Aledo U.S.A.
118 A4 Aleg Mauritania
142 C1 Alegre Espirito Santo Brazil
145 J5 Alegre r. Brazil
145 F3 Alegre, Pord Brazil
146 E2 Alegrete Brazil
146 E2 Alegranza i. Canary Is.
24 A4 Alegranza i. Canary Is.
79 □ Alegre, Monte r. Brazil
143 A6 Alegria Brazil
79 □ Alegre, Pto pt Sao Tome and Principe
64 D4 Aleksandra Bekovicha-Cherkasskogo, Zaliv b. Kazak.
14 E3 Aleksandrov Rus. Fed.
14 E3 Aleksandrov Gay Rus. Fed.
28 D3 Aleksandrovac Yugo.
29 K2 Aleksandrovo Bulgaria
13 H6 Aleksandrovsk Rus. Fed.
65 Q4 Aleksandrovsk-Sakhalinskiy Rus. Fed.
19 J3 Aleksandrów Kujawski Poland
19 K4 Aleksandrów Łódzki Poland
14 E4 Alekseyevka Rus. Fed.
13 G5 Alekseyevka Rus. Fed.
14 E4 Alekseyevka Rus. Fed.
12 F4 Alekseyevskoye Rus. Fed.
14 E4 Aleksin Rus. Fed.
28 C3 Aleksinac Yugo.
131 H4 Alemán, Presa, M. resr Mexico
142 C3 Além Paraíba Brazil
79 □ Alenço France
79 □ Alençon France
79 □ Alenuihaha Channel chan. U.S.A.
76 D5 Alépé Côte d'Ivoire
140 A2 Alerta Peru
110 D4 Alert Bay Can.
21 G4 Alès France
28 D1 Aleşd Romania
26 D3 Alessandria Italy
11 B3 Ålesund Norway
108 C3 Aleutian Islands is U.S.A.
108 B4 Aleutian Range mt. ra. U.S.A.
151 J2 Aleutian Trench Pac. Oc.
65 R3 Alevina, Mys c. Rus. Fed.
121 J2 Alexander U.S.A.
108 C4 Alexander Archipelago is U.S.A.

154

82 B4 Alexander Bay R.S.A.
119 C5 Alexander City U.S.A.
152 A2 Alexander I. i. Ant.
98 E3 Alexandra r. Aust.
97 F4 Alexandra Aust.
93 B6 Alexandra N.Z.
147 G7 Alexandra, C. c. Atlantic Ocean
29 E4 Alexandreia Greece
98 D3 Alexandria Aust.
115 H4 Alexandria Can.
73 E1 Alexandria Egypt
28 E3 Alexandria Romania
122 E5 Alexandria U.S.A.
125 E6 Alexandria U.S.A.
124 E2 Alexandria U.S.A.
120 E5 Alexandria U.S.A.
121 F2 Alexandria Bay U.S.A.
96 D3 Alexandrina, L. l. Aust.
29 C4 Alexandroupoli Greece
113 J3 Alexis r. Can.
122 B5 Alexis U.S.A.
110 E4 Alexis Creek Can.
24 A3 'Aley Lebanon
65 K2 Aleysk Rus. Fed.
65 K2 Aleysk Rus. Fed.
25 F2 Alfambra r. Spain
25 F1 Alfaro Spain
60 F4 Al Farwānīyah Kuwait
28 F1 Alfatar Bulgaria
60 E3 Al Fatḩah Iraq
60 G4 Al Fāw Iraq
80 D2 Al Fayj Yemen
18 D3 Alfeld (Leine) Germany
145 F4 Alfenas Brazil
19 K5 Alföld plain Hungary
26 D3 Alfonsine Italy
115 H4 Alfred Can.
121 H3 Alfred U.S.A.
145 H4 Alfredo Chaves Brazil
57 D4 Al Fuḩayʻil Kuwait
57 J4 Al Fujayrah U.A.E.
64 E3 Alga Kazak.
64 D2 Algabas Kazak.
11 B4 Algård Norway
146 B2 Algarrobo Atacama Chile
146 C4 Algarrobo del Aguilla Arg.
24 B4 Algarve reg. Portugal
14 E3 Algasovo Rus. Fed.
24 D4 Algeciras Spain
25 F3 Algemesi Spain
80 C1 Algena Eritrea
75 E1 Alger Algeria
123 E3 Alger U.S.A.
68 D3 Algeria country Africa
56 E1 Al Ghammas Iraq
59 H6 Al Ghaydah Yemen
27 B5 Alghero Italy
82 D5 Algoa Bay b. R.S.A.
122 D3 Algoma U.S.A.
124 E3 Algona U.S.A.
123 F4 Algona U.S.A.
115 J4 Algonquin Park Can.
115 F4 Algonquin Provincial Park res. Can.
42 A4 Alguada Reef reef Myanmar
73 H3 Al Ḩadbah reg. Saudi Arabia
57 B4 Al Ḩadd Saudi Arabia
73 H2 Al Ḩadhālīl plat. Saudi Arabia
61 G4 Al Ḩadīdīyah Syria
61 D4 Al Ḩadīthah Iraq
61 D4 Al Ḩadīthah Iraq
60 E3 Al Ḩaḑr Iraq
73 H2 Al Ḩafār well Saudi Arabia
74 B3 Al Ḩaggounina Western Sahara
60 D3 Al Ḩamad plain Jordan/Saudi Arabia
72 B2 Al Ḩamādah al Ḩamrā' desert Libya
24 E4 Alhama de Granada Spain
25 F4 Alhama de Murcia Spain
61 C4 Al Ḩamīdīyah Syria
60 F4 Al Ḩammār marsh Iraq
74 C3 Al Ḩamra Western Sahara
61 D2 Al Ḩamrāt Syria
73 H3 Al Ḩanākīyah Saudi Arabia
73 J2 Al Ḩarf Saudi Arabia
73 G1 Al Ḩarrah h. Saudi Arabia
72 C2 Al Ḩarūj al Aswad mt. ra. Libya
60 E2 Al Ḩasakah Syria
60 F3 Al Ḩāshimīyah Iraq
73 J2 Al Ḩatīfah plain Saudi Arabia
73 H3 Al Ḩawīyah Saudi Arabia
73 G2 Al Ḩawjā' Saudi Arabia
60 F3 Al Ḩayy Iraq
61 B5 Al Ḩazm Saudi Arabia
60 F3 Al Ḩillah Iraq
57 B4 Al Ḩinw mt. Saudi Arabia
61 D4 Al Ḩinw mt. Saudi Arabia
74 D1 Al Hoceima Morocco
24 E5 Al Hoceima, Baie d' b. Morocco
80 D2 Al Ḩudaydah Yemen
73 G2 Al Ḩufrah reg. Saudi Arabia
57 B4 Al Hufūf Saudi Arabia
61 C5 Al Ḩumayshah Yemen
57 B4 Al Ḩunayy Saudi Arabia
61 D4 Al Ḩusayn Syria
54 D2 Ali China
57 E3 'Alīābād Iran
57 C1 'Alīābād Iran
57 C1 'Alīābād Iran
60 A2 Aliağa Turkey
29 D4 Aliakmonas r. Greece
60 F4 'Alī al Gharbī Iraq
29 D5 Aliartos Greece
54 B4 Alībāg India
54 B4 Ali Bandar Pakistan
60 D2 Āli Bayramlı Azerbaijan
29 E5 Alibey Adası i. Turkey
77 F4 Alibori r. Benin
24 D2 Alibunar Yugo.
25 F3 Alicante Spain
99 F4 Alice r. Aust.
99 F4 Alice r. Aust.
54 E4 Alice U.S.A.
125 D7 Alice U.S.A.
110 D3 Alice Arm Can.
27 F6 Alice, Punta pt Italy
132 C3 Alice Shoal Caribbean
98 C4 Alice Springs Aust.
132 C1 Alice Town The Bahamas
115 H5 Aliceville U.S.A.
41 A5 Alick Cr. r. Aust.
27 E6 Alicudi, Isola i. Italy
54 D4 Aligarh India
25 E2 Alijó Portugal
80 D2 'Ali Sabieh Socotra Yemen
14 F3 Alikovo Rus. Fed.
78 C4 Alima r. Congo
78 D2 Alimia i. C.A.R.
40 D2 Alindao C.A.R.
14 D4 Alīpur India
29 H5 Aliaga r. Turkey
11 B4 Alingsås Sweden
55 G4 Alipur Duar India
54 C4 Aliquippa U.S.A.
80 D2 'Ali Sabieh Djibouti
61 D4 'Alī Şabḩ Syria
127 E6 Alisos r. Mexico
29 E5 Aliveri Greece
82 D5 Aliwal North R.S.A.

110 G4 Alix Can.
54 B2 Alizai Pakistan
72 D1 Al Jabal al Akhḑar mts Libya
57 B4 Al Jāfūrah desert Saudi Arabia
60 F4 Al Jahrah Kuwait
57 B4 Al Jamalīyah Qatar
72 D3 Al Jawf Libya
72 D3 Al Jawf Libya
60 E3 Al Jawsh Libya
60 E3 Al Jafrah reg. Iraq/Syria
57 B4 Al Jibān reg. Saudi Arabia
60 F4 Al Jil well Iraq
73 H2 Al Jilh escarpment Saudi Arabia
57 B4 Al Jishshah Saudi Arabia
60 F3 Al Jithāmīyah Saudi Arabia
73 H2 Al Jithāmīyah Saudi Arabia
73 D3 Al Jumūm Saudi Arabia
73 H3 Al Junaynah Saudi Arabia
73 D3 Al Jurayd i. Saudi Arabia
24 B4 Aljustrel Portugal
61 D3 Al Juwayf depression Syria
61 D5 Al Kabid waterhole Jordan
77 G4 Alkamari Niger
59 J5 Al Khābūrah Oman
73 H2 Al Khaḑrā' well Saudi Arabia
60 F3 Al Khālis Iraq
80 D1 Al Kharāb Yemen
73 H3 Al Khāṣirah Saudi Arabia
57 B4 Al Khawr Qatar
57 B4 Al Khīṣah well Saudi Arabia
72 D3 Al Khufrah Libya
72 D3 Al Khufrah Oasis oasis Libya
61 A5 Al Khums Libya
61 C3 Al Khushnīyah Syria
61 D3 Al Kir'ānah Qatar
61 D3 Al Kiswah Syria
18 B2 Alkmaar Netherlands
61 C4 Al Kūfah Iraq
73 H2 Al Kuhayfīyah Saudi Arabia
61 C4 Al Kumayt Iraq
60 F3 Al Kūt Iraq
60 F4 Al Kuwayt Kuwait
73 H2 Al Labbah plain Saudi Arabia
61 C2 Al Lādhiqīyah Syria
121 J1 Allagash r. U.S.A.
121 J1 Allagash U.S.A.
121 J1 Allagash Lake l. U.S.A.
55 G4 Allahabad India
61 D3 Al Lajā lava Syria
63 F3 Allakh-Yun' Rus. Fed.
24 C1 Allariz Spain
73 H3 Alldays R.S.A.
122 E4 Allegan U.S.A.
120 D4 Allegany U.S.A.
120 D4 Alleghany U.S.A.
73 H4 Al Qaḑārif Sudan
121 F4 Allegheny r. U.S.A.
120 D4 Allegheny Mountains U.S.A.
120 D4 Allegheny Reservoir resr U.S.A.
133 ¨5 Allegre, Pte pt Guadeloupe Caribbean
119 D5 Allendale U.S.A.
131 E3 Allende Coahuila Mexico
131 E3 Allende Nuevo León Mexico
114 E4 Allenford Can.
17 B4 Allen, Lough l. Rep. of Ire.
93 A7 Allen, Mt h. N.Z.
121 F4 Allentown U.S.A.
56 B4 Alleppey India
25 F2 Allepuz Spain
18 E2 Aller r. Germany
18 D3 Aller r. Germany
139 G2 Alliance Surinam
124 C3 Alliance U.S.A.
120 C4 Alliance U.S.A.
21 F4 Allier r. France
133 ¨1 Alligator Pond Jamaica
11 ¨2 Allinge-Sandvig Denmark
10 F1 Allisjav'ri l. Norway
10 F1 Alløjohka Norway
114 F4 Alliston Can.
73 H3 Al Lith Saudi Arabia
16 F3 Allschwil Switz.
99 H5 Allora Aust.
40 D1 Allu Indon.
80 D1 Al Luḩayyah Yemen
56 C3 Allur India
141 A2 Alluru Kottapatnam India
60 E4 Al Lussuf well Iraq
24 D3 Alma, Sierra de mt. ra. Spain
93 B6 Alma, Mt mt. N.Z.
37 F5 Almaard Mongolia
48 D2 Altanbulag Mongolia
48 C2 Altanbulag Mongolia
130 C2 Altar Mexico
130 B2 Altar, Desierto de desert Mexico
128 D3 Altata Mexico
125 C5 Altavista U.S.A.
65 J5 Altay China
48 A3 Altay Mongolia
65 J1 Altay, Respublika div. Rus. Fed.
51 E4 Altayskiy Rus. Fed.
65 K2 Altayskiy Kray div. Rus. Fed.
21 J3 Altdorf Switz.
73 J2 Altamira Spain
73 J2 Altamira reg. Spain
19 F3 Altenberg Germany
55 H1 Altentreptow Germany
24 C3 Alter do Chão Portugal
29 F5 Altınova Turkey
144 E4 Altınópolis Brazil
144 E4 Altınópolis Brazil
147 D5 Altınova Turkey
54 C2 Altıntaş Turkey
56 M4 Altınyayla Turkey
60 F2 Altınova Rus. Fed.
138 D4 Altiplanicie de Hakelhuincul plat. Arg.
138 D2 Altiplano plain Bolivia
18 E4 Altkirch France
18 E2 Altmärsen Germany
79 C6 Alto Chicapa Angola
143 B2 Alto Araguaia Brazil
131 E3 Alto del Moncayo mt. Spain
79 C6 Alto Molócuè Mozambique
146 A5 Alto Río Senguer Arg.
142 E2 Alto Parnaiba Brazil
145 G4 Alto Rio Doce Brazil
146 A5 Alto Río Verde Brazil
130 ¨7 Altotonga Mexico
83 H2 Alto Vista h. Aruba Caribbean
14 B3 Altukhovo Rus. Fed.

115 G4 Almonte Can.
24 E1 Almonte r. Spain
24 C4 Almonte Spain
25 F3 Almora India
25 F3 Almoradí Spain
64 E3 Almaty Kazak.
77 E3 Almoustarat Mali
57 E3 Almoutzarat Saudi Arabia
73 G2 Al Mudarraj Saudi Arabia
60 C4 Al Mudawwara Jordan
57 B4 Al Muharraq Bahrain
61 D5 Al Muḩṭaṭab depression Saudi Arabia
72 C1 Al 'Uqaylah Libya
80 D2 Al 'Uqayr Saudi Arabia
73 G2 Al Urayq desert Saudi Arabia
57 B4 Al 'Uthmānīyah Saudi Arabia
72 D3 Al 'Uwaynāt Libya
72 B2 Al 'Uwaynāt Libya
73 G2 Al 'Uwaynīdīyah i. Saudi Arabia
73 H3 Al 'Uwayqilah Saudi Arabia
73 H3 Al 'Uyūn Saudi Arabia
73 H2 Al 'Uyūn Saudi Arabia
57 B4 Al Khawr Qatar
57 B4 Al Khīṣah well Saudi Arabia
24 B2 Alva r. Portugal
125 D4 Alva U.S.A.
131 G5 Alvarado Mexico
21 G3 Alvaredos i. Brazil
11 C3 Älvdal Norway
11 D3 Älvdalen Sweden
11 C4 Ålvik Norway
125 E6 Alvin U.S.A.
145 G4 Alvinópolis Brazil
10 F2 Älvsbyn Sweden
73 J2 Al Wajh Saudi Arabia
57 B4 Al Wannān Saudi Arabia
40 C3 Al Wannān Saudi Arabia
54 D3 Alwar India
60 E4 Al Widyān desert Iraq/Saudi Arabia
75 G2 Al Widyān desert Iraq/Saudi Arabia
72 B3 Al Wīgh Libya
73 J2 Al Wusayṭ well Saudi Arabia
48 B5 Alxa Youqi China
48 B5 Alxa Zuoqi China
11 G5 Alytus Lithuania
11 G5 Alytus Lithuania
128 B4 Alzada U.S.A.
18 D4 Alzey Germany
138 C4 Amacayacu, Parque Nacional nat. park Colombia
131 H5 Amada Gaza C.A.R.
98 B5 Amadeus, Lake salt flat Aust.
72 C1 Al Qaddāḩīyah Libya
60 F4 Al Qādisīyah div. Iraq
73 H3 Al Qā'īyah Saudi Arabia
73 H3 Al Qalībah Saudi Arabia
72 D1 Al Qāmishlī Syria
73 H3 Al Qaraar Saudi Arabia
72 B1 Al Qaṣabāt Libya
59 G6 Al Qaṭn Yemen
72 B3 Al Qaṭrūn Libya
73 H2 Al Qāysūmah well Saudi Arabia
61 C3 Al Qunayṭirah div. Syria
73 H4 Al Qunfidhah Saudi Arabia
73 H2 Al Qurayn Yemen
60 F4 Al Qurnah Iraq
61 D3 Al Quṭayfah Syria
21 H2 Alsace div. France
111 H4 Alsask Can.
18 D3 Alsfeld Germany
65 H4 Al'shana Rus. Fed.
17 F4 Alston U.K.
11 G4 Alsunga Latvia
10 F1 Alta r. Norway
61 C3 Alta Gracia Venezuela
138 C2 Altagracia de Orituco Venezuela
44 E2 Altai Mountains mt. ra. Asia
119 D6 Altamaha r. U.S.A.
142 C2 Altamira Brazil
138 B3 Altamira Colombia
131 E3 Altamira Costa Rica
24 D3 Altamira, Sierra de mt. ra. Spain
93 D4 Alta, Mt mt. N.Z.
27 F5 Altamura Italy
48 C2 Altan Mongolia
48 D2 Altan Mongolia
128 B4 Altar Mexico
46 B7 Amakusa-nada b. Japan
46 B7 Amakusa-Shimo-shima i. Japan
11 D4 Åmål Sweden
138 C2 Amalapuram India
138 B2 Amalfi Colombia
27 E4 Amalfi Italy
29 C6 Amaliada Greece
120 D6 Amalner India
144 A5 Amambaí Brazil
46 A7 Amami-guntō is Japan
46 A7 Amami-Ōshima i. Japan
78 E4 Amamula r. Dem. Rep. Congo
144 A3 Amaná, Lago l. Brazil
26 D4 Amandola Italy
46 B7 Amangel'dy Aktyubinsk Kazak.
56 A4 Amindivi Islands is India
80 F4 Aminius Namibia
41 ¨10 Amanu i. Fr. Poly. Pac. Oc.
82 D2 Amanzimyama r. Zimbabwe
82 B2 Amanzimtoti R.S.A.
139 J3 Amapá, Brazil
139 G3 Amapá Brazil
139 G3 Amapari r. Brazil
73 H3 Amara Sudan
138 B3 Amaramba, Lagoa l. Moz.
142 E2 Amarante Brazil
142 D2 Amarante do Maranhão Brazil
42 A2 Amarapura Myanmar
42 D3 Amargo Mongolia
24 F3 Amarillo Portugal
128 C4 Amargosa Desert desert U.S.A.
128 C4 Amargosa Range mts U.S.A.
128 C4 Amargosa Valley U.S.A.
125 C5 Amarillo U.S.A.
74 B3 Amasine Western Sahara
60 C1 Amasra Turkey
60 E1 Amasya Turkey
131 E5 Amatán Mexico
138 D2 Amataurá Brazil
130 ¨6 Amatique, B. de b. Guatemala
130 D4 Amatlán de Cañas Mexico
49 G1 Amazar r. Rus. Fed.
139 H4 Amazonas div. Brazil
138 D4 Amazonas r. S. America
40 C2 Amazonas, Parque Nacional nat. park Brazil
139 H4 Amazon, Mouths of the river mouth Brazil
139 G4 Amazon, Source of the river source Peru
54 D3 Āmb India
54 C3 Amba Farīt mt. Ethiopia
83 H2 Ambahikily Madagascar
83 H3 Ambahy Madagascar
83 H3 Ambaja India
56 B4 Ambala India
41 B5 Ambalakida Madagascar
83 H3 Ambalangoda Sri Lanka
83 H3 Ambalavao Madagascar
83 H2 Ambalindum Madagascar
78 C3 Ambam Cameroon
83 H2 Amban r. Madagascar
83 H3 Ambanja Madagascar
63 R3 Ambarchik Rus. Fed.
83 H1 Ambararata Madagascar
138 B4 Ambato Ecuador
83 H2 Ambato Boeny Madagascar
83 H3 Ambato Finandrahana Madagascar
83 H2 Ambato-Sofia Madagascar
83 H2 Ambatolampy Madagascar
83 H2 Ambatomainty Madagascar
83 H2 Ambatondrazaka Madagascar

131 H5 Altun Ha Belize
44 E4 Altun Shan mt. ra. China
126 B3 Alturas U.S.A.
125 D5 Altus U.S.A.
61 G4 Altynasar Kazak.
15 F1 Altynivka Ukraine
14 H2 Altyshevo Rus. Fed.
60 D1 Alucra Turkey
11 G4 Alūksne Latvia
83 E5 Al 'Ulā Saudi Arabia
83 H3 Ambila Madagascar
83 H3 Ambilobe Madagascar
120 D4 Alum Creek Lake l. U.S.A.
83 H3 Alupka Ukraine
15 E6 Alushta Ukraine
57 B4 Al Uthaylī Saudi Arabia
29 D5 Almyros Greece
131 F6 Alta Haina U.S.A.
130 ¨5 Alvarado Mexico
129 J3 Alva U.S.A.
42 A2 Aloja i. Myanmar
55 H3 Along India
48 C3 Alongshan China
29 D5 Alonnisos i. Greece
24 C3 Alonso r. Brazil
39 H8 Alor i. Indon.
24 D4 Álora Spain
39 H8 Alor, Kepulauan is Indon.
24 D4 Alosno Spain
18 B3 Alost Belgium
90 ¨1 Alotau P.N.G.
128 C4 Aloysius, Mt mt. Aust.
123 F3 Alpena U.S.A.
25 F3 Alpera Spain
144 C2 Alpercatas r. Brazil
21 J4 Alpes du Dauphiné mts France
21 H4 Alpes Maritimes mt. ra. France/Italy
21 H4 Alpi Cozie mt. ra. France/Italy
26 C2 Alpi Dolomitiche mt. ra. Italy
26 C2 Alpi Lepontine mt. ra. Italy/Switz.
129 B5 Alpine U.S.A.
126 E3 Alpine U.S.A.
145 E4 Alpinópolis Brazil
26 B2 Alpi Orobie mt. ra. Italy
16 E4 Alpi Pennine mt. ra. Italy/Switz.
22 E2 Alps Europe
59 G6 Al Qa'āmīyāt reg. Saudi Arabia
98 B5 Amadeus, Lake salt flat Aust.
72 C1 Al Qaddāḩīyah Libya
109 M3 Amadjuak Lake l. Can.
129 G6 Amado U.S.A.
24 B3 Amadora Portugal
46 C7 Amagi Japan
46 C7 Amakusa-Kami-shima i. Japan
46 B7 Amakusa-nada b. Japan
138 B3 Amalfi Colombia
27 E4 Amalfi Italy
25 F2 Amelía Italy
29 D5 Amfilochia Greece
29 D5 Amfissa Greece
63 P4 Amga Rus. Fed.
63 P3 Amga r. Rus. Fed.
63 P4 Amgun' r. Rus. Fed.
121 J2 Amherst U.S.A.
113 H4 Amherst U.S.A.
114 D5 Amherstburg Can.
100 D3 Amherst, Mt h. Aust.
51 N6 Amahan N. Korea
78 E4 Amiens r. Dem. Rep. Congo
60 E3 Amij, Wādī w Iraq
146 C2 Amincha Arg.
29 C5 Amfilochia Greece
21 F2 Amiens France
56 A4 Amindivi Islands is India
56 M4 Aminuis Namibia
29 C5 Amīndelta Dem. Rep. Congo
141 H5 'Amīr, Amir Chah Pakistan
147 H5 Amirante Islands is Seychelles
147 H5 Amirante Trench sea feature Indian Ocean
10 E2 Amli Norway
17 C5 Amlwch U.K.
60 C3 'Ammān Jordan
10 G2 Ämmänsaari Finland
10 E2 Ammarnäs Sweden
43 C4 Ammassalik Greenland
18 F2 Amalme well Mali
61 C4 Ammōchostos Cyprus
61 C4 Ammōchostos Bay b. Cyprus
83 H2 Ampasimanolotra Madagascar

20 E4 Ambazac France
18 E4 Amberg Germany
133 G2 Ambergris Cays is Turks and Caicos Is Caribbean
21 G4 Ambérieu-en-Bugey France
94 C4 Amberley N.Z.
21 F4 Ambert France
76 B4 Ambidédi Mali
55 E5 Ambikapur India
83 H3 Ambila Madagascar
83 H3 Ambilobe Madagascar
83 H3 Ambinanindrano Madagascar
80 D3 Ambition, Mt mt. Can.
18 B3 Amblève r. Belgium
140 A2 Ambo Peru
83 H3 Amboasary Madagascar
83 H3 Ambodifotatra Madagascar
83 H3 Ambodimanga Madagascar
83 H3 Ambohimahasoa Madagascar
83 H1 Ambohitra mt. Madagascar
83 H2 Ambohipaky Madagascar
83 H3 Ambohitralanana Madagascar
20 E3 Amboise France
39 J7 Ambon Indon.
39 J7 Ambon Indon.
83 H3 Ambondromampy Madagascar
81 C6 Amboseli National Park nat. park Kenya
83 H3 Ambositra Madagascar
83 H3 Ambovombe Madagascar
83 H2 Amboy U.S.A.
128 D4 Amboy U.S.A.
122 C5 Amboy U.S.A.
18 D5 Amboy Center U.S.A.
81 ¨4 Ambre, Isle d' i. Mauritius
79 B5 Ambriz Angola
91 J1 Ambrym i. Vanuatu
40 C3 Ambrim Indon.
80 C3 Ambur India
54 B4 Amderma Chad
62 H2 Amderma Rus. Fed.
73 H3 Amdilis well Saudi Arabia
72 C5 Am Djémena Chad
54 D2 Amdo China
42 B3 Ameca Mexico
131 F5 Amecameca Mexico
18 B2 Ameland i. Netherlands
120 E4 American Court House U.S.A.
126 D3 American Falls U.S.A.
126 D3 American Falls Res. resr U.S.A.
126 E3 American Fork U.S.A.
87 L6 American Samoa terr. Pac. Oc.
119 C5 Americus U.S.A.
18 C2 Amersfoort Netherlands
111 J1 Amery Can.
152 D5 Amery Ice Shelf ice feature Ant.
124 E3 Ames U.S.A.
121 H3 Amesbury U.S.A.
54 C4 Amet India
29 E5 Amethi U.S.A.
29 C5 Amfilochia Greece
29 D5 Amfissa Greece
63 P4 Amga Rus. Fed.

152 C5 Amundsen, Mt mt. Ant.
152 A2 Amundsen Sea sea Ant.
152 A2 Amundsen-Scott U.S.A. Base Ant.
40 C2 Amuntai Indon.
49 H1 Amur r. Rus. Fed.
45 P2 Amursk Rus. Fed.
21 F4 Ambert France
29 C5 Amvrakikos Kolpos b. Greece
13 F6 Amvrosiyivka Ukraine
29 C5 Amyntaio Greece
114 C2 Amyot Can.
42 A3 Am-Zoer Chad
42 A3 An Myanmar
29 C5 Ana r. Turkey
140 A2 Anabanua Indon.
63 N2 Anabar r. Rus. Fed.
63 N2 Anabarskiy Zaliv b. Rus. Fed.
83 H3 Anadia Brazil
15 C5 Andriyivka Kharkiv Ukraine
15 G5 Andriyivka Zaporizhzhya Ukraine
142 B2 Anadolu Dağları mt. ra. Turkey
128 A3 Anadyr' r. Rus. Fed.
63 T3 Anadyr' Rus. Fed.
63 T3 Anadyrskiy Zaliv b. Rus. Fed.
29 E6 Anafi i. Greece
60 E3 'Ānah Iraq
128 D5 Anaheim U.S.A.
110 E4 Anahim Lake Can.
54 C4 Anaimalai Hills mts India
54 C4 Anai Mudi Pk mt. India
142 C3 Anajás Brazil
142 C2 Anajás, Ilha i. Brazil
77 F3 Anéfis Mali
83 H3 Analalava Madagascar
83 H3 Analavelona mts Madagascar
142 A2 Anamã Brazil
139 H4 Anambé div. Nigeria
77 F5 Anambra div. Nigeria
123 F4 Anamosa U.S.A.
60 C2 Anamur Turkey
60 C2 Anamur Br. pt Turkey
46 C6 Anan Japan
54 B5 Anand India
55 F5 Anandapur India
54 C2 Anantapur India
54 B4 Anantnag India
13 D5 Anan'yiv Ukraine
13 F6 Anapa Rus. Fed.
145 C1 Anápolis Brazil
57 C2 Anār Iran
57 C2 Anārak Iran
57 G2 Anasco Puerto Rico
39 M3 Anatahan i. Northern Mariana Is Pac. Oc.
60 B2 Anatolia reg. Turkey
131 H6 Anatoliki Makedonia kai Thraki div. Greece
80 C2 Añgerweh Wenz r. Ethiopia
90 ¨2 Anatom i. Vanuatu
146 D2 Añatuya Arg.
146 C3 Anauá r. Brazil
19 G2 Angermünde Germany
11 C4 Ånge Sweden
131 F4 Angel, Pto Mexico
83 H3 Angeles Phil.
138 B2 Angel Falls waterfall Venezuela
11 C4 Ängelholm Sweden
99 J2 Angellala Cr. r. Aust.

83 G3 Andranopasy Madagascar
83 H3 Andranovondronina Madagascar
83 H3 Andranovory Madagascar
83 H1 Andravida Greece
61 H1 An Nabk Saudi Arabia
60 H3 An Nabk Syria
73 H2 An Nafūd desert Saudi Arabia
104 A4 Andreanof Is U.S.A.
14 A1 Andreapol' Rus. Fed.
78 D2 Andre Felix, Parc National de nat. park C.A.R.
145 F4 André Fernandes Brazil
145 E4 Andrelândia Brazil
145 F4 Andrequicé Brazil
125 C5 Andrews U.S.A.
65 K3 Andreyevka Kazak.
14 E2 Andreyevo Rus. Fed.
65 H1 Andreyevskoye Rus. Fed.
27 F5 Andria Italy
83 H2 Androna reg. Madagascar
14 D3 Androniki Rus. Fed.
21 H3 Annemasse France
29 E6 Andros i. Greece
132 C1 Andros i. The Bahamas
121 H3 Androscoggin r. U.S.A.
132 C1 Andros Town The Bahamas
56 A4 Āndrott i. India
15 C1 Andrushivka Ukraine
19 J4 Andrychów Poland
10 E1 Andselv Norway
24 D2 Andújar Spain
79 C6 Andulo Angola
133 ¨3 Anegada i. Virgin Is Caribbean
133 ¨3 Anegada Passage chan. Virgin Is Caribbean
147 C6 Anegada, Bahía b. Arg.
63 P4 Anegan U.S.A.
77 E5 Aného Togo
78 B4 Anenguié, Lac l. Gabon
15 C2 Anenii Noi Moldova
21 H2 Aneth U.S.A.
77 G3 Anfile Bay b. Eritrea
51 H4 Anfu China
73 G3 'Anezah mt. Iraq/Saudi Arabia
98 B2 Angalarri r. Aust.
63 L4 Angara r. Rus. Fed.
48 D1 Angarsk Rus. Fed.
48 D1 Angarsk Rus. Fed.
144 B5 Angatuba Brazil
146 D5 Angaur U.S.A.
29 C7 Ano Viannos Greece
51 E4 Anpu Gang b. China
45 J3 Anren China
83 H1 Anosibe An'Ala Madagascar
83 H1 Ao Sawi b. Thailand
10 E1 Andselv Norway

83 H1 Antsirañana div. Madagascar
83 H1 Antsirañana Madagascar
83 H1 Antsohihy Madagascar
10 F2 Anttis Sweden
10 F2 Anttola Finland
146 B4 Antuco Chile
141 D2 Antuerpia Brazil
80 D1 Antufush I. i. Yemen
18 B3 Antwerpen Belgium
91 ¨10 Anuanu Raro i. Fr. Poly. Pac. Oc.
112 E2 Anuc, Lac l. Can.
55 F5 Anugul India
56 C4 Anuppur India
56 C4 Anuradhapura Sri Lanka
57 C4 Anveh Iran
51 E3 Anxi China
50 D2 An Xian China
51 E3 Anxi China
49 E5 Anxiang China
50 D2 Anxue China
40 A3 Anyar Indon.
55 E4 Anydros i. Greece
50 E3 A'nyêmaqên Shan mt. ra. China
51 F2 Anyi China
51 F3 Anyuan Jiangxi China
51 F3 Anyuan Jiangxi China
50 D2 Anyue China
62 H4 Anzhero-Sudzhensk Rus. Fed.
27 D5 Anzio Italy
90 ¨2 Aoba i. Vanuatu
49 F4 Aohan Qi China
46 E3 Aomori Japan
26 A3 Aosta Italy
93 B6 Aoraki mt. N.Z.
93 E4 Aorangi Mts mts N.Z.
90 ¨2 Aorere r. N.Z.
26 A3 Aosta Italy
25 H3 Aoste France
40 C3 Aouderas Niger
74 ¨3 Aouhinet bel Egra well Algeria
78 D2 Aouk-Aoakole, Réserve de Faune de l' res. C.A.R.
74 C4 Aoukâr reg. Mali/Mauritania
74 C4 Aoulef Algeria
74 C3 Aoulime, Jbel mt. Morocco
46 E4 Aoya Japan
50 A4 Aoxi China
42 C4 Apa r. Uganda
129 H6 Apache Creek U.S.A.
129 G5 Apache Junction U.S.A.
129 G6 Apache Peak summit U.S.A.
144 D1 Apahida Romania
144 C4 Apaiaí r. Brazil
81 ¨2 Apaiang atoll Kiribati
131 H5 Apalachee Bay b. U.S.A.
119 C6 Apalachicola U.S.A.
131 H5 Apan Mexico
124 D3 Anson U.S.A.
144 C4 Aparecida do Tabuado Brazil
93 B6 Aparima r. N.Z.
42 C2 Aparri Phil.
29 C5 Apatin Yugo.
62 E3 Apatity Rus. Fed.
130 D5 Apatzingán Mexico
11 G4 Ape Latvia
18 F3 Apeldoorn Netherlands
18 F2 Apen Germany
140 E4 Api mt. Nepal
91 ¨12 Apia Western Samoa
15 D1 Apia Ukraine
90 ¨1 Apinipan Solomon Is
92 E3 Apiti N.Z.
144 C3 Apodi Brazil
142 E2 Apodi r. Brazil
18 E3 Apolda Germany
96 C3 Apollo Bay Aust.
140 D3 Apolo Bolivia
119 D6 Apopka, L. l. U.S.A.
144 D2 Aporé Brazil
144 B1 Aporé r. Brazil
122 B2 Apostle Islands National Lakeshore res. U.S.A.
146 E2 Apóstoles Arg.
133 ¨5 Apostolos Andreas, C. hd Cyprus
15 E3 Apostolove Ukraine
139 J3 Apoteri Guyana
124 C4 Appalachia U.S.A.
120 C6 Appalachian Mountains mt. ra. U.S.A.
26 E4 Appennino mt. ra. Italy
22 E2 Appennino mt. ra. Italy
26 D3 Appennino Abruzzese mt. ra. Italy
27 D4 Appennino Lucano mt. ra. Italy
26 C4 Appennino Tosco-Emiliano mts Italy
26 D4 Appennino Umbro-Marchigiano mt. ra. Italy
17 F4 Appleby-in-Westmorland U.K.
16 ¨1 Applecross U.K.
124 E4 Apple Valley U.S.A.
139 G3 Approuague r. French Guiana
41 F4 Apra Harb. inlet Guam Pac. Oc.
41 ¨2 Apra Heights Guam Pac. Oc.
14 D5 Aprelevka Rus. Fed.
26 E4 Aprilia Italy
14 A1 Apsley Str. chan. Can.
21 G5 Apt France
144 B5 Apucarana Brazil
144 A5 Apucarana, Serra da h. Brazil
144 A5 Apuau r. N.Z.
144 A2 Apuí Brazil
145 C5 Apuiarés Brazil
41 A4 Apurahuan Phil.
140 C2 Apurimac r. Peru
138 C2 Apure r. Venezuela
60 G5 'Aqaba Jordan
61 C6 'Aqaba, Gulf of chan. Africa/Asia
57 B2 'Aqdā Iran
100 E3 Aqdoghmish r. Iran
73 H3 Aqla well Saudi Arabia
55 G3 Aqqikkol Hu salt l. China
129 G3 Aquarius Mts mts U.S.A.
129 G3 Aquarius Plateau plat. U.S.A.

B

27 F5 Aquaviva delle Fonti Italy
141 E4 Aquidabán mi r.
12 J3 Aquidauana r. Brazil
141 E3 Aquidauana r. Brazil
143 A5 Aquidauana Brazil
130 E5 Aquila Mexico
142 E1 Aquiraz Brazil
131 F4 Aquismón Mexico
20 D4 Aquitaine div. France
55 F4 Ara Jap.
25 G1 Ara r. Sudan
80 D3 Ära Ärba Ethiopia
57 F3 Arab r. Afghanistan
119 C5 Arab U.S.A.
50 D2 'Arabābād Iran
80 D3 Ara Bacalle well Ethiopia
139 E3 Arabelo Venezuela
149 J3 Arabian Basin Indian Ocean
149 J2 Arabian Sea sea Indian Ocean
139 E2 Arabopó Venezuela
60 C1 Araç Turkey
139 E3 Araça r. Brazil
142 E3 Aracaju Brazil
61 C4 'Arad Israel
72 D5 Arad Romania
72 D5 Arada Chad
39 K8 Arafura Sea sea Aust./Indonesia
144 B1 Araçarçás Brazil
47 H5 Aragats Lerr mt. Armenia
47 G5 Ara-gawa r. Japan
25 F1 Aragón r. Spain
25 E2 Aragón div. Spain
27 D7 Aragona Italy
142 C2 Aragoncillo mt. Spain
142 C2 Araguacema Brazil
142 C2 Araguaçu Brazil
139 E2 Aragua de Barcelona Venezuela
142 C2 Araguaia r. Brazil
142 B3 Araguaia, Braço Menor do r. Brazil
142 B3 Araguaia, Parque Nacional de nat. park Brazil
142 C2 Araguaína Brazil
142 B2 Araguana Brazil
133 G5 Araguapiche, Pta pt Venezuela
139 G3 Araguari r. Amapá Brazil
144 D3 Araguari r. Minas Gerais Brazil
142 C2 Araguatins Brazil
74 C5 Arāgūbh reg. Mali/Mauritania
13 H7 Aragvi r. Georgia
47 G5 Arai Japan
142 E1 Araioses Brazil
75 E3 Arak Algeria
57 B2 Arāk Iran
61 □1 Arakabesan i. Palau
133 G6 Arakaka Guyana
42 A3 Arakan div. Myanmar
42 A3 Arakan Yoma mt. ra. Myanmar
47 □2 Arakawa Japan
92 J3 Arakihi h. N.Z.
56 B3 Arakkonam India
64 E4 Aral Sea salt l. Asia
64 F3 Aral'sk Kazak.
64 D3 Aralsor, Ozero salt l. Zapadno-Kazakhstan Kazak.
64 C3 Aralsor, Ozero l. Zapadno-Kazakhstan Kazak.
64 F3 Aralsul'fat Kazak.
99 F4 Aramac r. Aust.
99 F4 Aramac w. Aust.
144 C3 Aramberri Mexico
90 □1 Aramia r. P.N.G.
56 B1 Aran r. India
146 C3 Arancibia Arg.
24 E2 Aranda de Duero Spain
72 C4 Aranđelovac Yugo.
17 F5 Aran Fawddwy h. U.K.
56 B3 Arani India
17 C4 Aran Islands i. Rep. of Ire.
17 C5 Aran Islands i. Rep. of Ire.
24 E2 Aranjuez Spain
82 B3 Aranos Namibia
125 D7 Aransas Pass U.S.A.
144 C3 Arantes r. Brazil
46 C7 Arao Japan
76 D3 Araouane Mali
75 D2 Arapahoe U.S.A.
93 E4 Arapawa i. N.Z.
146 E3 Arapey Grande r. Uruguay
142 E2 Arapiraca Brazil
60 D2 Arapkir Turkey
142 C2 Arapongas Brazil
142 D4 Arapoti Brazil
55 F4 A Rapti Doon r. Nepal
144 B4 Arapuá Brazil
92 E3 Arapuni N.Z.
143 G2 Araquari Brazil
143 G1 Arara Brazil
138 C4 Araracuara Colombia
143 D5 Araranguá Brazil
144 D4 Araraquara Brazil
142 B2 Araras Pará Brazil
143 C4 Araras São Paulo Brazil
60 F2 Ararat Aust.
97 F4 Ararat Aust.
142 E1 Arari Brazil
55 F4 Arari India
142 C1 Arari, Lago l. Brazil
142 D2 Araripina Brazil
145 D5 Araruama Brazil
143 D5 Araruama, Lago de lag. Brazil
60 E4 'Ar'ar, Wādī w Iraq/Saudi Arabia
60 E4 'Ar'ar Saudi Arabia
48 C2 Ar Asgat Mongolia
132 J5 Arasji Aruba Caribbean
131 E5 Arataca Mexico
130 D2 Arataúi r. Brazil
138 C3 Arauca Colombia
133 D4 Araúca r. Venezuela
146 B4 Arauco Chile
138 C2 Arauquita Colombia
21 H1 Aravis mts France
90 □1 Arawa P.N.G.
92 F3 Arawhana mt. N.Z.
143 C4 Araxá Minas Gerais Brazil
139 E1 Araya, Pta de pt Venezuela
133 F5 Araya, Pta de pt Venezuela
60 E2 Araz r. Azerbaijan/Iran
13 J7 Ara-zaki c. Japan
49 E5 Arbagar Rus. Fed.

80 C3 Árba Minch Ethiopia
60 F3 Arbat r. Iraq
12 J3 Arbazh Rus. Fed.
14 G2 Arbekovo Rus. Fed.
60 F3 Arbil Iraq
11 D4 Arboga Sweden
21 D4 Arbois France
16 F3 Arbroath U.K.
111 J4 Arborfield Can.
118 A2 Arbuckle U.S.A.
15 D3 Arbuzynka Ukraine
20 D4 Arcachon France
119 D7 Arcadia U.S.A.
126 A3 Arcata U.S.A.
128 D2 Arc Dome summit U.S.A.
131 E6 Arcelia Mexico
29 G6 Archangelos Greece
99 F3 Archer r. Aust.
99 F2 Archer Bend Nat. Park nat. park Aust.
129 H2 Arches Nat. Park nat. park U.S.A.
76 H2 Arch Henda well Mali
21 D4 Arc-sur-Aube France
96 C1 Arckaringa w Aust.
12 G1 Arkhangel'sk Rus. Fed.
15 G3 Arkhangel'skoye Ukraine
15 E3 Arkhanhel's'ke Ukraine
49 J2 Arkhara r. Rus. Fed.
17 D5 Arklow Rep. of Ire.
29 F6 Arkoi i. Greece
14 F1 Arkhipovka Rus. Fed.
18 E1 Arkona, Kap hd Germany
62 J1 Arkticheskogo Instituta, Ostrova is Rus. Fed.
121 F3 Arkville U.S.A.
21 F4 Arlanc France
21 G5 Arles France
77 E4 Arli Burkina
126 B2 Arlington U.S.A.
124 D2 Arlington U.S.A.
122 A4 Arlington Heights U.S.A.
77 F3 Arlit Niger
18 B4 Arlon Belgium
21 H4 Arly r. France
78 F3 Aru Zaire
41 C5 Armadores i. Indon.
17 D4 Armagh U.K.
61 □5 Armant' Egypt
21 G3 Armançon r. France
73 F2 Armant Egypt
29 F7 Armathia i. Greece
13 G6 Armavir r. Rus. Fed.
13 G6 Armavir Rus. Fed.
138 B3 Armenia Colombia
60 E1 Armenia country Asia
138 C3 Armero Colombia
29 B4 Armidale Bulgaria
111 L2 Armit Lake l. Can.
65 G1 Armizonskoye Rus. Fed.
54 E5 Armori India
110 B3 Armour, Mt mt. Can./U.S.A.
98 B3 Armstrong r. Aust.
110 F4 Armstrong Can.
114 A1 Armstrong Can.
56 B2 Armur India
15 E3 Armyans'k Ukraine
20 E3 Arnac r. France
29 C4 Arnaia Greece
61 B2 Arnaoutis, C. hd Cyprus
10 □2 Arnarfjörður b. Iceland
21 G3 Arnay-le-Duc France
17 C4 Arnaud r. Can.
54 B2 Arnawai Pak.
21 G3 Arnay-le-Duc France
13 H7 Ar-Rass Saudi Arabia
24 E2 Ar Rastan Syria
49 J2 Ar Rawdah Yemen
73 H3 Ar Rawdah Saudi Arabia
73 H3 Ar Rawnah Saudi Arabia
57 D7 Ar Rayyān Qatar
128 D4 Argus Range mts U.S.A.
57 B4 Ar Rifā'ī Iraq
138 D3 Arrecife Canary Is Spain
25 □ Arrecifes Canary Is Spain
146 D3 Arrecifes Arg.
20 B2 Arrée, Monts d'h.
14 J5 Ar Horqin Qi China
11 A5 Aria Denmark
92 E3 Aria N.Z.
82 B4 Ariake-b. Namibia
138 D3 Ariano Irpino Italy
138 C2 Ariari r. Colombia
53 D10 Ari Atoll Atoll Maldives
142 A1 Ariaú Brazil
140 B3 Arica Chile
138 C4 Arica Peru
140 D3 Arida r. Brazil
47 H3 Arida Japan
21 G4 Ariège r. France
29 E5 Arigni Gol r. Mongolia
126 B2 Arikaree r. U.S.A.

141 D1 Aripuanã Brazil
141 D1 Aripuanã r. Brazil
144 B2 Ariranhá r. Brazil
61 B4 'Arīsh, W. el w Egypt
133 E5 Arismendi Venezuela
131 G6 Arista, Pto Mexico
110 D4 Aristazabal I. i. Can.
147 C6 Aristizábal, c. pt Arg.
129 G4 Arizona div. U.S.A.
130 C2 Arizpe Mexico
40 C3 Arjasa Indon.
10 E2 Arjeplog Sweden
138 B1 Arjona Colombia
24 D4 Arjona Spain
40 □2 Arjuna, G. vol Indon.
11 H4 Arkadak Rus. Fed.
125 E5 Arkadelphia U.S.A.
17 L6 Arkaig, Loch l. U.K.
65 G2 Arkalyk Kazak.
125 E5 Arkansas r. U.S.A.
125 E5 Arkansas div. U.S.A.
125 F5 Arkansas City U.S.A.
55 G1 Arkatag Shan mt. ra. China
72 D3 Arkenu, Jabal mt. Libya
21 D4 Arkhangel'sk div. Rus. Fed.
15 K3 Arthur Can.
120 C4 Arthur, Lake l. U.S.A.
93 G4 Arthur Pt pt Aust.
93 C5 Arthur's Pass pass N.Z.
93 C5 Arthur's Pass National Park nat. park N.Z.
132 D1 Arthur's Town The Bahamas
64 E1 Arti Rus. Fed.
152 B1 Artigas Uruguay Base Ant.
60 E1 Art'ik Armenia
90 □2 Art, Île i. Pac. Oc.
111 H2 Artillery Lake l. Can.
21 F4 Artois reg. France
25 G5 Artrutx, Cap d' pt Spain
48 B3 Arts Bogd Uul mts Mongolia
28 G2 Artsyz Ukraine
65 J5 Artux China
60 E1 Artvin Turkey
78 E3 Aru Zaire
80 B4 Arua Uganda
133 E4 Aruba i. Caribbean
25 □ Arucas Canary Is Spain
20 D5 Arudy France
39 K8 Aru, Kepulauan is Indon.
139 E4 Arumã Brazil
67 C2 Arume Japan
49 G2 Arun r. Rus. Fed.
55 F4 Arun r. Nepal
55 H4 Arunachal Pradesh div. India
49 G2 Arun Qi China
13 J6 Aruppukkottai India
81 C5 Arusha Tanzania
81 C5 Arusha div. Tanzania
40 E1 Arus, Tg pt Indon.
40 B2 Arut r. Indon.
78 E3 Aruwimi r. Zaire
124 B4 Arvada U.S.A.
48 C2 Arvayheer Mongolia
55 F4 Arvi India
111 L2 Arviat Can.
10 E2 Arvidsjaur Sweden
11 D4 Arvika Sweden
128 C3 Arvin U.S.A.
49 E3 Arxan China
63 D2 Ary r. Rus. Fed.
64 G4 Arykbalyk Kazak.
64 G4 Arys' r. Kazak.
64 G4 Arys' Kazak.
65 H4 Arys, Oz. salt l. Kazak.
27 B5 Arzachena Italy
14 G2 Arzamas Rus. Fed.
14 F2 Arzgir Rus. Fed.
73 G5 'Asab Eritrea
60 D4 Aş Şafirah Syria
73 H4 As Safirah Syria
54 B4 As Sabkhah Syria
73 H4 Aş Şabyā Saudi Arabia
60 F4 As Safirah Syria
42 D1 Asadābād Afghanistan
57 B3 Asadābād Iran
54 C2 Asadābād Hamadan Iran
57 B2 Asadābād Khordsān Iran
43 B7 Asahan r. Indon.
46 J2 Asahi r. Japan
46 J2 Asahi-dake vol Japan
46 G6 Asahi-dake mt. Japan
46 J2 Asahikawa Japan
46 H5 Asaka Japan
74 B5 Asaka Uzbekistan
76 D5 Asamankese Ghana
47 G5 Asama-yama vol Japan
77 F4 Asankranguaa Ghana
76 D5 Asan Man b. S. Korea
55 G5 Asansol India
93 □12 Asau Western Samoa
64 F1 Asbest Rus. Fed.
115 F4 Asbestos Can.
124 B4 Asbury Park U.S.A.
55 D4 Ascension Bolivia
130 C2 Ascension Mexico
132 □2 Ascension Curaçao Netherlands Ant.
131 J5 Ascensión, B. de la b. Mexico
18 D4 Aschaffenburg Germany
18 C3 Aschersleben Germany
27 E4 Ascoli Piceno Italy
27 E4 Ascoli Satriano Italy
27 B6 Ascope Peru
140 C3 Ascotán, S. de mt. Chile
80 D3 Åsdabot mt. Ethiopia
80 D2 Aseb Eritrea
29 D5 Asedjrad plat. Algeria
10 E2 Åsele Sweden
72 D4 Asenovgrad Bulgaria
18 D2 Aşfāk Turkey
57 D2 Ashanti div. Ghana
62 C4 Ashburn U.S.A.
76 D3 Ashburton w. Aust.
93 C5 Ashburton r. N.Z.
65 J5 Ashchikol', salt l. Kazak.
125 D4 Ashdown U.S.A.
11 E3 Ashdod Israel
119 D5 Ashdown U.S.A.
125 E5 Asheville U.S.A.
93 □1 Asheweig r. Can.
93 F2 Ashford Aust.
73 H4 Ash Fork U.S.A.
73 H4 Ash Fork U.S.A.
57 F2 Ashgabat Turkmenistan
59 B5 Ashibetsu Japan
47 H5 Ashikaga Japan
47 H3 Ashiro Japan
46 D7 Ashizuri-misaki c. Japan

97 G2 Ashley Aust.
93 D5 Ashley r. N.Z.
124 D2 Ashley U.S.A.
91 □1 Atā'ita, J. el mt. Jordan
61 C4 Ashmūn Egypt
54 D4 Ashoknagar India
46 J2 Ashoro Japan
129 H5 Ash Peak U.S.A.
61 C4 Ashqelon Israel
73 H4 Ash Shabakah Iraq
60 E3 Ash Shaddādah Syria
73 H3 Ash Sha'rā' Saudi Arabia
80 D1 Ash Sharafī Yemen
57 C4 Ash Shāriqah U.A.E.
61 D3 Ash Sharqāt Iraq
73 G4 Ash Shaykh 'Uthmān Yemen
59 G7 Ash Shiḥr Yemen
60 F4 Ash Shinăfīyah Iraq
57 D4 Ash Shināş Oman
73 H2 Ash Shu'aybah Saudi Arabia
73 H4 Ash Shuqayq Saudi Arabia
72 B2 Ash Shuwayrif Libya
120 C4 Ashtabula U.S.A.
60 F1 Ashtarak Armenia
54 D5 Ashti India
56 A2 Ashti India
57 C3 Ashtiān Iran
126 E2 Ashton U.S.A.
109 M4 Ashuanipi Lake l. Can.
119 C5 Ashville U.S.A.
61 D3 'Āşī r. Lebanon/Syria
61 D1 'Āsī r. Turkey
130 E4 Asientos Mexico
56 D2 Asika India
17 C5 Asilah Morocco
115 H4 Asinara, Isola i. Italy
54 C4 Asind India
62 K4 Asino Rus. Fed.
12 D4 Asipovichy Belarus
73 H4 Asīr r. Saudi Arabia
60 E2 Aşkale Turkey
15 E3 Askaniya Nova Ukraine
11 C4 Askersund Sweden
13 G6 Askino Rus. Fed.
54 E3 Askot India
11 B4 Askøy i. Norway
11 B4 Askvoll Norway
61 B5 Asl Egypt
73 H3 Aslam, W. w Saudi Arabia
60 C1 Asmara Eritrea
73 G5 Asmera Eritrea
11 D4 Åsnen l. Sweden
140 B3 Atico Peru
17 C5 Athenry Rep. of Ire.
115 H4 Athens U.S.A.
119 C5 Athens U.S.A.
120 A5 Athens U.S.A.
125 E5 Athens U.S.A.
99 F3 Atherton Aust.
43 H3 Athi r. Kenya
28 D5 Athina Greece
56 A2 Athni India
93 B6 Athol N.Z.
121 G3 Athol U.S.A.
119 D7 Athol, The Bahamas
16 F3 Atholl, Forest of reg. U.K.
28 C4 Athos mt. Greece
17 E4 Athy Rep. of Ire.
77 D3 Ati Chad
81 D5 Atiak Uganda
145 G2 Atibaia Brazil
125 E4 Atichamba Mexico
140 B3 Atico Peru
24 D2 Atienza Spain
73 G4 Atiedo Sudan
91 □11 Atimaono Fr. Poly. Pac. Oc.
86 M7 Atiu i. Cook Islands
63 R3 Atka Rus. Fed.
13 G4 Atkarsk r. Rus. Fed.
13 G5 Atkarsk Rus. Fed.
125 E5 Atlanta U.S.A.
123 E3 Atlanta U.S.A.
124 D3 Atlantic U.S.A.
121 F5 Atlantic City U.S.A.
149 H5 Atlantic-Indian Antarctic Basin Atlantic Ocean
148 K9 Atlantic-Indian Ridge Indian Ocean
60 C2 Atlanti Turkey
125 E5 Atlanta U.S.A.
75 E1 Atlas Saharien mt. ra. Algeria
75 E1 Atlas Tellien mt. ra. Algeria
110 C2 Atlin Can.
110 C3 Atlin Lake l. Can.
110 C3 Atlin Prov. Park Can.
61 C4 At Tafilah Jordan
72 C2 Attapa Libya
111 M4 Attawapiskat Can.
114 C1 Attawapiskat r. Can.
114 C1 Attawapiskat L. l. Can.
73 H3 At Taysiyah plat. Saudi Arabia
27 E4 Attersee l. Austria
29 C5 Attica U.S.A.
122 C5 Attica U.S.A.
29 D5 Attiki div. Greece
120 A5 Attleboro U.S.A.
54 C2 Attock Pakistan
42 A3 Attu India
150 G2 Attu Island i. U.S.A.
54 E6 Attur India
56 B3 Attur India
80 C2 Ātu Tuwwayih well Saudi Arabia

61 B5 Atairtir el Dahami, G. mt. Egypt
124 D2 Ashley U.S.A.
120 E3 Auburn U.S.A.
99 G5 Auburn Ra. h. Aust.
91 □1 Atairt Fr. Poly. Pac. Oc.
54 A4 Ashmūn Egypt
73 H4 Ata Xang La pass China
77 E5 Atakpamé Togo
142 E2 Atalaia Brazil
138 C4 Atalaia do Norte Brazil
60 E3 Atalanti Greece
130 K8 Atalaya Panama
140 B2 Atalaya Peru
145 H3 Atáléia Brazil
48 E2 Atamanovka Rus. Fed.
42 B3 Ataran r. Myanmar
129 H4 Atarque U.S.A.
73 H3 Atasu Kazak.
90 H3 Atasu r. Kazak.
115 H4 Atascadero U.S.A.
73 G4 Atbara r. Sudan
73 G4 Atbara Sudan
65 G1 Atbasar Kazak.
125 E6 Atchafalaya b. U.S.A.
124 E4 Atchison U.S.A.
76 D5 Atebubu Ghana
25 E2 Ateca Spain
27 E4 Atessa Italy
18 C3 Ath Belgium
108 G4 Athabasca r. Can.
110 G4 Athabasca Can.
111 H3 Athabasca, Lake l. Can.
28 E5 Athboy Rep. of Ire.
17 C5 Athenry Rep. of Ire.
115 H4 Athens U.S.A.
120 E3 Auburn U.S.A.
99 G5 Auburn Ra. h. Aust.
80 C3 Āwasa Ethiopia
80 D3 Āwash Ethiopia
47 G4 Awa-shima i. Japan
80 D3 Āwash National Park nat. park Ethiopia
140 C4 Auca Mahuida, Sa de mt. Arg.
140 C4 Aucanquilcha, Co mt. Chile
20 E5 Auch France
76 F4 Auchi Nigeria
92 E2 Auckland N.Z.
92 E2 Auckland div. N.Z.
145 H3 Auckland I. i. Auckland Is N.Z.
48 E2 Atamanovka Rus. Fed.
92 □1 Auckland I. i. N.Z.
114 E4 Auden Can.
121 F2 Audet Can.
20 B2 Audierne France
20 B2 Audierne, Baie d' b. France
129 H4 Atarque U.S.A.
21 H3 Audincourt France
80 D3 Audo Range mt. h. Ethiopia
20 F1 Audruicq France
18 F3 Auersberg mt. Germany
99 F5 Augathella Aust.
21 F4 Aughrabies Falls waterfall R.S.A.
27 E7 Augusta Italy
121 J2 Augusta U.S.A.
125 D5 Augusta U.S.A.
122 B4 Augusta U.S.A.
123 B5 Augusta, Golfo di b. Italy
138 C1 Augustín Cadazzi Colombia
145 F3 Augusto de Lima Brazil
19 L2 Augustów Poland
100 D2 Augustus, L. l. Aust.
101 B5 Augustus, Mt mt. Aust.
21 F1 Aulnoye-Aymeries France
20 B2 Aulne r. France
91 □13 Aunu'u i. American Samoa Pac. Oc.
113 G2 Aupaluk Can.
57 F3 Aqcha Afghanistan
11 F3 Aura Finland
21 F4 Aura r. Finland
55 G4 Aurangābād India
56 A2 Aurangābād India
20 E4 Auray France
18 C2 Aurich Germany
144 C2 Auriflama Brazil
20 F4 Aurillac France
41 B5 Aurkuning Indon.
28 C3 Aurora Peru
139 E2 Aurora Surinam
126 F4 Aurora U.S.A.
125 F4 Aurora U.S.A.
124 C3 Aurora U.S.A.
122 C5 Aurora U.S.A.
99 E5 Aurukun Aust.
113 G2 Aupaluk Can.
82 A3 Aus Namibia
60 G2 Au Sable r. U.S.A.
120 E3 Au Sable Pt pt U.S.A.
122 E3 Au Sable Pt pt U.S.A.
11 B4 Aust-Agder div. Norway
10 □2 Austari-Jökulsá r. Iceland
122 A4 Austin U.S.A.
131 K5 Austin U.S.A.
125 D6 Austin U.S.A.
128 D2 Austin, L. salt flat Aust.
98 B4 Austral Downs Aust.
87 L7 Australes, Îles is Fr. Poly.
152 C6 Australia, I. i. Kerguelen Indian Ocean
149 J3 Australian Antarctic Territory reg. Ant.
97 G3 Australian Capital Territory reg. Ant.
10 D1 Austvågøy i. Norway
139 H4 Autazes Brazil
20 E3 Auterive France
20 E1 Authier r. France
20 E1 Authie r. France
130 E5 Autlán Mexico
21 G3 Autun France
20 G3 Auvergne reg. France
20 G3 Auvergne div. France
20 F2 Auxerre France
24 A4 Auxi-le-Château France
24 A4 Avaí r. Brazil
144 D2 Avaí Brazil
20 F2 Avallon France
145 D4 Avaré Brazil
55 F3 Avān Iran
91 □11 Avarua Cook Islands
119 □3 Avatiu r. Fr. Poly.
29 F6 Avcilar Turkey
29 D5 Avdira Greece
28 D4 Aveiro Brazil
24 B2 Aveiro Port.
24 B2 Aveiro div. Port.
57 B3 Āvej Iran
146 E3 Avellaneda Buenos Aires Arg.
146 E2 Avellaneda Santa Fe Arg.
27 E4 Avellino Italy
128 C4 Avenal U.S.A.
14 E3 Aversa Italy
126 C2 Avesta Sweden
11 D3 Avesta Sweden
21 G5 Aveyron r. France
27 E4 Avezzano Italy
16 F3 Aviemore U.K.
93 C6 Aviemore, L. l. N.Z.
27 E4 Avigliano Italy
21 G5 Avignon France
24 D2 Ávila Spain
24 D1 Avilés Spain
56 A4 Avinurme Estonia
24 B3 Avis Port.
21 G5 Avignon France
146 F3 Aviz Port.
72 D4 Avola Italy
27 E7 Avola Italy
121 E3 Avon r. U.K.
17 G6 Avon r. U.K.
124 C3 Avon U.S.A.
121 E3 Avon U.S.A.
129 E6 Avondale U.S.A.
126 D3 Avon Park U.S.A.
119 D6 Avon Park U.S.A.
20 D2 Avranches France
20 E2 Avre r. France
21 G3 Avrieux France
20 D2 Aubigny-sur-Nère France
14 A2 Avvil Fin.
60 F4 Awaji-shima i. Japan
47 G4 Awa-shima i. Japan
80 D3 Āwash West Wildlife Reserve res. Ethiopia
93 B6 Awarua Pt pt N.Z.
80 D4 Aw Dheegle Somalia
81 B4 Aweil Sudan
17 D4 Awe, Loch l. U.K.
76 F4 Awgu Nigeria
80 E2 Awssard Western Sahara
80 D4 Awo r. Indon.
74 B4 Awserd Western Sahara
80 C3 Āwasa Ethiopia

50 J6 Ba r. China
90 □8 Ba r. Fiji
90 □8 Ba r. Fiji
90 □2 Baábaa i. Pac. Oc.
40 D1 Baani r. Indon.
61 C3 Baalbek Lebanon
80 E3 Baardheere Somalia
54 D4 Bab India
74 B3 Bababé Mauritania
29 F5 Baba Burnu pt Turkey
28 G2 Babadag Romania
29 G6 Babadağ Turkey
57 D1 Babadurmaz Turkmenistan
142 C3 Babaçulândia Brazil
138 B4 Babahoyo Ecuador
138 B4 Babahoyo Ecuador
54 D5 Babai r. India
41 C5 Babar i. Indon.
39 J8 Babar i. Indon.
81 C5 Babati Tanzania
12 D4 Babayevo Rus. Fed.
13 H7 Babayurt Rus. Fed.
122 B2 Babbitt U.S.A.
41 □1 Babelthuap i. Palau
50 A3 Baber u India
12 F3 Baberu India
130 C2 Babiacora Mexico
130 D2 Babicora, L. de salt l. Mexico
90 D1 Bäbil div. Iraq
19 G2 Babimost Poland
110 D4 Babinda Aust.
39 K7 Babo Iran
110 D4 Babine r. Can.
110 D4 Babine Lake l. Can.
39 K7 Babo Indon.
57 B2 Bābol Iran
57 B2 Bābol Sar Iran
129 G6 Baboquivari Peak summit U.S.A.
77 G6 Baboua C.A.R.
12 C4 Babruysk Belarus
54 D3 Babstovo India
29 C4 Babuna Planina mt. ra. Macedonia
41 A5 Babu Indon.
41 B2 Babuyan i. Phil.
41 B2 Babuyan Channel chan. Phil.
41 B2 Babuyan Islands is Phil.
60 E3 Babylon Iraq
63 L3 Babyonga Rus. Fed.
80 D2 Bacaadweyn Somalia
142 E1 Bacabal Brazil
131 H5 Bacalar Mexico
41 C4 Bacan i. Indon.
72 D6 Băcău Romania
131 □3 Baccarat France
99 F3 Bacchus Marsh Aust.
42 D2 Bắc Giang Vietnam
42 D2 Bắc Kạn Vietnam
77 E4 Baco, mt. mt. Phil.
41 B3 Bacolod Phil.
131 H4 Bacqueville, Lac l. Can.
19 J5 Bácsalmás Hungary
54 B4 Bada India
80 D3 Bada mt. Ethiopia
41 B4 Bada i. Myanmar
42 A3 Badagara India
19 E2 Badajós Brazil
141 D2 Badajós Brazil
141 D2 Badajós, Lago l. Brazil
24 C3 Badajoz Spain
56 A3 Badami India
73 H1 Badanah Saudi Arabia
56 A4 Badarinath India
146 D3 Badavel Arg.
57 F2 Bādghīsāt div. Afghanistan
18 E3 Bad Berka Germany
18 D3 Bad Berleburg Germany
18 D3 Bad Bevensen Germany
113 J4 Baddeck Can.
18 E3 Bad Doberan Germany
18 D4 Bad Ems Germany
27 F2 Badén Switz.
146 E3 Baden-Baden Germany
18 D4 Baden-Württemberg div. Germany
19 G2 Bad Freienwalde Germany
72 E3 Badgastein Austria
113 J4 Badger Can.
18 E3 Bad Gleichenberg Austria
18 E3 Bad Harzburg Germany
18 E3 Bad Hersfeld Germany
18 E4 Bad Homburg vor der Höhe Germany
26 D2 Badia Polesine Italy
80 E3 Badiguera Swamp Somalia
130 C2 Badiraguato Mexico
18 E4 Bad Kissingen Germany
18 D4 Bad Kreuznach Germany
129 G2 Badlands reg. U.S.A.
124 C2 Badlands Nat. Park nat. park U.S.A.
18 E3 Bad Langensalza Germany
18 D4 Bad Lauterberg im Harz Germany
18 D4 Bad Mergentheim Germany
18 D4 Bad Nauheim Germany
18 D4 Bad Neuenahr-Ahrweiler Germany
18 E4 Bad Neustadt an der Saale Germany

156

54 C4 Badnor India
51 E2 Badong China
43 D5 Ba Đông Vietnam
77 E5 Badou Togo
64 C5 Bădovan Burnu pt Azerbaijan
28 B2 Badovinci Yugo.
18 D3 Bad Pyrmont Germany
60 F3 Badrah Iraq
18 F5 Bad Reichenhall Germany
73 G3 Badr Ḥunayn Saudi Arabia
54 D3 Badrinath Peaks mts India
19 G5 Bad St Leonhard im Lavanttal Austria
18 D2 Bad Salzuflen Germany
18 E3 Bad Salzungen Germany
18 D3 Bad Schwalbach Germany
18 E2 Bad Schwartau Germany
18 E2 Bad Segeberg Germany
95 H1 Badu I. i. Aust.
56 C5 Badulla Sri Lanka
18 D5 Bad Waldsee Germany
49 K2 Badzhal Rus. Fed.
18 D2 Bad Zwischenahn Germany
10 L2 Bæir Iceland
24 D4 Baena Spain
118 B4 Baeza Ecuador
24 E4 Baeza Spain
78 B2 Bafang Cameroon
76 B4 Bafatá Guinea-Bissau
54 C2 Baffa Pakistan
109 N2 Baffin Bay sea Can./Greenland
109 L2 Baffin Island i. Can.
78 B3 Bafia Cameroon
77 E5 Bafilo Togo
76 B4 Bafing r. Guinea/Mali
76 B4 Bafing, Parc National du nat. park Mali
61 D1 Bafliyun Syria
76 B4 Bafoulabé Mali
78 B2 Bafoussam Cameroon
57 C3 Bāfq Iran
60 C1 Bafra Turkey
60 C1 Bafra Burun pt Turkey
57 D3 Bāft Iran
78 E3 Bafwamboma Zaire
78 E3 Bafwasende Zaire
142 C3 Bagagem r. Brazil
55 E4 Bagaha India
56 A2 Bagalkot India
81 C6 Bagamoyo Tanzania
43 C7 Bagan Datuk Malaysia
82 C2 Bagani Namibia
41 B5 Baganian Peninsula pen. Phil.
43 C6 Bagan Serai Malaysia
43 C7 Bagansiapiapi Indon.
29 F6 Bağarası Turkey
77 F3 Bagaré well Niger
77 F3 Bagaroua Niger
75 G3 Bagata Zaire
50 B1 Bag Belqer China
129 F4 Bagdad U.S.A.
146 F3 Bagé Brazil
126 F3 Baggs U.S.A.
55 E4 Bagh India
60 F3 Baghdād Iraq
57 B3 Bāgh-e Malek Iran
27 C6 Bagheria Italy
57 H2 Bāghīn Iran
57 G2 Baghlān Afghanistan
57 F2 Baghlān Afghanistan
124 E2 Bagley U.S.A.
55 E3 Baglung Nepal
20 E5 Bagnères-de-Bigorre France
20 E5 Bagnères-de-Luchon France
26 C4 Bagno di Romagna Italy
21 G4 Bagnols-sur-Cèze France
55 F4 Bagmati r. Nepal
48 D5 Bas Nur I. China
41 B4 Bago Phil.
76 C4 Bagoé r. Côte d'Ivoire/Mali
11 F5 Bagrationovsk Rus. Fed.
142 B1 Bagre Brazil
138 B5 Bagua Grande Peru
77 E4 Bagudo Nigeria
41 B2 Baguio Phil.
77 E4 Bagzane, Monts mts Niger
55 E4 Bahadurganj Nepal
54 D3 Bahadrgarh India
104 L7 Bahamas, The country Caribbean
133 ¬4 Baham, Pte pt Martinique Caribbean
55 G4 Baharampur India
54 B4 Bahardipur Pakistan
73 E2 Bahariya Oasis oasis Egypt
43 C7 Bahau Malaysia
40 C2 Bahaur Indon.
54 C3 Bahawalnagar Pakistan
54 B3 Bahawalpur Pakistan
60 D2 Bahçe Turkey
81 C4 Baheri Tanzania
81 C6 Bahi Tanzania
145 H1 Bahia div. Brazil
146 D4 Bahía Blanca Arg.
130 J5 Bahia, Islas de la is Honduras
130 C2 Bahia Kino Mexico
147 C6 Bahía Laura Arg.
141 E4 Bahía Negra Paraguay
80 C2 Bahir Dar Ethiopia
57 B3 Bahmanyārī ye Pā'īn Iran
73 H4 Bahr Saudi Arabia
61 A4 Bahra el Burullus lag. Egypt
73 F1 Bahra el Manzala lag. Egypt
55 E4 Bahraich India
32 K7 Bahrain country Asia
57 B4 Bahrain, Gulf of g. Asia
55 E4 Bahramghat India
57 D3 Bahrāmjerd Iran
78 D2 Bahr Aouk r. C.A.R./Chad
61 D2 Bahrat Ḥimş resr Syria
72 D5 Bahr el Arab w Chad
72 D5 Bahr el Azraq w Chad
78 C5 Bahr Bola w Chad
80 B2 Bahr Dosséo r. Chad
78 E1 Bahr el Abiad r. Sudan/Uganda
78 H1 Bahr el Arab w Sudan
80 C2 Bahr el Ghazal r. Chad
78 E2 Bahr el Ghazal div. Sudan
80 B3 Bahr el Jebel r. Sudan/Uganda
78 C2 Bahr Kéita r. Chad
54 C4 Bahr Korom w Chad
80 B2 Bahr Salamat r. Chad
61 D3 Baḥret Yaqqal I. Syria
61 A5 Bahr Yūsef r. Egypt
51 F1 Bai China
28 D2 Baia Romania
28 D2 Baia de Aramă Romania

28 D1 Baia de Arieş Romania
142 F2 Baia de Traição Brazil
79 B7 Baia dos Tigres Angola
28 D1 Baia Mare Romania
142 C1 Baião Brazil
28 D1 Baia Sprie Romania
57 C2 Bājgīrān Iran
72 D4 Baïbokoum Chad
78 C2 Baïbokoum Chad
65 K4 Baicheng China
49 G3 Baicheng China
49 G3 Baicheng China
28 D2 Baile Herculane Romania
24 E3 Bailén Spain
28 D2 Băileşti Romania
28 E2 Băile Tuşnad Romania
101 C6 Bailey R. b. Aust.
133 D3 Bailique Brazil
111 H2 Baillie r. Can.
133 D3 Baillif Guadeloupe Caribbean
50 C1 Bailong r. China
79 C6 Bailundo Angola
50 C1 Baima China
119 C6 Bainbridge U.S.A.
121 F3 Bainbridge U.S.A.
20 D3 Bain-de-Bretagne France
133 D3 Bainet Haiti
55 G3 Baingoin China
24 B1 Baiona Spain
49 H3 Baiquan China
50 E2 Baisha Co I. China
51 E5 Baisha China
51 E5 Baisha China
49 H4 Baishan China
51 E5 Baishui r. China
49 F4 Baishui r. China
11 F5 Baisogala Lithuania
11 G3 Baisong Guan pass China
42 D3 Bai Thương Vietnam
49 F4 Baitle r. China
28 E2 Baixa de Banheira Portugal
29 G3 Baixingt China
80 D3 Baixo Guandu Brazil
79 C7 Baixo-Longa Angola
50 D2 Baiyin China
19 J5 Baja Hungary
130 B2 Baja California pen. Mexico
130 B2 Baja California Norte div. Mexico
130 B3 Baja California Sur div. Mexico
131 E3 Bajan Mexico
54 E3 Bajang Nepal
91 ¬16 Baja, Pta pt Easter I. Chile
130 A2 Baja, Pta pt Mexico
39 H8 Bajawa Indon.
54 E5 Baj Baj India
28 D2 Bajina Bašta Yugo.
55 G4 Bajitpur Bangladesh
29 F4 Bajram Curri Albania
64 C2 Baka Kazak.
72 B4 Bakaoré Chad
76 B4 Bakau The Gambia
40 C2 Bakau Indon.
13 F4 Bakal Rus. Fed.
78 D4 Bakala C.A.R.
15 E1 Bakan India
65 H2 Bakanas Kazak.
64 D4 Bakei Senegal
131 G4 Bakel Senegal
128 C5 Baker U.S.A.
87 R4 Baker I. i. Pac. Oc.
110 D3 Baker I. i. U.S.A.
111 K2 Baker Lake I. Can.
111 K2 Baker Lake Can.
147 Mt vol. U.S.A.
112 E2 Bakers Dozen Islands is Can.
32 B2 Bakersfield U.S.A.
43 D4 Bá Kêv Cambodia
14 G2 Bakhmach Rus. Fed.
64 E5 Bakharden Turkmenistan
57 C2 Bākharz mt. ra. Iran
54 B4 Bākharz India
13 E6 Bakhchysaray Ukraine
15 E1 Bakhmach Ukraine
57 B2 Bakhtiari Country reg. Iran
97 F2 Bākhtyārī Iran
17 C4 Bakhty Kazak.
57 B2 Bakhtyzino Rus. Fed.
81 G5 Bakı Azer.
65 J2 Bakırköy Turkey
80 C4 Bakki Iceland
60 C1 Bakkejord Norway
10 E2 Bako Côte d'Ivoire
80 C3 Bako Ethiopia
18 D4 Bakony h. Hungary
17 D4 Bakool div. Somalia
78 B4 Bakouma Gabon
72 B4 Bakor r. Mali
13 G7 Baksan Rus. Fed.
80 B1 Baktálorántháza Hungary
78 F3 Baku Zaire
61 D4 Bakung i. Indon.
125 C6 Bakur Rus. Fed.
60 C1 Bakut Yemen
40 D2 Bakongan Indon.
17 D5 Balachna India (?)
17 D5 Balā U.K.
41 A5 Balabac i. Phil.
41 A5 Balabac Strait str. Malaysia/Phil.

40 D2 Balabalangan, Kep. atolls Indon.
14 C2 Balabanovo Rus. Fed.
90 ¬2 Balabio i. Pac. Oc.
133 ¬1 Balaclava Jamaica
57 B3 Bālādeh Iran
57 B1 Bālādeh Iran
54 E5 Balaghat India
54 D3 Balaghat Range h. India
25 G2 Balaguer Spain
57 D3 Bālā Ḥowẓ Iran
40 B2 Balaiberkuak Indon.
40 B2 Balaiaranga Indon.
40 B2 Balaiariam Indon.
83 E1 Balaka Malawi
14 D1 Balakhna Rus. Fed.
14 F1 Balakirevo Rus. Fed.
54 C2 Balakot Pakistan
15 F6 Balakleya Ukraine
13 G2 Balakliya Ukraine
41 A5 Balambangan i. Malaysia
57 E2 Bālā Morghāb Afghanistan
57 B4 Bālān India
28 E1 Bălan Romania
29 G6 Balan Dağı mt. Turkey
41 B3 Balanga Phil.
81 C5 Balangida, Lake I. Tanzania
56 C5 Balangoda Sri Lanka
40 E2 Balasar r. Indon.
13 G5 Balashov Rus. Fed.
139 G3 Balashika r. Rus. Fed.
19 J4 Balassagyarmat Hungary
19 H5 Balaton I. Hungary
19 H5 Balatonfüred Hungary
19 H5 Balatonlelle Hungary
25 E3 Balazote Spain
19 L1 Balbieriškis Lithuania
139 F4 Balbina Brazil
32 B2 Balbriggan Rep. of Ire.
96 D2 Balcanoona Aust.
146 E4 Balcarce Arg.
32 D2 Balchik Bulgaria
93 B7 Balclutha N.Z.
101 B7 Bald Hd hd Aust.
144 G3 Baldim Brazil
125 F5 Bald Knob U.S.A.
55 F4 Baldnath India
111 K3 Baldock Lake I. Can.
115 F4 Baldwin U.S.A.
119 D6 Baldwin U.S.A.
122 A3 Baldwin i. U.S.A.
121 E3 Baldwinsville U.S.A.
129 H5 Baldy Peak mt. U.S.A.
47 L1 Bal'dzhikan Rus. Fed.
76 B4 Baléa Mali
25 H3 Baleares, Islas is Spain
40 C1 Baleh r. Malaysia
113 G2 Baleine, Rivière à la r. Can.
20 D3 Baleines, Pte des pt France
152 ¬ Baleiniers, Golfe de b. Kerguelen Indian Ocean
80 C3 Bale Mts National Park nat. park Ethiopia
41 B3 Baler Phil.
41 B3 Baler Bay b. Phil.
55 F5 Bāleshwar India
49 F2 Baley r. China
77 E4 Baleyara Niger
99 E4 Balfe's Creek Aust.
93 B6 Balfour N.Z.
57 A4 Bālgatay Mongolia
40 D2 Balgatpani Indon.
100 D4 Balgo Mission Aust.
81 C5 Balgo well Kenya
65 L4 Baguntay r. China
80 D2 Bālḥāf Yemen
56 C4 Bali div. Indon.
38 C6 Balige Indon.
54 E5 Baliguda India
49 F4 Balihan China
55 H4 Balik r. Turkey
57 D1 Balikesir Turkey
29 E5 Balıkesir Turkey
29 F5 Balıklıçeşme Turkey
40 D2 Balikpapan Indon.
40 D2 Balikpapan, Tk b. Indon.
41 A5 Balimbing Phil.
90 ¬3 Balimo P.N.G.
18 D4 Balingen Germany
43 C4 Bali Sea g. Indon.
73 H4 Balitondo C.A.R. (?)
74 A4 Banc d'Arguin, Parc National du nat. park Mauritania
57 C1 Balkan div. Turkmenistan
65 H2 Balkashino Kazak.
57 F1 Balkh Afghanistan
65 H3 Balkhash Kazak.
65 H3 Balkhash, Ozero I. Kazak.
17 C5 Balkuduk Kazak.
13 K4 Ballachulish U.K.
126 E2 Ballantine U.S.A.
77 E4 Ballantrae U.K.
78 E3 Ballarat Aust.
33 D5 Ballard, L. salt flat Aust.
54 B2 Ballater U.K.

28 E2 Balş Romania
115 F3 Balsam Creek Can.
144 B4 Balsas Brazil
25 G2 Balsareny Spain
130 E5 Balsas r. Mexico
131 F5 Balsas Mexico
142 C3 Balsas, Rio das r. Brazil
15 C3 Balta Ukraine
28 C2 Balta Berilovac Yugo.
12 J3 Baltasi Rus. Fed.
14 H3 Baltay Rus. Fed.
15 B3 Bălţi Moldova
4 G3 Baltic Sea g. Europe
61 A4 Baltîm Egypt
54 C2 Baltistan reg. Pakistan
11 E5 Baltiysk Rus. Fed.
138 ¬ Baltra, I. i. Galapagos Is Ecuador
55 H4 Balu India
57 D3 Baluch Ab well Iran
55 G4 Balurghat India
28 F1 Bălușeni Romania
41 B1 Balut i. Phil.
11 G4 Balvi Latvia
100 D4 Balwina Abor. Reserve res. Aust.
29 F5 Balya Turkey
48 C3 Balyaga Rus. Fed.
65 L2 Balyksa Rus. Fed.
65 H1 Balykshi Kazak.
48 A2 Balyktyg-Khem r. Rus. Fed.
57 B3 Bām Iran
57 D3 Bām Iran
50 D3 Bama China
78 A4 Bama Nigeria
99 E1 Bamaga Aust.
112 B3 Bamaji L. I. Can.
76 C4 Bamako Mali
76 D3 Bamba Mali
78 B3 Bambama Congo
41 C5 Bamban Phil.
79 D6 Bambangando Angola
78 D2 Bambari C.A.R.
18 E6 Bamberg Germany
119 D5 Bamberg U.S.A.
78 E3 Bambesa Zaire
76 A4 Bambey Senegal
78 E3 Bambili Zaire
78 E3 Bambio C.A.R.
82 D5 Bamboesberg mts R.S.A.
76 B4 Bambouk reg. Mali
81 ¬4 Bamboo Mts h. Mauritius
78 E3 Bambouti C.A.R.
80 B2 Bambudi Ethiopia
145 H4 Bambuí Brazil
78 B2 Bamenda Cameroon
78 B2 Bamendjing, Lac de I. Cameroon
57 F2 Bāmīān Afghanistan
49 H3 Bamiancheng China
78 C2 Bamingui C.A.R.
78 D2 Bamingui r. C.A.R.
78 D2 Bamingui-Bangoran div. C.A.R.
78 D2 Bamingui-Bangoran, Parc National du nat. park C.A.R.
42 C4 Bamnet Narong Thailand
57 E4 Bam Posht reg. Iran
57 E4 Bam Posht, Kūh-e mt. ra. Iran
57 D4 Bampūr r. Iran
57 D4 Bampūr Iran
57 D4 Bamrūd Iran
40 D2 Bamsalsepulun Indon.
86 H5 Banaba i. Kiribati
142 E2 Banabuiu, Açude resr Brazil
10 C2 Banagher Rep. of Ire.
78 E3 Banalia Zaire
76 C4 Banamba Mali
99 G5 Banana Aust.
42 A6 Bananga Andaman and Nicobar Is India
56 D2 Banapur India
29 F4 Banarli Turkey
54 D4 Banas r. India
80 W. Y Bana, W. w Yemen
40 D3 Banawaya s. Indon.
60 B2 Banaz Turkey
42 D3 Ban Ban Laos
43 C6 Banbar China
43 D4 Ban Betong Thailand
18 D6 Banbridge U.K.
43 C4 Ban Bua Chum Thailand
74 A4 Ban Bua Yai Thailand
17 G5 Banbury U.K.
42 C4 Ban Channabot Thailand
43 B5 Ban Chiang Dao Thailand
42 B3 Banchory U.K.
131 J5 Banco Chinchorro is Mexico
132 B4 Banco Gorda sand bank Honduras
17 C5 Bancroft Can.
115 G4 Bancroft Can.
57 D2 Band Iran
78 B2 Banda Cameroon
55 F4 Banda India
39 J8 Banda Aceh Indon.
54 B2 Banda Daud Shah Pakistan
42 B3 Ban Dan Lan Hin Thailand

39 J8 Banda Sea sea Indon.
57 D4 Band Bonī Iran
57 C4 Band-e Chārak Iran
145 H1 Bandeira Brazil
144 A3 Bandeirantes Mato Grosso do Sul Brazil
144 C5 Bandeirantes São Paulo Brazil
145 H4 Bandeirantes, Pico de mt. Brazil
15 C3 Banderola Brazil
118 E3 Bandera Arg.
130 C2 Banderas Mexico
130 D4 Banderas, Bahía de b. Mexico
57 E2 Band-e Sar Qom Iran
54 C4 Bandi r. Rajasthan India
56 D2 Bandia r. India
76 D4 Bandiagara Mali
57 F2 Band-i-Amir r. Afghanistan
52 ? Bandikui India
54 C2 Bandipur Nepal
60 B1 Bandırma Turkey
57 E2 Band-i-Turkestan mt. ra. Afghanistan
17 C6 Bandon Rep. of Ire.
79 C4 Bandundu Zaire
40 A3 Bandung Indon.
101 C5 Banbury r. Indon. (Banjar)
28 F2 Băneasa Romania
60 F3 Bāneh Iran
132 D2 Banes Cuba
114 C4 Banff Can.
16 F3 Banff U.K.
114 C4 Banff National Park nat. park Can.
76 C4 Banfora Burkina
42 B3 Ban Sut Ta Thailand
42 B3 Banswada India
54 C5 Banswara India
40 D3 Banggai Indon.
39 H7 Banggai, Kepulauan is Indon.
41 A5 Banggi i. Malaysia
72 D1 Banghāzī Libya
40 A2 Bangil Indon.
40 A2 Bangka i. Indon.
40 A3 Bangkalan Indon.
50 E1 Bangkir Indon.
50 E1 Bangko Co I. China
43 C4 Bangkok Thailand
43 C4 Bangkok, Bight of b. Thailand
32 K7 Bangladesh country Asia
50 B4 Bangma Shan mt. ra. China
43 B5 Bang Saphan Yai Thailand
129 F3 Bangs, Mt mt. U.S.A.
10 C2 Bangsund Norway
41 B2 Bangued Phil.
81 B2 Bangui C.A.R.
81 B2 Bangui-Motaba Congo
42 D2 Ban Hà Vietnam
42 B3 Ban Hat Yai Thailand
83 B3 Banhine, Parque Nacional de nat. park Mozambique
43 C6 Ban Lôc Vietnam
49 K3 Banhoïng China (?)
78 C3 Bani C.A.R.
133 D3 Baní Dominican Rep.
76 C4 Baní r. Mali
51 C1 Baocheng China
51 F1 Baoding China
51 F4 Baofeng China
42 D2 Bao Hà Vietnam
50 D2 Baoji China
51 E2 Baoji China
51 F5 Ba Ria Vietnam
75 F1 Barika Algeria

42 D4 Ban Nakham Laos
42 C3 Ban Na Noi Thailand
43 B5 Ban Na San Thailand
43 C6 Ban Na Thawi Thailand
138 C1 Banoa Colombia
110 B3 Baranof Island I. U.S.A.
14 H3 Baranovka Rus. Fed.
42 B3 Ban Noi Myanmar
76 B4 Banora Guinea
28 E1 Baraolt Romania
139 F6 Bararuelli Mali
14 F2 Barashevo Rus. Fed.
39 J8 Barat Daya, Kepulauan is Indon.
96 D3 Baraut India
54 D3 Baraut India
79 B5 Barca do Cuanza Brazil
144 B1 Barra do Garças Brazil
104 N8 Barbados country Caribbean
114 B2 Barbara Lake I. Can.
61 B5 Barbar, G. el mt. Egypt
25 G3 Barbaria, Cap de pt Spain
25 G1 Barbastro Spain
24 D4 Barbate de Franco Spain
114 E2 Barber's Bay Can.
127 ¬1 Barbers Pt pt U.S.A.
120 C4 Barberton U.S.A.
20 D4 Barbezieux-St-Hilaire France
138 C2 Barbosa Colombia
111 L2 Barbour Bay b. Can.
120 B6 Barbourville U.S.A.
41 B4 Barboza Phil.
133 G3 Barbuda i. Antigua and Barbuda
28 D3 Bârca Romania
132 ¬1 Barcadera Aruba
99 F4 Barcaldine Aust.
26 E4 Barcelona Pozzo di Gotto Italy
25 H2 Barcelona Spain
139 F1 Barcelona Venezuela
119 ¬3 Barceloneta Puerto Rico
21 H4 Barcelonnette France
139 E4 Barcelos Brazil
19 H2 Barcin Poland
76 C6 Barclayville Liberia
142 B3 Barreiro r. Brazil
17 E5 Bardsey Island i. U.K.
118 C4 Barcoo w Aust.
99 F4 Barcoo w Aust.
19 K2 Barczewo Poland
43 A4 Bareen I. i. Andaman and Nicobar Is India
72 C3 Bardaï Chad
100 D2 Bárðarbunga mt. Iceland
110 C4 Barerhead Can.
119 D6 Bari India
11 D4 Barr Pte i. Can.
97 E2 Barrier Range h. Aust.
43 A4 Bar Đôn Vietnam
26 A3 Bardonecchia Italy
17 E5 Bardsey Island i. U.K.
118 B5 Bardstown U.S.A.
120 B5 Bardwell U.S.A.
54 D3 Bareilly India
97 F3 Barellan Aust.
20 E2 Barentin France
20 E2 Barenton France
62 D2 Barentsøya i. Svalbard
62 C2 Barents Sea sea Arctic Ocean
80 C1 Barentu Eritrea
20 D2 Barfleur France
20 D2 Barfleur, Pte de pt France
78 B2 Banyo Cameroon
25 H1 Banyoles Spain
40 B2 Banyuasin r. Indon.
40 B2 Banyuwangi Indon.
149 K7 Banzare Seamount Indian Ocean
18 E2 Barganehaide Germany
17 D4 Bargi div. Somalia
18 D3 Baoying China
42 D2 Baoji Vietnam
50 D4 Ba Oaj China

76 D4 Barani Burkina
63 5 Barankha Rus. Fed.
15 B1 Baranivka Ukraine
57 E2 Bārān, Kūh-e mt. ra. Iran
138 C1 Baranoa Colombia
110 B3 Baranof Island I. U.S.A.
14 H3 Baranovka Rus. Fed.
122 C5 Banner U.S.A.
132 C1 Bannerman Town The Bahamas
128 D5 Banning U.S.A.
42 B3 Ban Noi Myanmar
76 B4 Banora Guinea
28 E1 Baraolt Romania
76 B4 Baraouéli Mali
139 F5 Baranelli i. Brazil
14 F2 Barashevo Rus. Fed.
39 J8 Barat Daya, Kepulauan is Indon.
96 D3 Baraut India
54 D3 Baraut India
54 D3 Barat India
138 B2 Baraya Colombia
145 H4 Barbacena Colombia
138 B3 Barbacoas Colombia
104 N8 Barbados country Caribbean
114 B2 Barbara Lake I. Can.
61 B5 Barbar, G. el mt. Egypt
25 G3 Barbaria, Cap de pt Spain
25 G1 Barbastro Spain
24 D4 Barbate de Franco Spain
114 E2 Barber's Bay Can.
127 ¬1 Barbers Pt pt U.S.A.
120 C4 Barberton U.S.A.
20 D4 Barbezieux-St-Hilaire France
138 C2 Barbosa Colombia
111 L2 Barbour Bay b. Can.
120 B6 Barbourville U.S.A.
41 B4 Barboza Phil.
133 G3 Barbuda i. Antigua and Barbuda
28 D3 Bârca Romania
132 ¬1 Barcadera Aruba
99 F4 Barcaldine Aust.
55 H2 Barcelona Spain
25 H2 Barcelona Spain
139 F1 Barcelona Venezuela
121 G2 Barcelonnette France
146 C3 Barrel Arg.
142 D3 Barreiras Brazil
142 D1 Barreirinha Brazil
142 D2 Barreiro r. Brazil
142 B3 Barreiro Brazil
99 G5 Barcoo w Aust.
142 E2 Barreiros Brazil
19 K2 Barczewo Poland
43 A4 Barren I. i. Andaman and Nicobar Is India
72 C3 Bardaï Chad
100 D3 Barrett, Mt h. Aust.
110 C4 Barrhead Can.
114 D4 Barrie Can.
92 E2 Barrier, Cape c. N.Z.
97 E2 Barrier Range h. Aust.
43 A4 Bar Đôn Vietnam
111 J3 Barrington Lake I. Can.
17 E5 Barrington, Mt mt. U.S.A.
120 B5 Barrow r. Rep. of Ire.
144 D1 Barro Alto Brazil
54 D3 Bareilly India
93 F3 Barrell Aust.
20 E2 Barenton France (Barr)
99 F3 Barrow Falls waterfall Aust.
62 D2 Barentsøya i. Svalbard
110 C2 Barrow U.S.A.
80 C1 Barrow r. U.S.A.
108 ¬ Barrow c. U.S.A.
98 C2 Barrow, Pt c. U.S.A.
100 A4 Barrow I. i. Aust.
17 F4 Barrow-in-Furness U.K.

16 I3 Barra i. U.K.
97 G2 Barraba Aust.
144 D5 Barra Bonita Brazil
142 B1 Barraca da Bôca Brazil
141 E1 Barração do Barreto Brazil
25 F2 Barracas Spain
145 E6 Barra de Santos inlet Brazil
145 H3 Barra de São Francisco Brazil
145 G5 Barra de São João Brazil
142 A4 Barra de Bugres Brazil
96 D3 Baratta Can.
54 D3 Baraut India
142 C2 Barra do Corda Brazil
79 B5 Barra do Cuanza Brazil
144 B1 Barra do Garças Brazil
145 G5 Barra do Pirai Brazil
104 N8 Barbados country Caribbean
143 B7 Barra do Ribeiro Brazil
139 F5 Barra do São Manuel Brazil
144 Da Barra Falsa, Pta da pt Mozambique
145 G4 Barra Longa Brazil
145 F5 Barra Mansa Brazil
138 B4 Barranca Peru
140 A2 Barranca Peru
138 C2 Barranca-bermeja Colombia
138 C1 Barrancas r. Corrientes Arg.
138 C2 Barrancas Colombia
139 F2 Barrancas Venezuela
24 C4 Barranco Velho Portugal
146 E2 Barranqueras Arg.
138 C1 Barranquilla Colombia
146 B4 Barraux France (?)
16 I3 Barra, Sound of chan. U.K.
115 G2 Barraute Can.
25 E3 Barrax Spain
121 G2 Barre U.S.A.
146 C3 Barreal Arg.
142 D3 Barreiras Brazil
142 D1 Barreirinha Brazil
142 D2 Barreirinhas Brazil
142 B3 Barreiro r. Brazil
145 G2 Barreiro Nascimento Brazil
142 E2 Barreiros Brazil
142 E2 Barretos Brazil
144 A1 Barro Alto Brazil
145 G2 Barrocão Brazil
122 B3 Barron U.S.A.
99 F4 Barron Falls waterfall Aust.
125 D7 Barroterán Mexico
146 D4 Barrow Arg.
108 C2 Barrow U.S.A.
98 C2 Barrow Creek Aust.
100 A4 Barrow I. i. Aust.
17 F4 Barrow-in-Furness U.K.

17 G6 Basingstoke U.K.
55 G5 Basirhat India
121 K2 Baskahegan Lake I. U.S.A.
14 B2 Baskakovka Rus. Fed.
60 F2 Başkale Turkey
115 H3 Baskatong, Réservoir resr Can.
61 B1 Başköy Turkey
13 H5 Baskunchak, Ozero I. Rus. Fed.
40 A2 Baso i. Indon.
54 D6 Basoda India
78 D3 Basoko Zaire
25 E1 Basque Country div. Spain
26 C3 Bassano del Grappa Italy
77 E5 Bassar Togo
69 J8 Bassas da India i. Indian Ocean
42 A3 Bassein Myanmar
42 A4 Bassein r. Myanmar
78 D3 Basse-Kotto div. C.A.R.
20 D4 Basse-Normandie div. France
133 ¬4 Basse Pointe Martinique Caribbean
76 B4 Basse Santa Su The Gambia
133 ¬5 Basse Terre i. Guadeloupe Caribbean
133 ¬5 Basse Terre Guadeloupe Caribbean
133 ¬6 Basse Terre Trin. and Tobago
124 D3 Bassett U.S.A.
129 G5 Bassett Peak summit U.S.A.
121 J2 Bass Harbor U.S.A.
74 C5 Bassikounou Mauritania
77 E5 Bassila Benin
72 D4 Basso, Plateau de plat. Chad
16 I3 Bass Rock i. U.K.
97 F4 Bass Strait str. Aust.
11 D4 Båstad Sweden
57 C4 Bastak Iran
60 F2 Bāstānābād Iran
18 E3 Bastheim Germany
21 J5 Bastia France
142 E2 Bastião r. Brazil
18 B3 Bastogne Belgium
125 F6 Bastrop U.S.A.
125 D6 Bastrop i. U.S.A.
57 F4 Basul r. Pakistan
40 A2 Basu, Tg i. Indon.
79 B5 Bas-Zaïre div. Zaire
41 B2 Batac Phil.
63 P3 Batagay Rus. Fed.
63 P3 Batagay-Alyta Rus. Fed.
48 L1 Batagol r. Rus. Fed.
144 B4 Bataguaçu Brazil
28 E4 Batak Bulgaria
54 E3 Batakan Indon.
21 F4 Batala Portugal
40 A1 Batam i. Indon.
78 E3 Batama Zaire
63 O3 Batamay Rus. Fed.
65 J4 Batamshinskiy Kazak.
41 B1 Batan i. Phil.
50 B2 Batang China
78 C3 Batangafo C.A.R.
41 B3 Batangas Phil.
40 A2 Batanghari r. Indon.
144 C5 Batatais Brazil
122 C5 Batavia U.S.A.
120 D3 Batavia U.S.A.
14 A3 Batayeva Rus. Fed.
14 H3 Batayevskaya Rus. Fed.
13 F6 Bataysk Rus. Fed.
114 C1 Batchawana Bay Can.
114 C1 Batchawana Bay b. Can.
114 C1 Batchawana Mtn h. Can.
98 B2 Batchelor Aust.
43 C4 Bătdâmbâng Cambodia
79 B4 Batéké, Plateaux plat. Congo
97 G3 Batemans Bay Aust.
95 ¬1 Bates, Mt h. Norfolk I. Pac. Oc.
101 C5 Bates Ra. h. Aust.
125 F5 Batesville U.S.A.
11 J3 Batetskiy Rus. Fed.
113 G4 Bath Can.
17 F6 Bath U.K.
121 J2 Bath U.S.A.
120 E3 Bath U.S.A.
72 C4 Batha w Chad
72 C4 Batha div. Chad
17 G6 Bathgate U.K.
54 D3 Bathinda India
113 G4 Bathurst Can.
109 J2 Bathurst I. Abor. Land res. Aust.
108 H3 Bathurst Inlet inlet Can.
80 C2 Batī Ethiopia
40 B2 Batikala, Tg pt Indon.
90 ¬8 Bätiki i. Fiji
29 F6 Batı Menteşe Dağları mt. Turkey
57 B2 Bāţlāq-e Gavkhūnī salt marsh Iran
77 D5 Batié Burkina
60 C1 Batman Turkey
75 F1 Batna Algeria
142 D3 Batovi Brazil
73 G5 Batrā, J. el mt. Saudi Arabia
61 C5 Batrā, Jebel el mt. Jordan
61 C4 Batroûn Lebanon
10 H1 Båtsfjord Norway
43 A5 Bat-Sot Rus. Fed.
56 C5 Batticaloa Sri Lanka
81 A5 Batti Malv i. Andaman and Nicobar Is India
26 D4 Battipaglia Italy
111 G4 Battle r. Can.
122 C2 Battle Creek U.S.A.
111 H4 Battleford Can.
126 C3 Battle Mountain U.S.A.
54 C1 Battura Gl. gl. Jammu and Kashmir
80 C3 Batu mt. Ethiopia
40 A2 Batuata i. Indon.
40 C1 Batubetumbang, Bukit mt. Indon.
40 A2 Batu Gajah Malaysia

17 G6 Basingstoke U.K.
55 G5 Basirhat India
121 K2 Baskahegan Lake I. U.S.A.
14 B2 Baskakovka Rus. Fed.
60 F2 Başkale Turkey
115 H3 Baskatong, Réservoir resr Can.
61 B1 Başköy Turkey
13 H5 Baskunchak, Ozero I. Rus. Fed.
40 A2 Baso i. Indon.
54 D6 Basoda India
78 D3 Basoko Zaire
25 E1 Basque Country div. Spain

40 C4 Batukau, G. vol Indon.
41 C5 Batulaki Phil.
40 D4 Batulanteh mt. Indon.
40 C2 Batulicin Indon.
40 C1 Batulilangmembang, G.
  mt. Indon.
13 G7 Bat'umi Georgia
43 C7 Batu Pahat Malaysia
38 C7 Batu, P.P. is Indon.
43 C6 Batu Puteh, Gunung mt.
  Malaysia
40 A3 Baturaja Indon.
40 B3 Baturetno Indon.
142 E1 Baturité Brazil
142 E1 Baturite, Sa h. Brazil
15 F1 Baturyn Ukraine
14 H2 Batyrevo Rus. Fed.
20 B2 Batz, Île de l. France
21 H4 Bau r. Brazil
90 ⁻8 Bau i. Fiji
39 H8 Baubau Indon.
77 H4 Bauchi Nigeria
77 G4 Bauchi div. Nigeria
55 F5 Bauda India
124 E1 Baudette U.S.A.
94 ⁻3 Bauer Bay b. Macquarie I.
  Pac. Oc.
80 E3 Bauet well Ethiopia
20 D3 Baugé France
21 H4 Bauges mts France
99 G5 Bauhinia Downs Aust.
113 K3 Bauld, C. hd Can.
21 H3 Baume-l.-Dames
  France
140 D2 Baures Bolivia
144 D5 Bauru Brazil
144 B5 Baús Brazil
11 G4 Bauska Latvia
19 G3 Bautzen Germany
18 E4 Bavaria div. Germany
130 C2 Bavispe r. Mexico
64 D2 Bavly Rus. Fed.
78 C3 Bavula Zaire
42 A2 Baw Myanmar
40 B2 Bawal i. Indon.
40 B2 Bawang, Tg pt Indon.
40 C3 Bawean i. Indon.
73 E2 Bawiti Egypt
76 D4 Bawku Ghana
42 B3 Bawlake Myanmar
50 C2 Bawolung China
50 C2 Ba Xian China
49 F5 Ba Xian China
119 D6 Baxley U.S.A.
50 B2 Baxoi China
80 D4 Bay div. Somalia
132 C2 Bayamo Cuba
119 ⁻3 Bayamón Puerto Rico
49 H3 Bayan Indon.
40 D4 Bayan Indon.
48 D2 Bayan Mongolia
48 B3 Bayan Mongolia
54 D4 Bayana India
65 J2 Bayanaul Kazak.
48 A3 Bayanbulag Bayan-
  Hongor Mongolia
48 B3 Bayanbulag Bayan-
  Hongor Mongolia
48 B3 Bayanbulag Hentiy
  Mongolia
48 D3 Bayandelger Mongolia
78 C3 Bayanga C.A.R.
78 C2 Bayanga-Didi C.A.R.
48 B2 Bayangol Mongolia
50 A1 Bayan Har Shan mt. ra.
  China
50 B1 Bayan Har Shankou pass
  China
48 A3 Bayan-Hongor div.
  Mongolia
48 B3 Bayanhongor Mongolia
48 B3 Bayanhushuu Mongolia
48 A4 Bayan Mod China
48 D2 Bayan Obo China
48 B2 Bayan-Ovoo Mongolia
48 D2 Bayan-Ovoo Mongolia
48 D2 Bayan Qagan China
48 A3 Bayansumküre China
65 K4 Bayasgalan Mongolia
48 E3 Bayasgalan Mongolia
60 B2 Bayat Turkey
53 F3 Bayat Iran
41 C4 Baybay Phil.
123 F4 Bay City U.S.A.
125 D6 Bay City U.S.A.
62 H3 Baydaratskaya Guba b.
  Rus. Fed.
80 D4 Baydhabo Somalia
48 A3 Baydrag Gol r. Mongolia
18 E4 Bayerischer Wald mt. ra.
  Germany
18 E4 Bayern div. Germany
20 C2 Bayeux France
65 H2 Bayevo Rus. Fed.
122 B2 Bayfield U.S.A.
64 E3 Baygaín Kazak.
80 E2 Bayhan al Qişab Yemen
60 D4 Bayir Jordan
65 H4 Baykadam Kazak.
48 C2 Baykal Rus. Fed.
48 C2 Baykal, Ozero l. Rus. Fed.
63 L3 Baykal'sk Rus. Fed.
65 J3 Baykonur Kazak.
41 B3 Bay, Laguna de lag. Phil.
64 E2 Baymak Rus. Fed.
92 F3 Bay of Plenty div. N.Z.
41 B4 Bayombong Phil.
138 B5 Bayóvar Peru
64 F5 Bayramaly Turkmenistan
60 A2 Bayramiç Turkey
76 D4 Bay, Réserve de res. Mali
18 E4 Bayreuth Germany
125 F6 Bay St Louis U.S.A.
73 H4 Baysh w. Saudi Arabia
121 G4 Bay Shore U.S.A.
115 F4 Baysun Uzbekistan
80 E2 Bayt al Faqīh Yemen
80 D2 Bayt al Faqīh Yemen
73 F4 Bayuda Desert desert
  Sudan
40 A2 Bayunglincir Indon.
92 F3 Bay View N.Z.
25 E4 Baza Spain
15 C1 Bazar Ukraine
57 B1 Bäzär-e Māsäl Iran
14 H3 Bazarnaya Ken'sha
  Rus. Fed.
14 H3 Bazarnyy Karabulak
  Rus. Fed.
14 H3 Bazarnyy Syzgan
  Rus. Fed.
64 D2 Bazarsak Rus. Fed.
83 F3 Bazaruto, Ilha do i.
  Mozambique
24 E4 Bazas France
25 E4 Baza, Sierra de mt. ra.
  Spain
57 B3 Bazdar Pakistan
52 B3 Bazhong China
115 H3 Bazin r. Iran
57 E3 Bazmān Iran
57 E3 Bazmán, Küh-e mt. Iran
43 D5 Be r. Vietnam
124 C2 Beach U.S.A.
115 H4 Beach Haven U.S.A.
121 E4 Beach Haven U.S.A.
17 H6 Beachy Head hd U.K.
101 B6 Beacon Aust.
45 ⁻1 Beacon Hill h.
  Hong Kong
79 ⁻2 Beaconsfield
  Zimbabwe
100 C3 Beagle Bay Abor. Reserve
  res. Aust.

98 B2 Beagle Gulf b. Aust.
83 H1 Bealanana Madagascar
83 H3 Beampingaratra mts
  Madagascar
120 B6 Bean Station U.S.A.
126 E3 Bear r. U.S.A.
111 N2 Bear Cove b. Can.
114 B2 Beardmore Can.
152 B4 Beardmore Gl. gl. Ant.
99 G5 Beardmore Res. resr
  Aust.
122 B5 Beardstown U.S.A.
112 D3 Bear Island I. Can.
126 E3 Bear L. l. U.S.A.
110 D3 Bear Lake Can.
56 A3 Bearma r. India
126 E1 Bear Paw Mtn mt. U.S.A.
152 A3 Bear Pen. pen. Ant.
19 K5 Bearskin Lake Can.
83 H3 Bekily Madagascar
46 B2 Bekkai Japan
48 E2 Beklemishevo Rus. Fed.
14 F3 Bekovo Rus. Fed.
76 D5 Bekyem Ghana
28 D3 Belovo Bulgaria
14 M2 Belovod'ye Rus. Fed.
12 F1 Beloye r. Rus. Fed.
12 F2 Beloye, Ozero l. Rus. Fed.
12 F2 Beloye More g. Rus. Fed.
12 F1 Beloye More sea
  Rus. Fed.
126 E2 Bel Air U.S.A.
24 E4 Belalcázar Spain
25 G5 Bela Palanka Yugo.
97 F3 Belaraboon Aust.
5 H3 Belarus country Europe
14 G1 Belasovka Rus. Fed.
96 D2 Beltana Aust.

29 D3 Bistreț Romania
28 F1 Bistrița r. Romania
28 E1 Bistrița Romania
54 E4 Biswan India
19 K1 Bisztynek Poland
78 B3 Bitam Gabon
18 C4 Bitburg Germany
21 H2 Bitche France
64 D2 Bitik Kazak.
78 C1 Bitkine Chad
60 E2 Bitlis Turkey
29 C4 Bitola Macedonia
27 F5 Bitonto Italy
53 D8 Bitra Par i. India
129 H2 Bitter Creek r. U.S.A.
82 B5 Bitterfontein R.S.A.
73 F1 Bitter Lakes lakes Egypt
126 D2 Bitterroot Range mt. ra. U.S.A.

14 E4 Bityug r. Rus. Fed.
77 G4 Biu Nigeria
54 E4 Bivolari Romania
28 E1 Bixad Romania
65 L2 Biya r. Rus. Fed.
61 A4 Biyala Egypt
51 F1 Biyang China
54 D5 Biyavra India
80 D2 Biye K'obē Ethiopia
65 L2 Biysk Rus. Fed.
46 E6 Bizen Japan
75 F1 Bizerte Tunisia
K2 Bjargtangar hd Iceland
65 G3 Bjästa Sweden
28 B3 Bjelasica mts Yugo.
26 F3 Bjelašnica mts Bos.-Herz.
26 F3 Bjelovar Croatia
11 C4 Bjerringbro Denmark
10 E1 Bjerkvik Norway
10 E1 Björkliden Sweden
11 E3 Björklinge Sweden
11 C3 Bjorli Norway
10 E3 Björna Sweden
10 E3 Bjurholm Sweden
76 C4 Bla Mali
28 Blace Yugo.
19 J3 Blachownia Poland
133 ☐1 Black r. Jamaica
129 H5 Black r. U.S.A.
125 F5 Black r. U.S.A.
123 F4 Black r. U.S.A.
99 F5 Blackall Aust.
114 A2 Black Bay b. Can.
112 B3 Blackbear r. Can.
99 E3 Blackbull Aust.
17 F5 Blackburn U.K.
128 A2 Black Butte summit U.S.A.

128 A2 Black Butte L. l. Can.
129 E4 Black Canyon U.S.A.
129 F4 Black Canyon City U.S.A.
22 E5 Blackduck U.S.A.
110 G4 Blackfalds Can.
126 D3 Blackfoot U.S.A.
126 D2 Black Foot r. U.S.A.
18 D4 Black Forest forest Germany

124 C2 Black Hills reg. U.S.A.
115 K3 Black Lake Can.
111 K3 Black Lake l. Can.
111 H3 Black Lake l. U.S.A.
123 E3 Black Lake l. U.S.A.
133 ☐9 Blackman's Barbados Caribbean
129 G3 Black Mesa plat. U.S.A.
17 F6 Black Mountain h. U.K.
128 D4 Black Mt mt. U.S.A.
127 D5 Black Mts mts U.S.A.
129 E4 Black Mts mts U.S.A.
82 B3 Black Nossob w Namibia
17 F5 Blackpool U.K.
87 B3 Black Pt pt Hong Kong
133 ☐1 Black River Jamaica
122 B3 Black River Falls U.S.A.
126 C3 Black Rock Desert desert U.S.A.
120 C6 Blacksburg U.S.A.
60 D1 Black Sea sea Asia/Europe
17 B4 Blacksod Bay b. Rep. of Ire.
120 E6 Blackstone U.S.A.
114 A2 Black Sturgeon Lake l. Can.
97 G2 Black Sugarloaf mt. Aust.

97 G2 Blackville Aust.
99 F4 Blackwater Aust.
17 C5 Blackwater r. Rep. of Ire.
120 E6 Blackwater r. U.S.A.
110 E2 Blackwater Lake l. Can.
125 D4 Blackwell U.S.A.
101 A7 Blackwood r. Aust.
13 G6 Blagodarnyy Rus. Fed.
28 D3 Blagoevgrad Bulgaria
65 J2 Blagoveshchenka Rus. Fed.
64 E1 Blagoveshchensk Rus. Fed.
49 H2 Blagoveshchensk Rus. Fed.
65 H4 Blagoveshchenskoye Kazak.
15 F3 Blahodatne Kherson Ukraine
15 D3 Blahodatne Mykolayiv Ukraine
20 D3 Blain France
120 F4 Blain U.S.A.
126 E3 Blaine U.S.A.
111 H4 Blaine Lake Can.
124 D3 Blair U.S.A.
122 B3 Blair U.S.A.
99 F4 Blair Athol Aust.
16 F3 Blair Atholl U.K.
16 F4 Blairgowrie U.K.
28 D1 Blaj Romania
119 C6 Blakely U.S.A.
122 C1 Blake Pt pt U.S.A.
147 K4 Blanca, Bahía b. Arg.
140 A1 Blanca, Cord. mt. ra. Peru
147 C5 Blanca de la Totora, Sa h. Arg.
146 D3 Blanca, Lag. La l. Arg.
127 F4 Blanca Peak summit U.S.A.

96 C3 Blanche, C. hd Aust.
96 D2 Blanche, L. salt flat Aust.
100 C4 Blanche, L. salt flat Aust.
120 B5 Blanchester U.S.A.
96 B3 Blanchetown Aust.
133 ☐3 Blanchisseuse Trin. and Tobago
21 H4 Blanc, Mont mt. France/Italy
140 D2 Blanco r. Bolivia
130 J7 Blanco, C. c. Costa Rica
126 A3 Blanco, C. c. U.S.A.
113 J3 Blanc-Sablon Can.
8 N2 Blanda r. Iceland
17 F6 Blandford Forum U.K.
129 H3 Blanding U.S.A.
25 H2 Blanes Spain
122 E2 Blaney Park U.S.A.
20 D4 Blangy-sur-Bresle France
139 E1 Blanquilla, Isla i. Venezuela
26 D2 Blansko Czech Rep.
83 F2 Blantyre Malawi
19 J3 Blaszki Poland
26 E2 Blatná Czech Rep.
10 E2 Blåviksjön Sweden
20 D4 Blaye France
97 G3 Blayney Aust.
92 ☐2 Blaze, Pt pt Aust.
18 B1 Blážowa Poland
19 L4 Błażowa Poland
40 C3 Bled Indon.
11 D4 Blekinge div. Sweden

93 D4 Blenheim N.Z.
17 D5 Blessington Lakes lakes Rep. of Ire.
78 F3 Bleus, Monts mt. ra. Zaire
78 F3 Blida Algeria
75 E1 Blida Algeria
93 A6 Bligh Sd inlet N.Z.
90 ☐8 Bligh Water sea Fiji
114 D3 Blind River Can.
94 ☐4 Blinkenthorpe B. b. Lord Howe I. Pac. Oc.
96 D2 Blinman Aust.
126 D3 Bliss U.S.A.
123 F5 Blissfield U.S.A.
76 C4 Blitta Togo
121 H4 Block I. i. U.S.A.
121 H4 Block Island Sound chan. U.S.A.
82 D4 Bloemfontein R.S.A.
20 E3 Blois France
10 L2 Blönduós Iceland
19 K2 Błonie Poland
121 E5 Bloodsworth I. i. U.S.A.
111 K4 Bloodvein r. Can.
17 C4 Bloody Foreland hd Rep. of Ire.
115 G5 Bloomfield Can.
118 C4 Bloomfield U.S.A.
122 A5 Bloomfield U.S.A.
127 E4 Bloomfield U.S.A.
122 C5 Bloomington U.S.A.
118 D3 Bloomington U.S.A.
122 A3 Bloomington U.S.A.
121 E4 Bloomsburg U.S.A.
99 G4 Bloomsbury Aust.
40 B3 Blora Indon.
120 E4 Blossburg U.S.A.
109 ☐3 Blosseville Kyst Greenland
18 D5 Bludenz Austria
129 H5 Blue r. U.S.A.
129 G3 Bluebell U.S.A.
129 G2 Blue Bell Knoll summit U.S.A.
124 E3 Blue Earth U.S.A.
120 C6 Bluefield U.S.A.
133 H6 Bluefields Jamaica
131 H6 Bluefields Nicaragua
121 J2 Blue Hill U.S.A.
61 D1 Bluğürtlen Turkey
133 ☐1 Blue Mountain Peak summit Jamaica
40 C1 Blue Mountain h. Indon.
126 C2 Blue Mountain Lake l. Can.
138 ☐3 Blue Mountains mt. ra. Jamaica
133 ☐1 Blue Mts mts Jamaica
97 G3 Blue Mts mts Aust.
97 G3 Blue Mts Nat. Park nat. park Aust.
108 G3 Bluenose Lake l. Can.
119 C5 Blue Ridge U.S.A.
120 D6 Blue Ridge mt. ra. U.S.A.
110 F4 Blue River Can.
128 D2 Blue Springs U.S.A.
17 C4 Blue Stack mt. Rep. of Ire.
120 C6 Bluestone Lake l. U.S.A.
93 B7 Bluff N.Z.
93 B7 Bluff U.S.A.
129 H3 Bluff U.S.A.
15 L1 Bluff I. i. Hong Kong
129 E4 Bluff Knoll mt. Aust.
101 A5 Bluff Pt pt Aust.
132 C1 Bluff, The Bahamas
120 B4 Bluffton U.S.A.
118 D4 Bluffton U.S.A.
144 D3 Blumenau Brazil
144 C3 Bois r. Brazil
81 ☐5 Bois Blanc Réunion Indian Ocean
123 F3 Bois Blanc I. i. U.S.A.
15 D1 Blystova Ukraine
98 C2 Bly r. Aust.
126 D3 Boise City U.S.A.
17 G4 Blyth U.K.
129 E5 Blythe U.S.A.
125 F5 Blytheville U.S.A.
101 B5 Blyth Ra. h. Aust.
15 G2 Blyznyuky Ukraine
11 C4 Bø Norway
76 B5 Bo Sierra Leone
130 J6 Boaco Nicaragua
142 D2 Boa Esperança Brazil
145 F4 Boa Esperança Brazil
55 G1 Bokadaban Feng mt. China
144 D4 Boa Esperança do Sul Brazil
51 F1 Bo'ai China
50 D1 Bo'ai China
76 B5 Boajibu Sierra Leone
24 C1 Boal Spain
42 A3 Boalemo Indon.
120 C4 Boardman U.S.A.
92 ☐2 Boat Harbour inlet Aust.
99 F5 Boatman Aust.
82 ☐1 Boatswain-bird I. i. Ascension Atlantic Ocean
142 E1 Boa Viagem Brazil
139 G4 Boa Vista Brazil
76 ☐ Boa Vista i. Cape Verde
138 D4 Boa Vista, Ilha b. Brazil
97 F3 Bobadah Aust.
83 H1 Bobai China
54 C2 Bobbili India
20 F2 Bobigny France
76 B4 Bobo-Dioulasso Burkina
83 D3 Bobonong Botswana
45 F2 Bobo Chad
28 D2 Bobota Romania
19 L4 Bobowa Poland
28 D3 Bobovdol Bulgaria
15 D1 Bóbr r. Poland
13 F5 Bobrov Rus. Fed.
15 D2 Bobrovo-Dvorskoye Rus. Fed.
15 D2 Bobrovytsya Ukraine
15 E2 Bobrynets Ukraine
83 H3 Boby mt. Madagascar
139 E2 Boca Araguari river mouth Venezuela
131 J5 Boca Bacalar Chico chan. Mexico
139 E2 Boca del Pao Venezuela
142 E2 Bôca do Acre Brazil
139 E2 Bôca do Moaco Brazil
139 E2 Boca Grande river mouth Venezuela
145 F5 Bocaina de Minas Brazil
96 C3 Bocaiúva Brazil
133 ☐3 Bocas del Toro Panama
21 H4 Boce C.A.R.
140 D2 Boco Angola
138 D3 Bocono Venezuela
28 E2 Bocșa Romania
60 C2 Boçsa Romania
17 ☐ Böda Sweden
54 B4 Bodalla Aust.
63 M4 Bodaybo Rus. Fed.
125 D6 Bodcau Lake l. U.S.A.
132 B3 Bodden Town Cayman Is Caribbean
78 A2 Bodega Head hd U.S.A.
45 A2 Bodélé reg. Chad
10 D5 Bodensee l. Germany/Switz.
77 E5 Bode-Sadu Nigeria
28 F1 Bodeşti Romania

56 B2 Bodhan India
56 B4 Bodinayakkanur India
78 B3 Bodmin U.K.
17 E6 Bodmin Moor reg. U.K.
10 D2 Bodø Norway
143 A4 Bodoquena Brazil
60 A2 Bodrum Turkey
17 C5 Bodträskfors Sweden
78 D4 Boende Zaire
43 D4 Boeng Lvea Cambodia
76 B4 Boffa Guinea
55 H3 Boga India
42 A3 Bogale Myanmar
125 F6 Bogalusa U.S.A.
77 F4 Bogan r. Aust.
146 C2 Bogan Gate Aust.
77 F3 Bogandé Burkina
97 F3 Bogan Gate Aust.
99 F4 Bogantungan Aust.
28 B2 Bogatić Yugo.
21 G4 Boğazlıyan Turkey
78 C2 Bogbonga Zaire
42 C3 Bogcang r. China
29 D4 Bogdanci Macedonia
44 E3 Bogda Shan mt. ra. China
99 G6 Boggabilla Aust.
97 G2 Boggabri Aust.
17 C5 Boggeragh Mts h. Rep. of Ire.
101 A6 Boggola h. Aust.
133 ☐7 Boggy Pk mt. Antigua Caribbean
90 ☐1 Bogia P.N.G.
78 C3 Bogo Cameroon
41 C4 Bogo Phil.
42 A2 Bogolyubovo Rus. Fed.
14 E1 Bogolyubovo Rus. Fed.
97 F4 Bogong, Mt mt. Aust.
40 A3 Bogor Indon.
14 G2 Bogoroditsk Rus. Fed.
14 E1 Bogorodskoye Rus. Fed.
14 F1 Bogorodsk Rus. Fed.
13 J3 Bogorodskoye Rus. Fed.
72 C4 Bogoroud well Chad
138 C3 Bogotá Colombia
55 G4 Bogra Bangladesh
63 L4 Boguchany Rus. Fed.
13 G5 Boguchar Rus. Fed.
76 B4 Bogué Mauritania
61 D1 Boğürtlen Turkey
133 ☐1 Bog Walk Jamaica
40 C1 Boh r. Indon.
49 G5 Bohai Haixia chan. China
21 F2 Bohain-en-Vermandois France
49 F4 Bohai Wan b. China
28 E1 Bohan Romania
18 F4 Bohemia reg. Czech Rep.
83 D4 Bohlokong R.S.A.
18 F4 Böhmer Wald mts Germany
49 F4 Bohodukhiv Ukraine
41 C4 Bohol i. Phil.
41 C4 Bohol Sea sea Phil.
41 C4 Bohol Str. chan. Phil.
15 C2 Bohorodchany Ukraine
48 D3 Böhöt Mongolia
29 D4 Bohuslav Ukraine
139 E4 Boiaçu r. Brazil
83 D4 Boichoko R.S.A.
125 G2 Boice U.S.A.
111 K5 Boileau, C. c. Aust.
131 G6 Boima, Cape c. Phil.
142 J1 Boim Brazil
42 A2 Boinu r. Myanmar
142 E3 Boipeba, i r. Brazil
142 C3 Bois r. Brazil
81 ☐5 Bois Blanc Réunion Indian Ocean
123 F3 Bois Blanc I. i. U.S.A.
14 G2 Bol'shoye Murashkino Rus. Fed.
14 G1 Bol'shoye Popovo Rus. Fed.
125 F4 Boise U.S.A.

21 G2 Bologne France
138 C5 Bolognesi Peru
14 C2 Bologoye Rus. Fed.
78 C3 Bolomba Zaire
78 C3 Bolombo r. Zaire
131 H4 Bolonchén de Rejón Mexico
78 C4 Bolondo Zaire
41 B5 Bolong Phil.
27 B5 Bolotana Italy
65 K1 Bolotnoye Rus. Fed.
43 D4 Bolovens, Plateau des plat. Laos
146 C2 Bolsa, Co mt. Arg.
26 C4 Bolsena, Lago di l. Italy
14 G3 Bol'shaya Arya Rus. Fed.
11 F5 Bol'shakovo Rus. Fed.
64 D2 Bol'shaya Glushitsa Rus. Fed.
10 J2 Bol'shaya Imandra, Oz. l. Rus. Fed.
62 C3 Bol'shaya Kandarat' Rus. Fed.
12 H3 Bol'shaya Kokshaga r. Rus. Fed.
14 E3 Bol'shaya Lipovitsa Rus. Fed.
13 G6 Bol'shaya Martinovka Rus. Fed.
13 G6 Bol'shaya Orlovka Rus. Fed.
12 J1 Bol'shaya Pyssa Rus. Fed.
14 G2 Bol'shaya Tsivil' r. Rus. Fed.
64 E1 Bol'shaya Usa Rus. Fed.
27 B5 Bol'shaya Vladimirovka Kazak.
14 G3 Bol'shaya Yelan' Rus. Fed.
14 G2 Bol'shaya Yelkhovka Rus. Fed.
65 J2 Bol'shegrivskoye Rus. Fed.
65 K3 Bol'shenarymskoye Kazak.
21 H3 Bol'sherech'ye Rus. Fed.
15 G1 Bol'shetroitskoye Rus. Fed.
63 M2 Bolshevik, O. i. Rus. Fed.
14 G2 Bol'shiye Algashi Rus. Fed.
14 A1 Bolshoio Rus. Fed.
46 C8 Bōno-misaki pt Japan
43 D5 Bonom Mhai mt. Vietnam
12 H2 Bol'shiye Chirki Rus. Fed.
14 C3 Bol'shiye Kozly Rus. Fed.
14 C3 Bol'shiye Medvedki Rus. Fed.
14 F3 Bol'shiye Mozhary Rus. Fed.
14 G2 Bol'shiye Soli Rus. Fed.
13 H6 Bol'shoy Altsyn, Ozero l. Rus. Fed.
63 S3 Bol'shoy Aluy r. Rus. Fed.
63 N2 Bol'shoy Begichev, Ostrov i. Rus. Fed.
14 G2 Bol'shoye Boldino Rus. Fed.
14 G2 Bol'shoye Beresnevo Rus. Fed.
14 G2 Bol'shoye Gorodishche Rus. Fed.
15 G1 Bol'shoye Soldatskoye Rus. Fed.
14 G2 Bol'shoye Yeravnoye, Ozero l. Rus. Fed.
48 D1 Bol'shoy Lug Rus. Fed.
21 B5 Bol'shoy Lyakhovskiy, O. i. Rus. Fed.
15 D3 Bol'shoy V'yas r. Rus. Fed.
14 G2 Bol'shoy V'yas Rus. Fed.
14 G2 Bol'shoye Mikhaylovskoye Rus. Fed.
17 F5 Bolton U.K.
78 B3 Bokode Zaire
78 E3 Bokoko Zaire
14 A2 Boltuno r. Rus. Fed.
80 A4 Bokora Corridor Game Reserve res. Uganda
72 C5 Bokoro Chad
78 B3 Bokote Zaire
14 C1 Bokovaya Rus. Fed.
14 C3 Bokovskaya Rus. Fed.
76 B5 Boké Guinea
78 B3 Bokungu Zaire
28 D2 Bokujevo r. Rus. Fed.
42 B2 Bokpyin Myanmar
82 C4 Boksburg R.S.A.
83 H2 Boksitogorsk Rus. Fed.
78 C4 Bokungu Zaire
78 B3 Bokwankusu Zaire
78 C3 Bolaiti Zaire
79 D4 Bolama Guinea-Bissau
78 E2 Bolanda, Jebel mt. Sudan
130 B4 Bolaños Mexico
130 C4 Bolaños r. Mexico
24 E1 Bolaños de Calatrava Spain
54 A3 Bolan Pass Pakistan
28 E2 Bolbec, Cape c. Phil.
140 C1 Boldești-Scăeni Romania
14 F2 Boldovo Rus. Fed.
28 F2 Boldu Romania
65 K4 Bole China
13 G5 Bole Ghana
28 D2 Bolesti r. Rus. Fed.
28 D2 Bolena Zaire
14 F2 Boleslawiec Poland
74 D4 Bolgar Rus. Fed.
76 D3 Bolgatanga Ghana
14 C2 Bolhrad Ukraine
78 C4 Boli China
14 G2 Bolia Sudan
10 D2 Boliden Sweden
140 D3 Bolintin-Vale Romania
14 C2 Bolívar Colombia
119 C5 Bolívar U.S.A.
138 C4 Bolívar Peru
138 C2 Bolívar Venezuela

21 G2 Bologne France
76 D5 Bondoukou Côte d'Ivoire
76 D4 Bondoukui Burkina
40 C3 Bondowoso Indon.
119 ☐7 Bonefish Pond I. The Bahamas
40 E3 Bone Lake l. Indon.
40 E3 Bonerate i. Indon.
40 E3 Bonerate, Kep. is Indon.
77 G4 Borno r. Nigeria
42 A2 Boruwa r. Sudan
40 C4 Bone, Co mt. Indon.
40 E3 Bone, Teluk b. Indon.
62 K3 Borodino Rus. Fed.
145 H2 Bonfim r. Brazil
145 H4 Bonfim Brazil
80 D3 Bonga Ethiopia
55 G4 Bongaigaon India
78 C3 Bongandanga Zaire
76 B5 Bong Co salt l. China
76 B5 Bongo Mts h. Liberia
41 B5 Bongo i. Phil.
83 H2 Bongolava mts Madagascar
78 D2 Bongo, Massif des mts C.A.R.
79 C5 Bongor Chad
79 C5 Bongo, Serra de mts Angola
76 D5 Bonguanou Côte d'Ivoire
13 G6 Bongville Italy
55 G1 Boni Mali
26 E3 Bonifacio France
26 G1 Bonifacio, Strait of str. France/Italy
143 A5 Bonito Mato Grosso do Sul Brazil
145 F1 Bonito Minas Gerais Brazil
28 C1 Bonn r. Brazil
18 C3 Bonn Germany
28 E1 Borsec Romania
93 ☐2 Bounty Is is Rep. of Ire.
65 K3 Bonners Ferry U.S.A.
21 H3 Bonneville France
48 D2 Bonney, L. l. Aust.
126 E3 Bonneville France
21 G3 Bonneville France
45 E3 Bono Italy
27 B5 Bono Italy
13 G6 Bonorva Italy
120 B6 Boone U.S.A.
124 E3 Boone U.S.A.
120 B6 Boone U.S.A.
125 F4 Boonesborough U.S.A.
118 D4 Boonville U.S.A.
121 F3 Boonville U.S.A.
48 A5 Böön Tsagaan Nuur salt l. Mongolia
116 C4 Booneville U.S.A.
124 E3 Boonville U.S.A.
121 F3 Boonville U.S.A.
93 B6 Bōōn Pt pt Antigua Caribbean
48 A5 Böön Tsagaan Nuur salt l. Mongolia
119 H4 Boonville U.S.A.
26 F3 Boona r. Bos.-Herz.
4 G Bosnia-Herzegovina country Europe
56 D5 Boorama Somalia

76 D5 Bondoukou Côte d'Ivoire
11 D3 Borlänge Sweden
76 C4 Bornay Germany
13 L5 Bornholm i. Denmark
11 D5 Bornholm div. Denmark
77 G4 Borno r. Nigeria
42 A2 Boro r. Sudan
62 K3 Borodino Rus. Fed.
11 H3 Borodinskoye Rus. Fed.
63 R3 Borogontsy Rus. Fed.
65 K4 Borohoro Shan mt. ra. China
14 D3 Borok Rus. Fed.
12 H3 Borok-Sulezhskiy Rus. Fed.
78 D1 Boromata C.A.R.
15 F1 Boromlya Ukraine
15 F1 Boromlya Ukraine
76 C4 Boromo Burkina
76 C4 Boron Mali
76 C5 Borotou Côte d'Ivoire
78 B3 Boumba r. Cameroon
78 D5 Bouna Côte d'Ivoire
15 C3 Borova Kharkiv Ukraine
12 E1 Borova Kyyiv Ukraine
12 E1 Borovichi Rus. Fed.
14 D3 Borovoy Rus. Fed.
65 H2 Borovoye Kazak.
65 H3 Borovskiy Kazak.
64 F2 Borovskoy Kazak.
65 G1 Borovskiy Kazak.
78 D2 Borovaya Rus. Fed.
57 B3 Borūjen Iran
57 B3 Borūjerd Iran
48 E1 Bor Uul Shan mt. ra. China
13 B5 Boryslav Ukraine
15 C1 Boryspil' Ukraine
15 E1 Borzenka r. Ukraine
28 E2 Borzna Ukraine
49 F2 Borzya Rus. Fed.
26 F3 Bosa Italy
26 F3 Bosanska Dubica Bos.-Herz.
26 F3 Bosanska Gradiška Bos.-Herz.
26 F3 Bosanska Kostajnica Bos.-Herz.
26 F3 Bosanska Krupa Bos.-Herz.
26 F3 Bosanski Novi Bos.-Herz.
26 F3 Bosanski Petrovac Bos.-Herz.
26 F3 Bosansko Grahovo Bos.-Herz.
26 D2 Boskovice Czech Rep.
42 B5 Bose China
50 D4 Bose China
50 D4 Bose China
57 D2 Bosenge Zaire
48 K9 Bosnyakovo i. Atlantic Ocean
4 G Bosnia-Herzegovina country Europe
56 D5 Boorama Somalia
78 D2 Bosobolo C.A.R.
78 C3 Bosobolo Zaire
42 B4 Bosom Somalia
80 E2 Bosobolo Somalia
55 H4 Bosporos Somalia
45 F3 Bossangoa C.A.R.
78 C3 Bossembélé C.A.R.
78 C3 Bossentélé C.A.R.
125 E5 Bossier City U.S.A.
82 A3 Bossiesvlei Namibia
47 F5 Bōsō-hantō pen. Japan
24 E1 Bossóst Spain
79 H1 Bosten Hu l. China
125 F5 Boston U.S.A.
17 G5 Boston U.K.
121 H3 Boston U.S.A.
125 E5 Boston Mts mts U.S.A.
115 G5 Boswell Can.
54 A3 Botad India
28 E2 Botany B. b. Aust.
82 C3 Botev mt. Bulgaria
28 D3 Botevgrad Bulgaria
28 D3 Botevgrad Bulgaria
82 C3 Bothaville R.S.A.
10 F3 Bothnia, Gulf of g. Finland/Sweden
99 G3 Botany B. b. Aust.
97 G3 Botany B. b. Aust.
42 B3 Botou China
28 F1 Botoşani Romania
139 J4 Boto-Pasi Surinam
78 C3 Botro Côte d'Ivoire
139 F4 Botum Brazil
13 H5 Botkul', Ozero l. Rus. Fed.
57 B3 Borjomi Georgia
51 F3 Botou China
42 B3 Botou China
72 C4 Botro Côte d'Ivoire

76 D5 Bondoukou Côte d'Ivoire
77 E3 Boughessa Mali
76 C4 Bougouni Mali
76 C4 Bougtob Algeria
133 ☐5 Bouillante Guadeloupe Caribbean
18 B4 Bouillon Belgium
75 E1 Bouira Algeria
74 B3 Boujdour Western Sahara
74 B3 Boukra Western Sahara
45 A3 Boukra Chad
62 K3 Borodino Rus. Fed.
145 G5 Brahman Baria Bangladesh
145 G5 Brahmapur India
126 F3 Boulder U.S.A.
126 F3 Boulder U.S.A.
101 C6 Boulder Aust.
129 E3 Boulder U.S.A.
129 E3 Boulder Canyon U.S.A.
129 E4 Boulder City U.S.A.
128 D5 Boulevard U.S.A.
14 D3 Borok Rus. Fed.
20 F1 Boulogne-Billancourt France
20 E1 Boulogne-sur-Mer France
78 D2 Boulsa Burkina
78 B4 Boumango Gabon
78 B3 Boumba r. Cameroon
78 D5 Bouna Côte d'Ivoire
128 C3 Boundary Peak summit U.S.A.
76 C5 Boundiali Côte d'Ivoire
42 C2 Boundji Congo
42 C2 Boung r. Vietnam
78 D2 Boung r. Vietnam
43 D4 Boun Nua Laos
42 C2 Boun Nua Laos
74 B5 Boû Nâga Mauritania
121 H2 Boundary Mountains mt. ra. U.S.A.
15 C1 Bourail Pac. Oc.
21 G3 Bourbince r. France
152 Bourbon, C. c. Kerguelen Indian Ocean
21 G3 Bourbon-Lancy France
21 F3 Bourbonne-les-Bains France
20 C2 Bourbriac France
20 E3 Bourem Mali
21 G3 Bourg r. France
20 F3 Bourges France
21 G3 Bourg-en-Bresse France
115 H4 Bourget Can.
18 E3 Bourgogne div. France
21 H4 Bourg-St-Maurice France
21 H4 Bourke Aust.
17 G6 Bournemouth U.K.
98 C4 Brassey, Mt mt. Aust.
78 D1 Bourtoutou Chad
75 E1 Bou Saâda Algeria
75 F1 Bou Salem Tunisia
78 D1 Bouar C.A.R.
17 G6 Bourmerdes Algeria
40 B3 Bovet Norway
139 H4 Bossu r. Bos.-Herz.
118 C4 Boswell U.S.A.
40 D2 Boven Kapuas Mts mt. ra. Malaysia
4 G Bosnia-Herzegovina country Europe
76 Boa Vista i. Cape Verde
130 D2 Bravo del Norte r. Mexico/U.S.A.
14 G1 Bovrovitsa Ukraine
15 E2 Bovtyshka Ukraine
139 J4 Boto-Pasi Surinam
100 B4 Bow r. Aust.
110 G4 Bow r. Can.
17 D5 Bray Rep. of Ire.
15 D2 Brayiiv Ukraine
119 D5 Braidwood U.S.A.
64 E1 Braga div. Portugal
28 E1 Brăhnea div. Romania
11 C5 Brande Denmark
18 F2 Brandenburg div. Germany
18 F2 Brandenburg Germany
21 J5 Brandon France
21 J5 Brandon France
124 D3 Brandon U.S.A.
123 G3 Brandon U.S.A.
121 G3 Brandon U.S.A.
17 A5 Brandon Head hd Rep. of Ire.
24 E1 Braña r. U.S.A.
82 C4 Brandvlei R.S.A.
11 C5 Brande Denmark
18 F2 Brandenburg div. Germany
18 F2 Brandenburg Germany

110 B3 Brady Gl. gl. U.S.A.
23 B2 Braemar U.K.
24 B2 Braga Portugal
146 D4 Bragado Arg.
142 C1 Bragança Brazil
24 C1 Bragança Portugal
145 E5 Bragança Paulista Brazil
15 D1 Brahin Belarus
55 H4 Brahmakund India
55 G5 Brahman Baria Bangladesh
55 G5 Brahmani r. India
55 F5 Brahmapur India
120 B6 Brady Gl. gl. U.S.A.
128 D5 Boulevard U.S.A.
83 D3 Brak r. R.S.A.
98 D3 Bravía div. Czech Rep.
20 F2 Braine-le-Château France
11 C5 Brämön i. Sweden
11 E3 Bramming Denmark
21 J5 Brampton Can.
17 F4 Brampton U.K.
54 C2 Bramwell Aust.
139 H3 Branco r. Brazil
139 E3 Branco r. Arg.
139 E3 Branco r. Brazil
139 E4 Branco r. Brazil
82 A3 Brandberg mt. Namibia
11 C5 Brandbu Norway
11 C5 Brande Denmark
18 F2 Brandenburg div. Germany
18 F2 Brandenburg Germany
21 J5 Brandon France
124 D3 Brandon U.S.A.
121 G3 Brandon U.S.A.
17 A5 Brandon Head hd Rep. of Ire.
144 B4 Brasiléia Brazil
144 C1 Brasília Brazil
142 A3 Brasília Legal Brazil
145 G3 Braúnas Brazil
18 F2 Braunau am Inn Austria
18 E2 Braunschweig Germany
76 ☐ Brava i. Cape Verde
130 D2 Bravo del Norte r. Mexico/U.S.A.
129 E5 Brawley U.S.A.
17 D5 Bray Rep. of Ire.
15 D2 Brayiiv Ukraine
143 A4 Brazil country S. America
126 F4 Brazil Basin Atlantic
121 H3 Breakseá Sd inlet N.Z.
108 G4 Bream Bay b. N.Z.
93 A6 Breaksea Sd inlet N.Z.
93 E2 Bream Bay b. N.Z.
93 E2 Bream Head hd N.Z.
93 E2 Bream Tail c. N.Z.
40 B3 Brebes Indon.
14 G2 Brebes Indon.
16 E3 Brechin U.K.
18 B3 Brecht Belgium
109 K2 Brodeur Peninsula pen. Can.
122 C4 Breckenridge U.S.A.
124 D2 Breckenridge U.S.A.
125 D5 Breckenridge U.S.A.
26 D2 Břeclav Czech Rep.
17 E6 Brecon U.K.
17 E6 Brecon Beacons U.K.
18 C2 Breda Netherlands
82 C5 Bredasdorp R.S.A.
98 D4 Bredbo Aust.
10 E3 Bredbyn Sweden
82 A3 Bredstedt Germany
65 G3 Bredy Rus. Fed.
18 C4 Bree Belgium
65 G3 Bregance Austria
18 D5 Bregenz Austria
28 F2 Bregovo Bulgaria
8 N2 Breiðafjörður b. Iceland
8 N2 Breiðdalsvík Iceland
21 H5 Breil-sur-Roya France
18 C4 Breisach am Rhein Germany
15 B1 Brejinha de Nazaré Brazil
142 D1 Brejo Brazil
145 G3 Brejo da Porta Brazil
145 F2 Brejo de Goiás Brazil

28 E2 Brezoi Romania
28 E3 Brezovo Bulgaria
78 D2 Bria C.A.R.
21 H4 Briançon France
21 F3 Briare France
99 H5 Bribie I. i. Aust.
15 B2 Briceni Moldova
20 D2 Bricquebec France
129 G1 Bridgeland U.S.A.
121 G4 Bridgeport U.S.A.
124 C3 Bridgeport U.S.A.
126 F3 Bridger Peak summit U.S.A.
121 F5 Bridgeton U.S.A.
101 A7 Bridgetown Aust.
133 ☐9 Bridgetown Barbados Caribbean
110 H4 Bridgewater Can.
121 H3 Bridgewater U.S.A.
121 K1 Bridgewater U.S.A.
121 G4 Bridgwater U.K.
121 G4 Bridgwater Bay b. U.K.
17 G4 Bridlington U.K.
97 G4 Bridport Aust.
17 E6 Bridport U.K.
20 C2 Briec France
21 G2 Brienne-le-Château France
21 G2 Brienne-le-Château France
21 H3 Brig Switz.
126 D3 Brigham City U.S.A.
93 C6 Brighton N.Z.
21 J5 Brighton France
17 G6 Brighton U.K.
123 F4 Brighton U.S.A.
142 E2 Brigida, R. da r. Brazil
121 G3 Brandon U.S.A.
17 B5 Brandon Head hd Rep. of Ire.
144 A3 Brikama The Gambia
18 E3 Brilhante r. Brazil
18 D3 Brilon Germany
14 F1 Brilyakovo Rus. Fed.
26 E3 Brindisi Italy
26 E3 Brioni Croatia
146 D3 Brinkmann Arg.
96 D3 Brinkworth Aust.
113 H4 Brion, Île i. Can.
20 F3 Brionne France
21 G3 Brioude France
20 E2 Briouze France
113 H4 Briouze France
113 J3 Brisay Can.
99 H5 Brisbane Aust.
17 F6 Bristol U.K.
121 K2 Bristol U.S.A.
108 B4 Bristol Bay b. U.S.A.
17 E6 Bristol Channel est. U.K.
152 C1 Bristol I. i. S. Sandwich Is Atlantic Ocean
121 G4 Bristol Lake l. U.S.A.
129 E4 Bristol Lake l. U.S.A.
92 ☐1 Bristow Pt pt Auckland Is N.Z.
82 C4 Britstown R.S.A.
110 D3 British Columbia div. Can.
109 L1 British Empire Range mt. ra. Can.
24 E1 Brihuega Spain
65 H4 Brno Czech Rep.
26 D2 Brno Czech Rep.
121 J5 Broad r. U.S.A.
119 D5 Broad r. U.S.A.
123 F4 Broad Arrow Aust.
112 D3 Broadback r. Can.
121 K4 Broadford U.K.
99 G4 Broad Sound Channel chan. Aust.
126 F2 Broadus U.S.A.
111 H4 Broadview Can.
113 J4 Broadwater U.S.A.
112 E4 Brochet, Lac l. Can.
111 H3 Brock r. U.S.A.
108 F2 Brock I. i. Can.
123 F4 Brockport U.S.A.
121 H3 Brockton U.S.A.
115 H4 Brockville Can.
120 D4 Brockway U.S.A.
109 K2 Brodeur Peninsula pen. Can.
16 D5 Brodick U.K.
19 J2 Brodnica Poland
15 C1 Brody Ukraine
125 E4 Broken Arrow U.S.A.
97 F3 Broken Hill Aust.
96 E2 Broken Hill Aust.
139 F3 Brokopondo Surinam
12 H2 Brokopondo Surinam
142 C1 Brejo Brazil
125 F5 Brownfield U.S.A.
121 J2 Brewer U.S.A.
125 C5 Brownfield U.S.A.
121 J5 Brewster U.S.A.
18 E2 Bronzone U.S.A.
101 B6 Brown, L. salt flat Aust.
125 D6 Brownsville U.S.A.
122 C3 Browns Mills U.S.A.

C

133 □1 Brown's Town Jamaica
119 B5 Brownsville U.S.A.
125 D7 Brownsville U.S.A.
121 J2 Brownsville U.S.A.
121 J2 Brownsville Junction U.S.A.
125 D6 Brownwood U.S.A.
100 C2 Browse I. i. Aust.
24 J3 Brozas Spain
53 D4 Brozha Belarus
20 F1 Bruay-en-Artois France
133 □9 Bruce Barbados Caribbean
93 B5 Bruce Bay b. N.Z.
122 C2 Bruce Crossing U.S.A.
100 B4 Bruce, Mt mt. Aust.
114 E4 Bruce Pen. pen. Can.
114 E4 Bruce Peninsula National Park nat. park Can.
101 B6 Bruce Rock Aust.
18 D4 Bruchsal Germany
18 □ Bruck an der Leitha Austria
19 G5 Bruck an der Mur Austria
18 A3 Brugge Belgium
129 G2 Bruin Pt summit U.S.A.
53 G4 Bruini India
61 B4 Brŭk, W. el w Egypt
122 B2 Brule U.S.A.
145 F4 Brumadinho Brazil
142 D3 Brumado Brazil
11 □ Brumunddal Norway
126 D3 Bruneau r. U.S.A.
126 D3 Bruneau U.S.A.
33 N9 Brunei country Asia
98 C3 Brunette Downs Aust.
10 □3 Brunflo Sweden
26 C2 Brunico Italy
93 C5 Brunner, L. l. N.Z.
111 H4 Bruno Can.
18 D2 Brunsbüttel Germany
119 D6 Brunswick U.S.A.
121 J3 Brunswick U.S.A.
120 C4 Brunswick U.S.A.
100 D2 Brunswick Bay b. Aust.
101 A7 Brunswick Jct. Aust.
114 D2 Brunswick Lake l. Can.
147 B7 Brunswick, Península de pen. Chile
19 H4 Bruntál Czech Rep.
152 E1 Brunt Ice Shelf ice feature Ant.
97 F5 Bruny I. i. Aust.
28 C3 Brus Yugo.
12 G2 Brusenets Rus. Fed.
126 G3 Brush U.S.A.
114 E5 Brussels Can.
122 D3 Brussels U.S.A.
19 H2 Brusy Poland
15 C1 Brusyliv Ukraine
97 F4 Bruthen Aust.
18 B3 Bruxelles Belgium
120 A4 Bryan U.S.A.
125 D6 Bryan U.S.A.
152 A3 Bryan Coast Ant.
96 D3 Bryan, Mt h. Aust.
14 A3 Bryansk Rus. Fed.
13 H6 Bryanskaya div. Rus. Fed.
129 F3 Bryce Canyon National Park nat. park U.S.A.
129 H5 Bryce Mt mt. U.S.A.
15 E3 Brylivka Ukraine
13 F6 Bryne Norway
13 H5 Bryukhovetskaya Rus. Fed.
19 H3 Brzeg Poland
19 H3 Brzeg Dolny Poland
19 J4 Brzozów Krosno Poland
73 J4 Bū Fiji
90 □6 Bua r. Malawi
81 B7 Bua r. Malawi
80 D4 Bu'aale Somalia
90 □1 Buala Solomon Is.
94 D1 Bua, Tg pt Indon.
72 D2 Bū Athiah w/l Libya
72 C1 Bu'ayrāt al Ḩasūn Libya
76 A4 Buba Guinea-Bissau
81 A5 Bubanza Burundi
76 A4 Bubaque Guinea-Bissau
83 E3 Bubi r. Zimbabwe
41 B5 Bubiyan I. i. Kuwait
90 □6 Buca Fiji
29 F5 Buca Turkey
60 B2 Bucak Turkey
61 B1 Bucakkışla Turkey
133 C2 Bucaramanga Colombia
41 C4 Bucas Grande i. Phil.
100 C3 Buccaneer Archipelago is Aust.
27 E4 Buccino Italy
15 A2 Buchach Ukraine
97 G4 Buchan Aust.
76 B5 Buchanan Liberia
122 D5 Buchanan U.S.A.
120 D6 Buchanan U.S.A.
99 F4 Buchanan, L. salt flat Aust.
101 C5 Buchanan, L. salt flat Aust.
125 D6 Buchanan, L. l. U.S.A.
109 L2 Buchan Gulf b. Can.
113 J4 Buchans Can.
18 D2 Buchholz in der Nordheide Germany
128 B4 Buchon, Point pt U.S.A.
97 F2 Buckambool Mt h. Aust.
129 F5 Buckeye U.S.A.
120 B5 Buckeye Lake l. U.S.A.
120 C5 Buckhannon r. U.S.A.
120 C5 Buckhannon U.S.A.
115 F4 Buckhorn Can.
129 H5 Buckhorn U.S.A.
115 F4 Buckhorn Lake l. Can.
16 F3 Buckie U.K.
115 H4 Buckingham Can.
17 G5 Buckingham U.K.
98 C2 Buckingham B. b. Aust.
99 G5 Buckland Tableland reg. Aust.
152 A6 Buckle I. i. Ant.
94 □3 Buckley Bay b. Macquarie I. Pac. Oc.
128 D3 Buckley U.S.A.
129 F4 Buckskin Mts mts U.S.A.
121 K2 Bucks Mt mt. U.S.A.
121 J2 Bucksport U.S.A.
19 H4 Bučovice Czech Rep.
79 B4 Buco-Zau Cabinda Angola
28 E2 Bucureşti Romania
122 B4 Bucyrus U.S.A.
14 B3 Buda Rus. Fed.
25 G2 Buda, Illa de i. Spain
42 A2 Budalin Myanmar
19 J5 Budapest Hungary
54 D3 Budaun India
80 E4 Budd Coast Ant.
152 G6 Budd Coast Ant.
80 D3 Buddi Ethiopia
27 B5 Budduso Italy
17 E6 Bude U.K.
125 F6 Bude U.S.A.
13 H6 Budennovsk Rus. Fed.
28 F2 Budeşti Romania
54 B4 Budhapur India
61 B5 Budhīya, G. mt. i. Egypt
54 C3 Budjala India
54 C5 Budini India
12 E3 Budogoshch' Rus. Fed.
55 H2 Budongquan China
27 B5 Budoni Italy
28 B3 Budva Yugo.
21 B4 Buech r. France
128 B4 Buellton U.S.A.
146 C3 Buena Esperanza Arg.
138 B3 Buenaventura Colombia
130 D2 Buenaventura Mexico
138 B3 Buenaventura, B. de b. Colombia

127 F4 Buena Vista U.S.A.
120 D6 Buena Vista U.S.A.
132 C2 Buena Vista, B. de b. Cuba
24 D1 Buenavista de Valdavia Spain
25 E2 Buendia, Embalse de resr Spain
79 C5 Buenga r. Angola
76 □ Bueno r. Chile
147 B5 Buenópolis Brazil
146 D4 Buenos Aires div. Arg.
146 E3 Buenos Aires Arg.
140 B1 Buenos Aires Brazil
147 B6 Buenos Aires, L. l. Arg.
133 □3 Buenos Ayres Trin. & Tobago
147 B5 Buen Pasto Arg.
147 C7 Buen Tiempo, C. hd Arg.
145 J1 Buerarema Brazil
24 D1 Bueu Spain
130 D3 Búfalo Mexico
110 D3 Buffalo r. Can.
125 D4 Buffalo r. U.S.A.
124 C2 Buffalo U.S.A.
125 D6 Buffalo U.S.A.
122 B3 Buffalo U.S.A.
122 B3 Buffalo r. U.S.A.
126 F2 Buffalo U.S.A.
110 F3 Buffalo Head Hills h. Can.
110 F2 Buffalo Lake l. Can.
111 H3 Buffalo Narrows Can.
133 □1 Buff Bay Jamaica
82 B4 Buffels r. R.S.A.
119 D5 Buford U.S.A.
28 □ Buftea Romania
19 K2 Bug r. Poland
138 B3 Buga Colombia
77 F5 Bugana Nigeria
48 C2 Bugant Mongolia
19 □ Bugel, Tg pt Indon.
24 □ Bugojno Bos.-Herz.
62 F3 Bugrino Rus. Fed.
14 □ Bugsuk i. Phil.
49 E2 Bugt China
62 J1 Bugul'deyka Rus. Fed.
64 D2 Bugul'ma r. Rus. Fed.
78 B1 Buguruma Rus. Fed.
64 F3 Bugun' w/l Sudan
62 G2 Buguruslan Rus. Fed.
28 A3 Buh r. China
59 K6 Bühabad Iran
60 C3 Buḩayrat al Asad resr Syria
61 D3 Buḩayrat ath Tharthār l. Iraq
60 E3 Buhera Zimbabwe
41 B3 Buhi Phil.
18 D4 Bühl Germany
99 F4 Buhl U.S.A.
122 A2 Bühtan r. Turkey
81 C6 Buhu r. Tanzania
28 F1 Buhuşi Romania
17 F5 Builth Wells U.K.
90 □1 Buin P.N.G.
76 D5 Bui National Park nat. park Ghana
12 J4 Buinsk Rus. Fed.
57 B2 Bu'in Zahrā Iran
49 F3 Buir Nur l. Mongolia
82 A2 Buitepos Namibia
18 E1 Burg Sachsen-Anhalt Germany
24 D4 Bujalance Spain
28 E3 Bujanovac Yugo.
28 E3 Bujoru Romania
19 H2 Buk Poland
81 A5 Bujumbura Burundi
81 A5 Buka, I. i. P.N.G.
82 C2 Bukalo Namibia
14 B3 Bukan' Rus. Fed.
57 D3 Būkānd Iran
64 F5 Bukhara Uzbekistan
65 K3 Bukhtarminskoye Vdkhr. resr Kazak.
41 B4 Bukide I. i. Indon.
11 E4 Bukovsik Sweden
44 A4 Burhan Budai Shan mt. ra. China
43 □ Bukit Batok Singapore
54 D5 Bukit Fraser Malaysia
43 □ Bukittinggi Indon.
38 D7 Bukit Panjang Singapore
43 □ Bukit Timah Singapore
53 H4 Bükk mts Hungary
81 B5 Bukka, J. el mt. Jordan
81 B5 Bukoba Tanzania
81 B5 Bukombekombe Tanzania
14 D2 Bukrino Rus. Fed.
94 D1 Bukum, P. i. Singapore
77 F5 Bukuru Nigeria
15 D2 Buky Ukraine
42 B2 Bula Myanmar
21 K7 Bülach Switz.
144 D2 Bulagtay Mongolia
48 B1 Bulan r. Mongolia
41 B3 Bulan Phil.
60 D1 Bulancak Turkey
54 D3 Bulandshahr India
73 E2 Būlaq Egypt
83 E3 Bulawayo Zimbabwe
65 H2 Bulayevo Kazak.
54 D4 Buldan India
78 B3 Buldana India
80 C3 Bulei well Ethiopia
28 □ Bulgan Mongolia
48 B3 Bulgan Bulgan Mongolia
48 B3 Bulgan Hövsgöl Mongolia
48 B3 Bulgan Ömnögovĭ Mongolia
48 A2 Bulgan div. Mongolia
28 E3 Bulgaria country Europe
5 H4 Bullaregh Somalia
133 □1 Bull Bay Jamaica
124 F3 Bulle U.S.A.
21 H7 Bulle Switz.
97 H3 Bullen Baai b. Curaçao
132 □2 Bullenbaai b. Curaçao
121 J2 Bullhead City U.S.A.
129 E4 Bullhead City U.S.A.
128 C4 Bullion Mts mts U.S.A.
99 E6 Bulloo watercourse Aust.
99 E6 Bulloo Downs Aust.
99 E6 Bulloo L. salt flat Aust.
92 □ Bull Rock i. Campbell I. N.Z.
65 H4 Bulnayn Range mt. ra. Mongolia
111 H1 Bulun Rus. Fed.
43 □ Bulolo P.N.G.
29 G4 Bulqizë Albania
108 E3 Bulukumba Indon.
119 F7 Bulwell well Malawi
78 B4 Bulukutu Indon.
42 A2 Bum Cameroon
79 C4 Bulungu Bandundu Zaire
78 B4 Bulungu Kasai-Occidental Zaire
65 G5 Bulunqu Uzbekistan
41 □ Bulusan Phil.
78 B3 Bulwark Cameroon
81 B5 Bumba Équateur Zaire
79 D4 Bumba Bandundu Zaire
42 B2 Bumbat-Jiu Romania
81 B5 Bumbire I. i. Tanzania
129 F4 Bumble Bee U.S.A.
42 A2 Bum-Bum i. Malaysia
42 A2 Bumkhang Myanmar
79 C4 Buna Zaire

81 B5 Bunazi Tanzania
101 A7 Bunbury Aust.
17 D4 Buncrana Rep. of Ire.
81 B5 Bunda Tanzania
99 H5 Bundaberg Aust.
97 G2 Bundarra Aust.
98 C4 Bundey w Aust.
54 C4 Bundi India
81 B4 Bundibugyo Uganda
17 C4 Bundoran Rep. of Ire.
80 B3 Bunduqiya Sudan
77 F4 Bunga w Nigeria
17 H5 Bungay U.K.
69 G6 Bungku Indon.
81 A5 Bunguu Burundi
18 E4 Bunia Zaire
79 D4 Buniania Zaire
54 D2 Buni-Yadi Nigeria
54 C2 Bunji Jammu and Kashmir
99 H4 Bunker Group atolls Aust.
129 E3 Bunkerville U.S.A.
125 E6 Bunkie U.S.A.
119 D6 Bunnell U.S.A.
25 F3 Buñol Spain
40 C2 Buntok Indon.
40 C2 Buntokecil Indon.
78 C4 Bununu Nigeria
40 C2 Bünyan Turkey
41 A6 Bunyu i. Indon.
77 G6 Bunza Nigeria
61 D3 Buoʻai al Kheyr Iran
43 E4 Buôn Mê Thuột Vietnam
63 P2 Buorkhaya, Guba b. Rus. Fed.
28 E2 Buşteni Romania
130 D2 Bustillos, L. l. Mexico
80 D3 Buto Arsizio Italy
41 A3 Busuanga Phil.
41 A3 Busuanga i. Phil.
78 D3 Büsum Germany
78 D3 Buta Zaire
145 J2 Buranhaém r. Brazil
145 H2 Buranhaém Brazil
80 C3 Buraq Syria
14 H3 Burasy Rus. Fed.
41 B3 Burauen U.K.
73 H2 Buraydah Saudi Arabia
16 E4 Bute i. U.K.
110 D4 Butedale Can.
78 E3 Butembo Zaire
83 D4 Butha-Buthe Lesotho
79 C4 Buthidaung Myanmar
122 B5 Butler U.S.A.
120 C4 Butler U.S.A.
39 H8 Buton i. Indon.
15 G1 Butovo Rus. Fed.
128 B1 Butte Meadows U.S.A.
82 B5 Butterworth Malaysia
82 D5 Butterworth R.S.A.
16 F5 Butt of Lewis hd U.K.
109 M3 Button Is is Can.
128 C2 Buttonwillow U.S.A.
101 C7 Butty Hd pt Aust.
40 A2 Butuan Indon.
41 C4 Butuan Phil.
13 G5 Buturlino Rus. Fed.
13 G5 Buturlinovka Rus. Fed.
54 E3 Butwal Nepal
14 E2 Butylitsy Rus. Fed.
18 E1 Bützow Germany
80 E4 Buulobarde Somalia
80 B4 Buur Gaabo Somalia
80 D4 Buurhabaka Somalia
81 B4 Buvuma I. i. Uganda
80 D4 Buwāh, J. mt. Saudi Arabia
18 D4 Buxar India
18 D4 Buxtehude Germany
17 G4 Buxton U.K.
12 G3 Buy r. Rus. Fed.
62 G4 Buy U.S.A.
48 B3 Buyant Mongolia
48 A3 Buyant Gol r. Mongolia
48 B3 Buyant-Ovoo Mongolia
48 C3 Buyant-Uhaa Mongolia
122 A1 Buyck U.S.A.
13 H7 Buynaksk Rus. Fed.
76 B4 Buyo, Lac de l. Côte d'Ivoire
50 C4 Buyuan r. China
60 E1 Büyük Ağrı mt. Turkey
61 B1 Büyük Egri D. mt. Turkey
29 G6 Büyükkarıştıran Turkey
29 G5 Büyükmenderes r. Turkey
28 □ Büyükorhan Turkey
54 C2 Buyun Shan mt. China
80 D3 Buzachi, Pov. pen. Kazak.
20 E3 Buzançais France
28 E2 Buzău Romania
73 B4 Buzaymah oasis Libya
47 H6 Buzen Japan
83 E3 Búzi r. Mozambique
146 D4 Buzios, Ilha dos i. Brazil
145 H5 Buzios, Cabo dos hd Brazil
80 □ Caddabassa l. Ethiopia
18 □ Cadenberge Germany
128 C4 Cadibarrawirracanna, L. salt flat Aust.
96 C2 Cadibarrawirracanna, L. salt flat Aust.
115 H2 Cadillac Can.
20 D4 Cadillac France
122 E3 Cadillac U.S.A.
41 B4 Cadiz Phil.
24 C4 Cádiz Spain
129 E4 Cádiz U.S.A.
24 C4 Cádiz, Golfo de g. Spain
128 D4 Cadiz Lake l. U.S.A.
20 D2 Caen France
17 C5 Caernarfon U.K.
17 C5 Caernarfon Bay b. U.K.
120 D6 Caesar Creek Lake l. U.S.A.
61 C3 Caesarea Israel
142 D3 Caetité Brazil
146 C3 Cafayate Arg.
139 E4 Cafelândia Brazil
139 F4 Cafifos Brazil
140 B1 Cafuni Brazil
140 B1 Cafuni r. Brazil
80 C2 Cafuni r. Brazil
48 □2 Cagayan r. Phil.
41 B4 Cagayan de Oro Phil.
41 B5 Cagayan Islands is Phil.
29 □ Cagli Italy
27 B6 Cagliari Italy
27 B6 Cagliari, Golfo di b. Italy
21 H5 Cagnes-sur-Mer France
133 E3 Caguán r. Colombia
133 E5 Caguas Puerto Rico
119 C6 Cahaba r. U.S.A.
17 C5 Caha Mts h. Rep. of Ire.
17 C6 Cahir Rep. of Ire.
17 B6 Cahirciveen Rep. of Ire.
119 □2 Cahokia U.S.A.
20 E4 Cahors France
138 B3 Cahuapanas Peru
24 E3 Cahul Moldova
83 D2 Cahora Bassa, Barragem de dam Mozambique
83 D2 Cahora Bassa, Lago de resr Mozambique
17 D6 Cahore Point pt Rep. of Ire.
20 E4 Cahors France
138 B3 Cahuapanas Peru

60 B1 Bursa Turkey
73 F2 Bûr Safâga Egypt
15 A2 Burshtyn Ukraine
73 E2 Bûr Taufiq Egypt
122 D3 Burt Lake l. U.S.A.
123 F4 Burton U.S.A.
112 E3 Burton, Lac l. Can.
17 C4 Burtonport Rep. of Ire.
17 G5 Burton upon Trent U.K.
42 A3 Burtrisk Sweden
121 K1 Burtts Corner Can.
97 E3 Burtundy Aust.
39 J7 Buru i. Indon.
81 A5 Burundi country Africa
81 A5 Bururi Burundi
100 B2 Burwash Landing Can.
16 F2 Burwick U.K.
115 K4 Bury Can.
17 G4 Bury U.K.
48 B2 Buryatiya div. Rus. Fed.
15 E1 Buryn' Ukraine
17 H5 Bury St Edmunds U.K.
54 C2 Burzil Pass pass Jammu & Kashmir
74 □ Busanga Zaire
15 C2 Busha Ukraine
81 D5 Bushush r. Kenya/Somalia
80 D2 Bûshâd Qaadir Somalia
14 A3 Bushcha Ukraine
57 B3 Būshehr div. Iran
57 B3 Būshehr Iran
55 E2 Bushēngcaka China
81 B5 Bushenyi Uganda
122 B5 Bushnell U.S.A.
49 F1 Bushuley Rus. Fed.
78 D3 Businga Zaire
79 B5 Busina Italy
14 C3 Busk r. Poland
61 D3 Buşrá ash Shām Syria
49 H2 Busse Rus. Fed.
97 F2 Busselton Aust.
78 E2 Bustamante, B. b. Arg.
147 C6 Bustamante, B. b. Arg.
28 E2 Buşteni Romania
130 D2 Bustillos, L. l. Mexico
80 D3 Buto Arsizio Italy
41 A3 Busuanga Phil.
41 A3 Busuanga i. Phil.
78 D3 Büsum Germany
78 D3 Buta Zaire
145 J2 Butajira Ethiopia
43 B6 Butang Group is Thailand
81 A5 Butare Rwanda
16 E4 Bute i. U.K.
78 E3 Butea Romania
110 D4 Butedale Can.
78 E3 Butembo Zaire
83 D4 Butha-Buthe Lesotho
79 C4 Buthidaung Myanmar
122 B5 Butler U.S.A.
120 C4 Butler U.S.A.
39 H8 Buton i. Indon.
15 G1 Butovo Rus. Fed.
128 B1 Butte Meadows U.S.A.
82 B5 Butterworth Malaysia
82 D5 Butterworth R.S.A.
16 F5 Butt of Lewis hd U.K.
109 M3 Button Is is Can.
128 C2 Buttonwillow U.S.A.
101 C7 Butty Hd pt Aust.
40 A2 Butuan Indon.
41 C4 Butuan Phil.
13 G5 Buturlino Rus. Fed.
13 G5 Buturlinovka Rus. Fed.
54 E3 Butwal Nepal
14 E2 Butylitsy Rus. Fed.
18 E1 Bützow Germany
80 E4 Buulobarde Somalia
80 B4 Buur Gaabo Somalia
80 D4 Buurhabaka Somalia
81 B4 Buvuma I. i. Uganda
80 D4 Buwāh, J. mt. Saudi Arabia
18 D4 Buxar India
18 D4 Buxtehude Germany
17 G4 Buxton U.K.
12 G3 Buy r. Rus. Fed.
62 G4 Buy U.S.A.
48 B3 Buyant Mongolia
48 A3 Buyant Gol r. Mongolia
48 B3 Buyant-Ovoo Mongolia
48 C3 Buyant-Uhaa Mongolia
122 A1 Buyck U.S.A.
13 H7 Buynaksk Rus. Fed.
76 B4 Buyo, Lac de l. Côte d'Ivoire
50 C4 Buyuan r. China
60 E1 Büyük Ağrı mt. Turkey
61 B1 Büyük Egri D. mt. Turkey
29 G6 Büyükkarıştıran Turkey
29 G5 Büyükmenderes r. Turkey
28 □ Büyükorhan Turkey
54 C2 Buyun Shan mt. China
80 D3 Buzachi, Pov. pen. Kazak.
20 E3 Buzançais France
28 E2 Buzău Romania
73 B4 Buzaymah oasis Libya
47 H6 Buzen Japan
83 E3 Búzi r. Mozambique
146 D4 Buzios, Ilha dos i. Brazil
145 H5 Buzios, Cabo dos hd Brazil
80 □ Caddabassa l. Ethiopia
18 □ Cadenberge Germany
132 □3 California Trin. & Tobago
131 E3 Californía Mexico
96 C2 Caiabirrawirranna, L. salt flat Aust.
130 D2 California, Golfo de g. Mexico
119 □2 California Hot Springs U.S.A.
57 C2 Cālīābād Azerbaijan
28 □ Cālimăneşti Romania
28 E1 Cālimani, Munţii mt. ra. Romania
127 F5 Calipatria U.S.A.
128 B3 Calistoga U.S.A.
82 B5 Calitzdorp R.S.A.
57 C2 Calkini Mexico
97 G4 Callabonna Cr. w. Aust.
96 C2 Callabonna, L. salt flat Aust.
20 □2 Callac France
17 D5 Callan Rep. of Ire.
131 G4 Callander U.K.
138 C4 Callao Peru
140 C3 Callao U.S.A.
121 G4 Calloway U.S.A.
99 G5 Calliope Aust.
28 □ Câmpia Moldovei de Nord plain Moldova
15 B3 Câmpia Moldovei de Sud plain Moldova
28 □ Câmpia Turzii Romania
27 F4 Cagli Italy
27 B6 Cagliari Italy

43 D5 Cai Be Vietnam
139 D2 Caicara Venezuela
133 E5 Caicó Brazil
133 D2 Caicos Is is Turks and Caicos Is Caribbean
133 D2 Caicos Passage chan. The Bahamas/Turks and Caicos Is Caribbean
140 D3 Cailloma Peru
41 A3 Caiman Point pt. Phil.
40 A3 Cái Nước Vietnam
16 F3 Cairngorm Mts mt. ra. U.K.
99 F3 Cairns Aust.
61 E4 Cairo Egypt
61 E4 Cairo Egypt
26 C3 Cairo Montenotte Italy
79 B6 Caiundo Angola
79 C7 Caiundo Angola
99 F5 Caiwarro Aust.
51 G2 Caizi Hu l. China
119 □3 Caja de Muertos, I. i. Puerto Rico
138 B5 Cajamarca div. Peru
20 E4 Cajarc France
138 B5 Cajari Peru
142 D2 Cajatambo Peru
142 □2 Cajàzeiras Brazil
28 B2 Cajetina Yugo.
28 B2 Cajnice Bos.-Herz.
138 B5 Cajuru Brazil
140 B2 Cajuru Brazil
79 □ Caka Yanhu salt l. China
48 A5 Cakovec Croatia
60 C1 Çakırlar Turkey
26 F2 Çakovec Croatia
60 A1 Çakit r. Turkey
26 F2 Çakovec Croatia
79 C4 Cal Turkey
60 B1 Çal Turkey
115 H2 Calabar Nigeria
79 □ Calabozo Can.
145 E3 Calabozo Venezuela
27 F5 Calabria div. Italy
24 D3 Calaceite Italy
28 □ Calafat Romania
147 B7 Calafate Arg.
25 H3 Calaig Figuera, Cap de pt Spain
25 F1 Calahorra Spain
25 F1 Calais France
25 E1 Calais France
121 K2 Calais U.S.A.
140 C3 Calalaste, Sierra de mt. ra. Arg.
141 D1 Calama Brazil
140 C1 Calama Chile
146 C1 Calama Chile
138 C2 Calamar Bolívar Colombia
138 C3 Calamar Guaviare Colombia
41 A4 Calamian Group is Phil.
119 □3 Calamocha Spain
24 C4 Calamocha Spain
41 A3 Calamian Group is Phil.
24 F2 Calanda Spain
24 F2 Calanda mt. Spain
79 C6 Calandula Angola
72 D2 Calanscio Sand Sea desert Libya
41 B3 Calapan Phil.
41 B3 Calapayog Phil.
28 E2 Călăraşi Moldova
15 B3 Călăraşi Moldova
28 F2 Călăraşi Romania
25 F2 Calasparra Spain
27 E6 Calatafimi Italy
25 F2 Calatayud Spain
41 B3 Calauag Phil.
41 B4 Calavá, Cape c. Phil.
41 A3 Calayan i. Phil.
41 B3 Calbayog Phil.
28 B4 Calbuco Chile
139 G4 Calçado r. Brazil
79 C5 Calçoene Brazil
55 G5 Calcutta India
24 B3 Caldas da Rainha Portugal
142 D2 Caldas Novas Brazil
147 C4 Caldera Arg.
146 B2 Caldera Chile
82 □ Caldera, Cape c. Lesotho/R.S.A.
82 D4 Caldon r. R.S.A.
126 C2 Caldwell U.S.A.
140 C4 Caledon r. Lesotho/R.S.A.
82 □ Caledon R.S.A.
126 C2 Caledon B. b. Aust.
142 A2 Caledon Turkey
130 E3 Cadoux France
24 C2 Caledonia U.S.A.
127 F5 Cali Colombia
78 A3 Cali Colombia
138 B3 Cali Colombia
54 A4 Calicut India
56 C4 Caliente U.S.A.
129 E3 Caliente U.S.A.
128 B3 California U.S.A.
128 B4 California div. U.S.A.
130 B2 California, Golfo de g. Mexico

80 F2 Caluula Somalia
129 G5 Calva U.S.A.
98 D3 Calvert r. Aust.
146 D2 Calvert Hills Aust.
110 D4 Calvert I. i. Can.
101 C4 Calvert Ra. h. Aust.
21 J5 Calvi France
25 C4 Calviá Spain
130 E4 Calvillo Mexico
82 B5 Calvinia R.S.A.
27 E5 Calvo, Monte mt. Italy
24 D2 Calzada de Calatrava Spain
17 H5 Cam r. U.K.
79 B5 Camabatela Angola
145 J1 Camacã Brazil
142 C2 Camaçari Brazil
129 H2 Camache Reservoir resr U.S.A.
130 C3 Camacho Mexico
79 C6 Camacupa Angola
99 □6 Caiwarro Aust.
51 G2 Caizi Hu l. China
119 □3 Caja de Muertos, I. i. Puerto Rico
133 C2 Camaguán Venezuela
132 C2 Camagüey Cuba
132 C2 Camagüey, Arch. de is Cuba
143 C3 Camah, Gunung mt. Malaysia
145 E3 Camamu Brazil
146 B3 Camaná Peru
144 A3 Camanongue Angola
143 A3 Camapuã Brazil
143 B7 Camaquã r. Brazil
24 □ Câmara de Lobos Madeira Portugal
142 B1 Camaraipí r. Brazil
141 E2 Camaret-sur-Mer France
131 E4 Camargo Mexico
21 G5 Camargue reg. France
132 B2 Camarioca Cuba
147 B7 Camarones, C. c. Honduras
147 C6 Camarones Arg.
147 C6 Camarones, Bahía b. Arg.
24 C2 Camarzana de Tera Spain
35 M8 Cambodia country Asia
79 B6 Cambongo r. Angola
20 F1 Cambrai France
141 E2 Cambrian Mountains mt. ra. U.K.
114 C5 Cambridge Can.
92 □2 Cambridge N.Z.
17 H5 Cambridge U.K.
122 B5 Cambridge U.S.A.
121 J2 Cambridge U.S.A.
121 F5 Cambridge U.S.A.
120 C4 Cambridge U.S.A.
109 H3 Cambridge Bay Can.
133 E2 Cambridge Gulf b. Aust.
76 C4 Cambribs de Mar Spain
145 J5 Cambulo Angola
141 A3 Cambundi-Catembo Angola
145 H4 Cambuquira Brazil
97 G3 Camden Aust.
79 C5 Camden U.S.A.
125 E5 Camden U.S.A.
121 J2 Camden U.S.A.
121 F5 Camden U.S.A.
120 E5 Camden U.S.A.
99 F6 Camden Sd chan. Aust.
80 C3 Cameia, Parque Nacional de nat. park Angola
15 C2 Camena Moldova
138 B4 Camenca Moldova
146 C4 Cameron Arg.
124 D3 Cameron U.S.A.
125 D6 Cameron U.S.A.
121 □ Cameron U.S.A.
114 □ Cameron U.S.A.
110 A2 Cameron Falls Can.
111 J3 Cameron Highlands Malaysia
115 J3 Cameron Hills h. Can.
115 J3 Cameron Mts mts N.Z.
140 D4 Cameron country Africa
78 A3 Cameroun, Mont mt. Cameroon
142 A2 Cametá Brazil
141 B3 Camiguin i. Phil.
41 B4 Camiguin i. Phil.
41 B2 Camiguin i. Phil.
130 □ Camila U.S.A.
119 C6 Camilla U.S.A.
24 □ Caminha Portugal
142 B1 Camiranga Brazil
146 C1 Camiri Bolivia
142 B1 Camocim Brazil
98 D3 Camooweal Aust.
54 C5 Camorta i. Andaman and Nicobar Is India
24 □ Camotes i. Phil.
131 J4 Campana Mexico
119 D7 Campana Mexico
147 A7 Campana, I. i. Chile
138 B3 Campamento Honduras
24 D2 Campana div. Spain
25 G2 Campanet Spain
147 A7 Campana, I. i. Chile
111 G4 Campbell, Cape c. N.Z.
92 □2 Campbell, Cape c. N.Z.
94 □2 Campbell Island i. N.Z.
124 D1 Campbell, L. l. U.S.A.
100 □ Campbell Plateau Pac. Oc.
128 B2 Campbellpore Pakistan
93 □ Campbell River Can.
110 D4 Campbell River Can.
120 B6 Campbellsville U.S.A.
113 G4 Campbellton Can.
97 G3 Campbell Town Aust.
79 B5 Camabatela Angola
131 G4 Campeche Mexico
131 G5 Campeche, Bahía de g. Mexico
97 E4 Camperdown Aust.
119 □ Camperdown The Netherlands
28 D2 Câmpia Băileştilor plain Romania
140 C3 Campillos Spain
24 D4 Campina Romania
28 E2 Câmpina Romania
131 E5 Campoalegre Colombia
142 E2 Campina Grande Brazil
142 □2 Campina Verde Brazil
140 B2 Campinas Brazil
142 □2 Campina Verde Brazil
79 C6 Campo Cameroon
79 D6 Campoalegre Colombia
138 B3 Campo de Criptana Spain
142 D3 Campo Dolocino Italy
142 E2 Campo Esperanza Paraguay

80 F2 Caluula Somalia
144 D3 Campo Florido Brazil
142 D2 Campo Formoso Brazil
146 D2 Campo Gallo Arg.
141 E1 Campo Grande Amazonas Brazil
144 A4 Campo Grande Mato Grosso do Sul Brazil
142 D2 Campo Maior Brazil
24 C3 Campo Maior Portugal
143 B6 Campo Mourão Brazil
78 B3 Campo, Reserva de res. Cameroon
145 J1 Campos Altos Brazil
142 C3 Campos Belos Brazil
143 C7 Campos de Palmas reg. Brazil
142 D3 Campos do Jordão Brazil
142 B3 Campos Erê reg. Brazil
142 B3 Campos Gerais Brazil
139 G6 Campo Maceió r. Brazil
144 B6 Campos Novos Brazil
144 D5 Campos Novos Paulista Brazil
142 D2 Campos Sales Brazil
25 H1 Camprodon Spain
126 D6 Campton U.S.A.
119 E6 Campton U.S.A.
28 E1 Câmpulung Moldovenesc Romania
140 B3 Camana Angola
144 A3 Camanongue Angola
143 B7 Camaquã r. Brazil
111 G2 Camsell Lake l. Can.
111 H3 Camsell Portage Can.
119 □3 Camuy Puerto Rico
133 □2 Canaan Tobago Trin. & Tobago
121 G3 Canaan U.S.A.
146 B2 Cana Brava r. Brazil
142 B2 Cana Brava r. Brazil
145 H3 Canabrava Brazil
104 Canada country N. America
111 J4 Canada Falls Lake l. U.S.A.
125 C5 Canadian r. U.S.A.
125 C5 Canadian U.S.A.
121 H2 Canajoharie U.S.A.
29 F5 Çanakkale div. Turkey
29 F5 Çanakkale Boğazı str. Turkey
90 □ Canala Pac. Oc.
147 A7 Canal Beagle chan. Arg.
147 A7 Canal Concepción chan. Chile
147 B7 Canal de Trasvase canal Spain
133 □ Canal do Norte chan. Brazil
142 B2 Canal do Sul chan. Brazil
76 C4 Canal du Sahel canal Mali
122 D4 Canalejas Arg.
147 B6 Canal Moraleda chan. Chile
126 B3 Canyonville U.S.A.
121 G4 Canandaigua U.S.A.
121 G4 Canandaigua L. l. U.S.A.
130 D2 Cananea Mexico
139 E4 Canápolis Brazil
138 B4 Cañar Ecuador
148 H4 Canary Basin Atlantic Ocean
72 A2 Canarias, Islas is Atlantic Ocean
72 A2 Canarias, Islas div. Spain
79 B5 Canzar r. Angola
131 J4 Cancún Mexico
28 □ Candé France
130 C2 Candelaria Chihuahua Mexico
131 G4 Candelaria Campeche Mexico
142 C2 Cândido Mendes Brazil
142 D2 Cândido Sales Brazil
111 G4 Candle Lake l. Can.
121 G4 Candlewood, L. l. U.S.A.
124 D1 Cando U.S.A.
28 □ Candon Phil.
146 C3 Candás Spain
24 E1 Candás Spain
147 A7 Cape Barren Island i. Aust.
148 K8 Cape Basin Atlantic Ocean
100 D2 Cape Bougainville Abor. Land res. Aust.
113 H4 Cape Breton Highlands Nat. Park nat. park Can.
113 J4 Cape Breton Island i. Can.
119 □7 Cape Charles U.S.A.
76 D5 Cape Coast Ghana
121 H4 Cape Cod B. b. U.S.A.
121 H4 Cape Cod National Seashore res. U.S.A.
119 □7 Cape Coral U.S.A.
109 L3 Cape Dorset Can.
152 B5 Cape Evans Antarctic Base Ant.
125 F4 Cape Girardeau U.S.A.
150 □ Cape Johnson Depth depth Pac. Oc.
101 C7 Cape Le Grand Nat. Park nat. park Aust.
145 G2 Capelinha Brazil
78 B4 Capella Angola
100 A4 Cape Range Nat. Park nat. park Aust.
113 H5 Cape Sable Island i. Can.
82 □ Cape St George Can.
133 □5 Capesterre Guadeloupe Caribbean
113 H4 Cape Tormentine Can.
82 B5 Cape Town R.S.A.
76 □ Cape Verde country Africa
148 J5 Cape Verde Basin Atlantic Ocean
148 H5 Cape Verde Fracture Atlantic Ocean
148 H4 Cape Verde Plateau Atlantic Ocean
121 E4 Cape Vincent U.S.A.
99 F2 Cape York Peninsula pen. Aust.
132 □ Cap-Haïtien Haiti
142 □2 Capim r. Brazil
142 B1 Capim Brazil
152 B2 Capitán Arturo Prat Chile Base Ant.
141 E4 Capitán Bado Paraguay
146 □ Capitán Leónidas Escobar Paraguay
127 F5 Capitan Peak summit U.S.A.
129 H2 Capitol Reef National Park nat. park U.S.A.

160

142 D2 Capivara, Parque Nacional da Serra da nat. park. Brazil
142 D3 Capivari r. Brazil
142 D3 Capixaba Brazil
26 F4 Čapljina Bos.-Herz.
83 E1 Capoche r. Mozambique/Zambia
27 E6 Capo d'Orlando Italy
139 F5 Capoeira Brazil
27 E7 Capo Passero, Isola i. Italy
26 B4 Capraia, Isola di i. Italy
99 G4 Capricorn, C. c. Aust.
99 H4 Capricorn Channel chan. Aust.
99 H4 Capricorn Group atolls Aust.
27 E5 Capri, Isola di i. Italy
82 C2 Caprivi div. Namibia
82 C2 Caprivi Strip reg. Namibia
127 □2 Captain Cook U.S.A.
97 G3 Captain's Flat Aust.
20 C5 Captieux France
81 □2 Caquin Pt pt Seychelles
138 C4 Caquetá r. Colombia
41 B3 Carabao i. Phil.
140 B2 Carabaya, Cord. de mt. ra. Peru
28 E2 Caracal Romania
139 E3 Caracaraí Brazil
138 D1 Caracas Venezuela
142 D2 Caracol Bolivia
140 C3 Caracollo Bolivia
41 C5 Caraga Phil.
142 F5 Caraguatatuba Brazil
147 B4 Carahue Chile
145 H2 Caraí Brazil
142 B1 Carajarí r. Brazil
41 B3 Caramoan Pen. pen. Phil.
141 E2 Caraná r. Brazil
139 E5 Caranapatuba Brazil
145 G4 Carandaí Brazil
141 D4 Carandaití Bolivia
145 H4 Carangola Brazil
28 D2 Caransebeş Romania
144 A6 Carapá r. Paraguay
113 H4 Caraquet Can.
138 A4 Caráquez Ecuador
138 A4 Caráquez, B. de b. Ecuador
28 C2 Carasova Romania
130 K6 Caratasca Honduras
130 K6 Caratasca, Laguna lag. Honduras
145 G3 Caratinga Brazil
138 D4 Carauari Brazil
25 F3 Caravaca de la Cruz Spain
133 □4 Caravelle, Presqu'île de la pen. Martinique Caribbean
140 A1 Caraz Peru
143 B6 Carazinho Brazil
24 B1 Carballiño Spain
24 B1 Carballo Spain
124 D1 Carberry Can.
130 C2 Carbó Mexico
27 B6 Carbonara, Capo pt Italy
118 B4 Carbondale U.S.A.
121 F4 Carbondale U.S.A.
113 K4 Carbonear Can.
25 F4 Carbonero El Mayor Spain
27 B6 Carbonia Italy
145 G2 Carbonita Brazil
25 F3 Carcaixent Spain
21 B4 Carcar r. Phil.
20 F5 Carcassonne France
25 F1 Carcastillo Spain
97 G3 Carcoar Aust.
101 A4 Cardabia Aust.
56 B4 Cardamon Hills mts India
24 D3 Cárdena Spain
132 B2 Cárdenas Cuba
131 F4 Cárdenas San Luis Potosí Mexico
131 E5 Cárdenas Tabasco Mexico
97 E2 Cardenyabba w Aust.
147 B6 Cardiel, L. l. Arg.
17 F6 Cardiff U.K.
17 E5 Cardigan U.K.
17 E5 Cardigan Bay b. U.K.
115 H4 Cardinal Can.
120 B4 Cardington U.S.A.
25 G2 Cardona Spain
146 E3 Cardona Uruguay
144 C4 Cardoso Brazil
142 D1 Cardoso, Ilha i. Brazil
93 B6 Cardrona N.Z.
93 B6 Cardrona, Mt mt. N.Z.
110 C5 Cardston Can.
99 F3 Cardwell Aust.
28 D1 Carei Romania
139 H4 Careiro Brazil
20 D2 Carentan France
120 B4 Carey U.S.A.
101 A5 Carey Downs Aust.
96 E2 Carey, L. salt flat Aust.
111 J2 Carey Lake l. Can.
149 J5 Cargados Carajos is Mauritius
20 C2 Carhaix-Plouguer France
146 D4 Carhué Arg.
142 E3 Cariacá r. Brazil
145 H4 Cariacica Brazil
139 E1 Cariaco Venezuela
138 B4 Cariaí r. Brazil
138 B4 Carianamga Ecuador
79 C6 Cariango Angola
27 E6 Cariati Italy
132 B3 Caribbean Sea sea
110 E4 Cariboo Mts mt. ra. Can.
111 K3 Caribou r. Can.
111 J3 Caribou Can.
110 D2 Caribou l. Can.
114 C3 Caribou Can.
110 D3 Caribou Mountains mts Can.
131 E5 Carichíc Mexico
130 D3 Carigara Mexico
115 J3 Carignan France
21 G4 Carignan France
97 E2 Carinda Aust.
25 F2 Cariñena Spain
142 C3 Carinhanha Brazil
142 C3 Carinhanha r. Brazil
139 E1 Caripito Venezuela
139 E1 Cariré Brazil
115 H4 Carleton Place Can.
99 □2 Carletonville R.S.A.
111 J5 Carlin U.S.A.
110 B2 Carlisle U.K.
26 A3 Carmagnola Italy
111 K5 Carman Can.

17 E6 Carmarthen U.K.
17 E6 Carmarthen Bay b. U.K.
20 F4 Carmaux France
121 I2 Carmel U.S.A.
17 E5 Carmel Head hd U.K.
131 H5 Carmelita Guatemala
146 E3 Carmelo Uruguay
138 B2 Carmen Colombia
41 C4 Carmen i. Mexico
140 C4 Carmen Alto Chile
147 G6 Carmen de Patagones Arg.
131 F5 Carmen, I. del i. Mexico
146 D4 Carmensa Arg.
118 B4 Carmi U.S.A.
99 G4 Carmila Aust.
145 G4 Carmo Brazil
145 F4 Carmo da Cachoeira Brazil
145 F5 Carmo de Minas Brazil
145 E5 Carmo do Paranaíba Brazil
24 D4 Carmona Spain
101 A5 Carnarvon Aust.
82 C5 Carnarvon R.S.A.
99 F5 Carnarvon Nat. Park nat. park. Aust.
99 G5 Carnarvon Ra. mt. ra. Aust.
101 C5 Carnarvon Ra. mt. ra. Aust.
17 D4 Carndonagh Rep. of Ire.
101 C5 Carnegie, L. salt flat Aust.
151 D6 Carnegie Ridge Pac. Oc.
152 D4 Carney I. i. Ant.
43 A5 Car Nicobar i. Andaman and Nicobar Is India
92 □1 Carnley Harb. inlet Auckland Is N.Z.
78 C2 Carnot C.A.R.
99 F5 Carnot, C. hd Aust.
17 D5 Carnsore Point pt Rep. of Ire.
111 H4 Carnwood Can.
123 F4 Caro U.S.A.
119 D7 Carol City U.S.A.
142 C2 Carolina Brazil
119 □3 Carolina Puerto Rico
131 H5 Caroline Cove b. Macquarie I. Pac. Oc.
121 □2 Caroline l. atoll Kiribati
86 F4 Caroline Islands is Pac. Oc.
93 A6 Caroline Pk summit N.Z.
133 □3 Caroni div. Trinidad Trin. & Tobago
133 □3 Caroni r. Trin. & Tobago
139 E2 Caroní r. Venezuela
133 □3 Caroni Swamp swamp Trinidad Trin. & Tobago
139 E2 Carora Venezuela
115 H4 Carp Can.
5 H4 Carpathian Mts mt. ra. Europe
28 D2 Carpaţii Meridionali mts Romania
99 F3 Carpentaria, Gulf of g. Aust.
21 G4 Carpentras France
142 E2 Carpina Brazil
128 C4 Carpinteria U.S.A.
17 C6 Carquefou France
110 E4 Carp Lake Prov. Park res. Can.
27 E6 Carrara Italy
27 E5 Castèl di Sangro Italy
26 C3 Castelfiorentino Italy
26 D3 Castelfranco Veneto Italy
21 D5 Cavan Rep. of Ire.
21 F4 Cavarzere Italy
142 D1 Caxias Brazil
142 D2 Caxias do Sul Brazil
79 B5 Caxito Angola
138 B4 Çay Turkey
138 B3 Cayambe Ecuador
138 B4 Cayambe-Coca, Parque Nacional nat. park Ecuador
138 B4 Cayambe, Volcán vol Ecuador
119 D5 Cayce U.S.A.
60 D2 Caycuma Turkey
60 E1 Çayeli Turkey
139 G3 Cayenne French Guiana
119 □3 Cayey Puerto Rico
60 D3 Çayıran Turkey
132 C3 Cayman Brac i. Cayman Is Caribbean
132 B3 Cayman Islands terr. Caribbean
151 L6 Cayman Trench Caribbean Sea
80 E3 Caynabo Somalia
146 B3 Cayo Anelitas i. Cuba
131 H4 Cayo Arcas reef Gulf of Mexico
132 C2 Cayo Breton i. Cuba
132 C3 Cayo del Rosario i. Cuba
133 F5 Cayo de Sal i. Venezuela
132 C2 Cayo Gde i. Cuba
132 C2 Cayo Largo i. Cuba
131 H5 Cayon St Kitts-Nevis
131 F3 Cayo Nuevo reef Gulf of Mexico
132 D2 Cayo Romano i. Cuba
132 C2 Cayo Sabinal i. Cuba
132 B4 Cayos Becerro reef Honduras
132 B3 Cayos Cinco-Balas is Cuba
132 B4 Cayos de Albuquerque atolls Colombia
132 B4 Cayos Miskitos atolls Nicaragua

125 E6 Catahoula L. l. U.S.A.
122 A4 Cedar r. U.S.A.
29 G4 Çatalca Turkey
41 B3 Catalão Brazil
29 G4 Çatalca Turkey
29 G4 Çatalca Yarımadası pen. Turkey
41 □2 Catalina, Pta pt Guam Pac. Oc.
147 C3 Catalina Chile
25 G2 Catalonia div. Spain
25 G2 Cataluña div. Spain
146 D2 Catamarca Arg.
146 C2 Catamarca div. Arg.
41 C3 Catanduanes i. Phil.
144 D6 Catanduva Brazil
144 B4 Catanduvas Brazil
27 E7 Catania Italy
27 E7 Catania, Golfo di g. Italy
27 F6 Catanzaro Italy
125 D6 Catarina U.S.A.
41 C3 Catarman Phil.
41 B4 Catarroja Spain
96 C3 Catastrophe, C. hd Aust.
138 C2 Catatumbo r. Venezuela
43 A3 Cataxa Mozambique
12 □ Catbalogan Phil.
12 □ Cat Cays is The Bahamas
41 B4 Cateel Phil.
41 B4 Cateel Bay b. Phil.
79 B5 Catete Angola
83 E1 Catete Mozambique
41 B4 Cauayan Phil.
138 B2 Cauca r. Colombia
138 B2 Caucaia Brazil
138 B2 Caucasia Colombia
5 L4 Caucasus mt. ra. Asia/Europe
146 C4 Caucete Arg.
121 J4 Caucomgomoc Lake l. U.S.A.
25 F3 Caudete Spain
20 F1 Caudry France
83 E2 Cauese Mts mts Mozambique
41 C4 Cauit Point pt Phil.
20 C2 Caulnes France
79 C5 Caungula Angola
147 B4 Cauquenes Chile
138 C2 Caura r. Venezuela
115 J2 Causapscal Can.
28 D2 Căuşeni Moldova
140 D2 Cautário r. Brazil
147 B5 Cautín r. Chile
21 G5 Cavaillon France
142 C3 Cavalcante Brazil
25 J2 Cavalleria, Cap de pt Spain
92 □1 Cavalli Is is N.Z.
122 B4 Cavalier U.S.A.
76 B4 Cavalla r. Côte d'Ivoire/Liberia
76 B4 Cavally r. Côte d'Ivoire/Liberia
17 D5 Cavan Rep. of Ire.
125 F4 Cave City U.S.A.
146 B6 Caveira r. Brazil
143 B6 Cavernoso, Sa do mt. ra. Brazil
41 □2 Cavern Pk h. Auckland Is N.Z.
41 B3 Caviana, Ilha i. Brazil
41 B4 Cavili reef Phil.
140 C3 Cavinas Bolivia
41 B3 Cavite Phil.
142 D1 Caxambu Brazil

24 C3 Ceclavín Spain
28 E2 Cecina Romania
29 G4 Cedarburg U.S.A.
129 F3 Cedar City U.S.A.
122 A4 Cedar Falls U.S.A.
120 C5 Cedar Grove U.S.A.
133 □7 Cedar Grove Antigua
11 J4 Cedar L. l. U.S.A.
122 D5 Cedar Lake l. U.S.A.
26 D3 Cesenatico Italy
11 J4 Cedar L. l. Can.
122 B5 Cedar Rapids U.S.A.
121 F5 Cedar Run U.S.A.
114 D5 Cedar Springs U.S.A.
119 D5 Cedartown U.S.A.
122 E3 Cedarville U.S.A.
132 C3 Cedral Jamaica
122 E3 Cedarville U.S.A.
26 C2 Cedegolo Italy
24 E1 Cedeira Spain
24 D4 Cedillo, Embalse de l. Spain
24 B4 Cedros i. Mexico
140 B3 Ceduna Australia
96 C3 Ceduna Aust.
80 E4 Ceelbuur Somalia
80 E4 Ceeldheere Somalia
80 E2 Ceel Gaal Bari Somalia
80 D2 Ceel Gaal Woqooyi Galbeed Somalia
80 E4 Ceel Garas well Somalia
80 D4 Ceel Qoonhato well Somalia
80 D4 Ceel Waalaq well Somalia
80 E2 Ceerigaabo Somalia
27 E6 Cefalù Italy
142 D2 Cegléd Hungary
24 D2 Cegrane Macedonia
50 D3 Cehena r. Rus. Fed.
21 J5 Ceheng China
129 F4 Cehu Silvaniei Romania
119 □3 Ceiba Puerto Rico
60 C1 Çekerek Turkey
54 C2 Celah, Gunung mt. Malaysia
27 D4 Celano Italy
24 D2 Celanova Spain
79 H6 Celebes i. Indon./Philippines
138 B5 Celendín Peru
120 B4 Celina U.S.A.
26 E2 Celje Slovenia
19 H5 Celldömölk Hungary
19 H5 Celle Niedersachsen Germany
17 C6 Celtic Sea Rep. of
39 L7 Cenderawasih, Teluk g. Indon.
41 C4 Cenei Romania
40 D2 Cenrana Phil.
40 D2 Centelles Spain
144 C2 Centenário do Sul Brazil
83 C2 Centenary Zimbabwe
129 F5 Centennial Wash r. U.S.A.
121 E6 Center U.S.A.
120 B5 Center Point U.S.A.
119 C6 Centerville U.S.A.
122 E3 Centerville U.S.A.
82 D3 Central div. Botswana
81 B5 Central div. Ghana
81 B5 Central div. Kenya
83 D1 Central div. Malawi
78 C3 Central div. Sudan
79 B5 Central div. Zambia
78 C3 Central African Republic country Africa

24 C3 Ceclavín Spain
19 H3 Červená Voda Czech Rep.
28 E2 Cervena Romania
28 D2 Cedarburg U.S.A.
26 D3 Cerveteri Italy
25 D5 Cerveteri Italy
26 D3 Cervia Italy
26 D3 Cervignano del Friuli Italy
21 J5 Cervione France
24 C1 Cervo r. Italy
24 C1 Cervo Spain
26 D3 Cesena Italy
26 D3 Cesenatico Italy
11 G4 Cēsis Latvia
19 G4 Česká Lípa Czech Rep.
19 G4 České Budějovice Czech Rep.
19 G4 Českomoravská Vysočina reg. Czech Rep.
19 G4 Český Krumlov Czech Rep.
18 F4 Český les mts Czech Rep./Germany
26 F3 Česma r. Croatia
26 C2 Cessnock Aust.
97 G3 Cessnock Aust.
20 E4 Cestas France
76 C5 Cestos r. Liberia
26 F4 Cetina r. Croatia
27 E6 Cetraro Italy
24 D5 Ceuta Spain
25 F5 Cévennes mts France
61 J3 Cevizli Turkey
60 C2 Ceyhan Turkey
60 C2 Ceyhan r. Turkey
60 G3 Ceylanpınar Turkey
54 C3 Chaadayevka Rus. Fed.
57 F3 Chaacha Turkmenistan
14 G3 Chaadayevka Rus. Fed.
133 □3 Chacachacare I. i. Trinidad Trin. & Tobago
146 C3 Chacharramendi Arg.
147 B5 Chacao Chile
122 C3 Chachapoyas r. Arg.
140 B2 Chachapoyas Peru
54 D2 Chaco div. Arg.
144 D3 Chaco Boreal reg. Paraguay
110 C4 Chacon, C. c. U.S.A.
78 B2 Chad country Africa
131 H5 Chadan Rus. Fed.
51 K1 Chadron U.S.A.
124 C3 Chaeryŏng N. Korea
49 H4 Chafarinas, Is is Spain
128 B1 Chaffee U.S.A.
57 F3 Chagai Pakistan
57 F3 Chagai Hills mt. ra. Afghanistan/Pakistan
51 G5 Chagda Rus. Fed.
57 F2 Chaghcharān Afghanistan
57 H2 Chagny France
55 E4 Chagos Archipelago is British Indian Ocean Territory
54 D2 Chagoyan Rus. Fed.
49 H4 Chagrayskoye Plato plat. Kazak.
59 G1 Chaguanas Trin. & Tobago
133 □3 Chaguaramas Trin. & Tobago
139 E2 Chaguaramas Venezuela
57 F2 Chagai Turkmenistan
55 G3 Ch'ang'ubinoba China
130 C6 Chahar Turkmenistan
54 A3 Chagai Afghanistan

20 E3 Château-Renault France
20 E3 Châteauroux Centre France
21 H2 Château-Salins France
21 F2 Château-Thierry France
133 □5 Châteaubelair Guadeloupe Caribbean
18 B3 Châtelet Belgium
21 F2 Châtellerault France
21 G2 Châtenois Lorraine France
113 A4 Chatfield Can.
114 C5 Chatham Can.
121 H4 Chatham U.S.A.
114 D5 Chatham Can.
120 D5 Chatham U.S.A.
93 □1 Chatham I. i. Chatham Is N.Z.
93 □1 Chatham Is is N.Z.
104 C4 Chatham Sd chan. Can.
110 C3 Chatham Str. chan. Can.
20 D3 Châtillon-sur-Indre France
20 F3 Châtillon-sur-Seine France
65 H4 Chatkal r. Kyrgzstan
65 H4 Chatkal Range mt. ra. Kyrgzstan
147 B5 Chato mt. Chile
55 F4 Chatra India
98 E1 Chatsworth Aust.
122 C5 Chatsworth U.S.A.
119 C5 Chattanooga U.S.A.
43 A4 Chatturat Thailand
65 H2 Chatyr-Tash Kyrgyzstan
65 J3 Châu Đốc Vietnam
21 G3 Chauffailles France
54 B4 Chauhtan India
42 A2 Chauka r. India
42 A2 Chaumont France
42 A2 Chaungwa Myanmar
63 S3 Chaunskaya G. b. Rus. Fed.
21 F2 Chauny France
42 A2 Chausey, Îles is France
120 D3 Chautauqua, Lake l. U.S.A.
56 C4 Chavakachcheri Sri Lanka
60 F1 Chavār Iran
24 C2 Chaves Portugal
142 C1 Chaves Brazil
79 D6 Chavuma Zambia
12 D4 Chavusy Belarus
54 A3 Chāwāl r. Vietnam
54 C2 Chhay r. Vietnam
130 D3 Charcas Mexico
131 B4 Chard Can.
19 G2 Chazy U.S.A.
120 D3 Cheaha Mt mt. U.S.A.
19 E4 Cheb Czech Rep.
14 H2 Cheboksarskoye Vdkhr. resr Rus. Fed.
118 E3 Cheboygan U.S.A.
60 A1 Chech, Erg desert Algeria/Mali
133 □5 Chechen', O. i. Rus. Fed.
49 J5 Chech'ŏn S. Korea
19 J4 Chęciny Poland
125 E5 Checotah U.S.A.
42 A3 Cheduba Myanmar
42 A3 Cheduba I. i. Myanmar
42 A3 Cheduba Str. chan. Myanmar
99 F5 Cheepie Aust.
104 C4 Cheektowaga U.S.A.
108 B3 Chefornak U.S.A.
74 C3 Chegga Mauritania
83 C2 Chegutu Zimbabwe
57 P2 Chehardar P. pass Afghanistan
57 D3 Chehardeh Iran
74 B5 Chéhel'āyeh Iran
74 B5 Cheikria well Algeria
46 N5 Chêju-haehyŏp chan. S. Korea
49 J5 Chēju S. Korea
14 G3 Chekhov Rus. Fed.
54 D1 Chekhov Rus. Fed.
50 F4 Chekiang div. China
79 D6 Chelan, Lake l. U.S.A.
74 C3 Chelarevo Yugo.
14 G2 Cheleken Turkmenistan
126 B2 Chelforó Arg.
20 D2 Chelghoum el Aïd Algeria
20 D2 Chéliff, Massif de mts Algeria
130 J6 Cheliff, Oued r. Algeria
19 L3 Chełm Poland
19 J2 Chełmno Poland
17 H6 Chelmsford U.K.
17 H6 Chelmsford U.K.
17 F6 Cheltenham U.K.
25 F3 Chelva Spain
14 M2 Chelyabinsk Rus. Fed.
63 M2 Chelyuskin, Mys c. Rus. Fed.
83 E1 Chemba Mozambique
74 B2 Chemaïa Morocco
74 D2 Chemora Algeria
19 F4 Chemnitz Germany
74 C3 Chenachane Algeria
74 C3 Chenachane, Oued w. Algeria
49 G3 Chen Barag Qi China
57 D2 Chenārān Iran
49 G5 Cheney Res. resr U.S.A.
49 H5 Chengalpattu India
50 E1 Cheng'an China
50 D2 Chengde China
49 D4 Chengdu China
50 D4 Chenggu China
51 H2 Chenghai China
51 E3 Cheng Xian China
50 E3 Chenzhou China
14 H1 Chepes Arg.
57 D4 Chepel'ev Ukraine
130 L7 Chepo Panama
122 D5 Chequamegon Bay b. U.S.A.

20 F3 Cher r. Auvergne/Limousin France

20 E3 Cher r. Centre France
119 E5 Cheraw U.S.A.
20 D2 Cherbourg France
12 J4 Cherdakly Rus. Fed.
14 C4 Cheremkhovo Rus. Fed.
65 M2 Cheremushki Rus. Fed.
44 H1 Cherepanovo Rus. Fed.
12 F3 Cherepovets Rus. Fed.
12 H2 Cherevkovo Rus. Fed.
75 F1 Chéria Algeria
15 G2 Cherkas'ke Ukraine
14 H3 Cherkasskoye Rus. Fed.
15 E2 Cherkasy Ukraine
15 D2 Cherkasy div. Ukraine
13 G6 Cherkessk Rus. Fed.
14 C1 Cherkutino Rus. Fed.
56 C2 Cherla India
65 H2 Cherlak Rus. Fed.
48 D3 Cherlen Gol r. Mongolia
15 B2 Cherlenivka Ukraine
14 C3 Chern' Rus. Fed.
65 G4 Chernak Kazak.
14 D3 Chernava Rus. Fed.
14 D3 Chernava Rus. Fed.
62 K2 Chernaya r. Rus. Fed.
15 E1 Chernecha Sloboda Ukraine
15 F2 Cherneshchyna Ukraine
14 D2 Chernevo Rus. Fed.
49 K3 Chernigovka Rus. Fed.
15 D1 Chernihiv Ukraine
15 G3 Cherninivka Ukraine
15 A2 Chernivtsi Chernivtsi Ukraine
15 G3 Chernivtsi Vinnytsya Ukraine
15 A2 Chernivtsi Ukraine
14 D1 Chernogolovka Rus. Fed.
65 M2 Chernogorsk Rus. Fed.
12 K2 Chernorechenskiy Rus. Fed.
48 E2 Chernovskiye Rus. Fed.
14 F3 Chernoyar Rus. Fed.
65 G1 Chernoye, Oz. l. Rus. Fed.
14 F2 Chernushka Rus. Fed.
64 E1 Chernyakhiv Ukraine
15 C1 Chernyakhiv Ukraine
11 F5 Chernyakhovsk Rus. Fed.
15 G1 Chernyayeve Rus. Fed.
49 H1 Chernyayevo Rus. Fed.
49 F1 Chernyshevsk Rus. Fed.
13 H6 Chernyye Zemli reg. Rus. Fed.
15 H5 Chernyy Yar Rus. Fed.
23 E3 Cherokee U.S.A.
125 D4 Cherokee U.S.A.
125 E4 Cherokees, Lake o' the l. U.S.A.
132 C1 Cherokee Sound The Bahamas
55 G4 Cherrapunji India
129 E2 Cherry Creek U.S.A.
129 E1 Cherry Creek Mts mts U.S.A.
121 K2 Cherryfield U.S.A.
86 J6 Cherry Island i. Solomon Islands
115 G5 Cherry Valley Can.
121 F3 Cherry Valley U.S.A.
63 S3 Cherskiy Rus. Fed.
63 Q3 Cherskogo, Khrebet mt. ra. Rus. Fed.
13 G5 Chertkovo Rus. Fed.
93 C5 Chertsey N.Z.
12 J2 Cherva Rus. Fed.
28 E3 Cherven Bryag Bulgaria
14 B4 Chervone Rus. Fed.
15 C2 Chervone Ukraine
15 C1 Chervonoarmiys'k Ukraine
15 A1 Chervonohrad Ukraine
15 E1 Chervonozavods'ke Ukraine
15 D3 Chervonoznam"yanka Ukraine
15 G2 Chervonyy Donets' Ukraine
15 E3 Chervonyy Mayak Ukraine
12 J4 Chervyen' Belarus
123 E4 Chesaning U.S.A.
121 E6 Chesapeake U.S.A.
121 E5 Chesapeake Bay b. U.S.A.
121 G3 Cheshire U.S.A.
64 F5 Cheshme 2-y Turkmenistan
62 F3 Cheshskaya Guba b. Rus. Fed.
57 E2 Chesht-e Sharif Afghanistan
64 F2 Chesma Rus. Fed.
17 F5 Chester U.K.
128 B1 Chester U.S.A.
118 B4 Chester U.S.A.
121 E5 Chester U.S.A.
126 E1 Chester U.S.A.
121 F5 Chester r. U.S.A.
119 D5 Chester U.S.A.
133 □1 Chester Cas. Jamaica
95 L2 Chesterfield, Îles is Pac. Oc.
111 L2 Chesterfield Inlet Can.
111 L2 Chesterfield Inlet inlet Can.
121 G3 Chestertown U.S.A.
121 G3 Chestertown U.S.A.
115 H4 Chesterville Can.
120 D4 Chestnut Ridge ridge U.S.A.
121 J1 Chesuncook U.S.A.
121 J1 Chesuncook Lake l. U.S.A.
75 F1 Chetaïbi Algeria
43 A5 Chetamale Andaman and Nicobar Is
83 D2 Chete Safari Area res. Zimbabwe
83 H4 Chéticamp Can.
50 B2 Cheti La pass China
53 D8 Chetlat i. India
131 H5 Chetumal Mexico
93 E4 Chetwode Is Is N.Z.
114 D3 Chetwynd Can.
49 J2 Cheugda Rus. Fed.
45 □5 Cheung Chau i. Hong Kong
45 □5 Cheung Chau Hong Kong
140 C2 Chevejecure Bolivia
93 D5 Cheviot N.Z.
17 F4 Cheviot Hills h. U.K.
17 F4 Cheviot, The h. U.K.
80 C4 Chew Bahir salt l. Ethiopia
80 C3 Chew Bahir Wildlife Reserve res. Ethiopia
126 C1 Chewelah U.S.A.
83 D2 Chewore Safari Area res. Zimbabwe
125 D5 Cheyenne U.S.A.
124 C2 Cheyenne r. U.S.A.
124 C3 Cheyenne U.S.A.
124 C4 Cheyenne Wells U.S.A.
101 B7 Cheyne B. b. Aust.
110 E4 Chezacut Can.
54 D4 Chhapara India
54 D4 Chhapra India
55 G4 Chhatak Bangladesh
54 D4 Chhatarpur India
54 D5 Chhindwara India
43 J4 Chhlong, P. r. Cambodia
54 A5 Chhota Udepur India
51 H4 Chhukha Bhutan
79 B7 Chiange Angola
42 B2 Chiang Kham Thailand
42 B2 Chiang Khan Thailand
131 G5 Chiapas div. Mexico

26 B3 Chiari Italy
26 D4 Chiasco r. Italy
131 F5 Chiautla Mexico
26 B3 Chiavari Italy
26 B2 Chiavenno Italy
47 H6 Chiba Japan
47 H6 Chiba div. Japan
47 □2 Chiba Japan
79 B7 Chibemba Angola
79 B7 Chibia Angola
83 E3 Chiboma Mozambique
115 H2 Chibougamau Can.
115 H2 Chibougamau, L. l. Can.
115 J2 Chibougamau, Parc de res. Can.
46 D5 Chibu Japan
46 D6 Chiburi-jima i. Japan
47 F5 Chibu-Sangaku Nat. Park nat. park. Japan
55 G2 Chibuzhang Hu salt l. China
122 D5 Chicago airport U.S.A.
122 D5 Chicago U.S.A.
122 D5 Chicago Heights U.S.A.
122 C5 Chicago Ship Canal canal U.S.A.
79 D6 Chicapa r. Angola
138 B5 Chicama r. Peru
138 B5 Chicama r. Peru
83 E2 Chicamba Real, Barragem de dam Mozambique
79 C6 Chicapa r. Angola
72 C4 Chicha well Chad
110 B3 Chichagof i. U.S.A.
110 B3 Chichagof Island i. U.S.A.
140 C4 Chichas, Cord. de mt. ra. Bolivia
49 E4 Chicheng China
131 H4 Chichén Itzá Mexico
17 G6 Chichester U.K.
100 B4 Chichester Ra. Nat. park nat. park Aust.
100 B4 Chichester Range mt. ra. Aust.
47 G6 Chichibu Japan
47 G6 Chichibu-Tama National Park nat. park. Japan
120 E6 Chickahominy r. U.S.A.
119 C5 Chickamauga L. l. U.S.A.
125 D5 Chickasha U.S.A.
24 C4 Chiclana de la Frontera Spain
138 B5 Chiclayo Peru
147 C5 Chico r. Chubut Arg.
147 B5 Chico r. Santa Cruz/Chubut Arg.
147 C6 Chico r. Santa Cruz Arg.
147 B7 Chico r. Chubut/Río Negro Arg.
126 B2 Chico U.S.A.
83 E2 Chicoa Mozambique
115 F2 Chicobi, Lac l. Can.
79 B6 Chicomba Angola
131 G5 Chicomucelo Mexico
121 G3 Chicopee U.S.A.
41 B2 Chico Sapocoy, Mt mt. Phil.
81 □5 Chicots, Pl. des plain Réunion Indian Ocean
115 J4 Chicoutimi Can.
83 E3 Chicualacuala Mozambique
79 C6 Chicupo Angola
56 B4 Chidambaram India
83 E3 Chidenguele Mozambique
113 H1 Chidley, C. c. Can.
119 D6 Chiefland U.S.A.
18 F5 Chiemsee l. Germany
79 E5 Chiengi Zambia
26 A3 Chieri Italy
27 E4 Chieti Italy
131 F5 Chietla Mexico
49 F4 Chifeng China
65 H4 Chiganak Kazak.
65 H3 Chiganak Kazak.
113 G4 Chignecto B. b. Can.
83 E2 Chigorodó Colombia
108 C4 Chignik U.S.A.
140 C4 Chiguana Bolivia
83 D3 Chigubo Mozambique
55 G3 Chigu Co l. China
130 D2 Chihuahua div. Mexico
130 D2 Chihuahua Mexico
130 C3 Chihuahua, Medio mt. Arg.
56 C4 Chik India
51 H4 Chikballapur India
46 J2 Chikhachevo Rus. Fed.
56 A3 Chikmagalur India
48 C2 Chikoy Rus. Fed.
47 G6 Chikuma-gawa r. Japan
47 G6 Chikura Japan
81 B7 Chikwawa Zambia
46 H2 Chikyū-misaki pt Japan
83 E2 Chila Angola
110 E4 Chilanko Forks Can.
54 C2 Chilas Pakistan
65 H5 Chilas Jammu and Kashmir
56 B4 Chilaw Sri Lanka
140 B3 Chilca, Cord. de mt. ra. Peru
128 B2 Chilcoot U.S.A.
110 E4 Chilcotin r. Can.
99 G3 Chilcott Island i. Coral Sea Islands Terr. Pac. Oc.
99 H5 Childers Aust.
125 C5 Childress U.S.A.
136 C7 Chile country S. America
148 B8 Chile Basin Pac. Oc.
147 B6 Chile Chico Chile
147 B6 Chilecito La Rioja Arg.
140 B2 Chilete Peru
79 E6 Chililabombwe Zambia
110 E4 Chilko l. Can.
110 E4 Chilko r. Can.
110 E4 Chilko Lake l. Can.
146 E4 Chillán Chile
146 E4 Chillar Arg.
124 E4 Chillicothe U.S.A.
120 B5 Chillicothe U.S.A.
110 E4 Chilliwack Can.
147 B5 Chiloé, Isla de i. Chile
147 B5 Chiloé, Parque Nacional nat. park Chile
131 F5 Chilpancingo Mexico
54 C1 Chilpi India
17 G6 Chiltern Hills h. U.K.
79 D6 Chilubi Zambia
83 D1 Chilumba Malawi
54 D2 Chilung Pass India
83 F2 Chilwa, Lake l. Malawi
81 B6 Chimala Tanzania
131 H6 Chimaltenango Guatemala
130 □7 Chimán Panama
83 D3 Chimanimani Zimbabwe
83 D3 Chimanimani Mountains mts Mozambique/Zimbabwe
146 C3 Chimbas Arg.
64 F4 Chimbay Uzbekistan
138 B4 Chimborazo mt. Ecuador
138 B5 Chimbote Peru
138 C2 Chimichaguá Colombia

81 □1 Chimney Rocks is Seychelles
83 E2 Chimoio Mozambique
42 A2 Chin div. Myanmar
33 L6 China country Asia
131 F3 China Mexico
138 C2 Chinácota Colombia
131 H5 Chinajá Guatemala
54 E4 China Lake I. U.S.A.
121 J2 China Lake l. U.S.A.
130 J6 Chinandega Nicaragua
128 C5 China Pt pt U.S.A.
140 A2 Chincha Alta Peru
140 A2 Chincha, Islas de is Peru
99 G5 Chinchilla Aust.
121 F6 Chincoteague B. b. U.S.A.
83 F2 Chinde Mozambique
49 H6 Chin Do i. S. Korea
50 B1 Chindu China
42 A2 Chindwin r. Myanmar
47 □2 Chineni Japan
54 C2 Chineni India
49 H5 Chinghwa N. Korea
64 D2 Chingirlau Rus. Fed.
65 J3 Chingiz-Tau, Khr. mt. ra. Kazak.
79 E6 Chingola Zambia
79 C6 Chingue r. Angola
74 B4 Chinguetti Mauritania
78 C1 Chinguil Chad
83 □1 Chinhoyi Zimbabwe
54 C3 Chiniot Pakistan
130 C3 Chinipas Mexico
49 H6 Chinju S. Korea
64 E4 Chink Kaplankyr h. Asia
78 D2 Chinko r. C.A.R.
123 H3 Chinle U.S.A.
129 H3 Chinle Valley v. U.S.A.
129 H3 Chinle Wash r. U.S.A.
51 G3 Chinmen Taiwan
80 D2 Chinnile well Djibouti
56 B2 Chinnur India
47 □2 Chino Japan
129 F4 Chino Valley U.S.A.
81 B7 Chinsali Zambia
56 B3 Chintamani India
132 D5 Chinú Colombia
46 A6 Chinyang-ho l. S. Korea
64 D4 Chin Zap. escarpment Kazak.
26 D3 Chioggia Italy
29 F5 Chios i. Greece
29 F5 Chios Greece
81 B7 Chipata Zambia
147 C5 Chipchihua, Sa de mt. ra. Arg.
79 E6 Chipili Zambia
79 C6 Chipindo Angola
49 F5 Chiping China
83 E3 Chipinge Zimbabwe
83 D3 Chipinge Zimbabwe
114 B2 Chipman Lake l. Can.
79 C6 Chipoia Angola
17 F6 Chippenham U.K.
122 B3 Chippewa r. U.S.A.
122 B3 Chippewa Falls U.S.A.
122 B2 Chippewa, Lake l. U.S.A.
17 G6 Chipping Norton U.K.
28 D3 Chiprovtsi Bulgaria
121 K2 Chiputneticook Lakes lakes Can.
131 H6 Chiquimula Guatemala
138 C2 Chiquinquira Colombia
13 G5 Chir r. Rus. Fed.
56 C3 Chirada India
83 F2 Chiradzulu Malawi
56 A4 Chirakkal India
83 D2 Chiramba Mozambique
57 F2 Chiras Afghanistan
65 G4 Chirchik Uzbekistan
83 E3 Chiredzi Zimbabwe
77 D2 Chirfa Niger
48 A2 Chirgalandy Rus. Fed.
129 H6 Chiricahua National Monument res. U.S.A.
129 H5 Chiricahua Peak summit U.S.A.
138 B3 Chiriguaná Colombia
55 H5 Chiringa Bangladesh
130 K7 Chiriquí, Golfo de b. Panama
130 □7 Chiriquí, L. de b. Panama
146 B3 Chiripó mt. Chile
83 D2 Chirisa Safari Area res. Zimbabwe
83 F2 Chiromo Malawi
28 E3 Chirpan Bulgaria
130 K7 Chirripó mt. Costa Rica
79 E6 Chirundu Zambia
79 E6 Chisamba Zambia
131 H6 Chisec Guatemala
46 H3 Chishima Japan
83 E2 Chishui China
54 C1 Chita India
15 B1 Chișinău Moldova
15 C1 Chișinău-Criș Romania
63 J2 Chistoozernoye Rus. Fed.
14 H4 Chistopol' Rus. Fed.
128 B3 Chita Bolivia
110 F4 Chitina U.S.A.
89 E1 Chitato Angola
48 D2 Chitayevo Rus. Fed.
12 J2 Chita Rus. Fed.
114 E4 Chitek L. l. Can.
111 J4 Chitek Lake Can.
148 B7 Chile Basin
147 F1 Chiloé Chico Chile
55 G4 Chitipa Malawi
146 E4 Chitose Japan
54 D5 Chitradurga India
54 C1 Chitrakoot India
54 B2 Chitral Pakistan
130 K8 Chitré Panama
55 H5 Chittagong Bangladesh
55 G5 Chittagong div. Bangladesh
54 C4 Chittaurgarh India
56 B4 Chittoor India
56 B3 Chittur India
81 B7 Chitungulu Zambia
83 □1 Chitungwiza Zimbabwe
79 D6 Chiume Angola/Zaire
83 D1 Chiúre Novo Mozambique
54 C4 Chiusi Italy
147 B5 Chiuta, Lake l. Malawi/Mozambique
140 C3 Chiva Bolivia
83 D3 Chive Bolivia
83 D3 Chivhu Zimbabwe
146 E3 Chivilcoy Arg.
50 B2 Chizarira National Park nat. park Zimbabwe
46 J2 Chizha Rus. Fed.
46 J3 Chizu Japan
54 D2 Chkalovo Kazak.
14 F3 Chkalovsk Rus. Fed.
14 F3 Chmielnik Poland
65 J2 Chkalovskoye Rus. Fed.
49 H6 Ch'o i. S. Korea
45 □ Choa Chu Kang h. Singapore
45 □ Choa Chu Kang Singapore
43 C4 Choâm Khsant Cambodia
19 G2 Chociwel Poland

129 E5 Chocolate Mts mts U.S.A.
138 C2 Chocontá Colombia
19 H2 Chodzież Poland
147 C4 Choele Choel Arg.
83 E1 Chofombo Mozambique
54 C2 Chogo Lungma Gl. gl. Pakistan
13 H6 Chograyskoye Vdkhr. resr Rus. Fed.
111 J4 Choiceland Can.
90 □1 Choiseul i. Solomon Is.
147 E7 Choiseul Sound chan. Falkland Is.
130 C3 Choix Mexico
19 G2 Chojna Poland
19 H2 Chojnice Poland
19 G3 Chojnów Poland
47 H4 Chōkai-san vol Japan
129 D6 Choke Canyon L. l. U.S.A.
80 C2 Ch'ok'ē Mountains mt. ra. Ethiopia
54 E3 Chokala mt. China
65 H4 Chokpar Kazak.
55 F3 Choksum China
49 E7 Chŏk Shan mt. ra. China
50 B1 Chola Shan mt. ra. China
20 D3 Cholet France
147 B5 Cholila Arg.
65 J4 Cholpon-Ata Kyrgyzstan
130 J6 Choluteca Honduras
79 E7 Choma Zambia
55 G4 Chomo Lhari mt. Bhutan
42 B2 Chom Thong Thailand
54 C4 Chomun India
18 F3 Chomutov Czech Rep.
63 S3 Chona r. Rus. Fed.
49 H5 Ch'ŏnan S. Korea
43 C4 Chon Buri Thailand
138 A4 Chone Ecuador
51 G3 Chong'an China
49 H5 Chongchon r. N. Korea
49 J4 Chongjin N. Korea
49 H5 Ch'ŏngju S. Korea
49 H5 Ch'ŏngju S. Korea
43 C4 Chŏng Kal Cambodia
50 B2 Chongkü China
51 □ Chongming Dao i. China
79 B6 Chongoroi Angola
49 H5 Ch'ŏngp'yŏng N. Korea
50 D2 Chongqing China
51 □ Chongqing China
50 C2 Chongqing China
49 G6 Chŏngŭp S. Korea
49 G6 Chongyang China
49 G5 Chongyang Xi r. China
51 F3 Chongyi China
49 F2 Chŏngŭp S. Korea
48 E2 Chonogol Mongolia
15 D3 Chonhar Ukraine
15 D2 Chonhar, Pivostriv pen. Ukraine
43 D5 Chon Thanh Vietnam
43 C5 Chop Ukraine
74 B4 Choûm Mauritania
128 B3 Chowchilla U.S.A.
110 F4 Chown, Mt mt. Can.
48 B3 Choybalsan Mongolia
19 J4 Choynice (no) Choszczno Poland
138 C3 Chiquinquirá
93 D5 Christchurch N.Z.
139 G3 Christianburg Guyana
109 M2 Christian, C. pt Can.
111 H4 Chitek Lake
83 E2 Chitipa Mozambique
54 D2 Chitkul India
81 B6 Chitipa Malawi
81 □4 Chitose (no)
110 E4 Chitose Japan
54 D5 Chitradurga India
54 C1 Chitorgarh India
119 □3 Christiansted Virgin Is
43 □ Christina i. (no)
100 A3 Christina r. Can.
41 B4 Christina, Mt mt. N.Z.
91 □14 Christian, Pt pt Pitcairn I. Pac. Oc.
24 D3 Chitina Embalse de resr Spain
110 □ Christian Sound chan. U.S.A.
28 E3 Chitradurga (no) Christmas Cr. r. Aust.
13 G7 Christmas Cr. r. Aust.
43 □ Christmas Creek Aust.
149 M4 Christmas Island i. Indian Ocean
18 D2 Christmas i. (no) Chrudim Czech Rep.
29 F7 Chrysi i. Greece
29 F5 Chrysoupoli Greece
65 G4 Chu r. Kazak.
16 D div. Kyrgyzstan
55 G5 Chuadanga Bangladesh
79 D7 Chu div. Angola/Zaire
51 F2 Chuansha China
54 E2 Chubarivka Ukraine
55 C4 Chubbuck U.S.A.
147 C5 Chubut div. Arg.
147 C5 Chubut r. Arg.
14 E2 Chuchkovo Rus. Fed.
138 B4 Chuckwalla Mts mts U.S.A.

12 H1 Chulasa Rus. Fed.
128 D5 Chula Vista U.S.A.
14 F1 Chulkovo Rus. Fed.
138 A5 Chulucanas Peru
48 B2 Chuluut Gol r. Mongolia
65 L2 Chulyshmanskiy Khr. mt. ra. Rus. Fed.
140 C3 Chuma Bolivia
80 C4 Chumba Ethiopia
55 G3 Chumar India
146 C2 Chumbicha Arg.
65 L3 Chumek Kazak.
43 B5 Chumphon Thailand
42 C4 Chum Saeng Thailand
12 G2 Chumsya r. Rus. Fed.
49 H4 Ch'un'an China
49 H5 Ch'ungju S. Korea
49 J6 Ch'ungmu S. Korea
81 C7 Chungu Tanzania
51 H3 Chunut Tso l. China
65 M3 Chunya r. Rus. Fed.
81 B6 Chunya Tanzania
43 D5 Chuŏr Phnum Dâmrei mt. ra. Cambodia
43 D4 Chuŏr Phnum Dângrêk mt. ra. Cambodia/Thailand
43 C4 Chuŏr Phnum Krâvanh mt. ra. Cambodia
50 B2 Chuosijia China
12 E1 Chupa Rus. Fed.
133 □3 Chupara Pt pt Trinidad Trin. & Tobago
140 B3 Chupra Peru
140 C4 Chuquibamba Peru
140 D3 Chuquicamata Chile
140 C4 Chuquisaca div. Bolivia
21 J3 Chur Switz.
55 H4 Churachandpur India
14 H2 Churachki Rus. Fed.
63 R3 Churapcha Rus. Fed.
15 F2 Churayevo Rus. Fed.
111 L3 Churchill r. Can.
113 H3 Churchill r. Can.
111 L3 Churchill, Cape c. Can.
113 H3 Churchill Falls Can.
111 J3 Churchill Lake l. Can.
110 D3 Churchill Peak summit Can.
112 E2 Churchill Sound chan. Can.
27 C4 Churchs Ferry U.S.A.
120 D5 Churchville U.S.A.
55 F4 Churia Ghati Hills mt. ra. Nepal
60 B2 Çıvril Turkey (no) Churu India
54 C3 Churu India
138 D1 Churuguara Venezuela
24 B3 Cívıl (no)
14 H2 Chusovoy Rus. Fed.
65 G4 Chushka-Köl l. Kazak.
115 G3 Chute-des-Passes Can.
115 H3 Chute-Rouge Can.
115 F4 Chute-St-Philippe Can.
51 H3 Chu-tung Taiwan
86 G4 Chuuk is Fed. States of Micronesia
14 H2 Chuvashiya div. Rus. Fed.
50 D1 Chuxiong China
43 E4 Chu Yang Sin mt. Vietnam
15 D3 Chychykliya r. Ukraine
15 D2 Chyhyryn Ukraine
15 C2 Chyhyryn Ukraine
49 K2 Chyulu Range h. Kenya
60 B2 Çivril Turkey
51 F2 Cixi China
50 D2 Ci Xian China
20 E3 Cizre Turkey
129 F4 Clovis U.S.A.
20 E2 Cléry-sur-le-Loir France
111 H4 Cluff Lake Can.
111 L2 Cold Lake Can.
60 D1 Cide Turkey
19 L2 Ciechanów Poland
19 L2 Ciechanowiec Poland
-19 J2 Ciechocinek Poland
133 □5 Ciego de Ávila Cuba
138 C1 Ciénaga Colombia
133 □5 Ciénaga de Oro Colombia
133 □5 Ciénaga Grande l. Colombia
125 C7 Ciénega de Flores Mexico
127 C6 Cieneguita Mexico
132 C5 Cienfuegos Cuba
19 J4 Cieszanów Poland
27 D4 Cieszyn Poland
19 L4 Ciechocinek (no)
25 F3 Cieza Spain
60 C2 Çifteler Turkey
60 B2 Çiftlikköy Turkey
25 E3 Cifuentes Spain
24 E2 Cigüela r. Spain
60 C2 Çihanbeyli Turkey
131 E5 Cihuatlán Mexico
24 D3 Cijara, Embalse de resr Spain
40 B3 Cikalong Indon.
91 □14 Christian (no) Çikobia i. Fiji
91 □1 Çikobia-i-Ra i. Fiji
60 B1 Çili Turkey
51 E2 Cili China
60 C2 Cilicia reg. Turkey
60 E2 Cilician Gates pass Turkey
13 H7 Çıldır Gölü l. Turkey
13 H7 Çıldır Turkey
51 E2 Cili China
24 E3 Cilleruelo de Bezana Spain
41 B2 Cilongozi (no)
27 □ Cima i. Italy
128 D4 Cima U.S.A.
40 B3 Cimahi Indon.
17 D6 Cill Mhantáin (no)
125 D4 Cimarron r. U.S.A.
125 C4 Cimarron U.S.A.
14 D2 Çımışlia Moldova
125 D4 Cimone, Monte mt. Italy
26 D3 Çınarcık Turkey
138 B2 Cinaruco-Capanaparo, Parque Nacional nat. park Venezuela
25 G2 Cinca r. Spain
132 B4 Cinco Chañares (no) Arg.
25 G2 Cinco Balas, Cayos de is Cuba
26 A3 Çine Turkey
60 B2 Çine Turkey
146 C2 Cinco Chañares Arg.
18 D4 Ciney Belgium
131 G5 Cintalapa Mexico
144 C3 Cinzas r. Brazil
26 B2 Cipo r. Brazil
145 G3 Cipo r. Brazil
146 D4 Cipolletti Arg.
111 H4 Cipu (no)
118 C4 Circle U.S.A.
124 F2 Circle U.S.A.
120 B5 Circleville U.S.A.
129 F3 Circleville U.S.A.
40 B3 Cirebon Indon.
27 □ Cirella (no) Ciremay, G. vol. Indon.
40 C3 Ciremay, G. vol. Indon.
17 F6 Cirencester U.K.
44 A1 Cires (no)
26 A3 Ciriè Italy
15 D2 Cirípcău Moldova

27 F6 Cirò Marina Italy
119 D6 Clermont U.S.A.
21 F4 Clermont-Ferrand France
26 C2 Cisco U.S.A.
125 D5 Cisco U.S.A.
28 E2 Cisnădie Romania
147 B5 Cisnes r. Chile
99 E3 Cisterna di Latina Italy
122 D2 Citaré r. Brazil
131 F5 Citlaltépetl, Vol. vol Mexico
26 F4 Çıtluk Bos.-Herz.
139 G3 Citron French Guiana
82 B5 Citrusdal R.S.A.
26 C4 Città della Pieve Italy
26 D4 Città di Castello Italy
28 D1 Ciucea Romania
131 E5 Ciudad Acuña Mexico
131 E5 Ciudad Altamirano Mexico
139 E2 Ciudad Bolívar Venezuela
130 D3 Ciudad Camargo Mexico
131 H5 Ciudad del Carmen Mexico
141 F5 Ciudad del Este Paraguay
130 D2 Ciudad Delicias Mexico
130 D2 Ciudad del Maíz Mexico
138 D2 Ciudad de Nutrias Venezuela
130 C3 Ciudad de Valles Mexico
139 E2 Ciudad Guayana Venezuela
130 D2 Ciudad Guerrero Mexico
130 C3 Ciudad Guzmán Mexico
131 E5 Ciudad Hidalgo Mexico
131 E5 Ciudad Ixtepec Mexico
130 D2 Ciudad Juárez Mexico
130 D2 Ciudad Lerdo Mexico
131 H4 Ciudad Madero Mexico
130 D3 Ciudad Mante Mexico
130 D3 Ciudad Mendoza Mexico
130 C3 Ciudad Mier Mexico
130 D2 Ciudad Obregón Mexico
24 D3 Ciudad Real Spain
131 E5 Ciudad Río Bravo Mexico
24 C2 Ciudad Rodrigo Spain
28 E1 Ciudad Rodrigo (no)
28 E1 Ciumani Romania
27 D4 Cividale del Friuli Italy
26 C4 Civita Castellana Italy
26 D4 Civitanova Marche Italy
26 C4 Civitavecchia Italy
20 D3 Civray Poitou-Charentes France
60 B2 Çivril Turkey
51 F2 Cixi China
50 D2 Ci Xian China
20 E3 Cizre Turkey
111 J4 Cluff Lake Can.
111 L2 Cladich U.K.
113 G2 Clair Engle L. resr U.S.A.
17 D4 Claire U.K.
17 D4 Claire, Lake l. Can.
126 B3 Clair Engle L. resr U.S.A.
20 F3 Clairton U.S.A.
21 F3 Clamecy France
26 D2 Clanwilliam R.S.A.
93 B6 Clapham N.Z.
17 C5 Clara Rep. of Ire.
99 F3 Clara r. Aust.
43 B5 Clara I. i. Myanmar
17 D5 Claraville r. Aust.
122 E4 Clare U.S.A.
96 C3 Clare Aust.
17 D5 Clare U.S.A.
17 B4 Clare Island i. Rep. of Ire.
17 C5 Clarecastle Rep. of Ire.
100 C4 Claremont U.S.A.
121 G3 Claremont U.S.A.
133 □1 Claremont Jamaica
17 C4 Claremorris Rep. of Ire.
125 E4 Claremore U.S.A.
99 G6 Clarence r. N.Z.
93 D5 Clarence N.Z.
93 D5 Clarence r. N.Z.
147 B7 Clarence I. i. Chile
147 B7 Clarence I. i. Chile
82 A4 Clarence Bay b. Ascension Atlantic Ocean
147 B7 Clarence I. i. Chile
133 □1 Clarence Str. chan. Aust.
98 C2 Clarence Str. chan. Aust.
133 E5 Clarence Town The Bahamas
120 D4 Clarendon U.S.A.
133 □1 Clarendon div. Jamaica
133 □3 Clarendon Peak Jamaica
113 J3 Clarenville Can.
110 G4 Claresholm Can.
123 F5 Clarington U.S.A.
138 D1 Clarines Venezuela
124 E3 Clarinda U.S.A.
122 A4 Clarion U.S.A.
120 D4 Clarion r. U.S.A.
150 B4 Clarión, Isla i. Mexico
151 L4 Clarion Fracture Zone Pac. Oc.
124 D2 Clark U.S.A.
115 G4 Clark, Pt pt Can.
110 D4 Clarke City Can.
99 G4 Clarke r. Aust.
99 F3 Clarke Ra. mt. ra. Aust.
120 C4 Clarke Cr. r. U.S.A.
110 F4 Clark Fork r. U.S.A.
110 F4 Clark Fork U.S.A.
126 D1 Clark Fork r. U.S.A.
119 C5 Clark Hill Res. resr U.S.A.
128 D3 Clark Mtn mt. U.S.A.
147 B7 Clarke I. i. Chile
120 D4 Clarksburg U.S.A.
125 F5 Clarksdale U.S.A.
115 K2 Clark's Harbour Can.
127 C6 Clarkston U.S.A.
126 C2 Clarks Summit U.S.A.
125 F5 Clarksville U.S.A.
119 C4 Clarksville U.S.A.
144 C1 Claro r. Brazil
144 C2 Claro r. Goiás Brazil
145 G3 Claro r. Goiás Brazil
147 B4 Claro r. Chile
99 G5 Clarrie (no)
120 C4 Clarington (no)
126 B2 Clayton U.S.A.
120 E3 Claverack U.S.A.
125 C4 Clayton U.S.A.
119 D5 Clayton U.S.A.
121 F2 Clayton U.S.A.
119 C6 Clayton U.S.A.
128 C3 Clayton Valley v. U.S.A.
120 C6 Claytor Lake l. U.S.A.
120 D6 Clear Fork Reservoir resr U.S.A.
17 B6 Clear, Cape c. Rep. of Ire.
129 E4 Clearfield U.S.A.
120 D4 Clearfield U.S.A.
110 F4 Clear Lake l. Can.
111 G4 Clear Lake l. Can.
128 A2 Clear Lake l. U.S.A.
124 E3 Clear Lake U.S.A.
124 D2 Clear Lake U.S.A.
128 A2 Clear Lake Res. resr U.S.A.
126 C3 Clearwater r. U.S.A.
114 F4 Clearwater Can.
119 D7 Clearwater U.S.A.
114 F4 Clearwater r. Can.
111 J3 Clearwater Lake Provincial Park res. Can.
110 F3 Clearwater Mountains mts U.S.A.
133 □3 Clearwater Town The Bahamas
126 D2 Cle Elum U.S.A.
17 F5 Cleethorpes U.K.
126 E1 Cleft (no)
129 H2 Clements (no) Clements U.S.A.
45 □ Clementi Singapore
45 □ Clementi Singapore

99 F4 Clermont Aust.
119 D6 Clermont U.S.A.
21 F4 Clermont-Ferrand France
26 C2 Cles Italy
96 D3 Cleve Aust.
125 F5 Cleveland U.S.A.
122 C4 Cleveland U.S.A.
119 C5 Cleveland U.S.A.
99 F3 Cleveland, C. hd Aust.
122 D2 Cleveland Cliffs Basin l. U.S.A.
143 B6 Clevelândia Brazil
139 G3 Clevelândia do Norte Brazil
110 G5 Cleveland, Mt mt. U.S.A.
17 C5 Clew Bay b. Rep. of Ire.
17 C5 Clifden Rep. of Ire.
129 H5 Cliff U.S.A.
98 D3 Cliffdale r. Aust.
93 D5 Clifford Bay b. N.Z.
99 G5 Clifton Aust.
119 □2 Clifton The Bahamas
129 H5 Clifton U.S.A.
96 D1 Clifton Hills Aust.
119 □2 Clifton Pt pt The Bahamas
119 C5 Clinch r. U.S.A.
119 C5 Clinch Mountain mt. ra. U.S.A.
114 F4 Clinton Can.
121 H4 Clinton U.S.A.
126 C2 Clinton U.S.A.
122 B5 Clinton U.S.A.
121 H4 Clinton U.S.A.
122 A5 Clinton U.S.A.
119 E5 Clinton U.S.A.
125 D5 Clinton U.S.A.
111 H2 Clinton-Colden Lake l. Can.
26 A3 Cloates (no)
122 A5 Clintonville U.S.A.
97 G3 Clints Well U.S.A.
151 M5 Clipperton Fracture Zone Pac. Oc.
130 □ Coiba, Isla i. Panama
151 M5 Clipperton I. i. Pac. Oc.
20 D3 Clisson France
146 D3 Cliza Bolivia
101 A4 Cloates, Pt pt Aust.
56 B4 Coimbatore India
17 C6 Clonakilty Rep. of Ire.
99 E4 Cloncurry Aust.
24 E2 Coín Spain
17 D5 Clonmel Rep. of Ire.
18 E2 Cloppenburg Germany
114 G2 Cloquet U.S.A.
144 D1 Clorinda Brazil
97 F4 Cloud Peak summit U.S.A.
128 B2 Cloverdale U.S.A.
17 H6 Clovelly U.K.
129 F4 Clovis U.S.A.
127 C5 Clovis U.S.A.
28 D1 Cluj-Napoca Romania
21 F3 Cluny France
21 G3 Cluses France
26 C3 Clusone Italy
93 B6 Clutha r. N.Z.
17 E5 Clwydian Range h. U.K.
93 C5 Clyde N.Z.
17 E4 Clyde, Firth of est. U.K.
109 L3 Clyde River Can.
93 C6 Clyde N.Z.
17 E5 Clyde r. U.K.
122 E4 Clyde U.S.A.
121 F3 Clyde U.S.A.
17 E4 Clyde, Firth of est. U.K.
28 E2 Coala r. Romania
146 C3 Coalcoman Mexico
99 F4 Coalcoman Mexico
17 F5 Coalville U.K.
126 E3 Coal r. Can.
21 G3 Coal River Can.
97 E3 Coaldale U.S.A.
126 E3 Coalgate U.S.A.
130 D4 Coalinga U.S.A.
128 B3 Coalville U.S.A.
21 G3 Coari Brazil
142 D2 Coari r. Brazil
142 D2 Coari Brazil
80 C4 Coast div. Kenya
99 G5 Coast Ra. h. Aust.
100 A3 Coast Range mt. ra. Aust.
110 D3 Coast Mountains mt. ra. Can.
128 A2 Coast Ranges mts U.S.A.
17 E4 Coatbridge U.K.
115 G5 Coaticook Can.
152 C4 Coats Land Ant.
128 B3 Coatzacoalcos Mexico
131 G5 Coatzacoalcos Mexico
95 □ Collins Hd hd Norfolk I. Pac. Oc.
112 D3 Coats Island i. Can.
121 H2 Colebrook U.S.A.
131 G5 Coatzacoalcos Mexico
130 □ Cobán Guatemala
131 G5 Cobán Guatemala
99 G4 Cobar Aust.
121 G3 Cobargo Aust.
99 G6 Cobargo Aust.
97 F4 Cobar Aust.
98 C4 Cobb (no)
115 G4 Cobden Can.
17 C6 Cobh Rep. of Ire.
142 D3 Cobija Bolivia
121 F3 Cobleskill U.S.A.
121 F3 Cobourg Can.
98 C2 Cobourg Pen. pen. Aust.
99 F5 Cobram Aust.
79 D6 Cóbuè Mozambique
18 E3 Coburg Germany
140 C4 Cocachacra Peru
142 D3 Cocalinho Brazil
140 C4 Cochabamba Bolivia
140 C4 Cochabamba div. Bolivia
50 C3 Coche, I. i. Venezuela
56 B4 Cochin India
56 B4 Cochin reg. Vietnam
56 B4 Cochin India
129 H6 Cochise U.S.A.
126 E2 Cochrane Chile
120 D4 Cochran U.S.A.
114 E4 Cochrane Can.
110 G4 Cochrane r. Can.
147 B6 Cochrane Chile
147 B6 Cochrane, L. l. Arg./Chile
99 F4 Cockburn Aust.
133 □2 Cockburn Harbour Turks and Caicos Is Caribbean
147 C7 Cockburn, Mt mt. Aust.
133 □5 Cockburn Town The Bahamas
133 E4 Cockburn Town Turks and Caicos Is Caribbean
17 E4 Cockermouth U.K.
17 F4 Cockermouth U.K.
133 □1 Cockpit Country reg. Jamaica
130 K7 Coco r. Honduras/Nicaragua
130 □ Coco, Isla del i. Costa Rica
146 C2 Codegua (no)
43 A5 Coco Channel chan. India
41 A4 Coco, Isla i. Phil.

97 F3 Cocoparra Range h. Aust.
138 B2 Cocorná Colombia
142 D3 Côcos Brazil
133 □3 Cocos Bay b. Trin. & Tobago
41 □2 Cocos I. i. Guam Pac. Oc.
145 G1 Cocos i. is Indian Ocean
148 C6 Cocos Ridge Pac. Oc.
138 C2 Cocula Mexico
138 C2 Cocuy, Parque Nacional nat. park Colombia
138 C2 Codajás Brazil
124 C2 Cod, Cape c. U.S.A.
121 F2 Codera, C. c. Venezuela
93 A7 Codfish I. i. N.Z.
26 B3 Codigoro Italy
26 D3 Codogno Italy
142 D1 Codó Brazil
126 B3 Codroipo Italy
15 C3 Codru Moldova
126 E2 Cody U.S.A.
98 D2 Coen r. Aust.
99 E2 Coen r. Aust.
126 B1 Coeroeni r. Surinam
149 H4 Coëtivy Island i. Seychelles
110 F4 Coeur d'Alene U.S.A.
126 C2 Coeur d'Alene L. l. U.S.A.
126 C2 Coeur d'Alene U.S.A.
82 B5 Coffee Bay R.S.A.
125 E4 Coffeyville U.S.A.
99 C5 Coffin B. b. Aust.
96 C3 Coffin Bay Aust.
115 J5 Coffs Harbour Aust.
15 C2 Cogâlniceni Moldova
122 B4 Cogealac Romania
122 B4 Coggon U.S.A.
20 D3 Cognac France
26 A3 Cogne Italy
24 E2 Cogolludo Spain
28 □ Cohocton r. U.S.A.
121 F3 Cohoes U.S.A.
96 D2 Cohuna Aust.
130 □ Coiba, Isla i. Panama
147 B6 Coihaique Chile
147 B6 Coihueco Chile
56 B4 Coimbatore India
24 B2 Coimbra div. Portugal
24 B2 Coimbra Portugal
24 D4 Coín Spain
142 D3 Coipasa, L. de l. Bolivia
140 C4 Coipasa, Salar de salt flat Bolivia
133 □2 Cojimíes Ecuador
130 □ Cojutepeque El Salvador
93 C6 Col (no)
97 C4 Colac Aust.
145 H2 Colares Brazil
26 D3 Colatina Brazil
17 H6 Colchester U.K.
121 G4 Colchester U.S.A.
111 H4 Cold Lake Can.
111 H4 Cold Lake l. Can.
17 F4 Coldstream U.K.
115 F5 Coldwater Can.
122 E5 Coldwater U.S.A.
126 A2 Coldwater r. U.S.A.
17 D5 Coleraine U.K.
97 C4 Coleraine Aust.
17 E4 Coleraine U.K.
93 C5 Coleridge, L. l. N.Z.
82 D5 Colesberg R.S.A.
93 C5 Coles Bay Aust.
82 D3 Coligny R.S.A.
131 E5 Colima div. Mexico
131 E5 Colima Mexico
17 C4 Coll i. U.K.
99 F5 Collarenebri Aust.
99 E3 College Park U.S.A.
97 E3 College Station U.S.A.
101 B5 Collie Aust.
101 B5 Collier Ra. mt. ra. Aust.
101 B5 Collier Ranges h. Aust.
101 B5 Collier Range Nat. Park res. Aust.
17 D5 Collin Top h. U.K.
92 □ Collingwood N.Z.
93 C4 Collingwood N.Z.
93 C4 Collins Hd hd Norfolk I. Pac. Oc.
99 F4 Collinsville Aust.
122 C6 Collinsville U.S.A.
138 C3 Colmena Arg.
138 C3 Colmenar Spain
24 E2 Colmenar de Oreja Spain
24 E2 Colmenar Viejo Spain
55 H4 Colne r. U.K.
55 H4 Colne U.K.
138 C2 Coloma U.S.A.
138 C3 Colombia Colombia
136 C2 Colombia country S. America
144 C3 Colombo Brazil
56 B5 Colombo Sri Lanka
146 D3 Colón Buenos Aires Arg.
146 D3 Colón Entre Ríos Arg.
133 □5 Colón Cuba
130 □ Colón Panama
151 M6 Colón, Archipiélago de is Ecuador
127 C7 Colonet, C. c. Mexico
146 D3 Colonia Agrippina (no)
146 E4 Colonia Choele Choel Arg.
146 E4 Colonia del Sacramento Uruguay
146 D2 Colonia Dora Arg.
146 E3 Colonia Emilio Mitre Arg.
24 C2 Colonia Las Heras Arg.
146 B2 Colonia Lavalleja Arg.
145 H2 Colónia Leopoldina Brazil
120 E5 Colonial Heights U.S.A.
120 C5 Colonna, Capo pt Italy
24 E2 Colonsay i. U.K.
133 □ Colquechaca Bolivia
140 C4 Colquiri Bolivia
24 D4 Colsterworth U.K.
121 H2 Colton U.S.A.
120 E4 Columbia r. Can./U.S.A.
124 E4 Columbia U.S.A.
119 D5 Columbia U.S.A.
120 E5 Columbia U.S.A.
119 C5 Columbia U.S.A.
109 L1 Columbia, C. c. Can.
122 C5 Columbia, District of div. U.S.A.
121 K2 Columbia Falls U.S.A.
126 D1 Columbia Falls U.S.A.
126 C2 Columbia Mountains mt. ra. Can.
110 F4 Columbia, Mt mt. Can.
126 C2 Columbia Plateau plat. U.S.A.
82 B5 Columbine, Cape c. R.S.A.
119 C5 Columbus U.S.A.
118 C5 Columbus U.S.A.
124 D3 Columbus U.S.A.
127 F6 Columbus U.S.A.
122 E5 Columbus U.S.A.
120 A5 Columbus U.S.A.
132 D2 Columbus Bank sand bank The Bahamas
122 D5 Columbus Jct U.S.A.
133 □2 Columbus Point pt The Bahamas
132 D1 Columbus Pt pt The Bahamas
128 D4 Columbus Salt Marsh salt marsh U.S.A.
128 B2 Colusa U.S.A.
108 C3 Colville U.S.A.
126 C1 Colville U.S.A.
92 E2 Colville Channel chan. N.Z.
110 F4 Columbia (no)
108 B3 Colville Lake Can.
126 C1 Colville r. U.S.A.
17 F5 Colwyn Bay U.K.
26 D3 Comacchio, Valli di lag. Italy
55 G2 Comai China
26 A3 Comachio (no)
130 J6 Comalcalco Mexico
131 G5 Comalcalco Mexico
146 E3 Comallo r. Arg.
140 D3 Comarapa Bolivia
42 A3 Combermere Bay b. Myanmar
97 G3 Comboyne Aust.
142 D3 Comercinho Brazil
119 □2 Comerio Puerto Rico
99 E4 Comet Aust.
99 G5 Comet r. Aust.
27 C5 Comino, Capo pt Italy
55 G5 Comilla Bangladesh
27 G7 Comino i. Malta
131 G5 Comitán de Domínguez Mexico
20 F3 Commentry France
41 E5 Commerce U.S.A.
144 E2 Compostela Brazil
122 D4 Commerce U.S.A.
120 B6 Commissioner's Pt pt Bermuda
109 L3 Committee Bay b. Can.
152 B6 Commonwealth Territory div. Aust.
26 D2 Como Italy
147 C6 Comodoro Rivadavia Arg.
147 C6 Como Chamling l. China
76 B4 Comoé, Parc National de la nat. park Côte d'Ivoire
130 □ Comondú Mexico
56 B4 Comorin, Cape c. India
149 G7 Comoros country Africa
20 E2 Compiègne France
24 D2 Compostela Brazil
130 □ Compostela Mexico
146 E3 Comrat Moldova
141 E3 Comrie U.K.
55 H4 Comilla Bangladesh
146 E4 Conakry Guinea
145 G3 Conara Aust.
130 □ Concarneau France
145 G3 Conceição Brazil
142 D3 Conceição da Barra Brazil
145 H2 Conceição das Alagoas Brazil
145 H2 Conceição de Macabu Brazil
144 D3 Conceição do Araguaia Brazil
142 D2 Conceição do Coité Brazil
145 G3 Conceição do Mato Dentro Brazil
144 C2 Concepción Beni Bolivia
140 D3 Concepción Santa Cruz Bolivia
146 E2 Concepción Arg.
146 E2 Concepción Paraguay
146 E4 Concepción del Uruguay Uruguay
82 A3 Conception Bay b. Namibia
113 K4 Conception Bay South Can.
119 F7 Conception I. i. The Bahamas
128 B4 Conception, Pt pt U.S.A.
138 C2 Conchas Brazil
142 D2 Conchas São Paulo Brazil
140 C4 Conches-en-Ouche France
130 D2 Conchos r. Mexico
128 A3 Concord U.S.A.
121 H3 Concord U.S.A.
119 D5 Concord U.S.A.
146 E3 Concordia Arg.

138 B2 Concordia *Antioquia* Colombia
138 C3 Concordia *Meta* Colombia
138 C4 Concordia Peru
124 D4 Concordia U.S.A.
99 G5 Condamine Aust.
99 G5 Condamine r. Aust.
43 D5 Côn Đao Vietnam
142 E3 Conde Brazil
83 E2 Condédezi r. Mozambique
130 J6 Condega Nicaragua
20 D2 Condé-sur-Noireau France
145 H1 Condeúba Brazil
97 F3 Condobolin Aust.
20 E5 Condom France
126 B2 Condon U.S.A.
138 B4 Condor, Cord. del mt. ra. Peru
119 C6 Conecuh r. U.S.A.
26 D3 Conegliano Italy
130 E3 Conejos Mexico
120 D4 Conemaugh r. U.S.A.
114 E5 Conestogo Lake l. Can.
120 E3 Conesus Lake l. U.S.A.
21 H3 Coney r. France
121 G4 Coney I. i. U.S.A.
90 □1 Conflict Group is P.N.G.
20 E3 Confolens France
129 F2 Confusion Range mts U.S.A.
141 E4 Confuso r. Paraguay
51 E3 Congjiang China
69 F5 Congo country Africa
78 C4 Congo r. Congo/Zaire
145 G4 Congonhas Brazil
144 C5 Congonhinhas Brazil
129 F4 Congress U.S.A.
147 B4 Conguillo, Parque Nacional nat. park Chile
147 B5 Cónico, Co mt. Arg.
24 C4 Conil de la Frontera Spain
114 E3 Coniston Can.
17 F4 Coniston U.K.
111 G3 Conklin Can.
79 B4 Conkouati, Réserve de Faune res. Congo
146 C3 Conlara Arg.
114 E2 Connaught Can.
17 C5 Connaught reg. Rep. of Ire.
120 C4 Conneaut U.S.A.
121 G4 Connecticut div. U.S.A.
118 F3 Connecticut r. U.S.A.
120 D4 Connellsville U.S.A.
99 E5 Connemara Aust.
17 C5 Connemara reg. Rep. of Ire.
121 J1 Conners Can.
118 C4 Connersville U.S.A.
17 C4 Conn, Lough l. Rep. of Ire.
99 G4 Connors Ra. h. Aust.
42 D2 Co Nôi Vietnam
121 E5 Conowingo U.S.A.
144 E3 Conquista Brazil
126 E1 Conrad U.S.A.
125 E6 Conroe U.S.A.
145 G4 Conselheiro Lafaiete Brazil
145 H3 Conselheiro Pena Brazil
43 D5 Côn Sơn i. Vietnam
111 G4 Consort Can.
18 D5 Constance, L. l. Germany/Switz.
139 E5 Constância dos Baetas Brazil
28 G2 Constanța Romania
24 D4 Constantina Spain
75 F1 Constantine Algeria
122 E5 Constantine U.S.A.
108 C4 Constantine, C. c. U.S.A.
133 □1 Constant Spring Jamaica
129 E6 Constitución de 1857, Parque Nacional nat. park Mexico
99 G5 Consuelo Aust.
126 D3 Contact U.S.A.
145 F3 Contagem Brazil
138 B5 Contamana Peru
142 D3 Contas r. Brazil
129 G6 Continental U.S.A.
121 H3 Contoocook r. U.S.A.
131 J4 Contoy, I. i. Mexico
115 J4 Contrecoeur Can.
25 F3 Contreras, Embalse de resr Spain
147 B7 Contreras, I. i. Chile
20 E3 Contres France
145 F3 Contria Brazil
138 B5 Contumazá Peru
111 G1 Contwoyto Lake l. Can.
27 F5 Conversano Italy
125 E5 Conway U.S.A.
121 H3 Conway U.S.A.
119 E5 Conway U.S.A.
96 C2 Conway, L. salt flat Aust.
96 C2 Coober Pedy Aust.
96 B2 Cook Aust.
122 A2 Cook U.S.A.
147 B7 Cook, B. de b. Chile
110 D4 Cook, C. c. Can.
101 B7 Cooke, Mt h. Aust.
119 C4 Cookeville U.S.A.
108 C3 Cook Inlet chan. U.S.A.
87 L6 Cook Islands terr. Pac. Oc.
93 C5 Cook, Mt mt. N.Z.
121 F3 Cooksburg U.S.A.
113 J3 Cook's Harbour Can.
115 K4 Cookshire Can.
93 E4 Cook Strait str. N.Z.
99 F2 Cooktown Aust.
97 F2 Coolabah Aust.
99 F5 Cooladdi Aust.
97 G2 Coolah Aust.
101 C6 Coolgardie Aust.
129 G5 Coolidge U.S.A.
129 G5 Coolidge Dam U.S.A.
97 G4 Cooma Aust.
96 E3 Coombah Aust.
97 G2 Coonabarabran Aust.
96 D3 Coonalpyn Aust.
97 G2 Coonamble Aust.
101 C6 Coonana Aust.
96 C2 Coondambo Aust.
99 F5 Coongoola Aust.
96 D2 Cooper Cr. w Aust.
93 A6 Cooper I. i. N.Z.
97 H2 Coopernook Aust.
121 J2 Coopers Mills U.S.A.
132 C1 Coopers Town The Bahamas
124 D2 Cooperstown U.S.A.
121 F3 Cooperstown U.S.A.
133 □3 Coora Trin. & Tobago
96 C2 Coorabie Aust.
101 B6 Coorow Aust.
99 H5 Cooroy Aust.
126 A3 Coos Bay U.S.A.
17 D4 Cootehill Rep. of Ire.
99 G5 Cooyar Aust.
146 C2 Copacabana Arg.
146 B4 Copahue, Volcán mt. Chile
131 G5 Copainalá Mexico
131 F5 Copala Mexico
131 F5 Copalillo Mexico
130 H6 Copán Honduras
126 G4 Cope U.S.A.
27 G5 Copertino Italy
146 B2 Copiapo r. Chile
146 B2 Copiapo Chile
96 D2 Copley Aust.
26 C3 Copparo Italy
114 D2 Coppell Can.
79 E6 Copperbelt div. Zambia
114 E3 Copper Cliff Can.
99 F3 Copperfield r. Aust.
122 D2 Copper Harbor U.S.A.
108 G3 Coppermine Can.
108 G3 Coppermine r. Can.
114 C3 Coppermine Pt pt Can.
28 E1 Copșa Mică Romania
55 F3 Coqên China
146 B3 Coquimbo div. Chile
146 B2 Coquimbo Chile
28 E3 Corabia Romania
145 F2 Coração de Jesus Brazil
140 B2 Coracora Peru
114 E1 Coral Can.
119 D7 Coral Gables U.S.A.
109 K3 Coral Harbour Can.
119 □2 Coral Harbour The Bahamas
150 F7 Coral Sea sea Pac. Oc.
150 E6 Coral Sea Basin Pac. Oc.
86 G6 Coral Sea Islands Territory div. Pac. Oc.
122 B5 Coralville Reservoir resr U.S.A.
97 E4 Corangamite, L. l. Aust.
139 F3 Corantijn r. Surinam
27 F5 Corato Italy
74 A4 Corbeiro, Cap pt *Western Sahara*
144 B6 Corbélia Brazil
146 D4 Corbett Arg.
111 L2 Corbett Inlet inlet Can.
20 F2 Corbie France
120 A6 Corbin U.S.A.
24 D4 Corbones r. Spain
28 G2 Corbu Romania
128 C3 Corcoran U.S.A.
147 B5 Corcovado Arg.
147 B5 Corcovado, G. de chan. Chile
147 B5 Corcovado, V. vol Chile
142 C2 Corda r. Brazil
145 G5 Cordeiro Brazil
119 D6 Cordele U.S.A.
138 C3 Cordillera de los Picachos, Parque Nacional nat. park Colombia
41 B4 Cordilleras Range mt. ra. Phil.
96 E1 Cordillo Downs Aust.
145 F3 Cordisburgo Brazil
146 D3 Cordoba div. Arg.
146 D3 Córdoba Arg.
147 C5 Cordoba Arg.
131 F5 Cordoba Mexico
130 E3 Córdoba Mexico
24 D4 Córdoba *Córdoba* Spain
146 D3 Cordoba, Sierras de mt. ra. Arg.
140 A2 Cordova Peru
108 D3 Cordova U.S.A.
110 C4 Cordova Bay b. U.S.A.
121 K2 Corea U.S.A.
142 D1 Coreaú Brazil
98 E4 Corella r. Aust.
98 C3 Corella L. salt flat Aust.
99 E4 Corfield Aust.
144 A3 Corguinho Brazil
24 C3 Coria Spain
27 F6 Corigliano Calabro Italy
99 G3 Coringa Is is *Coral Sea Islands Terr.* Pac. Oc.
97 F5 Corinna Aust.
121 J2 Corinna U.S.A.
111 J4 Corinne Can.
125 F5 Corinth U.S.A.
121 G3 Corinth U.S.A.
145 F3 Corinto Brazil
141 E3 Corixa Grande r. Bolivia
141 E3 Corixinha r. Brazil
17 C6 Cork Rep. of Ire.
27 D7 Corleone Italy
60 A1 Çorlu Turkey
139 G3 Cormontibo French Guiana
41 □1 Cormoran Reef reef Palau
111 J4 Cormorant Can.
144 C5 Cornélio Procópio Brazil
139 F2 Corneliskondre Surinam
122 B3 Cornell U.S.A.
113 J4 Corner Brook Can.
97 F4 Corner Inlet b. Aust.
15 C3 Cornești Moldova
128 A2 Corning U.S.A.
120 E3 Corning U.S.A.
26 D4 Corno, Monte mt. Italy
20 B2 Cornouaille reg. France
115 H4 Cornwall Can.
109 J2 Cornwall I. i. Can.
109 J2 Cornwallis I. i. Can.
96 D3 Corny Pt pt Aust.
138 D1 Coro Venezuela
145 G3 Coroaci Brazil
142 D1 Coroatá Brazil
140 C3 Corocoro Bolivia
133 E5 Coro, Golfete de b. Venezuela
140 C3 Coroico Bolivia
144 E3 Coromandel Brazil
56 C4 Coromandel Coast India
92 E2 Coromandel Peninsula pen. N.Z.
92 E2 Coromandel Range h. N.Z.
41 B3 Coron Phil.
96 E2 Corona Aust.
128 D5 Corona U.S.A.
128 D5 Coronado U.S.A.
130 K7 Coronado, B. de b. Panama
147 B5 Coronados, G. de los inlet Chile
111 G4 Coronation Can.
108 G3 Coronation Gulf b. Can.
152 B1 Coronation I. i. *S. Orkney Is* Atlantic Ocean
100 D2 Coronation Is is Aust.
110 C3 Coronation Island i. U.S.A.
41 B4 Coron Bay b. Phil.
146 D3 Coronda Arg.
146 D4 Coronel Dorrego Arg.
145 G3 Coronel Fabriciano Brazil
145 G2 Coronel Murta Brazil
141 E5 Coronel Oviedo Paraguay
142 B4 Coronel Ponce Brazil
146 D4 Coronel Pringles Arg.
144 A5 Coronel Sapucaia Brazil
146 D4 Coronel Suárez Arg.
146 E4 Coronel Vidal Arg.
140 A1 Corongo Peru
29 C4 Çorovodë Albania
97 F3 Corowa Aust.
131 H5 Corozal Belize
132 D5 Corozal Colombia
133 □3 Corozal Pt pt *Trinidad* Trin. & Tobago
125 D7 Corpus Christi U.S.A.
125 D6 Corpus Christi, L. l. U.S.A.
140 C3 Corque Bolivia
24 E3 Corral de Almaguer Spain
24 D3 Corral de Cantos mt. Spain
25 □ Corralejo *Canary Is* Spain
144 C2 Córrego do Ouro Brazil
145 G3 Córrego Novo Brazil
142 D3 Corrente r. *Bahia* Brazil
142 C3 Corrente *Goiás* Brazil
144 C3 Corrente r. *Goiás* Brazil
145 G3 Corrente Grande r. Brazil
144 A2 Correntes Brazil
143 B4 Correntes r. Brazil
142 D3 Correntina Brazil
20 E4 Corrèze r. France
17 C5 Corrib, Lough l. Rep. of Ire.
146 E2 Corrientes r. Arg.
146 E2 Corrientes Arg.
146 E2 Corrientes div. Arg.
146 E4 Corrientes, C. c. Arg.
130 D4 Corrientes, C. c. Mexico
138 B2 Corrientes, Cabo pt Colombia
132 A2 Corrientes, Cabo pt Cuba
125 E6 Corrigan U.S.A.
101 B7 Corrigin Aust.
139 F2 Corriverton Guyana
120 D4 Corry U.S.A.
97 F4 Corryong Aust.
21 J5 Corse div. France
21 J5 Corse, Cap c. France
125 D5 Corsicana U.S.A.
21 J5 Corte France
24 C4 Cortegana Spain
129 H3 Cortez U.S.A.
128 D1 Cortez Mts mts U.S.A.
26 D2 Cortina d'Ampezzo Italy
121 E3 Cortland U.S.A.
26 C4 Cortona Italy
24 B3 Coruche Portugal
60 E1 Çoruh r. Turkey
60 C1 Çorum Turkey
144 D2 Corumbá r. Brazil
141 E3 Corumbá Brazil
144 D1 Corumbá de Goiás Brazil
144 D3 Corumbaíba Brazil
144 C6 Corumbataí r. Brazil
145 J2 Corumbaú, Pta pt Brazil
28 E1 Corund Romania
142 E3 Coruripe Brazil
126 B2 Corvallis U.S.A.
17 F5 Corwen U.K.
130 D3 Cosalá Mexico
140 C3 Cosapa Bolivia
140 C3 Coscaya Chile
27 F6 Cosenza Italy
120 C4 Coshocton U.S.A.
144 E5 Cosmópolis Brazil
20 F3 Cosne-Cours-sur-Loire France
146 D3 Cosquín Arg.
20 D3 Cossé-le-Vivien France
25 F3 Costa Blanca Spain
25 H2 Costa Brava France/Spain
24 C4 Costa de la Luz reg. Spain
25 F3 Costa del Azahar Spain
24 D4 Costa del Sol Spain
130 K6 Costa de Mosquitos reg. Nicaragua
25 H2 Costa Dorada Spain
140 D2 Costa Marques Brazil
141 E2 Costa Pinheiro, Cap r. Brazil
144 B3 Costa Rica Brazil
104 K8 Costa Rica country Central America
130 D3 Costa Rica Mexico
24 C1 Costa Verde reg. Spain
15 B3 Costești Moldova
28 F1 Costești Romania
121 J2 Costigan U.S.A.
41 C5 Cotabato Phil.
140 C4 Cotagaita Bolivia
140 B3 Cotahuasi Peru
145 H3 Cotaxé r. Brazil
21 H5 Côte d'Azur reg. France
69 D5 Côte d'Ivoire country Africa
142 D3 Cotegipe Brazil
110 C3 Cote, Mt mt. U.S.A.
20 D2 Cotentin reg. France
21 G2 Côtes de Meuse ridge France
28 E2 Cotești Romania
25 G1 Cotiella mt. Spain
139 E3 Cotingo r. Brazil
15 C3 Cotiujeni Moldova
15 C3 Cotiujenii Mici Moldova
28 F1 Cotnari Romania
77 E5 Cotonou Benin
81 □3 Coton, Pt pt *Rodrigues I.* Mauritius
138 B4 Cotopaxi, Vol. vol Ecuador
17 F6 Cotswold Hills h. U.K.
126 B3 Cottage Grove U.S.A.
19 G3 Cottbus Germany
56 B3 Cotteliar r. India
152 □ Cotter, C. c. *Kerguelen* Indian Ocean
139 G3 Cottica Surinam
129 H5 Cotton City U.S.A.
129 F4 Cottonwood U.S.A.
129 G4 Cottonwood Wash r. U.S.A.
133 E3 Cotuí Dominican Rep.
125 D6 Cotulla U.S.A.
20 D4 Coubre, Pte de la pt France
120 D4 Coudersport U.S.A.
96 D4 Couëdic, C. de c. Aust.
20 D3 Couëron France
152 B1 Coulman I. i. Ant.
20 E1 Coulogne France
75 F3 Couloir 1 well Algeria
21 F2 Coulommiers France
21 G5 Coulon r. France
115 G3 Coulonge r. Can.
20 D3 Coulonges-sur-l'Autize France
128 B3 Coulterville U.S.A.
126 C2 Council U.S.A.
124 E3 Council Bluffs U.S.A.
111 G2 Courageous Lake l. Can.
139 F3 Courantyne r. Guyana
152 □ Courbet, Péninsule pen. *Kerguelen* Indian Ocean
11 F5 Courland Lagoon Lithuania/Rus. Fed.
92 □2 Courrejolles Pt pt *Campbell I.* N.Z.
110 E5 Courtenay Can.
17 C6 Courtmacsherry Rep. of Ire.
18 A3 Courtrai Belgium
125 E5 Coushatta U.S.A.
81 □1 Cousin Is is Seychelles
79 B5 Coutada do Ambriz res. Angola
79 D7 Coutada Pública do Longa-Mavinga res. Angola
79 D7 Coutada Pública do Luengué res. Angola
79 D7 Coutada Pública do Luiana res. Angola
79 D7 Coutada Pública do Mucusso res. Angola
20 D2 Coutances France
145 G3 Couto de Magalhães de Minas Brazil
142 C2 Couto Magalhães Brazil
20 D4 Coutras France
112 E2 Couture, Lac l. Can.
133 □3 Couva Trin. & Tobago
18 B3 Couvin Belgium
20 E4 Couzeix France
25 E2 Covaleda Spain
28 F2 Covasna Romania
77 E5 Covè Benin
129 F2 Cove Fort U.S.A.
114 E4 Cove I. i. Can.
120 E5 Cove Mts h. U.S.A.
17 G5 Coventry U.K.
121 E5 Cove Point U.S.A.
24 C2 Covilhã Portugal
119 D5 Covington U.S.A.
122 D5 Covington U.S.A.
120 A5 Covington U.S.A.
119 B5 Covington U.S.A.
120 D6 Covington U.S.A.
114 D3 Cow r. Can.
97 F3 Cowal, L. l. Aust.
101 C6 Cowan, L. salt flat Aust.
115 J4 Cowansville Can.
50 B1 Cowargarze China
101 B6 Cowcowing Lakes salt flat Aust.
16 F3 Cowdenbeath U.K.
96 D3 Cowell Aust.
97 F4 Cowes Aust.
99 F5 Cowley Aust.
120 D5 Cowpasture r. U.S.A.
97 G3 Cowra Aust.
142 D3 Coxá r. Brazil
146 E3 Coxilha de Santana h. Brazil/Uruguay
143 B6 Coxilha Grande h. Brazil
144 A3 Coxim Brazil
144 A3 Coxim r. Brazil
98 C2 Cox R. r. Aust.
121 G3 Coxsackie U.S.A.
55 G5 Cox's Bazar Bangladesh
76 B5 Coyah Guinea
147 C7 Coy Aike Arg.
128 D4 Coyote Lake l. U.S.A.
129 E5 Coyote Peak summit U.S.A.
128 C3 Coyote Peak summit U.S.A.
130 C3 Coyote, Pta pt Mexico
130 D4 Coyotitán Mexico
131 E5 Coyuca de Benitez Mexico
55 F2 Cozhê China
127 D6 Cozón, Co mt. Mexico
131 J4 Cozumel Mexico
131 J4 Cozumel, I. de i. Mexico
27 F6 Cozzo del Pellegrino mt. Italy
99 E1 Crab I. i. Aust.
81 □3 Crab I. i. *Rodrigues I.* Mauritius
97 G3 Craboon Aust.
99 G5 Cracow Aust.
97 F5 Cradle Mountain Lake St Clair Nat. Park nat. park Aust.
96 D2 Cradock Aust.
82 D5 Cradock R.S.A.
92 E2 Cradock Channel chan. N.Z.
110 C3 Craig U.S.A.
126 F3 Craig U.S.A.
97 F4 Craigieburn Aust.
120 D5 Craigsville U.S.A.
18 E4 Crailsheim Germany
28 D2 Craiova Romania
17 G4 Cramlington U.K.
121 F2 Cranberry L. l. U.S.A.
121 F2 Cranberry Lake U.S.A.
97 F4 Cranbourne Aust.
101 B7 Cranbrook Aust.
110 F5 Cranbrook Can.
122 C3 Crandon U.S.A.
126 C3 Crane U.S.A.
125 C6 Crane U.S.A.
122 A1 Crane Lake U.S.A.
133 □9 Crane, The *Barbados* Caribbean
121 H4 Cranston U.S.A.
20 D3 Craon France
152 B4 Crary Ice Rise ice feature Ant.
152 A4 Crary Mts mts Ant.
15 C3 Crasnoe Moldova
126 B3 Crater L. l. U.S.A.
126 B3 Crater Lake Nat. Pk nat. park. U.S.A.
126 D3 Craters of the Moon Nat. Mon. res. U.S.A.
142 D2 Crateús Brazil
142 E2 Crato Brazil
141 E2 Cravari r. Brazil
144 E4 Cravinhos Brazil
138 C2 Cravo Norte Colombia
124 C3 Crawford U.S.A.
122 D5 Crawfordsville U.S.A.
119 C6 Crawfordville U.S.A.
17 G6 Crawley U.K.
119 □1 Crawl, The pt Bermuda
126 E2 Crazy Mts mt. ra. U.S.A.
111 H4 Crean L. l. Can.
17 F6 Crediton U.K.
111 H3 Cree r. Can.
130 D3 Creel Mexico
111 H3 Cree Lake l. Can.
111 J4 Creighton Can.
20 F2 Creil France
26 B3 Crema Italy
26 C3 Cremona Italy
26 E3 Cres i. Croatia
26 E3 Cres Croatia
126 A3 Crescent City U.S.A.
45 □ Crescent I. i. Hong Kong
129 H2 Crescent Junction U.S.A.
128 B1 Crescent Mills U.S.A.
129 E4 Crescent Peak summit U.S.A.
122 A4 Cresco U.S.A.
146 D3 Crespo Arg.
98 C3 Cresswell w Aust.
110 F5 Creston Can.
124 E3 Creston U.S.A.
126 F3 Creston U.S.A.
119 C6 Crestview U.S.A.
121 F5 Crestwood Village U.S.A.
97 E4 Creswick Aust.
21 H3 Crêt Monniot mt. France
25 H1 Creus, Cap de pt Spain
20 E3 Creuse r. France
25 F3 Crevillente Spain
17 F5 Crewe U.K.
120 D6 Crewe U.S.A.
16 E3 Crianlarich U.K.
143 C6 Criciúma Brazil
15 C3 Cricova Moldova
16 F3 Crieff U.K.
26 E3 Crikvenica Croatia
28 G2 Crișan Romania
121 F6 Crisfield U.S.A.
142 C3 Cristalândia Brazil
144 E2 Cristalina Brazil
139 F5 Cristalino r. Brazil
78 B3 Cristal, Monts de mt. ra. Equatorial Guinea/Gabon
144 D2 Cristianópolis Brazil
142 D2 Cristino Castro Brazil
130 L7 Cristóbal Panama
138 C1 Cristóbal Cólon, P. mt. Colombia
138 □ Cristóbal, Pta pt *Galapagos Is* Ecuador
28 E1 Cristuru Secuiesc Romania
15 C3 Criuleni Moldova
142 C3 Crixás r. Brazil
142 C3 Crixás Brazil
142 C3 Crixás Açu r. Brazil
142 B3 Crixás Mirim r. Brazil
28 C3 Crna Gora mts Macedonia/Yugo.
28 B3 Crna Gora div. Yugo.
28 D3 Crna Trava Yugo.
28 D2 Crni Vrh mt. Yugo.
26 E3 Črnomelj Slovenia
97 G4 Croajingolong Nat. Park nat. park Aust.
4 G4 Croatia country Europe
125 E6 Crockett U.S.A.
121 F3 Croghan U.S.A.
21 G5 Croisette, Cap c. France
98 C1 Croker I. i. Aust.
16 E3 Cromarty U.K.
17 H5 Cromer U.K.
93 B6 Cromwell N.Z.
93 C5 Cronadun N.Z.
120 D4 Crooked Creek Reservoir resr U.S.A.
45 □ Crooked I. i. Hong Kong
132 D2 Crooked I. i. The Bahamas
132 D2 Crooked I. Passage chan. The Bahamas
122 B1 Crooked Lake l. Can./U.S.A.
124 D2 Crookston U.S.A.
97 G3 Crookwell Aust.
97 G2 Croppa Cr. Aust.
99 E2 Crosbie r. Aust.
111 J5 Crosby U.S.A.
77 F5 Cross r. Nigeria
111 L2 Cross Bay b. Can.
119 D6 Cross City U.S.A.
121 K1 Cross Creek Can.
125 E5 Crossett U.S.A.
17 F4 Cross Fell h. U.K.
111 K4 Cross Lake Can.
111 K4 Cross Lake l. Can.
120 E3 Cross Lake l. U.S.A.
93 D5 Crossley, Mt mt. N.Z.
129 E4 Crossman Peak summit U.S.A.
77 F5 Cross River div. Nigeria
110 B3 Cross Sound chan. U.S.A.
122 E3 Cross Village U.S.A.
119 C5 Crossville U.S.A.
123 F4 Croswell U.S.A.
27 F6 Crotone Italy
97 F2 Crowal w Aust.
97 F2 Crowl w Aust.
125 E6 Crowley U.S.A.
128 C3 Crowley, Lake l. U.S.A.
133 □2 Crown Point pt *Tobago* Trin. & Tobago
122 D5 Crown Point U.S.A.
121 G3 Crown Point U.S.A.
152 D4 Crown Prince Olav Coast Ant.
152 C3 Crown Princess Martha Coast Ant.
99 H5 Crows Nest Aust.
110 G5 Crowsnest Pass Can.
99 E3 Croydon Aust.
152 □ Croy, I. de i. *Kerguelen* Indian Ocean
149 H6 Crozet Basin Indian Ocean
149 H7 Crozet, Îles is Indian Ocean
149 G6 Crozet Plateau Indian Ocean
108 F2 Crozier Chan. chan. Can.
152 □ Crozier, Mt h. *Kerguelen* Indian Ocean
20 B2 Crozon France
28 E1 Crucea Romania
140 B2 Crucero Peru
131 F3 Cruillas Mexico
143 B6 Cruz Alta Brazil
119 □3 Cruz Bay *Virgin Is* Caribbean
132 C3 Cruz, Cabo c. Cuba
146 D3 Cruz del Eje Arg.
145 F5 Cruzeiro Brazil
144 B5 Cruzeiro do Oeste Brazil
140 B1 Cruzeiro do Sul *Acre* Brazil
144 B5 Cruzeiro do Sul *Paraná* Brazil
129 H5 Cruzville U.S.A.
28 B2 Crvenka Yugo.
110 E3 Crysdale, Mt mt. Can.
96 D3 Crystal Brook Aust.
125 D6 Crystal City U.S.A.
122 C2 Crystal Falls U.S.A.
122 C4 Crystal Lake U.S.A.
19 L5 Csenger Hungary
19 J5 Cserhát h. Hungary
19 K5 Csongrád Hungary
19 H5 Csorna Hungary
19 H5 Csurgó Hungary
133 F5 Cúa Venezuela
147 C5 Cuadrada, Sierra h. Arg.
24 C2 Cualedro Spain
43 D5 Cửa Lớn r. Vietnam
83 F1 Cuamba Mozambique
79 D7 Cuando r. Angola
79 C7 Cuando Cubango div. Angola
79 C7 Cuangar Angola
79 C5 Cuango *Lunda Norte* Angola
79 C5 Cuango *Uíge* Angola
79 C5 Cuango r. Angola
79 C5 Cuanza r. Angola
79 C5 Cuanza Norte div. Angola
79 C6 Cuanza Sul div. Angola
146 D3 Cuarto r. Arg.
79 C7 Cuatir r. Angola
130 E3 Cuatro Ciénegas Mexico
140 D3 Cuatro Ojos Bolivia
130 D2 Cuauhtémoc Mexico
131 F5 Cuautla Mexico
138 B2 Cuayabal Colombia
104 L8 Cuba country Caribbean
24 C3 Cuba Portugal
122 B5 Cuba U.S.A.
127 F4 Cuba U.S.A.
129 F6 Cubabi, Cerro summit Mexico
133 F5 Cubagua, I. i. Venezuela
79 B6 Cubal r. Angola
79 B6 Cubal Angola
79 C7 Cubango r. Angola/Namibia
138 C2 Cubara Colombia
145 E5 Cubatão Brazil
111 J4 Cub Hills h. Can.
60 C1 Çubuk Turkey
79 C6 Cuchi r. Angola
79 C6 Cuchi Angola
146 E3 Cuchilla de Haedo h. Uruguay
146 E3 Cuchilla del Daymán h. Uruguay
146 E3 Cuchilla de Montiel h. Arg.
146 E3 Cuchilla Grande h. Uruguay
146 E3 Cuchilla Grande del Durazno h. Uruguay
146 E3 Cuchilla Grande Inferior h. Uruguay
146 D4 Cuchillo-Có Arg.
120 E6 Cuckoo U.S.A.
138 D3 Cucuí Brazil
79 C6 Cucumbi Angola
138 C2 Cúcuta Colombia
56 B4 Cuddalore India
56 B3 Cuddapah India
111 H4 Cudworth Can.
101 B5 Cue Aust.
79 C7 Cuebe r. Angola
79 C6 Cuelei r. Angola
24 D2 Cuéllar Spain
79 C6 Cuemba Angola
138 B4 Cuenca Ecuador
25 E2 Cuenca Spain
130 E3 Cuencamé Mexico
131 F5 Cuernavaca Mexico
125 D6 Cuero U.S.A.
21 H5 Cuers France
128 B4 Cuesta Pass pass U.S.A.
131 F4 Cuetzalán Mexico
28 D2 Cugir Romania
27 B5 Cuglieri Italy
20 E5 Cugnaux France
79 C5 Cugo r. Angola
139 F5 Cuiaba Brazil
141 E3 Cuiabá r. Brazil
142 A4 Cuiabá Brazil
142 A3 Cuiabá de Larga Brazil
131 F5 Cuicatlan Mexico
91 □16 Cuidado, Pta pt *Easter I.* Chile
131 H6 Cuilapa Guatemala
16 D3 Cuillin Hills mts U.K.
16 D3 Cuillin Sound chan. U.K.
79 C5 Cuilo Angola
49 J3 Cuiluan China
79 B5 Cuimba Angola
79 B6 Cuio Angola
145 H3 Cuité r. Brazil
142 E2 Cuité Brazil
79 C7 Cuito r. Angola
79 C7 Cuito Cuanavale Angola
131 E5 Cuitzeo, L. de l. Mexico
139 E4 Cuiuni r. Brazil
28 D2 Cujmir Romania
43 C6 Cukai Malaysia
60 E2 Çukurca Turkey
42 E4 Cu Lao Cham i. Vietnam
42 E4 Cu Lao Re i. Vietnam
43 E5 Cu Lao Thu i. Vietnam
126 F1 Culbertson U.S.A.
124 C3 Culbertson U.S.A.
97 F3 Culcairn Aust.
119 □3 Culebra, Isla de i. Puerto Rico
24 C2 Culebra, Sierra de la mt. ra. Spain
60 F2 Culfa Azerbaijan
97 F2 Culgoa r. Aust.
130 D3 Culiacán Mexico
130 D3 Culiacancito Mexico
41 A4 Culion i. Phil.
41 A4 Culion Phil.
142 B3 Culiseiu r. Brazil
25 E4 Cúllar-Baza Spain
99 E1 Cullen Pt pt Aust.
25 F3 Cullera Spain
119 C5 Cullman U.S.A.
60 E2 Çullu Turkey
120 D5 Culpeper U.S.A.
138 □ Culpepper, I. i. *Galapagos Is* Ecuador
140 D4 Culpina Bolivia
142 B3 Culuena r. Brazil
142 B3 Culuene r. Brazil
93 D5 Culverden N.Z.
101 D7 Culver, Pt pt Aust.
139 E1 Cumaná Venezuela
138 C3 Cumare, Cerro h. Colombia
144 D3 Cumari Brazil
118 C4 Cumberland r. U.S.A.
120 D5 Cumberland U.S.A.
122 A3 Cumberland U.S.A.
91 □15 Cumberland, Bahía b. *Juan Fernandez Is* Chile
111 J4 Cumberland House Can.
99 G4 Cumberland Is is Aust.
111 J4 Cumberland Lake l. Can.
120 B6 Cumberland Mtn mt. ra. U.S.A.
109 M3 Cumberland Peninsula pen. Can.
118 C4 Cumberland Plateau plat. U.S.A.
122 C2 Cumberland Pt pt U.S.A.
109 M3 Cumberland Sound chan. Can.
139 F3 Cuminapanema r. Brazil
128 A2 Cummings U.S.A.
96 C3 Cummins Aust.
17 E4 Cumnock U.K.
130 C2 Cumpas Mexico
60 C2 Çumra Turkey
130 C2 Cumuripa Mexico
145 J2 Cumuruxatiba Brazil
132 C2 Cunagua Cuba
101 B6 Cunderdin Aust.
131 H6 Cunén Guatemala
79 B7 Cunene r. Angola
79 C7 Cunene div. Angola
26 A3 Cuneo Italy
43 E4 Cung Sơn Vietnam
79 C6 Cunhinga r. Angola
15 C3 Cunicea Moldova
99 F6 Cunnamulla Aust.
133 □3 Cunupia Trin. & Tobago
26 A3 Cuorgnè Italy
16 F3 Cupar U.K.
142 A1 Cupari r. Brazil
15 B2 Cupcina Moldova
138 B2 Cupica Colombia
138 B2 Cupica, Golfo de b. Colombia
26 D4 Cupra Marittima Italy
28 C3 Ćuprija Yugo.
142 E2 Curaçá Brazil
138 C5 Curaçá r. Brazil
142 E2 Curaçá r. Brazil
132 □2 Curaçao airport *Curaçao* Netherlands Ant.
132 □2 Curaçao i. Netherlands Ant.
147 B4 Curacautín Chile
146 C4 Curacó r. Arg.
138 C4 Curaray r. Peru
146 B3 Curaumilla, Punta pt Chile
127 F4 Curecanti Nat. Rec. Area res. U.S.A.
81 □4 Curepipe Mauritius
146 B3 Curicó Chile
138 D4 Curieuriari r. Brazil
81 □1 Curieuse I. i. Seychelles
142 D3 Curimata Brazil
142 E2 Curimataú r. Brazil
144 D6 Curitiba Brazil
143 B6 Curitibanos Brazil
144 C6 Curiúva Brazil
96 D2 Curnamona Aust.
79 B7 Curoca r. Angola
142 E2 Currais Novos Brazil
142 C1 Curralinho Brazil
76 □ Curral Velho Cape Verde
123 F3 Curran U.S.A.
17 B6 Currane, Lough l. Rep. of Ire.
129 E2 Currant U.S.A.
99 E5 Currawilla Aust.
119 E7 Current The Bahamas
97 E4 Currie Aust.
129 E1 Currie U.S.A.
28 E2 Curtea de Argeș Romania
28 C1 Curtici Romania
99 H5 Curtis Channel chan. Aust.
97 F4 Curtis Group is Aust.
99 G4 Curtis I. i. Aust.
92 □4 Curtis I. i. *Kermadec Is* N.Z.
142 B2 Curuá r. Brazil
142 B1 Curuá do Sul r. Brazil
142 B2 Curuaés r. Brazil
139 G3 Curuá, Ilha i. Brazil
139 G4 Curuapanema r. Brazil
142 B1 Curuá Una r. Brazil
142 C1 Curuçá Brazil
142 B1 Curumu Brazil
139 F5 Cururu r. Brazil
139 F5 Cururu Açu r. Brazil
142 D1 Cururupu Brazil
146 E2 Curuzú Cuatiá Arg.
145 F3 Curvelo Brazil
140 B2 Cusco Peru
125 D4 Cushing U.S.A.
130 D2 Cusihuiráchic Mexico
119 C5 Cusseta U.S.A.
122 A1 Cusson U.S.A.
112 E1 Cusson, Pte pt Can.
126 F2 Custer U.S.A.
124 C3 Custer U.S.A.
79 C6 Cutato r. Angola
126 D1 Cut Bank U.S.A.
138 B5 Cutervo, Parque Nacional nat. park Peru
119 C6 Cuthbert U.S.A.
111 H4 Cut Knife Can.
121 K2 Cutler U.S.A.
119 D7 Cutler Ridge U.S.A.
147 C4 Cutral-Co Arg.
55 F5 Cuttack India
129 G5 Cutter U.S.A.
79 C7 Cuvelai Angola
78 C4 Cuvette div. Congo
101 A5 Cuvier, C. hd Aust.
115 G2 Cuvillier, Lac l. Can.
18 D2 Cuxhaven *Niedersachsen* Germany
138 B4 Cuyabeno Ecuador
120 C4 Cuyahoga Falls U.S.A.
120 C4 Cuyahoga Valley National Recreation Area res. U.S.A.
128 C4 Cuyama r. U.S.A.
41 B3 Cuyapo Phil.
41 B4 Cuyo i. Phil.
41 B4 Cuyo Phil.
41 B4 Cuyo East Pass. chan. Phil.
41 B4 Cuyo Islands is Phil.
41 B4 Cuyo West Pass. chan. Phil.
139 F2 Cuyuni r. Guyana
26 F4 Čvrsnica mts Bos.-Herz.
81 A5 Cyangugu Rwanda
19 G2 Cybinka Poland
120 A5 Cynthiana U.S.A.
111 G5 Cypress Hills mt. ra. Can.
32 E6 Cyprus country Asia
72 D2 Cyrenaica reg. Libya
19 H2 Czaplinek Poland
111 G4 Czar Can.
19 L2 Czarna Białostocka Poland
19 H2 Czarne Poland
19 H2 Czarnków Poland
4 G4 Czech Republic country Europe
19 H2 Czempiń Poland
19 L2 Czeremcha Poland
19 H2 Czersk Poland
19 G2 Czerwieńsk Poland
19 J3 Częstochowa Poland
19 H2 Człopa Poland
19 H2 Człuchów Poland
19 L2 Czyżew-Osada Poland

D

49 H3 Da'an China
61 D4 Dab'a Jordan
138 C1 Dabajuro Venezuela
76 D5 Dabakala Côte d'Ivoire
48 B5 Daban Shan mt. ra. China
19 J5 Dabas Hungary
50 E1 Daba Shan mt. ra. China
80 C2 Dabat Ethiopia
76 B4 Dabatou Guinea
138 B2 Dabeiba Colombia
42 B3 Dabein Myanmar
54 C5 Dabhoi India
56 A2 Dabhol India
51 F2 Dabie Shan mt. ra. China
61 D5 Dabl, W. w Saudi Arabia
54 D4 Daboh India
76 B4 Dabola Guinea
76 D5 Dabou Côte d'Ivoire
54 D4 Dabra India
19 L2 Dąbrowa Białostocka Poland
19 J3 Dąbrowa Górnicza Poland
19 K3 Dąbrowa Tarnowska Poland
51 G3 Dabu China
28 E3 Dăbuleni Romania
80 B2 Dabus Wenz r. Ethiopia
80 D3 Dacarbudhug Somalia
18 E4 Dachau Germany
48 B5 Dachechang China
56 B2 Dachepalle India
115 G4 Dacre Can.
139 F3 Dadanawa Guyana
80 D2 Daddato Djibouti
119 D6 Dade City U.S.A.
54 A3 Dadhar Pakistan
54 C5 Dadra India
54 C5 Dadra and Nagar Haveli div. India
50 C2 Dadu r. China
54 A4 Dadu Pakistan
43 D5 Đa Dung r. Vietnam
73 G3 Daedalus Reef reef Saudi Arabia
41 B3 Daet Phil.
50 D3 Dafang China
61 C5 Dafdaf, J. mt. Saudi Arabia
51 H1 Dafeng China
80 D3 Daferur well Ethiopia
55 H4 Dafla Hills mt. ra. India
80 D3 Daga Medo Ethiopia
76 A3 Dagana Senegal
50 C1 Dagcanglhamo China
13 H6 Dagestan div. Rus. Fed.
93 A6 Dagg Sd inlet N.Z.
75 F2 Daglet Lagrouba Algeria
49 G5 Dagu r. China
50 C3 Daguan China
45 □ D'Aguilar Peak h. Hong Kong
41 B2 Dagupan Phil.
55 H1 Dagur China
55 G3 Dagzê China
55 F3 Dagzê Co salt l. China
55 G3 Dagzhuka China
73 F2 Dahab Egypt
73 G3 Dahabān Saudi Arabia
56 A2 Dahanu India
48 D4 Dahei r. China
49 J3 Daheiding Shan mt. China
51 G3 Daheng China
49 K3 Dahezhen China
49 F3 Da Hinggan Ling mts China
80 D1 Dahlak Archipelago is Eritrea
80 C1 Dahlak Marine National Park nat. park Eritrea
18 C3 Dahlem Germany
54 C5 Dāhod India
54 D2 Dahongliutan China/Jammu and Kashmir
60 E2 Dahūk Iraq
60 E2 Dahūk div. Iraq
49 H4 Dahuofang Sk. resr China
48 E4 Dai Hai l. China
40 A2 Daik Indon.
42 B3 Daik-u Myanmar
49 E3 Dailamin Sum China
55 E3 Dailekh Nepal
57 D2 Daim Iran
46 D5 Daimanji-san h. Japan
24 E3 Daimiel Spain
47 F6 Dainichiga-take vol Japan
50 B1 Dainkog China
50 B1 Dainkognubma China
99 F3 Daintree Nat. Park nat. park. Aust.
47 F6 Daiō Japan
47 F6 Daiō-zaki pt Japan
146 D4 Daireaux Arg.
73 F2 Dairût Egypt
122 A2 Dairyland U.S.A.
46 D6 Daisen vol Japan
51 H2 Daishan China
86 E2 Daito-jima is Japan
48 E5 Dai Xian China
51 G3 Daiyun Shan mt. ra. China
98 D4 Dajarra Aust.
50 C2 Dajin Chuan r. China
48 B5 Dajing China
55 H1 Da Juh China
76 D5 Daka r. Ghana
76 A4 Dakar Senegal
73 E4 Dakar el Arāk well Sudan
55 G3 Dakelangsi China
80 D3 Daketa Shet' w Ethiopia
55 G5 Dakhin Shabazpur I. i. Bangladesh
73 E2 Dakhla Oasis oasis Egypt
74 A4 Dakhlet Nouâdhibou div. Mauritania
77 E4 Dakingari Nigeria
43 D4 Dak Kon Vietnam
43 A6 Dakoank *Andaman and Nicobar Is* India
13 D4 Dakol'ka r. Belarus
76 C4 Dakoro Burkina
77 F4 Dakoro Niger
124 D3 Dakota City U.S.A.
28 C3 Đakovica Yugo.
26 G3 Đakovo Croatia
49 H1 Daktuy Rus. Fed.
80 D2 Dal well Djibouti
79 D6 Dala Angola
76 B4 Dalaba Guinea
48 D4 Dalad Qi China
49 F4 Dalai Nur l. China
61 B5 Dalal, G. mt. Egypt
48 E4 Dalamamiao China
60 B2 Dalaman Turkey
60 B2 Dalaman r. Turkey
48 C4 Dalandzadgad Mongolia
41 B4 Dalanganem Islands is Phil.
43 E5 Đa Lat Vietnam
48 B4 Dalay Mongolia
57 F3 Dalbandin Pakistan
99 G5 Dalby Aust.
11 B3 Dale *Hordaland* Norway
11 B3 Dale *Sogn og Fjordane* Norway
120 E5 Dale City U.S.A.
125 G4 Dale Hollow Lake l. U.S.A.
42 A3 Dalet Myanmar
42 A2 Daletme Myanmar
11 D3 Dalfors Sweden
57 D4 Dalgān Iran
101 B5 Dalgaranger, Mt h. Aust.
125 C4 Dalhart U.S.A.
113 G4 Dalhousie Can.
51 E1 Dali *Shaanxi* China
50 C3 Dali *Yunnan* China
49 G5 Dalian China
50 C2 Daliang Shan mt. ra. China
49 G4 Dalin China
49 F4 Daling r. China
49 H4 Dalizi China
55 F4 Dālkola India
99 H5 Dallarnil Aust.
121 F4 Dallas U.S.A.
125 D5 Dallas U.S.A.
122 B5 Dallas City U.S.A.
126 B2 Dalles, The U.S.A.
110 C4 Dall I. i. U.S.A.
77 E3 Dallol Bosso w Mali/Niger
57 C4 Dalmā i. U.A.E.
26 F4 Dalmacija reg. Croatia
146 D3 Dalmacio Vélez Sarsfield Arg.
54 E4 Dalman India
64 F1 Dalmatovo Rus. Fed.
17 E4 Dalmellington U.K.
49 K3 Dal'nerechensk Rus. Fed.
14 G2 Dal'neye Konstantinovo Rus. Fed.
76 C5 Daloa Côte d'Ivoire
50 D3 Dalou Shan mt. ra. China
99 F4 Dalrymple, L. l. Aust.
99 G4 Dalrymple, Mt mt. Aust.
55 F4 Daltenganj India
114 C2 Dalton Can.
119 C5 Dalton U.S.A.
121 G3 Dalton U.S.A.
114 C2 Dalton Mills Can.
50 C4 Da Luo China
41 B2 Dalupiri i. Phil.
10 M2 Dalvík Iceland
98 B2 Daly r. Aust.
128 A3 Daly City U.S.A.
98 B2 Daly River Abor. Land res. Aust.
98 C3 Daly Waters Aust.
19 L3 Damachava Belarus
77 F4 Damagaram Takaya Niger
79 E6 Damalisques de Leshwe res. Zaire
54 C5 Daman India
54 C5 Damān and Diu div. India
61 A4 Damanhûr Egypt
57 B2 Damaq Iran
49 E4 Damaqun Shan mt. ra. China
39 J8 Damar i. Indon.
41 C6 Damar Indon.
78 C3 Damara C.A.R.
82 B3 Damaraland reg. Namibia
77 G4 Damasak Nigeria
146 B3 Damas, P. de las Arg./Chile
77 G4 Damaturu Nigeria
57 C2 Damāvand Iran
57 C2 Damāvand mt. Iran
79 C5 Damba Angola
77 E5 Dambai Ghana
77 F4 Dambatta Nigeria
77 G4 Damboa Nigeria
56 C5 Dambulla Sri Lanka
132 D3 Dame Marie Haiti
132 D3 Dame Marie, Cap c. Haiti
57 C1 Damghan Iran
49 E5 Daming China
61 C3 Dāmiya Jordan
50 A1 Damjong China
54 D5 Damoh India
76 D5 Damongo Ghana
40 D1 Dampelas, Tg pt Indon.
100 B4 Dampier Aust.
100 B4 Dampier Arch. is Aust.
90 □1 Dampier Strait chan. P.N.G.
40 C4 Dampit Indon.
55 H2 Dam Qu r. China
55 H3 Damroh India
55 G3 Damxung China
55 E3 Dana Nepal
76 C5 Danané Côte d'Ivoire
42 E3 Đa Nẵng Vietnam
41 C4 Danao Phil.
40 E2 Danau Poso l. Indon.
50 C2 Danba China
121 G4 Danbury U.S.A.
121 H3 Danbury U.S.A.
121 G3 Danby U.S.A.
129 E4 Danby Lake l. U.S.A.
51 F1 Dancheng China
101 A6 Dandaragan Aust.
79 B5 Dande r. Angola
80 C4 Dande Ethiopia
54 E3 Dandel'dhura Nepal
56 A3 Dandeli India
97 F4 Dandenong Aust.
49 H4 Dandong China
115 H3 Dandurand, Lac l. Can.
109 Q2 Daneborg Greenland
28 D3 Daneți Romania
51 E1 Danfeng China
121 K2 Danforth U.S.A.
51 F4 Dangan Liedao is China
49 J3 Dangbizhen Rus. Fed.
50 D1 Dangchang China
79 C5 Dange Angola
150 J6 Danger Islands is *Cook Islands* Pac. Oc.
82 B5 Danger Pt pt R.S.A.
65 G5 Danghara Tajikistan
80 C2 Dangila Ethiopia
55 G3 Dangqên China
131 H5 Dangriga Belize
51 G1 Dangshan China
51 G2 Dangtu China
77 F4 Dan-Gulbi Nigeria
80 C2 Dangur Ethiopia
51 E2 Dangyang China
126 E3 Daniel U.S.A.
12 G3 Danilov Rus. Fed.
28 B3 Danilovgrad Yugo.
14 G3 Danilovka Rus. Fed.
13 H5 Danilovka Rus. Fed.
12 F3 Danilovskaya Vozvyshennost' h. Rus. Fed.
48 D5 Daning China
51 E1 Danjiangkou Sk. resr China
46 B7 Danjo-guntō is Japan
54 D2 Dankhar India
14 D3 Dankov Rus. Fed.
50 C2 Danleng China
130 J6 Danlí Honduras
76 C5 Dan, Mts des mts Côte d'Ivoire
121 G2 Dannemora U.S.A.
18 E2 Dannenberg (Elbe) Germany
92 F4 Dannevirke N.Z.
76 D4 Dano Burkina
42 C3 Dan Sai Thailand
120 E3 Dansville U.S.A.
54 C4 Danta India
56 C2 Dantewara India
42 A3 Danubyu Myanmar
40 C1 Danumparai Indon.
115 J4 Danville Can.
122 D5 Danville U.S.A.
122 D6 Danville U.S.A.
118 C4 Danville U.S.A.
123 J5 Danville U.S.A.
120 D6 Danville U.S.A.
51 E5 Dan Xian China
51 G2 Danyang China
77 E5 Danyi, Plateau de plat. Togo
50 D3 Danzhai China
19 J1 Danzig, Gulf of g. Poland/Rus. Fed.
41 B4 Dao Phil.
42 D2 Đao Bach Long Vi i. Vietnam
42 D2 Đao Cai Bâu i. Vietnam
42 D2 Đao Cat Ba i. Vietnam
50 C2 Daocheng China
43 C5 Đao Phu Quôc i. Vietnam
48 B5 Daotanghe China
43 C5 Đao Thô Chư i. Vietnam
74 C5 Daoudi well Mauritania
76 D5 Daoukro Côte d'Ivoire
43 C5 Đao Vây i. Vietnam
51 E3 Dao Xian China
50 D2 Daozhen China
41 C4 Dapa Phil.
77 E4 Dapaong Togo
55 H4 Daphabum mt. India
61 B4 Daphnae Egypt
41 B4 Dapiak, Mt mt. Phil.
41 B4 Dapitan Phil.
44 G4 Da Qaidam China
49 H3 Daqing China
48 D4 Daqing Shan mt. ra. China
57 C2 Daqq-e Dombūn Iran
60 F3 Dāqūq Iraq
51 H2 Daqu Shan i. China
76 A3 Dara Senegal
61 D3 Dar'ā Syria
61 D3 Dar'a div. Syria
57 C3 Dārāb Iran
54 B3 Daraban Pakistan
28 F1 Darabani Romania
72 B1 Daraj Libya
57 C3 Dārākūyeh Iran
59 H3 Dārān Iran
65 H3 Darat Kazak.
28 C3 Đaravica mt. Yugo.
73 F3 Daraw Egypt
77 G4 Darazo Nigeria
57 D3 Darband Iran
54 B1 Darband Pakistan
24 D5 Dar Ben Karricha el Behri Morocco
55 F4 Darbhanga India
50 B1 Darcang China
24 D5 Dar Chaoui Morocco
26 G3 Darda Croatia
128 C2 Dardanelle U.S.A.
125 E5 Dardanelle, Lake l. U.S.A.
60 D2 Darende Turkey
81 C6 Dar es Salaam Tanzania
93 D5 Darfield N.Z.
26 C3 Darfo Boario Terme Italy
72 D4 Darfur div. Sudan
54 B2 Dargai Pakistan
64 F4 Dargan-Ata Turkmenistan
92 D1 Dargaville N.Z.
97 F4 Dargo Aust.
77 E4 Dargol Niger
48 C2 Darhan Mongolia
48 D4 Darhan Muminggan Lianheqi China
119 D6 Darien U.S.A.
138 B2 Darién, Golfo del g. Colombia
130 L8 Darién, Parque Nacional de nat. park Panama
65 H3 Dar'inskiy Kazak.
130 J6 Darío Nicaragua
55 G4 Dārjiling India
101 B7 Darkan Aust.

50 B1 Darlag China
97 E3 Darling r. Aust.
95 G2 Darling Downs reg. Aust.
101 B7 Darling Range h. Aust.
17 G4 Darlington U.K.
122 B4 Darlington U.S.A.
97 F3 Darlington Point Aust.
101 C5 Darlot, L. salt flat Aust.
19 H1 Darłowo Poland
54 E3 Darma Pass pass China/India
56 B2 Darmaraopet India
57 D2 Dar Mazār Iran
18 E4 Darmstadt Germany
54 A2 Darna r. India
72 D1 Darnah Libya
97 E3 Darnick Aust.
108 F3 Darnley Bay b. Can.
152 D5 Darnley, C. c. Ant.
25 F2 Daroca Spain
65 H5 Daroot-Korgan Kyrgyzstan
12 G3 Darovka Rus. Fed.
12 H3 Darovskoye Rus. Fed.
99 E4 Darr w Aust.
146 D4 Darregueira Arg.
54 D2 Darreh Bid Iran
57 D1 Darreh Gaz Iran
57 G2 Darri-i-Shikar r. Afghanistan
80 □ Darsa i. Socotra Yemen
56 H5 Darsi India
18 F1 Darß pen. Germany
18 F1 Darßer Ort c. Germany
17 F6 Dart r. U.K.
17 H6 Dartford U.K.
96 E4 Dartmoor Aust.
17 F6 Dartmoor reg. U.K.
113 H5 Dartmouth Can.
17 F6 Dartmouth U.K.
99 F5 Dartmouth, L. salt flat Aust.
90 □1 Daru P.N.G.
76 B5 Daru Sierra Leone
73 F4 Daru waterhole Sudan
55 G3 Darum Tso I. China
26 F3 Daruvar Croatia
64 E4 Darvaza Turkmenistan
57 B3 Darvīša r.
57 F3 Darwazagi Afghanistan
57 F3 Darweshan Afghanistan
98 B2 Darwin Aust.
147 E7 Darwin Arg.
147 C7 Darwin, Mte mt. Chile
138 □ Darwin, Vol. vol Galápagos Is Ecuador
57 C3 Daryächeh-ye Bakhtegan salt l. Iran
57 C3 Daryächeh-ye Mahārlū salt l. Iran
57 B2 Daryächeh-ye Namak salt flat Iran
60 F2 Daryächeh-ye Orūmīyeh salt l. Iran
57 E3 Daryächeh-ye Sīstan marsh Afghanistan
57 C3 Daryächeh-ye Tashk Iran
57 D3 Dārzīn Iran
57 C4 Dās i. U.A.E.
48 E2 Dashbalbar Mongolia
51 E2 Dashennongjia mt. China
15 C2 Dashiv Ukraine
49 G3 Dashköwuz Turkmenistan
64 E4 Dashkhovuz div. Turkmenistan
57 D1 Dasht Iran
57 E4 Dasht r. Pakistan
57 D1 Dasht Āb Iran
57 E2 Dasht-e-Daqq-e-Tundi depression Afghanistan
57 C2 Dasht-e Kavīr desert Iran
57 D2 Dasht-e Lut desert Iran
57 E2 Dasht-e Naomid plain Afghanistan/Iran
57 B3 Dasht-i-Palang r. Iran
57 F3 Dasht-i-Arbu Lut desert Afghanistan
57 E4 Dashtiari Iran
57 E3 Dasht-i-Margo desert Afghanistan
48 C5 Dashuikeng China
48 C5 Dashuitou China
54 C2 Daska Pakistan
55 B3 Daşkäsän Azerbaijan
54 C1 Daspar mt. Pakistan
77 E5 Dassa Benin
57 D2 Dastgardān Iran
29 J4 Da Suife r. China
40 C1 Datadian Indon.
42 A2 Datça Turkey
46 H2 Date Japan
129 F5 Dateland U.S.A.
54 D4 Datia India
48 B5 Datian China
54 B1 Datian Pakistan
48 C4 Datong China
48 H3 Datong China
48 A5 Datong Shan mt. ra. China
40 C1 Datu i. Indon.
40 A2 Datuk, Tg pt Indon.
40 B1 Dau Piang Phil.
40 B1 Datu, Tg c. Indon./Malaysia
54 D4 Daud Khel Pakistan
54 C3 Daudnagar India
12 G3 Dauga r. Latvia
12 G3 Daugava r. Latvia
11 G5 Daugavpils Latvia
57 F1 Daulatabad Afghanistan
18 C2 Daun Germany
43 B4 Daung Kyun i. Myanmar
42 A2 Daungyu r. Myanmar
21 J4 Dauphin France
111 J4 Dauphin Can.
125 F6 Dauphin U.S.A.
21 H4 Dauphin I. L. U.S.A.
77 F4 Daura Nigeria
101 A5 Daurie Cr. r. Aust.
49 F2 Dauriya Rus. Fed.
49 D2 Daurskiy Khrebet mt. ra. Rus. Fed.
54 D4 Dausa India
60 G1 Dāvāci Azerbaijan
56 A3 Davangere India
41 C5 Davao Phil.
41 C5 Davao Gulf b. Phil.
57 D2 Dāvar Panāh Iran
57 D1 Dāvarzan Iran
128 A3 Davenport U.S.A.
122 B4 Davenport U.S.A.
99 E5 Davenport Downs Aust.
98 B4 Davenport, Mt h. Aust.
98 C3 Davenport Ra. h. Aust.
130 K7 David Panama
111 H4 Davidson Can.
96 E3 Davies, Mt mt. Aust.
144 E3 Davinópolis Brazil
152 D5 Davis Australia Base Ant.
128 B2 Davis U.S.A.
129 E4 Davis Dam U.S.A.
113 H2 Davis Inlet Can.
152 D5 Davis Sea sea Ant.
109 N3 Davis Strait str. Can./Greenland
64 D2 Davlekanovo Rus. Fed.
29 D5 Davlia Greece
21 J3 Davos Switz.
15 G3 Davydiv Brid Ukraine
80 B4 Dawa China
54 C2 Dawan China
50 C2 Dawe China
57 B4 Dawhat Salwah b. Qatar/Saudi Arabia

80 D2 Dawi well Ethiopia
15 C1 Dawlyady Belarus
42 B3 Dawna Range mt. ra. Myanmar/Thailand
59 H6 Dawqah Oman
73 H4 Dawqah Saudi Arabia
80 D2 Dawrān Yemen
99 G5 Dawson r. Aust.
119 C6 Dawson U.S.A.
124 D2 Dawson Can.
111 J4 Dawson Bay b. Can.
110 E3 Dawson Creek Can.
111 L2 Dawson Inlet inlet Can.
110 B2 Dawson Range mt. ra. Can.
50 C2 Dawu China
51 F2 Dawu China
20 D5 Dax France
50 D2 Daxian China
50 D4 Daxin China
49 F5 Daxing China
54 □ Daxue Shan mt. ra. China
51 F2 Dayang r. India
49 H2 Dayangshu China
65 L3 Dayan Nuur I. Mongolia
50 C3 Daye China
51 E4 Dayao Shan mt. ra. China
51 F2 Daye China
50 C2 Dayi China
51 F3 Dayu Ling mt. ra. China
49 E5 Da Yunhe r. Hebei China
51 F3 Da Yunhe r. Jiangsu China
126 C2 Dayville U.S.A.
46 C7 Dazaifu Japan
50 D2 Dazu China
82 C5 De Aar R.S.A.
122 D2 Dead r. U.S.A.
81 D7 Deadman's Cay The Bahamas
48 A2 Delger Mörön r. Mongolia
61 C4 Dead Sea salt l. Israel/Jordan
17 H6 Deal U.K.
51 F2 De'an China
51 F6 Dean, Forest of forest U.K.
146 D3 Dean Funes Arg.
123 H4 Dearborn U.S.A.
108 F3 Dease Arm b. Can.
110 E3 Dease Lake Can.
128 D3 Death Valley v. U.S.A.
128 D3 Death Valley Junction U.S.A.
128 D3 Death Valley National Monument res. U.S.A.
40 B1 Debak Malaysia
54 D4 Debao China
80 C2 Debark Ethiopia
19 H2 Dębica Poland
19 K3 Dęblin Poland
133 □2 Debe Trin. & Tobago
80 D3 Débo, Lac l. Mali
101 B6 Deborah, L. salt flat Aust.
80 C2 Debre Birhan Ethiopia
80 C2 Debrecen Hungary
80 C2 Debre Markos Ethiopia
80 C2 Debre Sīna Ethiopia
29 C4 Debreşte Macedonia
80 C2 Debre Tabor Ethiopia
80 C2 Debre Werk' Ethiopia
80 C2 Debre Zeyit Ethiopia
28 C2 Deçani Yugo.
119 C5 Decatur U.S.A.
119 C5 Decatur U.S.A.
122 C5 Decatur U.S.A.
122 E4 Decatur U.S.A.
20 E4 Decazeville France
115 G3 Decelles, Réservoir resr Can.
54 B5 Deccan plat. India
82 C2 Deception r. Botswana
83 E1 Deception Pans salt pan Botswana
50 C3 Dechang China
139 E4 Décin Czech Rep.
60 B2 Décines-Charpieu France
21 F3 Decize France
23 F2 Decorah U.S.A.
122 B4 Decorah U.S.A.
54 D2 Dêdang China
41 □2 Dededo Guam Pac. Oc.
18 □ Dedemsvaart Netherlands
80 D2 Deder Ethiopia
11 D4 Dedinovo Rus. Fed.
147 B6 Dedo, Co. mt. Chile
144 E4 Dedo de Deus mt. Brazil
15 A2 Dedovichi Ukraine
83 D5 Dedza Malawi
83 E1 Dedza Mountain mt. Malawi
17 E4 Dee est. U.K.
17 E4 Dee r. U.K.
45 Dee r. India
115 G4 Deep Bay b. Hong Kong
120 D6 Deep Creek Lake l. U.S.A.
129 F2 Deep Creek Range mts U.S.A.
115 G3 Deep River Can.
111 K1 Deep Rose Lake l. Can.
128 B2 Deep Springs U.S.A.
82 A5 Deep Valley B. b. St Helena Atlantic Ocean
97 G2 Deepwater Aust.
120 D5 Deer Cr. r. U.S.A.
101 A5 Deeral Aust.
80 E4 Deeri Somalia
54 D4 Deesa India
113 J2 Deer Lake Can.
126 D2 Deer Lodge U.S.A.
18 C2 Defiance U.S.A.
77 G2 Défirou well Niger
56 A5 De Funiak Springs U.S.A.
54 C4 Degê China
80 D2 Degeh Bur Ethiopia
80 D3 Degodia reg. Ethiopia
18 E4 Deggendorf Germany
80 D4 Degodia reg. Ethiopia
57 C2 Dehaj Iran
57 C3 Dehak Iran
57 E3 Deh Bīd Iran

57 B3 Deh-Dasht Iran
121 □ Dehdez Iran
57 B3 Deh-e Khalīfeh Iran
75 G2 Dehiba Tunisia
56 B5 Dehiwala-Mount Lavinia Sri Lanka
57 A2 Dehkūyeh Iran
57 A2 Dehlonān Iran
55 F4 Dehri India
57 D3 Deh Salm Iran
57 E3 Deh Sard Iran
57 E3 Deh Shū Afghanistan
51 G3 Dehua China
78 B2 Dehui China
28 D1 Dej Romania
50 E2 Dejiang China
80 B2 Dejen Ethiopia
25 □ De Kalb U.S.A.
125 E5 De Kalb U.S.A.
121 F2 De Kalb Junction U.S.A.
45 Q1 De-Kastri Rus. Fed.
80 C1 Dekemhare Eritrea
79 D4 Dekese Zaire
76 B3 Dekina Nigeria
78 C2 Dékoa C.A.R.
129 F2 Delano Peak summit U.S.A.
57 E2 Delārām Afghanistan
146 E3 Delareyville R.S.A.
111 H4 Delaronde Lake l. Can.
122 C5 Delavan U.S.A.
121 F4 Delaware r. U.S.A.
120 B4 Delaware U.S.A.
121 F5 Delaware div. U.S.A.
121 F5 Delaware Bay b. U.S.A.
121 F4 Delaware Water Gap National Recreational Area res. U.S.A.
28 D4 Delčevo Macedonia
97 G4 Delegate Aust.
21 H3 Delémont Switz.
145 E4 Delfinópolis Brazil
18 B2 Delft Netherlands
56 B4 Delft I. i. Sri Lanka
18 C2 Delfzijl Netherlands
81 D7 Delgado, Cabo pt Mozambique
73 F3 Delgo Sudan
114 E5 Delhi Can.
127 F4 Delhi U.S.A.
40 A3 Deli i. Indon.
21 H5 Delice r. Turkey
139 G3 Délices French Guiana
57 B2 Delījān Iran
110 E1 Déline Can.
18 C2 Delitzsch Germany
124 D3 Dell Rapids U.S.A.
75 E1 Dellys Algeria
128 B5 Del Mar U.S.A.
129 E3 Delmar U.S.A.
18 D2 Delmenhorst Germany
26 E3 Delnice Croatia
63 R2 De-Longa, O-va is Rus. Fed.
108 B3 De Long Mts mt. ra. U.S.A.
97 G5 Deloraine Aust.
114 A4 Deloraine Can.
122 E5 Delphi U.S.A.
120 A4 Delphos U.S.A.
119 D6 Delray Beach U.S.A.
127 E6 Del Rio Mexico
125 C6 Del Rio U.S.A.
63 R3 Delta div. U.S.A.
122 D5 Delta U.S.A.
129 F2 Delta U.S.A.
99 E3 Delta Downs Aust.
76 A4 Delta du Saloum, Parc National du nat. park Senegal
108 D3 Delta Junction Can.
121 F3 Delta Reservoir resr U.S.A.
119 C6 Deltona U.S.A.
97 G2 Delungra Aust.
29 C5 Delvinë Albania
15 A2 Delyatyn Ukraine
64 E2 Dema r. Rus. Fed.
24 □1 Demanda, Sierra de la mt. ra. Spain
79 D4 Demba Zaire
80 C2 Dembech'a Ethiopia
78 B2 Dembia C.A.R.
80 C2 Dembi Dolo Ethiopia
14 E2 Demidov Rus. Fed.
125 C5 Deming U.S.A.
139 E2 Demini r. Brazil
42 B2 Demirci Turkey
42 A1 Demirköprü Baraji resr Turkey
21 H3 Demirköy Turkey
18 F2 Demmin Germany
76 D2 Demnate Morocco
122 B4 Demotte U.S.A.
41 □2 Dempo, G. vol Indon.
101 C7 Dempster, Pt pt Aust.
14 A3 Dëmovo Rus. Fed.
15 D1 Demydiv Ukraine
15 E2 Demydivka Ukraine
60 F2 Denali see McKinley, Mt
80 C3 Denan Ethiopia
111 H3 Denare Beach Can.
65 H5 Denau Uzbekistan
115 G4 Denbigh Can.
110 C2 Denbigh, C. c. U.S.A.
17 E4 Denbigh U.K.
43 B5 Den Burg Netherlands
42 B2 Den Chai Thailand
74 C4 Dendâra Mauritania
18 C2 Denge Nigeria
77 F4 Dengkou China
48 D4 Dêngqên China
54 D2 Deng Xian China
50 E2 Den Helder Netherlands
18 B2 Denia Spain
25 Denial B. b. Aust.
96 C3 Deniliquin Aust.
97 F4 Denio U.S.A.
126 C3 Denison U.S.A.
125 D5 Denison U.S.A.
100 C3 Denison Plains plain Aust.
42 A2 Denizli Turkey
42 A2 Denizli div. Turkey
97 H3 Denman Aust.
54 C4 Denman Glacier gl. Ant.
101 A7 Denmark Aust.
11 C4 Denmark country Europe
109 Q3 Denmark Strait str. Greenland/Iceland
129 F5 Dennehotso U.S.A.
121 E5 Dennis U.S.A.
121 H4 Dennysville U.S.A.
57 C2 Denpasar Indon.
57 B3 Dent du Bid Iran

92 □2 Dent I. i. Campbell I. N.Z.
121 G3 Denton U.S.A.
125 D5 Denton U.S.A.
90 □1 D'Entrecasteaux Islands is P.N.G.
101 A7 D'Entrecasteaux, Pt pt Aust.
90 □2 D'Entrecasteaux, Récifs reef Pac. Oc.
126 F4 Denver U.S.A.
121 F3 Deoband India
55 F4 Deobhog India
55 F5 Deogarh India
55 F4 Deogarh India
55 F4 Deogarh mt. India
55 F4 Deoghar India
21 H3 Déols France
54 D5 Deori India
55 F5 Deoria India
54 C2 Deosai, Plains of plain Pakistan
55 F5 Deosil India
122 C3 De Pere U.S.A.
121 F3 Deposit U.S.A.
115 G3 Depot-Forbes Can.
114 E2 Depot-Rowanton Can.
122 C5 Depue U.S.A.
63 P3 Deputatskiy Rus. Fed.
51 E3 Dêqên China
50 C3 Deqing China
51 F4 Deqing China
51 G3 Dequ China
125 E5 De Queen U.S.A.
54 B3 Dera Bugti Pakistan
54 C2 Dera Ghazi Khan Pakistan
54 B3 Dera Ismail Khan Pakistan
54 B3 Derajat reg. Pakistan
54 B3 Derawar Fort Pakistan
55 E4 Derazhne Ukraine
15 B2 Derazhnya Ukraine
13 J7 Derbent Rus. Fed.
29 G5 Derbent Turkey
65 G5 Derbent Uzbekistan
78 B2 Derbissaka C.A.R.
100 D3 Derby Aust.
17 G5 Derby U.K.
121 G4 Derby U.S.A.
125 D4 Derby U.S.A.
72 D5 Déréssa Chad
13 J5 Dergachi Rus. Fed.
20 C2 Derg, Lough l. Rep. of Ire.
17 C5 Derrachi Ukraine
126 B6 De Ridder U.S.A.
60 E2 Derik Turkey
42 C1 Derinkuyu Turkey
80 D3 Derio well Ethiopia
57 D3 Deriyivka Ukraine
80 D4 Derkali well Kenya
13 F5 Derkul r. Rus. Fed.
82 B4 Dernberg, Cape c. Namibia
15 A1 Dërono Ukraine
50 B2 Dêrong China
16 □ Déroute, Passage de la str. Channel Is./France
83 F2 Derre Mozambique
121 H3 Derry U.S.A.
73 G4 Derudeb Sudan
26 G3 Derventa Bos.-Herz.
97 F5 Derwent r. Aust.
14 B1 Derwent r. U.K.
13 G6 Derza r. Rus. Fed.
29 E7 Dia i. Greece
133 □1 Diablo, Mt h. Jamaica
128 B3 Diablo Range mts U.S.A.
81 C7 Diaca Mozambique
78 B4 Diafarabé Mali
76 A3 Diagbe C.A.R.
79 C5 Diakalaou Senegal
78 B4 Diallassagou Mali
146 D3 Diamante Arg.
146 D3 Diamantina r. Brazil
145 G1 Diamantina Brazil
142 E3 Diamantina Lakes Aust.
144 B2 Diamantino Mato Grosso Brazil
144 B2 Diamantino Mato Grosso Brazil
55 G5 Diamond Harb. India
126 D3 Diamond hd hd U.S.A.
99 E3 Diamond Islets is Coral Sea Islands Terr. Pac. Oc.
129 E2 Diamond Peak summit U.S.A.
82 B5 Diana's Pk h. St Helena Atlantic Ocean
51 E4 Diancang Shan l. China
50 C4 Dian Chi l. China
76 C3 Diandioumé Mali
139 E4 Dianópolis Brazil
142 D2 Diánopolis Brazil
74 D3 Diaoling China
43 A4 Diaoya China
74 D3 Diapaga Burkina
80 D3 Diavolo, Mt h. Andaman and Nicobar Is India
57 D2 Dīāz Pt pt Namibia
146 C3 Dibaya-Lubwe Zaire
78 C4 Dibbis Sudan
78 B2 Dibdibah plain Saudi Arabia

56 A2 Devrukh India
40 D3 Dewakang Besar i. Indon.
54 D3 Dewangiri Bhutan
54 D5 Dewas India
120 B6 Dewey Lake l. U.S.A.
126 F3 De Witt U.S.A.
122 B5 De Witt U.S.A.
121 J2 Dexter U.S.A.
121 F2 Dexter U.S.A.
121 E2 Dexter U.S.A.
50 D2 Deyang China
96 B2 Dey-Dey L. salt flat Aust.
57 D2 Deyhuk Iran
57 D2 Deynau Turkmenistan
39 L8 Deyong, Tg pt Indon.
57 B2 Dezfūl Iran
57 B3 Dez Dasht Iran
108 A3 Dezhneva, Mys c. Rus. Fed.
80 C3 Dhaba India
39 J8 Dhaka Bangladesh
55 H4 Dhalbhum reg. India
80 C2 Dhamār Yemen
55 F5 Dhāmara India
54 D3 Dhamnod India
55 F5 Dhampur India
55 G5 Dhamtari India
54 B3 Dhana Sar Pakistan
55 F5 Dhandhuka India
55 F4 Dhangarhi Nepal
55 G4 Dhang Ra. mt. ra. Nepal
55 F4 Dhankuta Nepal
54 D4 Dhar India
56 B4 Dharan Bazar Nepal
56 A4 Dharapuram India
56 A4 Dhari India
56 B3 Dharmapuri India
55 F5 Dharmavaram India
55 F5 Dharmjaygarh India
56 A4 Dharmshala India
74 C5 Dharoor r. Somalia
80 F2 Dharoor r. Somalia
74 C5 Dhar Oualâta h. Mauritania
74 C5 Dhar Tichît h. Mauritania
54 D5 Dhārwad India
56 B3 Dharwas India
54 D3 Dhasan r. India
55 F4 Dhaulagiri mt. Nepal
54 D3 Dhaulpur India
55 G5 Dhebar L. l. India
60 C4 Dhībān Jordan
54 D5 Dhing India
60 C4 Dhī Qār div. Iraq
55 F4 Dhone India
55 F5 Dhoraji India
55 F4 Dhrangadhra India
80 D2 Dhubāb Yemen
55 F4 Dhule India
60 B2 Dinar Turkey
55 G4 Dhuburi India
80 D2 Dhunche Nepal
80 E3 Dhuusa Marreeb Somalia
73 G2 Dhuwaybān basin Saudi Arabia
29 F7 Dia i. Greece
133 □1 Diablo, Mt h. Jamaica

55 F5 Digha India
21 H4 Digne-les-Bains France
21 F3 Digoin France
41 C5 Digras India
57 J3 Digul r. Indon.
76 D5 Digya National Park nat. park Ghana
55 H3 Dihang r. India
15 E1 Dihtyari Ukraine
80 D4 Dinsoor Somalia
60 D3 Dīyālá r. Iraq
21 G3 Dijon France
80 D2 Dikhil Djibouti
57 C2 Diz Chah Iran
19 J3 Dobczyce Poland
60 A2 Dikili Turkey
61 A4 Dikirnis Egypt
77 G4 Dikwa Nigeria
79 B4 Djambala Congo
75 F4 Djanet Algeria
83 E1 Djamâa Algeria
21 H3 Dilijan Armenia
60 F1 Di Linh Vietnam
93 D5 Dilion Cone mt. N.Z.
18 D3 Dillenburg Germany
55 F5 Dilley U.S.A.
73 E5 Dilling Sudan
18 E4 Dillingen an der Donau Germany
110 C4 Dillingham U.S.A.
111 H3 Dillon Can.
126 D2 Dillon U.S.A.
119 E5 Dillon U.S.A.
79 C6 Dilolo Zaire
29 E5 Dilos i. Greece
80 D3 Dimako Cameroon
55 H4 Dimapur India
61 D3 Dimashq Syria
61 C3 Dimashq div. Syria
79 D5 Dimbelenge Zaire
76 C4 Dimbokro Côte d'Ivoire
99 E5 Dimboola Aust.
28 E3 Dimitrovgrad Bulgaria
64 D2 Dimitrovgrad Rus. Fed.
28 D3 Dimitrovo Bulgaria
61 C4 Dimona Israel
82 D3 Dimpho Pan salt pan Botswana
16 I1 Dimunarfjörður chan. Faeroes
41 C4 Dinagat i. Phil.
80 D3 Dinajpur Bangladesh
20 C2 Dinan France
18 B3 Dinant Belgium
42 B2 Dinar Turkey
26 F4 Dinara mt. ra. Croatia
20 C2 Dinard France
55 F4 Dindori India

76 D6 Dixcove Ghana
121 H2 Dixfield U.S.A.
115 H3 Dix Milles, Lac des l. Can.
121 J2 Dixmont U.S.A.
128 B2 Dixon U.S.A.
122 C5 Dixon U.S.A.
110 B3 Dixon Entrance chan. Can./U.S.A.
110 F3 Dixonville Can.
115 K4 Dixville Can.
60 E3 Diyadin Turkey
60 F3 Diyarbakir Turkey
57 D2 Diz Chah Iran
19 J3 Dja r. Iraq
83 H1 Djamandjary Madagascar
79 B4 Djambala Congo
75 F4 Djanet Algeria
75 F4 Djelfa Algeria
78 C2 Djéma C.A.R.
78 B3 Djenné Mali
76 D4 Djérem r. Cameroon
76 D4 Djerma Mali
77 G4 Djibo Burkina
68 J4 Djibouti country Africa
80 D2 Djibouti Djibouti
74 C5 Djiguéni Mauritania
21 J3 Djénné Benin
78 B3 Djoua r. Congo
19 K5 Djombang Indon.
10 N2 Djúpivogur Iceland
11 D3 Djūrás Sweden
152 C5 Dome Circle ice feature Ant.
65 L2 Dmitriyevka Respublika Altay Rus. Fed.
14 B3 Dmitriyev-L'govskiy Rus. Fed.
14 E2 Dmitrovskiy Rus. Fed.
14 C2 Dmitrovskoye Rus. Fed.
14 C2 Dmitrov Rus. Fed.
14 C2 Dmitrovo Rus. Fed.
20 D2 Dmitrovskiy Pogost Rus. Fed.
15 F2 Dmitriyevskaya Rus. Fed.
15 E1 Dmytrivka Chernihiv Ukraine
15 F3 Dmytrivka Kherson Ukraine
15 F3 Dmytrivka Zaporizhzhya Ukraine
15 F2 Dnepr r. Rus. Fed.
15 F2 Dneprovskoye Vodoskhovyshche resr Ukraine
81 D7 Dnipro r. Ukraine
15 F2 Dniprodzerzhyns'k Ukraine
15 F2 Dniprodzerzhyns'ke Vodoskhovyshche resr Ukraine
15 F2 Dnipropetrovs'k Ukraine
15 F2 Dnipropetrovs'k div. Ukraine
15 G2 Dniprorudne Ukraine
15 F2 Dniprovs'ke Vodoskhovyshche resr Ukraine
15 C2 Dnister r. Ukraine
12 D4 Dno Rus. Fed.
14 A2 Dnyapro r. Belarus
15 F2 Dobele Latvia
18 E3 Döbeln Germany
19 G2 Dobiegniew Poland
26 G3 Doboj Bos.-Herz.
28 E3 Dobrich Bulgaria
14 B3 Dobrinka Rus. Fed.
78 D3 Dobrovelychkivka Ukraine
15 E2 Dobromyl' Ukraine

110 B2 Donjek r. Can.
26 G3 Donji Miholjac Croatia
26 F3 Donji Milanovac Yugo.
26 F3 Donji Vakuf Bos.-Herz.
55 G5 Donmanick Is. is Bangladesh
125 C7 Don Martín Mexico
81 A4 Donnacona Can.
110 F3 Donnelly Can.
92 E1 Donnellys Crossing N.Z.
128 B2 Donner Pass pass U.S.A.
15 F1 Donnybrook Aust.
25 I1 Donostia–San Sebastián Spain
29 E6 Donoussa i. Greece
15 G3 Dons'ke Ukraine
12 G4 Donskoye Rus. Fed.
12 F4 Donskoye Rus. Fed.
19 J3 Donskoye Rus. Fed.
100 B4 Dooleena h. Aust.
98 D3 Doomadgee Aust.
98 D3 Doomadgee Abor. Land Aust.
122 B3 Door Peninsula pen. U.S.A.
80 E3 Dooxo Nugaaleed v. Somalia
50 C1 Do Qu r. China
57 E3 Dor w Afghanistan
26 F3 Dora, L. salt flat Aust.
100 C4 Dora, L. salt flat Aust.
49 H3 Dorah India
17 F6 Dorchester U.K.
83 E3 Dordabis Namibia
20 E4 Dordives France
21 J3 Dordogne r. France
18 B3 Dordrecht Netherlands
83 E5 Dordrecht R.S.A.
18 B3 Dore, L. L. Can.
21 F4 Doré L. l. Can.
20 F4 Doré Lake l. Can.
111 H4 Dore Lake Can.
145 H3 Dores do Indaiá Brazil
18 F4 Dorfen Germany
147 A7 Dorgali Italy
77 E3 Dori Burkina
82 B5 Doring r. R.S.A.
21 F2 Dormans France
78 C2 Dormaa-Ahenkro Ghana
15 G2 Dormans France
55 G3 Dorna Watra Romania
18 D5 Dornbirn Austria
20 E4 Dornogovĭ div. Mongolia
49 E2 Dornoch div. Mongolia
17 E3 Dornoch U.K.
145 H4 Doro Mali
76 D3 Dorobantu Romania
28 F2 Dorobantu Romania
145 G4 Dorohoi Romania
15 C1 Dorohoi Romania
28 G1 Dorohusk Poland
14 G1 Dorokhsh Iran
14 C1 Doroshkh Iran
57 D1 Dörötölö Nuur salt l. Mongolia
44 F2 Dorotea Sweden
101 A5 Dorre i. Aust.
97 H2 Dorrigo Aust.
128 B1 Dorris U.S.A.
115 H4 Dorset U.K.
18 C3 Dortmund Germany
120 B6 Dorton U.S.A.
60 B1 Dörtyol Turkey
43 Doruma Zaire
14 D3 Dorval Can.
147 C5 Dos Bahías, C. c. Arg.
129 H5 Dos Cabezas U.S.A.
138 A5 Doschadero Peru
78 B3 Dos Hermanas Spain
138 B5 Dos de Mayo Peru
128 Dos Palos U.S.A.
29 C7 Dospat Bulgaria
76 A4 Dossé r. France
77 F3 Dosso div. Niger
77 F4 Dosso Niger
77 E3 Dosso, Réserve Partielle du Niger
119 C5 Dothan U.S.A.
76 D4 Douai France
78 B3 Douala Cameroon
78 B3 Douarnenez France
20 B2 Douarnenez, Baie de b. France
128 H5 Double I. i. Hong Kong
99 E4 Double Island Pt pt Aust.
128 Double Peak summit U.S.A.
99 E5 Double Pt pt Aust.
21 G3 Doubs r. France/Switz.
93 A6 Doubtful Sound inlet N.Z.
92 E1 Doubtless Bay b. N.Z.
20 D3 Doué-la-Fontaine France
92 C5 Douglas Isle of Man
83 C4 Douglas R.S.A.
17 E4 Douglas U.K.
124 F3 Douglas U.S.A.
119 D6 Douglas U.S.A.
129 H5 Douglas U.S.A.
110 C3 Douglas Can.
99 E3 Douglas Cr. w Aust.
127 E6 Douglas Creek r. U.S.A.
76 D4 Doullens France
78 B3 Doumé Cameroon
78 B3 Doumé r. Cameroon
76 D4 Douna Mali
144 A2 Dourada, Cach. waterfall Brazil
144 A2 Dourada Brazil
144 A2 Dourados Brazil
24 B2 Douro r. Portugal
24 C2 Douro Litoral reg. Portugal
21 F4 Douvaine France
113 J3 Douville Can.
75 F2 Douz Tunisia
15 C1 Dovbysh Ukraine
14 F3 Dovhe Ukraine
14 E2 Dovsk Belarus
122 E5 Dowagiac U.S.A.
57 G3 Dowlatabad Afghanistan
57 D2 Dowlatābād Iran
57 C3 Dowlatābād Iran
57 D2 Dowlatābād Iran
57 E1 Dowshī Afghanistan
14 E2 Downham Market U.K.
57 □ Dowrān at Yâr Afghanistan
21 G3 Downieville U.S.A.
121 F3 Downsville U.S.A.

57 B2 Dow Rūd Iran
57 D3 Dowsārī Iran
57 G2 Dowshī Afghanistan
128 B1 Doyle U.S.A.
121 F4 Doylestown U.S.A.
28 E3 Doyrentsi Bulgaria
57 D3 Dozdān r. Iran
46 D5 Dōzen i. Japan
115 G3 Dozois, Réservoir resr Can.
15 E2 Drabiv Ukraine
15 D2 Drabivka Ukraine
144 C4 Dracena Brazil
14 E2 Drachevo Rus. Fed.
18 C2 Drachten Netherlands
28 F2 Dragalina Romania
28 E2 Drăgănești-Olt Romania
28 E2 Drăgănești-Vlașca Romania
28 E2 Drăgășani Romania
29 F7 Dragonada i. Greece
29 E6 Dragonisi i. Greece
133 □3 Dragon's Mouths str. Trinidad/Venezuela
11 F3 Dragsfjärd Finland
21 H5 Draguignan France
28 F1 Drăgușeni Romania
13 C4 Drahichyn Belarus
129 F4 Drake U.S.A.
111 J5 Drake U.S.A.
83 D5 Drakensberg mt. ra. Lesotho/R.S.A.
83 D3 Drakensberg mt. ra. R.S.A.
152 A1 Drake Passage str. Ant.
29 E4 Drama Greece
11 C4 Drammen Norway
11 C4 Drangedal Norway
54 C2 Dras India
54 C1 Drasan Pakistan
19 G5 Drau r. Austria
26 E2 Dravograd Slovenia
19 G2 Drawsko Pomorskie Poland
110 G4 Drayton Valley Can.
27 A7 Dréan Algeria
18 D3 Dreieich Germany
18 C2 Drenthe div. Netherlands
19 F3 Dresden Germany
20 E2 Dreux France
11 D3 Drevsjø Norway
19 G2 Drezdenko Poland
50 B2 Dri China
114 E2 Driftwood Can.
120 D4 Driftwood U.S.A.
15 D1 Drimaylivka Ukraine
28 B2 Drina r. Bos.-Herz./Yugo.
29 C4 Drino r. Albania
26 F4 Drniš Croatia
28 D2 Drobeta-Turnu Severin Romania
15 B2 Drochia Moldova
17 D5 Drogheda Rep. of Ire.
19 L2 Drohiczyn Poland
13 B5 Drohobych Ukraine
17 F5 Droitwich U.K.
55 G4 Drokung India
26 A3 Dronero Italy
20 E4 Dronne r. France
109 Q2 Dronning Louise Land reg. Greenland
152 C3 Dronning Maud Land reg. Ant.
54 B2 Drosh Pakistan
14 C3 Droskovo Rus. Fed.
48 E2 Drovyanaya Rus. Fed.
114 B1 Drowning r. Can.
15 B1 Drozdyn' Ukraine
90 □6 Drua Drua i. Fiji
132 □1 Druif Aruba Caribbean
55 H3 Druk La China
110 G4 Drumheller Can.
126 D2 Drummond U.S.A.
122 B2 Drummond U.S.A.
123 F3 Drummond Island i. U.S.A.
98 D3 Drummond, Mt h. Aust.
99 F4 Drummond Range h. Aust.
115 J4 Drummondville Can.
11 G5 Druskininkai Lithuania
14 A3 Druzhba Ukraine
15 F3 Druzhbivka Ukraine
63 Q3 Druzhina Rus. Fed.
15 G2 Druzhkivka Ukraine
28 E3 Dryanovo Bulgaria
14 D3 Dryazgi Rus. Fed.
110 B3 Dry Bay b. U.S.A.
112 B4 Dryberry L. l. Can.
122 E2 Dryburg U.S.A.
112 B4 Dryden Can.
152 D5 Drygalski I. i. Ant.
152 B5 Drygalski Ice Tongue ice feature Ant.
133 □1 Dry Harbour Mts mts Jamaica
128 D2 Dry Lake l. U.S.A.
100 D2 Drysdale r. Aust.
98 C1 Drysdale I. i. Aust.
100 D2 Drysdale River Nat. Park nat. park Aust.
132 B1 Dry Tortugas is U.S.A.
19 K3 Drzewica Poland
78 B2 Dschang Cameroon
51 E1 Du r. China
78 D3 Dua r. Zaire
57 B2 Dūāb r. Iran
50 E4 Du'an China
121 F2 Duane U.S.A.
99 G4 Duaringa Aust.
55 G4 Duars reg. India
73 G2 Ḍubā Saudi Arabia
15 C3 Dubăsari Moldova
15 C3 Dubău Moldova
111 J2 Dubawnt r. Can.
111 J2 Dubawnt Lake l. Can.
57 C4 Dubayy U.A.E.
61 C6 Dubbagh, J. ad mt. Saudi Arabia
97 G3 Dubbo Aust.
21 J3 Dübendorf Switz.
14 H2 Dubenki Rus. Fed.
14 D1 Dubets Rus. Fed.
19 L3 Dubienka Poland
14 H4 Dubki Rus. Fed.
114 B2 Dublin Can.
17 D5 Dublin Rep. of Ire.
119 D5 Dublin U.S.A.
14 C1 Dubna r. Rus. Fed.
14 C1 Dubna Rus. Fed.
14 C2 Dubna Rus. Fed.
15 A1 Dubno Ukraine
126 D2 Dubois U.S.A.
120 D4 Du Bois U.S.A.
126 E3 Dubois U.S.A.
14 C3 Dubovaya Roshcha Rus. Fed.
28 D1 Dubove Ukraine
15 F2 Dubovi Hryady Ukraine
14 D3 Dubovka Rus. Fed.
13 H5 Dubovka Rus. Fed.
13 G5 Dubovka Rus. Fed.
13 G6 Dubovskoye Rus. Fed.
15 E1 Dubov"yazivka Ukraine
76 B5 Dubréka Guinea
15 B1 Dubrivka Ukraine
14 A3 Dubrovka Rus. Fed.
14 F3 Dubrovki Rus. Fed.
26 G4 Dubrovnik Croatia
15 B1 Dubrovytsya Ukraine
12 D4 Dubrowna Belarus
78 D3 Dubulu Zaire
122 B4 Dubuque U.S.A.
15 D2 Dubynove Ukraine
91 □10 Duc de Gloucester, Îles is Fr. Poly. Pac. Oc.
51 G2 Duchang China
129 G1 Duchesne U.S.A.
98 D4 Duchess Aust.
151 L7 Ducie Island i. Pitcairn Islands Pac. Oc.
119 C5 Duck r. U.S.A.
111 J4 Duck Bay Can.
100 B4 Duck Cr. r. Aust.
111 H4 Duck Lake Can.
122 E4 Duck Lake U.S.A.
129 E2 Duckwater U.S.A.
129 E2 Duckwater Peak summit U.S.A.
133 □4 Ducos Martinique Caribbean
43 E4 Đưc Pho Vietnam
43 E5 Đưc Trong Vietnam
15 E3 Dudchany Ukraine
18 E3 Duderstadt Germany
55 E4 Dudhi India
55 G4 Dudhnai India
54 E3 Dudhwa India
62 K3 Dudinka Rus. Fed.
17 F5 Dudley U.K.
56 B2 Dudna r. India
14 B3 Dudorovskiy Rus. Fed.
76 C5 Duékoué Côte d'Ivoire
24 C2 Duero r. Spain
115 F2 Dufault, Lac l. Can.
152 B4 Dufek Coast Ant.
112 E2 Dufferin, Cape hd Can.
120 B6 Duffield U.S.A.
86 H5 Duff Is is Solomon Is.
16 F3 Dufftown U.K.
112 E1 Dufrost, Pte pt Can.
61 D5 Dughdash mt. ra. Saudi Arabia
26 E4 Dugi Otok i. Croatia
26 F4 Dugi Rat Croatia
14 C2 Dugna Rus. Fed.
26 F4 Dugopolje Croatia
48 D5 Dugui Qarag China
72 C3 Duhūn Tārsū mts Chad/Libya
139 D3 Duida, Co mt. Venezuela
138 D3 Duida-Marahuaca, Parque Nacional nat. park Venezuela
99 E2 Duifken Pt pt Aust.
18 C3 Duisburg Germany
138 C2 Duitama Colombia
63 R3 Dukat Rus. Fed.
82 D5 Dukathole R.S.A.
29 B4 Dukat i Ri Albania
110 C4 Duke I. i. U.S.A.
80 B3 Duk Fadiat Sudan
80 B3 Duk Faiwil Sudan
57 B4 Dukhān Qatar
73 H2 Dukhnah Saudi Arabia
14 A2 Dukhovshchina Rus. Fed.
54 B3 Duki Pakistan
77 G4 Dukku Nigeria
19 K4 Dukla Poland
50 C3 Dukou China
11 G5 Dūkštas Lithuania
48 C2 Dulaanhaan Mongolia
44 G4 Dulan China
146 D2 Dulce r. Arg.
130 K7 Dulce, Golfo b. Costa Rica
130 J6 Dulce Nombre de Dios Honduras
48 E2 Dul'durga Rus. Fed.
28 F3 Dŭlgopol Bulgaria
99 E1 Dulhunty r. Aust.
55 E2 Dulishi Hu salt l. China
55 H4 Dullabchara India
28 F3 Dulovo Bulgaria
122 A2 Duluth U.S.A.
122 A2 Duluth/Superior airport U.S.A.
14 E1 Dulyapino Rus. Fed.
60 D3 Dūmā Syria
41 B4 Dumaguete Phil.
43 C7 Dumai Indon.
41 B4 Dumaran i. Phil.
97 G2 Dumaresq r. Aust.
125 F5 Dumas U.S.A.
125 C5 Dumas U.S.A.
61 D3 Ḍumayr Syria
61 D3 Ḍumayr, J. mt. ra. Syria
16 E4 Dumbarton U.K.
90 □2 Dumbéa Pac. Oc.
19 J4 Ďumbier mt. Slovakia
28 E1 Dumbrăveni Sibiu Romania
28 F2 Dumbrăveni Vrancea Romania
28 E2 Dumbrăvița Romania
24 B1 Dumbría Spain
54 D2 Dumchele India
40 A1 Dumdum i. Indon.
55 H4 Dum Duma India
17 F4 Dumfries U.K.
14 B3 Duminichi Rus. Fed.
28 E1 Dumitra Romania
55 F4 Dumka India
18 F2 Dummerstorf Germany
115 G3 Dumoine, L. l. Can.
152 □ Dumont d'Urville France Base Ant.
152 B6 Dumont d'Urville Sea sea Ant.
61 A4 Dumyât Egypt
19 J5 Dunaföldvár Hungary
19 H5 Dunaj r. Hungary
19 K4 Dunajec r. Poland
19 H5 Dunajská Streda Slovakia
19 J5 Dunakeszi Hungary
97 F5 Dunalley Aust.
17 D5 Dunany Point pt Rep. of Ire.
28 G2 Dunării, Delta delta Romania
28 B1 Dunaszekcső Hungary
19 J5 Dunaújváros Hungary
28 F3 Dunav r. Bulgaria/Romania
19 J5 Duna-völgyi-főcsatorna canal Hungary
28 D3 Dunavtsi Bulgaria
15 B2 Dunayivtsi Khmel'nyts'kyy Ukraine
15 B2 Dunayivtsi Khmel'nyts'kyy Ukraine
93 C6 Dunback N.Z.
99 E3 Dunbar Aust.
110 E5 Duncan Can.
129 H5 Duncan U.S.A.
125 D5 Duncan U.S.A.
112 D3 Duncan, Cape c. Can.
112 E3 Duncan, L. l. Can.
120 E4 Duncannon U.S.A.
43 A5 Duncan Passage chan. Andaman and Nicobar Is India
133 □1 Duncans Jamaica
16 F2 Duncansby Head hd U.K.
122 B5 Duncans Mills U.S.A.
132 D2 Duncan Town The Bahamas
11 F4 Dundaga Latvia
114 E4 Dundalk Can.
17 D4 Dundalk Rep. of Ire.
120 E5 Dundalk U.S.A.
17 D5 Dundalk Bay b. Rep. of Ire.
110 C4 Dundas I. i. Can.
101 C7 Dundas, L. salt flat Aust.
98 B1 Dundas Str. chan. Aust.
48 D3 Dundbürd Mongolia
83 E4 Dundee R.S.A.
16 F3 Dundee U.K.
123 F5 Dundee U.S.A.
120 E3 Dundee U.S.A.
48 C3 Dundgovĭ div. Mongolia
99 F5 Dundoo Aust.
55 E4 Dundwa Ra. mt. ra. Nepal
93 C6 Dunedin N.Z.
119 D6 Dunedin U.S.A.
112 F2 Dune, Lac l. Can.
65 J3 Dunenbay Kazak.
75 F2 Dunes de Dokhara sand dunes Algeria
16 F3 Dunfermline U.K.
54 C3 Dungargarh India
54 C5 Dungarpur India
17 D5 Dungarvan Rep. of Ire.
17 H6 Dungeness hd U.K.
147 C7 Dungeness, Pta pt Arg.
97 G3 Dungog Aust.
78 E3 Dungu Zaire
43 C6 Dungun Malaysia
73 G3 Dungunab Sudan
49 J4 Dunhua China
44 F3 Dunhuang China
16 F3 Dunkeld U.K.
20 F1 Dunkerque France
120 D3 Dunkirk U.S.A.
76 D5 Dunkwa Ghana
17 D5 Dún Laoghaire Rep. of Ire.
17 C6 Dunmanway Rep. of Ire.
98 C3 Dunmarra Aust.
119 E7 Dunmore Town The Bahamas
128 D3 Dunmovin U.S.A.
119 E5 Dunn U.S.A.
16 F2 Dunnet Head hd U.K.
128 B2 Dunnigan U.S.A.
124 C3 Dunning U.S.A.
115 F5 Dunnville Can.
97 E4 Dunolly Aust.
16 F4 Duns U.K.
93 D5 Dunsandel N.Z.
124 C1 Dunseith U.S.A.
126 B3 Dunsmuir U.S.A.
93 B6 Dunstan Mts mt. ra. N.Z.
93 C6 Duntroon N.Z.
54 B3 Dunyapur Pakistan
49 H2 Duobukur r. China
49 F4 Duolon China
51 E3 Dupang Ling mt. ra. China
115 F2 Duparquet Can.
115 F2 Duparquet, Lac l. Can.
124 C2 Dupree U.S.A.
100 A4 Dupuy, C. c. Aust.
145 G5 Duque de Caxias Brazil
147 A7 Duque de York, I. i. Chile
118 B4 Du Quoin U.S.A.
61 C4 Dura Israel
100 D3 Durack r. Aust.
100 D3 Durack Range h. Aust.
60 C1 Durağan Turkey
123 F4 Durand U.S.A.
122 B3 Durand U.S.A.
90 □2 Durand, Récif reef Pac. Oc.
130 D3 Durango div. Mexico
130 D3 Durango Mexico
25 E1 Durango Spain
127 F4 Durango U.S.A.
57 F3 Durani reg. Afghanistan
28 G3 Durankulak Bulgaria
125 D5 Durant U.S.A.
146 E3 Durazno Uruguay
83 E4 Durban R.S.A.
20 F5 Durban-Corbières France
82 B5 Durbanville R.S.A.
120 D5 Durbin U.S.A.
18 B3 Durbuy Belgium
24 E4 Dúrcal Spain
18 C3 Düren Germany
55 E5 Durg India
55 G4 Durgapur Bangladesh
55 F5 Durgapur India
114 E4 Durham Can.
17 G4 Durham U.K.
128 B2 Durham U.S.A.
119 E4 Durham U.S.A.
121 H3 Durham U.S.A.
99 E5 Durham Downs Aust.
80 D3 Durhi well Ethiopia
15 C3 Durlești Moldova
16 E2 Durness U.K.
49 F2 Duroy Rus. Fed.
29 B4 Durrës Albania
98 E5 Durrie Aust.
17 B6 Dursey Island i. Rep. of Ire.
60 B2 Dursunbey Turkey
20 D3 Durtal France
57 E2 Dūruḥ Iran
80 E3 Durukhsi Somalia
61 D3 Durūz, Jabal ad mt. Syria
92 D4 D'Urville Island i. N.Z.
39 L7 D'Urville, Tanjung pt Indon.
57 F2 Durzab Afghanistan
73 F3 Dûsh Egypt
54 A3 Dushai Pakistan
57 D1 Dushak Turkmenistan
50 D3 Dushan China
65 G5 Dushanbe Tajikistan
93 A6 Dusky Sound inlet N.Z.
18 C3 Düsseldorf Germany
57 G1 Dusti Tajikistan
65 G4 Dustlik Uzbekistan
19 H3 Duszniki-Zdrój Poland
129 F1 Dutch Mt mt. U.S.A.
77 F4 Dutsan-Wai Nigeria
77 F4 Dutse Nigeria
77 F4 Dutsin-Ma Nigeria
99 E4 Dutton r. Aust.
129 F3 Dutton, Mt mt. U.S.A.
64 E1 Duvan Rus. Fed.
133 E3 Duvergé Dominican Rep.
113 F2 Duvert, Lac l. Can.
60 F2 Duwin Iraq
50 D3 Duyun China
57 E4 Duzab Pakistan
60 B1 Düzce Turkey
28 E3 Dve Mogili Bulgaria
12 F1 Dvinskaya Guba g. Rus. Fed.
15 B1 Dvirets' Ukraine
15 G2 Dvorichna Ukraine
14 D2 Dvoyni Rus. Fed.
54 B5 Dwarka India
101 B7 Dwellingup Aust.
122 C5 Dwight U.S.A.
126 C2 Dworshak Res. resr U.S.A.
14 B3 Dyat'kovo Rus. Fed.
16 F3 Dyce U.K.
122 D5 Dyer U.S.A.
128 C3 Dyer U.S.A.
114 E4 Dyer Bay Can.
109 M3 Dyer, C. c. Can.
119 B4 Dyersburg U.S.A.
122 B4 Dyersville U.S.A.
17 F5 Dyfi r. U.K.
19 H4 Dyje r. Austria/Czech Rep.
15 F2 Dykan'ka Ukraine
13 G7 Dykh Tau mt. Georgia
15 D1 Dymer Ukraine
15 G2 Dymytrov Ukraine
15 E2 Dymytrove Ukraine
99 F6 Dynevor Downs Aust.
19 L4 Dynów Poland
122 A4 Dysart U.S.A.
82 C5 Dysselsdorp R.S.A.
29 C5 Dytiki Ellas div. Greece
29 C4 Dytiki Makedonia div. Greece
64 F3 Dyurmen'tyube Kazak.
64 D1 Dyurtyuli Rus. Fed.
28 G2 Dyviziya Ukraine
48 B3 Dzaanhushuu Mongolia
48 A3 Dzag Gol r. Mongolia
48 A3 Dzalaa Mongolia
48 D4 Dzamïn Üüd Mongolia
81 E7 Dzaoudzi Mayotte Africa
48 A2 Dzavhan div. Mongolia
48 B3 Dzegstey Mongolia
15 B2 Dzelentsi Ukraine
48 C2 Dzelter Mongolia
14 F1 Dzerzhinsk Rus. Fed.
65 K3 Dzerzhinskoye Kazak.
15 B1 Dzerzhyns'k Ukraine
64 F3 Dzhalagash Kazak.
49 G1 Dzhalinda Rus. Fed.
64 D2 Dzhambeyty Kazak.
65 H3 Dzhambul Kazak.
64 D4 Dzhanga Turkmenistan
64 D3 Dzhangala Kazak.
64 F4 Dzhankel'dy Uzbekistan
13 E6 Dzhankoy Ukraine
65 J3 Dzhansugurov Kazak.
13 H5 Dzhanybek Rus. Fed.
65 G5 Dzharkurgan Uzbekistan
15 E3 Dzharylhats"ka Zatoka b. Ukraine
59 H2 Dzhebel Turkmenistan
64 F2 Dzhetygara Kazak.
65 G3 Dzhezdy Kazak.
65 G3 Dzhezkazgan Kazak.
48 C2 Dzhida Rus. Fed.
48 C2 Dzhida Rus. Fed.
48 B2 Dzhidinskiy, Khrebet mt. ra. Mongolia/Rus. Fed.
63 R3 Dzhigudzhak Rus. Fed.
65 G4 Dzhizak Uzbekistan
57 E1 Dzhu-Dzhu-Klu Turkmenistan
63 P4 Dzhugdzhur, Khrebet mt. ra. Rus. Fed.
15 C2 Dzhulynka Ukraine
65 G5 Dzhuma Uzbekistan
65 J4 Dzhungarskiy Alatau, Khr. mt. ra. China/Kazak.
64 E3 Dzhurun Kazak.
15 C2 Dzhuryn Ukraine
64 F3 Dzhusaly Kazak.
19 K2 Działdowo Poland
131 H5 Dzibalchén Mexico
19 J2 Dzierzgoń Poland
19 H3 Dzierżoniów Poland
131 H4 Dzilam de Bravo Mexico
75 F2 Dzioua Algeria
77 E5 Dzodze Ghana
48 C3 Dzogsool Mongolia
48 A2 Dzöölön Mongolia
65 K3 Dzungarian Gate pass China/Kazak.
48 A2 Dzur Mongolia
48 D3 Dzüünbayan Mongolia
48 C2 Dzüünharaa Mongolia
48 C3 Dzuunmod Mongolia
12 C4 Dzyarzhynsk Belarus

E

112 C3 Eabamet L. l. Can.
129 H4 Eagar U.S.A.
113 J3 Eagle r. Can.
127 F4 Eagle U.S.A.
121 F3 Eagle Bay U.S.A.
111 H4 Eagle Cr. r. Can.
128 D4 Eagle Crags summit U.S.A.
112 B4 Eagle L. l. Can.
126 B3 Eagle L. l. U.S.A.
121 J1 Eagle Lake l. U.S.A.
121 J1 Eagle Lake U.S.A.
122 B2 Eagle Mtn h. U.S.A.
125 C6 Eagle Pass U.S.A.
108 E3 Eagle Plain plain Can.
122 C2 Eagle River U.S.A.
122 C3 Eagle River U.S.A.
110 F3 Eaglesham Can.
129 F5 Eagle Tail Mts mts U.S.A.
47 H4 Eai-gawa r. Japan
101 C5 Earaheedy Aust.
112 B3 Ear Falls Can.
128 C4 Earlimart U.S.A.
115 F3 Earlton Can.
16 E3 Earn, L. l. U.K.
93 B6 Earnslaw, Mt mt. N.Z.
125 C5 Earth U.S.A.
119 D5 Easley U.S.A.
98 C2 East Alligator r. Aust.
115 K4 East Angus Can.
152 C5 East Antarctica reg. Ant.
121 F4 East Ararat U.S.A.
120 D3 East Aurora U.S.A.
98 B2 East Baines r. Aust.
125 F6 East Bay b. U.S.A.
121 G2 East Berkshire U.S.A.
93 E4 Eastbourne N.Z.
17 H6 Eastbourne U.K.
120 D4 East Branch Clarion River Reservoir resr U.S.A.
121 H4 East Brooklyn U.S.A.
115 K3 East Broughton Station Can.
92 G2 East Cape c. N.Z.
129 G2 East Carbon U.S.A.
122 D5 East Chicago U.S.A.
45 M6 East China Sea sea Asia
92 E2 East Coast Bays N.Z.
121 G2 East Corinth U.S.A.
17 H5 East Dereham U.K.
119 □2 East End Pt pt The Bahamas
41 □1 East Entrance chan. Palau
91 □16 Easter I. i. Chile
151 M7 Easter Island Fracture Zone Pac. Oc.
76 D5 Eastern div. Ghana
80 C4 Eastern div. Kenya
76 B5 Eastern div. Sierra Leone
73 G4 Eastern div. Sudan
81 B7 Eastern div. Zambia
82 D5 Eastern Cape div. R.S.A.
73 F2 Eastern Desert desert Egypt
56 B3 Eastern Ghats mt. ra. India
93 □2 Eastern Group is Bounty Is N.Z.
111 K4 Easterville Can.
147 E7 East Falkland i. Falkland Is.
121 H4 East Falmouth U.S.A.
128 D2 Eastgate U.S.A.
124 D2 East Grand Forks U.S.A.
121 G3 Easthampton U.S.A.
121 G4 East Hampton U.S.A.
99 E3 East Haydon Aust.
120 D4 East Hickory U.S.A.
121 G3 East Jamaica U.S.A.
148 J1 East Jan Mayen Ridge Atlantic Ocean
122 E3 East Jordan U.S.A.
122 D3 Eastlake U.S.A.
45 □ East Lamma Channel chan. Hong Kong
17 G6 Eastleigh U.K.
120 C4 East Liverpool U.S.A.
82 D5 East London R.S.A.
120 B5 East Lynn Lake l. U.S.A.
112 E3 Eastmain Can.
112 F3 Eastmain r. Can.
115 J4 Eastman Can.
119 D5 Eastman U.S.A.
99 F4 Eastmere Aust.
121 J2 East Millinocket U.S.A.
122 B5 East Moline U.S.A.
122 C5 Easton U.S.A.
121 E5 Easton U.S.A.
121 F4 Easton U.S.A.
151 M8 East Pacific Ridge Pac. Oc.
151 N5 East Pacific Rise Pac. Oc.
128 A2 East Park Res. resr U.S.A.
82 A5 East Point pt Tristan da Cunha Atlantic Ocean
113 H4 East Point pt Prince Edward I. Can.
119 □3 East Point pt Virgin Is Caribbean
119 □3 East Point pt Virgin Is Caribbean
94 □4 East Point pt Lord Howe I. Pac. Oc.
119 C5 East Point U.S.A.
121 K2 Eastport U.S.A.
122 E3 Eastport U.S.A.
128 D1 East Range mts U.S.A.
118 B4 East St Louis U.S.A.
97 G4 East Sister I. i. Aust.
55 E4 East Tons r. India
122 C4 East Troy U.S.A.
121 F6 Eastville U.S.A.
128 C2 East Walker r. U.S.A.
121 G3 East Wallingford U.S.A.
120 A5 Eaton U.S.A.
119 D5 Eatonton U.S.A.
122 B3 Eau Claire U.S.A.
122 B3 Eau Claire r. U.S.A.
112 F2 Eau Claire, Lac á l' l. Can.
150 E5 Eauripik - New Guinea Rise Pac. Oc.
20 E5 Eauze France
99 E2 Ebagoola Aust.
77 E5 Eban Nigeria
131 F4 Ebano Mexico
17 F6 Ebbw Vale U.K.
78 B3 Ebebiyin Equatorial Guinea
120 D4 Ebensburg U.S.A.
19 F2 Eberswalde-Finow Germany
114 D5 Eberts Can.
46 H2 Ebetsu Japan
50 C2 Ebian China
65 K4 Ebinur Hu salt l. China
61 D2 Ebla Syria
78 D3 Ebola r. Zaire
27 E5 Eboli Italy
78 B3 Ebolowa Cameroon
82 B3 Ebony Namibia
25 F2 Ebro r. Spain
133 □3 Ecclesville Trin. & Tobago
60 A1 Eceabat Turkey
41 B2 Echague Phil.
25 E1 Echarri-Aranaz Spain
75 E1 Ech Chélif Algeria
25 E1 Echegárate, Pto pass Spain
51 F2 Echeng China
29 E4 Echinos Greece
47 E6 Echizen-misaki pt Japan
110 F1 Echo Bay Can.
114 C3 Echo Bay Can.
129 G3 Echo Cliffs cliff U.S.A.
112 B3 Echoing r. Can.
97 F5 Echo, L. l. Aust.
115 H3 Échouani, Lac l. Can.
18 C4 Echternach Luxembourg
97 F4 Echuca Aust.
24 D4 Écija Spain
122 E2 Eckerman U.S.A.
18 D1 Eckernförde Germany
109 L2 Eclipse Sound chan. Can.
145 H3 Ecoporanga Brazil
136 C3 Ecuador country S. America
112 E2 Écueils, Pte aux pt Can.
80 D2 Ed Eritrea
11 C4 Ed Sweden
111 H4 Edam Can.
16 F2 Eday i. U.K.
78 E1 Ed Da'ein Sudan
73 F5 Ed Dair, Jebel mt. Sudan
80 B2 Ed Damazin Sudan
73 F4 Ed Damer Sudan
73 F4 Ed Debba Sudan
73 F5 Ed Dueim Sudan
97 G5 Eddystone Pt pt Aust.
122 A5 Eddyville U.S.A.
77 E5 Ede Nigeria
78 B3 Edéa Cameroon
111 K2 Edehon Lake l. Can.
144 D2 Edéia Brazil
97 G4 Eden Aust.
17 F4 Eden r. U.K.
120 D6 Eden U.S.A.
125 D6 Eden U.S.A.
82 D4 Edenburg R.S.A.
93 B7 Edendale N.Z.
17 D5 Edenderry Rep. of Ire.
96 E4 Edenhope Aust.
119 E4 Edenton U.S.A.
29 D4 Edessa Greece
100 C4 Edgar, Mt h. Aust.
100 C3 Edgar Ra. h. Aust.
121 H4 Edgartown U.S.A.
124 D2 Edgeley U.S.A.
124 C3 Edgemont U.S.A.
122 C4 Edgerton U.S.A.
122 A5 Edina U.S.A.
122 C6 Edinburg U.S.A.
125 D7 Edinburg U.S.A.
16 F4 Edinburgh U.K.
82 A5 Edinburgh, Settlement of Tristan da Cunha Atlantic Ocean
15 B2 Edineț Moldova
60 A1 Edirne Turkey
29 F4 Edirne div. Turkey
110 F4 Edith Cavell, Mt mt. Can.
72 A2 Edjeleh Libya
77 E3 Édjérir w Mali
101 C6 Edjudina Aust.
126 B2 Edmonds U.S.A.
110 G4 Edmonton Can.
111 K5 Edmore U.S.A.
122 B4 Edmund U.S.A.
111 L4 Edmund L. l. Can.
113 G4 Edmundston Can.
125 D6 Edna U.S.A.
110 C3 Edna Bay U.S.A.
77 F5 Edo div. Nigeria
61 C4 Edom reg. Israel/Jordan
60 A2 Edremit Turkey
29 F5 Edremit Körfezi b. Turkey
48 A3 Edrengiyn Nuruu mt. ra. Mongolia
11 D3 Edsbyn Sweden
110 F4 Edson Can.
146 D4 Eduardo Castex Arg.
97 F3 Edward r. Aust.
99 E2 Edward r. Aust.
98 C2 Edward I. i. Aust.
114 A2 Edward I. i. Can.
81 A5 Edward, Lake l. Uganda/Zaire
98 B4 Edward, Mt mt. Aust.
99 E2 Edward River Aust.
99 E2 Edward River Abor. Land res. Aust.
121 F2 Edwards U.S.A.
96 C2 Edward's Cr. Aust.
125 C6 Edwards Plateau plat. U.S.A.
118 B4 Edwardsville U.S.A.
152 D4 Edward VIII Ice Shelf ice feature Ant.
152 A4 Edward VII Pen. pen. Ant.
110 C3 Edziza Pk mt. Can.
78 B4 Edzouga Congo
128 A1 Eel r. U.S.A.
82 C4 Eenzamheid Pan l. R.S.A.
90 □2 Éfaté i. Vanuatu
118 B4 Effingham U.S.A.
77 E5 Effon-Alaiye Nigeria
28 G2 Eforie Romania
48 D2 Eg Mongolia
129 E2 Egan Range mts U.S.A.
115 G4 Eganville Can.
19 K5 Eger Hungary
11 B4 Egersund Norway
18 F4 Eggenfelden Germany
10 N2 Egilsstaðir Iceland
100 B4 Eginbah Aust.
65 J2 Egindy Kazak.
60 B2 Eğirdir Turkey
60 B2 Eğirdir Gölü l. Turkey
48 B2 Egiyn Gol r. Mongolia
20 F4 Égletons France
108 G2 Eglinton I. i. Can.
92 D3 Egmont, Cape c. N.Z.
92 E3 Egmont, Mt vol N.Z.
92 E3 Egmont National Park nat. park N.Z.
29 G5 Eğrigöz Dağı mts Turkey
142 C3 Éguas r. Brazil
108 A3 Egvekinot Rus. Fed.
68 G3 Egypt country Africa
46 D7 Ehime div. Japan
129 E5 Ehrenberg U.S.A.
98 B4 Ehrenberg Ra. h. Aust.
25 E1 Eibar Spain
18 C2 Eibergen Netherlands
18 E4 Eichstätt Germany
18 D1 Eider r. Germany
11 B3 Eidfjord Norway
16 D1 Eiði Faeroes
99 G5 Eidsvold Aust.
11 C3 Eidsvoll Norway
16 D3 Eigg i. U.K.
53 D9 Eight Degree Channel chan. India/Maldives
152 A3 Eights Coast Ant.
100 C3 Eighty Mile Beach beach Aust.
16 K1 Eikelandsosen Norway
97 F4 Eildon, Lake l. Aust.
111 H2 Eileen Lake l. Can.
18 F3 Eilenburg Germany
139 F3 Eilerts de Haan Geb. mt. ra. Surinam
41 □1 Eil Malk i. Palau
99 F3 Einasleigh Aust.
99 E3 Einasleigh r. Aust.
18 D3 Einbeck Germany
18 B3 Eindhoven Netherlands
73 E4 Ein Mansur well Sudan
42 A3 Einme Myanmar
21 J3 Einsiedeln Switz.
138 D5 Eirunepé Brazil
82 C3 Eiseb w Botswana/Namibia
18 E3 Eisenach Germany
19 G5 Eisenerz Austria
19 G2 Eisenhüttenstadt Germany
19 H5 Eisenstadt Austria
16 K1 Eivinvik Norway
25 G3 Eivissa i. Islas Baleares Spain
25 G3 Eivissa Spain
25 F1 Ejea de los Caballeros Spain
83 G3 Ejeda Madagascar
130 C3 Ejido Insurgentes Mexico
48 D5 Ejin Horo Qi China
48 B4 Ejin Qi China
60 F1 Ejmiadzin Armenia
76 D5 Ejura Ghana
131 F5 Ejutla Mexico
11 F4 Ekenäs Finland
77 F6 Eket Nigeria
92 E4 Eketahuna N.Z.
65 J2 Ekibastuz Kazak.
63 M3 Ekonda Rus. Fed.
78 C3 Ekouamou Congo
11 D3 Ekshärad Sweden
11 D4 Eksjö Sweden
78 D4 Ekuku Zaire
112 D3 Ekwan r. Can.
112 D3 Ekwan Point pt Can.
42 B3 Ela Myanmar
75 E2 El Abiodh Sidi Cheikh Algeria
29 D6 Elafonisos i. Greece
73 F5 El Agaliyin r. Sudan
74 C5 El Aghlâf well Mauritania
61 C4 El 'Agrûd well Egypt
73 E1 El 'Alamein Egypt
75 F2 El Alia Algeria
131 G5 El Almendro Mexico
60 B4 El 'Amirîya Egypt
83 D4 Elands r. Mpumalanga R.S.A.
24 D4 El Arahal Spain
130 B2 El Arco Mexico
61 B4 El 'Arîsh Egypt
29 F7 Elasa i. Greece
73 F2 El Ashmûnein Egypt
29 D5 Elassona Greece
24 E1 El Astillero Spain
61 C5 Elat Israel
74 A4 El 'Aṭf reg. Western Sahara
60 D2 Elazığ Turkey
61 D4 El Azraq Jordan
61 A5 El Badrshein Egypt
26 C4 Elba, Isola d' i. Italy
73 F2 El Balyana Egypt
45 P1 El'ban Rus. Fed.
138 C2 El Banco Colombia
138 C2 El Barranquitas Venezuela
80 B2 El Barun Sudan
29 C4 Elbasan Albania
73 F4 El Bauga Sudan
138 D2 El Baúl Venezuela
75 E2 El Bayadh Algeria
18 E2 Elbe r. Germany
122 D3 Elberta U.S.A.
129 G2 Elberta U.S.A.
127 F4 Elbert, Mount mt. U.S.A.
119 D5 Elberton U.S.A.
80 C4 El Bes well Kenya
20 E2 Elbeuf France
61 D1 Elbeyli Turkey
74 B4 El Beyyeḍ well Mauritania
61 B5 El Bilaiyim b. Egypt
60 D2 Elbistan Turkey
19 J1 Elbląg Poland
80 C4 Elbojtong well Kenya
147 B5 El Bolsón Arg.
75 F2 El Borma Tunisia
119 □1 Elbow Bay b. Bermuda
132 C1 Elbow Cay i. The Bahamas
13 G7 Elbrus mt. Rus. Fed.
13 G7 El'brusskiy Rus. Fed.
24 E2 El Burgo de Osma Spain
57 B1 Elburz Mountains mt. ra. Iran
74 B3 El Cabiño hd Western Sahara
147 C5 El Cain Arg.
128 D5 El Cajon U.S.A.
139 E2 El Callao Venezuela
125 D6 El Campo U.S.A.
133 E5 El Carmelo Venezuela
140 D2 El Carmen Bolivia
129 E5 El Centro U.S.A.
141 D3 El Cerro Bolivia
139 D2 El Chaparro Venezuela
25 F3 Elche Spain
131 G5 El Chichón vol Mexico
130 D2 El Chilicote Mexico
98 C1 Elcho I. i. Aust.
138 C2 El Cocuy Colombia
24 D2 El Cubo de Tierra del Vino Spain
130 D2 El Cuervo Mexico
131 J4 El Cuyo Mexico
25 F3 Elda Spain
60 B4 El Dab'a Egypt
18 E2 Elde r. Germany
80 D4 El Debb well Ethiopia
115 F3 Eldee Can.
94 □3 Elder, Mt h. Macquarie I. Pac. Oc.
128 D5 El Descanso Mexico
138 C2 El Difícil Colombia
63 P3 El'dikan Rus. Fed.
61 A4 El Dilingat Egypt
138 B3 El Diviso Colombia
129 E6 El Doctor Mexico
122 A5 Eldon U.S.A.
124 E4 Eldon U.S.A.
146 F2 Eldorado Arg.
144 A5 Eldorado Mato Grosso do Sul Brazil
144 D6 Eldorado São Paulo Brazil
130 D3 El Dorado Mexico
125 E5 El Dorado U.S.A.
125 D4 El Dorado U.S.A.
125 C6 Eldorado U.S.A.
139 E2 El Dorado Venezuela
81 C4 Eldoret Kenya
61 C2 Eleaia, C. pt Cyprus
126 E2 Electric Peak summit U.S.A.
74 D3 El Eglab mts Algeria
73 E4 El 'Ein well Sudan
25 E4 El Ejido Spain
12 F4 Elektrostal' Rus. Fed.
28 E3 Elena Bulgaria
138 C4 El Encanto Colombia
127 F5 Elephant Butte Res. resr U.S.A.
152 B1 Elephant I. i. Ant.
83 F2 Elephant Marsh marsh Malawi
55 H5 Elephant Pt pt Bangladesh
79 D5 Eléphants de Kaniama, Réserve d' res. Zaire
79 E6 Éléphants de Sakania, Réserve partielle à res. Zaire
24 D2 El Espinar Spain
131 H6 El Estor Guatemala
75 F1 El Eulma Algeria
132 C1 Eleuthera i. The Bahamas
27 B7 El Fahs Tunisia
61 A5 El Faiyûm Egypt
72 E5 El Fasher Sudan
73 F2 El Fashn Egypt
24 D5 El Fendek Morocco
61 A6 El Fikriya Egypt
80 D3 El Fud Ethiopia
130 C3 El Fuerte Mexico
76 C2 El Gçaib well Mali
72 D5 El Geneina Sudan
73 F5 El Geteina Sudan
74 B4 El Ghallâouîya well Mauritania
61 A4 El Ghayata Egypt
61 C4 El Ghor v. Israel/Jordan
16 F3 Elgin U.K.
122 C4 Elgin U.S.A.
124 C2 Elgin U.S.A.
129 E3 Elgin U.S.A.
129 G2 Elgin U.S.A.
99 F4 Elgin Down Aust.
63 Q3 El'ginskiy Rus. Fed.
73 E4 El Gir well Sudan
73 F5 El Gir w Sudan
61 A4 El Gîza Egypt
75 E2 El Goléa Algeria
130 B2 El Golfo de Santa Clara Mexico
81 B4 Elgon, Mount mt. Uganda
76 D2 El Guettâra well Mali
75 F1 El Hadjar Algeria
75 F2 El Hamma Tunisia
73 E1 El Hammâm Egypt
74 B4 El Ḥammâmi reg. Mauritania
74 C4 El Ḥank escarpment Mali/Mauritania
73 F5 El Hasira Sudan
130 K7 El Hato del Volcán Panama
73 F5 El Hawata Sudan
73 E2 El Heiz Egypt
25 □ El Hierro i. Canary Is Spain
131 F4 El Higo Mexico
73 E5 El Hilla Sudan
75 E3 El Homr Algeria
74 B5 El Houeïtat well Mauritania
77 F3 Eli well Niger
133 E3 Elías Piña Dominican Rep.
93 C5 Elie de Beaumont mt. N.Z.
79 E4 Elila Zaire
79 E4 Elila r. Zaire
108 B3 Elim U.S.A.
61 D5 El 'Inâb h. Jordan
28 D3 Elin Pelin Bulgaria
113 H2 Eliot, Mount mt. Can.
25 F1 Eliozondo Spain
78 D4 Elipa Zaire
142 D2 Eliseu Martins Brazil
13 H6 Elista Rus. Fed.
122 B4 Elizabeth U.S.A.
121 F4 Elizabeth U.S.A.
120 C5 Elizabeth U.S.A.
82 B4 Elizabeth Bay b. Namibia
119 E4 Elizabeth City U.S.A.
121 H4 Elizabeth Is is U.S.A.
119 D4 Elizabethton U.S.A.
118 C4 Elizabethtown U.S.A.
119 E5 Elizabethtown U.S.A.
121 G2 Elizabethtown U.S.A.
120 E4 Elizabethtown U.S.A.
63 Q4 Elizavety, Mys c. Rus. Fed.
74 C2 El Jadida Morocco
60 D4 El Jafr Jordan
61 D4 El Jafr l. Jordan
130 D3 El Jaralito Mexico
73 F5 El Jebelein Sudan
75 G1 El Jem Tunisia
130 J6 El Jicaral Nicaragua
110 G4 Elk r. Can.
19 L2 Ełk Poland
128 A2 Elk U.S.A.
120 C5 Elk r. U.S.A.
73 F4 El Kab Sudan
27 B7 El Kala Algeria
73 F4 El Kamlin Sudan
125 D5 Elk City U.S.A.
128 A2 Elk Creek U.S.A.
98 C4 Elkedra Aust.
98 C4 Elkedra w Aust.
74 C2 El Kelaâ des Srarhna Morocco
80 D3 Ēl Kerē Ethiopia
128 B2 Elk Grove U.S.A.
73 F4 El Khandaq Sudan
61 A4 El Khânka Egypt
73 F2 El Khârga Egypt
122 E5 Elkhart U.S.A.
76 D2 El Khnâchîch escarpment Mali
124 D3 Elkhorn r. U.S.A.
122 C4 Elkhorn U.S.A.
28 F3 Elkhovo Bulgaria
120 D5 Elkins U.S.A.
110 G4 Elk Island Nat. Park nat. park. Can.
114 E3 Elk Lake Can.
122 E3 Elk Lake l. U.S.A.
120 E4 Elkland U.S.A.
110 F5 Elko Can.
126 D3 Elko U.S.A.
111 G4 Elk Point Can.
124 E2 Elk River U.S.A.
121 F5 Elkton U.S.A.
120 D5 Elkton U.S.A.
60 D3 El Kubar Syria
61 C5 El Kuntilla Egypt
78 E1 El Lagowa Sudan
61 A5 El Lâhûn Egypt
111 M2 Ell Bay b. Can.
108 H2 Ellef Ringnes I. i. Can.
80 C4 Ēl Lēh Ethiopia
81 D5 El Lein well Kenya
101 B7 Elleker Aust.
72 C4 Elléloyé well Chad
54 C3 Ellenabad India
124 D2 Ellendale U.S.A.
129 G2 Ellen, Mt mt. U.S.A.
126 B2 Ellensburg U.S.A.
121 F4 Ellenville U.S.A.
97 G4 Ellery, Mt mt. Aust.
109 K2 Ellesmere Island i. Can.
93 D5 Ellesmere, Lake l. N.Z.
108 H3 Ellice r. Can.
120 D3 Ellicottville U.S.A.
131 F4 El Limón Mexico
90 □8 Ellington Fiji
98 C3 Elliot Aust.
114 D3 Elliot Lake Can.
99 F3 Elliot, Mt mt. Aust.
94 □3 Elliot Reef reef Macquarie I. Pac. Oc.
126 D2 Ellis U.S.A.
61 C4 El Lişān reg. Jordan
82 D3 Ellisras R.S.A.
96 C3 Elliston Aust.
16 F3 Ellon U.K.
121 J2 Ellsworth U.S.A.
122 A3 Ellsworth U.S.A.
152 A3 Ellsworth Land reg. Ant.
152 B3 Ellsworth Mountains mts Ant.
18 E4 Ellwangen (Jagst) Germany
61 A4 El Mahalla el Kubra Egypt
61 A4 El Mahmudiya Egypt
60 B2 Elmalı Turkey
73 F5 El Manaqil Sudan
128 D6 El Maneadero Mexico
75 D3 El Mannsour Algeria
61 A4 El Mansûra Egypt
133 G6 El Manteco Venezuela
61 A4 El Manzala Egypt
24 D5 El Manzla Morocco
73 F2 El Marâgha Egypt
61 A4 El Matarîya Qalyubīya Egypt
60 C4 El Matarîya Sharqîya Egypt
61 B4 El Mazâr Egypt
74 B5 El Mechoual well Mauritania
75 F2 El Meghaïer Algeria
74 B5 El Melḥes well Mauritania
139 E2 El Miamo Venezuela
73 F2 El Minya Egypt
61 A5 El Minya Egypt
122 E3 Elmira U.S.A.
120 E3 Elmira U.S.A.
129 F5 El Mirage U.S.A.
140 B3 El Misti mt. Peru
74 B5 El Moïnane well Mauritania
140 C2 El Mojar Bolivia
24 D3 El Molinillo Spain
25 E4 El Moral Spain
97 F4 Elmore Aust.
146 C3 El Morro mt. Arg.
129 H4 El Morro National Monument res. U.S.A.
76 D3 El Mraïti well Mali
74 C5 El Mreyyé reg. Mauritania
18 D2 Elmshorn Germany
78 E1 El Muglad Sudan
114 E4 Elmwood Can.
122 C5 Elmwood U.S.A.
122 A3 Elmwood U.S.A.
76 C2 El Mzereb well Mali
10 B3 Elnesvågen Norway
138 C3 El Nevado, Cerro mt. Colombia
41 A4 El Nido Phil.
73 F5 El Obeid Sudan
61 D1 Eloglu Turkey
130 E3 El Oro Mexico
138 D2 Elorza Venezuela
75 F2 El Oued Algeria
129 G5 Eloy U.S.A.
138 B4 Eloy Alfaro Ecuador
139 E2 El Palmar Venezuela
130 D3 El Palmito Mexico
139 E2 El Pao Bolívar Venezuela
138 D2 El Pao Cojedes Venezuela
122 C5 El Paso U.S.A.
125 B6 El Paso U.S.A.
25 G2 El Perelló Catalunya Spain
140 C2 El Perú Bolivia
133 G5 El Pilar Venezuela
128 C3 El Portal U.S.A.
140 A1 El Portugues Peru
130 D2 El Porvenír Mexico
130 L7 El Porvenír Panama
25 H2 El Prat de Llobregat Spain
131 H6 El Progreso Guatemala
141 D3 El Puente Bolivia
24 C4 El Puerto de Santa María Spain
61 B5 El Qâ' v. Egypt
61 B4 El Qantara Egypt
61 C3 El Qasimiye r. Lebanon
73 E2 El Qasr Egypt
73 F2 El Qurna Egypt
61 C4 El Quşeima Egypt
60 C4 El Quweira Jordan
130 L7 El Real Panama
125 D5 El Reno U.S.A.
131 E4 El Retorno Mexico
73 F3 El Ridisîya Bahari Egypt
122 B4 Elroy U.S.A.
110 B2 Elsa Can.
26 C4 Elsa r. Italy
73 F2 El Saff Egypt
147 C6 El Salado Arg.
131 E3 El Salado Mexico
61 B4 El Sâlhîya Egypt
130 D4 El Salto Mexico
104 K8 El Salvador country Central America
146 C2 El Salvador Chile
131 E3 El Salvador Mexico
41 C4 El Salvador Phil.
133 E6 El Samán de Apure Venezuela
114 D2 Elsas Can.
130 D2 El Sauz Mexico
133 E3 El Seibo Dominican Rep.
55 H2 Elsen Nur l. China
73 E3 El Shab well Egypt
61 B4 El Shallûfa Egypt
60 C4 El Shatt Egypt
61 A4 El Simbillâwein Egypt
146 F2 El Soberbio Arg.
130 B2 El Socorro Mexico
138 D2 El Sombrero Venezuela
146 C4 El Sosneado Arg.
18 F3 Elsterwerda Germany
130 D2 El Sueco Mexico
131 F4 El Tajin Ruins Mexico
75 F1 El Tarf Algeria
24 C1 El Teleno mt. Spain
133 G5 El Temblador Venezuela
92 E3 Eltham N.Z.
61 C5 El Thamad Egypt
139 E2 El Tigre Venezuela
61 B4 El Tîna Egypt
138 D2 El Tocuyo Venezuela
13 H5 El'ton Rus. Fed.
13 H5 El'ton, Ozero l. Rus. Fed.
126 C2 Eltopia U.S.A.
146 B2 El Toro Chile
139 E2 El Toro Venezuela
146 B2 El Tránsito Chile
146 D3 El Trébol Arg.
130 C4 El Triunfo Mexico
133 □3 El Tucuche h. Trinidad Trin. & Tobago
138 D2 El Tuparro, Parque Nacional nat. park Colombia
61 B5 El Tûr Egypt
147 B7 El Turbio Chile
25 G1 El Turbón mt. Spain
56 C2 Eluru India
73 F4 El 'Uteishān well Sudan
11 G4 Elva Estonia
138 B2 El Valle Colombia
24 C3 Elvas Portugal
20 C3 Elven France
11 C3 Elverum Norway
138 C2 El Vigía Venezuela
138 C5 Elvira Brazil
100 E3 Elvire r. Aust.
26 B3 Elvo r. Italy
80 D4 El Wak Kenya
61 A5 El Wasta Egypt
122 E5 Elwood U.S.A.
78 E1 El Wurail well Sudan
73 E5 El Wurl w Sudan
73 F5 El Wuz Sudan
17 H5 Ely U.K.
122 B2 Ely U.S.A.
129 E2 Ely U.S.A.
80 C4 El Yibo well Kenya
120 B4 Elyria U.S.A.
91 □15 El Yunque h. Juan Fernandez Is Chile
119 □3 El Yunque mt. Puerto Rico
61 A4 El Zarqa Egypt
90 □2 Émaé i. Vanuatu
57 C1 Emāmrūd Iran
57 G1 Emām Sahēb Afghanistan
57 D1 Emām Taqī Iran
11 E4 Emån r. Sweden
90 □2 Emao i. Vanuatu
144 B3 Emas, Parque Nacional das nat. park Brazil
64 E3 Emba r. Kazak.
64 E3 Emba Kazak.
146 D1 Embarcación Arg.
111 G3 Embarras Portage Can.
78 C3 Embondo Zaire
115 H4 Embrun Can.
145 E5 Embu Brazil
81 C5 Embu Kenya
18 C2 Emden Niedersachsen Germany
50 C2 Emei China
50 C2 Emei Shan mt. China
65 K3 Emel' r. Kazak.
99 G4 Emerald Aust.
108 G2 Emerald I. i. Can.
113 G3 Emeril Can.
111 K5 Emerson Can.
60 B2 Emet Turkey
129 E3 Emigrant Valley v. U.S.A.
83 E4 eMijindini R.S.A.
72 C4 Emi Koussi mt. Chad
131 H5 Emiliano Zapata Mexico
26 C3 Emilia Romagna div. Italy
65 K3 Emin r. China
65 K3 Emin China
81 B5 Emin Pasha Gulf b. Tanzania
28 F3 Eminska Planina h. Bulgaria
60 B2 Emirdağ Turkey
97 F5 Emita Aust.
11 D4 Emmaboda Sweden
132 □2 Emmastad Curaçao Netherlands Ant.
11 F4 Emmaste Estonia
14 C1 Emmaus Rus. Fed.
97 G2 Emmaville Aust.
18 C2 Emmen Netherlands
21 J3 Emmen Switz.
18 C4 Emmendingen Germany
99 F5 Emmet Aust.
56 B3 Emmiganuru India
125 C6 Emory Pk summit U.S.A.
130 C3 Empalme Mexico
83 E4 Empangeni R.S.A.
146 E2 Empedrado Arg.
150 G3 Emperor Seamount Chain Pac. Oc.
26 C4 Empoli Italy
124 D4 Emporia U.S.A.
120 E6 Emporia U.S.A.
120 D4 Emporium U.S.A.
111 G4 Empress Can.
83 D2 Empress Mine Zimbabwe
57 D2 'Emrānī Iran
18 C2 Ems r. Germany
115 F4 Emsdale Can.
99 G4 Emu Park Aust.
49 G1 Emur r. China
49 G1 Emur Shan mt. ra. China
10 D3 Enafors Sweden
39 L7 Enarotali Indon.
47 F6 Ena-san mt. Japan
46 H1 Enbetsu Japan
25 G2 Encanadé mt. Spain
130 B2 Encantada, Co de la mt. Mexico
143 B7 Encantadas, Sa das h. Brazil
41 B3 Encanto, Cape c. Phil.
130 E4 Encarnación Mexico
141 E5 Encarnación Paraguay
76 D5 Enchi Ghana
25 F3 Encina r. Spain
125 D6 Encinal U.S.A.
128 D5 Encinitas U.S.A.
127 F5 Encino U.S.A.
138 C2 Encontrados Venezuela
96 D3 Encounter Bay b. Aust.
145 H1 Encruzilhada Brazil
143 B7 Encruzilhada do Sul Brazil
19 K4 Encs Hungary
110 D4 Endako Can.
43 C7 Endau Malaysia
99 E1 Endeavour Str. chan. Aust.
39 H8 Endeh Indon.
92 □1 Enderby I. i. Auckland Is N.Z.
152 D4 Enderby Land reg. Ant.
121 E3 Endicott U.S.A.
110 C3 Endicott Arm inlet U.S.A.
108 C3 Endicott Mts mt. ra. U.S.A.
101 A6 Eneabba Aust.
65 J4 Energeticheskiy Kazak.
64 E2 Energetik Rus. Fed.
146 E4 Energía Arg.
15 F3 Enerhodar Ukraine
60 A1 Enez Turkey
79 B7 Enfião, Pta do pt Angola
121 G3 Enfield U.S.A.
122 E2 Engadine U.S.A.
10 C3 Engan Norway
133 E3 Engaño, Cabo pt Dominican Rep.
41 B2 Engaño, Cape c. Phil.
46 J1 Engaru Japan
14 H4 Engel's Rus. Fed.
145 G2 Engenheiro Navarro Brazil
96 C2 Engenina w Aust.
38 D8 Enggano i. Indon.
40 B1 Engkilili Malaysia
17 G5 England div. U.K.
113 J3 Englee Can.
119 F5 Englehard U.S.A.
115 F3 Englehart Can.
20 C1 English Channel str. France/U.K.
98 D1 English Company's Is., The is Aust.
133 □7 English Harbour b. Antigua Caribbean
133 □7 English Harbour Town Antigua Caribbean
12 E1 Engozero Rus. Fed.
13 G7 Enguri r. Georgia
61 C4 'En Hazeva Israel
125 D4 Enid U.S.A.
29 D5 Enipefs r. Greece
46 H2 Eniwa Japan
63 Q4 Enkan, M. pt Rus. Fed.
11 E4 Enköping Sweden
139 F2 Enmore Guyana
27 E7 Enna Italy
111 J2 Ennadai Lake l. Can.
73 E5 En Nahud Sudan
77 F3 E-n-Nassamé well Niger
72 D4 Ennedi, Massif mts Chad
77 G2 Enneri Achelouma w Niger
72 C4 Enneri Maro w Chad
72 C3 Enneri Modragué w Chad
97 F2 Enngonia Aust.
124 C2 Enning U.S.A.
17 C5 Ennis Rep. of Ire.
126 E2 Ennis U.S.A.
125 D5 Ennis U.S.A.
17 D5 Enniscorthy Rep. of Ire.
17 D4 Enniskillen U.K.
17 C5 Ennistymon Rep. of Ire.
61 C3 Enn Nâqoûra Lebanon
19 G5 Enns r. Austria
19 G4 Enns Austria
10 H3 Eno Finland
129 F3 Enoch U.S.A.
40 A2 Enok Indon.
10 F1 Enontekiö Finland
51 F4 Enping China
40 D2 Enrekang Indon.
41 B2 Enrile Phil.
133 E3 Enriquillo, Lago de l. Dominican Rep.
97 F4 Ensay Aust.
18 C2 Enschede Netherlands
130 A2 Ensenada Mexico
119 □3 Ensenada Puerto Rico
132 B2 Ensenada de la Broa b. Cuba
51 E2 Enshi China
81 B4 Entebbe Uganda
110 F2 Enterprise Can.
115 G4 Enterprise Can.
119 C6 Enterprise U.S.A.
126 C2 Enterprise U.S.A.
129 F3 Enterprise U.S.A.
21 G4 Entraigues-sur-Sorgues France
110 F4 Entrance Can.
81 □5 Entre-Deux Réunion Indian Ocean
25 E2 Entrepeñas, Embalse de resr Spain
146 E3 Entre Ríos div. Arg.
140 D4 Entre Rios Bolivia
142 B2 Entre Rios Brazil
145 F4 Entre Rios de Minas Brazil
24 B3 Entroncamento Portugal
77 F5 Enugu Nigeria
77 F5 Enugu div. Nigeria

108 A3 Enurmino Rus. Fed.
140 B1 Envira Brazil
79 D4 Enyamba Zaire
78 C3 Enyéllé Congo
93 C5 Enys, Mt mt. N.Z.
26 C3 Enza r. Italy
47 G6 Enzan Japan
90 □2 Eo i. Pac. Oc.
78 C3 Epéna Congo
21 F2 Épernay France
129 G2 Ephraim U.S.A.
121 E4 Ephrata U.S.A.
126 C2 Ephrata U.S.A.
90 □2 Epi i. Vanuatu
21 G3 Épinac France
21 H2 Épinal France
139 F2 Epira Guyana
61 B2 Episkopi Cyprus
61 B2 Episkopi B. b. Cyprus
27 D5 Epomeo, Monte h. Italy
17 H6 Epping U.K.
17 G6 Epsom U.K.
146 D4 Epu-pel Arg.
57 C3 Eqlīd Iran
78 C3 Équateur div. Zaire
80 B3 Equatoria div. Sudan
69 E5 Equatorial Guinea country Africa
139 E2 Equeipa Venezuela
99 F5 Erac Cr. w Aust.
76 D3 Erakchiouene well Mali
41 A4 Eran Phil.
54 C5 Erandol India
60 D1 Erbaa Turkey
73 G3 Erba, Jebel mt. Sudan
18 F4 Erbendorf Germany
18 C4 Erbeskopf h. Germany
60 E2 Erçek Turkey
60 E2 Erciş Turkey
60 C2 Erciyes Daği mt. Turkey
19 J5 Érd Hungary
49 H4 Erdao r. China
55 H2 Erdaogou China
60 A1 Erdek Turkey
61 C1 Erdemli Turkey
48 C2 Erdenet Mongolia
48 A2 Erdenet Mongolia
48 C4 Erdenetsogt Mongolia
72 D4 Erdi reg. Chad
18 E4 Erding Germany
152 B5 Erebus, Mt mt. Ant.
60 F4 Erech Iraq
143 B6 Erechim Brazil
49 E2 Ereentsav Mongolia
60 C2 Ereğli Konya Turkey
60 B1 Ereğli Zonguldak Turkey
29 B5 Ereikoussa i. Greece
27 E7 Erei, Monti mts Italy
48 E4 Erenhot China
57 D2 Eresk Iran
24 D2 Eresma r. Spain
29 D5 Eretria Greece
74 D2 Erfoud Morocco
18 E3 Erfurt Germany
60 D2 Ergani Turkey
76 C2 Erg Atouila sand dunes Mali
74 C4 'Erg Chech sand dunes Algeria/Mali
72 C4 Erg du Djourab sand dunes Chad
77 G3 Erg du Ténéré sand dunes Niger
48 D4 Ergel Mongolia
60 A1 Ergene r. Turkey
74 D2 Erg er Raoui sand dunes Algeria
74 D3 Erg labès sand dunes Algeria
74 C3 Erg Iguidi sand dunes Algeria/Mauritania
75 F3 Erg Issaouane sand dunes Algeria
11 G4 Ergļi Latvia
78 C1 Erguig r. Chad
49 G2 Ergun Yougi China
49 G2 Ergun Zuoqi China
50 C3 Er Hai l. China
49 H4 Erhulai China
24 B3 Ericeira Portugal
16 E3 Ericht, Loch l. U.K.
122 B5 Erie U.S.A.
125 E4 Erie U.S.A.
120 C3 Erie U.S.A.
123 F5 Erie, Lake l. Can./U.S.A.
76 C3 'Erîgât sand dunes Mali
46 J2 Erimo Japan
46 J3 Erimo-misaki c. Japan
96 C1 Eringa Aust.
133 □3 Erin Point pt Trinidad Trin. & Tobago
68 H4 Eritrea country Africa
19 F2 Erkner Germany
73 G4 Erkowit Sudan
18 E4 Erlangen Germany
98 C5 Erldunda Aust.
49 J4 Erlong Shan mt. China
49 H4 Erlongshan Sk. resr China
48 E2 Ermana, Khr. mt. ra. Rus. Fed.
83 D4 Ermelo R.S.A.
61 B1 Ermenek Karaman Turkey
60 C2 Ermenek Turkey
29 D6 Ermioni Greece
29 E6 Ermoupoli Greece
56 B4 Ernakulam India
101 C5 Ernest Giles Ra. h. Aust.
93 A7 Ernest Is is N.Z.
56 B4 Erode India
99 E5 Eromanga Aust.
82 A3 Erongo div. Namibia
82 B3 Erongo Mts mts Namibia
74 D2 Er Rachidia Morocco
73 F5 Er Rahad Sudan
83 F2 Errego Mozambique
80 B2 Er Renk Sudan
17 C4 Errigal h. Rep. of Ire.
17 B4 Erris Head hd Rep. of Ire.
121 H2 Errol U.S.A.
90 □2 Erromango i. Vanuatu
80 B2 Er Roseires Sudan
73 F5 Er Rua'at Sudan
61 D3 Er Ruseifa Jordan
29 C4 Ersekë Albania
124 D2 Erskine U.S.A.
10 F3 Ersmark Sweden
14 E4 Ertil' Rus. Fed.
65 L3 Ertix r. China
96 D2 Erudina Aust.
60 E2 Eruh Turkey
146 F3 Erval Brazil
145 G4 Ervália Brazil
120 D5 Erwin U.S.A.
29 C6 Erymanthos r. Greece
29 D5 Erythres Greece
50 B3 Eryuan China
18 F3 Erzgebirge mt. ra. Czech Rep./Germany
49 H2 Erzhan China
48 A2 Erzin Rus. Fed.
61 D1 Erzin Turkey
60 D2 Erzincan Turkey
60 E2 Erzurum Turkey
90 □1 Esa-ala P.N.G.
46 H3 Esan-misaki pt Japan
46 J1 Esashi Japan
47 H4 Esashi Japan
46 H3 Esashi Japan
46 D7 Esawasaki Japan
11 C5 Esbjerg Denmark
142 E2 Escada Brazil
129 G3 Escalante U.S.A.
129 G3 Escalante r. U.S.A.
129 F3 Escalante Desert desert U.S.A.
25 G1 Escaló Spain
130 D3 Escalón Mexico
122 D3 Escanaba U.S.A.
131 H5 Escárcega Mexico
41 B2 Escarpada Point pt Phil.
25 F2 Escatrón Spain
21 F1 Escaut r. France
18 E2 Eschede Germany
18 B4 Esch-sur-Alzette Luxembourg
18 E3 Eschwege Germany
18 C3 Eschweiler Germany
133 E3 Escocesa, Bahía b. Caribbean
140 C3 Escoma Bolivia
128 D5 Escondido U.S.A.
130 D4 Escuinapa Mexico
131 H6 Escuintla Guatemala
131 G6 Escuintla Mexico
133 E5 Escuque Venezuela
145 E2 Escurso r. Brazil
138 C2 Escutillas Colombia
78 B3 Eséka Cameroon
57 C1 Esenguly Turkmenistan
18 C2 Esens Germany
57 B2 Eşfahan Iran
57 B2 Eşfahan div. Iran
57 C3 Esfandāran Iran
57 B3 Esfarjan Iran
64 E5 Eshāqābād Iran
57 C4 Eshkanān Iran
61 C4 Esh Sharā reg. Jordan
57 B2 Eshtehārd Iran
83 D3 Esigodini Zimbabwe
83 E4 Esikhawini R.S.A.
99 H5 Esk Aust.
97 F5 Esk r. Aust.
57 B2 Eskandarī Iran
92 F3 Eskdale N.Z.
113 G3 Esker Can.
15 G2 Eskhar Ukraine
10 N2 Eskifjörður Iceland
11 E4 Eskilstuna Sweden
60 C1 Eskipazar Turkey
60 B2 Eskişehir Turkey
24 D1 Esla r. Spain
60 F3 Eslamābād e Gharb Iran
11 D5 Eslöv Sweden
60 B2 Eşme Turkey
132 C2 Esmeralda Cuba
147 A6 Esmeralda, I. i. Chile
138 B3 Esmeraldas Ecuador
114 B1 Esnagami Lake l. Can.
114 C2 Esnagi Lake l. Can.
57 E4 Espakeh Iran
20 F4 Espalion France
114 E3 Espanola Can.
127 F4 Espanola U.S.A.
138 □ Española, I. i. Galapagos Is Ecuador
25 G2 Esparraguera Spain
128 A2 Esparto U.S.A.
101 C7 Esperance Aust.
101 C7 Esperance B. b. Aust.
92 □4 Espérance Rock, L' i. Kermadec Is N.Z.
142 D1 Esperantinópolis Brazil
152 B2 Esperanza Argentina Base Ant.
147 B7 Esperanza Santa Cruz Arg.
146 D3 Esperanza Santa Fé Arg.
130 C3 Esperanza Mexico
140 B1 Esperanza Peru
41 C4 Esperanza Phil.
119 □3 Esperanza Puerto Rico
130 J6 Esperanza, Sa de la mt. ra. Honduras
24 B3 Espichel, Cabo hd Portugal
24 D3 Espiel Spain
24 D1 Espigüete mt. Spain
125 C7 Espinazo Mexico
24 B2 Espinho Portugal
143 B6 Espinilho, Sa do h. Brazil
145 G1 Espinosa Brazil
145 H3 Espírito Santo div. Brazil
41 B2 Espiritu Phil.
90 □2 Espíritu Santo i. Vanuatu
131 J5 Espíritu Santo, B. del b. Mexico
130 C3 Espíritu Sto i. Mexico
142 E3 Esplanada Brazil
11 G3 Espoo Finland
83 E3 Espungabera Mozambique
147 B5 Esquel Arg.
110 E5 Esquimalt Can.
146 E3 Esquina Arg.
61 D3 Es Samrā Jordan
41 C5 Essang Indon.
74 C2 Essaouira Morocco
74 B3 Es Semara Western Sahara
18 C3 Essen Germany
101 C5 Essendon, Mt h. Aust.
139 F2 Essequibo r. Guyana
114 D5 Essex Can.
129 E4 Essex U.S.A.
121 G2 Essex Junction U.S.A.
123 F4 Essexville U.S.A.
18 D4 Esslingen am Neckar Germany
63 R4 Esso Rus. Fed.
73 F5 Es Suki Sudan
78 B3 Est div. Cameroon
24 C1 Estaca de Bares, Pta da pt Spain
147 D7 Estados, I. de los i. Arg.
57 C3 Eşţahbānāt Iran
114 E3 Estaire Can.
142 E3 Estância Brazil
147 C7 Estancia Camerón Chile
25 E4 Estancias, Sierra de las mt. ra. Spain
20 E5 Estats, Pic d' mt. France/Spain
83 D4 Estcourt R.S.A.
26 C3 Este Italy
146 D2 Esteban Rams Arg.
24 B2 Estela Portugal
130 J6 Estelí Nicaragua
25 E1 Estella Spain
24 D3 Estena r. Spain
24 D4 Estepa Spain
24 D4 Estepona Spain
119 □3 Este, Pta pt Puerto Rico
25 E2 Esteras de Medinaceli Spain
21 H5 Esterel reg. France
111 J4 Esterhazy Can.
78 A3 Esterias, Cap pt Gabon
128 B4 Estero Bay b. U.S.A.
141 D4 Esteros Paraguay
146 E2 Esteros del Iberá marsh Arg.
111 J5 Estevan Can.
124 E3 Estherville U.S.A.
113 H4 Est, Île de l' i. Can.
119 D5 Estill U.S.A.
142 D2 Estiva r. Brazil
145 E5 Estiva Brazil
121 J1 Est, Lac de l' l. Can.
142 D2 Estolado r. Brazil
5 H3 Estonia country Europe
145 F3 Estrêla do Indaiá Brazil
144 E3 Estrêla do Sul Brazil
24 C2 Estrela, Serra da mt. ra. Portugal
24 E3 Estrella mt. Spain
24 B3 Estremadura reg. Portugal
24 C3 Estremoz Portugal
78 B3 Estuaire div. Gabon
19 J5 Esztergom Hungary
20 C2 Étables-sur-Mer France
96 D2 Etadunna Aust.
54 D4 Etah India
21 G2 Étain France
20 F2 Étampes France
96 D1 Etamunbanie, L. salt flat Aust.
20 D4 Étang de Biscarrosse et de Parentis l. France
20 D4 Étang de Cazaux et de Sanguinet l. France
20 D4 Étang d'Hourtin-Carcans l. France
81 □5 Étang Salé Réunion Indian Ocean
20 E1 Étaples France
54 D4 Etawah India
83 E4 eThandakukhanya R.S.A.
101 C4 Ethel Creek Aust.
90 □8 Ethel Reefs reef Fiji
82 C4 E'Thembini R.S.A.
99 E3 Etheridge r. Aust.
69 H5 Ethiopia country Africa
60 C2 Etimesğut Turkey
16 E3 Etive, Loch inlet U.K.
27 E7 Etna, Monte vol Italy
11 B4 Etne Norway
110 C3 Etolin I. i. U.S.A.
99 G4 Eton Aust.
82 B2 Etosha National Park nat. park Namibia
82 B2 Etosha Pan salt pan Namibia
78 B3 Etoumbi Congo
28 E3 Etropole Bulgaria
56 B4 Ettaiyapuram India
18 C4 Ettelbruck Luxembourg
18 B3 Etten-Leur Netherlands
74 A5 Et Tîdra i. Mauritania
78 E4 Etumba Zaire
130 D4 Etzatlán Mexico
90 □4 'Eua i. Tonga
97 F3 Euabalong Aust.
90 □4 'Eua Iki i. Tonga
90 □3 Euakafa i. Tonga
101 E6 Eucla Aust.
120 C4 Euclid U.S.A.
142 E3 Euclides da Cunha Brazil
97 G4 Eucumbene, L. l. Aust.
96 D3 Eudunda Aust.
119 C6 Eufaula U.S.A.
125 E5 Eufaula Lake resr U.S.A.
126 B2 Eugene U.S.A.
141 E2 Eugênia r. Brazil
130 B3 Eugenia, Pta c. Mexico
97 G3 Eugowra Aust.
99 F6 Eulo Aust.
97 G2 Eumungerie Aust.
99 G4 Eungella Nat. Park Aust.
125 E6 Eunice U.S.A.
60 F4 Euphrates r. Iraq
11 F3 Eura Finland
20 E2 Eure r. France
126 A3 Eureka U.S.A.
126 D1 Eureka U.S.A.
129 E2 Eureka U.S.A.
145 J2 Euriápolis Brazil
96 E2 Eurinilla w Aust.
96 E2 Euriowie Aust.
97 F4 Euroa Aust.
99 G5 Eurombah Aust.
99 G5 Eurombah Cr. r. Aust.
149 G5 Europa, Île i. Indian Ocean
24 D1 Europa, Picos de mt. ra. Spain
24 D4 Europa Point hd Gibraltar
97 E3 Euston Aust.
110 D4 Eustuk Lake l. Can.
119 C5 Eutaw U.S.A.
18 E1 Eutin Germany
98 C3 Eva Downs Aust.
119 □1 Evans Bay Bermuda
110 F4 Evansburg Can.
97 H2 Evans Head Aust.
152 B3 Evans Ice Stream ice feature Ant.
112 E3 Evans, L. l. Can.
127 F4 Evans, Mt mt. U.S.A.
126 D2 Evans, Mt mt. U.S.A.
109 K3 Evans Strait chan. Can.
122 D4 Evanston U.S.A.
126 E3 Evanston U.S.A.
114 D4 Evansville Can.
118 C4 Evansville U.S.A.
122 C4 Evansville U.S.A.
126 F3 Evansville U.S.A.
122 E4 Evart U.S.A.
82 D4 Evaton R.S.A.
57 C4 Evaz Iran
122 A2 Eveleth U.S.A.
63 R3 Evensk Rus. Fed.
93 □1 Eveque, Cape L' c. Chatham Is N.Z.
96 C2 Everard, L. salt flat Aust.
96 C1 Everard, Mt mt. Aust.
96 C1 Everard Park Aust.
96 C1 Everard Range h. Aust.
55 F4 Everest, Mt mt. China
121 K1 Everett Can.
126 B1 Everett U.S.A.
119 D7 Everglades Nat. Park nat. park. U.S.A.
119 D7 Everglades, The swamp U.S.A.
125 G6 Evergreen U.S.A.
139 F2 Everton Guyana
99 E4 Evesham Aust.
17 G5 Evesham U.K.
10 F3 Evijärvi Finland
78 B3 Evinayong Equatorial Guinea
11 B4 Evje Norway
24 C3 Évora Portugal
24 C3 Évora div. Portugal
45 P1 Evoron, Ozero l. Rus. Fed.
20 E2 Évreux France
20 D2 Évron France
29 F4 Evros r. Greece/Turkey
29 D6 Evrotas r. Greece
20 F2 Évry France
29 E5 Evvoia i. Greece
127 □1 Ewa Beach U.S.A.
133 □1 Ewarton Jamaica
81 C5 Ewaso Ngiro r. Kenya
49 F2 Ewenkizu Zizhiqi China
152 B2 Ewing I. i. Ant.
92 □1 Ewing I. i. Auckland Is N.Z.
78 B4 Ewo Congo
140 C2 Exaltación Bolivia
128 C2 Excelsior Mtn mt. U.S.A.
128 C2 Excelsior Mts mts U.S.A.
124 E4 Excelsior Springs U.S.A.
152 A4 Executive Committee Range mt. ra. Ant.
97 G3 Exeter Aust.
114 E5 Exeter Can.
17 F6 Exeter U.K.
128 C3 Exeter U.S.A.
121 H3 Exeter U.S.A.
17 F6 Exmoor reg. U.K.
121 F6 Exmore U.S.A.
100 A4 Exmouth Aust.
17 F6 Exmouth U.K.
100 A4 Exmouth Gulf b. Aust.
149 M5 Exmouth Plateau Indian Ocean
99 G5 Expedition Range mt. ra. Aust.
90 □7 Exploring Is is Fiji
24 D3 Extremadura div. Spain
78 B1 Extrême-Nord div. Cameroon
142 E2 Exú Brazil
132 C1 Exuma Sound chan. The Bahamas
78 D4 Eyangu Zaire
81 B5 Eyasi, Lake salt l. Tanzania
16 F4 Eyemouth U.K.
10 M2 Eyjafjörður b. Iceland
80 E3 Eyl Somalia
20 E4 Eymoutiers France
57 C2 Eyn or Rashid Iran
98 D5 Eyre Cr. w Aust.
93 B6 Eyre Mountains mt. ra. N.Z.
96 D2 Eyre (North), Lake salt flat Aust.
96 C3 Eyre Peninsula pen. Aust.
96 D2 Eyre (South), L. salt flat Aust.
18 D2 Eystrup Germany
16 D1 Eysturoy i. Faeroes
81 C5 Eyuku waterhole Kenya
78 A2 Eyumojok Cameroon
83 E4 Ezakheni R.S.A.
147 C4 Ezequil Ramos Mexia, Embalse resr Arg.
12 J2 Ezhva Rus. Fed.
60 A2 Ezine Turkey

F

91 □11 Faaa Fr. Poly. Pac. Oc.
53 D9 Faadhippolhu Atoll atoll Maldives
80 D4 Faafxadhuun Somalia
91 □10 Faaite i. Fr. Poly. Pac. Oc.
91 □11 Faaone Fr. Poly. Pac. Oc.
125 B6 Fabens U.S.A.
110 F2 Faber Lake l. Can.
43 □ Faber, Mt h. Singapore
24 C1 Fabero Spain
11 C5 Fåborg Denmark
26 D4 Fabriano Italy
138 C3 Facatativá Colombia
77 G3 Fachi Niger
99 G4 Facing I. i. Aust.
41 □2 Facpi Pt pt Guam Pac. Oc.
121 F4 Factoryville U.S.A.
147 B6 Facundo Arg.
72 D4 Fada Chad
77 E4 Fada-Ngourma Burkina
80 E2 Faḑli reg. Yemen
75 F3 Fadnoun, Plateau du plat. Algeria
26 C3 Faenza Italy
16 D1 Faeroes is Atlantic Ocean
78 C2 Fafa r. C.A.R.
90 □4 Fafa i. Tonga
39 K7 Fafanlap Indon.
24 B2 Fafe Portugal
80 D3 Fafen Shet' w Ethiopia
91 □12 Fagaloa Bay b. Western Samoa
91 □12 Fagamalo Western Samoa
28 E2 Făgăraş Romania
11 C3 Fagernes Norway
11 D4 Fagersta Sweden
28 D2 Făget Romania
77 F4 Faggo Nigeria
147 C7 Fagnano, L. l. Arg.
76 D3 Faguibine, Lac l. Mali
10 M3 Fagurhólsmýri Iceland
80 B3 Fagwir Sudan
57 D3 Fahraj Iran
24 □ Faial Madeira Portugal
115 G2 Faillon, Lac l. Can.
108 D3 Fairbanks U.S.A.
120 B5 Fairborn U.S.A.
124 D3 Fairbury U.S.A.
120 E5 Fairfax U.S.A.
128 A2 Fairfield U.S.A.
122 B5 Fairfield U.S.A.
120 A5 Fairfield U.S.A.
125 D6 Fairfield U.S.A.
121 G3 Fair Haven U.S.A.
41 A4 Fairie Queen sand bank Phil.
16 G2 Fair Isle i. U.K.
99 F2 Fairlight Aust.
124 E3 Fairmont U.S.A.
120 C5 Fairmont U.S.A.
127 F4 Fairplay U.S.A.
122 D3 Fairport U.S.A.
120 C4 Fairport Harbor U.S.A.
99 F2 Fairview Aust.
110 F3 Fairview Can.
123 E3 Fairview U.S.A.
125 D4 Fairview U.S.A.
129 G2 Fairview U.S.A.
45 □ Fairview Park Hong Kong
110 B3 Fairweather, Cape c. U.S.A.
110 B3 Fairweather, Mt mt. Can./U.S.A.
39 M5 Fais i. Fed. States of Micronesia
54 C3 Faisalabad Pakistan
124 C2 Faith U.S.A.
16 G1 Faither, The pt U.K.
55 E4 Faizabad India
119 □3 Fajardo Puerto Rico
91 □10 Fakaina i. Fr. Poly. Pac. Oc.
90 □3 Fakalele i. Tonga
87 K5 Fakaofo i. Tokelau Pac. Oc.
91 □10 Fakarava i. Fr. Poly. Pac. Oc.
17 H5 Fakenham U.K.
10 D3 Fåker Sweden
39 K7 Fakfak Indon.
57 C3 Fakhrabad Iran
49 G4 Faku China
76 B5 Falaba Sierra Leone
77 E4 Falagountou Burkina
20 D2 Falaise France
72 C4 Falaise d'Angamma cliff Chad
76 D4 Falaise de Bandiagara escarpment Mali
76 D4 Falaise de Banfora escarpment Burkina
77 F3 Falaise de Tiguidit escarpment Niger
55 G4 Falakata India
42 A2 Falam Myanmar
57 B2 Falavarjan Iran
28 G1 Fălciu Romania
26 D4 Falconara Marittima Italy
125 D7 Falcon Lake l. Mexico/U.S.A.
91 □12 Falealupo Western Samoa
91 □12 Faleasiu Western Samoa
91 □12 Falelima Western Samoa
76 B4 Falémé r. Mali/Senegal
12 J3 Falenki Rus. Fed.
91 □12 Falerai Western Samoa
15 B3 Făleşti Moldova
91 □12 Faleula Western Samoa
125 D7 Falfurrias U.S.A.
110 F3 Falher Can.
80 C1 Falkat r. Eritrea
11 D4 Falkenberg Sweden
18 F2 Falkensee Germany
16 F4 Falkirk U.K.
147 E7 Falkland Islands is Atlantic Ocean
147 D7 Falkland Sound chan. Falkland Is.
29 D6 Falkonera i. Greece
11 D4 Falköping Sweden
128 D5 Fallbrook U.S.A.
128 C2 Fallon U.S.A.
121 H4 Fall River U.S.A.
126 F3 Fall River Pass U.S.A.
124 E3 Falls City U.S.A.
77 E4 Falmey Niger
133 □7 Falmouth Antigua Caribbean
133 □1 Falmouth Jamaica
17 E6 Falmouth U.K.
120 A5 Falmouth U.S.A.
121 H3 Falmouth U.S.A.
122 E3 Falmouth U.S.A.
82 B5 False Bay b. R.S.A.
11 D5 Falster i. Denmark
28 F1 Fălticeni Romania
11 D3 Falun Sweden
146 C2 Famatina Arg.
146 C2 Famatina, Sa de mt. ra. Arg.
79 C4 Fambono Zaire
111 K4 Family L. l. Can.
76 C4 Fana Mali
83 H2 Fanandrana Madagascar
51 G2 Fanchang China
83 H3 Fandriana Madagascar
42 B3 Fang Thailand
91 □10 Fangatau i. Fr. Poly. Pac. Oc.
90 □4 Fanga Uta lag. Tonga
51 F1 Fangchēng China
50 E4 Fangcheng China
50 E2 Fangdou Shan mt. ra. China
51 H4 Fang-liao Taiwan
49 F5 Fangshan China
48 D5 Fangshan China
51 H4 Fangshan Taiwan
51 E1 Fang Xian China
49 J3 Fangzheng China
45 □ Fanling Hong Kong
16 E3 Fannich, Loch l. U.K.
57 D4 Fannūj Iran
26 D4 Fano Italy
51 H3 Fanshan China
48 E5 Fanshi China
42 C2 Fan Si Pan mt. Vietnam
49 E6 Fan Xian China
64 F5 Farab Turkmenistan
76 B4 Faraba Mali
152 B2 Faraday Ukraine Base Ant.
78 E3 Faradje Zaire
83 H3 Farafangana Madagascar
76 A4 Farafenni The Gambia
73 E2 Farafra Oasis oasis Egypt
57 C3 Farāgheh Iran
57 E2 Farah w Afghanistan
57 E2 Farāh Afghanistan
57 E2 Farah Rud r. Afghanistan
57 G2 Farakhulm Afghanistan
39 M2 Farallon de Pajaros i. Northern Mariana Is Pac. Oc.
76 B4 Faranah Guinea
92 D4 Farewell, Cape c. N.Z.
92 D4 Farewell Spit spit N.Z.
11 D4 Färgelanda Sweden
124 D2 Fargo U.S.A.
124 E2 Faribault U.S.A.
113 F2 Faribault, Lac l. Can.
54 D3 Faridabad India
54 C3 Faridkot India
55 G5 Faridpur Bangladesh
54 D3 Faridpur India
83 H2 Farihy Alaotra l. Madagascar
83 G3 Farihy Ihotry l. Madagascar
83 H2 Farihy Kinkony l. Madagascar
83 H2 Farihy Tsiazompaniry l. Madagascar
83 G3 Farihy Tsimanampetsotsa l. Madagascar
24 B3 Farilhões i. Portugal
57 D2 Farīmān Iran
142 C2 Farinha r. Brazil
61 A4 Fâriskûr Egypt
11 E4 Färjestaden Sweden
29 D5 Farkadonas Greece
65 G5 Farkhor Tajikistan
29 F6 Farmakonisi i. Greece
122 C5 Farmer City U.S.A.
112 D2 Farmer Island i. Can.
110 E3 Farmington Can.
122 B5 Farmington U.S.A.
122 B5 Farmington U.S.A.
121 H2 Farmington U.S.A.
121 H3 Farmington U.S.A.
129 H3 Farmington U.S.A.
126 E3 Farmington U.S.A.
110 D4 Far Mt. mt. Can.
120 D6 Farmville U.S.A.
17 G4 Farne Islands is U.K.
110 F4 Farnham, Mt mt. Can.
142 A1 Faro Brazil
110 C2 Faro Can.
24 C4 Faro Portugal
24 B4 Faro div. Portugal
11 E4 Fårö i. Sweden
78 B2 Faro, Réserve du res. Cameroon
24 C1 Faro, Serra do mt. ra. Spain
11 E4 Fårösund Sweden
69 K7 Farquhar Group is Seychelles
99 E5 Farrars Cr. w Aust.
57 C3 Farrāshband Iran
120 C4 Farrell U.S.A.
115 H4 Farrellton Can.
57 D2 Farrokhī Iran
57 C3 Fārs div. Iran
57 C2 Farsakh Iran
29 D5 Farsala Greece
57 E2 Fārsī Afghanistan
126 E3 Farson U.S.A.
11 B4 Farsund Norway
79 B6 Farta, Baia Angola
28 F2 Fărţăneşti Romania
144 C2 Fartura r. Brazil
143 B6 Fartura, Sa da mt. ra. Brazil
125 C5 Farwell U.S.A.
57 C3 Fasā Iran
27 F5 Fasano Italy
120 E4 Fassett U.S.A.
15 C1 Fastiv Ukraine
15 E1 Fastivtsi Ukraine
78 F3 Fataki Zaire
54 C3 Fatehabad India
54 D4 Fatehgarh India
54 C2 Fatehjang Pakistan
54 C4 Fatehnagar India
54 C4 Fatehpur Rajasthan India
54 E4 Fatehpur Uttar Pradesh India
54 B3 Fatehpur Pakistan
54 D4 Fatehpur Sikri India
14 B3 Fateyevka Rus. Fed.
14 B3 Fatezh Rus. Fed.
57 C3 Fatḩābād Iran
114 E4 Fathom Five National Marine Park nat. park Can.
76 A4 Fatick Senegal
144 A5 Fátima do Sul Brazil
90 □3 Fatumanga i. Tonga
79 C4 Fatundu Zaire
114 D2 Fauquier Can.
101 A5 Faure I. i. Aust.
28 F2 Făurei Romania
10 D2 Fauske Norway
129 F1 Faust U.S.A.
27 D7 Favignana, Isola i. Italy
110 G4 Fawcett Can.
112 C3 Fawn r. Can.
73 H2 Fawwārah Saudi Arabia
10 L2 Faxaflói b. Iceland
10 E3 Faxälven r. Sweden
50 C3 Faxian Hu l. China
72 C4 Faya Chad
122 D3 Fayette U.S.A.
125 E4 Fayetteville U.S.A.
119 E5 Fayetteville U.S.A.
119 C5 Fayetteville U.S.A.
73 H4 Fayfā Saudi Arabia
61 B4 Fâyid Egypt
60 G4 Faylakah i. Kuwait
61 D5 Fazair al Ghrazi w Saudi Arabia
77 E5 Fazao Malfakassa, Parc National de nat. park Togo
54 C3 Fazilka India
54 B3 Fazilpur Pakistan
57 B4 Fazrān, J. h. Saudi Arabia
74 B4 Fdérik Mauritania
119 E5 Fear, Cape c. U.S.A.
119 E5 Fear, Cape r. U.S.A.
128 B2 Feather Falls U.S.A.
93 E4 Featherston N.Z.
97 F4 Feathertop, Mt mt. Aust.
20 E2 Fécamp France
146 E3 Federación Arg.
77 F5 Federal Capital Territory div. Nigeria
16 K1 Fedje Norway
65 J2 Fedorovka Kazak.
64 F2 Fedorovka Kazak.
64 D2 Fedorovka Kazak.
15 F3 Fedotova Kosa spit Ukraine
19 L5 Fehérgyarmat Hungary
18 E1 Fehmarn i. Germany
145 H5 Feia, Lagoa lag. Brazil
51 G2 Feidong China
51 H1 Feihuanghe Kou river mouth China
140 B1 Feijó Brazil
92 E4 Feilding N.Z.
144 C4 Feio ou Aguapei r. Brazil
142 E3 Feira de Santana Brazil
24 C1 Feira do Monte Spain
61 B5 Feirân well Egypt
61 B5 Feirân, W. w Egypt
51 G2 Feixi China
51 G1 Fei Xian China
60 C2 Feke Turkey
25 H3 Felanitx Spain
122 D3 Felch U.S.A.
18 F2 Feldberg Mecklenburg-Vorpommern Germany
18 D5 Feldberg mt. Germany
18 D5 Feldkirch Austria
19 G5 Feldkirchen in Kärten Austria
28 E1 Feldru Romania
90 □3 Feletoa Tonga
146 E3 Feliciano r. Arg.
81 □1 Félicité I. i. Seychelles
53 D10 Felidu Atoll atoll Maldives
131 H5 Felipe C. Puerto Mexico
145 F3 Felixlândia Brazil
17 H6 Felixstowe U.K.
130 D2 Félix U. Gómez Mexico
26 D2 Fella r. Italy
133 □1 Fellowship Jamaica
26 C2 Feltre Italy
142 C3 Femeas r. Brazil
18 E1 Femer Bælt str. Denmark/Germany
11 C3 Femunden l. Norway
48 D5 Fen r. China
83 G4 Fenambosy, Lohatanjona pt Madagascar
129 H4 Fence Lake U.S.A.
115 F4 Fenelon Falls Can.
15 D1 Fenevychi Ukraine
29 E4 Fengari mt. Greece
49 H4 Fengcheng China
51 F2 Fengcheng China
50 D2 Fengdu China
50 D3 Fenggang China
51 H2 Fenghua China
51 E3 Fenghuang China
51 E2 Fengjie China
51 E4 Fengkai China
51 H4 Fenglin Taiwan
49 F5 Fengnan China
49 F4 Fengning China
50 B3 Fengqing China
51 F1 Fengqiu China
49 F5 Fengrun China
50 D3 Fengshan China
51 G4 Fengshun China
51 G1 Fengtai China
50 D1 Feng Xian China
51 F2 Fengxin China
51 G1 Fengyang China
48 E4 Fengzhen China
55 G5 Feni Bangladesh
90 □1 Feni Is is P.N.G.
122 B4 Fennimore U.S.A.
83 H2 Fenoarivo Atsinanana Madagascar
83 H2 Fenoarivo Be Madagascar
21 J6 Feno, Capo di pt France
17 G5 Fens, The reg. U.K.
123 F4 Fenton U.S.A.
151 J7 Fenua Ura is Fr. Poly. Pac. Oc.
48 D5 Fenxi China
48 D5 Fenyang China
13 E6 Feodosiya Ukraine
75 F1 Fer, Cap de hd Algeria
57 D2 Ferdows Iran
29 F4 Feres Greece
65 H4 Fergana Uzbekistan
65 H4 Fergana Too Tizmegi mt. ra. Kyrgyzstan
114 E5 Fergus Can.
124 D2 Fergus Falls U.S.A.
90 □1 Fergusson I. i. P.N.G.
75 F2 Fériana Tunisia
76 C5 Ferkessédougou Côte d'Ivoire
19 G5 Ferlach Austria
114 A1 Ferland Can.
76 B4 Ferlo Sud, Réserve de Faune du res. Senegal
76 A3 Ferlo, Vallée du w Senegal
26 D4 Fermo Italy
113 G3 Fermont Can.
24 C2 Fermoselle Spain
17 C5 Fermoy Rep. of Ire.
146 D2 Fernández Arg.
119 D6 Fernandina Beach U.S.A.
138 □ Fernandina, I. i. Galapagos Is Ecuador
147 B7 Fernando de Magallanes, Parque Nacional nat. park Chile
148 G6 Fernando de Noronha i. Atlantic Ocean
144 C4 Fernandópolis Brazil
145 F2 Fernão Dias Brazil
83 G1 Fernão Veloso, Baia de b. Mozambique
126 B1 Ferndale U.S.A.
17 G6 Ferndown U.K.
110 F5 Fernie Can.
128 C2 Fernley U.S.A.
121 F4 Fernridge U.S.A.
126 C2 Fernwood U.S.A.
26 C3 Ferrara Italy
27 B6 Ferrato, Capo pt Italy
24 B3 Ferreira do Alentejo Portugal
139 G3 Ferreira-Gomes Brazil
144 B4 Ferreiros Brazil
138 B5 Ferreñafe Peru
125 F6 Ferriday U.S.A.
142 B3 Ferro r. Brazil
27 B5 Ferro, Capo pt Italy
24 B1 Ferrol Spain
129 G2 Ferron U.S.A.
145 G3 Ferros Brazil
14 C2 Ferzikovo Rus. Fed.
74 D2 Fès Morocco
79 C5 Feshi Zaire
111 K5 Fessenden U.S.A.
124 F4 Festus U.S.A.
76 B4 Fété Bowé Senegal
28 F2 Feteşti Romania
60 B2 Fethiye Turkey
16 G1 Fetlar i. U.K.
113 F2 Feuilles, Rivière aux r. Can.
21 G4 Feurs France
61 D1 Fevzipaşa Turkey
57 G1 Feyzābād Afghanistan
57 D2 Feyẕābād Iran
146 C2 Fiambalá Arg.
76 D4 Fian Ghana
83 H3 Fianarantsoa Madagascar
83 H3 Fianarantsoa div. Madagascar
78 C2 Fianga Chad
80 C3 Fichē Ethiopia
142 D2 Fidalgo r. Brazil
26 C3 Fidenza Italy
110 F4 Field Can.
114 E3 Field Can.
98 C2 Field I. i. Aust.
28 E2 Fieni Romania
29 B4 Fier Albania
98 D3 Fiery Cr. r. Aust.
122 E3 Fife Lake U.S.A.
16 F3 Fife Ness pt U.K.
97 F3 Fifield Aust.
122 B3 Fifield U.S.A.
73 F4 5th Cataract rapids Sudan
20 F4 Figeac France
133 □6 Fig Tree St Kitts-Nevis Caribbean
24 B2 Figueira da Foz Portugal
144 B3 Figueirão Brazil
25 H1 Figueres Spain
75 D2 Figuig Morocco
78 B2 Figuil Cameroon
61 D5 Fiha al 'Ināb reg. Saudi Arabia
80 E2 Fi'i reg. Yemen
86 J6 Fiji country Pac. Oc.
83 D3 Filabusi Zimbabwe
130 J7 Filadelfia Costa Rica
141 D4 Filadélfia Paraguay
19 J4 Fiľakovo Slovakia
76 C4 Filamana Mali
152 B3 Filchner Ice Shelf ice feature Ant.
28 D2 Filiaşi Romania
29 C5 Filiates Greece
29 C6 Filiatra Greece
27 E6 Filicudi, Isola i. Italy
77 E4 Filingué Niger
14 F2 Filinskoye Rus. Fed.
29 C5 Filippiada Greece
11 D4 Filipstad Sweden
10 C3 Fillan Norway
128 C4 Fillmore U.S.A.
129 F2 Fillmore U.S.A.
80 D3 Fīltu Ethiopia
152 C3 Fimbulheimen mt. ra. Ant.
152 C3 Fimbulisen ice feature Ant.
26 B3 Finale Ligure Italy
115 H4 Finch Can.
80 C3 Finch'a'ā Hayk' l. Ethiopia
16 E3 Findhorn r. U.K.
61 C1 Fındıkpınarı Turkey
120 B4 Findlay U.S.A.
97 G5 Fingal Aust.
112 E5 Finger Lakes lakes U.S.A.
83 E2 Fingoè Mozambique
60 B2 Finike Turkey
61 A1 Finike Kör. b. Turkey
98 C5 Finke w Aust.
98 C5 Finke Aust.
98 C5 Finke Gorge Nat. Park nat. park. Aust.
96 C2 Finke, Mt h. Aust.
5 H2 Finland country Europe
11 F4 Finland, Gulf of g. Europe
110 D3 Finlay r. Can.
110 D3 Finlay, Mt mt. Can.
97 F3 Finley Aust.
18 E3 Finne ridge Germany
99 F2 Finnigan, Mt h. Aust.
96 C3 Finniss, C. c. Aust.
62 D3 Finnland Finland
10 F1 Finnmark div. Norway
10 E1 Finnsnes Norway
90 □1 Finschhafen P.N.G.
11 D4 Finspång Sweden
19 F3 Finsterwalde Germany
17 D4 Fintona U.K.
76 D3 Fintrou well Mali
99 E4 Finucane Ra. h. Aust.
93 A6 Fiordland National Park nat. park N.Z.
26 B3 Fiorenzuola d'Arda Italy
60 D2 Fırat r. Turkey
128 B3 Firebaugh U.S.A.
111 J2 Firedrake Lake l. Can.
121 G4 Fire Island National Seashore res. U.S.A.
26 C4 Firenze Italy
114 D2 Fire River Can.
77 G3 Firkachi well Niger
146 D3 Firmat Arg.
145 J1 Firmino Alves Brazil
144 C2 Firminópolis Brazil
21 G4 Firminy France
12 E3 Firovo Rus. Fed.
54 B3 Firoza Pakistan
54 D4 Firozabad India
57 F2 Firozkoh reg. Afghanistan
54 D4 Firozpur India
54 C3 Firozpur India
73 F3 1st Cataract rapids Egypt
121 H2 First Connecticut L. l. U.S.A.
99 F2 1st Three Mile Opening chan. Aust.
92 E2 Firth of Thames b. N.Z.
57 C3 Fīrūzābād Iran
57 D1 Fīrūzeh Iran
57 C2 Fīrūzkūh Iran
57 D1 Firyuza Turkmenistan
82 B4 Fish w Namibia
150 E10 Fisher Bay b. Ant.
121 F6 Fisherman I. i. U.S.A.
121 H4 Fishers I. i. U.S.A.
111 N2 Fisher Strait chan. Can.
17 E6 Fishguard U.K.
110 E2 Fish Lake l. Can.
122 A2 Fish Lake l. U.S.A.
129 G2 Fish Lake l. U.S.A.
45 □ Fish Ponds lakes Hong Kong
123 F4 Fish Pt pt U.S.A.
152 B3 Fiske, C. c. Ant.
21 F2 Fismes France
24 B1 Fisterra, Cabo c. Spain
121 H3 Fitchburg U.S.A.
16 K2 Fitjar Norway
91 □12 Fito mt. Western Samoa
72 C5 Fitri, Lac l. Chad
140 B2 Fitzcarrald Peru
111 G3 Fitzgerald Can.
119 D6 Fitzgerald U.S.A.
101 B7 Fitzgerald River Nat. Park nat. park Aust.
98 B2 Fitzmaurice r. Aust.
147 C6 Fitz Roy Arg.
99 G4 Fitzroy r. Aust.
100 C3 Fitzroy r. Aust.
147 B6 Fitz Roy, Co mt. Arg.
100 D3 Fitzroy Crossing Aust.
114 E4 Fitzwilliam I. i. Can.
93 A6 Five Fingers Peninsula pen. N.Z.
26 C3 Fivizzano Italy
92 □2 Fizeau, Mt h. Campbell I. N.Z.
28 D1 Fizeşu Gherlii Romania
79 E4 Fizi Zaire
16 K1 Fjell Norway
74 C2 Fkih Ben Salah Morocco
11 C3 Flå Norway
129 G4 Flagstaff U.S.A.
82 A5 Flagstaff Bay b. St Helena Atlantic Ocean
121 H2 Flagstaff Lake l. U.S.A.
112 E2 Flaherty Island i. Can.
122 B3 Flambeau r. U.S.A.
17 G4 Flamborough Head hd U.K.
18 F2 Fläming h. Germany
126 E3 Flaming Gorge Res. l. U.S.A.
82 C5 Flaminksvlei l. R.S.A.
133 □3 Flanagin Town Trin. & Tobago
20 F1 Flandre reg. France
78 C4 Flandria Zaire
16 D2 Flannan Isles is U.K.
10 D2 Flåsjön l. Sweden
122 E4 Flat r. U.S.A.
126 D2 Flathead L. l. U.S.A.
81 □4 Flat I. i. Mauritius
93 E4 Flat Point pt N.Z.
99 F2 Flattery, C. c. Aust.
126 A1 Flattery, C. c. U.S.A.
119 □1 Flatts Village Bermuda
119 □2 Fleeming Pt pt The Bahamas
17 F5 Fleetwood U.K.
121 F4 Fleetwood U.S.A.
11 B4 Flekkefjord Norway
120 E3 Fleming U.S.A.
120 B5 Flemingsburg U.S.A.
11 E4 Flen Sweden
18 D1 Flensburg Germany
20 D2 Flers France
114 E4 Flesherton Can.
111 H2 Fletcher Lake l. Can.
94 □3 Fletcher, Mt h. Macquarie I. Pac. Oc.
123 F3 Fletcher Pond l. U.S.A.
152 B3 Fletcher Prom. hd Ant.
20 E5 Fleurance France
21 F5 Fleury France
20 E3 Fleury-les-Aubrais France
18 B2 Flevoland div. Netherlands
99 E3 Flinders r. Aust.
101 A7 Flinders B. b. Aust.
96 D3 Flinders Chase Nat. Park nat. park Aust.
99 F2 Flinders Grp is Aust.
97 G4 Flinders I. i. Aust.
99 G3 Flinders Passage chan. Aust.
96 D2 Flinders Ranges mt. ra. Aust.
96 D2 Flinders Ranges Nat. Park nat. park Aust.
99 G3 Flinders Reefs reef Coral Sea Islands Terr. Pac. Oc.
111 J4 Flin Flon Can.
17 F5 Flint U.K.
119 C6 Flint r. U.S.A.
123 F4 Flint U.S.A.
123 F4 Flint r. U.S.A.
87 M6 Flint Island i. Kiribati
99 G5 Flinton Aust.
11 D3 Flisa Norway
25 G2 Flix Spain
20 F1 Flixecourt France
18 F3 Flöha Germany
152 A4 Flood Ra. mt. ra. Ant.
122 A2 Floodwood U.S.A.
118 B4 Flora U.S.A.
21 F4 Florac France
99 F3 Flora Reef reef Coral Sea Islands Terr. Pac. Oc.
98 D3 Floraville Aust.
114 D5 Florence Can.
119 C5 Florence U.S.A.
129 G5 Florence U.S.A.
124 D4 Florence U.S.A.
120 C5 Florence U.S.A.
126 A3 Florence U.S.A.
119 E5 Florence U.S.A.
129 G5 Florence Junction U.S.A.
121 K1 Florenceville Can.
138 B3 Florencia Colombia
147 C5 Florentino Ameghino Arg.
147 C5 Florentino Ameghino, Embalse resr Arg.
146 E4 Flores r. Arg.
142 E2 Flores Pernambuco Brazil
142 D2 Flores Piauí Brazil
142 D2 Flores r. Brazil
131 H5 Flores Guatemala
40 E4 Flores i. Indon.
40 D3 Flores Sea sea Indon.
142 E2 Floresta Brazil
15 C3 Floreşti Moldova
142 D2 Floriano Brazil
140 C1 Floriano Peixoto Brazil
143 C6 Florianopolis Brazil
140 D3 Florida Bolivia
146 E3 Florida Uruguay
119 D6 Florida div. U.S.A.
119 D7 Florida Bay b. U.S.A.
119 D7 Florida City U.S.A.
90 □1 Florida Is is Solomon Is.
144 C4 Flórida Paulista Brazil
132 B2 Florida, Straits of str. The Bahamas/U.S.A.
29 C4 Florina Greece
144 C5 Florínia Brazil
11 B3 Florø Norway
113 H3 Flour Lake l. Can.
122 A4 Floyd U.S.A.
120 C6 Floyd U.S.A.
125 C5 Floydada U.S.A.
129 F4 Floyd, Mt mt. U.S.A.
25 F2 Flúmen r. Spain
27 B6 Flumendosa r. Italy
21 J3 Flums Switz.
25 H1 Fluvià r. Spain
90 □1 Fly r. P.N.G.
120 C5 Fly U.S.A.
94 □2 Flying Fish Cove Christmas I. Indian Ocean
90 □5 Foa i. Tonga
26 G4 Foča Bos.-Herz.
29 F5 Foça Turkey
152 □ Foch, I. i. Kerguelen Indian Ocean
28 F2 Focşani Romania
78 D2 Fodé C.A.R.
98 D3 Foelsche r. Aust.
90 □3 Fofoa i. Tonga
51 F4 Fogang China
65 G4 Fogelevo Kazak.
75 E3 Foggâret ez Zoûa Algeria
27 E5 Foggia Italy
76 □ Fogo i. Cape Verde
113 K4 Fogo I. i. Can.
77 F4 Fogolawa Nigeria
18 D1 Föhr i. Germany
20 E5 Foix France
14 B3 Fokino Rus. Fed.
77 E4 Fokku Nigeria
10 D2 Folda chan. Norway
10 D2 Foldereid Norway
10 C2 Foldfjorden chan. Norway
29 E6 Folegandros i. Greece
114 D2 Foleyet Can.
26 D4 Foligno Italy
17 H6 Folkestone U.K.
119 D6 Folkston U.S.A.
11 C3 Folldal Norway
26 C4 Follonica Italy
128 B2 Folsom Lake l. U.S.A.
81 D7 Fomboni Comoros
14 F2 Fominki Rus. Fed.
12 J1 Fominskaya Rus. Fed.
12 J2 Fominskiy Rus. Fed.
12 G3 Fominskoye Rus. Fed.
111 H3 Fond-du-Lac Can.
111 J3 Fond du Lac r. Can.
122 C4 Fond du Lac U.S.A.
81 □4 Fond du Sac Mauritius
24 B2 Fondevila Spain
27 D5 Fondi Italy
76 C5 Fon Going ridge Guinea
27 B5 Fonni Italy
130 H6 Fonseca, G. de b. Central America
20 F2 Fontainebleau France
113 F3 Fontanges Can.
110 E3 Fontas Can.
110 E3 Fontas r. Can.
139 D4 Fonte Boa Brazil
141 E2 Fonte do Pau-d'Agua Brazil
20 D3 Fontenay-le-Comte France
10 N2 Fontur pt Iceland
90 □5 Fonuafo'ou i. Tonga
90 □3 Fonua Unga i. Tonga
19 H5 Fonyód Hungary
115 F4 Foot's Bay Can.
50 E1 Foping China
97 G3 Forbes Aust.
55 F4 Forbesganj India
126 C1 Forbes, Mt mt. Can.
93 A6 Forbes, Mt mt. N.Z.
18 E4 Forchheim Germany
113 G2 Ford r. Can.
122 D2 Ford r. U.S.A.
11 B3 Førde Norway
111 K2 Forde Lake l. Can.
152 A4 Ford Ra. mt. ra. Ant.
97 F2 Fords Bridge Aust.
125 E5 Fordyce U.S.A.
76 B5 Forécariah Guinea
110 D4 Foresight Mtn mt. Can.
114 E5 Forest Can.
125 F5 Forest U.S.A.
120 B4 Forest U.S.A.
121 G3 Forest Dale U.S.A.
128 B2 Foresthill U.S.A.
97 G5 Forestier, C. hd Aust.
122 A3 Forest Lake U.S.A.
119 C5 Forest Park U.S.A.
113 G4 Forestville Can.
21 F2 Forêt d'Othe forest France
16 F3 Forfar U.K.
20 E2 Forges-les-Eaux France
126 A2 Forks U.S.A.
121 J2 Forks, The U.S.A.
120 E4 Forksville U.S.A.
26 D3 Forlì Italy
25 G3 Formentera i. Spain
25 H3 Formentor, Cap de pt Spain
27 D5 Formia Italy
145 F4 Formiga Brazil
146 E2 Formosa Arg.
146 D1 Formosa div. Arg.
144 E1 Formosa Brazil
142 C3 Formosa do R. Prêto Brazil
142 D3 Formoso r. Bahia Brazil
144 B3 Formoso r. Goiás Brazil
145 E1 Formoso Goiás Brazil
144 B4 Formoso Mato Grosso do Sul Brazil
142 C3 Formoso r. Tocantins Brazil
142 C3 Formoso Tocantins Brazil
16 F3 Forres U.K.
97 E4 Forrest Aust.
101 E6 Forrest Aust.
100 D2 Forrest r. Aust.
122 C5 Forrest U.S.A.
125 F5 Forrest City U.S.A.
122 C4 Forreston U.S.A.
100 D2 Forrest River Abor. Reserve res. Aust.
10 E3 Fors Sweden
99 E3 Forsayth Aust.
10 F2 Forsnäs Sweden
11 F3 Forssa Finland
19 G3 Forst Germany
97 H3 Forster Aust.
125 E4 Forsyth U.S.A.
126 F2 Forsyth U.S.A.
115 G2 Forsythe Can.
99 E4 Forsyth Ra. h. Aust.
54 C3 Fort Abbas Pakistan
112 D3 Fort Albany Can.
140 C2 Fortaleza Bolivia
142 E1 Fortaleza Brazil
129 H5 Fort Apache U.S.A.
110 G4 Fort Assiniboine Can.
122 C4 Fort Atkinson U.S.A.
16 E3 Fort Augustus U.K.
82 D5 Fort Beaufort R.S.A.
126 E2 Fort Benton U.S.A.
111 H3 Fort Black Can.
128 A2 Fort Bragg U.S.A.
111 G3 Fort Chipewyan Can.
125 D5 Fort Cobb Res. resr U.S.A.
126 F3 Fort Collins U.S.A.
98 E4 Fort Constantine Aust.
115 G4 Fort-Coulonge Can.
121 F2 Fort Covington U.S.A.
125 C6 Fort Davis U.S.A.
133 □4 Fort-de-France Martinique Caribbean
133 □4 Fort de France, Baie de b. Martinique Caribbean
119 C5 Fort Deposit U.S.A.
124 E3 Fort Dodge U.S.A.
141 E3 Forte Coimbra Brazil
100 B4 Fortescue r. Aust.
124 E1 Fort Frances U.S.A.
112 E3 Fort George Can.
108 F3 Fort Good Hope Can.
16 E3 Forth r. U.K.
16 F3 Forth, Firth of est. U.K.
115 J3 Fortierville Can.
129 E2 Fortification Range mts U.S.A.
141 D4 Fortín Ávalos Sánchez Paraguay
141 D4 Fortín Capitán Demattei Paraguay
141 E4 Fortín Carlos Antonio López Paraguay
141 E4 Fortín Coronel Bogado Paraguay
141 D4 Fortín Coronel Eugenio Garay Paraguay
141 E4 Fortín Falcón Paraguay
141 E3 Fortín Galpón Paraguay
141 E4 Fortín General Caballero Paraguay
141 D4 Fortín General Mendoza Paraguay
141 D4 Fortin Hernandarías Paraguay
141 D4 Fortin Infante Rivarola Paraguay
141 E4 Fortín Juan deZalazar Paraguay
146 D2 Fortín Lavalle Arg.
141 D4 Fortín Linares Paraguay
141 E4 Fortín Madrejón Paraguay
141 E3 Fortín Paredes Bolivia
146 D1 Fortín Pilcomayo Arg.
141 E4 Fortín Presidente Ayala Paraguay
141 D3 Fortín Ravelo Bolivia
141 D3 Fortín Suárez Arana Bolivia
141 D4 Fortin Tte. Juan E. López Paraguay
121 J1 Fort Kent U.S.A.
119 D7 Fort Lauderdale U.S.A.
110 E2 Fort Liard Can.
133 E3 Fort Liberté Haiti
111 G3 Fort Mackay Can.
110 G5 Fort Macleod Can.
122 B5 Fort Madison U.S.A.
122 B3 Fort McCoy U.S.A.
111 G3 Fort McMurray Can.
108 E3 Fort McPherson Can.
126 G3 Fort Morgan U.S.A.
54 B3 Fort Munro Pakistan
119 D7 Fort Myers U.S.A.
110 E3 Fort Nelson r. Can.
110 E3 Fort Nelson Can.
110 D2 Fort Norman Can.
119 C5 Fort Payne U.S.A.
126 F1 Fort Peck U.S.A.
126 F2 Fort Peck Res. resr U.S.A.
119 D7 Fort Pierce U.S.A.
124 C2 Fort Pierre U.S.A.
81 B4 Fort Portal Uganda
110 F2 Fort Providence Can.
111 J4 Fort Qu'Appelle Can.
110 G2 Fort Resolution Can.
83 D2 Fort Rixon Zimbabwe
93 B7 Fortrose N.Z.
16 E3 Fortrose U.K.
128 A2 Fort Ross U.S.A.
112 E3 Fort Rupert Can.
110 E4 Fort St James Can.
110 E3 Fort St John Can.
110 G4 Fort Saskatchewan Can.
125 E4 Fort Scott U.S.A.
112 C2 Fort Severn Can.
110 E2 Fort Simpson Can.
111 G2 Fort Smith Can.
125 E5 Fort Smith U.S.A.
125 C6 Fort Stockton U.S.A.
127 F5 Fort Sumner U.S.A.
126 A3 Fortuna U.S.A.
124 C1 Fortune U.S.A.
113 J4 Fortune B. b. Can.
110 F3 Fort Vermilion Can.
119 C6 Fort Walton Beach U.S.A.
122 E5 Fort Wayne U.S.A.
139 F2 Fort Wellington Guyana
42 A2 Fort White Myanmar
16 E3 Fort William U.K.
125 D5 Fort Worth U.S.A.
93 □1 Forty Fours, The is Chatham Is N.Z.
108 D3 Fort Yukon U.S.A.
10 D2 Forvik Norway
51 F4 Foshan China
76 D5 Foso Ghana
26 A3 Fossano Italy
97 F4 Foster Aust.
110 B3 Foster, Mt mt. Can./U.S.A.
120 B4 Fostoria U.S.A.
83 H3 Fotadrevo Madagascar
78 B1 Fotokol Cameroon
81 □3 Fouce, Pte de la pt Rodrigues I. Mauritius
20 B3 Fouesnant France
78 B4 Fougamou Gabon
20 D2 Fougères France

16 F1 Foula i. U.K.
73 G3 Foul Bay b. Egypt
78 A4 Foulenzem Gabon
42 A3 Foul I. i. Myanmar
17 H6 Foulness Point pt U.K.
56 C4 Foul Pt pt Sri Lanka
93 C4 Foulwind, Cape c. N.Z.
78 B2 Foumban Cameroon
74 C2 Foum Zguid Morocco
152 B3 Foundation Ice Stream ice feature Ant.
122 A4 Fountain U.S.A.
20 D4 Fouras France
21 F3 Fourchambault France
128 D4 Four Corners U.S.A.
93 ¹ Fournier, C. c. Chatham Is N.Z.
29 F6 Fournoi i. Greece
133 ¹ Four Paths Jamaica
122 C2 Fourteen Mile Pt pt U.S.A.
73 F4 4th Cataract rapids Sudan
76 B4 Fouta Djallon reg. Guinea
93 A7 Foveaux Strait str. N.Z.
132 C1 Fowl Cay i. The Bahamas
122 C4 Fowler U.S.A.
124 F4 Fowler U.S.A.
152 B3 Fowler U.S.A.
96 C3 Fowlers B. b. Aust.
96 C2 Fowlers Bay Aust.
113 L1 Fox r. Can.
122 C4 Fox r. U.S.A.
110 F4 Fox Creek Can.
109 L3 Foxe Basin g. Can.
109 K3 Foxe Channel str. Can.
109 L3 Foxe Peninsula pen. Can.
93 C5 Fox Glacier N.Z.
108 B4 Fox Islands is U.S.A.
110 G3 Fox Lake Can.
122 C4 Fox Lake U.S.A.
92 E4 Foxton N.Z.
92 E4 Foxton Beach N.Z.
17 D4 Foyle, Lough inlet Rep. of Ire./U.K.
17 C5 Foynes Rep. of Ire.
24 C1 Foz Spain
138 C5 Foz de Gregório Brazil
143 B6 Foz do Cunene Angola
138 D4 Foz do Jutaí Brazil
25 G2 Fraga Spain
152 D4 Framnes Mts mts Ant.
144 E4 Franca Brazil
90 ⁻² Français, Récif des reef Pac. Oc.
27 F5 Francavilla Fontana Italy
4 F4 France country Europe
109 R2 France, Île de i. Greenland
96 F4 Frances Aust.
110 D2 Frances r. Can.
110 D2 Frances Lake Can.
110 D2 Frances Lake l. Can.
138 C4 Francés, Pta pt Cuba
122 D5 Francesville U.S.A.
78 B4 Franceville Gabon
21 H3 Franche-Comté div. France
124 D3 Francis Case, Lake l. U.S.A.
138 C4 Francisco de Orellana Peru
130 D3 Francisco I. Madero Mexico
145 G2 Francisco Sá Brazil
121 H2 Francis, Lake l. U.S.A.
82 D3 Francistown Botswana
145 E5 Franco da Rocha Brazil
110 D4 François Lake l. Can.
126 E3 Francs Peak summit U.S.A.
75 F2 Frane Algeria
18 F3 Frankenberg Germany
18 D3 Frankenberg (Eder) Germany
123 F4 Frankenmuth U.S.A.
18 E4 Frankenwald forest Germany
133 ¹ Frankfield Jamaica
122 B5 Frankfort U.S.A.
118 C4 Frankfort U.S.A.
121 H3 Frankfort U.S.A.
18 D3 Frankfurt am Main Germany
19 G2 Frankfurt (Oder) Germany
129 E1 Franklin U.S.A.
18 E4 Fränkische Alb h. Germany
18 E4 Fränkische Schweiz reg. Germany
101 B7 Frankland r. Aust.
126 E3 Franklin U.S.A.
125 C6 Franklin U.S.A.
121 H4 Franklin U.S.A.
119 D5 Franklin U.S.A.
121 H3 Franklin U.S.A.
121 K3 Franklin U.S.A.
120 D6 Franklin U.S.A.
119 C5 Franklin U.S.A.
120 D5 Franklin U.S.A.
108 F2 Franklin Bay b. Can.
126 C1 Franklin D. Roosevelt Lake l. U.S.A.
96 D3 Franklin Harb. b. Aust.
152 B1 Franklin I. i. Ant.
110 E2 Franklin Mountains mt. ra. Can.
93 A6 Franklin Mts mts N.Z.
97 F5 Franklin Sd chan. Aust.
109 J2 Franklin Str. chan. Can.
11 B3 Fränsta Sweden
114 C2 Franz Can.
93 C5 Franz Josef Glacier N.Z.
27 B6 Frasca, Capo della pt Italy
27 D5 Frascati Italy
110 F4 Fraser r. Can.
112 H2 Fraser r. Can.
82 B5 Fraser R.S.A.
25 F3 Fraserburg R.S.A.
16 F3 Fraserburgh U.K.
99 H4 Fraserdale Can.
99 H5 Fraser I. i. Aust.
99 H5 Fraser I. Nat. Park nat. park Aust.
110 E4 Fraser Lake Can.
93 B6 Fraser, Mt h. N.Z.
110 E4 Fraser Plateau plat. Can.
92 F3 Frasertown N.Z.
114 C2 Frater Can.
28 E3 Frăteşti Romania
21 J3 Frauenfeld Switz.
146 E3 Fray Bentos Uruguay
122 A3 Frederic U.S.A.
122 A3 Frederic U.S.A.
11 C5 Fredericia Denmark
101 B5 Frederick U.S.A.
125 D5 Frederick U.S.A.
127 F5 Frederick U.S.A.
99 H4 Frederick Reef reef Coral Sea Islands Terr. Pac. Oc.
125 D6 Fredericksburg U.S.A.
127 E5 Fredericksburg U.S.A.
110 C3 Frederick Sound chan. U.S.A.
113 H3 Fredericton Can.
109 P3 Frederik E. Hyde Fjord inlet Greenland
11 C4 Frederikshavn Denmark
119 ⁻³ Frederikshåb Virgin Is Caribbean
133 F3 Frederiksted Virgin Is Caribbean
11 D5 Frederiksværk Denmark
123 F4 Fredonia U.S.A.
120 D5 Fredonia U.S.A.
11 C4 Fredrika Sweden
11 C4 Fredrikstad Norway
121 F3 Freehold U.S.A.
121 F3 Freeland U.S.A.

96 D2 Freeling Heights mt. Aust.
98 C4 Freeling, Mt mt. Aust.
128 C2 Freel Peak summit U.S.A.
124 D3 Freeman U.S.A.
122 D5 Freeman, Lake l. U.S.A.
132 C1 Freeport The Bahamas
122 D5 Freeport U.S.A.
121 H4 Freeport U.S.A.
125 E6 Freeport U.S.A.
132 C1 Freeport City The Bahamas
125 D7 Freer U.S.A.
133 ¹ Free State div. R.S.A.
133 ¹ Freetown Antigua Caribbean
76 B5 Freetown Sierra Leone
25 C3 Fregenal de la Sierra Spain
18 F3 Freiberg Germany
18 D3 Freiburg im Breisgau Germany
21 G2 Freistadt Austria
18 D3 Freinsheim Germany
146 B2 Freirina Chile
18 E4 Freising Germany
19 F3 Freistadt Austria
24 C2 Freixo de Espada à Cinta Portugal
21 H5 Fréjus France
16 K1 Frekhaug Norway
101 A7 Fremantle Aust.
124 D3 Fremont U.S.A.
120 B4 Fremont U.S.A.
129 G2 Fremont U.S.A.
124 D4 Fremont r. U.S.A.
97 F4 Frenchman r. Can./U.S.A.
128 C2 Frenchman U.S.A.
93 F5 Frenchman Cap mt. Aust.
128 B2 Frenchman L. l. U.S.A.
123 F3 Frenchman L. l. U.S.A.
93 D4 French Pass N.Z.
87 N6 French Polynesia terr. Pac. Oc.
121 J1 Frenchville U.S.A.
75 E1 Frenda Algeria
19 J4 Frenštát pod Radhoštěm Czech Rep.
76 B4 Fresco Côte d'Ivoire
142 B2 Fresco r. Brazil
129 G6 Fresnal Canyon U.S.A.
130 E4 Fresnillo Mexico
128 C3 Fresno r. U.S.A.
128 C3 Fresno U.S.A.
25 E3 Freu, Cap des pt Spain
18 E4 Freudenstadt Germany
20 F1 Frévent France
98 C3 Frewena Aust.
101 A5 Freycinet Est. b. Aust.
97 G5 Freycinet Nat. Park nat. park Aust.
21 H2 Freyming-Merlebach France
146 D3 Freyre Arg.
76 B4 Fria Guinea
82 A2 Fria, Cape c. Namibia
146 D2 Frías Arg.
21 H3 Fribourg Switz.
18 D5 Friedrichshafen Germany
133 ¹ Friendship Jamaica
121 J3 Friendship U.S.A.
18 E2 Friesack Germany
18 F2 Friesland div. Netherlands
18 C2 Friesoythe Germany
81 ⁻¹ Frigate I. i. Seychelles
125 D6 Frio r. U.S.A.
24 C1 Friol Spain
129 F2 Frisco Mt mt. U.S.A.
26 E2 Friuli - Venezia Giulia div. Italy
109 M3 Frobisher Bay b. Can.
111 H3 Frobisher Lake l. Can.
10 C3 Frohavet b. Norway
18 F3 Frohburg Germany
19 G5 Frohnleiten Austria
13 F5 Frolishch Rus. Fed.
12 K2 Frolovskaya Rus. Fed.
19 J1 Frombork Poland
17 F6 Frome U.K.
96 D2 Frome Downs Aust.
96 D2 Frome, lake salt flat Aust.
80 D3 Frontera Mexico
25 ⁻¹ Frontera, i. Canary Is Spain
131 G5 Frontera, Pta pt Mexico
130 C2 Fronteras Mexico
21 F5 Frontignan France
127 E5 Front Royal U.S.A.
27 D5 Frosinone Italy
10 C3 Frostburg U.S.A.
10 C3 Frøya i. Norway
21 H3 Frutigen Switz.
19 H4 Frýdek-Místek Czech Rep.
21 H2 Freyburg Germany
11 H2 Fryeburg U.S.A.
50 D1 Fu'an China
90 ⁻³ Fua'amotu Tonga
90 ⁻³ Fuamotu i. Tonga
51 D5 Fu'an China
26 C4 Fucecchio Italy
19 H5 Fudai Japan
51 D4 Fuding China
24 D4 Fuengirola Spain
24 D4 Fuenlabrada Spain
25 F3 Fuente-Álamo Spain
25 E3 Fuente-Álamo Spain
119 C5 Fuente de Cantos Spain
24 D3 Fuente Obejuna Spain
24 D3 Fuentesaúco Spain
25 F2 Fuentes de Ebro Spain
147 B7 Fuerte Bulnes Chile
146 D4 Fuerte Olimpo Paraguay
25 ⁻¹ Fuerteventura i. Canary Is Spain
17 H2 Fuga i. Phil.
16 D1 Fuglafjørdur Faeroes
51 D3 Fugou China
51 C1 Fugu China
51 F1 Fuhai China
65 H3 Fuji r. Japan
47 G6 Fujian div. China
47 G6 Fujieda Japan
47 G6 Fuji-Hakone-Izu National Park nat. park Japan
47 G6 Fujin China
47 G6 Fujinomiya Japan
47 G6 Fujisawa Japan
47 G6 Fujiyoshida Japan
47 G6 Fūka Japan
47 G6 Fukagawa Japan
46 H4 Fukuchiyama Japan
47 F6 Fukue Japan
47 F6 Fukue-jima i. Japan
47 F6 Fukui Japan
46 C7 Fukuoka Japan

46 C7 Fukuoka div. Japan
47 H5 Fukushima div. Japan
46 H3 Fukushima Japan
47 H5 Fukushima Japan
46 C8 Fukuyama Japan
76 A4 Fulacunda Guinea-Bissau
57 C1 Fūlād Mairalleh Iran
90 ⁻³ Fulaga i. Fiji
21 J2 Fulda r. Germany
18 D3 Fulda Germany
50 D2 Fuling China
133 ⁻³ Fullarton Trin. & Tobago
111 M2 Fullerton, Cape hd Can.
128 D5 Fullerton U.S.A.
19 H4 Fulnek Czech Rep.
122 B5 Fulton U.S.A.
118 B4 Fulton U.S.A.
124 F4 Fulton U.S.A.
121 E3 Fulton U.S.A.
21 G2 Fumay France
20 E4 Fumel France
47 H6 Funabashi Japan
86 J5 Funafuti i. Tuvalu
24 ⁻¹ Funchal Madeira Portugal
138 C1 Fundación Colombia
140 B3 Fundão Brazil
24 C2 Fundão Portugal
130 D3 Fundición Mexico
28 F2 Fundulea Romania
113 G5 Fundy, Bay of g. Can.
113 G4 Fundy Nat. Park nat. park Can.
128 C2 Funeral Peak summit U.S.A.
83 E3 Funhalouro Mozambique
51 D4 Funing China
51 C1 Funing China
51 E1 Funiu Shan mt. ra. China
76 C3 Funtua Nigeria
51 D3 Fuping China
51 C1 Fuping China
50 D3 Fuquan China
83 E1 Furancungo Mozambique
46 J2 Furano Japan
46 K2 Füren-ko l. Japan
14 E1 Furmanov Rus. Fed.
64 C3 Furmanovo Kazak.
128 D3 Furnace Creek U.S.A.
97 G5 Furneaux Group is Aust.
18 F2 Fürstenberg Brandenburg Germany
18 E2 Fürstenwalde Germany
18 E4 Fürth Bayern Germany
18 E4 Furth im Wald Germany
46 H2 Furubira Japan
47 H4 Furukawa Japan
47 H4 Furukawa Japan
109 K3 Fury and Hecla Strait Can.
138 C1 Fusagasugá Colombia
49 G4 Fushun China
50 A4 Fushun China
50 A4 Fushun China
51 E2 Fushun China
48 B3 Fusong China
49 H3 Fusui China
51 H3 Fuxin China
51 G2 Fuxin China
49 H3 Fuyang China
51 E2 Fuyang China
51 G2 Fuyu China
49 H3 Fuyu China
49 J2 Fuyuan China
50 D3 Fuyuan China
19 K5 Füzesabony Hungary
51 D3 Fuzhou China
51 D3 Fuzhou Jiangxi China
11 C5 Fyn i. Denmark
29 C5 Fyteies Greece
133 ⁻³ Fyzabad Trin. & Tobago

54 A4 Gajar Pakistan
80 C4 Gajos well Kenya
78 C2 Gakarorai mt. R.S.A.
77 F5 Gakem Nigeria
54 C1 Gakuch Pakistan
65 H5 Gakuch Jammu and Kashmir
55 G3 Gala China
64 F5 Galaasiya Uzbekistan
61 A5 Galāla el Bahariya, G. el plat. Egypt
73 E5 Galāla el Qibliya, G. el plat. Egypt
81 C5 Galana r. Kenya
146 C2 Galán, Co mt. Arg.
19 H4 Galanta Slovakia
41 ⁻¹ Galap Palau
138 ⁻¹ Galápagos, Islas is Ecuador
17 F4 Galashiels U.K.
28 F2 Galaţi Romania
29 D4 Galatista Greece
120 C6 Galax U.S.A.
99 E3 Galbraith Aust.
25 ⁻¹ Gáldar Canary Is Spain
10 C3 Galdhøpiggen summit Norway
130 D3 Galeana Mexico
57 C4 Galeh Dār Iran
122 B4 Galena U.S.A.
133 ⁻³ Galeota Pt pt Trinidad Trin. & Tobago
96 D4 Galeothe, C. hd Aust.
131 F6 Galera, Pta pt Mexico
147 B5 Galera, Punta hd Chile
82 C4 Galeshewe R.S.A.
118 B4 Galesville U.S.A.
120 E4 Galeton U.S.A.
81 ⁻⁵ Galets, Pte des pt Réunion Indian Ocean
80 E3 Galgaduud div. Somalia
142 C3 Galheirão r. Brazil
13 G7 Gali Georgia
144 D5 Gália Brazil
28 D2 Galicea Mare Romania
12 G3 Galich Rus. Fed.
12 G3 Galicheskaya Vozvyshennost' h. Rus. Fed.
24 C1 Galicia div. Spain
51 E3 Galilee, L. salt flat Aust.
49 F5 Galion Brazil
80 E3 Galiraw Mts mts U.S.A.
73 G5 Gallabat Sudan
126 E2 Gallatin r. U.S.A.
119 C4 Gallatin U.S.A.
56 C5 Galle Sri Lanka
147 B7 Gallegos r. Arg.
54 B2 Gālēli, Massif mts China
75 F4 Gallinas, Pta pt Colombia
27 G5 Gallipoli Italy
120 B5 Gallipolis U.S.A.
10 F2 Gällivare Sweden
25 F2 Gállego r. Spain
129 H4 Gallo, Capo c. Italy
121 E3 Gallo I. i. U.S.A.
129 H5 Gallup U.S.A.
81 D5 Galma Galla waterhole Kenya
56 D3 Galong China
56 D3 Galoya Sri Lanka
80 E2 Gal Oya in Sri Lanka
80 E2 Gal Shiikh Somalia
74 B3 Galt U.K.
74 B3 Galtat Zemmour Western Sahara
17 C5 Galtee Mountains h. Rep. of Ire.
57 C4 Galūgāh-e Āslyeh Iran
122 B5 Galva U.S.A.
125 E6 Galveston U.S.A.
125 E6 Galveston Bay b. U.S.A.
140 C3 Galway Arg.
55 H2 Galwa Nepal
17 C5 Galway Rep. of Ire.
17 C5 Galway Bay g. Rep. of Ire.
42 D2 Gâm r. Vietnam
54 B1 Gamā Brazil
22 D1 Gamaches France
47 F6 Gamagōri Japan
138 C1 Gamarra Colombia
77 G4 Gamawa Nigeria
76 B4 Gamba Angola
79 A4 Gamba China
80 B3 Gambaga Ethiopia
80 B3 Gambela Ethiopia
80 B3 Gambela National Park nat. park Ethiopia
122 D5 Gambell U.S.A.
76 A3 Gambia, The country Africa
75 F4 Garet El Djenoun mt. Algeria
76 A3 Gambia r. Senegal
98 B1 Gambier, Îles is Fr. Poly. Pac. Oc.
90 ⁻⁴ Gambier, Îles is Fr. Poly. Pac. Oc.
96 D3 Gambier Is is Aust.
113 K4 Gambo Can.
78 B3 Gamboma Congo
133 K4 Gamboa Panama
78 B3 Gambos Angola
54 D2 Gamerco U.S.A.
11 E4 Gamleby Sweden
80 D2 Gammams well Sudan
10 F2 Gammelstaden Sweden
24 D2 Gamonal Spain
56 D4 Gampola Sri Lanka
54 B3 Gamud mt. Ethiopia
54 D4 Gamut China
54 D4 Ganado U.S.A.
129 H4 Gananoque Can.
57 C4 Gānāveh Iran
13 G7 Gäncä Azerbaijan
78 B3 Gangala-na-Bodio Zaire

55 G5 Ganga, Mouths of the Bangladesh
54 C3 Ganganagar India
54 C3 Gangapur India
54 C4 Gangapur India
77 F4 Gangara Niger
42 A2 Gangaw Myanmar
42 B1 Gangaw Range mt. ra. Myanmar
55 E3 Gangca China
55 E3 Gangdisê Shan mt. ra. China
21 F5 Ganges France
56 C3 Gangotri India
50 D1 Gangtok India
50 D1 Gangu China
56 D2 Ganjam India
57 B3 Gangjān Iran
24 C2 Ganluo China
97 F3 Gannan India
24 C2 Gannat France
21 F3 Gannat France
126 E3 Gannett Peak summit U.S.A.
15 B1 Gannopil' Ukraine
120 B6 Gansu div. China
48 D5 Ganquan China
19 H4 Gänserndorf Austria
80 D4 Gansu div. China
80 D4 Gantamaa Somalia
96 D4 Gantheaume, C. hd Aust.
13 H6 Gant'iadi Georgia
40 B2 Gantung China
49 H5 Ganwan India
80 D5 Gan Xian China
77 G5 Ganye Nigeria
50 D1 Ganyu China
64 C3 Ganyushkino Kazak.
51 D3 Ganzhou China
76 B3 Gao Mali
77 E3 Gao Mali
77 E3 Gao'an China
80 B2 Gaocheng China
82 D4 Gaohebu China
51 F2 Gaolan China
50 B3 Gaoligong Shan mt. ra. China
49 F5 Gaomi China
51 E3 Gaomutang China
49 F5 Gaoqing China
48 A5 Gaotai China
55 F2 Gaotang China
76 B4 Gaoua China
76 A3 Gaoual Guinea
50 D2 Gao Xian China
48 E5 Gaoyang China
51 E3 Gaoyi China
51 E3 Gaoyou China
51 E3 Gaoyou Hu l. China
51 D3 Gaozhou China
21 H4 Gap France
54 D2 Gar China
75 G2 Gar India
54 B2 Gar India
49 E4 Gar r. China
80 E3 Garaad Somalia
80 D3 Garachiné Panama
138 B2 Garadag Somalia
75 F4 Garagheh Iran
19 G4 Garah Aust.
76 C4 Gara, Lough l. Rep. of Ire.
78 C3 Garamba r. Zaire
78 C3 Garamba, Parc National de la nat. park Zaire
142 E2 Garanhuns Brazil
145 E2 Garanuns Brazil
78 B2 Gara C.A.R.
80 D4 Garbahaarrey Somalia
81 D4 Garba Tula Kenya
128 A1 Garberville U.S.A.
18 D2 Garbsen Niedersachsen Germany
144 D5 Garça Brazil
142 D2 Garças r. Brazil
144 B4 Garças, R. das r. Brazil
131 F5 Garcia Sola, Embalse de resr Spain
26 D2 Garda, Lago di l. Italy
75 F1 Garde, Cap de c. Algeria
124 C4 Garden City U.S.A.
122 D5 Garden City U.S.A.
128 C5 Garden Grove U.S.A.
119 C6 Garden Hill Can.
111 L4 Garden I. i. Aust.
121 J3 Garden I. i. U.S.A.
76 C3 Gardēz Afghanistan
121 J2 Gardiner U.S.A.
126 E2 Gardiner U.S.A.
128 C4 Gardner I. i. U.S.A.
121 G3 Gardner U.S.A.
150 H4 Gardner Pinnacles is U.S.A.
128 C3 Gardnerville U.S.A.
129 E5 Gardony Hungary
80 E3 Garēn r. India
75 F4 Garet El Djenoun mt. Algeria
72 E2 Garet el Gorane depres. Algeria
96 D3 Gargano, Promontorio del hd Italy
56 C3 Gargždai Lithuania
54 C5 Garhakota India
55 F5 Garhi Khairo Pakistan
54 C4 Garhi Malehra India
55 E5 Garibaldi, Mt mt. U.S.A.
112 E5 Garibaldi Prov. Park nat. park Can.
57 C4 Ge'gyai China
82 B5 Garies R.S.A.
81 C5 Garissa Kenya
54 B1 Garkalne Latvia
11 H4 Garland U.S.A.
125 D5 Garland U.S.A.
126 D3 Garland U.S.A.
18 E5 Garmisch-Partenkirchen Germany
57 D3 Garmsar reg. Afghanistan
57 D3 Garmsel reg. Afghanistan
122 E6 Garnett U.S.A.
54 E4 Garnett Lake l. Aust.
20 E4 Garonne r. France
80 E3 Garoowe Somalia
78 B2 Garoua Cameroon
78 B2 Garoua Boulai Cameroon
76 C3 Garouga, Mt Mali
57 C4 Gārpenberg Sweden
76 B3 Garu China
54 E5 Garut India
93 B6 Garut Indon.
93 B6 Garvie Mts mts N.Z.
54 D5 Garwolin Poland
122 D5 Gary U.S.A.
54 D3 Garyarsa China
54 D3 Garyi China
131 H4 Garza García Mexico
57 D2 Gar Zangbo r. China
50 B2 Garzê China
138 B3 Garzón Colombia
20 D4 Gascogne reg. France
20 D5 Gascogne, Golfe de g. France/Spain

124 E4 Gasconade r. U.S.A.
101 A5 Gascoyne r. Aust.
101 B5 Gascoyne Junction Aust.
101 B5 Gascoyne, Mt h. Aust.
54 D2 Gasherbrum mt. China/Jammu and Kashmir
147 B3 Gashua Nigeria
77 G4 Gashua Nigeria
77 F4 Gangara Niger
42 A2 Gangaw Range mt. ra. Myanmar
113 H4 Gaspé Can.
113 G4 Gaspé, C. c. Can.
113 G4 Gaspé, Péninsule de pen. Can.
113 G4 Gaspésie, Parc de la nat. park Can.
21 E5 Gassan vol Japan
47 H4 Gassan vol Japan
76 A4 Gassane Senegal
119 D5 Gastonia U.S.A.
29 C6 Gastouni Greece
24 C2 Gastre Arg.
25 E4 Gata, C. c. Cyprus
25 E4 Gata, Cabo de c. Spain
25 E4 Gata, Sierra de mt. ra. Spain
11 H4 Gatchina Rus. Fed.
120 B6 Gate City U.S.A.
12 D3 Gateshead U.K.
125 D6 Gatesville U.S.A.
129 F2 Gateway U.S.A.
121 F4 Gateway National Recreational Area res. U.S.A.
115 H3 Gatineau r. Can.
14 C2 Gatineau Can.
57 C3 Gatrūyeh Iran
19 H5 Gatton Aust.
130 K7 Gatún L. l. Panama
145 G4 Gatvand Iran
90 ⁻⁸ Gau i. Fiji
111 K3 Gauer Lake l. Can.
10 C3 Gaula r. Norway
55 E5 Gauley Bridge U.S.A.
146 D2 Gaurella India
82 D4 Gauteng div. R.S.A.
57 C4 Gavāter Iran
54 C4 Gāvbandī Iran
54 C4 Gāvbūs, Kūh-e mt. ra. Iran
29 D7 Gavdopoula i. Greece
29 D7 Gavdos i. Greece
60 F3 Gaveh r. Iran
60 E3 Gavilan r. U.S.A.
80 D3 Gäviko India
138 C4 Gaviota U.S.A.
11 E3 Gävle Sweden
10 E3 Gävleborg div. Sweden
14 F3 Gavrilovka Vtoraya Rus. Fed.
14 E1 Gavrilov Posad Rus. Fed.
14 F1 Gavrilov-Yam Rus. Fed.
72 B2 Gawai Myanmar
18 D2 Gawler Aust.
96 C3 Gawler Ranges h. Aust.
91 C3 Gaxun Nur salt l. China
21 H4 Gay U.S.A.
64 E2 Gay Rus. Fed.
54 D4 Gaya r. China
49 J4 Gaya r. China
76 D3 Gaya Niger
54 B1 Gaya India
26 B3 Gaya Niger
26 B3 Genoa r. Aust.
145 G4 Gaza div. Mozambique
61 B4 Gaza Gaza
64 E5 Gazak Iran
128 A1 Gazalkent Uzbekistan
18 D2 Gazandzhyk Turkmenistan
80 E3 Gazawa Cameroon
98 B4 George Gills Ra. mt. ra. Aust.
142 D2 Garça Brazil
142 D2 Garças r. Brazil
144 B4 Garças, R. das r. Brazil
142 D2 Garcias Brazil
60 D2 Gaziantep Turkey
60 D2 Gaziantep div. Turkey
49 E2 Gazimur r. Rus. Fed.
49 E2 Gazimuro-Ononskiy Khrebet mt. ra. Rus. Fed.
49 E2 Gazimurskiy Kr. mt. ra.
57 D2 Gazimurskiy Zavod Rus. Fed.
60 C2 Gazipaşa Turkey
54 F3 Gazli India
54 D2 Gazni Uzbekistan
57 A4 Gaz Māhū Iran
57 A4 Gaz Sāleh Iran
78 C3 Gbaaka Zaire
76 D4 Gbarnga Liberia
78 B3 Gbadolite Zaire
76 B4 Gbangbatok Sierra Leone
76 D4 Gbarnga Liberia
77 F5 Gboko Nigeria
76 D4 Gbova Liberia
19 J1 Gdańsk Poland
11 G5 Gdańsk, Gulf of g. Poland
19 J1 Gdov Rus. Fed.
19 H1 Gdynia Poland
80 E3 Gdyñ div. Somalia
80 E3 Gebeit Sudan
73 G5 Gedaref Sudan
73 G5 Gedid Ras el Fil Sudan
60 A2 Gediz r. Turkey
60 B2 Gediz Turkey
139 E3 Gedney Guyana
80 D2 Gedo div. Somalia
80 D4 Gedo Somalia
11 D5 Gedser Denmark
18 A4 Geel Belgium
97 E4 Geelong Aust.
101 B5 Geelvink Channel chan. Aust.
18 D2 Geeste r. Germany
18 E2 Geesthacht Germany
82 E3 Gefersa Ethiopia
18 F3 Gehren Germany
18 E3 Geilenkirchen Germany
10 C3 Geilo Norway
57 D2 Geishing Iran
60 F3 Geit r. Iran
57 D2 Geislingen an der Steige Germany
18 E4 Geislingen Germany
81 B4 Geita Tanzania
80 E3 Gejiu China
50 C3 Gejiu China
80 D3 Geladī Ethiopia
55 E3 Ge'gyai China
57 C4 Geklengkui, Ozero l. China
18 D3 Geldern Germany
60 B2 Gelembe Turkey
60 B2 Gelendost Turkey
13 F6 Gelendzhik Rus. Fed.
60 A1 Gelibolu Turkey
60 B3 Gelidonya Burnu pt Turkey
18 E3 Gelnhausen Germany
18 D3 Gelsenkirchen Germany
42 C5 Gemas Malaysia
18 A4 Gembloux Belgium
78 B3 Gemena Zaire
60 C2 Gemerek Turkey
60 B1 Gemlik Turkey
60 B1 Gemlik Körfezi b. Turkey
26 E2 Gemona del Friuli Italy
20 D4 Gémozac France

73 F2 Gemsa Egypt
82 C4 Gemsbok National Park nat. park Botswana
49 E2 Gen r. China
101 A5 Gen r. China
80 C2 Genalē Wenz r. Ethiopia
80 C2 Gendoa r. Ethiopia
146 D4 General Acha Arg.
19 F5 General Alvear Mendoza Arg.
141 E5 General Artigas Paraguay
146 E3 General Belgrano Arg.
146 E3 General Belgrano II Argentina Base Ant.
152 B2 General Bernardo O'Higgins Chile Base Ant.
125 D7 General Bravo Mexico
144 B1 General Carneiro Brazil
147 B5 General Carrera, L. l. Chile
131 D7 General Cepeda Mexico
146 C4 General Conesa Buenos Aires Arg.
147 D5 General Conesa Rio Negro Arg.
11 H4 Ghanādah, Rās pt U.A.E.
146 E3 General Guido Arg.
146 E4 General J. Madariaga Arg.
140 C3 General Lagos Chile
146 C3 General La Madrid Arg.
146 E4 General Lavalle Arg.
146 D4 General Levalle Arg.
130 K7 General Luna Phil.
130 K7 General MacArthur Phil.
146 D1 General Martin Miguel de Güemes Arg.
146 D3 General Pico Arg.
146 D3 General Pinedo Arg.
146 C4 General Pinto Arg.
146 E3 General Roca Arg.
57 C4 General Santos Phil.
130 E4 General Terán Mexico
28 F3 General Toshevo Bulgaria
146 C3 General Villegas Arg.
120 D3 Geneseo U.S.A.
122 B5 Geneseo U.S.A.
80 C3 Geneva U.S.A.
121 E3 Geneva U.S.A.
124 D3 Geneva U.S.A.
120 C4 Geneva U.S.A.
21 H3 Genève Switz.
24 D4 Genil r. Spain
18 A4 Genk Belgium
46 C7 Genkai-nada b. Japan
26 B3 Gennargentu, Monti del mt. ra. Italy
18 D3 Gennep Germany
79 D4 Gennes France
147 B5 Genoa r. Aust.
26 B3 Genova Italy
4 E5 Genova, Golfo di g. Italy
40 A3 Genteng i. Indon.
42 C7 Genteng Indon.
18 F2 Genthin Germany
120 A4 Genthin Germany
20 F4 Gentioux, Plateau de plat. France
48 B3 Gichgeniyn Nuruu mt. ra. Mongolia
80 D3 Gidda Ethiopia
54 C1 Gidda Ethiopia
113 G3 George r. Can.
82 C6 George R.S.A.
121 H2 George, C. c. Kerguelen Indian Ocean
96 E1 George, L. salt flat Aust.
81 A4 George, L. l. Uganda
121 G3 George, Lake l. U.S.A.
119 D6 George, Lake l. U.S.A.
92 F4 George Sd inlet N.Z.
97 G4 George Town Ascension Atlantic Ocean
42 C4 George Town Malaysia
133 G4 Georgetown Cayman Is Caribbean
99 E2 Georgetown Aust.
115 J4 Georgetown Can.
139 F2 Georgetown Guyana
119 E5 Georgetown U.S.A.
118 B4 Georgetown U.S.A.
125 D6 Georgetown U.S.A.
120 A5 Georgetown U.S.A.
119 E5 Georgetown U.S.A.
119 F5 Georgetown U.S.A.
76 B3 George V Ld chan. Ant.
98 D1 George V Ld chan. Ant.
152 B6 George V Sd chan. Ant.
152 A1 George VI Sound g. Ant.
97 G5 George Town Aust.
72 E1 Georgia div. Asia
119 D5 Georgia div. U.S.A.
115 F4 Georgian Bay b. Can.
114 E4 Georgian Bay Island National Park nat. park Can.
54 C3 Georgina w. Aust.
98 D4 Georgina w. Aust.
64 D2 Georgiyevka Kazak.
64 E2 Georgiyevka Kazak.
13 G6 Georgiyevsk Rus. Fed.
14 G2 Georgiyevskoye Rus. Fed.
18 F3 Gera Germany
18 A4 Geraardsbergen Belgium
21 J5 Gérardmer France
60 B1 Gerede r. Turkey
60 C1 Gerede Turkey
57 E3 Gereshk Afghanistan
60 A2 Gerihun Sierra Leone
60 C1 Germencik Turkey
18 D4 Germersheim Germany
18 D3 Gernsheim Germany
80 B1 Geronimo U.S.A.
11 F4 Gers div. France
51 C2 Gêrzê China
73 F2 Gerze Turkey
80 E3 Gesira div. Somalia
18 E2 Gesthacht Germany
18 E3 Gescher Germany
18 D3 Geseke Germany
19 J4 Gešir Iran
19 J4 Getafe Spain
57 D2 Gettysburg U.S.A.
124 D2 Gettysburg U.S.A.
120 E5 Gettysburg National Military Park res. U.S.A.
152 A4 Getz Ice Shelf ice feature Ant.
18 D2 Getestthal Germany

29 D4 Gevgelija Macedonia
21 G3 Gevrey-Chambertin France
25 E1 Gexto Spain
61 A1 Geydik D. mts Turkey
61 A1 Geyik Dağ mt. Turkey
43 F5 Geylang Singapore
60 B1 Geyve Turkey
83 C1 Gezhouba China
73 G3 Geziret Mukawwar i. Sudan
138 B4 Girón Ecuador
20 D4 Gironde est. France
25 G1 Gironella Spain
16 F3 Girvan U.K.
92 G3 Gisborne N.Z.
72 A4 Ghādāmis Libya
72 A4 Ghaddūwah Libya
73 F3 Ghafurov Tajikistan
56 B2 Ghaghara r. India
55 B3 Ghana country Africa
11 H4 Ghanādah, Rās pt U.A.E.
82 C3 Ghanzi Botswana
82 C3 Ghanzi div. Botswana
60 C4 Gharandal Jordan
72 B2 Ghārb, jebel mt. Egypt
54 B4 Gharo Pakistan
57 B4 Ghār, Ras al pt Saudi Arabia
54 B1 Gharyan Libya
72 B1 Gharyān Libya
72 B2 Ghāt Libya
54 C4 Ghātampur India
57 E2 Ghazaabad India
57 E2 Ghazaouet Algeria
55 E4 Ghaziabad India
55 F4 Ghazipur India
54 B2 Ghazluna Pakistan
57 E3 Ghaznī Afghanistan
57 F2 Ghazzālah Saudi Arabia
18 A4 Gheorgheni Romania
19 D4 Gherla Romania
113 K4 Ghisoonaccia France
57 E2 Ghizao Afghanistan
54 C1 Ghitzai reg. Afghanistan
25 J5 Ghisonaccia France
28 F3 Ghizar Pakistan
54 D2 Ghod r. India
54 C4 Ghotāru India
54 B3 Ghotki Pakistan
57 C3 Ghudāf, Wādī al w Iraq
80 E3 Ghugus India
61 B1 Ghunthur Syria
57 F2 Ghurian Afghanistan
29 G5 Giannitsa Greece
122 C4 Giannutri, Isola di i. Italy
40 C4 Gianyar Indon.
42 D3 Gia Rai Vietnam
43 E5 Giardini-Naxos Italy
43 E5 Giarre Italy
26 B2 Giaveno Italy
124 C3 Gibbon U.S.A.
119 ⁻¹ Gibb's Hill h. Bermuda
80 C3 Gibē Shet' r. Ethiopia
18 F2 Gibeon Namibia
25 D4 Gibraltar terr. Europe
24 D5 Gibraltar, Strait of str. Morocco/Spain
96 F2 Gid a. l. Aust.
101 A5 Gibson Desert Aust.
16 G4 Giddalur India
12 D4 Gidea r. U.S.A.
114 C4 Gidgi, L. salt flat Aust.
80 C3 Gīdolē Ethiopia
21 F3 Gien France
18 D3 Gießen Germany
47 F6 Gifu Japan
47 F6 Gifu div. Japan
130 C3 Giganta, Sierra de la mt. ra. Mexico
138 B3 Gigante Colombia
16 D5 Giglio, Isola del i. Italy
24 D1 Gijón Spain
129 F5 Gila r. U.S.A.
129 G5 Gila Bend U.S.A.
129 G5 Gila Bend Mts mts U.S.A.
57 A4 Gīlān div. Iran
54 B3 Gilan Garb Iraq
90 ⁻⁴ Gilbert Islands is Kiribati
86 J4 Gilbert r. Aust.
99 E2 Gilbert r. Aust.
129 G5 Gilbert, Mt mt. U.S.A.
99 E3 Gilbert River Aust.
142 C3 Gilbués Brazil
101 B3 Gil Chashmeh Iran
60 B2 Gilgandra Aust.
81 B5 Gil Gil Cr. r. Aust.
54 C1 Gilgit Pakistan
65 H5 Gilgit Jammu and Kashmir
54 C1 Gilgunnia Aust.
111 K4 Gillam Can.
10 D4 Gilleleje Denmark
96 D1 Gilles, L. salt flat Aust.
111 H4 Gillette U.S.A.
129 G6 Gila Rock U.S.A.
57 D3 Gilmour Island i. Can.
55 F4 Gilo r. Ethiopia
129 G2 Gilroy U.S.A.
128 B3 Gilroy U.S.A.
128 E1 Gimli Can.
80 C3 Gīmi r. Ethiopia
11 D4 Gimo Sweden
20 D5 Gimont France
80 C3 Ginir Ethiopia
80 C3 Gīnīr Ethiopia
27 F5 Ginosa Italy
82 A5 Gīnīr St Helena Atlantic Ocean
27 F5 Gioia del Colle Italy
27 F5 Gioia, Golfo di b. Italy
61 C1 Girard U.S.A.

29 D4 Girdao Pakistan
57 F4 Girdar Dhor r. Pakistan
57 F4 Girdi Iran
57 C4 Gireh, Kūh-e mt. Iran
54 B5 Gir Forest forest India
72 F2 Girga Egypt
81 J1 Gizycko Poland
138 B4 Girón Ecuador
54 C2 Girna r. India
138 B4 Girón Ecuador
20 D4 Gironde est. France
25 G1 Gironella Spain
16 F3 Girvan U.K.
49 F2 Giruno Switz.
92 G3 Gisborne N.Z.
92 G3 Gisborne div. N.Z.
110 E2 Giscome Can.
81 A5 Giseinyi Rwanda
11 D4 Gislaved Sweden
20 E2 Gisors France
81 A4 Gissar Range mt. ra. Tajikistan/Uzbekistan
81 A5 Gitarama Rwanda
81 A5 Gitega Burundi
26 D2 Giulianova Italy
21 G4 Givors France
83 E3 Giyani R.S.A.
80 C3 Giyon Ethiopia
61 A4 Gizai Egypt
73 F2 Giza Pyramids Egypt
73 F2 Gizhduvan Uzbekistan
63 S3 Gizhiga Rus. Fed.
90 ⁻¹ Gizo Solomon Is.
19 J1 Giżycko Poland
29 B4 Gjiri i Drinit b. Albania
29 A4 Gjiri i Karavastasë b. Albania
29 B4 Gjirokastër Albania
109 J3 Gjoa Haven Can.
11 C3 Gjøra Norway
10 C3 Gjøvik Norway
113 J4 Glace Bay Can.
110 B3 Glacier Bay National Park and Preserve nat. park. U.S.A.
152 Glacier Cook gl. Kerguelen Indian Ocean
110 F4 Glacier Nat. Park nat. park Can.
126 D1 Glacier Nat. Park nat. park U.S.A.
126 B1 Glacier Peak vol U.S.A.
114 E3 Gladstone Can.
99 G4 Gladstone Aust.
96 D2 Gladstone Aust.
122 D3 Gladstone U.S.A.
122 D4 Gladwin U.S.A.
16 E4 Gladwin U.S.A.
11 C3 Glåma r. Norway
26 E2 Glamoč Bos.-Herz.
114 E5 Glanworth Can.
21 J3 Glärnisch mt. Switz.
21 J3 Glarner Alpen mt. ra. Switz.
133 ¹ Glasgow Jamaica
16 E4 Glasgow U.K.
118 C4 Glasgow U.S.A.
126 F1 Glasgow U.S.A.
120 E5 Glasgow U.S.A.
17 F6 Glastonbury U.K.
15 E5 Glazov Rus. Fed.
12 J3 Glazov Rus. Fed.
19 H5 Gleisdorf Austria
114 D3 Glen Afton Can.
92 E2 Glen Afton N.Z.
122 E4 Glen Arbor U.S.A.
92 E4 Glen Canyon gorge U.S.A.
129 H3 Glen Canyon National Recreation Area res. U.S.A.
114 E5 Glencoe Can.
128 C4 Glendale U.S.A.
129 G5 Glendale U.S.A.
128 C4 Glendale U.S.A.
126 F2 Glendale Lake l. U.S.A.
126 F2 Glendive U.S.A.
126 F3 Glendo Res. l. U.S.A.
101 B5 Glenelg Ra. h. Aust.
97 E4 Glengyle Aust.
123 F4 Glen Innes Aust.
99 G6 Glen More r. U.K.
16 E3 Glenmorgan Aust.
99 G5 Glenns U.S.A.
126 F4 Glenns Ferry U.S.A.
101 B6 Glenora Can.
99 G4 Glenorchy Aust.
99 H5 Glenormiston Aust.
114 D3 Glen Robertson Can.
121 F3 Glens Falls U.S.A.
17 D4 Glen Shee U.K.
129 H5 Glenwood U.S.A.
121 G2 Glenwood U.S.A.
124 E3 Glenwood U.S.A.
127 F4 Glenwood Springs U.S.A.
122 A2 Glidden U.S.A.
19 H3 Glina Croatia
10 H3 Glinishevo Moldova
11 D4 Glinjeni Moldova
19 J2 Glodeanu-Sărat Romania
28 E2 Glodeni Moldova
28 E1 Glodeni Romania
19 J2 Głogów Yugo.
19 H3 Głogów Poland
19 H3 Głogów Małopolski Poland
10 D2 Glomfjord Norway
11 E4 Glomma r. Norway
143 A5 Glommersträsk Sweden
144 A4 Glória de Dourados Brazil
13 J3 Glotovka Rus. Fed.
19 J1 Gloucester P.N.G.
90 ⁻¹ Gloucester P.N.G.
17 F6 Gloucester U.K.
121 H3 Gloucester U.S.A.
120 E6 Gloucester U.S.A.
19 J3 Głowno Poland
19 J2 Głubczyce Poland
13 G5 Glubokiy Rus. Fed.
19 J2 Głuchołazy Poland
14 B2 Glukhov Rus. Fed.
18 E1 Glückstadt Germany
57 D4 Glushkovo Rus. Fed.
18 E3 Gmelinka Rus. Fed.
18 F5 Gmünd Niederösterreich Austria
18 F5 Gmünd Kärnten Austria
18 F5 Gmunden Austria
11 D3 Gnarp Sweden
19 J2 Gniew Poland
19 H2 Gniezno Poland
28 B3 Gnjilane Yugo.
11 D4 Gnosjö Sweden
54 B5 Goa India
54 B5 Goa div. India
97 E3 Goalen Head hd Aust.

55 G4 Goalpara India
40 D4 Goang Indon.
76 D5 Goaso Ghana
80 D3 Goba Ethiopia
82 B3 Gobabis Namibia
146 C4 Gobernador Duval Arg.
147 B6 Gobernador Gregores Arg.
146 E2 Gobernador Virasoro Arg.
48 B3 Gobi desert Mongolia
14 A3 Gobiki Rus. Fed.
46 E7 Goch Germany
18 C3 Gochas Namibia
82 B3 Gochas Namibia
43 D5 Go Công Vietnam
56 C2 Godavari r. India
56 C2 Godavari, Mouths of the India
113 G4 Godbout Can.
55 F4 Godda India
128 C3 Goddard, Mt mt. U.S.A.
139 F3 Goddo Surinam
80 D3 Godē Ethiopia
28 D3 Godech Bulgaria
61 A1 Gödek Turkey
80 D4 Godere Ethiopia
21 E5 Goderich Can.
54 C5 Godhra India
80 E3 Godinlabe Somalia
19 J5 Gödöllő Hungary
111 L3 Gods r. Can.
111 L4 Gods Lake l. Can.
111 M2 Gods Mercy, Bay of b. Can.
54 C4 Godwar reg. India
14 H3 Godyaykino Rus. Fed.
115 G2 Goéland, Lac au l. Can.
113 H2 Goéland, Lac aux l. Can.
18 A3 Goes Netherlands
123 E2 Goetzville U.S.A.
129 E4 Goffs U.S.A.
13 G6 Gofitskoye Rus. Fed.
114 E3 Gogama Can.
64 D6 Gogaru r. Japan
122 C2 Gogebic, Lake l. U.S.A.
122 C2 Gogebic Range h. U.S.A.
100 D3 Gogoi Sudan
77 E4 Gogounou Benin
78 E2 Gogrial Sudan
54 D4 Gohad India
142 F2 Goiana Brazil
144 D3 Goianésia Brazil
144 C1 Goiánia Brazil
144 C1 Goiás Brazil
144 C3 Goiás div. Brazil
144 D3 Goiatuba Brazil
41 □1 Goikul Palau
50 B2 Goinxab China
144 B5 Goio r. Brazil
144 B5 Goio-Erê Brazil
80 D3 Gojeb Wenz r. Ethiopia
47 H4 Gojôme Japan
54 C3 Gojra Pakistan
56 A2 Gokak India
46 C7 Gokase-gawa r. Japan
61 B1 Gök Çay r. Turkey
60 A1 Gökçeada i. Turkey
29 G5 Gökdere r. Turkey
61 B1 Gökdere r. Turkey
55 G3 Gokhar La China
60 C1 Gökirmak r. Turkey
57 E4 Gokprosh Hills mt. ra. Pak.
61 B1 Göksun Turkey
60 D2 Göksu r. Turkey
83 D2 Gokwe Zimbabwe
11 C3 Gol Norway
54 E3 Gola India
19 H2 Golaghat India
57 D4 Golashkerd Iran
57 G2 Golbāhār Afghanistan
60 D2 Gölbaşı Turkey
62 K2 Gol'chikha Rus. Fed.
29 G5 Gölcük Bolkessi Turkey
29 G5 Gölcük r. Turkey
19 G2 Golczewo Poland
19 L1 Goldap Poland
18 E2 Goldberg Germany
19 H6 Gold Coast Aust.
76 D6 Gold Coast Ghana
110 F4 Golden Can.
92 E4 Golden Bay b. N.Z.
128 A3 Golden Gate National Recreation Area res. U.S.A.
110 D5 Golden Hinde mt. Can.
133 □6 Golden Rock airport St Kitts-Nevis Caribbean
128 D3 Goldfield U.S.A.
128 D3 Gold Point U.S.A.
119 E5 Goldsboro U.S.A.
100 B4 Goldsworthy Aust.
125 D6 Goldthwaite U.S.A.
60 E1 Göle Turkey
19 E2 Goleniów Poland
57 C3 Golestán Afghanistan
57 C3 Golestának Iran
128 C4 Goleta U.S.A.
48 C1 Golets-Davydov, G. mt. Rus. Fed.
130 K7 Golfito Costa Rica
29 G6 Gölgeli Dağları mt. ra. Turkey
125 D6 Goliad U.S.A.
28 D3 Golija mt. ra. Yugo.
28 C3 Golija Planina mts Yugo.
49 G3 Golin Baixing China
14 G3 Golitsyno Rus. Fed.
14 G3 Golitsyno Rus. Fed.
60 D1 Gölköy Turkey
29 F5 Gölmarmara Turkey
55 H1 Golmud r. China
21 J5 Golo r. France
41 B3 Golo i. Phil.
14 E2 Golobino Rus. Fed.
14 E2 Golovanovo Rus. Fed.
46 E3 Golovino Rus. Fed.
57 B2 Golpāyegān Iran
19 J2 Golub-Dobrzyń Poland
65 H2 Golubovka Kazak.
57 E4 Golun' Iran
14 F2 Goly'tsvka Rus. Fed.
83 C2 Goma Zaire
29 G4 Gölyazı Turkey
13 F5 Golyshmanovo Rus. Fed.
78 B4 Goma Zaire
55 G3 Gomang Co l. China
43 □1 Gombak, Bukit h. Singapore
77 E4 Gombe Nigeria
81 B5 Gombe r. Tanz.
77 G4 Gombi Nigeria
81 □3 Gombrani I. i. Rodrigues I. Mauritius
77 F5 Gómez Nigeria
25 □1 Gomera, La i. Canary Is Spain
130 D2 Gómez Farías Mexico
130 D2 Gómez Palacio Mexico
131 F3 Gómez, Presa M. R. resr Mexico
57 C1 Gomišan Iran
57 E2 Gomo Co l. China
133 D3 Gonaïves Haiti
83 E2 Gonarezhou National Park nat. park Zimbabwe
133 D3 Gonâve, Île de la i. Haiti
57 C1 Gonbad-e Kavus Iran
80 E3 Gonda Ethiopia
80 D3 Gonda Libah well Ethiopia
80 C2 Gonder Ethiopia

54 E5 Gondia India
60 A1 Gönen Turkey
20 E2 Gonfreville-l'Orcher France
51 F2 Gong'an China
53 H3 Gongga'gyamda China
51 E3 Gongcheng China
55 G3 Gonggar China
50 C2 Gongga Shan mt. China
48 B5 Gonghe China
65 K4 Gonghui China
142 E3 Gongogi r. Brazil
77 G4 Gongola r. Nigeria
97 F2 Gongolgon Aust.
78 A4 Gongoué Gabon
50 B3 Gongshan China
50 C3 Gongwang Shan mt. ra. China
51 F1 Gong Xian China
50 D2 Gong Xian China
19 L2 Goniądz Poland
77 F4 Goniri Nigeria
50 B2 Gonjo China
27 B6 Gonnesa Italy
46 H3 Gonohe Japan
46 B7 Gōnoura Japan
131 F4 Gonzáles Mexico
124 C3 Gonzales U.S.A.
125 D6 Gonzales U.S.A.
120 E6 Good U.S.A.
152 C6 Goodenough, C. c. Ant.
90 □1 Goodenough I. i. P.N.G.
115 F4 Goodenham Can.
122 E3 Good Harbor Bay b. Can.
82 B5 Good Hope, Cape of R.S.A.
126 D3 Gooding U.S.A.
124 C4 Goodland U.S.A.
81 □4 Goodlands Mauritius
97 F2 Goodooga r. Aust.
99 H5 Goodnight Aust.
99 G6 Goodiwindi Aust.
101 C6 Goongarrie, L. salt flat Aust.
113 H3 Goose r. Can.
147 E7 Goose Green Falkland Is
126 B3 Goose L. l. U.S.A.
56 B3 Gooty India
55 F4 Gopālganj India
19 H3 Góra Leszno Poland
13 H7 Góra Bazardyuzi mt. Rus. Fed.
19 K3 Góra Kalwaria Poland
55 E4 Gora Lopatina mt. Rus. Fed.
45 Q1 Gora Lopatina mt. Rus. Fed.
45 P2 Gora Medvezh'ya mt. China/Rus. Fed.
45 P2 Gora Tardoki-Yani mt. Rus. Fed.
76 D4 Gourcy Burkina
20 E4 Gourdon France
77 G4 Gouré Niger
20 C2 Gourin France
54 F4 Gouripur Bangladesh
82 C5 Gouritz r. R.S.A.
76 B3 Gourma-Rharous Mali
72 D4 Gourmeur well Chad
20 F2 Gournay-en-Bray France
72 C4 Gouro Chad
97 G4 Gourock Range mt. ra. U.K.
20 F2 Goussainville France
145 G3 Gouvêa Brazil
24 C2 Gouveia Portugal
121 F2 Gouverneur U.S.A.
133 □8 Gouyave Grenada Caribbean
63 S4 Govena, Mys hd Rus. Fed.
111 H5 Govenlock Can.
145 H3 Governador Valadares Brazil
41 C5 Governor Generoso Phil.
119 E7 Governor's Harbour The Bahamas
48 A3 Govĭaltay div. Mongolia
48 B4 Govĭaltay Nuruu mt. ra. Mongolia
55 E4 Govind Ballash Pant Sägar resr India
146 E4 Goya Arg.
133 □5 Goyave Guadeloupe Caribbean
19 K4 Goyatz Germany
59 G1 Göyçay Azerbaijan
98 C5 Goyder w Aust.
60 B1 Göynük Turkey
29 G5 Göynük Turkey
47 H4 Goyō-zan mt. Japan
78 D2 Goz-Beïda Chad
75 D5 Gozareh Afghanistan
55 H3 Gozha Co salt l. China
61 C1 Gözne Turkey
26 E7 Gozo i. Malta
132 B2 Goz Regeb Sudan
82 C4 Graaff-Reinet R.S.A.
76 D5 Grabo Côte d'Ivoire
28 D2 Grabovica Yugo.
28 C2 Grabovo R.S.A.
18 F2 Grabow Germany
19 J3 Grabów nad Prosną Poland
28 E3 Gračac Croatia
28 C3 Gračanica Bos.-Herz.
115 G2 Gracefield Can.
124 E2 Graceville U.S.A.
130 H6 Gracias Honduras
130 H6 Gracias a Dios, Cabo pt Nic./Honduras
25 □5 Graciosa i. Canary Is Spain
25 □ Graciosa i. Azores Port.
39 H6 Gorontalo Indon.
18 F4 Görwihl Germany
19 K1 Górowo Iławeckie Poland
13 F5 Gorshechnoye Rus. Fed.
17 B4 Gort Rep. of Ire.
13 F6 Goryachiy Klyuch Rus. Fed.
65 F4 Gory Akkyr. h. Turkmenistan
64 F4 Gory Baysuntau mt. ra. Uzbekistan
65 F4 Gory Bukantau h. Uzbekistan
63 L2 Gory Byrranga mt. ra. Rus. Fed.
64 F2 Gory Koymatdag h. Turkmenistan
64 D2 Gory Kul'dzhuktau h. Uzbekistan
64 E3 Gory Nuratau mt. ra. Uzbekistan
19 K3 Gory Świętokrzyskie h. Poland

65 G3 Gory Ulutau mt. ra. Kazak.
65 H2 Gory Yerementau h. Kazak.
19 G2 Gorzów Wielkopolski Poland
47 G5 Gosen Japan
97 G3 Gosford Aust.
122 E5 Goshen U.S.A.
121 F4 Goshen U.S.A.
46 H3 Goshogawara Japan
18 E3 Goslar Germany
124 C3 Gosnells Aust.
26 E3 Gospić Croatia
17 G6 Gosport U.K.
98 C3 Gosse w Aust.
76 D3 Gossi Mali
28 C3 Gostivar Macedonia
19 H3 Gostyń Leszno Poland
19 J2 Gostynin Poland
80 D3 Gota Ethiopia
11 C4 Götaälv r. Sweden
11 C4 Göteborg Sweden
11 C4 Göteborg och Bohus div. Sweden
78 B2 Gotel Mountains mt. ra. Cameroon/Nigeria
11 D4 Götene Sweden
18 E3 Gotha Germany
124 C3 Gothenburg U.S.A.
77 F3 Gotheye Niger
11 E4 Gotland div. Sweden
11 E4 Gotland i. Sweden
132 □3 Gotomeer l. Bonaire Netherlands Ant.
46 B7 Gotō-rettō is Japan
29 D4 Gotse Delchev Bulgaria
11 E4 Gotska Sandön i. Sweden
46 D6 Gōtsu Japan
18 D3 Göttingen Germany
110 E4 Gott Peak summit Can.
129 F3 Gouan r. U.S.A.
114 E3 Goulburn r. N.S.W. Aust.
114 C3 Goulais River r. Can.
114 C3 Goulbin Kaba w Niger
97 G3 Goulburn r. N.S.W. Aust.
97 G4 Goulburn r. Aust.
98 C1 Goulburn Is i. Aust.
154 B4 Gould City U.S.A.
78 B1 Goulféy Cameroon
76 C4 Goumbou Mali
78 C2 Goundi Chad
133 □5 Gourbeyre Guadeloupe Caribbean
76 D4 Gouré Niger
129 F3 Grand Canyon gorge U.S.A.
129 F3 Grand Canyon U.S.A.
129 F3 Grand Canyon Nat. Park nat. park U.S.A.
132 B3 Grand Cayman i. Cayman Is Caribbean
114 C4 Grand Centre Can.
76 C6 Grand Cess Liberia
126 C2 Grand Coulee U.S.A.
133 □5 Grand Cul-de Sac Marin b. Guadeloupe Caribbean
146 C4 Grande r. Arg.
140 D3 Grande r. Bolivia
142 E3 Grande r. Bahia Brazil
144 D4 Grande r. São Paulo Brazil
130 D2 Grande r. Mexico
130 J6 Grande r. Nicaragua
140 A2 Grande r. Peru
112 E3 Grande 2, Réservoir de La resr Can.
112 E3 Grande 3, Réservoir de La resr Can.
112 F3 Grande 4, Réservoir de La resr Can.
133 □5 Grande Anse Guadeloupe Caribbean
147 C7 Grande, Bahía b. Arg.
81 □4 Grande Baie Mauritius
110 F4 Grande Cache Can.
142 B1 Grande de Gurupa, Ilha i. Brazil
140 C4 Grande de Jujuy r. Arg.
139 E4 Grande de Manacapuru, Lago l. Brazil
130 D4 Grande de Santiago r. Mexico
140 D4 Grande de Tarija r. Arg./Bolivia
145 G4 Grande, Ilha i. Brazil
141 G2 Grande o'Guapay r. Bolivia
110 F3 Grande Prairie Can.
72 D2 Grand Erg de Bilma sand dunes Niger
75 D2 Grand Erg Occidental desert Algeria
72 B2 Grand Erg Oriental desert Algeria
113 H4 Grande-Rivière Can.
133 □3 Grande Rivière Trinidad Trin. & Tobago
112 F3 Grande Rivière de la Baleine r. Can.
126 C2 Grande Ronde r. U.S.A.
115 J3 Grandes-Piles Can.
133 □5 Grande Terre i. Guadeloupe Caribbean
133 □5 Grande Vigie, Pointe de la pt Guadeloupe Caribbean
125 F5 Grand Falls Can.
113 J4 Grand Falls Can.
110 F5 Grand Forks Can.
124 D2 Grand Forks U.S.A.
121 F2 Grand Gorge U.S.A.
132 C1 Grand Harbour Can.
122 E4 Grand Haven U.S.A.
122 D2 Grand I. i. U.S.A.
110 D2 Grandin, Lac l. Can.
114 E2 Grand Island U.S.A.
125 F6 Grand Isle U.S.A.
121 J1 Grand L. l. U.S.A.
129 H2 Grand Junction U.S.A.
113 G4 Grand L. l. Can.
125 E6 Grand L. l. U.S.A.
76 C5 Grand-Lahou Côte d'Ivoire
113 J4 Grand Lake l. Can.
113 H3 Grand Lake l. Can.
121 J1 Grand Lake l. U.S.A.
123 E3 Grand Lake l. U.S.A.
123 F3 Grand Lake l. U.S.A.
120 A4 Grand Lake Matagamon l. U.S.A.
121 J1 Grand Lake St Marys l. U.S.A.
122 E5 Grand Lake Seboeis l. U.S.A.
120 A4 Grand Lake Stream U.S.A.
122 E4 Grand Ledge U.S.A.
113 G5 Grand Manan I. i. U.S.A.
114 E2 Grand Marais U.S.A.
122 E2 Grand Marais U.S.A.
115 G3 Grand-Mère Can.
24 B3 Grândola Portugal
114 E2 Grand Portage U.S.A.
114 E3 Grand Rapids Can.
122 D4 Grand Rapids U.S.A.
122 A2 Grand Rapids U.S.A.
124 E2 Grand Rapids U.S.A.
126 E3 Grand Teton mt. U.S.A.
126 E3 Grand Teton Nat. Park nat. park U.S.A.
133 □4 Grand Turk i. Turks and Caicos Is Caribbean
133 □4 Grand Turk Turks and Caicos Is Caribbean
110 D2 Grandview Can.
129 H3 Grandview U.S.A.
129 F4 Grand Wash r. U.S.A.
129 E4 Grand Wash Cliffs U.S.A.
25 F2 Grañén Spain
133 □1 Grange Hill Jamaica
11 C3 Granger U.S.A.
11 D3 Grängesberg Sweden
126 C2 Grangeville U.S.A.
110 C3 Granisle Can.
112 F4 Granite Falls Can.
113 H4 Granite Lake l. Can.
126 F3 Granite Mts U.S.A.
126 F3 Granite Peak summit U.S.A.
129 F1 Granite Peak summit U.S.A.

16 E3 Grampian Mts mt. ra. U.K.
97 E4 Grampians mt. ra. Aust.
29 C4 Gramsh Albania
138 C3 Granada Colombia
130 J7 Granada Nicaragua
25 □ Granadilla de Abona Canary Is Spain
147 C6 Gran Altiplanicie Central Seco reg. Arg.
146 C4 Gran Bajo Salitroso salt marsh Arg.
136 D5 Gran Chaco reg. Arg.
133 □3 Gran Couva Trin. & Tobago
147 C5 Gran Laguna Salada l. Arg.
138 C1 Granada Colombia
130 J7 Granada Nicaragua
25 □ Gran Canaria i. Canary Is Spain
136 D5 Gran Chaco reg. Arg.
118 C3 Grand r. U.S.A.
113 J4 Grand r. U.S.A.
132 C1 Grand Bahama i. The Bahamas
113 J4 Grand Bank Can.
148 F2 Grand Banks Atlantic Ocean
76 D5 Grand-Bassam Côte d'Ivoire
81 □5 Grand Bassin Réunion Indian Ocean
113 G4 Grand Bay Can.
114 E5 Grand Bend Can.
76 C6 Grand-Béréby Côte d'Ivoire
133 □5 Grand Bourg Guadeloupe Caribbean
81 □5 Grand Brûlé pt Réunion Indian Ocean

27 D7 Granitola, Capo c. Italy
93 C4 Granity N.Z.
142 D1 Granja Brazil
147 C5 Gran Laguna Salada l. Arg.
11 D4 Gränna Sweden
25 F2 Granollers Spain
140 B2 Gran Pajonal plain Peru
26 A3 Gran Paradiso mt. Italy
26 C2 Gran Pilastro mt. Austria/Italy
17 G5 Grantham U.K.
152 C1 Grant I. i. Ant.
98 C1 Grant L. l. U.S.A.
83 E2 Grantley Adams airport Barbados Caribbean
128 C2 Grant, Mt mt. U.S.A.
128 D2 Grant, Mt mt. U.S.A.
16 F3 Grantown-on-Spey U.K.
129 F2 Grant Range mts U.S.A.
127 F5 Grants U.S.A.
20 D2 Granville France
122 C5 Granville U.S.A.
121 G3 Granville U.S.A.
111 J3 Granville Lake l. Can.
145 G2 Grão Mogol Brazil
128 C4 Grapevine U.S.A.
128 D3 Grapevine Mts mts U.S.A.
121 G3 Graphite U.S.A.
111 G2 Gras, Lac de l. Can.
121 F2 Grass r. U.S.A.
115 H5 Grasse France
115 F2 Grasset, Lac l. Can.
115 H5 Grasslands Nat. Park nat. park Can.
111 J4 Grass River Prov. Park res. Can.
128 C3 Grass Valley U.S.A.
97 F5 Grassy Aust.
119 E7 Grassy r. The Bahamas
11 D4 Grästorp Sweden
122 B4 Gratiot U.S.A.
19 G5 Gratkorn Austria
19 H4 Graulhet France
90 □1 Graus Spain
142 F2 Gravata r. Brazil
142 F2 Gravatá Brazil
111 J2 Gravel Hill Lake l. Can.
97 G2 Gravesend U.K.
20 F2 Grave, Pte de pt France
27 E5 Gravina in Puglia Italy
122 E3 Grawn U.S.A.
21 J3 Gray France
121 H3 Gray U.S.A.
126 E3 Grays L. l. U.S.A.
120 B5 Grayson r. U.S.A.
111 H3 Gray Strait chan. Can.
118 B4 Grayville U.S.A.
15 F1 Grayvoron Rus. Fed.
23 G2 Graz Austria
14 D2 Grazhdanovka Rus. Fed.
132 C1 Great Abaco i. The Bahamas
90 □7 Great Astrolabe Reef reef Fiji
96 B3 Great Australian Bight g. Aust.
133 □8 Great Bacolet Bay b. Grenada Caribbean
92 E2 Great Barrier Island i. N.Z.
99 F3 Great Barrier Reef reef Aust.
99 F3 Great Barrier Reef Marine Park (Cairns Section) nat. park Aust.
99 G4 Great Barrier Reef Marine Park (Capricorn Section) nat. park Aust.
99 G3 Great Barrier Reef Marine Park (Central Section) nat. park Aust.
99 F2 Great Barrier Reef Marine Park (Far North Section) nat. park Aust.
121 G3 Great Barrington U.S.A.
127 C4 Great Basin reg. U.S.A.
129 E2 Great Basin Nat. Park nat. park U.S.A.
55 F2 Great Bay b. U.S.A.
26 C3 Guà r. Italy
132 B4 Great Bear r. Can.
108 F3 Great Bear Lake l. Can.
124 D4 Great Bend U.S.A.
82 B5 Great Berg r. R.S.A.
17 B5 Great Blasket I. i. Rep. of Ire.
43 A4 Great Coco i. Cocos Is Indian Ocean
99 F4 Great Dividing Range mt. ra. Aust.
17 G5 Great Driffield U.K.
114 C4 Great Duck I. i. Can.
121 H4 Great Egg Harbor inlet U.S.A.
132 B2 Greater Antilles is Caribbean
92 D1 Great Exhibition Bay b. N.Z.
132 C1 Great Exuma i. The Bahamas
126 E2 Great Falls U.S.A.
82 D5 Great Fish r. R.S.A.
121 H4 Great Fish Pt pt R.S.A.
55 H4 Great Gandak r. India
132 C1 Great Guana Cay i. The Bahamas
119 E7 Great Harbour Cay i. The Bahamas
55 G4 Great Himalaya mt. ra. India
132 D2 Great Inagua i. The Bahamas
82 C5 Great Karoo plat. R.S.A.
82 D5 Great Kei r. R.S.A.
97 F5 Great Lake l. Aust.
92 E4 Great Mercury I. i. N.Z.
43 A6 Great Nicobar i. Andaman and Nicobar Is India
90 □2 Great North East Channel chan. Aust./P.N.G.
17 H5 Great Oasis, The oasis Egypt
17 H5 Great Ormes Head hd U.K.
17 H6 Great Ouse r. U.K.
99 F3 Great Palm Is is Aust.
83 B4 Great Peconic Bay b. U.S.A.
130 D2 Great Pedro Bluff hd Jamaica
81 C6 Great Ruaha r. Tanzania
121 G4 Great Sacandaga l. U.S.A.
128 B3 Great St Bernard Pass pass Italy/Switz.
14 E5 Great Sale Cay i. The Bahamas
126 D3 Great Salt Lake l. U.S.A.
127 D4 Great Salt Lake Desert desert U.S.A.
72 D3 Great Sand Sea desert Egypt/Libya
100 C4 Great Sandy Desert desert Aust.
97 G2 Great Scarcies r. Guinea/Sierra Leone
108 G3 Great Slave Lake l. Can.
119 D5 Great Smoky Mts mt. ra. U.S.A.
119 D5 Great Smoky Mts Nat. Park U.S.A.

110 E3 Great Snow Mtn mt. Can.
119 □1 Great Sound inlet Bermuda
121 G4 Great South Bay b. U.S.A.
121 E6 Great Torrington U.K.
101 C5 Great Victoria Desert desert Aust.
48 D5 Great Wall China
121 K2 Great Wass I. i. U.S.A.
17 H5 Great Yarmouth U.K.
60 E2 Great Zab r. Iraq
83 E2 Great Zimbabwe Zimbabwe
27 D5 Greco, Monte mt. Italy
24 D2 Gredos, Sa de mt. ra. Spain
147 C7 Greece Chile
5 H5 Greece country Europe
126 F3 Greeley U.S.A.
109 K1 Greely Fiord inlet Can.
62 H1 Greem Bell, O. i. Rus. Fed.
118 C4 Green r. U.S.A.
129 H2 Green r. U.S.A.
115 H3 Greenbank Can.
82 C4 Green Bay b. U.S.A.
122 C3 Green Bay U.S.A.
97 G4 Green C. hd Aust.
118 C4 Greencastle U.S.A.
132 C1 Green Cay i. The Bahamas
119 D6 Green Cove Springs U.S.A.
121 J2 Greene U.S.A.
119 D4 Greeneville U.S.A.
128 B3 Greenfield U.S.A.
121 G3 Greenfield U.S.A.
120 B5 Greenfield U.S.A.
118 C4 Greenfield U.S.A.
101 A6 Green Head hd Aust.
133 □3 Green Hill Trin. & Tobago
133 □1 Green Island Jamaica
41 A4 Green Island Bay b. Phil.
90 □1 Green Islands is P.N.G.
111 H4 Green Lake l. Can.
124 C4 Green Lake l. U.S.A.
104 O2 Greenland terr. Arctic Ocean
133 □9 Greenland Barbados Caribbean
148 J1 Greenland Basin Arctic Ocean
133 □9 Greenland Sea sea Greenland/Svalbard
109 R2 Green Mountains mt. ra. U.S.A.
82 A4 Green Mt h. Ascension Atlantic Ocean
16 E4 Greenock U.K.
17 B6 Greenore Rep. of Ire.
17 A6 Greenough Aust.
126 E3 Green River U.S.A.
129 H2 Green River U.S.A.
119 C4 Greensboro U.S.A.
118 C4 Greensburg U.S.A.
120 D5 Greensburg U.S.A.
110 D3 Greenstone Point pt U.K.
120 C4 Green Valley U.S.A.
119 C5 Greenville Liberia
118 B5 Greenville U.S.A.
128 B1 Greenville U.S.A.
121 J2 Greenville U.S.A.
125 F5 Greenville U.S.A.
119 E5 Greenville U.S.A.
118 C4 Greenville U.S.A.
121 H3 Greenville U.S.A.
119 D5 Greenville U.S.A.
119 C5 Greenwood U.S.A.
118 C4 Greenville U.S.A.
125 F5 Greenwood U.S.A.
121 J2 Greers Ferry Lake l. U.S.A.
132 □ Grenada Caribbean
126 E2 Gregory r. U.S.A.
124 A5 Gregory Aust.
98 B2 Gregory, L. salt flat Aust.
99 G3 Gregory Downs Aust.
98 B3 Gregory, L. salt flat Aust.
100 D4 Gregory Nat. Park nat. park Aust.
99 F3 Gregory Range mt. ra. Aust.
18 F1 Greifswald Germany
18 F3 Greiz Germany
61 C2 Greko, C. c. Cyprus
15 F5 Gremyachka Rus. Fed.
14 E5 Gremyachinsk Rus. Fed.
133 □8 Grenville Grenada Caribbean
18 D3 Grenville Can.
130 D2 Gresik Indon.
40 C3 Gresik Indon.
43 A6 Great Nicobar i. India
42 D2 Greymouth N.Z.
132 B3 Grey Hunter Pk summit Can.
118 B2 Grey Is Can.
121 J3 Grey r. N.Z.
21 G4 Grey Range mt. ra. Aust.
83 B4 Grey R.S.A.
130 D3 Greytown R.S.A.
78 C3 Gribingui-Bamingui, Réserve de Faune du res. C.A.R.
128 D2 Gridley U.S.A.
15 G5 Grigorievka Rus. Fed.
19 M2 Grigoriopol Moldova

16 K2 Grindafjord Norway
10 L3 Grindavik Iceland
11 D3 Grindsted Denmark
28 G2 Grindul Romania
28 G2 Grindul Chituc spit Romania
122 A5 Grinnell U.S.A.
28 E1 Grinţieş Romania
130 C3 Griqualand East reg. R.S.A.
82 C5 Griqualand West reg. R.S.A.
82 C4 Griquatown R.S.A.
20 E1 Gris Nez, Cap c. France
13 G6 Gritsovskiy Rus. Fed.
14 G4 Grivki Rus. Fed.
74 D3 Grizim well Algeria
11 F5 Grömbing Austria
19 L2 Gródek Poland
49 J3 Grodekovo Rus. Fed.
19 H3 Grodków Poland
19 K2 Grodzisk Mazowiecki Poland
19 H2 Grodzisk Wielkopolski Poland
50 D2 Grong Norway
18 C2 Groningen Netherlands
139 F3 Groningen Surinam
18 C2 Groningen div. Netherlands
139 E2 Groote Eylandt i. Aust.
98 D2 Groote Eylandt Abor. Land res. Aust.
82 B2 Grootfontein Namibia
82 B4 Groot Karas Berg plat. Namibia
82 C3 Groot Laagte w Botswana/Namibia
82 B4 Groot Letaba r. R.S.A.
82 C5 Groot Swartberg mt. ra. R.S.A.
82 D1 Grootvloer salt pan R.S.A.
133 □9 Gros Cap Martinique
133 □9 Gros Morne Martinique Caribbean
113 J3 Gros Morne Nat. Pk nat. park Can.
115 E1 Grosne r. France
133 □5 Grosse Pointe pt Guadeloupe Caribbean
18 F3 Großenhain Germany
132 D2 Guantánamo, B. de b. Cuba
23 F2 Grosser Beerberg mt. Germany
19 G5 Grosser Speikkogel mt. Austria
26 D3 Grosseto Italy
23 F4 Groß-Gerau Germany
18 F5 Großglockner mt. Austria
18 D3 Groß Ums Namibia
23 E3 Gros Ventre Range mt. ra. U.S.A.
113 J3 Groswater Bay b. Can.
121 F3 Groton U.S.A.
115 H3 Grottaglie Italy
110 F3 Grouard Can.
115 G2 Groundhog r. Can.
120 C4 Grove City U.S.A.
119 C6 Grove Hill U.S.A.
128 B4 Grover Beach U.S.A.
25 E4 Groves U.S.A.
129 G5 Growler Mts U.S.A.
129 G5 Growler Mts U.S.A.
18 F3 Grudziądz Poland
145 J2 Gruaramá Brazil
82 B4 Grünau Namibia
122 A4 Grundy Center U.S.A.
15 H6 Gryazi Rus. Fed.
12 G3 Gryazovets Rus. Fed.
19 K4 Grybów Poland
19 G2 Gryfice Poland
19 G2 Gryfino Poland
19 G3 Gryfów Śląski Poland
149 D7 Grytviken Atlantic Ocean
55 E4 Gua India
26 C3 Guà r. Italy
132 D3 Guacara Venezuela
138 C2 Guachucal Colombia
143 □3 Guadalajara Mexico
139 G3 Guadalaviar r. Spain
90 □1 Guadalcanal i. Solomon Is
25 D3 Guadalcanal Spain
25 E3 Guadalajara div. Spain
25 E4 Guadalhorce r. Spain
24 D4 Guadalquivir r. Spain
130 E4 Guadalupe Zacatecas Mexico
130 E4 Guadalupe Mexico
125 B6 Guadalupe Mts Nat. Park nat. park U.S.A.
24 D3 Guadalupe, Sierra de mt. ra. Spain
130 D3 Guadalupe Victoria Mexico
130 D3 Guadalupe Aguilera Mexico
133 □5 Guadeloupe terr. Caribbean
104 M8 Guadeloupe Caribbean
133 G3 Guadeloupe Passage chan. Guadeloupe Caribbean
25 E2 Guadiana r. Spain
24 C3 Guadiana, B. b. b. Spain
24 D4 Guadiana, B. de b. Spain
25 E4 Guadix Spain
147 B5 Guafo, I. i. Chile
138 C2 Guainía r. Colombia
132 D3 Guaira Brazil
132 A4 Guaico Trin. & Tobago
142 D2 Guaiçuí Brazil
132 A5 Guáimaro Cuba
145 J2 Guaira Brazil
147 B5 Guaitecas, Islas is Chile
138 C3 Guaje, Llano de plain Mexico
142 C2 Guajará Brazil
141 E2 Guajará Mirim Brazil
138 C1 Guajira, Península de pen. Colombia
143 □3 Gualaceo Ecuador
130 J7 Gualán Guatemala
132 A4 Gualeguay Arg.
90 □1 Gualalcanal i.
146 E3 Gualeguay Arg.
146 E3 Gualeguay r. Arg.
146 E3 Gualeguaychú Arg.
90 □1 Guam terr. Pac. Oc.
146 D3 Gualjaina Arg.
80 C3 Guban plain Somalia
80 D4 Gubbi India
80 C3 Gubed Rugguuda b. Somalia
18 G3 Guben Germany
19 G3 Gubin Poland
61 A1 Gubulan Turkey
80 C3 Gudaal Ethiopia
80 C3 Gudamoji Ethiopia
59 F3 Gudbandsdalen v. Norway
11 C3 Gudbrandsdalen v. Norway
56 B3 Gudiyattam India
80 C3 Gudmaji Ethiopia
56 B2 Gudur India
11 B3 Gudvangen Norway
74 B5 Guebwiller France
21 H2 Guéckédou Guinea
76 C5 Guédi, Massif du mts Chad
133 □3 Gueiba Trin. & Tobago
74 D2 Guelb er Richât h. Mauritania
75 F1 Guelma Algeria
74 B4 Guelmim Morocco
75 E2 Guelta Zemmur Western Sahara
114 E5 Guelph Can.
130 D3 Guémez Mexico
80 C2 Guéna r. Ethiopia
21 H4 Guérande France
21 G3 Guéret France
17 E7 Guernsey i. Channel Is
17 E7 Guernsey U.S.A.

74 B5 Guérou Mauritania
75 F1 Guerrah Et-Tarf salt pan Algeria
131 E5 Guerrero div. Mexico
131 F3 Guerrero Mexico
130 B3 Guerrero Negro Mexico
21 G3 Gueugnon France
76 C5 Guéyo Côte d'Ivoire
80 C3 Guge mt. Ethiopia
57 C2 Gügerd, Küh-e mt. ra. Iran
80 C3 Gugu Mountains mt. ra. Ethiopia
40 A3 Guhakolak, Tg pt Indon.
51 E3 Gui r. China
25 □ Guía de Isora Canary Is Spain
148 F5 Guiana Basin Atlantic Ocean
20 D3 Guiana France
51 G2 Guichi China
146 E3 Guichón Uruguay
77 F4 Guidan-Roumji Niger
78 C2 Guidari Chad
20 C3 Guide France
78 B2 Guider Cameroon
78 B1 Guidiguis Cameroon
74 B5 Guidimaka div. Mauritania
50 D3 Guiding China
51 F3 Guidong China
27 D5 Guidonia-Montecelio Italy
74 A3 Guier, Lac de l. Senegal
21 F2 Guignicourt France
51 H2 Guiji Shan mt. ra. China
24 D2 Guijuelo Spain
17 G6 Guildford U.K.
121 J2 Guilford U.S.A.
51 E3 Guilin China
112 E2 Guillaume-Delisle, Lac l. Can.
21 H4 Guillaumes France
21 H4 Guillestre France
25 □ Güímar Canary Is Spain
24 B3 Guimarães Portugal
41 B4 Guimaras Str. chan. Phil.
48 B6 Guinan China
128 A2 Guinda U.S.A.
76 B4 Guinea country Africa
148 H5 Guinea Basin Atlantic Ocean
68 C4 Guinea-Bissau country Africa
148 K5 Guinea, Gulf of g. Africa
75 B4 Guinée-Maritime div. Guinea
132 B2 Güines Cuba
20 E1 Guînes France
20 B2 Guingamp France
20 B2 Guipavas France
51 F2 Guiping China
144 B2 Guiratinga Brazil
142 E2 Guarabira Brazil
139 E2 Güiria Venezuela
139 G3 Guisanbourg French Guiana
21 F2 Guise France
25 F3 Guissona Spain
141 D4 Güitiri Spain
54 C1 Gujar Khan Pakistan
54 C2 Gujranwala Pakistan
54 C2 Gujrat Pakistan
129 G5 Gu Komelik U.S.A.
144 E2 Guda Mor Brazil
14 F2 Gudariagrafsk U.S.A.
148 F2 Guariba r. Brazil
138 D2 Guárico r. Venezuela
14 G5 Gulcha Kyrgyzstan
55 E4 Gulbarga India
11 G4 Gulbene Latvia
64 F4 Gulistan Uzbekistan
54 C2 Gulistan Pakistan
54 F2 Guliya Shan mt. ra. China
142 B2 Gull Bay Can.
14 E2 Gulkana U.S.A.
111 H4 Gull Lake Can.
29 F4 Gullträsk Sweden
29 E1 Güllük Turkey
11 F2 Güllük Körfezi b. Turkey
29 F5 Güllük Turkey
81 D4 Gulpan Indon.
11 G4 Gülpınar Turkey
31 F4 Gülşehir Turkey
62 F3 Gul'shad Kazak.
29 E1 Gülşheher Turkey
81 B4 Gulu Uganda
81 B4 Gumare Botswana
14 G3 Gumdag Turkmenistan
57 F4 Gumel Nigeria
54 F5 Gumia India
25 F2 Gumiel de Izán Spain
54 E5 Gumla India
83 D2 Gumy Indon.
19 K4 Gumundia Hungary
46 F6 Gumma div. Japan
61 E1 Gümüşhacıköy Turkey
61 F1 Gümüşhane Turkey
54 C4 Guna India
97 F3 Gunbar Aust.
97 G3 Gundagai Aust.
78 C3 Gundji Zaire
61 A1 Gündoğmuş Turkey
29 E5 Güney Kütahya Turkey
29 F5 Güney Denizli Turkey
72 B1 Gunib Rus. Fed.
46 J4 Gunma div. Japan
11 D4 Gunnarn Sweden
81 □2 Gunner's Quoin i. Mauritius
152 □ Gunnerus Ridge Ant.
127 F4 Gunnison U.S.A.
129 G2 Gunnison U.S.A.
129 H2 Gunnison r. U.S.A.
56 C2 Guntakal India
119 C5 Guntersville U.S.A.
119 C5 Guntersville L. l. U.S.A.
56 C2 Guntur India
40 A2 Gunungsitoli Indon.
40 A3 Gunungsugih Indon.
54 C5 Gunupur India
50 C3 Gunza China
40 C3 Gunza Indon.
51 H1 Gunzan Korea
51 E2 Guojiaba China
48 E5 Guoyang China
54 D2 Gupis Jammu and Kashmir
19 K3 Gura Galbenei Moldova
28 E1 Gura Humorului Romania

H

54 C2 Gurais Jammu and Kashmir
77 F5 Gurara r. Nigeria
78 E3 Gurba r. Zaire
48 B5 Gurban Hudag China
48 E4 Gurban Obo China
54 C2 Gurdaspur India
57 E4 Gurdim Iran
29 G5 Güre Turkey
54 D3 Gurgaon India
72 D5 Gurgei, Jebel mt. Sudan
142 D2 Gurgueia r. Brazil
54 B4 Gurha India
139 E2 Guri, Embalse de resr Venezuela
98 C1 Gurig Nat. Park nat. park Aust.
144 D3 Gurinhatã Brazil
13 H7 Gurjaani Georgia
57 D3 Gur Khar Iran
54 E3 Gurla Mandhata mt. China
64 F4 Gurlen Uzbekistan
83 E2 Guro Mozambique
29 G4 Gürsu Turkey
55 G3 Guru China
83 F2 Gurué Mozambique
29 G4 Gürün Turkey
142 B1 Gurupá Brazil
142 C3 Gurupi Brazil
142 C1 Gurupi r. Brazil
54 C4 Guru Sikhar mt. India
83 E2 Guruve Zimbabwe
65 L2 Gur'yevsk Rus. Fed.
11 F5 Gur'yevsk Rus. Fed.
14 E2 Gus' r. Rus. Fed.
77 F4 Gusau Nigeria
15 P4 Gusev Rus. Fed.
49 G5 Gushan China
129 H1 Gusher U.S.A.
57 E2 Gushgy Afghanistan
64 F5 Gushgy Turkmenistan
51 F1 Gushi China
76 D5 Gushiregu Ghana
47 □2 Gushikami Japan
47 □2 Gushikawa Japan
41 A5 Gusi Malaysia
63 M2 Gusikha Rus. Fed.
48 C2 Gusinoozersk Rus. Fed.
48 C2 Gusinoye Ozero l. Rus. Fed.
48 C2 Gusinoye, Ozero l. Rus. Fed.
14 E2 Gus'-Khrustal'nyy Rus. Fed.
27 B6 Guspini Italy
19 H5 Güssing Austria
109 P3 Gustav Holm, Kap c. Greenland
110 B3 Gustavus U.S.A.
128 B3 Gustine U.S.A.
19 G2 Güstrow Germany
14 E2 Gus'-Zheleznyy Rus. Fed.
50 A2 Gutang China
18 D3 Gütersloh Germany
123 H5 Guthrie U.S.A.
125 C4 Guthrie U.S.A.
125 C5 Guthrie U.S.A.
51 G3 Gutian Fujian China
51 G3 Gutian Fujian China
18 D3 Gutsuo China
122 B4 Guttenberg U.S.A.
83 E2 Gutu Zimbabwe
55 G4 Guwahati India
60 E2 Guwēr Iraq
48 D5 Gu Xian China
136 E2 Guyana country S. America
48 D4 Guyang China
20 D4 Guyenne reg. France
125 C4 Guymon U.S.A.
57 C3 Güyom Iran
92 G3 Guyra Aust.
49 E4 Guyuan China
48 C6 Guyuan China
65 G5 Guzar Uzbekistan
29 F5 Güzelhisar Baraji resr Turkey
61 A1 Güzelsu Turkey
51 E2 Guzhang China
51 G1 Guzhen China
130 D2 Guzmán Mexico
130 D2 Guzmán, L. de l. Mexico
11 F5 Gvardeysk Rus. Fed.
42 A3 Gwa Myanmar
92 G2 Gwabegar Aust.
77 F4 Gwadabawa Nigeria
57 E4 Gwadar Pakistan
57 E4 Gwadar West B. b. Pakistan
77 E4 Gwadu Nigeria
54 D3 Gwaldam India
54 D4 Gwalior India
83 E3 Gwanda Zimbabwe
78 E3 Gwane Zaire
54 A3 Gwash Pakistan
57 E4 Gwatar Bay b. Pakistan
93 B7 Gwawele Zaire
82 D2 Gwayi r. Zimbabwe
17 G4 Gwda r. Poland
42 A1 Gwedaukkon Myanmar
17 C4 Gweebarra Bay b. Rep. of Ire.
17 C4 Gweedore Rep. of Ire.
83 D2 Gweru r. Zimbabwe
83 D2 Gweru Zimbabwe
81 A5 Gweshe Zaire
82 D3 Gweta Botswana
122 D2 Gwinn U.S.A.
54 A3 Gwoza Nigeria
92 G2 Gwydir r. Aust.
55 H3 Gyaca China
50 C1 Gyagartang China
29 F6 Gyali i. Greece
55 F3 Gyangrang China
55 F3 Gyaring China
55 G3 Gyaring China
55 G3 Gyaring Co l. China
50 B1 Gyaring Hu l. China
29 E6 Gyaros i. Greece
55 F3 Gyarubtang China
62 J2 Gydanskiy Poluostrov pen. Rus. Fed.
55 F3 Gyimda China
55 F3 Gyirong China
55 F3 Gyirong China
55 G2 Gyitang China
50 A1 Gyiza China
109 O3 Gyldenløves Fjord inlet Greenland
99 H5 Gympie Aust.
42 A3 Gyobingauk Myanmar
17 K5 Gyomaendröd Hungary
19 J5 Gyöngyös Hungary
111 K4 Gypsumville Can.
113 G2 Gyrfalcon Is l. Can.
29 E6 Gytheio Greece
19 J5 Gyula Hungary
61 H1 Gyumri Armenia
64 E5 Gyzylarbat Turkmenistan
14 B2 Gzhat' r. Rus. Fed.

H

18 C3 Haarstrang ridge Germany
93 B5 Haast N.Z.
93 B5 Haast r. N.Z.
98 B4 Haast Bluff Aust.
98 B4 Haasts Bluff Aboriginal Land res. Aust.
90 □4 Ha'atua Tonga
54 A4 Hab r. Pakistan
18 C3 Habahe China
132 B2 Habana Cuba
56 C4 Habarane Sri Lanka
81 C4 Habar Cirir Somalia
81 C4 Habaswein Kenya
73 H4 Habawnāh, W. w. Saudi Arabia
110 F3 Habay Can.
59 G7 Habbān Yemen
60 E3 Habbānīyah Iraq
54 A4 Hab Chauki Pakistan
61 C4 Habesor w Israel
55 G4 Habiganj Bangladesh
49 G4 Habirag China
61 C4 Habis, W. el w Jordan
138 B4 Hacha Colombia
147 B4 Hachado, Pico de pass Arg./Chile
47 G7 Hachijō-jima i. Japan
46 D3 Hachimori Japan
46 H3 Hachinohe Japan
47 G6 Hachiōji Japan
47 G3 Hachiryū Japan
60 □1 Hacı Zeynalabdin Azerbaijan
96 D2 Hack, Mt mt. Aust.
83 E3 Hacufera Mozambique
65 K4 Hadadong China
56 A3 Hadagalli India
47 G2 Hadano Japan
49 H2 Hadayang China
73 G3 Hadd' Saudi Arabia
16 F4 Haddington U.K.
81 □1 Haddon Pt pt Seychelles
53 D10 Haddummahti Atoll atoll Maldives
49 J4 Hadejia r. Nigeria
77 G4 Hadejia Nigeria
61 C3 Hadera Israel
11 C5 Haderslev Denmark
73 H4 Hadīboh Saudi Arabia
80 □ Hadībū Socotra Yemen
61 D3 Hādi, J. el mts Jordan
60 C2 Hadim Turkey
108 H2 Hadley Bay b. Can.
46 A6 Hadong S. Korea
11 C4 Hadsund Denmark
49 H5 Hadyach Ukraine
46 B5 Haeju N. Korea
46 B5 Haeju-man b. S. Korea
152 A5 Haeju S. Korea
114 F3 Hafford Can.
60 D2 Hafik Turkey
73 G2 Hafirat al'Aydā Saudi Arabia
61 D4 Hafira, W. w Jordan
52 H4 Hafizabad Pakistan
55 H4 Haflong India
10 12 Hafnarfjörður Iceland
57 B3 Haft Gel Iran
10 12 Hafursfjörður b. Iceland
73 F5 Hag Abdullah Sudan
114 E3 Hagar r. Can.
80 C1 Hagar Nish Plateau plat. Eritrea
108 B4 Hagemeister I. i. U.S.A.
18 E2 Hagenow Germany
80 D3 Hāgere Hiywet Ethiopia
80 D3 Hāgere Selam Ethiopia
120 E5 Hagerstown U.S.A.
20 D5 Hagetmau France
11 D3 Hagfors Sweden
42 D2 Ha Giang Vietnam
17 C5 Hag's Head hd Rep. of Ire.
111 H4 Hague Can.
20 D2 Hague, Cap de la pt France
21 H2 Haguenau France
39 M1 Hahajima-rettō is Japan
50 B2 Hai'an China
51 E4 Hai'an China
81 C4 Hai r. Tanzania
51 H1 Hai'an China
54 D4 Haidargarh India
42 D2 Hai Duong Vietnam
61 C3 Haifa, B. of b. Israel
51 F4 Haifeng China
51 F4 Haikang China
10 D1 Haikou China
73 H2 Hamāta, Gebel mt. Egypt
46 H3 Hailar r. China
49 F2 Hailar r. China
115 F3 Haileybury Can.
49 H4 Hailin China
49 H3 Hailun China
10 H2 Hailuoto Finland
51 F5 Haimen China
51 H1 Haimen China
51 F4 Hainan i. China
51 F4 Hainan div. China
15 □ Hainaut div. Belgium
42 D2 Hai Phong Vietnam
61 D3 Haiqing Rus. Fed.
49 J3 Hairag China
51 □ Hairhan Namag China
23 H4 Haitan Dao i. China
104 L8 Haiti country Caribbean
51 E5 Haitou China
44 H3 Haivana Nakya U.S.A.
128 D3 Haiwee Reservoir U.S.A.
49 F2 Haixing China
73 G4 Haiya Sudan
48 D5 Haiyan China
48 B5 Haiyan China
48 B5 Haiyang China
49 F5 Haiyang Dao i. China
19 K5 Hajdúböszörmény Hungary
19 K5 Hajdúdorog Hungary
19 K5 Hajdúszoboszló Hungary
57 B6 Hajjāk P. pass Afghanistan
47 H4 Hajiki-zaki pt Japan
55 H4 Hajipur India
55 F3 Hajjah Yemen
57 C4 Hajjīābād Iran
57 C3 Hajjīābād-e Zarrīn Iran
57 C3 Hajmah Iran
19 J2 Hajnówka Poland
42 A2 Haka Myanmar
80 □ Hakabi Socotra Yemen
47 G7 Hakalau U.S.A.
79 E5 Hakansson, Monts mts Zaire
90 □5 Hakau Fusi reef Tonga
60 C1 Hakkâri Turkey
60 C1 Hakkas Sweden
46 H3 Hakken-zan mt. Japan
46 H3 Hakodate Japan

82 B3 Hakos Mts mts Namibia
122 C6 Hakseenpan l. R.S.A.
125 F6 Hakui Japan
47 F5 Haku-san National Park nat. park. Japan
54 B4 Hala Pakistan
61 D1 Halab div. Syria
61 D1 Halab Syria
73 H3 Halabān Saudi Arabia
21 J3 Halabjah Iraq
49 H3 Halahai China
54 D3 Halaib Sudan
61 B4 Halāl, G. h. Egypt
61 D5 Hālat 'Ammār Saudi Arabia
127 □2 Halawa U.S.A.
61 C3 Halba Lebanon
48 A2 Halban Mongolia
18 E3 Halberstadt Germany
92 E4 Halcomb N.Z.
41 B3 Halcon, Mt mt. Phil.
11 C4 Halden Norway
18 E2 Haldensleben Germany
55 F5 Haldi r. India
55 G5 Haldia India
55 G4 Haldibari India
54 D3 Haldwani India
98 C4 Hale w Aust.
123 F3 Hale U.S.A.
60 D3 Halebiye Syria
76 D5 Half Assini Ghana
54 B4 Halfeti Turkey
93 B7 Halfmoon Bay N.Z.
12 C4 Halfway r. Can.
49 F3 Halhgol Mongolia
120 D5 Hancock U.S.A.
122 C2 Hancock U.S.A.
121 F4 Hancock U.S.A.
54 A3 Handan China
73 H4 Handan China
81 C6 Handeni Tanzania
80 D5 Handowr Sd chan. The Bahamas
94 □3 Handspike Pt pt Macquarie I. Pac. Oc.
128 C3 Hanford U.S.A.
56 A3 Hangal India
41 H5 Hangang r. S. Korea
91 □16 Hanga Roa Easter I. Chile
48 A3 Hangayn Nuruu mt. ra. Mongolia
48 D1 Hanggin Houqi China
49 D5 Hanggin Qi China
49 F5 Hangu China
54 B2 Hangu Pakistan
28 E1 Hangu Romania
51 H2 Hangzhou China
51 H2 Hangzhou Wan b. China
60 D2 Hani Turkey
73 H3 Hanīdh Saudi Arabia
29 G4 Hanife r. Turkey
73 G2 Hanīsh Kabir i. Eritrea
48 C5 Hanjiahukou China
73 □2 Hanjiaoshui China
11 F4 Hanko Finland
129 G2 Hanksville U.S.A.
54 D2 Hanle India
93 D5 Hanmer Springs N.Z.
99 E2 Hann r. Aust.
100 D3 Hann r. Aust.
11 C4 Hann, Mt mt. Aust.
112 H2 Hannah Bay b. Can.
122 B6 Hannibal U.S.A.
73 F4 Hannik well Sudan
15 E2 Hannivka Ukraine
100 D2 Hann, Mt mt. Aust.
18 D2 Hannover Germany
42 D2 Ha Nôi Vietnam
115 F2 Hanover div. Can.
133 □1 Hanover div. Jamaica
121 G3 Hanover U.S.A.
120 E5 Hanover U.S.A.
152 F3 Hansen Mts mts Ant.
115 F1 Hanshou China
121 G5 Hanshou China
42 D2 Han Shui r. China
48 C4 Hansi India
100 E4 Hanson r. Aust.
93 □1 Hanson w Aust.
96 D2 Hanson, L. salt flat Aust.
11 D5 Hanstholm Denmark
42 D2 Ha Nôi Vietnam

111 G4 Hardisty Can.
110 F2 Hardisty Lake l. Can.
121 G2 Hardwick U.S.A.
96 D3 Hardwicke B. b. Aust.
125 F4 Hardy U.S.A.
122 E4 Hardy Reservoir resr U.S.A.
61 C4 Haredin, W. w Egypt
18 C2 Haren (Ems) Germany
80 D3 Härer Ethiopia
80 D3 Härer Wildlife Sanctuary res. Ethiopia
61 □3 Harf el Mreffi mt. Lebanon
121 F4 Harford U.S.A.
80 D3 Hargant China
80 D3 Hargeysa Somalia
61 C4 Har Harif mt. Israel
48 C5 Harhatum China
73 G2 Hāmūn-i-Lora salt flat Pakistan
57 C3 Hārīb Yemen
56 A3 Haridwar India
46 E6 Harima-nada b. Japan
55 G5 Haringhat r. Bangladesh
54 C2 Haripur Pakistan
73 H4 Harjab, W. w Saudi Arabia
11 D3 Harjavalta Finland
124 E3 Harlan U.S.A.
120 B6 Harlan U.S.A.
28 E1 Hârlău Romania
126 E1 Harlem U.S.A.
18 B2 Harlingen Netherlands
125 D7 Harlingen U.S.A.
17 H6 Harlow U.K.
126 E2 Harlowton U.S.A.
60 B2 Harmancık Turkey
80 D1 Harmil i. Eritrea
122 A4 Harmony U.S.A.
61 C4 Har Nafha h. Israel
54 A3 Harnai Pakistan
126 B3 Harney Basin basin U.S.A.
133 □9 Hastings Barbados
11 E3 Hässleholm Sweden
97 F4 Hastings Aust.
92 F3 Hawke Bay b. N.Z.
92 F3 Hawke's Bay div. N.Z.
115 H4 Hawkesbury Can.
129 F3 Hawkins Peak summit U.S.A.
123 F3 Hawks U.S.A.
121 K2 Hawkshaw Can.
18 E3 Hawksnest Aust.
121 F4 Hawley U.S.A.
42 B2 Hawng Luk Myanmar
60 E4 Hawr al 'Awdah l. Iraq
60 F4 Hawr al Habbānīyah l. Iraq
60 F4 Hawr al Hammār l. Iraq
60 E3 Hawrān, Wādī w Iraq
73 H4 Hawshah, Jabal h. Saudi Arabia
97 F3 Hay Aust.
98 A4 Hay w Aust.
110 F2 Hay r. Can.
123 F5 Hay U.S.A.
15 G3 Haylaastay Mongolia
60 C2 Haymana Turkey
120 E5 Haymarket U.S.A.

131 J5 Herrero, Pta pt Mexico
97 F5 Herrick r. Aust.
120 E4 Hershey U.S.A.
17 G6 Hertford U.K.
99 H5 Hervey Bay Aust.
151 J7 Hervey Islands is Cook Is Pac. Oc.
115 J3 Hervey-Jonction Can.
99 F3 Hervey Ra. mt. ra. Aust.
133 □1 Hellshire Hills h. Jamaica
61 C3 Herzliyya Israel
18 E4 Herzogenaurach Germany
19 G4 Herzogenburg Austria
20 F1 Hesdin France
42 E2 Heshan China
51 F2 Heshengqiao China
48 E5 Heshun China
128 D4 Hesperia U.S.A.
112 C2 Hess r. Can.
18 D3 Hessen div. Germany
42 C2 Het r. Laos
128 B3 Hetch Hetchy Aqueduct canal U.S.A.
51 E4 Hetou China
124 C2 Hettinger U.S.A.
18 E3 Hettstedt Germany
20 E1 Hève, Cap de la pt France
19 K5 Heves Hungary
51 E3 Hexham U.K.
51 H4 He Xian China
51 G2 He Xian China
54 E5 Hexigten Qi China
51 E1 Heyang China
57 E3 Heydarābād Iran
57 B3 Heydarābād Iran
17 F4 Heywood Aust.
96 E4 Heywood Aust.
122 C5 Heyworth U.S.A.
51 F1 Heze China
51 E3 Hezhang China
50 C3 Hezheng China
51 H4 Hialeah U.S.A.
119 D7 Hialeah U.S.A.
124 E4 Hiawatha U.S.A.
73 H4 Hibata reg. Saudi Arabia
122 A2 Hibbing U.S.A.
97 F5 Hibbs, Pt hd Aust.
100 C2 Hibernia Reef reef Pac. Oc.
46 J2 Hibiki-nada b. Japan
119 D5 Hickory U.S.A.
131 K2 Hicks Bay N.Z.
120 A4 Hicksville U.S.A.
125 D5 Hico U.S.A.
46 J2 Hidaka Japan
47 H2 Hidaka-sanmyaku mt. ra. China
131 H4 Hidalgo div. Mexico
131 H3 Hidalgo Mexico
130 D3 Hidalgo del Parral Mexico
18 F1 Hiddensee i. Germany
144 D2 Hidrolândia Brazil
144 D1 Hidrolina Brazil
90 □2 Hienghène Pac. Oc.
47 □6 Higashi-iwa is Japan
47 G6 Higashi-izu Japan
47 H4 Higashine Japan
47 E6 Higashi-ōsaka Japan
47 □6 Higashi-suidō chan. Japan
121 J5 Higgins Bay U.S.A.
122 J3 Higgins Lake l. U.S.A.
126 B3 High Desert desert U.S.A.
122 C2 High Falls Reservoir resr U.S.A.
92 □3 High I. i. Snares Is N.Z.
121 K2 High I. i. Can.
45 High Island Res. resr Hong Kong
43 A4 Highland Park U.S.A.
128 C2 Highland Peak summit U.S.A.
114 E6 Hensall Can.
82 A3 Hentiesbaai Namibia
110 F3 High Level U.S.A.
82 A5 High Pk h. St Helena Atlantic Ocean
110 D3 High Point U.S.A.
114 G4 High Prairie Can.
132 C1 High Rock The Bahamas
111 J3 Highrock Lake l. Can.
97 F5 High Rocky Pt hd Aust.
128 C2 Hightstown U.S.A.
17 G6 High Wycombe U.K.
80 D3 Higlale well Ethiopia
80 D3 Higlokaghadcday well Somalia
130 C3 Higuera de Zaragoza Mexico
139 D4 Higueras Venezuela
133 □5 Higüey Dom. Rep.
131 K7 Hihya Egypt
10 S5 Hiidenportin kansallispuisto nat. park Finland
10 S1 Hiiumaa i. Estonia
73 G2 Hijaz reg. Saudi Arabia
129 F1 Hiko U.S.A.
47 F6 Hikone Japan
92 E2 Hikueru i. Fr. Poly.
92 F2 Hikurangi mt. N.Z.
92 F1 Hikurangi N.Z.
128 D3 Hildale U.S.A.
18 D2 Hildburghausen Germany
18 D2 Hildesheim Germany
152 B5 Hillary Coast Ant.
124 D3 Hill City U.S.A.
152 B5 Heritage Ra. mt. ra. Ant.
18 B2 Hillegom Netherlands
124 E3 Hillsboro U.S.A.
119 D5 Hilton Head Island U.S.A.

10 F1 Hammerfest Norway
122 D5 Hammond U.S.A.
125 F6 Hammond U.S.A.
123 E3 Hammond b. U.S.A.
121 F5 Hammonsport U.S.A.
121 F5 Hammonton U.S.A.
61 D1 Ham-Nord Can.
73 H3 Hampden N.Z.
121 J2 Hampden U.S.A.
125 G4 Hampton U.S.A.
121 H3 Hampton U.S.A.
121 E6 Hampton U.S.A.
101 D6 Hampton Tableland reg. Aust.
73 E5 Hamrat esh Sheikh Sudan
43 D3 Ham Tân Vietnam
57 D2 Hamta P. pass India
57 D4 Hāmūn-i Jaz Mūriān salt marsh Iran
57 B3 Hāmūn Helmand marsh Iran
59 L4 Hāmūn-i-Lora salt flat Pakistan
57 B3 Hāmūn Pu salt l. Afghanistan
122 E7 Hana U.S.A.
82 C3 Hanahai r. Botswana/Namibia
47 H4 Hanamaki Japan
73 H4 Hanare-iwa is Japan
15 C3 Hâncești Moldova
51 E1 Hancheng China
51 F2 Hanchuan China

111 G4 Hardisty Can.

56 B3 Hassan India
110 F2 Hassayampa r. U.S.A.
94 □3 Hasselborough Bay b. Macquarie I. Pac. Oc.
18 B3 Hasselt Belgium
74 B3 Hassi Aridal well Western Sahara
75 F3 Hassi Bedjedjene well Algeria
75 F2 Hassi Bel Guebbour Algeria
74 D3 Hassi Bou Bernous well Algeria
75 F3 Hassi Bourahla well Algeria
75 F3 Hassi Doumas well Western Sahara
75 F3 Hassi el Ahmar well Algeria
75 E2 Hassi el Krenig well Algeria
75 F3 Hassi Fahl well Algeria
75 E3 Hassi Habadra well Algeria
75 F2 Hassi I-n-Belrem well Algeria
75 E3 Hassi Inifel Algeria
77 D3 Hāssi Karkabane well Mali
74 D3 Hassi Mdakane well Algeria
75 F2 Hassi Messaoud Algeria
75 F2 Hassi M'Rara well Algeria
75 F2 Hassi Msegguem well Algeria
75 E2 Hassi Nebka well Algeria
73 H4 Hassis Saudi Arabia
75 F2 Hassi Sebbakh well Algeria
75 F3 Hassi Tabelbalet well Algeria
74 B4 Hassi Teraga well Algeria
75 F2 Hassi Tiguentourine well Algeria
73 H4 Hassi Ti-n-Fouchaye well Algeria
11 D4 Hässleholm Sweden
97 F4 Hastings Aust.
133 □9 Hastings Barbados
126 C3 Harney L. l. U.S.A.
11 E3 Hästveden Sweden
29 H4 Hasanoğlan Turkey
17 H6 Hastings U.K.
92 D1 Hastings N.Z.
80 □1 Hasty Yemen
110 F2 Hay River Can.
124 D4 Hays U.S.A.
80 D3 Hays Yemen
15 E2 Haysyn Ukraine
15 C2 Hayvoron Ukraine
128 A3 Hayward U.S.A.
122 B2 Hayward U.S.A.
17 G6 Haywards Heath U.K.
57 F2 Hazar-Gyaur Afghanistan
121 F3 Hazard U.S.A.
55 F5 Hazārībāg India
119 B5 Hazlehurst U.S.A.
28 D2 Hațeg Romania
20 F1 Hazebrouck France
110 D3 Hazelton Can.
121 F4 Hazleton U.S.A.
108 G2 Hazen Strait chan. Can.
15 F3 Henichesk Ukraine
93 C6 Henley N.Z.
17 G6 Henley-on-Thames U.K.
121 F5 Henlopen, Cape pt U.S.A.
47 □2 Henna Japan
20 □3 Hennebont France
18 □3 Hennef (Sieg) Germany
121 H3 Henniker U.S.A.
120 C5 Henrietta U.S.A.
112 D2 Henrietta Maria, Cape c. Can.
149 J7 Heard Island i. Indian Ocean

18 C1 Helgoland i. Germany
18 D1 Helgoländer Bucht b. Germany
10 L3 Hella Iceland
81 □5 Hell-Bourg Réunion Indian Ocean
57 B3 Helleh r. Iran
25 F3 Hellín Spain
126 C2 Hells Canyon gorge U.S.A.
123 F5 Helm U.S.A.
57 B3 Helmand r. Afghanistan
57 B3 Helmand div. Afghanistan
18 B3 Helmond Netherlands
16 F2 Helmsdale r. U.K.
18 E2 Helmstedt Germany
83 H2 Helodrano Antongila b. Madagascar
83 H2 Helodrano Mahajamba b. Madagascar
49 J4 Helong China
129 G2 Helper U.S.A.
11 D4 Helsingborg Sweden
11 D4 Helsingør Denmark
11 G3 Helsinki Finland
14S J2 Helvécia Brazil
17 F4 Helvellyn mt. U.K.
61 A5 Helwân Egypt
128 D5 Hemet U.S.A.
114 C2 Hemlo Can.
122 B3 Hay r. U.S.A.
48 B4 Haya China
46 C7 Hayasui-seto chan. Japan
50 C1 Hayachine-san mt. Japan

(continued)

47 H4 Himekami-dake mt. Japan
46 C7 Hime-shima i. Japan
47 G4 Hime-zaki pt Japan
47 F5 Himi Japan
18 D2 Himmelpforten Germany
61 D2 Ḥimṣ Syria
61 D2 Ḥimṣ div. Syria
41 C4 Hinatuan Phil.
133 D3 Hinche Haiti
99 F3 Hinchinbrook I. i. Aust.
122 A2 Hinckley U.S.A.
129 F2 Hinckley U.S.A.
121 F3 Hinckley Reservoir resr U.S.A.
79 B4 Hinda Congo
54 D3 Hindan r. India
54 D3 Hindaun India
120 B6 Hindman U.S.A.
96 E4 Hindmarsh, L. l. Aust.
55 F5 Hindola India
93 C6 Hindu N.Z.
57 G2 Hindu Kush mt. ra. Asia
56 B3 Hindupur India
61 C5 Hindu, W. al w Saudi Arabia
110 F3 Hines Creek Can.
119 D6 Hinesville U.S.A.
54 D5 Hinganghat India
57 F4 Hinglaj Pakistan
54 B2 Hingoli India
57 F2 Hinis Turkey
128 D4 Hinkley U.S.A.
10 D1 Hinnøya i. Norway
46 D6 Hino Japan
41 B4 Hinobaan Phil.
24 D3 Hinojosa del Duque Spain
46 C7 Hino Japan
46 D6 Hino-misaki pt Japan
121 G3 Hinsdale U.S.A.
11 G4 Hinton Can.
120 C6 Hinton U.S.A.
79 C4 Hippopotames de Mangai, Réserve de Faune de res. Zaire
79 E6 Hippopotames de Sakania, Réserve de res. Zaire
60 F2 Hirabit Dağ mt. Turkey
46 B7 Hirado Japan
46 B7 Hirado-shima i. Japan
47 F5 Hirakud Reservoir resr India
81 C5 Hiraman w Kenya
54 D4 Hirapur India
46 D6 Hirata Japan
76 C5 Hiré-Watta Côte d'Ivoire
46 J2 Hiroo Japan
46 H3 Hirosaki Japan
46 D6 Hiroshima div. Japan
18 E4 Hirschaid Germany
18 D3 Hirschberg Germany
15 F3 Hirsova Ukraine
15 D2 Hirs'kyy Tikych r. Ukraine
21 G2 Hirson France
21 C4 Hirtshals Denmark
54 B7 Hisaka-jima i. Japan
60 C1 Hisarönü Turkey
29 F6 Hisarönü Körfezi b. Turkey
65 G5 Hisor Tajikistan
133 E2 Hispaniola i. Caribbean
54 C1 Hispur Gl gl. Pakistan
54 F4 Hissua India
61 D2 Hisyah Syria
46 E3 Hita Japan
46 C7 Hita Japan
47 H5 Hitachi Japan
47 H5 Hitachi-ōta Japan
7 □11 Hitiaa Fr.Poly.Pac.Oc.
46 C7 Hitoyoshi Japan
10 C3 Hitra i. Norway
90 □2 Hiu i. Vanuatu
46 D6 Hiuchiga-take vol Japan
46 D6 Hiuchi-nada b. Japan
151 K6 Hiva Oa i. Fr.Poly.Pac.Oc.
110 E4 Hixon Can.
61 C4 Hiyon w Israel
60 E2 Hizan Turkey
11 E4 Hjälmaren l. Sweden
111 H2 Hjalmar Lake l. Can.
11 D3 Hjerkinn Norway
11 D4 Hjo Sweden
11 C4 Hjørring Denmark
42 B2 Hkok r. Myanmar
42 B1 Hkring Bum mt. Myanmar
42 A3 Hlaing r. Myanmar
55 F3 Hlako Kangri mt. China
83 E4 Hlatikulu Swaziland
14 A3 Hlazove Ukraine
42 B3 Hlegu Myanmar
19 G4 Hlinsko Czech Rep.
15 E2 Hlobyne Ukraine
19 H4 Hlohovec Slovakia
82 D4 Hlotse Lesotho
19 J4 Hluboká Czech Rep.
19 L4 Hlukhiv Ukraine
42 A2 Hlung-Tan Myanmar
15 B1 Hlushkavichy Belarus
12 C4 Hlybokaye Belarus
15 F2 Hlyns'k Ukraine
15 C2 Hnivan' Ukraine
19 J4 Hnúšťa Slovakia
15 G1 Hnylytsya Ukraine
15 D2 Hnylyy Tikych r. Ukraine
77 F5 Ho Ghana
42 D2 Hoa Binh Vietnam
82 B3 Hoachanaa Namibia
82 A2 Hoanib w Namibia
82 A2 Hoarusib w Namibia
97 F5 Hobart Aust.
125 D5 Hobart U.S.A.
125 C5 Hobbs U.S.A.
119 B7 Hobe Sound U.S.A.
65 L3 Hoboksar China
11 C4 Hobro Denmark
80 E3 Hobyo Somalia
82 B3 Hochfeld Namibia
43 D5 Hô Chi Minh Vietnam
19 G5 Hochschwab mt. Austria
120 B6 Hocking r. U.S.A.
131 H4 Hoctún Mexico
74 C5 Hodh reg. Mauritania
80 F2 Hodda mt. Somalia
121 K5 Hodgdon U.S.A.
74 C5 Hodh ech Chargui div. Mauritania
74 C5 Hodh El Gharbi div. Mauritania
19 K5 Hódmezővásárhely Hungary
19 H4 Hodonín Czech Rep.
9 W2 Hodh w Somalia
19 A4 Hödrögö Mongolia
45 A2 Hödrögö Mongolia
16 C2 Hoek van Holland Netherlands
9 J4 Hoengsŏng N. Korea
49 H5 Hoeryŏng N. Korea
115 H5 Hoffman Mt. mt. U.S.A.
18 E3 Hofheim in Unterfranken Germany
10 N2 Höfn Iceland
10 M2 Hofsjökull ice cap Iceland
10 M2 Hofsós Iceland
46 C6 Hōfu Japan
11 E4 Höganäs Sweden
99 F5 Hoganthulla Cr. r. Aust.
74 C2 Hoggar plat. Algeria
11 E4 Högsby Sweden
18 D4 Hohenloher Ebene plain Germany

19 F5 Hoher Dachstein mt. Austria
18 D3 Hohe Rhön mt. ra. Germany
18 F5 Hohe Tauern mt. ra. Austria
77 E5 Hohhot China
77 E5 Hohoe Ghana
15 E2 Hoholiv Ukraine
15 D1 Hoholiv Ukraine
55 G2 Hoh Xil Hu salt l. China
55 G2 Hoh Xil Shan mt. ra. China
42 E4 Hôi An Vietnam
81 B4 Hoima Uganda
42 D2 Hôi Xuân Vietnam
55 H4 Hojai India
47 D6 Hōjo Japan
50 B4 Hoke r. Myanmar
92 D1 Hokianga Harbour inlet N.Z.
47 G5 Hōki-gawa r. Japan
93 C5 Hokitika N.Z.
46 K1 Hokkaidō i. Japan
46 J2 Hokkaidō div. Japan
11 C4 Hokksund Norway
46 H2 Hokkōku Japan
47 F6 Hokuriku Tunnel tunnel Japan
11 C3 Hol Norway
56 B3 Holalkere India
140 D2 Holanda Bolivia
15 C1 Hola Prystan' Ukraine
16 D2 Holborne I. i. Aust.
99 G3 Holbrook Aust.
97 F3 Holbrook U.S.A.
129 G4 Holbrook U.S.A.
122 B3 Holcombe Flowage resr U.S.A.
11 G4 Holden Can.
129 F2 Holden U.S.A.
125 D5 Holdenville U.S.A.
124 D3 Holdrege U.S.A.
56 B3 Hole Narsipur India
133 □9 Holetown Barbados
132 C2 Holguín Cuba
19 H4 Holíč Slovakia
11 D3 Höljes Sweden
19 H4 Hollabrunn Austria
16 C2 Holland Netherlands
133 □11 Holland Bay b. Jamaica
120 D4 Hollidaysburg U.S.A.
125 D5 Hollis U.S.A.
128 B3 Hollister U.S.A.
123 F4 Holly U.S.A.
125 F5 Holly Springs U.S.A.
122 B4 Hollywood U.S.A.
108 G2 Holman Can.
10 N3 Hólmavík Iceland
11 C4 Holmestrand Vestfold Norway
11 C4 Holmön i. Sweden
109 N2 Holms Ø i. Greenland
15 A1 Holoby Ukraine
15 A2 Holohory h. Ukraine
61 C3 Holon Israel
90 □3 Holong Indonesia
82 B4 Holoog Namibia
15 D2 Holovanivs'k Ukraine
15 E2 Holovkivka Ukraine
15 D1 Holovyne Ukraine
99 E2 Holroyd r. Aust.
15 E4 Holsnøy i. Norway
11 C4 Holstebro Denmark
119 D4 Holston r. U.S.A.
120 C6 Holston Lake l. U.S.A.
122 E4 Holt U.S.A.
124 E4 Holton U.S.A.
15 D2 Holubivka Ukraine
17 E5 Holyhead U.K.
16 G4 Holy Island i. U.K.
17 E5 Holy Island i. U.K.
126 G3 Holyoke U.S.A.
121 G3 Holyoke U.S.A.
18 E5 Holzkirchen Germany
18 D3 Holzminden Germany
81 B5 Homa Bay Kenya
42 A1 Homalin Myanmar
57 B2 Homāyūnshahr Iran
18 D3 Homberg (Efze) Germany
20 F4 Hombori Mali
76 D3 Hombori Mali
18 C4 Homburg Germany
109 M3 Home Bay b. Can.
99 F1 Home Hill Aust.
94 □1 Home I. i. Cocos Is Indian Ocean
108 C4 Homer U.S.A.
125 E5 Homer U.S.A.
119 D6 Homerville U.S.A.
119 D7 Homestead Aust.
99 F4 Homestead U.S.A.
125 F5 Homewood U.S.A.
56 B2 Homnabad India
28 F1 Homocea Romania
77 G3 Homodji well Niger
83 F3 Homoine Mozambique
41 C4 Homonhon pt Phil.
15 C2 Homyel' Belarus
12 D4 Homyel' div. Belarus
56 A3 Honavar India
60 B2 Honaz Turkey
15 D1 Honcharivs'ke Ukraine
15 D1 Honchnytsya Ukraine
138 C2 Honda Colombia
16 C3 Hondeklip Baai b. S. Africa
49 H5 Hondlon Ju China
48 D1 Hon Ju China
47 H4 Hondo Japan
130 D6 Hondo r. China
141 A3 Honduras country Central America
11 C3 Hønefoss Norway
121 F4 Honesdale U.S.A.
128 B1 Honey Lake l. U.S.A.
92 □2 Honey, Mt h. Campbell I. N.Z.
121 G3 Honeoye Lake l. U.S.A.
51 F2 Hong r. China
51 F2 Hong r. China
49 G5 Hông Gai China
49 F4 Hông Hai b. China
51 H3 Honghai Wan b. China
48 C4 Honghe China
51 F2 Honghu China
51 G2 Honghu China
49 E4 Hong Kong terr. Asia
77 H3 Hong Kong Island i. China
51 E2 Hongliu r. China
49 G4 Hongliugou China
48 B4 Hongliuyuan China
48 A5 Honglong Shen China
42 D2 Hông Ngư Vietnam
48 D2 Hongor China
48 D2 Hong or Red River, Vietnam
15 B1 Horodok Ukraine
49 H4 Hongshansi China
49 G3 Hongshui r. China
57 H3 Hongtong China
48 B3 Honguedo, Détroit d' chan. Can.
49 H5 Hongwŏn N. Korea
51 G1 Hongze China
48 E2 Hongze Hu l. China
91 F3 Honiara Solomon Is.
17 F7 Honiton U.K.
46 H3 Honjō Japan
11 T3 Honkajoki Finland
47 G6 Honkawane Japan

147 D5 Hon Khoai i. Vietnam
43 E4 Hon Lon i. Vietnam
42 D3 Hon Mê i. Vietnam
56 A3 Honnali India
10 G1 Honningsvåg Norway
127 □2 Honokaa U.S.A.
7 □1 Honolulu U.S.A.
43 D5 Hon Rai i. Vietnam
24 E2 Honrubia de la Cuesta Spain
46 D6 Honshū i. Japan
126 B2 Hood, Mt vol U.S.A.
101 B7 Hood Pt pt Aust.
16 C2 Hoogeveen Netherlands
125 C4 Hooker U.S.A.
98 B3 Hooker Creek Abor. Reserve Aust.
17 D6 Hook Head hd Rep.of Ire.
99 G4 Hook I. i. Aust.
99 G3 Hook Rf reef Aust.
110 B3 Hoonah U.S.A.
108 B3 Hooper Bay U.S.A.
122 C5 Hoopeston U.S.A.
11 D5 Höör Sweden
16 E1 Hoorn Netherlands
150 H6 Hoorn, Îsles de Wallis & Futuna Pac. Oc.
121 G3 Hoosick U.S.A.
129 E3 Hoover Dam dam U.S.A.
120 B4 Hoover Memorial Reservoir resr U.S.A.
48 B3 Höövör Mongolia
60 E1 Hopa Turkey
121 F4 Hope Bottom U.S.A.
110 E5 Hope Can.
129 F5 Hope U.S.A.
125 E5 Hope U.S.A.
133 □11 Hope Bay Jamaica
13 J2 Hopedale Can.
44 F2 Hovd Mongolia
48 B3 Hovd Mongolia
57 B3 Hoveyzeh Iran
48 A2 Hövsgöl div. Mongolia
48 D4 Hövsgöl Mongolia
48 B2 Hövsgöl Nuur l. Mongolia
62 D2 Howar r. Sudan/Arctic Ocean
108 B3 Howe, Point c. U.S.A.
93 D4 Howe Saddle pass N.Z.
113 G2 Hopes Advance, Baie b. Can.
84 B4 Hövüün Mongolia
80 D1 Howakil I. i. Eritrea
15 E2 Hovtva r. Ukraine
15 E2 Hovtva Ukraine
18 B4 Höxter Germany
42 D3 Huê Vietnam
147 B5 Huehuecuicui, Pta pt Chile
114 C2 Hoyle U.S.A.
10 H3 Höytiäinen l. Finland
60 D1 Hoytla Aust.
44 E2 Hozat Turkey
19 H3 Hradec Králové Czech Rep.
15 E2 Hradyz'k Ukraine
15 C1 Hranitne Ukraine
24 D4 Hrasnica Bos.-Herz.
19 G4 Hranice Czech Rep.
15 D2 Hrebinky Ukraine
14 A3 Hrem''yach Ukraine
15 E3 Hreyhove Ukraine
19 L3 Hrodna Belarus
19 L3 Hrubieszów Poland
57 E2 Hromai r. Iran
15 F1 Hrun' r. Ukraine
15 E1 Hrushuvakha Ukraine
15 E1 Hryhorivka Chernihiv Ukraine
15 E3 Hryhorivka Kherson Ukraine
5 H4 Hufrany L. Norway
98 G5 Hugh w Aust.
99 F4 Hughenden Aust.
120 E4 Hughesville U.S.A.
54 D1 Hunza, L. take l. Can./U.S.A.
55 G5 Hugli r. India
55 G5 Hugli-Chunchura India
125 C5 Hugo U.S.A.
125 C4 Hugoton U.S.A.
49 H3 Hui'an China
49 J3 Hui'an China
92 F3 Huiarau Range mt. ra. N.Z.
82 C4 Huib-Hoch Plateau plat. S. Africa
51 H4 Huichang China
49 H4 Huich'ŏn N. Korea
51 F5 Huidong China
48 E3 Huifa r. China
51 E4 Huijue China
43 □ Huila Indon.
49 H4 Huili China
51 E4 Huili China
51 E2 Huimin China
49 H4 Huinan China
146 C3 Huinca Renancó Arg.
49 H4 Huining China
51 G6 Huishui China
48 C4 Huitong China
11 T3 Huittinen Finland
130 E5 Hui Xian China
48 D3 Hui Xian China
131 F5 Huixtla Mexico
48 C4 Huize China
51 H3 Huizhou China
49 J2 Hujirt Mongolia
48 H1 Hukawng Valley v. Myanmar
49 C5 Hukou China
82 B4 Hukuntsi Botswana
49 H1 Hulan China
49 H1 Hulan Ergi China
73 H3 Hulayfah Saudi Arabia
61 C5 Huldon Israel
11 D6 Huludao China
6 E5 Hulhaye Sudan
82 A2 Hulul r. Angola
63 G2 Hulwan Egypt
49 J2 Hulstfred Sweden
11 □ Hulun Nur l. China
15 E2 Hulyaypole Ukraine
77 E5 Huma r. China
61 C6 Humā w Iran
61 C6 Humaidan India
138 C2 Humaitá Brazil
140 D1 Humaitá Bolivia
141 A5 Humaitá Brazil
147 F2 Humaitá Paraguay
82 B4 Humansdorp R.S.A.
138 C2 Humbebe Brazil
141 F3 Humberto de Campos Brazil
79 B5 Humbe Angola
79 B5 Humbe, Serra de mts Angola
111 E4 Humboldt Can.
124 D3 Humboldt r. U.S.A.
124 E3 Humboldt U.S.A.
128 C1 Humboldt Bay b. U.S.A.
128 C1 Humboldt Lake l. U.S.A.
128 C2 Humboldt, Mt mt. Pac. Oc.

51 F2 Huangshaije China
51 G2 Huang Shan mt. China
51 G2 Huangshan China
51 F2 Huangshi China
48 B5 Huang Shui r. China
49 G5 Huang Xian China
51 H2 Huangyan China
48 B5 Huangyuan China
51 G3 Huanjiang China
49 H4 Huanren China
51 F5 Huantai China
140 C3 Huanuco Peru
140 C3 Huanuni Bolivia
140 B2 Huanzo, Cord. de mt. ra. Peru
72 C2 Huar Bolivia
51 H3 Hua-ping Hsü i. Taiwan
140 C3 Huara Chile
140 A2 Huaral Peru
140 A1 Huaráz Peru
140 D3 Huarina Bolivia
140 A2 Huarmey Peru
51 H2 Huarong China
140 A1 Huascarán, Parque Nacional nat. park Peru
146 B2 Huasco r. Chile
146 B2 Huasco Chile
130 C4 Huatabampo Mexico
131 E5 Huatusco Mexico
131 F4 Huauchinango Mexico
131 F5 Huautla Mexico
48 E4 Hua Xian China
51 E1 Hua Xian China
140 A2 Huayhuash, Cord. mt. ra. Peru
140 A1 Huaylas Peru
140 A2 Huayllay Peru
51 F2 Huayuan China
51 E4 Huazhou China
124 D2 Hubbard r. U.S.A.
123 F3 Hubbard, Mt mt. Can./U.S.A.
113 G2 Hubbard, Pointe hd Can.
51 F2 Hubei div. China
56 B3 Hubli India
15 F2 Hubynykha Ukraine
49 H4 Huch'ang N. Korea
17 G5 Huddersfield U.K.
120 B6 Huddy U.S.A.
49 G2 Huder China
11 E3 Hudiksvall Sweden
121 G3 Hudson r. U.S.A.
124 C2 Hudson r. U.S.A.
115 H4 Hudson Can.
96 F1 Hudson, L. salt flat Aust.
97 F4 Hudson, Mt mt. Aust.
122 A3 Hudson U.S.A.
123 H3 Hudson Bay Can.
115 J3 Hudson Bay b. Can.
121 G3 Hudson Falls U.S.A.
111 K3 Hudson Hope Can.
109 L3 Hudson Strait str. Can.
28 E2 Huedin Romania
131 H6 Huehuetenango Guatemala
130 D3 Huehueto, Co mt. Mexico
131 F5 Huejotzingo Mexico
131 F4 Huejutla Mexico
24 E4 Huelma Spain
25 B4 Huelva r. Spain
25 C4 Huelva Spain
25 F3 Huéneja Spain
146 B3 Huentelauquén Chile
131 F5 Huércal-Overa Spain
25 F3 Huéscar, Cabo de c. Chile
25 G2 Huesca Spain
25 E4 Huéscar Spain
131 E5 Huexotla Mexico
24 E2 Huete Spain
131 F5 Huexotla Mexico
24 E2 Huezna r. Spain
16 K1 Hufrany L. Norway
114 A2 Hugett Can.
122 D2 Hurley U.S.A.
124 D2 Huron U.S.A.
122 C2 Huron r. U.S.A.
130 C5 Huron Mts h. U.S.A.
128 B3 Hurricane U.S.A.
40 C1 Hurung, G. mt. Indon.
83 D7 Hurungwe Safari Area res. Zimbabwe
131 D5 Hur'yan China
126 B3 Hurst U.S.A.
54 B3 Husainiwala India
45 B3 Husavik Norðurland eystra Iceland
10 L2 Húsavík Vestfirðir Iceland
46 D2 Hush Al 'Abr Yemen
79 C7 Huila div. Angola
48 B4 Huilai China
76 B4 Huila Plateau plat. Angola

54 B4 Hyderabad Pakistan
21 H5 Hyères France
21 H5 Hyères, Îles d' is France
49 J4 Hyesan N. Korea
99 F5 Humedán Iran
57 D4 Humboldt Iran
51 F4 Hu man r. China
19 K4 Humenné Slovakia
97 F3 Hume Res Aust.
93 C6 Hummock h. N.Z.
79 B7 Humpata Angola
128 C3 Humphreys, Mt mt. U.S.A.
128 C3 Humphreys Peak summit U.S.A.
19 G4 Humpolec Czech Rep.
49 H4 Hun r. China
49 H4 Hun r. China
82 B2 Hun Xian China
140 B2 Huanzo, Cord. de mt. ra. Peru
50 D3 Huang Yen Vietnam
49 H4 Hunjiang China
17 H5 Hunstanton U.K.
57 H1 Hunsur India
18 C5 Hunsrück mt. ra. Germany
57 H1 Hunsur India
10 E2 Hunnebostrand Sweden
121 F3 Hunter r. Aust.
93 B7 Hunter r. N.Z.
121 F3 Hunter r. Aust.
97 G4 Hunter I. i. Aust.
93 B6 Hunters Hills, The h. N.Z.
75 G5 Hunters Is is Aust.
150 G7 Hunter I. i. Pac. Oc.
57 H2 Hunter r. India
18 D2 Hunte r. Germany
115 H4 Huntingdon Can.
119 C5 Huntingdon U.S.A.
122 D5 Huntington U.S.A.
120 B5 Huntington U.S.A.
128 D5 Huntington Beach U.S.A.
92 E2 Huntly N.Z.
16 F3 Huntly U.K.
115 H4 Huntsville Can.
119 C5 Huntsville U.S.A.
125 E6 Huntsville U.S.A.
48 B5 Hunyuan China
54 D1 Hunza China
50 D4 Huocheng China
49 G3 Huojia China
65 K4 Huocheng China
49 G5 Huolin r. China
110 D3 Huolongmen China
90 □2 Hunt I. Pac. Oc.
51 H4 Huolu China
42 D3 Huong Khê Vietnam
42 D3 Huong Thuy Vietnam
90 □1 Huon Peninsula pen. P.N.G.
97 F5 Huonville Aust.
48 D3 Huoqiu China
48 E3 Huoshan China
51 G2 Huoshan China
51 G2 Huo Shan mt. China
49 G5 Huo-shao Tao i. Taiwan
48 D5 Hua Xian China
49 H4 Hupik r. China
73 D3 Hūr Iran
37 J5 Hurbanovo Slovakia
61 B1 İçel div. Turkey
129 E3 Iceberg Canyon U.S.A.
8 E5 Iceland country Europe
144 D4 Icana Brazil
61 A1 İçel Turkey
61 B1 İçel div. Turkey
54 C3 Ichalkaranji India
82 E3 Ichchapuram India
73 F2 Ichifusa-yama mt. Japan
20 F4 Ichinomiya Japan
47 G5 Ichinoseki Japan
47 H3 Ichinoseki Japan
15 E1 Ichnya Ukraine
49 J3 Ich'ŏn S. Korea
49 H4 Ich'ŏn S. Korea
46 C7 Ichu w Yemen
76 B4 Idd el Asoda well Sudan
78 D1 Idd el Chanam well Sudan

130 D2 Ignacio Zaragoza Mexico
11 G5 Ignalina Lithuania
49 L1 Ignashino Rus. Fed.
60 B1 İğneada Turkey
28 G4 İğneada Burnu pt Turkey
45 A5 Ignoitijala Andaman and Nicobar Is India
81 B6 Igoma Tanzania
81 B5 Igombe r. Tanzania
29 C5 Igoumenitsa Greece
62 H3 Igrim Rus. Fed.
143 B6 Iguaçu r. Brazil
144 B6 Iguaçu, Parque Nacional do nat. park Arg.
145 H1 Iguaí Brazil
131 F5 Iguala Mexico
25 G2 Igualada Spain
144 E6 Iguape Brazil
142 C1 Iguará r. Brazil
144 A5 Iguatemi Brazil
144 A5 Iguatemi r. Brazil
142 E2 Iguatu Brazil
12 H3 Iguazú, Cataratas del waterfall Arg./Brazil
78 A4 Iguéla Gabon
78 A4 Iguéla, Lagune lag. Gabon
24 C1 Igueña Spain
81 B3 Igunga Tanzania
83 H1 Iharaña Madagascar
74 C2 Ihbulag Mongolia
75 E3 Iherir Algeria
77 F5 Ihiala Nigeria
77 F5 Ihnàsya el Madina Egypt
83 H3 Ihosy Madagascar
75 F3 Ihsuyi Mongolia
49 A4 Ih Tal China
47 F6 Iida Japan
48 E3 Iide-san mt. Japan
10 H1 Iijärvi l. Finland
47 G5 Iisalmi Finland
47 G5 Iiyama Japan
47 E6 Iizuka Japan
77 F5 Ijebu-Ode Nigeria
18 B2 Ijmuiden Netherlands
78 D3 Ijnàouene well Mauritania
55 H4 Imphal India
29 E4 Imralı Adası i. Turkey
29 E4 Imroz Turkey
60 B1 İmtan Syria
54 D3 Imuris Mexico
41 A4 Imuruan Bay b. Phil.
74 A4 Imza r. Rus. Fed.
24 D5 Imzouren Morocco
19 G2 Ina r. Poland
46 B4 Ina Japan
77 F5 In-Abalene well Mali
82 A5 Inaccessible I. i. Tristan da Cunha Atlantic Ocean
144 C6 Inácio Martins Brazil
75 F4 In Afaleleh well Algeria
46 D6 Ina-gawa r. Japan
47 F6 Ina-gawa r. Japan
142 B2 Inajá Brazil
75 F4 In-Akhmed well Mali
76 B3 In-Aki well Mali
77 F4 In-Alchig well Mali
77 F4 In-Aleï well Mali
77 F3 In-Amar well Mauritania
75 E4 In Aménas Algeria
77 F5 In Amguel Algeria
93 A7 In Amaguna Junction N.Z.
77 F4 Inanwatan Indon.
39 F7 Iñapari Peru
77 F5 Inari Finland
10 G1 Inari Finland
10 G1 Inarijärvi l. Finland
77 F4 In-Atankarer well Mali
138 D5 Inauini r. Brazil
47 F6 Inawashiro-ko l. Japan
77 F2 In-Azzoua well Libya
75 E2 In Azar well Libya
46 D6 Inazawa Japan
15 F3 In Azzaf well Mali
51 H1 In-lan Taiwan
77 F5 In Belbel Algeria
15 G1 Ianova r. Madagascar
146 C2 Inca, Paso del pass Arg./Chile
29 F4 Ince Burnu pt Turkey
28 G4 İnce Burun hd Turkey
29 G4 İncekum Burnu pt Turkey
80 C4 İn'inïi Terara mt. Ethiopia
6 G6 Inchiri div. Mauritania
49 H5 Inch'ŏn S. Korea
76 C2 İn-n-Daguober well Mali
145 H4 Indaiá r. Brazil
144 C6 Indaiá Grande r. Brazil
11 E3 Indalsälven r. Sweden
42 A2 Indaw Myanmar
74 C2 Indawgyi, L. l. Myanmar
122 C3 Independence U.S.A.
124 E4 Independence U.S.A.
124 E3 Independence U.S.A.
122 B5 Independence U.S.A.
122 B4 Independence U.S.A.
128 C3 Independence U.S.A.
140 C2 Independencia Bolivia
140 D2 Independencia, B. de b. Peru
28 E2 Independenţa Călăraşi Romania
28 F2 Independenţa Galaţi Romania
80 C2 Inderacha Ethiopia
64 D3 Inder, Oz. salt l. Kazak.
52 D2 Indi India
32 J7 India country Asia
115 H4 Indian r. U.S.A.
122 C5 Indiana div. U.S.A.
120 D4 Indiana U.S.A.
122 C6 Indianapolis U.S.A.
119 B7 Indianapolis airport U.S.A.
149 D6 Indian-Antarctic Ridge Pac. Oc.
122 A4 Indianola U.S.A.
125 F5 Indianola U.S.A.
145 F2 Indianópolis Brazil
127 □2 Indian Springs U.S.A.
24 E2 Indíbil Spain
62 H3 Indiga Rus. Fed.
37 N2 Indigirka r. Rus. Fed.
26 F2 Indija Yugo.
128 D5 Indio U.S.A.
32 J7 Indonesia country Asia
54 D4 Indore India
43 C7 Indramayu Indon.
43 C7 Indramayu, Tg pt Indon.
56 B2 Indravati r. India
20 E3 Indre r. France
54 A4 Indus r. Asia
54 B4 Indus, Mouths of the river mouth Pakistan

46 D6 Imabari Japan
139 F4 Imaru Brazil
146 C4 Imaichi Japan
47 F6 Imajō Japan
83 F1 Imala Mozambique
62 E3 Imandra, Ozero l. Rus. Fed.
83 H3 Imamombo Madagascar
146 E2 Iman, Sa del h. Arg.
46 B7 Imari Japan
143 C6 Imaruí Brazil
143 B6 Imbé Brazil
140 B3 Imata Peru
143 C6 Imbituba Brazil
144 C6 Imbituva Brazil
64 F5 im. Chapayeva Turkmenistan
12 G3 Imeni Babushkina Rus. Fed.
15 F1 Imeni Karla Libknekhta Rus. Fed.
12 H3 Imeni Stepana Razina Rus. Fed.
14 E2 Imeni Vorovskogo Rus. Fed.
15 F2 Imeni Lenina, Ozero l. Ukraine
80 D3 Imi Ethiopia
74 C2 Imi-n-Tanoute Morocco
74 B3 Imirikliy Labyad reg. Western Sahara
60 G2 Imişli Azerbaijan
77 F5 Imlili Western Sahara
24 A4 Imilchil Morocco
26 C3 Imo r. Nigeria
26 C3 Imola Italy
142 C2 Imotski Croatia
142 B2 Imperatriz Brazil
26 B4 Imperia Italy
124 C3 Imperial U.S.A.
128 D5 Imperial U.S.A.
128 D5 Imperial Beach U.S.A.
128 D5 Imperial Valley v. U.S.A.
78 C3 Impfondo Congo

60 B1 İnegöl Turkey
75 F4 In Ekker Algeria
40 E4 Inerie vol Indon.
28 C1 Ineu Romania
120 B6 Inez U.S.A.
75 G4 In Ezzane well Algeria
131 E5 Infiernillo, L. l. Mexico
24 D1 Infiesto Spain
12 E1 Inga Rus. Fed.
42 A3 Ingabu Myanmar
77 F3 Ingal Niger
122 D3 Ingalls U.S.A.
111 J2 Ingalls Lake l. Can.
128 B2 Ingalls, Mt. U.S.A.
65 H1 Ingaly Rus. Fed.
78 C4 Ingende Zaire
146 D1 Ingeniero Guillermo Nueva Juárez Arg.
147 C5 Ingeniero Jacobacci Arg.
25 □ Ingenio Canary Is Spain
114 E3 Ingersoll Can.
48 B2 Ingettolgoy Mongolia
99 F3 Ingham Aust.
109 L2 Inglefield Land reg. Greenland
99 G6 Inglewood Aust.
97 E4 Inglewood Aust.
92 E3 Inglewood N.Z.
6 E2 Ingoda r. Rus. Fed.
18 E4 Ingolstadt Germany
113 H4 Ingonish Can.
55 G4 Ingrāj Bāzār India
110 F2 Ingray Lake l. Can.
140 D4 Ingre Bolivia
152 D5 Ingrid Christensen Coast Ant.
75 F5 I-n-Guezzam Algeria
13 H7 Ingushetiya div. Rus. Fed.
83 F3 Inhambane Mozambique
83 F3 Inhambane div. Mozambique
83 F3 Inhambane, Baia de b. Mozambique
142 E3 Inhambupe Brazil
83 F2 Inhaminga Mozambique
145 G3 Inhapim Brazil
83 F3 Inharrime Mozambique
142 D3 Inhaúmas Brazil
145 H1 Inhobim Brazil
15 E3 Inhul r. Ukraine
15 E3 Inhulets' r. Ukraine
15 E3 Inhulets' r. Ukraine
144 D2 Inhumas Brazil
25 F3 Iniesta Spain
145 F3 Inimutaba Brazil
139 G3 Inini French Guiana
138 D3 Inírida r. Colombia
11 B5 Inishbofin i. Rep. of Ire.
17 C5 Inishmore i. Rep. of Ire.
17 C5 Inishmurray i. Rep. of Ire.
17 D4 Inishowen pen. Rep. of Ire.
17 D4 Inishtrahull i. Rep. of Ire.
17 B5 Inishturk i. Rep. of Ire.
49 F3 Injgan Sum China
99 G5 Injune Aust.
99 E3 Inkerman Aust.
57 E1 Inkylap Turkmenistan
93 D5 Inland Kaikoura Range mt. ra. N.Z.
42 B2 Inle, L. l. Myanmar
18 F4 Inn r. Austria/Germany
96 E1 Innamincka Aust.
10 D2 Inndyr Norway
16 E3 Inner Sound chan. U.K.
99 E3 Innisfail Aust.
49 J2 Innoken'yevka Rus. Fed.
46 D6 Innoshima Japan
18 E5 Innsbruck Austria
44 A3 Inocência Brazil
78 C4 Inongo Zaire
76 D3 I-n-Ouchef well Mali
19 J2 Inowrocław Poland
140 D3 Inquisivi Bolivia
75 E3 In Salah Algeria
62 E2 Insar r. Rus. Fed.
52 G4 Insar Rus. Fed.
101 A5 Inscription, C. c. Aust.
42 B3 Insein Myanmar
28 F2 Însurăţei Romania
83 E3 Insuza r. Zimbabwe
42 C3 Inta r. Rus. Fed.
77 F3 I-n-Tabakat well Niger
77 F2 I-n-Tadéra well Niger
77 E3 I-n-Talak well Mali
77 F3 I-n-Tebezas Mali
77 F3 I-n-Tédébni well Niger
146 D4 Intendente Alvear Arg.
29 F4 İntepe Turkey
124 E1 International Falls U.S.A.
43 A4 Interview I. i. Andaman and Nicobar Is India
146 D2 Intiyaco Arg.
28 F2 Întorsura Buzăului Romania
131 G2 Intracoastal Waterway canal U.S.A.
12 G1 Intsy Rus. Fed.
82 D2 Intundhla Zimbabwe
138 C4 Intutu Peru
47 H6 Inubō-zaki pt Japan
46 C7 Inukai Japan
112 E2 Inukjuak Can.
108 C3 Inuvik Can.
16 E3 Inveraray U.K.
79 B4 Inverbervie U.K.
93 B7 Invercargill N.Z.
92 G2 Inverell Aust.
113 H4 Invermere Can.
16 E3 Inverness U.K.
119 D6 Inverness U.S.A.
98 B3 Inverway Aust.
43 B4 Investigator Chan. chan. Myanmar
96 C3 Investigator Group is Aust.
96 D3 Investigator Strait chan. Aust.
65 L2 Inya r. Rus. Fed.
65 K1 Inya r. Rus. Fed.
83 E2 Inyanga mts Zimbabwe
127 C5 Inyokern U.S.A.
128 C3 Inyo Mts mts U.S.A.
80 C4 Inyonga Tanzania
14 H3 Inza r. Rus. Fed.
62 F2 Inza Rus. Fed.
64 E2 Inzer Rus. Fed.
52 H3 Inzhavino Rus. Fed.
79 C5 Inzia r. Zaire
29 G5 Ioannina Greece
39 M2 Iō-jima i. Japan
125 E4 Iola U.S.A.
28 E2 Ioneşti div. Romania
79 J4 Ipel' r. Hungary/Slovakia
28 E2 Ipeleqeng R.S.A.
138 B3 Ipiales Colombia
19 J4 Ipel' r. Hungary/Slovakia
138 D3 Ipiales Colombia
142 B3 Ipiaú Brazil
144 C6 Ipiranga Brazil
140 B1 Ipixuna Amazonas Brazil

142 D1 Ipixuna Maranhão Brazil
142 B1 Ipixuna r. Brazil
43 C6 Ipoh Malaysia
142 E2 Ipojuca r. Brazil
144 B5 Iporá Brazil
144 D6 Iporanga Brazil
78 D2 Ippy C.A.R.
29 F4 İpsala Turkey
99 H5 Ipswich Aust.
133 ¹ Ipswich Jamaica
17 J5 Ipswich U.K.
142 D1 Ipu Brazil
144 D4 Ipuã Brazil
142 D3 Ipueiras Brazil
142 D3 Ipupiara Brazil
109 M3 Iqaluit Can.
141 E2 Iqué r. Brazil
146 B3 Iquique Chile
138 C4 Iquitos Peru
14 F3 Ira r. Rus. Fed.
78 D2 Ira Banda C.A.R.
139 G2 Iracoubo French Guiana
57 E4 Īrafshān reg. Iran
142 E1 Irajuba Brazil
143 B6 Irai Brazil
29 D4 Irakleia Kentriki Makedonia Greece
29 E6 Irakleia i. Greece
29 E7 Irakleio Greece
142 D3 Iramaia Brazil
59 H3 Iran Iran
60 F2 Īrānshāh Iran
57 E4 Īrānshahr Iran
14 D2 Irapa Ven.
130 D4 Irapuato Mexico
32 F6 Iraq country Asia
59 J3 Irara Brazil
139 G4 Iratapuru r. Brazil
144 C6 Irati Brazil
12 K1 Irayel' Rus. Fed.
60 C3 Irbid Jordan
142 D3 Irecê Brazil
78 C4 Ireko Zaire
119 ¹ Ireland Island i. Bermuda
4 ¹ Ireland, Republic of country Europe
78 D4 Irema Zaire
139 F3 Ireng r. Brazil
146 B6 Iretama Brazil
64 F3 Irgiz Kazak.
64 F3 Irgiz r. Kazak.
62 B3 Irgiz, B. r. Rus. Fed.
74 C2 Irhil M'Goun mt. Morocco
75 F3 Irhzer Ediessane w Algeria
49 H6 Iri S. Korea
39 L8 Irian Jaya div. Indon.
72 D2 Iriba Chad
41 A3 Iriga Phil.
75 G3 Irigui reg. Mali/Mauritania
81 B6 Iringa div. Tanzania
81 C6 Iringa Tanzania
56 B4 Irinjalakuda India
51 J3 Iriri r. Brazil
142 B2 Iriri Novo r. Brazil
17 G5 Irish Sea sea Rep. of Ire./U.K.
142 C1 Irituia Brazil
15 E2 Irkestam Kyrgyzstan
15 E2 Irkliyiv Ukraine
48 C1 Irkut r. Rus. Fed.
48 C1 Irkutsk Rus. Fed.
48 C1 Irkutsk div. Rus. Fed.
72 B2 Iro, Lac l. Chad
96 D3 Iron Baron Aust.
96 D3 Iron Bridge Can.
120 E3 Irondequoit U.S.A.
96 D3 Iron Knob Aust.
122 C3 Iron Mountain U.S.A.
127 D3 Iron Mt mt. U.S.A.
99 E2 Iron Range Nat. Park nat. park Aust.
122 C2 Iron River U.S.A.
125 F4 Ironton U.S.A.
120 B5 Ironton U.S.A.
122 B2 Ironwood U.S.A.
114 E2 Iroquois Can.
115 J3 Iroquois r. U.S.A.
114 J2 Iroquois Falls Can.
47 G6 Irosin Phil.
47 H6 Irō-zaki hd Japan
15 D1 Irpin' Ukraine
15 D1 Irpin' r. Ukraine
73 H3 'Irq Subay sand dunes Saudi Arabia
42 A4 Irrawaddy r. China/Myanmar
42 A4 Irrawaddy div. Myanmar
42 A4 Irrawaddy, Mouths of the river mouth Myanmar
15 C1 Irsha r. Ukraine
14 J3 Irshad P. Afghanistan/Pakistan
12 J2 Irta Rus. Fed.
65 H1 Irtysh r. Kazak./Rus. Fed.
65 H1 Irtyshsk Kazak.
78 E3 Irumu Zaire
25 F1 Irún Spain
140 C3 Irupana Bolivia
17 E4 Irvine U.K.
128 C4 Irvine U.S.A.
125 D6 Irving U.S.A.
101 A6 Irwin r. Aust.
77 F4 Isa Nigeria
64 E1 Isaac r. Aust.
41 B5 Isabela Phil.
137 ¹ Isabela Puerto Rico
133 E2 Isabela, Cabo pt Dominican Rep.
138 ¹ Isabela, Isla i. Galapagos Is Ecuador
138 ¹ Isabela, Isla i. Galapagos Is Ecuador
130 K6 Isabelia, Cordillera mt. ra. Nicaragua
122 B2 Isabella de Sagua Cuba
145 H4 Isabelle, Pt pt U.S.A.
119 ¹ Isabel Segunda Puerto Rico
28 G3 Ísafjörður est. Iceland
10 ¹² Ísafjörður Iceland
54 C4 Isagarh India
46 D7 Isahaya Japan
78 C3 Isaka Zaire
81 A6 Isaka Tanzania
14 E2 Īshsbet Pakistan
142 E1 Isaka Rus. Fed.
54 B2 Isalo, Parc National de l' nat. park Madagascar
55 F5 Itaki India
4 ¹² Italy country Europe
145 J2 Itamaraju Brazil
77 H4 Isanlu Nigeria
79 B4 Isandja Zaire

46 H2 Ishikari-wan b. Japan
47 F5 Ishikawa div. Japan
47 F5 Ishikawa Japan
65 G2 Ishim r. Kazak./Rus. Fed.
65 H1 Ishim Rus. Fed.
46 H5 Ishimbay Rus. Fed.
64 E2 Ishimbay Rus. Fed.
65 H1 Ishimskaya Step' plain Rus. Fed.
65 G2 Ishimskoye Kazak.
47 H4 Ishinomaki Japan
46 H5 Ishinomaki-wan b. Japan
47 H5 Ishioka Japan
46 D7 Ishizuchi-san mt. Japan
65 H5 Ishkoshim Tajikistan
14 D1 Ishnya Rus. Fed.
122 D2 Ishpeming U.S.A.
65 G5 Ishtykhan Uzbekistan
55 G4 Ishurdi Bangladesh
140 D3 Isiboro Sécure, Parque Nacional nat. park Bolivia
20 D2 Isigny-sur-Mer France
46 H3 Isil'kul' Rus. Fed.
65 G2 Isil'kul' Rus. Fed.
81 E4 Isinga Rus. Fed.
83 E1 Isingiro Uganda
61 C1 İskenderun Turkey
61 C1 İskenderun Körfezi b. Turkey
61 C1 İskilip Turkey
64 D3 İskine Kazak.
14 E4 Iski r. Rus. Fed.
15 E2 İskrivka Kirovohrad Ukraine
15 E2 İskrivka Poltava Ukraine
14 B1 İskür r. Bulgaria
80 F2 İskushuban Somalia
110 C3 İskut r. Can.
110 C3 İskut Can.
24 C4 Isla Cristina Spain
60 D2 İslahiye Turkey
78 E4 Isiro Zaire
99 F5 Isisford Aust.
78 D3 Isiro Zaire
99 F5 Isisford Aust.
61 C1 İskenderun Turkey
61 C1 İskenderun Körfezi b. Turkey
119 D4 Islamorada U.S.A.
41 A4 Island Bay b. Phil.
121 J1 Island Falls U.S.A.
111 L4 Island Lake l. Can.
96 D2 Island Lagoon salt flat Aust.
111 L4 Island Lake Can.
122 A2 Island Lake l. U.S.A.
128 A1 Island Mountain U.S.A.
121 H2 Island Pond U.S.A.
92 E1 Islands, Bay of b. N.Z.
17 D5 Islay i. U.K.
20 E3 Isle r. France
21 H3 Isle of Wight U.K.
114 A1 Isle Royale National Park nat. park U.S.A.
25 ² Isleta, La pen. Canary Is Spain
133 ³ Islote Pt pt Trinidad Trin. & Tobago
73 F1 Ismâ'ilîya Egypt
13 G1 İsmayıllı Azerbaijan
73 F1 Isna Egypt
11 F3 Isojoki Finland
81 B7 Isoka Zambia
10 F3 Isokylä Finland
26 D3 Isola della Scala Italy
27 F6 Isola di Capo Rizzuto Italy
139 F2 Isparta Bulgaria
57 B4 İsperih Bulgaria
72 E4 İspir Turkey
141 E5 Ituri r. Paraguay
78 E4 Ituri r. Zaire
43 B3 İsquiluac, I. i. Chile
32 E6 Israel country Asia
75 E3 Israelândia Brazil
74 A4 Issa r. Mordoviya Rus. Fed.
14 G3 Issa Rus. Fed.
78 A3 Issanguele Cameroon
139 F2 Issano Guyana
76 C5 Issia Côte d'Ivoire
20 E3 Issoudun France
21 D3 Is-sur-Tille France
65 J4 Issyk' India
144 C1 Ivaiporã Brazil

145 F4 Itapecerica Brazil
145 H4 Itapemirim Brazil
145 H3 Itapetinga Brazil
145 H1 Itapetininga Brazil
144 D5 Itaperuna Brazil
139 F3 Itapi r. Brazil
142 E1 Itapicuru r. Bahia Brazil
142 D1 Itapicuru r. Maranhão Brazil
142 D1 Itapicuru Mirim r. Brazil
142 D1 Itapipoca Brazil
145 E3 Itápira Brazil
139 F4 Itapiranga Brazil
144 C1 Itapirapuã Brazil
144 C1 Itápolis Brazil
144 D5 Itaporanga São Paulo Brazil
144 B1 Itapuranga Goiás Brazil
145 E5 Itaquaquecetuba Brazil
143 A5 Itaquari Brazil
144 A6 Itaquyri Paraguay
144 D1 Itarana Brazil
145 H1 Itarantim Brazil
143 D6 Itararé Brazil
54 D5 Itarsi India
144 C3 Itarumã Brazil
145 H1 Itati r. Brazil
142 E1 Itatiba Brazil
145 E3 Itatinga Brazil
142 B1 Itatupã Brazil
144 D2 Itauçu Brazil
142 E1 Itauaara r. Brazil
144 A5 Itaum Brazil
141 E3 Itaúna Brazil
145 J3 Itaúnas r. Brazil
145 J3 Itaúnas r. Brazil
41 B1 Itbayat i. Phil.
110 H5 Itchen Lake l. Can.
140 B3 Ite Peru
29 D5 Itea Sterea Ellas Greece
78 E4 Itebero Zaire
79 E7 Itezhi-Tezhi Dam Zambia
122 E4 Ithaca U.S.A.
120 E3 Ithaca U.S.A.
29 C5 Ithaki i. Greece
61 D5 Ithl, W. al w Saudi Arabia
61 D4 Ithriyat, Jebel h. Jordan
78 D3 Itimbiri r. Zaire
145 H2 Itinga Brazil
78 D2 Itiquira r. Brazil
144 A2 Itiquira Brazil
144 E4 Itirapuã Brazil
144 B5 Itiruçu Brazil
64 D3 Itmurinkol', Oz. l. Kazak.
47 G6 Itō Japan
47 G6 Itoigawa Japan
78 D4 Itoko Zaire
47 ² Itoman Japan
61 B5 Itsa Egypt
61 A3 Ittiri Italy
109 Q2 Ittoqqortoormiit Greenland
138 D2 Ituango Colombia
138 D5 Itui r. Brazil
144 D3 Ituiutaba Brazil
144 D3 Itumbiara, Barragem resr Brazil
139 F3 Ituni Guyana
144 C2 Itupiranga Brazil
144 C3 Ituporanga Brazil
144 C3 Iturama Brazil
141 E5 Iturbe Paraguay
78 E4 Ituri r. Zaire
45 D3 Iturup, Ostrov i. Rus. Fed.
146 D2 Ituzaingo Arg.
18 D2 Itzehoe Germany
14 E2 Itzer Germany
142 D2 Iuaretê Brazil
108 B3 Iultin U.S.A.
54 B5 Iúna Brazil
146 E1 Iúna Brazil
131 F4 Ivaí r. Brazil
144 C3 Ivaí r. Brazil
28 E2 Ivajlovgrad Bulgaria
26 D3 Ivanava Belarus
97 G4 Ivanec Croatia
97 G4 Ivanhoe Aust.
111 J3 Ivanhoe Can.
114 D1 Ivanhoe Lake l. Can.
54 C2 Ivanishchi Rus. Fed.
15 F1 Ivanivka Kherson Ukraine
15 E2 Ivanivka Kherson Ukraine
15 D3 Ivanivka Odesa Ukraine
28 E2 Ivanjica Yugo.
14 C1 Ivankovo Rus. Fed.
14 C1 Ivan'kovo Vdkhr. resr Rus. Fed.
14 C1 Ivan'kovskoye Vdkhr. resr Rus. Fed.
15 C2 Ivano-Frankivs'k div. Ukraine
15 C2 Ivano-Frankivs'k Ukraine
15 G2 Ivanopil' Ukraine
142 D1 Ivanov Rus. Fed.
142 D1 Ivanovo Brazil
14 H1 Ivanovo div. Rus. Fed.
14 H1 Ivanovo Rus. Fed.
26 F2 Ivanovo Bos.-Herz.
26 F2 Ivanovskoye Rus. Fed.
52 H3 Ivanteyevka Rus. Fed.
15 C2 Ivanychi Ukraine
72 B1 İvanyns'ke Ukraine
54 C4 Ivanya Yugo.
20 F3 Ivato Madagascar
14 G3 Ivedal Brazil
9 H3 Ivdel' Rus. Fed.
142 B3 Ivinhema Brazil
83 ¹ Ivohibe Madagascar
83 ¹ Ivohibe Madagascar
142 ¹ Ivolândia Brazil
4 ¹ Ivot r. Rus. Fed.
146 D2 Ivrea Italy
29 F4 İvrindi Turkey
116 Can. Ivujivik Can.
47 H4 Iwaizumi Japan
47 G5 Iwaki Japan
47 F5 Iwaki-san vol Japan
46 B6 Iwakuni Japan
47 H4 Iwamizawa Japan
47 H3 Iwanai Japan
47 H4 Iwanuma Japan
47 G5 Iwata Japan
77 F5 Iwo Nigeria
130 C3 Ixmiquilpan Mexico
131 F4 Ixtaba, L. l. Guatemala
131 H5 Izabal, L. de l. Guatemala
131 E5 Izamal Mexico
131 E5 Izapa Mexico
46 H2 Ishikari-gawa r. Japan

81 C6 Izazi Tanzania
13 H7 Izberbash Rus. Fed.
14 A2 Izberb'evo Rus. Fed.
57 B3 Īzeh Iran
73 F3 Izgagane well Niger
54 C2 Izhar India
62 G4 Izhevsk Rus. Fed.
62 G4 Izhevsk Rus. Fed.
62 G3 Izhma r. Rus. Fed.
62 G3 Izhma Rus. Fed.
15 C3 Izmalkovo Rus. Fed.
28 D2 Izmayil Ukraine
14 H3 Izmayilovo Rus. Fed.
60 A2 İzmir Turkey
29 F5 İzmir div. Turkey
29 F5 İzmir Körfezi b. Turkey
24 E5 İznajar Spain
24 E4 İznalloz Spain
73 D3 Izra' Syria
29 E4 Iztochni Rodopi mt. ra. Bulgaria
72 G6 Izu-hantō pen. Japan
46 C7 Izumi Japan
47 E6 Izumo Japan
46 D6 Izumo Japan
47 G6 Izu-Shotō is Japan
15 J2 Izvestkovy Rus. Fed.
15 B1 Izyaslav Ukraine
15 G2 Izyum Ukraine

J

57 D2 Jaba r. Iran
24 E3 Jabalón r. Spain
98 C3 Jabalpur India
73 H4 Jabbārah Fara Is i. Saudi Arabia
98 C3 Jabiru Aust.
60 C3 Jabla Syria
54 C3 Jablanica r. Yugo.
19 G3 Jablonec nad Nisou Czech Rep.
19 J4 Jabłonków Czech Rep.
19 K3 Jabłonowo Pomorskie Poland
142 E2 Jaboatão Brazil
144 D4 Jaboticabal Brazil
26 E4 Jabuka i. Bos.-Herz.
54 D1 Jabuka r. Yugo.
78 C4 Jabukovac Yugo.
142 B3 Jacaré r. Brazil
142 E1 Jacaré r. Brazil
144 D3 Jacarezinho Brazil
145 F5 Jacareí Brazil
145 G4 Jacaraú Brazil
144 D5 Jaceaba Brazil
96 A5 Jackaranca Aust.
99 G5 Jackson Aust.
122 E4 Jackson U.S.A.
124 D2 Jackson U.S.A.
120 B6 Jackson U.S.A.
122 D4 Jackson U.S.A.
56 A2 Jackson India
93 B6 Jackson Bay b. N.Z.
93 E4 Jackson, Cape c. N.Z.
93 B5 Jackson Head hd N.Z.
121 G3 Jackson, L. l. U.S.A.
122 D5 Jackson, Lake U.S.A.
122 D5 Jacksonport U.S.A.
119 D6 Jacksonville U.S.A.
118 B4 Jacksonville U.S.A.
119 E5 Jacksonville U.S.A.
125 E5 Jacksonville U.S.A.
119 D6 Jacksonville Beach U.S.A.
133 D3 Jacmel Haiti
130 D2 Jaco Mexico
54 C2 Jacobabad Pakistan
129 F3 Jacob Lake U.S.A.
25 ¹ Jacquemart I. i. Campbell I. N.Z.
113 H3 Jacques-Cartier, Détroit de chan. Can.
113 G3 Jacques Cartier, Mt mt. Can.
113 G3 Jacques Cartier, Parc de la res. Can.
113 G4 Jacquet River Can.
54 A3 Jacuba r. Brazil
142 C1 Jacui r. Minas Gerais Brazil
142 C1 Jacundá Brazil
142 C1 Jacundá r. Brazil
145 H2 Jacupiranga Brazil
138 Jacura Venezuela
26 F3 Jadar r. Bos.-Herz.
26 F2 Jadovnik mt. Bos.-Herz.
72 B1 Jādū Libya
24 E4 Jaén Peru
24 E4 Jaén Spain
33 P6 Ja'farābād Iran
14 J3 Jaffa, C. c. Aust.
121 G3 Jaffna Sri Lanka
121 G3 Jaffrey U.S.A.
54 D3 Jagadhri India
56 B2 Jagdalpur India
54 C3 Jagdaqi China
54 C4 Jagdispur India
14 H5 Jagersfontein R.S.A.
14 A3 Jagodina Yugo.
131 F4 Jaggang China

110 C2 Jakes Corner Can.
54 B5 Jakhan India
72 D2 Jakharrah Libya
11 U3 Jäkkvik Sweden
81 D5 Jasiird Jofay i. Somalia
125 C5 Jal U.S.A.
49 G3 Jalaid Qi China
57 G2 Jalālābād Afghanistan
54 C3 Jalalabad India
55 H4 Jalalabad India
65 H4 Jalal-Abad div. Kyrgyzstan
65 H4 Jalal-Abad Kyrgyzstan
54 C3 Jalalpur India
77 G4 Jalam Nigeria
131 G6 Jalapa Guatemala
131 F5 Jalapa Mexico
130 J6 Jalapa Nicaragua
11 F5 Jalasjärvi Finland
55 G2 Jaldhaka r. Bangladesh
55 B2 Jaldrug India
144 D4 Jales Brazil
55 F5 Jaleshwar India
55 D5 Jalgaon India
54 D4 Jalgaon India
77 G4 Jalingo Nigeria
56 A2 Jalna India
54 D4 Jaloi Pakistan
25 F2 Jalón r. Spain
54 C4 Jalor India
54 C4 Jalor India
130 E4 Jalostotitlán Mexico
28 E4 Jalovik Yugo.
130 E4 Jalpa Mexico
55 G4 Jalpaiguri India
131 F4 Jalpan Mexico
72 D2 Jālū Oasis oasis Libya
57 E2 Jām r. Iran
57 E2 Jām r. Iran
72 D2 Jālū Iraq
60 F3 Jalūlā' Iraq
145 F5 Jaú Brazil
132 D3 Jamaica country Caribbean
132 D3 Jamaica Channel chan. Haiti/Jamaica
57 B2 Jamālābād Iran
55 G4 Jamalpur Bangladesh
144 B3 Jamanxim r. Brazil
132 ¹ Jamanota mt. Aruba
141 D1 Jamari r. Brazil
138 A4 Jambeli, Can. de chan. Ecuador
40 A2 Jambi Indon.
40 A2 Jambi div. Indon.
25 G3 Jávea Spain
54 C4 Jambo India
19 J4 Jambongan i. Malaysia
19 J4 Jambusar India
124 D2 James r. U.S.A.
122 E4 James Bay b. Can.
147 B6 James, I. i. Chile
109 Q2 Jameson Land reg. Greenland
93 B6 James Pk mt. N.Z.
98 C5 James Ranges mt. ra. Aust.
152 B2 James Ross I. i. Ant.
121 H2 Jamestown St Helena Atlantic Ocean
121 H2 Jamestown U.S.A.
96 D3 Jamestown Aust.
119 E5 Jamestown U.S.A.
124 D2 Jamestown U.S.A.
120 D3 Jamestown U.S.A.
121 H3 Jamestown U.S.A.
120 B6 Jamestown U.S.A.
55 G4 Jamkhandi India
54 B2 Jamkhed India
56 A2 Jammalamadugu India
54 D1 Jammu and Kashmir terr. Asia
54 B5 Jamnagar India
54 C3 Jamni r. India
40 A3 Jampang Kulon Indon.
54 C3 Jampur Pakistan
11 U3 Jämsä Finland
11 G3 Jämsänkoski Finland
55 G4 Jamshedpur India
55 F4 Jamtari Nigeria
11 G5 Jämtland div. Sweden
55 G4 Jamuna r. Bangladesh
80 B3 Janaale Somalia
55 H4 Janakpur Nepal
145 G1 Janaúba Brazil
139 E4 Janaucú, Ilha i. Brazil
24 D5 Jand Pakistan
54 D1 Jandaq Iran
144 C5 Jandaia do Sul Brazil
77 G4 Jandaí Nigeria
25 ¹ Jandía, Pta de pt Canary Is Spain
25 ¹ Jandía, Pta de pt Canary Is Spain
144 D5 Jandira Brazil
138 ¹ Jangamo Mozambique
78 B3 Jangany Madagascar
54 C3 Jangaon India
55 H5 Janghai India
145 G1 Jangipur India
14 H2 Janikowo Poland
19 J5 Janjanbureh Gambia
28 E3 Jánoshalma Hungary
19 H5 Jánosháza Hungary
19 J5 Janów Lubelski Poland
19 L5 Janów Podlaski Poland
72 B1 Jādū Libya
19 J5 Januária Brazil
145 G1 Januária Brazil
143 E6 Janúario Cicco Brazil
54 C4 Jaora India
33 P6 Japan country Asia
150 E4 Japan, Sea of sea Asia
46 C6 Japan Tr. Pac. Oc.
138 C4 Japurá r. Brazil
138 E4 Japurá Brazil
132 C2 Jaqué Panama
19 G3 Jaraguá Brazil
19 G3 Jaraguá do Sul Brazil
145 G4 Jaraguari Brazil
24 D3 Jaraicejo Spain
24 D3 Jaral de la Vera Spain
54 B3 Jarash Jordan
144 D2 Jaraguá Brazil
142 C2 Jardim Brazil
144 C4 Jardinópolis Brazil
142 D3 Jaraguá do Sul Brazil
132 C2 Jardines de la Reina is Cuba
144 A3 Jardinópolis Brazil
18 ¹ Jaraucú, Rio r. Brazil
99 F3 Jardine River Nat. Park nat. park Aust.
132 C2 Jardines de la Reina is Cuba

120 E4 Jersey Shore U.S.A.
118 B4 Jerseyville U.S.A.
98 C4 Jervois Ra. h. Aust.
27 B6 Jerzu Italy
26 E2 Jesenice Slovenia
19 H3 Jeseník Czech Rep.
26 D3 Jesi Italy
18 F3 Jessen Germany
55 G5 Jessore Bangladesh
11 C3 Jessheim Norway
119 D6 Jesup U.S.A.
131 G5 Jesús Carranza Mexico
146 D3 Jesús María Arg.
76 H4 Jetalsar India
54 B5 Jetalsar India
124 D3 Jetmore U.S.A.
115 K6 Jewett City U.S.A.
19 K2 Jeziorany Poland
26 E3 Jeziorsko, Jez. l. Poland
19 H2 Jeziorsko l. Poland
19 H1 Jezioro Dargin l. Poland
19 H1 Jezioro Jamno lag. Poland
19 J2 Jezioro Jeziorak l. Poland
19 J3 Jezioro Jeziorsko l. Poland
19 J1 Jezioro Łebsko lag. Poland
19 K1 Jezioro Mamry l. Poland
19 J2 Jezioro Miedwie l. Poland
19 K2 Jezioro Narie l. Poland
19 J4 Jezioro Śniardwy l. Poland
19 J2 Jezioro Sulejowskie l. Poland
19 K2 Jezioro Zegrzyńskie l. Poland
61 C3 Jezzine Lebanon
54 D4 Jhabua India
54 B4 Jha Jha India
54 C4 Jhajju India
49 E2 Jhajjar India
55 G5 Jhalakati Bangladesh
54 C4 Jhalawar India
54 A4 Jhal Jhao Pakistan
80 E2 Jhalrapatan India
54 C3 Jhang Maghiana Pakistan
54 D4 Jhansi India
55 F5 Jharsuguda India
54 D5 Jhatpat Pakistan
55 H5 Jhawani Nepal
54 C3 Jhelum r. India
54 C3 Jhelum Pakistan
130 J6 Jhenida Bangladesh
130 J7 Jhudo Pakistan
50 D3 Jhunjhunün India
51 ¹ Jiading China
51 ¹ Jiahe China
49 J3 Jiajiang China
51 ¹ Jiamusi China
49 H4 Ji'an China
80 C4 Jiangcheng China
50 C4 Jiangchuan China
51 ¹ Jiangdong China
50 E2 Jiangdu China
48 ¹ Jiange China
51 ¹ Jiangkou China
51 ¹ Jiangkou China
51 ¹ Jiangling China
50 E2 Jiangmen China
49 F5 Jiangshan China
51 ¹ Jiangsu div. China
51 ¹ Jiangtaibu China
51 ¹ Jiangxi div. China
51 ¹ Jiangyan China
51 ¹ Jiangyin China
51 ¹ Jiangyong China
51 ¹ Jiangyou China
51 ¹ Jianhu China
51 ¹ Jiaojiang China
48 ¹ Jiaozhou Wan b. China
50 D3 Jiaozuo China
49 G4 Jiaxing China

130 D3 Jiménez Chihuahua Mexico
131 E3 Jiménez Coahuila Mexico
131 F3 Jiménez Tamaulipas Mexico
77 G5 Jimeta Nigeria
90 ¹ Jimi r. P.N.G.
49 G5 Jimo China
44 E3 Jimsar China
121 F4 Jim Thorpe U.S.A.
51 F2 Jin r. China
49 F5 Jin'an China
48 B5 Jincheng China
52 F1 Jincheng China
50 D2 Jinchuan China
51 F1 Jinchuan China
97 G4 Jindabyne Aust.
19 G4 Jindřichův Hradec Czech Rep.
50 A5 Jinfosi China
51 H3 Jing r. China
48 A5 Jingbian China
48 D5 Jingchuan China
51 G2 Jingde China
50 D1 Jingdezhen China
51 G2 Jingdong China
51 G3 Jinggangshan China
51 G2 Jinggongqiao China
49 G4 Jinggu China
50 D2 Jinghai China
49 F5 Jinghe China
65 K4 Jinghong China
51 F3 Jingle China
48 D5 Jingmen China
52 ¹ Jingning China
19 ¹ Jingpo Hu resr China
50 D1 Jingpo China
49 J4 Jingtai China
51 H4 Jingtai China
50 D4 Jingxi China
51 ¹ Jing Xian China
48 B4 Jingyang China
50 ¹ Jingyu China
49 J4 Jingyuan China
51 H4 Jinhe China
51 ¹ Jinhua China
49 J4 Jinhua China
48 ¹ Jining China
80 B3 Jinja Uganda
81 B4 Jinja Uganda
50 C4 Jinotega Nicaragua
130 J7 Jinotepe Nicaragua
50 D3 Jinping Yunnan China
51 ¹ Jinping Shan r. China
50 D3 Jinsha r. China
50 C2 Jinsha China
51 ¹ Jinshan China
50 E2 Jintang China
51 ¹ Jintotolo i. Phil.
41 M Jintotolo Channel chan. Phil.

56 B2 Jintur India
51 ¹ Jinxi China
51 ¹ Jinxi China
51 ¹ Jinxian China
49 G5 Jinxiang China
48 ¹ Jinxiang China
51 ¹ Jinyun China
48 ¹ Jinzhai China
48 A5 Jinzhong China
49 G4 Jinzhou China
81 C5 Jipe, L. l. Kenya/Tanzania
138 ¹ Jipijapa Ecuador
65 K3 Jirgatal Tajikistan
75 ¹ Jirin Gol China
57 D3 Jiroft Iran
80 E3 Jirriiban Somalia
51 ¹ Jishou China
51 ¹ Jishui China
60 E3 Jisr ash Shughūr Syria
43 C6 Jitra Malaysia
51 ¹ Jiujiang China
51 ¹ Jiuling Shan mt. ra. China
50 C2 Jiuquan China
50 E2 Jiujiang China
51 H2 Jiuling Shan mt. ra. China
50 D2 Jiuquan China
51 ¹ Jiutai China
51 H2 Jiuxu China
51 ¹ Jiwani Pakistan
73 H4 Jīzān Saudi Arabia
73 H4 Jīzān Saudi Arabia
73 ¹ Jizl, Wādī al w Saudi Arabia
61 ¹ Jīzl, Wādī al w Saudi Arabia
65 ¹ Jizzax Uzbekistan
143 ¹ Joaíma Brazil
142 ¹ João Pessoa Brazil
143 ¹ João Pinheiro Brazil
145 ¹ Joaquim Felício Brazil
146 ¹ Joaquín V. González Arg.
128 C2 Job Peak summit U.S.A.
55 F5 Joda India
54 B4 Jodhpur India
11 G4 Jõelähtme Estonia
10 ¹ Joensuu Finland
47 G5 Jõetsu Japan
130 ¹ Jofane Mozambique
54 B4 Jogbani India
11 G4 Jõgeva Estonia
54 C4 Jodhpur India
82 D3 Johannesburg R.S.A.
128 C4 Johannesburg U.S.A.
133 ¹ Johilla r. India
133 ¹ John Crow Mts Jamaica
120 D6 John Day U.S.A.
126 B2 John Day r. U.S.A.
126 B2 John Day U.S.A.
110 F3 John H. Kerr Res. resr U.S.A.
16 F2 John o'Groats U.K.
119 D4 John's Pass U.S.A.
125 C5 Johnson City U.S.A.
119 C4 Johnson City U.S.A.
131 ³ Johnsons Crossing Can.
100 ¹ Johnston I. i. Pac. Oc.
150 E2 Johnston I. Pac. Oc.
150 E2 Johnston, L. salt flat Aust.
49 ¹ Jilin China
121 F3 Johnstown U.S.A.
123 C4 Johnstown U.S.A.
43 C7 Johor, Selat str. Malaysia
43 ¹ Johor Bahru Malaysia
142 ¹ Joinville Brazil
143 ¹ Joinville Brazil
152 B2 Joinville I. i. Ant.
10 E2 Jokkmokk Sweden
10 N2 Jökulsá á Brú r. Iceland

10 M2 Jökulsá á Fjöllum r. Iceland
10 N2 Jökulsá í Fljótsdal r. Iceland
60 F2 Jolfa Iran
122 C5 Joliet U.S.A.
115 J3 Joliette U.S.A.
41 B5 Jolo Phil.
41 B5 Jolo i. Phil.
41 B3 Jomalig i. Phil.
40 C3 Jombang Indon.
11 G5 Jonava Lithuania
50 C1 Jonê China
125 F5 Jonesboro U.S.A.
121 K2 Jonesboro U.S.A.
152 A3 Jones Mts mts Ant.
121 K2 Jonesport U.S.A.
94 □2 Jones Pt pt Christmas I. Indian Ocean
109 K2 Jones Sound chan. Can.
120 B6 Jonesville U.S.A.
80 B3 Jonglei Sudan
80 B3 Jonglei Canal canal Sudan
55 K1 Jonk r. India
11 D4 Jönköping Sweden
11 D4 Jönköping div. Sweden
115 K2 Jonquière Can.
131 G5 Jonuta Mexico
20 D4 Jonzac France
125 E4 Joplin U.S.A.
54 D4 Jora India
61 C3 Jordan r. Asia
32 E6 Jordan country Asia
126 F2 Jordan U.S.A.
126 E3 Jordan r. U.S.A.
99 F4 Jordan Cr. w Aust.
145 H1 Jordânia Brazil
126 C3 Jordan Valley U.S.A.
143 B6 Jordet Norway
11 D3 Jordet Norway
65 J5 Jor Hu l. China
57 G1 Jorm Afghanistan
10 F2 Jörn Sweden
11 G3 Joroinen Finland
11 B4 Jørpeland Norway
77 F5 Jos Nigeria
140 C2 José A de Palacios Bolivia
142 B2 José Bispo r. Brazil
141 D2 José Bonifácio Rondônia Brazil
144 D4 José Bonifácio São Paulo Brazil
131 F5 José Cardel Mexico
147 B5 José de San Martin Arg.
143 A4 Joselândia Brazil
146 F3 José Pedro Varela Uruguay
100 E2 Joseph Bonaparte Gulf g. Aust.
129 G4 Joseph City U.S.A.
113 G3 Joseph, Lac l. Can.
54 D3 Joshimath India
47 G5 Jöshinetsu-kögen National Park nat. park. Japan
129 E5 Joshua Tree National Monument res. U.S.A.
77 F5 Jos Plateau plat. Nigeria
20 C3 Josselin France
119 □3 Jost Van Dyke I. i. Virgin Is Caribbean
82 D4 Joubertan R.S.A.
61 C3 Joûnié Lebanon
115 F2 Joutel Can.
11 G3 Joutsa Finland
11 H3 Joutseno Finland
55 H4 Jowai India
19 L3 Józefów Zamość Poland
74 A5 Jreïda Mauritania
130 E3 Juan Aldama Mexico
49 E6 Juancheng China
126 A1 Juan de Fuca, Str. of chan. U.S.A.
83 G2 Juan de Nova i. Indian Ocean
151 □8 Juan Fernández, Islas is Chile
133 G5 Juangriego Venezuela
138 B5 Juanjuí Peru
10 H3 Juankoski Finland
130 J7 Juan Santamaria airport Costa Rica
131 E3 Juárez Mexico
130 A1 Juárez, Sierra de mt. ra. Mexico
142 D2 Juàzeiro Brazil
142 E2 Juàzeiro do Norte Brazil
76 C5 Juazohn Liberia
55 E5 Juba r. Zaire
80 B4 Juba Sudan
81 D4 Jubba r. Somalia
81 D4 Jubba Dhexe div. Somalia
81 D4 Jubba Hoose div. Somalia
101 D6 Jubilee L. salt flat Aust.
128 D4 Jubilee Pass pass U.S.A.
74 B3 Juby, Cap pt Morocco
25 F3 Júcar r. Spain
132 C2 Jucaro Cuba
131 F5 Juchatengo Mexico
131 G5 Juchipila Mexico
130 D4 Juchitán Mexico
144 C1 Jucuara Brazil
145 J2 Jucururu r. Brazil
60 E4 Judaidat al Hamir Iraq
60 E4 Judayyidat 'Ar'ar well Iraq
19 G5 Judenburg Austria
11 C5 Juelsminde Denmark
145 J2 Juerana Brazil
48 D5 Juh China
73 G2 Juhaynah reg. Saudi Arabia
49 G4 Juhua Dao i. China
130 J6 Juigalpa Nicaragua
141 E2 Juína r. Brazil
141 E2 Juinamarim r. Brazil
18 C2 Juist i. Germany
145 G4 Juiz de Fora Brazil
146 C1 Jujuy div. Arg.
140 C4 Julaca Bolivia
126 E3 Julesburg U.S.A.
140 C3 Juli Peru
55 G4 Juliaca Peru
99 F4 Julia Cr. r. Aust.
99 E4 Julia Creek Aust.
139 F3 Juliana Top summit Surinam
26 D2 Julijske Alpe mts Slovenia
146 D4 Julio, 9 de Arg.
98 D4 Julius, Lake l. Aust.
20 F5 Jullouville France
50 B1 Jumaggoin China
138 B5 Jumbilla Peru
25 F3 Jumilla Spain
55 E3 Jumla Nepal
61 C4 Jum Suwwāna mt. Jordan
54 B1 Junagadh India
56 C2 Junagarh India
51 G1 Junan China
49 E3 Jun Bulen China
146 B3 Juncal mt. Chile
147 D5 Juncal, L. l. Arg.
119 □3 Juncos Puerto Rico
127 C6 Junction U.S.A.
99 E5 Junction B. b. Aust.
123 F4 Junction City U.S.A.
124 D4 Junction City U.S.A.
145 G5 Jundiaí Brazil
110 E4 Juneau U.S.A.
97 G3 Junee Aust.
54 D2 Jungar Pendi basin China
120 E4 Juniata r. U.S.A.

146 D3 Junín Arg.
140 A2 Junín Peru
147 B4 Junín de los Andes Arg.
121 K1 Juniper Can.
128 B3 Junipero Serro Peak summit U.S.A.
47 H3 Jūnishō reg. Japan
50 D2 Junlian China
56 A2 Junnar India
10 E3 Junsele Sweden
51 G2 Junshan Hu l. China
126 C3 Juntura U.S.A.
51 E1 Jun Xian China
50 B1 Ju'nyunggoin China
11 G4 Juodupė Lithuania
145 H3 Juparanã, Lagoa l. Brazil
144 C4 Jupiá Brazil
146 E6 Juquiá r. Brazil
146 E6 Juquiá Brazil
78 E2 Jur r. Sudan
16 E4 Jura i. U.K.
79 D5 Jurakumba Zaire
77 F5 Jurakumba Nigeria
76 A4 Kaffrine Senegal
78 D2 Kafia Kingi Sudan
61 D2 Kafr Buhum Syria
73 F1 Kafr el Sheik Egypt
61 A4 Kafr Sa'd Egypt
80 B4 Kafu r. Egypt
79 E7 Kafue r. Zambia
79 E6 Kafue Zambia
79 E6 Kafue National Park nat. park Zambia
47 F5 Kaga Japan
78 C2 Kaga Bandoro C.A.R.
54 C2 Kagan Pakistan
64 F5 Kagan Uzbekistan
50 C1 Kagang China
77 F5 Kagarko Nigeria
48 A3 Kagawa, div. Japan
51 G2 Jurong China
43 □ Jurong Singapore
139 D4 Juruá Brazil
138 D5 Juruá r. Brazil
138 C5 Juruá Mirim r. Brazil
141 E1 Juruena r. Brazil
142 B3 Juruna r. Brazil
11 F3 Jurva Finland
46 H3 Jūsan-ko l. Japan
133 G5 Jusepín Venezuela
61 D2 Jūsīyah Syria
21 E3 Justo Daraž Brazil
138 D5 Jutaí Brazil
138 D5 Jutaí r. Brazil
142 B1 Jutaí, L. do Brazil
18 F3 Jüterbog Germany
144 A5 Juti Brazil
127 □1 Jutiapa Guatemala
130 J6 Juticalpa Honduras
43 A3 Jutis Sweden
10 H3 Juuka Finland
11 G3 Juva Finland
132 B2 Juventud, Isla de la i. Cuba
11 G3 Jyväskylä Finland
11 G3 Jyväskylän mlk Finland

K

54 D2 K2 mt. China/Jammu and Kashmir
77 F4 Ka r. Nigeria
49 H5 Ka i. N. Korea
64 E5 Kaakhka Turkmenistan
127 □1 Kaala mt. U.S.A.
80 D5 Kaaboon Kenya
11 F3 Kaarina Finland
76 C4 Kaarta reg. Mali
10 H3 Kaavi Finland
39 H8 Kabaena i. Indon.
64 F5 Kabakly Turkmenistan
76 B5 Kabala Sierra Leone
81 A5 Kabale Uganda
79 E5 Kabalo Zaire
79 E5 Kabamba, Lac l. Zaire
48 C2 Kabansk Rus. Fed.
51 E1 Kabara i. Fiji
60 F2 Kabardino–Balkariya div. Rus. Fed.
78 E4 Kabare Zaire
46 D6 Kaba–shima i. Japan
54 B3 Kabdalis Sweden
46 D6 Kabe Japan
114 C2 Kabenung Lake l. Can.
74 E5 Kabertene Algeria
114 C2 Kabinakagami Lake l. Can.
79 D5 Kabinda Zaire
78 C2 Kabo C.A.R.
79 D6 Kabompo r. Zambia
79 D6 Kabompo Zambia
40 B1 Kabong Malaysia
77 E5 Kabongo Zaire
57 D1 Kabūdeh Iran
57 D1 Kabūd Gonbad Iran
60 F3 Kabud Rahang Iran
81 A2 Kabugao Phil.
56 B2 Kabul r. Afghanistan
57 H3 Kābul Afghanistan
79 E6 Kabunda Zaire
40 A4 Kabunduk Indon.
73 H4 Kabushiya Sudan
79 E5 Kabwe, Lac l. Zaire
79 D6 Kabwe Zambia
28 C3 Kačanik Yugo.
90 □4 Kadavu i. Fiji
90 □4 Kadavu Passage chan. Fiji
92 F2 Kadena Japan
54 B5 Kadi India
96 D3 Kadina Aust.
76 E4 Kadiolo Mali
60 C2 Kadirli Turkey
80 D5 Kadjabi well Niger
124 C2 Kadoka U.S.A.
83 E2 Kadoma Zimbabwe
78 D2 Kadugli Sudan
77 F4 Kaduna Nigeria
77 F4 Kaduna r. Nigeria
50 E2 Kadusam mt. China
12 F3 Kaduy Rus. Fed.
56 A2 Kadwa r. India
14 H2 Kadykchev Rus. Fed.
12 G3 Kady Rus. Fed.
49 H5 Kaechon N. Korea
76 B3 Kaédi Mauritania
78 B1 Kaélé Cameroon
127 □1 Kaena Pt pt U.S.A.
92 D1 Kaeo N.Z.
49 H5 Kaesŏng N. Korea
73 G1 Käf Saudi Arabia
79 D5 Kafakumba Zaire
77 F5 Kafanchan Nigeria
14 G2 Kadoshkino Rus. Fed.
42 B1 Kadu Myanmar
78 E1 Kadugli Sudan
77 F4 Kaduna Nigeria

92 E1 Kakatahi N.Z.
55 H4 Kakching India
46 D6 Kake Japan
110 C3 Kake U.S.A.
47 G6 Kakegawa Japan
79 E4 Kakenge Zaire
15 E3 Kakhovka Ukraine
15 E3 Kakhovs'ke Vodoskhovyshche resr Ukraine
12 H2 Kadyshevo Rus. Fed.
12 G3 Kadyi Rus. Fed.
49 H5 Kaechon N. Korea
76 B3 Kaédi Mauritania
57 B3 Kākī Iran
56 C2 Kākināda India
110 F2 Kakisa r. Can.
110 F2 Kakisa Lake l. Can.
46 E6 Kakogawa Japan
19 L3 Kąkolewnica Wschodnia Poland
54 E4 Kakori India
78 E4 Kakoswa Zaire
76 D5 Kakpin Côte d'Ivoire
54 D4 Kakrala India
76 B4 Kakrima r. Guinea
47 H5 Kakuda Japan
15 C1 Kakwa r. Can.
30 F6 Kalymnos i. Greece
29 F6 Kalymnos Greece
15 D1 Kalynivka Kyiviv Ukraine
15 D1 Kalynivka Vinnytsya Ukraine
15 E1 Kalyta Ukraine
57 G5 Kam Myanmar
42 A3 Kama Myanmar
12 K3 Kama r. Rus. Fed.
43 H4 Kamashi Japan
47 G6 Kamakura Japan
76 B5 Kamakwie Sierra Leone
72 C3 Kamal Chad
54 A2 Kamalia Pakistan
81 B4 Kamananga Myanmar
78 E4 Kamanyola Zaire
72 A2 Kamanjab Namibia
80 D1 Kamaran Yemen
80 D1 Kamarān i. Yemen
57 G2 Kamard reg. Afghanistan
56 B2 Kamareddi India
29 C5 Kamares Dytiki Ellas Greece

56 A4 Kalpeni i. India
55 J4 Kalpin China
108 C3 Kaltag U.S.A.
65 L2 Kaltan Rus. Fed.
18 C2 Kaltenkirchen Germany
77 G5 Kaltungo Nigeria
15 E3 Kakhovka Ukraine
14 B2 Kaluga r. Rus. Fed.
12 F3 Kalugino Rus. Fed.
15 E3 Kaluha Ukraine
77 E6 Kalukundi i. Indon.
100 D2 Kalumburu Aust.
100 D2 Kalumburu Abor. Land Reserve res. Aust.
11 D5 Kalundborg Denmark
79 E6 Kalungwishi r. Zambia
54 B2 Kalur Kot Pakistan
15 A2 Kalush Ukraine
19 K2 Kalvarija Lithuania
11 L1 Kālviä Finland
29 F6 Kalymnos i. Greece
45 □ Kai Kung Leng h. Hong Kong
76 B5 Kailahun Sierra Leone
54 D5 Kailashahar India
50 D3 Kaili China
80 C4 Kailongong waterhole Kenya
49 G4 Kaihu N.Z.
127 □2 Kailua Kona U.S.A.
39 H7 Kaimana Indon.
92 D1 Kaimana N.Z.
92 E1 Kaimanawa Mountains mt. ra. N.Z.
50 A1 Kaimar China
54 E4 Kaimganj India
54 E5 Kaimur Range h. India
11 F4 Käina Estonia
40 C2 Kainan Japan
47 F6 Kainan Japan
47 G5 Kainokuni Japan
77 E4 Kaingiwa Nigeria
77 F4 Kainji Lake National Park nat. park Nigeria
77 F4 Kainji Lake National Park nat. park resr Nigeria
56 B2 Kaintarāgarh India
N.Z.
129 G3 Kaiparowits Plateau plat. U.S.A.
51 F4 Kaiping China
113 J3 Kaipokok Bay inlet Can.
54 A3 Kairana India
74 D1 Kairouan Tunisia
18 D5 Kaiserslautern Germany
49 J4 Kaishantun China
81 J3 Kaitaia N.Z.
93 B7 Kaitangata N.Z.
54 D3 Kaithal India
51 E1 Kaixiangkou China
10 □ Kaixian China
11 F5 Kajaani Finland
98 E4 Kajabbi Aust.
99 F4 Kajan r. Indon.
54 A3 Kajang Malaysia
81 B5 Kajiado Kenya
77 G4 Kajuru Nigeria
77 F4 Kajy-Say Kyrgyzstan
96 D2 Kadina India
98 D4 Kadina Lake l. China
13 H6 Kalmykiya div. Rus. Fed.
13 J5 Kalmykovo Kazak.
55 G4 Kalni r. Bangladesh
21 J5 Kalocsa Hungary
27 H4 Kaloma r. Andaman and Nicobar Is India
79 B5 Kaloma l. Zaire
79 C4 Kalomo r. Zaire
79 E5 Kalomo Zambia
110 B2 Kaloma Pk summit U.S.A.
29 E5 Kalpáki Greece
54 D3 Kalpa India

56 A4 Kalpeni i. India
15 B1 Kam"yane Rivne Ukraine
15 F1 Kam"yane Sumy Ukraine
15 B2 Kam"yanets'-Podil's'kyy Ukraine
15 E2 Kam"yanka Cherkosy Ukraine
15 D3 Kam"yanka Kharkiv Ukraine
15 D3 Kam"yanka Odesa Ukraine
15 S1 Kam"yanka-Buz'ka Ukraine
15 F3 Kam"yanka-Dniprov'ska Ukraine
15 B1 Kam"yanyy Brid Ukraine
15 D3 Kam"yanyy Mist Ukraine
15 E1 Kamyshevakhskaya Rus. Fed.
13 H5 Kamyshin Rus. Fed.
64 F3 Kamyshlybash Kazak.
65 L3 Kamyshlybas, Oz. l. Kazak.
57 D4 Kamzar Oman
80 B3 Kan Sudan
78 F3 Kan Zaire
80 B3 Kanab U.S.A.
129 F3 Kanab Creek r. U.S.A.
90 □1 Kanacea i. Fiji
46 D7 Kanagawa div. Japan
54 A3 Kanak Pakistan
29 C5 Kanallaki Greece
79 D5 Kananga Zaire
12 K3 Kanash Rus. Fed.
120 C5 Kanawha r. U.S.A.
43 H4 Kanashi Japan
54 D4 Kanauj India
43 B4 Kanazawa Japan
54 B3 Kanbalu Myanmar
78 E4 Kamande Zaire
54 A3 Kamanjab Namibia
56 B3 Kanchipuram India
21 J2 Kańczuga Poland
54 A2 Kand mt. Afghanistan
54 B2 Kandahar Afghanistan
10 J2 Kandalaksha Rus. Fed.
10 J2 Kandalakshskiy g. Rus. Fed.
40 C2 Kandangan Indon.
56 A3 Kanderi Mposhi Zambia
77 F4 Kandi Benin
54 A4 Kandiaro Pakistan
60 B1 Kandıra Turkey
56 A1 Kandla India
54 E4 Kannauj India
29 D6 Kanni Kona U.S.A.
54 E4 Kannur India
73 H4 Kantharalak Thailand
13 J5 Kanal r. Bangladesh
56 A2 Kannur India

15 B2 Kam-onji Japan
46 D6 Kanowit Malaysia
46 C8 Kanoya Japan
54 E4 Kanpur India
56 B3 Kanrach reg. Pakistan
54 E2 Kansas r. U.S.A.
124 D4 Kansas div. U.S.A.
124 E4 Kansas City U.S.A.
65 G2 Kansu Kazak.
63 L4 Kansk Rus. Fed.
65 J1 Kansu r. Kyrgyzstan
80 D3 Kanta mt. Ethiopia
42 C3 Kantang Thailand
54 E4 Kantchari Burkina
14 F2 Kantemirovka Rus. Fed.
55 F4 Kanti Hill India
150 H6 Kanton Island i. Kiribati
47 G6 Kanto-sanchi mt. ra. Japan
54 E4 Kanpur India
57 H4 Kanuku Mts mts Guyana
47 G5 Kanuma Japan
82 A4 Kanus Namibia
47 G6 Kanuwe r. P.N.G.
83 G4 KaNyamazane R.S.A.
55 F2 Kanye Botswana
10 G1 Kanyutino Rus. Fed.
64 F2 Kanzou Kazak.
129 F3 Kao i. Tonga
43 C5 Kaoh Kông i. Cambodia
43 D6 Kaoh Rūng i. Cambodia
51 E4 Kao-hsiung Taiwan
43 D5 Kaoh Smăch i. Cambodia
80 D5 Kaokoveld plat. Namibia
76 A4 Kaolack Senegal
76 A4 Kaoma Zambia
74 B2 Kaortchi well Chad
78 D2 Kaouadja C.A.R.

40 C3 Karamian i. Indon.
55 F1 Karamiran China
55 F1 Karamiran Shankou pass China
12 D3 Karamyshevo Rus. Fed.
57 K1 Karan r. Afghanistan
72 F1 Karan i. Saudi Arabia
57 E4 Karand Iran
40 C4 Karangagung Indon.
29 F4 Karangasem Indon.
40 C4 Karangbolong, Tg pt Indon.
54 E2 Karanja r. India
56 B2 Karanja India
56 D1 Karanja r. India
54 D3 Karasjok Norway
64 F2 Karasu r. Kazak.
60 D2 Karasu r. Turkey
60 C1 Karasu Turkey
15 F3 Karasubazar Ukraine
64 F2 Karasuk Rus. Fed.
15 E3 Karatau China
60 A2 Karatax Shan mt. ra. Kazak.
54 E2 Karatat Shan mt. ra. China
57 L2 Karāt Iran
60 B1 Karatta Turkey
78 E2 Karatobe Kazak.
65 H5 Karatobe, Mys pt Kazak.
60 C1 Karatol r. Kazak.
65 J5 Karasu r. Kazak.
80 E2 Karossa Indon.
80 B1 Karossa, Tg pt Indon.
29 F7 Karpathos i. Greece
25 C5 Karpenísi Greece
12 H1 Karpogory Rus. Fed.
29 F4 Karpuzlu Aydin Turkey
29 E4 Karpuzlu Edirne Turkey
15 E1 Karpylivka Ukraine
100 B4 Karratta Aust.
57 K2 Karrukh Afghanistan
15 E1 Karrychivka Turkmenistan
60 E1 Kars Turkey
11 G4 Kärsämäki Finland
11 F4 Kärsava Latvia
65 G5 Karshi Turkmenistan
57 F5 Karsiyaka Turkey
62 G2 Karskiye Vorota, Proliv chan. Rus. Fed.
62 J2 Karskoye More sea
18 E2 Karstädt Germany
11 G3 Karstula Finland
14 H2 Karsun Rus. Fed.
81 D7 Kartala crater Comoros
21 H4 Kartayev Hungary
14 E1 Kartayel' Rus. Fed.
10 G3 Karttula Finland
19 H3 Kartuzy Poland
99 E3 Karumba Aust.
57 B3 Kārūn r. Iran
80 D4 Karungu Bay b. Kenya
11 F3 Karuni Indon.
56 B4 Karur India
11 F3 Karvia Finland
11 F3 Karvianjoki r. Finland
19 J4 Karviná Czech Rep.
82 E3 Karwar India
48 E2 Karymskoye Rus. Fed.
29 E5 Karystos Greece
14 G3 Karzhimant Rus. Fed.
112 J3 Kasabonika Can.
112 J3 Kasabonika Lake l. Can.
46 E5 Kasai Japan
79 D5 Kasai r. Zaire
79 D5 Kasai Occidental div. Zaire
79 D5 Kasai Oriental div. Zaire
79 E6 Kasama Japan
41 B7 Kasama Zambia
82 D2 Kasane Botswana
78 B4 Kasanga Tanzania
76 B4 Kasanza Zaire
79 C5 Kasenye Zaire
78 E4 Kasese Uganda
78 E4 Kasese Zaire
54 D4 Kasganj India
79 E5 Kashan r. Iran
112 D5 Kashechewan Can.
46 C7 Kashima-nada b. Japan
47 H5 Kashima r. Japan
11 G4 Kashinka r. Rus. Fed.
12 D3 Kashino Rus. Fed.
79 C5 Kashira Rus. Fed.
47 G5 Kashiwazaki Rus. Fed.
47 G5 Kashiwazaki Japan
57 E2 Kashman r. Iran
54 C2 Kashmir India
54 C2 Kashmir, Vale of valley India
54 A3 Kashmore Pakistan

91 □16 Katiki h. Easter I. Chile
82 C2 Katima Mulilo Namibia
76 C5 Katiola Côte d'Ivoire
91 □10 Katiu i. Fr. Poly. Pac. Oc.
29 C5 Kato Achaïa Greece
23 A5 Katochi Greece
29 C6 Kato Figaleia Greece
54 D5 Katol India
29 D4 Kato Nevrokopi Greece
43 □1 Katong Singapore
81 B4 Katonga r. Uganda
97 G3 Katoomba Aust.
29 C5 Kato Tithorea Greece
19 J3 Katowice Poland
55 G5 Katoya India
11 E4 Katrineholm Sweden
83 H2 Katsepy Madagascar
73 F4 Katsina Nigeria
77 F4 Katsina div. Nigeria
77 F5 Katsina-Ala Nigeria
46 B7 Katsumoto Japan
47 □2 Katsuren-zaki c. Japan
47 H5 Katsuta Japan
47 H4 Katsuura Japan
46 D6 Katsuyama Japan
47 F5 Katsuyama Japan
113 G2 Kattaktoc, Cap hd Can.
65 G5 Kattakurgan Uzbekistan
29 F7 Kattavia Greece
114 E2 Kattawagami Lake l. Can.
11 C4 Kattegat str. Denmark/Sweden
65 L2 Katun' r. Rus. Fed.
15 L1 Katunki Rus. Fed.
57 E4 Katur Pakistan
65 L2 Katunskiy Khrebet mt. ra. Rus. Fed.
54 B3 Katuri Pakistan
19 H3 Katy Wrocławskie Poland
127 □2 Kau i. Indon.
127 □2 Kau i. Indon.
82 C2 Kaudom Game Park res. Namibia
91 □10 Kauehi i. Fr. Poly. Pac. Oc.
18 E5 Kaufbeuren Germany
11 F3 Kauhajoki Finland
10 F3 Kauhava Finland
42 B1 Kaukkwè Hills mt. ra. Myanmar
10 G2 Kaukonen Finland
91 □10 Kaukura i. Fr. Poly. Pac. Oc.
127 □2 Kaula i. U.S.A.
127 □2 Kaulakahi Channel chan. U.S.A.
113 H2 Kaumajet Mts mt. ra. Can.
127 □2 Kaunakakai U.S.A.
11 F5 Kaunas Lithuania
11 G4 Kaunata Latvia
77 F4 Kaura-Namoda Nigeria
45 □1 Kau Sai Chau i. Hong Kong
10 F3 Kaustinen Finland
10 F1 Kautokeino Norway
43 B5 Kau-ye Kyun i. Myanmar
29 D4 Kavadarci Macedonia
83 A6 Kavajë Albania
29 F4 Kavak Çanakkale Turkey
60 C1 Kavak Samsun Turkey
29 G6 Kavaklıdere Turkey
29 E4 Kavala Greece
57 □3 Kavār Iran
53 D8 Kavaratti i. India
28 D3 Kavarna Bulgaria
4A A2 Kavel'shchino Rus. Fed.
76 B4 Kavendou, Mt mt. Guinea
56 B4 Kāverī r. India
14 E2 Kaverino Rus. Fed.
90 □1 Kavieng P.N.G.
82 C2 Kavimba Botswana
57 D2 Kavīr-e Namak-e salt flat Iran
57 B2 Kavīr-e Namak-e Miqalan salt flat Iran
64 D3 Kavzhshanbas Kazak.
139 G3 Kaw French Guiana
47 H4 Kawabe Japan
47 G6 Kawaguchi Japan
47 H4 Kawai Japan
127 □2 Kawaihae Japan
46 D6 Kawajiri Japan
92 E1 Kawakawa N.Z.
79 E5 Kawambwa Zambia
47 E6 Kawanishi Japan
112 E5 Kawartha Lakes lakes Can.
47 G6 Kawasaki Japan
46 C6 Kawashiri-misaki pt Japan
46 B7 Kawauchi Japan
92 E2 Kawau I. i. N.Z.
46 C7 Kawaura Japan
113 G2 Kawawachikamach Can.
92 F3 Kaweka mt. N.Z.
47 G5 Kawerau N.Z.
92 E3 Kawhia Japan
92 E3 Kawhia Harbour inlet N.Z.
128 D3 Kawich Range mts U.S.A.
40 D4 Kawkareik Myanmar
42 A3 Kawlin Myanmar
42 A2 Kawludo Myanmar
43 B4 Kawmapyin Myanmar
42 A2 Kawngmeum Myanmar
43 A5 Kawthaung Myanmar
65 K4 Kax r. China
65 J5 Kaxgar China
55 E1 Kaxtax Shan mt. ra. China
76 D4 Kaya Burkina
63 M2 Kayak Rus. Fed.
81 B6 Kayambi Zambia
40 C2 Kayan r. Kalimantan Barat Indon.
40 D1 Kayan r. Kalimantan Timur Indon.
81 A5 Kayanza Burundi
127 □1 Kayangel Islands is Palau
127 □1 Kayangel Passage chan. Palau
56 B4 Kayankulam India
65 G2 Kaybagar, Oz. l. Kazak.
126 F3 Kayenta U.S.A.
76 B4 Kayes div. Mali
76 B4 Kayes Mali
64 F2 Kayga Kazak.
55 J3 Kayin State div. Myanmar
60 D2 Kaynar Kazak.
47 G6 Kayo Japan
13 H5 Kaysatskoye Rus. Fed.
65 P3 Kazach'ye Rus. Fed.
63 P2 Kazach'ye Rus. Fed.
64 D4 Kazakhskiy Zaliv b. Kazak.
32 G5 Kazakhstan country Asia
64 E3 Kazalinsk Kazak.
32 E4 Kazandzhik Turkm.
111 K2 Kazan r. Can.
12 J4 Kazan' Rus. Fed.
60 C2 Kazancı Turkey
64 C1 Kazanka Kazak.
13 G5 Kazanka Ukraine
29 M1 Kazanlŭk Bulgaria
65 H4 Kazarman Kyrgyzstan

13 H7 Kazbek mt. Georgia
29 E5 Kaz Dağı mts Turkey
57 □2 Kāzerūn Iran
12 J2 Kazhim Rus. Fed.
57 F4 Kazhmak r. Pakistan
15 F3 Kazhovs'kyy Mahistral'nyy Kanal r. Ukraine
19 K3 Kazimierz Dolne Poland
19 K4 Kazincbarcika Hungary
15 G1 Kazinka Rus. Fed.
47 □2 Kazo Japan
64 C3 Kaztalovka Kazak.
79 D5 Kazumba Zaire
79 E7 Kazungula Zambia
47 H3 Kazuno Japan
67 Kazymskiy Mys Rus. Fed.
29 E6 Kea i. Greece
127 □2 Kealakekua Bay b. U.S.A.
129 G4 Keams Canyon U.S.A.
124 D3 Kearney U.S.A.
129 G5 Kearny U.S.A.
60 B4 Keban Turkey
60 B4 Keban Baraji dam Turkey
40 B2 Kebatu i. Indon.
76 A3 Kébémèr Senegal
77 G4 Kebili Tunisia
60 D3 Kebir r. Lebanon/Syria
72 D5 Kebkabiya Sudan
10 E2 Kebnekaise mt. Sweden
80 D3 K'ebrī Dehar Ethiopia
54 B2 Kebumen Indon.
57 E4 Kech reg. Pakistan
80 C3 K'ech'a Terara mt. Ethiopia
110 D3 Kechika r. Can.
19 J5 Kecskemét Hungary
43 C6 Kedah div. Malaysia
11 F5 Kėdainiai Lithuania
19 K3 Kedarnath India
54 D3 Kedarnath Pk. mt. India
43 C6 Kedgwick Can.
40 C3 Kediri Indon.
49 H3 Kedong China
76 B3 Kédougou Senegal
40 B3 Keduanguwni Indon.
12 F2 Kedva r. Rus. Fed.
12 K1 Kedvavom Rus. Fed.
19 J4 Kędzierzyn-Koźle Poland
110 C2 Keele r. Can.
108 C3 Keele Pk summit Can.
41 A5 Keenapusan i. Phil.
121 G3 Keene U.S.A.
99 C2 Geer-weer, C. c. Aust.
82 B2 Keetmanshoop Namibia
112 B4 Keewatin Can.
111 L5 Keewatin U.S.A.
29 C5 Kefallonia i. Greece
29 F6 Kefalos Greece
39 H8 Kefamenanu Indon.
77 F5 Keffi Nigeria
60 D4 Keflavik Iceland
56 C5 Kegalla Sri Lanka
65 J5 Kegen' Kazak.
113 G2 Keglo, Baie de b. Can.
13 H6 Kegul'ta Rus. Fed.
73 F4 Keheili Sudan
18 C4 Kehl Germany
74 C5 Kehoula well Mauritania
11 G4 Kehra Estonia
42 B2 Kehsi Mansam Myanmar
15 F2 Kehychivka Ukraine
11 G4 Keila Estonia
82 C4 Keimoes R.S.A.
74 C5 Kéran, Parc National de la nat. park Togo
29 D6 Keratea Greece
11 G3 Kerava Finland
13 F6 Kerch Ukraine
12 K2 Kerchem'ya Rus. Fed.
73 G5 Kereaba Sudan
42 B2 Kereidila pool Sudan
90 □1 Kerema P.N.G.
110 F5 Keremeos Can.
60 C1 Kerempe Burun pt Turkey
80 C1 Keren Eritrea
92 F2 Kerepehi N.Z.
74 B5 Kerewan The Gambia
57 D1 Kergeli Turkmenistan
152 □ Kerguelen, Îles is Indian Ocean
149 J7 Kerguelen Ridge Indian Ocean
81 C5 Kericho Kenya
81 C4 Kerihun mt. Indon.
92 D1 Kerikeri N.Z.
38 D7 Kerinci, G. volc. Indon.
81 D4 Kerio r. Kenya
57 C1 Keriya Shankou China
55 G2 Kerkenah, Îles is Tunisia
65 G5 Kerki Turkmenistan
57 E1 Kerkichi Turkmenistan
29 B5 Kerkyra i. Greece
29 B5 Kerkyra Greece
73 F4 Kerma Sudan
92 □4 Kermadec Is is N.Z.
150 H8 Kermadec Tr. Pac. Oc.
57 D2 Kermān Iran
57 D2 Kermān div. Iran
128 B3 Kerman U.S.A.
57 D3 Kermān Desert desert Iran
57 C2 Kermānshāh Iran
57 B2 Kermānshāhān div. Iran
15 B2 Kermis' Rus. Fed.
127 C6 Kermit U.S.A.
128 D4 Kern r. U.S.A.
113 G2 Kernertut, Cap pt Can.
29 E6 Keros i. Greece
77 F4 Kérou Benin
76 C5 Kérouané Guinea
152 B5 Kerr, C. c. Ant.
111 J4 Kerrobert Can.
18 E4 Kerry div. Rep. of Ire.
17 B5 Kerry Head hd Rep. of Ire.
43 □1 Kerteh Malaysia
11 C5 Kerteminde Denmark
63 M3 Kerulen r. Mongolia
60 E4 Keryneia Cyprus
75 D3 Kerzaz Algeria
12 H2 Kerzhenets r. Rus. Fed.
112 E1 Kesagami Lake l. Can.
29 F5 Keşan Turkey
47 H4 Kesennuma Japan
54 D5 Keshod India
14 G1 Keshu Rus. Fed.
60 E2 Keskin Turkey
11 H2 Keski-Suomi div. Finland
10 G3 Keskozero Rus. Fed.
67 Kesten'ga Rus. Fed.
10 D2 Kestilä Finland
17 F4 Keswick Can.
16 E3 Keswick U.K.
19 H5 Keszthely Hungary
63 L2 Ket' r. Rus. Fed.
76 D5 Keta Ghana
40 B3 Ketapang i. Indon.
43 □1 Ketam, P. i. Singapore
40 C3 Ketapang Indon.
108 C3 Ketchikan U.S.A.
129 F4 Ketchum U.S.A.
40 B3 Ketepang Indon.
77 F4 Kétou Benin
19 K1 Kętrzyn Poland

93 D4 Kendall, Mt mt. N.Z.
122 E5 Kendallville U.S.A.
40 A3 Kendang, G. vol Indon.
39 H7 Kendari Indon.
40 B2 Kendawangan Indon.
55 F6 Kendrapara India
126 C3 Kendrick U.S.A.
129 G4 Kendrick Peak summit U.S.A.
55 F5 Kendujhargarh India
65 H4 Kendyrlı mt. ra. Kazak.
64 D4 Kendyrli-Kayasanskoye, Plato plat. Kazak.
125 D6 Kenedy U.S.A.
76 B5 Kenema Sierra Leone
79 C4 Keneurgench Turkm.
79 C4 Kenge Zaire
42 B2 Keng Hkam Myanmar
42 B2 Keng Lon Myanmar
42 B2 Keng Tawng Myanmar
42 B2 Kengtung Myanmar
82 C4 Kenhardt R.S.A.
74 B4 Kéniéba Mali
74 C2 Kénitra Morocco
49 F5 Kenli China
17 C6 Kenmare Rep. of Ire.
17 B6 Kenmare River inlet Rep. of Ire.
23 G5 Kenna U.S.A.
121 J2 Kennebec r. U.S.A.
121 J2 Kennebunk U.S.A.
121 H3 Kennebunkport U.S.A.
99 F2 Kennedy r. Aust.
101 A5 Kennedy Ra. h. Aust.
125 F6 Kenner U.S.A.
101 B4 Kenneth Ra. h. Aust.
125 F4 Kennett U.S.A.
126 C2 Kennewick U.S.A.
114 E2 Kenogami Lake l. Can.
114 E2 Kenogamissi Lake l. Can.
110 B3 Keno Hill Can.
86 □ Kenora Can.
122 C4 Kenosha U.S.A.
12 F2 Kenozero, Ozero l. Rus. Fed.
121 G3 Kent U.S.A.
125 B6 Kent U.S.A.
17 H6 Kent div. U.K.
65 G4 Kentau Kazak.
97 F4 Kent Group is Aust.
122 D5 Kentland U.S.A.
122 E5 Kenton U.S.A.
29 D4 Kentriki Makedonia div. Greece
122 C6 Kentucky div. U.S.A.
119 B4 Kentucky Lake l. U.S.A.
113 H4 Kentville Can.
125 F6 Kenwood U.S.A.
73 □5 Kenya country Africa
81 C5 Kenya, Mt mt. Kenya
122 A4 Kenyon U.S.A.
152 B2 Kenyon Pen. pen. Ant.
65 J2 Kenzharyk Rus. Fed.
65 H3 Kenzharyk Kazak.
65 K3 Keokuk U.S.A.
42 D3 Keo Neua, Col de pass Laos/Vietnam
122 B5 Keosauqua U.S.A.
125 E5 Kepala Batas Malaysia
60 D2 Kepçe Turkey
29 F4 Kepi i Gjuhëzës pt Albania
12 G1 Kepina r. Rus. Fed.
99 G4 Keppel B. b. Aust.
43 □1 Keppel Harbour chan. Singapore
74 C5 Kepsut Turkey
57 D3 Kerah Iran
56 A4 Kerala div. India
97 F2 Kerang Aust.
57 C2 Kerend-e Gharb Iran
13 G6 Keradzhensk Rus. Fed.
73 H4 Keren Eritrea
13 F6 Kerch Ukraine
72 D1 Khalïg Abu Qîr b. Egypt
72 D1 Khalïg el 'Arab b. Egypt

78 C3 Ketta Congo
78 B3 Kétté Cameroon
78 B3 Kette Congo
57 E3 Khash Afghanistan
120 A5 Kettering U.K.
110 F5 Kettle r. U.S.A.
122 A2 Kettle Creek r. U.S.A.
126 C1 Kettle River Ra. ra. U.S.A.
126 C1 Kettleman City U.S.A.
55 H4 Kendujhargarh India
65 H4 Kendyarla mt. ra. Kazak.
64 D4 Kendyrli-Kayasanskoye, Plato plat. Kazak.
14 F3 Kevdo-Vershina Rus. Fed.
133 D2 Kew Turks and Caicos Is Caribbean
122 C5 Kewanee U.S.A.
122 D3 Kewanee U.S.A.
122 C2 Keweenaw Bay b. U.S.A.
122 C2 Keweenaw Peninsula pen. U.S.A.
122 D2 Keweenaw Pt pt U.S.A.
139 E2 Keweigek Guyana
80 B4 Keyala Sudan
112 F3 Keyano Can.
114 E4 Key Harbour Can.
49 G2 Keyihe China
17 C4 Key, Lough l. Rep. of Ire.
120 D5 Keyser U.S.A.
129 G6 Keystone Peak summit U.S.A.
125 F4 Keysville U.S.A.
93 A6 Key, The N.Z.
119 D7 Key West U.S.A.
122 B4 Key West U.S.A.
121 H3 Kezar Falls U.S.A.
19 K3 Kežmarok Slovakia
82 D3 Kgalagadi div. Botswana
82 D3 Kgatleng div. Botswana
82 C3 Kgomofatshe Pan salt pan Botswana
82 C3 Kgoro Pan salt pan Botswana
82 D4 Kgotsong Botswana
49 E2 Khabarovsk div. Rus. Fed.
49 E2 Khabarovsk Rus. Fed.
65 J2 Khabary Rus. Fed.
73 H4 Khabb, W. w. Yemen
57 C5 Khabrā al'Arn salt pan Saudi Arabia
61 D3 Khabrat Abu al Ḩusain reg. Jordan
61 D5 Khabrat Umm ar Raqabah l. Saudi Arabia
57 C2 Khabur r. Syria
73 H4 Khaḑārah Saudi Arabia
78 E1 Khadari w Sudan
13 H6 Khadyzhensk Rus. Fed.
57 E4 Khadro Pakistan
54 B4 Khagaria India
54 E4 Khagaria India
54 C5 Khairagarh India
54 B4 Khairgarh Pakistan
54 B3 Khairpur India
54 B3 Khairpur Pakistan
54 C5 Khairthal India
57 E4 Khajuri Kach Pakistan
60 G2 Khakasiya, Resp. div. Rus. Fed.
14 G1 Khakhaly Rus. Fed.
82 D1 Khakhea Botswana
57 E2 Khakir Afghanistan
57 F2 Khakrêz reg. Afghanistan
57 F2 Khakrîz reg. Afghanistan
64 E4 Khalach Turkmenistan
82 C3 Khalagari reg. Iran
54 C5 Khalidabad Iran
54 B3 Khalifat mt. Pakistan
61 A4 Khalïg Abu Qîr b. Egypt
12 D3 Khalïg el 'Arab b. Egypt
61 A5 Khalïg el Tina b. Egypt
72 D1 Khalïg Bumbah b. Libya
72 C1 Khalïj Surt g. Libya
57 D2 Khaliabad Iran
54 B3 Khalkhal Iran
56 D2 Khallikot India
48 B2 Khaman-Daban, Khrebet mt. ra. Rus. Fed.
54 C5 Khambhat India
54 C5 Khambhat, Gulf of g. India
54 C5 Khamgaon India
54 D4 Khamir Yemen
81 B4 Khamis Mushayt Saudi Arabia
42 C3 Khamkkeut Laos
54 D3 Khammam India
54 C5 Khamra r. Rus. Fed.
61 B4 Khamsa Egypt
12 G3 Khamseh reg. Iran
40 D3 Khanabad Afghanistan
57 E2 Khan Afghanistan
57 E2 Khan r. Afghanistan
60 F2 Khan az Zabib Jordan
57 D2 Khānabad Iran
54 D4 Khānaqīn Iraq
54 C4 Khandela India
54 C5 Khand P. pass Afghanistan/Pakistan
54 C5 Khandud Afghanistan
54 C5 Khandwa India
54 B3 Khanewal Pakistan
42 D4 Khanh Dương Vietnam
54 D3 Khanino r. Rus. Fed.
54 B4 Khanpur Pakistan
57 B2 Khānpur Iran
57 C2 Khorāsān div. Iran
54 B2 Khordha India
61 C1 Khān az Zabib Jordan
61 C4 Khān Shaykhūn Syria
73 F4 Khān Yūnis Gaza
43 B5 Khao Chum Thong Thailand
43 A5 Khao Luang Kha Toek mt. Thailand
43 A5 Khao Sai Dao Tai mt. Thailand
55 D5 Khapa India
13 H5 Khar r. Iran
54 A3 Kharadari Rus. Fed.
54 C5 Kharaghoda India
54 B3 Kharan r. Pakistan
57 E3 Kharan Afghanistan
57 E3 Kharān Pakistan
57 E3 Khārān r. Iran
54 B3 Kharari Pakistan
54 C4 Kharda India
72 C2 Khārga Oasis oasis Egypt
54 C5 Kharghar India
54 D4 Khargon India
54 B4 Khari r. Rajasthan India
54 C4 Khari r. Rajasthan India
57 E4 Kharian Pakistan
57 F4 Kharif, W. w. Pakistan
54 C5 Kharim, G. h. Egypt
54 B4 Khari div. Ukraine
13 G5 Kharkiv r. Ukraine
13 G5 Kharkiv Ukraine
13 G5 Kharkiv div. Ukraine
10 H3 Kharlu Rus. Fed.
28 D3 Kharmanli Bulgaria
12 H3 Kharovsk Rus. Fed.
57 D2 Khorramdar Iran
55 F4 Kharsia India
54 B4 Khartoum div. Sudan
73 F4 Khartoum Sudan
73 F4 Khartoum North Sudan
12 H1 Khasav'yurt Rus. Fed.

57 E3 Khash Afghanistan
57 E3 Khāsh Iran
57 E3 Khash Desert desert Afghanistan
73 G5 Khashm el Girba Sudan
57 B3 Khashm Rud r. Afghanistan
13 G7 Khashuri Georgia
55 G4 Khāsi Hills India
28 E3 Khaskovo div. Bulgaria
63 M2 Khatanga r. Rus. Fed.
13 H4 Khvatynsk Rus. Fed.
74 A5 Khatt el Toueïrja w Mauritania
57 D2 Khātūnābād Iran
63 T3 Khatyrka r. Rus. Fed.
54 B4 Khavda India
57 D2 Khawd Nārvan Iran
57 C2 Khvoy Iran
12 E3 Khvoynaya Rus. Fed.
57 E3 Khawak P. pass Afghanistan
54 B2 Khawr Fakkan U.A.E.
73 F4 Khawsa Sudan
54 B3 Khaybar Saudi Arabia
73 H5 Khaybar Saudi Arabia
57 G1 Khwaja Muhammad Ra. mt. ra. Afghanistan
54 B2 Khyber Pass pass Afghanistan/Pakistan
63 M2 Kheta r. Rus. Fed.
55 H5 Kheyrābād Iran
57 D3 Khezerābād Iran
55 D5 Khilchipur India
54 C4 Khilok r. Rus. Fed.
14 E2 Khimki Rus. Fed.
12 G3 Khirbat Isriyah Syria
60 E4 Khirr, Wādī al w Saudi Arabia
28 E3 Khisarya Bulgaria
14 E3 Khitrovo Rus. Fed.
60 E2 Khiva Uzbekistan
64 F3 Khiyāv Iran
14 B2 Khlepen' Rus. Fed.
13 B3 Khlevnoye Rus. Fed.
15 B2 Khmel'nyts'ky div. Ukraine
15 B2 Khmel'nyts'kyy Ukraine
79 E6 Khmil'nyk Ukraine
57 B2 Khobda Afghanistan
57 E2 Khodā Afarïn Iran
29 D5 Khodoriv Ukraine
64 E4 Khodzheyli Uzbekistan
78 E2 Khogali Sudan
72 E3 Khojak P. pass Pakistan
73 B5 Khokhol'sky Rus. Fed.
12 D3 Khoksar India
57 F4 Kholm Afghanistan
81 B5 Kholmech' Rus. Fed.
13 B3 Kholmogory Rus. Fed.
65 H3 Kholmsk Rus. Fed.
11 H5 Kholmy Ukraine
47 F6 Kholtoson Rus. Fed.
47 F6 Kii-sanchi mt. ra. Japan
82 B3 Khomas div. Namibia
82 B3 Khomas Highland reg. Namibia
57 B2 Khomeyn Iran
57 C2 Khomeynīshahr Iran
78 E3 Khomra r. Uzbekistan
54 C4 Khonj Iran
54 D4 Khonsa India
57 E3 Khor r. Iran
57 E2 Khor Anghar Djibouti
63 F5 Khoper r. Volgograd Rus. Fed.
60 D1 Khopyor Rus. Fed.
63 Q2 Khor r. Rus. Fed.
57 E3 Khor Iran
73 G4 Khora Sudan
57 C2 Khorāsān div. Iran
54 B2 Khordha India
55 F4 Khorixas Namibia
82 B3 Khorol Ukraine
15 E1 Khorol r. Ukraine
57 D2 Khoroshe Ukraine
15 E1 Khorostkiv Ukraine
13 G5 Khorramābād Iran
57 B2 Khorramshahr Iran
81 B5 Khorugh Tajikistan
57 B2 Khosf Iran
12 D3 Khoshoyeh Rus. Fed.
57 B2 Khosravi Iran
54 C4 Khosrowābād Iran
57 C2 Khost Pakistan
57 F2 Khost Afghanistan
57 F2 Khost div. Afghanistan
15 D2 Khotetovo Rus. Fed.
14 E3 Khot'kovo Rus. Fed.
15 C1 Khotymsk Rus. Fed.
57 D3 Khouribga Morocco
57 B2 Khowai India
57 B2 Khowrjān Iran
15 B2 Khoyniki Belarus
72 D3 Khrami r. Georgia
13 G7 Khristoforovka Ukraine
13 F5 Khromtau Kazak.
15 E2 Khrystoforivka Ukraine
54 C4 Khrystynivka Ukraine
125 D6 Khudan r. Rus. Fed.
54 B4 Khude Hills mt. ra. Pakistan
73 G5 Khudubais Khr. mt. ra. Rus. Fed.
73 G5 Khuff Saudi Arabia
57 B3 Khūjand Tajikistan
57 C2 Khu Khan Thailand
54 B3 Khulm r. Afghanistan
55 G5 Khulna Bangladesh
55 G5 Khulna div. Bangladesh
57 D3 Khunayzir, J. al mt. ra. Syria
54 C4 Khunjerab pass China/Jammu and Kashmir
54 E4 Khunti India
54 B4 Khur India
57 D2 Khur Iran
55 E2 Khūran chan. Iran
54 C5 Khurja India
57 F4 Khurmalik Afghanistan
54 B3 Khusab Pakistan

57 D3 Khushk Rud Iran
61 D5 Khush Shah, W. el w Jordan
57 E2 Khuspas Afghanistan
73 G5 Khust Ukraine
13 G6 Khutorskoy Rus. Fed.
78 C3 Khuzdar Pakistan
57 B3 Khūzestān div. Iran
57 C2 Khvāf Iran
57 C2 Khvājeh Iran
57 D3 Khvalynsk Rus. Fed.
14 D2 Khvashchevka Rus. Fed.
14 H3 Khvatovich Rus. Fed.
57 C2 Khvor Iran
57 D2 Khvor Nārvan Iran
57 C2 Khvormūj Iran
57 C2 Khvoy Iran
14 E3 Khvorostnyanka Rus. Fed.
12 E3 Khvoynaya Rus. Fed.
57 E3 Khwaja Ali Afghanistan
41 A5 Khwaja Amran mt. Pakistan
57 G1 Khwaja Muhammad Ra. mt. ra. Afghanistan
54 B2 Khyber Pass pass Afghanistan/Pakistan
92 □3 Kia i. Fiji
97 G3 Kiama Aust.
41 C5 Kiamba Phil.
79 E5 Kiambi Zaire
81 C5 Kiambu Kenya
41 C5 Kiamichi r. U.S.A.
81 C4 Kiamusze Uganda
10 H2 Kiantajärvi l. Finland
29 C5 Kiasti Iran
74 D2 Kiato Greece
81 B4 Kibaha Tanzania
81 A4 Kibale Uganda
78 E3 Kibali r. Zaire
79 D4 Kibangou Congo
79 C5 Kibawe Phil.
81 C6 Kibaya Tanzania
81 C5 Kibiti Tanzania
80 D4 Kiboga Uganda
81 B5 Kibombo Zaire
80 D4 Kibondo Tanzania
80 C3 Kibre Mengist Ethiopia
79 D4 Kičevo Macedonia
72 C4 Kichi-Kichi well Chad
12 J3 Kichmengsky Gorodok Rus. Fed.
77 D4 Kidal Mali
77 D3 Kidal div. Mali
16 E4 Kidderminster U.K.
80 B4 Kidepo Valley National Park nat. park Uganda
76 B3 Kidira Senegal
92 F3 Kidnappers, Cape c. N.Z.
74 B2 Kidnaz w Egypt
18 E1 Kiel Germany
122 C4 Kiel U.S.A.
19 K4 Kielce Poland
17 F4 Kielder Water resr U.K.
79 E4 Kieler Bucht b. Germany
17 E6 Kienge Zaire
19 L2 Kietrz Poland
76 B3 Kiffa Mauritania
29 D5 Kifisia Greece
29 D5 Kifisos r. Greece
57 C2 Kifrī Iraq
80 D4 Kigali Rwanda
78 E4 Kigezi Game Reserve res. Zaire
60 D2 Kiği Turkey
113 H2 Kiglapait Mts mt. ra. Can.
94 □4 King Pt pt Lord Howe I. Pac. Oc.
76 B4 Kignan Mali
17 F6 Kigoma Tanzania
81 B5 Kigoma div. Tanzania
10 H1 Kihlanki Finland
55 H3 Kihniö Finland
11 G4 Kihnu i. Estonia
47 E6 Kii-nagashima Japan
47 F6 Kii-sanchi mt. ra. Japan
47 E6 Kiire Japan
81 C5 Kiisi Nigeria
19 J5 Kiiskila Hungary
80 D4 Kijabe Kenya
73 F5 Kijungu Well well Tanzania
11 H4 Kikerino Rus. Fed.
77 F6 Kikinda Yugo.
47 H4 Kikonai Japan
46 H3 Kikonai Japan
79 D4 Kikondja Zaire
79 B5 Kikori r. P.N.G.
90 □1 Kikori P.N.G.
79 B5 Kikwit Zaire
11 J3 Kil Norway
81 C5 Kilafors Sweden
56 B4 Kilakkarai India
81 D6 Kilauea U.S.A.
127 □1 Kilauea Crater crater U.S.A.
60 E3 Kilboghamn Norway
60 E3 Kilbrannan Sound chan. U.K.
60 E3 Kilcar Rep. of Ire.
60 B4 Kilchu N. Korea
17 E5 Kilcoole Rep. of Ire.
17 E5 Kilcormac Rep. of Ire.
99 G5 Kilcoy Aust.
17 E5 Kildare div. Rep. of Ire.
17 E5 Kildare Rep. of Ire.
10 H1 Kil'dinstroy Rus. Fed.
10 H1 Kil'demary Rus. Fed.
125 E5 Kilgore U.S.A.
16 G3 Kilham U.K.
81 C6 Kilibo Benin
81 C5 Kilifi Kenya
81 C5 Kilimanjaro div. Tanzania
81 C5 Kilimanjaro National Park nat. park Tanzania
81 B5 Kilindoni Tanzania
11 G4 Kilingi-Nõmme Estonia
60 E3 Kilis Turkey
13 C6 Kiliya Ukraine
17 B5 Kilkee Rep. of Ire.
17 F3 Kilkeel U.K.
17 D5 Kilkenny div. Rep. of Ire.
17 D5 Kilkenny Rep. of Ire.
17 B5 Kilkieran Bay b. Rep. of Ire.
29 D4 Kilkis Greece
17 C4 Kilkieran Rep. of Ire.
99 □1 Killala Bay b. Rep. of Ire.
17 C4 Killala Rep. of Ire.
17 C5 Killaloe Rep. of Ire.
114 E4 Killaloe Station Can.
111 H4 Killam Can.
99 G5 Killarney Aust.
114 D4 Killarney Can.
17 B5 Killarney Rep. of Ire.
17 B5 Killarney, Lake l. The Bahamas
17 B5 Killarney National Park nat. park Can.
125 D6 Killary Harbour b. Rep. of Ire.
125 D5 Killeen U.S.A.
16 E2 Killin U.K.
16 D3 Killin U.K.
17 C4 Killinaule Rep. of Ire.
113 H1 Killiniq Island i. Can.
17 C5 Killorglin Rep. of Ire.
17 D4 Killybegs Rep. of Ire.
16 D3 Kilmarnock U.K.
14 G2 Kil'mez' r. Rus. Fed.
14 G2 Kil'mez' Rus. Fed.
81 C6 Kilmore Aust.
81 C6 Kilosa Tanzania
81 B5 Kipini Tanzania
81 C6 Kiloza Tanzania
81 C5 Kilwa Zaire
81 C6 Kilwa Kivinje Tanzania
81 C6 Kilwa Masoko Tanzania
17 C5 Kilrush Rep. of Ire.
81 C6 Kimamba Tanzania
78 C4 Kimba Congo
57 E3 Kimba Aust.
124 C3 Kimball U.S.A.
81 B6 Kimbe P.N.G.
82 D4 Kimberley R.S.A.
100 D3 Kimberley Downs Aust.

100 D3 Kimberley Plateau plat. Aust.
92 E4 Kimbolton N.Z.
49 J4 Kimch'aek N. Korea
49 J5 Kimch'ŏn S. Korea
46 B6 Kimhae S. Korea
11 F3 Kimito Finland
29 E6 Kimje S. Korea
79 B4 Kimongo Congo
29 E6 Kimolos i. Greece
12 F4 Kimovsk Rus. Fed.
79 B4 Kimpanzou Congo
78 B4 Kimpese Zaire
46 C8 Kimshima-yama vol Japan
14 C1 Kimry Rus. Fed.
42 A5 Kinabalu, G. mt. Malaysia
41 A5 Kinabatangan r. Malaysia
81 C5 Kinango Kenya
29 E5 Kinaros i. Greece
110 G4 Kinbasket Lake l. Can.
16 E2 Kinbrace U.K.
42 A5 Kincardine Can.
129 J2 Kincardine U.K.
114 C4 Kincardine Can.
79 C4 Kinda Zaire
42 A2 Kindat Myanmar
42 B3 Kinder Myanmar
42 B3 Kinder Scout h. U.K.
114 H4 Kindersley Can.
76 B4 Kindia Guinea
64 D4 Kindu Zaire
64 D1 Kinel' Rus. Fed.
64 D1 Kinel'-Cherkasy Rus. Fed.
14 F1 Kineshma Rus. Fed.
98 E4 Kingaroy Aust.
80 F5 King r. Aust.
81 C6 Kingani r. Aust.
81 B6 Kingarooy Aust.
120 D2 Kinghorn U.K.
64 D2 Kingir Rus. Fed.
64 E1 Kingfield U.S.A.
125 D5 Kingfisher U.S.A.
147 D7 King George B. b. Falkland Is.
152 B2 King George Islands is Ant.
57 E1 King George Sound b. Aust.
100 C4 King Hill h. Aust.
100 D4 King I. i. Can.
114 E1 Kingi i. i. N.Z.
122 C4 Kingisepp Rus. Fed.
58 D5 Kingisepp Rus. Fed.
97 F4 King I. i. Aust.
115 J4 King Kirkland Can.
55 L2 King Leopold and Queen Astrid Coast Ant.
100 D3 King Leopold Ranges h. Aust.
129 E4 Kingman U.S.A.
129 J2 Kingman U.S.A.
121 J2 Kingman U.S.A.
47 □2 Kingo Japan
47 F6 Kingo-misaki c. Japan
47 G4 Kiryū Japan
47 J2 Kirzhach Rus. Fed.
79 C4 Kisangani Zaire
81 C6 Kisangani Aust.
47 H4 Kisanji Japan
28 E3 Kisar i. Indon.
46 D6 Kisarazu Japan
111 J4 Kisbey Can.
65 H2 Kiselevsk Rus. Fed.
82 C3 Kisel'sk Rus. Fed.
55 F4 Kishanganj India
54 C4 Kishangarh India
77 F4 Kishi Nigeria
81 C5 Kishiwada Japan
47 E6 Kishiwada Japan
81 C5 Kisii Kenya
81 C5 Kisiju Tanzania
19 L3 Kiskörös Hungary
19 K5 Kiskőrösi-Szék Hungary
19 J5 Kiskunfélegyháza Hungary
19 J5 Kiskunhalas Hungary
19 J5 Kiskunlacháza Hungary
19 J5 Kiskunmajsa Hungary
13 H7 Kislovodsk Rus. Fed.
80 E4 Kismaayo Somalia
47 G5 Kiso-gawa r. Japan
47 F6 Kiso-sanmyaku mt. ra. Japan
76 C5 Kissidougou Guinea
119 D6 Kissimmee U.S.A.
119 D7 Kissimmee, L. l. U.S.A.
111 J3 Kississing L. l. Can.
54 A4 Kishorganj Bangladesh
76 C4 Kissawa Nigeria
19 J5 Kistelek Hungary
19 J5 Kisújszállás Hungary
81 C5 Kisumu Kenya
19 J4 Kisvárda Hungary
76 C4 Kita Mali
81 C5 Kita Uganda
65 H5 Kitab Uzbekistan
47 H4 Kitagami-gawa r. Japan
47 H4 Kitaibaraki Japan
47 H4 Kitakami Japan
47 H4 Kitakami-gawa r. Japan
46 C6 Kita-Kyūshū Japan
47 H4 Kitami Japan
47 G5 Kitanga-yama vol Japan
47 □2 Kitano-shima i. Japan
47 G5 Kitano-ura inlet Japan
81 B4 Kitanda Tanzania
81 B5 Kitangari Tanzania
81 B5 Kitangiri, Lake l. Tanzania
47 F6 Kitano-kawa r. Japan
81 B4 Kitaraba Tanzania
114 E4 Kitchener Can.
80 D4 Kitgum Uganda
72 D5 Kitgum Uganda
114 D4 Kithira i. Greece
81 B5 Kitona Zaire
81 B4 Kitope Tanzania
29 E5 Kitros Greece
81 B5 Kitunda Tanzania
79 D6 Kitwe Zambia
18 E5 Kitzbüheler Alpen mts Austria
18 E5 Kitzingen Germany
72 C4 Kirdimi Chad
72 C4 Kivi r. Chad
81 A5 Kivu div. Rwanda/Zaire

15 C1 Kocheriv Ukraine
14 G4 Kochetovka Rus. Fed.
14 E3 Kochetovka Rus. Fed.
40 D7 Kōchi Japan
47 □2 Kochinada Japan
65 K2 Kochki Rus. Fed.
65 J4 Kochkor Kyrgyzstan
13 G4 Kochubey Rus. Fed.
13 H6 Kochubey Rus. Fed.
13 G6 Kochubeyevskoye Rus. Fed.
19 L3 Kock Poland
56 B4 Kodaikanal India
15 D1 Kodaky Ukraine
50 D2 Kodala India
55 F4 Kodari Nepal
55 F4 Kodarma India
6 Kodeń Poland
108 C4 Kodiak U.S.A.
108 C4 Kodiak Island i. U.S.A.
12 F2 Kodino Rus. Fed.
80 B3 Kodok Sudan
46 H3 Kodomari-misaki pt Japan
13 G7 Kodori r. Georgia
15 C1 Kodra Ukraine
15 C3 Kodyma r. Ukraine
15 C2 Kodyma Ukraine
29 E4 Kodzhaele mt. Bulgaria/Greece
55 E4 Koel r. India
55 F5 Koel, S. r. India
82 B4 Koës Namibia
129 F5 Kofa Mts mts U.S.A.
28 F4 Kofçaz Turkey
82 C4 Koffiefontein R.S.A.
19 G5 Köflach Austria
76 D5 Koforidua Ghana
40 E6 Kōfu Japan
112 E2 Kogaluc r. Can.
113 E2 Kogaluc, Baie de b. Can.
113 H2 Kogaluk r. Can.
11 D5 Køge Denmark
77 F5 Kogi div. Nigeria
76 B4 Kogon r. Guinea
46 A6 Kogūm do i. S. Korea
46 C6 Koguchi Japan
54 A4 Kohan Pakistan
54 B2 Kohat Pakistan
57 F2 Koh-i-Hisar mt. ra. Afghanistan
11 G4 Kohila Estonia
55 H4 Kohima India
57 F2 Koh-i-Mazar mt. Afghanistan
54 A4 Koh-i-Patandar mt. Pakistan
57 F2 Koh-i-Sangan mt. Afghanistan
57 G2 Kohistan reg. Afghanistan
54 C2 Kohistan reg. Pakistan
57 E3 Koh-i-Sultan mt. Pakistan
57 B3 Kohkīlūyeh w Būyer Ahmadī div. Iran
152 A3 Kohler Ra. mt. ra. Ant.
54 B3 Kohlu Pakistan
57 E2 Kohsan Afghanistan
11 G4 Kohtla-Järve Estonia
92 E2 Kohukohunui h. N.Z.
49 H6 Kohŭng S. Korea
93 C6 Kohurau mt. N.Z.
47 G5 Koide Japan
110 A2 Koidern Can.
43 A5 Koihoa Andaman and Nicobar Is India
56 B3 Koilkuntla India
60 F2 Koi Sanjaq Iraq
49 J6 Kōje do i. S. Korea
47 G7 Ko-jima i. Japan
47 □2 Ko-jima i. Japan
101 B7 Kojonup Aust.
42 B3 Kok r. Thailand
121 J2 Kokadjo U.S.A.
64 F3 Kokalaat Kazak.
65 H4 Kokand Uzbekistan
11 H4 Kökar Finland
54 A3 Kokcha r. Afghanistan
11 F3 Kokemäenjoki r. Finland
80 C3 K'ok' Häyk' l. Ethiopia
14 E1 Kokhma Rus. Fed.
76 A3 Koki Senegal
56 B3 Kokita India
10 F3 Kokkola Finland
63 L3 Kok Kuduk well China
77 E4 Koko Nigeria
76 C4 Kokofata Mali
127 □1 Koko Hd hd U.S.A.
122 D5 Kokomo U.S.A.
14 C1 Kokoreva Rus. Fed.
14 B3 Kokorevka Rus. Fed.
77 E5 Kokpekty Rus. Fed.
65 J4 Koksaray Kazak.
65 G4 Kokshaal-Tau mt. ra. China/Kyrgyzstan
65 G2 Kokshetau div. Kazak.
65 G2 Kokshetau Kazak.
113 G2 Koksoak r. Can.
10 D2 Kokstad R.S.A.
42 A3 Koktal Thailand
46 C3 Kokterek Kazak.
46 D6 Kokubu Japan
45 C4 Ko Kut i. Thailand
43 C6 Kokuy Rus. Fed.
10 J1 Kola Rus. Fed.
54 A4 Kolachi r. Pakistan
54 C2 Kolahoi mt. India
39 H7 Kolaka Indon.
43 B6 Ko Lanta Thailand
43 B6 Ko Lanta i. Thailand
56 C2 Kolar India
56 C2 Kolaras India
56 B3 Kolar Gold Fields India
10 F2 Kolari Finland
55 F4 Kolayat India
19 K3 Kolbuszowa Poland
14 F3 Kol'chugino Rus. Fed.
76 A3 Kolda Senegal
11 C5 Kolding Denmark
78 B3 Kole Kasai-Oriental Zaire
78 C3 Kole Haute-Zaire Zaire
10 F2 Koler Sweden
62 F2 Kolguyev, O. i. Rus. Fed.
55 F5 Kolhan India
54 A2 Kolhapur India
43 B6 Ko Libong i. Thailand
76 B3 Kolimbiné w Mali/Mauritania
19 J3 Kolín Czech Rep.
80 C3 K'olíto Ethiopia
11 H4 Kõljala Estonia
11 F4 Kolkasrags pt Latvia
65 H4 Kolkhozobod Tajikistan
15 A1 Kolky Ukraine
56 C2 Kollegal India
56 D3 Kolleru L. l. India
18 C3 Köln Germany
19 L2 Koło Poland
79 D5 Koloa i. Tonga
14 F2 Kolobovo Rus. Fed.
14 F2 Kologriv Rus. Fed.
76 C4 Kolokani Mali
15 F2 Kolomak Ukraine
15 A2 Kolomyya Ukraine
14 G2 Kolomna Rus. Fed.
90 □1 Kolombangara i. Solomon Is.
90 Kolonga Tonga
29 B4 Kolonjë Albania

15 F2 Kolontayiv Ukraine
65 H1 Kolosovka Rus. Fed.
90 □4 Kolovai Tonga
64 D7 Koloverstnoye Kazak.
14 E2 Kolp' r. Rus. Fed.
62 K4 Kolpashevo Rus. Fed.
14 C3 Kolpny Rus. Fed.
29 D4 Kolpos Agiou Orous b. Greece
29 D7 Kolpos Chanion b. Greece
29 D4 Kolpos Ierissou b. Greece
29 E7 Kolpos Irakleiou b. Greece
29 D4 Kolpos Kassandras b. Greece
29 E4 Kolpos Kavalas b. Greece
29 D7 Kolpos Kissamou b. Greece
29 D4 Kolpos Orfanou b. Greece
29 D6 Kolpos Ydras chan. Greece
14 G3 Koltovskoye Rus. Fed.
28 B2 Kolubara r. Yugo.
80 D2 Koluli Eritrea
53 D10 Kolumadulu Atoll atoll Maldives
65 G2 Koluton Kazak.
56 A2 Kolvan India
10 C2 Kolvereid Norway
10 G1 Kolvik Norway
12 E1 Kolvitskoye, Ozero l. Rus. Fed.
57 F4 Kolwa reg. Pakistan
79 E6 Kolwezi Zaire
14 D3 Kolybel'skoye Rus. Fed.
63 R3 Kolyma r. Rus. Fed.
63 R3 Kolymskaya Nizmennost' lowland Rus. Fed.
63 S3 Kolymskiy, Khrebet mt. ra. Rus. Fed.
14 G3 Kolyshley Rus. Fed.
14 G3 Kolyshley Rus. Fed.
65 K1 Kolyvan' Rus. Fed.
77 G4 Komadugu-gana w Nigeria
47 F6 Komagane Japan
46 H7 Komaga-take vol Japan
82 B4 Komaggas Mts mts Namibia
19 L4 Komańcza Poland
63 S4 Komandorskiye Ostrova is Rus. Fed.
14 B3 Komarichi Rus. Fed.
15 B2 Komariv Ukraine
29 J5 Komárno Slovakia
15 A1 Komarove Ukraine
47 F5 Komatsu Japan
46 E6 Komatsushima Japan
79 E4 Kombe Zaire
76 D4 Kombissiri Burkina
76 D4 Kombongou Burkina
55 H3 Komdi mt. India
41 □1 Komebail Lagoon lag. Palau
81 B5 Kome Channel chan. Uganda
81 B5 Kome i. Uganda
81 B5 Kome Island i. Tanzania
40 A2 Komering r. Indon.
12 J2 Komi div. Rus. Fed.
46 H3 Kominato Japan
14 D3 Kominternivs'ke Ukraine
112 E1 Komiža Croatia
16 □ Komló Hungary
14 E1 Kommunar Rus. Fed.
65 L2 Kommunar Rus. Fed.
40 D4 Komodo i. Indon.
76 C5 Komodou Guinea
76 D5 Komoé r. Côte d'Ivoire
76 D5 Komoé r. Côte d'Ivoire
73 F3 Kôm Ombo Egypt
79 B4 Komono Congo
47 G5 Komoro Japan
29 E4 Komotini Greece
14 F2 Kompaniyivka Ukraine
82 C5 Komsberg mts R.S.A.
63 M1 Komsomolets, O. i. Rus. Fed.
62 H4 Komsomolets, Zaliv b. Rus. Fed.
14 F5 Komsomol'sk Rus. Fed.
14 F5 Komsomol'sk Turkmenistan
15 E2 Komsomol's'k Ukraine
15 G2 Komsomol's'ke Ukraine
12 H4 Komsomol'skiy Rus. Fed.
45 P1 Komsomol'sk-na-Amure Rus. Fed.
64 E4 Komsomol's'ka-Ustyurte Uzbekistan
14 F2 Komsomol'skoye Rus. Fed.
48 D1 Komsomol'skoye Rus. Fed.
28 B4 Komunga Bulgaria
13 G7 Kömürlü Turkey
14 F2 Komyshnya Ukraine
15 D1 Komyshuvakha Ukraine
55 F1 Konakovo Rus. Fed.
55 F5 Konar Res. India
55 G5 Konār Tahkteh Dālakī Iran
54 D4 Konda India
55 H5 Konārak India
76 B3 Kondagaon India
76 B3 Kondembaia Sierra Leone
115 G3 Kondiaronk, Lac l. Can.
101 B7 Kondinin Aust.
12 F2 Kondopoga Rus. Fed.
14 F2 Kondrovo Rus. Fed.
55 G4 Kondūz Afghanistan
57 G1 Kondūz Afghanistan
90 □2 Kone New Caledonia
76 B3 Koné Mali
81 B5 Kong Cameroon
109 □ Kong Christian IX Land reg. Greenland
109 Q2 Kong Christian X Land reg. Greenland
109 Q2 Kong Frederik VIII Land reg. Greenland
109 O3 Kong Frederik VI Kyst Greenland
152 □2 Kong Håkon VII Sea sea Ant.
62 □ Kong Karl's Land is Svalbard Arctic Ocean
82 □2 Kongola Namibia
109 Q2 Kong Oscar Fjord inlet Greenland
76 □4 Kongoussi Burkina
11 C4 Kongsberg Norway
11 C3 Kongsvinger Norway
65 J5 Kongur Shan mt. China
109 Q2 Kong Wilhelm Land reg. Greenland

15 E1 Konotop Ukraine
43 E4 Kon Plong Vietnam
41 □1 Konrei Palau
19 L3 Końskie Poland
80 C3 Konso Ethiopia
49 H2 Konstantinovka Rus. Fed.
14 D1 Konstantinovo Rus. Fed.
13 G6 Konstantinovsk Rus. Fed.
14 D1 Konstantinovskiy Rus. Fed.
18 E4 Konstanz Germany
77 F4 Kontagora Nigeria
42 B2 Kontha Myanmar
10 H3 Kontiolahti Finland
10 G2 Konttila Finland
43 D4 Kon Tum Vietnam
42 D4 Kon Tum, Plateau du plat. Vietnam
72 G1 Konushin, Mys pt Rus. Fed.
61 N1 Konya div. Turkey
60 C2 Konya Turkey
15 C4 Konyshevka Rus. Fed.
101 C6 Kookynie Aust.
127 □1 Koolau Range mt. ra. U.S.A.
98 D5 Koolivoo, L. salt flat Aust.
101 B6 Koolyanobbing Aust.
97 F3 Koondrook Aust.
96 C2 Koonibba Aust.
120 D5 Koontz Lake l. U.S.A.
101 B6 Koorda Aust.
82 A3 Koos waterhole Namibia
126 C2 Kooskia U.S.A.
110 F5 Kootenay r. Can./U.S.A.
110 F4 Kootenay L. l. Can.
110 F4 Kootenay Nat. Park nat. park Can.
56 A2 Kopargaon India
77 E5 Kopargo Benin
10 M2 Kópasker Iceland
65 J3 Kopbirlik Kazak.
26 D3 Koper Slovenia
11 C3 Kopervik Norway
64 E5 Kopet Dag, Khrebet mt. ra. Turkmenistan
54 D4 Kosi r. India
43 C5 Ko Phangan i. Thailand
43 B5 Ko Phra Thong i. Thailand
43 B6 Ko Phuket i. Thailand
11 E4 Köping Sweden
29 B5 Koplik Albania
10 E3 Köpmanholmen Sweden
14 B2 Koporikha Rus. Fed.
56 C3 Koppal India
11 D4 Kopparberg Sweden
26 F2 Koprivnica Croatia
60 B2 Köprübaşı Turkey
15 B2 Kopychyntsi Ukraine
57 B3 Kor w Iran
14 E3 Korablino Rus. Fed.
80 D3 K'orahē Ethiopia
44 A4 Korak Pakistan
112 E1 Korak, Baie b. Can.
56 B2 Korangal India
57 G1 Korān w Monjan Afghanistan
76 D3 Koraput India
79 B4 Korba India
75 G1 Korba Tunisia
82 D2 Korbach Germany
78 C2 Korbol Chad
40 A3 Korbu, Gunung mt. Malaysia
29 C4 Korçë Albania
26 F4 Korchivka Ukraine
26 F4 Korčula i. Croatia
26 F4 Korčulanski Kanal chan. Croatia
57 A2 Kördestan div. Iran
57 C1 Kord Kūy Iran
73 E3 Kordofan div. Sudan
57 D2 Kords reg. Iran
80 C3 Kordi Sheykh Iran
49 H4 Korea Bay g. China/North Korea
49 H4 Korea Strait str. Japan/South Korea
76 D4 Koréba Burkina
56 A2 Koregaon India
15 E1 Koren' r. Rus. Fed.
14 D2 Korenevo Rus. Fed.
13 G6 Korenovsk Rus. Fed.
15 C1 Korets' Ukraine
57 C1 Korf Iran
60 E1 Körfez Turkey
152 B3 Korff Ice Rise ice feature Ant.
54 B4 Korgan Turkey
76 B4 Korhogo Côte d'Ivoire
19 H5 Kőris-hegy mt. Hungary
29 H5 Koriyama Japan
47 G5 Korkino Rus. Fed.
60 C1 Korkuteli Turkey
63 G2 Korla China
78 C3 Kormakitis, C. c. Cyprus
19 H4 Körmend Hungary
26 E4 Kornat i. Croatia
15 G2 Kornyn Ukraine
90 □8 Koro i. Fiji
76 C4 Koro Mali
15 G1 Korocha Rus. Fed.
60 E1 Köroğlu Tepesi mt. Turkey
81 E7 Korogwe well Ethiopia
90 □8 Korogwe Tanzania
90 □ Korolevu Fiji
29 B4 Koronia, L. l. Greece
29 D4 Koroni Greece
15 E2 Koronowo Poland
29 H5 Körös r. Hungary
19 J5 Köröshegy Hungary
90 □8 Koro Sea sea Fiji
78 D3 Korosten' Ukraine
78 E4 Korostyshiv Ukraine
78 D3 Koro Toro Chad
14 A2 Korovyntsi Ukraine
90 □8 Korovou Fiji
11 G3 Korpo Finland
90 □ Korsakov Rus. Fed.
48 H2 Korsakov Rus. Fed.
76 D5 Korsimoro Burkina
11 D5 Korsør Denmark
15 D1 Korsun'-Shevchenkivs'kyy Ukraine

19 K1 Korsze Poland
10 F3 Kortesjärvi Finland
73 F4 Korti Sudan
12 K2 Kortkeros Rus. Fed.
18 A3 Kortrijk Belgium
78 A2 Korup, Parc National de nat. park Cameroon
10 G2 Korvala Finland
54 D4 Korwai India
63 R4 Koryakskaya Sopka vol Rus. Fed.
63 S3 Koryakskiy Khrebet mt. ra. Rus. Fed.
12 H2 Koryazhma Rus. Fed.
19 L2 Korycin Poland
15 E1 Koryukivka Ukraine
15 E1 Koryzhevka Rus. Fed.
29 F6 Kos i. Greece
29 F6 Kos Greece
13 E6 Kosa Arabats'ka Strilka spit Ukraine
15 D1 Kosachivka Ukraine
43 C5 Ko Samui i. Thailand
14 C2 Kosaya Gora Rus. Fed.
64 D3 Koschagyl Kazak.
19 H1 Kościerzyna Poland
125 F5 Kosciusko U.S.A.
110 C3 Kosciusko I. i. U.S.A.
97 G4 Kosciusko, Mt mt. Aust.
97 G4 Kosciusko National Park nat. park Aust.
60 D1 Köse Dağı mt. Turkey
56 B2 Kosgi India
44 E2 Kosh-Agach Rus. Fed.
15 E1 Koshary Ukraine
46 B8 Koshikijima-rettō is Japan
46 B8 Koshiki-kaikyō chan. Japan
57 E2 Koshimizu Japan
57 E2 Koshk Iran
57 E2 Koshk-e-Kohneh Afghanistan
12 J4 Koshki Rus. Fed.
122 C4 Koshkonong, Lake l. U.S.A.
15 B2 Koshlyaky Ukraine
14 E1 Koshmanivka Ukraine
46 C6 Koshoba Turkmenistan
47 G5 Kōshoku Japan
54 D4 Kosi r. India
13 J4 Kosi r. India
56 B3 Kosigi India
65 J4 Kos-Istek Kazak.
28 B3 Kosiv Ukraine
63 L4 Košice Slovakia
14 A2 Kosiv Ukraine
65 J4 Koskol' Kazak.
65 H4 Koskuduk Kazak.
11 D4 Koskullskulle Sweden
55 F5 Koslan Rus. Fed.
14 E1 Kosmynino Rus. Fed.
49 H6 Kosŏng N. Korea
49 J5 Kosŏng S. Korea
28 B3 Kosovo div. Yugo.
28 B3 Kosovo Polje plain Yugo.
28 B3 Kosovska Kamenica Yugo.
28 B3 Kosovska Mitrovica Yugo.
86 H4 Kosrae i. Fed. States of Micronesia
65 J5 Kosrap China
72 D4 Kossanto well Niger
41 □1 Kossol Passage chan. Palau
41 □1 Kossol Reef reef Palau
76 C5 Kossou, Lac de l. Côte d'Ivoire
28 D3 Kostenets Bulgaria
14 D2 Kosterevo Rus. Fed.
73 F5 Kosti Sudan
28 D3 Kostinbrod Bulgaria
62 K3 Kostino Rus. Fed.
25 G7 Kostolac Yugo.
10 H2 Kostomuksha Rus. Fed.
15 C1 Kostopil' Ukraine
12 G3 Kostroma r. Rus. Fed.
12 G3 Kostroma div. Rus. Fed.
14 E1 Kostroma Rus. Fed.
19 G4 Kostrzyn Poland
13 G5 Kostyantynivka Donets'k Ukraine
15 F2 Kostyantynivka Kharkiv Ukraine
15 D2 Kostyantynivka Zaporizhzhya Ukraine
14 A2 Kostyri Rus. Fed.
19 H3 Koszalin Poland
19 H5 Kőszeg Hungary
55 E5 Kota India
54 C4 Kota India
40 A3 Kotaagung Indon.
40 B2 Kotabaru Indon.
40 C2 Kotabesi Indon.
40 B3 Kota Bharu Malaysia
38 G5 Kota Kinabalu Malaysia
54 B4 Kotapārh India
40 B2 Kotapinang Indon.
43 C6 Kota Tinggi Malaysia
54 B4 Kotawaringin Indon.
12 J3 Kotel'nich Rus. Fed.
13 G6 Kotel'nikovo Rus. Fed.
63 P2 Kotel'nyy, O. i. Rus. Fed.
18 E3 Köthen Germany
81 □ Kotido Uganda
80 B4 Kotikala India
103 B3 Kot Kapura India
10 H3 Kotka Finland
12 J2 Kotlas Rus. Fed.
10 □ Kötlutangi pt Iceland
11 H4 Kotly Rus. Fed.
77 F5 Koton-Karifi Nigeria
28 B3 Kotor Yugo.
76 C5 Kotouba Côte d'Ivoire
13 H5 Kotovo Rus. Fed.
14 F3 Kotovras Rus. Fed.
15 C2 Kotovsk Ukraine
14 G3 Kotovsk Rus. Fed.
54 B4 Kot Putli India
54 B3 Kotri Pakistan
54 B4 Kotri r. India
56 E2 Kottagudem India
54 C4 Kotra India
56 C4 Kottarakara India
56 C4 Kottayam India
56 C4 Kotte Sri Lanka
78 C3 Kotto r. C.A.R.
90 □5 Kotu Fiji
90 □5 Kotu Group is Tonga
13 G4 Koturdepe Turkmenistan
29 J4 Kötürpınar Turkey
108 B3 Kotzebue U.S.A.
108 B3 Kotzebue Sound b. U.S.A.

78 B2 Koum Cameroon
78 C2 Kouma r. C.A.R.
90 □2 Koumac Pac. Oc.
99 G4 Kouma r. Rus. Fed.
76 B4 Koumbia Guinea
76 B4 Koumbia Burkina
78 C2 Koumra Chad
76 B4 Koundara Guinea
76 A4 Koundougou Burkina
84 B4 Koungheul Senegal
76 B4 Kounoupi r. Greece
65 H3 Kounradskiy Kazak.
65 K2 Kourak Rus. Fed.
76 C4 Kouroussa Guinea
72 D4 Kourti well Chad
72 C4 Kousseri Cameroon
76 C4 Koutiala Mali
90 □2 Koutoumo i. Pac. Oc.
29 F6 Koutsomyti i. Greece
28 C2 Kovačica Yugo.
79 C6 Kovari r. Congo
10 H2 Kovdor Rus. Fed.
15 B1 Kovel' Ukraine
14 H1 Kovernino Rus. Fed.
56 B4 Kovilpatti India
28 C2 Kovin Yugo.
14 E1 Kovrov Rus. Fed.
15 E1 Kov'yahy Ukraine
14 E2 Kovylkino Rus. Fed.
14 E1 Kovzhskoye, Ozero l. Rus. Fed.
99 E2 Kowanyama Aust.
82 A2 Kowares waterhole Namibia
93 C5 Kowhitirangi N.Z.
114 B1 Kowkash Can.
45 □ Kowloon Hong Kong
45 □ Kowloon Pk h. Hong Kong
65 K5 Koxlax China
49 G5 Koxtag China
46 C6 Kōyama-misaki pt Japan
43 E4 Ko Yao Yai i. Thailand
60 B2 Köyceğiz Turkey
29 E6 Köyceğiz Gölü l. Turkey
12 J2 Koygorodok Rus. Fed.
57 D1 Koyda Rus. Fed.
65 J2 Koylyk Kazak.
56 A2 Koyna Res. resr India
13 H6 Koynas Rus. Fed.
47 G4 Koyoshi-gawa r. Japan
15 G2 Kozacha Lopan' Ukraine
13 F6 Kö-zaki pt Japan
14 E1 Kozan Rus. Fed.
29 C4 Kozan Turkey
29 D4 Kozani Greece
26 F3 Kozara mt. ra. Bos.-Herz.
15 D1 Kozara Dubica Bos.-Herz.
65 J2 Kozats'ke Ukraine
15 D1 Kozelets' Ukraine
14 C2 Kozel'shchyna Ukraine
14 B2 Kozel'sk Rus. Fed.
15 F2 Kozhabakhy Kazak.
45 D4 Kozhikode India
14 C1 Kozhva Rus. Fed.
15 B2 Kozienice Poland
15 E1 Kozin Ukraine
28 C3 Kozloduy Bulgaria
15 G2 Kozlovo Rus. Fed.
60 B1 Kozlu Turkey
26 F3 Kozluk Bos.-Herz.
14 H1 Koz'modem'yansk Rus. Fed.
15 B2 Kozova Ukraine
19 O4 Kožuł mt. Poland
19 J4 Kožuchów Poland
46 G3 Kōzu-shima i. Japan
15 D2 Kozyatyn Ukraine
15 D2 Kozyilvka Ukraine
29 H4 Kozyörük Turkey
60 E1 Kozyin Rus. Fed.
76 D5 Kpalimé Togo
77 E5 Kpandae Ghana
77 F5 Kpandu Ghana
43 B5 Kra Buri Thailand
43 □1 Krächeh Cambodia
10 D3 Kraddsele Sweden
40 B3 Kragan Indon.
28 B3 Kragerø Norway
28 C2 Kragujevac Yugo.
42 B4 Kra, Isthmus of isth. Thailand
19 K2 Krajenka Poland
43 D4 Krakatau i. Indon.
43 D4 Krâkôr Cambodia
19 K3 Kraków Poland
132 □1 Kralendijk Bonaire Netherlands Ant.
15 J3 Kralovice Czech Rep.
28 B3 Kraljeviča Croatia
28 C2 Kraljevo Yugo.
19 J3 Králův hof a m. Slovakia
19 J3 Kralovice Czech Rep.
19 H3 Kráľovský Chlmec Slovakia
19 J4 Kralupy nad Vltavou Czech Rep.
29 C5 Kramers Greece
15 C2 Kramators'k Ukraine
11 E3 Kramfors Sweden
29 D6 Kranidi Greece
26 E3 Kranj Slovenia
78 A3 Kranji Res. resr Singapore
26 F2 Krapina r. Croatia
26 F2 Krapina Croatia
19 H3 Krapkowice Poland
12 H2 Krasavino Rus. Fed.
14 C4 Krasna, Zaliv b. Rus. Fed.
12 J4 Krasavino Rus. Fed.
26 E3 Krasnaja Gora Bos.-Herz.
13 G4 Krasnaya Gorbatka Rus. Fed.

14 H2 Krasnoarmeyskoye Rus. Fed.
15 G2 Krasnoarmiys'k Ukraine
13 F5 Krasnobrodskiy Rus. Fed.
13 H5 Krasnodar div. Rus. Fed.
13 F6 Krasnodar Rus. Fed.
15 D1 Krasnodon Ukraine
15 G1 Krasnogorodskoye Rus. Fed.
14 C2 Krasnogorskoye Rus. Fed.
45 Q2 Krasnogorskiy Rus. Fed.
42 B4 Krasnogvardeyskoye Rus. Fed.
13 G6 Krasnogvardeyskoye Rus. Fed.
15 F2 Krasnohrad Ukraine
15 E1 Krasnohvardiys'ke Ukraine
49 F2 Krasnokamensk
14 D2 Krasnokutsk Rus. Fed.
15 F2 Krasnokuts'k Ukraine
14 D4 Krasnolesnyy Rus. Fed.
14 H1 Krasnooktyabr'skiy Rus. Fed.
13 G6 Krasnopavlivka Ukraine
15 G2 Krasnoperekops'k Ukraine
14 C2 Krasnopillya Ukraine
15 F1 Krasnopillya Ukraine
14 D2 Krasnorechenskiy Rus. Fed.
15 E2 Krasnoselka Ukraine
64 F3 Krasnoturinsk Rus. Fed.
64 E1 Krasnoufimsk Rus. Fed.
15 D1 Krasnousol'skiy Rus. Fed.
14 E1 Krasnovishersk Rus. Fed.
64 D4 Krasnovodsk Turkmenistan
64 D5 Krasnovodskiy Zaliv b. Turkmenistan
64 D4 Krasnovodsk, Mys pt Turkmenistan
64 D5 Krasnovodskoye Plato plat. Turkmenistan
64 F2 Krasnoyarovo Rus. Fed.
49 J1 Krasnoyarovo Rus. Fed.
65 M2 Krasnoyarskoye Vdkhr. resr Rus. Fed.
19 K4 Krynica Poland
15 J1 Krychaw Belarus
15 C2 Kryms'k Rus. Fed.
13 F6 Krym' pen. Ukraine
49 H6 Krym'ki Hori mt. ra. Ukraine
19 K4 Krynica Poland
19 J1 Krynica Morska Poland
15 F2 Krynychky Ukraine
29 D4 Kryoneri Greece
15 E2 Kryve Ozero l. Ukraine
15 E1 Kryve Ozero Ukraine
14 E1 Kryvyy Rih Ukraine
19 J3 Krzepice Poland
19 K3 Krzyż Wielkopolski Poland
14 B3 Kroma r. Rus. Fed.
15 B1 Kromy Rus. Fed.
18 E3 Kronach Germany
43 C5 Krŏng Kaôh Kŏng Cambodia
10 F3 Kronoby Finland
55 H4 Kulat, G. mt. Indon.
109 Q1 Kronprins Christian Ld reg. Greenland
109 P3 Kronprins Frederik Bjerge nunatak Greenland
42 B4 Kronshagen Germany
82 D4 Kroonstad R.S.A.
13 G6 Kropotkin Rus. Fed.
19 H4 Kroměříž Czech Rep.
19 G2 Krosno Odrzańskie Poland
19 H3 Krotoszyn Poland
10 B3 Kroya Indon.
26 E3 Krško Slovenia
14 G3 Kruchi Rus. Fed.
15 A1 Krasnuts'k Ukraine
14 D4 Krasnolesnyy Rus. Fed.
83 E3 Kruger National Park nat. park R.S.A.
40 A3 Krui Indon.
82 C5 Kruisfontein R.S.A.
28 C4 Krujë Albania
29 F4 Krumbach Germany
28 E4 Krumovgrad Bulgaria
42 C4 Krung Thep (Bangkok) Thailand
19 H4 Krupanj Yugo.
15 J1 Krupets Rus. Fed.
19 J4 Krupina Slovakia
12 D4 Krupki Belarus
15 F1 Krupodernytsi Ukraine
28 C3 Kruševac Yugo.
29 C4 Kruševo Macedonia
19 J3 Krušné Hory mt. ra. Czech Rep.

65 J4 Kulanak Kyrgyzstan
64 E3 Kulandy Kazak.
57 E4 Kulaneh reg. Pakistan
60 F1 Kulat Azerbaijan
14 H2 Kulatkino Rus. Fed.
55 H4 Kulat, G. mt. Indon.
81 B5 Kulassein i. Phil.
55 H4 Kulaura Bangladesh
11 H4 Kuldīga Latvia
11 F4 Kuldīga Latvia
14 F2 Kulebaki Rus. Fed.
43 D4 Kulen Cambodia
57 J4 Kuleshi Rus. Fed.
19 K4 Kulesze Kościelne Poland
14 E2 Kulevatovo Rus. Fed.
60 C1 Kürdämir Azerbaijan
98 C4 Kulgera Aust.
12 J3 Kulikovo Rus. Fed.
43 C6 Kulim Malaysia
65 H5 Kuli Sarez l. Tajikistan
64 D1 Kulja Kazak.
64 F4 Kulkuduk Uzbekistan
97 F2 Kulkyne w Aust.
54 D3 Kullu India
18 D2 Kulmbach Germany
65 G5 Kūlob Tajikistan
12 G1 Kuloy r. Rus. Fed.
12 G2 Kuloy Rus. Fed.
54 B4 Kuri India
11 F4 Kurikka Finland
47 H4 Kurikoma-yama vol Japan
13 K5 Kurilovka Rus. Fed.
49 F1 Kuril'sk Japan
63 Q5 Kuril'skiye Ostrova is
19 J3 Kruszwica Poland
49 F1 Kukalin Rus. Fed.
64 E4 Krutikha Rus. Fed.
65 H1 Krutinka Rus. Fed.
14 E2 Krutoye Rus. Fed.
19 J3 Kruty Ukraine
110 B3 Kruzof I. i. U.S.A.
15 A2 Krychaw Belarus
19 J3 Kryly' Ukraine
15 A2 Kryms'k Rus. Fed.
15 D1 Krym' pen. Ukraine

101 B4 Kurabura r. Aust.
46 D6 Kurahashi-jima i. Japan
60 F1 Kurakh Rus. Fed.
13 G3 Kurakhove Ukraine
14 H2 Kurakino Rus. Fed.
14 F3 Kurakino Rus. Fed.
14 Kura Kurk chan. Estonia/Latvia
46 D6 Kurashiki Japan
55 E5 Kurasia India
65 L2 Kurayskiy Khr. mt. ra. Rus. Fed.
48 L1 Kurba r. Rus. Fed.
48 D2 Kurba, Nov. Rus. Fed.
14 E2 Kurchum Rus. Fed.
19 E2 Kurchatov Rus. Fed.
60 C1 Kürdämir Azerbaijan
56 A4 Kurduvadi India
14 E1 Kurdyum Rus. Fed.
28 E4 Kŭrdzhali Bulgaria
60 D1 Küre Turkey
87 K2 Kure Atoll atoll U.S.A.
11 F4 Kuressaare Estonia
65 H2 Kurgal'dzhinskiy Kazak.
65 G3 Kurgasyn Kazak.
62 J4 Kurgan Rus. Fed.
54 B4 Kuri India
11 F4 Kurikka Finland
47 H4 Kurikoma-yama vol Japan
13 K5 Kurilovka Rus. Fed.
49 F1 Kuril'sk Japan
63 Q5 Kuril'skiye Ostrova is Rus. Fed.
14 G5 Kuroshany r. Ukraine
19 K1 Kurovskiy Rus. Fed.
14 G2 Kurovskoye Rus. Fed.
92 D4 Kurow N.Z.
19 J3 Kurów Poland
54 B2 Kurram r. Afghanistan/Pakistan
97 A3 Kurri Kurri Aust.
13 G6 Kursavka Rus. Fed.
55 F4 Kursela India
14 F4 Kuršių Marios b. Lithuania
14 C4 Kursk Rus. Fed.
14 B4 Kursk div. Rus. Fed.
14 B4 Kurskoye Vdkhr. resr Rus. Fed.
60 C1 Kurşunlu Turkey
60 C1 Kuršumlija Yugo.
64 F2 Kurtamysh Rus. Fed.
60 C2 Kurtoğlu Burnu pt Turkey
78 D4 Kurty r. Kazak.
78 G4 Kuru r. Bhutan
14 B4 Kuru r. Sudan
44 D3 Kurukshetra India
82 C4 Kuruman R.S.A.
82 C4 Kuruman w R.S.A.
46 D6 Kurume Japan
56 D5 Kurunegala Sri Lanka
64 C4 Kunar r. Afghanistan
73 T3 Kurūsh, Jebel h. Sudan
110 B2 Kusawa Lake l. Can.
14 C1 Kushalino Rus. Fed.
55 G4 Kushchevskaya Rus. Fed.
47 K4 Kushida-gawa r. Japan
46 K2 Kushikino Japan
46 D6 Kushima Japan
47 K4 Kushimoto Japan
46 K2 Kushiro-Shitsugen National Park nat. park Japan
64 F5 Kushka r. Turkmenistan
54 C1 Kushmurun Kazak.
55 G4 Kushtagi India
55 G5 Kushtia Bangladesh
14 E1 Kushum r. Kazak.
64 F2 Kushum Rus. Fed.
82 A2 Kuskovo Rus. Fed.
51 J4 Kusong N. Korea
108 C3 Kuskokwim Bay U.S.A.
108 C3 Kuskokwim Mountains mt. ra. U.S.A.
46 D5 Kuskharo-ko l. Japan
110 D4 Kustanay div. Kazak./Kyrgyzstan
49 H5 Kustanay Rus. Fed.
14 H1 Kusnacht Switz.
60 C1 Kütahya Turkey
13 G7 K'ut'aisi Georgia
56 B3 Kutigi Nigeria
55 G4 Kutina Croatia/Slovenia
26 G3 Kutjevo Croatia
19 J3 Kutná Hora Czech Rep.
19 J2 Kutno Poland
79 B4 Kutu Zaire
55 H4 Kutubdia I. i. Bangladesh
78 D2 Kutum Sudan
79 C6 Kutvikumbi Angola
37 □2 Kuujjua r. Can.
113 G3 Kuujjuaq Can.
111 J3 Kuujjuarapik Can.
10 H2 Kuusamo Finland
47 H3 Kuusankoski Finland
47 □1 Kuuli-Mayak Rus. Fed.
79 C6 Kuvango Angola
14 F1 Kuvshinovo Rus. Fed.
14 F1 Kuwait country Asia
37 F2 Kuya Rus. Fed.
14 E2 Kuybyshev Rus. Fed.
65 H1 Kuybyshev Rus. Fed.
15 D2 Kuybysheve Zaporizhzhya Ukraine
15 F1 Kuybyshevka Rus. Fed.
14 H2 Kuybyshevskoye Vdkhr. resr Rus. Fed.
15 F1 Kuzemyn Ukraine

65 M2 Kuzhe-Baza Rus. Fed.
14 G2 Kuzhutki Rus. Fed.
14 A2 Kuz'minichi Rus. Fed.
14 D2 Kuz'minskoye Rus. Fed.
15 B2 Kuz'myn Ukraine
11 H3 Kuznechnoye Rus. Fed.
14 H3 Kuznetsk Rus. Fed.
65 L1 Kuznetskiy Alatau, Khrebet mt. ra. Rus. Fed.
15 A1 Kuznetsovs'k Ukraine
19 L2 Kuźnica Poland
12 F1 Kuzomen' Rus. Fed.
14 G2 Kuzovatovo Rus. Fed.
14 D3 Kuzovka Rus. Fed.
61 C1 Kuzucubelen Turkey
10 F1 Kvænangen chan. Norway
10 E1 Kvaleya i. Norway
10 F1 Kvalsund Norway
26 E3 Kvarnerić chan. Croatia
28 E1 Kvasy Ukraine
15 B1 Kvasyliv Ukraine
108 C4 Kvichak Bay b. U.S.A.
16 K2 Kvitsøy Norway
110 D3 Kwadacha Wilderness Prov. Park res. Can.
45 □ Kwai Tau Leng h. Hong Kong
139 F2 Kwakoegron Surinam
139 F2 Kwakwani Guyana
81 C5 Kwale Kenya
77 F5 Kwale Nigeria
83 E4 KwaMashu R.S.A.
76 D5 Kwame Danso Ghana
81 C6 Kwa Mtoro Tanzania
49 H6 Kwangju S. Korea
79 C4 Kwango r. Zaire
80 B4 Kwania, Lake I. Uganda
82 D5 Kwanobuhle R.S.A.
82 D5 Kwanojoli R.S.A.
77 E5 Kwara div. Nigeria
82 D5 Kwatinidubu R.S.A.
83 E4 Kwazulu-Natal div. R.S.A.
83 D2 Kwekwe Zimbabwe
82 C3 Kweneng div. Botswana
79 C5 Kwenge r. Zaire
19 J2 Kwidzyn Poland
90 □1 Kwigillingok U.S.A.
79 C4 Kwikila P.N.G.
39 K7 Kwilu r. Angola/Zaire
39 K7 Kwoka mt. Indon.
45 □ Kwun Tong Hong Kong
78 C2 Kyabé Chad
99 E5 Kyabra Aust.
99 E5 Kyabra w Aust.
42 A2 Kyadet Myanmar
42 A3 Kyaikkami Myanmar
42 B3 Kyaiklat Myanmar
42 B3 Kya-in-Seikkyi Myanmar
48 C2 Kyakhta Rus. Fed.
97 E3 Kyalite Aust.
96 C3 Kyancutta Aust.
42 A3 Kyangin Myanmar
42 B3 Kyaukhnyat Myanmar
115 J3 Kyaukkyi Myanmar
42 A2 Kyaukme Myanmar
42 A2 Kyaukpadaung Myanmar
42 A2 Kyaukpyu Myanmar
42 A2 Kyaukse Myanmar
42 A3 Kyauktan Myanmar
42 A2 Kyauktaw Myanmar
42 A2 Kyaukyit Myanmar
42 A2 Kyaunggon Myanmar
11 F5 Kybartai Lithuania
42 A3 Kyeintali Myanmar
81 B4 Kyela Tanzania
54 D2 Kyelang India
81 B4 Kyenjojo Uganda
48 B5 Kyikug China
19 H4 Kyjov Czech Rep.
29 E6 Kyklades is Greece
111 H4 Kyle Can.
16 E3 Kyle of Lochalsh U.K.
18 D3 Kyll r. Germany
29 E6 Kyllini mt. Greece
11 G3 Kymi div. Finland
29 E5 Kymi Greece
99 F4 Kynuna Aust.
47 □2 Kyoda Japan
80 B4 Kyoga, Lake I. Uganda
47 E6 Kyōga-misaki pt Japan
97 H2 Kyogle Aust.
78 E2 Kyom w Sudan
42 C3 Kyomachi Japan
42 B3 Kyonpyaw Myanmar
49 F4 Kyong Aust.
42 B2 Kyong Myanmar
49 J6 Kyōngju S. Korea
47 F6 Kyōto div. Japan
29 C6 Kyparissia Greece
29 C6 Kyparissiakos Kolpos b. Greece
48 E2 Kyra Rus. Fed.
29 F5 Kyra Panagia i. Greece
48 E2 Kyren Rus. Fed.
32 J3 Kyrgyzstan country Asia
18 F2 Kyritz Germany
10 C3 Kyrksæterøra Norway
15 F3 Kyrnasivka Ukraine
28 G2 Kyrnychky Ukraine
15 F3 Kyrykivka Ukraine
15 F2 Kyrylivka Ukraine
15 F2 Kyselil Ukraine
15 F3 Kyslivka Ukraine
65 J1 Kyshtovka Rus. Fed.
12 H1 Kyssa Rus. Fed.
19 H3 Kysucké Nové Mesto Slovakia
63 F3 Kytalyktakh Rus. Fed.
29 E6 Kythira i. Greece
29 E6 Kythnos i. Greece
61 B2 Kythrea Cyprus
42 A2 Kyunhla Myanmar
42 A2 Kyushe Aust.
46 C7 Kyūshū i. Japan
149 D2 Kyūshū - Palau Ridge Pac. Oc.
46 C7 Kyūshū-sanchi mts Japan
28 D3 Kyustendil Bulgaria
97 F3 Kywong Aust.
15 D1 Kyyiv Ukraine
62 H4 Kyyiv'ske Vdskh. resr Ukraine
10 G3 Kyyjärvi Finland
64 D4 Kyzan Kazak.
64 F4 Kyzyl Rus. Fed.
65 H5 Kyzyl-Art P. Kyrgyzstan
65 G3 Kyzyldyykan Kazak.
65 G2 Kyzyl-Khaya Rus. Fed.
48 A2 Kyzyl-Khem r. Rus. Fed.
65 H4 Kyzyl-Kiya Kyrgyzstan
64 F4 Kyzyl-Kya Kyrgyzstan
44 F1 Kyzyl-Mazhalyk Rus. Fed.
65 H5 Kyzylrabot Rus. Fed.
65 H2 Kyzylshaikha Kazak.
65 G2 Kyzyltu Kazak.
65 F4 Kyzylzhar Kazak.
65 G4 Kzyl-Dzhar Kazak.
65 G4 Kzyl-Orda Kazak.
65 G3 Kzyltu Kazak.
65 G3 Kzyluy Rus. Fed.

L

18 F2 Laage Germany
11 G4 Laagri Estonia
132 D5 La Aguja, Cabo de pt Colombia
25 F2 La Almunia de Doña Godina Spain
10 U1 Laanila Finland
80 E3 Laanle well Somalia
147 B4 La Araucania div. Chile
80 E3 Laascaanood Somalia
80 E2 Laasgoray Somalia
139 E1 La Asunción Venezuela
74 B3 Laâyoune Western Sahara
28 C3 Lab r. Yugo.
13 G6 Laba r. Rus. Fed.
125 C6 La Babia Mexico
115 K2 La Baie Can.
146 D2 La Banda Arg.
126 E3 La Barge U.S.A.
90 □6 Labasa Fiji
20 E5 Labastide-St-Pierre France
20 C3 La Baule-Escoublac France
20 C2 La Bazoge France
19 G3 Labe r. Czech Rep.
76 B4 Labé Guinea
115 H3 Labelle Can.
122 B5 La Belle U.S.A.
110 B2 Laberge, Lake I. Can.
41 A5 Labian, Tg pt Malaysia
21 H4 La Biche r. Can.
26 E3 Labin Croatia
13 G6 Labinsk Rus. Fed.
43 C7 Labis Malaysia
41 B3 Labo Phil.
78 F3 Labo Zaire
115 J4 La Boquilla Mexico
101 B5 Labouchere, Mt h. Aust.
20 D4 Labouheyre France
146 D3 Laboulaye Arg.
20 D3 La Bourboule France
113 H3 Labrador Can.
113 H3 Labrador City Can.
120 A6 La Follette U.S.A.
81 □5 La Fontaine Réunion Indian Ocean
109 N3 Labrador Sea sea Can./Greenland
139 E1 Lábrea Brazil
133 □1 La Brea Trin. & Tobago
130 C3 La Brecha Mexico
113 J3 Labuanhaju Indon.
138 C2 Labuhanbilik Indon.
39 J7 Labuan r. Indon.
47 □2 Labuan Malaysia
41 A5 Labuk r. Malaysia
41 A5 Labuk, Telukan b. Malaysia
39 J7 Labuna Indon.
21 J3 Labutta Myanmar
41 A2 Labytnangi Rus. Fed.
11 C4 Lac r. Albania
72 B5 Lac div. Chad
115 J3 Lac-à-Beauce Can.
115 J3 Lac-à-la-Tortue Can.
115 J3 La Calera Can.
146 B3 La Calera Chile
28 C3 La Calera Canary Is Spain
20 D4 Lacanau France
133 G5 La Canoa Venezuela
147 B5 Lacar, L. l. Arg.
24 E3 La Carlota Arg.
24 D4 La Carlota Spain
24 E3 La Carolina Spain
72 C5 Lac Lakha Chad
112 G5 La Bouchette Can.
115 J2 Laccadive Islands is India
53 D8 Laccadive Islands is India
113 J3 Lac-Chat Can.
115 J2 Lac-des-Commissaires Can.
111 K4 Lac du Bonnet Can.
113 J3 Lac-Édouard Can.
131 J6 La Ceiba Honduras
133 E5 La Ceiba Venezuela
76 D5 Lacepede B. b. Aust.
100 C3 Lacepede B. b. Aust.
77 E5 Lacey U.S.A.
121 H1 Lac Frontière Can.
131 E4 Lacha, Ozero l. Rus. Fed.
20 D3 La Châtaigneraie France
20 E3 La Châtre France
21 G4 La Chaux-de-Fonds Switz.
55 G4 Lachen India
55 G4 Lachhmangarh India
123 F3 Lachine Can.
115 H4 Lachlan r. Aust.
133 G4 La Chorrera Colombia
130 L7 La Chorrera Panama
115 H4 Lachute Can.
21 H5 La Ciotat France
130 D3 La Ciudad Mexico
133 D3 La Concepción Venezuela
111 G4 La Biche r. Can.
110 F2 La Loche Can.
110 F2 La Ronge Can.
113 H3 Lac la Ronge Provincial Park res. Can.
20 D4 Lac Mégantic Can.
113 H4 Lac-Nominingue Can.
115 J4 Lacolle Can.
130 C4 La Colorada Mexico
130 D3 La Concordia Mexico
130 D3 La Concordia Mexico
122 B3 Laconi Italy
121 H3 Laconia U.S.A.
133 □1 Lacovia Jamaica
20 E2 Lacre Pt pt Bonaire Netherlands Ant.
122 A2 La Crescent U.S.A.
122 A4 La Crosse U.S.A.
146 B4 La Cruz Arg.
25 D6 La Cruz Corrientes Arg.
146 B4 La Cruz Chile
146 B4 La Cruz Costa Rica
130 C3 La Cruz Sinaloa Mexico
131 F3 La Cruz Tamaulipas Mexico
130 J6 La Cruz Nicaragua
113 H3 Lac-Ste-Thérèse Can.
128 C2 Lacunas Res. resr U.S.A.
140 A3 La Cygne U.S.A.
139 E2 La Dada Bolivia
54 D2 Ladakh reg. Jammu and Kashmir
54 D2 Ladakh Range mt. ra. India
15 E1 Ladan Ukraine
43 A6 Lada, Tk b. Indon.
19 H3 Ladek-Zdrój Poland
81 □ La Désirade i. Guadeloupe Caribbean
81 □ La Digue I. i. Seychelles
82 C5 Ladismith R.S.A.
54 D4 Lādiz Iran
55 E4 Ladnun India
42 A2 Lai-Hka Myanmar
42 A2 Lai-Hsak Myanmar
49 F5 Laibin China
80 C3 Laisamis Kenya
18 F2 Laage Germany
138 C5 Laguna Mts mts U.S.A.

109 K2 Lady Ann Strait chan. Can.
97 G5 Lady Barron Aust.
114 E3 Lady Evelyn Lake I. Can.
110 E5 Ladysmith Can.
83 D4 Ladysmith R.S.A.
122 B3 Ladysmith U.S.A.
65 G2 Ladyzhenka Kazak.
15 C2 Ladyzhyn Ukraine
15 C2 Ladyzhynka Ukraine
80 C1 Lae P.N.G.
43 C4 Laem Ngop Thailand
43 B3 Laem Pho pt Thailand
11 B3 Lærdalsøyri Norway
141 D4 La Esmeralda Bolivia
139 D3 La Esmeralda Venezuela
11 C4 Læsø i. Denmark
141 D2 La Esperanza Bolivia
130 H6 La Esperanza Honduras
146 D1 La Estrella Salta Arg.
146 D3 La Estrella Bolivia
146 D3 La Falda Arg.
80 D2 Lafarug Somalia
20 E5 Lafayette France
119 C5 La Fayette U.S.A.
125 E6 Lafayette U.S.A.
125 E6 Lafayette U.S.A.
41 □ Lafayette, Pt pt Mauritius
21 D7 La Ferté-Bernard France
21 F2 La Ferté-Gaucher France
21 F2 La Ferté-Macé France
21 F2 La-Ferté-Milon France
21 F2 La Ferté-sous-Jouarre France
20 E3 La Ferté-St-Aubin France
54 B4 Laffan, Ra's pt Qatar
77 F5 Lafia Nigeria
77 F5 Lafiagi Nigeria
115 F4 Laflamme r. Can.
21 G2 La Foa Pac. Oc.
120 A6 La Follette U.S.A.
21 □5 La Fontaine Réunion Indian Ocean
115 F3 Laforce Can.
114 E3 Laforest Can.
139 G2 La Forestière French Guiana
113 F3 Laforge Can.
138 C2 La Fria Venezuela
57 C4 Laft Iran
84 A6 Laful Andaman and Nicobar Is India
20 C3 La Gacilly France
23 H7 La Galite i. Tunisia
31 H6 Lagan r. U.K.
77 G4 Lagané well Niger
142 E3 Lagarto Brazil
76 B3 Lagbar Senegal
78 B2 Lagdo, Lac de l. Cameroon
11 C4 Lågen r. Norway
80 C4 Lagh Bogal w Kenya
80 C4 Lagh Bor w Kenya/Somalia
80 D3 Lagh Dima w Kenya/Somalia
80 D4 Lagh Kutulo w Kenya
28 C3 La Gineta Spain
29 E4 Lagkadas Greece
21 G4 Lagkor Co salt l. China
72 C5 Lag Lakha Chad
12 G4 La Gloria Colombia
145 F4 Lagoa da Prata Brazil
145 G3 Lagoa Santa Brazil
146 F2 Lagoa Vermelha Brazil
142 D3 Lago da Pedra Brazil
13 H7 Lagodekhi Georgia
41 B3 Lagonoy Gulf b. Phil.
43 L1 Lagong r. Indon.
147 B6 Lago Posadas Arg.
21 G4 Lago Ranco Chile
77 E5 Lagos Nigeria
24 B4 Lagos Portugal
81 A6 Lagosa Tanzania
131 F5 Lagos de Moreno Mexico
112 E3 La Grande r. Can.
21 G4 La Grande-Combe France
119 C2 La Grange U.S.A.
122 E5 Lagrange U.S.A.
121 J2 La Grange U.S.A.
122 D5 La Grange U.S.A.
100 C3 Lagrange Aust.
139 F3 La Grande Sabana plain Venezuela
147 B6 Laguna Chile
146 D5 Laguna Brazil
138 D5 Lagunas Peru
130 C3 Laguna San Rafael, Parque Nacional nat. park Chile
146 B4 Laguna de Laja, Parque nac. nat. park Chile
146 E3 Laguna Grande Brazil
142 E3 Laguna, Ilha da i. Brazil
146 A6 Laguna Chile
49 E5 Lalin China
24 E1 Lalín Spain
55 H4 Lalaghat India
146 A3 La Laja Chile

81 C5 Laivera well Tanzania
26 C2 Laives Italy
49 F5 Laiwu China
49 G5 Laixi China
49 G5 Laiyang China
49 E5 Laiyuan China
49 F5 Laiyang China
146 B4 Laja r. Chile
132 A2 La Jagua Colombia
146 B4 Laja, Lago la l. Chile
98 B3 Lajamanu Aust.
143 G7 La Jigua Colombia
142 E2 Lajes Rio Grande do Norte Brazil
143 B6 Lajes Santa Catarina Brazil
145 H4 Lajinha Brazil
129 F4 Lajitas U.S.A.
19 H5 Lajosmizse Hungary
147 B6 La Junta Mexico
127 G4 La Junta U.S.A.
74 C4 Lakamané Mali
83 H3 Lakandrano Ampangalana canal Madagascar
14 E2 Lakash Rus. Fed.
126 E2 Lake i. U.S.A.
92 E4 Lake Alice N.Z.
97 F3 Lake Cargelligo Aust.
126 B1 Lake Chelan Nat. Recreation Area res. U.S.A.
119 D6 Lake City U.S.A.
122 A3 Lake City U.S.A.
122 A3 Lake City U.S.A.
119 E5 Lake City U.S.A.
128 D5 Lake Elsinore U.S.A.
96 D2 Lake Eyre Nat. Park nat. park Aust.
77 F5 Lakefield Aust.
99 F4 Lakefield Nat. Park nat. park Aust.
101 B7 Lake Grace Aust.
129 E4 Lake Havasu City U.S.A.
115 F3 Lake Isabella U.S.A.
101 B7 Lake King Aust.
119 D6 Lakeland U.S.A.
119 D6 Lake Linden U.S.A.
110 F4 Lake Louise Can.
98 A4 Lake Mackay Aboriginal Land res. Aust.
101 C5 Lake, Lake l. Phil.
130 D2 La Mula Mexico
99 F4 Lana r. Aust.
26 C2 Lana Italy
127 □2 Lanai i. U.S.A.
127 □2 Lanai City U.S.A.
41 C5 Lanao, Lake l. Phil.
115 G4 Lanark U.K.
16 F5 Lanark U.K.
122 C4 Lanark U.S.A.
121 E3 Lanark U.S.A.
41 B5 Lanas Malaysia
43 B5 Lanbi Kyun i. Myanmar
50 C4 Lancang China
50 C4 Lancang r. China
17 E4 Lancaster U.K.
128 D4 Lancaster U.S.A.
121 F3 Lancaster U.S.A.
120 B5 Lancaster U.S.A.
119 D5 Lancaster U.S.A.
122 B4 Lancaster U.S.A.
112 F4 Lancaster Sound str. Can.
109 K2 Lancaster Sound str. Can.
133 □8 Lance aux Épines Grenada Caribbean
26 B3 Lanciano Italy
147 B4 Lanco Italy
130 D2 La Perla Mexico
91 □14 La Pérouse, Bahía b. Easter I. Chile
46 J2 La Pérouse Strait str. Japan/Rus. Fed.
131 F4 La Pesca Mexico

133 ⌐4 Lamentin Martinique Caribbean
113 H4 Langwedel Germany
140 A2 La Merced Peru
96 E3 Lameroo Aust.
128 D5 La Mesa U.S.A.
25 G2 L'Ametlla de Mar Spain
29 D5 Lamia Greece
99 H6 Lamington Nat. Park nat. park Aust.
127 E6 La Misa Mexico
128 D5 La Misión Mexico
41 B5 Lamitan Phil.
45 ⌐ Lamma I. i. Hong Kong
74 C3 Lammaylthiyine w Western Sahara
93 B6 Lammerlaw Ra. mt. ra. N.Z.
93 B6 Lammerlaw Top mt. N.Z.
16 F4 Lammermuir Hills h. U.K.
11 D4 Lammhult Sweden
55 F3 Lamma La pass China
122 C5 La Moille U.S.A.
122 B1 La Moine r. U.S.A.
81 B3 Lamon Bay b. Phil.
40 C3 Lamongan Indon.
124 E3 Lamoni U.S.A.
80 B3 Lamotrek i. Pac. Oc.
51 J4 Lam Yü i. Taiwan
25 □ Lanzarote i. Canary Is Spain
125 B6 La Morita Mexico
115 F2 La Motte Can.
20 F3 Lamotte-Beuvron France
42 C3 Lam Pao Res. resr Thailand
43 B4 Lampang Thailand
131 E3 Lampazos, Isola di i. Italy
27 D7 Lampedusa, Isola di i. Italy
17 E5 Lampeter U.K.
42 B2 Lam Plai Mat r. Thailand
12 H1 Lampozhnya Rus. Fed.
40 A3 Lampung div. Indon.
14 D3 Lamskoye Rus. Fed.
81 □6 Lamu Kenya
81 D5 Lamu Kenya
42 E3 La Mure France
99 F4 Lana Aust.
49 J4 Laoye Ling mt. a. China
143 C6 Lapa Brazil
41 B5 Lapac i. Phil.
122 C4 Lapeer U.S.A.
130 D4 La Pedrera Colombia
123 F4 Lapeer U.S.A.
79 C7 Lapi Angola
21 F3 Lapalisse France
130 L7 La Palma Panama
24 C4 La Palma del Condado Spain
25 □ Las Palmas de Gran Canaria Canary Is Spain
146 F3 La Palma Rocha Uruguay
124 B3 La Pampa div. Arg.
146 F3 Las Petas Bolivia
141 E3 Las Petas Bolivia
26 B3 La Spezia Italy
128 A6 La Panza Range mts U.S.A.
121 H1 Lapeer U.S.A.
139 E2 La Paragua Venezuela
41 A5 Lapinig r. Phil.
145 F3 Lapa Brazil
146 D3 La Paz Mendoza Arg.
146 E3 La Paz Entre Rios Arg.
141 D3 La Paz div. Bolivia
141 D3 La Paz Bolivia
132 B2 La Paz Honduras
130 C4 La Paz Mexico
146 D3 La Paz Mexico

10 F2 Långvattnet Sweden
61 B2 Larnaca Bay b. Cyprus
51 G2 Langxi China
61 B2 Larnaca Cyprus
50 D2 Langzhong China
17 E4 Larne U.K.
111 H4 Lanigan Can.
124 D4 Larned U.S.A.
111 H4 Lanigan Can.
78 B2 Laro Cameroon
127 □1 Lanihuli mt. U.S.A.
25 D1 La Robla Spain
147 B4 Lanin, V. vol Arg.
20 D3 La Roche France
15 B2 Lanivtsi Ukraine
20 C3 La Roche-sur-Yon France
40 B1 Lanjak, Bukit mt. Malaysia
25 E3 La Roda Spain
133 E3 La Romana Dominican Rep.
51 F1 Lankao China
40 F2 Larompong Indon.
60 D2 Länkäran Azerbaijan
111 H3 La Ronge Can.
20 E5 Lannemezan France
125 C7 La Rosa Mexico
20 C2 Lannion France
131 E2 La Rosita Mexico
115 H3 L'Annonciation Can.
40 D2 Laut i. Indon.
25 G2 L'Anoia r. Spain
21 H3 Lauterbrunnen Switz.
130 D4 La Noria Mexico
18 D3 Lautersbach (Hessen) Germany
12 D3 Lansån Sweden
40 C3 Laut Kecil, Kepulauan is Indon.
122 C1 L'Anse U.S.A.
110 C2 Lansing r. Can.
15 G2 Laryne Ukraine
122 B4 Lansing U.S.A.
16 E2 La Sabana Arg.
122 E4 Lansing U.S.A.
12 D3 La Sal Junction U.S.A.
51 F4 Lantau I. i. Hong Kong
115 J4 La Salle Can.
45 ⌐ Lantau Peak h. Hong Kong
129 G2 La Salle U.S.A.
122 C5 La Salle U.S.A.
138 D7 La Sarre Can.
138 D7 Las Aves, Is is Venezuela
133 F6 Las Bonitas Venezuela
121 F5 Laurel U.S.A.
34 C1 Lawit, G. mt. Indon./Malaysia
125 F6 Laurel U.S.A.
126 E2 Laurel U.S.A.
124 D1 Laurel Hill h. U.S.A.
120 A6 Laurel River Lake l. U.S.A.
16 F3 Laurencekirk U.K.
115 K3 Laurentides, Réserve faunique des res. Can.
54 E4 Lauria Italy
27 E5 Lauria Italy
119 E5 Laurinburg U.S.A.
122 C2 Laurium U.S.A.
21 H3 Lausanne Switz.
43 E6 Laut i. Indon.
40 D2 Laut i. Indon.
40 D2 Laut i. Indon.

121 F5 Laurel U.S.A.
125 F6 Laurel U.S.A.
126 E2 Laurel U.S.A.
124 D1 Laurel Hill h. U.S.A.
120 A6 Laurel River Lake l. U.S.A.
16 F3 Laurencekirk U.K.
115 K3 Laurentides, Réserve faunique des res. Can.
54 E4 Lauria India
27 E5 Lauria Italy
119 E5 Laurinburg U.S.A.
122 C2 Laurium U.S.A.
21 H3 Lausanne Switz.
43 E6 Laut i. Indon.
40 D2 Laut i. Indon.
40 D2 Laut i. Indon.
21 H3 Lauterbrunnen Switz.
18 D3 Lautersbach (Hessen) Germany
40 C3 Laut Kecil, Kepulauan is Indon.
90 □8 Lautoka Fiji
10 H3 Lauvuskylä Finland
82 A4 Lava Fields lava Ascension Atlantic Ocean
133 F6 Las Bonitas Venezuela
133 F6 Las Cabras Chile
146 C3 Las Cañas Arg.
20 E4 Lavardac France
57 B3 Lāvar Kabkān Iran
20 E5 Lavaur France
113 J4 La Scie Can.
131 G5 Las Cruces U.S.A.
133 D3 La Selle mt. Haiti
27 D2 La Serena Spain
146 B2 La Serena Chile
125 C7 Las Esperanças Mexico
25 G1 La Seu d'Urgell Spain
24 D4 La Solana Spain
25 G1 Las Nieves Mexico
125 B7 Las Nieves Mexico
21 G3 La Souterraine France
146 E2 Las Palmas Arg.
120 E6 Lawrenceville U.S.A.
146 F3 La Paragua Venezuela
121 G3 Lawton U.S.A.
125 D5 Lawton U.S.A.
73 G2 Lawz, J. al mt. Saudi Arabia
11 D4 Laxå Sweden
140 B3 La Yarada Peru
141 E3 Las Petas Bolivia
141 E3 Las Petas Bolivia
26 B3 La Spezia Italy
146 E4 Las Piedras Uruguay
128 A2 Laytonville U.S.A.
28 C2 Lazarevac Yugo.
54 B3 Las Plumas Arg.
131 H6 Las Quebradas Guatemala
14 C3 Lazarevo Rus. Fed.
140 C3 La Paz Bolivia
140 D3 La Paz Honduras
20 D2 Lassay-les-Châteaux France
127 D6 Lázaro Cárdenas Mexico

19 L3 Łęczna Poland
19 J2 Łęczyca Poland
43 C7 Ledang, Gunung mt. Malaysia
17 F5 Ledbury U.K.
24 D2 Ledesma Spain
133 □4 Le Diamant Martinique Caribbean
76 D4 Lédigué Burkina
12 E1 Ledmozero Rus. Fed.
40 B1 Ledo Indon.
152 □ le Dôme summit Kerguelen Indian Ocean
51 E5 Ledong China
51 E6 Le Dorat France
48 B5 Ledu China
110 G4 Leduc Can.
121 G3 Lee U.S.A.
122 A3 Lee r. U.S.A.
121 H2 Leeds U.S.A.
17 F5 Leeds U.K.
120 D4 Leeper U.S.A.
18 C2 Leer (Ostfriesland) Germany
119 D6 Leesburg U.S.A.
120 E5 Leesburg U.S.A.
93 C5 Leeston N.Z.
125 E6 Leesville U.S.A.
120 C4 Leesville Lake l. U.S.A.
97 F3 Leeton Aust.
18 B2 Leeuwarden Friesland Netherlands
101 A7 Leeuwin, C. c. Aust.
128 C3 Lee Vining U.S.A.
93 □3 Leeward I. i. Antipodes Is N.Z.
133 G3 Leeward Islands is Caribbean
20 C4 Le Faouët France
21 H3 Lefedzha r. Bulgaria
79 C4 Léfini, Réserve de Chasse de la res. Congo
61 B2 Lefka Cyprus
29 C5 Lefkada i. Greece
29 C5 Lefkada Greece
29 C5 Lefkimmi Greece
61 B2 Lefkonikon Cyprus
61 B2 Lefkosia Cyprus
133 □4 Le François Martinique Caribbean
101 C6 Lefroy, L. salt flat Aust.
113 □ Légaré, Lac l. Can.
41 B3 Legaspi Phil.
20 D3 Legé France
100 B4 Legendre I. i. Aust.
97 F5 Legges Tor mt. Aust.
98 B3 Legune Aust.
128 A2 Leggett U.S.A.
76 D4 Legmoin Burkina
19 H3 Legnago Italy
133 □5 Le Gosier Guadeloupe Caribbean
21 G5 Le Grau-du-Roi France
140 C4 Leguena Chile
78 E3 Léguga Zaire
98 B2 Leguar Aust.
54 D2 Leh India
121 G3 Lehi U.S.A.
121 F4 Le Havre Canada
18 E2 Lehighton U.S.A.
45 □ Lehua i. U.S.A.

19 L1 Leipalingis Lithuania
18 F2 Leipzig Germany
18 F3 Leira Portugal
18 F3 Leirvik Norway
18 F3 Leirvik Norway
18 F3 Leister U.K.
92 □1 Leith Hill h. U.K.
118 E4 Leith U.K.
16 F4 Leith U.K.
17 E5 Leixlip Rep. of Ire.
78 C3 Lékana Congo
79 C4 Le Kef Tunisia
78 B2 Lékila Gabon
78 B3 Lékoni Gabon
78 B3 Lékoumou div. Congo
11 C4 Leksand Sweden
12 E2 Leksozero, Oz. l. Rus. Fed.
133 □4 Le Lamentin Martinique Caribbean
122 A3 Leland U.S.A.
18 F3 Leland U.S.A.
18 E2 Lelystad Netherlands
147 C7 Le Maire, Estrecho de chan. Arg.
133 □4 Le Marin Martinique Caribbean
133 □4 Le Mars U.S.A.
124 E3 Le Mars U.S.A.
144 A3 Leme Brazil
80 B4 Lemera Zaire
77 G3 Lemi Finland
10 G1 Lemmenjoen Kansallispuisto nat. park Finland
124 C2 Lemmon U.S.A.
129 G5 Lemmon, Mt mt. U.S.A.
132 D3 Le Môle St Nicolas Haiti
128 C3 Lemoore U.S.A.
133 □4 Le Morne Rouge Martinique Caribbean
130 H6 Lempa r. El Salvador
11 H3 Lempäälä Finland
42 A2 Lemro r. Myanmar
28 D2 Lemvig Denmark
42 A2 Lemyethna Myanmar
90 □7 Lénakel Vanuatu
55 H4 Lengaung Bok Is India
142 A4 Lençóis Maranhenses, Parque Nacional dos nat. park Brazil
144 A4 Lençóis Paulista Brazil
78 E3 Lenda r. Brazil

19 L3 Łęczna Poland
19 J2 Łęczyca Poland
43 C7 Ledang, Gunung mt. Malaysia
17 F5 Ledbury U.K.
24 D2 Ledesma Spain

26 F2 Lendava Slovenia
57 D3 Lengbarüt Iran
65 G4 Lenger Kazak.
48 B5 Lenglong Ling mt. ra. China
78 C3 Lengoué r. Congo
51 E3 Lengshuijiang China
51 E3 Lengshuitan China
146 B3 Lengua de Vaca, Pta hd Chile
11 D4 Lenhovda Sweden
65 G5 Lenin Tajikistan
64 E4 Leninabad Uzbekistan
13 E6 Lenine Krym Ukraine
15 E3 Lenine Mykolayiv Ukraine
11 H3 Leningrad div. Rus. Fed.
63 T3 Leningradskaya Rus. Fed.
65 H5 Leningradskiy Tajikistan
65 K2 Leninogorsk Kazak.
64 D2 Leninogorsk Rus. Fed.
64 F3 Leninsk Kazak.
13 H5 Leninsk Rus. Fed.
14 C2 Leninskiy Rus. Fed.
65 L2 Leninsk-Kuznetskiy Rus. Fed.
65 G4 Leninskoye Kazak.
65 G2 Leninskoye Kazak.
65 H2 Leninskoye Rus. Fed.
12 H3 Leninskoye Rus. Fed.
18 C3 Lenne r. Germany
147 C7 Lennox, I. i. Chile
115 K4 Lennoxville Can.
119 D5 Lenoir U.S.A.
121 G3 Lenox U.S.A.
63 N3 Lensk Rus. Fed.
60 E1 Lentekhi Georgia
19 H5 Lenti Hungary
76 D4 Léo Burkina
17 F5 Leominster U.K.
121 H3 Leominster U.S.A.
20 D5 Léon France
131 E4 León Mexico
130 J6 León Nicaragua
24 D1 León Spain
82 B3 Leonardville Namibia
61 C2 Leonarissos Cyprus
91 Leone American Samoa Pac. Oc.
27 E7 Leonforte Italy
97 F4 Leonga Aust.
29 D6 Leonidi Greece
24 C1 Léon, Montes de mt. ra. Spain
100 C6 Leonora Aust.
100 D3 Leopold r. Aust.
145 G4 Leopoldina Brazil
144 D2 Leopoldo de Bulhões Brazil
28 F1 Leorda Romania
15 C3 Leova Moldova
111 H4 Leoville Can.
20 C3 Le Palais France
40 A2 Lepar i. Indon.
82 D3 Lephepe Botswana
51 G2 Leping China
14 J4 L'Épiphanie Can.
21 G4 Le Pont-de-Claix France
81 Le Port Réunion
28 C3 Leposavić Yugo.
10 G3 Leppävirta Finland
65 J3 Lepsy Kazak.
29 D4 Leptokarya Greece
21 F4 Le-Puy-en-Velay France
133 Le Raizet airport Guadeloupe Caribbean
27 D7 Lercara Friddi Italy
78 B2 Leré Chad
77 F4 Lere Nigeria
138 C4 Lerida Colombia
25 G2 Lérida Spain
60 G2 Lerik Azerbaijan
24 E1 Lerma Spain
13 G6 Lermontov Rus. Fed.
49 K3 Lermontovka Rus. Fed.
76 D3 Lernéb Mali
133 Le Robert Martinique Caribbean
29 F6 Leros i. Greece
122 C5 Le Roy U.S.A.
11 D4 Lerum Sweden
16 G1 Lerwick U.K.
78 E1 Ler Zerai well Sudan
133 Les Abymes Guadeloupe Caribbean
133 Le St Esprit Martinique Caribbean
20 F3 Les Aix-d'Angillon France
133 Les Anses d'Arlets Martinique Caribbean
81 C5 Lesatima mt. Kenya
81 Les Avirons Réunion Indian Ocean
25 G2 Les Borges Blanques Spain
25 H1 L'Escala Spain
81 L'Escalier Mauritius
132 D3 Les Cayes Haiti
20 D2 Les Coëvrons h. France
21 H3 Le Sentier Switz.
25 G1 Les Escaldes Andorra
13 G4 Les Escoumins Can.
121 J1 Les Etroits Can.
50 C2 Leshan China
72 H1 Leshukonskoye Rus. Fed.
78 E2 Lesi w Sudan
91 Lesiaceva Pt pt Fiji
27 E5 Lesina, Lago di lag. Italy
19 J4 Lesko Poland
28 C3 Leskovac Yugo.
29 C4 Leskovik Albania
15 E2 Les'ky Ukraine
133 Les Mangles Guadeloupe Caribbean
14 D1 Lesnaya Polyana Rus.
20 B2 Lesneven France
12 E4 Lesnoy Rus. Fed.
13 G5 Lesnoy Rus. Fed.
12 F2 Lesnoye Rus. Fed.
14 F2 Lesogorsk Rus. Fed.
62 L4 Lesosibirsk Rus. Fed.
83 K3 Lesotho country Africa
49 K3 Lesozavodsk Rus. Fed.
20 D4 Lesparre-Médoc France
13 Les Ponts-de-Cé France
20 D3 Les Sables-d'Olonne France
133 G3 Lesser Antilles is Caribbean
110 L3 Lesser Slave Lake l. Can.
110 G3 Lesser Slave Lake Provincial Park res. Can.
10 G3 Lestijärvi Finland
10 G3 Lestijärvi r. Finland
133 Les Trois Îlets is Martinique Caribbean
152 Les Trois Swains is Kerguelen Indian Ocean
100 D2 Lesueur r. Aust.
101 A6 Lesueur, Mt h. Aust.
21 G4 Les Vans France
29 C5 Lesvos i. Greece
19 H3 Leszno Poland
19 H5 Letenye Hungary
54 D4 Leteri India
42 H2 Letha Range mt. ra. Myanmar
110 G5 Lethbridge Can.
139 F3 Lethem Guyana
21 H3 Le Thillot France
138 C4 Leticia Colombia
39 J8 Leti, Kepulauan is Indon.
82 D3 Letlhakane Botswana
82 D3 Letlhakeng Botswana
12 F1 Letniy Navolok Rus. Fed.
12 H1 Letnyaya Baza Rus. Fed.
20 E1 Le Touquet-Paris-Plage France
42 A3 Letpadan Myanmar

20 E1 Le Tréport France
43 B5 Letsok-aw Kyun i. Myanmar
17 D4 Letterkenny Rep. of Ire.
43 D7 Letung Indon.
15 B2 Letychiv Ukraine
79 D6 Léua Angola
28 E1 Leu Romania
129 G4 Leupp Corner U.S.A.
99 G4 Leura Aust.
18 E5 Leutkirch im Allgäu Germany
18 C4 Leuven Belgium
29 D5 Levadeia Greece
29 B4 Levan Albania
129 G2 Levan U.S.A.
10 C3 Levanger Norway
26 B3 Levanto Italy
27 D6 Levanzo, Isola di i. Italy
13 H7 Levashi Rus. Fed.
133 Le Vauclin Martinique Caribbean
125 C5 Levelland U.S.A.
93 C6 Levels N.Z.
16 F3 Leven U.K.
21 H5 Levens France
100 C3 Lévêque, C. c. Aust.
122 E3 Levering U.S.A.
18 C3 Leverkusen Germany
20 F4 Lévézou mts France
21 J4 Levice Slovakia
29 D6 Levidi Greece
92 E4 Levin N.Z.
115 K3 Lévis Can.
29 F6 Levitha i. Greece
121 F4 Levittown U.S.A.
121 F4 Levittown U.S.A.
19 K4 Levoča Slovakia
20 E3 Levroux France
28 E3 Levski Bulgaria
90 Levuka Fiji
20 D2 Lévy, Cap pt France
40 D4 Lewa Indon.
42 B3 Lewe Myanmar
17 H6 Lewes U.K.
121 F5 Lewes U.S.A.
19 H3 Lewin Brzeski Poland
16 D2 Lewis i. U.K.
120 E4 Lewisburg U.S.A.
120 C6 Lewisburg U.S.A.
93 D5 Lewis Pass N.Z.
100 E4 Lewis Ra. h. Aust.
126 D1 Lewis Range mt. ra. U.S.A.
119 C5 Lewis Smith, L. l. U.S.A.
129 G6 Lewis Springs U.S.A.
126 C2 Lewiston U.S.A.
121 H2 Lewiston U.S.A.
126 C3 Lewistown U.S.A.
120 E4 Lewistown U.S.A.
124 E4 Lewistown U.S.A.
125 E5 Lewisville U.S.A.
119 C6 Lewisville, Lake l. U.S.A.
122 C5 Lexington U.S.A.
118 C4 Lexington U.S.A.
124 E4 Lexington U.S.A.
119 D5 Lexington U.S.A.
119 B5 Lexington U.S.A.
120 D6 Lexington U.S.A.
120 E5 Lexington U.S.A.
120 E5 Lexington Park U.S.A.
50 D3 Leye China
152 Leygues, Is is Kerguelen Indian Ocean
41 C4 Leyte i. Phil.
41 C4 Leyte Gulf g. Phil.
19 L3 Lezajsk Poland
28 B4 Lezhë Albania
50 D2 Lezhi China
12 E1 Leznevo Rus. Fed.
20 E4 Lezoux France
51 G4 L'gov Rus. Fed.
55 H3 Lhari China
55 F3 Lhasa Tibet China
54 C3 Lhazê China
54 D3 Lhazhong China
20 C3 L'Herbaudière, Pte de pt France
38 C5 Lhokseumawe Indon.
50 A2 Lhorong China
55 G3 Lhünzê China
55 G3 Lhünzhub China
81 L'Ilot L. i. Seychelles
82 C2 Liambezi, Lake l. Namibia
51 G3 Liancheng China
41 C4 Lianga Phil.
41 C4 Lianga Bay b. Phil.
48 E4 Liangcheng China
50 D1 Liangdang China
51 E3 Lianghekou China
40 C1 Liangpran, Bukit mt. Indon.
49 J3 Liangshan China
49 G4 Liangtian China
50 C3 Liangwang Shan mt. ra. China
48 D5 Liangzhou China
51 F3 Lianhua China
51 F2 Lianhua Shan mt. ra. China
51 G3 Lianjiang China
51 E4 Lianjiang China
51 F3 Liannan China
51 F3 Lianping China
51 E3 Lianshan China
51 G1 Lianshui China
51 F3 Lian Xian China
51 G3 Lianyin China
51 G2 Lianyuan China
51 F1 Lianyungang Jiangsu China
51 G1 Lianyungang Jiangsu China
49 J3 Lianzhushan China
50 E4 Liao r. China
50 E4 Liaocheng China
49 G4 Liaodong Bandao pen. China
49 G4 Liaodong Wan b. China
49 G4 Liaoning div. China
49 G4 Liaoyang China
49 G4 Liaoyuan China
49 G4 Liaozhong China
29 E5 Liapades Greece
110 E2 Liard r. Can.
54 A4 Liard Plateau Can.
61 C3 Liban, Jebel mt. ra. Lebanon
138 C3 Libano Colombia
120 C5 Libby U.S.A.
78 B3 Libenge Zaire
125 D4 Liberal U.S.A.
142 B2 Liberdade r. Brazil
142 E2 Liberdade Brazil
69 C5 Liberia country Africa
131 H6 Liberia Costa Rica
138 D2 Libertad Venezuela
140 B2 Libertad Venezuela

146 B3 Licantén Chile
27 D7 Licata Italy
60 E2 Lice Turkey
27 B6 Licenza, Monte mt. Italy
48 E5 Licheng China
17 G5 Lichfield U.K.
81 C5 Lichinga Mozambique
18 E3 Lichte Germany
82 B4 Lichtenburg R.S.A.
18 E3 Lichtenfels Germany
51 E2 Lichuan China
51 F2 Lichuan China
128 B2 Lick Observatory U.S.A.
121 J2 Licking r. U.S.A.
123 F3 Licking r. U.S.A.
124 D3 Licking r. U.S.A.
121 H2 Lick Park U.S.A.
145 G1 Licinio de Almeida Brazil
120 B5 Licking r. U.S.A.
26 E3 Lički Osik Croatia
12 C4 Lida Belarus
128 D3 Lida U.S.A.
11 D4 Lidköping Sweden
11 D4 Lidsjöberg Sweden
19 J2 Lidzbark Poland
19 K1 Lidzbark Warmiński Poland
18 F2 Liebenwalde Germany
98 M4 Liebig, Mt h. Aust.
4 F4 Liechtenstein country Europe
18 B3 Liège div. Belgium
18 B3 Liège Belgium
11 G4 Lieksa Finland
11 G4 Lievärde Latvia
10 E3 Lien Sweden
78 E3 Lienart r. Zaire
18 F5 Lienz Austria
11 F4 Liepāja Latvia
11 F4 Liepna Latvia
78 B4 Liévin France
115 H3 Lièvre r. Can.
29 G5 Liezen Austria
49 H3 Lifanga r. Zaire
17 D5 Liffey r. Rep. of Ire.
17 D5 Lifford Rep. of Ire.
20 D2 Liffré France
147 C5 Lifi Mahuida mt. Arg.
90 Lifou i. Pac. Oc.
65 K2 Lifuka i. Tonga
41 B3 Ligao Phil.
11 G4 Ligatne Latvia
11 G4 Ligatne Latvia
97 F2 Lightning Ridge Aust.
83 F2 Ligonha r. Mozambique
122 E5 Ligonier U.S.A.
26 B3 Liguria div. Italy
26 B4 Ligurian Sea sea Italy
48 E6 Lihe r. China
81 C7 Lihehe Tanzania
90 Lihir Group is P.N.G.
99 G3 Lihou Reef & Cays reef Coral Sea Islands Terr. Pac. Oc.
127 Lihue Hawaii U.S.A.
50 C3 Lijiang China
49 F5 Lijin China
79 E6 Likasi Zaire
78 D3 Likati r. Zaire
78 D3 Likati Zaire
110 E4 Likely Can.
14 B1 Likhoslavl' Rus. Fed.
78 D4 Likia Zaire
78 D3 Likoto Zaire
78 C3 Likouala div. Congo
78 C3 Likouala r. Congo
78 C3 Likouala aux Herbes r. Congo
76 B4 Likuri Harb. b. Fiji
90 Liku Indon.
41 B3 Likupang Indon.
90 Likuri Harb. b. Fiji
48 D5 Lili China
40 D2 Liliendal Austria
18 D2 Lilienthal Germany
50 D3 Liling China
54 C2 Lilla Pakistan
11 D4 Lilla Edet Sweden
21 F1 Lille Nord France
11 C4 Lille Bælt chan. Denmark
11 C4 Lillehammer Norway
11 C4 Lillesand Norway
11 D4 Lillestrøm Norway
11 D4 Linjiang China
11 D4 Lillholmsjö Sweden
101 H5 Lillian, Pt h. Aust.
110 E4 Lillooet Can.
110 E4 Lillooet r. Can.
81 B4 Lilongwe Malawi
81 B5 Lilongwe r. Malawi
81 Liloy Phil.
147 B5 Lilpela, P. pass Arg./Chile
97 Lilydale Aust.
140 A2 Lima Peru
18 B3 Lima r. Port.
122 D4 Lima U.S.A.
145 G4 Lima Duarte Brazil
13 H6 Liman Rus. Fed.
19 K4 Limanowa Poland
54 C3 Lima Ringma Tso l. China
40 A1 Limas Indon.
147 B5 Limay r. Arg.
146 C4 Limay Mahuida Arg.
18 F3 Limbach-Oberfrohna Germany
82 C2 Linyanti Swamp swamp Botswana/Namibia
77 F5 Limbani Peru
27 B6 Limbara, Monte mt. ra. Italy
11 F4 Limbaži Latvia
78 A3 Limbe Cameroon
40 D2 Limbungan Indon.
18 C4 Limburg div. Belgium
18 C4 Limburg div. Netherlands
18 D3 Limburg an der Lahn Germany
43 Lim Chu Kang h. Singapore
43 Lim Chu Kang Singapore
82 C4 Lime Acres R.S.A.
93 B7 Limehills N.Z.
17 C5 Limeira Brazil
17 C5 Limerick Rep. of Ire.
121 A4 Lime Springs U.S.A.
121 K1 Limestone U.S.A.
24 C1 Limia r. Spain
10 D2 Limingen l. Norway
10 D2 Limingen Norway
10 F3 Limington Finland
10 H3 Limka r. Rus. Fed.
11 J2 Limmen Bight b. Aust.
98 C3 Limmen Bight R. r. Aust.
29 D4 Limni Greece
29 C5 Limni Aliakmonas l. Greece
29 C5 Limni Kerkinitis l. Greece
29 C5 Limni Trichonida l. Greece
29 E5 Limni Vistonida lag. Greece
29 E5 Limnos i. Greece
142 E1 Limoeiro Brazil
115 H4 Limoges Can.
20 E4 Limoges France
131 H6 Limón Costa Rica
130 J6 Limón Honduras
19 J4 Limon U.S.A.
81 Limoni, Mt h. Rodrigues I. Mauritius
20 E4 Limousin reg. France
20 D4 Limousin, Monts du h. France
20 E5 Limoux France
83 F3 Limpopo r. Africa
41 B3 Linapacan i. Phil.
41 A4 Linapacan Strait chan. Phil.
146 B4 Linares Chile

131 F3 Linares Mexico
24 D3 Linares Spain
27 B6 Linas, Monte mt. Italy
51 G2 Lincang China
43 C6 Linchuan China
51 G3 Linchuan China
146 D3 Lincoln Arg.
93 C5 Lincoln N.Z.
17 G5 Lincoln U.K.
128 B2 Lincoln U.S.A.
121 J2 Lincoln U.S.A.
121 J2 Lincoln U.S.A.
123 F3 Lincoln U.S.A.
124 D3 Lincoln U.S.A.
121 H2 Lincoln U.S.A.
126 E4 Lincoln City U.S.A.
123 F4 Lincoln Park U.S.A.
109 M1 Lincoln Sea sea Can./Greenland
17 G5 Lincolnshire Wolds reg. U.K.
121 J2 Lincolnville U.S.A.
11 G1 Linda Rus. Fed.
11 G1 Linda Sweden
16 K1 Lindas Norway
142 D3 Lindau (Bodensee) Germany
139 F2 Linden Guyana
119 C5 Linden U.S.A.
119 C5 Linden U.S.A.
122 A2 Linden Grove U.S.A.
101 B7 Lindenow Fjord inlet Greenland
109 O3 Lindenow Fjord inlet Greenland
101 B7 Lindesay, Mt h. Aust.
11 B4 Lindesnes c. Norway
81 C6 Lindi r. Tanzania
78 E4 Lindi r. Zaire
81 C6 Lindi Tanzania
49 H4 Lindian China
141 E4 Lindo, Monte r. Paraguay
29 G6 Lindos Greece
121 K1 Lindsay Can.
115 F4 Lindsay Can.
128 C3 Lindsay U.S.A.
87 M5 Line Islands is Pac. Oc.
65 K2 Linevo Rus. Fed.
48 D5 Linfen China
56 B6 Linganamakki Reservoir resr India
51 E3 Lingao China
41 B3 Lingayen Phil.
41 B3 Lingayen Gulf b. Phil.
51 E1 Lingbao China
51 G2 Lingchuan China
51 E2 Lingchuan China
48 E6 Lingchuan China
82 D5 Lingelihle R.S.A.
18 C2 Lingen (Ems) Germany
39 D7 Lingga i. Indon.
40 A1 Lingga Malaysia
40 A2 Lingga, Kepulauan is Indon.
41 C4 Lingig Phil.
126 F3 Lingle U.S.A.
78 D3 Lingomo Zaire
51 G2 Lingqiu China
51 E3 Lingshan China
51 E3 Lingshan Dao i. China
48 D5 Lingshi China
55 F3 Lingshi China
48 E4 Lingshou China
48 E5 Lingtai China
51 E4 Lingtou China
76 A3 Linguère Senegal
51 G1 Lingui China
51 G1 Lingwu China
51 G2 Lingyuan China
51 F2 Lingyun China
50 D3 Lingyun China
51 G3 Linhai China
48 E5 Linhares Brazil
48 D4 Linhe China
11 D4 Linköping Sweden
49 H4 Linjiang China
11 D4 Linköping Sweden
49 J4 Linkou China
16 E3 Linlithgow U.K.
51 E2 Linli China
16 D3 Linnhe, Loch inlet U.K.
128 C4 Linn, Mt mt. U.S.A.
27 D7 Linosa, Isola di i. Italy
49 G3 Linqing China
54 B5 Linqu China
93 D5 Linru China
51 F1 Linru China
144 D4 Lins Brazil
10 D2 Linshu China
50 D2 Linshui China
133 Linstead Jamaica
83 D3 Linta r. Madagascar
21 J3 Lintan Switz.
50 E1 Lintong China
48 E5 Linxi China
48 C5 Linxia China
51 E2 Lin Xian China
51 F2 Linxiang China
81 Linyanti r. Botswana/Namibia
49 F5 Linyi China
51 E1 Linyi China
51 F1 Linyi China
51 F2 Linying China
18 F4 Linz Germany
18 H6 Linz Austria
51 G1 Lioboml' Ukraine
48 C6 Linze China
81 Linzi China

24 B3 Lisboa Portugal
24 B3 Lisboa Portugal
122 C5 Lisbon U.S.A.
121 H2 Lisbon U.S.A.
124 D2 Lisbon U.S.A.
121 H2 Lisbon U.S.A.
120 C4 Lisbon U.S.A.
17 D4 Lisburn U.K.
17 C5 Liscannor Bay b. Rep. of Ire.
17 C5 Lisdoonvarna Rep. of Ire.
51 E2 Lishi China
51 E2 Lishi China
49 H4 Lishu China
51 G2 Lishui China
51 F2 Li Shui r. China
20 E2 Lisieux France
13 F5 Liski Rus. Fed.
54 D3 Liskot India
99 H2 Lismore Aust.
17 E4 Lismore Rep. of Ire.
114 C5 Listowel Can.
99 F5 Listowel Downs Aust.
17 C5 Listowel Rep. of Ire.
48 C2 Listvyanka Rus. Fed.
10 D3 Lit Sweden
51 E4 Litang China
51 F4 Litang China
50 C2 Litang China
50 C2 Litang Qu r. China
61 C3 Lītāni r. Lebanon
139 G3 Litani r. Surinam
128 B1 Litchfield U.S.A.
118 B4 Litchfield U.S.A.
81 C6 Lit-et-Mixe France
20 D4 Lit-et-Mixe France
97 G3 Lithgow Aust.
5 H3 Lithuania country Europe
28 D3 Litochoro Greece
19 G3 Litoměřice Czech Rep.
19 H3 Litovel Czech Rep.
13 D5 Litovko Rus. Fed.
114 E2 Little Abitibi r. Can.
114 E2 Little Abitibi L. l. Can.
80 D2 Little Aden Yemen
56 E6 Little Andaman i. Andaman and Nicobar Is India
132 C1 Little Bahama Bank sand bank The Bahamas
54 C2 Little Barrier i. N.Z.
122 D3 Little Bay de Noc b. U.S.A.
126 E2 Little Belt Mts mt. ra. U.S.A.
132 B3 Little Cayman i. Cayman Is Caribbean
43 A4 Little Coco i. Cocos Is Indian Ocean
129 H4 Little Colorado r. U.S.A.
114 D2 Little Current Can.
112 C3 Little Current r. Can.
96 E4 Little Desert Nat. Park nat. park Aust.
121 F5 Little Egg Harbor inlet U.S.A.
119 F7 Little Exuma i. The Bahamas
124 E2 Little Falls U.S.A.
121 F3 Little Falls U.S.A.
125 C5 Littlefield U.S.A.
124 E2 Littlefork U.S.A.
122 A1 Little Fork r. U.S.A.
111 K4 Little Grand Rapids Can.
132 D2 Little Inagua i. The Bahamas
17 H6 Littlehampton U.K.
114 B2 Little Mecatina r. Can.
113 H3 Little Mecatina i. Can.
16 D3 Little Minch str. U.K.
126 F2 Little Missouri r. U.S.A.
56 A6 Little Nicobar i. Andaman and Nicobar Is India
114 E2 Little Pic r. Can.
110 D2 Little Rancheria r. Can.
54 B5 Little Rann h. India
93 D5 Little River N.Z.
125 E5 Little Rock U.S.A.
122 D3 Little Sable Pt pt U.S.A.
119 F7 Little San Salvador i. The Bahamas
110 F4 Little Smoky r. Can.
119 Little Sound inlet Bermuda
133 Little Tobago i. Tobago Trin. & Tobago
127 F4 Littleton U.S.A.
121 H2 Littleton U.S.A.
120 C5 Littleton U.S.A.
60 E1 Little Zab r. Iraq
81 Littoral div. Cameroon
83 Little Rancheria Afghanistan
50 D2 Litunde Mozambique
10 D1 Lituya Bay b. U.S.A.
15 C2 Lityn Ukraine
51 G4 Liu r. China
49 H4 Liu r. China
51 E4 Liubou r. China
50 D2 Liuchong r. China
49 H4 Liugu r. China
51 H4 Liuhe China
51 E4 Liujiachang China
50 D2 Liujiang China
48 E5 Liujia Sk. l. China
99 G4 Liupan Shan mt. ra. China
110 D2 Liupanshui China
83 Liuwa Plain Nat. Park nat. park Zambia
50 D1 Liuyang China
48 E5 Liuzhi China
51 E4 Liuzhou China
15 C2 Livada Ukraine
28 B3 Livani Latvia
76 Livanjsko Polje plain Bos.-Herz.
147 Lively i. Falkland Is
90 Live Oak U.S.A.
119 D6 Live Oak U.S.A.
119 C6 Livermore U.S.A.
128 B3 Livermore, Mt mt. U.S.A.
121 H2 Livermore Falls U.S.A.
17 F5 Liverpool U.K.
17 F5 Liverpool U.S.A.
108 Liverpool Bay b. Can.
99 G3 Liverpool Plains plain Aust.
99 Liverpool Ra. mts Aust.
131 H2 Livingston Guatemala
125 E6 Livingston U.S.A.
126 D2 Livingston U.S.A.
119 C5 Livingston U.S.A.
152 Livingston I. i. S. Shetland
93 A6 Livingston N.Z.
81 A5 Livingstone Zambia
81 A5 Livingstonia Malawi
79 C6 Livingston Mts mts N.Z.
26 F4 Livno Bos.-Herz.
14 C3 Livny Rus. Fed.
12 G2 Livojoki r. Finland
10 G2 Livonia U.S.A.
26 C3 Livorno Livorno Italy
78 C4 Livradois, Monts du mt. France
78 C4 Liwa Zaire
131 H5 Liwa' w Syria
78 D4 Liwale Tanzania

78 C4 Lokolo r. Zaire
78 C3 Lokomo Cameroon
78 D4 Lokona Zaire
78 D4 Lokosafa C.A.R.
77 F5 Lokossa Benin
14 B3 Lokot' Rus. Fed.
78 E2 Lol Sudan
78 C2 Lokoti Sudan
76 C5 Lola Guinea
81 C5 Lola Tanzania
24 E4 Lolland i. Denmark
80 B3 Lolle w Sudan
81 C5 Lollondo Tanzania
81 C5 Lolomalasin crater Tanzania
28 D3 Lom Bulgaria
11 C3 Lom Norway
11 D3 Lomami r. Zaire
146 C4 Loma Negra, Planicie de la plain Arg.
131 H4 Loma del Real Mexico
130 E3 Lomas de Zamora Arg.
90 Lomawai Fiji
79 D7 Lomba r. Angola
26 B3 Lombardia div. Italy
100 C4 Lombadina Aust.
40 C4 Lombok i. Indon.
40 A4 Lombok i. Indon.
77 F5 Lomé Togo
78 C4 Lomela r. Zaire
78 D4 Lomela Zaire
18 C4 Lommel Belgium
16 E3 Lomond, Loch l. U.K.
65 G2 Lomonosovka Kazak.
21 H3 Lomont reg. France
11 H4 Lomonosov Rus. Fed.
12 C1 Lomovoye Rus. Fed.
146 D2 Lonavai mt. Chile
128 B4 Lompoc U.S.A.
49 F1 Lomy Rus. Fed.
14 C3 Lom r. Rus. Fed.
19 L2 Łomża Poland
128 B4 Lompoc U.S.A.
17 G5 London U.K.
114 D5 London Can.
124 D4 London U.S.A.
120 A6 Londonderry U.K.
147 B7 Londonderry, C. c. Chile
100 D2 Londonderry, I. i. Chile
144 C4 Londrina Brazil
17 G5 Lone Pine U.S.A.
131 H4 Long r. China
79 B6 Longa Angola
79 C6 Longa Angola
93 E4 Longa, Proliv chan. Rus. Fed.
16 E2 Longa, Firth of est. U.K.
51 F4 Long an Vietnam
119 E6 Long Bay b. Jamaica
119 E5 Long Bay b. U.S.A.
128 C5 Long Beach U.S.A.
121 G4 Long Beach U.S.A.
50 D2 Longchang China
51 F2 Longchuan China
51 E4 Longchuan r. China
17 G5 Long Eaton U.K.
79 C6 Longfellow, Mt mt. N.Z.
17 D4 Longford Rep. of Ire.
99 Longford Aust.
51 F1 Longgang China
51 E4 Longhai China
51 F2 Longhua China
51 F2 Longhui China
51 E4 Longjiang China
51 G3 Longju China
51 E4 Longlac Can.
113 H4 Longli China
50 C3 Longling China
54 Long Island i. India
51 G1 Long Island i. Aust.
99 Long Island i. P.N.G.
93 Long Island i. N.Z.
119 F7 Long Island i. The Bahamas
121 G4 Long Island i. U.S.A.
121 G4 Long Island Sound chan. U.S.A.
114 D2 Longlac Can.
126 Longmont U.S.A.
50 D3 Longnan China
51 G2 Longnan China
51 E4 Longnawan Indon.
51 G4 Longping China
51 F2 Long Pt pt China
119 Long Point pt The Bahamas
114 Long Range Mts h. Can.
126 Longs Peak summit U.S.A.
42 Long Tan China
45 Longtian China
51 G3 Longtian China
51 F4 Longtou China
51 G3 Longtou China
99 Longreach Aust.
50 D1 Longtian China
51 E4 Longwu China
51 G3 Longxi China
81 Long Xian China
50 D1 Longxian China
43 Long Xuyên Vietnam
51 F3 Longyan China

49 H2 Longzhen China
78 D3 Longzhou China
26 F3 Lonjsko Polje plain Croatia
21 G3 Lons-le-Saunier France
10 N2 Lónsvík b. Iceland
42 B1 Lonton Myanmar
144 B4 Lontra r. Brazil
142 C2 Lontra r. Brazil
113 C6 Looc Phil.
122 E4 Looking Glass r. U.S.A.
121 F4 Lookout, Cape c. U.S.A.
112 D2 Lookout, Cape c. Can.
119 E5 Lookout, Cape c. U.S.A.
110 C4 Lookout, Mt mt. U.S.A.
121 H2 Lookout, Pt pt Aust.
123 F3 Lookout, Pt pt U.S.A.
81 C5 Loolmalasin crater Tanzania
114 A2 Loon r. Can.
110 G4 Loon Can.
111 H4 Loon Lake Can.
121 J1 Loon Lake Can.
17 C5 Loop Head hp Rep. of Ire.
54 D1 Lop China
31 China Lopatina, Mys c. Rus. Fed.
15 A1 Lopatyn Ukraine
42 B1 Lop Buri Thailand
54 G4 Lopbukhöa China
10 F1 Lopphavet b. Norway
78 B4 Lopori r. Zaire
145 Lora r. Afghanistan
57 F3 Lora r. Afghanistan
24 D4 Lora del Río Spain
120 B4 Lorain U.S.A.
57 E3 Loralai r. Pakistan
54 A3 Loralai Pakistan
25 F4 Lorca Spain
41 A4 Lord Auckland sand bank Phil.
94 Lord Howe Island i. Aust.
149 P6 Lord Howe Rise r. Pac. Oc.
17 F5 Lord Loughborough I. i. Myanmar
128 B4 Lordsburg U.S.A.
145 H5 Lorena Brazil
99 G3 Lorengau P.N.G.
144 D2 Loreto Bolivia
130 C3 Loreto Mexico
130 C3 Loreto Mexico
140 B2 Loreto Peru
128 B2 Loreto div. Peru
139 E3 Loretto U.S.A.
79 Long r. China
20 D2 Lorient France
99 Lorne Aust.
43 Lorraine Aust.
79 Lorraine reg. France
21 H2 Lorrain, Plateau plat. France
145 D2 Longavi mt. Chile
120 C6 Los Alamos U.S.A.
146 D2 Los Alerces, Parque Nacional nat. park Arg.
146 D2 Los Amores Arg.
146 B4 Los Angeles Chile
128 C5 Los Angeles U.S.A.
128 C4 Los Angeles Aqueduct canal U.S.A.
130 C3 Los Banos U.S.A.
131 H4 Los Blancos Arg.
146 Los Canarios Canary Is
146 Los Cardones, Parque Nacional nat. park Chile
147 A6 Los Chonos, Archipiélago de is Chile
146 Los Cisnes, Lagunas de salt l. Arg.
130 Los Coronados, Islas de is Mexico
147 Los Corrales de Buelna Spain
140 B2 Los Cusis Bolivia
79 Losevo Rus. Fed.
81 Loseya well Tanzania
128 B4 Los Gatos U.S.A.
142 C3 Lošinj i. Croatia
140 Los Lagos div. Chile
130 Los Llanos de Aridane Canary Is Spain
147 A5 Los Menucos Arg.
130 D3 Los Mochis Mexico
131 E4 Los Molinos U.S.A.
130 Los Palacios Cuba
24 Los Palacios y Villafranca Spain
130 Los Pedrones Spain
24 Los Realejos Canary Is Spain
130 Los Reyes Mexico
138 C2 Los Roques, Is is Venezuela
16 F2 Lossiemouth U.K.
120 Lossburg Germany
25 Los Santos de Maimona Spain
128 Lost Hills U.S.A.
126 Lost Trail Pass pass U.S.A.
146 Los Vientos Chile
146 Los Vilos Chile
24 D4 Los Yébenes Spain
79 Lota r. Zaire
147 Loubomo Congo
57 Loubs L. i. Can.

20 E3 Loudun France
79 B4 Louéssé r. Congo
152 l'Ouest, I. de i. Kerguelen Indian Ocean
76 Louga Senegal
17 G5 Loughborough U.K.
108 Lougheed I. i. Can.
17 C5 Loughrea Rep. of Ire.
120 B5 Louisa U.S.A.
120 C5 Louisa U.S.A.
110 C4 Louise I. i. Can.
90 Louisiade Archipelago is P.N.G.
125 E6 Louisiana div. U.S.A.
125 D6 Louis Trichardt R.S.A.
83 D1 Louisville U.S.A.
125 F5 Louisville U.S.A.
112 E3 Louisville U.S.A.
118 B4 Louisville U.S.A.
112 E3 Louis-XIV, Pointe c. Can.
10 C3 Loukhi Rus. Fed.
78 C4 Loukoléla Congo
78 A3 Loum Cameroon
24 B3 Louná r. Congo
77 Loungoundou well Niger
113 Lourdes Can.
143 Lourdes France
139 Lourenço Brazil
24 Louriçocha, Lago l. Peru
140 Lourinhã Portugal
24 Lousã Portugal
18 Lousy Belgium
10 Louvain Belgium
20 Louviers France
10 Lövånger Sweden
12 Lovat r. Rus. Fed.
28 Lovech Bulgaria
126 Lovech div. Bulgaria
126 Loveland U.S.A.
126 Lovell U.S.A.
11 Lovelock U.S.A.
11 Lovisa Finland
120 Lovington U.S.A.
12 Lovozero Rus. Fed.
142 Lowa r. Zaire
79 Lowa r. Zaire
110 Lowa, Cape c. Can.
121 Lowell U.S.A.
121 Lowell U.S.A.
129 Lower Arrow L. l. Can.
93 Lower Granite Gorge gorge U.S.A.
93 Lower Hutt N.Z.
17 Lower Lough Erne l. U.K.
43 Lower Peirce Res. resr Singapore
110 Lower Sackville Can.
79 Lower Zambezi National Park nat. park Zambia
17 Lowestoft U.K.
57 Loya r. Afghanistan
57 Loya, Lac l. Can.
94 Low Pt pt Christmas I.
97 Low Rocky Pt hd Aust.
121 Lowther U.S.A.
121 Lowville U.S.A.
96 Loxton Aust.
82 Loxton R.S.A.
16 Loyal, Loch l. U.K.
15 Loyalsock Creek r. U.S.A.
12 Loyalton U.S.A.
21 Loyew Belarus
15 Lozère, Mont mt. France
28 Loznica Yugo.
15 Lozova Ukraine
15 Lozovaya Ukraine
65 Lozovatka r. Ukraine
79 Lua r. Zaire
79 Luacano Angola
79 Luahiapu i. Tonga
110 Luala r. Mozambique
79 Luampa r. Zambia
147 Luampa Zambia
79 Luán Angola
79 Lualaba r. Zaire
79 Luancheng China
51 Luanco Spain
51 Luanda Angola
79 Luanginga r. Angola
79 Luangwa r. Central/Eastern Zambia
79 Luangwa r. Northern Zambia
55 Luanhaizi China
51 Luanping China
51 Luanshya Zambia
51 Luan Xian China
79 Luanza Zaire
79 Luao Angola
79 Luapula r. D. I. Indon.
79 Luar, Danau l. Indon.
79 Luarca Spain
79 Luashi Zaire
79 Luatfito i. Tonga
51 Luau Angola
131 Lubang Islands is Phil.
131 Lubango Angola
79 Lubao Zaire
18 Lübbecke Germany
18 Lübben Germany
18 Lübbenau Germany
125 Lubbock U.S.A.
18 Lübeck Germany
79 Lubefu Zaire
79 Lubero Zaire
20 Lubersac France
19 Lubień Kujawski Poland
19 Lubiń Legnica Poland
15 Lubimówka Poland
19 Lubin Poland
15 Lubliniec Poland
15 Lubny Ukraine
40 Lubok Antu Malaysia
19 Lubon Poland
11 Lubonos Rus. Fed.

19 J2 Lubraniec Poland
25 E4 Lubrín Spain
19 G3 Lubsko Poland
18 E2 Lübtheen Germany
41 B2 Lubuagan Phil.
79 E5 Lubudi Zaire
40 A2 Lubukbalang Indon.
38 D7 Lubuklinggau Indon.
79 E6 Lubumbashi Zaire
79 E6 Lubungu Zambia
78 E4 Lubutu Zaire
14 B3 Lubyanki Rus. Fed.
19 L3 Lubycza Królewska Poland
79 C5 Lucala Angola
110 A2 Lucania, Mt mt. Can.
79 D5 Lucapa Angola
142 A3 Lucas Brazil
119 E7 Lucaya The Bahamas
26 C4 Lucca Italy
17 E4 Lucea Jamaica
144 C4 Lucélia Brazil
41 B3 Lucena Phil.
24 D4 Lucena Spain
19 J4 Lučenec Slovakia
27 E6 Lucera Italy
140 C2 Lucerna Peru
15 C1 Luchanky Ukraine
49 K3 Luchegorsk Rus. Fed.
48 E5 Lucheng China
81 C7 Lucheringo r. Mozambique
14 D1 Luchki Rus. Fed.
51 E4 Luchuan China
50 C4 Lüchun China
139 F3 Lucie r. Surinam
115 F1 Lucie, Lac l. Can.
93 E4 Lucinda Aust.
79 B6 Lucira Angola
19 F3 Luckau Germany
55 F4 Luckeesarai India
19 F2 Luckenwalde Germany
114 E5 Lucknow Can.
54 E4 Lucknow India
132 D2 Lucrecia, Cabo hd Cuba
79 D6 Lucusse Angola
12 F1 Luda Rus. Fed.
82 B4 Lüderitz Namibia
81 E7 Ludewe Tanzania
51 D3 Ludian China
122 D4 Ludington U.S.A.
17 F5 Ludlow U.K.
128 D4 Ludlow U.S.A.
121 J1 Ludlow U.S.A.
121 G3 Ludlow U.S.A.
28 F3 Ludogorsko Plato plat. Bulgaria
28 E1 Ludus Romania
13 D4 Ludvika Sweden
18 D4 Ludwigsburg Germany
18 F2 Ludwigsfelde Germany
18 D4 Ludwigshafen am Rhein Germany
18 E2 Ludwigslust Germany
15 C5 Ludza Latvia
79 D5 Luebo Zaire
79 C4 Lueki Zaire
79 E4 Luema r. Zaire
79 C6 Luena Angola
79 D6 Luena r. Zambia
79 D6 Luena Flats plain Zambia
79 D7 Luengue r. Angola
83 E2 Luenha r. Mozambique/Zimbabwe
139 E2 Luepa Venezuela
50 D1 Lüeyang China
51 F4 Lufeng China
50 C3 Lufeng China
79 E5 Lufira r. Zaire
79 E6 Lufira, Lac de retenue de la resr Zaire
125 E6 Lufkin U.S.A.
81 B6 Lufubu r. Zambia
12 D3 Luga Rus. Fed.
12 D3 Luga r. Rus. Fed.
21 J3 Lugano Switz.
79 D6 Luganville Vanuatu
83 F2 Lugela Mozambique
83 F2 Lugela r. Mozambique
81 C7 Lugenda r. Mozambique
80 D2 Lughaye Somalia
26 C3 Lugo Italy
24 C1 Lugo Spain
62 D2 Lugoj Romania
65 H4 Lugovoy Kazak.
65 H4 Lugovoye Kazak.
41 B5 Lugus i. Phil.
13 F5 Luhans'k Ukraine
51 G1 Luhe China
49 F3 Luhin Sum China
81 C6 Luhombero Tanzania
50 C2 Luhuo China
15 C1 Luhyny Ukraine
79 C6 Luia r. Angola
83 F2 Luia r. Mozambique
79 D7 Luiana Angola
78 D4 Luilaka r. Zaire
26 B3 Luino Italy
79 C6 Luio r. Angola
10 G2 Luiro r. Finland
142 D1 Luís Correia Brazil
130 E4 Luis Moya Mexico
79 D5 Luiza Zaire
131 H5 Luján de Cuyo Arg.
51 G2 Lujiang China
15 E1 Luka Ukraine
79 B5 Lukala Zaire
26 G3 Lukavac Bos.-Herz.
101 B5 Luke, Mt h. Aust.
123 F6 Lukenie r. Zaire
14 F1 Lukh r. Rus. Fed.
14 D2 Lukhovitsy Rus. Fed.
14 G2 Lukhovka Rus. Fed.
28 F3 Lūki Bulgaria
79 D4 Lukibu r. Zaire
54 E1 Lukino Rus. Fed.
15 A1 Lukiv Ukraine
78 C4 Lukolela Zaire
28 E3 Lukovit Bulgaria
19 J3 Łuków Poland
65 J1 Lukovnikovo Rus. Fed.
19 L3 Luków Poland
79 B5 Lukula Zaire
81 B7 Lukulu Zambia
81 B7 Lukulu r. Zambia
81 C6 Lukumburu Tanzania
79 F6 Lukusuzi National Park nat. park Zambia
10 F2 Luleå Sweden
10 F2 Luleälven r. Sweden
60 A1 Lüleburgaz Turkey
50 C3 Luliang China
48 C5 Lüliang Shan mt. ra. China
79 E4 Lulimba Zaire
125 E6 Luling U.S.A.
49 F5 Lulong China
78 C3 Lulonga r. Zaire
78 C3 Lulonga r. Zaire
55 F3 Lulu r. Zaire
101 B5 Lulworth, Mt h. Aust.
91 □14 Lumā American Samoa Pac. Oc.
55 F3 Lumachomo China
40 C4 Lumajang Indon.
55 F3 Lumajangdong Co salt l. China
79 D6 Lumbala Kaquengue Angola
79 D6 Lumbala N'guimbo Angola
79 E5 Lumbe r. Zambia
119 E5 Lumberton U.S.A.
55 H4 Lumding India

81 C7 Lumecha Tanzania
26 C3 Lumezzane Italy
10 G2 Lumijoki Finland
145 H4 Luminárias Brazil
43 D4 Lumphăt Cambodia
93 B6 Lumsden N.Z.
40 C2 Lumut, G. mt. Indon.
40 A2 Lumut, Tg pt Indon.
48 C3 Lün Mongolia
129 H5 Luna U.S.A.
50 C3 Lunan China
123 F5 Luna Pier U.S.A.
54 C5 Lunavada India
28 E1 Luncu Ilvei Romania
54 B4 Lund Pakistan
11 D5 Lund Sweden
129 F2 Lund U.S.A.
79 C5 Lunda Norte div. Angola
111 K4 Lundar Can.
79 D6 Lunda Sul div. Angola
81 B7 Lundazi Zambia
17 E6 Lundy Island i. U.K.
18 E2 Lüneburg Germany
21 G5 Lunel France
21 H2 Lunéville France
81 B7 Lunga r. Zambia
55 F2 Lungdo China
79 B6 Lunggar China
79 B6 Lungué-Bungo r. Angola
79 D6 Lungwebungu r. Zambia
54 C4 Luni r. India
128 C2 Luni India
54 B4 Luni r. India
48 D6 Luni r. Shaanxi China
62 D3 Luninyets Belarus
13 C4 Luninyets Belarus
20 E5 L'Union France
54 C3 Lunkaransar India
76 B5 Lunsar Sierra Leone
79 E6 Lunsemfwa r. Zambia
65 K4 Luntai China
40 D4 Lunyuk Indon.
51 E1 Luo r. Henan China
48 D6 Luo r. Shaanxi China
51 G2 Luocheng China
51 E3 Luocheng China
48 D6 Luochuan China
50 D3 Luoci China
51 E4 Luoding China
51 E4 Luodou Sha China
51 E1 Luohe r. China
51 F1 Luohe China
51 B6 Luombe r. Zambia
51 F2 Luoning China
50 D3 Luoping China
51 E2 Luoshan China
51 F2 Luotian China
51 F1 Luoyang China
51 G2 Luoyuan China
79 C4 Luozi Zaire
82 D2 Lupane Zimbabwe
40 B1 Lupar r. Malaysia
28 D2 Lupeni Romania
81 C7 Lupilichi Mozambique
41 C5 Lupon Phil.
129 H4 Lupton U.S.A.
50 C3 Luqu China
50 D3 Luquan China
119 □3 Luquillo Puerto Rico
20 H2 Lûrä Shîrîn Iran
51 F4 Lure France
79 C5 Lureco r. Mozambique
79 C5 Luremo Angola
17 D4 Lurgan U.K.
140 D3 Luribay Bolivia
140 A2 Lurin Peru
81 D7 Lúrio Mozambique
83 F1 Lurio r. Mozambique
83 F1 Lúrio, Baía do b. Mozambique
81 B5 Lusahunga Tanzania
79 F7 Lusaka Zambia
79 D4 Lusaka div. Zambia
79 D4 Lusambo Zaire
90 □1 Lusancay Islands and Reefs is P.N.G.
81 B5 Lusangi Zaire
110 C4 Luscar Can.
111 H4 Luseland Can.
78 C3 Lusengo Zaire
50 C2 Lushan China
51 E1 Lushi China
100 D3 Lush, Mt h. Aust.
29 B4 Lushnjë Albania
81 C5 Lushoto Tanzania
49 G5 Lüshun China
78 E4 Lusika Zaire
94 □3 Lusitania Bay b. Macquarie I. Pac. Oc.
126 F3 Lusk U.S.A.
51 C5 Lushima r. Zaire
15 A1 Luts'k Ukraine
152 D4 Lützow-Holmbukta b. Ant.
41 B1 Luuk Phil.
11 G3 Luumäki Finland
80 D4 Luuq Somalia
124 D3 Luverne U.S.A.
142 C1 Luwuka r. R.S.A.
81 C5 Luwegu r. Tanzania
79 C6 Luwemba Zambia
39 H7 Luwuk Indon.
18 B3 Luxembourg div. Belgium
F4 Luxembourg country Europe
18 C4 Luxembourg Luxembourg
18 C4 Luxeuil-les-Bains France
50 B3 Luxi China
50 D3 Luxi China
50 D3 Luxi China
71 F3 Luxor Egypt
21 G5 Luy r. France
142 D3 Luz Brazil
12 J2 Luza r. Rus. Fed.
13 F6 Luzern Switz.
21 F3 Luzhai China
50 D2 Luzhi China
50 D2 Luzhou China
142 D2 Luziânia Brazil
41 B2 Luzon i. Phil.
41 B2 Luzon Strait str. Phil.
21 G4 Luy France
15 F1 L'va Tolstogo Ukraine
15 A1 L'viv Ukraine
15 A1 L'viv div. Ukraine
15 E1 L'vovskiy Rus. Fed.
13 H4 L'vovskiy Rus. Fed.
19 G3 Lwówek Poland
19 H2 Lwówek Śląski Poland
114 C3 Lyall, Mt mt. Can.
15 E2 Lyamtsa Rus. Fed.
110 C4 Lyangar Tajik.
14 D2 Lyantor Rus. Fed.

28 E3 Lyaskovets Bulgaria
15 F2 Lychkove Ukraine
61 A1 Lycia reg. Turkey
10 C2 Lycksele Sweden
152 C5 Lyddan I. i. Ant.
83 E4 Lydenburg R.S.A.
29 G5 Lydia reg. Turkey
15 C1 Lyel'chytsy Belarus
98 B4 Lyell, Mt mt. N.Z.
110 C4 Lyell I. i. Can.
128 C3 Lyell, Mt mt. U.S.A.
12 C4 Lyepyel' Belarus
119 □2 Lyford Cay The Bahamas
29 D6 Lygourio Greece
15 G2 Lyhivka Ukraine
120 E4 Lykens U.S.A.
15 C1 Lykhachiv Ukraine
15 E2 Lykhivka Ukraine
29 D5 Lyman Ukraine
126 E3 Lyman U.S.A.
15 C3 Lyman's'k Ukraine
17 F6 Lyme Bay b. U.K.
120 D6 Lynchburg U.S.A.
121 H2 Lynchville U.S.A.
99 F3 Lynd r. Aust.
99 F3 Lyndhurst Aust.
99 F3 Lyndhurst Aust.
99 F3 Lynd Junction, The r. Aust.
54 A3 Lyndon r. Aust.
121 G2 Lyndonville U.S.A.
89 □4 Lyngdal Norway
100 C2 Lynher Reef reef Aust.
55 H5 Lynn U.S.A.
110 H3 Lynn Canal chan. U.S.A.
129 F2 Lynndyl U.S.A.
15 F1 Lynne r. Ukraine
15 F1 Lynove Ukraine
111 H2 Lynx Lake l. Can.
21 G4 Lyon France
121 G3 Lyon Mountain U.S.A.
21 G4 Lyonnais, Monts du h. France
96 C2 Lyons Aust.
101 A5 Lyons r. Aust.
119 D5 Lyons U.S.A.
121 F3 Lyons U.S.A.
121 F3 Lyons Falls U.S.A.
12 D4 Lyozna Belarus
15 C1 Lypova Ukraine
15 C1 Lypova Dolyna Ukraine
15 G1 Lypovets' Ukraine
15 G1 Lyptsi Ukraine
11 C4 Lysa Hora Ukraine
11 C4 Lysekil Sweden
15 D2 Lyster Can.
15 D2 Lysyanka Ukraine
13 F5 Lysychans'k Ukraine
14 G4 Lysyye Gory Rus. Fed.
12 D4 Lytkarino Rus. Fed.
93 D5 Lyttelton N.Z.
110 E4 Lytton Can.
15 D2 Lyuban' Belarus
15 D2 Lyubar Ukraine
15 B1 Lyubashivka Ukraine
15 B2 Lyubazh Rus. Fed.
14 C2 Lyubertsy Rus. Fed.
15 C1 Lyubeshiv Ukraine
15 D1 Lyubim Rus. Fed.
28 E4 Lyubimets Bulgaria
65 H1 Lyubinskiy Rus. Fed.
15 D2 Lyubokhna Rus. Fed.
15 D2 Lyubotyn Ukraine
15 G2 Lyubymivka Ukraine
14 H1 Lyul'pari Rus. Fed.
28 F3 Lyulyakovo Bulgaria
79 C5 Lyunda r. Angola
15 F1 Lyutens'ki Budyshchyna Ukraine

M

53 D9 Maalosmadulu Atoll atoll Maldives
79 E7 Maamba Zambia
78 B3 Ma'an Cameroon
61 C4 Ma'ān Jordan
10 G3 Maaninka Finland
10 H2 Maaninkavaara Finland
51 G2 Ma'anshan China
48 D3 Maanyt Mongolia
48 B2 Maanyt Mongolia
11 H4 Maardu Estonia
18 C3 Ma'arrat an Nu'mān Syria
18 B3 Maas r. Netherlands
18 B3 Maaseik Belgium
18 B3 Maasin Phil.
75 F5 Maastsuyker Is is Aust.
82 C2 Mababe Depression Botswana
41 B3 Mabalacat Phil.
41 B3 Mabalane Mozambique
78 B4 Mabana Zaire
79 B4 Mabanda Gabon
80 D2 Ma'bar Yemen
139 F2 Mabaruma Guyana
78 E4 Mabenge Zaire
81 C5 Mabira Tanzania
17 G6 Mablethorpe U.K.
83 E3 Mabote Mozambique
79 D6 M.A.B., Réserve res. Zaire
77 D2 Mabrous well Niger
70 C2 Mabruk Libya
82 C4 Mabuasehube Game Reserve res. Botswana
93 B6 McKerrow, L. l. N.Z.
122 C3 Mackinac I. i. U.S.A.
122 C3 Mackinac, Straits of chan. U.S.A.
122 C3 Mackinaw City U.S.A.
99 F4 McKinlay Aust.
99 F4 McKinlay r. Aust.
108 C3 McKinley, Mt. mt. U.S.A.
125 D5 McKinney U.S.A.
121 G5 McKittrick U.S.A.
101 D5 McKittrick Ra. h. Aust.
114 H4 Macklin Can.
97 H2 Macksville Aust.
128 C2 McLaughlin U.S.A.
97 G4 Maclean Aust.
97 H2 Macleay r. Aust.
110 F3 McLeod r. Can.
100 A5 McLeod, Lake l. Aust.
110 F4 McLeod Lake Can.
114 E3 McLoughlin, Mt mt. U.S.A.
110 C2 Macmillan r. Can.
122 B4 McMillan U.S.A.
114 D5 McMinnville U.S.A.
119 C5 McMinnville U.S.A.
152 D4 McMurdo U.S.A. Base Ant.
129 H4 McNary U.S.A.
110 F4 McNaughton Lake l. Can.

17 F5 Macclesfield U.K.
100 D3 McClintock Ra. h. Aust.
28 C3 McCluer I. i. U.S.A.
90 □1 McCluer I. i. U.S.A.
108 F2 McClure Strait str. Can.
125 F6 McComb U.S.A.
29 C4 McConaughy, L. l. U.S.A.
120 E5 McConnellsburg U.S.A.
98 B4 McConnell, Mt h. U.S.A.
124 C3 McCook U.S.A.
111 K4 McCreary Can.
129 E4 McCullough Range mts U.S.A.
110 D3 McDame Can.
25 □1 McDermitt U.S.A.
114 A2 Macdiarmid Can.
100 E4 Macdonald, L. salt flat Aust.
126 D2 McDonald Peak summit U.S.A.
92 □4 Macdonald Rock i. Kermadec Is N.Z.
98 C4 Macdonnell Ranges mt. ra. Aust.
112 B3 MacDowell L. l. Can.
129 G5 McDowell Peak summit U.S.A.
16 F3 Macduff U.K.
24 C2 Macedo de Cavaleiros Portugal
5 H4 Macedonia country Europe
142 E2 Maceió Brazil
76 B4 Macenta Guinea
26 D4 Macerata Italy
128 C3 McFarland U.S.A.
113 H3 McFarlane r. Can.
96 D3 Macfarlane, L. salt flat Aust.
85 B3 McFarlane, Mt mt. N.Z.
129 E2 McGill U.S.A.
119 □4 Macgillycuddy's Reeks mt. ra. Rep. of Ire.
108 C3 McGregor U.S.A.
122 A2 McGregor r. Can.
114 E3 McGregor Bay Can.
99 E5 McGregor Ra. h. Aust.
126 D2 McGuire, Mt mt. U.S.A.
15 A5 Mach Pakistan
145 H2 Machacalis Brazil
140 C3 Machacamarca Bolivia
140 A2 Machachi Ecuador
141 D1 Machadinho r. Brazil
145 H4 Machado Brazil
81 C5 Machaila Mozambique
81 C5 Machakos Kenya
138 B4 Machala Ecuador
141 D4 Machareti Bolivia
80 B3 Machar Marshes marsh Sudan
98 D5 Machattie, L. salt flat Aust.
20 D3 Machecoul France
51 C2 Macheng China
56 B2 Macherla India
55 E4 Machhakund Dam dam India
55 E4 Machhlishahr India
121 H3 Machias r. U.S.A.
120 D3 Machias U.S.A.
25 E1 Machichaco, Cabo pt Spain
24 □3 Machico Madeira Portugal
56 B2 Machilipatnam India
81 D6 Machinga Malawi
75 C5 Machuhy Ukraine
140 B2 Machupicchu ru. Peru
79 C6 Macia Mozambique
99 E2 McIlwraith Ra. h. Aust.
28 G2 Măcin Romania
121 G2 McIndoe Falls U.S.A.
124 C2 McIntosh U.S.A.
71 H4 Mack U.S.A.
99 G4 Mackay Aust.
22 C3 Mackay Aust.
100 E4 Mackay, Lake salt flat Aust.
12 C3 McKay Lake l. Can.
100 C4 McKay Ra. h. Aust.
150 H6 McKean Island i. Kiribati
120 A6 McKee r. U.S.A.
79 G6 McKeesport U.S.A.
121 F3 McKever U.S.A.
110 F4 Mackenzie r. Can.
98 B4 Mackenzie r. Can.
108 D3 Mackenzie Bay b. Can.
152 B3 Mackenzie Bay b. Ant.
108 G2 Mackenzie Bison Sanctuary res. Can.
110 E2 Mackenzie King I. i. Can.
110 E2 Mackenzie Mountains mt. ra. Can.

90 □6 Macuata-i-wai i. Fiji
138 C1 Macuira, Parque Nacional nat. park Colombia
28 C4 Macukull Albania
96 D1 Macuma w Aust.
140 B2 Macusani Peru
131 G5 Macuspana Mexico
130 C3 Macuzari, Psa resr Mexico
28 B2 Mačvanska Mitrovica Yugo.
40 B3 Mad r. U.S.A.
77 F5 Mada r. Nigeria
83 E4 Madadeni R.S.A.
69 J8 Madagascar country Africa
149 H5 Madagascar Basin Indian Ocean
73 G2 Madā'in Şālih Saudi Arabia
56 B3 Madakasira India
54 D4 Madalai Palau
29 C4 Madan Bulgaria
56 B3 Madanapalle India
90 □1 Madang P.N.G.
77 F4 Madaoua Niger
55 G5 Madaripur Bangladesh
77 F4 Madarounfa Niger
27 G5 Madaula r. Cam.
115 G4 Madawaska r. Can.
121 J1 Madawaska r. Can.
42 B2 Madaya Myanmar
27 E7 Maddalena, Penisola della pen. Italy
24 □ Madeira r. Brazil
20 D2 Madeira i. Atlantic Ocean
113 H4 Madeleine, Îles de la is Can.
21 F3 Madeline, Monts de la mts France
122 B2 Madeline I. i. U.S.A.
60 D2 Maden Turkey
125 E6 Madera Mexico
128 B3 Madera r. U.S.A.
130 C3 Madero, F. I. r. Mexico
56 B1 Madgaon India
54 □1 Madge Rocks i. Seychelles
55 F4 Madhepura India
55 F4 Madhubani India
55 F5 Madhupur India
54 D5 Madhya Pradesh India
56 A3 Madikeri India
78 C3 Madimba Zaire
75 G4 Madinani Côte d'Ivoire
78 B4 Madingou Congo
78 C2 Madingrin Cameroon
140 C2 Madini r. Bolivia
78 B4 Madirovalo Madagascar
118 C4 Madison r. U.S.A.
124 D3 Madison U.S.A.
120 D5 Madison r. U.S.A.
124 D3 Madison U.S.A.
122 C5 Madison U.S.A.
120 C5 Madison U.S.A.
118 C4 Madison r. U.S.A.
122 B6 Madisonville U.S.A.
125 E6 Madison U.S.A.
83 H1 Madiso Shet' w Ethiopia
40 B3 Madiun Indon.
40 B3 Madjingo Gabon
101 D5 Madley, Mt h. Aust.
81 C4 Mado Gashi Kenya
55 D5 Madoi China
11 G4 Madona Latvia
54 D4 Madpura India
56 B2 Madra Dağı mt. ra. Turkey
41 C4 Madras Phil.
56 B2 Madras India
145 F4 Madre de Deus de Minas Brazil
140 C2 Madre de Dios, I. i. Chile
131 F3 Madre, Laguna lag. Mexico
125 D7 Madre, Laguna lag. U.S.A.
41 A4 Madrid Phil.
24 E2 Madrid Spain
24 E2 Madrid div. Spain
41 B3 Madridejos Phil.
24 E3 Madridejos Spain
56 C2 Maduga India
101 D6 Madura i. Indon.
43 A4 Madura i. Indon.
56 B4 Madurai India
56 B4 Madwas India
54 B3 Madyan Pakistan
15 A5 Madzhalis Rus. Fed.
83 D2 Madzhwadzo Zimbabwe
28 F2 Mădzhwadzo Bulgaria
43 B5 Mae-ho Thailand
83 E2 Mae Hong Son Thailand
47 □2 Mae-jima i. Japan
42 C4 Mae Khlong r. Thailand
42 C4 Mae La r. Thailand
92 C3 Mae Li r. Thailand
42 C4 Mae Nam Ing r. Thailand
42 C4 Mae Nam Mun r. Thailand
42 C4 Mae Nam Nan r. Thailand
42 C4 Mae Nam Pa Sak r. Thailand
42 C4 Mae Nam Ping r. Thailand
42 C4 Mae Nam Song Khram r. Thailand
42 C4 Mae Nam Wang r. Thailand
42 C4 Mae Nam Yom r. Thailand
42 C4 Mae Rim Thailand
42 C4 Mae Sai Thailand
42 C4 Mae Sariang Thailand
42 C4 Mae Suai Thailand
42 B2 Mae Tuen Thailand
82 B2 Maevatanana Madagascar
90 □1 Maéwa i. Vanuatu
42 C4 Mae Yuam r. Thailand
111 H4 Mafeking Can.
83 E4 Mafeteng Lesotho
81 D5 Mafia Channel chan. Tanzania
81 D6 Mafia I. i. Tanzania
83 E3 Mafinga Tanzania
143 C6 Mafra Brazil
61 B3 Mafraq Jordan
81 C5 Magadan Rus. Fed.
45 Q4 Magadan Rus. Fed.
81 C4 Magadi Kenya
140 C4 Magadi salt l. Bolivia
132 C3 Magangué Colombia
77 G4 Magaria Niger
78 B4 Magburaka Sierra Leone
81 □2 Magdala Ethiopia
138 C2 Magdalena r. Colombia
140 D2 Magdalena Bolivia
139 E2 Magdalena Bolivia

138 C2 Magdalena r. Colombia
138 C1 Magdalena Mexico
130 C2 Magdalena Mexico
127 F5 Magdalena, B. Mexico
127 G7 Magdalena, B. Mexico
147 B5 Magdalena, Isla i. Chile
96 D1 Macduma w Aust.
18 A5 Magdaleno, mt. Malaysia
18 E2 Magdeburg Germany
99 G3 Magdelaine Cays atoll Coral Sea Islands Terr. Pac. Oc.
40 B3 Magelang Indon.
150 F4 Magellan Seamounts Pac. Oc.
26 B3 Magenta Italy
101 B7 Magenta, L. salt flat Aust.
10 G1 Mageroya i. Norway
26 B3 Maggiorasca, Monte mt. Italy
26 C3 Maggiore, Lago l. Italy
61 C5 Maghā'ir Shu'ayb Saudi Arabia
71 D1 Maghâgha Egypt
17 D4 Maghera U.K.
17 D4 Magherafelt U.K.
17 E4 Maghull U.K.
26 F4 Magione Italy
46 A3 Maglai Bos.-Herz.
27 G5 Máglić mt. Bos.-Herz.
27 G5 Maglie Italy
132 D4 Magnetic I. i. Aust.
99 F3 Magnetic I. i. Aust.
152 E4 Magnet Bay b. Ant.
55 G5 Maiskhal I. i. Bangladesh
13 H3 Magnitnyy Rus. Fed.
14 J3 Magnitogorsk Rus. Fed.
125 E5 Magnolia U.S.A.
128 D3 Magrath Can.
65 K3 Magtang div. Yemen
74 B5 Magta' Lahjar Mauritania
81 B5 Magu Tanzania
15 H3 Magoca i. Spain
25 H3 Magocra i. Spain
130 C2 Magosa Cyprus
60 D4 Magosa Cyprus
113 H4 Magpie Can.
113 H3 Magpie r. Can.
121 J1 Magpie, L. Can.
28 D2 Magura i. Yugo.
145 G5 Magé Brazil
55 G5 Magura Bangladesh
55 E4 Mahabaleshwar India
56 A2 Mahabaleshwar India
82 B3 Mahabo Madagascar
56 A2 Mahabobo Madagascar
54 C4 Mahad India
81 C5 Mahaddayweyne Somalia
54 D3 Mahadeo Hills India
90 □11 Mahaena Fr. Poly. Pac. Oc.
78 B4 Magwe Myanmar
40 D2 Mahagi Port Zaire
54 E2 Mahajan India
82 B2 Mahajanga Madagascar
82 B2 Mahajanga div. Madagascar
40 C2 Mahakam r. Indon.
82 C3 Mahalapye Botswana
83 □2 Mahalevona Madagascar
54 C4 Mahamid, G. vol Indon.
83 □3 Mahanoro Madagascar
54 E2 Maharajganj India
56 A2 Maharashtra div. India
54 C3 Mahasamund India
42 B2 Maha Sarakham Thailand
82 □3 Mahavavy r. Madagascar
82 □3 Mahavelona Madagascar
55 □1 Mahaweli Ganga r. Sri Lanka
56 A2 Mahbubabad India
56 B2 Mahbubnagar India
73 F3 Mahd adh Dhahab Saudi Arabia
131 H4 Mahdah Oman
15 F2 Mahdalynivka Ukraine
82 □2 Mahdia Guyana
56 A2 Mahé i. Seychelles
54 D3 Mahendragiri mt. India
83 E3 Mahenge Tanzania
93 C6 Maheno N.Z.
54 C5 Mahesana India
54 C4 Mahi r. India
93 D5 Mahia Peninsula pen. N.Z.
12 D4 Mahilyow Belarus
73 G5 Mahirija Fr. Poly. Pac. Oc.
91 □11 Mahina Fr. Poly. Pac. Oc.
14 H3 Mahino Rus. Fed.
56 B2 Mahi r. India
78 B4 Mahdia div. India
93 C4 Maian N.Z.
28 B2 Mahni Tanzania
93 A7 Mahia Tunisia
55 G4 Maibong India
139 E2 Maicao Colombia
143 B6 Maicasagi, Lac l. Can.
138 B4 Maichen China
18 D3 Maidstone U.K.
77 G3 Maiduguri Nigeria
13 □1 Maidstone Can.
54 E4 Maihar India
55 F5 Maijdi Court Bangladesh
14 □3 Maiko r. Zaire
79 D4 Maiko, Parc National de le nat. park Zaire
54 D4 Maikala Range India
81 □2 Maiko r. Zaire
52 □4 Main r. Germany
55 H4 Main r. Germany
14 □1 Maina Ina r. Rus. Fed.
67 □6 Ma'în Yemen

55 G4 Mainaguri India
113 J3 Main Brook Can.
18 E4 Mainburg Germany
114 E4 Main Channel chan. Can.
78 C4 Mai-Ndombe, Lac l. Zaire
115 G5 Main Duck I. i. Can.
121 J2 Maine div. U.S.A.
138 C4 Mainé Hanari, Co h. Colombia
83 □1 Mainé-Soroa Niger
42 B1 Maingkwan Myanmar
43 B4 Maingy I. i. Myanmar
16 G1 Mainit Phil.
16 G1 Mainland (Orkney) i. U.K.
16 G1 Mainland (Shetland) i. U.K.
54 D4 Mainpat reg. India
55 E4 Mainpuri India
16 G2 Maintirano Madagascar
18 D3 Mainz Germany
76 □1 Maio i. Cape Verde
146 C4 Maipó, Vol. vol Chile
146 E4 Maipú Buenos Aires Arg.
139 F3 Maipuri Landing Guyana
145 H1 Maiquetia Venezuela
145 H1 Maiquinique Brazil
94 □3 Maitland r. N.Z.
96 D3 Maitland r. Aust.
97 G2 Maitland Aust.
60 E5 Maitland r. Aust.
152 C3 Maitri India Base Ant.
49 K3 Maiyu, Mt h. Aust.
130 D3 Maíz, Is del i. Colombia
47 G6 Maizuru Japan
28 B2 Maja i. Albania
29 C4 Maja e Tomorit mts Albania
120 D5 Majagual Colombia
113 H3 Majdanpek Yugo.
28 D2 Majene Indon.
145 G5 Majé Brazil
82 □3 Majevica mts Bos.-Herz.
54 E4 Majia r. China
49 F5 Majiang China
128 D3 Majia r. China
25 H3 Majorca i. Spain
28 B2 Major Lake I. Macquarie I. Pac. Oc.
94 □3 Major I. i. India
149 J4 Maldive Ridge Indian Ocean
53 D10 Maldives country Maldives
146 E4 Maldonado Uruguay
127 J1 Makaha i. Fiji
40 D2 Makak Cameroon
78 B3 Makale Indon.
42 A2 Makalu, Mt mt. China
65 K3 Makapuu Hd U.S.A.
93 B7 Makarewa N.Z.
12 J2 Makar-Ib Rus. Fed.
12 J3 Makar'ye Rus. Fed.
14 G3 Makarov Rus. Fed.
25 H3 Makarska Croatia
12 J3 Makar'ye Rus. Fed.
14 G3 Makaryev Rus. Fed.
14 G2 Makatini Flats plain R.S.A.
83 E4 Makatini Flats plain R.S.A.
90 □11 Makatea i. Fr. Poly. Pac. Oc.
76 A4 Makeni Sierra Leone
78 B4 Makete Tanzania
82 D2 Makgadikgadi salt pan Botswana
82 C3 Makgadikgadi Pans Game Reserve res. Botswana
14 G3 Makhachkala Rus. Fed.
14 H3 Makhalino Rus. Fed.
65 K1 Makhmal Turkmenistan
60 E3 Makhmur Iraq
93 □2 Makikihi N.Z.
78 B4 Makindu Kenya
65 H2 Makinsk Kazak.
15 F2 Makiivka Donets'k Ukraine
73 F3 Makkah Saudi Arabia
13 H7 Makkaveyevo Rus. Fed.
113 J2 Makkovik Can.
113 J2 Makkovik, Cape c. Can.
19 K5 Makó Hungary
82 D2 Makoua i. Fiji
78 B4 Makokou Gabon
81 B6 Makongolosi Tanzania
78 B4 Makoua Congo
15 F2 Makoshyne Ukraine
19 J2 Maków Mazowiecki Poland
78 B3 Makrakomi Greece
54 B4 Makran reg. Iran/Pakistan
56 A2 Makrana India
54 B4 Makran Coast Range mt. ra. Pakistan
29 E6 Makronisi i. Notio Aigaio Greece
29 G5 Makronisi i. Voreio Aigaio Greece
12 G4 Maksatikha Rus. Fed.
14 H3 Maksimovka Rus. Fed.
14 H3 Maksotag Rus. Fed.
54 □2 Maktau Mt mt. India
54 C3 Makthar Tunisia
54 □2 Makum India
81 B6 Makumbako Tanzania
81 C6 Makunduchi Tanzania
47 □2 Makurazaki Japan
77 F5 Makurdi Nigeria
65 □5 Makushino Rus. Fed.
81 C6 Makuyuni Tanzania
80 □1 Makwassie R.S.A.
55 G4 Mal India
130 C4 Mala Guinea
15 B2 Mala r. Peru
11 □5 Mala Sweden
54 B4 Malá Fatra mts Slovakia
146 A3 Malabar Coast India
78 C3 Malabo Equatorial Guinea
55 G4 Maladz India

41 □1 Malakal Palau
80 B3 Malakal Sudan
40 □1 Malakal Passage chan. Indon.
78 C4 Malake i. Fiji
90 □8 Malake i. Fiji
11 B4 Malakula i. Vanuatu
54 C2 Malakwal Pakistan
139 F2 Malali Guyana
54 C2 Malakwal Pakistan
139 E2 Malali Guyana
40 A1 Mala Moshchanytsya Ukraine
15 A1 Mala Moshchanytsya Ukraine
40 D3 Malang Indon.
40 D2 Malangwa Nepal
55 F4 Malangwa Nepal
79 C5 Malanje Angola
77 F4 Malanville Benin
146 C3 Malanzán, Sa. de mt. ra. Arg.
54 C4 Malappuram India
130 18 Mala, Pta pt Panama
146 C4 Malargüe Arg.
115 F2 Malartic Can.
115 F2 Malartic, Lac l. Can.
110 A3 Malaspina Glacier gl. U.S.A.
60 D2 Malatya Turkey
60 □1 Malatya Turkey
94 □3 Malaut India
139 G3 Malavate French Guiana
57 A2 Malāvi Iran
15 D2 Mala Vil'shanka Ukraine
69 H7 Malawi country Africa
55 □1 Malawi i. Malaysia
63 M2 Malaya reg. Malaysia
43 C6 Malaya reg. Malaysia
12 K1 Malaya Pera Rus. Fed.
54 □1 Malaya Serdoba Rus. Fed.
12 E3 Malaya Vishera Rus. Fed.
41 C4 Malaybalay Phil.
57 B2 Malāyer Iran
38 B1 Malaysia country Asia
61 A1 Malazgirt Turkey
19 J1 Malbork Poland
19 J1 Malbork Poland
18 D2 Malchin Germany
65 H4 Malden U.S.A.
99 J1 Malbon Aust.
53 D10 Male Atoll atoll Maldives
54 D3 Malegaon India
54 C4 Malegaon India
19 H4 Malé Karpaty h. Slovakia
54 D3 Malegaon India
79 C5 Male Mozambique
81 B6 Malemba Nkulu Zaire
81 B6 Malema Mozambique
145 G5 Malema Mozambique
83 □3 Malemba Nkulu Zaire
63 □3 Maléndoio i. Greece
20 F2 Malesherbes France
29 D6 Maléstan Afghanistan
25 H3 Maleta Spain
64 D3 Makat Kazak.
91 □1 Makau Mama'o i. Tonga Pac. Oc.
49 K2 Makarov Rus. Fed.
76 B5 Makete Tanzania
79 B6 Malanje Angola
54 C4 Malappuram India
54 C5 Malia Fiji
56 A2 Mahe i. Seychelles
83 E4 Maleme Mozambique
90 □1 Manam I. i. P.N.G.
83 □3 Mananara Avaratra Madagascar
76 B5 Malema Tanzania
54 D4 Maliai India
72 D3 Mala India
40 A2 Mali r. Myanmar
14 H1 Mali Hka r. Myanmar
76 B4 Mali country Africa
90 □8 Mali i. Fiji
76 B4 Mali Guinea
42 B1 Mali Hka r. Myanmar
79 D4 Mali Kyun i. Myanmar
43 B4 Mali Kyun i. Myanmar
28 C3 Malili i. Thatë mt. Albania
15 F2 Malin Ukraine
39 G7 Malili Indon.
40 D1 Malimping Indon.
80 B4 Malindi Kenya
81 D5 Malindi Kenya
90 □1 Malines Belgium
18 B3 Malines Belgium
17 D4 Malin Head hd Rep. of Ire.
15 C1 Malyn Ukraine

151 D5 Malpelo, I. de i. Colombia
24 E1 Malpica Spain
56 B3 Malprabha r. India
54 C4 Malpura India
11 H4 Malta Latvia
126 F1 Malta U.S.A.
27 E7 Malta Channel chan. Mediterranean Sea
82 B4 Maltahöhe Namibia
54 D4 Malthone India
17 G4 Malton U.K.
91 □12 Malua Western Samoa
61 A3 Ma'lūlā, J. mt. ra. Syria
11 D3 Malung Sweden
83 D4 Maluti Mts mts Lesotho
90 □1 Malu'u Solomon Is.
56 A2 Malvan India
133 □1 Malvern Jamaica
125 E5 Malvern U.S.A.
15 D2 Malvyntsi Ukraine
90 J4 Malyy Irgiz r. Rus. Fed.
57 F6 Malyy Kavkaz mt. ra.
48 C2 Malyy Kunaley Rus. Fed.
63 Q2 Malyy Lyakhovskiy, Ostrov i. Rus. Fed.
63 M2 Malyy Taymyr, Ostrov i. Rus. Fed.
13 H5 Malyy Uzen' r. Kazak./Rus. Fed.
12 K1 Malyya Pera Rus. Fed.
48 A2 Malyy Yenisey r. Rus. Fed.
12 J4 Malyye Derbety Rus. Fed.
57 G2 Māmā Khēyl Afghanistan
56 C3 Māmaluanga India
59 □1 Mamanuca Group is Fiji
14 D2 Mamasa Indon.
33 □9 Mamaia Indon.
11 A5 Mambahenauhan i. Phil.
78 B3 Mambasa Zaire
78 B3 Mambéré r. C.A.R.
90 □1 Mambéré-Kadéi div. C.A.R.
144 B6 Mamborê Brazil
41 B3 Mamburao Phil.
81 □1 Mamelle I. i. Seychelles
83 D4 Mametodi
140 C4 Mamers France
78 F4 Mamfé Cameroon
140 C4 Mamfé Cameroon
65 L2 Mamlyutka Rus. Fed.
129 G5 Mammoth U.S.A.
128 C3 Mammoth Cave Nat. Park nat. park U.S.A.
145 G1 Mammoth Lakes U.S.A.
81 □4 Mamoré r. Bolivia/Brazil
138 B4 Mamoriá Brazil
140 C1 Mamou Guinea
76 B4 Mamou Guinea
83 D2 Mamoudzou Mayotte Africa
83 H2 Mampikony Madagascar
76 D5 Mampong Ghana
147 B4 Mamuil Malal, P. pass Arg./Chile
40 D2 Mamuju Indon.
78 □3 Man Côte d'Ivoire
90 □1 Mana i. Fiji
139 G2 Mana r. French Guiana
92 □5 Mana French Guiana
139 G2 Mana r. French Guiana
25 H3 Manacor Spain
139 H3 Manacapuru Brazil
130 D3 Managua Nicaragua
130 D3 Managua, L. de l. Nicaragua
29 D5 Manakaros Kolpos b. Greece
83 □3 Manakara Madagascar
83 H3 Manakau mt. N.Z.
80 D2 Manākhah Yemen
83 H3 Manambato i. Madagascar
83 □3 Manambato Madagascar
83 □3 Manambolo r. Madagascar
83 □3 Mananara Avaratra Madagascar
83 □3 Mananara r. Toamasina Madagascar
83 H3 Mananjary Madagascar
76 B4 Manankoro Mali
90 □1 Manam i. P.N.G.
83 □3 Manantantely Madagascar
83 □3 Manantenina Madagascar
15 A1 Malyn Ukraine
83 D2 Mana Pools National Park nat. park Zimbabwe
93 A6 Manapouri N.Z.
93 A6 Manapouri, L. l. N.Z.
83 H3 Manarantsandry Madagascar
65 L3 Manas Hu l. China
54 □1 Manaslu mt. Nepal
121 F5 Manasquan U.S.A.
119 □3 Manassas U.S.A.
96 □1 Manati Bay b. St Helena Atlantic Ocean
39 F4 Manatuto Indon.
54 □2 Manaus Brazil
60 A2 Manavgat Turkey
93 □4 Manawatu r. N.Z.
93 □4 Manawatu-Wanganui div. N.Z.
41 C5 Manay Phil.
15 □4 Manbazar India
60 □2 Manbij Syria
49 E5 Mancheng China
17 E4 Manchester U.K.
133 □1 Manchester Jamaica
121 G3 Manchester U.S.A.
122 A4 Manchester U.S.A.
120 A6 Manchester U.S.A.
119 □5 Manchester U.S.A.
122 D4 Manchester U.S.A.
121 G2 Manchester U.S.A.
54 A4 Manchhar L. l. Pakistan
51 □1 Manchioneal Jamaica
49 G3 Manchuria reg. China
54 C4 Manchuria reg. China
45 N2 Mancho Rus. Fed.
129 H3 Mancos U.S.A.
129 H3 Mancos r. U.S.A.
57 □4 Mand r. Iran
81 C6 Manda Tanzania
78 □2 Manda, Jebel mt. Sudan
78 D2 Manda, Jebel mt. Sudan

57 E2 Mandal Afghanistan
54 C4 Mandal India
48 C2 Mandal Mongolia
11 B4 Mandal Norway
39 M7 Mandala, Pk mt. Indon.
42 A2 Mandalay Myanmar
42 B2 Mandalay div. Myanmar
48 C3 Mandalgovĭ Mongolia
48 E3 Mandalt Sum China
124 C2 Mandan U.S.A.
81 B3 Mandaon Phil.
78 C2 Manda, Parc National de nat. park Chad
78 B1 Mandara Mountains mts Cameroon/Nigeria
40 D2 Mandar, Teluk b. Indon.
27 B6 Mandas Italy
26 B3 Mandello del Lario Italy
80 D4 Mandera Kenya
129 F2 Mandeville Jamaica
133 ¹¹ Mandeville Jamaica
93 B6 Mandeville N.Z.
54 B4 Mandha India
80 D3 Mandheera Somalia
54 D3 Mandi India
76 C4 Mandiana Mali
54 C3 Mandi Burewala Pakistan
83 E2 Mandié Mozambique
83 F1 Mandimba Mozambique
78 C3 Manding, Mts Mali
141 E3 Mandioré, Lagoa l. Bolivia
55 F5 Mandira Dam India
78 B4 Mandji Gabon
54 E5 Mandla India
40 B1 Mandor Indon.
83 H2 Mandoro Madagascar
77 F4 Mandouri Togo
83 H3 Mandrare r. Madagascar
83 H2 Mandritsara Madagascar
54 C4 Mandsaur India
101 A7 Mandurah Aust.
27 F5 Manduria Italy
54 B5 Mandvi India
54 B5 Mandvi India
56 B3 Mandya India
41 ² Manell Pt pt Guam
56 B2 Maner r. India
26 C3 Manerbio Italy
15 A1 Manevychi Ukraine
73 F2 Manfalūt Egypt
27 F5 Manfredonia Italy
27 F5 Manfredonia, Golfo di g. Italy
145 G1 Manga Brazil
76 D4 Manga Burkina
79 C4 Mangai Zaire
151 J7 Mangaia i. Cook Islands
92 E3 Mangakino N.Z.
56 C2 Mangaldai India
55 H4 Mangaldai India
28 G3 Mangalia Romania
72 C5 Mangalmé Chad
56 A3 Mangalvedha India
54 B4 Mangan India
56 C2 Mangapet India
41 C6 Mangarang Indon.
92 D4 Manganui N.Z.
92 F3 Mangaweka mt. N.Z.
92 E3 Mangaweka N.Z.
54 G4 Mangde r. Bhutan
79 E4 Mangembe Zaire
16 K1 Manger Norway
93 ¹¹ Mangere I. i. Chatham Is N.Z.
40 B2 Manggar Indon.
41 ² Mangilao Guam Pac. Oc.
64 D4 Mangistau Kazak.
40 D1 Mangkalihat, Tg pt Indon.
40 C2 Mangkutup r. Indon.
42 B1 Mangkyi Myanmar
44 F4 Mangnai China
83 F1 Mangochi Malawi
76 D5 Mangodara Burkina
83 G3 Mangoky r. Toliara Madagascar
83 H3 Mangoky r. Toliara Madagascar
39 J7 Mangole i. Indon.
92 D1 Mangonui N.Z.
92 A7 Mangoro r. Madagascar
54 B5 Mangral India
54 D4 Mangrol India
132 C1 Mangrove Cay The Bahamas
24 C2 Mangualde Portugal
54 D4 Manguchar Pakistan
78 B1 Manguéigne Chad
146 F3 Mangueira, L. l. Brazil
143 B6 Mangueirinha Brazil
77 E2 Manguéni, Plateau du plat. Niger
142 C3 Mangui r. Brazil
49 E1 Mangui China
142 E3 Manguinha, Pontal do pt Brazil
41 C5 Mangupung i. Indon.
48 E2 Mangut Rus. Fed.
64 D4 Mangyshlak, Pov. pen. Kazak.
64 D4 Mangyshlakskiy Zal. b. Kazak.
48 A2 Manhan Mongolia
124 D4 Manhattan U.S.A.
128 D2 Manhattan U.S.A.
83 G3 Manhiça Mozambique
145 K3 Manhuaçu r. Brazil
145 J4 Manhuaçu Brazil
142 D2 Manhumirim Brazil
138 D1 Mani Colombia
83 H2 Mania r. Madagascar
26 D2 Maniago Italy
81 B7 Maniamba Mozambique
83 E3 Manica div. Mozambique
83 E2 Manicaland div. Mozambique
139 E5 Manicoré Brazil
113 J3 Manicouagan Can.
113 J3 Manicouagan r. Can.
113 J3 Manicouagan, Réservoir resr Can.
57 A4 Manifah Saudi Arabia
99 C4 Manifold, C. pt Aust.
50 B2 Maniganggo China
55 F4 Manihari India
91 ¹¹ Manihi i. Fr. Poly. Pac. Oc.
150 J6 Manihiki atoll Cook Islands Pac. Oc.
109 N3 Maniitsoq Greenland
79 E6 Manika, Plateau de la plat. Zaire
55 G5 Manikganj Bangladesh
54 E4 Manikpur India
83 E2 Manjacaze Mozambique
126 B3 Manis U.S.A.
41 B3 Manila Bay b. Phil.
97 G2 Manilla Aust.
90 ¹³ Maninita i. Tonga
55 H4 Manipur r. India/Myanmar
29 F4 Manisa div. Turkey
29 F4 Manisa Turkey
17 L4 Man, Isle of terr. Europe
54 D3 Manismata India
142 B3 Manissauá Missu r. Brazil
122 E3 Manistee r. U.S.A.
122 E3 Manistee U.S.A.
122 D2 Manistique Lake l. U.S.A.
108 J4 Manitoba div. Can.
111 H4 Manito L. l. Can.

111 K5 Manitou Can.
120 E3 Manitou Beach U.S.A.
112 B3 Manitou Falls Can.
112 B3 Manitou Island i. U.S.A.
118 C2 Manitou Island i. U.S.A.
114 E4 Manitou, Lake l. Can.
114 E4 Manitoulin I. i. Can.
114 D4 Manitouwadge Can.
122 D3 Manitowoc U.S.A.
115 H3 Maniwaki Can.
138 B2 Manizales Colombia
83 H2 Manja Madagascar
83 H3 Manjak Madagascar
73 ¹ Manjam Umm Qurayyāt waterhole Egypt
56 A4 Manjeri India
101 B7 Manjimup Aust.
55 G3 Manjo r. India
56 B2 Manjra r. India
42 B1 Man Kabat Myanmar
55 G4 Mankachar India
124 E2 Mankato U.S.A.
54 B3 Mankera Pakistan
78 B2 Mankim Cameroon
76 C5 Mankono Côte d'Ivoire
56 C4 Mankulam Sri Lanka
42 B1 Manlc Myanmar
25 H2 Manlleu Spain
42 B2 Man Na Myanmar
96 D3 Mannahill Aust.
56 B4 Mannar Sri Lanka
56 B4 Mannar, Gulf of g. India/Sri Lanka
56 B3 Mannera r. India
54 D3 Mannheim Germany
97 C2 Manning r. Aust.
110 F3 Manning Can.
119 D5 Manning U.S.A.
96 B1 Mann Ranges mt. ra. Aust.
27 B6 Mannu r. Italy
27 B5 Mannu, Capo pt Italy
96 D3 Mannum Aust.
76 B5 Mano r. Liberia/Sierra Leone
140 C1 Manoa Bol.
97 G4 Mansel I. i. Can.
97 F4 Mansfield U.S.A.
17 G5 Mansfield U.K.
120 B4 Mansfield U.S.A.
120 C4 Mansfield U.S.A.
142 D1 Marajó, Baía de est. Brazil
142 B1 Marajó, Ilha de i. Brazil
56 B3 Marakkanam India
78 C2 Maralal C.A.R.
78 C2 Maralinga Aust.
90 ¹¹ Maramasike i. Solomon Is.
41 C5 Marampit i. Indon.
132 K2 Maramureşului, Munţii mt. ra. Romania
43 C7 Maran Malaysia
122 D3 Marana U.S.A.
144 C5 Maranã Brazil
83 E2 Maranguape Brazil
142 E1 Maranhão r. Brazil
142 B1 Maranhão div. Brazil
142 B1 Maranoa r. Aust.
140 C2 Marañón r. Peru
76 C5 Maraoué, Parc National de la nat. park Côte d'Ivoire
142 A3 Marapanim Brazil
138 D5 Marari r. Brazil
93 A6 Maramaroa r. N.Z.
96 D2 Marasende i. Indon.
28 F2 Mârâşeşti Romania
142 C2 Marathon Can.
114 D4 Marathon Can.
125 C6 Marathon U.S.A.
142 E3 Marathonas Greece
142 B2 Marau Brazil
133 ¹³ Maraval Trin. and Tobago
141 A4 Marawá Brazil
61 C3 Marawih i. U.A.E.
50 A2 Marcapata Peru
100 B4 Marble Bar Aust.
129 H3 Marble Canyon U.S.A.
129 H3 Marble Canyon gorge U.S.A.
120 A5 Marblehead U.S.A.
121 H3 Marble I. i. Can.
152 Marble I. i. Ant.
18 G3 Marburg Germany
18 D3 Marburg R.S.A.
115 J5 Markham r. Can.
19 H5 Marcali Hungary
29 J6 Markopoulo Greece
17 H5 March U.K.
56 B3 Marcha reg. India
26 C4 Marche reg. Italy
18 B3 Marche-en-Famenne Belgium
23 F4 Marche, Plateaux de la plat. France
133 ⁹ Marchena Barbados
20 D3 Marchena, I. i. Galápagos Is Ecuador
23 G4 Marche, Plateaux de la plat. France
139 B3 Marco Peru
127 F5 Marco Island U.S.A.
146 B3 Marcos Juárez Arg.
121 G2 Marcy, Mt mt. U.S.A.
54 C2 Mardan Pakistan
146 E4 Mar del Plata Arg.
29 F5 Marmaris Turkey
60 E1 Mardin Turkey
90 ¹⁰ Mardzad Mongolia
92 B7 Mare r. N.Z.
83 E3 Mareeba Aust.

50 C3 Maotou Shan mt. China
54 E2 Mapai Mozambique
120 B3 Mapam Yumco l. China
55 E3 Mapam Yumco l. China
131 A5 Mapane Indon.
130 D3 Mapimí Mexico
41 A5 Mapin i. Phil.
83 F3 Mapinhane Mozambique
139 E2 Mapire Venezuela
140 C3 Mapiri Bolivia
122 E4 Maple r. U.S.A.
111 H5 Maple Creek Can.
99 E1 Mapoon Aust.
99 E1 Mapoon Abor. Reserve res. Aust.
40 A1 Mapor i. Indon.
90 ¹¹ Maprik P.N.G.
139 F4 Mapuera r. Brazil
83 E3 Mapulanguene Mozambique
83 E3 Maputo Mozambique
83 E3 Maputo r. Mozambique
83 E4 Maputo Mozambique
83 E3 Maputo r. Mozambique/R.S.A.
60 D4 Maqar an Na'am well Iraq
50 C1 Maqèn China
50 B1 Maqèn Gangri mt. China
65 L4 Maqiao China
61 C5 Maqla, J. al mt. Saudi Arabia
60 E4 Maqna Saudi Arabia
65 H4 Maqtēir reg. Mauritania
50 C1 Maqu China
55 E3 Maquan r. China
41 C3 Maqueda Channel chan. Phil.
79 C5 Maquela do Zombo Angola
147 C5 Maquinchao r. Arg.
147 C5 Maquinchao Arg.
122 A4 Maquoketa r. U.S.A.
122 B4 Maquoketa U.S.A.
54 A4 Mar r. Pakistan
111 H1 Mara r. India
139 F2 Mara Guyana
55 E5 Mära India
83 D4 Mara R.S.A.
81 B5 Mara div. Tanzania
83 E2 Mara Brazil
130 K8 Maria van Diemen, Cape c. N.Z.
91 ¹¹ Maraa Fr. Poly. Pac. Oc.
142 B3 Maraba Brazil
144 D1 Marabá Paulista Brazil
144 A4 Marabbat Brazil
76 A4 Maraboon, L. resr Aust.
110 F2 Maricao Arg.
141 B4 Maricopa U.S.A.
119 C6 Maricopa U.S.A.
128 C4 Maricopa Mts mts U.S.A.
142 C1 Maracaçumé r. Brazil
144 C5 Maracaí Brazil
138 D2 Maracaibo Venezuela
138 C2 Maracaibo, Lago de l. Venezuela
81 ¹¹ Maraini-Anne I. i. Seychelles
52 A4 Marie Byrd Land reg. Ant.
133 ¹⁵ Marie Galante i. Guadeloupe Caribbean
11 E3 Mariehamn Finland
14 H1 Mari-El div. Rus. Fed.
142 B3 Mariembero r. Brazil
26 D4 Marienbad Namibia
11 D4 Mariestad Sweden
120 C5 Marietta U.S.A.
125 C5 Marietta U.S.A.
21 G5 Marignane France
152 Marigny, C. c. Kerguelen Indian Ocean
133 G3 Marigot Guadeloupe Caribbean
133 ¹⁵ Marigot Martinique Caribbean
11 F5 Marijampolė Lithuania
100 A4 Marilla Aust.
144 D4 Mariluz Brazil
139 E4 Marimari r. Angola
11 U6 Marimba Angola
11 M4 Marimari r. Indon.
125 C7 Marin Mexico
25 F5 Marín Spain
133 G3 Marina di Gioiosa Ionica Italy
27 F6 Marina di Gioiosa Ionica Italy
121 E4 Mar'ina Horka Belarus
41 B3 Marinduque i. Phil.
122 D3 Marinette U.S.A.
144 C5 Maringá Brazil
83 E2 Maringué Mozambique
24 B2 Marinha Grande Portugal
118 B4 Marion U.S.A.
122 C5 Marion U.S.A.
120 C4 Marion U.S.A.
119 E5 Marion U.S.A.
120 B5 Marion U.S.A.
99 D4 Marion Downs Aust.
119 D5 Marion, L. l. U.S.A.
98 D4 Marion Reef reef Coral Sea Islands Terr. Pac. Oc.
139 D2 Maripa Venezuela
139 G3 Maripasoula French Guiana
128 C3 Mariposa U.S.A.
141 D4 Mariscal Estigarribia Paraguay
28 E3 Mârişelu Romania
28 F3 Maritsa r. Bulgaria
15 F6 Mariupol' Ukraine
65 J5 Marjanyoh r. Lebanon
80 C3 Marka Somalia
54 D1 Markam China
56 B2 Markapur India
11 C4 Markaryd Sweden
110 D3 Marken U.S.A.
122 E3 Market Drayton U.K.
17 H5 Market Harborough U.K.
17 G5 Market Weighton U.K.
63 O3 Markha r. Rus. Fed.
115 G5 Markham Can.
152 Markham, Mt mt. Ant.
29 J6 Markopoulo Greece
13 J6 Markovo Rus. Fed.
77 E4 Markoye Burkina
18 D3 Marktheidenfeld Germany
18 E3 Marktoberdorf Germany
18 F3 Marktredwitz Germany
122 B4 Mark Twain Lake l. U.S.A.
18 D2 Marl Germany
99 E4 Marlborough Aust.
93 D5 Marlborough div. N.Z.
17 G6 Marlborough U.K.

20 D3 Mareuil-sur-Lay-Dissais France
14 A1 Marevo Rus. Fed.
125 B6 Marfa U.S.A.
55 F2 Margai Caka salt l. China
96 D2 Margaret w Aust.
100 D3 Margaret r. Aust.
101 A7 Margaret River Aust.
139 E1 Margarita, I. de i. Venezuela
17 H6 Margate U.K.
21 F4 Margeride, Monts de la mts France
55 H4 Margherita India
28 D1 Marghita Romania
65 H4 Margilan Uzbekistan
28 E1 Marginea Romania
41 B5 Margosatubig Phil.
122 E3 Margrethe, Lake l. U.S.A.
152 Marguerite Bay b. Ant.
55 G3 Margyang China
15 F3 Marhanets' Ukraine
75 D2 Marhoum Algeria
42 B1 Mari r. Myanmar
144 A4 Maria r. Brazil
140 C4 Maria Cleofas, I. i. Mexico
140 C4 María Elena Chile
98 C2 Maria I. i. Aust.
97 G5 Maria I. i. Aust.
151 J7 María, Îles i. Fr. Poly. Pac. Oc.
130 D4 María Madre, I. i. Mexico
55 E3 Maquan r. China
41 C3 María Magdalena, I. i. Mexico
130 D4 María Madre Mexico
99 G4 Mariana Brazil
145 G4 Mariana Brazil
132 B2 Mariano Cuba
150 E4 Marianas Ridge Pac. Oc.
150 E5 Marianas Tr. Pac. Oc.
26 C3 Mariani r. India
110 F2 Mariano Lake U.S.A.
125 F5 Marianna U.S.A.
119 C6 Marianna U.S.A.
146 E2 Mariano Loza Arg.
18 F4 Mariánské Lázně Czech Rep.
130 D4 Marías, Islas is Mexico
130 K8 Mariato, Pta pt Panama
92 B7 Maria van Diemen, Cape c. N.Z.
19 G5 Mariazell Austria
80 E1 Ma'rib Yemen
26 F2 Maribor Slovenia
129 F5 Maricopa U.S.A.
128 C4 Maricopa U.S.A.
72 C4 Maridi r. Sudan
78 C3 Maridi w Sudan
81 ¹¹ Maraini-Anne I. i. Seychelles
52 A4 Marie Byrd Land reg. Ant.
133 ¹⁵ Marie Galante i. Guadeloupe Caribbean
83 F2 Marromeu Mozambique
83 F2 Marromeu, Reserva de res. Mozambique
81 C7 Marropino Mozambique
73 ¹ Marsa Alam Egypt
72 C1 Marsa al Burayqah Libya
80 C4 Marsabit Kenya
80 C4 Marsabit National res. Kenya
61 C5 Marsa Dahab b. Egypt
10 F1 Marsala Italy
72 E1 Marsa Matrūh Egypt
82 A4 Marsassoum Senegal
82 A4 Mars Bay b. Ascension Atlantic Ocean
26 D4 Marsberg Germany
26 D3 Marsciano Italy
26 D4 Marsdenia Namibia
11 D4 Marstrand Sweden
120 C5 Marietta U.S.A.
110 F2 Marsfjället mt. Sweden
21 G5 Marseille France
122 C5 Marseilles U.S.A.
132 B1 Marsh Harbour The Bahamas
121 J1 Marshall r. Aust.
98 C4 Marshall r. Aust.
114 A2 Marshall Can.
128 A2 Marshall U.S.A.
124 E3 Marshall U.S.A.
125 E5 Marshall U.S.A.
124 E3 Marshall U.S.A.
150 F5 Marshall Islands country Pac. Oc.
114 B1 Marshall Lake l. Can.
122 B5 Marshall, B. b. Aust.
124 E3 Marshalltown U.S.A.
122 C3 Marshfield U.S.A.
120 A4 Marshfield U.S.A.
132 C1 Marsh Harbour The Bahamas
115 K4 Massawippi, Lac l. Can.
121 F2 Massena U.S.A.
110 C3 Massena U.S.A.
110 C3 Masset Can.
119 B4 Massey U.S.A.
21 F4 Massif Central mts France
54 A3 Massilah w Pakistan
93 A6 Martins Bay b. N.Z.
120 D5 Martinsburg U.S.A.
120 C4 Martins Ferry U.S.A.
83 E3 Massinga Mozambique
83 F2 Massingir Mozambique
83 E3 Massingir, Barragem de resr Mozambique
15 F3 Matviyivka Mykolayiv Ukraine
152 D5 Masson I. i. Ant.

20 F2 Marne-la-Vallée France
78 C2 Maro Chad
83 H2 Maroantsetra Madagascar
145 J2 Maroba r. Brazil
91 ¹⁰ Marokau i. Fr. Poly. Pac. Oc.
54 D2 Marol Pakistan
65 J6 Marol Jammu and Kashmir
83 H3 Marolambo Madagascar
83 H1 Maromokotro mt. Madagascar
83 E2 Maromony, Lohatanjona pt Madagascar
81 C5 Masai Mara National Reserve res. Kenya
81 C5 Masai Steppe plain Tanzania
20 F4 Maronne r. France
99 H5 Maroochydore Aust.
133 ¹ Maroon Town Jamaica
40 D3 Maros Indon.
83 H2 Maroseranana Madagascar
19 K5 Maros-Körös Köze plain Hungary
81 N7 Maroriri i. Fr. Poly. Pac. Oc.
81 C5 Marsabit National res. Kenya
74 C2 Marrakech Morocco
83 F2 Marrah, Jebel mt. Sudan
82 A4 Marra r. Brazil
81 C5 Marra div. Tanzania
83 D4 Mara R.S.A.
145 G4 Marrecha Brazil
145 G4 Marromeu Mozambique
83 F2 Marromeu, Reserva de res. Mozambique
81 C7 Marropino Mozambique
83 F2 Marra Plateau plat. Sudan
97 F5 Marrawah Aust.
83 C7 Marromeu, Reserva de res. Mozambique
130 D4 Marías, Islas is Mexico
130 K8 Mariato, Pta pt Panama
96 D2 Marree Aust.
125 F6 Marrero U.S.A.
83 F1 Marrupa Mozambique
81 B7 Marsabit div. Kenya
80 C4 Marsabit National res. Kenya
65 L1 Marsden r. Pakistan
55 J3 Marshall r. Aust.
76 B5 Marshall Liberia
57 B3 Masjed Soleymān Iran
65 D2 Maskanah Syria
115 J3 Maskhong r. Can.
17 G5 Mask, Lough l. Rep. of Ire.
57 C4 Maskūtān Iran
13 G5 Maslova Pristan' Rus. Fed.
57 D3 Masmok r. Iran
83 G2 Masoala, Tanjona c. Madagascar
83 G2 Masoarivo Madagascar
122 C5 Masomb Cameroon
24 B3 Masotnos Portugal
80 C2 Maych'ew Ethiopia
80 C2 Maydān Ikbī Iraq
26 C3 Matati India
145 G3 Mateus Leme Brazil
130 E4 Matehuala Mexico
27 F5 Matera Italy
19 J5 Mátészalka Hungary
82 D3 Matetsi r. Zimbabwe
74 C1 Mateur Tunisia
145 F3 Matias Barbosa Brazil
130 E3 Matias Romero Mexico
131 G4 Matina Costa Rica
140 D1 Matisea Peru
83 E3 Matlabas r. R.S.A.
119 B6 Matamoros Coahuila Mexico
83 ¹⁴ Matola Mozambique
42 B2 Matala Sri Lanka
80 E2 Matam N.Z.
92 F3 Matamata N.Z.
130 C2 Matamoros Coahuila Mexico

128 B2 Marysville U.S.A.
120 B5 Marysville U.S.A.
120 A4 Marysville U.S.A.
99 F3 Maryvale Aust.
124 E4 Maryville U.S.A.
144 D2 Marzagão Brazil
79 C6 Matala Angola
56 A4 Matale Sri Lanka
92 F2 Matam N.Z.
61 A4 Masabb Dumyāt river mouth Egypt
61 A4 Masabb Rashid river mouth Egypt
130 K7 Masachapa Nicaragua
81 C5 Masai Mara National Reserve res. Kenya
81 C5 Masai Steppe plain Tanzania
83 E3 Masaka Uganda
82 C3 Masalanyane Pan salt pan Botswana
40 C3 Masalembu Besar i. Indon.
40 D3 Masalembu Kecil i. Indon.
19 K5 Maros-Körös Köze plain Hungary
81 C5 Masasi Bolivia
141 D3 Masavi Bolivia
130 K7 Masaya Nicaragua
81 B3 Masbate Phil.
81 B3 Masbate i. Phil.
60 D3 Masjid ash Syria
50 C1 Maqèn China
72 C5 Maskin div. Zimbabwe
74 B1 Maskara Algeria
25 H2 Mascaro r. Spain
149 H5 Mascarene Basin Indian Ocean
149 H5 Mascarene Ridge Indian Ocean
115 J4 Mascot Brazil
81 A4 Maseno Kenya
115 G2 Masères, Lac l. Can.
82 B4 Maseru Lesotho
16 K1 Masfjorden Norway
83 E2 Mashala r. Tanzania
55 H3 Mashar i. Phil.
83 H2 Mashava R.S.A.
54 D2 Masherbrum mt. Pakistan
57 D1 Mashhad Iran
46 C4 Mashike Japan
15 E6 Mashkivka Ukraine
57 C3 Mashīz r. Iran
57 E4 Mashket r. Pakistan
81 B5 Mashra Chah Pakistan
57 E4 Mäshkīd r. Iran
83 E2 Mashonaland Central div. Zimbabwe
83 E2 Mashonaland East div. Zimbabwe
83 E2 Mashonaland West div. Zimbabwe
57 B3 Masjed Soleymān Iran
60 D2 Maskanah Syria
115 J3 Maskhong r. Can.
17 G5 Mask, Lough l. Rep. of Ire.
57 C4 Maslova Pristan' Rus. Fed.
80 C3 Masmaslebo Somalia
125 D6 Mason U.S.A.
122 E4 Mason U.S.A.
124 D3 Mason City U.S.A.
93 A7 Mason Bay b. N.Z.
110 D3 Mason Bay U.S.A.
57 D4 Masqaţ, Gulf of b. Oman
83 H2 Masoarivo Madagascar
83 B4 Masombo Cameroon
24 B3 Masotnos Portugal
55 G3 Massarosa Italy
83 E2 Massangena Mozambique
79 C5 Massango Angola
81 B5 Massangulo Mozambique
80 C1 Massawa Eritrea
80 C1 Massawa Channel chan. Eritrea
21 F5 Masseube France
124 D3 Masset Can.
83 C7 Massif Central mts France
42 B1 Massilah w Pakistan
82 A4 Massinga Mozambique
83 E3 Massingir Mozambique

61 A5 Matāi Egypt
91 ¹¹ Mataiva I. Fr. Poly. Pac. Oc.
43 D7 Matak i. Indon.
124 E3 Matakana I. i. N.Z.
144 D2 Matam N.Z.
79 C6 Matala Angola
56 A4 Matale Sri Lanka
61 A4 Matam N.Z.
92 F2 Matam N.Z.
77 F4 Matamey Niger
92 E2 Matamata N.Z.
92 E2 Matangi N.Z.
131 F3 Matamoros Tamaulipas Mexico
43 B4 Maungmagan Is is Myanmar
43 B4 Maungmagon Myanmar
43 B4 Maungmagan Is is Myanmar
72 D3 Ma'ţan as Sārah well Libya
72 D3 Ma'ţan Bishrah well Libya
130 D4 Matamoros r. Tanzania
113 G4 Matane Can.
132 B2 Matanzas Cuba
144 D4 Matão Brazil
130 K7 Matapalo, C. c. Costa Rica
113 G4 Matapédia r. Can.
24 D1 Mataporquera Spain
146 B4 Mataquito r. Chile
56 C5 Matara Sri Lanka
29 C5 Mataragka Dytiki Ellas Greece
141 D3 Masavi Bolivia
81 A4 Masasi Tanzania
41 B3 Masbate i. Phil.
60 C3 Mascara Syria
50 C1 Maqèn China
25 H2 Mataró Spain
40 A3 Masiri i. Indon.
73 E4 Mava well Sudan
81 C7 Mavago Mozambique
81 C7 Mavengue Angola
79 D7 Mavinga Angola
83 D3 Mavuya r. India
92 D3 Mawhai Pt pt N.Z.
57 C1 Mawlaik Myanmar
42 A2 Mawlaik Myanmar
92 E3 Mawhiti N.Z.
90 ¹³ Mata'utuliki i. Tonga
90 ¹³ Mata'utu Wallis and Futuna Western Samoa
91 ¹⁶ Matavera i. Fr. Poly.
92 Q3 Mawai N.Z.
141 D2 Matawi r. Bolivia
115 J3 Matawin r. Can.
141 D2 Mategua Bolivia
131 E4 Matehuala Mexico
133 ¹ Matelot Trin. and Tobago
78 C3 Matemanga Tanzania
81 B6 Matemanga Tanzania
83 F2 Matemo, Ilha i. Mozambique
27 F5 Matera Italy
19 J5 Mátészalka Hungary
82 D3 Matetsi r. Zimbabwe
74 C1 Mateur Tunisia
145 F3 Matias Barbosa Brazil
130 E3 Matias Romero Mexico
131 G4 Matina Costa Rica
140 D1 Matisea Peru
83 E2 Mathanga r. Zimbabwe
83 E2 Matetsi Zimbabwe
140 A2 Matisea Peru
83 E2 Matlabas r. R.S.A.
55 H3 Matli Pakistan
54 B4 Matli Pakistan
82 C1 Matlabas r. R.S.A.
145 G4 Matipó Brazil
55 E3 Matisi India

39 H8 Maumere Indon.
82 C1 Matau Botswana
127 ² Mauna Kea vol U.S.A.
127 ² Mauna Loa vol U.S.A.
127 ² Maunalua B. b. U.S.A.
79 C6 Matala Angola
92 C6 Maungahautu mt. N.Z.
92 F3 Maungapohatu mt. N.Z.
92 F3 Maungataniwha mt. N.Z.
92 F2 Maunganui N.Z.
92 E2 Matamata N.Z.
92 E2 Maungaturoto N.Z.
92 E2 Maungaw N.Z.
43 B4 Maungmagan Is is Myanmar
43 B4 Maungmagon Myanmar
72 D3 Ma'ţan as Sārah well Libya
54 D4 Mau Rampur India
21 H5 Maures, Massif des reg. France
140 C2 Mauri r. Bolivia
113 G4 Mauriac France
144 D4 Matão Brazil
130 K7 Matapalo, C. c. Costa Rica
115 J3 Maurice, Parc National res. Can.
68 C4 Mauritania country Africa
69 K7 Mauritius country Indian Ocean
113 G4 Matapédia r. Can.
24 D1 Mataporquera Spain
146 B4 Mataquito r. Chile
91 ¹⁶ Matavera i. Fr. Poly.
92 Q3 Mawai N.Z.
93 Q3 Mataura r. N.Z.
115 J3 Matawin r. Can.
141 D2 Mategua Bolivia
131 E4 Matehuala Mexico
133 ¹ Matelot Trin. and Tobago
80 D2 Mawqa' Yemen
42 A2 Mawlaik Myanmar
43 B4 Maw Taung mt. Myanmar
124 D2 Max U.S.A.
54 A4 Maxbass Somalia
54 A2 Maxán Arg.
131 H4 Maxcanú Mexico
131 H4 Maxia, Punta mt. Italy
122 D5 Maxinkuckee, Lake l. U.S.A.
10 F1 Maxmo Finland
123 F2 Maxton U.S.A.
19 E5 Maxville Can.
144 A2 Maxwelton Aust.
99 E4 Maxwelton Aust.
83 F3 Maya r. Rus. Fed.
63 Q4 Maya r. Rus. Fed.
15 E5 Mayachka Ukraine
142 D2 Mayaguana i. The Bahamas
132 D2 Mayaguana Passage The Bahamas
74 D4 Mcherrah reg. Algeria
21 C6 Mchinga Tanzania
81 B7 Mchinji Malawi
108 C3 McKinley, Mount mt. U.S.A.
57 C1 Mayamey Iran
81 B6 Mdandu Tanzania
81 B6 Mdantsane R.S.A.
75 F1 M'Daourouch Algeria
75 F1 Mdennah reg. Mali/Mauritania

128 B2 Marysville U.S.A.
120 B5 Marysville U.S.A.
120 A4 Marysville U.S.A.
99 F3 Maryvale Aust.
124 E4 Maryville U.S.A.
144 D2 Marzagão Brazil
57 B3 Masabb Dumyāt river mouth Egypt
130 J7 Masachapa Nicaragua
81 B5 Masai Mara National Reserve res. Kenya
83 E3 Masat Syria
72 D3 Ma'ţan Bishrah well Libya
72 D3 Ma'ţan as Sārah well Libya
130 D4 Matane r. Tanzania
113 G4 Matane Can.
132 B2 Matanzas Cuba
144 B4 Matão Brazil
130 K7 Matapalo, C. c. Costa Rica
113 G4 Matapédia r. Can.
24 D1 Mataporquera Spain
146 B4 Mataquito r. Chile
56 C5 Matara Sri Lanka
29 C5 Mataragka Dytiki Ellas Greece
145 F4 Mauá Brazil
145 G4 Mauá Brazil
55 H4 Mau Aimma India
78 B2 Maubeuge France
21 E5 Maubourguet France
92 F3 Maud, Pt pt Aust.
152 Maud Seamount Ant.
139 G3 Maués Brazil
54 D3 Mauganj India
114 C4 Maughold Head U.K.
113 J4 Maugyi r. Myanmar
91 ¹¹ Maui i. U.S.A.
146 C3 Maule, C. i. Chile
114 A2 Maumee r. U.S.A.
114 A2 Maumee Bay b. U.S.A.
122 E5 Maumee U.S.A.
122 E5 Maumee Bay b. U.S.A.
39 H8 Maumere Indon.
82 C1 Maun Botswana
14 D1 Maunath Bhanjan India
83 D2 Maunatlala Botswana
92 D4 Maungataniwha mt. N.Z.
147 A5 Maullín Chile
57 D1 Mawlaw-e Sharif Afghanistan
57 D1 Maxäräbishi mt. Afghanistan
13 K4 May Day Mts mts Jamaica
129 G3 Mayer U.S.A.
129 G4 Mayfield N.Z.
114 A2 Mayfield U.S.A.
48 C3 Maych'ew Mongolia
92 C6 Mayhill U.S.A.
129 F5 Maymana Afghanistan
42 B2 Maymyo Myanmar
92 C6 Mayh N.Z.
115 K2 Mayo r. Can.
108 D3 Mayo r. Can.
78 B2 Mayo Daga Nigeria
131 F5 Mayo, 25 de Buenos Aires Arg.
147 C5 Mayo, 25 de La Pampa Arg.
146 C3 Mayor Buratovich Arg.
139 E2 Maturín Venezuela
139 E2 Mayor Pablo Lagerenza Paraguay

25 F4 Mazarrón, Golfo de b. Spain
65 K5 Maartagh mts China
139 F2 Mazaruni r. Guyana
131 H6 Mazatenango Guatemala
130 C4 Mazatlán Mexico
129 G4 Mazatzal Peak summit U.S.A.
11 F4 Mažeikiai Lithuania
77 F3 Mazelet well Niger
64 D3 Mazhambet Kazak.
29 F6 Mazı Turkey
120 C2 Mazīkeh Latvia
130 C2 Mazocahui Mexico
140 C3 Mazocruz Peru
83 E2 Mazomora Tanzania
83 E3 Mazowe r. Zimbabwe
61 C4 Mazra Jordan
83 E2 Mazunga Zimbabwe
27 F7 Mazzarino Italy
73 E4 Mba well Sudan
76 A4 Mbacké Senegal
78 C3 Mbaiki C.A.R.
78 C3 Mbaïki C.A.R.
81 B5 Mbala Zambia
83 D3 Mbalabala Zimbabwe
78 B2 Mbalam Cameroon
81 B4 Mbale Uganda
78 B3 Mbalmayo Cameroon
78 B3 Mbam r. Cameroon
78 C4 Mbandaka Zaire
79 C4 Mbandjok Zaire
79 B5 M'banza Congo Angola
79 B5 Mbanza-Ngungu Zaire
81 B5 Mbarara Uganda
81 C6 Mbarika Mountains mts Tanzania
78 B7 Mbati Zambia
78 C3 Mbé Cameroon
81 C6 Mbemkuru r. Tanzania
78 B2 Mbengwi Cameroon
76 C4 Mbenqué Côte d'Ivoire
81 C6 Mberengwa Zimbabwe
81 B6 Mbeya Tanzania
81 B6 Mbeya div. Tanzania
78 B3 Mbi r. C.A.R.
78 B4 Mbigou Gabon
78 A4 Mbilapé Gabon
78 B3 Mbinda Congo
78 A3 Mbinga Tanzania
78 A3 Mbini Equatorial Guinea
81 B6 Mbizi Mts mts Tanzania
78 C3 Mbomo Congo
78 C3 Mbomou r. C.A.R.
78 B3 Mbouda Cameroon
76 A3 Mbour Senegal
76 A3 Mbout Mauritania
78 C4 Mbrès C.A.R.
79 C5 Mbuji-Mayi Zaire
81 C5 Mbuyuni Tanzania
108 H2 McClintock Channel chan. Can.
74 D4 Mcherrah reg. Algeria
81 C6 Mchinga Tanzania

63 H8 Mazarrón, Golfo de b. Spain
82 C2 Maun Botswana
79 C6 Matala Angola
127 ² Mauna Kea vol U.S.A.
127 ² Mauna Loa vol U.S.A.
127 ² Maunalua B. b. U.S.A.
79 C6 Matala Angola
92 C6 Maungahautu mt. N.Z.
92 F3 Maungapohatu mt. N.Z.
92 F3 Maungataniwha mt. N.Z.
11 F4 Mažeikiai Lithuania
77 F3 Mazelet well Niger
64 D3 Mazhambet Kazak.
29 F6 Mazı Turkey
120 C2 Mazu Taiwan
130 C2 Mazocahui Mexico
140 C3 Mazocruz Peru
83 E2 Mazomora Tanzania
83 E3 Mazowe r. Zimbabwe
61 C4 Mazra Jordan
83 E2 Mazunga Zimbabwe
27 F7 Mazzarino Italy
83 F1 Mbamba Bay Tanzania
83 D2 Mbalabala Zimbabwe
78 B2 Mbalam Cameroon
81 B4 Mbale Uganda
78 B3 Mbalmayo Cameroon
78 B3 Mbam r. Cameroon
78 C4 Mbandaka Zaire
79 C4 Mbandjok Zaire
79 B5 M'banza Congo Angola
79 B5 Mbanza-Ngungu Zaire
81 B5 Mbarara Uganda
81 C6 Mbarika Mountains mts Tanzania
78 B7 Mbati Zambia
78 C3 Mbé Cameroon
81 C6 Mbemkuru r. Tanzania
78 B2 Mbengwi Cameroon
76 C4 Mbenqué Côte d'Ivoire
81 C6 Mberengwa Zimbabwe
81 B6 Mbeya Tanzania
81 B6 Mbeya div. Tanzania
78 B3 Mbi r. C.A.R.
78 B4 Mbigou Gabon
78 A4 Mbilapé Gabon
78 B3 Mbinda Congo
78 A3 Mbinga Tanzania
78 A3 Mbini Equatorial Guinea
81 B6 Mbizi Mts mts Tanzania
78 C3 Mbomo Congo
78 C3 Mbomou r. C.A.R.
78 B3 Mbouda Cameroon
76 A3 Mbour Senegal
76 A3 Mbout Mauritania
78 C4 Mbrès C.A.R.
79 C5 Mbuji-Mayi Zaire
81 C5 Mbuyuni Tanzania
74 D4 Mcherrah reg. Algeria
81 C6 Mchinga Tanzania
81 B7 Mchinji Malawi
108 C3 McKinley, Mount mt. U.S.A.
81 B6 Mdandu Tanzania
81 B6 Mdantsane R.S.A.
75 F1 M'Daourouch Algeria

39 H8 Maumere Indon.
82 C2 Maun Botswana
50 D5 Mayan China
151 J7 Mayan Fr. Poly. Pac. Oc.
132 B1 Mayaguana I. The Bahamas
74 C3 Mchelta reg. Algeria
50 C1 Mchinga r. Can.
143 C4 Mayo r. Can.
47 G4 Maya-san mt. Japan
125 C6 Meade U.S.A.
110 F3 Meadow Lake Provincial Park res. Can.
129 F3 Meadow Valley Wash r. U.S.A.
120 C4 Meadville U.S.A.
114 E4 Meaford Can.
46 A2 Meaken-dake vol Japan
24 B2 Mealhada Portugal
113 J3 Mealy Mountains mt. ra. Can.
142 C5 Mearim r. Brazil
79 B5 Mebridege r. Angola
114 C2 Mechanic Falls U.S.A.
120 D4 Mechanicsburg U.S.A.
122 E5 Mechanicsville U.S.A.
18 B3 Mechelen Belgium
75 D2 Mecheria Algeria
29 H4 Mechmèra Turkey
60 C1 Mecidiye Turkey
18 E1 Mecklenburger Bucht b. Germany
18 E1 Mecklenburg-Vorpommern div. Germany
83 F1 Meconta Mozambique
81 C7 Mecubúri Mozambique
81 C7 Mecubúri r. Mozambique
81 C7 Mecula Mozambique
56 A4 Meda r. Aust.
24 B2 Meda Portugal
56 A2 Medak India
54 C5 Medan Indon.
40 A1 Medang i. Indon.
147 C6 Médanos de Coro, Parque Nacional nat. park Venezuela
56 C4 Medawachchiya Sri Lanka
56 B2 Medchal India
121 K2 Meddybemps L. l. U.S.A.
126 E6 Medebal Indon.
138 B2 Medellín Colombia
74 D1 Medenine Tunisia
126 A3 Medford U.S.A.
122 C3 Medford Farms U.S.A.
28 G2 Medgidia Romania
28 D2 Mediaş Romania
126 F3 Medicine Bow U.S.A.
126 F3 Medicine Bow Peak summit U.S.A.
111 G4 Medicine Hat Can.
126 D3 Medicine Lodge U.S.A.
144 A2 Medina Brazil
28 E1 Mediaş Romania
126 F3 Medicine Bow Peak summit U.S.A.
60 D5 Medina Saudi Arabia
120 D3 Medina U.S.A.
24 D2 Medina del Campo Spain
24 D1 Medina de Pomar Spain
76 A4 Médina Gounas Senegal
76 A4 Médina Sabach Senegal
24 D2 Medina-Sidonia Spain

81 ⁻4 Medine Mauritius
55 F5 Médiclim India
22 D4 Mediterranean Sea sea
27 A7 Medjerda, Monts de la mts Algeria
64 E2 Mednogorsk Rus. Fed.
14 B1 Mednoye Rus. Fed.
150 G2 Medny, Ostrov i. Rus. Fed.
20 D4 Médoc reg. France
78 B3 Médouneu Gabon
28 C3 Medveđa Yugo.
14 H1 Medvedevo Rus. Fed.
14 C1 Medveditsa r. Tver' Rus. Fed.
13 H5 Medveditsa r. Volgograd Rus. Fed.
14 G3 Medvedok Rus. Fed.
26 E3 Medvednica mts Croatia
15 G1 Medvezh'i, O−va is
63 S2 Medvezh'i, O−va is Rus. Fed.
12 E2 Medvezh'yegorsk Rus. Fed.
17 H6 Medway r. U.K.
94 ⁻2 Medwin Pt pt Christmas I. Indian Ocean
14 H2 Medyana Rus. Fed.
19 L4 Medyka Poland
14 G2 Medyn' Rus. Fed.
29 D6 Medzhybizh Ukraine
101 A5 Meeberrie Aust.
101 B5 Meekatharra Aust.
129 H1 Meeker U.S.A.
128 B2 Meeks Bay U.S.A.
21 J4 Meelpaeg Res. resr Can.
54 D3 Meerut India
126 E2 Meeteetse U.S.A.
80 C4 Mēga Ethiopia
80 C4 Mega Escarpment escarpment Ethiopia/Kenya
29 D4 Megali Panagia Greece
80 D3 Megalo Ethiopia
29 D6 Megalopoli Greece
29 C5 Meganisi i. Greece
29 D5 Megara Greece
28 B2 Meget Rus. Fed.
54 S4 Meghalaya India
55 F5 Meghāsani mt. India
61 C3 Megiddo Israel
10 G1 Mehamn Norway
54 A4 Mehar Pakistan
54 D5 Mehekar India
55 G5 Meherpur Bangladesh
120 E6 Meherrin r. U.S.A.
91 ⁻10 Mehetia i. Fr. Poly. Pac. Oc.
42 A2 Mehndawal India
60 F2 Mehrābān Iran
57 C4 Mehrān r. Iran
60 F3 Mehrān Iran
57 C3 Mehriz Iran
57 G2 Mehtar Lām Afghanistan
20 F3 Mehun-sur-Yèvre France
51 F3 Mei r. China
144 D3 Meia Ponte r. Brazil
78 B2 Meiganga Cameroon
109 J2 Meighen I. i. Can.
72 C2 Meigu China
42 A2 Meiktila Myanmar
21 J3 Meilen Switz.
18 E3 Meiningen Germany
24 C1 Meira Spain
21 J3 Meiringen Switz.
72 D2 Meishan China
18 F3 Meißen Germany
50 E3 Meitan China
49 J3 Meixi China
50 D1 Mei Xian China
51 G3 Meizhou China
74 C4 Mejauyi well Mauritania
146 C2 Mejicana mt. Arg.
140 B4 Mejillones Chile
140 B4 Mejillones del Sur, B. de b. Chile
73 G4 Mekadio well Sudan
78 B3 Mékambo Gabon
80 C2 Mek'elē Ethiopia
76 A3 Mékhé Senegal
54 B3 Mekhtar Pakistan
74 C2 Meknès Morocco
43 D5 Mekong, Mouths of the river mouth Vietnam
43 C7 Melaka div. Malaysia
43 C7 Melaka Malaysia
40 A2 Melalo, Tg pt Indon.
150 F6 Melanesia is Pac. Oc.
40 C2 Melawi r. Indon.
97 F4 Melbourne Aust.
119 D6 Melbourne U.S.A.
131 H5 Melchor de Mencos Guatemala
147 B6 Melchor, I. i. Chile
18 D1 Meldorf Germany
114 D4 Meldrum Bay Can.
41 ⁻1 Melekeiok Palau
14 E1 Melekhovo Rus. Fed.
14 E2 Melenki Rus. Fed.
64 E2 Meleuz Rus. Fed.
113 F2 Mélèzes, Rivière aux r. Can.
78 B1 Melfi Chad
27 E5 Melfi Italy
111 J4 Melfort Can.
142 E1 Melgaço Brazil
24 D1 Melgar de Fernamental Spain
10 C3 Melhus Norway
40 B2 Meliau Indon.
24 C1 Melide Spain
29 C6 Meligalas Greece
90 ⁻6 Melilla, Ilha do i. Brazil
75 D1 Melilla Spain
27 E7 Melilli Italy
147 B5 Melimoyu, Mte mt. Chile
93 B6 Melina, Mt mt. N.Z.
40 C2 Melintang, D. l. Indon.
15 F2 Melioratyvne Ukraine
146 B3 Melipilla Chile
111 J5 Melita Can.
27 E7 Melito di Porto Salvo Italy
15 D2 Melitopol' Ukraine
19 G4 Melk Austria
80 C4 Melka Guba Ethiopia
65 H3 Melkosopochnik reg. Kazak.
10 G2 Mellakoski Finland
10 E3 Mellansel Sweden
18 D2 Melle Germany
122 B2 Mellen U.S.A.
11 D4 Mellerud Sweden
147 B6 Mellizo Sur, C. mt. Chile
76 B3 Mellit Sudan
146 F3 Melo Uruguay
87 C7 Meloco Mozambique
12 H1 Melogorskoye Rus. Fed.
80 E3 Melolo Indon.
18 D3 Melsungen Germany
10 G2 Meltaus Finland
17 G5 Melton Mowbray U.K.
22 D4 Mel'tsany Rus. Fed.
40 B1 Meluan Indon.
40 C2 Melucco Mozambique
73 G5 Melut Sudan
111 J4 Melville Can.
98 D2 Melville B. b. Aust.
109 M2 Melville Bugt b. Greenland
99 F3 Melville, C. c. Aust.
40 D1 Melville, C. c. Phil.
98 B1 Melville I. i. Aust.
98 B1 Melville I. i. Abor. Land res. Aust.
108 G2 Melville Island i. Can.
113 J3 Melville, Lake l. Can.

109 K3 Melville Peninsula pen. Can.
17 C4 Melvin, Lough l. Rep. of Ire.
11 G5 Melyuveyem Rus. Fed.
63 T3 Melyuveyem Rus. Fed.
29 B4 Memaliaj Albania
55 E2 Mêmar Co salt l. China
83 G1 Memba Mozambique
83 G1 Memba, Baía de b. Mozambique
39 L7 Memberamo r. Indon.
40 D4 Memboro Indon.
18 E5 Memmingen Germany
40 B1 Mempawah Indon.
122 C3 Memphis div. U.S.A.
122 D5 Memphis U.S.A.
124 C3 Memphis U.S.A.
119 D6 Memphis U.S.A.
119 D6 Memphis U.S.A.
97 G2 Memphrémagog, Lac l.
115 J4 Memphrémagog, Lac l. Can.
46 J2 Memuro-dake mt. Japan
15 E1 Mena Ukraine
125 E5 Mena U.S.A.
83 G3 Menabe reg. Madagascar
77 E3 Ménaka Mali
42 C3 Nam Khong r. Asia
83 G4 Menarandra r. Madagascar
125 D6 Menard U.S.A.
122 C4 Menasha U.S.A.
40 A2 Mendanau i. Indon.
145 G3 Mendanha Brazil
40 A1 Mendarik i. Indon.
40 C2 Mendawai r. Indon.
21 H4 Mende France
80 C3 Mendebo Mountains mt. ra. Ethiopia
110 C3 Mendenhall Glacier gl. U.S.A.
29 F5 Menderes r. Turkey
131 F3 Méndez Mexico
10 G3 Mendi P.N.G.
17 F6 Mendip Hills h. U.K.
128 A2 Mendocino U.S.A.
126 A3 Mendocino, C. c. U.S.A.
151 K3 Mendocino Seascape Pac. Oc.
122 E4 Mendon U.S.A.
128 B3 Mendota U.S.A.
122 C5 Mendota U.S.A.
122 C4 Mendota, Lake l. U.S.A.
146 C3 Mendoza div. Arg.
146 C3 Mendoza Arg.
138 C1 Mene de Mauroa Venezuela
147 D5 Mene Grande Venezuela
60 A2 Menemen Turkey
27 D7 Menfi Italy
78 B2 Meng r. Cameroon
51 G1 Mengcheng China
72 D4 Mengen Turkey
40 A3 Menggala Indon.
97 E3 Menghai China
113 G3 Mengjin China
80 C2 Mengkatip Indon.
20 F2 Mengkia, G. mt. Indon.
122 C3 Mengkofu Indon.
122 D3 Mengla China
122 B3 Menglian China
78 B3 Mengyin China
25 H2 Mengzi China
25 H2 Menihek Can.
38 C7 Menihek Lakes lakes Can.
40 C2 Menindee Aust.
43 C7 Menindee L. l. Aust.
129 H4 Meningie Aust.
109 L3 Menkere Rus. Fed.
21 H5 Menna r. Ethiopia
120 C4 Mennecy France
40 B1 Menominee U.S.A.
14 D2 Menominee Falls U.S.A.
40 E1 Menomonie U.S.A.
40 C2 Menongue Angola
48 B5 Menorca i. Islas Baleares Spain
48 D2 Mensalong Indon.
75 F1 Mentawai, Kepulauan is Indon.
27 C6 Mentaya r. Indon.
101 C6 Mentekab Malaysia
152 D4 Mentiras mt. Spain
75 F2 Mentmore U.S.A.
81 B7 Mentoka Incognita Pen. pen. Can.
18 C2 Menton France
18 D2 Mentor U.S.A.
81 C7 Menukung Indon.
26 E3 Menya r. Rus. Fed.
25 G2 Menyapa, G. mt. Indon.
12 S3 Menyuan China
40 D1 Menza r. Rus. Fed.
10 D3 Menza r. Rus. Fed.
56 B4 Menzel Bourguiba Tunisia
12 C2 Menzel Temime Tunisia
39 M8 Menzies Aust.
97 E3 Menzies, Mt mt. Ant.
25 J3 Menzel Chaker Tunisia
83 D4 Meponda Mozambique
146 C3 Meppel Netherlands
142 C2 Meppen Germany
146 E3 Meqlieng Slovenia
146 E3 Mequinenza, Embalse de resr Spain
146 D2 Mera r. Rus. Fed.
146 E3 Merah Indon.
125 D7 Meråker Norway
120 A4 Meram Turkey
122 B2 Merano Italy
35 Merauke Indon.
61 C1 Merbein Aust.
65 J3 Mercadal Spain
92 E4 Mercaderes Col.
109 M3 Mercedario, Co mt. Arg.
17 F5 Mexiana, Ilha i. Brazil
147 D7 Mercedes San Luis Arg.
125 C5 Mercedes Arg.
125 C5 Mercedes Arg.

41 ⁻2 Merizo Guam Pac. Oc.
65 H4 Merke Kazak.
125 C5 Merkel U.S.A.
11 G5 Merkys r. Lithuania
43 Merlimau, P. i. Singapore
15 F1 Merlo r. Ukraine
99 E2 Merluna Aust.
100 B3 Mermaid Reef reef Aust.
28 C3 Merošina Yugo.
73 H4 Merowe Sudan
101 B6 Merredin Aust.
17 F4 Merrick h. U.K.
114 E3 Merrickville Can.
122 C3 Merrill U.S.A.
122 C5 Merrillville U.S.A.
124 C3 Merriman U.S.A.
57 E4 Merrimack r. U.S.A.
119 D6 Merritt Island U.S.A.
97 G2 Merrygoen Aust.
80 D2 Mersa Fatma Eritrea
18 C4 Mersch Luxembourg
18 E3 Merseburg Germany
17 F5 Mersey est. U.K.
54 C4 Mersrags Latvia
17 F5 Merta India
81 C4 Merti Kenya
152 B6 Mertz Gl. gl. Ant.
20 F2 Méru France
81 C4 Meru Kenya
81 C4 Meru crater Tanzania
57 E3 Merui Pakistan
43 C6 Merutai Malaysia
60 C1 Merzifon Turkey
18 E4 Merzig Germany
99 F3 Merz Pen. pen. Ant.
25 F2 Mesa r. Spain
128 D5 Mesa U.S.A.
122 A2 Mesabi Range h. U.S.A.
138 D2 Mesa de Iguaje h. Colombia
127 D6 Mesa de S. Carlos h. Mexico
138 C3 Mesa de Yambi h. Colombia
27 E6 Mesagne Italy
40 A1 Mesanak i. Indon.
129 H3 Mesa Verde Nat. Park U.S.A.
18 D3 Mesa Volcánica de Somuncurá plat. Arg.
18 D3 Meschede Germany
10 E2 Mesefinto Sweden
139 E2 Meseta del Co Jáua plat. Venezuela
147 C5 Meseta de Montemayor plat. Arg.
80 C2 Mesfinto Ethiopia
122 D2 Mesgouez L. l. Can.
122 D5 Meshcherskaya Nizmennost' lowland Rus. Fed.
124 A4 Meshchovsk Rus. Fed.
114 C3 Meshchura Rus. Fed.
114 C3 Meshkan Iran
114 C3 Meshra'er Req Sudan
131 E5 Mesihovina Bos.-Herz.
28 F3 Mesimeri Greece
14 E5 Meski Morocco
14 C5 Mesolongi Greece
78 C3 Mesopotamia reg. Iraq
122 C2 Mesquita Brazil
150 E5 Mesquite U.S.A.
86 G4 Mesquite U.S.A.
57 D1 Mesquite Lake l. U.S.A.
148 G4 Messaad Algeria
18 A3 Messalo r. Mozambique
85 D5 Messina Italy
85 G5 Messina R.S.A.
11 C5 Messina, Stretta di str. Italy
18 B3 Messini Italy
43 Messiniakos Kolpos b. Greece
128 C1 Mesta r. Bulgaria
148 C5 Mesters Vig Greenland
112 B4 Mestre Italy
121 E4 Mesuji r. Indon.
114 E5 Meta r. Colombia/Venezuela
121 F3 Metaline Falls U.S.A.
99 E3 Métabetchouan Can.
42 A1 Metagama Can.
93 C6 Metairie U.S.A.
120 D6 Metallifere, Colline mts Italy
17 G4 Metán Arg.
124 E3 Metangai Indon.
17 H4 Metangula Mozambique
128 B1 Metarica Mozambique
121 F5 Metema Ethiopia
121 G4 Meteor depth Atlantic Ocean
120 A5 Methoni Greece
120 E5 Methuen U.S.A.
93 B6 Metković Croatia
74 B2 Metlakatla U.S.A.
80 D3 Metlaoui Tunisia
80 D1 Metlika Slovenia
149 K4 Metoro Mozambique
149 K6 Metro Indon.
20 E4 Metropolis U.S.A.
115 F3 Mettawee r. U.S.A.
120 E4 Mettler U.S.A.
125 C6 Mettu India
83 D2 Metundo, Ilha i. Mozambique

14 A3 Mglin Rus. Fed.
83 E2 Mhangura Zimbabwe
54 D4 Mhasvad India
83 E4 Mhlume Swaziland
54 D5 Mhow India
49 F5 Mi r. China
42 A2 Mi r. Myanmar
131 H5 Miahuatlán Mexico
24 E2 Miajadas Spain
129 G5 Miami U.S.A.
119 D7 Miami U.S.A.
125 E4 Miami U.S.A.
119 D7 Miami Beach U.S.A.
57 B3 Miān Āb Iran
50 D1 Miānābād Iran
57 E4 Mianaz Pakistan
48 A6 Miancaowan China
51 E1 Mianchi China
57 D1 Mīāndarreh Iran
57 D1 Mīāndasht Iran
60 E2 Miāndowāb Iran
83 H2 Miandrivazo Madagascar
60 E2 Mīāneh Iran
54 A4 Miani Hor b. Pakistan
57 D1 Mianjoi Afghanistan
54 B2 Mian Kalai Pakistan
72 B2 Mianmian Shan mt. ra. China
50 C2 Mianning China
54 B2 Mianwali Pakistan
50 D1 Mian Xian China
50 C2 Mianyang China
50 D2 Mianyang China
50 D2 Mianzhu China
49 G5 Miao Dao i. China
49 G5 Miaodao Qundao is China
65 K3 Miao'ergou China
29 B4 Miaoli Taiwan
83 H2 Miarinarivo Antananarivo Madagascar
83 H2 Miarinarivo Toamasina Madagascar
19 H1 Miastko Poland
129 G5 Mica Mt mt. U.S.A.
50 C2 Micang Shan mt. China
12 J1 Michaichmon' Rus. Fed.
19 J4 Michalovce Slovakia
111 H3 Michel Can.
122 C2 Michigamme Lake l. U.S.A.
122 C2 Michigamme Reservoir resr U.S.A.
122 D3 Michigan div. U.S.A.
122 D5 Michigan City U.S.A.
122 D4 Michigan, Lake l. U.S.A.
114 C3 Michipicoten Bay b. Can.
114 C3 Michipicoten I. i. Can.
114 C3 Michipicoten River Can.
131 E5 Michoacán div. Mexico
28 F3 Michurin Bulgaria
14 E5 Michurinsk Rus. Fed.
14 C5 Mici Moldova
78 C3 Micomeseng Equatorial Guinea
150 E5 Micronesia is Pac. Oc.
86 G4 Micronesia, Federated States of country Pac. Oc.
57 D1 Midai i. Indon.
148 G4 Mid-Atlantic Ridge Atlantic Ocean
18 A3 Middelburg Netherlands
85 D5 Middelburg R.S.A.
85 G5 Middelburg R.S.A.
11 C5 Middelfart Denmark
18 B3 Middelharnis Netherlands
18 B3 Middelharnis Netherlands
21 ⁻2 Millau The Bahamas
121 F4 Mill Creek r. U.S.A.
48 B5 Millwood, Lake l. U.S.A.
128 C1 Middle Alkali Lake l. U.S.A.
148 C5 Middle America Trench Pac. Oc.
112 B4 Middle Andaman i. Andaman and Nicobar Is India
121 E4 Middleboro U.S.A.
8 D5 Middleburg R.S.A.
15 H2 Middleburg U.S.A.
121 E4 Middleburgh U.S.A.
99 E3 Middle Cr. r. Aust.
42 A1 Middle I. i. Tristan da Cunha Atlantic Ocean
93 C6 Middlemarch N.Z.
120 D6 Middlesboro U.S.A.
17 G4 Middlesbrough U.K.
124 E3 Middlesex Belize
17 H4 Middleton Aust.
128 B1 Middleton Aust.
121 F5 Middletown U.S.A.
121 G4 Middletown U.S.A.
120 A5 Middletown U.S.A.
120 E5 Middleville U.S.A.
93 B6 Mid Dome mt. N.Z.
74 B2 Midelt Morocco
80 D3 Midhisho well Somalia
80 D1 Midi Yemen
149 K4 Mid-Indian Basin Indian Ocean
149 K6 Mid-Indian Ridge Indian Ocean
20 E4 Midi-Pyrénées div. France
115 F3 Midland Can.
120 E4 Midland U.S.A.
125 C6 Midland U.S.A.
83 D2 Midlands div. Zimbabwe
83 H3 Midongy Atsimo Madagascar
46 C7 Midori r. Japan
74 C3 Midouze r. France
150 H4 Mid-Pacific Mountains Pac. Oc.
50 C3 Midu China
16 C1 Miðvágur Faeroes
122 A3 Midway Islands is U.S.A.
119 B5 Midwest U.S.A.
125 D6 Midwest City U.S.A.
28 D3 Đurđ, Mt mt. Bulgaria/Yugo.
74 B2 Mie div. Japan
46 F6 Mie div. Japan
19 J2 Miechów Poland
17 H5 Mildenhall U.K.
18 J3 Międzychód Poland
19 K2 Międzylesie Poland
19 K2 Międzyrzec Podlaski Poland
11 G5 Międzyrzecz Poland
10 F3 Miehikkälä Finland
10 G2 Miekojärvi l. Finland
81 D5 Mielec Poland
146 A5 Miena Aust.
57 H3 Mien-hua Hsü i. Taiwan
11 E4 Meynypil'gyno Rus. Fed.
28 E1 Miercurea-Ciuc Romania
24 D1 Mieres Spain
61 D4 Miéso Ethiopia

47 F6 Mikawa-wan b. Japan
12 F4 Mikhaylov Rus. Fed.
28 D3 Mikhaylovgrad div. Bulgaria
152 D5 Mikhaylov I. i. Ant.
65 H4 Mikhaylovka Kazak.
65 J2 Mikhaylovka Rus. Fed.
14 B2 Mikhaylovka Rus. Fed.
13 G5 Mikhaylovka Rus. Fed.
48 D2 Mikhaylovka Rus. Fed.
28 D3 Mikhaylovo Bulgaria
64 E1 Mikhaylovsk Rus. Fed.
65 J2 Mikhaylovskiy Rus. Fed.
14 G1 Mikhaylovskoye Rus. Fed.
14 C2 Miki Japan
46 E6 Miki Japan
47 H6 Miki Japan
11 G3 Mikkeli div. Finland
11 G3 Mikkeli Finland
11 G3 Mikkelin mlk Finland
110 G3 Mikkwa r. Can.
16 D1 Mikladalur Faeroes
14 J2 Mikulov Czech Rep.
81 C6 Mikumi Tanzania
81 C6 Mikumi National Park nat. park Tanzania
12 H2 Mikun' Rus. Fed.
47 G5 Mikuni-sammyaku mt. Japan
75 F1 Mikura-jima i. Japan
124 E2 Mila Algeria
53 D9 Milaca U.S.A.
142 E2 Miladhunmadulu Atoll atoll Maldives
119 B5 Milagres Brazil
81 B7 Milan U.S.A.
81 B7 Milando, Reserva Especial do res. Angola
96 D3 Milang Aust.
83 H2 Milange Mozambique
26 B3 Milan Italy
81 B7 Milanoa Madagascar
60 A2 Milas Turkey
27 E6 Milazzo Italy
124 D2 Milbank U.S.A.
115 H2 Milbridge U.S.A.
97 G5 Mildura Aust.
99 F6 Mile China
19 L2 Mile Gully Jamaica
133 ⁻1 Mileiz, W. el w Egypt
99 G5 Miles Aust.
80 D2 Miles City U.S.A.

41 C5 Mindanao i. Phil.
42 A2 Mindat Sakan Myanmar
76 ⁻ Mindelheim Germany
152 D5 Mindelo Cape Verde
65 H5 Min Wali Jammu and Kashmir
64 F5 Miryang S. Korea
55 E4 Mirzachirla Turkmenistan
57 B3 Mirzapur India
65 H4 Misaki Japan
47 H6 Misaki Japan
55 H1 Misalay China
99 F4 Misato Japan
46 H3 Misawa Japan
147 D5 Misery, Mt mt. St. Kitts-Nevis Caribbean
14 B2 Misgar Pakistan
43 A6 Misha Andaman and Nicobar Is India
78 D3 Mishash al Hādī well Saudi Arabia
122 D5 Mishawaka U.S.A.
47 F5 Misheronskiy Rus. Fed.
51 D1 Mishicot U.S.A.
75 F1 Mishmi Hills mt. ra. India
90 ⁻11 Misima I. i. P.N.G.
146 F2 Misiones div. Arg.
147 D3 Misiones, Sa de h. Arg.
61 C1 Misión Fagnano Arg.
43 A6 Misis Dağ h. Turkey
74 D2 Miskah Saudi Arabia
19 K4 Miskolc Hungary
81 C7 Mismā, Jibāl al mt. ra. Saudi Arabia
39 J7 Misoöl i. Indon.
18 A3 Misrātah Libya
72 C1 Mişrātah Libya
80 B2 Missanabie Can.
114 C3 Missinaibi r. Can.
114 C3 Missinaibi Lake l. Can.
111 J3 Missinipe Can.
113 H3 Mission Can.
110 F5 Mission City Can.
112 D3 Mississagi r. Can.
114 D3 Mississauga Can.
122 D4 Mississinewa Lake l. U.S.A.
122 C5 Mississippi r. Can.
125 F6 Mississippi div. U.S.A.
119 C5 Mississippi r. U.S.A.
125 F6 Mississippi Delta delta U.S.A.
126 D2 Missoula U.S.A.
124 E4 Missouri div. U.S.A.
124 E4 Missouri r. U.S.A.
122 A3 Missouri Valley U.S.A.
113 H2 Mistassibi r. Can.
113 H2 Mistassini Can.
113 H2 Mistassini, L. l. Can.
113 H3 Mistastin L. l. Can.
19 H4 Mistelbach Austria
132 B3 Misteriosa Bank sand bank Caribbean Sea
110 D3 Misty Fjords National Monument res. U.S.A.
78 B2 Mitanga Cameroon
54 C1 Mitha Tiwana Pakistan
54 B3 Mithi Pakistan
54 B4 Mitkof I. i. U.S.A.
61 C1 Mitla Pass pass Egypt
59 M4 Mitole Tanzania
46 D5 Mito Japan
47 H5 Mitre mt. N.Z.
92 E4 Mitsamiouli Comoros
81 C5 Mitsamiouli Comoros
92 E4 Mitsinjo Madagascar
54 D1 Mittagong Aust.
54 B4 Mitterteich Germany
18 F4 Mittweida Germany
138 C3 Mitú Colombia
138 C4 Mitumba, Chaîne des mt. ra. Zaire
81 B7 Mitumba, Monts mt. ra. Zaire
78 B2 Mitwaba Zaire
81 C4 Mityana Uganda
59 M3 Mitzic Gabon
138 C3 Miura Japan
46 H3 Miyagawa r. Japan
47 H5 Miyagi div. Japan
60 D3 Miyah, Wādī el w Syria
46 H3 Miyah, W. al w Saudi Arabia
14 A2 Miyake-jima i. Japan
47 H4 Miyako Japan
47 H4 Miyakonojō Japan
59 M4 Miyazaki div. Japan
81 D5 Miyazaki Japan
79 E6 Miyazu Japan
79 F6 Miyi China
60 D3 Miyoshi Japan
54 D3 Miyun China
28 F3 Miyun Shuiku resr China
57 D3 Mizdah Libya
17 B6 Mizen Hd hd Rep. of Ire.
15 B1 Mizhhir"ya Ukraine
28 E2 Mizil Romania
79 E5 Miziya Bulgaria
55 H4 Mizoram div. India
142 D2 Mizpe Ramon Israel
146 E2 Mizushima Japan
63 O3 Mizusawa Japan
81 D5 Mjällby Sweden
10 E3 Mjölby Sweden
90 H2 Mjøsa l. Norway
92 D4 Mkata Tanzania
92 E4 Mkokotoni Tanzania
81 C5 Mkomazi Game Reserve res. Tanzania
92 D4 Mkushi Zambia
79 E6 Mladá Boleslav Czech Rep.
28 C2 Mladenovac Yugo.
19 K2 Mława Poland

28 C2 Mlava r. Yugo.
19 K2 Mława Poland
26 F4 Mljet i. Croatia
26 F4 Mljetski Kanal chan. Croatia
82 D3 Mlungisi R.S.A.
15 C2 Mlyniv Ukraine
82 D4 Mmabatho R.S.A.
82 D3 Mmadinare Botswana
28 B3 Mmamabula mts Yugo.
14 A1 Mo r. Norway
79 H1 Mo r. Aust.
79 H6 Moa i. Indon.
78 B4 Moa i. Aust.
95 H1 Moa i. Fiji
57 C2 Mo'alla Iran
14 H3 Moama r. Rus. Fed.
14 G3 Moamba Gabon
79 F5 Moamba Mozambique
78 E6 Moanda Gabon
13 H5 Moanda r. Rus. Fed.
14 G3 Mobara Japan
78 D3 Mobaye C.A.R.
78 D3 Mobayi-Mbongo Zaire
122 A6 Moberly U.S.A.
119 B6 Mobile U.S.A.
119 B6 Mobile Bay b. U.S.A.
124 C2 Mobridge U.S.A.
141 C3 Moçambique Moçambique
42 B2 Môc Châu Vietnam
44 A2 Moce i. Fiji
139 E1 Mochirma, Parque Nacional nat. park Venezuela
82 D3 Mochudi Botswana
81 D7 Mocimboa da Praia Mozambique
81 D7 Mocímboa do Rovuma Mozambique
130 C6 Mocorito Colombia
130 D2 Moctezuma Chihuahua Mexico
131 E4 Moctezuma San Luis Potosí Mexico
130 C2 Moctezuma Sonora Mexico
83 F2 Mocuba Mozambique
21 H4 Modane France
54 C5 Modasa India
82 D4 Modder r. R.S.A.
26 C3 Modena Italy
128 D3 Modesto U.S.A.
27 E7 Modica Italy
19 H4 Mödling Austria
82 B3 Modung China
92 F4 Moe Aust.
128 C3 Moehau h. N.Z.
14 A1 Moelv Norway
10 C3 Moen Norway
17 E3 Moffat U.K.
54 A1 Moga India
19 J6 Mogadishu Somalia
28 D3 Mogador Morocco
79 H4 Mogami-gawa r. Japan
80 C1 Mogaung Myanmar
92 E2 Moggerah N.Z.
83 F2 Mogincual Mozambique
125 J2 Mogi das Cruzes Brazil
144 D3 Mogi-Guaçu r. Brazil
128 E4 Mogilev see Mahilyow
81 C4 Mogi-Mirim Brazil
143 C5 Mogincual Mozambique
82 D4 Mogincual Mozambique
129 H5 Mogocha Rus. Fed.
142 A2 Mogoditshane Botswana
12 K4 Mogojtuj Rus. Fed.
55 H3 Mogok Myanmar
129 H5 Mogollon Mts mts U.S.A.
129 G4 Mogollon Baldy mt. U.S.A.
74 B3 Mogollon Rim plat. U.S.A.
82 D3 Mogotoev, L. l. Rus. Fed.
10 E3 Moguer Spain
82 D4 Mogwase R.S.A.
24 B2 Mohács Hungary
79 G5 Mohali's Hoek Lesotho
61 C2 Mohammad Iran
75 G1 Mohammadia Algeria
121 J1 Mohawk r. U.S.A.
129 H5 Mohawk Mts mts U.S.A.
46 A2 Mohe China
91 ⁻14 Mohéli i. Comoros
81 B6 Mohon Peak summit U.S.A.
79 E6 Mohoro Tanzania
15 C1 Mohyliv Podil's'kyy Ukraine
10 A2 Moi Norway
28 E1 Moineşti Romania
10 F2 Mo i Rana Norway
72 D5 Mointy Kazak.
28 F1 Mogoşeşti-Siret Romania

82 D3 Mokobela Pan salt pan Botswana
92 E1 Mokohinau Is is N.Z.
55 H4 Mokokchung India
78 B1 Mokolo Cameroon
28 C3 Mokra Gora mts Yugo.
15 D2 Mokra Kalyhirka Ukraine
28 B3 Mokrous r. Rus. Fed.
13 H5 Mokrous r. Rus. Fed.
14 G3 Mokroye r. Rus. Fed.
14 F3 Mokry Karay r. Rus. Fed.
127 ⁻1 Mokuauia I. i. U.S.A.
127 ⁻1 Mokuola I. i. U.S.A.
85 F5 Møksy Finland
131 ⁻4 Molango Mexico
102 ⁻2 Molaoi Greece
26 D3 Molat i. Croatia
10 D2 Molde Norway
10 D2 Moldjord Norway
5 H4 Moldova country Europe
28 C2 Moldova Nouă Romania
22 F4 Moldovei Centrale, Podişul reg. Moldova
42 A3 Mole Chuang r. Myanmar
76 D3 Mole National Park nat. park Ghana
82 D3 Molepolole Botswana
11 G5 Moletai Lithuania
27 F5 Molfetta Italy
25 F2 Molina de Aragón Spain
25 F3 Molina de Segura Spain
122 B5 Moline U.S.A.
79 E6 Molise div. Italy
10 G3 Molkom Sweden
140 B3 Mollendo Peru
101 B6 Mollerin, L. salt flat Aust.
18 E2 Mölln Germany
11 D4 Mölnlycke Sweden
15 D2 Molochans'k Ukraine
15 E3 Molochne Ukraine
10 J1 Molochnyy Rus. Fed.
15 C2 Molochnyy Lyman est. Ukraine
19 H2 Molodechno see Maladzyechna
152 D4 Molodëzhnaya Rus. Fed. Base Ant.
97 H4 Moe Aust.
14 A1 Molodoy Tud Rus. Fed.
127 ⁻2 Molokai i. U.S.A.
151 K4 Molokai Fracture Zone Pac. Oc.
12 J3 Moloma r. Rus. Fed.
97 G3 Molong Aust.
85 G3 Molopo r. Botswana/R.S.A.
145 H4 Moloporivier Brazil
81 B4 Moloundou Cameroon
18 C2 Moloundou Cameroon
113 J2 Molson L. l. Can.
85 G4 Molteno R.S.A.
39 J6 Moluccas is Indon.
39 H7 Molucca Sea sea Indon.
87 D5 Moma Mozambique
122 D2 Momba r. Tanzania
145 H4 Mombaça Brazil
81 C5 Mombasa Kenya
80 C4 Mombo Tanzania
28 E3 Momchilgrad Bulgaria
122 D5 Momi Zaire
81 D5 Mompono Zaire
78 D3 Mompós Colombia
11 C5 Møn i. Denmark
42 A2 Mon Myanmar
133 ⁻1 Mona Jamaica
17 D4 Monaghan Rep. of Ire.
125 C6 Monahans U.S.A.
133 E3 Monapo Mozambique
137 E4 Monapo Mozambique
133 ⁻1 Mona Passage chan. Dominican Rep.
87 E5 Monapo Mozambique
17 D4 Monaragala Sri Lanka
17 D4 Monarch Mt. mt. Can.
110 F4 Monarch Pass pass U.S.A.
17 D4 Monashee Mts mts Can.
17 B5 Monastir Tunisia
15 D2 Monastyrshche Ukraine
15 C2 Monastyrys'ka Ukraine
21 H4 Monasterio mt. Cameroon
46 J2 Monbetsu Japan
26 B3 Moncalieri Italy
24 B3 Monchique Portugal
122 D4 Moncks Corner U.S.A.
131 E3 Monclova Mexico
114 C3 Moncton Can.
24 C2 Mondego, Cabo pt Portugal
24 C2 Mondego r. Portugal
78 C4 Mondjamboli Zaire
78 B3 Mondjoku Zaire
78 C4 Mondombe Zaire
78 C3 Mondoñedo Spain
78 C4 Mondoro Zimbabwe
21 H4 Mondorf r. Can.
26 B3 Mondoví Italy
78 C4 Mondragone Italy
133 C5 Mondragone Italy
82 B1 Monduli Tanzania
147 D5 Mondy Rus. Fed.
29 B4 Monemvasia Greece
81 C5 Moneron, Ostrov i. Rus. Fed.
120 D4 Monessen U.S.A.
24 D2 Monesterio Spain
27 E5 Monestier-de-Clermont France
27 B4 Monfalcone Italy
24 C1 Monforte Portugal
78 D3 Monga Zaire
82 B3 Mongala r. Zaire
145 H4 Mongaguá Brazil
81 B7 Mongandjo Zaire
40 E4 Mongar Bhutan
122 C2 Mongers Lake salt flat Aust.
122 C2 Monggon Qulu China
101 B6 Mongo Chad
78 B1 Mongo Chad
42 A2 Mongol Myanmar
42 A2 Mongol Myanmar
72 C3 Mongo Chad

Column 1

33 L5 Mongolia country Asia
78 B3 Mongomo Equatorial Guinea
77 G4 Mongonu Nigeria
54 C2 Mongora Pakistan
72 D5 Mongororo Chad
78 C3 Mongoumba C.A.R.
42 B2 Mong Pan Myanmar
42 B2 Mong Pat Myanmar
42 B2 Mong Pu Myanmar
42 B2 Mong Pu-awn Myanmar
42 B2 Mong Ton Myanmar
79 D7 Mongu Zambia
42 C2 Mong Un Myanmar
42 B2 Mong Yang Myanmar
42 B2 Mong Yawng Myanmar
42 C2 Mong Yawng Myanmar
121 J3 Monhegan I. i. U.S.A.
21 G4 Monistrol-sur-Loire France
128 D2 Monitor Mt mt. U.S.A.
128 D2 Monitor Range mts U.S.A.
145 F3 Monjolos Brazil
83 F1 Monkey Bay Malawi
19 J2 Mońki Poland
98 E5 Monkira Aust.
78 D4 Monkoto Zaire
114 E5 Monkton Can.
122 B5 Monmouth U.S.A.
110 H4 Monmouth U.S.A.
17 E5 Monmouth U.K.
77 E5 Mono r. Benin/Togo
128 C3 Mono Lake l. U.S.A.
121 H4 Monomoy Pt pt U.S.A.
122 D5 Monon U.S.A.
122 B4 Monona U.S.A.
145 I4 Monopoli Italy
19 J5 Monor Hungary
125 C5 Monroe La. U.S.A.
133 ⁻³ Monos I. i. Trinidad Trin. and Tobago
72 D4 Monou Chad
25 F3 Monóvar Spain
25 F2 Monreal del Campo Spain
27 D6 Monreale Italy
125 E5 Monroe U.S.A.
123 F5 Monroe U.S.A.
119 D5 Monroe U.S.A.
121 F4 Monroe U.S.A.
129 F2 Monroe U.S.A.
122 C4 Monroe U.S.A.
122 B6 Monroe City U.S.A.
119 C6 Monroeville U.S.A.
76 B5 Monrovia Liberia
18 C3 Mons Belgium
26 C3 Monselice Italy
18 E3 Montabaur Germany
83 H1 Montagne d'Ambre, Parc National de la nat. park Madagascar
122 D4 Montague U.S.A.
101 B5 Montague Ra. h. Aust.
100 D2 Montague Sd b. Aust.
152 C1 Montagu I. i. S. Sandwich Is Atlantic Ocean
25 E3 Montalbán Spain
21 G4 Montalieu-Vercieu France
27 E6 Montalto mt. Italy
27 F6 Montalto Uffugo Italy
138 B4 Montalvo Ecuador
28 D3 Montana Bulgaria
126 E2 Montana div. U.S.A.
24 C2 Montánchez, Sierra de mt. ra. Spain
145 I4 Montanha Brazil
20 F3 Montargis France
20 E4 Montauban Midi-Pyrénées France
121 G4 Montauk U.S.A.
121 H4 Montauk Pt pt U.S.A.
21 G3 Montbard France
21 H3 Montbéliard France
25 G2 Montblanc Spain
21 G4 Mont Blanche Mauritius
21 G4 Montbrison France
21 G3 Montceau-les-Mines France
20 E4 Montcuq France
20 D5 Mont-de-Marsan France
20 F5 Montech France
140 D3 Monteagudo Bolivia
142 E1 Monte Alegre Brazil
142 D3 Monte Alegre de Goiás Brazil
144 D3 Monte Alegre de Minas Brazil
145 G4 Monte Aprazível Brazil
145 G4 Monte Azul Brazil
144 D4 Monte Azul Paulista Brazil
115 H4 Montebello Can.
100 A4 Montebello Is is Aust.
26 D3 Montebelluna Italy
146 F2 Montecarlo Arg.
21 H5 Monte Carlo Monaco
144 E3 Monte Carmelo Brazil
146 E3 Monte Caseros Arg.
26 C4 Montecatini Terme Italy
146 C5 Monte Comán Arg.
133 E3 Monte Cristi Dominican Rep.
138 A4 Montecristi Ecuador
27 C4 Montecristo, Isola di i. Italy
147 D7 Monte Dinero Arg.
26 D4 Montefiascone Italy
133 □¹ Montego Bay b. Jamaica
133 □¹ Montego Bay Jamaica
24 C2 Montehermoso Spain
98 B3 Monteith Aust.
21 G4 Montélimar France
146 E2 Monte Lindo r. Arg.
27 E5 Montella Italy
24 C2 Montellano Spain
122 C4 Montello U.S.A.
131 F3 Montemorelos Mexico
24 B3 Montemor-o-Novo Portugal
20 D4 Montendre France
143 B6 Montenegro Brazil
145 H2 Montenegro Mozambique
81 C7 Montepuez r. Mozambique
26 C4 Montepulciano Italy
146 D2 Monte Quemado Arg.
20 F2 Montereau-faut-Yonne France
128 B3 Monterey U.S.A.
120 D5 Monterey U.S.A.
128 B3 Monterey Bay b. U.S.A.
138 B2 Montería Colombia
140 D3 Montero Bolivia
141 D3 Monteros Arg.
27 C4 Montevarchi Italy
146 E4 Montevideo Uruguay
124 E2 Montevideo U.S.A.
127 D4 Monte Vista U.S.A.
122 A5 Montezuma U.S.A.
129 G4 Montezuma Castle National Monument res. U.S.A.
129 H3 Montezuma Creek U.S.A.
128 D3 Montezuma Peak summit U.S.A.
20 D2 Montfort-le-Gesnois France

Column 2

17 F5 Montgomery U.K.
119 C5 Montgomery U.S.A.
21 H3 Monthey Switz.
27 B5 Monti Italy
125 F5 Monticello U.S.A.
119 D6 Monticello U.S.A.
122 D5 Monticello U.S.A.
122 B4 Monticello U.S.A.
121 K1 Monticello U.S.A.
121 F4 Monticello U.S.A.
129 H3 Monticello U.S.A.
122 C4 Monticello U.S.A.
20 E4 Montignac France
24 C3 Montijo Spain
130 K8 Montijo, G. de b. Panama
24 D4 Montilla Spain
144 C2 Montividiu Brazil
20 E2 Montivilliers France
113 G4 Mont Joli Can.
115 H3 Mont-Laurier Can.
20 F3 Montlouis France
113 F4 Montmagny Can.
21 F2 Montmirail Champagne-Ardenne France
22 D5 Montmorency r. Can.
115 K3 Montmorency r. Can.
20 E3 Montmorillon France
99 G5 Monto Aust.
24 D3 Montoro Spain
76 C5 Mont Peko, Parc National du nat. park Côte d'Ivoire
133 □¹ Montpelier Jamaica
126 E3 Montpelier U.S.A.
122 C5 Montpelier U.S.A.
120 A4 Montpelier U.S.A.
121 G2 Montpelier U.S.A.
21 F5 Montpellier Hérault France
20 E4 Montpon-Ménestérol France
114 E3 Montréal r. Can.
114 D3 Montréal r. Can.
115 J4 Montréal Can.
114 C3 Montreal l. i. Can.
111 H4 Montreal L. l. Can.
111 H4 Montreal Lake Can.
121 F2 Montréal-Mirabel Can.
20 E1 Montreuil France
20 D3 Montreuil-Bellay France
21 H3 Montreux Switz.
20 E3 Montrichard France
20 E3 Montrose well R.S.A.
16 F3 Montrose U.K.
121 F4 Montrose U.S.A.
127 G4 Montrose U.S.A.
121 F4 Montrose U.S.A.
20 E3 Monts France
76 C5 Mont Sangbé, Parc National du nat. park Côte d'Ivoire
104 M8 Montserrat terr. Caribbean
139 G3 Montsinéry French Guiana
21 G3 Monts, Pte des pt Can.
20 E2 Mont-St-Aignan France
115 H3 Mont-Tremblant, Parc du res. Can.
92 □² Monument Harb. inlet Campbell I. N.Z.
129 G3 Monument Valley reg. U.S.A.
78 D3 Monveda Zaire
42 A2 Monywa Myanmar
26 B3 Monza Italy
79 E7 Monze Zambia
140 H1 Monzón Peru
25 G2 Monzón Spain
73 C5 Mookane Botswana
83 H3 Mookgopong R.S.A.
96 D2 Moolawatana Aust.
114 D2 Moonbeam Can.
97 G2 Moonbi Ra. mt. ra. Aust.
99 G5 Moonda L. salt flat Aust.
82 C4 Moonie r. Aust.
82 C4 Moonie Aust.
83 G3 Moorabel Madagascar
132 C2 Moorcroft Can.
126 F2 Moorcroft U.S.A.
120 D5 Moorefield U.S.A.
101 B6 Moore, Lake salt flat Aust.
119 E7 Moores I. i. The Bahamas
16 F4 Moorfoot Hills h. U.K.
80 B4 Moorhead U.S.A.
124 D2 Moorhead U.S.A.
97 A6 Mooroopna Aust.
112 D3 Moose r. Can.
114 D2 Moose Factory Can.
114 E5 Morpeth Can.
111 H4 Moose Jaw Can.
111 H4 Moose Lake l. Can.
121 H2 Mooselookmeguntic Lake l. U.S.A.
111 H4 Moose River Can.
111 J4 Moosomin Can.
112 D3 Moosonee Can.
83 F2 Mopeia Mozambique
76 D3 Mopti Mali
76 D3 Mopti div. Mali
140 D3 Moquegua Peru
19 J5 Mór Hungary
76 C3 Mora Cameroon
24 B3 Mora Portugal
14 D3 Mora Sweden
124 E2 Mora U.S.A.
55 G4 Morādābād India
146 B4 Mora Campanario, Cerro summit Chile
54 D3 Morad r. Pakistan
54 D3 Moradabad India
133 □¹ Morant Pt pt Jamaica
145 F3 Morada Nova de Minas Brazil

Column 3

14 F2 Mordoviya div. Rus. Fed.
14 E3 Mordovo Rus. Fed.
14 D2 Mordves Rus. Fed.
97 G3 Mordy Poland
124 C2 Moreau r. U.S.A.
17 F4 Morecambe U.K.
17 F4 Morecambe Bay b. U.K.
97 G2 Moree Aust.
90 □¹ Morehead P.N.G.
120 E5 Morehead City U.S.A.
54 D4 Morel r. India
131 E5 Morelia Mexico
25 F2 Morella Spain
25 E2 Morella Aust.
131 H5 Morelos div. Mexico
131 H5 Morelos Mexico
82 C2 Moremi Wildlife Reserve res. Botswana
54 D4 Morena India
24 D3 Morena, Sierra mt. ra. Spain
29 H5 Morenci U.S.A.
123 F5 Morenci U.S.A.
28 E2 Moreni Romania
127 E6 Moreno Mexico
128 D5 Moreno Valley U.S.A.
10 B3 Møre og Romsdal div. Norway
141 E2 Morerú r. Brazil
110 C4 Moresby Gory Rus. Fed.
82 C3 Moreswe Pan salt pan Botswana
96 H5 Moreton B. b. Aust.
99 H5 Moreton I. i. Aust.
20 F2 Moreuil France
21 H3 Morez France
14 E2 Morki Rus. Fed.
133 □² Moriah Tobago Trin. and Tobago
129 E2 Moriah, Mt mt. U.S.A.
127 F6 Moriarty U.S.A.
99 F6 Moriarty's Ra. h. Aust.
76 C5 Moribaya Guinea
54 C1 Morich Pakistan
138 C2 Morichal Colombia
77 F4 Morið Nigeria
49 H4 Morin Dawa China
47 H4 Morioka Japan
16 E3 Moriston r. U.K.
47 H4 Moriyama Japan
47 H4 Moriyoshi Japan
47 H4 Moriyoshi-zan vol Japan
10 F2 Morjärv Sweden
57 E3 Morjen r. Pakistan
12 J3 Morki Rus. Fed.
54 A1 Morkiny Gory Rus. Fed.
20 C2 Morlaix France
129 G4 Mormon Lake l. U.S.A.
133 □² Morne-à-l'Eau Guadeloupe Caribbean
133 □¹ Morne Constant h. Guadeloupe Caribbean
133 G4 Morne Diablotin vol Dominica
92 □² Morne, Pte pt Kerguelen Indian Ocean
133 □¹ Morne Seychellois h. Seychelles
99 F5 Morney r. Aust.
98 D3 Mornington, I. i. Aust.
147 A6 Mornington, I. i. Chile
54 A4 Moro r. Aust.
90 □¹ Morobe P.N.G.
80 B3 Morocco country Africa
72 C2 Morocco U.S.A.
140 A2 Morococha Peru
81 D6 Morogoro Tanzania
81 D6 Morogoro div. Tanzania
47 □¹ Moro-yama h. Japan
46 E2 Moroleón Mexico
80 E2 Moromet well Somalia
83 E3 Morombe Madagascar
132 C2 Morón Cuba
79 □⁷ Morón Ecuador
138 B4 Morona Ecuador
83 H3 Morondava Madagascar
24 C4 Morón de la Frontera Spain
81 □⁷ Moroni I. i. Fr. Poly. Pac. Oc.
81 C5 Moroni Comoros
39 J6 Morotai i. Indon.
80 B4 Moroto, Mt mt. Uganda
14 E3 Morozovsk Rus. Fed.
14 E3 Morozovy-Borki Rus. Fed.
143 D3 Morpara Brazil
114 E5 Morpeth U.K.
17 F4 Morpeth U.K.
144 D6 Morretes Brazil
92 F2 Morrinsville N.Z.
111 K5 Morris r. Can.
124 E2 Morris U.S.A.
122 C5 Morris U.S.A.
119 C6 Morris U.S.A.
111 K5 Morrisburg Can.
109 L2 Morris Jessup, Kap c. Greenland
122 C4 Morris, Mt mt. U.S.A.
121 E3 Morristown U.S.A.
121 F4 Morristown U.S.A.
121 F3 Morrisville U.S.A.
120 D6 Morrisville U.S.A.
145 F2 Morro r. Brazil
143 B4 Morro Agudo Brazil
128 B4 Morro Bay U.S.A.
133 E5 Morrocoy, Parque Nacional nat. park Venezuela
138 C1 Morrosquillo, G. de b. Colombia
83 F2 Morrumbala Mozambique
83 F3 Morrumbene Mozambique
122 D5 Morse Reservoir resr U.S.A.

Column 4

97 H3 Morundah Aust.
80 B4 Morungole mt. Uganda
97 G3 Moruya Aust.
142 E3 Morvan reg. France
99 F5 Morven Aust.
93 C6 Morven N.Z.
97 F4 Morwell Aust.
12 G1 Morzhovets, O. i. Rus. Fed.
18 E4 Mosbach Germany
120 C5 Moscow U.S.A.
152 C6 Moscow Univ. Ice Shelf ice feature Ant.
126 C2 Moscow U.S.A.
15 B2 Moşana Moldova
18 D4 Mosbach Germany
126 C2 Moscow U.S.A.
82 D3 Mosetse Botswana
52 H1 Moseyevo Rus. Fed.
65 N2 Mosgiel N.Z.
114 C2 Mosher Can.
81 C5 Moshi Tanzania
15 D2 Moshny Ukraine
12 K1 Mosh'yuga Rus. Fed.
19 H2 Mosina Poland
122 C3 Mosinee U.S.A.
65 H2 Mosjøen Norway
10 F2 Moskalenki Rus. Fed.
11 E4 Moskenesøy i. Norway
14 D2 Moskva r. Rus. Fed.
14 C2 Moskva Rus. Fed.
14 D2 Moskvy, Kanal imeni canal Rus. Fed.
28 C1 Mosonmagyaróvár Hungary
26 F4 Mosor mts Croatia
142 C1 Mosqueiro Brazil
138 B3 Mosquera Colombia
127 F5 Mosquero U.S.A.
130 K6 Mosquitia reg. Honduras
145 H1 Mosquito r. Brazil
122 F4 Mosquito Creek Lake l. U.S.A.
130 K7 Mosquitos, Golfo de los b. Panama
11 J2 Mosquito Lake l. Can.
14 D3 Moss Norway
78 C4 Mossaka Congo
144 C2 Mossâmedes Brazil
82 C5 Mossbank R.S.A.
79 B4 Mossendjo Congo
78 A4 Mossendjo Congo
82 C5 Mossel Bay R.S.A.
82 C5 Mossel Bay b. R.S.A.
92 □² Mossburn N.Z.
99 F4 Mossman Aust.
142 E2 Mossoró Brazil
83 G1 Mossuril Mozambique
97 G3 Moss Vale Aust.
79 C6 Mossyrebland Angola
142 E2 Moxotó r. Brazil
80 D4 Moyale Ethiopia
76 B4 Moyamba Sierra Leone
74 C2 Moyar r. Aust.
72 C2 Moyen-Chari div. Chad
82 D5 Moyeni Lesotho
76 B4 Moyenne-Guinée div. Guinea
78 D4 Moyen-Ogooué div. Gabon
14 D3 Moyero r. Rus. Fed.
80 B4 Moyo Uganda
38 D2 Moyo i. Indon.
140 A1 Moyobamba Peru
50 C1 Moyu China
80 B4 Moyo Uganda
65 J5 Moyynty Kazak.
83 G2 Mozambique country Africa
144 F4 Mozambique Channel str. Africa
149 G5 Mozambique Ridge Indian Ocean
15 H7 Mozdok Rus. Fed.
57 E1 Mozdūrān Iran
14 C2 Mozhaysk Rus. Fed.
51 B2 Mozhga Rus. Fed.
57 D3 Mozhnābād Iran
42 A2 Mozo Myanmar
42 A2 Mpala Zaire
80 C4 Mpanda Tanzania
76 A3 Mpé Congo
76 C4 Mpessoba Mali
81 B5 Mpigi Uganda
81 □⁷ Mpika Zambia
81 B7 Mpoko Zambia
79 D6 Mporokoso Zambia
79 C4 Mpouya Congo
79 C4 Mpulungu Zambia
83 H2 Mpumalanga div. R.S.A.
81 C5 Mpwapwa Tanzania
24 C3 Mqanduli R.S.A.
120 C5 Mrągowo Poland
120 C4 Mreäuld U.S.A.
26 F3 Mrkonjić-Grad Bos.-Herz.
75 C4 M'Saken Tunisia
75 E4 Msambweni Kenya
75 E4 M'Sila Algeria
81 C5 Mshinskaya Rus. Fed.
79 E5 Msta r. Rus. Fed.
14 C1 Mstera Rus. Fed.
14 C1 Mstislavl' Belarus
14 D1 Mstsislaw Belarus
14 C4 Mtama Tanzania
80 C4 Mtelo mt. Kenya
14 C2 Mtsensk Rus. Fed.
81 D7 Mtwara Tanzania
81 D7 Mtwara div. Tanzania
42 A2 Mu r. Myanmar
90 □⁴ Muaguide Mozambique
38 C5 Muar r. Malaysia
38 C5 Muarabunga Indon.
38 C3 Muarabungo Indon.

Column 5

97 F3 Mount Hope Aust.
96 C3 Mount Hope Aust.
120 C6 Mount Hope U.S.A.
99 E5 Mount Howitt Aust.
98 D4 Mount Isa Aust.
121 G4 Mount Kisco U.S.A.
114 E3 Mount MacDonald Can.
101 B6 Mount Magnet Aust.
97 F3 Mount Manara Aust.
92 F2 Mount Maunganui N.Z.
42 C4 Mount Meadows Reservoir resr U.S.A.
99 F3 Mount Molloy Aust.
99 G4 Mount Morgan Aust.
99 G5 Mount Perry Aust.
99 G5 Mount Pleasant Aust.
98 D3 Mount Pleasant Aust.
119 D5 Mount Pleasant U.S.A.
122 E4 Mount Pleasant U.S.A.
118 D1 Mount Pleasant U.S.A.
123 F4 Mount Pleasant U.S.A.
125 E5 Mount Pleasant U.S.A.
129 G2 Mount Pleasant U.S.A.
122 C5 Mount Pulaski U.S.A.
126 B2 Mount Rainier Nat. Park nat. park U.S.A.
110 F4 Mount Robson Prov. Park res. Can.
120 C6 Mount Rogers National Recreation Area res. U.S.A.
17 E6 Mount's Bay b. U.K.
93 C5 Mount Somers N.Z.
122 B6 Mount Sterling U.S.A.
120 B5 Mount Sterling U.S.A.
120 D5 Mount Storm U.S.A.
99 F3 Mount Surprise Aust.
97 G4 Mount Swan Aust.
120 E4 Mount Union U.S.A.
101 B5 Mount Vernon Aust.
118 B3 Mount Vernon U.S.A.
122 B6 Mount Vernon U.S.A.
121 G4 Mount Vernon U.S.A.
120 B4 Mount Vernon U.S.A.
126 B1 Mount Vernon U.S.A.
97 G5 Mount William Nat. Park nat. park Aust.
99 E4 Moura Aust.
139 E4 Moura Brazil
72 D5 Moura Chad
24 C3 Moura Portugal
78 D1 Mouraya Chad
76 C4 Mourdiah Mali
72 D4 Mourdi, Dépression du depression Chad
40 A3 Mouraenim Indon.
40 A3 Muaratembesi Indon.
40 D3 Muarajawa Indon.
40 A3 Muarakaman Indon.
40 D1 Muaralakitan Indon.
40 D1 Muaralaksan Indon.
40 A3 Muaramawai Indon.
38 C2 Muarasabak Indon.
40 D1 Muaratebo Indon.
40 A3 Muaratuang Malaysia
40 D1 Muarawahau Indon.
57 F4 Mauri, B. r. Iran
61 C5 Mubārak, J. mt. Jordan/Saudi Arabia
81 B4 Mubende Uganda
77 G4 Mubi Nigeria
142 E2 Muxotó r. Brazil
80 C4 Moyale Ethiopia
74 C2 Moyen Atlas mt. ra. Morocco
82 D5 Moyeni Lesotho
76 B4 Moyenne-Guinée div. Guinea
139 F2 Mucajaí r. Brazil
138 C3 Mucajaí Brazil
81 B7 Muchinga Escarpment escarpment Zambia
46 C7 Munakata Japan
18 D5 München Germany
138 B3 Munchique, Co mt. Colombia
110 D3 Muncho Lake Provincial Park res. Can.
49 H5 Munch'ŏn N. Korea
122 D5 Muncie U.S.A.
99 F4 Munconung, L. salt flat Aust.
12 J3 Munda Rus. Fed.
90 □⁴ Munda Solomon Is.
54 B5 Mundakayam India
145 J3 Mucuri r. Brazil
143 E6 Mucuri Brazil
138 C2 Mucumpora Venezuela
83 E2 Mucumbura Mozambique
81 B7 Mucussueje Angola
60 C2 Mucur Turkey
90 □¹ Munda Solomon Is.
145 J3 Mucuri r. Brazil
43 C6 Muda r. Malaysia
80 C4 Mudanjiang China
49 J3 Mudan Jiang r. China
60 A1 Mudanya Turkey
23 E5 Mudaybī Oman
54 D3 Muddabidri India
49 J3 Mudan Jiang r. China
129 E3 Muddy Creek r. U.S.A.
127 G4 Muddy Peak summit U.S.A.
57 D3 Müd-e-Dahanāb Iran
61 D4 Mudhol India
79 B6 Mudilube r. Zaire
14 E3 Mududu Rus. Fed.
81 C7 Mueda Mozambique
100 C3 Mueller Ra. h. Aust.
42 B2 Mumedu Myanmar

Column 6

46 J2 Mu-kawa r. Japan
42 B3 Mukdahan Thailand
54 C3 Mukerian India
41 □¹ Mukeru Palau
91 H1 Mukhino Rus. Fed.
48 E1 Mukhor-Konduy Rus. Fed.
48 D2 Mukhorshibir' Rus. Fed.
51 N3 Mukhtolovo Rus. Fed.
54 A3 Mukhtuddin Pakistan
38 D7 Mukinbudin Aust.
81 B6 Mukono Uganda
65 G5 Mukry Turkmenistan
55 F3 Muktinath Nepal
25 G3 Mula r. Pakistan
54 D5 Mula r. India
25 F3 Mula Spain
54 A2 Mulaku Atoll atoll Maldives
49 J3 Mulan China
41 B3 Mulanay Phil.
83 F2 Mulanje Malawi
83 F2 Mulanje, Mt mt. Malawi
142 B1 Mulata Brazil
125 F5 Mulberry r. U.S.A.
146 B4 Mulchén Chile
18 E5 Mulde r. Germany
18 D5 Müldeim Germany
131 H4 Mule Creek U.S.A.
126 F3 Mule Creek U.S.A.
46 D2 Mulegé Mexico
40 A4 Mules i. Indon.
16 D3 Mulhacén mt. Spain
21 H3 Mulhouse France
50 D5 Muli China
79 E6 Muli r. China
91 □² Mulifanua Western Samoa
49 J3 Muling China
49 J3 Muling China
49 J3 Muling r. China
16 E3 Mull i. U.K.
54 C4 Mullaittivu Sri Lanka
54 C4 Mullaley Aust.
17 B4 Mullet, The b. Rep. of Ire.
122 E3 Mullett Lake l. U.S.A.
101 A6 Mullewa Aust.
120 D5 Mullens U.S.A.
18 D5 Müllheim Germany
17 D4 Mullingar Rep. of Ire.
16 D3 Mull, Sound of chan. U.K.
97 H2 Mullumbimby Aust.
79 C7 Mulobezi Zambia
79 D7 Mulonga Plain plain Zambia
20 E3 Mulsanne France
56 A2 Mulshi L. l. India
18 C5 Mûnchen Germany
76 E4 Multan Pakistan
14 H3 Multia Finland
10 H3 Mulubwu, Monts mts China
79 C5 Mulumbe, Monts mts Zaire
40 C1 Mulurulu L. l. Aust.
41 B7 Muchinga Escarpment escarpment Zambia
40 C1 Murung r. Kalimantan Tengah Indon.
40 C1 Murung r. Kalimantan Tengah Indon.
18 D5 Münchberg Germany
18 D5 München Germany
138 B3 Munchique, Co mt. Colombia

Column 7

80 B4 Murchison Falls National Park nat. park Uganda
114 A1 Murchison I. i. Can.
101 B5 Murchison, Mt. h. Aust.
93 C5 Murchison, Mt. N.Z.
25 E4 Murcia Spain
20 C2 Mûr-de-Bretagne France
124 C3 Murdo U.S.A.
113 G4 Murdochville Can.
47 G5 Mure Japan
83 E2 Murewha Zimbabwe
28 D2 Mureş r. Romania
20 E5 Muret France
119 C5 Murfreesboro U.S.A.
119 D5 Murfreesboro U.S.A.
111 K4 Murgab r. Turkmenistan
122 C4 Mukwonago U.S.A.
57 E1 Murgab Turkmenistan
57 F2 Murghab r. Afghanistan
57 E2 Murghab r. Afghanistan
65 H5 Murgob Tajikistan
54 A3 Murgha Pass pass Afghanistan
99 G5 Murgon Aust.
54 B3 Muri China
48 A5 Muri China
57 D1 Mûrî Iran
12 J3 Muriaé Brazil
145 G4 Muriaé Brazil
79 C5 Muriege Angola
18 F3 Müritz l. Germany
11 G3 Murjärv Finland
57 C3 Mûrjän Iran
14 F2 Murmansk Rus. Fed.
10 H1 Murmansk div. Rus. Fed.
12 E2 Murmino Rus. Fed.
14 C2 Muro, Capo di pt France
14 F3 Murom Rus. Fed.
81 B5 Muromtsevo Rus. Fed.
14 F2 Muron Rus. Fed.
24 B1 Muros Spain
46 J2 Muroto Japan
46 J2 Muroto-zaki pt Japan
15 B2 Murovani Kurylivtsi Ukraine
122 D4 Murphey Lake, J. C. l. U.S.A.
119 C5 Murphy U.S.A.
128 B2 Murphys U.S.A.
99 F6 Murra Murra Aust.
47 □¹ Murray r. Aust.
96 D3 Murray r. Aust.
110 E3 Murray r. Can.
121 E4 Murray Bridge Aust.
96 C3 Murray Downs Aust.
94 □² Murray Hill h. Christmas I. Indian Ocean
119 D5 Murray, Lake l. P.N.G.
151 L3 Murray Seascarp Pac. Oc.
96 E3 Murrville Aust.
99 F2 Murree Pakistan
97 F3 Murrumbidgee r. Aust.
97 H3 Murrumburrah Aust.
83 F2 Murrupula Mozambique
97 H3 Murrurundi Aust.
56 A3 Murtajāpur India
26 F4 Murter Croatia
26 C2 Murtosa Aust.
28 C2 Murtoa Aust.
54 D4 Musa Khel Bazar Pakistan
57 D2 Musa Qala Afghanistan
57 C2 Musa Qala, Rud-r Afghanistan
54 D4 Musallam r. Saudi Arabia
61 D5 Musallam r. Saudi Arabia
23 F5 Muscat Oman
122 B5 Muscatine U.S.A.
123 F4 Musgrave Bay b. U.S.A.
96 B1 Musgrave Ranges mt. ra. Aust.
78 B4 Mushie Zaire
38 C3 Musi r. Indon.
129 F5 Music Mt mt. U.S.A.
14 F2 Musina R.S.A.
110 E3 Muskeg r. Can.
121 H4 Musket Channel chan. U.S.A.
122 D4 Muskegon r. U.S.A.
122 C4 Muskegon U.S.A.
120 C5 Muskingum r. U.S.A.
125 E5 Muskogee U.S.A.
114 E4 Muskoka, Lake l. Can.
110 D3 Muskwa r. Can.
54 B1 Muslim Bagh Pakistan
61 D5 Muslimīyah Syria
54 D1 Musmar Sudan
81 C5 Musoma Tanzania
90 □⁶ Mussau I. i. P.N.G.
14 C2 Musselburgh U.K.
120 D5 Musselshell r. U.S.A.
79 B6 Mussende Angola
20 D3 Mussidan France
79 B7 Mussuma Angola
60 B1 Mustafakemalpaşa Turkey
13 H3 Mustang Draw r. U.S.A.
147 B7 Musters, L. l. Arg.
14 D4 Mustvee Estonia
97 G3 Muswellbrook Aust.
57 □¹ Mût Egypt
60 C3 Mut Turkey
83 D2 Mutare Zimbabwe
66 C3 Muting Indon.
46 D6 Muto Japan
79 E5 Mutshatsha Zaire
47 H4 Mutsu Japan
47 H4 Mutsu-wan b. Japan
99 F4 Muttaburra Aust.

Column 8

94 □⁴ Mutton Bird I. i. Lord Howe I. Pac. Oc.
93 B7 Muttonbird Is is N.Z.
93 A7 Muttonbird Islands is N.Z.
83 F1 Mutuali Mozambique
139 E5 Mutum Amazonas Brazil
145 H3 Mutum Minas Gerais Brazil
77 G5 Mutum Biyu Nigeria
142 C3 Mutunópolis Brazil
56 C4 Mutur Sri Lanka
10 G1 Mutusjärvi l. Finland
10 H2 Mutyn Ukraine
10 H2 Muurola Finland
79 B5 Muxaluando Angola
79 B6 Muxima Angola
12 E2 Muyezerskiy Rus. Fed.
65 G4 Muynak Uzbekistan
79 E6 Muyumba Zaire
50 D2 Muyuping China
54 C2 Muzaffarabad Pakistan
54 B3 Muzaffargarh Pakistan
54 C3 Muzaffarnagar India
55 F4 Muzaffarpur India
145 H4 Muzambinho Brazil
65 K4 Muzat r. China
110 C4 Muzon, C. c. U.S.A.
131 E3 Múzquiz Mexico
50 C1 Muztag mt. China
50 B1 Muztagata mt. China
50 B1 Muztagata mt. China
54 B2 Mvadi Gabon
78 B3 Mvangan Cameroon
78 E2 Mvolo Sudan
83 C2 Mvomero Tanzania
79 B4 Mvouti Congo
83 E2 Mvuma Zimbabwe
81 B5 Mwali i. Comoros
81 B5 Mwanza Tanzania
78 B5 Mwanza Zaire
79 C4 Mweka Zaire
79 D5 Mwene-Ditu Zaire
79 E5 Mwenezi r. Zimbabwe
83 E3 Mwenezi Zimbabwe
79 C4 Mwenga Zaire
79 E5 Mweru, Lake l. Zambia
79 E5 Mweru Wantipa, Lake l. Zambia
79 E5 Mweru Wantipa Nat. Park nat. park Zambia
79 C6 Mwimba Zaire
79 D5 Mwinilunga Zambia
54 B4 Myājlār India
15 E1 M'yakoty Ukraine
97 F3 Myall L. l. Aust.
42 A3 Myanaung Myanmar
42 A3 Myanmar country Asia
14 D2 Myatlevo Rus. Fed.
42 A3 Myaungmya Myanmar
42 A3 Myawadi Thailand
42 A2 Mybon Myanmar
42 A2 Myedu Myanmar
42 A2 Myingyan Myanmar
42 B1 Myitkyina Myanmar
42 B2 Myitson Myanmar
42 A2 Myinmoletkat mt. Myanmar
42 A2 Myinmu Myanmar
42 B2 Myittha r. Myanmar
55 H5 Myittha r. Myanmar
19 H6 Myjava Slovakia
15 E1 Mykhailivka Ukraine
15 F2 Mykhailivka Zaporizhzhya Ukraine
15 F2 Mykhaylivka Zaporizhzhya Ukraine
15 D1 Mykhaylo-Kotsyubyns'ke Ukraine
15 D2 Mykolayiv Mykolayiv Ukraine
15 C2 Mykolayiv Lviv Ukraine
15 E2 Mykolayivka Kherson Ukraine
15 D2 Mykolayivka Odesa Ukraine
15 E2 Mykolayivka-Novorosiys'ka Ukraine
29 E6 Mykonos i. Greece
29 E6 Mykonos Greece
54 D2 Mymensingh Bangladesh
14 A1 Mynämäki Finland
17 F5 Mynydd Eppynt h. U.K.
17 E5 Mynydd Preseli h. U.K.
49 H5 Myŏkø-san vol Japan
49 J4 Myonggan N. Korea
10 M3 Mýrdalsjökull ice cap Iceland
10 D1 Myre Norway
10 F2 Myrheden Sweden
29 E6 Myrhorod Ukraine
29 G4 Myrina Greece
15 E1 Myronivka Kyiv Ukraine
15 D1 Myropil Ukraine
15 F1 Myropillya Ukraine
119 E5 Myrtle Beach U.S.A.
126 A3 Myrtle Point U.S.A.
65 J3 Myshkin Rus. Fed.
19 L2 Myślenice Poland
19 G4 Myślibórz Poland
54 D5 Mysore India
15 D2 Myszków Poland
43 C5 My Tho Vietnam
29 E5 Mytilini Greece
29 F5 Mytilini Strait chan. Greece
14 C2 Mytishchi Rus. Fed.
15 M2 Myyeldino Rus. Fed.
83 F1 Mzimba Malawi
83 F1 Mzuzu Malawi

Column 9 (N)

78 C1 Naala Chad
127 C2 Naalehu U.S.A.
76 A3 Naama Algeria
10 G1 Näätämö Finland
10 D5 Naba Myanmar
114 E3 Nabagamsag r. Can.
56 B2 Nabari Japan
61 C3 Nabatiye et Tahta Lebanon
91 □⁵ Nabavatu Fiji
14 D4 Naberera Tanzania
14 E4 Naberezhnyye Chelny Rus. Fed.
75 G1 Nabeul Tunisia

180

54 D3 Nabha India
57 D3 Nabid Iran
141 E4 Nabileque r. Brazil
39 L7 Nabire Indon.
61 C3 Nablus West Bank
76 D4 Nabolo Ghana
90 □8 Naboutini Fiji
90 □6 Nabouwalu Fiji
61 C5 Nabq Egypt
54 D2 Nabra r. India
43 B4 Nabule Myanmar
83 G1 Nacala Mozambique
130 J6 Nacaome Honduras
83 F1 Nacaroa Mozambique
126 B2 Naches U.S.A.
81 C7 Nachingwea Tanzania
54 B4 Nachna India
19 H3 Náchod Czech Rep.
90 □8 Nacilau Pt pt Fiji
128 B4 Nacimiento Reservoir resr U.S.A.
125 E6 Nacogdoches U.S.A.
130 C2 Nacozari de García Mexico
47 G5 Nadachi Japan
90 □8 Nadarivatu Fiji
90 □8 Nadi Fiji
54 C5 Nadiad India
90 □8 Nadi B. b. Fiji
57 D3 Nadik Iran
28 C1 Nădlac Romania
76 D1 Nador Morocco
90 □8 Nadrau Plateau plat. Fiji
90 □6 Nadroga Fiji
15 A2 Nadvirna Ukraine
12 E2 Nadvoitsy Rus. Fed.
62 J3 Nadym Rus. Fed.
54 C4 Naenwa India
11 C5 Næstved Denmark
77 G4 Nafada Nigeria
29 C5 Nafpaktos Greece
29 D6 Nafplio Greece
65 J4 Naft r. Iraq
57 B3 Naft-e Safid Iran
60 F3 Naft Khaneh Iraq
60 F3 Naft Shahr Iraq
73 H7 Nafud al 'Urayq sand dunes Saudi Arabia
72 B1 Nafūsah, Jabal h. Libya
73 H7 Nafy Saudi Arabia
41 B3 Naga Phil.
114 C2 Nagagami r. Can.
114 C2 Nagagami Lake l. Can.
114 C2 Nagagamisis Lake l. Can.
114 C2 Nagagamisis Provincial Park res. Can.
47 H8 Nagagusuku-wan b. Japan
46 D3 Nagahama Japan
47 G4 Naga Hills mt. ra. India
47 H4 Nagai Japan
55 H4 Nagaland India
47 □3 Nagannu-jima i. Japan
47 G5 Nagano Japan
47 F5 Nagano div. Japan
47 G5 Nagaoka Japan
55 H4 Nagaon India
56 B4 Nagappattinam India
54 D4 Nagar India
52 E4 Nagar India
56 B2 Nāgārjuna Sāgar Reservoir resr India
54 B4 Nagar Parkar Pakistan
55 G3 Nagarzê China
46 B7 Nagasaki Japan
46 B7 Nagasaki div. Japan
46 C7 Nagashima Japan
46 C7 Naga-shima i. Japan
46 D7 Naga-shima i. Japan
46 C6 Nagato Japan
54 C4 Nagaur India
56 C2 Nagavali r. India
56 C2 Nag, Lo salt l. China
54 C5 Nagda India
56 B4 Nagercoil India
57 F4 Nagha Kalat Pakistan
73 F2 Nag 'Hammâdi Egypt
80 B2 Nagichot Sudan
54 D3 Nagina India
55 E3 Nagma Nepal
47 □2 Nago Japan
54 E4 Nagod India
50 A2 Nagong Chu r. China
12 J3 Nagor'ye Rus. Fed.
14 D1 Nagor'ye Rus. Fed.
47 F2 Nago-wan b. Japan
47 F6 Nagoya Japan
55 H3 Nagqu China
119 □3 Naguabo Puerto Rico
41 C3 Nagumbuaya Point pt Phil.
62 F1 Nagurskoye Rus. Fed.
19 H5 Nagyatád Hungary
19 K6 Nagyhalász Hungary
19 K6 Nagykálló Hungary
19 H5 Nagykanizsa Hungary
19 J5 Nagykáta Hungary
19 J5 Nagykőrös Hungary
47 □2 Naha Japan
57 F4 Nahang r. Iran/Pakistan
124 M1 Nahanni Butte Can.
110 D2 Nahanni National Park nat. park Can.
61 C3 Naharayim Israel
61 C3 Nahariyya Israel
18 E4 Nahe r. Germany
90 □2 Nahoï, Cap c. Vanuatu
61 D1 Nahr Sājūr r. Syria
146 B4 Nahuelbuta, Parque nacional nat. park Chile
147 B5 Nahuel Huapi L. l. Arg.
147 B5 Nahuel Huapi, Parque nacional nat. park Arg.
119 D6 Nahunta U.S.A.
57 F1 Naibabad Afghanistan
28 C2 Naidâş Romania
90 □6 Naidi Fiji
42 B1 Nai Ga Myanmar
90 □8 Naigani i. Fiji
54 D2 Naij Tal China
90 □6 Nailotha Pk. h. Fiji
73 F5 Na'īma Sudan
49 G4 Naiman Qi China
113 H2 Nain Can.
57 C2 Nā'īn Iran
54 D3 Naini Tal India
54 E4 Nainpur India
90 □8 Nairai i. Fiji
16 F3 Nairn U.K.
114 E3 Nairn Centre Can.
81 C5 Nairobi Kenya
90 □6 Naisara i. Fiji
81 C5 Naitauba i. Fiji
81 C4 Naivasha Kenya
81 C5 Naivasha, L. l. Kenya
49 H4 Naizishan China
57 B2 Najafābād Iran
57 B2 Najafābād Iran
73 K5 Najd reg. Saudi Arabia
25 E2 Nájera Spain
54 D3 Najibabad India
49 J4 Najin N. Korea
73 H4 Najrān Saudi Arabia
46 A5 Naju S. Korea
46 H3 Nakadôri-shima i. Japan
46 H1 Nakagawa Japan
47 H5 Naka-gawa r. Japan
46 D7 Naka-gawa r. Japan
47 G7 Nakagusuku-wan b. Japan
46 C7 Nakama Japan
46 D4 Nakambé w Burkina/Ghana
47 H4 Nakamura Japan
63 H3 Nakano Rus. Fed.
47 G5 Nakano Japan
46 H3 Nakano-shima i. Japan
46 D6 Nakanoumi lag. Japan
46 H3 Nakaoshi Japan
81 B4 Nakasongola Uganda
46 H3 Nakasato Japan
46 J2 Nakasatsunai Japan
46 H3 Nakashibetsu Japan
46 C7 Nakatsu Japan

47 F6 Nakatsugawa Japan
40 C1 Nakfa Eritrea
73 F2 Nakhl Egypt
45 C3 Nakhodka Rus. Fed.
55 H4 Nakhola India
43 C4 Nakhon Nayok Thailand
43 C4 Nakhon Pathom Thailand
43 C4 Nakhon Ratchasima Thailand
43 B5 Nakhon Si Thammarat Thailand
42 C2 Nakhon Thai Thailand
55 H4 Nakhtarana India
110 C3 Nakina Can.
114 B1 Nakina r. Can.
19 H2 Nakło nad Notecią Poland
108 C4 Naknek U.S.A.
81 B6 Nakonde Zambia
11 C5 Nakskov Denmark
49 J6 Naktong r. S. Korea
81 C5 Nakuru Kenya
110 F4 Nakusp Can.
54 A4 Nal r. Pakistan
57 F4 Nal r. Pakistan
48 C3 Nalayh Mongolia
55 G4 Nalbari India
13 G7 Nal'chik Rus. Fed.
56 B2 Nalgonda India
55 F4 Nalhati India
56 B3 Nallamala Hills h. India
60 B1 Nallıhan Turkey
72 B1 Nālūt Libya
90 □8 Namacu Fiji
79 C7 Namacunde Angola
83 F2 Namacurra Mozambique
83 D4 Namahadi S. Africa
41 □1 Namai Bay b. Palau
57 D3 Namakzār-e Shadad salt flat Iran
40 A2 Namang India
55 H4 Namanga Kenya
65 H4 Namangan Uzbekistan
90 □6 Namanu-i-Ra i. Fiji
82 B4 Namaqualand reg. R.S.A.
82 B4 Namaqualand reg. Namibia
90 □1 Namatanai P.N.G.
42 C2 Nam Beng r. Laos
55 H4 Nambol India
99 H5 Nambour Aust.
97 H2 Nambucca Heads Aust.
42 B2 Năm Căn Vietnam
20 D3 Namche Bazar Nepal
49 H5 Namch'ŏn N. Korea
55 G5 Nam Co salt l. China
10 C2 Namdalen v. Norway
42 D2 Nam Đinh Vietnam
122 B3 Namekagon l. U.S.A.
41 □1 Namelakl Passage chan. Palau
90 □8 Namena Barrier Reef reef Fiji
90 □8 Namenalala i. Fiji
19 J4 Námestovo Slovakia
49 J6 Namhae Do i. S. Korea
42 A2 Nam Hka r. Myanmar
42 B1 Nam Hsim r. Myanmar
82 A3 Namib Desert desert Namibia
79 B7 Namibe Angola
79 B7 Namibe div. Angola
79 B7 Namibe, Reserva de res. Angola
69 F8 Namibia country Africa
82 B2 Namib-Naukluft Park res. Namibia
83 F2 Namie Mozambique
42 C3 Nam Khan r. Laos
42 B2 Namlan Myanmar
42 B2 Namlang r. Myanmar
39 J7 Namlea Indon.
42 C3 Nam Lik r. Laos
42 C2 Nam Loi r. Myanmar
42 A3 Nam Na r. China/Vietnam
42 B1 Nam Ngum r. Laos
97 G2 Namoi r. Aust.
110 F3 Nampa Can.
126 C3 Nampa U.S.A.
76 C3 Nampala Mali
42 C3 Nam Pat Thailand
42 C2 Nam Phong Thailand
49 H5 Nampʼo N. Korea
83 F2 Nampula Mozambique
83 F2 Nampula div. Mozambique
55 H4 Namru Co l. China
42 B2 Namsai Myanmar
42 A2 Nam Sam r. Laos/Vietnam
55 H3 Namsê La Nepal
55 H4 Namsi India
10 C2 Namsos Norway
42 A2 Nam Teng r. Myanmar
42 C2 Nam Tha r. Laos
42 B2 Nam Tok Myanmar
83 F2 Namton Myanmar
63 D3 Namtsy Rus. Fed.
42 B2 Namtu Myanmar
90 □7 Namuka-i-lau i. Fiji
76 C3 Namuka Mali
83 F2 Namuli, Monte mt. Mozambique
97 F3 Namur div. Belgium
18 A3 Namur Belgium
42 B3 Namur div. Belgium
82 A1 Namutoni Namibia
79 E7 Namwala Zambia
46 A5 Namwŏn S. Korea
42 B1 Namya Ra Myanmar
42 B2 Nam Yi Tu r. Myanmar
19 H3 Namysłów Poland
78 D2 Nana Bakassa C.A.R.
78 C2 Nana Barya r. C.A.R.
56 C2 Nanasagar India
56 C2 Nanasaropet India
78 C2 Nana-Grébizi div. C.A.R.
110 E5 Nanaimo Can.
127 □1 Nanakuli U.S.A.
56 C5 Nanam India
55 H4 Nanango Aust.
49 G5 Nanao Japan
47 F5 Nanao Japan
47 F5 Nanao-wan b. Japan
47 F5 Nanatsu-shima i. Japan
51 F2 Nanbu China
49 F5 Nancha China
51 E3 Nanchang China
51 F3 Nanchang China
50 C4 Nanchong China
50 D2 Nanchuan China
19 E2 Nancowry i. Andaman and Nicobar Is India
21 H2 Nancy France
54 C1 Nanda Devi mt. India
50 D3 Nandan China
54 C1 Nandan India
91 G5 Nandan China
47 H6 Nanded India
46 B2 Nandewar Range mt. ra. Aust.
63 M2 Nanding r. China/Myanmar

78 B3 Nanga Eboko Cameroon
40 C1 Nangahbunut Indon.
40 B2 Nangah Dedai Indon.
97 G4 Nangahembaloh Indon.
40 B1 Nangahkantuk Indon.
40 B1 Nangahketungau Indon.
40 B1 Nangah Merakai Indon.
40 B2 Nangahpinoh Indon.
49 J4 Nangahtempuai Indon.
54 C2 Nanga Parbat mt. Jammu and Kashmir
42 C2 Nangatayap Indon.
40 B2 Nangbéto, Retenue de res. Togo
43 B5 Nangin Myanmar
49 H5 Nangnim Sanmaek mt. China
46 C8 Nangô Japan
49 E5 Nangong China
50 B4 Nangqên China
55 H3 Nang Xian China
48 A5 Nanhua China
50 C3 Nanhua China
51 H2 Nanhui China
56 B3 Nanjangud India
50 D1 Nanjiang China
50 E3 Nanjing China
51 G3 Nanjing China
50 B4 Nanka r. China
79 C7 Nankova Angola
49 E5 Nanle China
50 B4 Nanlei r. China
51 E3 Nan Ling mt. ra. China
48 B3 Nanling China
50 D1 Nanliu Jiang r. China
10 E3 Nanna r. China
51 G1 Nanning China
50 D3 Nanning China
51 G3 Nanning China
55 G3 Nanniwan China
50 B4 Nannuo Jiang r. China
133 □6 Nanny Town Jamaica
109 L2 Nanortalik Greenland
50 D3 Nanpan r. China
50 D1 Nanpiao China
50 D3 Nanping China
51 G3 Nanping China
51 G3 Nanri Dao i. China
51 G3 Nansei China
16 □5 Nansei-shotō is Japan
149 N2 Nansei-shotō Trench Pac. Oc.
109 □1 Nansen Land reg. Greenland
109 J1 Nansen Sound chan. Can.
81 C5 Nansio Tanzania
20 D3 Nantes France
110 C4 Nanthi Kadal lag. Sri Lanka
40 A3 Nanti, Bukit mt. Indon.
114 E5 Nanticoke U.S.A.
110 C4 Nanton r. U.S.A.
51 H1 Nantong China
51 H1 Nantong China
51 H3 Nant'ou Taiwan
121 H4 Nantucket U.S.A.
121 H4 Nantucket I. i. U.S.A.
121 H4 Nantucket Sound g. U.S.A.
17 D4 Nantwich U.K.
90 □6 Nanuku Passage chan. Fiji
90 □6 Nanuku Reef reef Fiji
86 J5 Nanumanga i. Tuvalu
82 A3 Namib Desert desert Namibia
145 H2 Nanuque Brazil
44 A4 Nanusa, Kepulauan is Indon.
101 A4 Nanutarra Roadhouse Aust.
50 D2 Nanxi China
51 F3 Nan Xian China
51 E3 Nanxiong China
51 E3 Nanyang China
51 F1 Nanyang China
81 C4 Nanyuki Kenya
49 H4 Nanzamu China
51 E2 Nanzhang China
39 J7 Nanzhao China
25 G3 Nao, Cabo de la hd Spain
57 B2 Naqanz Iran
113 H3 Natashquan r. Can.
113 H3 Natashquan Can.
125 E6 Natchez U.S.A.
125 E6 Natchitoches U.S.A.
28 D1 Năsăud Romania
57 A4 Nathalia Aust.
96 E4 Natimuk Aust.
128 C5 National City U.S.A.
128 B2 National Park U.S.A.
92 E3 Naperville U.S.A.
82 A3 National West Coast Tourist Recreation Area res. Namibia
77 G4 Natitingou Benin
145 H1 Natividade Rio de Janeiro Brazil
142 C3 Natividade Tocantins Brazil
42 A2 Natogyi Myanmar
20 F4 Nátora Mexico
47 H4 Natori Japan
81 C5 Natron, Lake salt l. Tanzania
47 □5 Natsui-gawa r. Japan
42 A3 Nattalin Myanmar
57 E2 Na'tū Iran
40 A2 Natuna Besar i. Indon.
61 B5 Natuna, Kepulauan is Indon.
73 F2 Natrûn, Wādī an w Egypt
127 F3 Natural Bridge U.S.A.
129 G3 Natural Bridges National Monument res. U.S.A.
149 M6 Naturaliste Plateau Indian Ocean
43 C4 Naturita U.S.A.
20 F4 Naubinway U.S.A.
14 E4 Nauchas Namibia
18 F2 Nauen Germany
121 F4 Naugatuck U.S.A.
41 B3 Naujan Phil.
11 F4 Naujoji Akmenė Lithuania
54 B4 Naukh India
79 B7 Naulila Angola
42 B2 Naumburg Sachsen-Anhalt Germany
18 E3 Naumburg Hessen Germany
61 C4 Naur Jordan
61 C2 Nauroz Kalat Pakistan
60 D3 Naushahra Firoz Pakistan
57 E2 Nardin Iran
90 □7 Nausori Fiji
10 □8 Naustdal Norway
138 C4 Nauta Peru
131 H4 Nautla Mexico
40 A3 Navadwip India
40 C2 Navahermosa Spain
12 C4 Navahrudak Belarus
127 F4 Navajo Lake l. U.S.A.
80 D3 Navajo Mt. mt. U.S.A.
41 C4 Naval Phil.
24 D3 Navalcamero Spain
24 D3 Navalero Spain
24 D3 Navalmoral de la Mata Spain
24 D3 Navalvillar de Pela Spain
12 D4 Navapolatsk Belarus
45 R3 Navarin, Mys c. Rus. Fed.
147 C7 Navarino, I. i. Chile
25 E1 Navarra div. Spain
24 D1 Navarredonda Spain
25 F3 Navarrés Spain

15 C1 Narodychi Ukraine
14 C2 Naro-Fominsk Rus. Fed.
81 C5 Narok Kenya
97 G4 Narooma Aust.
15 C1 Narowlya Belarus
21 F3 Närpes Finland
97 G2 Narrabri Aust.
97 H4 Narragansett Bay b. U.S.A.
97 F2 Narran r. Aust.
97 F2 Narrandera Aust.
97 F2 Narran L. l. Aust.
101 B7 Narrogin Aust.
120 C6 Narrows U.S.A.
121 F4 Narrows U.S.A.
133 □6 Narrows, The chan. St Kitts-Nevis Caribbean
130 C1 Narsapur India
55 G5 Narsimhapur India
55 G5 Narsinghgarh India
56 C2 Narsipatnam India
48 E4 Nart China
48 C2 Nart Mongolia
60 E3 Narva Estonia
11 G4 Narva r. Estonia
11 G4 Narva Bay b. Estonia/Rus. Fed.
41 B2 Narvacan Phil.
10 E1 Narvik Norway
10 E1 Narvskoye Vdkhr. resr Rus. Fed.
54 D4 Narwana India
54 D4 Narwar India
62 G3 Nary'an-Mar Rus. Fed.
65 H3 Naryn div. Kyrgyzstan
65 J4 Naryn r. Kyrgyzstan
65 J4 Naryn Kyrgyzstan
54 B3 Naryshkino Rus. Fed.
14 B3 Näsåker Sweden
10 E3 Näsåud Romania
129 H3 Naschitti U.S.A.
93 C6 Naseby N.Z.
122 A5 Nashua U.S.A.
121 H3 Nashua U.S.A.
119 C4 Nashville U.S.A.
122 A2 Nashwauk U.S.A.
10 D2 Nasib Syria
10 D5 Näsijärvi l. Finland
11 F3 Näsijärvi l. Finland
54 C5 Nasik India
80 B1 Nasir Sudan
54 B3 Nasirabad India
54 A4 Nasirabad Pakistan
54 D4 Nasirabad Pakistan
60 E1 Naşîriyah Iraq
60 F3 Naşrābād Eşfahān Iran
57 D2 Naşrābād Khorāsān Iran
61 D3 Naşrîli, J. an mt. ra. Syria
60 D3 Nārsîan-e-Pā'īn Iran
110 D3 Nass r. Can.
77 F5 Nassarawa Nigeria
99 E2 Nassau r. Aust.
87 M5 Nassau i. Cook Islands Pac. Oc.
119 □2 Nassau airport The Bahamas
119 □2 Nassau The Bahamas
82 A5 Nassau, B. de b. Chile
147 C7 Nassau Village U.S.A.
73 □2 Nassau The Bahamas
73 F2 Nasser, Lake resr Egypt
11 D4 Nässjö Sweden
112 E2 Nastapoca r. Can.
112 E2 Nastapoka Islands is Can.
81 C5 Nasu-dake vol Japan
12 D3 Nasva r. Rus. Fed.
82 D3 Nata Botswana
138 B3 Natagaima Colombia
142 E2 Natal Brazil
149 H6 Natal Basin Indian Ocean
57 B2 Naţanz Iran

128 A2 Navarro U.S.A.
14 F2 Navashino Rus. Fed.
125 D6 Navasota U.S.A.
132 D3 Navassa I. terr. Caribbean
10 D3 Năverede Sweden
75 F2 Nègrine Algeria
146 B3 Navidad Chile
133 E2 Navidad Bank Caribbean
142 E2 Navio r. Brazil
144 A5 Naviraí Brazil
90 □8 Naviti I. Fiji
15 A1 Naviz Ukraine
14 B3 Navlya r. Rus. Fed.
14 B3 Navlya Rus. Fed.
130 C3 Navodari Romania
65 G4 Navoi Uzbekistan
130 C2 Navojoa Mexico
130 C3 Navolato Mexico
55 G4 Navsari India
90 □8 Navua r. Fiji
90 □8 Navua Fiji
90 □8 Nawa r. India
55 G4 Nawabganj Bangladesh
55 F4 Nawabganj India
54 B4 Nawabshah Pakistan
54 C4 Nawalgarh India
54 D3 Nawan Kot Pakistan
54 D3 Nawashahr India
42 A2 Nawnghkio Myanmar
42 B1 Nawngleng Myanmar
60 F2 Naxçivan Azerbaijan
50 D2 Naxi China
29 E6 Naxos i. Greece
53 A5 Nayagarh India
57 F2 Nayak Afghanistan
130 D4 Nayar Mexico
63 P4 Nel'kan Rus. Fed.
63 O4 Nel'kan Rus. Fed.
90 □7 Nayau i. Fiji
57 C4 Nây Band Iran
57 D2 Nayoro Japan
29 E6 Naxos i. Greece
130 D4 Nayarit div. Mexico
56 B3 Näyudupeta India
72 D2 Nayyäl, W. w Saudi Arabia
142 E3 Nazaré Bahia Brazil
142 E3 Nazaré Pará Brazil
61 C3 Nazareth Israel
142 C2 Nazário Brazil
12 J3 Nazas r. Mexico
138 C6 Nazca Peru
11 F3 Näzîl Iran
60 B2 Nazilli Turkey
54 A4 Nazimabad Pakistan
70 F1 Nazir Hat Bangladesh
110 E4 Nazko r. Can.
110 E4 Nazko Can.
75 F2 Nemencha, Monts des mts Algeria
13 H7 Nazran' Rus. Fed.
59 J5 Nazwá Oman
12 F3 Nazyvayevsk Rus. Fed.
81 B5 Nchelenge Zambia
82 B2 Ncojane Botswana
78 B4 Ncue Equatorial Guinea
79 B5 N'dalatando Angola
77 F5 Ndali Nigeria
77 F5 Ndeji Nigeria
90 □8 Ndelanathau Pk h. Fiji
78 C3 Ndélé C.A.R.
78 B4 Ndendé Gabon
76 A3 Ndiael, Réserve de Faune du res. Senegal
78 C2 Ndjamena Chad
77 D5 Ndji r. C.A.R.
76 A4 Ndofane Senegal
78 B4 Ndjolé Gabon
80 B4 Ndola Zambia
80 C4 Ndoto mt. Kenya
76 B3 Nduye Zaire
29 C5 Nea r. Greece
29 E7 Nea Alikarnassos Greece
29 E5 Nea Anchialos Greece
29 D5 Nea Artaki Greece
29 C5 Neabul Cr. r. Aust.
95 H2 Neagle country Asia
81 C5 Neah Bay U.S.A.
96 B3 Neale, L. salt flat Aust.
96 D5 Neales r. Aust.
29 D5 Nea Makri Greece
29 C6 Nea Moudania Greece
29 E7 Neapoli Attiki Greece
29 C7 Neapoli Peloponnisos Greece
29 E7 Neapoli Kriti Greece
78 B4 Ne Roda Greece
17 F6 Neath U.K.
29 C7 Nea Zichni Greece
80 D4 Nebbi Uganda
76 F3 Nebbou Burkina
12 J1 Nebdino Rus. Fed.
57 E1 Nebine Cr. r. Aust.
54 E1 Nebitdag Turkmenistan
99 D4 Nebo Aust.
129 H2 Nebo, Mount mt. U.S.A.
128 C4 Nebraska div. U.S.A.
124 C3 Nebraska City U.S.A.
27 F7 Nebrodi, Monti mt. ra. Italy
15 D3 Nechayne Ukraine
15 D2 Nechayevka Rus. Fed.
26 E5 Neches r. U.S.A.
138 C2 Nechí r. Colombia
80 C3 Nechisar National Park nat. park Ethiopia
18 D3 Neckar r. Germany
18 D4 Neckarsulm Germany
146 D7 Neckar i. U.S.A.
29 C7 Necochea Arg.
28 B2 Necula Brazil
112 E2 Nedouc I. i. Can.
13 F6 Nedryhayliv Ukraine
9 B3 Nedstrand Norway
10 F1 Nedre Soppero Sweden
17 □2 Needles, The stack U.K.
17 G6 Needles, The stack U.K.
129 E4 Needles U.S.A.
11 C4 Needles U.S.A.
11 B4 Neede Neth.
122 B4 Neenah U.S.A.
111 K4 Neepawa Can.
60 G1 Neftçala Azerbaijan
64 E2 Neftekamsk Rus. Fed.
61 G2 Neftkchala r. Rus. Fed.
111 N2 Neftekhala Cape c. Can.
62 H3 Nefteyugansk Rus. Fed.
76 B3 Nefza Tunisia
104 M8 Netherlands Antilles terr. Caribbean
78 C4 Négala Mali
40 C2 Negara Bali Indon.
40 B2 Negara Kalimantan Selatan Indon.
40 C2 Negara r. Indon.
80 C3 Negele Ethiopia
80 C3 Negele Ethiopia
90 □8 Negerabu i. Kiribati
43 A5 Negeri Sembilan div. Malaysia
61 C4 Negev reg. Israel
141 E3 Negla r. Paraguay
83 D4 Ngome Mozambique
18 E4 Neuburg an der Donau Germany
121 G3 Néguac Can.
28 D2 Negoiu mt. Romania
84 E5 Negomane Mozambique
56 B5 Negombo Sri Lanka
28 B3 Negotin Yugo.
21 H3 Negotino Macedonia
24 B3 Negra, Cord hd mt. ra. Peru
42 A2 Negrais, Cape c. Myanmar
138 A4 Negra, Pta pt Peru
21 G5 Negreira Spain
24 B1 Negreira Spain

20 E4 Nègrepelisse France
28 F1 Negreşti Romania
28 D1 Negreşti-Oaş Romania
28 F1 Negri Romania
133 □1 Negril Jamaica
75 F2 Négrine Algeria
18 E3 Negritos Peru
19 H5 Neunkirchen Austria
18 D4 Neunkirchen Saarland Germany
141 E3 Negro r. Mato Grosso do Sul Brazil
143 C6 Negro r. Paraná/Santa Catarina Brazil
141 E4 Negro r. Paraguay
138 D5 Negro r. S. America
24 D5 Negro, Cabo c. Morocco
74 C1 Negro, Cap hd Morocco
81 B4 Negros i. Phil.
28 G3 Negru Vodă Romania
57 B3 Nehbandān Iran
21 H2 Nehe China
79 D7 Nehone Angola
57 A3 Nehri Iran
50 D2 Neijiang China
122 B3 Neillsville U.S.A.
18 C3 Neiva Colombia
138 B3 Neiva Colombia
51 E1 Neixiang China
111 K3 Nejanilini Lake l. Can.
80 C3 Nek'emtē Ethiopia
15 F1 Nekhayevka Rus. Fed.
15 E1 Nekhayevka Ukraine
14 G1 Neklyudovo Rus. Fed.
14 E1 Neklyudovo Rus. Fed.
14 E1 Nekrasovskoye Rus. Fed.
11 D5 Neksø Denmark
99 E4 Nela i. Italy
55 F5 Naxos i. Greece
130 B3 Neixiang China
146 A5 Nelidovo Rus. Fed.
124 D3 Neligh U.S.A.
63 P4 Nel'kan Rus. Fed.
63 O4 Nel'kan Rus. Fed.
114 E2 Nellie Lake l. Can.
110 E5 Nelson r. Can.
111 L3 Nelson r. Can.
56 B3 Nelson r. India
93 D4 Nelson div. N.Z.
96 C4 Nelson, C. c. Aust.
147 A7 Nelson, Estrecho str. Chile
110 E5 Nelson Forks Can.
111 L3 Nelson House Can.
128 D5 Nesquit r. U.S.A.
110 E3 Nelson Forks Can.
130 B3 Nelson Reservoir resr U.S.A.
128 D5 Nelspoort S. Africa
140 A1 Nelspruit S. Africa
76 C3 Néma Mauritania
146 B4 Nemaiah Valley Can.
29 B6 Nemea Greece
12 D3 Nevel' Rus. Fed.
14 H3 Neverkino Rus. Fed.
21 F3 Nevers France
114 D4 Nemegos Can.
75 □ Nementcha, Monts des mts Algeria
26 G4 Nemesvadkert Hung.
59 J5 Nazrét Ethiopia
133 □6 Nevis i. St Kitts-Nevis
59 J5 Nazwá Oman
81 C4 Nazret Ethiopia
20 C2 Nemours France
60 C2 Nevşehir Turkey
49 K3 Nevte Rus. Fed.
46 K2 Nemuro-kaikyō chan. Japan
46 K2 Nemuro Japan
46 K2 Nemuro-wan b. Japan
15 D2 Nemyriv Vinnytsya Ukraine
15 A1 Nemyriv Ukraine
17 C5 Nenagh Rep. of Ire.
17 H6 Nene r. U.K.
91 □10 Nengonengo i. Fr. Poly.
50 B4 Nenjiang r. China
29 D6 Neo Greece
29 C5 Neochori Thessalia Greece
50 D2 Neo Karlovasi Greece
40 C2 Neos Marmaras Greece
29 E5 Neos Marmaras Greece
32 K7 Nepal country Asia
55 F4 Nepalganj Nepal
124 C3 Nephi U.S.A.
99 F2 Nepean r. Aust.
95 □1 Nepean i. Norfolk I. Pac. Oc.
16 E4 Ner r. Poland
17 □5 Nera r. Italy
17 □2 Nérac France
49 K3 Nerchinsk Rus. Fed.
49 J2 Nerchinskiy Khr. mt. ra. Rus. Fed.
49 J2 Nerchinsk Zavod Rus. Fed.
14 E1 Nerekhta Rus. Fed.
26 G3 Neretva r. Bos.-Herz./Croatia
79 D6 Neriquinha Angola
11 F5 Neris r. Lithuania
24 E4 Nerja Spain
21 F2 Nerl' r. Rus. Fed.
14 F1 Nerl' r. Rus. Fed.
83 E3 Neriquinha Angola
25 E4 Nerja Spain
127 □1 Nerpio Spain
61 G1 Nerskaya r. Rus. Fed.
12 F2 Nes' Rus. Fed.
9 B3 Nesbyen Norway
28 F3 Nesebŭr Bulgaria
110 D3 Nesna Norway
124 C3 Ness, Loch l. U.K.
10 D2 Nesna Norway
16 E3 Nestani Greece
131 G5 Nestório Greece
138 B1 Neth Colombia
75 □ Nestos r. Greece
29 E4 Nestos r. Greece
61 C3 Netanya Israel
111 M2 Netchek, Cape c. Can.
97 G2 Neath r. U.K.
108 A1 Netherlands country Europe
69 G4 Netherlands Antilles terr. Caribbean
97 D2 Neto r. Italy

18 D3 Neuhof Germany
111 K2 Neultin Lake l. Can.
18 E4 Neumarkt in der Oberpfalz Germany
19 H5 Neumünster Germany
19 H5 Neunkirchen Austria
18 D4 Neunkirchen Saarland Germany
146 B4 Neuquén r. Arg.
146 C4 Neuquén Arg.
146 B4 Neuquén div. Arg.
119 E5 Neuse r. U.S.A.
19 H5 Neusiedler See l. Austria/Hungary
18 D2 Neustadt an der Weinstraße Germany
18 E3 Neustadt in Holstein Germany
19 G3 Neustadt in Sachsen Germany
21 H2 Neuves-Maisons France
18 D3 Neuwerk i. Germany
18 C3 Neuwied Germany
125 D4 Nevada U.S.A.
128 D2 Nevada, Co mt. Arg.
126 B3 Nevada, Sierra mt. ra. Spain
24 E4 Nevada, Sierra mt. ra. Spain
140 B3 Nevado Auzangate mt. Peru
146 B4 Nevado Chillán mt. ra. Chile
146 C2 Nevado de Aconquija mt. ra. Arg.
140 B3 Nevado de Ampato mt. Peru
140 B3 Nevado de Chachani mt. Peru
146 C2 Nevado de Chañi mt. Arg.
130 E5 Nevado de Colima vol Mexico
138 B3 Nevado de Cumbal mt. Colombia
140 A1 Nevado Huascaran mt. Peru
140 B3 Nevado de Huila mt. Colombia
140 B3 Nevado Illampu mt. Bolivia
140 B3 Nevado de Illimani mt. Bolivia
138 B3 Nevado del Ruiz vol Colombia
130 E5 Nevado de Toluca vol Mexico
45 Q6 New Territories reg. Hong Kong
124 A2 Nevada, Sierra del mt. Arg.
146 C4 Nevado, Sierra del mt. ra. Arg.
12 D3 Nevel' Rus. Fed.
14 H3 Neverkino Rus. Fed.
21 H3 Nevertire Aust.
26 G4 Nevesinje Bos.-Herz.
13 G6 Nevinnomyssk Rus. Fed.
133 □6 Nevis i. St Kitts-Nevis Caribbean
133 □6 Nevis Pk mt. St Kitts-Nevis Caribbean
60 C2 Nevşehir Turkey
49 K3 Nev'yansk Rus. Fed.
60 E3 New r. Guyana
120 C6 New r. U.S.A.
128 D5 New r. U.S.A.
121 F4 New r. U.S.A.
86 J9 New Zealand country Australasia
149 Q7 New Zealand Plateau Pac. Oc.
97 F2 New Angledool Aust.
121 H3 Newark U.S.A.
120 E4 Newark U.S.A.
121 F4 Newark U.S.A.
120 A4 Newark U.S.A.
17 G5 Newark-on-Trent U.K.
121 E3 Newark Valley U.S.A.
121 H4 New Bedford U.S.A.
118 E5 New Bern U.S.A.
128 C4 Newberry U.S.A.
122 E3 Newberry U.S.A.
119 D5 Newberry U.S.A.
129 E4 Newberry Springs U.S.A.
121 F4 New Boston U.S.A.
120 C6 New Boston U.S.A.
125 D6 New Braunfels U.S.A.
90 □1 New Britain i. P.N.G.
121 G4 New Britain U.S.A.
115 H4 New Brunswick div. Can.
121 F4 New Brunswick U.S.A.
99 F2 New Broughton Jamaica
115 H4 New Brunswick div. Can.
17 G5 New Buckenham U.K.
122 A4 New Buffalo U.S.A.
16 F3 New Byth U.K.
120 A4 Newburgh U.S.A.
121 F4 Newburgh U.S.A.
17 G6 Newbury U.K.
121 H3 Newburyport U.S.A.
90 □2 New Bussa Nigeria
90 □2 New Caledonia terr. Pac. Oc.
113 G4 New Carlisle Can.
99 D4 New Carlisle Aust.
110 D4 New Castle Aust.
120 C4 Newcastle U.S.A.
119 D5 Newcastle U.S.A.
83 E4 Newcastle R.S.A.
114 D4 Newcastle Can.
17 C6 Newcastle Rep. of Ire.
17 D5 Newcastle Emlyn U.K.
17 E4 Newcastle-under-Lyme U.K.
16 F4 Newcastle upon Tyne U.K.
98 C3 Newcastle Waters Aust.
17 B5 Newcastle West Rep. of Ire.
17 F5 New Church U.S.A.
121 H4 New Denmark Can.
130 B3 New Don Pedro Reservoir resr U.S.A.
108 B4 New Eddystone Rock i. U.S.A.
123 F2 Newenham, C. c. U.S.A.
16 E4 New Galloway U.K.
90 □2 New Georgia i. Solomon Is.
90 □2 New Georgia Islands is Solomon Is.
113 G4 New Glasgow Can.
78 □ New Grant Trin. and Tobago
39 K8 New Guinea i.
50 A2 New Halfa Sudan
121 G4 New Hampshire div. U.S.A.
121 G3 New Hampshire U.S.A.
122 A4 New Hampton U.S.A.
83 E4 New Hanover R.S.A.
90 □1 New Hanover i. P.N.G.
121 G4 New Haven U.S.A.
120 B4 New Hazelton U.S.A.
128 B4 New Hogan Reservoir resr U.S.A.
122 C4 New Holstein U.S.A.

125 F6 New Iberia U.S.A.
83 E3 Newington R.S.A.
18 E4 New Ireland i. P.N.G.
121 F5 New Jersey div. U.S.A.
120 E6 New Kent U.S.A.
121 J2 New Lexington U.S.A.
122 B4 New Lisbon U.S.A.
115 F3 New Liskeard Can.
121 G4 New London U.S.A.
122 B6 New London U.S.A.
101 B4 New Norcia Aust.
122 D6 Newman U.S.A.
133 □1 Newmarket Jamaica
121 H3 Newmarket U.S.A.
115 F5 Newmarket Can.
120 C5 Newmarket-on-Fergus Rep. of Ire.
120 C5 New Martinsville U.S.A.
90 □6 New Melanes L. l. U.S.A.
128 B3 New Melanes L. l. U.S.A.
121 G3 New Mexico div. U.S.A.
119 C5 New Orleans U.S.A.
121 F4 New Paltz U.S.A.
121 J4 New Philadelphia U.S.A.
92 E3 New Plymouth N.Z.
133 □3 Newport Jamaica
132 □2 New Port Curaçao Netherlands Ant.
17 G6 Newport U.K.
17 F6 Newport U.K.
17 G6 Newport U.K.
120 A5 Newport U.S.A.
120 J2 Newport U.S.A.
123 G3 Newport U.S.A.
121 J3 Newport U.S.A.
121 G3 Newport U.S.A.
121 H2 Newport U.S.A.
121 G4 Newport U.S.A.
126 A2 Newport U.S.A.
128 D5 Newport Beach U.S.A.
120 E6 Newport News U.S.A.
119 □2 New Providence i. The Bahamas
17 C7 Newquay U.K.
113 G4 New Richmond Can.
122 A3 New Richmond U.S.A.
129 F5 New River U.S.A.
17 D4 New Ross Rep. of Ire.
17 D4 Newry U.K.
122 A5 New Sharon U.S.A.
119 D6 New Smyrna Beach U.S.A.
97 F2 New South Wales div. Aust.
124 D3 Newton U.S.A.
124 E4 Newton U.S.A.
125 F5 Newton U.S.A.
121 F4 Newton U.S.A.
120 E4 Newton U.S.A.
16 E4 Newton Stewart U.K.
17 C4 New Town U.S.A.
17 F4 Newtonabbey U.K.
17 E4 Newtonards U.K.
124 E2 New Ulm U.S.A.
17 E6 Newville U.S.A.
16 E4 New Westminster Can.
121 F3 New York div. U.S.A.
121 G4 New York U.S.A.
120 C4 New York U.S.A.
121 F4 New York-John F. Kennedy airport U.S.A.
121 F4 New York-Newark U.S.A.
86 J9 New Zealand country Australasia
149 Q7 New Zealand Plateau Pac. Oc.
12 D3 Neya r. Rus. Fed.
14 F1 Neya Rus. Fed.
57 C2 Neyrīz Iran
57 D1 Neyshābūr Iran
56 B4 Neyyattinkara India
15 C2 Nezhyn Ukraine
126 C2 Nez Perce U.S.A.
15 E2 Nezlobnaya Rus. Fed.
15 F2 Nezvys'ko Ukraine
40 D2 Ngabang Indon.
43 A6 Nga Chong, Kh. mt. Myanmar/Thailand
42 B3 Ngabordamlu, Tanjung pt Indon.
40 A3 Ngada mt. Indon.
77 G4 Ngadda w Nigeria
42 A3 Ngalaa mt. Myanmar
77 G4 Ngala Nigeria
90 □8 Ngalau Angola
77 G4 Ngalu Indon.
82 A3 Ngami, Lake l. Botswana
54 E2 Ngamring China
55 F3 Nganglong Kangri mt. China
55 E3 Nganglong Kangri mt. ra. China
55 F3 Ngangzê Co l. China
79 C5 Ngangola Angola
79 C5 Ngangola Co salt l. China
76 D4 Nganjuk Indon.
78 B3 Ngaoundal Cameroon
78 B3 Ngaoundéré Cameroon
78 D3 Ngara Tanzania
77 F4 Ngaras Indon.
93 C6 Ngarua N.Z.
92 D1 Ngaruawahia N.Z.
92 F3 Ngarururoro r. N.Z.
78 B3 Ngaundaba Cameroon
81 B4 Ngau i. Fiji
77 G4 Ngawi Indon.
81 B4 Ngawihi N.Z.
79 D5 Ngabé Congo
78 B4 Ngba Cameroon
42 A3 Ngape Myanmar
80 B4 Ngara Tanzania
78 B4 Ngo Congo
42 A3 Ngoako Ramalepe S. Africa
50 A1 Ngoin, Co l. China
78 B3 Ngol Bembo Nigeria
77 G4 Ngomdzap Cameroon
50 A1 Ngoin, Co l. China
78 B4 Ngomedzap Cameroon
42 A2 Ngop Sudan
81 C5 Ngorongoro Conservation Area res. Tanzania
78 B3 Ngong Cameroon
81 C5 Ngong Kenya
50 A1 Ngoqu China
48 C4 Ngoring Hu l. China
48 C5 Ngoring Hu l. China
81 C5 Ngorongoro Crater crater Tanzania
78 B4 Ngoto C.A.R.
77 G4 Ngourti Niger
78 C1 Ngouri Chad
78 C1 Ngoura Chad
78 C1 Ngouri Chad
77 G3 Ngoyi Niger
72 C4 Ngoutchou well Chad
78 E2 Ngol Niger
77 G4 Ngui Niger
39 L5 Ngulu i. Fed. States of Micronesia
90 □2 Nguna i. Vanuatu
83 D4 Ngungu Zimbabwe
40 C4 Ngunut Indon.
77 G4 Nguru Nigeria
42 D2 Nguyên Binh Vietnam
42 D2 Ngwaketse div. Botswana
82 C3 Ngwako Pan salt pan Botswana
79 E7 Ngweze r. Zambia
83 F3 Nhachengue Mozambique
83 G2 Nha Som Vietnam
83 G2 Nhamalabué Mozambique
83 G2 Nhamatanda Mozambique
141 E2 Nhambiquara Brazil
142 A1 Nhamundá Brazil
139 F4 Nhamundá r. Brazil
79 C6 N'harea Angola
79 C6 Nha Trang Vietnam
141 E3 Nhecolândia Brazil
79 B6 Nhia r. Angola
96 F4 Nhill Aust.
42 D2 Nho Quan Vietnam
98 D2 Nhulunbuy Aust.
111 J4 Niacam Can.
76 D3 Niafounké Mali
76 D3 Niagara U.S.A.
122 D3 Niagara Falls Can.
120 D3 Niagara Falls U.S.A.
123 H4 Niagara River r. U.S.A.
76 C4 Niagassola Guinea
76 C4 Niagouelé, Mt de h. Guinea
54 D2 Niagzu China/Jammu and Kashmir
76 C4 Niakaramandougou Côte d'Ivoire
77 F3 Niamey Niger
41 C5 Niamtougou Togo
76 C5 Niandan r. Guinea
78 B3 Niangara Zaire
76 D4 Nia-Nia Zaire
49 J3 Niangara Zaire
93 B4 Niapa mt. Indon.
44 B7 Nias i. Indon.
81 C7 Niassa div. Mozambique
11 F4 Nica Latvia
104 K8 Nicaragua country Central America
132 D4 Nicaragua, Lago de l. Nicaragua
27 F5 Nicastro Italy
21 H5 Nice France
113 G3 Nichicun, Lac l. Can.
46 C7 Nichihara Japan
132 B2 Nicholas Channel chan. The Bahamas/Cuba
132 □1 Nicholl's Town The Bahamas
120 D3 Nicholson r. Aust.
100 D3 Nicholson r. Aust.
101 B5 Nicholson Ra. h. Aust.
43 A5 Nicobar Islands is Andaman and Nicobar Is India
28 G2 Nicolae Bălcescu Romania
115 J3 Nicolet Italy
27 E4 Nicotera Italy
130 J7 Nicoya, G. de b. Mexico
121 K2 Nictau Can.
28 D2 Niculiţel Romania
11 J3 Nida Lithuania
19 J3 Nida r. Poland
18 E3 Nidda r. Germany
19 G2 Nidzica Poland
19 G4 Niedere Tauern mts Austria
18 D2 Niederösterreich div. Austria
18 D2 Niedersachsen div. Germany
77 G4 Nienburg (Weser) Germany
78 D3 Niemba Zaire
18 E2 Niemegk Germany
76 C4 Niéna Mali
18 D2 Nienburg (Weser) Germany
76 C4 Niénokoué, Mt h. Côte d'Ivoire
18 B2 Niers r. Germany
18 D3 Niesky Germany
18 C3 Nieuw Amsterdam Surinam
139 G3 Nieuw-Jacobkondre Surinam
18 B2 Nieuw Nickerie Surinam
147 □ Nieves, Pico de las mt. Canary Is
77 F4 Niéri Niger
77 G3 Niger country Africa
77 F3 Niger div. Nigeria
77 F4 Niger r. Africa
77 F4 Niger, Mouths of the river mouth Nigeria
76 B5 Niger, Source of the Guinea
93 C4 Nightcaps N.Z.
114 C1 Nighthawk Lake l. Can.
147 □ Nightingale Is. i. Tristan da Cunha Atlantic Ocean
46 D6 Nihommatsu Japan
47 G5 Niigata div. Japan
47 H5 Niigata Japan
46 D7 Nihino Japan
127 □1 Ni'ihau i. U.S.A.
46 J2 Niikappu Japan
47 G6 Niimi Japan
47 G5 Niitsu Japan
25 F2 Níjar Spain
18 C2 Nijkerk Netherlands
18 B2 Nijmegen Netherlands
10 H1 Nikel' Rus. Fed.
91 F3 Nikiniki Indon.
10 F1 Nikki Benin
47 G5 Nikkō Japan
47 G5 Nikkō National Park nat. park Japan
65 G2 Nikolayevka Kazak.
64 F2 Nikolayevka Rus. Fed.
13 H5 Nikolayevsk Rus. Fed.
63 Q4 Nikolayevsk-na-Amure Rus. Fed.
14 J3 Nikol'sk Rus. Fed.
14 H1 Nikol'sk Rus. Fed.
63 S4 Nikol'skoye Rus. Fed.

28 E3 Nikopol Bulgaria
15 F3 Nikopol' Ukraine
57 B1 Nik Pey Iran
60 D1 Niksar Turkey
57 E4 Nikshahr Iran
28 B3 Nikšić Yugo.
150 H6 Nikumaroro i. Kiribati
150 G6 Nikunau i. Kiribati
54 C2 Nila Pakistan
55 F5 Nilagiri India
129 E5 Niland U.S.A.
53 D10 Nilande Atoll atoll Maldives
54 D3 Nilang India
56 B2 Nilanga India
73 F2 Nile r. Africa
122 D5 Niles U.S.A.
56 A3 Nileswaram India
56 B4 Nilgiri Hills mts India
80 C2 Nili r. Ethiopia
57 F2 Nil P. pass Afghanistan
10 H3 Nilsiä Finland
131 G5 Niltepec Mexico
54 C4 Nimach India
54 C4 Nimbahera India
76 C5 Nimba, Monts mt. Côte d'Ivoire
21 G5 Nîmes France
97 G4 Nimmitabel Aust.
152 B4 Nimrod Gl. gl. Ant.
80 B4 Nimule Sudan
60 E3 Nīnawá div. Iraq
79 D6 Ninda Angola
99 G6 Nindigully Aust.
53 D9 Nine Degree Channel chan. India
128 D2 Ninemile Peak summit U.S.A.
45 □ Ninepin Group is Hong Kong
149 K5 Ninety-East Ridge Indian Ocean
97 F4 Ninety Mile Beach beach Aust.
92 D1 Ninety Mile Beach beach N.Z.
60 E2 Nineveh Iraq
121 F3 Nineveh U.S.A.
147 D5 Ninfas, Pta pt Arg.
49 J3 Ning'an China
51 H2 Ningbo China
49 F4 Ningcheng China
51 G3 Ningde China
51 F3 Ningdu China
51 F3 Ninggang China
51 G2 Ningguo China
51 H2 Ninghai China
49 F5 Ninghe China
51 G3 Ninghua China
77 F4 Ningi Nigeria
50 B2 Ningjing Shan mt. ra. China
50 C3 Ninglang China
51 F1 Ningling China
50 D4 Ningming China
50 C3 Ningnan China
50 D1 Ningqiang China
50 E1 Ningshan China
48 E5 Ningwu China
48 C5 Ningxia div. China
50 D1 Ning Xian China
51 F2 Ningxiang China
49 F6 Ningyang China
51 E3 Ningyuan China
42 D2 Ninh Binh Vietnam
43 E4 Ninh Hoa Vietnam
90 □5 Niniva i. Tonga
152 B6 Ninnis Gl. gl. Ant.
47 H3 Ninohe Japan
147 B6 Ninualac, Can. chan. Chile
143 A5 Nioaque Brazil
124 C3 Niobrara r. U.S.A.
78 F3 Nioka Zaire
79 C4 Nioki Zaire
55 H4 Nioko India
76 B4 Niokolo Koba, Parc National du nat. park Senegal
76 C4 Niono Mali
76 C3 Nioro Mali
76 A4 Nioro du Rip Senegal
20 D3 Niort France
74 C5 Nioût well Mauritania
90 □1 Nipa P.N.G.
56 A2 Nipani India
111 J4 Nipawin Can.
111 J4 Nipawin Provincial Park res. Can.
114 A2 Nipigon Can.
114 A2 Nipigon Bay b. Can.
114 A2 Nipigon, Lake l. Can.
113 H3 Nipishish Lake l. Can.
115 F3 Nipissing Can.
115 F3 Nipissing, L. l. Can.
128 B4 Nipomo U.S.A.
129 E4 Nipton U.S.A.
142 C3 Niquelândia Brazil
132 C2 Niquero Cuba
60 F2 Nir Iran
56 A2 Nira r. India
47 G6 Nirasaki Japan
73 H3 Nīr, J. an h. Saudi Arabia
56 B2 Nirmal India
55 F4 Nirmali India
56 B2 Nirmal Range h. India
28 C3 Niš Yugo.
24 C3 Nisa Portugal
27 E7 Niscemi Italy
46 H2 Niseko Japan
47 G5 Nishiaizu Japan
46 K2 Nishibetsu-gawa r. Japan
46 C8 Nishikata Japan
47 H4 Nishikawa Japan
46 E6 Nishino-shima i. Japan
46 D5 Nishino-shima i. Japan
46 B7 Nishi-Sonogi-hantō pen. Japan
46 B6 Nishi-suidō chan. S. Korea
46 E6 Nishiwaki Japan
19 L3 Nisko Poland
110 B2 Nisling r. Can.
15 C3 Nisporeni Moldova
11 D4 Nissan r. Sweden
15 C3 Nistru r. Moldova
110 C2 Nisutlin r. Can.
29 F6 Nisyros i. Greece
57 B4 Niţā Saudi Arabia
113 F3 Nitchequon Can.
145 G5 Niterói Brazil
17 F4 Nith r. U.K.
19 J4 Nitra Slovakia
120 C5 Nitro U.S.A.
90 □4 Niu' Aunofo pt Tonga
87 L6 Niue i. Pac. Oc.
150 G6 Niulakita i. Tuvalu
50 C3 Niulan r. China
86 J5 Niutao i. Tuvalu
49 G4 Niuzhuang China
10 G3 Nivala Finland
99 F5 Nive w Aust.
99 F5 Nive Downs Aust.
12 K2 Nivshera Rus. Fed.
54 C4 Niwāi India
128 C2 Nixon U.S.A.
65 K5 Niya r. China
46 D7 Niyodo-gawa r. Japan
40 B1 Niyut, G. mt. Indon.
56 B2 Nizamabad India
56 B2 Nizam Sagar l. India
64 D1 Nizhnekamsk Rus. Fed.
64 D1 Nizhnekamskoye Vdkhr. resr Rus. Fed.
63 S3 Nizhnekolymsk Rus. Fed.
63 L4 Nizhneudinsk Rus. Fed.
62 J3 Nizhnevartovsk Rus. Fed.
63 P2 Nizhneyansk Rus. Fed.
13 G5 Nizhniy Chir Rus. Fed.
14 F3 Nizhniy Lomov Rus. Fed.
14 F1 Nizhniy Novgorod div. Rus. Fed.
12 K2 Nizhniy Odes Rus. Fed.
14 F3 Nizhniy Shibryay Rus. Fed.
14 G3 Nizhniy Shkaft Rus. Fed.
62 G4 Nizhniy Tagil Rus. Fed.
49 E2 Nizhniy Tsasuchey Rus. Fed.
12 H3 Nizhniy Yenangsk Rus. Fed.
12 H1 Nizhnyaya Mgla Rus. Fed.
65 H1 Nizhnyaya Omka Rus. Fed.
49 F2 Nizhnyaya Shakhtama Rus. Fed.
12 G1 Nizhnyaya Zolotitsa Rus. Fed.
15 D1 Nizhyn Ukraine
19 K2 Nizina reg. Poland
60 D2 Nizip Turkey
61 D1 Nizip r. Turkey
19 K4 Nízke Beskydy reg. Slovakia
19 J4 Nízke Tatry mts Slovakia
26 B3 Nizza Monferrato Italy
10 E2 Njavve Sweden
81 D7 Njazidja i. Comoros
28 B3 Njegoš mts Yugo.
81 C6 Njinjo Tanzania
79 D7 Njoko r. Zambia
81 B6 Njombe Tanzania
81 B6 Njombe r. Tanzania
11 E3 Njurundabommen Sweden
78 B2 Nkambe Cameroon
81 B6 Nkasi Tanzania
76 D5 Nkawkaw Ghana
83 D2 Nkayi Zimbabwe
74 C5 Nkhaïlé well Mauritania
81 B7 Nkhata Bay Malawi
81 B7 Nkhotakota Malawi
81 B7 Nkhotakota Game Reserve res. Malawi
78 A4 Nkomi, Lagune lag. Gabon
81 B6 Nkondwe Tanzania
78 A3 Nkongsamba Cameroon
76 D5 Nkoranza Ghana
78 B3 Nkoteng Cameroon
81 B6 Nkundi Tanzania
82 B2 Nkurenkuru Namibia
82 D5 Nkwenkwezi R.S.A.
42 B1 Nmai Hka r. Myanmar
55 H4 Noa Dihing r. India
55 G5 Noakhali Bangladesh
55 F5 Noamundi India
46 C7 Nobeoka Japan
46 H2 Noboribetsu Japan
142 A3 Nobres Brazil
99 E5 Noccundra Aust.
99 E5 Nockatunga Aust.
114 E3 Noelville Can.
130 C2 Nogales Mexico
20 D5 Nogaro France
46 C7 Nōgata Japan
20 E2 Nogent-le-Rotrou France
20 F2 Nogent-sur-Oise France
20 F3 Nogent-sur-Vernisson France
14 D2 Noginsk Rus. Fed.
63 L3 Noginsky Rus. Fed.
99 G5 Nogo r. Aust.
99 F5 Nogoa r. Aust.
47 F6 Nōgōhaku-san mt. Japan
146 E3 Nogoyá Arg.
146 E3 Nogoya r. Arg.
25 G1 Noguera Pallaresa r. Spain
49 J5 Nogwak-san mt. S. Korea
54 C3 Nohar India
46 H3 Noheji Japan
18 C4 Nohfelden Germany
24 B1 Noia Spain
144 B1 Noidore r. Brazil
133 □5 Noire, Pointe pt Guadeloupe Caribbean
24 E5 Noire, Pte pt Morocco
20 C2 Noires, Montagnes h. France
20 C3 Noirmoutier-en-l'Île France
20 C3 Noirmoutier, Île de i. France
47 G6 Nojima-zaki c. Japan
54 C4 Nokha India
57 E3 Nok Kundi Pakistan
111 J3 Nokomis Lake l. Can.
72 B5 Nokou Chad
55 G4 Nokrek Pk. mt. India
78 C3 Nola C.A.R.
12 J3 Nolinsk Rus. Fed.
46 C8 Noma-misaki pt Japan
121 H4 No Mans Land i. U.S.A.
108 B3 Nome U.S.A.
48 C4 Nomgon Mongolia
46 D6 Nōmi-jima i. Japan
86 G4 Nomoi Islands is Fed. States of Micronesia
82 D5 Nomonde R.S.A.
46 B7 Nomo-zaki pt Japan
90 □5 Nomuka i. Tonga
90 □5 Nomuka Group is Tonga
90 □5 Nomuka Iki i. Tonga
12 G3 Nomzha Rus. Fed.
111 H2 Nonacho Lake l. Can.
49 H3 Nong'an China
42 D3 Nông Hèt Laos
43 C4 Nong Hong Thailand
42 C3 Nong Khai Thailand
55 G4 Nongstoin India
96 D3 Nonning Aust.
130 D3 Nonoava Mexico
150 G6 Nonouti i. Kiribati
49 H5 Nonsan S. Korea
43 C4 Nonthaburi Thailand
20 E4 Nontron France
82 C5 Nonzwakazi R.S.A.
101 B5 Nookawarra Aust.
96 D1 Noolyeanna L. salt flat Aust.
99 F6 Noorama Cr. w Aust.
18 A3 Noordbeveland i. Netherlands
18 B3 Noord-Brabant div. Netherlands
18 B2 Noord-Holland div. Netherlands
18 B2 Noordoost Polder reclaimed land Netherlands
132 □2 Noord Punt pt Curaçao Netherlands Ant.
110 D5 Nootka I. i. Can.
79 B5 Nóqui Angola
65 G5 Norak Tajikistan
41 C5 Norala Phil.
115 F2 Noranda Can.
11 D3 Norberg Sweden
78 B2 Nord div. Cameroon
109 R1 Nord Greenland
62 D2 Nordaustlandet i. Svalbard Arctic Ocean
18 C2 Norden Germany
63 L2 Nordenshel'da, Arkhipelag is Rus. Fed.
18 C2 Norderney i. Germany
18 C2 Norderney Germany
18 E2 Norderstedt Germany
11 B3 Nordfjordeid Norway
10 D2 Nordfold Norway
18 D1 Nordfriesische Inseln is Germany
18 E3 Nordhausen Germany
16 K1 Nordhorland chan. Norway
18 C2 Nordhorn Germany
10 G1 Nordkapp c. Norway
10 E1 Nordkjosbotn Norway
10 H1 Nordkynhalvøya i. Norway
10 D2 Nordland div. Norway
10 D2 Nordlii Norway
18 E4 Nördlingen Germany
10 E3 Nordmaling Sweden
78 B2 Nord-Ouest div. Cameroon
20 F1 Nord-Pas-de-Calais div. France
109 N3 Nordre Strømfjord inlet Greenland
18 C3 Nordrhein-Westfalen div. Germany
18 D1 Nordstrand i. Germany
10 C2 Nord-Trøndelag div. Norway
10 L2 Norðurland Vestra div. Iceland
63 N2 Nordvik Rus. Fed.
17 D5 Nore r. Rep. of Ire.
124 D3 Norfolk U.S.A.
121 F2 Norfolk U.S.A.
121 E6 Norfolk airport U.S.A.
95 □1 Norfolk I. i. Pac. Oc.
150 G7 Norfolk Island Ridge Pac. Oc.
150 F7 Norfolk Island Trough Pac. Oc.
125 E4 Norfork L. l. U.S.A.
11 B3 Norheimsund Norway
47 F5 Norikura-dake vol Japan
62 K3 Noril'sk Rus. Fed.
14 A3 Norino Rus. Fed.
115 F4 Norland Can.
122 C5 Normal U.S.A.
99 E3 Norman r. Aust.
125 D5 Norman U.S.A.
99 F2 Normanby r. Aust.
90 □1 Normanby I. i. P.N.G.
99 G4 Normanby Ra. h. Aust.
139 F3 Normandia Brazil
115 J2 Normandin Can.
119 □3 Norman I. i. Virgin Is Caribbean
92 □1 Norman Inlet inlet Auckland Is N.Z.
119 D5 Norman, L. l. U.S.A.
133 □1 Norman Manley airport Jamaica
99 E3 Normanton Aust.
110 D1 Norman Wells Can.
115 F2 Normétal Can.
152 □ Noroît, Baie b. Kerguelen Indian Ocean
141 E2 Noronha r. Brazil
147 B5 Ñorquinco Arg.
10 F3 Norra Kvarken str. Finland/Sweden
10 D2 Norra Storfjället mts Sweden
10 E2 Norrbotten div. Sweden
114 C2 Norris Can.
120 B6 Norris Lake l. U.S.A.
121 F4 Norristown U.S.A.
11 E4 Norrköping Sweden
11 E4 Norrtälje Sweden
101 C7 Norseman Aust.
92 F4 Norsewood N.Z.
10 E2 Norsjö Sweden
90 □2 Norsup Vanuatu
139 G3 Norte, Cabo pt Brazil
91 □16 Norte, Cabo c. Easter I. Chile
142 A3 Nortelândia Brazil
146 E4 Norte, Pta pt Buenos Aires Arg.
147 D5 Norte, Pta pt Chubut Arg.
121 G3 North Adams U.S.A.
17 G4 Northallerton U.K.
101 B6 Northam Aust.
148 F4 North American Basin Atlantic Ocean
101 A6 Northampton Aust.
17 G5 Northampton U.K.
121 G3 Northampton U.S.A.
99 F5 Northampton Downs Aust.
43 A4 North Andaman i. Andaman and Nicobar Is India
120 E5 North Anna r. U.S.A.
121 J2 North Anson U.S.A.
110 G2 North Arm b. Can.
90 □7 North Astrolabe Reef reef Fiji
119 D5 North Augusta U.S.A.
113 H2 North Aulatsivik Island i. Can.
41 A4 North Balabac Strait chan. Phil.
111 H4 North Battleford Can.
115 F3 North Bay Can.
112 E2 North Belcher Islands is Can.
126 A3 North Bend U.S.A.
16 F3 North Berwick U.K.
121 H3 North Berwick U.S.A.
122 A3 North Branch U.S.A.
152 A5 North, C. c. Ant.
147 G7 North C. c. Atlantic Ocean
113 H4 North, C. c. Can.
93 □3 North C. c. Antipodes Is N.Z.
113 H4 North Cape pt Prince Edward I. Can.
92 D1 North Cape c. N.Z.
112 B3 North Caribou Lake l. Can.
119 D5 North Carolina div. U.S.A.
126 B1 North Cascades Nat. Park U.S.A.
119 □2 North Cay i. The Bahamas
114 D3 North Channel chan. Can.
17 E4 North Channel str. U.K.
101 B7 Northcliffe Aust.
121 H2 North Conway U.S.A.
124 C2 North Dakota div. U.S.A.
17 G6 North Downs h. U.K.
82 D3 North East div. Botswana
120 D3 North East U.S.A.
82 □1 North East Bay b. Ascension Atlantic Ocean
80 D4 North-Eastern div. Kenya
148 H2 North-Eastern Atlantic Basin Atlantic Ocean
92 □2 North East Harb. inlet Campbell I. N.Z.
92 □3 North East Island i. Snares Is N.Z.
94 □2 North East Point pt Christmas I. Indian Ocean
133 □1 Northeast Point pt Jamaica
132 D2 Northeast Point pt The Bahamas
132 D2 Northeast Point pt The Bahamas
132 C1 Northeast Providence Chan. chan. The Bahamas
18 D3 Northeim Germany
132 D1 North End Pt pt The Bahamas
41 □1 North Entrance chan. Palau
76 D5 Northern div. Ghana
81 B7 Northern div. Malawi
76 B5 Northern div. Sierra Leone
73 E4 Northern div. Sudan
81 B7 Northern div. Zambia
54 C1 Northern Areas div. Pakistan
82 C5 Northern Cape div. R.S.A.
111 K3 Northern Indian Lake l. Can.
17 D4 Northern Ireland div. U.K.
112 B4 Northern Light L. l. Can.
86 F3 Northern Mariana Islands terr. Pac. Oc.
94 □2 Northern Plateau plat. Christmas I. Indian Ocean
83 D3 Northern Province div. R.S.A.
133 □3 Northern Range mt. ra. Trinidad Trin. and Tobago
98 C3 Northern Territory div. Aust.
16 F3 North Esk r. U.K.
121 G3 Northfield U.S.A.
122 A3 Northfield U.S.A.
121 G2 Northfield U.S.A.
17 H6 North Foreland c. U.K.
128 C3 North Fork U.S.A.
128 B2 North Fork American r. U.S.A.
128 B2 North Fork Feather r. U.S.A.
122 E3 North Fox I. i. U.S.A.
114 E1 North French r. Can.
133 □6 North Friar's Bay b. St Kitts-Nevis Caribbean
121 K2 North Head Can.
92 E2 North Head hd N.Z.
94 □3 North Head pt Macquarie I. Pac. Oc.
111 K2 North Henik Lake l. Can.
121 G3 North Hudson U.S.A.
94 □4 North I. i. Lord Howe I. Pac. Oc.
81 □1 North I. i. Seychelles
41 B1 North Is i. Phil.
92 E3 North Island i. N.Z.
41 B4 North Islet reef Phil.
129 G4 North Jadito Canyon U.S.A.
122 D5 North Judson U.S.A.
94 □1 North Keeling I. i. Cocos Is Indian Ocean
111 K3 North Knife r. Can.
33 O5 North Korea country Asia
55 H4 North Lakhimpur India
92 E1 Northland div. N.Z.
129 E3 North Las Vegas U.S.A.
125 E5 North Little Rock U.S.A.
81 B7 North Luangwa National Park nat. park Zambia
129 H2 North Mam Peak summit U.S.A.
122 E5 North Manchester U.S.A.
122 D3 North Manitou I. i. U.S.A.
114 E3 North Monetville Can.
110 D2 North Nahanni r. Can.
133 □1 North Negril Pt pt Jamaica
111 L5 Northome U.S.A.
128 C3 North Palisade summit U.S.A.
124 C3 North Platte r. U.S.A.
124 C3 North Platte U.S.A.
82 A4 North Point pt Ascension Atlantic Ocean
82 A5 North Point pt Tristan da Cunha Atlantic Ocean
97 F4 North Point pt Aust.
133 □9 North Point pt Barbados Caribbean
45 □ North Point Hong Kong
81 □2 North Point pt Seychelles
118 D2 North Point pt U.S.A.
122 E3 Northport U.S.A.
92 □3 North Promontory pt Snares Is N.Z.
43 A4 North Reef I. i. Andaman and Nicobar Is India
129 F3 North Rim U.S.A.
16 F2 North Ronaldsay i. U.K.
128 B2 North San Juan U.S.A.
111 G4 North Saskatchewan r. Can.
4 F3 North Sea sea Europe
111 J3 North Seal r. Can.
43 A5 North Sentinel I. i. Andaman and Nicobar Is India
128 D2 North Shoshone Peak summit U.S.A.
17 H5 North Somercotes U.K.
99 H5 North Stradbroke I. i. Aust.
121 H2 North Stratford U.S.A.
92 E3 North Taranaki Bight b. N.Z.
110 F4 North Thompson r. Can.
120 D3 North Tonawanda U.S.A.
54 D3 North Tons r. India
93 A7 North Trap reef N.Z.
121 G2 North Troy U.S.A.
112 D3 North Twin I. i. Can.
17 F4 North Tyne r. U.K.
16 D3 North Uist i. U.K.
99 G4 Northumberland Is is Aust.
113 H4 Northumberland Strait chan. Can.
110 E5 North Vancouver Can.
121 F3 Northville U.S.A.
17 H5 North Walsham U.K.
82 D4 North West div. R.S.A.
92 □2 North West B. b. Campbell I. N.Z.
100 A4 North West C. c. Aust.
92 □1 North West C. c. Auckland Is N.Z.
79 D6 North-Western div. Zambia
54 C2 North West Frontier Pakistan
94 □2 North West Point pt Christmas I. Indian Ocean
132 C1 Northwest Providence Chan. chan. The Bahamas
113 J3 North West River Can.
108 H3 Northwest Territories Can.
121 F5 North Wildwood U.S.A.
121 H2 North Woodstock U.S.A.
17 G4 North York Moors h. U.K.
113 G4 Norton Can.
124 D4 Norton U.S.A.
121 H2 Norton U.S.A.
120 B6 Norton U.S.A.
83 E2 Norton Zimbabwe
108 B3 Norton Sound b. U.S.A.
18 D1 Nortorf Germany
20 D3 Nort-sur-Erdre France
152 C2 Norvegia, C. c. Ant.
121 G4 Norwalk U.S.A.
120 B4 Norwalk U.S.A.
4 F2 Norway country Europe
121 H2 Norway U.S.A.
115 G4 Norway Bay Can.
111 K4 Norway House Can.
148 J1 Norwegian Basin Atlantic Ocean
109 J2 Norwegian Bay b. Can.
148 K1 Norwegian Sea Atlantic Ocean
114 E5 Norwich Can.
17 H5 Norwich U.K.
121 G4 Norwich U.S.A.
121 F3 Norwich U.S.A.
121 H3 Norwood U.S.A.
121 F2 Norwood U.S.A.
120 A5 Norwood U.S.A.
46 K2 Nosapu-misaki pt Japan
146 C1 Nos de Cachi mt. Arg.
111 H1 Nose Lake l. Can.
28 F3 Nos Emine pt Bulgaria
28 F3 Nos Galata pt Bulgaria
46 H1 Noshappu-misaki hd Japan
47 G3 Noshiro Japan
12 J2 Noshul' Rus. Fed.
15 D1 Nosivka Ukraine
28 G3 Nos Kaliakra pt Bulgaria
15 B2 Noskivtsi Ukraine
82 C4 Nosop r. Botswana
14 G1 Nosovaya Rus. Fed.
57 D3 Noşratābād Iran
142 E3 Nossa Senhora das Dores Brazil
143 A4 Nossa Senhora do Livramento Brazil
11 D4 Nossebro Sweden
18 F3 Nossen Germany
28 G3 Nos Shabla pt Bulgaria
16 G1 Noss, Isle of i. U.K.
82 C4 Nossob r. Namibia/R.S.A.
76 C4 Nossombougou Mali
83 H1 Nosy Bé i. Madagascar
83 H2 Nosy Boraha i. Madagascar
83 H1 Nosy Lava i. Madagascar
83 H1 Nosy Radama i. Madagascar
83 H3 Nosy Varika Madagascar
129 F2 Notch Peak summit U.S.A.
19 G2 Noteć r. Poland
29 C5 Notia Pindos mt. ra. Greece
29 E6 Notio Aigaio div. Greece
29 D5 Notios Evvoïkos Kolpos chan. Greece
29 C5 Notio Steno Kerkyras chan. Greece
47 F5 Noto Japan
11 C4 Notodden Norway
27 E7 Noto, Golfo di g. Italy
47 F5 Noto-hantō pen. Japan
47 F5 Noto-jima i. Japan
46 K1 Notoro-ko l. Japan
113 K4 Notre Dame Bay b. Can.
115 H4 Notre-Dame-de-la-Salette Can.
121 H2 Notre-Dame-des-Bois Can.
115 H3 Notre-Dame-du-Laus Can.
115 F3 Notre-Dame-du-Nord Can.
113 G4 Notre Dame, Monts mt. ra. Can.
77 E5 Notsé Togo
46 K2 Notsuke-saki pt Japan
46 K2 Notsuke-suidō chan. Japan
114 E4 Nottawasaga Bay b. Can.
112 E3 Nottaway r. Can.
17 G5 Nottingham U.K.
120 E6 Nottoway r. U.S.A.
111 H5 Notukeu Cr. r. Can.
74 A4 Nouâdhibou Mauritania
74 A5 Nouakchott Mauritania
74 C5 Noual well Mauritania
74 A5 Nouâmghâr Mauritania
42 D4 Nouei Vietnam
74 A5 Noueïch well Mauritania
90 □2 Nouméa Pac. Oc.
78 B3 Noun r. Cameroon
76 D4 Nouna Burkina
82 C5 Noupoort R.S.A.
10 H2 Nousu Finland
65 G4 Nov Tajikistan
145 H4 Nova Almeida Brazil
144 A4 Nova Alvorada Brazil
144 D1 Nova America Brazil
144 B5 Nova Andradina Brazil
13 F5 Nova Astrakhan' Ukraine
144 D3 Nova Aurora Brazil
19 J4 Nová Baňa Slovakia
15 C1 Nova Borova Ukraine
79 B5 Nova Caipemba Angola
28 D2 Novaci Romania
145 G3 Nova Era Brazil
144 B5 Nova Esperança Brazil
145 G5 Nova Friburgo Brazil
26 F3 Nova Gradiška Croatia
144 D4 Nova Granada Brazil
145 G5 Nova Iguaçu Brazil
15 E3 Nova Kakhovka Ukraine
145 G3 Nova Lima Brazil
144 B5 Nova Londrina Brazil
12 D4 Novalukoml' Belarus
83 F3 Nova Mambone Mozambique
15 E3 Nova Mayachka Ukraine
83 F2 Nova Nabúri Mozambique
15 D3 Nova Odesa Ukraine
19 G3 Nová Paka Czech Rep.
28 C2 Nova Pazova Yugo.
142 D2 Nova Pilão Arcado Brazil
144 E3 Nova Ponte Brazil
15 E2 Nova Praha Ukraine
26 B3 Novara Italy
142 D2 Nova Remanso Brazil
145 E4 Nova Resende Brazil
142 C3 Nova Roma Brazil
144 B6 Nova Santa Rosa Brazil
113 H5 Nova Scotia div. Can.
142 D2 Nova Sento Sé Brazil
145 F3 Nova Serrana Brazil
15 F1 Nova Sloboda Ukraine
142 E3 Nova Soure Brazil
128 A2 Novato U.S.A.
26 F3 Nova Topola Bos.-Herz.
15 B2 Nova Ushytsya Ukraine
28 B3 Nova Varoš Yugo.
145 H3 Nova Venécia Brazil
145 J2 Nova Viçosa Brazil
141 D2 Nova Vida Brazil
15 F2 Nova Vodolaha Ukraine
144 B1 Nova Xavantina Brazil
14 H3 Novaya Bekshanka Rus. Fed.
64 C3 Novaya Kazanka Kazak.
12 E2 Novaya Ladoga Rus. Fed.
14 E3 Novaya Lyada Rus. Fed.
63 R2 Novaya Sibir', O. i. Rus. Fed.
62 G2 Novaya Zemlya i. Rus. Fed.
28 E3 Nova Zagora Bulgaria
15 E3 Nova Zbur"yivka Ukraine
15 E2 Nove Ukraine
25 F3 Novelda Spain
19 H3 Nové Město nad Metuj Czech Rep.
19 J5 Nové Zámky Slovakia
12 D3 Novgorod div. Rus. Fed.
12 D3 Novgorod Rus. Fed.
15 E2 Novhorodka Ukraine
14 A4 Novhorod-Sivers'kyy Ukraine
28 C2 Novi Bečej Yugo.
15 C1 Novi Bilokorovychi Ukraine
15 D1 Novi Borovychi Ukraine
15 A1 Novi Chervyshcha Ukraine
28 D3 Novi Iskŭr Bulgaria
26 B3 Novi Ligure Italy
26 F2 Novi Marof Croatia
15 E1 Novi Mlyny Ukraine
28 F3 Novi Pazar Bulgaria
28 C3 Novi Pazar Yugo.
28 B2 Novi Sad Yugo.
15 F2 Novi Sanzhary Ukraine
26 E3 Novi Vinodolski Croatia
14 E1 Novki Rus. Fed.
14 E2 Novlyanka Rus. Fed.
142 B1 Novo r. Brazil
13 G6 Novoaleksandrovsk Rus. Fed.
14 B2 Novoaleksandrovskiy Rus. Fed.
64 E2 Novoalekseyevka Kazak.
65 K2 Novoaltaysk Rus. Fed.
13 G5 Novoanninskiy Rus. Fed.
139 E5 Novo Aripuanã Brazil
15 D2 Novoarkhanel's'k Ukraine
13 F6 Novoazovs'k Ukraine
15 F3 Novobohdanivka Ukraine
14 E3 Novobokino Rus. Fed.
14 H1 Novocheboksarsk Rus. Fed.
13 G6 Novocherkassk Rus. Fed.
145 H2 Novo Cruzeiro Brazil
15 F3 Novodanylivka Ukraine
14 F2 Novodmitriyevka Rus. Fed.
15 B2 Novodnistrovs'k Ukraine
65 H2 Novodolinka Kazak.
15 G2 Novodonets'ke Ukraine
14 B2 Novodugino Rus. Fed.
12 G1 Novodvinsk Rus. Fed.
15 C2 Novofastiv Ukraine
49 H2 Novogeorgiyevka Rus. Fed.
14 B3 Novognezdilovo Rus. Fed.
14 C2 Novogurovskiy Rus. Fed.
143 B6 Novo Hamburgo Brazil
144 D4 Novo Horizonte Brazil
15 E3 Novohradivka Ukraine
15 B1 Novohrad-Volyns'kyy Ukraine
15 G2 Novohrodivka Ukraine
48 D2 Novoil'insk Rus. Fed.
15 F3 Novoivanivka Ukraine
14 D4 Novokastornoye Rus. Fed.
64 F3 Novokazalinsk Kazak.
49 J2 Novokiyevskiy Uval Rus. Fed.
13 G6 Novokubansk Rus. Fed.
12 J4 Novokuybyshevsk Rus. Fed.
65 L2 Novokuznetsk Rus. Fed.
15 E3 Novokyyivka Ukraine
152 D3 Novolazarevskaya Rus. Fed. Base Ant.
63 M2 Novoletov'ye Rus. Fed.
15 F2 Novomar"yivka Ukraine
26 E3 Novo Mesto Slovenia
14 D2 Novomichurinsk Rus. Fed.
13 F6 Novomikhaylovskiy Rus. Fed.
12 F4 Novomoskovsk Rus. Fed.
15 F2 Novomoskovs'k Ukraine
15 F3 Novomykhaylivka Ukraine
15 F3 Novomykolayivka Ukraine
15 D2 Novomyrhorod Ukraine
15 E3 Novonatalivka Ukraine
13 G5 Novonikolayevskiy Rus. Fed.
13 H5 Novonikol'skoye Rus. Fed.
15 F3 Novooleksiyivka Ukraine
139 F4 Novo Olinda do Norte Brazil
64 E2 Novoorsk Rus. Fed.
15 E1 Novoorzhyts'ke Ukraine
15 C1 Novoozeryanka Ukraine
142 D2 Novo Parnarama Brazil
15 D3 Novopavlivka Ukraine
48 D2 Novopavlovka Rus. Fed.
14 E1 Novopistsovo Rus. Fed.
15 F2 Novopokrovka Ukraine
13 G6 Novopokrovskaya Rus. Fed.
14 F4 Novopokrovskoye Rus. Fed.
15 E3 Novopoltavka Ukraine
14 D3 Novopolyan'ye Rus. Fed.
13 F5 Novopskov Ukraine
49 J1 Novorossiyka Rus. Fed.
13 F6 Novorossiysk Rus. Fed.
63 M2 Novorybnoye Rus. Fed.
12 D3 Novorzhev Rus. Fed.
15 C3 Novoselivka Ukraine
14 F2 Novoselki Rus. Fed.
29 D4 Novo Selo Macedonia
15 B2 Novoselytsya Ukraine
64 D2 Novosergiyevka Rus. Fed.
13 F6 Novoshakhtinsk Rus. Fed.
65 K1 Novosibirsk Rus. Fed.
65 K2 Novosibirsk Rus. Fed.
63 P2 Novosibirskiye Ostrova is Rus. Fed.
14 C3 Novosil' Rus. Fed.
14 D4 Novosil'skoye Rus. Fed.
64 F1 Novosineglazovskiy Rus. Fed.
12 D3 Novosokol'niki Rus. Fed.
64 E2 Novotroitsk Rus. Fed.
65 H4 Novotroitskoye Kazak.
14 A3 Novotroitskoye Rus. Fed.
14 G2 Novotroitskoye Rus. Fed.
15 F3 Novotroyits'ke Ukraine
15 D2 Novoukrayinka Kirovohrad Ukraine
15 A1 Novoukrayinka Rivne Ukraine
13 J5 Novouzensk Rus. Fed.
15 F3 Novovasylivka Ukraine
15 A1 Novovolyns'k Ukraine
13 F5 Novovoronezh Rus. Fed.
15 E3 Novovorontsovka Ukraine
14 F1 Novovyazniki Rus. Fed.
14 D3 Novoye Dubovoye Rus. Fed.
14 E1 Novoye Leushino Rus. Fed.
14 E3 Novoyur'yevo Rus. Fed.
14 C1 Novozavidovskiy Rus. Fed.
15 C2 Novozhyvotiv Ukraine
13 D4 Novozybkov Rus. Fed.
19 G3 Nový Bor Czech Rep.
19 H4 Nový Jičín Czech Rep.
63 M2 Novyy Rus. Fed.
15 E3 Novyy Buh Ukraine
15 D1 Novyy Bykiv Ukraine
14 H2 Novyye Aybesi Rus. Fed.
14 H3 Novyye Burasy Rus. Fed.
14 A3 Novyye Ivaytenki Rus. Fed.
14 D1 Novyy Nekouz Rus. Fed.
15 G1 Novyy Oskol Rus. Fed.
62 J3 Novyy Port Rus. Fed.
14 C3 Novyy Sinets Rus. Fed.
15 E2 Novyystarodub Ukraine
12 J3 Novyy Tor'yal Rus. Fed.
62 J3 Novyy Urengoy Rus. Fed.
49 K2 Novyy Urgal Rus. Fed.
64 D4 Novyy Uzen' Kazak.
57 C3 Now Iran
19 K3 Nowa Dęba Poland
19 H3 Nowa Ruda Poland
19 G3 Nowa Sól Poland
125 E4 Nowata U.S.A.
57 B2 Nowbarān Iran
19 J2 Nowe Poland
19 K3 Nowe Miasło nad Pilicą Poland
19 G3 Nowe Miasteczko Poland
19 J2 Nowe Miasto Lubawskie Poland
54 D4 Nowgong India
60 G2 Nowjeh Deh Iran
57 C1 Now Kharegan Iran
111 J2 Nowleye Lake l. Can.
19 G2 Nowogard Poland
19 K2 Nowogród Poland
19 G3 Nowogród Bobrzański Poland
97 G3 Nowra Aust.
57 B1 Now Shahr Iran
60 G2 Nowshahr Iran
54 C2 Nowshera Pakistan
19 J1 Nowy Dwór Gdański Poland
19 K2 Nowy Dwór Mazowiecki Poland
19 K4 Nowy Sącz Poland
19 K4 Nowy Targ Poland
19 H2 Nowy Tomyśl Poland
121 E4 Noxen U.S.A.
62 J3 Noyabr'sk Rus. Fed.
110 C3 Noyes I. i. U.S.A.
20 F2 Noyon France
20 D3 Nozay France
78 C4 Nsambi Zaire
83 F2 Nsanje Malawi
76 D5 Nsawam Ghana
78 B3 Nsoc Equatorial Guinea
79 E6 Nsombo Zambia
76 D5 Nsuatre Ghana
77 F5 Nsukka Nigeria
74 A4 Ntalfa well Mauritania
78 C4 Ntandembele Zaire
83 E1 Ntcheu Malawi
81 B7 Ntchisi Malawi
78 B3 Ntem r. Africa
78 A3 Ntoum Gabon
78 B3 Ntui Cameroon
81 B5 Ntungamo Uganda
82 D3 Ntwetwe Pan salt pan Botswana
50 B3 Nu r. China
152 □ Nuageuses, Is is Kerguelen Indian Ocean
90 □3 Nuapapu i. Tonga
59 J5 Nu'aym reg. Oman
73 F3 Nuba, Lake l. Sudan
80 B2 Nuba Mountains mts Sudan
73 F3 Nubian Desert desert Sudan
146 B4 Nuble r. Chile
48 D4 Nüden Mongolia
140 B3 Nudo Coropuna mt. Peru
125 D6 Nueces r. U.S.A.
130 J6 Nueva Armenia Honduras
138 D2 Nueva Florida Venezuela
141 E4 Nueva Germania Paraguay
132 B2 Nueva Gerona Cuba
147 C7 Nueva, I. i. Chile
147 B4 Nueva Imperial Chile
138 B3 Nueva Loja Ecuador
147 B5 Nueva Lubecka Arg.
131 E3 Nueva Rosita Mexico
131 H6 Nueva San Salvador El Salvador
132 C2 Nuevitas Cuba
130 D2 Nuevo Casas Grandes Mexico
147 D5 Nuevo, G. g. Arg.
130 D3 Nuevo Ideal Mexico
131 F3 Nuevo Laredo Mexico
131 F3 Nuevo León div. Mexico
140 C2 Nuevo Mundo Bolivia
80 E3 Nugaal div. Somalia
80 E3 Nugaal w Somalia
93 B7 Nugget Pt pt N.Z.
73 F3 Nugrus, Gebel mt. Egypt
90 □1 Nuguria Is is P.N.G.
92 F3 Nuhaka N.Z.
150 G6 Nui i. Tuvalu
11 G4 Nuia Estonia
21 G3 Nuits-St-Georges France
96 C3 Nukey Bluff h. Aust.
90 □4 Nuku i. Tonga
90 □4 Nuku'alofa Tonga
90 □6 Nukubasaga reef Fiji
150 G6 Nukufetau i. Tuvalu
151 K6 Nuku Hiva i. Fr. Poly. Pac. Oc.
150 G6 Nukulaelae i. Tuvalu
90 □1 Nukumanu Is is P.N.G.
87 K5 Nukunono atoll Tokelau Pac. Oc.
64 E4 Nukus Uzbekistan
100 C4 Nullagine Aust.
100 C4 Nullagine r. Aust.
96 B2 Nullarbor Aust.
96 B2 Nullarbor Nat. Park nat. park Aust.
96 B2 Nullarbor Plain plain Aust.
49 F4 Nulu'erhu Shan mt. ra. China
77 G5 Numan Nigeria
73 G2 Nu'mān i. Saudi Arabia
47 G5 Numata Gunma Japan
46 H2 Numata Hokkaido Japan
78 E2 Numatinna w Sudan
47 G6 Numazu Japan
98 C2 Numbulwar Aust.
11 C3 Numedal v. Norway
39 K7 Numfor i. Indon.
49 H3 Numin r. China
97 F4 Numurkah Aust.
113 H2 Nunaksaluk Island i. Can.
109 O3 Nunarsuit i. Greenland
111 M2 Nunavut reg. Can.
120 E3 Nunda U.S.A.
79 E4 Nunda Zaire
97 G2 Nundle Aust.
112 B3 Nungesser L. l. Can.
49 F3 Nungnain Sum China
108 B4 Nunivak I. U.S.A.
54 D2 Nunkun mt. India
108 A3 Nunligran Rus. Fed.
24 C2 Nuñomoral Spain
49 G2 Nuomin r. China
27 B5 Nuoro Italy
73 H2 Nuqrah Saudi Arabia
138 B2 Nuquí Colombia
54 E1 Nur China
65 H2 Nura r. Kazak.
65 H3 Nura Kazak.
64 C5 Nūrābād Iran
57 B3 Nūrābād Iran
65 G4 Nurata Uzbekistan
65 G4 Nuratau, Khr. mt. ra. Uzbekistan
61 D1 Nur Dağları mt. ra. Turkey
26 B3 Nure r. Italy
57 G2 Nūr Gal Afghanistan
54 A3 Núr Gamma Pakistan
130 C2 Nuri Mexico
57 G2 Nuristan reg. Afghanistan
40 B2 Nuri, Tk b. Indon.
54 D2 Nurla India
12 J4 Nurlat Rus. Fed.
10 H3 Nurmes Finland
10 F3 Nurmo Finland
18 E4 Nürnberg Germany
54 B3 Nurpur Pakistan
97 F2 Nurri, Mt h. Aust.
55 H1 Nur Turu China
40 D4 Nusa Tenggara Barat div. Indon.
40 D4 Nusa Tenggara Timur div. Indon.
60 E2 Nusaybin Turkey
61 D2 Nuşayrīyah, Jabal al mt. ra. Syria
50 B3 Nu Shan mt. ra. China
54 A3 Nushki Pakistan
113 H2 Nutak Can.
129 H5 Nutrioso U.S.A.
54 B3 Nuttal Pakistan
98 C2 Nutwood Downs Aust.
109 N3 Nuuk Greenland
10 G2 Nuupas Finland
91 □11 Nuupéré, Pte pt Fr. Poly. Pac. Oc.
109 N2 Nuussuaq Greenland
109 N2 Nuussuaq pen. Greenland
91 □13 Nuuúli American Samoa Pac. Oc.
56 C5 Nuwara Eliya Sri Lanka
61 C5 Nuweiba el Muzeina Egypt
14 G2 Nuya r. Rus. Fed.
96 C3 Nuyts Arch. is Aust.
101 B7 Nuyts, Pt pt Aust.
101 B7 Nyabing Aust.
83 E2 Nyadire r. Zimbabwe
62 H3 Nyagan' Rus. Fed.
81 C4 Nyahururu Kenya
97 E3 Nyah West Aust.
55 G3 Nyainqêntanglha Feng mt. China
55 G3 Nyainqêntanglha Shan mt. ra. China
55 H2 Nyainrong China
81 B5 Nyakaliro Tanzania
10 E3 Nyaker Sweden
72 D5 Nyala Sudan
55 F3 Nyalam China
83 D2 Nyamandhiovu Zimbabwe
78 E2 Nyamlell Sudan
12 G2 Nyandoma Rus. Fed.
12 F2 Nyandomskiy Vozvyshennost' h. Rus. Fed.
79 B4 Nyanga Congo
79 B4 Nyanga div. Gabon
83 E2 Nyanga Zimbabwe
55 G3 Nyang Qu r. Tibet China
55 H3 Nyang Qu r. Tibet China
76 D5 Nyankpala Ghana
81 B5 Nyanza div. Kenya
81 A5 Nyanza Rwanda
40 D1 Nyapa, G. mt. Indon.
81 B6 Nyasa, Lake l. Africa
83 D2 Nyathi Zimbabwe
42 B3 Nyaunglebin Myanmar
42 A2 Nyaungu Myanmar
64 E1 Nyazepetrovsk Rus. Fed.
10 H1 Nyborg Norway
11 D4 Nybro Sweden
109 N1 Nyeboe Land reg. Greenland
55 G3 Nyêmo China
81 C5 Nyeri Kenya
81 B7 Nyika National Park nat. park Malawi
55 F3 Nyima China
81 B7 Nyimba Zambia
55 H3 Nyingchi China
19 L5 Nyírbátor Hungary
19 L5 Nyírbéltek Hungary
19 K5 Nyíregyháza Hungary
80 C4 Nyiru, Mount mt. Kenya
10 F3 Nykarleby Finland
11 C5 Nykøbing Denmark
11 C5 Nykøbing Sjælland Denmark
10 E3 Nyland Sweden
83 D3 Nylstroom R.S.A.
97 F3 Nymagee Aust.
97 H2 Nymboida r. Aust.
19 G3 Nymburk Czech Rep.
11 E4 Nynäshamn Sweden
97 F2 Nyngan Aust.
12 B4 Nyoman r. Belarus/Lithuania
21 H3 Nyon Switz.
19 H3 Nysa Poland
19 H3 Nysa Kłodzka r. Poland
12 J2 Nyuchpas Rus. Fed.
47 G4 Nyūdō-zaki pt Japan
12 H2 Nyukhcha Rus. Fed.
12 H2 Nyuksenitsa Rus. Fed.
79 E5 Nyunzu Zaire
63 N3 Nyurba Rus. Fed.
12 J2 Nyuvchim Rus. Fed.
19 L4 Nyzhankovychi Poland
15 F3 Nyzhni Sirohozy Ukraine
15 F3 Nyzhni Torhayi Ukraine
15 F1 Nyzhnya Syrovatka Ukraine
15 F1 Nyzy Ukraine
79 B4 Nzambi Congo
78 E3 Nzara Sudan
76 C5 Nzébéla Guinea
81 B5 Nzega Tanzania
76 C5 Nzérékoré Guinea
79 B5 N'zeto Angola
76 D5 Nzi r. Côte d'Ivoire
79 E6 Nzilo, Lac l. Zaire
79 E4 Nzingu Zaire
81 B4 Nzoia r. Kenya
78 E3 Nzoro r. Zaire
81 D7 Nzwani i. Comoros

O

124 C2 Oahe, Lake l. U.S.A.
127 □1 Oahu i. U.S.A.
96 E3 Oakbank Aust.
129 F2 Oak City U.S.A.
125 E6 Oakdale U.S.A.
124 D2 Oakes U.S.A.
99 G5 Oakey Aust.
17 G5 Oakham U.K.
126 B1 Oak Harbor U.S.A.
120 C6 Oak Hill U.S.A.
128 C3 Oakhurst U.S.A.
122 B2 Oak I. i. U.S.A.
128 A3 Oakland airport U.S.A.
128 A3 Oakland U.S.A.
120 D5 Oakland U.S.A.
124 D3 Oakland U.S.A.
126 B3 Oakland U.S.A.
122 D5 Oak Lawn U.S.A.
124 C4 Oakley U.S.A.
100 C4 Oakover r. Aust.
126 B3 Oakridge U.S.A.
119 C4 Oak Ridge U.S.A.
92 D3 Oakura N.Z.
115 F5 Oakville Can.
93 C6 Oamaru N.Z.
17 D4 Oa, Mull of hd U.K.
93 D5 Oaro N.Z.
41 B3 Oas Phil.
46 D6 Ōasa Japan
126 D3 Oasis U.S.A.
28 D1 Oaşului, Munţii mts Romania
152 B5 Oates Land reg. Ant.
97 F5 Oatlands Aust.
129 E4 Oatman U.S.A.
131 F5 Oaxaca div. Mexico
131 F5 Oaxaca Mexico
5 O3 Ob' r. Rus. Fed.
114 C2 Oba Can.
114 C2 Obakamiga Lake l. Can.
78 B3 Obala Cameroon
114 C2 Oba Lake l. Can.
47 E6 Obama Japan
77 F5 Oban Nigeria
16 E3 Oban U.K.
47 H4 Obanazawa Japan
77 F5 Oban Hills mt. Nigeria
24 C1 O Barco Spain
112 F4 Obatogama L. l. Can.
110 F4 Obed Can.
93 B6 Obelisk mt. N.Z.
18 E5 Oberau Germany
18 F5 Oberdrauburg Austria
124 C4 Oberlin U.S.A.
120 B4 Oberlin U.S.A.
21 H2 Obernai France
19 F4 Oberösterreich div. Austria
18 F4 Oberpfälzer Wald mts Germany
19 H5 Oberpullendorf Austria
15 A2 Obertyn Ukraine
19 H5 Oberwart Austria
14 B4 Obesta r. Rus. Fed.
39 J7 Obi i. Indon.
142 A1 Obidos Brazil
65 G5 Obigarm Tajikistan
46 J2 Obihiro Japan
13 H6 Obil'noye Rus. Fed.
46 H1 Obira Japan
138 C2 Obispos Venezuela
13 G5 Oblivskaya Rus. Fed.
49 J2 Obluch'ye Rus. Fed.
14 C2 Obninsk Rus. Fed.
78 E2 Obo C.A.R.
48 B5 Obo China
80 D2 Obock Djibouti
78 E4 Obokote Zaire
24 C1 O Bolo Spain
15 E2 Obolon' Ukraine
19 H2 Oborniki Poland
78 C4 Obouya Congo
15 G1 Oboyan' Rus. Fed.
12 G2 Obozerskiy Rus. Fed.
55 E4 Obra India
19 G2 Obra r. Poland
130 C3 Obregón, Psa resr Mexico
28 F3 Obrochishte Bulgaria
19 H2 Obrzycko Poland
94 □4 Observatory Rock i. Lord Howe I. Pac. Oc.
14 A2 Obsha r. Rus. Fed.
64 D2 Obshchiy Syrt h. Rus. Fed.
62 J3 Obskaya Guba chan. Rus. Fed.
15 E1 Obtove Ukraine
76 D5 Obuasi Ghana
15 D1 Obukhiv Ukraine
12 J2 Ob"yachevo Rus. Fed.
15 G3 Obytichna Kosa spit Ukraine
15 F3 Obytichna Zakota b. Ukraine
14 F1 Obzherikha Rus. Fed.
119 D6 Ocala U.S.A.
130 E3 Ocampo Coahuila Mexico
131 E3 Ocampo Coahuila Mexico
138 C2 Ocaña Colombia
24 E3 Ocaña Spain
26 C3 Occhiobello Italy
140 C3 Occidental, Cordillera mt. ra. Chile
138 B3 Occidental, Cordillera mt. ra. Colombia
140 A2 Occidental, Cordillera mt. ra. Peru
110 B3 Ocean Cape pt U.S.A.
121 F5 Ocean City U.S.A.
121 F5 Ocean City U.S.A.
110 D4 Ocean Falls Can.
148 G3 Oceanographer Fracture Atlantic Ocean
128 D5 Oceanside U.S.A.
125 F6 Ocean Springs U.S.A.
15 D3 Ochakiv Ukraine
13 G7 Och'amch'ire Georgia
46 D6 Ōchi Japan
46 K2 Ochiishi-misaki pt Japan
16 F3 Ochil Hills h. U.K.
14 A3 Ochkyne Ukraine
133 □1 Ocho Rios Jamaica
18 E4 Ochsenfurt Germany
29 E5 Ochthonia Greece
11 E3 Ockelbo Sweden
28 D2 Ocna Sibiului Romania
15 B2 Ocniţa Moldova
131 G5 Ococingo Mexico
122 C4 Oconomowoc U.S.A.
122 D3 Oconto U.S.A.
24 C1 O Corgo Spain
130 J6 Ocotal Nicaragua
130 H6 Ocotepeque Honduras
128 D5 Ocotillo Wells U.S.A.
130 E4 Ocotlán Mexico
76 D5 Oda Ghana
46 D6 Ōda Japan
10 M2 Ódáðahraun lava Iceland
73 G3 Oda, Jebel mt. Sudan
47 H3 Ōdate Japan
47 G6 Odawara Japan
11 B3 Odda Norway
24 B4 Odeceixe Portugal
111 K3 Odei r. Can.
122 C5 Odell U.S.A.
24 B4 Odemira Portugal
60 A2 Ödemiş Turkey
11 C5 Odense Denmark
19 G1 Oderbucht b. Germany
19 G2 Oderhaff b. Germany
26 D3 Oderzo Italy
15 C3 Odesa div. Ukraine
13 D6 Odesa Ukraine
11 D4 Ödeshog Sweden
125 C6 Odessa U.S.A.
65 H2 Odesskoye Rus. Fed.
24 C4 Odiel r. Spain
76 C5 Odienné Côte d'Ivoire
14 C2 Odintsovo Rus. Fed.
28 F2 Odobeşti Romania
19 H3 Odolanów Poland
43 D5 Ôdôngk Cambodia
28 E1 Odorheiu Secuiesc Romania
14 C3 Odoyev Rus. Fed.
19 H3 Odra r. Germany/Poland
28 B2 Odžaci Yugo.
83 E2 Odzi r. Zimbabwe
142 D2 Oeiras Brazil
139 G3 Oelemari r. Surinam
124 C3 Oelrichs U.S.A.
18 F3 Oelsnitz Sachsen Germany
122 B4 Oelwein U.S.A.
87 P7 Oeno atoll Pitcairn Islands Pac. Oc.
98 C2 Oenpelli Aust.
60 E1 Of Turkey
27 F5 Ofanto r. Italy
61 C4 Ofaqim Israel
77 E5 Offa Nigeria
18 D3 Offenbach am Main Germany
18 C4 Offenburg Germany
78 B4 Offoué r. Gabon
29 F6 Ofidoussa i. Greece
77 E5 Ofiki r. Nigeria
90 □5 Ofolanga i. Tonga
91 □13 Ofu i. American Samoa Pac. Oc.
90 □3 Ofu i. Tonga
47 H4 Ōfunato Japan
46 H2 Ofuyu-misaki pt Japan
40 C1 Oga r. Indon.
47 G4 Oga Japan
47 H4 Ogachi Japan
80 E3 Ogadēn reg. Ethiopia
47 G4 Oga-hantō pen. Japan
47 F6 Ōgaki Japan
124 C3 Ogallala U.S.A.
40 A2 Ogan r. Indon.
39 M1 Ogasawara-shotō is Japan
115 F3 Ogascanane, Lac l. Can.
47 H5 Ōgawa Japan
46 H3 Ogawara-ko l. Japan
77 E5 Ogbomoso Nigeria
124 E3 Ogden U.S.A.
126 E3 Ogden U.S.A.
110 C3 Ogden, Mt mt. Can.
121 F2 Ogdensburg U.S.A.
90 □7 Ogea i. Fiji
47 G5 Ogi Japan
14 H1 Ogibnoye Rus. Fed.
108 E3 Ogilvie r. Can.
47 □2 Ogimi Japan
74 D3 Oglat Sbot well Algeria
119 C5 Oglethorpe, Mt mt. U.S.A.
26 C3 Oglio r. Italy
99 G4 Ogmore Aust.
40 D1 Ogoamas, G. mt. Indon.
77 F5 Ogoja Nigeria
112 C3 Ogoki r. Can.
112 C3 Ogoki Res. resr Can.
78 B4 Ogooué r. Gabon
78 B3 Ogooué-Ivindo div. Gabon
78 B4 Ogooué-Lolo div. Gabon
78 A4 Ogooué-Maritime div. Gabon
46 C6 Ogōri Japan
46 C7 Ogōri Japan
11 G4 Ogre Latvia
26 E3 Ogulin Croatia
77 E5 Ogun r. Nigeria
77 E5 Ogun div. Nigeria
64 D5 Ogurchinskiy, O. i. Turkmenistan
60 F1 Oğuz Azerbaijan
61 D1 Oğuzeli Turkey
77 F5 Ohafia Nigeria
93 A6 Ohai N.Z.
92 E3 Ohakune N.Z.
75 F3 Ohanet Algeria
82 B2 Ohangwena div. Namibia
46 H3 Ōhata Japan
92 E4 Ohau N.Z.
93 B6 Ohau, L. l. N.Z.
92 E2 Ohaupo N.Z.
140 B4 O'Higgins Chile
146 B3 O'Higgins div. Chile
91 □16 O'Higgins, C. c. Easter I. Chile
147 B6 O'Higgins, L. l. Arg.
118 C4 Ohio r. U.S.A.
120 B4 Ohio div. U.S.A.
15 F2 Ohiyivka Ukraine
18 D3 Ohm r. Germany
90 □4 Ohonua Tonga
18 F3 Ohre r. Czech Rep.
18 E2 Ohre r. Germany
29 C4 Ohrid Macedonia
29 C4 Ohrid, Lake l. Albania/Macedonia
92 E3 Ohura N.Z.
139 G3 Oiapoque r. Brazil
139 G3 Oiapoque Brazil
55 H3 Oiga China
120 D4 Oil City U.S.A.
128 C4 Oildale U.S.A.
50 B2 Oi Qu r. China
46 H3 Oirase-gawa r. Japan
21 F2 Oise r. France
133 □9 Oistins Barbados Caribbean
46 C7 Ōita div. Japan
46 C7 Ōita Japan
29 D5 Oiti mt. Greece

182

72 C3 Oiuru well Libya
46 H2 Oiwake Japan
128 C4 Ojai U.S.A.
122 B3 Ojibwa U.S.A.
46 B7 Ojika-jima i. Japan
130 D2 Ojinaga Mexico
131 F5 Ojitlán Mexico
47 G5 Ojiya Japan
146 D2 Ojo de Água, Va. Arg.
130 D2 Ojo de Laguna Mexico
130 B3 Ojo de Liebre, L. b. Mexico
146 C2 Ojos del Salado mt. Arg.
77 F5 Oju Nigeria
77 F5 Oka Nigeria
14 F1 Oka r. Rus. Fed.
82 B3 Okahandja Namibia
92 E3 Okahukura N.Z.
92 D1 Okaihau N.Z.
77 E5 Okaka Nigeria
82 B3 Okakarara Namibia
113 H2 Okak Islands is Can.
110 F5 Okanagan Falls Can.
110 F4 Okanagan Lake l. Can.
78 B3 Okano r. Gabon
126 C1 Okanogan r. Can./U.S.A.
110 F5 Okanogan U.S.A.
126 B1 Okanogan Range mt. ra. U.S.A.
78 E3 Okapi, Parc National de la nat. park Zaire
82 B3 Okaputa Namibia
54 C3 Okara Pakistan
64 D5 Okarem Turkmenistan
93 C5 Okarito Lagoon lag. N.Z.
82 B3 Okasise Namibia
82 B2 Okaukuejo Namibia
82 B2 Okavango r. Botswana/Namibia
82 B2 Okavango div. Namibia
82 B2 Okavango Delta swamp Botswana
46 C7 Okawa Japan
47 G5 Ō-kawa-gawa r. Japan
93 ¹¹ Okawa Pt pt Chatham Is N.Z.
47 G5 Okaya Japan
46 D6 Okayama Japan
46 D6 Okayama div. Japan
47 F6 Okazaki Japan
119 D7 Okeechobee U.S.A.
119 D7 Okeechobee, L. l. U.S.A.
119 D6 Okefenokee Swamp swamp U.S.A.
17 E6 Okehampton U.K.
77 F5 Oke-Iho Nigeria
77 F5 Okene Nigeria
54 B5 Okha India
63 Q4 Okha Rus. Fed.
55 F4 Okhaldhunga Nepal
55 F5 Okha Rann India
14 C4 Okhochevka Rus. Fed.
14 C1 Okhotino Rus. Fed.
63 Q3 Okhotka r. Rus. Fed.
63 Q4 Okhotsk Rus. Fed.
63 Q4 Okhotskoye More sea Rus. Fed.
15 N6 Okhtyrka Ukraine
45 N6 Okinawa i. Japan
47 ¹² Okinawa Japan
45 N6 Okinawa-guntō is Japan
46 C6 Okino-shima i. Japan
46 C6 Okino-shima i. Japan
77 F5 Okitipupa Nigeria
42 A3 Okkan Myanmar
125 D5 Oklahoma div. U.S.A.
125 D5 Oklahoma City U.S.A.
125 D5 Okmulgee U.S.A.
78 B3 Okola Cameroon
78 B4 Okondja Gabon
19 H2 Okonek Poland
19 G4 Okotoks Can.
82 A2 Okotusu well Namibia
14 G2 Okovskiy Les forest Rus. Fed.
78 C4 Okoyo Congo
10 F1 Øksfjord Norway
14 E3 Oksko-Donskaya Ravnina plain Rus. Fed.
12 F2 Oksovskiy Rus. Fed.
25 H3 Oksskolten mt. Norway
65 H5 Oksu r. Tajikistan
42 B3 Oktwin Myanmar
14 C1 Oktyabr' Rus. Fed.
64 E3 Oktyabr'sk Kazak.
14 F1 Oktyabr'skaya Rus. Fed.
14 D2 Oktyabr'skiy Rus. Fed.
12 H3 Oktyabr'skiy Rus. Fed.
12 G3 Oktyabr'skiy Rus. Fed.
13 G6 Oktyabr'skiy Rus. Fed.
64 D2 Oktyabr'skiy Rus. Fed.
15 G1 Oktyabr'skiy Rus. Fed.
52 H3 Oktyabr'skoye Kazak.
62 H3 Oktyabr'skoye Rus. Fed.
63 ¹² Oktyabr'skoy Revolyutsii, Ostrov i. Rus. Fed.
47 Q4 Oku Japan
26 F3 Okučani Croatia
72 C4 Okuchi Japan
12 E3 Okulovka Rus. Fed.
46 G2 Okushiri-kaikyō chan. Japan
46 G2 Okushiri-tō i. Japan
77 E5 Okuta Nigeria
47 E6 Okutango-hantō pen. Japan
82 C2 Okwa w Botswana/Namibia
10 L2 Olafsvík Iceland
128 C3 Olancha U.S.A.
128 C3 Olancha Peak summit U.S.A.
130 J6 Olanchito Honduras
11 E4 Öland i. Sweden
40 C3 Olanga Rus. Fed.
124 E4 Olathe U.S.A.
146 D4 Olavarría Arg.
19 G3 Oława Poland
27 B5 Olbia Italy
120 D3 Olcott U.S.A.
132 C2 Old Bahama Channel chan. Bahamas/Cuba
108 F4 Old Bastar India
99 E4 Old Cork Aust.
108 E3 Old Crow Can.
18 E1 Oldenburg Germany
(Niedersachsen Germany)
18 E1 Oldenburg in Holstein Germany
120 F1 Olderdalen Norway
121 F2 Old Forge U.S.A.
119 ¹² Old Fort U.S.A.
119 ¹² Old Fort r. The Bahamas
120 F2 Old Fort Pt pt The Bahamas
17 F5 Oldham U.K.
133 ¹¹ Old Harbour Jamaica
17 G4 Old Head of Kinsale hd. Rep. of Ire.
121 G4 Old Lyme U.S.A.
16 F3 Oldmeldrum U.K.
121 H3 Old Orchard Beach U.S.A.
113 K4 Old Perlican Can.
133 ⁵6 Old Road Antigua Caribbean
133 ⁵6 Old Road Town St Kitts-Nevis Caribbean
110 G4 Olds Can.

121 J2 Old Town U.S.A.
111 H4 Old Wives L. l. Can.
129 E4 Old Woman Mts mts U.S.A.
48 B2 Öldziyt Mongolia
48 D3 Öldziyt Mongolia
120 D3 Olean U.S.A.
19 L1 Olecko Poland
63 O3 Olekminsk Rus. Fed.
15 E1 Oleksandrivka Chernihiv Ukraine
15 E2 Oleksandrivka Donets'k Ukraine
15 D2 Oleksandrivka Kirovohrad Ukraine
15 D2 Oleksandrivka Kirovohrad Ukraine
15 E2 Oleksandrivka Mykolayiv Ukraine
15 E2 Oleksandrivka Kirovohrad Ukraine
15 B1 Oleksandriya Rivne Ukraine
11 B4 Olema Rus. Fed.
10 B4 Olen Norway
10 J1 Olenegorsk Rus. Fed.
63 M3 Olenek r. Rus. Fed.
14 A1 Olenino Rus. Fed.
11 C2 Olenitsa Rus. Fed.
15 D3 Olenivka Ukraine
48 E2 Olentuy Rus. Fed.
65 H2 Olenty r. Rus. Fed.
20 D4 Oléron, Île d' i. France
15 F1 Oleshnya Ukraine
46 A3 Oles'ko Ukraine
19 H3 Oleśnica Poland
19 J3 Olesno Poland
15 B1 Olevs'k Ukraine
98 B5 Olga, Mt mt. Aust.
24 B6 Olhão Portugal
25 O1 Oliana Spain
26 E3 Olib i. Croatia
82 B5 Olifants r. R.S.A.
82 B3 Olifants r. R.S.A.
82 B5 Olifants r. R.S.A.
82 B5 Olifantsrivierberg mts R.S.A.
144 D4 Olímpia Brazil
131 F5 Olinalá Mexico
142 F2 Olinda Brazil
83 F2 Olinga Mozambique
146 D3 Oliva Arg.
25 F3 Oliva Spain
146 C2 Oliva, Cord. de mt. ra. Chile
146 C3 Olivares, Co del mt. Chile
120 B5 Olive Hill U.S.A.
24 B2 Oliveira do Douro Portugal
142 D3 Oliveira dos Brejinhos Brazil
24 C3 Olivenza Spain
20 E3 Olivet France
124 E2 Olivia U.S.A.
93 B6 Olivine Range mt. ra. N.Z.
81 C5 Oljoro Wells well Tanzania
14 E3 Ol'khi Rus. Fed.
14 D3 Ol'khovatka Rus. Fed.
14 D3 Ol'khovets Rus. Fed.
13 H5 Ol'khovka Rus. Fed.
140 C4 Ollagüe, Vol. vol Bolivia
146 B3 Ollita, Cord. de mt. ra. Chile
78 C4 Ollombo Congo
21 J6 Ollon France
138 B5 Olmos Peru
121 G3 Olmstedville U.S.A.
118 C4 Olney U.S.A.
11 D4 Olofström Sweden
19 H4 Olomouc Czech Rep.
14 D3 Olonets Rus. Fed.
41 B3 Olongapo Phil.
40 C2 Olongliko Indon.
20 D5 Oloron-Ste-Marie France
25 H1 Olot Spain
48 D2 Olovyannaya Rus. Fed.
54 C5 Olpad India
18 D4 Olpe Germany
19 J4 Olše r. Czech Rep.
15 D3 Ol'shanka Ukraine
19 K2 Olsztyn Poland
19 K2 Olsztynek Poland
21 H3 Olten Switz.
27 M2 Oltenița Romania
28 E2 Oltu Turkey
60 E1 Oltu r. Turkey
41 B5 Oluanpi i. Phil.
24 D5 Ölüdeniz Turkey
25 F3 Olula de Río Spain
139 F2 Olvera Spain
146 F2 Olympia U.S.A.
126 A2 Olympic Nat. Park nat. park U.S.A.
126 A2 Olympic Park U.S.A.
29 D4 Olympus mt. Greece
61 B4 Olympus Mt Cyprus
126 B2 Olympus, Mt mt. U.S.A.
15 D1 Olyshivka Ukraine
63 S3 Olyutorskiy Rus. Fed.
63 S4 Olyutorskiy, Mys c. Rus. Fed.
63 S3 Olyutorskiy Zaliv b. Rus. Fed.
65 J1 Om' r. Rus. Fed.
46 H3 Ōma Japan
12 H1 Oma Rus. Fed.
47 G5 Ōmachi Japan
12 H1 Oma r. Rus. Fed.
47 F5 Ōmae-zaki pt Japan
47 H4 Ōmagari Japan
17 D4 Omagh U.K.
138 C4 Omaguas Peru
124 E3 Omaha U.S.A.
82 B4 Omaheke div. Namibia
126 C1 Omak U.S.A.
12 H7 Omalo Georgia
82 A3 Omaruru r. Namibia
82 B3 Omaruru Namibia
82 B2 Omatako w Namibia
146 B3 Omaui N.Z.

75 D1 Oran Algeria
146 D1 Orán Arg.
15 D1 Orane Ukraine
43 D4 O Rang Cambodia
55 H3 Orang China
97 G3 Orange Aust.
21 G4 Orange France
82 B4 Orange r. Namibia/R.S.A.
123 E6 Orange U.S.A.
120 D5 Orange U.S.A.
119 D5 Orangeburg U.S.A.
139 G3 Orange, Cabo pt Brazil
114 E5 Orangeville U.S.A.
129 E2 Orangeville U.S.A.
131 H5 Orange Walk Belize
76 A4 Orango i. Guinea-Bissau
27 B5 Orani Italy
41 B3 Orani Phil.
72 C4 Orori well Chad
142 E2 Orós, Açude resr Brazil
27 B5 Orosei Italy
27 B5 Orosei, Golfo di b. Italy
19 K5 Orosháza Hungary
41 ¹² Orote Pen. pen. Guam Pac. Oc.
63 R3 Orotukan Rus. Fed.
129 G5 Oro Valley U.S.A.
10 F3 Oravais Finland
93 A7 Orawia N.Z.
21 F5 Orb r. France
54 E2 Orba Co l. China
20 E2 Orbec France
27 C4 Orbetello Italy
97 G4 Orbost Aust.
152 B1 Orcadas Argentina Base Ant.
25 E3 Orcera Spain
129 H2 Orchard Mesa U.S.A.
139 D1 Orchila, Isla i. Venezuela
26 C4 Orcia r. Italy
140 A2 Orcotuna Peru
128 B4 Orcutt U.S.A.
100 D3 Ord, Mt h. Aust.
124 C3 Orderville U.S.A.
100 D3 Ord, Mt h. Aust.
128 D4 Ord Mt mt. U.S.A.
60 D1 Ordu Turkey
60 F2 Ordubad Azerbaijan
124 C4 Ordway U.S.A.
65 K2 Ordzhonikidze Kazak.
15 F3 Ordzhonikidze Ukraine
15 E2 Ordzhonikidze Ukraine
27 E5 Ore Nigeria
139 F2 Orealla Guyana
11 D4 Örebro Sweden
11 D4 Örebro div. Sweden
122 C4 Oregon U.S.A.
120 B4 Oregon U.S.A.
122 A2 Oregon U.S.A.
126 B3 Oregon div. U.S.A.
126 B2 Oregon City U.S.A.
14 F2 Orekhovets Rus. Fed.
14 D2 Orekhovo-Zuyevo Rus. Fed.
14 C4 Orel Rus. Fed.
14 C4 Orel div. Rus. Fed.
15 F2 Orel' r. Ukraine
129 G2 Orem U.S.A.
60 B2 Ören Turkey
64 E2 Orenburg Rus. Fed.
64 E2 Orenburg div. Rus. Fed.
146 E4 Orense Arg.
24 C1 Orense Spain
93 A7 Orepuki N.Z.
15 B1 Orevy Ukraine
29 E4 Orestiada Greece
11 D5 Øresund str. Denmark
139 G3 Oretí r. N.Z.
92 E7 Orewa N.Z.
97 F5 Orford Aust.
17 H5 Orford Ness spit U.K.
139 G2 Organabo French Guiana
132 B2 Organos, Sierra de los h. Cuba
129 F5 Organ Pipe Cactus National Monument res. U.S.A.
48 D5 Orgil Mongolia
14 E1 Orgtrud Rus. Fed.
29 G5 Orhaneli Turkey
13 D7 Orhangazi Turkey
13 D7 Orhei Moldova
48 B2 Orhon Gol r. Mongolia
48 C2 Orhon Mongolia
12 J3 Orichi Rus. Fed.
121 K2 Orient U.S.A.
140 C3 Oriental, Cordillera mt. ra. Bolivia
138 D3 Oriental, Cordillera mt. ra. Colombia
140 B2 Oriental, Cordillera mt. ra. Peru
114 A2 Orient Bay Can.
25 F3 Orihuela Spain
15 G2 Orikhiv Ukraine
15 G2 Oril'ka r. Ukraine
15 G2 Oril'ka Ukraine
113 H5 Orillia Can.
139 E3 Orinduik Guyana
139 D2 Orinoco r. Colombia/Venezuela
55 F5 Orissa div. India
114 Orissaare Estonia
27 B5 Oristano Italy
27 B6 Oristano, Golfo di b. Italy
10 F3 Orivesi Finland
11 G3 Orivesi l. Finland
139 F4 Oriximiná Brazil
131 F5 Orizaba Mexico
131 F5 Orizaba, Pico de vol Mexico
144 D2 Orizona Brazil
10 C3 Orkanger Norway
10 C4 Örkelljunga Sweden
10 C3 Orkla r. Norway
16 F2 Orkney Islands is U.K.
80 A1 Orkney U.K.
145 ¹⁰ Orlândia Brazil
144 A4 Orlândia Brazil
119 D6 Orlando U.S.A.
20 E3 Orléans France
121 H3 Orleans U.S.A.
19 G2 Orlovo Poland
20 D5 Orléans, Île d' i. France
20 C3 Orly airport France
14 D3 Ormara Pakistan
54 B4 Ormara, Ras hd. Pakistan
41 B4 Ormoc Phil.
119 D6 Ormond Beach U.S.A.
17 F4 Ormskirk U.K.
121 F2 Ormstown Can.
20 D3 Ornans France
10 M2 Ørnes Norway
19 K1 Orneta Poland

10 D4 Örnsköldsvik Sweden
138 C3 Orocué Colombia
76 D4 Orodara Burkina
126 C2 Orofino U.S.A.
11 D4 Ostergötland div. Sweden
127 F5 Orogrande U.S.A.
91 ¹¹ Orohena mt. Fr. Poly. Pac. Oc.
28 B2 Orom Yugo.
113 G4 Oromocto Can.
61 C4 Oron Israel
77 F6 Oron Nigeria
150 H6 Orona i. Kiribati
121 J2 Orono U.S.A.
139 F3 Oronoque Guyana
133 ³ Oropuche r. Trinidad Trin. and Tobago
49 G2 Oroqen Zizhiqi China
13 F5 Orosháza Hungary
74 C4 Orori well Chad
142 E2 Orós, Açude resr Brazil
82 C5 Oudtshoorn R.S.A.
75 E4 Oued Adjelman w Algeria
16 G1 Ouessant, Île d' i. France
72 B4 Ouesso Congo
76 B3 Oufilé Côte d'Ivoire
73 E4 Ouham r. C.A.R./Chad
73 E4 Ouham-Pendé div. C.A.R.
76 C4 Ouidah Benin
74 D2 Oujda Morocco
75 E4 Oujeft Mauritania
72 D5 Ouled Djellal Algeria
72 D4 Oulad Teima Morocco
74 B3 Oulad Farès Algeria
74 C1 Oulad Naïl, Monts des mts Algeria
10 F3 Oulu Finland
10 F3 Oulujoki r. Finland
10 F3 Oulujärvi l. Finland
10 F3 Oulu div. Finland
26 A3 Oulx Italy
72 D5 Oum-Chalouba Chad
76 B4 Oumé Côte d'Ivoire
72 C5 Oum-Hadjer Chad
74 C1 Oum el A'sel well Algeria
72 C5 Ounianga Kébir Chad
72 B5 Ounianga Sérir Chad
74 C1 Oudadi Mauritania
72 D4 Ounianga Kébir Chad

76 D4 Pã Burkina
90 ² Paama i. Vanuatu
109 D3 Paamiut Greenland
42 B3 Pa-an Myanmar
82 B5 Paarl R.S.A.
55 G4 Pabna Bangladesh
11 G5 Pabradé Lithuania
54 A4 Pab Range mt. ra. Pakistan
141 D2 Pacaás Novos, Parque Nacional nat. park Brazil
144 C4 Pacaembu Brazil
138 B5 Pacasmayo Peru
138 B5 Pacaya Samiria, Reserva Nacional res. Peru
127 E6 Pacheco Chihuahua Mexico
130 E3 Pacheco Zacatecas Mexico
147 B7 Pacheco, I. i. Chile
29 E6 Pachia i. Greece
27 E7 Pachino Italy
140 A1 Pachitea r. Peru
54 D5 Pachmarhi India
29 E4 Pachni Greece
131 F4 Pachuca Mexico
128 B2 Pacific U.S.A.
41 C4 Pacijan i. Phil.
40 C2 Pacitan, Tg pt Indon.
142 B1 Pacoval Brazil
145 F2 Pacuí r. Brazil
19 H3 Paczków Poland
41 C5 Padada Phil.
40 B2 Padang Indon.
38 D7 Padang Indon.
40 B2 Padang Indon.
12 E2 Padang Indon.
139 E3 Padauiri r. Brazil
121 G3 Paden City U.S.A.
18 D3 Paderborn Germany
14 H3 Padilla Bolivia
28 F2 Padina Yugo.
14 H3 Padishchevo Rus. Fed.
10 E2 Padjelanta National Park nat. park Sweden
55 G5 Padma r. Bangladesh
26 D3 Padova Italy
79 B5 Padrão, Pt pt Angola
55 F4 Padrauna India
144 D1 Padre Bernardo Brazil
125 D7 Padre Island i. U.S.A.
20 C2 Padre River Can.
124 E2 Paducah U.S.A.
118 B4 Paducah U.S.A.
125 C5 Paducah U.S.A.
24 E4 Padul Spain
54 D4 Padum India
91 ¹¹ Paea Fr. Poly. Pac. Oc.
49 J4 Paegam N. Korea
49 J4 Paekdu San mt. N. Korea
49 H5 Paengnyong-do i. N. Korea
92 E2 Paeroa N.Z.
41 B3 Pagadian Phil.
38 D7 Pagai Selatan i. Indon.
38 D7 Pagai Utara i. Indon.
39 M3 Pagan i. Northern Mariana Is Pac. Oc.
54 A3 Pagara Pakistan
29 C5 Pagasitikos Kolpos b. Greece
40 C2 Pagatan Indon.
40 C2 Pagatan Indon.
129 G3 Page U.S.A.
11 F5 Pagégiai Lithuania
147 G7 Paget, Mt mt. Atlantic Ocean
91 ¹³ Pago Pago American Samoa Pac. Oc.
127 F4 Pagosa Springs U.S.A.
55 H4 Pagri China
114 C1 Pagwa River Can.
43 C7 Pahang r. Malaysia
43 C7 Pahang div. Malaysia
92 E1 Pahiatua N.Z.
127 ³ Pahoa U.S.A.
119 D7 Pahokee U.S.A.
54 C2 Pahrump U.S.A.
128 C3 Pahute Mesa plat. U.S.A.
11 G3 Päijänne l. Finland
55 H3 Paikü Co l. China
128 D3 Pailin Cambodia
147 B4 Paillaco Chile
110 D4 Painesdale U.S.A.
120 C4 Painesville U.S.A.
129 G3 Painted Desert desert U.S.A.
129 G5 Painted Rock Reservoir resr U.S.A.
111 K3 Paint Lake Provincial Recr. Park res. Can.
120 B6 Paintsville U.S.A.
16 E5 Paisley U.K.
147 A6 Pais Vasco div. Spain
138 B5 Paita Peru
43 D7 Paiton Indon.
140 A2 Paiva r. Peru
130 C3 Pajapan Mexico
74 C2 Pajara Spain
10 E2 Pajala Sweden
11 H4 Pakenham Can.
54 C4 Pakistan country Asia
54 A3 Pakokku Myanmar
41 B3 Pakpak N. Korea
42 A1 Pakokku Myanmar
55 F2 Pakokku Myanmar
43 D5 Pak Phanang Thai.
42 A3 Pakpattan Pakistan
93 C7 Pakotai N.Z.
26 F3 Pakrac Croatia
11 F5 Pakruojis Lithuania

P

19 J5 Paks Hungary
57 G2 Paktīkā Afghanistan
40 A2 Paku, Tg pt Indon.
43 D4 Pakxé Laos
78 B2 Pala Chad
43 B4 Pala Myanmar
40 A1 Palabuhanratu Indon.
40 A3 Palabuhanratu, Tk b. Indon.
133 F5 Palacios Venezuela
25 H2 Palafrugell Spain
26 F4 Palagruža i. Croatia
29 F7 Palaikastro Greece
29 D7 Palaiochora Greece
25 D2 Palairos Greece
20 F2 Palaiseau France
83 D3 Palala r. India
55 F5 Pāla Laharha India
A5 Palalankwe Andaman and Nicobar Is India
29 D5 Palamos Greece
25 H2 Palamós Spain
54 C2 Palana India
63 R4 Palana Rus. Fed.
41 B2 Palanan Phil.
41 B2 Palanan Point pt Phil.
57 E3 Palangän, Küh-e mt. ra. Iran
40 C2 Palangkaraya Indon.
56 B4 Palani India
54 C1 Palanpur India
57 F4 Palantak Pakistan
41 C3 Palapag Phil.
82 D3 Palapye Botswana
40 E1 Palas r. India
55 G4 Palasbari India
63 R3 Palatka Rus. Fed.
86 E4 Palau country Pac. Oc.
41 B2 Palaui i. Phil.
41 A3 Palauig Phil.
40 E1 Palaw Myanmar
91 ¹12 Palauli B. b. Western Samoa
150 E5 Palau Tr. Pac. Oc.
43 B4 Palaw Myanmar
41 A4 Palawan i. Phil.
41 A4 Palawan Passage str. Phil.
41 A4 Palayan Phil.
27 E7 Palazzolo Acreide Italy
11 G4 Paldiski Estonia
14 E1 Palekh Rus. Fed.
40 A2 Palembang Indon.
147 B5 Palena Los Lagos Chile
147 B5 Palena r. Chile
55 F5 Palena, L. l. Chile
131 G5 Palenque Mexico
24 D1 Palencia Spain
133 E3 Palenque, Pta pt Dominican Rep.
27 D6 Palermo Italy
56 B4 Palestina Chile
61 C4 Palestine reg. Asia
125 E6 Palestine U.S.A.
42 A2 Paletwa Myanmar
56 B4 Palghat India
101 H4 Palgrave, Mt h. Aust.
82 A3 Palgrave Point pt Namibia
41 C5 Palimbang Phil.
27 E5 Palinuro, Capo c. Italy
129 H2 Palisade U.S.A.
18 B4 Paliseul Belgium
54 B5 Palitana India
11 H4 Palivere Estonia
11 H4 Palk Bay b. Sri Lanka
11 H4 Palkino Rus. Fed.
56 C2 Palkohda India
56 B3 Palkonda Range mt. ra. India
56 B4 Palk Strait str. India/Sri Lanka
140 B2 Pallapalla mt. Peru
13 H5 Pallasovka Rus. Fed.
56 B3 Pallavaram India
54 B4 Palleru r. Aust.
101 B7 Palliup r. Aust.
83 H3 Pallisa Uganda
93 E4 Palliser Bay b. N.Z.
93 E4 Palliser, Cape c. N.Z.
91 ¹10 Palliser, Îles is Fr. Poly. Pac. Oc.
54 C3 Palma i. India
142 C3 Palma Mozambique
24 D4 Palma del Río Spain
25 H3 Palma de Mallorca Spain
27 D7 Palma di Montechiaro Italy
25 Palma, I. i. Canary Is Spain
140 D2 Palmares Acre Brazil
143 B7 Palmares do Sul Brazil
138 C2 Palmarito Venezuela
27 D5 Palmarola, Isola i. Italy
115 F2 Palmarolle Can.
142 A5 Palmas Paraná Brazil
143 B6 Palmas Tocantins Brazil
78 Palmas, Cape c. Liberia
142 D3 Palmas de Monte Alto Brazil
132 Palma Soriano Cuba
119 D7 Palm Bay U.S.A.
119 D7 Palm Beach U.S.A.
128 C4 Palmdale U.S.A.
143 B6 Palmeira das Missões Brazil
142 E2 Palmeira dos Índios Brazil
142 D2 Palmeirais r. Brazil
142 Palmeiras r. Brazil
144 D2 Palmeiras de Goiás Brazil
79 B5 Palmeirinhas, Pta das hd Angola
152 B2 Palmer U.S.A. Base Ant.
98 C5 Palmer r. Aust.
99 Palmer r. Aust.
108 D3 Palmer r. Aust.
152 B2 Palmer Land reg. Ant.
99 G4 Palmerston, C. c. Aust.
150 J7 Palmerston Island i. Cook Islands Pac. Oc.
92 E4 Palmerston North N.Z.
121 F4 Palmerton U.S.A.
99 F2 Palmerville Aust.
119 E7 Palmetto Pt pt The Bahamas
27 E6 Palmi Italy
131 H4 Palmillas Mexico
133 Palmira Colombia
144 B6 Palmital Brazil
144 C5 Palmital São Paulo Brazil
99 G5 Palm Tree Cr. r. Aust.
122 B6 Palmyra U.S.A.
128 C2 Palmyra U.S.A.
150 J5 Palmyra I. i. Pac. Oc.
128 A3 Palo Alto U.S.A.
24 Palo de las Letras Colombia
80 B2 Paloich Sudan
10 F1 Palojärvi Finland
10 F1 Palojoensuu Finland
140 C2 Palomani, Mt. Peru
140 C2 Palomani Peru
128 D5 Palomares U.S.A.
128 D5 Palomas U.S.A.
40 E2 Palopo Indon.
146 E2 Palo Santo Arg.
25 F4 Palos, Cabo de c. Spain
133 Palo Seco Trin. and Tobago

144 B6 Palotina Brazil
129 F5 Palo Verde U.S.A.
59 E5 Palo Verde U.S.A.
140 A2 Palpa Peru
99 E5 Paltamo Finland
28 F1 Pâltiniş Romania
14 B3 Pal'tso Rus. Fed.
40 D2 Palu Indonesia
60 E2 Palu Turkey
133 G5 Palúa Venezuela
41 B3 Paluan Phil.
64 F5 Pal'vart Turkmenistan
54 D3 Palwal India
63 T3 Palyavaam r. Rus. Fed.
78 E3 Pama r. C.A.R.
131 H6 Panzos Guatemala
142 E2 Pão de Açúcar Brazil
27 B6 Paola Italy
118 C4 Paoli U.S.A.
56 B4 Pamban Channel chan. India
97 G4 Pambula Aust.
40 C3 Pamekasan Indon.
40 A3 Pameungpeuk Indon.
19 H5 Pamhagen Austria
56 B3 Pamidi India
20 E5 Pamiers France
57 J3 Pamir mt. ra. Afghanistan
119 E5 Pamlico Sound chan. U.S.A.
125 C5 Pampa U.S.A.
140 C3 Pampa Aullagas Bolivia
147 C6 Pampa Chica Arg.
140 B2 Pampachiri Peru
140 B2 Pampa de la Salinas salt l. Arg.
147 C6 Pampa del Castillo h. Arg.
140 D3 Pampa Grande Bolivia
141 B4 Pampas reg. Arg.
140 B2 Pampas r. Peru
16 G1 Pampa Stour i. U.K.
93 B7 Papatowai N.Z.
91 ¹11 Papara r. Fr. Poly. Pac. Oc.
16 F2 Papa Westray i. U.K.
91 ¹11 Papeete Fr. Poly. Pac. Oc.
18 D2 Papenburg Germany
91 ¹11 Papenoo Fr. Poly. Pac. Oc.
91 ¹11 Papenoo r. Fr. Poly. Pac. Oc.
115 H3 Papineau-Labelle, Réserve faunique de res. Can.
129 E3 Papoose L. l. U.S.A.
147 A6 Paposo Chile
90 ¹1 Papua, Gulf of g. P.N.G.
86 F5 Papua New Guinea country Australasia
42 A3 Papun Myanmar
98 B4 Papunya Aust.
131 H4 Panabá Mexico
129 E3 Panaca U.S.A.
29 E4 Panagia i. Greece
41 A4 Panagtaran Point pt Phil.
28 E3 Panagyurishte Bulgaria
56 A3 Panaji India
56 K9 Panamá country Central America
130 L7 Panamá Panama
130 L7 Panamá, B. de b. Panama
130 L7 Panama Canal canal Panama
119 C6 Panama City U.S.A.
130 L8 Panamá, Golfo de g. Panama
128 D3 Panamint Range mt. ra. U.S.A.
128 D3 Panamint Springs U.S.A.
128 D3 Panamint Valley U.S.A.
140 A1 Panao Peru
41 C4 Panaon i. Phil.
43 E7 Panarea, Isola i. Italy
41 B4 Panay i. Phil.
41 B4 Panay Gulf b. Phil.
28 C2 Pancevo Yugo.
129 E2 Pancake Range mts U.S.A.
145 H3 Pancas Brazil
28 D2 Panciu Romania
40 C1 Pancingapan, Bukit mt. Indon.
41 C3 Pandan Phil.
41 C3 Pandan Phil.
43 Pandan Res. resr Singapore
55 G5 Pandaria India
145 F1 Pandeiros r. Brazil
54 D5 Pandharpur India
142 E2 Paraíba div. Brazil
142 E2 Paraíba do Sul r. Brazil
54 D5 Pandhurna India
96 D1 Pandie Pandie Aust.
54 D5 Pandoh India
146 B3 Pando Uruguay
130 ¹5 Pandora Costa Rica
54 A3 Pandran Pakistan
11 G5 Panevežys Lithuania
11 D5 Panfyly Ukraine
41 B4 Pang r. China
78 E3 Panga Zaire
78 B2 Pangai Tonga
62 J3 Pangody Rus. Fed.
54 D2 Pangi Range mt. ra. Pakistan
40 D2 Pangkajene Indon.
38 C6 Pangkalanbuun Indon.
40 B3 Pangkalpinang Indon.
39 H7 Pangkalsiang, Tg pt Indon.
42 A2 Panglang Myanmar
109 M3 Pangnirtung Can.
78 B2 Pango Aluquém Angola
62 J3 Pangody Rus. Fed.
54 D2 Pangong Tso l. India
40 A3 Pangpang vol. Indon.
147 B4 Panguipulli Chile
147 B4 Panguipulli, L. l. Chile
129 F3 Panguitch U.S.A.
41 B5 Pangutaran i. Phil.
41 B5 Pangutaran Group is Phil.
125 C5 Panhandle U.S.A.
79 B6 Pania-Mwanga Zaire
90 ¹2 Panié, Mt mt. N. Cal.
54 B5 Panikhaita i. India
54 D4 Panipat India
54 A3 Panjab Afghanistan
57 G3 Panjgur Pakistan
57 G1 Panjhra r. India
57 J2 Panjkora r. Pakistan
63 K3 Panjkent Tajikistan
43 Panjshir r. Afghanistan
55 F5 Pankrushikha Rus. Fed.
79 G5 Pankshin Nigeria
100 B4 Pannawonica Aust.
144 C4 Panorama Brazil
65 H1 Panovo Rus. Fed.
56 B4 Panruti India
49 H4 Panshan China
40 D2 Pantai Indon.
143 A4 Pantanal de São Lourenço marsh Brazil
143 A4 Pantanal do Rio Negro marsh Brazil
143 A4 Pantanal do Taquari marsh Brazil

143 A4 Pantanal Matogrossense, Parque Nacional do nat. park Brazil
28 F2 Pantelimon Romania
27 C7 Pantelleria Italy
27 D7 Pantelleria, Isola di i. Italy
39 H8 Pantemakassar Indon.
41 C5 Pantukan Phil.
131 H4 Pánuco Veracruz Mexico
131 F4 Pánuco r. Mexico
40 C3 Pare Indon.
142 A3 Parecis Brazil
141 E2 Parecis r. Brazil
24 D1 Paredes de Nava Spain
146 C3 Pareditas Arg.
79 C5 Panzi Zaire
131 H6 Panzos Guatemala
142 E2 Pão de Açúcar Brazil
92 D1 Parengarenga Harbour inlet N.Z.
92 D1 Parengarenga Brazil
115 H3 Parente r. Peru
13 J3 Pareora N.Z.
28 E1 Parhăuţi Romania
13 J3 Pari r. Rus. Fed.
14 B2 Pari Paris Can.
14 E3 Paris r. Rus. Fed.
142 A3 Parintins Brazil
114 E5 Paris Can.
20 F2 Paris France
119 B4 Paris U.S.A.
125 E5 Paris U.S.A.
114 C3 Parisienne, Île i. Can.
130 K8 Parita Panama
130 K8 Parita Panama
43 C6 Parit Buntar Malaysia
57 D4 Parkā Bandar Iran
54 B2 Parkal India
11 F3 Parkano Finland
113 J3 Parke Lake l. Can.
65 G4 Parkent Uzbekistan
129 E4 Parker U.S.A.
122 C5 Parker Dam dam U.S.A.
111 K2 Parker Lake l. Can.
14 E3 Pará r. Rus. Fed.
145 F3 Pará r. Brazil
101 A6 Paraburdoo Aust.
41 B3 Paracale Phil.
120 C5 Parkersburg U.S.A.
145 F4 Paracari r. Brazil
144 D3 Paracatu Minas Gerais Brazil
145 F2 Paracatu r. Brazil
38 F3 Paracel Islands is S. China Sea
96 D2 Parachilna Aust.
54 B2 Parachinar Pakistan
28 C3 Paraćin Yugo.
128 B2 Paradise U.S.A.
122 D3 Paradise U.S.A.
128 D3 Park Range mt. ra. U.S.A.
145 F2 Paradis Guyana
128 B2 Paradise U.S.A.
122 C2 Paradise U.S.A.
111 K4 Paradise Hill Can.
119 Paradise I. i. The Bahamas
128 D2 Paradise Peak summit U.S.A.
113 J3 Paradise River Can.
125 F4 Paragould U.S.A.
142 A2 Paraguá Bolivia
139 E2 Paragua r. Venezuela
142 D3 Paraguaçu Brazil
144 C5 Paraguaçu Paulista Brazil
138 D1 Paraguaná, Pen. de pen. Venezuela
141 C6 Paraguari Paraguay
136 D5 Paraguay country S. America
57 E4 Parahadab Pakistan
142 E2 Paraíba div. Brazil
142 E2 Paraíba do Sul r. Brazil
54 D5 Paraíba do Sul r. Brazil
142 D3 Paraibano Brazil
144 C3 Paraíso Mexico
142 C2 Paraíso do Norte Brazil
130 L7 Paraíso Mexico
131 G5 Paraíso Mexico
142 F5 Paraisópolis Brazil
79 G4 Parakou Benin
77 E5 Parakou Benin
110 J7 Paramaribo Surinam
19 H2 Paramé France
96 D2 Paramillo, Parque Nacional nat. park Colombia
142 A3 Paramirim r. Brazil
14 D3 Paramonovo Rus. Fed.
121 F4 Paramus U.S.A.
63 R4 Paramushir, O. i. Rus. Fed.
19 H4 Partizánske Slovakia
11 G3 Partsany Ukraine
144 B3 Paru r. Brazil
139 E3 Paru de Oeste r. Brazil
15 D5 Parutyne Ukraine
142 D2 Parvatipuram India
54 D4 Parvatsar India
40 C3 Parwan vol. Indon.
50 ¹5 Paryang China
82 D4 Paryś S. Africa
101 A7 Pasadena U.S.A.
128 C4 Pasadena U.S.A.
125 E6 Pasadena U.S.A.
138 B4 Pasado, Cabo c. Ecuador

145 J1 Pardo r. Bahia/Minas Gerais Brazil
144 B4 Pardo r. Mato Grosso do Sul Brazil
145 F1 Pardo r. Minas Gerais Brazil
144 D6 Pardo r. Paraná/São Paulo Brazil
19 G3 Pardubice Czech Rep.
50 D3 Pare Indon.
51 F4 Panyu China
79 C5 Panzi Zaire
131 H6 Panzos Guatemala
142 E2 Pão de Açúcar Brazil
92 D1 Parengarenga Harbour inlet N.Z.
152 Passe Royale l. Arg.
81 B4 Passi Phil.
143 B6 Passo Fundo Brazil
145 E4 Passos Brazil
12 C4 Pastavy Belarus
138 B4 Pasto Col.
141 B4 Pastaza r. Peru
111 J4 Pas, The Can.
138 B3 Pasto Colombia
129 H3 Pastora Peak summit U.S.A.
142 D2 Pastos Bons Brazil
41 B2 Pasuquin Phil.
111 J4 Pasu Pakistan
40 C3 Pasuruan Indon.
11 F3 Pasvalys Lithuania
139 E2 Pariaguán Venezuela
142 E2 Patos, Lagoa dos lag. Brazil
144 D1 Patos de Minas Brazil
144 A5 Patos, R. dos r. Brazil
146 C5 Patquía Arg.
29 C5 Patra Greece
28 F1 Pătrăuţi Romania
10 X2 Patreksfjördur Iceland
142 D3 Patrocínio Lynch, I. i. Chile
133 Patrocínio Brazil
145 E4 Patrocínio Brazil
14 F3 Patrovka Rus. Fed.
55 E4 Pedo Lung r. China
145 H1 Pedra Azul Brazil
143 C6 Pedra de Faria Brazil
145 H2 Pedras de Maria da Cruz Brazil
131 H4 Pedras Mexico
142 D1 Pedregulho Brazil
138 C2 Pedregal Venezuela
138 D2 Pedre Brazil
142 E4 Pedrões Maranhão Brazil
143 D5 Pedreiras São Paulo Brazil
131 G5 Pedro Mexico
145 H2 Pedro Avelino Brazil
133 Pedro Bank Caribbean
131 G5 Pedro Cays is Caribbean
131 G5 Pedro Chico Colombia
142 D1 Pedro de Valdívia Chile
144 B4 Pedro Gomes Mato Grosso do Sul Brazil
144 D1 Pedro Gomes Mato Grosso do Sul Brazil
144 A3 Pedro Juan Caballero Paraguay
144 E4 Pedro Leopoldo Brazil
145 D3 Pedro II, Ilha reg. Brazil
142 D1 Pedro Juan Caballero Paraguay
144 A3 Pedro Leopoldo Brazil
131 G5 Pedro Mártir, Sa S. mt. ra. Mexico
133 Pedro Osorio Brazil
133 Pedro P. de Jamaica
119 Pedro Pt pt Jamaica
17 F6 Pedro Toledo Brazil
142 D1 Pedro Velho Brazil
91 ¹5 Pee Dee r. U.S.A.
121 G4 Peekskill U.S.A.
16 E3 Peel Isle of Man
51 E4 Peel r. Can.
108 E3 Peel r. Can./U.S.A.
111 K2 Peel Sound chan. Can.
51 E4 Peel Pt pt Can.
10 E2 Peera Peera Poolanna L. salt flat Aust.
40 E4 Peers Can.
92 E4 Pegasus Bay b. N.Z.
40 C1 Pegunungan Barisan mt. ra. Indon.
40 C1 Pegunungan Iran mt. ra. Indon.
40 C1 Pegunungan Kapuas Hulu mt. ra. Indon./Malaysia
142 E2 Pegunungan Maoke mt. ra. Indon.
40 C1 Pegunungan Meratus mt. ra. Indon.
40 C1 Pegunungan Muller mt. ra. Indon.
39 L7 Pegunungan Van Rees mt. ra. Indon.
40 C1 Pegunungan Schwaner mt. ra. Indon.
43 B5 Pegu Yoma mt. ra. Myanmar
40 C2 Pegunungan Muller mt. ra. Indon.
131 F4 Pehuajó Arg.
51 H4 Peikang Taiwan
14 A1 Peipus, Lake l. Estonia/Rus. Fed.
14 E3 Peixe r. Goiás Brazil
144 A5 Peixe r. Goiás Brazil
142 D2 Peixe, Rio do r. São Paulo Brazil
144 B2 Peixe, Rio do r. Goiás Brazil

141 E2 Peixes r. Mato Grosso Brazil
145 G4 Peixes r. Minas Gerais Brazil
144 B1 Peixes, Rio do r. Mato Grosso Brazil
51 G1 Pei Xian China
51 G1 Pei Xian China
141 E3 Peixoto de Couro r. Brazil
141 E2 Peixoto de Azevedo r. Brazil
40 A1 Pejantan i. Indon.
40 B3 Pekalongan Indon.
43 C7 Pekan Malaysia
14 E3 Pekhlets Rus. Fed.
122 C5 Pekin U.S.A.
14 D1 Peksha r. Rus. Fed.
43 C7 Pelabuhan Kelang Malaysia
129 F5 Peoria U.S.A.
122 C5 Peoria U.S.A.
27 D7 Pelagie, Isole is Italy
29 C4 Pelagonia plain Macedonia
40 C2 Pelaihari Indon.
40 D1 Pelawanbesar Indon.
19 G2 Pelczyce Poland
114 C6 Pelee I. i. Can.
41 ¹1 Peleliu i. Palau
39 H7 Peleng i. Indon.
44 B4 Pe Myanmar
100 B4 Peak Hill Aust.
99 G4 Peak Ra. mt. ra. Aust.
84 A4 Peak, The summit Ascension Atlantic Ocean
129 H2 Peale, Mt mt. U.S.A.
129 H6 Pearce r. U.S.A.
110 B2 Pelly r. Can.
110 B2 Pelly Crossing Can.
111 J1 Pelly Lake l. Can.
110 C2 Pelly Mountains mt. ra. Can.
29 C6 Peloponnisos div. Greece
27 E7 Peloritani, Monti mts Italy
27 E7 Peloro, Capo c. Italy
93 A6 Pelorus Sd chan. N.Z.
146 B3 Pelotas Brazil
143 B7 Pelot, R. das r. Brazil
15 G2 Pelpin Poland
73 H1 Pelusium Egypt
28 C5 Peć Yugo.
143 D5 Peçanha Brazil
21 H4 Peçanha Brazil
142 D2 Peças, I. das i. Brazil
40 D3 Pelokang is Indon.
62 G3 Pechora Rus. Fed.
62 G2 Pechora r. Rus. Fed.
142 D1 Pedreiras Maranhão Brazil
62 F2 Pechorskoye More sea Rus. Fed.
11 G4 Pechory Rus. Fed.
28 E1 Pecineaga Romania
76 A4 Pechora, Ilha de i. Guinea-Bissau
123 F4 Peck U.S.A.
27 B6 Pecora, Capo pt Italy
125 C6 Pecos U.S.A.
125 C6 Pecos r. U.S.A.
19 J5 Pécs Hungary
130 K7 Penonomé Panama
51 F2 Pengshan China
49 G2 Pengxi China
51 F3 Pengshui China
122 D4 Pentwater U.S.A.
40 A2 Penuba India
99 E5 Pencawan Myanmar
56 B3 Penukonda India
64 E1 Penza div. Rus. Fed.
17 E7 Penzance U.K.
13 G6 Penza Rus. Fed.
63 R3 Penzhina, Mys pt Kazak.
63 S3 Penzhinskaya Guba b. Rus. Fed.
129 F5 Peoria U.S.A.
122 C5 Peoria U.S.A.
29 C4 Pelagonia plain Macedonia
40 C2 Pelaihari Indon.
144 B1 Peixes, Rio do r. Mato Grosso Brazil
16 F4 Pentland Hills h. U.K.
122 D4 Pentwater U.S.A.

90 ¹2 Pentecost I. i. Vanuatu
110 F5 Penticton Can.
17 E6 Pentire Point pt U.K.
26 D4 Pesaro Italy
14 C2 Pescado U.S.A.
16 G4 Pentland Firth chan. U.K.
129 H4 Pescado U.S.A.
16 F4 Pentland Hills h. U.K.
122 D4 Pentwater U.S.A.
28 C2 Pescara Italy
40 A2 Penuba India
26 F4 Pescara Italy
99 E5 Penwegon Myanmar
56 B3 Penukonda India
26 F4 Pescara r. Italy
64 E1 Penza div. Rus. Fed.
15 F1 Peschici Italy
27 F5 Pescia Italy
74 B3 Pesebre, Pta pt Canary Is Spain
43 Pesek, P. i. Singapore
54 B2 Peshawar Pakistan
28 C4 Peshkopi Albania
28 D3 Peshtera Bulgaria
122 C3 Peshtigo U.S.A.
122 C3 Peshtigo r. U.S.A.
14 C2 Peski Rus. Fed.
64 D4 Peski Rus. Fed.
64 D4 Peski Bol'shiye Barsuki desert Kazak.
64 D4 Peski Chil'mamedkum desert Turkmenistan
64 D4 Peski Karakumy desert Turkmenistan
64 D4 Peski Kyzylkum desert Uzbekistan
65 G3 Peski Moinkum desert Kazak.
65 G4 Peski Muyunkum desert Kazak.
64 F5 Peski Priaral'skiy Karakumy desert Kazak.
64 F5 Peski Sundukli desert Kazak.
65 H4 Peski Taukum desert Kazak.
64 D4 Peski Taysoygan desert Kazak.
12 K3 Peskova Rus. Fed.
26 S Peskova Slovenia
14 C1 Pesochnoye Rus. Fed.
14 E2 Pesochnya Rus. Fed.
138 B3 Pereira Colombia
24 D4 Peso da Regua Portugal
143 B6 Pereira Barreto Brazil
140 B4 Pesqueira Brazil
140 C2 Pessac France
143 B6 Pestovo Rus. Fed.
14 F1 Pestyaki Rus. Fed.
64 C4 Pet r. Rus. Fed.
130 K5 Petacalco, B. de b. Mexico
29 C6 Petalidi Greece
29 E5 Petalioi i. Greece
128 A2 Petaluma U.S.A.
115 K1 Pétange Lux.
131 H5 Petatlán Mexico
82 Petauke Zambia
115 G4 Petawawa Can.
114 D2 Petenwell Lake l. U.S.A.
98 B5 Petermann Aboriginal Land res. Aust.
98 B5 Petermann Ranges mt. ra. Aust.
146 A6 Petermann, Vol. vol Chile
111 H3 Peter Pond L. l. Can.
122 C1 Petersburg U.S.A.
120 D5 Petersburg U.S.A.
113 F2 Petershagen Nordrhein-Westfalen Germany
113 F2 Peters, Lac l. Can.
139 H2 Peters Mine Guyana
108 C3 Petersville U.S.A.
133 ¹5 Petite Italy Guadeloupe Caribbean
133 ¹5 Petit Cul de Sac Marin b. Guadeloupe Caribbean
81 ¹5 Petite-Île Réunion Indian Ocean
133 ¹3 Petite Rivière de la Baleine r. Can.
133 ¹5 Petite Terre, Îles de la is Guadeloupe Caribbean
114 E2 Petit Lac Manicouagan l. Can.
115 K2 Petit Mécatina r. Can.
113 J3 Petit Mécatina r. Can.
133 ¹5 Petit-Bourg Guadeloupe
131 H5 Petlalcingo Mexico
131 H4 Peto Mexico
26 Petersberg Jordan
60 C3 Petra Jordan
133 ¹5 Petit Cul de Sac Marin b. Guadeloupe Caribbean

40 B2 Pesaguan Indon.
40 A2 Pesaguan r. Indon.
26 D4 Pesaro Italy
14 C2 Pescado U.S.A.
26 F4 Pescara Italy
26 F4 Pescara r. Italy
27 F5 Pescia Italy
43 Pesek, P. i. Singapore
54 B2 Peshawar Pakistan
28 C4 Peshkopi Albania
28 D3 Peshtera Bulgaria
122 C3 Peshtigo U.S.A.
14 C2 Peski Rus. Fed.
64 D4 Peski Bol'shiye Barsuki desert Kazak.
64 D4 Peski Chil'mamedkum desert Turkmenistan
64 D4 Peski Karakumy desert Turkmenistan
64 D4 Peski Kyzylkum desert Uzbekistan
65 G3 Peski Moinkum desert Kazak.
65 G4 Peski Muyunkum desert Kazak.
64 F5 Peski Priaral'skiy Karakumy desert Kazak.
64 F5 Peski Sundukli desert Kazak.
65 H4 Peski Taukum desert Kazak.
64 D4 Peski Taysoygan desert Kazak.
12 K3 Peskova Rus. Fed.
26 Peskova Slovenia
14 C1 Pesochnoye Rus. Fed.
14 E2 Pesochnya Rus. Fed.
24 D4 Peso da Regua Portugal
143 B6 Pereira Barreto Brazil
140 B4 Pesqueira Brazil
140 C2 Pessac France
14 C1 Pestovo Rus. Fed.
14 F1 Pestyaki Rus. Fed.
64 C4 Pet r. Rus. Fed.
130 K5 Petacalco, B. de b. Mexico
29 C6 Petalidi Greece
29 E5 Petalioi i. Greece
128 A2 Petaluma U.S.A.
115 K1 Pétange Lux.
131 H5 Petatlán Mexico
82 Petauke Zambia
115 G4 Petawawa Can.
114 D2 Petenwell Lake l. U.S.A.
98 B5 Petermann Aboriginal Land res. Aust.
98 B5 Petermann Ranges mt. ra. Aust.
146 A6 Petermann, Vol. vol Chile
111 H3 Peter Pond L. l. Can.
122 C1 Petersburg U.S.A.
120 D5 Petersburg U.S.A.
113 F2 Petershagen Nordrhein-Westfalen Germany
113 F2 Peters, Lac l. Can.
139 H2 Peters Mine Guyana
108 C3 Petersville U.S.A.
18 D3 Petosega Brazil
92 ¹1 Perseverance Harbour inlet Campbell I. N.Z.
71 C6 Pertek Turkey
15 E2 Pertusato, Capo c. France
48 D2 Petrovsk-Zabaykal'skiy Rus. Fed.
13 H5 Petrozavodsk Rus. Fed.
141 F2 Petukhovo Rus. Fed.
65 G1 Petukhovo Rus. Fed.
14 C2 Pezek etc. Austria
63 F3 Pezek etc. Rus. Fed.
64 B1 Pezmog Rus. Fed.
141 F5 Pezones Bolivia
20 D4 Pézenas France
141 F2 Pfaffenhofen an der Ilm Germany
18 E4 Pfarrkirchen Germany
19 G4 Pforzheim Germany
18 F5 Pfunds Austria
82 B3 Phagameng R.S.A.
83 D1 Phalaborwa R.S.A.
54 C4 Phalodi India

54 B4 Phalsund India
56 A2 Phaltan India
43 B5 Phangnga Thailand
43 E5 Phan Rang Vietnam
43 F5 Phan Ri Vietnam
43 E5 Phan Thiêt Vietnam
125 D7 Pharr U.S.A.
42 D2 Phat Diêm Vietnam
43 D5 Phatthalung Thailand
43 C5 Phayuhakhiri Thailand
55 H4 Phek India
98 C2 Phelp r. Aust.
111 J3 Phelps Lake l. Can.
42 C3 Phen Thailand
119 C5 Phenix City U.S.A.
43 D4 Phiafai Laos
61 A5 Philadelphia Egypt
125 F5 Philadelphia U.S.A.
121 F2 Philadelphia U.S.A.
121 F4 Philadelphia airport U.S.A.
121 F5 Philadelphia U.S.A.
73 F3 Philae Egypt
124 C2 Philip U.S.A.
95 □1 Philip I. i. Norfolk I.
18 B3 Philippeville Belgium
120 C5 Philippi U.S.A.
98 D5 Philippi, Lake salt flat Aust.
33 O8 Philippines country Asia
41 B2 Philippine Sea sea Phil.
149 N3 Philippine Trench Pac. Oc.
133 Philipsburg Netherlands Ant.
120 D4 Philipsburg U.S.A.
108 D3 Philip Smith Mtns mt. U.S.A.
82 C5 Philipstown R.S.A.
54 C3 Phillaur India
97 F4 Phillip I. i. Aust.
94 □4 Phillip Pt pt Lord Howe I. Pac. Oc.
121 H2 Phillips U.S.A.
122 B3 Phillips U.S.A.
124 D4 Phillipsburg U.S.A.
121 F4 Phillipsburg U.S.A.
125 D4 Phillipston U.S.A.
111 J3 Philmont Can.
111 D3 Philomena Can.
120 C6 Philpot Reservoir resr U.S.A.
43 C4 Phimae
43 C4 Phnum Aôral mt. Cambodia
43 D4 Phnum Aôral mt. Cambodia
43 D5 Phnum Penh Cambodia
81 □4 Phoenix Mauritius
129 F5 Phoenix U.S.A.
150 H6 Phoenix Islands is Pac. Oc.
42 C2 Phôngsali Laos
42 C2 Phong Thô Vietnam
42 D2 Phon Phisai Thailand
43 B1 Phon Thai Laos
42 D3 Phou Cô Pi mt. Laos/Vietnam
42 C2 Phou Sam Sao mt. ra. Laos/Vietnam
42 B3 Phrao Thailand
43 C4 Phra Phutthabat Thailand
42 D2 Phuc Yên Vietnam
43 E4 Phu Hôi Vietnam
43 B6 Phuket Thailand
55 F5 Phulabani India
55 G5 Phultala Bangladesh
42 D2 Phu Ly Vietnam
43 D5 Phumĭ Banam Cambodia
43 C4 Phumĭ Bânhchok Kon Cambodia
43 C5 Phumĭ Chhuk Cambodia
43 D4 Phumĭ Kâmpóng Trâlach Cambodia
43 C5 Phumĭ Kaôh Kông Cambodia
43 D4 Phumĭ Kon Kriel Cambodia
43 C4 Phumĭ Mlu Prey Cambodia
43 C4 Phumĭ Prâmaôy Cambodia
43 D4 Phumĭ Sâmraông Cambodia
43 D4 Phumĭ Thalabârivât Cambodia
43 D4 Phumĭ Toêng Cambodia
43 E4 Phu My Vietnam
43 D5 Phung Hiêp Vietnam
43 D4 Phu Nhon Vietnam
55 G4 Phuntsholing Bhutan
43 E4 Phuoc Long Vietnam
43 D4 Phu Quôc Vietnam
83 D4 Phuthaditjhaba R.S.A.
42 D2 Phu Tho Vietnam
42 C3 Phu Wiang Thailand
51 G2 Pi r. China
144 C2 Piaca Brazil
26 B3 Piacenza Italy
26 C3 Piadena Italy
97 G2 Pian r. Aust.
48 D5 Pianguan China
50 B3 Pianma China
26 C4 Pianosa, Isola i. Italy
96 Pian-Upe Game Reserve res. Uganda
133 □3 Piarco Trin. Trinidad and Tobago
19 K2 Piaseczno Warszawa Poland
19 L3 Piaski Poland
23 E3 Piatra Romania
28 F1 Piatra-Neamţ Romania
28 E2 Piatra Olt Romania
142 D2 Piauí r. Brazil
142 D2 Piauí div. Brazil
26 D3 Piave r. Italy
27 E7 Piazza Armerina Italy
80 B3 Pibor r. Sudan
80 B3 Pibor Post Sudan
114 B2 Pic r. Can.
140 C4 Pica Chile
129 G5 Picacho U.S.A.
129 E5 Picacho U.S.A.
130 E2 Picacho del Centinela mt. Mexico
130 B3 Picachos, Co dos mt. Mexico
20 D2 Picardie reg. France
20 F2 Picardie div. France
25 F3 Picassent Spain
119 B6 Picayune U.S.A.
43 C4 Pichachen mt.
14 F3 Pichanal Arg.
41 A2 Pichanal
14 C2 Pichayevo Rus. Fed.
146 B3 Pichi Ciego Arg.
146 B3 Pichilemu Chile
130 E3 Pichina Mexico
147 D4 Pichor India
130 B2 Pichon Mexico
20 F2 Pichucalco Mexico
114 B2 Pic, I. i. Can.
17 K4 Pickering U.K.
17 K4 Pickering, Vale of v. U.K.
112 B2 Pickle Bank Caribbean
112 B3 Pickle Lake Can.
78 A3 Pico Basile mt. Equatorial Guinea
142 C1 Pico Bolívar mt. Venezuela
130 C3 Pico Cupula mt. Mexico
139 D3 Pico da Neblina mt. Brazil
139 Pico da Neblina, Parque Nacional do nat. park Brazil
131 E3 Pico del Toro mt. Mexico

147 C6 Pico de Salamanca Arg.
133 E3 Pico Duarte mt. Dominican Republic
24 □ Pico Ruivo mt. Madeira Portugal
142 D2 Picos Brazil
138 B5 Picota Peru
147 C6 Pico Truncado Arg.
114 B2 Pic River Can.
115 G2 Picton Can.
147 C7 Picton, I. i. Chile
97 F5 Picton, Mt mt. Aust.
113 H4 Pictou Can.
122 D2 Pictured Rocks National Lakeshore res. U.S.A.
147 C4 Picún Leufú r. Arg.
54 C3 Pidarak Pakistan
15 L2 Pidhaytsi Ukraine
15 D2 Pidhorodna Ukraine
15 F2 Pidhorodne Ukraine
15 A2 Pidkamin' Ukraine
56 C5 Pidurutalagala mt. Sri Lanka
15 B2 Pidvolochys'k Ukraine
144 E5 Piedade Brazil
138 C2 Piedecuesta Colombia
146 C3 Pie de Palo, Sa mt. ra. Arg.
27 E5 Piedimonte Matese Italy
25 D3 Piedmont U.S.A.
120 C4 Piedmont Lake l. U.S.A.
24 C3 Piedra r. Spain
24 D3 Piedrahenna Spain
24 D3 Piedrahíta Spain
24 D1 Piedras Blancas Spain
132 E3 Piedras Negras Coahuila Mexico
131 F5 Piedras Negras Veracruz Mexico
146 E4 Piedras, Punta pt Arg.
140 B2 Piedras, Río de las r. Peru
114 A2 Pie I. i. Can.
21 G4 Pierre France
139 □ Pieksämäki Finland
10 G3 Pielavesi Finland
10 H3 Pielinen l. Finland
26 A3 Piemonte div. Italy
19 K1 Pieniężno Poland
19 J3 Pieńsk Poland
52 B3 Pierceton U.S.A.
128 A2 Piercy U.S.A.
29 D4 Pieria mts Greece
54 C2 Pierre r. India
114 E2 Pierre Lake l. Can.
21 G4 Pierrelatte France
115 J3 Pierreville Can.
133 □1 Pierreville Trin. and Tobago
19 H4 Piešťany Slovakia
81 □4 Pieter Both i. Mauritius
83 D4 Pietermaritzburg R.S.A.
83 D3 Pietersburg R.S.A.
26 C4 Pietrasanta Italy
27 F6 Pietra Spada, Passo di pass Italy
83 E4 Piet Retief R.S.A.
26 D2 Pieve di Cadore Italy
26 C3 Pievepelago Italy
123 F4 Pigeon U.S.A.
115 G4 Pigeon Bay b. Can.
133 □2 Pigeon Pt pt Tobago Trin. and Tobago
120 D6 Pigg r. U.S.A.
125 F4 Piggott U.S.A.
83 E4 Pigg's Peak Swaziland
146 D4 Piguë Arg.
131 F4 Piguicas mt. Mexico
92 D3 Pihama N.Z.
90 □4 Piha Passage chan. Tonga
11 H3 Pihlajavesi l. Finland
11 H3 Pihlava Finland
10 G3 Pihtipudas Finland
10 N2 Pihujärvi Finland
131 G6 Pijijiapan Mexico
14 E3 Pikalevo Rus. Fed.
114 E2 Pike Bay Can.
86 F4 Pikelot I. Fed. States of Micronesia
82 B5 Piketberg R.S.A.
120 B6 Pikeville U.S.A.
65 K1 Pikhtovka Rus. Fed.
76 A4 Pikine Senegal
43 G5 Pikou China
19 H2 Piła Poland
146 E2 Pilagá r. Arg.
54 D4 Pilani India
146 B3 Pilão Arcado Brazil
146 E3 Pilar Buenos Aires Arg.
146 E2 Pilar Paraguay
147 B7 Pilar, C. c. Chile
146 D3 Pilar de Goiás Brazil
54 C5 Pilas i. Phil.
24 C4 Pilas Spain
25 F3 Pilas, Sierra de la mt. ra. Spain
21 G4 Pilat, Mt mt. France
140 A4 Pilaya r. Bolivia
147 B5 Pilcaneyu Arg.
141 E5 Pilcomayo r. Bolivia/Paraguay
54 C3 Pilibhit India
15 D3 Pilica r. Poland
92 E3 Piripiri N.Z.
82 A4 Pillar Bay b. Ascension Atlantic Ocean
65 K4 Pillar, C. c. Aust.
140 B2 Pillcopata Peru
97 G2 Pilliga Aust.
97 G2 Pilliga r. Aust.
146 C4 Pillo, Isla del i. Arg.
144 E4 Piquiri r. Paraná Brazil
128 D2 Pilot Peak summit U.S.A.
108 C4 Pilot Point U.S.A.
97 G4 Pilot, The mt. Aust.
144 A2 Piloto Arg.
138 B4 Pimampiro Ecuador
144 B2 Pimenta Bueno Brazil
55 G4 Pimpri India
138 D3 Pinacate, Cerro del summit Mexico
54 D4 Pinahat India
129 E5 Pinaleno Mts mts U.S.A.
41 B3 Pinamalayan Phil.
144 E4 Pinamar Arg.
41 B2 Pinang div. Malaysia
43 B6 Pinang i. Malaysia
25 H3 Pinar, Cap des pt Spain
133 B2 Pinar del Río Cuba
60 A1 Pinarhisar Turkey
28 F2 Piñas Ecuador
144 B1 Pindaíba Brazil
145 F5 Pindamonhangaba Brazil
101 A6 Pindar Aust.
142 C1 Pindaré r. Brazil
142 C1 Pindaré Mirim Brazil
54 C2 Pind Dadan Khan Pakistan
54 C2 Pindi Gheb Pakistan
143 A4 Pindobal Brazil
23 H4 Pindos mts Greece
55 G4 Pindwara India
126 B2 Pine U.S.A.
122 C3 Pine r. U.S.A.
122 D3 Pine r. U.S.A.
121 F4 Pine Bluff U.S.A.
126 C2 Pine City U.S.A.
98 D2 Pine Creek Aust.
126 C3 Pine Creek r. U.S.A.
126 D3 Pinedale U.S.A.
126 C3 Pine Falls Can.
12 J2 Pinega r. Rus. Fed.

121 E4 Pine Grove U.S.A.
119 D6 Pine Hills U.S.A.
111 H3 Pinehouse Can.
29 D5 Pineios r. Greece
132 B1 Pine Is is U.S.A.
122 A3 Pine Island U.S.A.
152 A3 Pine Island Bay b. Ant.
121 F3 Pine Lake U.S.A.
121 F3 Pineland U.S.A.
128 B4 Pine Mt mt. U.S.A.
129 F4 Pine Peak summit U.S.A.
121 F4 Pine Point U.S.A.
114 C2 Pine Portage Can.
128 D2 Pineridge U.S.A.
126 E3 Pine Ridge U.S.A.
26 A2 Pinerolo Italy
25 E5 Pines, Lake O' the l. U.S.A.
83 E4 Pinetown R.S.A.
125 C6 Pineville U.S.A.
27 F5 Pinetamare Italy
14 E1 Ping'an China
50 C4 Pingbian China
48 E5 Pingding China
49 F5 Pingdingshan China
101 B7 Pingelly Aust.
50 D4 Pingguo China
49 F4 Pinghe China
51 E3 Pingjiang China
51 E3 Pingle China
51 D3 Pingli China
50 D1 Pingliang China
50 D4 Pingma China
48 E5 Pingnan China
51 E3 Pingnan China
48 E5 Pingquan China
51 D3 Pingshan China
51 E3 Pingtan China
50 D3 Pingtang China
51 G4 P'ing-tun Taiwan
50 D4 Pingwu China
51 F3 Pingxiang Guangxi China
51 E3 Pingxiang Jiangxi China
48 E5 Pingyang China
48 E5 Pingyao China
49 F5 Pingyi China
51 F1 Pingyin China
49 F5 Pingyu China
49 F5 Pingyuan China
51 F5 Pingyuanjie China
72 Ping Yuen Ho r. China/Hong Kong
26 C4 Pinhal Brazil
145 E3 Pinhal Novo Portugal
142 C1 Pinheiro Brazil
145 H3 Pinheiro Machado Brazil
24 C2 Pinhel Portugal
40 A2 Pinhuá r. Brazil
101 A6 Pinjarra Aust.
101 C6 Pinjin Aust.
112 H5 Pinkafeld Austria
110 E3 Pink Mountain Can.
42 A1 Pinlaung Myanmar
42 A1 Pinlebu Myanmar
93 H4 Pinnacle mt. N.Z.
97 F5 Pinnaroo Aust.
18 D2 Pinneberg Germany
128 C4 Pinos, Mt mt. U.S.A.
131 F5 Pinotepa Nacional Mexico
40 D2 Pinrang Indon.
13 C4 Pinsk Belarus
114 C5 Pins, Pointe aux pt Can.
140 C4 Pintados Chile
138 □ Pinta, I. i. Galapagos Is Ecuador
114 D2 Pintsman Malaysia
146 D2 Pinto Arg.
26 E3 Pintura U.S.A.
19 K4 Pinzolo Italy
79 E5 Piodi Zaire
62 K1 Pioner, O. i. Rus. Fed.
92 E3 Pionerskiy Rus. Fed.
92 D3 Pionki Poland
19 J3 Piopio N.Z.
19 J3 Piórków Trybunalski Poland
146 E3 Pioro Arg.
57 D4 Pip r. Iran
54 D5 Pipar r. India
29 E5 Piperi i. Greece
54 D5 Pipar Rd. India
124 D3 Pipestone r. Can.
124 D3 Pipestone U.S.A.
92 E3 Pipiriki N.Z.
115 F4 Pipmuacan, Réservoir resr Can.
74 D2 Piqua China
145 F5 Piquete Brazil
97 F2 Pilliga Aust.
144 B4 Piquiri r. Paraná Brazil
144 C3 Piracanjuba Brazil
145 F3 Piracicaba r. Minas Gerais Brazil
145 F4 Piracicaba r. São Paulo Brazil
142 D1 Piraçununga Brazil
142 D1 Piracuruca Brazil
144 C1 Piraí do Sul Brazil
144 D5 Piraju Brazil
144 D5 Pirajuba Brazil
60 D1 Pirajuí Brazil
145 G4 Pirambóia Brazil
146 E2 Piraná r. Arg.
145 H1 Piranga r. Brazil
145 G1 Piranga Brazil
74 A3 Piranhas Goiás Brazil
142 E2 Piranhas r. Paraíba/Rio Grande do Norte Brazil
142 E2 Piranhas Brazil
142 D2 Pirapetinga Brazil
142 B3 Pirapó r. Brazil
142 B2 Pirapora Brazil
142 D2 Pirapozinho Brazil
145 F4 Pirassununga Brazil
145 F1 Piratini Brazil
144 B3 Piratininga Brazil
145 E3 Pirenópolis Brazil
144 C2 Pires do Rio Brazil
55 G4 Pirganj Bangladesh
145 H1 Piriá r. Brazil
143 D1 Pirítu Venezuela
19 J4 Pirmasens Germany
18 E3 Pirna Germany
55 F5 Pirojpur Bangladesh (Pirangia)
77 T5 Piranga N.Z.
29 C4 Plateau div. Congo
54 C2 Platičevo Yugo.
108 B4 Platinum U.S.A.
54 B2 Plato Colombia
139 D3 Platte r. U.S.A.
124 D2 Platte U.S.A.
12 K2 Plato China (Pisa)
10 H3 Pisa r. Rus. Fed.
140 C4 Pisagua Chile

93 B6 Pisa, Mt mt. N.Z.
75 F2 Piscataway U.S.A.
29 D4 Platy Greece
140 A2 Pisco r. Peru
140 A2 Pisco Peru
140 A2 Pisco, B. de b. Peru
121 F3 Piseco Lake l. U.S.A.
19 G4 Písek Czech Rep.
51 H2 Pishan China
65 J5 Pishan China
15 C2 Pischana Ukraine
15 D2 Pischane Ukraine
15 C2 Pischanka Ukraine
57 E4 Pishin Iran
54 B3 Pishin Pakistan
57 E4 Pishin Lora r. Afghanistan/Pakistan
15 C1 Piskivka Ukraine
140 D2 Piso Firme Bolivia
27 F5 Pisticci Italy
26 D3 Pistoia Italy
14 E1 Pistsovo Rus. Fed.
24 D2 Pisuerga r. Spain
9 P2 Pisz Poland
126 B3 Pit r. U.S.A.
76 B4 Pita Guinea
113 G3 Pitaga Can.
131 H5 Pital Mexico
138 B3 Pitalito Colombia
144 D4 Pitanga Brazil
145 F3 Pitangueiras Brazil
145 F3 Pitangui Brazil
97 J3 Pitarpunga L. l. Aust.
91 □14 Pitcairn Island terr. Pac. Oc.
133 □3 Pitch Lake Trinidad Trin. & Tobago
10 E2 Piteå Sweden
10 E2 Piteälven r. Sweden
15 C5 Pitelino Rus. Fed.
13 H5 Piterka Rus. Fed.
54 E3 Pithoragarh India
41 □3 Piti Guam Pac. Oc.
127 D6 Pitjantjatjara Lands Aboriginal Land res. Aust.
12 J2 Pitkyaranta Rus. Fed.
16 F3 Pitlochry U.K.
90 □6 Pitman Reefs reef Fiji
78 B2 Pitoa Cameroon
81 □4 Piton de la Fournaise mt. Réunion Indian Ocean
81 □4 Piton de la Petite R. Noire h. Mauritius
81 □5 Piton des Neiges mt. Réunion Indian Ocean
130 H6 Pito Solo Honduras
147 B4 Pitrufquén Chile
93 □1 Pitt I. i. Chatham Is N.Z.
138 □ Pitt, Pta pt Galapagos Is Ecuador
125 E4 Pittsburg U.S.A.
120 D4 Pittsburgh U.S.A.
122 B6 Pittsfield U.S.A.
121 H3 Pittsfield U.S.A.
121 H3 Pittsfield U.S.A.
121 G3 Pittsfield U.S.A.
121 F3 Pittston U.S.A.
93 □1 Pitt Strait str. Chatham Is N.Z.
121 G4 Pituri r. Aust.
97 F5 Pitz Lake l. Can.
142 B3 Piuí Brazil
138 B4 Pium Brazil
128 C4 Piute Peak summit U.S.A.
54 D1 Piuthan Nepal
114 D1 Pivabiska r. Can.
15 D3 Pivdennyy Buh r. Ukraine
138 C1 Pivijay Colombia
23 E2 Pivka Slovenia
19 K4 Piwniczna Poland
54 D1 Pixa China
140 C3 Pixoval Mexico
140 B2 Pizacoma Peru
26 B2 Piz Bernina mt. Italy/Switz.
13 H5 Pizhi Nigeria
12 J3 Pizhma r. Rus. Fed.
12 J3 Pizhma Rus. Fed.
19 J3 Piotrków Trybunalski Poland
21 G3 Plabennec France
113 B4 Placentia B. b. Can.
113 J4 Placentia Can.
113 J4 Placentia B. b. Can.
128 B2 Placerville U.S.A.
128 B2 Placerville U.S.A.
133 C2 Placetas Cuba
140 D1 Plácido de Castro Brazil
18 D2 Plaine d'Alsace plain France
20 D2 Plaine de Caen plain France
78 D2 Plaine de Garar plain Chad
81 □4 Plaine des Roches plain Mauritius
74 D2 Plaine du Tamelet plain Morocco
75 E3 Plaine du Tidikelt plain Algeria
21 E4 Plaines de la Loire et de l'Allier plain France
20 D3 Plaines et Seuil du Poitou plain France
121 F4 Plainfield U.S.A.
122 C5 Plainfield U.S.A.
121 F3 Plainfield U.S.A.
122 D3 Plainfield U.S.A.
125 C5 Plainview U.S.A.
124 D3 Plainview U.S.A.
122 C5 Plainwell U.S.A.
21 F4 Plaisance France
54 D4 Plaisted U.S.A.
40 A2 Plaju Indon.
60 C4 Plakati, C. pt Cyprus
29 D5 Plamondon Can.
40 A2 Plampang Indon.
142 E2 Planaltina Brazil
145 F1 Planaltina Brazil
143 E2 Planalto da Borborema plat. Brazil
142 E3 Planalto de Mato Grosso plat. Brazil
142 B2 Planalto Maracanaquará plat. Brazil
83 D2 Planalto Moçambicano Moçambique
138 C1 Planeta Rica Colombia
124 D2 Plankinton U.S.A.
125 D5 Plano U.S.A.
119 D7 Plantation U.S.A.
133 □5 Plantain Garden r. Jamaica
125 F6 Plaquemine U.S.A.
24 D3 Plasencia Spain
26 E3 Plaški Croatia
131 H5 Plato Mexico

Finland
86 G4 Pohnpei i. Fed. States of Micronesia
15 E2 Pohreby Ukraine
83 D1 Pohrebyshche Ukraine
54 D4 Pohri India
18 F2 Plau Germany
18 F2 Plauen Germany
18 F2 Plauer See l. Germany
28 B3 Plav Yugo.
14 C3 Plavitsa r. Rus. Fed.
14 D3 Plavsk Rus. Fed.
79 E5 Poie Zaire
14 F3 Poim Rus. Fed.
90 □2 Poindimié Pac. Oc.
152 C2 Poinsett, C. c. Ant.
128 A2 Point Arena U.S.A.
96 D3 Point Broughton Aust.
115 H3 Point-Comfort Can.
24 C1 Ponferrada Spain
78 A3 Pongara, Pte pt Gabon
133 Pongaroa N.Z.
79 D5 Ponge r. Zaire
79 D4 Pongo r. Sudan
83 E4 Pongola r. R.S.A.
80 B3 Pongo de Manseriche Peru
19 L3 Poniatowa Poland
40 E2 Ponindilisa, Tg pt Indon.
15 B1 Poninka Ukraine
42 A2 Ponnaivar r. India
56 A4 Ponnani India
42 A2 Ponnyadaung Range mt. ra. Myanmar
110 G4 Ponoka Can.
15 E1 Ponornytsya Ukraine
40 B3 Ponorogo Indon.
114 E5 Ponoy r. Rus. Fed.
56 C5 Ponnani India
115 F4 Pont-à-Mousson France
21 H3 Ponta Grossa Brazil
142 D2 Pontal r. Brazil
144 C6 Ponta Grossa Brazil
144 C2 Pontalina Brazil
144 A2 Ponta Porã Brazil
21 H3 Pontarlier France
20 D4 Pontaudemer France
142 C1 Ponte Alta do Norte Brazil
26 B2 Pontebba Italy
24 B1 Ponte Caldelas Spain
26 D4 Pontecorvo Italy
24 B2 Pontedeume Spain
26 C4 Pontedera Italy
24 B1 Pontevedra Spain
144 C6 Ponte Serrada Brazil
24 C3 Pontevedra Spain
97 F5 Pont Hardy Aust.
115 G4 Pontiac U.S.A.
40 A2 Pontianak Indon.
40 B2 Pontinha Can.
20 D3 Pontivy France
20 B3 Pont-l'Abbé France
60 C1 Pontoise France
60 C2 Pontotoc U.S.A.
111 K4 Ponton w. Aust.
21 F5 Pont-St-Esprit France
115 H5 Pontypool U.K.
17 D6 Pontypool U.K.
17 D6 Pontypridd U.K.
14 F3 Ponyri Rus. Fed.
60 F2 Pool div. Congo
96 D1 Poolanna L. salt flat Aust.
96 D1 Poolawanna L. salt flat Aust.
97 G2 Poopelloe, L. salt l. Aust.
140 D4 Poopó, Lago de l. Bolivia
76 D4 Pooncarie Aust.
110 D3 Poona r. India
138 B3 Popayán Colombia
41 B2 Popoh Indon.
28 A2 Popovača Croatia
28 F3 Popovo Bulgaria
14 E3 Poppi Italy
19 J4 Poprad Slovakia
19 K4 Poprad r. Slovakia
54 D5 Porali r. Pakistan
56 A1 Porbandar India
110 C3 Porcher I. i. Can.
142 A2 Porciúncula Brazil
96 D2 Porcupine, Cape c. Can.
108 D3 Porcupine r. Can./U.S.A.
122 C2 Porcupine Mts mts U.S.A.
111 J4 Porcupine Prov. Forest res. Can.
138 C1 Porce r. Colombia
26 E3 Poreč Croatia
144 D2 Porecatu Brazil
14 G4 Porecatu r. Rus. Fed.
14 D1 Porech'ye-Rybnoye Rus. Fed.
14 H2 Poretskoye Rus. Fed.
76 B4 Pori Guinea
10 F3 Pori Finland
28 D1 Porkhov Rus. Fed.
72 Porkkala Finland
139 D1 Porlamar Venezuela
20 C2 Pornic France
21 H4 Poromaa Indon.
25 D6 Poronaysk Rus. Fed.
29 C6 Poros i. Greece
29 C6 Poros Greece
12 F2 Porosozero Rus. Fed.
61 D3 Porsangen chan. Norway
10 D1 Porsangerhalvøya pen. Norway
11 C4 Porsgrunn Norway
60 C1 Porsuk r. Turkey
147 B5 Portaceli Chile

119 D7 Pompano Beach U.S.A.
144 C5 Pompéia Brazil
83 D1 Pompuè r. Mozambique
26 C3 Ponazyrevo Rus. Fed.
125 D4 Ponce r. U.S.A.
119 □3 Ponce Puerto Rico
28 E1 Poiana Mare Romania
28 E1 Poiana Stampei Romania
14 F3 Poim Rus. Fed.
109 L2 Pond Inlet Can.
133 J3 Ponds, Island of i. Can.
56 B3 Pondicherry India
130 J6 Ponelya Nicaragua
128 D4 Poneloya Nicaragua
24 C1 Ponferrada Spain
78 A3 Pongara, Pte pt Gabon
126 B1 Port Angeles U.S.A.
133 E3 Port Antonio Jamaica
132 D3 Port-à-Piment Haiti
17 D5 Portarlington Rep. of Ire.
97 F5 Port Arthur Aust.
125 E6 Port Arthur U.S.A.
16 C4 Port Askaig U.K.
96 D2 Port Augusta Aust.
133 D3 Port-au-Prince Haiti
113 J3 Port aux Choix Can.
113 J3 Port Beaufort R.S.A.
82 D5 Port Bell Uganda
81 □4 Port Blair Andaman and Nicobar Is India
115 F4 Port Bolster Can.
25 H1 Portbou Spain
98 B3 Port Bradshaw b. Aust.
114 E5 Port Burwell Can.
54 C5 Port Canning India
115 F4 Port Carling Can.
93 C6 Port Chalmers N.Z.
121 F4 Port Charlotte U.S.A.
110 C4 Port Chester U.S.A.
110 C4 Port Clements Can.
120 B4 Port Clinton U.S.A.
114 E5 Port Colborne Can.
115 F5 Port Coquitlam Can.
115 F5 Port Credit Can.
76 □ Port Curieuse Kerguelen Indian Ocean
98 C2 Port Darwin b. Aust.
133 D3 Port Davey b. Aust.
133 D3 Port-de-Paix Haiti
43 C7 Port Dickson Malaysia
99 F4 Port Douglas Aust.
121 E4 Port Dover Can.
143 A2 Port dos Morts chan. U.S.A.
110 C4 Port Edward Can.
121 E4 Port Edwards U.S.A.
97 H3 Port Elgin Can.
14 □1 Port Elizabeth R.S.A.
16 C5 Port Ellen U.K.
146 C4 Porteña r. Arg.
146 F2 Porteirinha Brazil
17 F4 Port Erin Isle of Man
82 C5 Port Elizabeth R.S.A.
144 A2 Porto Esperidião Brazil
24 B2 Portel Portugal
142 B1 Portela Brazil
114 E4 Port Elgin Can.
110 C4 Porterville R.S.A.
97 H5 Port Fairy Aust.
92 F2 Port Fitzroy N.Z.
78 A4 Port-Gentil Gabon
96 E3 Port Germein Aust.
96 □5 Port Gibson U.S.A.
145 A2 Porto Ferreira Brazil
76 □4 Port Harcourt Nigeria
110 D4 Port Hardy Can.
113 H4 Port Hawkesbury Can.
97 H3 Port Hedland Aust.
133 □1 Port Henderson N.Z.
112 E2 Port Henry U.S.A.
20 B3 Port Henry France
25 F3 Portheni w. Aust.
17 E5 Porthmadog U.K.
29 C6 Porthmos Zakynthou chan. Greece
115 F4 Port Hope Can.
114 E4 Port Hope Simpson Can.
110 C4 Port Hope U.S.A.
115 F4 Port Hope Can.
115 H4 Port Hueneme U.S.A.
126 E1 Port Huron U.S.A.
17 C7 Porthleven U.K.
24 B4 Portimão Portugal
122 D3 Portis U.S.A.
114 B2 Portland Jamaica
99 F3 Portland r. Aust.
116 H6 Portland Aust.
92 E2 Portland N.Z.
121 H2 Portland U.S.A.
120 B5 Portland U.S.A.
126 B2 Portland U.S.A.
126 B2 Portland U.S.A.
114 E1 Portland Bight b. Jamaica
99 F3 Portland, C. c. Aust.
110 D3 Portland Canal inlet Can.
114 D1 Portland Creek Pond l. Can.
133 □1 Portland Pt pt Jamaica
133 □1 Portland Pt pt Ascension Atlantic Ocean
133 □1 Portland Ridge mt. Jamaica
21 F5 Port-la-Nouvelle France
17 D5 Portlaoise Rep. of Ire.
125 D6 Port Lavaca U.S.A.
76 A4 Port Loko Sierra Leone
81 □4 Port Louis Mauritius
133 □5 Port Maria Jamaica
110 D4 Port McNeill Can.
113 H4 Port-Menier Can.
99 F4 Port Moresby P.N.G.
81 □4 Port Mourant Guyana
96 D2 Port Neill Aust.
113 H4 Portneuf, Réserve faunique de res. Can.
115 H3 Port Nolloth R.S.A.
24 B1 Porto Portugal
147 □5 Porto Acre Amazonas Brazil
142 C2 Pôrto Alegre Pará Brazil
142 A2 Pôrto Alegre Rio Grande do Sul Brazil
144 A1 Pôrto Amboim Angola
145 A4 Pôrto Artur Brazil
84 C1 Porto Belo Brazil
144 C2 Portobelo Panama
143 B2 Porto de Mós Brazil
142 D1 Porto de Santa Cruz Brazil
26 C4 Porto do Meinacos Brazil
145 A2 Porto dos Gaúchos Brazil
140 D2 Porto Esperança Brazil
144 A1 Porto Esperidião Brazil
145 A2 Porto Ferreira Brazil
28 □ Portoferraio Italy
17 F4 Port of Ness U.K.
133 □1 Port of Spain Trin. and Tobago
26 D3 Portogruaro Italy
144 B4 Pôrto Guareí Brazil

76 □ Porto Inglês Cape Verde
143 A4 Pôrto Jofre Brazil
26 C3 Portomaggiore Italy
83 G2 Pôrto Mocambo b. Mozambique
24 □ Porto Moniz Madeira Portugal
141 E2 Pôrto Murtinho Brazil
142 C2 Pôrto Nacional Brazil
76 Porto-Novo Benin
76 □ Porto Novo Cape Verde
126 D4 Pôrto Orford U.S.A.
79 B5 Pôrto Rico Angola
26 D4 Porto Sant'Elpidio Italy
24 □ Porto Santo Madeira Portugal
24 □ Porto Santo, Ilha de i. Madeira Portugal
144 B5 Pôrto São José Brazil
145 J2 Pôrto Seguro Brazil
27 B5 Porto Torres Italy
143 J6 Pôrto-Vecchio France
140 C1 Pôrto Velho Brazil
138 A4 Portoviejo Ecuador
16 E5 Portpatrick U.K.
97 G4 Port Phillip Bay b. Aust.
96 E2 Port Pirie Aust.
16 D3 Portree U.K.
114 E5 Port Renfrew Can.
92 □1 Port Ross inlet Auckland Is N.Z.
98 B2 Port Roper Aust.
133 □1 Port Royal Jamaica
120 E5 Port Royal U.S.A.
17 D4 Portrush U.K.
73 F1 Port Said Egypt
119 C6 Port St Joe U.S.A.
95 D5 Port St Johns R.S.A.
123 F4 Port Sanilac U.S.A.
121 H2 Port Severn Can.
45 □ Port Shelter b. Hong Kong
83 D5 Port Shepstone R.S.A.
110 C4 Port Simpson Can.
133 G4 Portsmouth Dominica
121 H3 Portsmouth U.S.A.
120 B5 Portsmouth U.S.A.
120 E6 Portsmouth U.S.A.
17 G7 Portsmouth U.K.
81 □4 Port South East inlet Mauritius
97 H3 Port Stephens b. Aust.
147 D7 Port Stephens Falkland Is
73 G4 Port Sudan Sudan
119 B6 Port Sulphur U.S.A.
21 F5 Port-sur-Saône France
17 F6 Port Talbot U.K.
10 F4 Porttipahdan tekojärvi l. Finland
4 G1 Portugal country Europe
24 C2 Portugalete Spain
138 D2 Portuguesa r. Venezuela
17 C5 Portumna Rep. of Ire.
21 F5 Port-Vendres France
90 □2 Port-Vila Vanuatu
92 E3 Port Waikato N.Z.
96 D3 Port Wakefield Aust.
122 D4 Port Washington U.S.A.
122 D4 Port Wing U.S.A.
146 B7 Porvenir Chile
24 D1 Porzuna Spain
146 B3 Posadas Arg.
24 D4 Posadas Spain
152 □ Posel, I. du i. Kerguelen Indian Ocean
14 H3 Poselki Rus. Fed.
57 C2 Poshekhon'ye Rus. Fed.
57 C2 Posht-e Badam Iran
40 H2 Posht-e Kuh Iran
40 D2 Poso r. Indon.
19 M7 Poşta Romania
145 F5 Pôsto Alto Manissaua Brazil
113 J3 Postville Can.
122 B4 Postville U.S.A.
86 □ Post Weygand Algeria
14 H3 Pos'yet Rus. Fed.
145 F1 Poté Brazil
14 J2 Potapovo Rus. Fed.
145 A2 Potengi Brazil
122 B4 Poteau U.S.A.
27 F5 Potenza Italy
93 B7 Poteriteri, L. l. N.Z.
83 D4 Potgietersrus R.S.A.
83 D3 Poth U.S.A.
60 F1 Poti Georgia
76 D3 Potiskum Nigeria
15 □ Potoci Bos.-Herz./Croatia
126 B2 Potomac r. U.S.A.
120 D5 Potomac South Branch r. U.S.A.
140 D4 Potosí Bolivia
129 E3 Potosi Mt mt. U.S.A.
41 B4 Pototan Phil.
130 H5 Potrero Honduras
138 B3 Potrerillos Colombia
18 F2 Potsdam Germany
121 F2 Potsdam U.S.A.
120 E4 Pottstown U.S.A.
121 F4 Pottsville U.S.A.
110 C3 Pouce Coupe Can.
81 □4 Pouce, Pieter Both Mt mt. Mauritius
120 E4 Poughkeepsie U.S.A.
17 D5 Poulaphouca Reservoir resr Rep. of Ire.
145 J2 Pouso Alegre Brazil
91 □12 Pouvanaa Western Samoa
133 □1 Poŭthĭsăt Cambodia
43 □ Pouvanaa (cont.)
75 G2 Povenets Rus. Fed.
92 D1 Poverty Bay b. N.Z.
24 □ Póvoa de Varzim Portugal
13 G5 Povorino Rus. Fed.

49 G1 **Povorotnaya** Rus. Fed.
128 D5 **Poway** U.S.A.
126 F2 **Powder r.** U.S.A.
126 F3 **Powder River** U.S.A.
120 B6 **Powell r.** U.S.A.
126 E2 **Powell** U.S.A.
99 E5 **Powell Cr. w** Aust.
129 G3 **Powell, Lake resr** U.S.A.
128 C2 **Powell Mt mt.** U.S.A.
82 A5 **Powell Pt pt** *St Helena* Atlantic Ocean
132 C1 **Powell Pt** The Bahamas
110 E5 **Powell River** Can.
122 D3 **Powers** U.S.A.
120 E6 **Powhatan** U.S.A.
50 B1 **Powo** China
144 A1 **Poxoréu** Brazil
90 □2 **Poya** Pac. Oc.
51 G2 **Poyang Hu l.** China
43 □ **Poyan Res. resr** Singapore
49 J2 **Poyarkovo** Rus. Fed.
122 C3 **Poygan, Lake l.** U.S.A.
19 H4 **Poysdorf** Austria
141 E3 **Pozama** Bolivia
61 C1 **Pozantı** Turkey
28 C2 **Požarevac** Yugo.
131 F4 **Poza Rica** Mexico
49 J2 **Pozdeyevka** Rus. Fed.
28 C3 **Požega** Yugo.
49 K3 **Pozharskoye** Rus. Fed.
19 H2 **Poznań** Poland
25 E4 **Pozo Alcón** Spain
140 C4 **Pozo Almonte** Chile
24 D3 **Pozoblanco** Spain
141 E4 **Pozo Colorado** Paraguay
146 D2 **Pozo Hondo** Arg.
25 F3 **Pozohondo** Spain
147 C6 **Pozos, Pta pt** Arg.
27 E7 **Pozzallo** Italy
76 D5 **Pra r.** Ghana
14 E2 **Pra r.** Rus. Fed.
40 A2 **Prabumulih** Indon.
19 J2 **Prabuty** Poland
19 G4 **Prachatice** Czech Rep.
43 C4 **Prachin Buri** Thailand
43 B5 **Prachuap Khiri Khan** Thailand
142 B1 **Pracu r.** Brazil
19 H3 **Praděd mt.** Czech Rep.
20 F5 **Prades** France
145 J2 **Prado** Brazil
19 G3 **Praha** Czech Rep.
76 □ **Praia** Cape Verde
24 B2 **Praia de Mira** Portugal
145 E6 **Praia Grande** Brazil
142 A3 **Praia Rica** Brazil
142 B1 **Prainha** Brazil
99 F4 **Prairie** Aust.
122 E5 **Prairie Creek Reservoir resr** U.S.A.
125 C5 **Prairie Dog Town Fork r.** U.S.A.
122 B4 **Prairie du Chien** U.S.A.
43 C4 **Prakhon Chai** Thailand
29 C5 **Pramanta** Greece
43 B4 **Pran r.** Thailand
56 B2 **Pranhita r.** India
38 C6 **Prapat** Indon.
43 D4 **Prasat Preăh Vihear** Thailand
81 □1 **Praslin I. i.** Seychelles
19 J3 **Praszka** Poland
147 B6 **Prat i.** Chile
144 B3 **Prata r.** *Goiás* Brazil
144 D3 **Prata r.** *Minas Gerais* Brazil
142 D2 **Prata r.** *Piauí* Brazil
144 D3 **Prata** Brazil
54 C4 **Pratapgarh** India
145 E3 **Pratinha** Brazil
26 C4 **Prato** Italy
125 D4 **Pratt** U.S.A.
125 G5 **Prattville** U.S.A.
56 A2 **Pravara r.** India
11 F5 **Pravdinsk** Rus. Fed.
14 F1 **Pravdinsk** Rus. Fed.
15 E3 **Pravdyne** Ukraine
24 C1 **Pravia** Spain
40 D4 **Praya** Indon.
43 D4 **Preăh Vihear** Cambodia
14 A2 **Prechistoye** Rus. Fed.
26 C2 **Predazzo** Italy
28 E2 **Predeal** Romania
111 J4 **Preeceville** Can.
20 D2 **Pré-en-Pail** France
18 E1 **Preetz** Germany
11 F5 **Pregolya r.** Rus. Fed.
142 D1 **Preguiças r.** Brazil
11 G4 **Preiļi** Latvia
115 F2 **Preissac, Lac l.** Can.
28 E2 **Prejmer** Romania
28 B3 **Prekornica mts** Yugo.
43 D5 **Prêk Tnaôt l.** Cambodia
21 F3 **Prémery** France
18 F2 **Premnitz** Germany
26 F4 **Prenj mts** Bos.-Herz.
122 B3 **Prentice** U.S.A.
19 F2 **Prenzlau** Germany
15 F3 **Preobrazhenka** Ukraine
43 A4 **Preparis I. i.** *Cocos Is* Indian Ocean
43 A4 **Preparis North Channel chan.** *Cocos Is* Indian Ocean
43 A4 **Preparis South Channel chan.** *Cocos Is* Indian Ocean
19 H4 **Přerov** Czech Rep.
26 C2 **Presanella, Cima mt.** Italy
115 H4 **Prescott** Can.
129 F4 **Prescott** U.S.A.
129 F4 **Prescott Valley** U.S.A.
93 A7 **Preservation Inlet inlet** N.Z.
28 C3 **Preševo** Yugo.
124 C3 **Presho** U.S.A.
146 D2 **Presidencia Roque Sáenz Peña** Arg.
144 C5 **Presidente Bernardes** Brazil
146 E2 **Presidente de la Plaza** Arg.
142 D2 **Presidente Dutra** Brazil
144 B4 **Presidente Epitácio** Brazil
141 D2 **Presidente Hermes** Brazil
145 H1 **Presidente Jânio Quadros** Brazil
145 F3 **Presidente Juscelino** Brazil
144 B1 **Presidente Murtinho** Brazil
145 E3 **Presidente Olegário** Brazil
144 C5 **Presidente Prudente** Brazil
147 B6 **Presidente Rios, L. l.** Chile
144 C4 **Presidente Venceslau** Brazil
125 B6 **Presidio** U.S.A.
28 F3 **Preslav** Bulgaria
65 G2 **Presnogorkovka** Kazak.
65 G2 **Presnovka** Kazak.
19 K4 **Prešov** Slovakia
29 C4 **Prespa, Lake l.** Europe
121 K1 **Presque Isle** U.S.A.
122 D2 **Presque Isle Pt pt** U.S.A.
19 H4 **Pressbaum** Austria
76 D5 **Prestea** Ghana
18 F4 **Přeštice** Czech Rep.
17 F5 **Preston** U.K.
126 E3 **Preston** U.S.A.
122 A4 **Preston** U.S.A.
125 E4 **Preston** U.S.A.
129 E2 **Preston** U.S.A.
100 B4 **Preston, C. c.** Aust.
120 B6 **Prestonsburg** U.S.A.
17 E4 **Prestwick** U.K.
142 E3 **Prêto r.** *Bahia* Brazil
142 D3 **Prêto r.** *Bahia* Brazil
144 C3 **Preto r.** *Goiás* Brazil
145 E2 **Prêto r.** *Minas Gerais* Brazil
144 D4 **Preto r.** *São Paulo* Brazil
139 E5 **Prêto do Igapó Acu r.** Brazil
83 D4 **Pretoria** R.S.A.
120 E5 **Prettyboy Lake l.** U.S.A.
29 C5 **Preveza** Greece
43 D5 **Prey Vêng** Cambodia
49 K2 **Priamurskiy** Rus. Fed.
49 F2 **Priargunsk** Rus. Fed.
108 A4 **Pribilof Islands** U.S.A.
28 B3 **Priboj** Yugo.
113 G4 **Price** Can.
129 G2 **Price** U.S.A.
110 D4 **Price I. i.** Can.
119 B6 **Prichard** U.S.A.
24 D4 **Priego de Córdoba** Spain
11 F4 **Priekule** Latvia
11 G4 **Priekuļi** Latvia
11 F5 **Prienai** Lithuania
82 C4 **Prieska** R.S.A.
126 C1 **Priest L. l.** U.S.A.
133 □1 **Priestmans River** Jamaica
126 C1 **Priest River** U.S.A.
130 B2 **Prieta, Punta** Mexico
130 D3 **Prieto, Cerro** Mexico
19 J4 **Prievidza** Slovakia
14 A3 **Prigor'ye** Rus. Fed.
65 L2 **Priiskovyy** Rus. Fed.
49 F2 **Priiskovyy** Rus. Fed.
26 F3 **Prijedor** Bos.-Herz.
28 B3 **Prijepolje** Yugo.
64 C4 **Prikaspiyskaya Nizmennost' lowland** Kazak./Rus. Fed.
29 C4 **Prilep** Macedonia
131 F4 **Primavera** Mexico
142 D1 **Primeira Cruz** Brazil
146 D3 **Primero r.** Arg.
97 F5 **Prime Seal I. i.** Aust.
13 H5 **Primorsk** Rus. Fed.
49 J4 **Primorskiy** Rus. Fed.
13 F6 **Primorsko-Akhtarsk** Rus. Fed.
111 H3 **Primrose Lake l.** Can.
111 H4 **Prince Albert** Can.
82 C5 **Prince Albert** R.S.A.
152 B5 **Prince Albert Mts mts** Ant.
111 H4 **Prince Albert National Park nat. park** Can.
108 G2 **Prince Albert Peninsula pen.** Can.
108 G2 **Prince Albert Sound chan.** Can.
108 F2 **Prince Alfred, C. c.** Can.
109 L3 **Prince Charles Island i.** Can.
152 D4 **Prince Charles Mts mts** Ant.
113 H4 **Prince Edward Island div.** Can.
149 G7 **Prince Edward Islands is** Indian Ocean
115 G5 **Prince Edward Pt pt** Can.
120 E5 **Prince Frederick** U.S.A.
110 E4 **Prince George** Can.
108 H2 **Prince Gustaf Adolf Sea chan.** Can.
108 B3 **Prince of Wales, Cape c.** U.S.A.
99 E1 **Prince of Wales I. i.** Aust.
109 J2 **Prince of Wales Island i.** Can.
110 C3 **Prince of Wales Island i.** U.S.A.
108 G2 **Prince of Wales Strait chan.** Can.
108 F2 **Prince Patrick I. i.** Can.
100 D2 **Prince Regent r.** Aust.
109 J2 **Prince Regent Inlet chan.** Can.
110 C4 **Prince Rupert** Can.
111 K2 **Princes Mary Lake l.** Can.
121 F5 **Princess Anne** U.S.A.
152 D3 **Princess Astrid Coast** Ant.
99 E2 **Princess Charlotte Bay b.** Aust.
152 D5 **Princess Elizabeth Land reg.** Ant.
100 D2 **Princess May Ra. h.** Aust.
101 C5 **Princess Ra. h.** Aust.
152 D3 **Princess Ragnhild Coast** Ant.
110 D4 **Princess Royal I. i.** Can.
133 □3 **Prince's Town** *Trinidad* Trin. & Tobago
110 E5 **Princeton** Can.
128 A2 **Princeton** U.S.A.
122 C5 **Princeton** U.S.A.
118 C4 **Princeton** U.S.A.
118 C4 **Princeton** U.S.A.
121 K2 **Princeton** U.S.A.
124 E3 **Princeton** U.S.A.
121 F4 **Princeton** U.S.A.
122 C4 **Princeton** U.S.A.
120 C6 **Princeton** U.S.A.
115 K3 **Princeville** Can.
121 K2 **Prince William** Can.
108 D3 **Prince William Sound b.** U.S.A.
79 □ **Príncipe i.** Sao Tome and Principe
126 B2 **Prineville** U.S.A.
132 □1 **Prinses Beatrix airport** *Aruba* Caribbean
152 D4 **Prins Harald Coast** Ant.
62 B2 **Prins Karls Forland i.** *Svalbard* Arctic Ocean
130 K6 **Prinzapolca** Nicaragua
94 □3 **Prion Lake l.** *Macquarie I.* Pac. Oc.
24 B1 **Prior, Cabo pt** Spain
65 K3 **Priozerny** Kazak.
11 H3 **Priozersk** Rus. Fed.
10 H1 **Prirechnyy** Rus. Fed.
15 G1 **Pristen'** Rus. Fed.
28 C3 **Priština** *Kosovo* Yugo.
18 F2 **Pritzwalk** Germany
21 G4 **Privas** France
26 E3 **Privlaka** Croatia
14 B2 **Privokzal'nyy** Rus. Fed.
14 E1 **Privolzhsk** Rus. Fed.
14 G4 **Privolzhskaya Vozvyshennost' h.** Rus. Fed.
14 H4 **Privolzhskiy** Rus. Fed.
28 C3 **Prizren** Yugo.
26 F3 **Prnjavor** Bos.-Herz.
28 D3 **Probištip** Macedonia
40 C3 **Probolinggo** Indon.
19 H3 **Prochowice** Poland
122 A2 **Proctor** U.S.A.
121 G3 **Proctor** U.S.A.
139 F3 **Professor van Blommestein Meer resr** Surinam
130 J6 **Progreso** Honduras
125 C7 **Progreso** *Coahuila* Mexico
131 F4 **Progreso** *Hidalgo* Mexico
131 H4 **Progreso** *Yucatán* Mexico
49 J2 **Progress** Rus. Fed.
140 B1 **Progresso** Brazil
13 H7 **Prokhladnyy** Rus. Fed.
15 G1 **Prokhorovka** Rus. Fed.
15 E1 **Prokhory** Ukraine
28 B3 **Prokletije mt. ra.** Albania/Yugo.
65 L2 **Prokop'yevsk** Rus. Fed.
28 C3 **Prokuplje** Yugo.
12 D3 **Proletariy** Rus. Fed.
13 G6 **Proletarsk** Rus. Fed.
15 F1 **Proletarskiy** Rus. Fed.
14 C2 **Proletarskiy** Rus. Fed.
143 A4 **Promissão** *Mato Grosso do Sul* Brazil
144 D4 **Promissão** *São Paulo* Brazil
65 K2 **Promyshlennaya** Rus. Fed.
12 G3 **Pronino** Rus. Fed.
14 D2 **Pronsk** Rus. Fed.
14 E2 **Pronya r.** Rus. Fed.
108 F4 **Prophet r.** Can.
110 E3 **Prophet River** Can.
122 C5 **Prophetstown** U.S.A.
142 E3 **Propriá** Brazil
21 J6 **Propriano** France
99 G4 **Proserpine** Aust.
121 F3 **Prospect** U.S.A.
41 C4 **Prosperidad** Phil.
82 A5 **Prosperous B. b.** *St Helena* Atlantic Ocean
19 H4 **Prostějov** Czech Rep.
99 G5 **Proston** Aust.
65 H3 **Prostornoye** Kazak.
15 F2 **Prosyane** Ukraine
19 K3 **Proszowice** Poland
122 A4 **Protivin** U.S.A.
15 G2 **Protopopivka** Ukraine
14 C2 **Protva r.** Rus. Fed.
14 C2 **Protva** Rus. Fed.
14 C2 **Protvino** Rus. Fed.
28 F3 **Provadiya** Bulgaria
21 H5 **Provence-Alpes-Côte-d'Azur div.** France
121 H4 **Providence** U.S.A.
114 D4 **Providence Bay** Can.
93 A7 **Providence, Cape c.** N.Z.
125 F5 **Providence, Lake** U.S.A.
130 K6 **Providencia, I. de i.** Colombia
108 A3 **Provideniya** Rus. Fed.
121 H3 **Provincetown** U.S.A.
21 F2 **Provins** France
129 G1 **Provo** U.S.A.
111 G4 **Provost** Can.
26 F4 **Prozor** Bos.-Herz.
76 D5 **Pru r.** Ghana
13 E6 **Prubiynyy, Mys pt** Ukraine
28 E2 **Prudeni** Romania
144 C6 **Prudentópolis** Brazil
108 D2 **Prudhoe Bay** U.S.A.
99 G4 **Prudhoe I. i.** Aust.
19 H3 **Prudnik** Poland
15 G1 **Prudyanka** Ukraine
18 C3 **Prüm** Germany
28 F2 **Prundu** Romania
21 J5 **Prunelli-di-Fiumorbo** France
19 J1 **Pruszcz Gdański** Poland
19 K2 **Pruszków** Poland
28 G1 **Prut r.** Europe
26 E3 **Prvić i.** Croatia
14 B4 **Pryamitsyno** Rus. Fed.
15 F3 **Pryazovs'ke** Ukraine
152 D5 **Prydz Bay b.** Ant.
15 G1 **Prykolotne** Ukraine
15 E1 **Pryluky** Ukraine
15 G3 **Prymors'k** Ukraine
15 E3 **Prymors'ke** *Kherson* Ukraine
28 G2 **Prymors'ke** *Odesa* Ukraine
15 D1 **Pryp"yat'** Ukraine
15 D1 **Pryp"yat' r.** Ukraine
13 C4 **Prypyats' r.** Belarus
15 F3 **Pryshyb** Ukraine
15 A1 **Pryvitne** Ukraine
19 K2 **Przasnysz** Poland
19 J3 **Przedbórz** Poland
19 L4 **Przemyśl** Poland
19 L3 **Przeworsk** Poland
19 K3 **Przysucha** Poland
29 D5 **Psachna** Greece
29 E5 **Psara i.** Greece
13 G6 **Psebay** Rus. Fed.
15 F1 **Psel r.** Rus. Fed.
15 G1 **Pselets** Rus. Fed.
13 F6 **Pshekha r.** Rus. Fed.
13 F6 **Pshish r.** Rus. Fed.
11 H4 **Pskov** Rus. Fed.
12 D3 **Pskov div.** Rus. Fed.
11 G4 **Pskovskoye Ozero l.** Estonia/Rus. Fed.
26 F3 **Psunj mts** Croatia
19 J4 **Pszczyna** Poland
29 C4 **Ptolemaïda** Greece
72 D1 **Ptolemais** Libya
26 E2 **Ptuj** Slovenia
48 C6 **Pu r.** China
40 A2 **Pu r.** Indon.
146 D4 **Puán** Arg.
50 D3 **Pu'an** China
49 H6 **Puan** S. Korea
91 □12 **Puapua** Western Samoa
91 □12 **Puava, C. c.** Western Samoa
51 E4 **Pubei** China
140 B1 **Pucallpa** Peru
140 B3 **Pucara** Peru
140 B3 **Pucará r.** Peru
138 C4 **Puca Urco** Peru
51 E1 **Pucheng** China
51 G3 **Pucheng** China
14 F1 **Puchezh** Rus. Fed.
49 H5 **Puch'ŏn** S. Korea
28 E2 **Pucioasa** Romania
19 J1 **Puck** Poland
122 C4 **Puckaway Lake l.** U.S.A.
147 B4 **Pucón** Chile
57 C2 **Pūdanū** Iran
10 G2 **Pudasjärvi** Finland
12 F2 **Pudozh** Rus. Fed.
56 B4 **Pudukkottai** India
131 F5 **Puebla div.** Mexico
131 F5 **Puebla** Mexico
25 E4 **Puebla de Don Fadrique** Spain
127 F4 **Pueblo** U.S.A.
146 B2 **Pueblo Hundido** Chile
138 D1 **Pueblo Nuevo** Venezuela
131 G5 **Pueblo Viejo** Mexico
146 C4 **Puelches** Arg.
146 C4 **Puelén** Arg.
24 D4 **Puente-Genil** Spain
25 F1 **Puente la Reina** Spain
138 D1 **Puente Torres** Venezuela
50 C4 **Pu'er** China
141 F4 **Puerto Adela** Paraguay
141 D2 **Puerto Alegre** Bolivia
141 E4 **Puerto Antequera** Paraguay
130 K7 **Puerto Armuelles** Panama
138 B3 **Puerto Asís** Colombia
138 D2 **Puerto Ayacucho** Venezuela
138 □ **Puerto Ayora** *Galapagos Is* Ecuador
131 H6 **Puerto Barrios** Guatemala
140 B2 **Puerto Bermudez** Peru
138 C2 **Puerto Berrío** Colombia
138 D1 **Puerto Cabello** Venezuela
130 K6 **Puerto Cabezas** Nicaragua
130 K6 **Puerto Cabo Gracias á Dios** Nicaragua
142 A3 **Puerto Calueiro** Brazil
138 D2 **Puerto Carreño** Colombia
141 E4 **Puerto Casado** Paraguay
147 B5 **Puerto Cisnes** Chile
147 C7 **Puerto Coig** Arg.
141 E4 **Puerto Cooper** Paraguay
130 K7 **Puerto Cortés** Costa Rica
130 J6 **Puerto Cortés** Honduras
130 C3 **Puerto Cortés** Mexico
138 D1 **Puerto Cumarebo** Venezuela
25 F1 **Puerto de Ibañeta pass** Spain
25 □ **Puerto de la Cruz** *Canary Is* Spain
25 □ **Puerto de la Estaca** *Canary Is* Spain
25 □ **Puerto del Rosario** *Canary Is* Spain
131 J4 **Puerto de Morelos** Mexico
133 E5 **Puerto de Nutrias** Venezuela
141 D3 **Puerto de Pailas** Bolivia
24 D1 **Puerto de Pajares pass** Spain
24 D1 **Puerto de San Glorio pass** Spain
141 D2 **Puerto do Massaca** Brazil
141 E2 **Puerto dos Gauchos** Brazil
131 F6 **Puerto Escondido** Mexico
138 C1 **Puerto Estrella** Colombia
138 B5 **Puerto Eten** Peru
138 B4 **Puerto Francisco de Orellana** Ecuador
141 D2 **Puerto Frey** Bolivia
140 D3 **Puerto Grether** Bolivia
141 E4 **Puerto Guarani** Paraguay
138 D3 **Puerto Inírida** Colombia
146 D1 **Puerto Irigoyen** Arg.
141 E3 **Puerto Isabel** Bolivia
130 J7 **Puerto Jesus** Costa Rica
131 J4 **Puerto Juárez** Mexico
139 E1 **Puerto La Cruz** Venezuela
138 C4 **Puerto Leguizamo** Colombia
130 K6 **Puerto Lempira** Honduras
24 D3 **Puertollano** Spain
147 D5 **Puerto Lobos** Arg.
138 C3 **Puerto Lopéz** Colombia
133 E5 **Puerto Lopez Castilletes** Colombia
25 F4 **Puerto Lumbreras** Spain
147 C5 **Puerto Madryn** Arg.
140 C2 **Puerto Maldonado** Peru
140 D3 **Puerto Mamoré** Bolivia
132 C2 **Puerto Manatí** Cuba
138 A4 **Puerto Máncora** Peru
140 C3 **Puerto Marquez** Bolivia
141 F4 **Puerto Mendes** Paraguay
141 E4 **Puerto Mihanovich** Paraguay
138 D2 **Puerto Miranda** Venezuela
147 B5 **Puerto Montt** Chile
138 B5 **Puerto Morín** Peru
147 B7 **Puerto Natáles** Chile
138 D2 **Puerto Nuevo** Colombia
130 L7 **Puerto Obaldia** Panama
139 E2 **Puerto Ordaz** Venezuela
132 C2 **Puerto Padre** Cuba
138 D2 **Puerto Páez** Venezuela
138 B4 **Puerto Pardo** Peru
141 E4 **Puerto Pinasco** Paraguay
147 D5 **Puerto Pirámides** Arg.
133 F5 **Puerto Píritu** Venezuela
133 E3 **Puerto Plata** Dominican Rep.
140 B1 **Puerto Portillo** Peru
140 B2 **Puerto Prado** Peru
41 A4 **Puerto Princesa** Phil.
138 B2 **Puerto Rey** Colombia
140 C2 **Puerto Rico** Bolivia
104 M8 **Puerto Rico terr.** Caribbean
133 F3 **Puerto Rico Trench** Caribbean
132 D2 **Puerto Samá** Cuba
147 C7 **Puerto Santa Cruz inlet** Arg.
141 E4 **Puerto Sastre** Paraguay
141 D2 **Puerto Saucedo** Bolivia
24 D4 **Puerto Serrano** Spain
140 D2 **Puerto Siles** Bolivia
138 C4 **Puerto Socorro** Peru
141 E3 **Puerto Suárez** Bolivia
140 A2 **Puerto Supe** Peru
140 B2 **Puerto Tahuantisuyo** Peru
138 B3 **Puerto Tejado** Colombia
138 B4 **Puerto Tunigrama** Peru
140 A1 **Puerto Victoria** Peru
141 D2 **Puerto Villazon** Bolivia
147 C6 **Puerto Visser** Arg.
141 D4 **Puesto Estrella** Paraguay
91 □11 **Pueu** *Fr. Poly.* Pac. Oc.
13 J4 **Pugachev** Rus. Fed.
54 C3 **Pugal** India
83 F2 **Puga Puga, Ilha i.** Mozambique
50 C3 **Puge** China
40 C4 **Puger** Indon.
27 F5 **Puglia div.** Italy
40 A3 **Pugung, G. mt.** Indon.
57 C4 **Pūhāl-e Khamīr, Kuh-e mt. ra.** Iran
91 □16 **Puhi h.** *Easter I.* Chile
25 H3 **Puig Major mt.** Spain
20 F5 **Puigmal mt.** France/Spain
45 □ **Pui O Wan b.** Hong Kong
72 C5 **Puits 29 well** Chad
72 C5 **Puits 30 well** Chad
76 B5 **Pujehun** Sierra Leone
51 G2 **Pujiang** China
93 C6 **Pukaki, L. l.** N.Z.
87 O6 **Pukapuka atoll** *Fr. Poly.* Pac. Oc.
114 C2 **Pukaskwa r.** Can.
114 C2 **Pukaskwa National Park nat. park** Can.
111 J3 **Pukatawagan** Can.
49 J4 **Pukch'ŏng** N. Korea
28 B3 **Pukë** Albania
92 G2 **Pukeamara mt.** N.Z.
92 E2 **Pukekohe** N.Z.
93 D5 **Puketeraki Ra. mt. ra.** N.Z.
92 F4 **Puketoi Range h.** N.Z.
93 C6 **Pukeuri Junction** N.Z.
12 G2 **Puksoozero** Rus. Fed.
26 D3 **Pula** Croatia
27 B6 **Pula** Italy
140 C4 **Pulacayo** Bolivia
49 G5 **Pulandian Wan b.** China
41 C4 **Pulangi r.** Phil.
40 C2 **Pulangpisau** Indon.
140 C4 **Pular, Co mt.** Chile
40 E3 **Pulasi i.** Indon.
121 E3 **Pulaski** U.S.A.
119 C5 **Pulaski** U.S.A.
120 C6 **Pulaski** U.S.A.
122 C3 **Pulaski** U.S.A.
40 A2 **Pulaukijang** Indon.
19 K3 **Puławy** Poland
56 C3 **Pulicat L. b.** India
56 B3 **Pulivendla** India
56 B4 **Puliyangudi** India
10 G2 **Pulkkila** Finland
126 C2 **Pullman** U.S.A.
10 J1 **Pulozero** Rus. Fed.
130 C3 **Púlpito, Pta pt** Mexico
19 K2 **Pułtusk** Poland
55 E1 **Pulu** China
60 D2 **Pülümür** Turkey
41 C5 **Pulutan** Indon.
140 B2 **Pumasillo, Co mt.** Peru
55 G3 **Puma Yumco l.** China
146 D2 **Puna** Arg.
91 □11 **Punaauia** *Fr. Poly.* Pac. Oc.
138 A4 **Puná, Isla i.** Ecuador
55 G4 **Punakha** Bhutan
140 C3 **Punata** Bolivia
54 C2 **Punch** India
110 E4 **Punchaw** Can.
55 G3 **Püncogling** China
54 D3 **Pundri** India
56 A2 **Pune** India
43 □ **Punggol** Singapore
49 J4 **P'ungsan** N. Korea
83 E2 **Púnguè r.** Mozambique
78 E4 **Punia** Zaire
51 G4 **Puning** China
146 B3 **Punitaqui** Chile
54 C3 **Punjab** India
54 B3 **Punjab** Pakistan
54 D2 **Punmah Gl. gl.** China/Jammu and Kashmir
140 B3 **Puno** Peru
147 D4 **Punta Alta** Arg.
147 B7 **Punta Arenas** Chile
119 □3 **Punta, Cerro de mt.** Puerto Rico
147 D5 **Punta Delgada** Arg.
147 C7 **Punta Delgada** Chile
130 H5 **Punta Gorda** Belize
119 D7 **Punta Gorda** U.S.A.
25 □ **Puntallana** *Canary Is* Spain
147 D5 **Punta Norte** Arg.
130 J7 **Puntarenas** Costa Rica
24 C4 **Punta Umbría** Spain
132 □1 **Punt Basora pt** *Aruba* Caribbean
132 □2 **Punt Kanon pt** *Curaçao* Netherlands Ant.
138 C1 **Punto Fijo** Venezuela
120 D4 **Punxsutawney** U.S.A.
10 G2 **Puokio** Finland
10 G2 **Puolanka** Finland
51 F2 **Puqi** China
140 B2 **Puquio** Peru
146 C2 **Puquios** Chile
57 D4 **Pūr** Iran
62 J3 **Pur r.** Rus. Fed.
138 B3 **Puracé, Parque Nacional nat. park** Colombia
138 B3 **Purace, Volcán de vol** Colombia
54 E3 **Puranpur** India
90 □1 **Purari r.** P.N.G.
40 B3 **Purbalingga** Indon.
125 D5 **Purcell** U.S.A.
110 F4 **Purcell Mts mt. ra.** Can.
55 E2 **Pur Co l.** China
14 F2 **Purdoshki** Rus. Fed.
146 B4 **Purén** Chile
127 G4 **Purgatoire r.** U.S.A.
55 F6 **Puri** India
18 B2 **Purmerend** Netherlands
54 D6 **Purna r.** *Maharashtra* India
54 D5 **Purna r.** *Maharashtra* India
56 B2 **Purna** India
55 F4 **Pūrnia** India
147 B5 **Purranque** Chile
40 C2 **Purukcahu** Indon.
55 F5 **Puruliya** India
139 E4 **Purus r.** Brazil
11 H3 **Puruvesi l.** Finland
28 E3 **Pŭrvomay** Bulgaria
40 A3 **Purwakarta** Indon.
40 B3 **Purwareja** Indon.
40 B3 **Purwodadi** Indon.
40 B3 **Purwoketto** Indon.
49 J4 **Puryŏng** N. Korea
40 B1 **Pusa** Malaysia
56 B2 **Pusad** India
49 J6 **Pusan** S. Korea
40 B1 **Pusatdamai** Indon.
121 J2 **Pushaw Lake l.** U.S.A.
15 D1 **Pushcha-Vodytsya** Ukraine
14 C2 **Pushchino** Rus. Fed.
12 H2 **Pushemskiy** Rus. Fed.
12 D3 **Pushinskiye** Rus. Fed.
12 D3 **Pushkin** Rus. Fed.
14 C1 **Pushkino** *Moskva* Rus. Fed.
13 H5 **Pushkino** *Saratov* Rus. Fed.
57 E3 **Pusht-i-Rud reg.** Afghanistan
19 K5 **Püspökladány** Hungary
26 C2 **Pusteria, Val v.** Italy
115 G2 **Pusticamica, Lac l.** Can.
12 D3 **Pustoshka** Rus. Fed.
19 L2 **Puszcza Augustowska forest** Poland
19 G2 **Puszcza Natecka forest** Poland
42 B1 **Putao** Myanmar
92 E3 **Putaruru** N.Z.
18 F1 **Putbus** Germany
51 G3 **Putian** China
27 F5 **Putignano** Italy
14 C3 **Putimets** Rus. Fed.
140 C2 **Putina** Peru
40 B2 **Puting, Tg pt** Indon.
131 F5 **Putla** Mexico
57 F3 **Putla Khan** Afghanistan
18 F2 **Putlitz** Germany
28 F2 **Putna r.** Romania
121 H4 **Putnam** U.S.A.
121 G3 **Putney** U.S.A.
140 C3 **Putre** Chile
56 B4 **Puttalam** Sri Lanka
56 B4 **Puttalam Lagoon lag.** Sri Lanka
18 E1 **Puttgarden** Germany
138 C4 **Putumayo r.** Colombia/Peru
60 D2 **Pütürge** Turkey
40 C1 **Putusibau** Indon.
14 E2 **Putyatino** Rus. Fed.
15 A3 **Putyla** Ukraine
15 E1 **Putyvl'** Ukraine
11 H3 **Puumala** Finland
127 □2 **Puuwai** U.S.A.
112 E1 **Puvurnituq** Can.
48 D5 **Pu Xian** China
126 B2 **Puyallup** U.S.A.
49 E6 **Puyang** China
147 B5 **Puyehue** Chile
147 B5 **Puyehue, Parque Nacional nat. park** Chile
20 F5 **Puylaurens** France
20 E5 **Puymorens, Col de pass** France
138 B4 **Puyo** Ecuador
93 A7 **Puysegur Pt pt** N.Z.
12 K2 **Puzla** Rus. Fed.
81 C6 **Pwani div.** Tanzania
79 E5 **Pweto** Zaire
17 E5 **Pwllheli** U.K.
12 F1 **Pyalitsa** Rus. Fed.
12 E2 **Pyal'ma** Rus. Fed.
42 A3 **Pyalo** Myanmar
42 A4 **Pyamalaw r.** Myanmar
14 G2 **P'yana r.** Rus. Fed.
65 G5 **Pyandzh r.** Afghanistan/Tajikistan
12 D1 **Pyaozero, Ozero l.** Rus. Fed.
10 H2 **Pyaozerskiy** Rus. Fed.
42 A3 **Pyapon** Myanmar
62 K2 **Pyasina r.** Rus. Fed.
13 G6 **Pyatigorsk** Rus. Fed.
15 C1 **P''yatka** Ukraine
15 G1 **Pyatnitskoye** Rus. Fed.
14 C2 **Pyatovskiy** Rus. Fed.
15 E2 **P''yatykhatky** Ukraine
42 B2 **Pyawbwe** Myanmar
42 A3 **Pyè** Myanmar
93 B7 **Pye, Mt h.** N.Z.
13 D4 **Pyetrykaw** Belarus
10 G3 **Pyhäjärvi** Finland
10 G2 **Pyhäjoki r.** Finland
10 G2 **Pyhäjoki** Finland
10 G2 **Pyhäntä** Finland
10 H3 **Pyhäselkä l.** Finland
42 A2 **Pyingaing** Myanmar
42 B3 **Pyinmana** Myanmar
62 K3 **Pyl'karamo** Rus. Fed.
29 C6 **Pylos** Greece
120 C4 **Pymatuning Reservoir resr** U.S.A.
49 H5 **Pyŏksŏng** N. Korea
49 H4 **Pyŏktong** N. Korea
49 H5 **P'yŏnggang** N. Korea
49 H5 **P'yŏngsong** N. Korea
49 H5 **P'yŏngt'aek** S. Korea
49 H5 **P'yŏngyang** N. Korea
97 F4 **Pyramid Hill** Aust.
93 □1 **Pyramid I. i.** *Chatham Is* N.Z.
128 C1 **Pyramid Lake l.** U.S.A.
122 E3 **Pyramid Pt pt** U.S.A.
128 C2 **Pyramid Range mt. ra.** U.S.A.
20 D5 **Pyrenees mt. ra.** France
29 D5 **Pyrgetos** Greece
29 C6 **Pyrgos** *Dytiki Ellas* Greece
15 C1 **Pyrizhky** Ukraine
15 E2 **Pyrohy** Ukraine
15 E1 **Pyryatyn** Ukraine
19 G2 **Pyrzyce** Poland
12 H3 **Pyshchug** Rus. Fed.
64 F1 **Pyshma** Rus. Fed.
64 F1 **Pyshma r.** Rus. Fed.
11 G4 **Pytalovo** Latvia
42 B3 **Pyu** Myanmar

Q

109 M2 **Qaanaaq** Greenland
61 D4 **Qā 'Aẓamān** Saudi Arabia
61 C3 **Qabatiya** Israel
55 H3 **Qabnag** China
73 G3 **Qaḍīmah** Saudi Arabia
60 F3 **Qādir Karam** Iraq
60 E3 **Qadissiya Dam dam** Iraq
80 □ **Qādub** *Socotra* Yemen
61 D4 **Qā'el Hafīra salt flat** Jordan
61 D4 **Qa'el Jinz salt flat** Jordan
61 D4 **Qa'el 'Umarī salt flat** Jordan
49 F2 **Qagan** China
48 C4 **Qagan Ders** China
48 E4 **Qagan Nur l.** *Inner Mongolia* China
48 E4 **Qagan Nur** *Inner Mongolia* China
48 D5 **Qagan Nur** *Inner Mongolia* China
49 E4 **Qagan Nur resr** *Inner Mongolia* China
49 H3 **Qagan Nur l.** *Jilin* China
48 A5 **Qagan Nur** *Qinghai* China
49 F3 **Qagan Qulut** China
48 E4 **Qagan Teg** China
55 H2 **Qagan Tohoi** China
49 E4 **Qagan Us** China
55 H3 **Qagbasêrag** China
55 E2 **Qagcaka** China
109 O3 **Qagssimiut** Greenland
48 E4 **Qahar Youyi Qianqi** China
48 E4 **Qahar Youyi Zhongqi** China
73 H2 **Qahd, W. w** Saudi Arabia
73 H4 **Qahr, Jibāl al h.** Saudi Arabia
73 H3 **Qaḥṭān reg.** Saudi Arabia
44 F4 **Qaidam Pendi basin** China
57 F2 **Qaisar** Afghanistan
57 F1 **Qaisar r.** Afghanistan
54 E1 **Qakar** China
61 D3 **Qa Khanna reg.** Jordan
73 F5 **Qala'en Nahl** Sudan
65 H5 **Qal'aikhum** Tajikistan
80 □ **Qalansīyah** *Socotra* Yemen
57 F2 **Qala Shinia Takht** Afghanistan
57 F2 **Qalāt** Afghanistan
61 D2 **Qal'at al Ḥiṣn** Syria
61 C2 **Qal'at al Marqab** Syria
73 G2 **Qal'at al Mu'aẓẓam** Saudi Arabia
60 E3 **Qal'at as Sālihīyah** Syria
61 C4 **Qalat at Hasel** Jordan
73 H3 **Qal'at Bīshah** Saudi Arabia
60 F4 **Qal'at Sālih** Iraq
57 E2 **Qala Vali** Afghanistan
57 A2 **Qal'eh Safid** Iran
57 E2 **Qal 'eh-ve Now** Afghanistan
57 F3 **Qal 'eh-ye Bost** Afghanistan
60 F4 **Qalīb Bāqūr well** Iraq
72 E4 **Qalti Immaseri well** Sudan
61 A4 **Qalyûb** Egypt
50 B1 **Qamalung** China
54 B4 **Qambar** Pakistan
50 B2 **Qamdo** China
90 □6 **Qamea i.** Fiji
73 H4 **Qam Hadīl** Saudi Arabia
72 C1 **Qamīnis** Libya
54 B3 **Qamruddin Karez** Pakistan
57 B2 **Qamṣar** Iran
80 E2 **Qandala** Somalia
49 E4 **Qangdin Sum** China
57 C1 **Qapan** Iran
65 K4 **Qapqal** China
72 E2 **Qara** Egypt
61 C3 **Qaraaoun** Lebanon
60 F2 **Qarabağ div.** Azerbaijan
57 B2 **Qara Chai r.** Iran
57 G2 **Qarah Bāgh** Afghanistan
72 C2 **Qarārat an Nā'ikah depression** Libya
80 E3 **Qardho** Somalia
64 C5 **Qareh Sū r.** Iran
60 F3 **Qareh Su r.** Iran
55 H1 **Qarhan** China
61 B5 **Qarn el Kabsh, G. mt.** Egypt
57 F1 **Qarqīn** Afghanistan
61 C2 **Qartaba** Lebanon
60 F4 **Qaryat al Gharab** Iraq
57 A4 **Qaryat al Ulyā** Saudi Arabia
57 A4 **Qaryat as Sufla** Saudi Arabia
57 D2 **Qasamī** Iran
57 E2 **Qasa Murg mt. ra.** Afghanistan
57 D2 **Qāsemābād** Iran
61 D5 **Qa 'Sharawrā' salt pan** Saudi Arabia
57 B3 **Qash Qai reg.** Iran
109 N3 **Qasigiannguit** Greenland
73 H2 **Qasīm reg.** Saudi Arabia
61 D2 **Qasr al Ḥayr** Syria
60 E3 **Qasr al Khubbāz** Iraq
60 G4 **Qaṣr aş Şabīyah** Kuwait
60 D4 **Qasr el Azraq** Jordan
60 D3 **Qasr el Burqu'** Jordan
61 D4 **Qasr el Kharana** Jordan
57 E4 **Qaṣr-e-Qand** Iran
73 E2 **Qasr Farafra** Egypt
72 B1 **Qasr Khiyār** Libya
72 B2 **Qaṣr Larocu** Libya
80 D2 **Qa'tabah** Yemen
61 D4 **Qatafa, W. w** Jordan
60 D3 **Qaṭanā** Syria
32 G8 **Qatar country** Asia
57 D1 **Qatlish** Iran
61 D1 **Qaṭma** Syria
65 H5 **Qatorkŭhi Darvoz mt. ra.** Tajikistan
65 H5 **Qatorkŭhi Yazgulom mt. ra.** Tajikistan
65 G5 **Qatorkŭhi Zarafshon mt. ra.** Tajikistan
60 D4 **Qatrāna** Jordan
61 A5 **Qaṭrâni, Gebel escarpment** Egypt
73 E2 **Qattâra Depression depression** Egypt
73 G2 **Qā', W. al w** Saudi Arabia
60 F1 **Qax** Azerbaijan
57 D2 **Qāyen** Iran
60 E3 **Qayyarah** Iraq
60 F2 **Qazangöldag mt.** Armenia
60 F1 **Qazax** Azerbaijan
54 B4 **Qazi Ahmad** Pakistan
60 G1 **Qazımämmäd** Azerbaijan
57 B1 **Qazvīn** Iran
48 B4 **Qeh** China
90 □6 **Qeleni** Fiji
48 E3 **Qelin Ul** China
73 F2 **Qena** Egypt
109 N3 **Qeqertarsuatsiaat** Greenland
109 N3 **Qeqertarsuatsiaq i.** Greenland
109 N3 **Qeqertarsuup Tunua b.** Greenland
57 D4 **Qeshm** Iran
57 D4 **Qeshm i.** Iran
57 B1 **Qeydār** Iran
57 C4 **Qeys i.** Iran
60 G2 **Qezel Owzan r.** Iran
61 C4 **Qeẕi'ot** Israel
50 D1 **Qian r.** China
49 F5 **Qian'an** China
49 H3 **Qian'an** China
51 E3 **Qiancheng** China
51 G1 **Qiang r.** China
49 H3 **Qian Gorlos** China
50 E2 **Qianjiang** China
51 F2 **Qianjiang** China
49 K3 **Qianjin** China
50 C2 **Qianning** China
49 G3 **Qianqihao** China
49 G4 **Qian Shan mt. ra.** China
65 K4 **Qianshanlaoba** China
50 D3 **Qianxi** China
49 F4 **Qianxi** China
50 E1 **Qian Xian** China
51 G2 **Qianyang** China
50 D1 **Qianyang** China
51 E3 **Qianyang** China
48 E5 **Qiaocun** China
50 C3 **Qiaojia** China
82 D4 **Qibing** R.S.A.
51 H2 **Qidong** China
51 F3 **Qidong** China
50 A1 **Qidukou** China
44 E4 **Qiemo** China
49 F5 **Qihe** China
50 D2 **Qijiang** China
52 H2 **Qijiaojing** China
57 E4 **Qila Ladgasht** Pakistan
49 F4 **Qilaotu Shan mt. ra.** China
57 E3 **Qila Safed** Pakistan
54 B3 **Qila Saifullah** Pakistan
48 B5 **Qilian** China
48 A5 **Qilian Shan mt. ra.** China
48 A5 **Qilian Shan mt.** China
109 P3 **Qillak i.** Greenland
51 G2 **Qimen** China
48 E6 **Qin r.** China
50 D1 **Qin'an** China
51 E2 **Qing r.** China
49 H4 **Qing r.** China
49 H3 **Qing'an** China
49 G4 **Qingchengzi** China
50 D1 **Qingchuan** China
49 G5 **Qingdao** China
49 H3 **Qinggang** China
48 A5 **Qinghai div.** China
52 K3 **Qinghai Hu salt l.** China
48 A5 **Qinghai Nanshan mt. ra.** China
48 D5 **Qingjian** China
51 F2 **Qingjiang** China
51 G1 **Qingjiang** China
51 G3 **Qingliu** China
50 D3 **Qinglong** China
49 F4 **Qinglong** China
49 F5 **Qinglong r.** China
51 E4 **Qingping** China
51 H2 **Qingpu** China
48 B5 **Qingshizui** China
48 A5 **Qingshui** China
50 D1 **Qingshui** China
50 B1 **Qingshuihe** China
48 D5 **Qingshuihe** China
65 K4 **Qingshuihezi** China
51 H2 **Qingtian** China
49 F5 **Qing Xian** China
48 E5 **Qingxu** China
51 G2 **Qingyang** China
48 C5 **Qingyang** China
51 G3 **Qingyuan** China
51 F4 **Qingyuan** China
49 H4 **Qingyuan** China
49 F5 **Qinhuangdao** China
50 D1 **Qin Ling mt. ra.** China
48 E6 **Qinshui** China
48 C5 **Qintongxia** China
48 E5 **Qin Xian** China
51 F1 **Qinyang** China
48 E5 **Qinyuan** China
50 E4 **Qinzhou** China
50 E4 **Qinzhou Wan b.** China
51 E5 **Qionghai** China
50 C2 **Qionglai** China
50 C2 **Qionglai Shan mt. ra.** China
51 E5 **Qiongshan** China
51 E5 **Qiongzhong** China
51 E4 **Qiongzhou Haixia** China
50 D1 **Qipan Guan pass** China
49 G1 **Qiqian** China
49 G3 **Qiqihar** China
57 C3 **Qīr** Iran
54 E1 **Qira** China
61 C4 **Qiryat Gat** Israel
50 E4 **Qisha** China
61 C3 **Qishon r.** Israel
73 G3 **Qishrān I. i.** Saudi Arabia
61 D4 **Qitab ash Shāmah crater** Saudi Arabia
49 J3 **Qitaihe** China
50 D3 **Qiubei** China
51 F2 **Qiujin** China
49 G5 **Qixia** China
48 E6 **Qi Xian** China
48 E5 **Qi Xian** China
49 K3 **Qixing r.** China
51 E3 **Qiyang** China
48 C5 **Qiying** China
51 E5 **Qizhou Liedao** China
48 C4 **Qog Qi** China
57 A1 **Qojūr** Iran
57 B2 **Qom** Iran
50 A2 **Qomdo** China
57 B2 **Qomishēh** Iran
55 G3 **Qonggyai** China
48 D4 **Qongi** China
80 F2 **Qoor Hurdiyo b.** Somalia
80 E3 **Qooriga Neegro b.** Somalia
61 D2 **Qornet es Saouda mt.** Lebanon
57 A2 **Qorveh** Iran
80 E3 **Qoryale** Somalia
60 E2 **Qosh Tepe** Iraq
57 D4 **Qoṭbābād** Iran
60 F2 **Qotūr** Iran
50 D2 **Qu r.** China
121 G3 **Quabbin Reservoir resr** U.S.A.
128 D4 **Quail Mts mts** U.S.A.
101 B7 **Quairading** Aust.
121 F4 **Quakertown** U.S.A.
111 K2 **Quamarirjunq Lake l.** Can.
97 F2 **Quambone** Aust.
98 E4 **Quamby** Aust.
125 D5 **Quanah** U.S.A.
51 E1 **Quanbao Shan mt.** China
43 E4 **Quang Ngai** Vietnam
42 D3 **Quang Tri** Vietnam
42 D2 **Quang Yen** Vietnam
51 F3 **Quannan** China
51 E3 **Quanzhou** China
51 G3 **Quanzhou** China
111 J4 **Qu'Appelle r.** Can.
111 J4 **Qu'Appelle** Can.
109 M3 **Quaqtaq** Can.
146 E3 **Quaraí** Brazil
146 E3 **Quaraí r.** Brazil
79 C6 **Quarenta** Angola
45 □ **Quarry Bay** Hong Kong
24 B4 **Quarteira** Portugal
27 B6 **Quartu Sant'Elena** Italy
128 D3 **Quartzite Mt mt.** U.S.A.
129 E5 **Quartzsite** U.S.A.
81 □4 **Quatre Bornes** Mauritius
110 D4 **Quatsino Sound inlet** Can.
60 G1 **Quba** Azerbaijan
57 D1 **Quchan** Iran
97 G3 **Queanbeyan** Aust.
115 K3 **Québec** Can.
115 G3 **Québec div.** Can.
144 E3 **Quebra Anzol r.** Brazil
146 D2 **Quebracho Coto** Arg.
138 D1 **Quebrada del Toro, Parque Nacional de la nat. park** Venezuela
119 □3 **Quebradillas** Puerto Rico
147 B5 **Quedal, C. pt** Chile
144 B6 **Quedas do Iguaçu** Brazil
18 E3 **Quedlinburg** Germany
110 E4 **Queen Bess, Mt mt.** Can.
110 C4 **Queen Charlotte** Can.
147 D7 **Queen Charlotte B. b.** Falkland Is.
110 C4 **Queen Charlotte Islands is** Can.
110 D4 **Queen Charlotte Sound chan.** Can.
93 E4 **Queen Charlotte Sound chan.** N.Z.
110 D4 **Queen Charlotte Str. chan.** Can.
108 H2 **Queen Elizabeth Islands is** Can.
81 B5 **Queen Elizabeth National Park nat. park** Uganda
152 C5 **Queen Mary Land reg.** Ant.
82 A5 **Queen Mary's Peak mt.** *Tristan da Cunha* Atlantic Ocean
108 H3 **Queen Maud Gulf b.** Can.
152 B4 **Queen Maud Mts mts** Ant.
109 J2 **Queens Chan. chan.** Can.
98 B2 **Queens Channel chan.** Aust.
97 F4 **Queenscliff** Aust.
99 F4 **Queensland div.** Aust.
97 F5 **Queenstown** Aust.
93 B6 **Queenstown** N.Z.
43 □ **Queenstown** Singapore
82 D5 **Queenstown** R.S.A.
121 E5 **Queenstown** U.S.A.
126 A2 **Queets** U.S.A.
146 E3 **Queguay Grande r.** Uruguay
146 D4 **Quehué** Arg.
147 B5 **Queilén** Chile
142 E3 **Queimadas** Brazil
79 C5 **Quela** Angola
83 F2 **Quelimane** Mozambique
147 B5 **Quellón** Chile
129 H4 **Quemado** U.S.A.
79 C6 **Quembo r.** Angola
147 B5 **Quemchi** Chile
146 D4 **Quemú-Quemú** Arg.
146 E4 **Quequén Grande r.** Arg.
144 B5 **Querência do Norte** Brazil
131 E4 **Querétaro** Mexico
131 F4 **Querétaro div.** Mexico
18 E3 **Querfurt** Germany
130 C2 **Querobabi** Mexico
24 E4 **Quesada** Spain
74 B3 **Quesat w** *Western Sahara*
51 F1 **Queshan** China
110 E4 **Quesnel** Can.
110 E4 **Quesnel r.** Can.
110 E4 **Quesnel L. l.** Can.
20 C3 **Questembert** France
122 B1 **Quetico Provincial Park res.** Can.
54 A3 **Quetta** Pakistan
146 B4 **Queuco** Chile
147 B5 **Queulat, Parque Nacional nat. park** Chile
147 B4 **Queule** Chile
138 B4 **Quevedo** Ecuador
115 G2 **Quévillon, Lac l.** Can.
131 H6 **Quezaltenango** Guatemala
41 A4 **Quezon** Phil.
41 B3 **Quezon City** Phil.
80 D1 **Quflat al 'Udhr** Yemen
49 F6 **Qufu** China
79 B6 **Quibala** Angola
79 B5 **Quibaxe** Angola
138 B2 **Quibdó** Colombia
20 C3 **Quiberon** France
79 B5 **Quiçama, Parque Nacional do nat. park** Angola
42 D3 **Qui Châu** Vietnam
79 C5 **Quiculungo** Angola
141 E5 **Quiindy** Paraguay
129 F5 **Quijotoa** U.S.A.
147 B5 **Quilán, C. c.** Chile
79 B6 **Quilengues** Angola
146 D3 **Quilino** Arg.
140 B2 **Quillabamba** Peru
140 C3 **Quillacollo** Bolivia
140 C4 **Quillagua** Chile
65 G5 **Quillai Chimtargha mt.** Tajikistan
20 F5 **Quillan** France
111 J4 **Quill Lakes lakes** Can.
146 B3 **Quillota** Chile
146 E3 **Quilmes** Arg.
146 C2 **Quilmes, Sa del mt. ra.** Arg.
56 B4 **Quilon** India
99 F5 **Quilpie** Aust.
146 B3 **Quilpué** Chile
83 F2 **Quilua** Mozambique
79 C5 **Quimbele** Angola
146 D2 **Quimilí** Arg.
20 B3 **Quimper** France
20 C3 **Quimperlé** France
140 B2 **Quince Mil** Peru
128 B2 **Quincy** U.S.A.
119 C6 **Quincy** U.S.A.
122 B6 **Quincy** U.S.A.
121 H3 **Quincy** U.S.A.
146 C3 **Quines** Arg.
83 G2 **Quinga** Mozambique
76 A4 **Quinhámel** Guinea-Bissau
43 E4 **Qui Nhon** Vietnam
129 E3 **Quinn Canyon Range mts** U.S.A.
144 C5 **Quintana** Brazil
24 D3 **Quintana de la Serena** Spain
24 E3 **Quintanar de la Orden** Spain
25 F3 **Quintanar del Rey** Spain
131 H5 **Quintana Roo div.** Mexico
20 C2 **Quintin** France
146 D3 **Quinto r.** Arg.
25 F2 **Quinto** Spain
79 B5 **Quinzau** Angola
81 D7 **Quionga** Mozambique
79 B6 **Quipungo** Angola
146 B4 **Quirihue** Chile
79 C6 **Quirima** Angola
81 D7 **Quirimba, Ilha i.** Mozambique
97 G2 **Quirindi** Aust.
144 C3 **Quirinópolis** Brazil
146 D4 **Quiroga** Arg.
140 C3 **Quiroga** Bolivia
24 C1 **Quiroga** Spain
21 G5 **Quissac** France
81 D7 **Quissanga** Mozambique
83 E3 **Quissico** Mozambique
79 C6 **Quitapa** Angola
132 B4 **Quita Sueño Bank** Colombia
144 C3 **Quitéria r.** Brazil
79 C7 **Quiteve** Angola
119 D6 **Quitman** U.S.A.
119 B5 **Quitman** U.S.A.
138 B4 **Quito** Ecuador
127 D6 **Quitovac** Mexico
129 F4 **Quivero** U.S.A.
142 E1 **Quixadá** Brazil
142 E2 **Quixeramobim** Brazil
51 F3 **Qujiang** China
51 E4 **Qujie** China
50 C3 **Qujing** China
65 H5 **Qullai Garmo mt.** Tajikistan
50 A1 **Qumar r.** China
50 A1 **Qumarlêb** China
55 H2 **Qumarrabdün** China
55 H2 **Qumaryan** China
50 B2 **Qu'nyido** China
111 L2 **Quoich r.** Can.
98 B2 **Quoin I. i.** Aust.
82 B5 **Quoin Pt pt** R.S.A.
55 E2 **Quong Muztag mt.** China
96 D3 **Quorn** Aust.
82 C3 **Quoxo r.** Botswana
61 D5 **Qurayyah** Saudi Arabia
65 G5 **Qŭrghonteppa** Tajikistan
113 G2 **Qurlutu r.** Can.
60 G1 **Qusar** Azerbaijan
73 F2 **Quseir** Egypt
60 F2 **Qūshchi** Iran
51 E2 **Qutang Xia r.** China
57 B2 **Qūtīābād** Iran
73 H2 **Quṭn, J. h.** Saudi Arabia
73 H4 **Qutū' I. i.** Saudi Arabia
61 D1 **Quwayq r.** Syria
48 C5 **Quwu Shan mt. ra.** China
50 D2 **Qu Xian** China
55 G3 **Qüxü** China
42 D3 **Quynh Lưu** Vietnam
42 C2 **Quynh Nhai** Vietnam
115 G4 **Quyon** Can.
51 G2 **Quzhou** China
49 E5 **Quzhou** China
13 H7 **Qvareli** Georgia

R

19 G5 **Raab r.** Austria
10 G2 **Raahe** Finland
10 H3 **Rääkkylä** Finland
18 C2 **Raalte** Netherlands
10 G2 **Raanujärvi** Finland
40 C3 **Raas i.** Indon.
80 E2 **Raas Aantaara pt** Somalia
16 D3 **Raasay i.** U.K.
16 D3 **Raasay, Sound of chan.** U.K.
80 F2 **Raas Binna pt** Somalia
80 E3 **Raas Cabaad pt** Somalia
80 E2 **Raas Cadcadde pt** Somalia
80 F2 **Raas Caluula pt** Somalia
80 F2 **Raas Caseyr c.** Somalia
80 F3 **Raas Durdura pt** Somalia
80 F3 **Raas Gabbac pt** Somalia
80 E3 **Raas Ilig pt** Somalia
81 D5 **Raas Kaambooni pt** Somalia
80 E2 **Raas Khansiir pt** Somalia
80 F3 **Raas Macbar pt** Somalia
80 D2 **Raas Maskan pt** Somalia
81 D5 **Raas Matooni pt** Somalia
80 E2 **Raas Surud pt** Somalia
80 F2 **Raas Xaafuun pt** Somalia
80 E2 **Raas Xatiib pt** Somalia
80 F3 **Raas Xoor pt** Somalia
26 E3 **Rab i.** Croatia
40 D4 **Raba** Indon.
73 F5 **Rabak** Sudan
54 E2 **Rabang** China
20 E5 **Rabastens** France
27 E7 **Rabat** Malta
74 C2 **Rabat** Morocco
57 D2 **Rabāt-e Kamah** Iran
90 □1 **Rabaul** P.N.G.
26 C3 **Rabbi r.** Italy
110 D3 **Rabbit r.** Can.
90 □6 **Rabi i.** Fiji
73 G3 **Rābigh** Saudi Arabia
19 J4 **Rabka** Poland
55 G5 **Rabnabad Is. is** Bangladesh
15 C3 **Râbniţa** Moldova
12 E1 **Rabocheostrovsk** Rus. Fed.
57 D3 **Rābor** Iran
14 G1 **Rabotki** Rus. Fed.
72 D3 **Rabyānah oasis** Libya
26 A3 **Racconigi** Italy
120 B5 **Raccoon Creek r.** U.S.A.
113 K4 **Race, C. c.** Can.
121 H3 **Race Pt pt** U.S.A.
125 D7 **Rachal** U.S.A.
129 E3 **Rachel** U.S.A.
14 C1 **Rachevo** Rus. Fed.
43 D5 **Rach Gia** Vietnam
19 K2 **Raciąż** Poland
19 J3 **Racibórz** Poland
122 D4 **Racine** U.S.A.
114 D2 **Racine Lake l.** Can.
122 E2 **Raco** U.S.A.
28 E1 **Racoş** Romania
19 L2 **Raczki** Poland
80 D2 **Radā'** Yemen
28 E1 **Rădăuţi** Romania
14 C1 **Radchenko** Rus. Fed.
118 C4 **Radcliff** U.S.A.
49 J2 **Radde** Rus. Fed.
19 F3 **Radebeul** Germany
15 A1 **Radekhiv** Ukraine
120 C6 **Radford** U.S.A.
54 B5 **Radhanpur** India
14 H4 **Radishchevo** Rus. Fed.
112 E3 **Radisson** Can.
14 B3 **Raditsa-Krylovka** Rus. Fed.
110 F4 **Radium Hot Springs** Can.
15 G1 **Rad'kovka** Rus. Fed.
28 E3 **Radnevo** Bulgaria
138 B3 **Rado de Tumaco inlet** Colombia
19 K3 **Radom** Poland
78 D2 **Radom** Sudan
28 D3 **Radomir** Bulgaria
15 E1 **Radomka** Ukraine
78 D2 **Radom National Park nat. park** Sudan
19 J3 **Radomsko** Poland
15 C1 **Radomyshl'** Ukraine
28 F4 **Radovets** Bulgaria
28 D4 **Radoviš** Macedonia
14 D2 **Radovitskiy** Rus. Fed.
16 K1 **Radøy i.** Norway
96 C3 **Radstock, C. hd** Aust.
28 F1 **Răducăneni** Romania
15 D1 **Radul'** Ukraine
15 E3 **Radushne** Ukraine
11 F5 **Radviliškis** Lithuania
73 G3 **Raḍwá, J. mt.** Saudi Arabia
19 L4 **Radymno** Poland
15 A1 **Radyvyliv** Ukraine
19 J2 **Radziejów** Poland
19 L2 **Radziłów** Poland
19 L3 **Radzyń Podlaski** Poland
54 E4 **Rae Bareli** India
110 F2 **Rae-Edzo** Can.
91 □10 **Raeffsky, Îles is** *Fr. Poly.* Pac. Oc.
110 F2 **Rae Lakes** Can.
18 C3 **Raeren** Belgium
101 C6 **Raeside, Lake salt flat** Aust.
92 E3 **Raetihi** N.Z.
73 G2 **Rāf h.** Saudi Arabia
146 D3 **Rafaela** Arg.
61 C4 **Rafaḥ** *Gaza*
78 D3 **Rafaï** C.A.R.
15 B1 **Rafalivka** Ukraine
73 H2 **Rafḥā** Saudi Arabia
57 D3 **Rafsanjān** Iran
78 E2 **Raga** Sudan
78 D1 **Ragag** Sudan
41 C5 **Ragang, Mt vol** Phil.
41 B3 **Ragay Gulf b.** Phil.
132 D2 **Ragged I. i.** The Bahamas
121 J3 **Ragged I. i.** U.S.A.
101 C7 **Ragged, Mt h.** Aust.
133 □9 **Ragged Pt pt** *Barbados* Caribbean
54 D4 **Rāghogarh** India
80 D1 **Raghwān, W. w** Yemen
92 E2 **Raglan** N.Z.
27 E7 **Ragusa** Italy
50 C1 **Ra'gyagoinba** China
39 H7 **Raha** Indon.
23 K1 **Rahachow** Belarus
73 G5 **Rahad r.** Sudan
72 D4 **Rahad Wahal well** Sudan
60 E3 **Raḥḥālīyah** Iraq
56 A2 **Rahimatpur** India
54 B3 **Rahimyar Khan** Pakistan
57 B2 **Rāhjerd** Iran
92 D3 **Rahotu** N.Z.
56 A2 **Rahuri** India
57 E2 **Rahzanak** Afghanistan
91 □10 **Raiatea i.** *Fr. Poly.* Pac. Oc.
56 B2 **Raichur** India

```
55 G4  Raiganj India
55 E5  Raigarh India
90 □3  Raihifaihifa I. Tonga
129 E2 Railroad Valley v. U.S.A.
55 G5  Raimangal r. Bangladesh
113 G3 Raimbault, Lac l. Can.
129 G3 Rainbow Bridge Nat.
       Mon. res. U.S.A.
110 F3 Rainbow Lake Can.
99 F1  Raine Entrance chan.
       Aust.
99 E1  Raine I. i. Aust.
120 C6 Rainelle U.S.A.
128 C2 Rainier, Mt vol U.S.A.
54 B4  Raini N. r. Pakistan
112 B4 Rainy r. U.S.A.
117 H2 Rainy Lake l. Can./U.S.A.
112 B4 Rainy River Can.
54 C4  Raipur India
54 E5  Raipur India
55 F5  Rairangpur India
54 D3  Raisen India
54 C3  Raisinghnagar India
11 F3  Raisio Finland
151 K4 Raivavae i. Fr. Poly.
54 C3  Raiwind Pakistan
40 A3  Rajabasa, G. vol Indon.
55 F5  Rajagangapur India
56 C2  Rajahmundry India
10 H1  Raja-Jooseppi Finland
54 C3  Rajakhera India
54 C3  Rajaldesar India
56 B3  Rajampet India
40 C1  Rajang r. Malaysia
54 B3  Rajanpur Pakistan
56 B4  Rajapalaiyam India
56 A2  Rajapur India
54 C4  Rajasthan India
55 F4  Rajauli India
55 G5  Rajbari Bangladesh
54 D4  Rajgarh India
54 C3  Rajgarh India
19 J2  Rajgród Poland
40 A2  Rajik Indon.
55 E5  Rajim India
54 C5  Rajkot India
54 E5  Rajmahal India
54 E4  Rajmahal Hills h. India
54 E5  N. Nandgaon India
54 C4  Rajpipla India
54 C4  Rajsamand India
55 G5  Rajshahi div. Bangladesh
55 G4  Rajshahi Bangladesh
54 C4  Rajura India
55 F3  Raka China
87 L5  Rakahanga atoll Cook
       Islands Pac. Oc.
81 B5  Rakai Uganda
93 C5  Rakaia r. N.Z.
93 B6  Rakan, Ra's pt Qatar
54 C1  Rakaposhi mt. Pakistan
55 F3  Raka Zangbo r. China
49 J5  Rakdong r. S. Korea
28 E1  Rakhiv Ukraine
15 F5  Rakhmanivka Ukraine
54 B3  Rakhni Pakistan
57 H4  Rakhshan r. Pakistan
90 □8  Rakiraki Fiji
40 B3  Rakit i. Indon.
15 F1  Rakitnoye Rus. Fed.
11 G4  Rakke Estonia
19 F1  Rakkestad Norway
54 B3  Rakni r. Pakistan
19 F3  Rakovník Czech Rep.
28 E3  Rakovski Bulgaria
54 B3  Raksha Rus. Fed.
11 G4  Rakvere Estonia
119 E5 Raleigh U.S.A.
40 D3  Ralla Indon.
152    Rallier du Baty, Péninsule
       pen. Kerguelen
       Indian Ocean
122 D2 Ralph U.S.A.
110 E2 Ram r. Can.
61 C2  Ram Jordan
27 E7  Ramacca Italy
54 C4  Ramaltias Chile
113 H2 Ramah Can.
129 H4 Ramah U.S.A.
56 B3  Ramanagaram India
56 B4  Ramanathapuram India
56 B4  Ramanuj Ganj India
56 A3  Ramas, C. c. India
20 E2  Rambouillet France
90 □1  Rambutyo I. i. P.N.G.
56 A3  Ramdurg India
54 A2  Ramechhap Nepal
17 E6  Rame Head hd U.K.
83 H1  Ramena Madagascar
14 D2  Ramenki Rus. Fed.
14 D2  Ramenskoye Rus. Fed.
14 C1  Rameshki Rus. Fed.
56 B4  Rameswaram India
54 C3  Ramganga r. India
55 G4  Ramgarh Bangladesh
55 F4  Ramgarh India
57 G2  Ramgul reg. Afghanistan
57 B3  Ramhormoz Iran
57 B4  Ramis Shet' r. Ethiopia
60 C4  Ram, Jebel mt. Jordan
61 C4  Ramla Israel
72 C2  Ramlat al Wigh sand
       dunes Libya
73 H4  Ramlat Dahm sand
       dunes Saudi
       Arabia/Yemen
72 D2  Ramlat Rabyānah desert
       Libya
54 C3  Ramnagar India
54 D3  Ramnagar India
28 E2  Râmnicu Sărat Romania
28 E2  Râmnicu Vâlcea
       Romania
14 C4  Ramon' Rus. Fed.
128 D5 Ramona U.S.A.
20 E5  Ramonville-St-Agne
       France
114 E2 Ramore Can.
82 D4  Ramotswa Botswana
54 D3  Rampur India
54 D3  Rampur India
57 B3  Rampur India
54 E4  Rampura India
55 G4  Rampur Hat India
64 A3  Ramree Myanmar
42 A3  Ramree I. i. Myanmar
11 G5  Ramsele Sweden
17 E4  Ramsey U.K.
17 E6  Ramsey Island i. U.K.
17 H6  Ramsgate U.K.
54 D5  Ramshai Hat India
11 G5  Ramshir Iran
54 D4  Ramtha India
11 F3  Ramu r. P.N.G.
90 □1  Ramu r. P.N.G.
11 G5  Ramville, Îlet i.
       Martinique Caribbean
11 G6  Ramygala Lithuania
11 G3  Ramza Rus. Fed.
24 C1  Rañadoiro, Sierra de mt.
       ra. Spain
55 G5  Ranaghat India
55 G4  Ranakah, P. mt. Indon.
41 A5  Ranau Malaysia
54 D2  Ranau, D. l. Indon.
146 B3 Rancagua Chile
113 G3 Ranchi India
55 F5  Ranco, L. de l. Chile
27 E7  Rand Italy
11 D3  Randers Denmark
121 D3 Randolph U.S.A.
54 D2  Randow r. Germany
11 D3  Randsjö Sweden
43 E2  Rânĕa Sweden
76 B3  Rânérou Senegal
43 E2  Rangae Thailand
```

```
55 H5  Rangamati Bangladesh
147 C6 Rangapara North India
40 D2  Rangasa, Tg pt Sulawesi
       Selatan Indon.
40 D2  Rangas, Tg pt Sulawesi
       Selatan Indon.
93 □4  Rangatira I. i. Chatham Is
       N.Z.
92 D1  Rangaunu Bay b. N.Z.
121 H2 Rangeley U.S.A.
121 H2 Rangeley Lake l. U.S.A.
129 H1 Rangely U.S.A.
114 D3 Ranger Lake Can.
55 G4  Rangia Patharughat
       India
93 C6  Rangiora N.Z.
151 J6  Rangiroa atoll Fr. Poly.
91 □10 Rangiroa i. Fr. Poly.
92 F3  Rangitaiki r. N.Z.
92 E3  Rangitikei r. N.Z.
92 E4  Rangitkei r. N.Z.
92 E4  Rangitoto Is is N.Z.
40 A3  Rangkasbitung Indon.
42 B3  Rangoon r. Myanmar
55 G4  Rangpur Bangladesh
55 F5  Raniganj India
55 E5  Ranijula Pk. mt. India
54 B3  Ranikhet India
54 B4  Ranipur Pakistan
98 D4  Ranken w Aust.
125 C6 Rankin U.S.A.
111 L2  Rankin Inlet Can.
111 L2  Rankin Inlet inlet Can.
97 F3  Rankin's Springs Aust.
54 E4  Ranna Estonia
11 G5  Rannes Aust.
16 E3  Rannoch, L. l. U.K.
54 B4  Rann of Kachchh marsh
       India
77 F4  Rano Nigeria
83 G2  Ranohira Madagascar
83 H3  Ranohira Madagascar
91 □16 Rano Kito h. Easter I.
       Chile
83 H3  Ranomena Madagascar
90 □2  Ranoo Vanuatu
90 □1  Ranonga i. Solomon Is.
92 F3  Rano Raraku h. Easter I.
       Chile
14 D3  Ranot Thailand
14 C3  Ranova r. Rus. Fed.
57 B2  Rânsa Iran
11 D3  Ransby Sweden
39 K7  Ransiki Indon.
11 F3  Rantasalmi Finland
40 C2  Rantau Indon.
40 A2  Rantaupanjang Indon.
38 D6  Rantauprapat Indon.
       Indon.
40 D2  Rantepao Indon.
122 C5 Rantoul U.S.A.
14 E1  Rantsevo Rus. Fed.
10 G2  Rantsila Finland
10 G2  Ranua Finland
54 C5  Ranuj r. Iran (India?)
21 H2  Raon-l'Étape France
49 K3  Raohe China
24 D1  Raoping China
92 □4  Raoul I. i. Kermadec Is
       N.Z.
151 K5 Rapa i. Fr. Poly Pac. Oc.
54 B5  Rapar India
120 E5 Rapel r. U.S.A.
96 D2  Rapid Bay Aust.
124 C2 Rapid City U.S.A.
115 F3 Rapide-Deux Can.
115 F3 Rapide-Sept Can.
122 D3 Rapid River U.S.A.
11 G4  Rapla Estonia
120 E5 Rappahannock r. U.S.A.
40 D2  Rappang Indon.
54 C3  Rapti r. India
41 C3  Rapurapu i. Phil.
121 F2 Raquette r. U.S.A.
121 F2 Raquette Lake l. U.S.A.
19 H3  Rawicz Poland
120 D5 Rawley Springs U.S.A.
83 F2  Raraga r. Mozambique
91 □10 Raraka atoll Fr. Poly. Pac. Oc.
91 □10 Raroia atoll Fr. Poly.
       Pac. Oc.
151 J7  Rarotonga i. Cook Islands
       Pac. Oc.
146 C2 Rasa, Pta pt Arg.
50 B2  Ra's Abū Madd hd Saudi
       Arabia
73 G3  Ras Abu Shagara pt
       Sudan
74 A4  Râs Agâdîr pt Mauritania
60 A4  Râs 'Alam el Rûm c.
       Egypt
44 A1  Ray, C. hd Can.
119 D3 Raychikhinsk Rus. Fed.
72 D1  Ra's al Basīt c. Syria
73 G1  Ra's al Hilāl pt Libya
80 D1  Ra's al Kathīb pt Yemen
19 H3  Rawicz Poland
17 G6  Reigate U.K.
73 H3  Ra's al Khaymah U.A.E.
72 E1  Ra's al Murayssh pt
       Saudi Arabia
61 C3  Ras al Qasbah pt Saudi
       Arabia
147 D5 Rasa, Pta pt Arg.
54 C5  Ras at Tarfa pt Saudi
       Arabia
72 D1  Ra's at Tīn pt Libya
61 B4  Ras Banâs pt Egypt
73 G3  Ra's Barīdī hd Saudi
       Arabia
49 J4  Ra's Burūn pt Egypt
28 F1  Râșca r. Rus. Fed.
28 F1  Râșcani Moldova
73 H2  Râs Dashen mt. Ethiopia
61 A4  Ras Dib pt Egypt
61 B4  Râs el Barr pt Egypt
61 A4  Ras el Gilena mt. Egypt
73 H1  Râs el Kenâyis pt Egypt
73 G1  Râs el Mâ Mali
61 C5  Râs el Nafas mt. Egypt
61 C5  Ra's el Sudr pt Egypt
73 E8  Râs Ghârib Egypt
80 C2  Rashaant Mongolia
80 B2  Rashad Sudan
73 H5  Râs Hadarba pt Sudan
20 D4  Réalmont France
57 B2  Rasht Iran
80 B3  Rashid Qala Afghanistan
15 G6  Rashkiv Ukraine
57 D2  Rashm Iran
80 C2  Ra's Ibn Hānī' pt Syria
57 B2  Rasina r. Yugo.
43 E2  Rasipuram India
54 C4  Ra's 'Īsá pt Yemen
15 E5  Raska r. Rus. Fed.
142 F2 Recife Brazil
82 D6  Recife, Cape c. R.S.A.
82 □1  Récif l. i. Seychelles
57 H3  Raskoh mt. ra. Pakistan
54 C4  Ra's Koh mt. Pakistan
61 B5  Ra's Lānūf pt Libya
81 B5  Ras Mal'ab pt Egypt
61 B5  Râs Matarma pt Egypt
78 E4  Ra's Mkumbi pt Tanzania
61 B5  Ra's Momi pt Socotra
       Yemen
73 H2  Râs Muhammad c. Egypt
74 A4  Râs Nouâdhibou c.
       Western Sahara
28 E2  Râșnov Romania
```

```
81 C6  Ras Nungwi pt Tanzania
147 C6 Raso, C. pt Arg.
142 E2 Raso da Catarina reg.
       Brazil
99 H5  Rason L. salt flat Aust.
12 D4  Rasony Belarus
60 A4  Râs Qattâra Egypt
61 B5  Râs Ruahmi pt Egypt
73 G5  Rass Ajdir Tunisia
80 D2  Ras Shakhs pt Eritrea
54 E4  Ra's Shu'ab pt Socotra
       Yemen
121 F5 Redden U.S.A.
126 B3 Redding U.S.A.
17 F5  Redditch U.K.
75 F2  Redeyef Tunisia
124 D2 Redfield U.S.A.
121 F5 Redfield U.S.A.
133 □3 Redhead Trin. & Tobago
96 B3  Redhill Aust.
17 G6  Red Hill h. U.K.
74 A5  Red Hill, Mt h. Ascension
       Atlantic Ocean
125 D4 Red Hills h. U.S.A.
64 A4  Red Indian L. l. Can.
122 E5 Redkey U.S.A.
14 C1  Redkino Rus. Fed.
112 B2 Red L. l. Can.
129 E4 Red L. U.S.A.
124 E1 Red Lakes lakes U.S.A.
126 E2 Red Lodge U.S.A.
128 B2 Redmond U.S.A.
54 D4  Red Oak U.S.A.
111 J4  Red Deer r. L. Can.
121 F5 Redon France
24 A2  Redondo Portugal
114 A2 Red Rock Can.
107 D2 Red Rocks Pt pt Aust.
72 G3  Red Sea sea Africa/Asia
110 E4 Redstone Can.
110 D2 Redstone r. Can.
111 L4  Red Sucker L. l. Can.
110 G4 Redwater Can.
113 H3 Red Wine r. Can.
128 A3 Redwood City U.S.A.
122 E2 Redwood Falls U.S.A.
126 B3 Redwood Nat. Park
       U.S.A.
128 C4 Redwood Valley U.S.A.
122 E4 Reed City U.S.A.
128 C3 Reedley U.S.A.
126 C3 Reedsport U.S.A.
120 E6 Reedville U.S.A.
93 C5  Reefton N.Z.
17 D5  Ree, Lough l. Rep. of Ire.
20 D2  Refahiye Turkey
61 B4  Refa'i, T. mt.
       Jordan/Syria
147 B5 Refugio Chile
125 D6 Refugio U.S.A.
18 F4  Regen r. Germany
18 F4  Regen Germany
145 J3  Regência Brazil
18 F4  Regensburg Germany
18 F4  Regenstauf Germany
144 C5 Regente Feijó Brazil
75 E3  Reggane Algeria
27 E6  Reggio di Calabria Italy
26 D2  Reggio nell'Emilia Italy
28 D1  Reghin Romania
113 J3  Regina Brazil
111 J4  Régina Can.
139 H3 Régina French Guiana
57 F3  Registan reg.
       Afghanistan
144 D6 Registro Brazil
64 E5  Registro do Araguaia
       Brazil
10 H2  Regozero Rus. Fed.
54 D5  Rehli India
82 B3  Rehoboth Namibia
129 H4 Rehoboth U.S.A.
121 F5 Rehoboth Bay b. U.S.A.
121 F5 Rehoboth Beach U.S.A.
61 C4  Rehovot Israel
18 F3  Reichenbach Germany
19 K4  Reichshoffen France
90 □2  Reid Reef reef Fiji
119 E4 Reidsville U.S.A.
17 G6  Reigate U.K.
84 B3  Reilly Peak summit
       U.S.A.
21 G2  Reims France
147 B7 Reina Adelaida,
       Archipélago de la is
       Chile
21 H3  Reinach Basel Switz.
122 E4 Reinbek Germany
111 J4  Reindeer r. Can.
111 K4  Reindeer I. i. Can.
111 K3  Reindeer Lake l. Can.
10 L1  Reine Norway
92 D1  Reinga, Cape c. N.Z.
18 D4  Reinsfeld Germany
10 L2  Reipoldsfjøtl mt. Norway
11 □1  Reisdalsfjøtl mt. Norway
10 H1  Reisjärvi Finland
19 L3  Rejowiec Fabryczny
       Poland
139 F2 Rejunya Venezuela
54 B3  Rekhwah Pakistan
46 J2  Rekifune-gawa r. Japan
28 D2  Rekovac Yugo.
111 H2 Reliance Can.
75 E1  Relizane Algeria
93 □3  Remarkable Arch arch
       Antipodes Is N.Z.
73 G4  Remada Tunisia
73 G4  Rayyis Saudi Arabia
73 G3  Ra's Banās pt Egypt
28 E1  Razan r. Yugo.
28 E1  Razdol'noye Rus. Fed.
40 B3  Rembang Indon.
74 D4  Remesk r. Iran
139 G3 Rémire French Guiana
21 H2  Remiremont France
54 A1  Rempang i. Indon.
122 E4 Remus U.S.A.
80 B4  Rhino Camp Uganda
18 C4  Remscheid Germany
18 F3  Rena Norway
11 C3  Rena r. Norway
118 C4 Rend L. l. U.S.A.
10 H2  Rendova i. Solomon Is.
24 D1  Renedo Spain
92 F3  Renfrew Can.
114 E4 Rengat Indon.
146 B3 Rengo Chile
28 F2  Reni Ukraine
96 E3  Renmark Aust.
49 H3  Renmin Aust.
90 □1  Rennell i. Solomon Is.
20 D2  Rennes, Bassin de basin
       France
113 J2  Rennick L. Ant.
114 E2 Rennie Lake l. Can.
126 C2 Reno r. Italy
126 C3 Reno U.S.A.
120 D4 Renovo U.S.A.
49 F4  Renqiu China
49 E5  Renshou China
18 E4  Renswoude Neth.
18 F3  Rensselaer U.S.A.
141 F3 Rentería Spain
79 K4  Rentz U.S.A.
```

```
141 E5 Represa de Acaray resr
       Paraguay
139 F4 Represa de Balbina resr
       Brazil
144 D6 Reprêsa de Emborcação
       resr Brazil
144 A6 Represa de Itaipu resr
       Brazil/Paraguay
144 D5 Reprêsa de Jurumirim
       resr Brazil
144 D5 Reprêsa de São Simão
       resr Brazil
144 D5 Represa de Xavantes
       resr Brazil
145 E4 Reprêsa Furnas resr
       Brazil
144 B5 Reprêsa Ilha Grande resr
       Brazil
144 C4 Reprêsa Ilha Solteíra resr
       Brazil
144 C4 Reprêsa Jupiá resr Brazil
144 B4 Reprêsa Pôrto Primavera
       resr Brazil
144 C4 Reprêsa Promissão resr
       Brazil
144 C4 Reprêsa Três Irmãos resr
       Brazil
145 F3 Reprêsa Três Marias resr
       Brazil
142 C1 Reprêsa Tucuruí resr
126 C1 Republic U.S.A.
124 D3 Republican r. U.S.A.
99 G3  Repulse B. b. Aust.
111 K2 Repulse Bay Can.
138 C5 Requena Peru
25 F3  Requena Spain
60 A1  Resadiye Turkey
60 A1  Reşadiye Turkey
59 M2  Reshetikha Rus. Fed.
14 C1  Reshetnikovo Rus. Fed.
15 B3  Reshetylivka Ukraine
14 E1  Reshma Rus. Fed.
57 D1  Reshteh-ye Esfarayen
       mt. ra. Iran
146 E2 Resistencia Arg.
28 D2  Resko Poland
109 J2  Resolute Can.
109 M3 Resolution Island i. Can.
93 A6  Resolution Island i. N.Z.
18 E3  Resplendor Brazil
57 B3  Resseta r. Rus. Fed.
133 □1 Rest Jamaica
145 G5 Restinga de Marambaia
       beach Brazil
15 L3  Ret' r. Ukraine
131 H6 Retalhuleu Guatemala
43     Retan Laut, P. i.
       Singapore
146 B3 Retén Llico Chile
17 G5  Retford U.K.
21 G5  Rethel France
29 E7  Rethymno Greece
85 D1  Reus Spain
18 D4  Reutlingen Germany
128 D3 Reveille Peak summit
       U.S.A.
20 E5  Revel France
97 H2  Revelstoke Can.
110 F4 Revelstoke, L. l. Can.
138 B4 Reventazón Peru
21 F2  Revigny-sur-Ornain
       France
110 C3 Revillagigedo I. i. U.S.A.
130 □  Revillagigedo, Islas is
       Mexico
18 F3  Revin France
15 E4  Revna r. Rus. Fed.
83 E2  Revúboè r. Mozambique
19 K4  Revúca Slovakia
21 J2  Reyakina r. Phil.
90 □8  Rewa r. Fiji
54 D4  Rewa India
54 D3  Rewari India
14 D2  Rexburg U.S.A.
57 B3  Rezā, Kūh-e mt. Iran
28 D2  Rezé France
15 C1  Rezekne Latvia
11 F4  Rēzna, L. l. Latvia
57 C1  Rezvān Iran
21 G5  Rethel France
18 D4  Rhein r. Germany/Switz.
18 C3  Rhein r. Germany/Switz.
18 C4  Rheine Germany
18 C4  Rheinland-Pfalz div.
       Germany
18 D4  Rheinstetten Germany
126 C3 Riley U.S.A.
18 C3  Rhinow Germany
80 B4  Rhino Camp Uganda
125 J3  Rhodes, Isle de Is r. Arg.
152    Rhodes, Baie b. Kerguelen
       Indian Ocean
126 C4 Rhodes Pk summit U.S.A.
21 G4  Rhône r. France/Switz.
119 □3 Rhône-Alpes div. France
75 D3  Rhum, Oasis of oasis
       Syria
17 E5  Rhyl U.K.
130 C4 Rincón de Romos
       Mexico
11 C5  Ribe Denmark
144 D6 Ribeira Brazil
24 □  Ribeira Brava Madeira
       Portugal
144 D6 Ribeirão Branco Brazil
145 E3 Ribeirão das Neves
       Brazil
144 D5 Ribeirão do Pinhal Brazil
76 B4  Ribeira Prêto Brazil
27 D7  Ribera Italy
20 E4  Ribérac France
139 E3 Riberalta Bolivia
25 H1  Ribes de Freser Spain
26 E3  Ribnica Slovenia
18 F1  Ribnitz-Damgarten
       Germany
```

```
83 F1  Ribáuè Mozambique
17 F5  Ribble r. U.K.
11 C5  Ribe Denmark
139 E1 Rio Caribe Venezuela
144 D6 Ribeira Brazil
133 F5 Rio Chico Venezuela
133 E5 Rio Claro Brazil
133 E5 Rio Claro Trin. & Tobago
133 E5 Rio Claro Venezuela
139 E1 Rio Cobre r. Jamaica
76 B4  Rio Colorado Arg.
146 D3 Rio Cuarto Arg.
145 G5 Rio de Janeiro div.
       Brazil
145 G5 Rio de Janeiro Brazil
130 K8 Rio de Jesús Panama
18 F1  Rio de la Plata chan.
       Arg./Uruguay
19 G4  Rio do Sul Brazil
130 K7 Rio Frío Costa Rica
147 C7 Rio Gallegos Arg.
76 B4  Rio Gêba r. Guinea-
       Bissau/Senegal
122 A4 Riceville U.S.A.
120 D4 Richards r. Can.
147 C5 Rio Grande Brazil
146 F3 Rio Grande Piauí Brazil
146 F3 Rio Grande Rio Grande
       do Sul Brazil
133 □1 Rio Grande r. Jamaica
130 E4 Rio Grande Mexico
125 D7 Rio Grande Brazil
142 E4 Rio Grande do Norte div.
       Brazil
143 B6 Rio Grande do Sul div.
       Brazil
148 G8 Rio Grande Rise Atlantic
       Ocean
145 G1 Riohacha Colombia
138 B5 Rioja Peru
133 H4 Rio Lagartos Mexico
20 F4  Riom France
24 B3  Rio Maior Portugal
142 B3 Rio Manso r. Brazil
140 C3 Rio Mulatos Bolivia
78 B3  Rio Muni reg. Equatorial
       Guinea
147 C5 Rio Negro div. Arg.
143 B6 Rio Negro Mato Grosso
       do Sul Brazil
143 C6 Rio Negro Paraná Brazil
145 G4 Rio Novo Brazil
144 A3 Rio Novo do Sul Brazil
145 H3 Rio Pardo de Minas
       Brazil
145 D1 Rio Pescado Arg.
54 C3  Rio Piedras Arg.
146 E4 Rio Pomba Brazil
145 F2 Rio Primero Arg.
146 D3 Rio Rancho U.S.A.
146 D3 Rio Rancho U.S.A.
147 D5 Rio Tigre Ecuador
138 B4 Rio Tuba Phil.
120 C5 Rio Verde Brazil
147 B7 Rio Verde Chile
131 H4 Rio Verde Mexico
144 A3 Rio Verde de Mato
       Grosso Brazil
146 F2 Rio Vista U.S.A.
98 H4  Riddock, Mt mt. Aust.
141 E3 Riozinho r. Brazil
141 E3 Riozinho r. Brazil
128 D3 Ripanj Yugo.
15 D1  Ripky Ukraine
17 F4  Ripley U.S.A.
119 B5 Ripley U.S.A.
122 C5 Ripley U.S.A.
17 G4  Ripon U.K.
128 B3 Ripon U.S.A.
115 J3  Ripon Can.
27 E6  Riposto Italy
84 □4  Ritchie's Archipelago is
       Andaman and Nicobar Is
       India
11 G3  Ritsem Sweden
127 C4 Ritter, Mt mt. U.S.A.
126 C2 Ritzville U.S.A.
21 □1  Riva del Garda Italy
140 C2 Rivadavia Mendoza Arg.
146 D4 Rivadavia Pampas Arg.
146 C2 Rivadavia Salta Arg.
26 E3  Riva del Garda Italy
147 B6 Riva Palacio Mexico
130 J7  Rivas Nicaragua
147 D5 Rivera r. Netherlands
41 D3  Rivera div. Uruguay
75 C3  River Cess Liberia
78 E4  River Cess Liberia
77 F4  Rivers div. Nigeria
98 A3  Riversdale N.Z.
128 D5 Riverside U.S.A.
98 B3  Riversleigh Aust.
126 F3 Riverton Can.
92 A7  Riverton N.Z.
129 G2 Riverton U.S.A.
145 E2 Rivière-Bleue Can.
```

```
130 J5  Roatán Honduras
10 F3  Röbäck Sweden
139 E1 Rio Caribe Venezuela
145 G4 Rio Casca Brazil
51 E4  Roat i. Iran
82 D2  Robat-e Khān Iran
57 D2  Robat-e Karim Iran
55 F5  Robat Thana Pakistan
97 F5  Robbins I. i. Aust.
96 D4  Robe Aust.
100 A4 Robe r. Aust.
8 K6   Robe Ethiopia
96 E2  Robe, Mt h. Aust.
125 C6 Robert Lee U.S.A.
126 D2 Roberts U.S.A.
126 D2 Roberts Creek mt. U.S.A.
55 E4  Robertsganj India
11 G3  Robertsfors Sweden
82 B5  Robertson R.S.A.
76 B5  Robertsport Liberia
96 D3  Robertstown Aust.
96 D4  Robe, Mt mt. Aust.
26 D1  Robeck France
100 M1 Robeson Ch. chan.
       Can./Greenland
124 E4 Robin's Nest h.
       Hong Kong
133 □1 Robins U.S.A.
130 E4 Robinson U.S.A.
118 C4 Robinson U.S.A.
98 A3  Robinson Cr. r. Aust.
142 E2 Robinson Crusoe I. Juan
       Fernandez Is Chile
143 B6 Robinson Ranges h. Aust.
98 D3  Robinson River Aust.
97 E3  Robinvale Aust.
25 F2  Robledo Spain
129 G5 Robles Junction U.S.A.
129 G5 Robles Pass pass U.S.A.
111 J4  Roblin Can.
113 H3 Robore Bolivia
110 F4 Robson, Mt mt. Can.
125 D7 Robstown U.S.A.
24 B3  Roca, Cabo da c. Port.
27 D5  Rocca Imperiale Italy
146 F3 Rocha Uruguay
17 F5  Rochdale U.K.
144 A3 Rochedo Brazil
20 D4  Rochefort Belgium
112 F2 Rochefort France
20 D4  Rochefort, Lac l. Can.
122 B5 Rochelle U.S.A.
133 □4 Rocher du Diamant i.
       Martinique Caribbean
115 G1 Rocher River Can.
97 E5  Rochester Aust.
122 C5 Rochester U.S.A.
122 A5 Rochester U.S.A.
121 H3 Rochester U.S.A.
120 D3 Rochester U.S.A.
97 G3  Rock r. Aust.
129 H4 Rock r. U.S.A.
148 H2 Rockall Bank Atlantic
       Ocean
43 C7  Rompin r. Malaysia
122 B5 Rockford U.S.A.
119 E5 Rock Hill U.S.A.
101 B7 Rockingham Aust.
128 B3 Rockingham B. b. Aust.
99 G3  Rockingham Aust.
122 B5 Rock Island U.S.A.
122 B5 Rock Island l. U.S.A.
122 D2 Rockland U.S.A.
121 J2  Rockland U.S.A.
121 F2 Rockland U.S.A.
96 C4  Rocklands Reservoir resr
       Aust.
129 H2 Rock Point U.S.A.
100 D3 Rockport U.S.A.
124 D3 Rock Rapids U.S.A.
126 E2 Rock Springs U.S.A.
129 F2 Rock Springs U.S.A.
96 D3  Rockspring U.S.A.
98 H4  Rocky Chu r. China
111 J3  Rocky Ford U.S.A.
127 F4 Rocky Ford U.S.A.
114 E5 Rocky Island Lake l. Can.
124 F2 Rocky Mount U.S.A.
120 D6 Rocky Mount U.S.A.
110 G4 Rocky Mountain House
       Can.
126 E3 Rocky Mountain Nat.
       Park mt. park. U.S.A.
110 F4 Rocky Mountains Forest
       Reserve res. Can.
133 □1 Rocky Point h. Jamaica
82 B3  Rocky Point pt Namibia
117 J2  Rocky Point U.S.A.
128 B2 Rodalquilar U.S.A.
18 D3  Roddickton Can.
11 C3  Rødbyhavn Denmark
144 C2 Rodeio Brazil
130 C4 Rodeo Mexico
129 H5 Rodeo U.S.A.
20 F4  Rodez France
18 F3  Rödinghausen Germany
54 C3  Rodkhan Pakistan
91 □16 Rodney, Cape c. N.Z.
54 E3  Rodnei, Munţii mt. ra.
       Romania
11 E3  Rodney U.K.
28 F2  Rodniki Rus. Fed.
92 D2  Rodopi Planina mt. ra.
       Bulgaria/Greece
115 J3  Rodos i. Greece
29 G6  Rodos Greece
84 □5  Rodrigues I. i. Mauritius
149 L3  Rodrigues Fracture
       Indian Ocean
```

```
15 A2  Rohatyn Ukraine
15 D1  Rohizky Ukraine
128 A2 Rohnert Park U.S.A.
19 F4  Rohrbach in
       Oberösterreich Austria
54 B4  Rohri Pakistan
54 D3  Rohtak India
151 K6 Roi Georges, Îles du is Fr.
       Poly. Pac. Oc.
55 H3  Roing India
11 F4  Roja Latvia
25 G3  Roja, Pta hd Spain
146 D3 Rojas Arg.
54 B3  Rojhan Pakistan
11 C5  Rojo, Cabo c. Puerto Rico
43 C7  Rokan r. Indon.
99 E2  Rokeby Aust.
76 B5  Rokel r. Sierra Leone
11 G5  Rokiškis Lithuania
46 H3  Rokkasho Japan
15 D2  Rokytne Ukraine
19 F4  Rokycany Czech Rep.
15 D2  Rokytne Rivne Ukraine
15 B1  Rokytne Rivne Ukraine
55 G2  Rola Co salt l. China
152    Roland, C. I. Kerguelen
       Indian Ocean
11 C3  Rollag Norway
124 F4 Rolla, III. U.S.A.
93 C5  Rolleston N.Z.
99 G5  Rolleston Aust.
11 E1  Rolvsøya i. Norway
27 D5  Roma Italy
84 A3  Roma i. Indon.
27 D5  Roma Italy
25 □  Roma Sweden
119 E5 Roman, Cape c. U.S.A.
113 H3 Romaine r. Can.
28 F1  Roman Romania
148 H6 Romanche Gap
       Atlantic Ocean
61 B4  Romani Egypt
28 D1  Romania country Europe
41 B3  Romanovka Rus. Fed.
65 K1  Romanovo Rus. Fed.
21 G4  Romans-sur-Isère
       France
21 H2  Rombas France
21 H2  Romblon i. Phil.
41 B3  Romblon Phil.
41 B3  Romblon Pass. chan.
       Phil.
119 C5 Rome U.S.A.
121 C5 Rome U.S.A.
121 F3 Rome U.S.A.
122 E1 Romen r. Ukraine
123 F4 Romeo U.S.A.
17 G6  Romford U.K.
120 D5 Romilly-sur-Seine
       France
97 G5  Romney U.S.A.
15 E1  Romny Ukraine
11 C5  Rømø i. Denmark
20 E3  Romorantin-Lanthenay
       France
43 C7  Rompin r. Malaysia
21 H2  Romuli Romania
56 A3  Ron India
64 D4  Ron Vietnam
16 E2  Rona i. U.K.
11 C3  Ronan U.S.A.
146 B6 Roncador Arg.
132 B4 Roncador Cay i.
       Colombia
90 □1  Roncador Reef reef
       Solomon Is.
27 D4  Ronco r. Italy
24 D4  Ronda Spain
11 B3  Rønde, Is is Kerguelen
       Indian Ocean
144 B5 Rondon Colombia
140 C2 Rondônia div. Brazil
140 D2 Rondonópolis Brazil
54 C2  Rondu Jammu and
       Kashmir
51 E2  Rong'an China
11 B3  Rong'an China
49 G5  Rong Chu r. China
49 E5  Rongcheng China
49 G4  Rongcheng Wan b. China
147 K6 Rongelap atoll
       Myanmar
40 C2  Rongkong r. Indon.
55 H4  Rongklang Range mt. ra.
       Myanmar
50 D4  Rong Xian China
51 E2  Rong Xian China
11 E4  Rønne Denmark
11 B3  Ronneby Sweden
152 B3 Ronne Entrance str. Ant.
152 B3 Ronne Ice Shelf ice
       feature Ant.
21 B3  Ronnenberg Germany
21 B3  Ronse Belgium
146 C1 Roque Sáenz Peña Arg.
142 A3 Roraima div. Brazil
142 □1 Roraima, Mt mt. Guyana
11 C3  Røros Norway
21 □1  Rorschach Switz.
11 C3  Rørvik Norway
138    Rosa, C. c. Galapagos Is.
       Ecuador
133 B3 Rosalind Bank Caribbean
128 C4 Rosamond U.S.A.
11 D3  Rosamond Lake l. U.S.A.
26 A4  Rosa, Monte mt.
       Italy/Switz.
130 C4 Rosamorada Mexico
146 D3 Rosario Arg.
130 □  Rosario Baja California
       Norte Mexico
130 C4 Rosario Sinaloa Mexico
130 D4 Rosario Sonora Mexico
141 E4 Rosário Paraguay
141 F3 Rosário Brazil
138 C5 Rosario de la Frontera
       Arg.
132 B3 Rosario del Tala Arg.
146 E3 Rosario del Tala Arg.
146 F3 Rosário do Sul Brazil
```

142 A3 Rosário Oeste Brazil
130 B2 Rosarito Mexico
130 A1 Rosarito Mexico
130 C3 Rosarito *Sur* Mexico
27 E6 Rosarno Italy
138 B3 Rosa Zárate Ecuador
11 H3 Roschino Rus. Fed.
121 F4 Roscoe U.S.A.
20 C2 Roscoff France
17 C5 Roscommon Rep. of Ire.
122 E3 Roscommon U.S.A.
17 D5 Roscrea Rep. of Ire.
98 C2 Rose r. Aust.
133 G4 Roseau Dominica
111 K5 Roseau U.S.A.
81 □4 Rose Belle Mauritius
97 F5 Rosebery Aust.
113 J4 Rose Blanche Can.
126 B3 Roseburg U.S.A.
123 E3 Rose City U.S.A.
99 G5 Rosedale Aust.
133 □1 Rose Hall Jamaica
16 F3 Rosehearty U.K.
81 □4 Rose Hill Mauritius
80 B2 Roseires Reservoir resr Sudan
87 L6 Rose Island i. *American Samoa* Pac. Oc.
122 A3 Rosemount U.S.A.
128 C2 Rose, Mt mt. U.S.A.
125 E6 Rosenberg U.S.A.
11 B4 Rosendal Norway
18 F5 Rosenheim Germany
110 C4 Rose Pt pt Can.
25 H1 Roses Spain
119 F7 Roses The Bahamas
25 H1 Roses, Golf de b. Spain
26 E4 Roseto degli Abruzzi Italy
111 H4 Rosetown Can.
20 G2 Rosetti, C. A. Romania
111 J4 Rose Valley Can.
128 B2 Roseville U.S.A.
122 B5 Roseville U.S.A.
14 D2 Roshal' Rus. Fed.
57 D2 Roshkhvār Iran
82 B4 Rosh Pinah Namibia
26 C4 Rosignano Marittimo Italy
139 F2 Rosignol Guyana
28 E2 Rosiorii de Vede Romania
28 F3 Rositsa Bulgaria
11 D5 Roskilde Denmark
14 A3 Roslavl' Rus. Fed.
10 J1 Roslyakovo Rus. Fed.
12 H3 Roslyatino Rus. Fed.
114 B2 Roslyn Lake l. Can.
27 E7 Rosolini Italy
20 C3 Rosporden France
97 F5 Ross Aust.
110 C2 Ross r. Can.
93 C5 Ross N.Z.
27 F6 Rossano Italy
17 C4 Rossan Point pt Rep. of Ire.
125 F5 Ross Barnett Res. l. U.S.A.
113 G3 Ross Bay Junction Can.
152 A5 Ross Dependency reg. Ant.
115 F4 Rosseau Lake l. Can.
90 □1 Rossel I. i. P.N.G.
94 □2 Ross Hill h. *Christmas I.* Indian Ocean
152 B4 Ross Ice Shelf ice feature Ant.
113 H5 Rossignol, L. l. Can.
152 B5 Ross Island i. Ant.
17 D5 Rosslare Rep. of Ire.
115 G4 Rossmore Can.
152 □ Ross, Mt mt. *Kerguelen* Indian Ocean
93 E4 Ross, Mt mt. N.Z.
74 A5 Rosso Mauritania
21 J5 Rosso, Capo pt France
17 F6 Ross-on-Wye U.K.
13 F5 Rossosh' Rus. Fed.
114 B2 Rossport Can.
110 C2 Ross River Can.
152 A5 Ross Sea sea Ant.
10 D2 Røssvatnet l. Norway
122 D5 Rossville U.S.A.
110 D3 Rosswood Can.
57 G1 Rostāq Afghanistan
57 C4 Rostāq Iran
14 F4 Rostashi Rus. Fed.
15 C2 Rostavytsya r. Ukraine
111 H4 Rosthern Can.
18 F1 Rostock Germany
13 G6 Rostov div. Rus. Fed.
14 D1 Rostov Rus. Fed.
13 F6 Rostov-na-Donu Rus. Fed.
20 C2 Rostrenen France
10 F2 Rosvik Sweden
119 C5 Roswell U.S.A.
127 F5 Roswell U.S.A.
39 M4 Rota i. *Northern Mariana Is* Pac. Oc.
24 C4 Rota Spain
39 H8 Rote i. Indon.
18 D2 Rotenburg (Wümme) Germany
18 D5 Rote Wand mt. Austria
18 E4 Roth Germany
18 D3 Rothaargebirge h. Germany
17 G4 Rothbury U.K.
18 E4 Rothenburg ob der Tauber Germany
19 G3 Rothenburg (Oberlausitz) Germany
152 B2 Rothera U.K. Base Ant.
93 D5 Rotherham N.Z.
17 G5 Rotherham U.K.
16 E4 Rothesay U.K.
122 C3 Rothschild U.S.A.
152 B2 Rothschild I. i. Ant.
76 B5 Rotifunk Sierra Leone
97 F3 Roto Aust.
91 □10 Rotoava *Fr. Poly.* Pac. Oc.
92 F3 Rotoiti, L. l. N.Z.
93 C5 Rotomanu N.Z.
93 D4 Rotoroa, L. l. N.Z.
92 F3 Rotorua N.Z.
92 F3 Rotorua, L. l. N.Z.
18 F4 Rott r. Germany
19 G5 Rottenmann Austria
18 B3 Rotterdam Netherlands
101 A7 Rottnest I. i. Aust.
18 D4 Rottweil Germany
150 G6 Rotuma i. Fiji
10 D3 Rötviken Sweden
18 F4 Rötz Germany
21 F1 Roubaix France
19 G3 Roudnice nad Labem Czech Rep.
20 E2 Rouen *Seine-et-Marne* France
133 □3 Rouge, Point pt *Trinidad* Trin. & Tobago
93 B6 Rough Ridge ridge N.Z.
18 A3 Roulers Belgium
113 F3 Roundeyed, Lac l. Can.
81 □3 Round I. i. *Rodrigues I.* Mauritius
128 D2 Round Mountain U.S.A.
97 H2 Round Mt mt. Aust.
129 H3 Round Rock U.S.A.
126 E2 Roundup U.S.A.
49 J2 Rouny Rus. Fed.
139 G3 Roura French Guiana
16 F2 Rousay i. U.K.
121 G2 Rouses Point U.S.A.
21 G4 Roussillon France
115 F2 Rouyn Can.
10 G2 Rovaniemi Finland
13 F5 Roven'ki Rus. Fed.
26 C3 Rovereto Italy
43 D4 Rôviĕng Tbong Cambodia
26 C3 Rovigo Italy
28 D2 Rovinari Romania
26 D3 Rovinj Croatia
13 H5 Rovnoye Rus. Fed.
81 C7 Rovuma r. Mozambique
90 □2 Rowa is Vanuatu
57 B2 Row'ān Iran
97 G2 Rowena Aust.
100 B3 Rowley Shoals sand bank Aust.
41 B4 Roxas Phil.
41 B3 Roxas Phil.
41 B2 Roxas Phil.
41 B4 Roxas Phil.
41 A4 Roxas Phil.
119 E4 Roxboro U.S.A.
133 □2 Roxborough *Tobago* Trin. & Tobago
98 D4 Roxborough Downs Aust.
93 B6 Roxburgh N.Z.
96 D2 Roxby Downs Aust.
99 E2 Roxby Nat. Park nat. park Aust.
76 A4 Roxo, Cabo pt Senegal
115 J4 Roxton-Sud Can.
127 F4 Roy U.S.A.
17 D5 Royal Canal canal Rep. of Ire.
122 C1 Royale, Isle i. U.S.A.
114 A2 Royal, Mount h. Can.
123 F4 Royal Oak U.S.A.
20 D4 Royan France
20 F2 Roye France
15 D1 Royishche Ukraine
112 E2 Roy, Lac Le l. Can.
17 G5 Royston U.K.
28 C3 Rožaj Yugo.
19 K2 Różan Poland
15 D3 Rozdil'na Ukraine
13 E6 Rozdol'ne Ukraine
65 H2 Rozhdestvenka Kazak.
14 C1 Rozhdestveno Rus. Fed.
14 C1 Rozhdestveno Rus. Fed.
12 H3 Rozhdestvenskoye Rus. Fed.
14 H1 Rozhentsovo Rus. Fed.
15 A2 Rozhniv Ukraine
15 E1 Rozhnivka Ukraine
15 A1 Rozhyshche Ukraine
15 G3 Rozivka Ukraine
19 K4 Rožňava Slovakia
26 B3 Rozzano Italy
14 F3 Rtishchevo Rus. Fed.
26 D3 Rt Kamenjak pt Croatia
28 B3 Rt Platamon pt Yugo.
81 B6 Ruaha National Park nat. park Tanzania
92 E3 Ruapehu, Mt vol N.Z.
93 B7 Ruapuke I. i. N.Z.
92 F3 Ruarine Range mt. ra. N.Z.
93 C5 Ruatapu N.Z.
92 G2 Ruatoria N.Z.
59 G6 Rub' al Khālī desert Saudi Arabia
15 F3 Rubanivka Ukraine
81 C6 Rubeho Mountains mts Tanzania
145 G2 Rubelita Brazil
46 J2 Rubeshibe Japan
78 E3 Rubi Zaire
78 E3 Rubi r. Zaire
144 D1 Rubiataba Brazil
128 B2 Rubicon r. U.S.A.
13 F5 Rubizhne Ukraine
81 B5 Rubondo Island i. Tanzania
15 G2 Rubtsi Ukraine
65 K2 Rubtsovsk Rus. Fed.
108 C3 Ruby U.S.A.
129 E1 Ruby Lake l. U.S.A.
129 E1 Ruby Mountains mts U.S.A.
28 E2 Rucăr Romania
51 F3 Rucheng China
12 G1 Ruch'i Rus. Fed.
19 K2 Ruciane-Nida Poland
120 D5 Ruckersville U.S.A.
100 C4 Rudall w Aust.
100 C4 Rudall River Nat. Park nat. park Aust.
57 D4 Rudan Iran
55 E4 Rudarpur India
19 J3 Ruda Śląska Poland
55 E4 Rudauli India
57 E3 Rudbar Afghanistan
57 D1 Rūd-e Kāl-Shūr r. Iran
19 F2 Rüdersdorf Berlin Germany
57 D3 Rūd-e Shur w Iran
15 E1 Rudivka Ukraine
11 C5 Rudkøbing Denmark
28 C2 Rudna Glava Yugo.
46 K1 Rudnaya Rus. Fed.
45 P3 Rudnaya Pristan' China
12 K3 Rudnichnyy Rus. Fed.
19 L3 Rudnik Poland
12 D4 Rudnya Rus. Fed.
13 H5 Rudnya Rus. Fed.
14 G2 Rudnya r. Rus. Fed.
15 B1 Rudnya-Ivanivs'ka Ukraine
15 C2 Rudnytsya Ukraine
64 F2 Rudnyy Kazak.
62 G1 Rudolfa, O. i. Rus. Fed.
18 E3 Rudolstadt Germany
51 H1 Rudong China
14 F3 Rudovka Rus. Fed.
24 E1 Rudrón r. Spain
57 B1 Rūdsar Iran
122 E2 Rudyard U.S.A.
83 E2 Ruenya r. Zimbabwe
73 F5 Rufa'a Sudan
20 E3 Ruffec France
119 □3 Ruffing Pt pt *Virgin Is* Caribbean
81 C6 Rufiji r. Tanzania
146 D3 Rufino Arg.
76 A4 Rufisque Senegal
79 E7 Rufunsa Zambia
51 H1 Rugao China
17 G5 Rugby U.K.
124 C1 Rugby U.S.A.
18 F1 Rügen i. Germany
120 B4 Ruggles U.S.A.
81 A5 Ruhengeri Rwanda
11 F4 Ruhni i. Estonia
18 C3 Ruhr r. Germany
81 C6 Ruhudji r. Tanzania
51 H3 Rui'an China
51 F2 Ruichang China
51 E1 Ruicheng China
25 E3 Ruidera Spain
127 F5 Ruidoso U.S.A.
51 F3 Ruijin China
50 B3 Ruili China
111 N2 Ruin Point pt Can.
81 C6 Ruipa Tanzania
130 D4 Ruiz Mexico
11 G4 Rūjiena Latvia
57 B4 Rukbah well Saudi Arabia
78 C4 Ruki r. Zaire
55 E3 Rukumkot Nepal
81 A5 Rukungiri Uganda
90 □6 Rukuruku B. b. Fiji
81 B6 Rukwa div. Tanzania
81 B6 Rukwa, Lake l. Tanzania
57 D4 Rūl Ḍadnah U.A.E.
100 D2 Rulhieres, C. c. Aust.
57 D2 Rūm Iran
16 D3 Rum i. U.K.
28 B2 Ruma Yugo.
98 C5 Rumbalara Aust.
78 E2 Rumbek Sudan
19 G3 Rumburk Czech Rep.
132 D2 Rum Cay i. The Bahamas
121 H2 Rumford U.S.A.
19 J1 Rumia Poland
21 G4 Rumilly France
98 B2 Rum Jungle Aust.
73 H2 Rummān, J. ar mts Saudi Arabia
46 H2 Rumoi Japan
81 A5 Rumonge Burundi
81 B7 Rumphi Malawi
99 F3 Rumula Aust.
51 F1 Runan China
93 C5 Runanga N.Z.
133 □1 Runaway Bay Jamaica
92 F2 Runaway, Cape c. N.Z.
83 E3 Runde r. Zimbabwe
82 B2 Rundu Namibia
10 E3 Rundvik Sweden
40 C2 Rungan r. Indon.
78 E3 Rungu Zaire
81 B6 Rungwa *Rukwa* Tanzania
81 B6 Rungwa *Singida* Tanzania
81 B6 Rungwa r. Tanzania
81 B6 Rungwa Game Reserve res. Tanzania
51 G1 Runheji China
101 C4 Runton Ra. h. Aust.
50 C1 Ru'nying China
11 H3 Ruokolahti Finland
44 E4 Ruoqiang China
48 A4 Ruo Shui r. China
55 H4 Rupa India
97 E4 Rupanyup Aust.
28 E1 Rupea Romania
112 E3 Rupert r. Can.
126 D3 Rupert U.S.A.
112 E3 Rupert Bay b. Can.
152 A4 Ruppert Coast Ant.
139 F3 Rupununi r. Guyana
140 C2 Rurrenabaque Bolivia
87 N7 Rurutu i. *Fr. Poly.* Pac. Oc.
83 E2 Rusape Zimbabwe
28 E1 Ruscova Romania
28 E3 Ruse Bulgaria
55 F4 Rusera India
49 G5 Rushan China
122 B4 Rushford U.S.A.
83 E2 Rushinga Zimbabwe
122 C4 Rush Lake l. U.S.A.
55 H3 Rushon India
122 B5 Rushville U.S.A.
124 C3 Rushville U.S.A.
125 E6 Rusk U.S.A.
119 D7 Ruskin U.S.A.
28 F3 Rusokastro Bulgaria
142 E1 Russas Brazil
111 J4 Russell Can.
115 H4 Russell Can.
92 E1 Russell N.Z.
124 D4 Russell U.S.A.
110 F2 Russel Lake l. Can.
109 J2 Russell I. i. Can.
90 □1 Russell Is is Solomon Is.
101 C7 Russell Ra. h. Aust.
119 C4 Russellville U.S.A.
125 E5 Russellville U.S.A.
118 C4 Russellville U.S.A.
18 D3 Rüsselsheim Germany
62 G3 Russian Federation country Asia
14 C3 Russkiy Brod Rus. Fed.
14 H3 Russkiy Kameshkir Rus. Fed.
63 Q2 Russkoye Ust'ye Rus. Fed.
13 H7 Rust'avi Georgia
14 G1 Rustay Rus. Fed.
82 D4 Rustenburg R.S.A.
125 E5 Ruston U.S.A.
81 A5 Rutana Burundi
24 D4 Rute Spain
40 E4 Ruteng Indon.
129 E2 Ruth U.S.A.
115 F3 Rutherglen Can.
17 F5 Ruthin U.K.
14 H1 Rutka r. Rus. Fed.
121 G3 Rutland U.S.A.
43 A5 Rutland I. i. *Andaman and Nicobar Is* India
99 E2 Rutland Plains Aust.
17 G5 Rutland Water resr U.K.
111 G2 Rutledge Lake l. Can.
54 D2 Rutog China
114 E3 Rutter Can.
13 H7 Rutul Rus. Fed.
10 G2 Ruukki Finland
57 D4 Rū'us al Jibāl mts Oman
81 C7 Ruvuma div. Tanzania
81 C7 Ruvuma r. Tanzania
61 A5 Ruwayân, W. el depression Egypt
60 D3 Ruwayshid, Wādī w Jordan
61 C5 Ruweijil pt Saudi Arabia
57 C4 Ruweis U.A.E.
61 D5 Ruweita, W. w Jordan
81 A5 Ruwenzori Range mt. ra. Uganda/Zaire
51 F3 Ruyuan China
14 C2 Ruza r. Rus. Fed.
14 C2 Ruza Rus. Fed.
65 G2 Ruzayevka Kazak.
14 G2 Ruzayevka Rus. Fed.
14 B3 Ruzhnoye Rus. Fed.
15 C2 Ruzhyn Ukraine
19 J4 Ružomberok Slovakia
69 G6 Rwanda country Africa
81 B5 Rweru, Lake l. Burundi
57 C1 Ryābād Iran
12 H2 Ryadovo Rus. Fed.
15 F2 Ryas'ke Ukraine
15 D3 Ryasnopil' Ukraine
12 F4 Ryazan' div. Rus. Fed.
12 F4 Ryazan' Rus. Fed.
14 F3 Ryazanka Rus. Fed.
14 D2 Ryazanovskiy Rus. Fed.
14 D1 Ryazantsevo Rus. Fed.
14 E3 Ryazhsk Rus. Fed.
62 E2 Rybachiy, Poluostrov pen. Rus. Fed.
12 F3 Rybinskoye Vdkhr. resr Rus. Fed.
14 F2 Rybkino Rus. Fed.
19 J3 Rybnik Poland
12 F4 Rybnoye Rus. Fed.
19 H3 Rychnov nad Kněžnou Czech Rep.
110 F3 Rycroft Can.
11 D4 Ryd Sweden
152 B3 Rydberg Pen. pen. Ant.
15 A2 Rydomyl' Ukraine
17 H6 Rye U.K.
15 B1 Rykhal's'ke Ukraine
15 B2 Rykhta Ukraine
19 K3 Ryki Poland
14 B4 Ryl'sk Rus. Fed.
97 G3 Rylstone Aust.
19 K4 Rymanów Poland
19 H4 Rýmařov Czech Rep.
19 K2 Ryn Poland
64 C3 Ryn Peski desert Kazak.
47 H4 Ryōri-zaki pt Japan
47 G4 Ryōtsu Japan
19 J2 Rypin Poland
14 B3 Ryshkovo Rus. Fed.
16 K1 Rysjedal Norway
14 A3 Ryukhovo Rus. Fed.
19 G2 Rzepin Poland
19 L3 Rzeszów Poland
14 F3 Rzhaksa Rus. Fed.
14 B1 Rzhev Rus. Fed.
15 D2 Rzhyshchiv Ukraine

S

57 D2 Sa'ābād Iran
80 D4 Saacow Somalia
61 D5 Sa'ada al Barsa mt. ra. Saudi Arabia
57 C3 Sa'ādatābād *Fārs* Iran
57 C3 Sa'ādatābād *Hormozgān* Iran
57 C3 Sa'ādatābād *Kermān* Iran
18 E4 Saale r. Germany
18 E3 Saalfeld Germany
18 F5 Saalfelden am Steinernen Meer Austria
21 H3 Saanen Switz.
18 C4 Saarbrücken Germany
11 F4 Saaremaa i. Estonia
10 G2 Saarenkylä Finland
10 G3 Saarijärvi Finland
10 G2 Saari-Kämä Finland
10 F1 Saarikoski Finland
18 C4 Saarland div. Germany
60 G2 Saatli Azerbaijan
146 D4 Saavedra Arg.
133 G3 Saba i. Netherlands Ant.
61 B4 Saba'a Egypt
133 G3 Saba Bank Caribbean
60 D3 Sab' Ābār Syria
28 B2 Šabac Yugo.
25 H2 Sabadell Spain
47 F5 Sabae Japan
41 A5 Sabah div. Malaysia
43 C7 Sabak Malaysia
40 D3 Sabalana i. Indon.
40 D3 Sabalana, Kep. is Indon.
54 D4 Sabalgarh India
139 F2 Sabana Surinam
132 B2 Sabana, Arch. de is Cuba
130 J6 Sabana Gde Honduras
138 C1 Sabanalarga Colombia
133 E5 Sabaneta Venezuela
40 E2 Sabang Indon.
40 D1 Sabang Indon.
28 F1 Săbăoani Romania
145 G3 Sabará Brazil
56 C2 Sābari r. India
54 C5 Sabarmati r. India
40 D3 Sabaru i. Indon.
61 C3 Sabastiya Israel
27 D5 Sabaudia Italy
140 C3 Sabaya Bolivia
57 D2 Sabeh Iran
72 B2 Sabhā Libya
73 H3 Şabḩā' Saudi Arabia
54 D4 Sabi r. India
83 E4 Sabie r. Mozambique/R.S.A.
130 D2 Sabinal Mexico
25 F1 Sabiñánigo Spain
131 E3 Sabinas Mexico
131 E3 Sabinas Hidalgo Mexico
125 E6 Sabine L. l. U.S.A.
27 D4 Sabini, Monti mts Italy
145 G3 Sabinópolis Brazil
19 K4 Sabinov Slovakia
83 D3 Sabiwa Zimbabwe
74 B4 Sabkhat Aghzoumal salt flat *Western Sahara*
72 C1 Sabkhat al Hayshah salt pan Libya
61 D2 Sabkhat al Jabbūl salt flat Syria
61 D2 Sabkhat al Marāghah salt flat Syria
74 B3 Sabkhat Aridal salt pan *Western Sahara*
74 B3 Sabkhat Oum Dba salt pan *Western Sahara*
74 B3 Sabkhat Tah salt pan Morocco
61 B4 Sabkhet el Bardawîl lag. Egypt
41 B3 Sablayan Phil.
119 D7 Sable, Cape c. U.S.A.
90 □2 Sable, Î. de i. Pac. Oc.
113 J5 Sable Island i. Can.
114 D3 Sables, River aux r. Can.
20 D3 Sablé-sur-Sarthe France
142 E2 Saboeiro Brazil
77 F4 Sabon Kafi Niger
76 D4 Sabou Burkina
20 D4 Sabres France
152 C6 Sabrina Coast Ant.
41 B1 Sabtang i. Phil.
24 C2 Sabugal Portugal
122 B4 Sabula U.S.A.
40 E2 Sabulu Indon.
73 H4 Şabyā Saudi Arabia
57 D1 Sabzevār Iran
25 H3 Sa Cabaneta Spain
140 C3 Sacaca Bolivia
28 G2 Sacalinul Mare, Insula i. Romania
131 H5 Sacbecan Mexico
27 D5 Sacco r. Italy
28 E1 Săcel Romania
28 E2 Săcele Romania
79 C6 Sachanga Angola
112 B3 Sachigo r. Can.
112 B3 Sachigo L. l. Can.
54 C5 Sachin India
46 B6 Sach'ŏn S. Korea
54 D2 Sach P. pass India
18 F3 Sachsen div. Germany
18 E2 Sachsen-Anhalt div. Germany
108 F2 Sachs Harbour Can.
121 E3 Sackets Harbor U.S.A.
113 H4 Sackville Can.
121 H3 Saco U.S.A.
126 F1 Saco U.S.A.
41 B5 Sacol i. Phil.
144 E3 Sacramento Brazil
128 B2 Sacramento airport U.S.A.
128 B2 Sacramento r. U.S.A.
128 B2 Sacramento U.S.A.
127 F5 Sacramento Mts mt. ra. U.S.A.
126 B3 Sacramento Valley v. U.S.A.
141 E2 Sacre r. Brazil
28 D1 Săcueni Romania
141 E2 Sacuriuiná r. Brazil
82 D5 Sada R.S.A.
25 F1 Sádaba Spain
57 B3 Sa'dabad Iran
60 D3 Şadad Syria
73 H4 Şa'dah Yemen
57 B4 Sada, J. as h. Saudi Arabia
46 D7 Sada-misaki pt Japan
43 C6 Sadao Thailand
54 B2 Sadda Pakistan
99 F2 Saddle Hill h. Aust.
43 A4 Saddle Peak summit *Andaman and Nicobar Is* India
43 D5 Sa Đec Vietnam
55 H3 Sadêng China
54 D3 Sadhaura India
133 □3 Sadhoowa Trin. & Tobago
80 C3 Sadi Ethiopia
57 D4 Sadīj w Iran
54 B3 Sadiqabad Pakistan
54 C1 Sad Istragh mt. Afghanistan/Pakistan
55 H4 Sadiya India
73 G3 Sa'diya Saudi Arabia
57 C4 Sa'diyyat i. U.A.E.
57 D1 Sad-Kharv Iran
24 B3 Sado r. Portugal
47 G4 Sadoga-shima i. Japan
13 H7 Sadon Rus. Fed.
40 B1 Sadong r. Malaysia
13 H6 Sadovoye Rus. Fed.
25 H3 Sa Dragonera i. Spain
54 C4 Sadri India
61 C4 Sadût Egypt
11 C4 Sæby Denmark
61 D3 Safa lava Syria
91 □12 Safata B. b. Western Samoa
60 F4 Safayal Maqūf well Iraq
65 H5 Safed Khirs mts Afghanistan
57 G2 Safed Koh mt. ra. Afghanistan/Pakistan
11 D4 Säffle Sweden
129 H5 Safford U.S.A.
61 C4 Safi Jordan
74 C2 Safi Morocco
57 C2 Safid Ab Iran
57 E3 Safidabeh Iran
57 B2 Safid Dasht Iran
57 E2 Safīd Sagak Iran
145 G3 Safiras, Sa de mts Brazil
60 D3 Şāfītā Syria
14 A2 Safonovo Rus. Fed.
12 J1 Safonovo Rus. Fed.
10 J1 Safonovo Rus. Fed.
91 □12 Safotu Western Samoa
73 H2 Safrā' al Asyāḩ escarpment Saudi Arabia
73 H2 Safrā' as Sark escarpment Saudi Arabia
60 C1 Safranbolu Turkey
91 □12 Safune Western Samoa
60 F4 Safwān Iraq
55 F3 Saga China
46 C7 Saga div. Japan
46 C7 Saga Japan
64 F3 Saga Kazak.
47 H4 Sagae Japan
42 A2 Sagaing div. Myanmar
42 A2 Sagaing Myanmar
47 G6 Sagamihara Japan
47 G6 Sagami-nada g. Japan
47 G6 Sagami-wan b. Japan
138 C2 Sagamoso r. Colombia
77 E5 Sagamu Nigeria
114 D2 Saganash Lake l. Can.
65 J4 Sagankuduk China
43 B4 Saganthit Kyun i. Myanmar
56 B2 Sagar India
56 A3 Sagar India
54 D5 Sagar India
13 H7 Sagarejo Georgia
55 G5 Sagar I. i. India
63 O2 Sagastyr Rus. Fed.
55 F4 Sagauli India
57 C2 Saghand Iran
57 E2 Saghar Afghanistan
56 B3 Sagileru r. India
123 F4 Saginaw U.S.A.
123 F4 Saginaw Bay b. U.S.A.
29 G5 Sağırlar Turkey
64 D3 Sagiz r. Kazak.
64 D3 Sagiz Kazak.
76 C5 Sagleipie Liberia
113 H2 Saglek Bay b. Can.
21 J5 Sagone, Golfe de b. France
24 B4 Sagres Portugal
24 B4 Sagres, Pta de pt Portugal
48 A3 Sagsay w Mongolia
42 A2 Sagu Myanmar
127 F4 Saguache U.S.A.
132 D2 Sagua de Tánamo Cuba
132 B2 Sagua la Grande Cuba
129 G5 Saguaro National Monument res. U.S.A.
113 F4 Saguenay r. Can.
25 F3 Sagunto Spain
54 C5 Sagwara India
64 D4 Sagyndyk, Mys pt Kazak.
61 D4 Sahāb Jordan
60 G2 Şahağac Azerbaijan
138 B2 Sahagun Colombia
24 D1 Sahagún Spain
74 C4 Sahara desert Africa
61 C5 Sahara, G. mt. Egypt
54 D3 Saharanpur India
55 F4 Saharsa India
54 D3 Sahaswan India
60 F2 Şahbuz Azerbaijan
61 B5 Saheira, W. el w Egypt
76 D4 Sahel, Réserve partielle du res. Burkina
55 F4 Sahibganj India
54 C3 Sahiwal Pakistan
54 C3 Sahiwal Pakistan
57 D2 Sahlābād Iran
60 F3 Şaḩneh Iran
60 F4 Şaḩrā al Ḩijārah reg. Iraq
61 A5 Sahra esh Sharqiya desert Egypt
130 C2 Sahuaripa Mexico
129 G6 Sahuarita U.S.A.
130 E4 Sahuayo Mexico
73 H2 Şāḩūq reg. Saudi Arabia
73 H2 Şāḩūq, W. w Saudi Arabia
43 E4 Sa Huynh Vietnam
19 J4 Šahy Slovakia
54 C5 Sahyadriparvat h. India
61 D2 Sahyūn Syria
55 E4 Sai r. India
43 C6 Sai Buri r. Thailand
43 C6 Sai Buri Thailand
75 E2 Saïda Algeria
61 C3 Saïda Lebanon
57 C3 Sa'īdābād Iran
57 E4 Sa'īdī Iran
55 G4 Saidpur Bangladesh
55 E4 Saidpur India
46 D5 Saigō Japan
55 H5 Saiha India
48 B4 Saihan Toroi China
46 D7 Saijō Japan
46 C7 Saiki Japan
45 □ Sai Kung Hong Kong
54 C5 Sailana India
11 H3 Saimaa l. Finland
60 D2 Saimbeyli Turkey
57 C3 Sā'īn Iran
130 E4 Sain Alto Mexico
57 E3 Saindak Pakistan
60 F2 Sa'īndezh Iran
76 B4 Saïnsoubou Senegal
16 F4 St Abb's Head hd U.K.
20 F5 St-Affrique France
115 K3 St-Agapit Can.
20 E3 St-Aignan France
20 D4 St-Aigulin France
113 J4 St Alban's Can.
17 G6 St Albans U.K.
121 G2 St Albans U.S.A.
120 C5 St Albans U.S.A.
17 F6 St Alban's Head hd U.K.
110 G4 St Albert Can.
115 J3 Saint-Alexis-des-Monts Can.
20 F3 St-Amand-Montrond France
115 K2 St-Ambroise Can.
21 G3 St-Amour France
19 G5 St Andrä Austria
81 □5 St-André *Réunion* Indian Ocean
81 □4 Saint-André Mauritius
115 H4 St-André-Avellin Can.
115 K2 St-Andre-du-Lac Can.
133 □1 St Andrew div. Jamaica
133 □3 St Andrew div. *Trinidad* Trin. & Tobago
121 K2 St Andrews Can.
16 F3 St Andrews U.K.
133 □1 St Ann div. Jamaica
132 □2 St Anna'-baai b. *Curaçao* Netherlands Ant.
81 □2 St Anne I. i. Seychelles
133 □1 St Ann's Bay Jamaica
115 K3 St-Anselme Can.
122 A4 St Ansgar U.S.A.
113 J3 St Anthony Can.
126 E3 St Anthony U.S.A.
61 B5 St Anthony, Mon. of Egypt
115 K3 Saint-Apollinaire Can.
27 F5 St Arcangelo Italy
97 E4 St Arnaud Aust.
93 D5 St Arnaud Range mt. ra. N.Z.
20 E4 St-Astier *Aquitaine* France
113 J3 St-Augustin Can.
119 D6 St Augustine U.S.A.
17 E6 St Austell U.K.
20 C3 St-Avé France
20 E3 St-Avertin France
115 J3 St-Barthélémi Can.
133 G3 St Barthélémy i. *Guadeloupe* Caribbean
115 K3 Saint-Basile Can.
93 B6 St Bathans, Mt mt. N.Z.
17 F4 St Bees Head hd U.K.
81 □5 St-Benoît *Réunion* Indian Ocean
21 H4 St-Bonnet-en-Champsaur France
17 E6 St Bride's Bay b. U.K.
20 C2 St-Brieuc France
20 E3 St-Calais France
129 G5 St Carlos Lake l. U.S.A.
20 C2 St-Cast-le-Guildo France
115 F5 St Catharines Can.
119 □1 St Catharine's Pt pt Bermuda
133 □1 St Catherine div. Jamaica
61 B5 St Catherine, Mon. of Egypt
133 □8 St Catherine, Mt h. *Grenada* Caribbean
119 D6 St Catherines I. i. U.S.A.
17 G6 St Catherine's Point pt U.K.
20 E4 St-Céré France
115 J4 St-Césaire Can.
21 G4 St-Chamond France
126 E3 St Charles U.S.A.
120 E5 St Charles U.S.A.
122 A4 St Charles U.S.A.
124 F4 St Charles U.S.A.
21 F4 St-Chély-d'Apcher France
132 □2 St Christoffelberg h. *Curaçao* Netherlands Ant.
21 G4 St-Christol-lès-Alès France
123 F4 St Clair U.S.A.
114 D5 St Clair, Lake l. Can.
123 F4 St Clair Shores U.S.A.
133 □5 St Claude *Guadeloupe* Caribbean
21 G3 St-Claude France
124 E2 St Cloud U.S.A.
115 K2 St-Coeur-de-Marie Can.
113 G4 St Croix r. Can.
133 F3 St Croix i. *Virgin Is* Caribbean
122 A2 St Croix r. U.S.A.
122 A3 St Croix Falls U.S.A.
119 □3 St Croix I. i. *Virgin Is* Caribbean
133 □3 St David div. *Trinidad* Trin. & Tobago
129 G6 St David U.S.A.
17 E6 St David's Head hd U.K.
119 □1 St David's Island i. Bermuda
81 □5 St-Denis *Réunion* Indian Ocean
81 □5 St-Denis Mauritius
21 H2 St-Dié France
21 G2 St-Dizier France
115 H3 St-Donat Can.
115 H4 Ste-Adèle Can.
115 H3 Sainte-Agathe-des-Monts Can.
111 K5 Ste Anne Can.
115 K3 Ste-Anne r. Can.
133 □4 Ste Anne *Martinique* Caribbean
81 □5 Ste-Anne *Réunion* Indian Ocean
115 K3 Ste-Anne-de-Beaupré Can.
121 J1 Sainte-Anne-de-Madawaska Can.
115 H3 Sainte-Anne-du-Lac Can.
113 G3 Ste Anne, L. l. Can.
121 H1 Ste-Camille-de-Lellis Can.
115 K3 Sainte-Croix Can.
115 J3 Ste-Emélie-de-l'Energie Can.
115 K3 Ste-Foy Can.
20 E4 Ste-Foy-la-Grande France
21 G4 St-Égrève France
115 J4 Ste-Julienne Can.
121 H1 Sainte-Justine Can.
121 J1 St-Éleuthère Can.
108 D4 St Elias, C. c. U.S.A.
110 B2 St Elias Mountains mt. ra. Can.
139 G3 St Elie French Guiana
133 □1 St Elizabeth div. Jamaica
20 F3 St-Éloy-les-Mines France
133 □4 Ste Luce *Martinique* Caribbean
113 G3 Ste Marguerite r. Can.
115 K3 Sainte-Marie Can.
133 □4 Sainte Marie *Martinique* Caribbean
81 □5 Ste-Marie *Réunion* Indian Ocean
20 E3 Ste-Maure-de-Touraine France
21 H5 Ste-Maxime France
115 K2 Ste-Monique Can.
133 □5 Ste Rose *Guadeloupe* Caribbean
81 □5 Ste-Rose *Réunion* Indian Ocean
20 D4 Saintes France
133 □5 Saintes, Îles des is *Guadeloupe* Caribbean
21 G5 Stes-Maries-de-la-Mer France
81 □5 Ste-Suzanne *Réunion* Indian Ocean
115 J4 Ste-Thérèse Can.
21 G4 St-Étienne *Loire* France
20 E2 St-Étienne-du-Rouvray France
115 H4 St Eugene Can.
115 J4 St-Eustache Can.
133 G3 St Eustatius i. Netherlands Ant.
115 H3 Ste-Véronique Can.
115 J2 St-Félicien Can.
115 F2 St-Félix-de-Dalquier Can.
115 J3 St-Félix-de-Valois Can.
21 J5 St-Florent France
21 F2 St-Florentin France
20 F3 St-Florent-sur-Cher France
78 D2 St Floris, Parc National nat. park C.A.R.
21 F4 St-Flour France
121 J1 St-Francis r. Can./U.S.A.
124 C4 St Francis U.S.A.
121 J1 St Francis U.S.A.
125 F4 St Francis r. U.S.A.
113 K4 St Francis, C. c. Can.
115 J3 St-François r. Can.
133 □5 St François *Guadeloupe* Caribbean
121 J1 St Froid Lake l. U.S.A.
115 K2 St-Fulgence Can.
115 J3 Saint-Gabriel Can.
21 J3 St Gallen Switz.
20 E5 St-Gaudens France
20 E3 St-Gaultier France
121 H2 St-Gédéon Can.
99 G6 St George Aust.
119 □1 St George Bermuda
121 K2 St George Can.
133 □3 St George div. *Trinidad* Trin. & Tobago
108 B4 St George U.S.A.
119 D5 St George U.S.A.
129 F3 St George U.S.A.
90 □1 St George, C. pt P.N.G.
108 A4 St George I. i. U.S.A.
119 C6 St George I. i. U.S.A.
126 A3 St George, Pt pt U.S.A.
100 D3 St George Ra. h. Aust.
113 F4 St Georges Can.
133 □8 St George's *Grenada* Caribbean
139 G3 St Georges French Guiana
113 J4 St George's B. b. Can.
131 J5 St George's Cay i. Belize
90 □1 St George's Channel chan. P.N.G.
17 D6 St George's Channel chan. Rep. of Ire./U.K.
119 □1 St George's Island i. Bermuda
20 F3 St-Germain-du-Puy France
133 □2 St Giles Is i. *Tobago* Trin. & Tobago
20 D3 St-Gilles-Croix-de-Vie France
81 □5 St-Gilles-les-Bains *Réunion* Indian Ocean
17 E6 St Govan's Head hd U.K.
122 E3 St Helen U.S.A.
148 J7 St Helena i. Atlantic Ocean
128 A2 St Helena U.S.A.
82 B5 St Helena Bay b. R.S.A.
148 J6 St Helena Fracture Atlantic Ocean
97 G5 St Helens Aust.
17 F5 St Helens U.K.
126 B2 St Helens U.S.A.
126 B2 St Helens, Mt vol U.S.A.
97 G5 St Helens Pt pt Aust.
17 F7 St Helier *Jersey* Channel Is.
20 D2 St-Hilaire-du-Harcouët France
115 K2 St-Honoré Can.
18 B3 St-Hubert Belgium
115 J4 St-Hyacinthe Can.
122 E3 St Ignace U.S.A.
115 J3 St-Ignace-du-Lac Can.
114 A2 St Ignace I. i. Can.
17 E6 St Ives U.K.
121 J1 St-Jacques Can.
115 J4 St-Jacques Can.
115 F2 St-Jacques-de-Dupuy Can.
20 D2 St-James France
133 □1 St James div. Jamaica
122 E3 St James U.S.A.
110 C4 St James, Cape pt Can.
20 D4 St-Jean-d'Angély France
20 E3 St-Jean-de-la-Ruelle France
20 D5 St-Jean-de-Luz France
115 J3 Saint-Jean-de-Matha Can.
21 H4 St-Jean-de-Maurienne France
20 C3 St-Jean-de-Monts France
115 J2 St-Jean, Lac l. Can.
115 J4 St-Jean-sur-Richelieu Can.
115 H4 St-Jérôme Can.
126 C2 St Joe r. U.S.A.
18 F5 St Johann im Pongau Austria
113 G4 St John Can.
121 K2 St John r. Can./U.S.A.
133 F3 St John i. *Virgin Is* Caribbean
76 C5 St John r. Liberia
129 F1 St John U.S.A.
119 □3 St John I. i. *Virgin Is* Caribbean
113 K4 St John's Can.
133 □7 St John's *Antigua* Caribbean
129 H4 St Johns U.S.A.
119 D6 St Johns r. U.S.A.
122 E4 St Johns U.S.A.
121 H2 St Johnsbury U.S.A.
113 F4 St Joseph Can.
133 □4 St Joseph *Martinique* Caribbean
81 □5 St-Joseph *Réunion* Indian Ocean
133 □3 St Joseph Trin. & Tobago
122 E5 St Joseph r. U.S.A.
122 D4 St Joseph U.S.A.
124 E4 St Joseph U.S.A.
114 D3 St Joseph I. i. Can.
125 D7 St Joseph I. i. U.S.A.
112 B3 St Joseph, Lac l. Can.
115 H3 St Jovité Can.
132 □2 St Jozefsdal *Curaçao* Netherlands Ant.
115 J4 Saint-Jude Can.
20 E4 St-Junien France
20 F2 St-Just-en-Chaussée France
16 C3 St Kilda is U.K.
133 □6 St Kitts i. *St Kitts-Nevis* Caribbean
104 M8 St Kitts-Nevis country Caribbean
132 □2 St Kruis *Curaçao* Netherlands Ant.
152 □ St Lanne Gramont, I. i. *Kerguelen* Indian Ocean
139 G2 St Laurent French Guiana
99 G4 St Lawrence Aust.
113 K4 St Lawrence Can.
113 G4 St Lawrence inlet Can.
113 H4 St Lawrence, Gulf of g. Can./U.S.A.
108 B3 St Lawrence I. i. U.S.A.
115 H4 St Lawrence Islands National Park nat. park Can.
121 F2 St Lawrence Seaway chan. Can./U.S.A.
113 G4 St-Léonard Can.
115 J3 St-Léonard Can.
20 E4 St-Léonard-de-Noblat France
81 □5 St-Leu *Réunion* Indian Ocean
113 J3 St Lewis Can.
113 J3 Saint Lewis r. Can.
20 D2 St-Lô France
133 □5 St Louis *Guadeloupe* Caribbean
81 □5 St-Louis *Réunion* Indian Ocean
76 A3 St Louis Senegal
122 E4 St Louis U.S.A.
122 A2 St Louis r. U.S.A.
124 F4 St Louis U.S.A.
115 J3 Saint-Louis-de-France Can.
21 H3 St-Loup-sur-Semouse France
104 M8 St Lucia country Caribbean
133 G4 St Lucia Channel chan. Martinique/St Lucia
83 E4 St Lucia, Lake l. R.S.A.
21 G2 St-Lyé France
133 G3 St Maarten i. Netherlands Ant.
20 D3 St-Maixent-l'École France
20 C2 St-Malo France
20 C2 St-Malo, Golfe de g. France
133 D3 St Marc Haiti
115 J3 Saint-Marc-des-Carrières Can.
21 G4 St-Marcellin France
139 G3 St Marcel, Mt h. French Guiana
133 □1 St Margaret's Bay Jamaica
16 F2 St Margaret's Hope U.K.
133 □4 St Martin, Cap c. *Martinique* Caribbean
21 H4 St-Martin-de-Belleville France
20 D3 St-Martin-de-Ré France
122 D3 St Martin I. i. U.S.A.
111 K4 St Martin, L. l. Can.
55 H5 St Martin's I. i. Bangladesh
133 □1 St Mary div. Jamaica
93 B6 St Mary, Mt mt. N.Z.
96 D2 St Mary Pk mt. Aust.
97 G5 St Marys Aust.
114 E5 St Mary's Can.
133 □3 St Mary's Trin. & Tobago
17 D7 St Mary's i. U.K.
120 A4 St Marys r. U.S.A.
120 A4 St Marys U.S.A.
120 D4 St Marys U.S.A.
120 C5 Saint Marys U.S.A.
113 K4 St Mary's, C. hd Can.
115 F2 St-Mathieu Can.
108 A3 St Matthew I. i. U.S.A.
90 □1 St Matthias Group is P.N.G.
115 J3 St Maurice r. Can.
115 J3 St-Maurice, Parc du res. Can.
20 D4 St-Médard-en-Jalles France
19 F5 St Michael im Langau Austria
113 J3 St Michaels Bay b. Can.
133 D3 St Michel de l'Atalaye Haiti
21 H4 St-Michel-de-Maurienne France
115 J3 Saint-Michel-des-Saints Can.
132 □2 St Michiel *Curaçao* Netherlands Ant.
21 G2 St-Mihiel France
21 J3 St Moritz *Graubünden* Switz.
20 C3 St-Nazaire France
115 J4 St-Nicéphore Can.
133 E4 St Nicolaas *Aruba* Caribbean
21 H2 St-Nicolas-de-Port France
18 B3 St-Niklaas Belgium
21 H3 St Niklaus Switz.
20 F1 St-Omer France
20 D4 Saintonge reg. France
115 J4 St-Ours Can.
20 D5 St-Palais France
121 J1 St-Pamphile Can.
113 G4 St Pascal Can.
133 □3 St Patrick div. *Trinidad* Trin. & Tobago
111 G4 St Paul Can.
81 □5 St-Paul *Réunion* Indian Ocean
76 B5 St Paul r. Liberia
122 A3 St Paul U.S.A.
124 D3 St Paul U.S.A.
120 B6 St Paul U.S.A.
81 □5 St-Paul, B. de b. *Réunion* Indian Ocean
77 E5 St Paul, Cape c. Ghana
149 K6 St Paul, Île i. Indian Ocean
108 B4 St Paul Island U.S.A.
20 D5 St-Paul-lès-Dax France
61 B5 St Paul, Mon. of Egypt
91 □14 St Paul's Point pt *Pitcairn I.* Pac. Oc.
18 D1 St Peter-Ording Germany
17 F7 St Peter Port *Guernsey* Channel Is.
119 D7 St Petersburg U.S.A.
40 B1 St Petrus i. Indon.
20 D3 St-Philbert-de-Grand-Lieu France
81 □5 St-Philippe *Réunion* Indian Ocean
115 J4 St-Pie Can.
133 □4 St Pierre *Martinique* Caribbean
81 □5 St-Pierre *Réunion* Indian Ocean
81 □4 St Pierre Mauritius
113 J4 St-Pierre *St Pierre and Miquelon* N. America
133 □3 St Pierre Trin. & Tobago
104 N5 St Pierre and Miquelon terr. N. America
20 D4 St-Pierre-d'Oléron France
115 J3 St-Pierre, Lac l. Can.
21 F3 St-Pierre-le-Moûtier France
20 D2 St-Pierre-sur-Dives France
20 C2 St-Pol-de-Léon France
20 F1 St-Pol-sur-Ternoise France
19 G4 St Pölten Austria
21 F3 St-Pourçain-sur-Sioule France
121 H1 Saint-Prosper Can.
21 F2 St-Quentin France
21 H5 St-Raphaël France
121 F2 St Regis r. U.S.A.
121 F2 St Regis Falls U.S.A.
115 H3 St-Rémi Can.
115 J4 St-Rémi Can.
20 B2 St-Renan France
21 G3 St-Rigaud, Mont mt. France
115 H4 St-Sauveur-des-Monts Can.
121 H2 St-Sébastien Can.
113 G4 St Siméon Can.
119 D6 St Simons I. i. U.S.A.
121 K2 St Stephen Can.
119 E5 St Stephen U.S.A.
20 D4 St-Symphorien France
121 H2 St-Théophile Can.
111 L4 St Theresa Point Can.
114 E5 St Thomas Can.
133 F3 St Thomas i. *Virgin Is* Caribbean
133 □1 St Thomas div. Jamaica
119 □3 St Thomas I. i. *Virgin Is* Caribbean
115 J3 Saint-Tite Can.
21 H5 St-Tropez France
20 D2 St-Vaast-la-Hougue France
20 E2 St-Valery-en-Caux France
20 E1 St-Valery-sur-Somme France
21 G3 St-Vallier *Bourgogne* France
21 G4 St-Vallier *Rhône-Alpes* France
20 E3 St-Vaury France
19 G5 St Veit an der Glan Austria
21 H4 St-Véran France
26 A3 St-Vincent Italy
111 K5 St Vincent U.S.A.
104 M8 St Vincent and the Grenadines country Caribbean
96 D3 St. Vincent, Gulf b. Aust.
133 G4 St Vincent Passage chan. St Lucia/St Vincent
18 C3 St-Vith Belgium
111 H4 St Walburg Can.
18 C4 St Wendel Germany
132 □2 St Willebrordus *Curaçao* Netherlands Ant.
114 E5 St Williams Can.
20 E4 St-Yrieix-la-Perche France
55 E3 Saipal mt. Nepal
39 M3 Saipan i. *Northern Mariana Is* Pac. Oc.
41 □1 Saipan Palau
47 G6 Saitama div. Japan
42 A2 Saitlai Myanmar
46 C7 Saito Japan
45 □ Sai Wan Hong Kong
54 C3 Saiyidwala Pakistan
140 C3 Sajama Bolivia
73 H4 Sajīd Saudi Arabia
82 C5 Sak r. R.S.A.
80 C3 Saka Ethiopia
47 E6 Sakai Japan
46 D6 Sakaide Japan
46 D6 Sakaiminato Japan
73 H2 Sakākah Saudi Arabia
57 F4 Saka Kalat Pakistan
124 C2 Sakakawea, Lake l. U.S.A.
40 D3 Sakala i. Indon.
112 E3 Sakami Can.
112 F3 Sakami r. Can.
112 E3 Sakami, Lac l. Can.
28 F4 Sakar mts Bulgaria
83 G3 Sakaraha Madagascar
57 E1 Sakar-Chaga Turkmenistan
60 B1 Sakarya Turkey
60 B1 Sakarya r. Turkey
76 C5 Sakassou Côte d'Ivoire
47 G4 Sakata Japan
46 D7 Sakawa Japan
61 D1 Sakçagöze Turkey
49 H4 Sakchu N. Korea
43 C4 Sa Keo r. Thailand
77 E5 Sakété Benin
63 Q5 Sakhalin, O. i. Rus. Fed.
63 Q4 Sakhalinskiy Zaliv b. Rus. Fed.
14 C1 Sakharovo Rus. Fed.
54 C3 Sakhi India
83 D4 Sakhile R.S.A.
15 F2 Sakhnovshchyna Ukraine
57 B1 Sakht-Sar Iran
60 F1 Şäki Azerbaijan
77 E5 Şaki Nigeria
11 F5 Šakiai Lithuania
54 A3 Sakir mt. Pakistan
45 M7 Sakishima-guntō is Japan
42 B3 Sa-koi Myanmar
14 F2 Sakony Rus. Fed.
76 D5 Sakpiegu Ghana
54 B4 Sakrand Pakistan
43 □ Sakra, P. i. Singapore
82 C5 Sakrivier R.S.A.
64 F3 Saksaul'skiy Kazak.
47 G5 Saku Japan
47 F6 Sakuma Japan
47 H6 Sakura Japan
47 E6 Sakurai Japan
46 C8 Sakura-jima vol Japan
13 E6 Saky Ukraine
11 F3 Säkylä Finland
76 □ Sal i. Cape Verde
13 G6 Sal r. Rus. Fed.
19 H4 Šal'a Slovakia
11 E4 Sala Sweden
115 H4 Salaberry-de-Valleyfield Can.
11 G4 Salacgrīva Latvia
27 E5 Sala Consilina Italy
146 B2 Salada, Bahía b. Chile
130 B1 Salada, L. salt l. Mexico
129 E5 Salada, Laguna salt l. Mexico
146 E2 Saladas Arg.
61 C5 Saladih, W. w Jordan
146 E4 Saladillo *Buenos Aires* Arg.
146 D3 Saladillo r. *Córdoba* Arg.
146 D3 Saladillo r. *Santa Fé* Arg.
146 D2 Saladillo r. *Santiago del Estero* Arg.
146 E4 Salado r. *Buenos Aires* Arg.
146 E2 Salado r. *Formosa* Arg.
146 C2 Salado r. *La Rioja* Arg.
146 C3 Salado r. *Mendoza/San Luis* Arg.
147 C5 Salado r. *Río Negro* Arg.
146 D3 Salado r. *Santa Fé* Arg.
131 E3 Salado r. Mexico
24 D4 Salado r. *Andalucía* Spain
146 C2 Salado, Quebrada de r. Chile
76 C4 Saladou Guinea
76 D5 Salaga Ghana
60 E3 Şalāḩ ad Dīn div. Iraq
91 □12 Salailua Western Samoa
65 L2 Salair Rus. Fed.
82 C3 Salajwe Botswana
40 A3 Salak, G. vol Indon.
72 C5 Salal Chad
73 G3 Salâla Sudan
59 H6 Şalālah Oman
131 H6 Salamá Guatemala
130 J6 Salamá Honduras
146 B3 Salamanca Chile
131 E4 Salamanca Mexico
24 D2 Salamanca Spain
120 D3 Salamanca U.S.A.
78 D1 Salamat div. Chad
57 A2 Salamatabad Iran
40 C2 Salamban Indon.
138 B2 Salamina Colombia
29 D6 Salamina i. Greece
61 B2 Salamis Cyprus
60 D3 Salamīyah Syria
122 E5 Salamonie r. U.S.A.
122 E5 Salamonie Lake l. U.S.A.
55 F5 Salandi r. India
91 □12 Salani Western Samoa
11 F4 Salantai Lithuania
146 C1 Salar de Arizaro salt flat Arg.
140 C4 Salar de Atacama salt flat Chile
140 C3 Salar de Coipasa salt flat Bolivia
140 C4 Salar de Uyuni salt flat Bolivia
11 G4 Salaspils Latvia
40 B3 Salatiga Indon.
64 E2 Salavat Rus. Fed.
39 K7 Salawati i. Indon.
54 B5 Salaya India
40 E3 Salayar i. Indon.
151 N7 Sala y Gómez, Isla i. Chile
146 D4 Salazar Arg.
81 □5 Salazie *Réunion* Indian Ocean
20 F3 Salbris France
28 F1 Salcea Romania
28 F2 Sălciile Romania
11 G5 Šalčininkai Lithuania
138 B3 Saldana Colombia
24 D1 Saldaña Spain
82 B5 Saldanha R.S.A.
82 B5 Saldanha Bay b. R.S.A.
146 D4 Saldungaray Arg.
11 F4 Saldus Latvia
97 F4 Sale Aust.
42 A2 Sale Myanmar
133 □5 Salée r. *Guadeloupe* Caribbean
57 B2 Şāleḩābād Iran
57 C3 Şāleḩābād Iran
40 D4 Saleh, Teluk b. Indon.
62 H3 Salekhard Rus. Fed.
91 □12 Salelologa Western Samoa
56 B4 Salem India
121 H3 Salem U.S.A.
125 F4 Salem U.S.A.
118 F4 Salem U.S.A.
121 G3 Salem U.S.A.
120 C4 Salem U.S.A.
126 B2 Salem U.S.A.
118 D4 Salem U.S.A.
27 D7 Salemi Italy
16 E3 Salen U.K.
27 E5 Salerno Italy
27 E5 Salerno, Golfo di g. Italy
145 F5 Salesópolis Brazil
142 E2 Salgado r. Brazil
14 G2 Salgan Rus. Fed.
19 J4 Salgótarján Hungary
142 E2 Salgueiro Brazil
57 E3 Salian Afghanistan
41 C6 Salibabu i. Indon.
133 □3 Salibea Trin. & Tobago
20 D5 Salies-de-Béarn France
60 B2 Salihli Turkey
13 C4 Salihorsk Belarus
81 B7 Salima Malawi
81 C7 Salimo Mozambique
42 A2 Salin Myanmar
124 D4 Salina U.S.A.
129 G2 Salina U.S.A.
131 G5 Salina Cruz Mexico
146 C2 Salina de Antofalla salt flat Arg.
147 D5 Salina Gualicho salt flat Arg.
27 E6 Salina, Isola i. Italy
146 C3 Salina La Antigua salt flat Arg.
146 C4 Salina Llancanelo salt flat Arg.
132 D2 Salina Pt pt The Bahamas
145 G2 Salinas Brazil
138 A4 Salinas Ecuador
131 E4 Salinas Mexico
127 B4 Salinas r. U.S.A.
128 B3 Salinas U.S.A.
128 B3 Salinas r. U.S.A.
140 C3 Salinas de Garci Mendoza Bolivia

146 C1 Salinas Grandes salt flat Jujuy/Salta Arg.
146 C3 Salinas Grandes salt flat Arg.
127 F5 Salinas Peak summit U.S.A.
91 □15 Salinas, Punta pt Juan Fernandez Is Chile
133 E3 Salinas, Punta pt Dominican Rep.
79 B6 Salinas, Punta das pt Angola
125 E5 Saline r. U.S.A.
124 C4 Saline r. U.S.A.
133 □3 Saline Bay b. Trin. & Tobago
25 H3 Salines, Cap de ses pt Spain
133 □8 Salines, Pt pt Grenada Caribbean
128 D3 Saline Valley v. U.S.A.
42 A2 Salingyi Myanmar
142 C1 Salinópolis Brazil
140 A2 Salinosó Lachay, Pta pt Peru
17 G6 Salisbury U.K.
121 F5 Salisbury U.S.A.
119 D5 Salisbury U.S.A.
17 G6 Salisbury Plain plain U.K.
28 D2 Săliște Romania
142 D3 Salitre r. Brazil
60 D3 Şalkhad Syria
55 F5 Salki r. India
10 H2 Salla Finland
76 B5 Sallatouk, Pte pt Guinea
20 D4 Salles France
146 D4 Salliqueló Arg.
125 E5 Sallisaw U.S.A.
73 G4 Sallom Sudan
109 L3 Salluit Can.
55 E3 Sallyana Nepal
60 F2 Salmās Iran
110 F5 Salmo Can.
126 D2 Salmon r. U.S.A.
126 D2 Salmon U.S.A.
110 F4 Salmon Arm Can.
101 C7 Salmon Gums Aust.
121 F3 Salmon Reservoir resr U.S.A.
126 D2 Salmon River Mountains mts U.S.A.
18 C4 Salmtal Germany
11 F3 Salo Finland
26 C3 Salò Italy
141 E4 Salobra r. Brazil
133 □4 Salomon, Cap c. Martinique Caribbean
55 E4 Salon India
21 G5 Salon-de-Provence France
78 D4 Salonga r. Zaire
78 D4 Salonga Nord, Parc National de la nat. park Zaire
79 D4 Salonga Sud, Parc National de la nat. park Zaire
25 G2 Salou, Cap de hd Spain
76 A4 Saloum w Senegal
130 J6 Sal, Pta pt Honduras
20 F5 Salses-le-Château France
13 G6 Sal'sk Rus. Fed.
26 B3 Salsomaggiore Terme Italy
60 C4 Salt Jordan
129 G5 Salt r. U.S.A.
122 B6 Salt r. U.S.A.
146 C1 Salta Arg.
65 H1 Saltaim, Oz. l. Rus. Fed.
14 B3 Saltanovka Rus. Fed.
17 E6 Saltash U.K.
119 □2 Salt Cay i. The Bahamas
120 B5 Salt Creek r. U.S.A.
17 D5 Saltee Islands is Rep. of Ire.
10 D2 Saltfjellet Svartisen Nasjonalpark nat. park Norway
10 D2 Saltfjorden chan. Norway
125 B6 Salt Flat U.S.A.
120 C4 Salt Fork Lake l. U.S.A.
131 E3 Saltillo Mexico
126 E3 Salt Lake City U.S.A.
97 E2 Salt L., The salt flat Aust.
146 D3 Salto Arg.
144 E5 Salto Brazil
27 D4 Salto r. Italy
24 C2 Salto Portugal
146 E3 Salto Uruguay
145 J2 Salto da Divisa Brazil
144 A6 Salto del Guaíra Paraguay
144 D5 Salto Grande Brazil
129 E5 Salton Sea salt l. U.S.A.
76 D5 Saltpond Ghana
133 □1 Salt Ponds salt pan Jamaica
111 G2 Salt River Can.
133 □1 Salt River Jamaica
120 B5 Salt Rock U.S.A.
14 D3 Saltyki Rus. Fed.
14 G3 Saltykovka Rus. Fed.
14 F2 Saltykovo Rus. Fed.
14 F3 Saltykovo Rus. Fed.
14 G3 Saltykovo Rus. Fed.
91 □12 Saluafata Western Samoa
119 D5 Saluda U.S.A.
120 E6 Saluda U.S.A.
54 C4 Salumbar India
72 E1 Salûm, Gulf of b. Egypt
56 C2 Salur India
139 G2 Salut, Is du is French Guiana
26 A3 Saluzzo Italy
146 C3 Salvador Arg.
142 E3 Salvador Brazil
125 F6 Salvador, L. l. U.S.A.
146 D1 Salvador Mazza Arg.
142 C1 Salvaterra Brazil
131 E4 Salvatierra Mexico
129 G2 Salvation Creek r. U.S.A.
57 B4 Salwah Qatar
42 B3 Salween r. Myanmar/Thailand
60 G2 Salyan Azerbaijan
120 B6 Salyersville U.S.A.
18 F5 Salzburg Austria
18 F5 Salzburg div. Austria
18 E2 Salzgitter Germany
18 E2 Salzwedel Germany
54 B4 Sam India
48 A2 Samagaltay Rus. Fed.
57 A2 Samaida Iran
140 D3 Samaipata Bolivia
40 A2 Samak, Tg pt Indon.
41 C5 Samal i. Phil.
91 □12 Samalaeulu Western Samoa
40 B1 Samalantan Indon.
130 D2 Samalayuca Mexico
41 B5 Samales Group is Phil.
56 C2 Samalkot India
73 F2 Samâlût Egypt
133 E3 Samaná Dominican Rep.
133 E3 Samaná, Bahía de b. Mexico
132 D2 Samana Cay i. The Bahamas
60 C2 Samandağı Turkey
79 D4 Samangwa Zaire
46 J2 Samani Japan
29 G4 Samanlı Dağları mt. ra. Turkey
61 A4 Samannûd Egypt
41 C3 Samar i. Phil.
64 D2 Samara r. Rus. Fed.
12 J4 Samara div. Rus. Fed.
12 J4 Samara Rus. Fed.
15 G2 Samara r. Ukraine
90 □1 Samarai P.N.G.
138 D2 Samariapo Venezuela
40 D2 Samarinda Indon.
65 G5 Samarkand Uzbekistan
60 E3 Sāmarrā' Iraq
41 C4 Samar Sea g. Phil.
65 K3 Samarskoye Kazak.
65 H3 Samarskoye Kazak.
54 B3 Samasata Pakistan
55 F4 Samastipur India
91 □12 Samatau Western Samoa
60 G1 Şamaxı Azerbaijan
54 C2 Samba India
40 C2 Samba r. Indon.
78 D3 Samba Équateur Zaire
79 E4 Samba Kivu Zaire
79 C5 Samba Cajú Angola
76 B4 Sambaïlo Guinea
40 D1 Sambaliung mt. ra. Indon.
55 F5 Sambalpur India
40 B2 Sambar, Tg pt Indon.
40 B1 Sambas Indon.
83 H1 Sambava Madagascar
55 G4 Sambha India
54 D3 Sambhal India
54 C4 Sambhar India
54 C4 Sambhar L. l. India
13 B5 Sambir Ukraine
142 D2 Sambito r. Brazil
79 C6 Sambo Angola
40 D2 Sambo Indon.
40 D2 Samboja Indon.
146 E4 Samborombón, Bahía b. Arg.
21 F1 Sambre r. France
27 E7 Sambughetti, Monte mt. Italy
49 J5 Samch'ŏk S. Korea
49 J6 Samch'ŏnp'o S. Korea
28 D1 Şamcuta Mare Romania
81 C5 Same Tanzania
20 E1 Samer France
14 E1 Samet' Rus. Fed.
79 E6 Samfya Zambia
80 □ Samḩah i. Socotra Yemen
15 C2 Samhorodok Ukraine
54 B5 Sami India
73 H2 Samīrah Saudi Arabia
42 B2 Samka Myanmar
60 F1 Şämkir Azerbaijan
73 G2 Şamnah oasis Saudi Arabia
57 C2 Samnan & Damghan reg. Iran
72 B2 Samnū Libya
146 B3 Samo Alto Chile
26 E3 Samobor Croatia
12 G2 Samoded Rus. Fed.
28 D3 Samokov Bulgaria
19 H4 Šamorín Slovakia
29 F6 Samos i. Greece
29 F6 Samos Greece
29 E4 Samothraki i. Greece
40 D2 Sampaga Indon.
40 C3 Sampang Indon.
26 A3 Sampeyre Italy
40 C2 Sampit Indon.
40 C2 Sampit r. Indon.
40 C2 Sampit, Tk b. Indon.
14 E3 Sampur Rus. Fed.
79 E5 Sampwe Zaire
125 E6 Sam Rayburn Res. resr U.S.A.
61 B5 Samr el 'Abd, G. mt. Egypt
55 E3 Samsang China
11 C5 Samsø i. Denmark
42 D3 Sâm Sơn Vietnam
60 D1 Samsun Turkey
18 F1 Samtens Germany
54 D4 Samthar India
13 G7 Samtredia Georgia
98 C3 Samuel, Mt h. Aust.
13 J7 Samur r. Azerbaijan/Rus. Fed.
43 C4 Samut Sakhon Thailand
43 C4 Samut Songkhram Thailand
55 G3 Samyai China
76 D4 San Mali
19 L4 San r. Poland
80 D1 Şan'ā Yemen
80 E2 Sanaag div. Somalia
24 B1 San Adrián, Cabo de c. Spain
152 C3 Sanae South Africa Base Ant.
78 B3 Sanaga r. Cameroon
41 C5 San Agustin, Cape c. Phil.
108 B4 Sanak I. i. U.S.A.
136 C5 San Ambrosio i. Chile
60 F3 Sanandaj Iran
140 D4 Sanandita Bolivia
128 B2 San Andreas U.S.A.
140 D2 San Andrés Bolivia
41 C3 San Andres Phil.
24 D1 San Andrés del Rabanedo Spain
130 K6 San Andrés, I. de i. Colombia
127 F5 San Andres Mts mt. ra. U.S.A.
131 G5 San Andrés Tuxtla Mexico
125 C6 San Angelo U.S.A.
76 C4 Sanankoroba Mali
146 D2 San Antonio Catamarca Arg.
130 H5 San Antonio Belize
140 D2 San Antonio Bolivia
146 B2 San Antonio Atacama Chile
146 B3 San Antonio Valparaíso Chile
41 B3 San Antonio Phil.
125 D6 San Antonio U.S.A.
138 D3 San Antonio Venezuela
25 G3 San Antonio Abad Spain
41 A4 San Antonio Bay b. Phil.
132 A2 San Antonio, C. c. Cuba
146 E4 San Antonio, Cabo pt Arg.
25 G3 San Antonio, Cabo de pt Spain
138 C2 San Antonio de Caparo Venezuela
146 C1 San Antonio de los Cobres Arg.
139 D2 San Antonio de Tamanaco Venezuela
128 D4 San Antonio, Mt mt. U.S.A.
147 D5 San Antonio Oeste Arg.
128 B4 San Antonio Reservoir resr U.S.A.
128 B3 San Ardo U.S.A.
146 E4 San Augustín Arg.
146 C3 San Augustín de Valle Fértil Arg.
25 G2 Sanaüja Spain
54 D5 Sanawad India
131 E4 San Bartolo Mexico
25 □ San Bartolomé de Tirajana Canary Is Spain
26 D4 San Benedetto del Tronto Italy
130 □ San Benedicto, I. i. Mexico
142 D1 San Benedito do R. Prêto Brazil
128 B3 San Benito r. U.S.A.
125 D7 San Benito U.S.A.
128 B3 San Benito Mt mt. U.S.A.
128 D4 San Bernardino U.S.A.
127 C5 San Bernardino Mts mt. ra. U.S.A.
146 B3 San Bernardo Chile
130 D3 San Bernardo Mexico
132 C5 San Bernardo, I. de i. Colombia
46 D6 Sanbe-san vol Japan
130 D4 San Blas Nayarit Mexico
130 C3 San Blas Sinaloa Mexico
130 L7 San Blas, Archipiélago de is Panama
119 C6 San Blas, C. c. U.S.A.
130 L7 San Blás, Cord. de mt. ra. Panama
140 C2 San Borja Bolivia
121 H3 Sanbornville U.S.A.
131 E3 San Buenaventura Mexico
146 D1 San Camilo Arg.
26 D2 San Candido Italy
146 C3 San Carlos Mendoza Arg.
140 D3 San Carlos Bolivia
146 B4 San Carlos Chile
125 C6 San Carlos Coahuila Mexico
131 F3 San Carlos Tamaulipas Mexico
130 J7 San Carlos Nicaragua
141 E4 San Carlos r. Paraguay
41 B3 San Carlos Luzon Phil.
41 B4 San Carlos Negros Phil.
146 F3 San Carlos Uruguay
129 G5 San Carlos U.S.A.
138 D3 San Carlos Amazonas Venezuela
138 D2 San Carlos Cojedes Venezuela
146 D3 San Carlos C. Arg.
147 B5 San Carlos de Bariloche Arg.
146 D4 San Carlos de Bolívar Arg.
138 C2 San Carlos del Zulia Venezuela
147 B6 San Carlos, Pto Chile
27 D7 San Cataldo Italy
50 D3 Sancha r. China
48 D5 Sancha China
48 C5 Sancha China
49 H3 Sanchahe China
65 J5 Sanchakou China
54 B4 Sanchor India
48 D5 Sanchuan r. China
14 H1 Sanchursk Rus. Fed.
131 F4 San Ciro de Acosta Mexico
146 B4 San Clemente Chile
25 E3 San Clemente Spain
128 D5 San Clemente U.S.A.
128 C5 San Clemente I. i. U.S.A.
20 F3 Sancoins France
26 D4 San Costanzo Italy
146 D3 San Cristóbal Arg.
140 C4 San Cristóbal Bolivia
90 □1 San Cristobal i. Solomon Is.
138 C2 San Cristóbal Venezuela
25 □ San Cristóbal de la Laguna Canary Is Spain
131 G5 San Cristóbal de las Casas Mexico
138 □ San Cristóbal, I. i. Galapagos Is Ecuador
129 F5 San Cristobal Wash r. U.S.A.
81 □2 Sancta Maria Seychelles
132 C2 Sancti Spíritus Cuba
83 D3 Sand r. Northern R.S.A.
47 E6 Sanda Japan
40 B2 Sandai Indon.
17 E4 Sanda Island i. U.K.
41 A5 Sandakan Malaysia
11 B3 Sandane Norway
29 D4 Sandanski Bulgaria
76 B4 Sandaré Mali
16 F2 Sanday i. U.K.
16 K1 Sande Norway
11 C4 Sandefjord Norway
94 □3 Sandell Bay b. Macquarie I. Pac. Oc.
152 D4 Sandercock Nunataks nunatak Ant.
129 H4 Sanders U.S.A.
125 C6 Sanderson U.S.A.
140 C3 San de Surire Chile
100 C3 Sandfire Roadhouse Aust.
54 E4 Sandi India
122 B2 Sand I. i. U.S.A.
140 C2 Sandia Peru
130 C2 San Diego Mexico
127 C5 San Diego U.S.A.
147 D7 San Diego, C. c. Arg.
60 B2 Sandıklı Turkey
54 E4 Sandila India
119 □2 Sandilands Village The Bahamas
131 H5 San Dimas Campeche Mexico
130 D3 San Dimas Durango Mexico
114 C3 Sand Lake Can.
11 B4 Sandnes Norway
10 D2 Sandnessjøen Norway
79 D5 Sandoa Zaire
19 K3 Sandomierz Poland
28 E1 Sândominic Romania
138 B3 Sandoná Colombia
26 D3 San Donà di Piave Italy
98 C4 Sandover w Aust.
12 F3 Sandovo Rus. Fed.
42 A3 Sandoway Myanmar
17 G6 Sandown U.K.
16 D1 Sandoy i. Faeroes
126 C1 Sandpoint U.S.A.
83 H3 Sandrandahy Madagascar
98 D5 Sandringham Aust.
11 D3 Sandsjö Sweden
110 C4 Sandspit Can.
125 D4 Sand Springs U.S.A.
128 C2 Sand Springs Salt Flat salt flat U.S.A.
101 B5 Sandstone Aust.
122 A2 Sandstone U.S.A.
129 F5 Sand Tank Mts mts U.S.A.
51 F3 Sandu China
50 D3 Sandu China
123 F4 Sandusky U.S.A.
120 B4 Sandusky U.S.A.
120 B4 Sandusky Bay b. U.S.A.
82 B5 Sandveld mt. ra. R.S.A.
82 B4 Sandverhaar Namibia
11 C4 Sandvika Norway
10 D3 Sandvika Sweden
11 E3 Sandviken Sweden
113 J3 Sandwich Bay b. Can.
82 A3 Sandwich Bay b. Namibia
55 G5 Sandwip Bangladesh
55 G5 Sandwip Ch. chan. Bangladesh
121 H2 Sandy r. U.S.A.
82 A5 Sandy Bay reg. St Helena Atlantic Ocean
82 A5 Sandy Bay b. St Helena Atlantic Ocean
111 J3 Sandy Bay Can.
133 □1 Sandy Bay Jamaica
94 □3 Sandy Bay b. Macquarie I. Pac. Oc.
101 C7 Sandy Bight b. Aust.
97 F5 Sandy C. hd Aust.
99 H5 Sandy Cape c. Aust.
120 B5 Sandy Hook U.S.A.
121 F4 Sandy Hook pt U.S.A.
57 E1 Sandykachi Turkmenistan
112 B3 Sandy L. l. Can.
112 B3 Sandy Lake Can.
121 E3 Sandy Pond U.S.A.
133 □6 Sandy Pt Town St Kitts-Nevis Caribbean
21 G3 Sâne r. France
141 E4 San Estanislao Paraguay
41 B2 San Fabian Phil.
146 B3 San Felipe Chile
130 B2 San Felipe Norte Mexico
130 D3 San Felipe Chihuahua Mexico
131 E4 San Felipe Guanajuato Mexico
138 D1 San Felipe Venezuela
136 B5 San Félix i. Chile
146 E3 San Fernando Arg.
141 E3 San Fernando r. Bolivia
146 B3 San Fernando Chile
130 B2 San Fernando Mexico
131 F3 San Fernando Tamaulipas Mexico
41 B3 San Fernando Luzon Phil.
41 B2 San Fernando Luzon Phil.
24 C4 San Fernando Spain
133 □3 San Fernando Trin. & Tobago
128 C4 San Fernando U.S.A.
138 D2 San Fernando de Apure Venezuela
138 D3 San Fernando de Atabapo Venezuela
128 D5 San Filipe Creek r. U.S.A.
101 B5 Sanford r. Aust.
119 D6 Sanford U.S.A.
121 H3 Sanford U.S.A.
119 E5 Sanford U.S.A.
122 E4 Sanford Lake l. U.S.A.
133 □3 San Francique Trin. & Tobago
146 D3 San Francisco Arg.
130 B2 San Francisco Mexico
130 K7 San Francisco Panama
128 A3 San Francisco U.S.A.
128 A3 San Francisco airport U.S.A.
129 H5 San Francisco r. U.S.A.
128 A3 San Francisco Bay inlet U.S.A.
138 A3 San Francisco, Cabo de pt Ecuador
146 D2 San Francisco del Chañar Arg.
130 D3 San Francisco del Oro Mexico
133 E3 San Francisco de Macorís Dominican Rep.
143 B6 San Francisco de Paula Brazil
147 C6 San Francisco de Paula, C. c. Arg.
130 H6 San Francisco Gotera El Salvador
25 G3 San Francisco Javier Spain
146 C2 San Francisco, Paso de pass Arg.
138 B3 San Gabriel Ecuador
128 C4 San Gabriel Mts mts U.S.A.
130 B2 San Gabriel, Pta pt Mexico
40 A2 Sangaigerong Indon.
138 B4 Sangai, Parque Nacional nat. park Ecuador
56 A2 Sangamner India
122 C6 Sangamon r. U.S.A.
57 F2 Sangan Afghanistan
57 E3 Sangān Iran
54 C4 Sanganer India
63 O3 Sangar Rus. Fed.
56 B2 Sangāreddi India
54 C3 Sangaria India
40 D2 Sangasanga Indon.
27 B6 San Gavino Monreale Italy
57 D2 Sang Bast Iran
41 B5 Sangboy Islands is Phil.
40 D4 Sangeang i. Indon.
48 C4 Sangejing China
28 E1 Sângeorgiu de Pădure Romania
28 E1 Sângeorz-Băi Romania
128 C3 Sanger U.S.A.
15 C3 Sângerei Moldova
18 E3 Sangerhausen Germany
119 □3 San Germán Puerto Rico
48 E5 Sanggan r. China
50 C1 Sanggarmai China
40 D4 Sanggar, Tk b. Indon.
40 B1 Sanggau Indon.
49 G5 Sanggou Wan b. China
77 E4 Sangha Burkina
78 C3 Sangha div. Congo
78 C3 Sangha r. Congo
78 C3 Sangha-Mbaéré div. C.A.R.
54 B4 Sanghar Pakistan
138 C2 San Gil Colombia
48 A2 Sangilen, Nagor'ye mt. ra. Rus. Fed.
27 F6 San Giovanni in Fiore Italy
27 E5 San Giovanni Rotondo Italy
26 C4 San Giovanni Valdarno Italy
41 C6 Sangir i. Indon.
41 C6 Sangir, Kepulauan is Indon.
48 C3 Sangiyn Dalay Mongolia
48 A2 Sangiyn Dalay Nuur salt l. Mongolia
40 C3 Sangkapura Indon.
40 D3 Sangkarang, Kep. is Indon.
43 B4 Sangkhla Buri Thailand
40 D1 Sangkulirang Indon.
40 D1 Sangkulirang, Tk b. Indon.
56 A2 Sangli India
57 G1 Sanglich Afghanistan
78 B3 Sangmélima Cameroon
54 D3 Sangnam India
55 H3 Sangngagqoling China
83 E3 Sango Zimbabwe
54 D4 Sangod India
56 A2 Sāngole India
128 D4 San Gorgonio Mt mt. U.S.A.
50 B2 Sang Qu r. China
127 F4 Sangre de Cristo Range mt. ra. U.S.A.
133 □3 Sangre Grande Trin. & Tobago
54 C3 Sangrur India
55 F3 Sangsang China
133 □1 Sangster airport Jamaica
110 G4 Sangudo Can.
141 E2 Sangue r. Brazil
25 F1 Sangüesa Spain
83 E3 Sangutane r. Mozambique
51 E2 Sangzhi China
130 B3 San Hipólito, Pta pt Mexico
73 F2 Sanhûr Egypt
131 H5 San Ignacio Belize
140 C2 San Ignacio Beni Bolivia
140 D3 San Ignacio Santa Cruz Bolivia
141 D3 San Ignacio Santa Cruz Bolivia
130 B3 San Ignacio Mexico
141 E5 San Ignacio Paraguay
138 B5 San Ignacio Peru
112 E2 Sanikiluaq Can.
41 B3 San Ildefonso, Cape c. Phil.
41 B2 San Ildefonso Peninsula pen. Phil.
41 C4 San Isidro Phil.
18 F1 Sanitz Germany
72 C2 Sāniyat al Fawākhir well Libya
132 D5 San Jacinto Colombia
41 B3 San Jacinto Phil.
128 D5 San Jacinto U.S.A.
128 D5 San Jacinto Peak summit U.S.A.
146 E3 San Javier Santa Fé Arg.
146 E2 San Javier Arg.
140 D2 San Javier Bolivia
146 B4 San Javier de Loncomilla Chile
54 B3 Sanjawi Pakistan
81 C6 Sanje Tanzania
138 B2 San Jerónimo, Serranía de mt. ra. Colombia
51 E3 Sanjiang China
47 G5 Sanjō Japan
126 B3 San Joaquin r. U.S.A.
128 B3 San Joaquin U.S.A.
128 B3 San Joaquin Valley v. U.S.A.
146 D3 San Jorge Santa Fé Arg.
138 B2 San Jorge r. Colombia
147 C6 San Jorge, Golfo de g. Arg.
130 J7 San José Costa Rica
131 H6 San José Guatemala
130 C3 San José i. Mexico
41 B3 San Jose Phil.
41 B3 San Jose Phil.
128 B3 San Jose U.S.A.
139 E2 San José de Amacuro Venezuela
41 B4 San Jose de Buenavista Phil.
141 D3 San José de Chiquitos Bolivia
130 C2 San José de Dimas Mexico
146 E3 San José de Feliciano Arg.
130 B3 San José de Gracia Sur Mexico
130 D3 San José de Gracia Sinaloa Mexico
130 C2 San José de Gracia Sonora Mexico
139 E2 San José de Guanipa Venezuela
146 C3 San Jose de Jáchal Arg.
146 D3 San José de la Dormida Arg.
147 B4 San José de la Mariquina Chile
146 D2 San José del Boquerón Arg.
130 C4 San José del Cabo Mexico
138 C3 San José del Guaviare Colombia
146 E3 San José de Mayo Uruguay
138 C3 San José de Ocuné Colombia
131 E3 San José de Raíces Mexico
147 D5 San José, G. g. Arg.
130 L7 San José, I. i. Panama
146 C3 San José, Vol. vol Chile
65 J5 Sanju r. China
146 C3 San Juan San Juan Arg.
146 C3 San Juan div. Arg.
130 J7 San Juan r. Costa Rica/Nicaragua
132 B2 San Juan mt. Cuba
133 E3 San Juan Dominican Rep.
125 C7 San Juan Mexico
140 A3 San Juán Peru
41 C4 San Juan Phil.
119 □3 San Juan Puerto Rico
133 □3 San Juan Trin. & Tobago
128 B4 San Juan r. U.S.A.
129 H3 San Juan r. U.S.A.
139 D2 San Juan Venezuela
91 □15 San Juan Bautista Juan Fernandez Is Chile
141 E5 San Juan Bautista Paraguay
25 G3 San Juan Bautista Spain
131 F5 San Juan Bautista Tuxtepec Mexico
147 D7 San Juan, C. c. Arg.
78 A3 San Juan, Cabo c. Equatorial Guinea
130 J6 San Juancito Honduras
147 B5 San Juan dela Costa Chile
130 K7 San Juan del Norte Nicaragua
130 K7 San Juan del Norte, Bahía de b. Nicaragua
138 D1 San Juan de los Cayos Venezuela
138 D2 San Juan de los Morros Venezuela
130 D3 San Juan del Río Durango Mexico
131 F4 San Juan del Río Querétaro Mexico
130 J7 San Juan del Sur Nicaragua
147 D7 San Juan de Salvamento Arg.
130 B3 San Juanico, Pta pt Mexico
130 D4 San Juanito, I. i. Mexico
127 F4 San Juan Mts mt. ra. U.S.A.
131 H6 San Juan, Pta pt El Salvador
147 C6 San Julián Arg.
146 D3 San Justo Arg.
76 C4 Sankarani r. Côte d'Ivoire/Guinea
56 A2 Sankeshwar India
55 F5 Sankh r. India
11 H4 Sankt-Peterburg Rus. Fed.
79 D4 Sankuru r. Zaire
130 B3 San Lázaro, C. c. Mexico
60 D2 Şanlıurfa Turkey
146 D3 San Lorenzo Arg.
140 C3 San Lorenzo Beni Bolivia
140 D4 San Lorenzo Tarija Bolivia
138 B3 San Lorenzo Ecuador
130 B2 San Lorenzo i. Mexico
127 F6 San Lorenzo Mexico
140 C2 San Lorenzo Peru
119 □3 San Lorenzo Puerto Rico
147 B6 San Lorenzo, C. mt. Arg./Chile
140 A2 San Lorenzo, I. i. Peru
24 C4 Sanlúcar de Barrameda Spain
140 C4 San Lucas Bolivia
130 B3 San Lucas Sur Mexico
130 C4 San Lucas Sur Mexico
130 C4 San Lucas, C. c. Mexico
146 C3 San Luis div. Arg.
146 C3 San Luis Arg.
130 H5 San Luis Guatemala
130 D3 San Luis Mexico
129 G5 San Luis U.S.A.
129 E5 San Luis U.S.A.
133 E5 San Luis Venezuela
131 E4 San Luis de la Paz Mexico
146 E2 San Luis del Palmar Arg.
130 B2 San Luisito Mexico
140 D2 San Luis, Lago de l. Bolivia
128 B4 San Luis Obispo U.S.A.
128 B4 San Luis Obispo Bay b. U.S.A.
131 E4 San Luis Potosí Mexico
131 E4 San Luis Potosí div. Mexico
128 B3 San Luis Reservoir resr U.S.A.
130 B1 San Luis Río Colorado Mexico
146 C3 San Luis, Sa de mt. ra. Arg.
27 B6 Sanluri Italy
24 C1 San Mamede, Serra do mt. ra. Spain
27 B6 San Marco, Capo pt Italy
27 D7 San Marco, Capo c. Italy
27 E5 San Marco dei Cavoti Italy
131 H6 San Marcos Guatemala
131 F5 San Marcos Mexico
125 D6 San Marcos U.S.A.
26 D4 San Marino San Marino
146 C3 San Martín Arg.
146 C2 San Martin Arg.
141 D2 San Martin r. Bolivia
138 C3 San Martín Colombia
147 B5 San Martín de los Andes Arg.
24 D2 San Martín de Valdeiglesias Spain
147 B6 San Martin, L. l. Arg./Chile
21 J5 San-Martino-di-Lota France
128 A3 San Mateo U.S.A.
141 E3 San Matías Bolivia
147 D5 San Matías, Golfo g. Arg.
138 D2 San Mauricio Venezuela
51 H2 Sanmen China
51 H2 Sanmen Wan b. China
51 E1 Sanmenxia China
140 D2 San Miguel r. Bolivia
141 D3 San Miguel Bolivia
138 B3 San Miguel r. Colombia
130 H6 San Miguel El Salvador
130 C2 San Miguel r. Mexico
130 L7 San Miguel Panama
140 B2 San Miguel Peru
129 G6 San Miguel U.S.A.
128 B4 San Miguel U.S.A.
129 H2 San Miguel r. U.S.A.
41 B3 San Miguel Bay b. Phil.
131 E4 San Miguel de Allende Mexico
140 C3 San Miguel de Huachi Bolivia
146 E4 San Miguel del Monte Arg.
146 C2 San Miguel de Tucumán Arg.
142 B3 San Miguel do Araguaia Brazil
130 L7 San Miguel, G. de b. Panama
128 B4 San Miguel I. i. U.S.A.
41 A5 San Miguel Is. is Phil.
140 C2 San Miguelito Bolivia
130 L7 San Miguelito Panama
131 F5 San Miguel Sola de Vega Mexico
51 G3 Sanming China
41 B3 San Narciso Phil.
54 A3 Sanni Pakistan
27 E5 Sannicandro Garganico Italy
146 D3 San Nicolas de los Arroyos Arg.
25 □ San Nicolás de Tolentino Canary Is Spain
128 C5 San Nicolas I. i. U.S.A.
28 C1 Sânnicolau Mare Romania
76 C5 Sanniquellie Liberia
47 H3 Sannohe Japan
19 L4 Sanok Poland
140 C4 San Pablo Potosí Bolivia
141 D3 San Pablo Santa Cruz Bolivia
131 F4 San Pablo Mexico
41 B3 San Pablo Phil.
146 E3 San Pedro Buenos Aires Arg.
146 D1 San Pedro Jujuy Arg.
146 F2 San Pedro Misiones Arg.
131 J5 San Pedro Belize
141 D3 San Pedro Bolivia
76 C6 San-Pédro Côte d'Ivoire
132 C2 San Pedro r. Cuba
130 C4 San Pedro Mexico
141 E4 San Pedro Paraguay
41 B3 San Pedro Phil.
129 G5 San Pedro r. U.S.A.
128 C5 San Pedro Channel U.S.A.
138 C3 San Pedro de Arimena Colombia
140 C4 San Pedro de Atacama Chile
139 E2 San Pedro de las Bocas Venezuela
130 E3 San Pedro de las Colonias Mexico
25 F4 San Pedro del Pinatar Spain
133 E3 San Pedro de Macoris Dominican Rep.
24 C3 San Pedro, Sierra de mt. ra. Spain
130 H6 San Pedro Sula Honduras
27 B6 San Pietro, Isola di i. Italy
60 G1 Sanqaçal Azerbaijan
17 F4 Sanquhar U.K.
138 B3 Sanquianga, Parque Nacional nat. park Colombia
130 B2 San Quintín Mexico
130 A2 San Quintín, C. c. Mexico
146 C3 San Rafael Arg.
141 D3 San Rafael Bolivia
128 A3 San Rafael U.S.A.
129 G2 San Rafael r. U.S.A.
138 C1 San Rafael Venezuela
129 G2 San Rafael Knob summit U.S.A.
128 C4 San Rafael Mts mts U.S.A.
140 D2 San Ramón Beni Bolivia
141 D3 San Ramón Santa Cruz Bolivia
26 A4 San Remo Italy
138 C1 San Román, C. c. Venezuela
146 E2 San Roque Arg.
24 D4 San Roque Andalucía Spain
24 B1 San Roque Galicia Spain
125 D6 San Saba U.S.A.
76 B4 Sansalé Guinea
146 E3 San Salvador Arg.
130 H6 San Salvador El Salvador
132 D1 San Salvador i. The Bahamas
146 C1 San Salvador de Jujuy Arg.
138 □ San Salvador, I. i. Galapagos Is Ecuador
76 C4 Sansanding Mali
77 E4 Sansanné-Mango Togo
54 D5 Sansar India
147 C7 San Sebastián Arg.
130 B2 San Sebastian i. Mexico
119 □3 San Sebastián Puerto Rico
25 E1 San Sebastián Guipúzcoa Spain
147 C7 San Sebastián, B. de b. Arg.
25 □ San Sebastián de la Gomera Canary Is Spain
24 E2 San Sebastián de los Reyes Spain
26 D4 Sansepolcro Italy
27 E5 San Severo Italy
51 H3 Sansha China
51 F4 Sanshui China
133 E5 San Silvestre Venezuela
26 F3 Sanski Most Bos.-Herz.
133 □5 Sans Toucher mt. Guadeloupe Caribbean
50 E3 Sansui China
43 D4 San, T. r. Cambodia
28 E1 Sânț Romania
140 A1 Santa r. Peru
140 A1 Santa Peru
144 D4 Santa Adélia Brazil
140 C2 Santa Ana Beni Bolivia
140 C3 Santa Ana La Paz Bolivia
138 A4 Santa Ana Ecuador
131 H6 Santa Ana El Salvador
130 C2 Santa Ana Mexico
128 D5 Santa Ana U.S.A.
133 F5 Santa Ana Venezuela
125 D6 Santa Anna U.S.A.
145 G3 Santa Bárbara Brazil
138 B2 Sta Bárbara Colombia
130 H6 Sta Bárbara Honduras
130 D3 Santa Bárbara Mexico
25 E4 Santa Bárbara mt. Spain
128 C4 Santa Barbara U.S.A.
133 G5 Sta Bárbara Venezuela
128 B4 Santa Barbara Channel chan. U.S.A.
128 C5 Santa Barbara I. i. U.S.A.
143 B5 Sta Bárbara, Sa de h. Brazil
146 C2 Sta Catalina Chile
132 D5 Sta Catalina Colombia
130 C3 Sta Catalina i. Mexico
130 K7 Sta Catalina Panama
24 B1 Santa Catalina de Armada Spain
128 D5 Santa Catalina, Gulf of b. U.S.A.
128 C5 Santa Catalina I. i. U.S.A.
143 B6 Santa Catarina div. Brazil
130 B2 Sta Catarina Mexico
131 E3 Sta Catarina Nuevo León Mexico
143 C6 Sta Catarina, Ilha de i. Brazil
132 □2 Sta Catharina Curaçao Netherlands Ant.
91 □15 Santa Clara i. Juan Fernandez Is Chile
138 D4 Santa Clara Colombia
132 C2 Sta Clara Cuba
130 D2 Sta Clara Mexico
128 B3 Santa Clara U.S.A.
129 F3 Santa Clara U.S.A.
24 B4 Santa Clara-a-Velha Portugal
146 F3 Santa Clara de Olimar Uruguay
128 C4 Santa Clarita U.S.A.
138 C4 Santa Clotilde Peru
25 H2 Sta Coloma de Farners Spain
27 E7 Sta Croce, Capo c. Italy
147 C7 Santa Cruz r. Arg.
147 B6 Santa Cruz div. Arg.
141 D3 Santa Cruz Bolivia
141 D3 Santa Cruz div. Bolivia
142 B1 Santa Cruz Pará Brazil
142 E2 Sta Cruz Rio Grande do Norte Brazil
142 A1 Santa Cruz r. Brazil
146 B3 Sta Cruz Chile
133 □1 Sta Cruz Jamaica
130 C2 Sta Cruz Mexico
41 B3 Santa Cruz Luzon Phil.
41 B2 Santa Cruz Luzon Phil.
41 A3 Sta Cruz Luzon Phil.
127 E5 Santa Cruz r. U.S.A.
128 A3 Santa Cruz U.S.A.
131 H6 Sta Cruz Barillas Guatemala
145 J2 Santa Cruz Cabrália Brazil
144 D2 Santa Cruz de Goiás Brazil
25 □ Sta Cruz de la Palma Canary Is Spain
131 H6 Sta Cruz del Quiché Guatemala
132 C2 Santa Cruz del Sur Cuba
25 F3 Santa Cruz de Moya Spain
24 E3 Santa Cruz de Mudela Spain
25 □ Sta Cruz de Tenerife Canary Is Spain
144 D5 Santa Cruz do Rio Pardo Brazil
143 B6 Santa Cruz do Sul Brazil
138 □ Santa Cruz, I. i. Galapagos Is Ecuador
128 C4 Santa Cruz I. i. U.S.A.
150 G6 Santa Cruz Is is Solomon Is.
133 □1 Sta Cruz Mts mts Jamaica
147 C7 Santa Cruz, Pto Arg.
146 E3 Sta Elena Arg.
138 A4 Santa Elena Ecuador
139 E3 Sta Elena Venezuela
138 A4 Sta Elena, B. de b. Ecuador
130 J7 Sta Elena, C. hd Costa Rica
27 F6 Sta Eufemia, Golfo di g. Italy
24 B1 Santa Eugenia Spain
25 G3 Sta Eulalia del Río Spain
146 D3 Santa Fé Arg.
127 F5 Santa Fe U.S.A.
145 F2 Santa Fé de Minas Brazil
144 C4 Santa Fé do Sul Brazil
138 □ Santa Fé, I. i. Galapagos Is Ecuador
27 E6 Sant'Agata di Militello Italy
130 C4 Sta Genovéva mt. Mexico
142 C1 Santa Helena Maranhão Brazil
144 A6 Santa Helena Paraná Brazil
144 C2 Santa Helena de Goiás Brazil
50 D2 Santai China
147 B7 Santa Inés, Isla i. Chile
146 C4 Santa Isabel La Pampa Arg.
141 D2 Sta Isabel Brazil
119 □3 Santa Isabel Puerto Rico
90 □1 Santa Isabel i. Solomon Is.
140 B3 Sta Isabel de Sihuas Peru
144 B5 Santa Isabel do Ivaí Brazil
144 E3 Santa Juliana Brazil
146 D2 Sta Justina Arg.
54 B5 Santalpur India
146 E2 Sta Lucia Arg.
140 B4 Sta Lucia Chile
138 B4 Sta Lucia Ecuador
131 H6 Sta Lucia Guatemala
25 □ Sta Lucía de Tirajana Canary Is Spain
127 B4 Santa Lucia Range mt. ra. U.S.A.
143 B4 Sta Luisa, Sa de h. Brazil
76 □ Santa Luzia i. Cape Verde
28 F1 Santa Mare Romania
130 C3 Sta Margarita i. Mexico
146 C2 Sta Maria Arg.
139 F4 Santa Maria Amazonas Brazil
142 B1 Santa Maria Pará Brazil
143 B6 Santa Maria Rio Grande do Sul Brazil
146 F3 Santa Maria r. Brazil
145 E1 Santa Maria r. Brazil
76 □ Santa Maria Cape Verde
127 F6 Sta María r. Mexico
130 D3 Sta María Mexico
138 C4 Santa María Peru
128 B4 Santa Maria U.S.A.
83 E4 Santa Maria, Cabo de pt Mozambique
24 C4 Santa Maria, Cabo de c. Portugal
142 E2 Santa Maria da Boa Vista Brazil
142 C2 Santa Maria das Barreiras Brazil
142 D3 Santa Maria da Vitória Brazil
139 D2 Sta María de Ipire Venezuela
131 E4 Sta María del Río Mexico
138 C4 Sta Maria de Nanay Peru
27 G6 Sta Maria di Leuca, Capo c. Italy
145 H2 Santa Maria do Salto Brazil
145 G3 Santa Maria do Suaçuí Brazil
146 B4 Santa María, I. i. Chile
138 □ Santa María, I. i. Galapagos Is Ecuador
90 □2 Santa Maria I. i. Vanuatu
145 G4 Santa Maria Madalena Brazil
132 D2 Sta Marie, Cape c. The Bahamas
138 C1 Santa Marta Colombia
79 B6 Santa Marta, Cabo de c. Angola
143 C6 Sta Marta Grande, C. de Brazil
128 C4 Santa Monica U.S.A.
128 C5 Santa Monica Bay b. U.S.A.
40 D2 Santan Indon.
144 C3 Santana r. Brazil
142 D3 Santana Brazil
143 B7 Santana da Boa Vista Brazil
142 E2 Santana do Ipanema Brazil
138 B3 Santander Colombia
24 E1 Santander Spain
129 G5 Santan Mt mt. U.S.A.
27 B6 Sant'Antioco Italy
27 B6 Sant' Antioco, Isola di i. Italy
25 H3 Santanyí Spain
128 C4 Santa Paula U.S.A.
25 F3 Sta Pola Spain
25 F3 Santa Pola, Cabo de pt Spain
142 D1 Santa Quitéria Brazil
142 B1 Santarém Brazil
24 B3 Santarém Portugal
24 B3 Santarém div. Portugal
132 C2 Santaren Channel chan. The Bahamas
141 E1 Santa Rita Mato Grosso Brazil
142 F2 Santa Rita Paraíba Brazil
138 C3 Santa Rita Colombia
41 □2 Santa Rita Guam Pac. Oc.
138 C1 Sta Rita Venezuela
142 D3 Santa Rita de Cassia Brazil
144 B2 Santa Rita do Araguaia Brazil
145 F5 Santa Rita do Sapucaí Brazil
128 B3 Santa Rita Park U.S.A.
146 D4 Santa Rosa La Pampa Arg.
147 C5 Santa Rosa Rio Negro Arg.
140 C2 Santa Rosa Beni Bolivia
140 C2 Santa Rosa Beni Bolivia
140 B1 Santa Rosa Acre Brazil
143 B6 Santa Rosa Rio Grande do Sul Brazil
138 B4 Sta Rosa Ecuador
131 H5 Sta Rosa Mexico
140 B2 Sta Rosa Peru
128 A2 Santa Rosa U.S.A.
127 F5 Santa Rosa U.S.A.
130 H6 Sta Rosa de Copán Honduras
141 D3 Sta Rosa de la Roca Bolivia
144 E4 Santa Rosa de Viterbo Brazil
128 B5 Santa Rosa I. i. U.S.A.
130 B3 Sta Rosalia Mexico
126 C3 Sta Rosa Ra. mt. ra. U.S.A.
129 G5 Santa Rosa Wash r. U.S.A.
146 D2 Santa Sylvina Arg.
98 C5 Santa Teresa Aust.
142 C3 Santa Teresa r. Brazil
145 H3 Santa Teresa Brazil
133 F5 Sta Teresa Venezuela
27 B5 Sta Teresa di Gallura Italy
24 D2 Sta Teresa, Embalse de resr Spain
146 C1 Sta Victoria, Sierra mt. ra. Arg.
144 C3 Santa Vitória Brazil
146 F3 Sta Vitória do Palmar Brazil
27 B6 Sta Vittoria, Monte mt. Italy
25 G2 Sant Carles de la Ràpita Spain
128 D5 Santee U.S.A.
119 E5 Santee r. U.S.A.
130 A2 San Telmo Mexico
130 E5 San Telmo, Pta pt Mexico
26 C3 Santerno r. Italy
25 H2 Sant Feliu de Guíxols Spain
143 B6 Santiago Brazil
146 B3 Santiago div. Chile
146 B3 Santiago Chile
133 E3 Santiago Dominican Rep.
130 C4 Santiago Sur Mexico
130 D3 Santiago Durango Mexico
130 K7 Santiago Panama
138 B4 Santiago r. Peru
41 B2 Santiago Phil.
24 B1 Santiago Spain
131 G5 Santiago Astata Mexico
147 A7 Santiago, C. hd Chile
130 K7 Santiago, Co mt. Panama
138 B5 Santiago de Cao Peru
140 A2 Santiago de Chocorvos Peru
140 A1 Santiago de Chuco Peru
132 D2 Santiago de Cuba Cuba
25 E3 Santiago de la Espada Spain
146 D2 Santiago del Estero div. Arg.
24 B3 Santiago do Cacém Portugal
130 D4 Santiago Ixcuintla Mexico
78 A3 Santiago, Pta pt Equatorial Guinea
141 E3 Santiago, Sa de h. Bolivia
130 D3 Santiaguillo, L. de l. Mexico
111 N2 Santianna Point pt Can.
40 E1 Santigi Indon.
25 G2 Sant Jordi, Golf de g. Spain
142 E3 Santo Amaro Brazil
145 H4 Santo Amaro de Campos Brazil
144 C4 Santo Anastácio r. Brazil
144 C4 Santo Anastácio Brazil
145 E5 Santo André Brazil
143 B6 Sto Angelo Brazil
76 □ Santo Antão i. Cape Verde
145 G3 Sto Antônio r. Brazil
142 E3 Sto Antônio, C. c. Brazil
144 C2 Santo Antônio da Barra Brazil
144 C5 Santo Antônio da Platina Brazil
142 E3 Sto Antônio de Jesus Brazil
143 A4 Sto Antônio de Leverger Brazil
145 G4 Santo Antônio de Pádua Brazil
138 D4 Santo Antônio do Içá Brazil
145 F4 Santo Antônio do Monte Brazil
145 J2 Santo Antônio, Pta pt Brazil
141 E3 Santo Corazón Bolivia
133 E3 Santo Domingo Dominican Rep.
131 H6 Santo Domingo Guatemala
130 B2 Sto Domingo Mexico
130 C3 Sto Domingo Sur Mexico
131 E4 Sto Domingo San Luis Potosí Mexico
130 J6 Sto Domingo Nicaragua
140 C2 Santo Domingo Peru
25 □ Sto Domingo Canary Is Spain
133 E5 Sto Domingo r. Venezuela
138 B4 Sto Domingo de los Colorados Ecuador
145 F3 Santo Hipólito Brazil
142 D3 Santo Inácio Bahia Brazil
144 C5 Santo Inácio Paraná Brazil
24 E1 Santoña Spain
142 D3 Sto Onofre r. Brazil
145 E5 Santos Brazil
145 G4 Santos Dumont Brazil
24 B2 Sto Tirso Portugal
130 A2 Sto Tomás Mexico
130 D2 Sto Tomás Chihuahua Mexico
130 J6 Sto Tomás Nicaragua
140 B2 Santo Tomás Peru
146 E2 Santo Tomé Corrientes Arg.
24 D2 Santovenia Spain
129 F3 Sanup Plateau plat. U.S.A.
147 B6 San Valentín, Co mt. Chile
130 H6 San Vicente El Salvador
130 A2 San Vicente Mexico
41 B2 San Vicente Phil.
140 A2 San Vicente de Cañete Peru
24 D1 San Vicente de la Barquera Spain
138 C3 San Vicente del Caguán Colombia
25 F3 San Vicente del Raspeig Spain
26 C4 San Vincenzo Italy
27 D6 San Vito, Capo c. Italy
27 F5 San Vito dei Normanni Italy
56 A1 Sanwer India
51 E5 Sanya China
83 D2 Sanyati r. Zimbabwe
51 E1 Sanyuan China
79 C5 Sanza Pombo Angola
79 □ São Antônio Sao Tome and Principe
145 H2 São Antônio do Jacinto Brazil
144 E2 São Bartolomeu r. Brazil
139 F5 São Benedito r. Brazil
142 D1 São Benedito Brazil
140 C1 São Bento Amazonas Brazil
142 D1 São Bento Maranhão Brazil
144 C6 São Bento do Amparo Brazil
142 D1 São Bernardo Brazil

143 C5 São Bernardo do Campo Brazil
143 A6 São Borja Brazil
143 B6 São Carlos *Santa Catarina* Brazil
144 E5 São Carlos *São Paulo* Brazil
142 D3 São Desidério Brazil
142 D3 São Desidério r. Brazil
144 C3 São Domingos r. *Goiás* Brazil
144 B3 São Domingos r. *Mato Grosso do Sul* Brazil
145 E1 São Domingos r. *Minas Gerais* Brazil
142 C3 São Domingos Brazil
142 B3 São Félix *Mato Grosso* Brazil
142 B2 São Félix *Pará* Brazil
145 H4 São Fidélis Brazil
76 □ São Filipe Cape Verde
144 A6 São Francisco r. *Paraná* Brazil
142 E2 São Francisco r. Brazil
145 F1 São Francisco Brazil
143 A6 São Francisco de Assis Brazil
144 D1 São Francisco de Goiás Brazil
144 D3 São Francisco de Sales Brazil
143 C6 São Francisco do Sul Brazil
143 C6 São Francisco, I. de i. Brazil
146 F3 São Gabriel Brazil
145 H3 São Gabriel da Palha Brazil
144 E1 São Gabriel de Goiás Brazil
145 G5 São Gonçalo Brazil
145 F3 São Gonçalo do Abaeté Brazil
142 E1 São Gonçalo do Amirante Brazil
145 F4 São Gonçalo do Sapucaí Brazil
145 E3 São Gotardo Brazil
142 B3 São João r. *Mato Grosso* Brazil
143 B5 São João r. *Paraná* Brazil
144 E1 São João da Aliança Brazil
145 H4 São João da Barra Brazil
145 E4 São João da Boa Vista Brazil
24 B2 São João da Madeira Portugal
145 F1 São João da Ponte Brazil
144 C4 São João das Duas Pontas Brazil
145 F4 São João del Rei Brazil
142 C2 São João do Araguaia Brazil
142 E2 São João do Cariri Brazil
145 G1 São João do Paraíso Brazil
142 D2 São João do Piauí Brazil
142 D2 São João dos Patos Brazil
145 G3 São João Evangelista Brazil
145 G4 São João Nepomuceno Brazil
142 C1 São Joaquim *Pará* Brazil
143 C6 São Joaquim *Santa Catarina* Brazil
144 E4 São Joaquim da Barra Brazil
144 B5 São Jorge do Ivaí Brazil
138 D4 São José *Amazonas* Brazil
143 C6 São José *Santa Catarina* Brazil
142 C3 São José r. Brazil
142 D1 São José, Baia de b. Brazil
142 E2 São José de Mipibu Brazil
143 D5 São José do Calçado Brazil
145 H3 São José do Divino Brazil
145 G3 São José do Jacurí Brazil
146 F3 São José do Norte Brazil
145 E4 São José do Rio Pardo Brazil
144 D4 São José do Rio Prêto Brazil
145 F5 São José dos Campos Brazil
144 C4 São José dos Dourados r. Brazil
144 D6 São José dos Pinhais Brazil
143 B6 São Leopoldo Brazil
145 F5 São Lourenço Brazil
141 F3 São Lourenço r. Brazil
144 A2 São Lourenço Brazil
146 F3 São Lourenço do Sul Brazil
142 D1 São Luís Brazil
144 C2 São Luis de Montes Belos Brazil
145 F5 São Luís do Paraitinga Brazil
143 B6 São Luís Gonzaga Brazil
142 D1 São Luís, Ilha de i. Brazil
144 D5 São Manuel Brazil
144 E2 São Marcos r. Brazil
142 D1 São Marcos, Baia de b. Brazil
145 H3 São Mateus r. Brazil
145 J3 São Mateus Brazil
145 E1 São Miguel r. Brazil
144 E5 São Miguel Arcanjo Brazil
144 A6 São Miguel do Iguaçu Brazil
142 E2 São Miguel dos Campos Brazil
142 D2 São Miguel do Tapuio Brazil
21 G3 Saône r. France
140 A3 Sã Nicolás, Bahía b. Peru
142 D2 São Nicolau r. Brazil
143 A6 São Nicolãu Brazil
76 □ São Nicolau i. Cape Verde
145 E5 São Paulo Brazil
144 D4 São Paulo div. Brazil
138 D4 São Paulo de Olivença Brazil
139 F4 São Pedro *Amazonas* Brazil
144 C3 São Pedro *Mato Grosso do Sul* Brazil
141 D1 São Pedro *Rondônia* Brazil
144 E5 São Pedro *São Paulo* Brazil
142 D2 São Pedro r. Brazil
145 G5 São Pedro da Aldeia Brazil
144 C5 São Pedro do Ivaí Brazil
24 B2 São Pedro do Sul Portugal
148 H5 São Pedro e São Paulo is Atlantic Ocean
142 C2 São Raimundo das Mangabeiras Brazil
142 D2 São Raimundo Nonato Brazil
145 F2 São Romão Brazil
144 E5 São Roque Brazil
142 E2 São Roque, C. de c. Brazil
145 E4 São Roque de Minas Brazil
142 B2 São Sebastião *Pará* Brazil
141 D1 São Sebastião *Rondônia* Brazil
145 F5 São Sebastião *São Paulo* Brazil
142 C1 São Sebastião da Boa Vista Brazil
145 E4 São Sebastião do Paraíso Brazil
145 F5 São Sebastião, Ilha do i. Brazil
143 B7 São Sepé Brazil
144 E4 São Simão Brazil
144 C3 São Simão Brazil
144 C3 São Simão, Barragem de resr Brazil
39 J6 Sao-Siu Indon.
145 F4 São Tiago Brazil
76 □ São Tiago i. Cape Verde
79 □ São Tomé i. Sao Tome and Principe
79 □ São Tomé Sao Tome and Principe
69 E5 Sao Tome and Principe country Africa
145 H4 São Tomé, Cabo de c. Brazil
143 C5 São Vicente Brazil
76 □ São Vicente i. Cape Verde
24 B4 São Vicente, Cabo de c. Portugal
60 B1 Sapanca Turkey
142 C3 Sapão r. Brazil
39 J7 Saparua Indon.
77 F5 Sapele Nigeria
29 E4 Sapes Greece
147 C5 Sa Pire Mahuida mt. ra. Arg.
25 H3 Sa Pobla Spain
76 C5 Sapo National Park nat. park Liberia
144 C5 Sapopema Brazil
19 L2 Sapotskina Belarus
14 E3 Sapozhok Rus. Fed.
46 H2 Sapporo Japan
27 E5 Sapri Italy
145 F4 Sapucaí r. *Minas Gerais* Brazil
144 E4 Sapucaí r. *São Paulo* Brazil
40 C3 Sapudi i. Indon.
125 D4 Sapulpa U.S.A.
40 C3 Sapulu Indon.
57 D2 Sāqī Iran
109 N2 Saqqaq Greenland
60 F2 Saqqez Iran
138 B4 Saquisilí Ecuador
60 F2 Sarāb Iran
61 B5 Sarābīt el Khâdim Egypt
43 C4 Sara Buri Thailand
25 F2 Saragossa *Zaragoza* Spain
138 B4 Saraguro Ecuador
14 E3 Sarai Rus. Fed.
54 C3 Sarai Sidhu Pakistan
26 G4 Sarajevo Bos.-Herz.
57 E1 Sarakhs Iran
29 E5 Sarakino i. Greece
64 E2 Saraktash Rus. Fed.
65 L2 Sarala Rus. Fed.
55 H4 Saramati mt. India
65 H3 Saran' Kazak.
121 G2 Saranac r. U.S.A.
121 F2 Saranac Lake U.S.A.
112 E5 Saranac Lake lakes U.S.A.
29 C5 Sarandë Albania
143 B6 Sarandi Brazil
146 E3 Sarandí del Yí Uruguay
146 E3 Sarandí Grande Uruguay
40 B2 Saran, G. mt. Indon.
41 C5 Sarangani i. Phil.
41 C5 Sarangani Bay b. Phil.
41 C5 Sarangani Islands is Phil.
41 C5 Sarangani Str. chan. Phil.
55 E5 Sarangarh India
54 D5 Sarangpur India
14 G2 Saransk Rus. Fed.
64 D1 Sarapul Rus. Fed.
119 D7 Sarasota U.S.A.
54 B5 Saraswati r. India
15 C3 Sarata Ukraine
15 C3 Sărăteni Vechi Moldova
126 F3 Saratoga U.S.A.
121 G3 Saratoga Springs U.S.A.
40 B1 Saratok Malaysia
14 G4 Saratov Rus. Fed.
14 H4 Saratov div. Rus. Fed.
64 C2 Saratovskoye Vdkhr. resr Rus. Fed.
57 E4 Saravan Iran
42 D4 Saravan Laos
43 B4 Sarawa r. Myanmar
40 B1 Sarawak div. Malaysia
60 A1 Saray Turkey
76 B4 Saraya Senegal
61 C2 Sarāyā Syria
60 B2 Sarayköy Turkey
60 C2 Sarayönü Turkey
57 E4 Sarbāz Iran
57 E4 Sarbāz r. Iran
55 G4 Sarbhang Bhutan
57 D2 Sarbisheh Iran
19 J5 Sárbogárd Hungary
26 C3 Sarca r. Italy
146 B2 Sarco Chile
54 E3 Sarda r. India/Nepal
54 C5 Sardarpur India
54 C3 Sardarshahr India
60 F2 Sar Dasht Iran
27 C5 Sardegna i. Italy
27 B5 Sardegna div. Italy
138 C2 Sardinata Colombia
80 C4 Sardindida Plain plain Kenya
57 B4 Sareb, Rās-as pt U.A.E.
40 D3 Sarege i. Indon.
10 E2 Sareks National Park nat. park Sweden
10 E2 Sarektjåkkå mt. Sweden
40 C2 Sarempaka, G. mt. Indon.
57 F1 Sar-e Pol Afghanistan
57 C3 Sare Yazd Iran
148 E4 Sargasso Sea sea Atlantic Ocean
65 H1 Sargatskoye Rus. Fed.
54 C2 Sargodha Pakistan
78 C2 Sarh Chad
57 E3 Sarhad reg. Iran
74 C2 Sarhro, Jbel mts Morocco
57 C1 Sārī Iran
29 F7 Saria i. Greece
57 F2 Sar-i-Bum Afghanistan
28 G2 Sarichioi Romania
39 M3 Sarigan i. *Northern Mariana Is* Pac. Oc.
60 B2 Sarıgöl Turkey
60 E1 Sarıkamış Turkey
60 C2 Sarıkaya Turkey
29 F6 Sarıkemer Turkey
29 F4 Sarıköy Turkey
43 □ Sarimbun Res. resr Singapore
99 G4 Sarina Aust.
25 F2 Sariñena Spain
57 F2 Sar-i-Pul Afghanistan
57 C1 Sāri Qamīsh Iran
72 C3 Sarīr Tibesti desert Libya
72 D2 Sarir Water Wells' Field well Libya
49 H5 Sariwŏn N. Korea
60 B1 Sarıyer Turkey
55 E4 Sarju r. India
17 F7 Sark i. Channel Islands
65 K3 Sarkand Kazak.
54 B4 Sarkāri Tala India
60 B2 Şarkikaraağaç Turkey
60 D2 Şarkişla Turkey
60 A1 Şarköy Turkey
57 F3 Sarlath Ra. mt. ra. Afghanistan/Pakistan
20 E4 Sarlat-la-Canéda France
14 F2 Sarma r. Rus. Fed.
28 E1 Sărmaşu Romania
39 L7 Sarmi Indon.
147 C6 Sarmiento Arg.
11 D3 Särna Sweden
21 J3 Sarnen Switz.
114 D5 Sarnia Can.
27 E5 Sarno Italy
15 B1 Sarny Ukraine
38 D7 Sarolangun Indon.
46 J1 Saroma-ko l. Japan
29 D6 Saronikos Kolpos g. Greece
29 F4 Saros Körfezi b. Turkey
19 K4 Sárospatak Hungary
54 C4 Sarotra India
14 F2 Sarova Rus. Fed.
57 G2 Sarowbī Afghanistan
13 H6 Sarpa, Oz. l. *Kalmykiya* Rus. Fed.
13 H5 Sarpa, Ozero l. *Volgograd* Rus. Fed.
41 □1 Šar Passage chan. Palau
28 C4 Šar Planina mt. ra. Macedonia/Yugo.
11 C4 Sarpsborg Norway
21 H2 Sarrebourg France
21 H2 Sarreguemines France
24 C1 Sarria Spain
21 G2 Sarry France
21 J6 Sartène France
20 D3 Sarthe r. France
57 B2 Sarud r. Iran
46 J2 Saru-gawa r. Japan
29 F5 Saruhanlı Turkey
46 D6 Sarumasa-yama mt. Japan
54 A4 Saruna Pakistan
60 F2 Şărur Azerbaijan
61 D2 Sarūt r. Syria
19 H5 Sárvár Hungary
57 C3 Sarvestān Iran
54 C4 Sarwar India
65 G4 Saryagach Kazak.
64 F3 Sarybasat Kazak.
65 J3 Sary-Ishikotrau, Peski desert Kazak.
64 D3 Sarykamys Kazak.
64 E4 Sarykamyshkoye Ozero salt l. Turkmenistan
65 H2 Sarykiyak Kazak.
65 H5 Sarykol Range mt. ra. China/Tajikistan
65 H3 Sarykomey Kazak.
65 J4 Saryozek Kazak.
65 H3 Saryshagan Kazak.
65 G3 Sarysu r. Kazak.
65 H5 Sary Tash Kyrgyzstan
57 E1 Sary Yazïkskoye Vdkhr. resr Turkmenistan
26 B3 Sarzana Italy
20 C3 Sarzeau France
129 G6 Sasabe U.S.A.
55 F4 Sasaram India
40 E4 Sasar, Tg pt Indon.
15 E1 Saschnivka Ukraine
46 B7 Sasebo Japan
15 E2 Sasivka Ukraine
111 J4 Saskatchewan r. Can.
108 H4 Saskatchewan div. Can.
111 H4 Saskatoon Can.
63 N2 Saskylakh Rus. Fed.
130 J6 Saslaya mt. Nicaragua
14 E2 Sasovo Rus. Fed.
121 F5 Sassafras U.S.A.
76 C6 Sassandra Côte d'Ivoire
76 C5 Sassandra r. Côte d'Ivoire
27 B5 Sassari Italy
19 F1 Sassnitz Germany
26 D4 Sassocorvaro Italy
26 D4 Sassoferrato Italy
76 C6 Sass Town Liberia
26 C3 Sassuolo Italy
65 K3 Saskyyol', Oz. l. Kazak.
13 H6 Saskyoli Rus. Fed.
76 B4 Satadougou Mali
46 C8 Sata-misaki c. Japan
54 C5 Satana India
15 B2 Sataniv Ukraine
91 □12 Satapuala Western Samoa
56 A2 Satara India
91 □12 Satauа Western Samoa
40 D3 Satengar i. Indon.
14 E3 Satinka Rus. Fed.
140 B2 Satipo Peru
14 F2 Satis r. Rus. Fed.
14 F2 Satis Rus. Fed.
64 E1 Satka Rus. Fed.
55 G5 Satkhira Bangladesh
56 B2 Satmala Range h. India
54 E4 Satna India
19 K4 Sátoraljaújhely Hungary
65 G3 Satpayev Kazak.
54 C5 Satpura Range mt. ra. India
46 C8 Satsuma-hantō pen. Japan
46 J2 Satsunai-gawa r. Japan
47 G5 Satte Japan
54 D2 Satti *Jammu and Kashmir*
28 D1 Satu Mare Romania
43 C6 Satun Thailand
91 □12 Satupaitea Western Samoa
146 E3 Sauce Arg.
138 B5 Sauce Peru
125 C7 Sauceda Mexico
129 F5 Sauceda Mts mts U.S.A.
130 D2 Saucillo Mexico
11 B4 Sauda Norway
10 M2 Sauðárkrókur Iceland
32 F7 Saudi Arabia country Asia
141 E2 Sauêruiná r. Brazil
122 D4 Saugatuck U.S.A.
121 G3 Saugerties U.S.A.
21 F4 Saugues France
146 C2 Saujil Arg.
20 D4 Saujon France
124 E2 Sauk Center U.S.A.
122 C4 Sauk City U.S.A.
139 G3 Saul French Guiana
18 D4 Saulgau Germany
21 G3 Saulieu France
114 C3 Sault Ste Marie Can.
122 E2 Sault Ste Marie U.S.A.
99 H4 Saumarez Reef reef *Coral Sea Islands Terr.* Pac. Oc.
39 K8 Saumlakki Indon.
20 D3 Saumur France
93 C6 Saunders, Cape c. N.Z.
152 A4 Saunders Coast Ant.
152 C1 Saunders I. i. *S. Sandwich Is* Atlantic Ocean
98 B2 Saunders, Mt h. Aust.
43 B5 Saung Thailand
42 B1 Saungka Myanmar
64 D4 Saura Rus. Fed.
79 D5 Saurimo Angola
40 E2 Sausu Indon.
79 C6 Sautar Angola
133 □8 Sauters *Grenada* Caribbean
26 G3 Sava r. Europe
130 J6 Sava Honduras
91 □12 Savaii i. Western Samoa
14 E4 Savala r. Rus. Fed.
77 E5 Savalou Benin
122 B4 Savanna U.S.A.
119 D6 Savannah U.S.A.
119 D5 Savannah r. U.S.A.
119 B5 Savannah U.S.A.
119 E7 Savannah Sound The Bahamas
42 D3 Savannakhét Laos
133 □1 Savanna la Mar Jamaica
112 B3 Savant Lake Can.
56 A3 Savanur India
11 D3 Sävar Sweden
60 A2 Savaştepe Turkey
77 E5 Savè Benin
83 E3 Save r. Mozambique
57 B2 Sāveh Iran
76 D5 Savelugu Ghana
20 D3 Savenay France
28 F1 Săveni Romania
21 H2 Saverne France
10 H3 Saviaho Finland
28 F1 Săvineşti Romania
14 E1 Savino Rus. Fed.
12 G2 Savinskiy Rus. Fed.
28 B3 Šavnik Yugo.
26 B3 Savona Italy
11 H3 Savonranta Finland
15 D2 Savran' Ukraine
15 C2 Savranka r. Ukraine
11 D4 Sävsjö Sweden
39 H8 Savu i. Indon.
10 H2 Savukoski Finland
60 E2 Savur Turkey
90 □6 Savusavu Fiji
90 □6 Savusavu B. b. Fiji
82 C2 Savuti Botswana
49 F2 Savvo-Borzya Rus. Fed.
15 E1 Savynky Ukraine
15 G2 Savyntsi Ukraine
42 A2 Saw Myanmar
54 D4 Sawai Madhopur India
90 □8 Sawaleke Fiji
40 C2 Sawan Indon.
42 B3 Sawankhalok Thailand
47 G5 Sawasaki-bana pt Japan
47 G5 Sawata Japan
127 F4 Sawatch Mts mt. ra. U.S.A.
72 B2 Sawdā', Jabal as h. Libya
19 L3 Sawin Poland
122 B2 Sawtooth Mountains h. U.S.A.
39 H8 Sawu Sea g. Indon.
115 K4 Sawyerville Can.
99 E3 Saxby r. Aust.
10 D2 Saxnäs Sweden
18 F3 Saxony div. Germany
77 E4 Say Niger
65 J3 Sayak Kazak.
77 G4 Sayam well Niger
140 A2 Sayán Peru
65 M2 Sayanogorsk Rus. Fed.
64 F5 Sayat Turkmenistan
131 H5 Sayaxché Guatemala
73 H4 Şayḩ well Yemen
58 H6 Şayḩūt Yemen
13 H5 Saykhin Kazak.
80 D2 Sāylac Somalia
48 D3 Saynshand Mongolia
65 K4 Sayram Hu salt l. China
125 D5 Sayre U.S.A.
120 E4 Sayre U.S.A.
130 E5 Sayula *Jalisco* Mexico
131 G5 Sayula *Veracruz* Mexico
64 D4 Say-Utes Kazak.
29 B4 Sazan i. Albania
15 G1 Sazhnoye Rus. Fed.
54 C2 Sazin Pakistan
12 G2 Sazonovo Rus. Fed.
75 D3 Sbaa Algeria
75 F1 Sbeitla Tunisia
101 C7 Scaddan Aust.
17 F4 Scafell Pike mt. U.K.
27 E6 Scalea Italy
16 G1 Scalloway U.K.
26 C4 Scansano Italy
28 F2 Scânteia Romania
16 F2 Scapa Flow inlet U.K.
115 F5 Scarborough Can.
133 □2 Scarborough *Tobago* Trin. & Tobago
17 G4 Scarborough U.K.
41 A3 Scarborough Shoal sand bank Phil.
93 D5 Scargill N.Z.
43 D6 Scawfell Shoal sand bank S. China Sea
26 F4 Šćedro i. Croatia
21 J3 Schaffhausen Switz.
18 B2 Schagen Netherlands
57 E3 Schao w Afghanistan
18 E1 Scharbeutz Germany
18 F4 Schärding Austria
18 D2 Scharhörn sand bank Germany
113 G3 Schefferville Can.
19 G4 Scheibbs Austria
18 B3 Schelde r. Belgium
129 E2 Schell Creek Range mt. ra. U.S.A.
121 G3 Schenectady U.S.A.
18 D2 Schenefeld *Niedersachsen* Germany
18 D5 Schesaplana mt. Austria/Swit.
18 F4 Schierling Germany
18 C2 Schiermonnikoog i. Netherlands
29 D5 Schimatari Greece
26 C3 Schio Italy
28 F1 Schitu Duca Romania
18 C3 Schleiden Germany
18 E1 Schleswig Germany
18 D1 Schleswig-Holstein div. Germany
18 D3 Schlüchtern Germany
18 D2 Schneverdingen Germany
121 G3 Schodack Center U.S.A.
133 □4 Schoelcher *Martinique* Caribbean
122 C3 Schofield U.S.A.
127 □1 Schofield Barracks U.S.A.
18 E2 Schönebeck *Sachsen-Anhalt* Germany
18 E2 Schöningen Germany
121 J2 Schoodic Lake l. U.S.A.
122 E4 Schoolcraft U.S.A.
97 G5 Schouten I. i. Aust.
90 □1 Schouten Islands is P.N.G.
114 B2 Schreiber Can.
19 G4 Schrems Austria
18 E4 Schrobenhausen Germany
121 G3 Schroon Lake l. U.S.A.
129 F5 Schuchuli U.S.A.
17 C6 Schull Rep. of Ire.
111 K2 Schultz Lake l. Can.
128 C2 Schurz U.S.A.
121 G3 Schuylerville U.S.A.
18 E4 Schwabach Germany
18 D4 Schwäbische Alb mts Germany
18 D4 Schwäbisch Gmünd Germany
18 D4 Schwäbisch Hall Germany
18 D4 Schwabmünchen Germany
21 J3 Schwanden Switz.
18 F4 Schwandorf Germany
18 E5 Schwangau Germany
18 E2 Schwarzenbek Germany
18 F3 Schwarzenberg Germany
82 B4 Schwarzrand mts Namibia
18 D4 Schwarzwald mts Germany
18 E5 Schwaz Austria
19 G2 Schwedt Germany
18 E3 Schweinfurt Germany
18 D4 Schwenningen Germany
18 E2 Schwerin Germany
18 E2 Schweriner See l. Germany
21 J3 Schwyz Switz.
27 D7 Sciacca Italy
27 E7 Scicli Italy
17 D7 Scilly, Isles of is U.K.
120 B5 Scioto r. U.S.A.
129 F2 Scipio U.S.A.
126 F1 Scobey U.S.A.
97 G3 Scone Aust.
109 Q2 Scoresby Land reg. Greenland
109 Q2 Scoresby Sund chan. Greenland
28 E2 Scorniceşti Romania
152 B1 Scotia Ridge Atlantic Ocean
148 G9 Scotia Sea sea Atlantic Ocean
114 E5 Scotland Can.
16 E3 Scotland div. U.K.
115 K3 Scotstown Can.
115 K4 Scott Can.
152 B5 Scott Base N.Z. Base Ant.
83 E5 Scottburgh R.S.A.
98 B2 Scott, C. c. Aust.
110 D4 Scott, C. c. Can.
124 C4 Scott City U.S.A.
152 B5 Scott Coast Ant.
120 D4 Scottdale U.S.A.
152 B4 Scott Gl. gl. Ant.
109 L2 Scott Inlet inlet Can.
152 A5 Scott Island i. Ant.
111 H3 Scott Lake l. Can.
152 D4 Scott Mts mt. ra. Ant.
92 D1 Scott Pt pt N.Z.
100 C2 Scott Reef reef Aust.
124 C3 Scottsbluff U.S.A.
119 C5 Scottsboro U.S.A.
118 C4 Scottsburg U.S.A.
97 F5 Scottsdale Aust.
127 E5 Scottsdale U.S.A.
128 A3 Scotts Valley U.S.A.
122 D4 Scottville U.S.A.
128 D3 Scotty's Junction U.S.A.
16 E2 Scourie U.K.
121 F4 Scranton U.S.A.
17 G5 Scunthorpe U.K.
21 K3 Scuol Switz.
101 B6 Seabrook, L. salt flat Aust.
121 F5 Seaford U.S.A.
99 G4 Seaforth Aust.
114 E5 Seaforth Can.
133 □1 Seaforth Jamaica
41 A4 Seahorse Bank sand bank Phil.
111 K3 Seal r. Can.
97 E3 Sea Lake Aust.
82 A5 Seal Bay b. *Tristan da Cunha* Atlantic Ocean
82 C5 Seal, Cape c. R.S.A.
133 E2 Seal Cays is *Turks and Caicos Is* Caribbean
121 J3 Seal I. i. U.S.A.
113 H3 Seal Lake l. Can.
129 E3 Seaman Range mts U.S.A.
129 E4 Searchlight U.S.A.
125 F5 Searcy U.S.A.
128 D4 Searles Lake l. U.S.A.
122 E4 Sears U.S.A.
121 J2 Searsport U.S.A.
128 B3 Seaside U.S.A.
126 B2 Seaside U.S.A.
126 B2 Seattle U.S.A.
99 F3 Seaview Ra. mt. ra. Aust.
121 F5 Seaville U.S.A.
93 D5 Seaward Kaikoura Ra. mt. ra. N.Z.
121 H3 Sebago Lake l. U.S.A.
40 D2 Sebakung Indon.
40 C2 Sebangan, Tk b. Indon.
40 A1 Sebangka i. Indon.
130 B2 Sebastián Vizcaíno, B b. Mexico
121 J2 Sebasticook r. U.S.A.
41 A5 Sebatik i. Indon.
77 E4 Sebba Burkina
75 D2 Sebdou Algeria
76 C4 Sébékoro Mali
28 D2 Sebeş Romania
40 A3 Sebesi i. Indon.
123 F4 Sebewaing U.S.A.
12 D3 Sebezh Rus. Fed.
82 D3 Sebina Botswana
60 D1 Şebin Karahisar Turkey
28 D1 Sebiş Romania
75 E3 Sebkha Azzel Matti salt pan Algeria
74 B4 Sebkhet Chemchâm salt l. Mauritania
75 G1 Sebkhet de Sidi El Hani salt pan Tunisia
74 B3 Sebkhet Oum ed Droûs Telli salt flat Mauritania
74 B4 Sebkhet Oum ed Droûs Guebli salt l. Mauritania
74 A5 Sebkhet Te-n-Dghâmcha salt marsh Mauritania
121 J2 Seboeis Lake l. U.S.A.
121 J2 Seboomook U.S.A.
121 J2 Seboomook Lake l. U.S.A.
119 D7 Sebring U.S.A.
40 D2 Sebuku i. Indon.
40 B1 Sebuyau Malaysia
80 C3 Seccia Mts mts Ethiopia
14 G2 Sechenovo Rus. Fed.
138 A5 Sechura Peru
138 A5 Sechura, Bahía de b. Peru
73 F3 2nd Cataract rapids Sudan
121 H2 Second Lake l. U.S.A.
99 E2 2nd Three Mile Opening chan. Aust.
114 C5 Secord Lake l. U.S.A.
93 A6 Secretary Island i. N.Z.
56 B2 Secunderabad India
140 C3 Sécure r. Bolivia
124 E4 Sedalia U.S.A.
56 B2 Sedam India
96 D3 Sedan Aust.
21 G2 Sedan France
93 E4 Seddon N.Z.
93 C4 Seddonville N.Z.
60 A1 Seddülbahir Turkey
61 C4 Sede Boqer Israel
57 D2 Sedeh Iran
61 C4 Sederot Israel
121 J2 Sedgwick U.S.A.
76 A4 Sédhiou Senegal
19 G4 Sedlčany Czech Rep.
15 A1 Sedlyshche Ukraine
15 D1 Sedniv Ukraine
61 C4 Sedom Israel
129 G4 Sedona U.S.A.
27 A7 Sédrata Algeria
40 D1 Sedulang Indon.
11 F5 Šeduva Lithuania
19 G2 Seebad Heringsdorf Germany
18 E2 Seehausen Germany
82 B4 Seeheim Namibia
18 D4 Seeheim-Jugenheim Germany
129 E5 Seeley U.S.A.
152 B3 Seelig, Mt mt. Ant.
19 G2 Seelow Germany
20 E2 Sées France
18 E3 Seesen Germany
18 E2 Seevetal Germany
76 B5 Sefadu Sierra Leone
29 F5 Seferihisar Turkey
57 B2 Sefīd Dasht Iran
83 D3 Sefophe Botswana
74 D2 Sefrou Morocco
76 B4 Ségala Mali
11 C3 Segalstad Norway
41 A5 Segama r. Malaysia
43 C7 Segamat Malaysia
24 E5 Segangane Morocco
28 D2 Şegarcea Romania
77 E4 Ségbana Benin
40 D3 Segeri Indon.
12 E2 Segezha Rus. Fed.
57 G1 Seghnān Afghanistan
25 F3 Segorbe Spain
76 C4 Ségou Mali
76 C4 Ségou div. Mali
138 C2 Segovia Colombia
24 D2 Segovia Spain
12 E2 Segozerskoye, Oz. l. Rus. Fed.
20 D3 Segré France
77 G2 Séguédine Niger
76 C5 Séguéla Côte d'Ivoire
76 C5 Séguélon Côte d'Ivoire
125 D6 Seguin U.S.A.
146 D3 Segundo r. Arg.
25 E3 Segura r. Spain
25 E4 Segura, Sierra de mt. ra. Spain
82 C3 Sehithwa Botswana
54 D5 Sehore India
54 A4 Sehwan Pakistan
42 A2 Seikpyu Myanmar
10 F1 Seiland i. Norway
125 D4 Seiling U.S.A.
10 F3 Seinäjoki Finland
112 B4 Seine r. Can.
21 G3 Seine r. France
20 D2 Seine, Baie de b. France
20 F2 Seine, Val de v. France
28 D1 Seini Romania
40 C2 Seipinang Indon.
19 L1 Sejny Poland
40 B1 Sekadau Indon.
40 A2 Sekanak, Tk b. Indon.
41 A6 Sekatak Bengara Indon.
40 A2 Sekayu Indon.
47 F6 Seki Japan
76 D6 Sekondi Ghana
14 G3 Sekretarka Rus. Fed.
57 E3 Sekūheh Iran
40 B1 Sekura Indon.
80 C3 Sela Dingay Ethiopia
126 B2 Selah U.S.A.
40 B1 Selakau Indon.
43 C7 Selangor div. Malaysia
39 K8 Selaru i. Indon.
40 D3 Selat Alas chan. Indon.
40 C3 Selatan, Tg pt Indon.
40 C4 Selat Bali chan. Indon.
40 A2 Selat Bangka chan. Indon.
40 A2 Selat Berhala chan. Indon.
39 K7 Selat Dampir chan. Indon.
40 A2 Selat Gaspar chan. Indon.
43 □ Selat Johor chan. Malaysia/Singapore
43 □ Selat Jurong chan. Singapore
40 B2 Selat Karimata str. Indon.
40 C2 Selat Laut chan. Indon.
40 C4 Selat Lombok chan. Indon.
40 C3 Selat Madura chan. Indon.
43 □ Selat Pandan chan. Singapore
40 E3 Selat Salayar chan. Indon.
40 D4 Selat Sape chan. Indon.
40 D4 Selat Sumba chan. Indon.
40 A3 Selat Sunda chan. Indon.
39 L7 Selat Yapen chan. Indon.
108 B3 Selawik U.S.A.
10 C3 Selbekken Norway
10 C3 Selbu Norway
17 G5 Selby U.K.
124 C2 Selby U.S.A.
29 F6 Selçuk Turkey
27 E5 Sele r. Italy
82 D3 Selebi-Phikwe Botswana
29 C4 Selečka Planina mt. ra. Macedonia
29 G5 Selendi Turkey
48 C2 Selenduma Rus. Fed.
48 C1 Seleng r. Rus. Fed.
48 B2 Selenge Mongolia
48 C2 Selenge div. Mongolia
78 C4 Selenge Zaire
48 C2 Selenge Mörön r. Mongolia
48 C2 Selenginsk Rus. Fed.
29 B4 Selenicë Albania
21 H2 Sélestat France
43 □ Seletar Singapore
43 □ Seletar, P. i. Singapore
43 □ Seletar Res. resr Singapore
65 H2 Seletinskoye Kazak.
65 H2 Selety r. Kazak.
65 H2 Seletyteniz, Oz. salt l. Kazak.
124 C2 Selfridge U.S.A.
12 J2 Selib Rus. Fed.
74 B5 Sélibabi Mauritania
14 B3 Selichnya Rus. Fed.
14 A1 Seliger, Oz. l. Rus. Fed.
129 F4 Seligman U.S.A.
73 E3 Selîma Oasis oasis Sudan
40 C1 Selimbau Indon.
61 A1 Selimiye *Antalya* Turkey
29 F6 Selimiye *Muğla* Turkey
76 C4 Sélingué, Lac de l. Mali
123 J5 Selinsgrove U.S.A.
14 A1 Selishche Rus. Fed.
14 F2 Selishchi Rus. Fed.
13 H6 Selitrennoye Rus. Fed.
14 A1 Selizharovo Rus. Fed.
11 C4 Seljord Norway
111 K4 Selkirk Can.
110 F4 Selkirk Mountains mt. ra. Can.
129 G6 Sells U.S.A.
119 C5 Selma U.S.A.
128 C3 Selma U.S.A.
119 B5 Selmer U.S.A.
40 D4 Selong Indon.
21 G3 Selongey France
76 B4 Sélouma Guinea
81 C6 Selous Game Reserve res. Tanzania
57 E3 Selseleh-ye Pīr Shūrān mt. ra. Iran
17 G6 Selsey Bill hd U.K.
14 B3 Sel'tso *Bryansk* Rus. Fed.
14 B3 Sel'tso *Bryansk* Rus. Fed.
144 C4 Selvíria Brazil
111 J3 Selwyn Lake l. Can.
110 C2 Selwyn Mountains mt. ra. Can.
98 D4 Selwyn Range h. Aust.
15 A3 Selyatyn Ukraine
15 G2 Selydove Ukraine
29 B4 Seman r. Albania
40 A3 Semangka, Tk b. Indon.
40 B3 Semarang Indon.
40 B1 Sematan Malaysia
40 C2 Semayang, D. l. Indon.
41 A6 Sembakung r. Indon.
43 □ Sembawang Singapore
78 B3 Sembé Congo
40 C4 Semenanjung Blambangan pen. Indon.
79 C4 Semendua Zaire
14 D1 Semendyayevo Rus. Fed.
13 E4 Semenivka *Chernihiv* Ukraine
15 E2 Semenivka *Poltava* Ukraine
14 G1 Semenov Rus. Fed.
14 D1 Semibratovo Rus. Fed.
12 G3 Semigorodnyaya Rus. Fed.
14 G3 Semiley Rus. Fed.
14 F2 Semilovo Rus. Fed.
14 D4 Semiluki Rus. Fed.
126 F3 Seminoe Res. resr U.S.A.
125 C5 Seminole U.S.A.
119 C6 Seminole, L. l. U.S.A.
65 L2 Seminskiy Khrebet mt. ra. Rus. Fed.
14 E2 Semion Rus. Fed.
64 F2 Semiozernoye Kazak.
48 D2 Semiozer'ye Rus. Fed.
65 K2 Semipalatinsk Kazak.
65 J3 Semipalatinsk div. Kazak.
41 B3 Semirara i. Phil.
41 B3 Semirara Islands is Phil.
57 B3 Semīrom Iran
40 B1 Semitau Indon.
65 J2 Semiyarka Kazak.
65 H2 Semiz-Bugu Kazak.
57 C2 Semnān div. Iran
57 C2 Semnān Iran
48 B5 Sêmnyi China
18 B4 Semois r. Belgium
41 A5 Semporna Malaysia
40 C4 Sempu i. Indon.
142 B1 Sem Tripa Brazil
14 A3 Semtsy Rus. Fed.
21 G3 Semur-en-Auxois France
12 H1 Semzha Rus. Fed.
140 C2 Sena Bolivia
144 D2 Senador Canedo Brazil
142 E2 Senador Pompeu Brazil
41 A5 Senaja Malaysia
140 C1 Sena Madureira Brazil
56 C5 Senanayake Samudra l. Sri Lanka
79 D7 Senanga Zambia
40 B1 Senaning Indon.
21 G5 Sénas France
15 E1 Sencha Ukraine
47 H4 Sendai Japan
46 C8 Sendai Japan
46 C8 Sendai-gawa r. Japan
18 E4 Senden Germany
50 A2 Sêndo China
43 C7 Senebui, Tanjung pt Indon.
129 G5 Seneca U.S.A.
122 C5 Seneca U.S.A.
126 C2 Seneca U.S.A.
120 E3 Seneca Falls U.S.A.
120 E3 Seneca Lake l. U.S.A.
120 D5 Seneca Rocks U.S.A.
120 C5 Senecaville Lake l. U.S.A.
68 C4 Senegal country Africa
76 B3 Sénégal r. Mauritania/Senegal
122 E2 Seney U.S.A.
19 G3 Senftenberg Germany
81 B6 Senga Hill Zambia
54 D4 Sengar r. India
40 D1 Sengata Indon.
81 B5 Sengerema Tanzania
12 J4 Sengiley Rus. Fed.
64 D4 Sengiri, Mys pt Kazak.
147 B6 Senguerr r. Arg.
83 D2 Sengwa r. Zimbabwe
142 D3 Senhor do Bonfim Brazil
19 H4 Senica Slovakia
26 D4 Senigallia Italy
26 E3 Senj Croatia
10 E1 Senja i. Norway
76 C5 Senko Guinea
15 G2 Sen'kove Ukraine
54 D2 Senku India
20 F2 Senlis France
43 D4 Senmonorom Cambodia
47 E6 Sennan Japan
73 F5 Sennar Sudan
73 F5 Sennar Dam dam Sudan
115 G2 Senneterre Can.
14 H3 Sennoy Rus. Fed.
147 B7 Seno Otway b. Chile
83 D5 Senqu r. Lesotho
21 F2 Sens France
130 H6 Sensuntepeque El Salvador
28 C2 Senta Yugo.
129 F5 Sentinel U.S.A.
110 E3 Sentinel Pk summit Can.
152 B3 Sentinel Ra. mt. ra. Ant.
43 □ Sentosa i. Singapore
40 D1 Senyiur Indon.
60 E2 Şenyurt Turkey
46 C6 Senzaki Japan
46 D7 Sen-zaki pt Japan
54 D5 Seoni India
55 E5 Seorinarayan India
40 C3 Sepanjang i. Indon.
92 D4 Separation Pt pt N.Z.
40 D1 Sepasu Indon.
40 B1 Sepauk Indon.
143 D5 Sepetiba, Baía de b. Brazil
57 B3 Sepidān Iran
90 □1 Sepik r. P.N.G.
40 D1 Sepinang Indon.
27 E5 Sepino Italy
19 H2 Sępólno Krajeńskie Poland
141 E3 Sepotuba r. Brazil
113 G3 Sept-Îles Can.
20 C2 Sept-Îles, Les is France
40 A3 Seputih r. Indon.
128 C3 Sequoia National Park nat. park U.S.A.
13 G5 Serafimovich Rus. Fed.
57 E1 Serakhs Turkmenistan
39 J7 Seram i. Indon.
39 J7 Seram Sea g. Indon.
40 A3 Serang Indon.
43 □ Serangoon Harbour chan. Singapore
43 □ Serangoon, P. i. Singapore
43 E7 Serasan i. Indon.
43 E7 Seraya i. Indon.
43 □ Seraya, P. i. Singapore
61 B5 Serbāl, G. mt. Egypt
130 D2 Serdán Mexico
80 D2 Serdo Ethiopia
14 G3 Serdoba r. Rus. Fed.
14 G3 Serdobsk Rus. Fed.
65 K3 Serebryansk Kazak.
14 D2 Serebryanyye Prudy Rus. Fed.
19 H4 Sered' Slovakia
14 E1 Sereda Rus. Fed.
14 B2 Seredeyskiy Rus. Fed.
11 H4 Seredka Rus. Fed.
14 D2 Serednikovo Rus. Fed.
19 L4 Serednye Ukraine
14 B3 Seredyna-Buda Ukraine
60 C2 Şereflikoçhisar Turkey
21 F3 Serein r. France
43 C7 Seremban Malaysia
24 D3 Serena, Embalse de la resr Spain
81 B5 Serengeti National Park nat. park Tanzania
81 C5 Serengeti Plains plain Kenya
81 B7 Serenje Zambia
142 C2 Sereno r. Brazil
80 B4 Serere Uganda
15 A2 Seret r. Ukraine
14 F2 Serezha r. Rus. Fed.
14 G2 Sergach Rus. Fed.
48 D3 Sergelen Mongolia
48 E2 Sergelen Mongolia
65 G2 Sergeyevka Kazak.
142 E3 Sergipe div. Brazil
14 D1 Sergiyev Posad Rus. Fed.
64 D2 Sergiyevsk Rus. Fed.
14 C3 Sergiyevskoye Rus. Fed.
14 D3 Sergiyevskoye Rus. Fed.
15 E1 Serhiyivka *Chernihiv* Ukraine
15 D3 Serhiyivka *Odesa* Ukraine
15 D3 Serhiyivka *Odesa* Ukraine
38 F6 Seria Brunei
40 B1 Serian Malaysia
29 E6 Serifos i. Greece
113 G2 Sérigny, Lac l. Can.
60 B2 Serik Turkey
65 J5 Serikbuya China
100 C2 Seringapatam Reef reef Aust.
96 D2 Serle, Mt h. Aust.
39 J8 Sermata, Kepulauan is Indon.
12 J3 Sernur Rus. Fed.
64 E5 Sernyy Zavod Turkmenistan
132 □1 Seroe Colorado *Aruba* Caribbean
13 H6 Seroglazovka Rus. Fed.
25 E4 Serón Spain
82 C2 Seronga Botswana
75 F4 Serouenout well Algeria
62 H4 Serov Rus. Fed.
82 D3 Serowe Botswana
24 C4 Serpa Portugal
96 B2 Serpentine Lakes salt flat Aust.
139 E2 Serpent's Mouth chan. Trinidad/Venezuela
14 B2 Serpeysk Rus. Fed.
25 F3 Serpis r. Spain
15 C3 Serpneve Ukraine
14 E3 Serpovoye Rus. Fed.
14 C2 Serpukhov Rus. Fed.
145 H4 Serra Brazil
139 F3 Serra Acari h. Brazil/Guyana
144 A1 Serra Azul h. Brazil
145 E1 Serra Bonita Brazil
139 E3 Serra Curupira mt. ra. Brazil
143 B5 Serra da Apucarana h. Brazil
145 F5 Serra da Bocaina, Parque Nacional da nat. park Brazil
143 A5 Serra da Bodoquena h. Brazil
145 H2 Serra da Cana Brava h. Brazil
144 C1 Serra da Canastra mts *Goiás* Brazil
145 E3 Serra da Canastra mt. ra. *Minas Gerais* Brazil
145 E4 Serra da Canastra, Parque Nacional da nat. park Brazil
143 D4 Serra da Espinhaco mt. ra. Brazil
142 D1 Serra da Ibiapaba h. Brazil
145 F5 Serra da Mantiqueira mt. ra. Brazil
144 B3 Serra da Mombuca h. Brazil
144 B6 Serra das Araras mt. ra. Brazil
145 F1 Serra das Araras Brazil
144 B3 Serra das Araras h. Brazil
144 C2 Serra das Divisões ou de Santa Marta mt. ra. Brazil
142 D3 Serra da Tabatinga h. Brazil
141 E4 Serra de Amambaí h. Brazil/Paraguay
144 C6 Serra de Esperanca mt. ra. Brazil
142 C2 Serra de Itapicuru h. Brazil
144 A4 Serra de Maracaju h. Brazil
24 B1 Serra de Outes Spain
144 B4 Serra de Santa Bárbara h. Brazil
145 E1 Serra de Santa Maria h. Brazil
145 F1 Serra de São Felipe h. Brazil
144 A2 Serra de São Jerônimo h. Brazil
27 E7 Serra di Burgio h. Italy
142 B1 Serra do Almeirim h. Brazil
145 F2 Serra do Cabral mts Brazil
142 A2 Serra do Cachimbo h. Brazil
144 B2 Serra do Caiapó mts Brazil
145 H2 Serra do Chifre mt. ra. Brazil
140 B1 Serra do Divisor, Parque Nacional de nat. park Brazil
142 D2 Serra do Dois Irmãos h. Brazil
143 B6 Serra do Espigao mts Brazil
145 G2 Serra do Espinhaco mt. ra. Brazil
142 C1 Serra do Gurupi h. Brazil
144 B5 Serra do Lagarto h. Brazil
145 G5 Serra do Mar mt. ra. *Rio de Janeiro* Brazil
143 B6 Serra do Mar mt. ra. *Rio Grande do Sul/Santa Catarina* Brazil
145 F5 Serra do Mar mt. ra. *São Paulo* Brazil
139 E3 Serra do Mucajaí mt. ra. Brazil
139 G3 Serra do Navio Brazil
141 E2 Serra do Norte h. Brazil
142 D3 Serra do Ramalho h. Brazil
145 E2 Serra do Rio Prêto h. Brazil
142 B3 Serra do Roncador h. Brazil
145 H2 Serra dos Aimorés Brazil
142 A3 Serra dos Apiacas h. Brazil
142 A3 Serra dos Caiabis h. Brazil
142 B2 Serra dos Carajás h. Brazil
144 E2 Serra dos Cristais mts Brazil
144 B5 Serra dos Dourados h. Brazil
142 B2 Serra dos Gradaús h. Brazil
140 D2 Serra dos Pacaás h. Brazil
141 D2 Serra dos Parecis h. Brazil
144 E2 Serra dos Pilões mt. ra. Brazil
145 F1 Serra dos Tropeiros h. Brazil
142 B1 Serra do Tapara h. Brazil
144 B1 Serra do Taquaral h. Brazil
144 B3 Serra do Taquari h. Brazil
142 C1 Serra do Tiracambu h. Brazil
141 E2 Serra do Tombador h. Brazil
142 C3 Serra Dourada mt. ra. Brazil
144 C2 Serra Dourada h. Brazil
142 C2 Serra do Uruçuí h. Brazil
142 C2 Serra Estrondo h. Brazil
142 A3 Serra Formosa h. Brazil
144 C6 Serra Geral mt. ra. *Paraná* Brazil
143 B6 Serra Geral mt. ra. *Santa Catarina* Brazil
142 C3 Serra Geral de Goiás h. Brazil
144 E1 Serra Geral do Paraná h. Brazil
139 F3 Serra Iricoumé h. Brazil
139 G3 Serra Lombarda h. Brazil
132 B4 Serrana Bank Colombia
145 G3 Serra Negra mts Brazil
138 B2 Serranía de Abibe mt. ra. Colombia
138 B2 Serranía de Baudo mt. ra. Colombia
25 E2 Serranía de Cuenca mt. ra. Spain
139 E2 Serranía de Imataca mt. ra. Venezuela
138 D3 Serranía de la Neblina, Parque Nacional nat. park Venezuela
130 L7 Serranía del Darién mt. ra. Panama
132 C6 Serranía del Sapo mt. ra. Panama
24 D4 Serranía de Ronda mt. ra. Spain
131 E2 Serranías del Burro mt. ra. Mexico
139 E2 Serranía Turagua mt. Venezuela
147 B6 Serrano i. Chile
144 B3 Serranópolis Brazil
139 E3 Serra Pacaraima mt. ra. Brazil
144 D6 Serra Paranapiacaba mt. ra. Brazil
139 E3 Serra Parima mt. ra. Brazil
144 D1 Serra Pouso Alegre mts Brazil
142 E2 Serra Talhada Brazil
139 E3 Serra Tepequem mt. ra. Brazil
139 F3 Serra Tumucumaque h. Brazil
29 D4 Serres Greece
146 C3 Serrezuela Arg.
142 E3 Serrinha Brazil
145 G3 Sêrro Brazil
147 B5 Serrucho mt. Arg.
27 B7 Sers Tunisia
142 E2 Sertânia Brazil
144 C5 Sertanópolis Brazil
144 B3 Sertão de Camapuã reg. Brazil
144 E4 Sertãozinho Brazil
50 C1 Sêrtar China
11 H3 Sertolovo Rus. Fed.
40 A3 Sertung i. Indon.
39 L7 Serui Indon.
82 D3 Serule Botswana
40 C2 Seruyan r. Indon.
29 D4 Servia Greece
50 B1 Sêrxu China
41 A6 Sesayap r. Indon.
41 A6 Sesayap Indon.
112 B3 Seseganaga L. l. Can.
81 B5 Sese Is i. Uganda
114 E2 Sesekinika Can.
90 □6 Seseleka h. Fiji
82 A2 Sesfontein Namibia
14 A3 Seshcha Rus. Fed.
79 D7 Sesheke Zambia
29 F6 Sesklio i. Greece
47 □2 Sesoko Japan
47 □2 Sesoko-jima i. Japan
25 G3 S'Espalmador i. Spain
79 D6 Sessa Angola
27 D5 Sessa Aurunca Italy
26 B3 Sestri Levante Italy
11 H3 Sestroretsk Rus. Fed.
46 G2 Setana Japan
21 F5 Sète France
144 E6 Sete Barras Brazil
145 F3 Sete Lagoas Brazil
10 E1 Setermoen Norway
11 B4 Setesdal v. Norway
55 F3 Seti r. *Gandakhi* Nepal
54 E3 Seti r. *Seti* Nepal
75 F1 Sétif Algeria
73 G5 Setit r. Africa
47 F6 Seto Japan
46 D7 Seto-naikai sea Japan
42 A4 Setsan Myanmar
74 C2 Settat Morocco
79 A4 Setté Cama Gabon
26 B3 Settepani, Monte mt. Italy
26 A3 Settimo Torinese Italy
17 F4 Settle U.K.
98 D3 Settlement Cr. r. Aust.
145 G2 Setubal r. Brazil
24 B3 Setúbal Portugal
24 B3 Setúbal div. Portugal
24 B3 Setúbal, Baía de b. Portugal
122 E3 Seul Choix Pt pt U.S.A.
112 B3 Seul, Lac l. Can.
21 G3 Seurre France
14 B3 Sev r. Rus. Fed.
60 F1 Sevan Armenia
60 F1 Sevana Lich l. Armenia
13 E6 Sevastopol' Ukraine
113 H2 Seven Islands Bay b. Can.
21 F4 Sévérac-le-Château France
14 D2 Severka r. Rus. Fed.
97 G2 Severn r. Aust.
112 B3 Severn r. Can.
93 D5 Severn mt. N.Z.
17 F5 Severn r. U.K.
12 G2 Severnaya Dvina r. Rus. Fed.
13 G7 Severnaya Osetiya div. Rus. Fed.
63 M2 Severnaya Zemlya is Rus. Fed.
112 B3 Severn L. l. Can.
64 D2 Severnoye Rus. Fed.
65 J1 Severnoye Rus. Fed.
62 H3 Severnyy Rus. Fed.
14 G1 Severnyy Rus. Fed.
15 G1 Severnyy Rus. Fed.
64 E3 Severnyy Chink Ustyurta escarpment Kazak.
19 G3 Severočeský div. Czech Rep.
65 L2 Severo-Chuyskiy Khrebet mt. ra. Rus. Fed.
12 F1 Severodvinsk Rus. Fed.
65 G2 Severo-Kazakhstan div. Kazak.
63 R4 Severo-Kuril'sk Rus. Fed.
19 H4 Severomoravský div. Czech Rep.
10 J1 Severomorsk Rus. Fed.
12 F2 Severoonezhsk Rus. Fed.
63 L3 Severo-Yeniseyskiy Rus. Fed.
15 G1 Severskiy Donets r. Rus. Fed.
127 D4 Sevier r. U.S.A.
129 G2 Sevier Bridge Reservoir resr U.S.A.
129 F2 Sevier Desert desert U.S.A.
129 F2 Sevier Lake salt l. U.S.A.
138 B3 Sevilla Colombia
24 D4 Sevilla Spain
28 E3 Sevlievo Bulgaria
14 B3 Sevsk Rus. Fed.
76 B5 Sewa r. Sierra Leone
54 C3 Sewāni India
108 D3 Seward U.S.A.
124 D3 Seward U.S.A.
108 B3 Seward Peninsula pen. U.S.A.
110 F3 Sexsmith Can.
57 E2 Seyah Band Koh mt. ra. Afghanistan
62 J2 Seyakha Rus. Fed.
131 H5 Seybaplaya Mexico
81 □1 Seychelles country Indian Ocean
64 F5 Seydi Turkmenistan
60 B2 Seydişehir Turkey
10 N2 Seyðisfjörður Iceland
60 C2 Seyhan r. Turkey
61 C1 Seyhan Barajı resr Turkey
60 B2 Seyitgazi Turkey
14 B4 Seym r. Rus. Fed.
15 G1 Seym Rus. Fed.
15 E1 Seym r. Ukraine
63 R3 Seymchan Rus. Fed.
97 F4 Seymour Aust.
118 C4 Seymour U.S.A.
125 D5 Seymour U.S.A.
57 G2 Seyyedābād Afghanistan
21 F2 Sézanne France
14 B2 Sezha r. Rus. Fed.
27 D5 Sezze Italy
29 E7 Sfakia Greece
28 E2 Sfântu Gheorghe Romania
28 G2 Sfântu Gheorghe Romania
75 G2 Sfax Tunisia
18 B2 's-Gravenhage Netherlands
48 E5 Sha r. China
48 D6 Shaanxi div. China
79 E5 Shaba div. Zaire
80 E4 Shabeellaha Dhexe div. Somalia
80 D4 Shabeellaha Hoose div. Somalia
60 F2 Shabestar Iran
61 C5 Shabībī, J. esh mt. Jordan
28 G3 Shabla Bulgaria
14 B3 Shablykino Rus. Fed.
113 G3 Shabogamo Lake l. Can.
79 E4 Shabunda Zaire
65 J5 Shache China
152 B4 Shackleton Coast Ant.
152 B4 Shackleton Gl. gl. Ant.
152 D6 Shackleton Ice Shelf ice feature Ant.
152 C3 Shackleton Ra. mt. ra. Ant.
54 A4 Shadadkot Pakistan
57 F3 Shadikhak P. pass Afghanistan
57 C3 Shādkām w Iran
64 F1 Shadrinsk Rus. Fed.

73 F2 Shadwān Is i. Egypt
122 D5 Shafer, Lake l. U.S.A.
152 B5 Shafer Pk summit Ant.
57 D1 Shafi'abad Iran
128 C4 Shafter U.S.A.
93 C6 Shag r. N.Z.
64 E3 Shagan r. *Aktyubinsk* Kazak.
65 J3 Shagan r. *Semipalatinsk* Kazak.
14 G2 Shagayevo Rus. Fed.
108 C3 Shageluk U.S.A.
93 C6 Shag Pt pt N.Z.
152 B1 Shag Rocks is Atlantic Ocean
57 B1 Shah r. Iran
56 B2 Shahabad India
54 D4 Shahabad India
54 E4 Shahabad India
54 C5 Shahada India
43 C7 Shah Alam Malaysia
56 A3 Shahapur India
61 D3 Shahbā' Syria
54 A4 Shahbandar Pakistan
57 F4 Shahbaz Kalat Pakistan
55 G5 Shah bazpur chan. Bangladesh
57 D3 Shahdāb Iran
54 B4 Shahdadpur Pakistan
55 E5 Shahdol India
57 F2 Shah Fuladi mt. Afghanistan
54 B4 Shahgarh India
54 D4 Shahgarh India
72 D1 Shaḥḥāt Libya
57 F3 Shah Ismail Afghanistan
54 D4 Shahjahanpur India
57 D1 Shāh Jehān, Kuh-e mt. ra. Iran
57 F2 Shāh Jūy Afghanistan
64 D5 Shahmīrzād Iran
56 B2 Shahpur India
54 C2 Shahpur Pakistan
54 B3 Shahpur Pakistan
54 E5 Shahpura India
54 C4 Shahpura India
54 D4 Shahpura India
57 F2 Shahrak Afghanistan
57 E2 Shāhrakht Iran
73 H4 Shahran reg. Saudi Arabia
57 C3 Shahr-e Bābāk Iran
57 B2 Shahr-e Kord Iran
57 B2 Shahr Rey Iran
65 G5 Shahrtuz Tajikistan
57 C2 Shahrud Bustam reg. Iran
65 G4 Shaidara, Step' plain Kazak.
54 A3 Shaikh Husain mt. Pakistan
55 F4 Shaikhpura India
61 C5 Sha'īra, G. mt. Egypt
61 D2 Shā'īr, J. mt. ra. Syria
49 H4 Shajianzi China
114 A2 Shakespeare I. i. Can.
57 G1 Shakh Tajikistan
57 D2 Shākhen Iran
14 B1 Shakhovskaya Rus. Fed.
65 G5 Shakhrisabz Uzbekistan
65 H3 Shakhtinsk Kazak.
64 E3 Shakhty Kazak.
13 G6 Shakhty Rus. Fed.
122 A3 Shakopee U.S.A.
46 H2 Shakotan-hantō pen. Japan
46 H2 Shakotan-misaki c. Japan
12 H3 Shakun'ya Rus. Fed.
80 C3 Shala Hāyk' l. Ethiopia
12 G2 Shalakusha Rus. Fed.
14 G1 Shaldezh Rus. Fed.
65 H3 Shalginskiy Kazak.
64 F2 Shalkar Karashatau salt l. Kazak.
64 D2 Shalkar, Oz. salt l. Kazak.
64 F2 Shalkar-Yega-Kara, Oz. l. Rus. Fed.
57 B1 Shaltrak Iran
50 B2 Shaluli Shan mt. ra. China
55 H3 Shaluni mt. India
81 B6 Shama r. Tanzania
65 H4 Shamaldy-Say Kyrgyzstan
65 L2 Shaman, Khr. mt. ra. Rus. Fed.
111 L3 Shamattawa Can.
80 C3 Shambu Ethiopia
45 ▫ Sham Chun h. China/Hong Kong
54 C4 Shamgarh India
55 G4 Shamgong Bhutan
57 D4 Shamil Iran
57 C4 Shamis U.A.E.
13 H7 Shamkhal Rus. Fed.
73 H2 Shammar, Jabal reg. Saudi Arabia
120 E4 Shamokin U.S.A.
15 C2 Shamrayivka Ukraine
125 C5 Shamrock U.S.A.
83 E2 Shamva Zimbabwe
57 E3 Shand Afghanistan
57 E3 Shāndak Iran
48 B5 Shandan China
49 F4 Shandian r. China
57 D1 Shandiz Iran
128 B4 Shandon U.S.A.
49 F6 Shandong div. China
49 G5 Shandong Bandao pen. China
60 F3 Shandrūkh Iraq
54 C1 Shandur P. pass Pakistan
83 D2 Shangani r. Zimbabwe
51 F1 Shangcai China
50 E3 Shangchao China
51 F2 Shangcheng China
51 F4 Shangchuan Dao China
48 E4 Shangdu China
49 J3 Shangganling China
51 F2 Shanggao China
51 H2 Shanghai China
51 H2 Shanghai div. China
51 G3 Shanghang China
49 F5 Shanghe China
51 E1 Shangjin China
49 G2 Shangkuli China
50 E4 Shanglin China
51 E1 Shangman China
79 D7 Shangombo Zambia
51 F1 Shangqiu *Henan* China
51 F1 Shangqiu *Henan* China
51 G2 Shangrao *Jiangxi* China
51 G2 Shangrao *Jiangxi* China
51 F1 Shangshui China
50 E4 Shangsi China
51 F2 Shangtang China
48 E4 Shangyi China
51 F3 Shangyou China
65 K4 Shangyou Sk. salt flat China
51 H2 Shangyu China
49 H3 Shangzhi China
51 E1 Shangzhou China
49 H3 Shanhetun China
77 G4 Shani Nigeria
109 R2 Shannon i. Greenland
92 E4 Shannon N.Z.
17 C5 Shannon r. Rep. of Ire.
17 C5 Shannon, Mouth of the inlet Rep. of Ire.
44 F3 Shanshan China
49 H4 Shansonggang China
42 B2 Shan State div. Myanmar
63 P4 Shantarskiye Ostrova is Rus. Fed.
51 G4 Shantou China
48 D5 Shanxi div. China
51 G1 Shan Xian China
14 B2 Shanya r. Rus. Fed.
51 F1 Shanyang China
48 E5 Shanyin China
51 E3 Shaodong China
51 F3 Shaoguan China
51 G3 Shaowu China
51 H2 Shaoxing China
51 E3 Shaoyang *Hunan* China
51 E3 Shaoyang *Hunan* China
16 F2 Shapinsay i. U.K.
14 F4 Shapkino Rus. Fed.
15 E1 Shapovalivka Ukraine
65 L2 Shapshal'skiy Khrebet mt. ra. Rus. Fed.
73 E5 Shaqq el Khadir Sudan
73 J2 Shaqra' Saudi Arabia
60 E4 Sharaf well Iraq
73 E5 Sharafa Sudan
48 C2 Sharalday Rus. Fed.
14 H1 Sharanga Rus. Fed.
54 B3 Sharan Jogizai Pakistan
14 G2 Sharapovo Rus. Fed.
48 A2 Sharga Mongolia
15 C2 Sharhorod Ukraine
48 C3 Sharhulsan Mongolia
46 K2 Shari-dake vol Japan
61 D2 Sharīfah Syria
55 G3 Sharka-leb La China
12 C4 Sharkawshchyna Belarus
101 A5 Shark Bay b. Aust.
99 F2 Shark Reef reef *Coral Sea Islands Terr.* Pac. Oc.
64 E5 Sharlouk Turkmenistan
73 G2 Sharmah Saudi Arabia
73 F2 Sharm el Sheikh Egypt
73 G3 Sharm Yanbu b. Saudi Arabia
121 G4 Sharon U.S.A.
120 C4 Sharon U.S.A.
61 C3 Sharon, Plain of plain Israel
45 ▫ Sharp Peak h. Hong Kong
60 D3 Sharqi, Jebel esh mt. ra. Syria
48 A3 Shar U Gol r. Mongolia
12 H3 Shar'ya Rus. Fed.
83 D3 Shashe r. Botswana/Zimbabwe
80 C3 Shashemenē Ethiopia
51 F2 Shashi China
65 J3 Shashubay Kazak.
126 B3 Shasta L. l. U.S.A.
126 B3 Shasta, Mt vol U.S.A.
14 A2 Shatalovo Rus. Fed.
45 ▫ Sha Tin Hong Kong
14 G2 Shatki Rus. Fed.
64 F1 Shatrovo Rus. Fed.
14 E1 Shatsk Rus. Fed.
19 L3 Shats'k Ukraine
60 F3 Shatt al Hillah r. Iraq
57 B3 Shaṭṭ, Ra's osh pt Iran
14 D2 Shatura Rus. Fed.
60 C4 Shaubak Jordan
65 G4 Shaul'der Kazak.
111 H5 Shaunavon Can.
120 D5 Shavers Fork r. U.S.A.
100 B4 Shaw r. Aust.
121 F4 Shawangunk Mts h. U.S.A.
122 C3 Shawano U.S.A.
122 C3 Shawano Lake l. U.S.A.
115 J3 Shawinigan Can.
60 D3 Shawmarīyah, Jebel ash mt. ra. Syria
125 D5 Shawnee U.S.A.
51 G3 Sha Xi r. China
51 F2 Shayang China
72 G2 Shaybārā i. Saudi Arabia
100 C4 Shay Gap Aust.
60 D3 Shaykh, Jabal esh mt. Syria
61 D3 Shaykh Miskīn Syria
60 F3 Shaykh Sa'd Iraq
14 B2 Shaykovka Rus. Fed.
57 C3 Shaytūr Iran
73 H2 Shaẓāz, Jabal mt. Saudi Arabia
65 H5 Shazud Tajikistan
14 C2 Shchekino Rus. Fed.
15 B1 Shchekychyn Ukraine
14 D2 Shchelkovo Rus. Fed.
63 S3 Shcherbakovo Rus. Fed.
64 E2 Shcherbakty Kazak.
15 D2 Shcherbani Ukraine
14 E2 Shcherbatovka Rus. Fed.
14 C4 Shchigry Rus. Fed.
13 E6 Shcholkine Ukraine
15 D1 Shchors Ukraine
65 H2 Shchuchinsk Kazak.
64 F1 Shchuch'ye Rus. Fed.
14 E4 Shchuch'ye Rus. Fed.
12 C4 Shchuchyn Belarus
65 L2 Shebalino Rus. Fed.
15 G1 Shebekino Rus. Fed.
57 F1 Sheberghān Afghanistan
122 D4 Sheboygan U.S.A.
77 G5 Shebshi Mountains mt. ra. Nigeria
113 H4 Shediac Can.
110 D3 Shedin Pk summit Can.
17 D5 Sheelin, Lough l. Rep. of Ire.
17 D4 Sheep Haven b. Rep. of Ire.
129 E3 Sheep Peak summit U.S.A.
17 H6 Sheerness U.K.
113 H5 Sheet Harbour Can.
61 C3 Shefar'am Israel
93 D5 Sheffield N.Z.
17 G5 Sheffield U.K.
119 C5 Sheffield U.S.A.
122 C5 Sheffield U.S.A.
120 D4 Sheffield U.S.A.
125 C6 Sheffield U.S.A.
54 D5 Shegaon India
12 J1 Shegmas Rus. Fed.
114 E4 Sheguiandah Can.
50 D2 Shehong China
61 B5 Sheikh, W. es w Egypt
57 F3 Shekak r. Can.
54 C4 Shekhawati reg. India
14 E3 Shekhman' Rus. Fed.
54 C3 Shekhupura Pakistan
45 ▫ Shek Kwu Chau i. Hong Kong
45 ▫ Shek Pik Reservoir resr Hong Kong
12 F3 Sheksna Rus. Fed.
45 ▫ Shek Uk Shan h. Hong Kong
57 E3 Shelag r. Afghanistan/Iran
63 S2 Shelagskiy, Mys pt Rus. Fed.
122 A6 Shelbina U.S.A.
113 G5 Shelburne Can.
114 E4 Shelburne Can.
99 E1 Shelburne Bay b. Aust.
121 G3 Shelburne Falls U.S.A.
122 D4 Shelby U.S.A.
126 E1 Shelby U.S.A.
119 D5 Shelby U.S.A.
120 B4 Shelby U.S.A.
118 C4 Shelbyville U.S.A.
122 A6 Shelbyville U.S.A.
119 C5 Shelbyville U.S.A.
129 H5 Sheldon U.S.A.
122 D5 Sheldon U.S.A.
121 G2 Sheldon Springs U.S.A.
113 H3 Sheldrake Can.
48 B1 Shelekhov Rus. Fed.
63 R3 Shelikhova, Zaliv g. Rus. Fed.
108 C4 Shelikof Strait str. U.S.A.
111 H4 Shellbrook Can.
126 D3 Shelley U.S.A.
97 G3 Shellharbour Aust.
128 A1 Shell Mt mt. U.S.A.
49 F2 Shelopugino Rus. Fed.
110 F4 Shelter Bay Can.
128 A1 Shelter Cove U.S.A.
45 ▫ Shelter I. i. Hong Kong
121 G4 Shelter I. i. U.S.A.
93 B7 Shelter Pt pt N.Z.
57 B1 Shem Iran
65 K2 Shemonaikha Kazak.
61 C3 Shemona, Q. Israel
12 J3 Shemordan Rus. Fed.
14 H2 Shemursha Rus. Fed.
14 G3 Shemysheyka Rus. Fed.
124 E3 Shenandoah U.S.A.
121 E4 Shenandoah U.S.A.
120 D5 Shenandoah U.S.A.
120 D5 Shenandoah r. U.S.A.
120 D5 Shenandoah Mountains mt. ra. U.S.A.
120 D5 Shenandoah National Park nat. park U.S.A.
120 C4 Shenango River Lake l. U.S.A.
64 F3 Shenbertal Kazak.
77 F5 Shendam Nigeria
73 F4 Shendi Sudan
49 K3 Shending Shan mt. China
81 C5 Shengena mt. Tanzania
28 B4 Shëngjin Albania
49 H3 Shengping China
51 H2 Shengsi China
51 H2 Shengsi Liedao is China
51 H2 Sheng Xian China
12 G2 Shenkursk Rus. Fed.
48 D5 Shenmu China
51 E2 Shennongjia China
51 F1 Shenqiu China
49 J3 Shenshu China
101 C6 Shenton, Mt h. Aust.
49 F5 Shen Xian China
49 G4 Shenyang China
51 F4 Shenzhen China
54 C4 Sheoganj India
54 D4 Sheopur India
15 B1 Shepetivka Ukraine
90 ▫2 Shepherd Is is Vanuatu
97 F4 Shepparton Aust.
17 H6 Sheppey, Isle of i. U.K.
15 F1 Sheptukhovka Rus. Fed.
65 G5 Sherabad Uzbekistan
76 B5 Sherbro Island i. Sierra Leone
113 H4 Sherbrooke Can.
115 K4 Sherbrooke Can.
121 F3 Sherburne U.S.A.
72 C3 Sherda well Chad
57 G2 Sher Dahan P. pass Afghanistan
73 F4 Shereiq Sudan
54 C4 Shergarh India
55 F4 Sherghati India
125 E5 Sheridan U.S.A.
126 F2 Sheridan U.S.A.
109 M1 Sheridan, C. c. Can.
49 F2 Sherlovaya Gora Rus. Fed.
125 D5 Sherman U.S.A.
121 J2 Sherman Mills U.S.A.
129 E1 Sherman Mtn mt. U.S.A.
55 G4 Sherpur Bangladesh
111 J3 Sherridon Can.
18 B3 's-Hertogenbosch Netherlands
49 J2 Sheryshevo Rus. Fed.
110 C3 Sheslay Can.
14 D1 Shestikhino Rus. Fed.
64 D4 Shetpe Kazak.
45 ▫ Sheung Shui Hong Kong
45 ▫ Sheung Sze Mun chan. Hong Kong
56 B4 Shevaroy Hills mt. ra. India
15 G2 Shevchenkove Ukraine
14 C1 Shevlyakovo Rus. Fed.
80 C3 Shewa Gīmīra Ethiopia
51 G2 She Xian China
51 H1 Sheyang China
124 D2 Sheyenne r. U.S.A.
124 D2 Sheyenne U.S.A.
57 C4 Sheykh Sho'eyb i. Iran
63 R5 Shiashkotan, O. i. Rus. Fed.
123 E4 Shiawassee r. U.S.A.
59 G6 Shibām Yemen
47 G5 Shibata Japan
49 H1 Shibazhan China
46 J1 Shibetsu Japan
46 K2 Shibetsu Japan
73 F1 Shibīn el Kôm Egypt
46 L2 Shibotsu-jima i. Rus. Fed.
47 G5 Shibukawa Japan
46 B1 Shibushi-wan b. Japan
51 G3 Shicheng China
46 H3 Shichinohe Japan
121 E4 Shickshinny U.S.A.
49 G5 Shidao China
49 G5 Shidao Wan b. China
65 H2 Shiderty r. Kazak.
50 B3 Shidian China
98 D2 Shield, C. c. Aust.
16 E3 Shiel, Loch l. U.K.
73 G2 Shifa, Jabal ash mt. ra. Saudi Arabia
50 D2 Shifang China
47 E6 Shiga div. Japan
12 J4 Shigony Rus. Fed.
48 D4 Shiguaigou China
61 C4 Shīhān mt. Jordan
65 L4 Shihezi China
29 B4 Shijak Albania
48 E5 Shijiazhuang China
46 H2 Shikabe Japan
57 F3 Shikar r. Pakistan
56 A3 Shikarpur India
54 B4 Shikarpur Pakistan
14 H3 Shikhany Rus. Fed.
14 H2 Shikhazany Rus. Fed.
54 D4 Shikohabad India
46 D7 Shikoku i. Japan
46 D7 Shikoku-sanchi mt. ra. Japan
45 R3 Shikotan-tō i. Rus. Fed.
46 H2 Shikotsu-ko l. Japan
46 H2 Shikotsu-Tōya National Park Japan
12 H1 Shilega Rus. Fed.
55 G4 Shiliguri India
51 F2 Shilipu China
49 F2 Shilka Rus. Fed.
49 F1 Shilka r. Rus. Fed.
17 D5 Shillelagh Rep. of Ire.
114 E2 Shillington Can.
55 G4 Shillong India
13 J5 Shil'naya Balka Kazak.
121 F5 Shiloh U.S.A.
51 E1 Shilou China
14 E2 Shilovo Rus. Fed.
14 D3 Shilovo Rus. Fed.
46 C7 Shimabara Japan
46 C7 Shimabara-wan b. Japan
47 G6 Shimada Japan
46 D6 Shimane div. Japan
46 D6 Shimane-hantō pen. Japan
49 H1 Shimanovsk Rus. Fed.
80 E3 Shimbiris mt. Somalia
81 D4 Shimbirre waterhole Kenya
51 E2 Shimen China
50 C2 Shimian China
47 G6 Shimizu Japan
54 D3 Shimla India
47 G6 Shimoda Japan
47 G5 Shimodate Japan
56 A3 Shimoga India
46 H3 Shimokita-hantō pen. Japan
46 B8 Shimo-Koshiki-jima i. Japan
81 C5 Shimoni Kenya
46 C7 Shimonoseki Japan
14 F2 Shimorskoye Rus. Fed.
54 C1 Shimshal Pakistan
65 J5 Shimshal *Jammu and Kashmir*
12 D3 Shimsk Rus. Fed.
51 E4 Shinan China
47 G5 Shinano-gawa r. Japan
57 E2 Shindand Afghanistan
42 B1 Shingbwiyang Myanmar
42 B1 Shing-gai Myanmar
54 B3 Shinghar Pakistan
54 C1 Shinghshal P. pass Pakistan
122 D2 Shingleton U.S.A.
45 ▫ Shing Mun Res. resr Hong Kong
54 D2 Shingo P. pass India
65 K3 Shingozha Kazak.
47 F7 Shingū Japan
83 E3 Shingwedzi r. R.S.A.
114 E3 Shining Tree Can.
46 D6 Shinji-ko l. Japan
47 H4 Shinjō Japan
57 F3 Shīnkāy Afghanistan
16 E2 Shin, Loch l. U.K.
47 F5 Shinminato Japan
46 C6 Shin-nanyō Japan
121 J1 Shin Pond U.S.A.
61 D2 Shinshār Syria
46 J2 Shintoku Japan
81 B5 Shinyanga div. Tanzania
81 B5 Shinyanga Tanzania
47 H4 Shiogama Japan
47 F5 Shiojiri Japan
47 E7 Shiono-misaki c. Japan
47 H5 Shioya-zaki pt Japan
132 C1 Ship Chan Cay i. The Bahamas
14 D1 Shipilovo Rus. Fed.
50 C4 Shiping China
54 D3 Shipki Pass pass India
113 H4 Shippegan Can.
120 E4 Shippensburg U.S.A.
129 H3 Shiprock U.S.A.
129 H3 Shiprock Peak summit U.S.A.
51 H2 Shipu China
65 K2 Shipunovo Rus. Fed.
50 E3 Shiqian China
51 E1 Shiquan China
54 E2 Shiquan r. China
50 E1 Shiquan Sk. resr China
65 M2 Shira Rus. Fed.
47 E7 Shirahama Japan
46 H3 Shirakami-misaki pt Japan
47 H5 Shirakawa Japan
47 F5 Shirakawa Japan
47 G5 Shirane-san vol Japan
46 K2 Shiranuka Japan
46 H2 Shiraoi Japan
152 D4 Shirasebreen gl. Ant.
152 A4 Shirase Coast Ant.
46 J2 Shirataki Japan
57 C3 Shīrāz Iran
61 A4 Shirbîn Egypt
83 E2 Shire r. Malawi
48 E3 Shireet Mongolia
46 K2 Shiretoko-hantō pen. Japan
46 K1 Shiretoko-misaki c. Japan
64 F4 Shirikrabat Kazak.
54 A3 Shirinab r. Pakistan
14 F3 Shiringushi Rus. Fed.
46 H3 Shiriya-zaki c. Japan
64 E3 Shirkala reg. Kazak.
121 G4 Shirley U.S.A.
121 J2 Shirley Mills U.S.A.
47 H5 Shiroishi Japan
47 G5 Shirone Japan
77 F5 Shiroro Reservoir resr Nigeria
47 F6 Shirotori Japan
54 C5 Shirpur India
48 A4 Shirten Höloy Gobi desert China
57 D1 Shīrvān Iran
49 H2 Shisanzhan China
51 F2 Shishou China
51 G2 Shitai China
51 H2 Shitang China
47 F6 Shitara Japan
60 E3 Shithāthah Iraq
54 B4 Shiv India
118 C4 Shively U.S.A.
54 D4 Shivpuri India
61 C4 Shivta Israel
129 F3 Shivwits Plateau plat. U.S.A.
57 G1 Shiwal l. Afghanistan
50 D4 Shiwan Dashan mt. ra. China
81 B7 Shiwa Ngandu Zambia
51 F3 Shixing China
51 E1 Shiyan China
50 E2 Shizhu China
50 C3 Shizong China
47 H4 Shizugawa Japan
48 C5 Shizuishan China
47 G6 Shizuoka Japan
47 G6 Shizuoka div. Japan
60 E1 Shkhara mt. Rus. Fed.
12 D4 Shklow Belarus
28 B3 Shkodër *Shkodër* Albania
29 B4 Shkumbin r. Albania
15 G1 Shlyakhovo Rus. Fed.
63 L1 Shmidta, Ostrov i. Rus. Fed.
99 G4 Shoalwater B. b. Aust.
46 D6 Shōbara Japan
46 E6 Shōdo-shima i. Japan
47 F5 Shō-gawa r. Japan
64 E5 Shoghlābād Iran
46 H2 Shokanbetsu-dake mt. Japan
12 E1 Shomba r. Rus. Fed.
64 E3 Shomishkol' Kazak.
12 J2 Shomvukva Rus. Fed.
55 G4 Shongar Bhutan
61 A4 Shôni Egypt
14 D1 Shopsha Rus. Fed.
54 D2 Shor India
56 B4 Shoranur India
54 A4 Shorap Pakistan
57 F3 Shorawak reg. Afghanistan
64 E4 Shor Barsa-Kel'mes salt marsh Uzbekistan
54 C3 Shorkot Pakistan
90 ▫1 Shortland Is is Solomon Is.
46 H1 Shosanbetsu Japan
14 B1 Shosha r. Rus. Fed.
128 D4 Shoshone U.S.A.
126 D3 Shoshone U.S.A.
126 E2 Shoshone r. U.S.A.
126 E2 Shoshone L. l. U.S.A.
127 C4 Shoshone Mts mt. ra. U.S.A.
82 D3 Shoshong Botswana
126 E3 Shoshoni U.S.A.
15 E1 Shostka Ukraine
49 F5 Shouguang China
51 G3 Shouning China
51 G1 Shou Xian China
48 E5 Shouyang China
50 E1 Shouyang Shan mt. China
55 E3 Shovo Tso salt l. China
73 G5 Showak Sudan
129 G4 Show Low U.S.A.
62 F3 Shoyna Rus. Fed.
14 E4 Shpikulovo Rus. Fed.
15 D2 Shpola Ukraine
15 C2 Shpykiv Ukraine
15 E1 Shramkivka Ukraine
125 E5 Shreveport U.S.A.
17 F5 Shrewsbury U.K.
56 A2 Shrigonda India
54 B4 Shri Mohangarh India
51 G1 Shu r. China
50 C3 Shuangbai China
49 H3 Shuangcheng China
50 D2 Shuanghechang China
49 J2 Shuanghedagang Rus. Fed.
50 B4 Shuangjiang China
49 G4 Shuangliao China
51 E3 Shuangpai China
49 H4 Shuangyang China
49 J3 Shuangyashan China
64 E3 Shubarkuduk Kazak.
64 E3 Shubarshi Kazak.
61 D2 Shubayṭ, J. ash h. Syria
14 G2 Shubino Rus. Fed.
73 H3 Shubrāmīyāh well Saudi Arabia
51 G2 Shucheng China
55 H4 Shuganu India
14 H2 Shugurovo Rus. Fed.
51 G3 Shuiji China
48 B5 Shuiquanzi China
50 C2 Shuituo r. China
54 D5 Shujalpur India
57 B3 Shūl w Iran
49 H3 Shulan China
65 J5 Shule China
14 E3 Shul'gino Rus. Fed.
49 E5 Shulu China
108 C4 Shumagin Islands is U.S.A.
15 G1 Shumakovo Rus. Fed.
64 E4 Shumanay Uzbekistan
46 J1 Shumarinai-ko l. Japan
82 D2 Shumba Zimbabwe
28 F3 Shumen Bulgaria
14 H2 Shumerlya Rus. Fed.
64 F1 Shumikha Rus. Fed.
15 B1 Shums'k Ukraine
129 G4 Shumway U.S.A.
12 E4 Shumyachi Rus. Fed.
61 C4 Shuna Jordan
51 G3 Shunchang China
51 F4 Shunde China
14 E1 Shunga Rus. Fed.
108 C3 Shungnak U.S.A.
49 F4 Shunyi China
50 D4 Shuolong China
48 E5 Shuo Xian China
54 C2 Shupiyan India
80 E2 Shuqrah Yemen
57 C3 Shūr r. *Fārs/Būshehr* Iran
57 C3 Shūr r. *Fārs/Hormozgān* Iran
57 C4 Shūr r. *Fārs/Hormozgān* Iran
57 C3 Shūr r. *Kermān* Iran
57 D2 Shur r. *Khorāsān* Iran
57 D2 Shūr r. *Khorāsān* Iran
57 D3 Shūr Āb r. Iran
57 C2 Shūrāb Iran
57 B2 Shūrāb Iran
57 D2 Shūrāb Iran
57 B2 Shūr Āb Iran
65 G5 Shurchi Uzbekistan
57 D3 Shūr Gaz Iran
47 ▫2 Shuri Japan
57 C3 Shūrjestān Iran
12 J3 Shurma Rus. Fed.
83 E2 Shurugwi Zimbabwe
57 E3 Shusf Iran
57 B2 Shūsh Iran
12 G3 Shushkodom Rus. Fed.
57 B2 Shushtar Iran
14 B4 Shustovo Rus. Fed.
110 F4 Shuswap L. l. Can.
57 F2 Shutar Khun P. pass Afghanistan
14 G2 Shuvary Rus. Fed.
14 E1 Shuya Rus. Fed.
51 G1 Shuyang China
42 A3 Shwebandaw Myanmar
42 A1 Shwebo Myanmar
42 A3 Shwedaung Myanmar
42 A1 Shwedwin Myanmar
42 B3 Shwegun Myanmar
42 B3 Shwegyin Myanmar
42 B2 Shweli r. Myanmar
42 B2 Shweudaung mt. Myanmar
15 B2 Shybena Ukraine
65 G4 Shymkent Kazak.
54 D2 Shyok r. India
15 G2 Shypuvate Ukraine
15 E3 Shyroke *Dnipropetrovs'k* Ukraine
15 F2 Shyroke *Dnipropetrovs'k* Ukraine
15 D3 Shyrokolanivka Ukraine
15 D3 Shyryayeve Ukraine
15 F2 Shyshaky Ukraine
39 K8 Sia Indon.
54 D2 Siachen Gl. gl. *Jammu and Kashmir*
57 E4 Siahan Range mt. ra. Pakistan
60 F2 Siah Chashmeh Iran
57 F2 Siah Koh mt. ra. Afghanistan
57 C2 Siāh Kūh mt. ra. Iran
57 F3 Siah Sang P. pass Afghanistan
54 C2 Sialkot Pakistan
19 H1 Sianów Poland
43 D7 Siantan i. Indon.
57 E3 Sīāreh Iran
41 C4 Siargao i. Phil.
41 B5 Siasi Phil.
41 B5 Siasi i. Phil.
29 C4 Siatista Greece
41 B4 Siaton Phil.
11 F5 Šiauliai Lithuania
57 E4 Sib Iran
65 L3 Sibati China
41 B4 Sibay i. Phil.
64 E2 Sibay Rus. Fed.
83 E4 Sibayi, Lake l. R.S.A.
152 B5 Sibbald, C. c. Ant.
26 E4 Šibenik Croatia
32 L3 Siberia reg. Rus. Fed.
38 C7 Siberut i. Indon.
54 A3 Sibi Pakistan
80 C4 Sibiloi National Park nat. park Kenya
79 B4 Sibiti Congo
28 E2 Sibiu Romania
40 E1 Siboa Indon.
38 C6 Sibolga Indon.
40 E1 Siboluton Indon.
55 H4 Sibsagar India
38 F6 Sibu Malaysia
41 B5 Sibuco Phil.
41 B5 Sibuguey r. Phil.
41 B5 Sibuguey Bay b. Phil.
78 C2 Sibut C.A.R.
41 A5 Sibutu i. Phil.
41 A5 Sibutu Passage chan. Phil.
41 B3 Sibuyan i. Phil.
41 B3 Sibuyan Sea sea Phil.
41 B2 Sicapoo mt. Phil.
96 D2 Siccus w Aust.
50 C2 Sichuan div. China
50 D2 Sichuan Pendi basin China
21 G5 Sicié, Cap c. France
27 E7 Sicilia div. Italy
27 D7 Sicilia i. Italy
27 C7 Sicilian Channel chan. Mediterranean Sea
140 B2 Sicuani Peru
28 B2 Šid Yugo.
77 F3 Sidaouet Niger
54 C5 Siddhapur India
56 B2 Siddipet India
76 D4 Sidéradougou Burkina
55 E4 Sidhi India
75 E1 Sidi Ali Algeria
72 E1 Sidi Barrani Egypt
74 C2 Sidi Bel Abbès Algeria
74 B2 Sidi Bennour Morocco
75 F1 Sidi Bouzid Tunisia
74 B3 Sidi Ifni Morocco
74 C2 Sidi Kacem Morocco
75 E2 Sidi Khaled Algeria
76 C4 Sidikila Guinea
75 D3 Sidi Mannsour well Algeria
74 B4 Sidi Mhamed well Western Sahara
75 F2 Sidi Okba Algeria
29 D4 Sidirokastro *Kentriki Makedonia* Greece
61 A4 Sidi Sâlim Egypt
16 F3 Sidlaw Hills h. U.K.
152 A4 Sidley, Mt mt. Ant.
17 F6 Sidmouth U.K.
110 E5 Sidney Can.
126 F2 Sidney U.S.A.
124 C3 Sidney U.S.A.
121 F3 Sidney U.S.A.
120 A4 Sidney U.S.A.
119 D5 Sidney Lanier, L. l. U.S.A.
76 C4 Sido Mali
40 E1 Sidoan Indon.
40 C3 Sidoarjo Indon.
42 A2 Sidoktaya Myanmar
144 A4 Sidrolândia Brazil
19 L2 Siedlce Poland
19 L3 Siedliszcze Poland
18 D3 Siegen Germany
19 L2 Siemiatycze Poland
43 C4 Siĕmréab Cambodia
26 C4 Siena Italy
19 L3 Sieniawa Poland
19 J3 Sieradz Poland
19 H2 Sieraków Poland
19 J2 Sierpc Poland
125 B6 Sierra Blanca U.S.A.
147 C5 Sierra Colorada Arg.
139 E2 Sierra del Zamuro mt. ra. Venezuela
138 C2 Sierra de Perija mt. ra. Venezuela
129 F5 Sierra Estrella mts U.S.A.
140 C4 Sierra Gorda Chile
147 C5 Sierra Grande Arg.
138 D2 Sierra Guanay mts Venezuela
69 C5 Sierra Leone country Africa
148 H5 Sierra Leone Basin Atlantic Ocean
148 H5 Sierra Leone Rise Atlantic Ocean
131 G5 Sierra Madre mt. ra. Mexico
41 B2 Sierra Madre mt. Phil.
131 E5 Sierra Madre del Sur mt. ra. Mexico
128 C4 Sierra Madre Mts mts U.S.A.
130 C2 Sierra Madre Occidental mt. ra. Mexico
131 E3 Sierra Madre Oriental mt. ra. Mexico
139 D2 Sierra Maigualida mt. ra. Venezuela
130 E3 Sierra Mojada Mexico
127 B4 Sierra Nevada mt. ra. U.S.A.
138 C2 Sierra Nevada del Cocuy mt. Colombia
138 C1 Sierra Nevada de Santa Marta nat. park Colombia
138 C2 Sierra Nevada, Parque Nacional nat. park Venezuela
129 F5 Sierra Pinta summit U.S.A.
147 D5 Sierra, Pta pt Arg.
128 B2 Sierraville U.S.A.
129 G6 Sierra Vista U.S.A.
130 B3 Sierra Vizcaino mt. ra. Mexico
21 H3 Sierre Switz.
141 E4 Siete Puntas r. Paraguay
10 G3 Sievi Finland
50 D4 Sifang Ling mt. ra. China
49 H3 Sifangtai China
29 E6 Sifnos i. Greece
90 ▫8 Sigatoka Fiji
90 ▫8 Sigatoka r. Fiji
28 D1 Sighetu Marmaţiei Romania
28 E1 Sighişoara Romania
43 ▫ Siglap Singapore
53 J9 Sigli Indon.
10 M2 Siglufjörður Iceland
41 B4 Sigma Phil.
18 D4 Sigmaringen Germany
129 E5 Signal Peak summit U.S.A.
152 B1 Signy U.K. Base Ant.
122 A5 Sigourney U.S.A.
14 A1 Sig, Oz. l. Rus. Fed.
130 J6 Siguatepeque Honduras
25 E2 Sigüenza Spain
76 C4 Siguiri Guinea
11 G4 Sigulda Latvia
43 C5 Sihanoukville Cambodia
51 G1 Sihong China
54 E5 Sihora India
140 A1 Sihuas Peru
51 F4 Sihui China
10 G2 Siikajoki Finland
10 G3 Siilinjärvi Finland
60 E2 Siirt Turkey
38 D7 Sijunjung Indon.
54 B5 Sika India
110 E3 Sikanni Chief Can.
110 E3 Sikanni Chief r. Can.
54 C4 Sikar India
57 G2 Sikaram mt. Afghanistan
76 C4 Sikasso div. Mali
76 C4 Sikasso Mali
42 B2 Sikaw Myanmar
29 D4 Sikea Greece
125 F4 Sikeston U.S.A.
45 P3 Sikhote-Alin mt. ra. China/Rus. Fed.
29 E6 Sikinos i. Greece
55 G4 Sikkim div. India
19 J6 Siklós Hungary
10 E2 Siksjö Sweden
41 A5 Sikuati Malaysia
24 C1 Sil r. Spain
41 C4 Silago Phil.
11 F5 Šilalė Lithuania
26 C2 Silandro Italy
40 B1 Silantek, G. h. Indon./Malaysia
41 B4 Silay Phil.
26 E3 Silba i. Croatia
55 H4 Silchar India
56 C2 Sileru r. India
75 E4 Silet Algeria
54 E3 Silgarhi Nepal
55 H4 Silghat India
81 ▫1 Silhouette I. i. Seychelles
75 F1 Siliana Tunisia
61 B1 Silifke Turkey
55 G3 Siling Co salt l. China
54 D4 Silipur India
91 ▫12 Silisili mt. Western Samoa
28 F2 Silistea Nouă Romania
28 F2 Silistra Bulgaria
29 G4 Silivri Turkey
11 D3 Siljan l. Sweden
11 C4 Silkeborg Denmark
140 C3 Sillajhuay mt. Chile
11 G4 Sillamäe Estonia
24 B1 Silleda Spain
20 D2 Sillé-le-Guillaume France
54 C5 Sillod India
20 C2 Sillon de Talbert pen. France
55 G3 Silong China
125 E6 Silsbee U.S.A.
10 G1 Siltaharju Finland
72 C4 Siltou well Chad
40 B1 Siluas Indon.
77 F5 Siluko Nigeria
77 F5 Siluko r. Nigeria
57 E4 Sīlūp r. Iran
11 F5 Šilutė Lithuania
145 G5 Silva Jardim Brazil
60 E2 Silvan Turkey
144 D2 Silvânia Brazil
54 C5 Silvassa India
133 E2 Silver Bank *Turks and Caicos Is* Caribbean
133 E2 Silver Bank Passage chan. *Turks and Caicos Is* Caribbean
122 B2 Silver Bay U.S.A.
127 E5 Silver City U.S.A.
114 A2 Silver Islet Can.
128 D4 Silver Lake l. U.S.A.
122 D2 Silver Lake l. U.S.A.
126 B3 Silver Lake U.S.A.
17 C5 Silvermine Mts h. Rep. of Ire.
128 D3 Silver Peak Range mts U.S.A.
120 E5 Silver Spring U.S.A.
128 C2 Silver Springs U.S.A.
96 E2 Silverton Aust.
114 D4 Silver Water Can.
139 F4 Silves Brazil
24 B4 Silves *Faro* Portugal
131 H5 Silvituc Mexico
21 K3 Silvretta Gruppe mt. ra. Switz.
64 E2 Sim r. Rus. Fed.
64 E2 Sim Rus. Fed.
14 D1 Sima Rus. Fed.
40 B1 Simanggang Malaysia
15 C1 Simanichy Belarus
50 C4 Simao China
142 E3 Simão Dias Brazil
41 B3 Simara i. Phil.
115 F3 Simard, Lac l. Can.
60 F3 Sīmareh r. Iran
55 F4 Simaria India
60 B2 Simav Turkey
29 G5 Simav Dağları mt. ra. Turkey
78 D3 Simba Zaire
114 E5 Simcoe Can.
115 F4 Simcoe, Lake l. Can.
55 F5 Simdega India
80 C2 Simēn Mountains mt. ra. Ethiopia
28 D2 Simeria Romania
38 C6 Simeuluë i. Indon.
13 E6 Simferopol' Ukraine
55 E3 Simikot Nepal
19 K4 Siminy mt. Slovakia
138 C2 Simití Colombia
28 D4 Simitli Bulgaria
128 C4 Simi Valley U.S.A.
127 F4 Simla U.S.A.
28 D1 Şimleu Silvaniei Romania
18 C4 Simmern (Hunsrück) Germany
128 C4 Simmler U.S.A.
129 F4 Simmons U.S.A.
119 F7 Simms The Bahamas
119 ▫2 Simms Pt pt The Bahamas
19 L1 Simnas' Lithuania
10 G2 Simojärvi l. Finland
110 F4 Simonette r. Can.
111 J4 Simonhouse Can.
115 H4 Simon, Lac l. Can.
19 J5 Simontornya Hungary
40 A2 Simpang Indon.
142 D2 Simplício Mendes Brazil
21 J3 Simplon Pass pass Switz.
147 B6 Simpson r. Chile
98 D5 Simpson Desert desert Aust.
96 D1 Simpson Desert Conservation Park res. Aust.
98 D5 Simpson Desert Nat. Park nat. park Aust.
101 D5 Simpson Hill h. Aust.
114 B2 Simpson I. i. Can.
128 D2 Simpson Park Mts mts U.S.A.
11 D5 Simrishamn Sweden
40 B1 Simunjan Malaysia
41 A5 Simunul i. Phil.
63 R5 Simushir, O. i. Rus. Fed.
56 A2 Sina r. India
80 E3 Sina Dhaqa Somalia
61 C6 Sināfir i. Saudi Arabia
73 F2 Sinai pen. Egypt
28 E2 Sinaia Romania
21 G2 Sinai, Mont h. France
60 E2 Şınak Turkey
130 C3 Sinaloa div. Mexico
26 C4 Sinalunga Italy
50 E3 Sinan China
49 H5 Sinanju N. Korea
64 F1 Sinara r. Rus. Fed.
29 B5 Sinarades Greece
72 B1 Sīnāwin Libya
42 A3 Sinbaungwe Myanmar
42 B1 Sinbo Myanmar
42 A2 Sinbyugyun Myanmar
60 D2 Sincan Turkey
138 B2 Sincé Colombia
138 B2 Sincelejo Colombia
119 D5 Sinclair, L. l. U.S.A.
110 E4 Sinclair Mills Can.
54 D4 Sind r. India
41 B4 Sindañgan Phil.
40 A3 Sindangbarang Indon.
78 B4 Sindara Gabon
54 B4 Sindari India
18 D4 Sindelfingen Germany
56 B2 Sindgi India
54 B4 Sindh Pakistan
56 B3 Sindhnur India
29 G5 Sındırgı Turkey
56 B2 Sindkhed India
54 C5 Sindkheda India
12 J2 Sindor Rus. Fed.
55 F5 Sindri India
54 B3 Sind Sagar Doab low-land Pakistan
12 J3 Sinegor'ye Rus. Fed.
77 E4 Sinendé Benin
24 B4 Sines Portugal
24 B4 Sines, Cabo de pt Portugal
10 G2 Sinettä Finland
14 B3 Sinezerki Rus. Fed.
76 C5 Sinfra Côte d'Ivoire
42 B2 Sing Myanmar
73 F5 Singa Sudan
54 E3 Singahi India
50 B4 Singaingmyo Myanmar
49 H4 Sin'galp'a China
54 D2 Singa P. pass India
33 M9 Singapore country Asia
43 C7 Singapore Singapore
40 A1 Singapore, Str. of chan. Indon./Singapore
40 C4 Singaraja Indon.
43 C4 Sing Buri Thailand
18 D5 Singen (Hohentwiel) Germany
114 E4 Singhampton Can.
81 B5 Singida Tanzania
81 B6 Singida div. Tanzania
42 A1 Singkaling Hkamti Myanmar
40 E3 Singkang Indon.
40 B1 Singkawang Indon.
40 A2 Singkep i. Indon.
97 G3 Singleton Aust.
98 B4 Singleton, Mt h. Aust.
101 B6 Singleton, Mt h. Aust.
54 C4 Singoli India
42 A2 Singu Myanmar
28 E2 Singureni Romania
40 D2 Sinio, G. mt. Indon.
27 B5 Siniscola Italy
26 F4 Sinj Croatia
40 E3 Sinjai Indon.
28 B3 Sinjajevina Planina mt. ra. Yugo.
60 E2 Sinjār Iraq
60 E2 Sinjār, Jabal mt. Iraq
73 G4 Sinkat Sudan
49 H5 Sinmi i. N. Korea
139 G2 Sinnamary French Guiana
61 B5 Sinn Bishr, G. h. Egypt
61 A5 Sinnūris Egypt
28 G2 Sinoie, L. lag. Romania
60 C1 Sinop Turkey
49 J4 Sinp'o N. Korea
49 H5 Sinp'yŏng N. Korea
49 H5 Sinsang N. Korea
18 D4 Sinsheim Germany
40 B1 Sintang Indon.
132 ▫1 Sint Nicolaas *Aruba* Caribbean
125 D6 Sinton U.S.A.
138 B2 Sinú r. Colombia
49 H5 Sinŭiju N. Korea
80 E3 Sinujiif Somalia
41 B5 Siocon Phil.
79 D7 Sioma Ngwezi National Park nat. park Zambia
21 H3 Sion Switz.
124 D3 Sioux Center U.S.A.
124 D3 Sioux City U.S.A.
124 D3 Sioux Falls U.S.A.
112 B3 Sioux Lookout Can.
131 H6 Sipacate Guatemala
41 B4 Sipalay Phil.
139 F3 Sipaliwini r. Surinam
26 F4 Šipan i. Croatia
40 B1 Sipang, Tg pt Malaysia
133 ▫3 Siparia Trin. & Tobago
42 B2 Sipein Myanmar
49 H4 Siping China
111 K3 Sipiwesk Can.
111 K3 Sipiwesk L. l. Can.
152 B4 Siple Coast Ant.
152 A4 Siple, Mt mt. Ant.
54 C5 Sipra r. India
119 C5 Sipsey r. U.S.A.
38 C7 Sipura i. Indon.
80 ▫ Siqirah *Socotra* Yemen
144 D5 Siqueira Campos Brazil
41 B4 Siquijor i. Phil.
41 B4 Siquijor Phil.
57 G4 Sir r. Pakistan
56 B3 Sira India
11 B4 Sira r. Norway
57 C4 Şīr Abū Nu'āyr i. U.A.E.
27 E7 Siracusa Italy
55 G4 Sirajganj Bangladesh
110 E4 Sir Alexander, Mt mt. Can.
54 A4 Siranda L. l. Pakistan
77 E4 Sirba r. Burkina/Niger
57 C4 Şīr Banī Yās i. U.A.E.
98 D2 Sir Edward Pellew Group is Aust.
76 B5 Sirekude Sierra Leone
122 A3 Siren U.S.A.
28 F1 Siret Romania
57 E4 Sīrgān Iran
100 D2 Sir Graham Moore Is is Aust.
54 D3 Sirhind India
28 C1 Şiria Romania
42 C3 Siri Kit Dam dam Thailand
54 B3 Siritoi r. Pakistan
57 C3 Sīrīz Iran
110 D2 Sir James McBrien, Mt mt. Can.
57 C3 Sīrjan salt flat Iran
96 D3 Sir Joseph Banks Group is Aust.
57 D4 Sirk Iran
56 C2 Sironcha India
54 D4 Sironj India
74 C2 Siroua, Jbel mt. Morocco
56 B2 Sirpur India
128 C4 Sirretta Peak summit U.S.A.
54 C3 Sirsa *Haryana* India
55 E4 Sirsa *Madhya Pradesh* India
110 F4 Sir Sanford, Mt mt. Can.
56 A3 Sirsi *Karnataka* India
54 D3 Sirsi *Uttar Pradesh* India
56 B2 Sirsilla India
96 B1 Sir Thomas, Mt h. Aust.
56 A2 Sirur India
11 G5 Širvintos Lithuania
60 F3 Sīrwān r. Iraq
110 F4 Sir Wilfred Laurier, Mt mt. Can.
99 E2 Sir W. Thompson h. Aust.
26 F3 Sisak Croatia
43 D4 Sisaket Thailand
57 B3 Sīsakht Iran
131 H4 Sisal Mexico
25 E3 Sisante Spain
60 F2 Sisian Armenia
76 D4 Sisili r. Burkina/Ghana
109 N3 Sisimiut Greenland
122 C2 Siskiwit Bay b. U.S.A.
43 C4 Sisŏphŏn Cambodia
128 B4 Sisquoc r. U.S.A.
124 D2 Sisseton U.S.A.
121 K1 Sisson Branch Reservoir resr Can.
57 E3 Sīstān reg. Iran
57 E3 Sīstān va Balūchestān div. Iran
21 G4 Sisteron France
43 A5 Sisters i. *Andaman and Nicobar Is* India
82 A4 Sisters Pk h. *Ascension* Atlantic Ocean
93 ▫1 Sisters, The is *Chatham Is* N.Z.
81 ▫1 Sisters, The is Seychelles
55 F4 Sitamarhi India
54 C5 Sitamau India
83 H2 Sitampiky Madagascar
41 A5 Sitangkai Phil.
54 E4 Sitapur India
29 F7 Siteia Greece
83 E4 Siteki Swaziland
29 D4 Sithonia pen. Greece
145 E1 Sítio da Abadia Brazil
142 D3 Sítio do Mato Brazil
110 B3 Sitka U.S.A.
55 E4 Sitlaha India
28 C3 Sitnica r. Yugo.
42 B3 Sittang r. Myanmar
18 B3 Sittard Netherlands
42 A1 Sittaung Myanmar
42 A2 Sittwe Myanmar
40 C3 Situbondo Indon.
45 ▫ Siu A Chau i. Hong Kong
91 ▫12 Siumu Western Samoa
130 J6 Siuna Nicaragua
55 F5 Siuri India
56 B4 Sivaganga India
56 B4 Sivakasi India
49 H1 Sivaki Rus. Fed.
57 C3 Sivand Iran
60 D2 Sivas Turkey
60 B2 Sivaslı Turkey
60 D2 Siverek Turkey
12 D3 Siverskiy Rus. Fed.
14 F2 Sivin' r. Rus. Fed.
14 G2 Sivin' Rus. Fed.
60 B2 Sivrihisar Turkey
72 E2 Siwa Egypt
40 E2 Siwa Indon.
54 D3 Siwalik Range mt. ra. India
55 F4 Siwan India
54 C4 Siwana India
72 E2 Siwa Oasis oasis Egypt
21 G5 Six-Fours-les-Plages France
51 G1 Si Xian China
48 A5 Sixin China
122 E4 Six Lakes U.S.A.
83 D4 Siyabuswa R.S.A.
51 G1 Siyang China
60 G2 Siyäzän Azerbaijan
48 D4 Siyitang China
57 C2 Siyunī Iran
49 H2 Sizhan China
48 A2 Sizim Rus. Fed.
48 D4 Siziwang Qi China
11 C5 Sjælland i. Denmark
28 C3 Sjenica Yugo.
11 D5 Sjöbo Sweden
10 E1 Sjøvegan Norway
15 E3 Skadovs'k Ukraine
109 R2 Skærfjorden inlet Greenland
10 M2 Skaftafell nat. park Iceland
10 M3 Skaftárós b. Iceland
10 M2 Skagafjörður b. Iceland
11 C4 Skagen Denmark
11 C4 Skagerrak str. Denmark/Norway
126 B1 Skagit r. Can./U.S.A.
110 B3 Skagway U.S.A.
10 G1 Skaidi Norway
29 D6 Skala Greece
10 E1 Skaland Norway
15 B2 Skala-Podil's'ka Ukraine
15 A2 Skalat Ukraine
19 K3 Skalbmierz Poland
10 D2 Skalmodal Sweden
11 C4 Skanderborg Denmark
121 E3 Skaneateles Lake l. U.S.A.
122 C2 Skanee U.S.A.
29 E5 Skantzoura i. Greece
11 D4 Skara Sweden
11 D4 Skaraborg div. Sweden
99 E1 Skardon r. Aust.
54 C2 Skardu Pakistan
65 J5 Skardu *Jammu and Kashmir*
11 F4 Skargadshavets Nationalpark nat. park. Finland
11 C3 Skarnes Norway
19 J1 Skarszewy Poland
19 K3 Skaryszew Poland
15 B2 Skarzhyntsi Ukraine
19 K3 Skarżysko-Kamienna Poland
10 F2 Skaulo Sweden
19 J4 Skawina Poland
74 A4 Skaymat *Western Sahara*
110 D3 Skeena r. Can.
110 D3 Skeena Mountains mt. ra. Can.
17 H5 Skegness U.K.
82 A2 Skeleton Coast Game Park res. Namibia
10 F2 Skellefteå Sweden
10 E2 Skellefteälven r. Sweden
10 F2 Skelleftehamn Sweden
17 B6 Skellig Rocks is Rep. of Ire.
17 D5 Skerries Rep. of Ire.
11 C4 Ski Norway
29 D5 Skiathos i. Greece
29 D5 Skiathos Greece
17 C6 Skibbereen Rep. of Ire.
10 F1 Skibotn Norway
17 F4 Skiddaw mt. U.K.
11 C4 Skien Norway
19 K3 Skierniewice Poland
75 F1 Skikda Algeria
54 D2 Skio India
97 E4 Skipton Aust.
17 F5 Skipton U.K.
11 C4 Skive Denmark
10 M2 Skjálfandafljót r. Iceland
10 M2 Skjálfandi b. Iceland
11 C5 Skjern Denmark
11 B3 Skjolden Norway
14 C1 Sknyatino Rus. Fed.
10 B3 Skodje Norway
26 E2 Škofja Loka Slovenia
10 G1 Skoganvarre Norway
19 H2 Skoki Poland
122 D4 Skokie U.S.A.
17 E6 Skomer Island i. U.K.
29 D5 Skopelos *Thessalia* Greece
29 D5 Skopelos i. Greece
14 D3 Skopin Rus. Fed.
28 C4 Skopje Macedonia
16 D1 Skopun Faeroes
16 D1 Skopunarfjørður chan. Faeroes
19 J2 Skórcz Poland
15 G1 Skorodnoye Rus. Fed.
14 D1 Skoropuskovskiy Rus. Fed.
11 D4 Skövde Sweden
45 M1 Skovorodino Rus. Fed.
121 J2 Skowhegan U.S.A.
11 F4 Skrunda Latvia
110 B2 Skukum, Mt mt. Can.
128 D3 Skull Peak summit U.S.A.
16 K2 Skudenshavn Norway
122 B5 Skunk r. U.S.A.
11 F4 Skuodas Lithuania
11 D5 Skurup Sweden
11 E3 Skutskär Sweden
15 C2 Skvyra Ukraine
16 D3 Skye i. U.K.
29 E5 Skyropoula i. Greece
29 E5 Skyros i. Greece
29 E5 Skyros Greece
152 B3 Skytrain Ice Rise ice feature Ant.
11 C5 Slagelse Denmark
10 E2 Slagnäs Sweden
40 B3 Slamet, G. vol Indon.
17 D5 Slaney r. Rep. of Ire.
28 E2 Slănic Romania
28 F1 Slănic Moldova Romania
11 H4 Slantsy Rus. Fed.
19 G3 Slaný Czech Rep.
13 G5 Slashchevskaya Rus. Fed.
14 G4 Slastukha Rus. Fed.
114 B2 Slate Is is Can.
28 E2 Slatina Romania
15 G1 Slatyne Ukraine
111 G2 Slave r. Can.
77 E5 Slave Coast Africa
110 G3 Slave Lake Can.
65 J2 Slavgorod Rus. Fed.
15 F2 Slavhorod *Dnipropetrovs'k* Ukraine
15 F1 Slavhorod *Sumy* Ukraine
14 C1 Slavnoye Rus. Fed.
26 F3 Slavonija reg. Croatia
26 F3 Slavonska Požega Croatia
26 G3 Slavonski Brod Croatia
15 B1 Slavuta Ukraine
15 D1 Slavutych Ukraine
65 G4 Slavyanka Kazak.
49 J4 Slavyanka Rus. Fed.
28 E3 Slavyanovo Bulgaria
13 F6 Slavyansk-na-Kubani Rus. Fed.
19 H3 Sława Poland
19 H1 Sławno Poland
96 C3 Sleaford B. b. Aust.
17 B5 Slea Head hd Rep. of Ire.
16 E3 Sleat, Sound of chan. U.K.
112 E2 Sleeper Islands is Can.
122 D3 Sleeping Bear Dunes National Seashore res. U.S.A.
122 D3 Sleeping Bear Pt pt U.S.A.
13 H7 Sleptsovskaya Rus. Fed.
152 C3 Slessor Glacier gl. Ant.
125 F6 Slidell U.S.A.
17 D5 Slieve Bloom Mts h. Rep. of Ire.
17 B5 Slieve Mish Mts h. Rep. of Ire.
17 C4 Sligo Rep. of Ire.
17 C4 Sligo Bay b. Rep. of Ire.
11 E4 Slite Sweden
28 F3 Sliven Bulgaria
28 F3 Slivo Pole Bulgaria
15 C3 Slobidka Ukraine
12 H2 Sloboda Rus. Fed.
12 J2 Slobodchikovo Rus. Fed.
14 B2 Slobodka Rus. Fed.
12 J3 Slobodskoy Rus. Fed.
15 C3 Slobozia Moldova
28 F2 Slobozia Romania
110 F5 Slocan Can.
19 K3 Słomniki Poland
12 C4 Slonim Belarus
15 G1 Slonovka Rus. Fed.
90 ▫1 Slot, The chan. Solomon Is.
17 G6 Slough U.K.
14 A4 Slout Ukraine
4 G4 Slovakia country Europe
15 C1 Slovechne Ukraine
4 G4 Slovenia country Europe
26 E2 Slovenj Gradec Slovenia
26 E2 Slovenska Bistrica Slovenia
19 K4 Slovenské Rudohorie mt. ra. Slovakia
15 G2 Slov"yanohirs'k Ukraine
15 G2 Slov"yans'k Ukraine
15 C1 Slovyechna r. Belarus
15 B1 Sluch r. Ukraine
26 E3 Slunj Croatia
19 H2 Słupca Poland
19 H1 Słupsk Poland
10 E2 Slussfors Sweden
13 C4 Slutsk Belarus
17 B5 Slyne Head hd Rep. of Ire.
48 B2 Slyudyanka Rus. Fed.
121 J3 Small Pt pt U.S.A.
113 H3 Smallwood Reservoir resr Can.
12 C4 Smarhon' Belarus
111 J4 Smeaton Can.
28 C2 Smederevo Yugo.
28 C2 Smederevska Palanka Yugo.
28 F2 Smeeni Romania
120 D4 Smethport U.S.A.
49 K2 Smidovich Rus. Fed.

19 H2 Śmigiel Poland
15 D2 Smila Ukraine
15 E1 Smile Ukraine
11 G4 Smiltene Latvia
14 G2 Smirnovo Rus. Fed.
110 G3 Smith Can.
128 C2 Smith U.S.A.
120 C6 Smith r. U.S.A.
108 F3 Smith Arm b. Can.
110 D4 Smithers Can.
110 E5 Smithfield U.S.A.
126 E3 Smithfield U.S.A.
152 A3 Smith Glacier gl. Ant.
152 B2 Smith I. i.
  S. Shetland Is Ant.
43 A4 Smith I. i. Andaman and
  Nicobar Is India
121 E5 Smith I. i. U.S.A.
121 F6 Smith I. i. U.S.A.
120 D6 Smith Mountain Lake l.
  U.S.A.
110 D3 Smith River Can.
115 G4 Smiths Falls Can.
109 L2 Smith Sound str.
  Can./Greenland
97 F5 Smithton Aust.
128 C1 Smoke Creek Desert
  desert U.S.A.
110 F4 Smoky r. Can.
124 C4 Smoky r. U.S.A.
96 C3 Smoky Bay Aust.
97 H2 Smoky C. hd Aust.
114 D1 Smoky Falls Can.
114 D5 Smoky Hills h. U.S.A.
110 G4 Smoky Lake Can.
10 B3 Smøla i. Norway
14 A2 Smolensk Rus. Fed.
14 A2 Smolensk div. Rus. Fed.
14 A2 Smolenskaya
  Vozvyshennost' h.
  Rus. Fed.
65 K2 Smolenskoye Rus. Fed.
29 C4 Smolikas mt. Greece
14 F1 Smolino Rus. Fed.
29 E4 Smolyan Bulgaria
112 C3 Smooth Rock Falls Can.
77 E4 Smooth Rock l.
111 H4 Smoothstone Lake l.
  Can.
10 G1 Smørfjord Norway
15 D2 Smotrych Ukraine
14 A2 Smyadovo Bulgaria
15 A1 Smyha Ukraine
152 B3 Smyley I. i. Ant.
121 F5 Smyrna U.S.A.
119 C5 Smyrna U.S.A.
120 C4 Smyrna U.S.A.
121 J1 Smyrna Mills U.S.A.
15 G3 Smyrnove Ukraine
10 N2 Snæfell mt. Iceland
17 H4 Snaefell h. Isle of Man
110 A2 Snag Can.
126 D3 Snake r. U.S.A.
92 □3 Snares Is Is N.Z.
10 B2 Snåsa Norway
18 B2 Sneek Netherlands
17 C6 Sneem Rep. of Ire.
82 C5 Sneeuberg mts R.S.A.
113 H3 Snegamook Lake l. Can.
62 K3 Snezhnogorsk Rus. Fed.
25 H3 Snežnik mt. Slovenia
15 A1 Snihurivka Ukraine
19 L4 Snina Slovakia
16 D3 Snizort, Loch b. U.K.
126 B2 Snohomish U.S.A.
126 B2 Snoqualmie Pass pass
  U.S.A.
10 D2 Snøtinden mt. Norway
15 D1 Snov r. Ukraine
14 D3 Snova r. Rus. Fed.
111 J2 Snowbird Lake l. Can.
93 B6 Snowdon mt. N.Z.
17 D4 Snowdon mt. U.K.
129 C4 Snowflake U.S.A.
121 F5 Snow Hill U.S.A.
119 E5 Snow Hill U.S.A.
111 J4 Snow Lake Can.
110 D3 Snowtown Aust.
126 D3 Snowville U.S.A.
97 G4 Snowy r. Aust.
115 H5 Snow Mt. mt. U.S.A.
97 G4 Snowy Mts mt. ra. Aust.
132 D2 Snug Corner The
  Bahamas
113 J3 Snug Harbour Can.
114 E4 Snug Harbour Can.
43 D4 Snuöl Cambodia
15 D2 Snyatyn Ukraine
125 D5 Snyder U.S.A.
125 C5 Snyder U.S.A.
83 G2 Soahany Madagascar
93 A6 Soaker, Mt mt. N.Z.
83 H2 Soalala Madagascar
83 G3 Soalara Madagascar
83 G2 Soamanonga
  Madagascar
83 H2 Soanierana-Ivongo
  Madagascar
46 A6 Soan kundo i. S. Korea
83 H2 Soavinandriana
  Madagascar
80 B3 Sobat r. Sudan
19 G4 Sobéslav Czech Rep.
39 M7 Sobger r. Indon.
46 C7 Sobo-san mt. Japan
144 E1 Sobradinho Brazil
142 D3 Sobradinho, Barragem de
  resr Brazil
142 D1 Sobral Brazil
19 L4 Sobrance Slovakia
15 E1 Sobych Ukraine
15 F7 Sochi Rus. Fed.
91 □11 Société, Archipel de la is
  Fr. Poly. Pac. Oc.
28 C2 Socol Romania
140 C4 Socompa Chile
145 E5 Socorro Brazil
127 F5 Socorro U.S.A.
130 D5 Socorro, I. i. Mexico
25 J3 Socovos Spain
27 E6 Sochos Greece
91 □7 Soc Trăng Vietnam
25 E3 Socuéllamos Spain
128 D4 Soda Lake l. U.S.A.
12 D4 Sodankylä Finland
54 D2 Soda Plains plain
  China/Jammu and Kashmir
126 E3 Soda Springs U.S.A.
11 H4 Söderhamn Sweden
11 H4 Söderköping Sweden
11 H4 Södermanland div.
  Sweden
11 H4 Södertälje Sweden
80 D3 Sodiri Sudan
80 C3 Sodo Ethiopia
11 H3 Södra Kvarken str.
  Finland/Sweden
72 D4 Soëka well Chad
82 □4 Soekmekaar R.S.A.
18 D3 Soest Germany
29 D5 Sofades Greece
83 E2 Sofala div. Mozambique
83 E2 Sofala, Baia de b.
  Mozambique
29 D6 Sofiko Greece
14 F1 Sof'ino Rus. Fed.
28 D3 Sofiya Bulgaria
28 D3 Sofiya Bulgaria
15 F2 Sofiyivka Ukraine
10 H2 Sofporog Rus. Fed.
54 C1 Softnur Rus. Fed.
138 C2 Sogamoso Colombia
54 J6d Sōga Rus. Fed.
11 B4 Søgne Norway
11 K6 Sognesøen chan. Norway
11 B3 Sogn og Fjordane div.
  Norway
41 C4 Sogo Head
48 B4 Sogo Nur l. China
12 H2 Sogra Rus. Fed.

50 C1 Sogruma China
55 H3 Sog Xian China
73 F2 Sohâg Egypt
54 C2 Sohan r. Pakistan
90 □1 Sohano P.N.G.
55 E5 Sohela India
54 D3 Sohna India
18 B3 Soignies Belgium
56 B2 Soila China
10 G3 Soini Finland
21 F4 Soissons France
46 D6 Sōja Japan
54 C4 Sojat India
41 B4 Sojoton Point pt Phil.
64 D2 Sokr. Rus. Fed.
11 H6 Sokal' Ukraine
49 J5 Sokch'o S. Korea
81 D7 Soke Tanzania
65 H5 Sokh Tajikistan
48 D2 Sokhondo, G. mt. Rus.
  Fed.
13 G7 Sokhumi Georgia
28 C3 Sokobanja Yugo.
77 E5 Sokodé Togo
45 □1 Soko Islands is Hong
  Kong
12 G3 Sokol Rus. Fed.
25 H3 Sokolac Bos.-Herz.
15 D2 Sokolivka Cherkasy
  Ukraine
19 L2 Sokółka Poland
14 B1 Sokol'niki Rus. Fed.
64 D2 Sokol r. Rus. Fed.
76 C4 Sokolo Mali
18 F3 Sokolov Czech Rep.
19 J3 Sokołów Małopolski
  Poland
19 K2 Sokołów Podlaski Poland
14 F1 Sokol'skoye Rus. Fed.
76 A4 Sokone Senegal
47 □2 Sokoniya Japan
77 E4 Sokoto Nigeria
77 D4 Sokoto div. Nigeria
77 E4 Sokoto r. Nigeria
15 B2 Sokyrany Ukraine
54 D3 Solan India
93 A7 Solander I. i. N.Z.
14 C1 Solba Rus. Fed.
15 C3 doldăneşti Moldova
15 E5 Sölden Austria
19 J2 Solec Kujawski Poland
138 C1 Soledad Colombia
139 E2 Soledad Venezuela
130 D3 Soledad de Doblado
  Mexico
143 B6 Soledade Brazil
15 B2 Solenoye Rus. Fed.
17 G6 Solent, The inl. U.K.
21 G5 Solf'jellsjøen Norway
12 G2 Solginskiy Rus. Fed.
60 E2 Solhan Turkey
63 N4 Soligalich Rus. Fed.
14 C2 Solikamsk Rus. Fed.
13 J5 Sol'-Iletsk Rus. Fed.
139 E4 Solimões r. Brazil
18 C3 Solingen Germany
10 E3 Sollefteå Sweden
25 H3 Sóller Spain
18 D2 Solling h. Germany
14 F2 Solnechnogorsk
  Rus. Fed.
15 G1 Solntsevo Rus. Fed.
15 B2 Solo r. Ukraine
15 B2 Solobkivtsi Ukraine
15 J2 Sololá Guatemala
15 D2 Solonka Ukraine
86 H5 Solomon Islands country
  Pac. Oc.
90 □1 Solomon Sea sea
  P.N.G./Solomon Is.
49 G3 Solon China
64 F3 Solonchak Ghaklarteniz
  salt marsh Kazak.
64 D4 Solonchak Kendyrlisor l.
  Kazak.
64 E4 Solonchakovyye Vpadiny
  Unguz salt flat
  Turkmenistan
64 E4 Solonchak Shorkozakhly
  depression Turkmenistan
15 F2 Solone Ukraine
14 E1 Solonitsa r. Rus. Fed.
142 E2 Solonópole Brazil
122 B2 Solon Springs U.S.A.
39 H8 Solor, Kepulauan is
  Indon.
15 C2 Solotcha Rus. Fed.
21 H3 Solothurn Switz.
14 E5 Solotvyn Ukraine
12 E1 Solovetskiye Ostrova is
  Rus. Fed.
39 M5 Solovi I. Fed. States of
  Micronesia
39 K7 Solovo, Monte mt. Indon.
49 E2 Solov'yevsk Rus. Fed.
25 J2 Solsona Spain
80 B4 Soroti Uganda
19 J5 Šolta i. Croatia
26 E4 Solţānābād Iran
57 D3 Solţānābād Iran
57 C2 Solţānābād Iran
18 D2 Soltau Germany
19 F5 Solţānīyeh Iran
19 J3 Soltvadkert Hungary
121 E3 Solvay U.S.A.
11 G4 Sölvesborg Sweden
12 H2 Sol'vychegodsk Rus. Fed.
10 D1 Solvär Norway
79 E6 Solwezi Zambia
46 D6 Sōma Japan
60 A2 Soma Turkey
80 C4 Somali country Africa
131 J6 Somanya Ghana
29 B2 Sombor Yugo.
130 E4 Sombrerete Mexico
147 O2 Sombrero Chile
43 A4 Sombrero Channel chan.
  Andaman and Nicobar Is
  India
121 J2 Somerset Junction
  U.S.A.
11 F3 Somero Finland
11 □1 Somerset Bermuda
15 H2 Somerset U.S.A.
11 G2 Somerset U.S.A.
11 H3 Somerset div. U.K.
11 K3 Somerset I. i. Can.
82 D5 Somerset East R.S.A.
11 □3 Somerset Island i.
  Bermuda
109 J2 Somerset Island i. Can.
121 G3 Somerset Reservoir resr
  U.S.A.
125 D6 Somerville Res. resr
  U.S.A.
28 D1 Someş r. Romania
28 C1 Someşul Mare r. Rus. Fed.
47 F2 Sommen l. Sweden
11 D4 Sommen l. Sweden
18 E3 Sömmerda Germany
113 G3 Somoso, Lac du I. Can.
14 A5 Somonauk U.S.A.
130 J6 Somotillo Nicaragua
131 H4 Somoto Nicaragua
79 □2 Somosomo Str. chan. Fiji
78 E3 Somuéllamos Brazil
15 □2 Somovo Rus. Fed.
19 J2 Somovo Rus. Fed.
121 G3 Somovo Rus. Fed.
19 L2 Sompolno Poland
29 □4 Soufli Greece
130 K8 Soná Panama
65 H3 Sonaly Kazak.

55 G5 Sonamura India
55 G5 Sonapur India
54 D4 Sonar r. India
45 H5 Sŏnch'ŏn N. Korea
26 C2 Sondalo Italy
11 C5 Sønderborg Denmark
18 E3 Sondershausen Germany
26 B2 Sondrio Italy
56 B2 Sonepet India
54 B5 Songad India
51 F2 Songbu China
54 C4 Sông Cau Vietnam
42 D3 Sông Con r. Vietnam
42 C4 Sông Đa Răng r. Vietnam
81 C7 Songea Tanzania
43 D5 Sông Hau Giang r.
  Vietnam
49 J3 Songhua r. China
49 H4 Songhua Hu resr China
51 H2 Songhua Jiang China
46 A6 Songjŏng S. Korea
50 D2 Songkan China
43 C6 Songkhla Thailand
50 C3 Songling China
42 D3 Sông Ma r. Laos/Vietnam
42 C2 Sông Ma r. Myanmar
50 C3 Songming China
49 H5 Sŏngnam S. Korea
45 H5 Sŏngnam S. Korea
79 B5 Songo Angola
83 E2 Songo Mozambique
81 C6 Songo Mnara I. i.
  Tanzania
81 C6 Songo Songo I. i.
  Tanzania
15 C2 Songpan China
43 D5 Song Saigon r. Vietnam
55 G4 Songsak India
51 E2 Songtao China
51 G3 Songxi China
51 E2 Songzi China
43 E4 San Xian China
48 E4 Sonid Youqi China
48 E4 Sonid Zuoqi China
54 D3 Sonīpat India
14 C1 Sonkovo Rus. Fed.
42 C2 Son La Vietnam
54 A4 Sonmiani Pakistan
54 A4 Sonmiani Bay b. Pakistan
142 C2 Sono r. Brazil
145 F2 Sono r. Brazil
129 G6 Sonoita U.S.A.
130 C2 Sonora r. Mexico
128 B3 Sonora r. Mexico
125 C6 Sonora r. U.S.A.
129 F6 Sonoyta Mexico
130 B2 Sonoyta Mexico
57 A2 Sonqor Iran
26 C2 Sonsca Spain
139 H4 Sonsonate El Salvador
42 A2 Son Tây Vietnam
140 D3 Sopachuy Bolivia
78 E2 Sopo r. Sudan
28 E3 Sopot Bulgaria
27 D5 Sopot Poland
19 H5 Sopron Hungary
65 H4 Sopu-Korgon Kyrgyzstan
54 C2 Sopur India
27 D5 Sora Italy
11 C3 Sorada India
11 E3 Soraker Sweden
140 D3 Sorata Bolivia
25 E4 Sorbas Spain
11 C3 Sor Donyztau l. Kazak.
115 C7 Sorel Can.
97 F5 Sorell L. l. Aust.
97 F5 Sorell Aust.
60 C2 Soreq r. Israel
60 C2 Sorgun Turkey
27 D5 Soria Spain
62 C2 Sørkappøya i. Svalbard
64 D4 Sor Kaydak l. Kazak.
57 C2 Sorkheh Iran
57 C2 Sorkh, Küh-e mt. Iran
10 D1 Sørli Norway
93 C5 Soron N.Z.
111 K3 Soron India
78 D2 Sorong Indon.
39 J7 Sorong Indon.
39 J7 Sorong Indon.
80 B4 Soroti Uganda
12 G1 Sørøya i. Norway
10 G1 Sørraia r. Portugal
24 B2 Sorrento Italy
82 A3 Sorris Sorris Namibia
152 B3 Sør-Rondane mts Ant.
10 E2 Sørsele Sweden
27 B5 Sorso Italy
41 C3 Sorsogon Phil.
12 H2 Sortavala Rus. Fed.
10 D1 Sortland Norway
14 D2 Sosedka Rus. Fed.
15 G2 Sosna r. Rus. Fed.
10 D3 Sosna r. Rus. Fed.
146 B3 Sosneado mt. Arg.
15 A1 Sosnivka Ukraine
15 D2 Sosnovka Rus. Fed.
15 A1 Sosnove Ukraine
12 G2 Sosnovka Rus. Fed.
11 H3 Sosnovo Rus. Fed.
14 G3 Sosnovoborskoye
  Rus. Fed.
128 B2 Sosnovo-Ozerskoye
  Rus. Fed.
14 H4 Sosnovyy Bor Rus. Fed.
14 A1 Sosnytsya Ukraine
14 □2 Sosnytsya Ukraine
77 E4 Sota r. Benin
11 D7 Sotkamo Finland
11 H2 Soto la Marina Mexico
131 H4 Soto la Marina Mexico
130 D2 Sotuélamos Spain
131 H4 Sotuta Mexico
152 B1 Soufli Greece
13 G7 Souflion Greece
78 E5 Sofa r. Benin
29 E5 Souda Greece
29 D4 Soûfri Côte d'Ivoire
130 K8 Soná Panama
133 □5 Soufrière vol Guadeloupe
  Caribbean

133 G4 Soufrière vol St Vincent
76 B4 Sougueta Guinea
75 E1 Souguer Algeria
20 E4 Souillac France
81 □4 Souillac Mauritius
75 F1 Souk Ahras Algeria
74 C2 Souk el Arbaâ du Rharb
  Morocco
74 B1 Souk el Had el Rharbia
  Morocco
24 C5 Souk Khemis du Sahel
  Morocco
24 C5 Souk Tleta Taghramet
  Morocco
24 D5 Souk-Tnine-de-Sidi-el-
  Yamani Morocco
46 □5 Sŏul S. Korea
20 D4 Soulac-sur-Mer
  France
20 D5 Soulom France
43 A4 Sound I. i. Andaman and
  Nicobar Is India
76 A4 Soungrougrou r. Senegal
77 D3 Sountel well Niger
61 C3 Soûr Lebanon
142 C1 Soure Brazil
111 J5 Souris Can.
113 H4 Souris r. Prince Edward I.
  Can.
111 J5 Souris r. Can./U.S.A.
74 B5 Souroumelli well
  Mauritania
24 C2 Sousa Brazil
54 D2 Sousel Portugal
75 G1 Sousse Tunisia
25 D5 Soustons France
69 F9 South Africa, Republic of
  country Africa
98 C2 South Alligator r. Aust.
114 E4 Southampton Can.
121 G4 Southampton U.S.A.
111 M2 Southampton Island i.
  Can.
43 A4 South Andaman I.
  Andaman and Nicobar Is
  India
120 E6 South Aulatsivik Island i.
  Can.
136 F5 South Atlantic Ocean
  Atlantic Ocean
113 H2 South Aulatsivik Island i.
  Can.
96 C2 South Australia div.
  Aust.
114 E4 South Australian div.
  Aust.
148 N6 South Australian Basin
  Indian Ocean
125 F5 Southaven U.S.A.
125 F5 South Baldy mt. U.S.A.
120 B4 South Bass I. i. U.S.A.
111 N2 South Bay b. Can.
114 D4 South Baymouth Can.
122 D5 South Bend U.S.A.
126 B2 South Bend U.S.A.
132 C1 South Bight chan. The
  Bahamas
120 D6 South Boston U.S.A.
93 D5 Southbridge N.Z.
121 G3 Southbridge U.S.A.
59 L6 South C. c. Fiji
119 D5 South Carolina div.
  U.S.A.
121 D2 South China Sea sea
38 F3 Pac. Oc.
121 D2 South Dakota div. U.S.A.
121 D3 South Deerfield U.S.A.
17 H6 South Downs h. U.K.
82 A4 South East Bay b.
  Ascension Atlantic Ocean
97 F5 South East C. c. Aust.
92 □2 South East Harb. inlet i.
  Campbell I. N.Z.
82 A4 South East Head hd
  Ascension Atlantic Ocean
101 C7 South East Is is Aust.
148 D5 South-East Pacific Basin
  Pac. Oc.
94 □3 South East Reef reef
  Macquarie I. Pac. Oc.
94 □4 South East Rock i. Lord
  Howe I. Pac. Oc.
17 H6 Southend U.K.
17 H6 Southend-on-Sea U.K.
122 A5 South English U.S.A.
82 B5 Southern div. Malawi
76 B5 Southern div. Sierra
  Leone
79 E7 Southern div. Zambia
93 C5 Southern Alps mt. ra.
  N.Z.
111 K3 Southern Indian Lake l.
  Can.
79 D7 Southern Lueti r.
96 E4 Southern country Europe
79 B2 Southern National Park
  nat. park Sudan
152 A1 Southern Ocean ocean
119 □1 Southern Pines U.S.A.
152 C1 Southern Thule i.
  Sandwich Is Atlantic Ocean
119 E6 Southern Uplands h. U.K.
115 H4 South Esk r. U.K.
100 D4 South Esk Tableland reg.
  Aust.
119 D5 South Fabius r. U.S.A.
127 F5 South Fork U.S.A.
128 A2 South Fork r. U.S.A.
128 C4 South Fork Kern r. U.S.A.
121 G4 South Fork South Branch
  r. U.S.A.
122 B4 South Fox I. i. U.S.A.
133 □1 South Friar's Bay b.
  St Kitts-Nevis Caribbean
147 G7 South Geomagnetic Pole
  Ant.
147 G7 South Georgia i. Atlantic
  Ocean
16 D3 South Harris i. U.K.
55 G5 South Hatia I. i.
  Bangladesh
120 D4 South Haven U.S.A.
111 M2 South Henik Lake l. Can.
53 D5 South Hill U.K.
82 A5 South Hill h. Tristan da
  Cunha Atlantic Ocean
120 D6 South Hill U.S.A.
149 L6 South Honshu Ridge
  Pac. Oc.
80 C4 South Horr Kenya
111 M3 South Indian Lake Can.
94 □1 South Island i. Cocos Is
  Indian Ocean
93 C6 South Island i. N.Z.
80 C4 South Islet i. Antipodes Is
  N.Z.
41 A4 South Islet reef Phil.
81 C5 South Kitui National
  Reserve res. Kenya
3 D6 South Korea country
  Asia
128 B3 South Lake Tahoe U.S.A.
93 C6 Southland div. N.Z.
81 B7 South Luangwa National
  Park nat. park Zambia
149 G6 South Madagascar Ridge
  Indian Ocean
152 B6 South Magnetic Pole
  Ant.
28 D3 South Manitou I. i.
  U.S.A.
119 D7 South Miami U.S.A.
17 H6 South Molton U.K.
128 C3 South Moose L. l. U.S.A.
120 D5 South Nahanni r. Can.
18 D2 South Negril Pt pt
  Jamaica
152 B1 South Orkney Is is
  Atlantic Ocean
13 G7 South Ossetia div.
  Georgia
53 N8 South Pacific Ocean
  ocean
121 H2 South Paris U.S.A.
126 G3 South Platte r. U.S.A.

82 □1 South Point pt Ascension
  Atlantic Ocean
133 □9 South Point pt Barbados
132 D2 South Point pt The
  Bahamas
114 E2 South Porcupine Can.
17 F5 Southport U.K.
115 H5 South Portland U.S.A.
26 F4 South Ronaldsay i. U.K.
121 D3 South Royalton U.S.A.
82 B5 South Rukuru r. Malawi
152 C1 South Sandwich Islands
  is Atlantic Ocean
149 H9 South Sandwich Trench
  Atlantic Ocean
111 H4 South Saskatchewan r.
  Can.
111 K3 South Seal r. Can.
17 F4 South Shetland Is is Ant.
17 G4 South Shields U.K.
122 A5 South Skunk r. U.S.A.
92 E3 South Taranaki Bight b.
  N.Z.
129 G2 South Tent summit
  U.S.A.
55 E4 South Twin I. i. Can.
112 E3 South Twin I. i. Can.
17 H5 South Tyne r. U.K.
16 B3 South Uist i. U.K.
98 D3 South Wellesley Islands
  is Aust.
82 A4 South West Bay b.
  Ascension Atlantic Ocean
119 □2 South West Bay b. The
  Bahamas
97 F5 South West C. hd Aust.
92 □1 South West C. hd Aust.
119 □3 South West Cape Virgin
  Is Caribbean
80 D2 South West Pt pt St
  Helena Atlantic Ocean
149 H6 South-West Indian Ridge
  Indian Ocean
99 G3 South West Island i.
  Coral Sea Islands Terr. Pac.
  Oc.
97 F5 South West Nat. Park
  nat. park Aust.
148 D7 South-West Peru Ridge
  Pac. Oc.
82 A4 South West Pt pt St
  Helena Atlantic Ocean
133 □1 South West Pt Jamaica
94 □3 South West Pt pt
  Macquarie I. Pac. Oc.
132 C3 Southwest Rock i.
  Caribbean
17 J5 South Whitley U.S.A.
121 H3 South Windham U.S.A.
17 H5 Southwold U.K.
82 C5 Soutpansberg mt. ra.
  R.S.A.
28 E3 Sovata Romania
24 □4 Soverato Italy
61 B2 Sovereign Base Area
  Cyprus
61 B2 Sovereign Base Area
  Cyprus
12 J4 Sovetsk Rus. Fed.
27 F6 Sovetsk Rus. Fed.
17 J5 Spurn Head c. U.K.
15 H2 Soweto R.S.A.
45 J2 Soyetskaya Gavan'
  Rus. Fed.
62 H3 Sovetskiy Rus. Fed.
14 H3 Sovetskoye Rus. Fed.
14 H3 Sovetskoye Rus. Fed.
90 □8 Sovi B. b. Fiji
12 G2 Sovpol'ye Rus. Fed.
14 E2 Sovyets'kyy Ukraine
62 H3 Soyana r. Rus. Fed.
46 H1 Sōya-misaki c. Japan
46 H1 Sōya-wan b. Japan
79 B5 Soyo Angola
14 C2 Sozh r. Belarus
14 J2 Sozimskiy Rus. Fed.
28 F3 Sozopol Bulgaria
18 B3 Spa Belgium
96 E4 Spaatz I. i. Ant.
44 E4 Spain country Europe
96 E2 Spalding Can.
17 G5 Spalding U.K.
114 B3 Spanish r. Can.
119 □1 Spanish Fork U.S.A.
133 □1 Spanish Town Jamaica
133 □1 Spanish Town Virgin Is
  Caribbean
133 □1 Spanish Town Jamaica
120 C6 Sparta U.S.A.
122 B4 Sparta U.S.A.
49 L1 Sparta U.S.A.
32 K9 Sri Lanka country Asia
120 C5 Sparta U.S.A.
122 B4 Sparks U.S.A.
119 D5 Spartanburg U.S.A.
27 B7 Spartel, Cap pt Morocco
29 D6 Sparti Greece
27 B6 Spartivento, Capo pt
  Italy
27 F7 Spartivento, Capo c.
  Italy
28 B2 Spas-Demensk Rus. Fed.
14 D3 Spas-Klepiki Rus. Fed.
19 H2 Środa Śląska Poland
14 E2 Spasove Ukraine
14 D2 Spask-Demensk Rus. Fed.
14 D5 Spasovo Ukraine
14 D2 Spas-Ryazanskiy Rus.
  Fed.
99 D5 Staaten River Nat. Park
  nat. park Aust.
14 C1 Staara Luka r. Rus. Fed.
110 D3 Stadskanaal Netherlands
110 D3 Stadtallendorf Germany
18 D2 Stadthagen Germany
125 C4 Stadtlohn Germany
18 F3 Stadtroda Germany
110 D6 Spanish Fork U.S.A.
14 D2 Spassk-Dal'niy Rus. Fed.
99 D5 Spassk-Ryazanskiy Rus.
  Fed.
27 E5 Spercheios r. Greece
120 D5 Sperrgvile U.K.
29 D5 Spərt r. Germany
26 G1 Spessart reg. Germany
16 F3 Spey r. U.K.
18 C3 Speyer Germany
133 □2 Speyside Tobago Trin. &
  Tobago
97 F5 Spitze Greece
58 L6 Spiez Switz.
18 B2 Spijkenisse Netherlands
57 C3 Spīn Būldak Afghanistan
54 A2 Spīn Būldak Afghanistan
110 F3 Spirit Lake i. Kiribati
56 B4 Spirit River Flowage resr
  U.S.A.
111 H4 Spiritwood Can.
92 E3 Spirovo Rus. Fed.
14 B1 Spirovo Rus. Fed.

57 F2 Spīrsang P. pass
  Afghanistan
19 K4 Spišská Nová Ves
  Slovakia
54 D2 Spiti r. India
62 C2 Spitsbergen i. Svalbard
  Arctic Ocean
18 F5 Spittal an der Drau
  Austria
99 G6 Spittelthorpe Aust.
16 F3 Split Croatia
111 K3 Split Lake Can.
111 K3 Split Lake l. Can.
15 C2 Spodakhy Ukraine
116 F2 Spokane U.S.A.
43 D4 Spong Cambodia
126 E2 Spooner U.S.A.
118 D3 Spotted Horse U.S.A.
113 J2 Spotted Island Can.
24 A2 Spragge Can.
110 E4 Spranger, Mt mt. Can.
99 F1 Spratly Islands is
  S. China Sea
126 C2 Spray U.S.A.
19 D3 Sprēca r. Bos.-Herz.
18 F4 Spree r. Germany
18 F4 Spremberg Germany
12 H1 Spring Bay Aust.
82 B4 Springbok R.S.A.
93 A6 Spring Cr. w Aust.
93 D5 Spring Creek N.Z.
113 J4 Springdale Can.
118 D2 Springer U.S.A.
127 F4 Springerville U.S.A.
121 C6 Springfield U.S.A.
122 C6 Springfield U.S.A.
121 G3 Springfield U.S.A.
120 B5 Springfield U.S.A.
93 C5 Springfield N.Z.
118 D2 Springfield U.S.A.
124 E2 Springfield U.S.A.
124 E4 Springfield U.S.A.
113 H4 Springhill Can.
119 D6 Spring Hill U.S.A.
93 C5 Springs Junction N.Z.
15 J1 Springs, Mt h. Can.
99 E4 Springsure Aust.
98 E4 Springvale Aust.
93 C6 Springvale Aust.
122 A4 Spring Valley U.S.A.
126 D3 Springville U.S.A.
110 C4 Spruce Grove Can.
121 G3 Spruce Knob-Seneca
  Rocks National
  Recreation Area res.
  U.S.A.
17 G1 Sprucedale Can.
19 K2 Spytihněv Rus. Fed.
40 B4 Squamish Can.
24 G4 Squamish Can.
24 E3 Squillace Italy
24 F5 Squillace, Golfo di g.
  Italy
111 H3 Squaw Lake l. U.S.A.
121 J1 Squapan Lake l. U.S.A.
27 F6 Squillace Italy
127 H5 Squaw Peak mt. U.S.A.
17 F6 Start Point pt U.K.
16 G1 Startsya Ukraine
49 □2 Sragen Indon.
43 C4 Srē Âmbêl Cambodia
28 B3 Srbija div. Yugo.
28 B2 Srbobran Yugo.
43 C4 Srê Ambêl Cambodia
29 C4 Sreda No. 8 Bulgaria
29 C4 Sredna Gora mt. ra.
  Bulgaria
14 G2 Srednebelaya Rus. Fed.
14 G4 Srednekolymsk Rus. Fed.
14 C2 Sredne-Russkaya
  Vozvyshennost' h.
  Rus. Fed.
14 H3 Sredne-Sibirskoye
  Ploskogor'ye plat.
  Rus. Fed.
14 H2 Sredne Kuyto, Oz. l.
  Rus. Fed.
28 D3 Srednogorie Bulgaria
13 H5 Srednyaya Akhtuba
  Rus. Fed.
43 D4 Srêpôk, T. r. Cambodia
49 E1 Sretensk Rus. Fed.
15 E1 Sribne Ukraine
119 □1 Spanish Town Virgin Is
56 B2 Srīkakulam India
56 B3 Sri Kālāhasti India
32 K9 Sri Lanka country Asia
54 C2 Srinagar Jammu and
  Kashmir India
54 D3 Srinagar Himachal
  Pradesh India
56 B4 Srirangam India
54 D3 Sri Thep Thailand
56 B4 Srivaikuntam India
56 A2 Srivilliputtur India
19 H3 Šroda Śląska Poland
19 H2 Środa Wielkopolska
  Poland
82 B4 Strabane Bos.-Herz.
54 D3 Stefan Vodă Moldova
55 D5 Srikakulam India
56 A2 Srirangapatna India
56 B3 Stanley Reservoir resr
  India
56 B4 Stanton U.S.A.

14 D3 Stanovoye Rus. Fed.
63 N4 Stanovoye Nagor'ye mts
  Rus. Fed.
63 O4 Stanovoy Khrebet mt.
  Rus. Fed.
62 C2 Spitsbergen i. Svalbard
14 D3 Stanovoy Kolodez'
  Rus. Fed.
100 H4 Stanmore Ra. h. Aust.
99 G6 Stanthorpe Aust.
18 F5 Stanton U.S.A.
122 B6 Stanton U.S.A.
14 D3 Stanton U.S.A.
24 A2 Stapleton U.S.A.
19 K3 Staporków Poland
113 H5 Starachowice Poland
19 K3 Starachowice Poland
19 J3 Stará L'ubovňa Slovakia
28 E2 Stara Pazova Yugo.
28 E3 Stara Planina mt. ra.
  Bulgaria/Yugo.
15 G1 Stara Synyava Ukraine
15 A1 Stara Ushytsya Ukraine
15 A1 Stara Vyzhivka Ukraine
14 H1 Staraya Rudka Rus. Fed.
14 H1 Staraya Russa Rus. Fed.
14 E1 Staraya Vichuga
  Rus. Fed.
28 E3 Stara Zagora Bulgaria
23 J3 Stara Zagora Bulgaria
87 M5 Starbuck Island i. Kiribati
15 G3 Starchenkove Ukraine
28 D4 Starchiojd Romania
15 G2 Stare, Ozero l. Ukraine
19 J2 Stargard Szczeciński
  Szczecin Poland
15 E2 Staritsa Poland
14 C1 Staritsa Rus. Fed.
119 D6 Starke U.S.A.
93 □1 Star Keys is Chatham Is
  N.Z.
125 F5 Starkville U.S.A.
18 E5 Starnberger See l.
  Germany
65 K2 Staroaleyskoye Rus. Fed.
15 G2 Starobil's'k Ukraine
133 □1 Starodub Rus. Fed.
14 B2 Starodub Rus. Fed.
127 C7 Starke Ranges mt. ra.
  Can.
19 J2 Starogard Gdański
  Poland
15 C2 Starokonstantynov
  Ukraine
15 F3 Starokozache Ukraine
15 D1 Staroletovo Rus. Fed.
15 F3 Staromlynivka Ukraine
15 D2 Starominskaya Rus. Fed.
15 G3 Staroshcherbinovskaya
  Rus. Fed.
28 D3 Staro Selo Bulgaria
15 E3 Staroseslavino Rus. Fed.
15 F3 Staroshcherbinovskaya
64 E2 Starosubkhangulovo
  Rus. Fed.
14 G2 Staroyur'yevo Rus. Fed.
28 D3 Staro Selo Bulgaria
28 E3 Staro Selo Bulgaria
27 D6 Stilo, Punta pt Italy
98 B3 Staroye Drozhzhanoye
  Rus. Fed.
14 G2 Staroye Istomino
  Rus. Fed.
14 G2 Staroye Shaygovo
  Rus. Fed.
15 G1 Staroye-Sindrovo
  Rus. Fed.
15 G2 Starozhilovo Rus. Fed.
14 D3 Staryy Chirchim Rus. Fed.
15 F2 Staryy Oskol Rus. Fed.
15 G2 Staryy Ostropil' Ukraine
14 H3 Staryye Aybesi Rus. Fed.
15 A1 Staryy Olov Rus. Fed.
15 G1 Staryy Oskol Rus. Fed.
19 K2 Staryy Ostropil' Ukraine
20 E4 State College U.S.A.
11 B4 Stavanger Norway
15 D2 Stavertsi Bulgaria
15 H3 Stavropol' Rus. Fed.
15 G6 Stavropol' div. Rus. Fed.
13 G6 Stavropol'skaya
  Vovyshennost' reg.
  Rus. Fed.
29 D4 Stavros Greece
29 E6 Stavros Greece
26 D1 Stavyshche Ukraine
99 E4 Stawell Aust.
18 F4 Steamboat Springs
126 E3 U.S.A.
19 H2 Steblev Ukraine
110 C1 Steele U.S.A.
19 D2 Stefan Vodă Moldova
21 J3 Steenstrup gl. Greenland
111 K5 Steinbach Can.
82 B3 Steinhausen Namibia
82 A3 Steinkopf R.S.A.
18 D2 Steinkjer Norway
10 D3 Store Belt chan. Denmark
11 B4 Stavanger Norway

15 F3 Stepanivka Persha
  Ukraine
14 E1 Stepantsevo Rus. Fed.
14 C1 Stepanivka Rus. Fed.
92 D4 Stephens r. N.Z.
92 D4 Stephens I. i. N.Z.
113 J4 Stephenville Can.
113 J4 Stephenville Can.
122 E4 Stephenville U.S.A.
14 D3 Stepne Ukraine
65 H2 Stepnogorsk Kazak.
19 K3 Stepnoho's'k Ukraine
13 H5 Stepnove Yugo.
14 G1 Step'ne Basan' Ukraine
91 □13 Steps Pt pt American
  Samoa Pac. Oc.
126 G3 Sterling U.S.A.
126 G3 Sterling U.S.A.
126 G3 Sterling U.S.A.
125 C6 Sterling City U.S.A.
125 C6 Sterling Hgts U.S.A.
64 E2 Sterlitamak Rus. Fed.
18 F4 Šternberk Czech Rep.
19 H2 Stęszew Poland
122 C5 Steuben U.S.A.
23 G4 Steyr Austria
128 B4 Stevens r. U.S.A.
110 D4 Stevens L. l. Can.
122 C3 Stevens Point U.S.A.
100 D3 Stevens Village U.S.A.
118 F3 Stewart r. Can./U.S.A.
93 □1 Stewart I. i. N.Z.
147 B7 Stewart, L. i. Chile
110 B2 Stewart Lake l. Can.
110 A2 Stewart Town Jamaica
122 A4 Stewartville U.S.A.
114 E2 Stickney U.S.A.
11 G4 Štrenčí Latvia
110 B2 Stikine r. Can./U.S.A.
128 C4 Stikine Ranges mt. ra.
  Can.
27 F6 Stilo Italy
27 E6 Stilo, Punta pt Italy
19 K3 Stimlje Macedonia
29 C4 Štip Macedonia
98 B3 Stirling Cr. r. Aust.
16 E4 Stirling U.K.
101 B6 Stirling Range Nat. Park
  nat. park Aust.
18 D5 Stockerau Austria
11 H4 Stockholm div. Sweden
11 H4 Stockholm U.S.A.
122 C3 Stockbridge U.S.A.
17 F5 Stockport U.K.
17 G4 Stockton-on-Tees U.K.
128 B3 Stockton U.S.A.
124 E4 Stockton U.S.A.
110 A2 Stockton L. l. U.S.A.
119 C7 Stockton Springs U.S.A.
43 C4 Stoeng Trêng Cambodia
29 C4 Stoeng Planina mt. ra.
  Macedonia
11 B4 Stavanger Norway
17 F4 Stokesley U.K.
10 D1 Stokkvågen Norway
10 L1 Stokksnes Iceland
10 E1 Stokmarknes Norway
25 H3 Stolac Bos.-Herz.
19 H3 Stolin Belarus
18 A2 Stoltenhoff I. i. Tristan da
  Cunha Atlantic Ocean
18 D2 Stolzenau Germany
18 E3 Stone U.K.
17 F5 Stoneboro U.S.A.
113 J4 Stone Harbor U.S.A.
110 F4 Stone Mountain Prov.
  U.S.A.
111 K4 Stonewall Can.
122 B2 Stonewall Jackson Lake
  U.S.A.
29 C5 Stony Point U.S.A.
97 G1 Stony Rapids Can.
111 K3 Stora Lulevatten l.
  Sweden
10 E2 Stora Sjöfallets National
  Park nat. park Sweden
10 E2 Storavan l. Sweden
10 E2 Store Bælt chan.
82 A5 Stonewall U.K.
11 K6 Storfjellet mt. Norway
10 E3 Storfjorden chan. Norway
10 C2 Storforshei Norway
10 E3 Stornoway U.K.
29 E6 Storozhevsk Rus. Fed.
15 A2 Storozhynets' Ukraine
10 E2 Storsjön l. Jämtland
  Sweden
15 F1 Storslett Norway
10 D1 Storuman Sweden
10 E2 Storuman l. Sweden
124 E3 Story City U.S.A.
122 A4 Stoughton U.S.A.
17 H6 Stour r. U.K.
17 H6 Stour r. U.K.
17 G5 Stourbridge U.K.
17 G5 Stourport-on-Severn
  U.K.
110 F5 Stout Lake l. Can.
14 C2 Stowbtsy Belarus
17 H5 Stowmarket U.K.
17 J3 Strabane U.K.
11 F5 Strachur U.K.
28 D3 Stradella Italy

19 F4 Strakonice Czech Rep.
28 F1 Stralsund Germany
82 B5 Strand R.S.A.
11 B3 Stranda Norway
119 E7 Strangers Cay i. The
  Bahamas
17 J4 Strangford Lough inlet
  Rep. of Ire.
98 C1 Strangways r. Aust.
21 H2 Strasbourg Bas-Rhin
  France
120 D5 Strasburg U.S.A.
28 E1 Strășeni div. Moldova
28 E1 Strășeni Moldova
97 H4 Stratford Aust.
114 E5 Stratford Can.
92 E3 Stratford N.Z.
125 C4 Stratford U.S.A.
17 G5 Stratford-upon-Avon
  U.K.
96 D5 Strathcona Prov. Park
  res. Can.
110 G4 Strathmore Can.
114 E5 Strathnaver Can.
114 E5 Strathroy Can.
16 F3 Strathspey v. U.K.
121 F2 Stratton U.S.A.
18 E4 Straubing Germany
122 B4 Strawberry Point U.S.A.
127 H1 Strawberry resr U.S.A.
28 E3 Strazhitsa Bulgaria
28 D2 Streaha Romania
28 D3 Strehaia Romania
28 D2 Strelcha Bulgaria
28 D2 Strelcha Bulgaria
15 C1 Streltsy Moldova
63 R3 Strelka Rus. Fed.
100 B4 Strelley Aust.
11 G4 Streľna r. Rus. Fed.
11 G4 Strenčí Latvia
27 E7 Stretti di Messina str.
  Italy
15 E1 Streymoy i. Faeroes
35 E7 Strezhevoy Rus. Fed.
14 G2 Strezhevoy Rus. Fed.
114 E2 Strickland r. P.N.G.
29 □4 Strimonas r. Greece
147 D5 Stroeder Arg.
29 C5 Strofades i. Greece
15 C1 Stroitel' Rus. Fed.
27 E6 Stromboli, Isola i. Italy
147 G7 Stromness Atlantic
  Ocean
16 F2 Stromsburg U.K.
10 D3 Strömsund Sweden
120 C4 Strongsville U.S.A.
16 F2 Stronsay i. U.K.
19 K4 Stropkov Slovakia
17 F6 Stroud U.K.
97 G3 Stroud Road Aust.
17 F5 Struer Denmark
29 C4 Struga Macedonia
14 D2 Strugi-Krasnyye
  Rus. Fed.
17 J5 Strumble Head hd U.K.
29 C4 Strumica Macedonia
11 B3 Stryn Norway
11 B3 Stryy Ukraine
15 A2 Stryzhavka Ukraine
19 L2 Strzelce Opolskie Poland
19 H2 Strzelecki, Cr. w Aust.
19 H3 Strzelecki, Mt h. Aust.
19 H2 Strzelin Poland
19 H2 Strzelno Poland
19 J3 Strzyżów Poland
120 D5 Stuart U.S.A.
124 E3 Stuart U.S.A.
110 F4 Stuart Bluff Ra. mt. ra.
  Aust.
110 E4 Stuart L. l. Can.
93 A6 Stuart Mts mts N.Z.
96 C2 Stuart Ra. h. Aust.
122 A5 Stuarts Draft U.S.A.
17 F6 Stubber Germany
82 B5 Stubbings Pt pt
  Christmas I. Indian Ocean
93 C6 Studholme Junction
  N.Z.
11 C4 Studenka Rus. Fed.
14 H1 Studenka Rus. Fed.
19 J4 Stupava Slovakia
14 D2 Stupino Rus. Fed.
43 C6 Stung Treng Cambodia
152 A6 Sturge I. i. Ant.
111 G4 Sturgeon r. Can.
114 B2 Sturgeon Bay b. Can.
122 D3 Sturgeon Bay U.S.A.
114 D2 Sturgeon Bay Canal
  chan. U.S.A.
115 G2 Sturgeon Falls Can.
122 E5 Sturgeon L. l. Can.
12 E4 Sturgeon River Can.
120 D6 Sturgis U.S.A.
122 D5 Sturgis U.S.A.
118 C2 Sturt, Mt h. Aust.
96 E2 Sturt Nat. Park nat. park
  Aust.
98 C3 Sturt Plain plain Aust.
82 D5 Sturt R.S.A.
18 E5 Stuttgart Germany
125 F5 Stuttgart U.S.A.
10 L1 Stykkishólmur Iceland
15 C2 Styr r. Ukraine
145 G3 Suaçuí Grande r. Brazil
74 D2 Suakin Sudan
51 G3 Sua Taiwan
82 D3 Sua Pan salt pan
  Botswana
130 C2 Suaqui Mexico
127 E9 Suaqui Gde Mexico
42 A1 Suan N. Korea
51 □ Suata r. Venezuela
40 B3 Subang Indon.
55 H3 Subankhata India
55 H3 Subansiri r. India
43 E7 Subi Besar i. Indon.
73 H5 Subie Saudi Arabia
80 D2 Subic Eritrea
41 B2 Subic Phil.
79 □2 Subic Uganda
18 E5 Sucevita Romania
28 E1 Sucevita Romania
19 K3 Sucha Beskidzka Poland
19 J4 Suchdol nad Lužnicí
  Czech Rep.
15 K3 Suchowola Poland
19 J2 Suchowola Poland
15 F5 Sucre Bolivia
138 C2 Sucre Colombia
138 C3 Sucúa Ecuador
11 E3 Sucumbíos div. Ecuador
141 D2 Sucuriú r. Brazil
78 B3 Sud div. Cameroon

13 E6 Sudak Ukraine
68 G4 Sudan country Africa
12 G3 Suday Rus. Fed.
23 C3 Sudbishchi Rus. Fed.
114 C3 Sudbury Can.
17 H5 Sudbury U.K.
80 B3 Sudd swamp Sudan
139 F2 Suddie Guyana
19 H3 Sudety mt. ra. Czech Rep./Poland
14 B3 Sudimir Rus. Fed.
12 G3 Sudislavl' Rus. Fed.
121 F5 Sudlersville U.S.A.
14 E2 Sudogda Rus. Fed.
14 E2 Sudogda Rus. Fed.
14 A3 Sudost' r. Rus. Fed.
78 A3 Sud-Ouest div. Cameroon
81 ¬4 Sud Ouest, Pt pt Mauritius
61 B5 Sudr Egypt
10 M2 Suðurland div. Iceland
16 D1 Suðuroy i. Faeroes
15 F1 Sudzha Rus. Fed.
15 F1 Sudzha r. Rus. Fed.
78 E2 Sue w Sudan
54 C3 Sueca Spain
28 E3 Süedinenie Bulgaria
61 B5 Suez Egypt
73 F1 Suez Canal canal Egypt
73 F2 Suez, Gulf of g. Egypt
120 E6 Suffolk U.S.A.
53 H2 Süfîän Iran
122 C4 Sugar r. U.S.A.
121 H2 Sugarloaf Mt. mt. U.S.A.
94 ¬4 Sugarloaf Pass. chan. Lord Howe I. Pac. Oc.
82 A5 Sugar Loaf Pt pt St Helena Atlantic Ocean
97 H3 Sugarloaf Pt pt Aust.
41 C4 Sugbuhan Point pt Phil.
40 A1 Sugi i. Indon.
61 A1 Suğla Gölü l. Turkey
65 J5 Sugun China
41 A5 Sugut r. Malaysia
80 C4 Suguta r. Kenya
81 B5 Sugut B. b. Tanzania
41 A5 Sugut, Tg pt Malaysia
28 E3 Suhaia Romania
60 F2 Suhār Oman
59 J5 Sühbaatar Mongolia
48 C2 Sühbaatar Mongolia
48 E3 Sühbaatar div. Mongolia
18 E3 Suhl Germany
76 D5 Suhum Ghana
60 B2 Suhut Turkey
55 E3 Sui Pakistan
142 B3 Suiá Missur r. Brazil
49 J3 Suibin China
51 G2 Suichang China
51 E3 Suichuan China
48 D5 Suide China
49 J3 Suifenhe China
54 B4 Suigam India
49 H3 Suihua China
50 C2 Suijiang China
51 E2 Suileng China
50 D2 Suining China
51 G1 Suining China
51 E1 Suiping China
17 D5 Suir r. Rep. of Ire.
46 K2 Suishō-tō i. Rus. Fed.
51 G1 Suixi China
51 F1 Sui Xian China
50 D3 Suiyang China
51 G4 Suizhong China
51 F2 Suizhou China
48 C4 Suj China
54 C4 Sujangarh India
54 B4 Sujawal Pakistan
40 A3 Sukabumi Indon.
40 A3 Sukadana Indon.
40 B2 Sukadana Indon.
40 B2 Sukadana, Tk b. Indon.
40 A2 Sukagawa Japan
40 B2 Sukaramai Indon.
41 A5 Sukau Malaysia
49 H5 Sukch'ŏn N. Korea
28 F3 Sukha Reka r. Bulgaria
51 B4 Sukhaya Rus. Fed.
14 B2 Sukhinichi Rus. Fed.
14 F2 Sukhovzvodnoye Rus. Fed.
12 H2 Sukhona r. Rus. Fed.
42 B3 Sukhothai Thailand
49 H2 Sukhotino Rus. Fed.
14 B1 Sukhoverkovo Rus. Fed.
54 B4 Sukkur Pakistan
54 C3 Sukma India
72 C2 Süknah Libya
40 B2 Sukoharjo Indon.
53 H4 Sukri r. India
14 B1 Sukromny Rus. Fed.
72 B1 Sukrummy Rus. Fed.
82 B3 Sukses Namibia
46 D7 Sukumo Japan
11 B3 Sula i. Norway
62 C3 Suliljevt r. Estonia
54 E3 Sulaiman Ranges mt. ra. Pakistan
13 H7 Sulak Rus. Fed.
39 J7 Sula, Kepulauan is Indon.
61 C2 Sülär Iran
16 B2 Sula Sgeir i. U.K.
40 E2 Sulawesi i. Indon.
40 D2 Sulawesi Selatan div. Indon.
40 E1 Sulawesi Tengah div. Indon.
19 G2 Sulechów Poland
19 G2 Sulęcin Poland
76 B5 Suledeh Iran
15 E5 Sülüklü Turkey
19 J3 Sulejów Poland
16 E2 Sule Skerry i. U.K.
76 B5 Sulima Sierra Leone
28 C2 Sulina Romania
10 D2 Sulitjelma Norway
138 A4 Sullana Peru
124 F4 Sullivan U.S.A.
111 G4 Sullivan L. Can.
121 J1 Sully Can.
27 D4 Sulmona Italy
28 F4 Sülöğlu Turkey
125 E6 Sulphur U.S.A.
125 E5 Sulphur Springs U.S.A.
145 G4 Sul, Pico do mt. Brazil
51 C4 Sultan Can.
72 C1 Sultan Libya
61 A2 Sultanhanı Turkey
29 F4 Sultaniça Turkey
54 C3 Sultanpur India
41 B5 Sulu Archipelago is Phil.
54 B3 Sulung India
72 D1 Sülünköy Turkey
41 A4 Sulu Sea g. Phil.
15 D5 Sulymivka Ukraine
18 E4 Sulzbach-Rosenberg Germany
152 A4 Sulzberger Bay b. Ant.
28 C2 Sumadija reg. Yugo.
38 D6 Sumatera i. Indon.
18 H4 Šumava mt. ra. Czech Rep.
41 ¬2 Sumay Guam Pac. Oc.
16 D1 Sumba Denmark
40 D4 Sumba i. Indon.
40 D4 Sumba, Selat chan. Indon.
57 F2 Sumbar r. Turkmenistan
40 A4 Sumbawa i. Indon.
40 C4 Sumbawabesar Indon.
81 B6 Sumbawanga Tanzania
140 B3 Sumbay Peru
79 B6 Sumbe Angola
81 B6 Sumbu Nat. Park nat. park Zambia
16 D2 Sumburgh Head U.K.
50 C2 Sumdo China

54 D2 Sumdo China/Jammu and Kashmir
142 E2 Sumé Brazil
40 A3 Sumedang Indon.
19 H5 Sümeg Hungary
78 E2 Sumeih Sudan
40 C3 Sumenep Indon.
45 P5 Sumisu-jima Japan
55 E3 Sümiyn Bulag Mongolia
60 E2 Summāl Iran
112 C3 Summer Beaver Can.
113 K4 Summerford Can.
122 D3 Summer I. i. U.S.A.
113 H4 Summerside Prince Edward I. Can.
120 C5 Summersville U.S.A.
120 C5 Summersville Lake l. U.S.A.
92 F4 Summit N.Z.
110 E4 Summit Lake Can.
122 E4 Summit Lake l. U.S.A.
128 D2 Summit Mt. mt. U.S.A.
93 D5 Sumner N.Z.
122 A4 Sumner U.S.A.
93 D5 Sumner, L. l. N.Z.
110 C3 Sumner Strait chan. U.S.A.
47 G5 Sumon-dake mt. Japan
46 E6 Sumoto Japan
40 E2 Sumpangbinangae Indon.
19 H4 Šumperk Czech Rep.
42 B1 Sumprabum Myanmar
57 F3 Sumqayıt Azerbaijan
54 B4 Sumrahu Pakistan
65 H2 Sumskiy Posad Rus. Fed.
119 D5 Sumter U.S.A.
12 E3 Sumsar Rus. Fed.
15 E1 Sumy Ukraine
15 E1 Sumy div. Ukraine
126 D2 Sun r. U.S.A.
12 J3 Suna Rus. Fed.
46 H2 Sunaga Japan
13 H5 Sunam India
55 G4 Sunamganj Bangladesh
48 E5 Sunan China
49 H5 Sunan N. Korea
126 E1 Sunart, Loch inlet U.K.
126 E1 Sunburst U.S.A.
97 F4 Sunbury Aust.
120 A4 Sunbury U.S.A.
146 D3 Sunchales Arg.
49 H5 Sunch'ŏn N. Korea
49 H6 Sunch'ŏn S. Korea
82 D4 Sun City R.S.A.
121 H3 Suncook U.S.A.
126 F2 Sundance U.S.A.
55 G5 Sundarbans f. Bangladesh/India
44 C5 Sundarnagar India
149 M4 Sunda Trench Indian Ocean
11 C4 Sunde Norway
16 F4 Sunderland U.K.
40 B3 Sundoro, G. vol Indon.
11 E3 Sundsvall Sweden
83 E4 Sundumbili R.S.A.
51 G3 Sunduya Rus. Fed.
81 C5 Sunga Tanzania
40 A1 Sungaiapit Indon.
40 A1 Sungaikabung Indon.
40 A2 Sungailiat Indon.
40 A2 Sungaipenuh Indon.
40 A1 Sungaipinyuh Indon.
43 C6 Sungai Petani Malaysia
43 ¬ Sungei Seletar Res. resr Singapore
40 D1 Sunggumiasau Indon.
40 A3 Sungsang Indon.
78 C4 Sungu Zaire
60 C1 Sungurlu Turkey
26 F3 Sunj Croatia
55 F4 Sun Kosi r. Nepal
51 E1 Sunken China
12 J2 Suni r. China
64 D4 Sun, Mys pt Kazak.
47 F6 Suzu Japan
46 H2 Suzuka Japan
47 F6 Suzu-misaki pt Japan
26 E2 Suzun Rus. Fed.
26 D2 Suzzara Italy
11 H1 Sværholthalvøya pen. Norway
62 C2 Svalbard is Arctic Ocean
15 B4 Svalyava Ukraine
14 B4 Svapa r. Rus. Fed.
11 D5 Svappavaara Sweden
109 N2 Svartenhuk Halvø pen. Greenland
15 C4 Svatove Ukraine
43 C4 Svay Chek Cambodia
43 D5 Svay Rieng Cambodia
12 H3 Svecha Rus. Fed.
11 F3 Sveg Sweden
16 E2 Sveio Norway
10 T2 Svellingen Norway
12 E2 Svetl r. Rus. Fed.
11 H5 Švenčionys Lithuania
11 H5 Švenčionys Lithuania
11 F5 Svendborg Denmark
10 T1 Svensby Norway
11 F3 Svenstavik Sweden
11 H5 Šventoji r. Lithuania
14 B2 Sverchkovo Rus. Fed.
109 J2 Sverdrup Channel chan. Can.

47 ¬1 Suribachi-yama h. Japan
41 C4 Surigao Phil.
41 C4 Surigao Str. chan. Phil.
43 C4 Surin Thailand
81 ¬4 Surinam Mauritius
136 E2 Surinam country S. America
57 G2 Surkhab r. Afghanistan
55 E3 Surkhet Nepal
65 H5 Surkhob r. Tajikistan
72 B1 Surman Libya
57 C3 Surmãq Iran
60 E1 Sürmene Turkey
28 D4 Sürnitsa Bulgaria
14 F2 Surovikino Rus. Fed.
13 G5 Surovikino Rus. Fed.
90 ¬2 Surprise, Î. i. Pac. Oc.
128 B3 Sur, Pt pt U.S.A.
146 F4 Sur, Pta pt Arg.
19 J3 Surowo Poland
14 G3 Surra r. Rus. Fed.
14 H2 Surskoye Rus. Fed.
72 C1 Surt Libya
10 L3 Surtsey i. Iceland
142 C1 Surubiú r. Brazil
61 C3 Sürüç Turkey
46 D7 Suruga-wan b. Japan
41 C5 Surup Phil.
57 C1 Şuşa Azerbaijan
26 A3 Susa Italy
46 C6 Susa Japan
72 D1 Susac i. Croatia
72 D1 Süsah Libya
46 D7 Susaki Japan
46 D7 Susami Japan
138 B4 Susanino Rus. Fed.
15 E1 Susanino Rus. Fed.
18 F4 Susice Czech Rep.
12 J3 Suso Thailand
51 G2 Susong China
121 E4 Susquehanna r. U.S.A.
146 C1 Susques Arg.
113 J4 Sussex Can.
41 A5 Sussul Malaysia
63 O3 Susuman Rus. Fed.
60 B2 Susurluk Turkey
19 J2 Susz Poland
61 B1 Sutak India
128 C2 Sutcliffe U.S.A.
55 E3 Sutherland R.S.A.
124 C3 Sutherland U.S.A.
54 C3 Sutlej r. Pakistan
61 B1 Sütlüce Turkey
128 C2 Sutter Creek U.S.A.
112 D3 Sutton Can.
115 J4 Sutton r. Can.
17 G5 Sutton Coldfield U.K.
112 D3 Sutton L. l. Can.
128 B3 Sutton Lake l. U.S.A.
99 F4 Suttor r. Aust.
46 H2 Suttsu Japan
59 G4 Suugant Mongolia
11 E3 Suusamyr Kyrgyzstan
62 E3 Suva Fiji
15 C3 Suvorov Moldova
14 D3 Suvorov Rus. Fed.
28 D2 Suvorove Ukraine
87 L6 Suvorov Island i. Cook Islands Pac. Oc.
28 F3 Suvorovo Bulgaria
40 A2 Suwakong Indon.
19 K1 Suwałki Poland
42 A4 Suwannaphum Thailand
119 D6 Suwannee r. U.S.A.
73 H1 Suwar well Saudi Arabia
40 B3 Suweilih Jordan
41 S6 Suwŏn S. Korea
138 B2 Suyo Peru
65 G4 Suzak Kazak.
47 G5 Suzaka Japan
152 Suzanne, Pte pt Kerguelen Indian Ocean

17 F6 Swansea U.K.
17 F6 Swansea Bay b. U.K.
121 J2 Swans I. i. U.S.A.
121 G2 Swanton U.S.A.
129 E2 Swasey Peak summit U.S.A.
54 C2 Swat r. Pakistan
54 C2 Swat r. Pakistan
69 H8 Swaziland country Africa
4 G2 Sweden country Europe
126 B2 Sweet Home U.S.A.
119 C5 Sweetwater U.S.A.
125 C5 Sweetwater r. U.S.A.
126 E3 Sweetwater r. U.S.A.
82 C5 Swellendam R.S.A.
19 H3 Świdnica Wałbrzych Poland
19 J3 Świdnik Poland
19 G3 Świdwin Poland
19 G2 Świebodzice Poland
19 G2 Świebodzin Poland
19 J2 Świecie Poland
17 F5 Swift r. U.S.A.
111 H4 Swift Current Can.
111 H5 Swiftcurrent Cr. r. Can.
110 C2 Swift River Canada
17 C4 Swilly, Lough inlet Rep. of Ire.
17 G6 Swindon U.K.
19 G3 Świnoujście Poland
4 F4 Switzerland country Europe
17 D5 Swords Rep. of Ire.
99 E4 Swords Ra. h. Aust.
14 D2 Syamozero, Oz. l. Rus. Fed.
12 G2 Syamzha r. Rus. Fed.
14 C2 Syas'troy Rus. Fed.
12 G2 Sychevka Rus. Fed.
14 C2 Sychevka Rus. Fed.
97 G3 Sydney Aust.
113 H4 Sydney Can.
95 ¬1 Sydney B. b. Norfolk I.
113 J4 Sydney L. l. Can.
114 A3 Sydney Mines Can.
15 F5 Syeverodonets'k Ukraine
12 J2 Syktyvkar Rus. Fed.
54 E4 Sylacauga U.S.A.
10 D3 Sylarna mt. Norway/Sweden
55 E3 Sylhet Bangladesh
18 D1 Sylt i. Germany
119 D5 Sylvania U.S.A.
120 A4 Sylvania U.S.A.
111 G4 Sylvan Lake Can.
119 D6 Sylvester U.S.A.
98 C3 Sylvester, L. salt flat Aust.
110 D3 Sylvia, Mt mt. Can.
112 D3 Symi i. Greece
130 E3 Symon Mexico
15 F2 Synel'nykove Ukraine
15 D2 Syntul Rus. Fed.
15 D2 Synyukha r. Ukraine
152 D4 Syowa Japan Base Ant.
124 C4 Syracuse U.S.A.
121 E3 Syracuse U.S.A.
65 G2 Syrdar'ya r. Kazak.
65 G2 Syrdar'ya Kazak.
32 E6 Syria country Asia
29 H5 Syrna i. Greece
29 E6 Syria i. Greece
11 D3 Syrskiy Rus. Fed.
11 D3 Sysmä Finland
14 J3 Sysola r. Rus. Fed.
92 D1 Sysysy Rus. Fed.
15 C4 Sytkivtsi Ukraine
12 J4 Syumsi Rus. Fed.
14 G4 Syzran' Rus. Fed.
19 H2 Szamotuły Poland
19 K4 Szarvas Hungary
19 H2 Szczecin Poland
19 H2 Szczecinek Poland
19 J3 Szczuczyn Poland
19 J2 Szczytno Poland
19 J5 Szeged Hungary
19 H5 Szeghalom Hungary
19 J5 Székesfehérvár Hungary
19 J5 Szekszárd Hungary
19 K5 Szentes Hungary
19 J5 Szentgotthárd Hungary
19 K4 Szerencs Hungary
28 B1 Szeszka Góra h. Poland
19 H5 Szigetvár Hungary
19 J5 Szolnok Hungary
19 H5 Szombathely Hungary
19 H2 Szprotawa Poland
19 H2 Sztum Poland
19 H2 Szubin Poland
19 L1 Szydłowiec Poland
19 L1 Szypliszki Poland

T

76 C5 Taabo, Lac de l. Côte d'Ivoire
80 D3 Taagga Duudka reg. Somalia
61 C3 Taalabaya Lebanon
19 L2 Taal, L. l. Phil.
91 ¬1 Taapuma Fr. Poly. Pac. Oc.
19 J5 Tab Hungary
41 B3 Tabaco Phil.
60 D3 Tābah Saudi Arabia
40 D1 Tabajan Indon.
60 D3 Tabaqah Syria
11 F5 Tabaquite Trin. & Tobago
90 ¬1 Tabar Is i. P.N.G.
72 C1 Tabarka Tunisia
57 D2 Tabas Iran
57 E3 Tabas Iran
130 E4 Tabasco div. Mexico
57 D3 Tabāsīn Iran
138 E5 Tabatière r. Brazil
144 D4 Tabatinga Brazil
138 D5 Tabatinga Colombia
72 B2 Tabelbala Alg.
111 G5 Taber Can.
111 G5 Tabernas Spain
111 G5 Tabi Angola
90 ¬1 Tabiteuea i. Kiribati
41 B3 Tablas i. Phil.
41 B3 Tablas Strait chan. Phil.
93 C6 Table Cape c. N.Z.
81 ¬3 Table, Pointe de la pt Réunion Indian Ocean
125 E4 Table Rock Res. resr U.S.A.
129 E3 Tabletop, Mt h. U.S.A.
76 C4 Tabligbo Togo
82 B2 Taboco r. Brazil
18 F4 Tábor Czech Rep.
81 B6 Tabora Tanzania
81 B6 Tabora div. Tanzania
76 C5 Tabou Côte d'Ivoire
57 B1 Tabrīz Iran
60 D3 Tabūk Saudi Arabia
90 ¬1 Tabwémasana, h. mt. Vanuatu
11 D4 Täby Sweden
139 G3 Tacalé Brazil

131 H5 Tacámbaro Mexico
132 C5 Tacarcuna, Co mt. Panama
65 K3 Tacheng China
72 A2 Tachiumet well Libya
18 F4 Tachov Czech Rep.
40 E3 Tacipi Indon.
41 C4 Tacloban Phil.
140 C3 Tacna Peru
126 B2 Tacoma U.S.A.
140 D3 Tacopaya Bolivia
146 D2 Taco Pozo Arg.
140 D3 Tacora, Vol. vol Chile
147 C2 Tacuarembó Uruguay
130 C2 Tacupeto Mexico
144 A5 Tacuru Brazil
47 G5 Tadami-gawa r. Japan
75 ¬3 Tadamaït, Plateau du plat. Alg.
90 ¬2 Tadine Pac. Oc.
75 E3 Tadjmout Algeria
80 D2 Tadjoura Djibouti
80 D2 Tadjoura, Golfe de b. Djibouti
75 E2 Tadmour Algeria
60 D3 Tadmur Syria
111 K3 Tadoule Lake l. Can.
113 G4 Tadoussac Can.
45 H5 Taech'ŏn S. Korea
49 J6 Taedong man b. N. Korea
49 H5 Taehŭksan Do i. S. Korea
49 J5 Taejŏn S. Korea
49 J5 T'aepaek S. Korea
87 K6 Tafahi i. Tonga
99 E4 Tafassasset well Algeria
57 C3 Tafihān Iran
60 C4 Tafila Jordan
146 C2 Tafí Viejo Arg.
74 C3 Tafraoute Morocco
57 B2 Tafresh Iran
128 C4 Taft U.S.A.
57 D3 Taftān, Kūh-e mt. Iran
43 A6 Tafwap Andaman and Nicobar Is India
42 B2 Ta-Kaw Myanmar
46 H3 Takayama Japan
57 B3 Tak Bai Thailand
47 F6 Takefu Japan
47 F6 Takehara Japan
47 F6 Takeo Japan
57 B1 Takestān Iran
46 C7 Taketa Japan
43 C5 Takêv Cambodia
59 H1 Takhatatsh Uzbekistan
64 A4 Takhiatash Uzbekistan
43 K4 Takhmau Cambodia
64 C5 Takhta-Bazar Turkmenistan
65 G2 Takhtabrod Kazak.
64 A4 Takhtakupyr Uzbekistan
72 B1 Takhta Pul Post Afghanistan
54 B3 Takht-i-Sulaiman mt. Pakistan
111 G1 Takijuq Lake l. Can.
46 H2 Takikawa Japan
46 J2 Takinoue Japan
92 D2 Takitimu mts N.Z.
110 E4 Takla Lake l. Can.
65 K4 Takla Landing Can.
65 K5 Taklimakan Shamo des. China
110 A2 Takotna U.S.A.
90 ¬1 Takpa Shiri mt. China
46 D7 Taku r. China
46 H2 Taku Japan
91 ¬1 Takumé i. Fr. Poly. Pac. Oc.
41 ¬1 Takum Nigeria
77 F5 Takum Nigeria
28 B2 Tala Uruguay
146 E3 Tala Uruguay
12 D4 Talachyn Belarus
54 B4 Talagang Pakistan
54 C4 Talaimannar Sri Lanka
142 B2 Talaiassa r. Brazil
76 D4 Talamba r. Togo
57 C2 Talang r. Indon.
15 C1 Talalayivka Ukraine
40 D1 Talang Indon.
57 D4 Talangbetutu Indon.
138 A4 Talara Peru
138 A4 Talara Peru
141 H2 Talas r. Kazak./Kyrgyzstan
65 H3 Talas div. Kyrgyzstan
65 H3 Talas Kyrgyzstan
65 H3 Talas Ala-Too mt. ra. Kyrgyzstan
41 C5 Talaud, Kepulauan is Indon.
54 D3 Talavera de la Reina Spain
98 B3 Talawanta Aust.
54 D3 Talavera Myanmar
41 B3 Talavan Phil.
43 B5 Talayan Phil.

48 E5 Taiyuan China
48 E5 Taiyue Shan mt. ra. China
51 G1 Taizhou China
51 H2 Taizhou Wan b. China
80 D2 Ta'izz Yemen
40 E3 Tajem, G. h. Indon.
32 H6 Tajikistan country Asia
47 G5 Tajima Japan
45 H6 Tajimi Japan
130 E4 Tajito Mexico
42 B3 Tak Thailand
57 A1 Takāb Iran
80 C4 Takabba Kenya
46 D7 Takahashi Japan
47 H3 Takahagi Japan
80 D2 Takaka N.Z.
46 C7 Takamatsu Japan
47 H3 Takanosu Japan
80 D2 Takaoka Japan
92 E2 Takapau N.Z.
91 ¬1 Takapoto i. Fr. Poly. Pac. Oc.
92 E2 Takapuna N.Z.
91 ¬10 Takaroa i. Fr. Poly. Pac. Oc.
46 E6 Takasago Japan
46 E6 Takasaki Japan
82 C3 Takatokwane Botswana
54 B3 Takatsuki Japan
40 D2 Takatsukuri-yama mt. Japan
42 B2 Ta-Kaw Myanmar
46 H3 Takayama Japan
57 B3 Tak Bai Thailand
47 F6 Takefu Japan
47 F6 Takehara Japan
47 F6 Takeo Japan

54 C2 Tai Pass pass Pakistan
48 A3 Talshand Mongolia
11 F4 Talsi Latvia
146 B2 Taltal Chile
111 G2 Taltson r. Can.
60 D3 Talvār r. Iran
10 T1 Talvik Norway
99 G6 Talwood Aust.
40 A2 Tal'yanky Ukraine
12 K1 Talyy Rus. Fed.
122 A4 Tama U.S.A.
47 F5 Tamada Japan
14 F3 Tamala Rus. Fed.
138 C2 Tamalameque Colombia
76 D5 Tamale Ghana
40 C2 Tamalung Indon.
46 F7 Tamana Japan
72 B2 Tamanhint Libya
51 F1 Tamanthi Myanmar
75 F4 Tamanrasset Algeria
72 D3 Tamanrasset r. Algeria
138 C2 Tamar r. U.K.
81 ¬4 Tamarin Mauritius
28 E1 Tämäşeni Romania
19 J5 Tamási Hungary
19 J5 Tamási Hungary
131 E2 Tamaulipas div. Mexico
131 E4 Tamazula Mexico
131 E5 Tamazulápam Mexico
131 F4 Tamazunchale Mexico
76 B4 Tambacounda Senegal
80 C2 Tamba Kosi r. Nepal
40 D2 Tambalongang i. Indon.
57 B1 Tambangmunjul Indon.
142 A1 Tambaú Brazil
77 F4 Tambawel Nigeria
40 A1 Tambelan Besar i. Indon.
40 A1 Tembelan, Kepulauan is Indon.
54 B2 Tank Pakistan
57 D1 Tankse India
90 ¬2 Tanna i. Vanuatu
11 D3 Tännäs Sweden
142 C2 Tanô Ola, Khrebet mt. ra. China/Rus. Fed.
81 ¬4 Tanô Strait chan. Phil.
54 B4 Tañon Strait chan. Phil.
72 C2 Tanot India
54 C4 Tanout Niger

55 G2 Tanggula Shankou pass China
51 F1 Tanghe China
121 E6 Tangier I. i. U.S.A.
40 A3 Tangkittebak, G. mt. Indon.
55 G4 Tangla India
43 Tanglin Singapore
50 A2 Tangmai China
55 F3 Tango China
55 F3 Tangra Yumco salt l. China
122 A4 Tangshan China
41 B4 Tangub Phil.
77 F5 Tangueita Benin
49 J2 Tangwanghe China
51 Tang Xian China
96 C2 Tangxianzhen China
50 E2 Tangyan r. China
42 B2 Tangyin China
51 F1 Tangyin China
10 F2 Tanhua Finland
43 Tani Cambodia
138 C2 Taniantaweng Shan mt. ra. China
50 A2 Taniantaweng Shan mt. ra. China
39 K8 Tanimbar, Kepulauan is Indon.
41 B4 Tanjay Phil.
40 C3 Tanjung Indon.
40 D1 Tanjungbalai Indon.
40 D1 Tanjungbatu Indon.
40 A1 Tanjungbuaya i. Indon.
40 B2 Tanjungkarang Telukbetung Indon.
40 A2 Tanjungpandan Indon.
40 A2 Tanjungpinang Indon.
40 B2 Tanjungraja Indon.
40 A1 Tanjungredeb Indon.
40 A1 Tanjungsatai i. Indon.
40 A2 Tanjungselor Indon.
54 B2 Tank Pakistan
54 C2 Tankan India
90 ¬2 Tanna i. Vanuatu
11 D3 Tännäs Sweden
142 C2 Tannu Ola, Khrebet mt. ra. China/Rus. Fed.
81 ¬4 Tanô Strait chan. Phil.
54 B4 Tañon Strait chan. Phil.
72 C2 Tanot India
54 C4 Tanout Niger
54 C4 Tanout-ou-Fillali pass Morocco
140 C2 Tanta Egypt
54 C2 Tantan Morocco
40 D3 Tan-Tan Morocco
131 F4 Tantoyuca Mexico
49 G2 Tantu China
99 F5 Tanumshede Sweden
68 C5 Tanzania country Africa
51 B4 Tao'an China
48 B5 Tao'er r. China
51 B4 Taojiang China
50 C2 Taolanaro Madagascar
132 C1 Taos U.S.A.
76 D3 Taoudenni Mali
76 D3 Taouirt well Morocco
74 D2 Taounate well Mali
74 D2 Taourirt Morocco
93 B6 Taoxi China
41 B2 Taoyuan Taiwan
63 Q2 Taozhu China
62 J6 Tapa Estonia
131 G5 Tapachula Mexico
142 B1 Tapaiuna r. Brazil
139 F5 Tapajós r. Brazil
139 F6 Tapanahoni r. Surinam
131 F5 Tapanatepec Mexico
139 D4 Tapauá Brazil
139 D5 Tapauá r. Brazil

91 ¬11 Taravao Fr. Poly. Pac. Oc.
21 J6 Taravo r. France
92 F3 Tawarera N.Z.
92 F3 Tawarewa N.Z.
25 F2 Tarazona Spain
25 F2 Tarazona de la Mancha Spain
48 C2 Tarbagatay Rus. Fed.
65 K3 Tarbagatay, Khrebet mt. ra. China
16 F3 Tarbat Ness pt U.K.
16 D3 Tarbert U.K.
16 D3 Tarbert U.K.
20 E5 Tarbes France
119 E5 Tarboro U.S.A.
96 C2 Tarcoola Aust.
97 H2 Taree Aust.
80 E2 Tareifing Sudan
77 E3 Tarenkat well Mali
63 E1 Tarerya Rus. Fed.
74 B3 Tarfa, W. el w Egypt
74 B3 Tarfaya Morocco
74 B3 Tarfaya Morocco
29 J4 Targan China
126 F2 Targhee Pass pass U.S.A.
28 E1 Tîrgovişte Romania
28 F2 Tîrgu Bujor Romania
28 D2 Tîrgu Cărbuneşti Romania
28 D1 Tîrgu Jiu Romania
28 E1 Tîrgu Mureş Romania
28 E1 Tîrgu-Neamt Romania
28 E1 Tîrgu Ocna Romania
28 E2 Tîrgu Secuiesc Romania
72 B1 Tarhūnah Libya
48 D5 Tarian Gol China
57 C4 Tarif U.A.E.
54 D2 Tarifa Spain
140 E4 Tarija r. Bolivia
140 D4 Tarija Bolivia
39 J7 Tariku r. Indon.
65 J6 Tarim Yemen
81 B5 Tarime Tanzania
65 K5 Tarim Pendi basin China
61 C4 Tarin Kowt Afghanistan
51 B4 Tarıskay Shan mt. China
74 F3 Tarka, Vallée de w Niger
124 D3 Tarkio U.S.A.
12 K3 Tarko-Sale Rus. Fed.
76 D5 Tarkwa Ghana
20 D3 Tarlac Phil.
140 B2 Tarma Peru
20 F5 Tarn r. France
11 E3 Tärnaby Sweden
57 C2 Tarnak r. Afghanistan
28 E1 Tîrnaveni Romania
28 F1 Tarnawa Duża Poland
19 J3 Tarnobrzeg Poland
19 J3 Tarnogród Poland
12 G2 Tarnogskiy Gorodok Rus. Fed.
19 J3 Tarnos France
19 K3 Tarnów Tarnów Poland
19 J3 Tarnowskie Góry Poland
57 D3 Tarok Tso l. China
57 C1 Tārom Iran
74 C2 Taroom Aust.
130 C3 Tarra France
74 C2 Taroudant Morocco
132 C1 Tarpon Springs U.S.A.

55 G2 Tanggula Shan mt. ra. China
57 B2 Tarq Iran
27 C5 Tarquinia Italy
25 G2 Tarragona Spain
11 F4 Tärrajaur Sweden
25 H2 Tàrrega Spain
72 C2 Tarso Emissi mt. Chad
72 D1 Tarsumdo China
61 C1 Tarsus Turkey
146 C1 Tartagal Santa Fé Arg.
140 E4 Tartagal Arg.
57 B1 Tărtăr r. Azerbaijan
20 D5 Tartas France
61 C2 Ţarţūs div. Syria
61 C2 Ţarţūs Syria
145 J4 Tarumirim Brazil
143 B6 Tarumovka Rus. Fed.
13 H6 Tarumovka Rus. Fed.
142 B1 Tarun Hka r. Myanmar
14 E4 Tarusa Rus. Fed.
57 D1 Tarvo r. Bolivia
57 F2 Tarz Iran
61 B1 Taşağıl Turkey
60 C2 Tasbuget Kazak.
115 F2 Taschereau Can.
60 C2 Tashanta Rus. Fed.
62 G3 Tashigang Bhutan
61 C1 Tashir Armenia
57 D2 Tashk Iran
57 C3 Taskesken Uzbekistan
57 F2 Taskesir Turkmenistan
61 C1 Tashkömür Kyrgyzstan
114 E3 Tashota Can.
62 E6 Tasiilaq Greenland
40 A2 Tasikmalaya Indon.
113 G4 Tasiujaq, Lac l. Can.
75 G3 Tassili n'Ajjer f. Algeria
75 E3 Tassili-oua-n-Ahaggar plat. Algeria
74 D3 Tassara Niger
113 F2 Tasserest Mauritania
57 C1 Tastagal Kazak.
57 C3 Tashigang Bhutan

91 ¬11 Taravao Fr. Poly. Pac. Oc.
21 J6 Taravo r. France
92 F3 Tawerera N.Z.
97 H2 Taree Aust.
80 B2 Tareifing Sudan
77 E3 Tarenkat well Mali
14 E4 Tarusa Rus. Fed.
57 D1 Tarvo r. Bolivia
57 F2 Tarz Iran
61 B1 Taşağıl Turkey
60 C2 Tasbuget Kazak.
115 F2 Taschereau Can.
60 C2 Tashanta Rus. Fed.
62 G3 Tashigang Bhutan
61 C1 Tashir Armenia
57 D2 Tashk Iran
57 C3 Taskesken Uzbekistan
57 F2 Taskesir Turkmenistan
61 C1 Tashkömür Kyrgyzstan
114 E3 Tashota Can.
62 E6 Tasiilaq Greenland
40 A2 Tasikmalaya Indon.
113 G4 Tasiujaq, Lac l. Can.
75 G3 Tassili n'Ajjer f. Algeria
75 E3 Tassili-oua-n-Ahaggar plat. Algeria
74 D3 Tassara Niger
113 F2 Tasserest Mauritania
149 L5 Tasman Basin Pac. Oc.
93 C5 Tasman Bay b. N.Z.
149 K5 Tasman Sea sea Pac. Oc.
92 E2 Tasman I. i. Aust.
92 E2 Tasmania div. Aust.
92 E2 Tasman Mountains mts N.Z.
149 O7 Tasman Plateau Pac. Oc.
149 O7 Tasman Sea sea Pac. Oc.
28 E1 Tăşnad Romania
28 E1 Taşova Romania
128 B3 Tassajara Hot Springs U.S.A.
72 C2 Tassili Sudan
113 F2 Tassili n'Ajjer Algeria

21 J6 Taravo r. France
92 F3 Taverny France
41 B2 Tawau Malaysia
41 A5 Tawau Malaysia
16 D3 Tarbert U.K.
16 D3 Tarbert U.K.
20 E5 Tarbes France
119 E5 Tarboro U.S.A.
96 C2 Tarcoola Aust.
97 H2 Taree Aust.
80 E2 Tareifing Sudan
77 E3 Tarenkat well Mali
63 E1 Tarerya Rus. Fed.
74 B3 Tarfa, W. el w Egypt
92 F3 Tatara N.Z.
51 C1 Tate Aust.
99 F3 Tate r. Aust.
48 D2 Tatei China
48 B5 Tateshima well Rus. Fed.
47 H3 Tate-yama vol Japan
47 H3 Tateyama Japan

110 F2 **Tathlina Lake l.** Can.
73 H4 **Tathlīth** Saudi Arabia
73 H3 **Tathlīth, W. w** Saudi Arabia
74 B5 **Tâtîlt well** Mauritania
111 K2 **Tatinnai Lake l.** Can.
14 G4 **Tatishchevo** Rus. Fed.
42 B2 **Tatkon** Myanmar
126 A1 **Tatla Lake** Can.
110 D3 **Tatlatui Prov. Park res.** Can.
19 J4 **Tatry mts** Poland/Slovakia
110 B3 **Tatshenshini r.** Can.
13 G5 **Tatsinskiy** Rus. Fed.
46 E6 **Tatsuno** Japan
54 A4 **Tatta** Pakistan
65 H4 **Tatty** Kazak.
144 E5 **Tatuí** Brazil
110 E4 **Tatuk Mtn mt.** Can.
125 C5 **Tatum** U.S.A.
60 E2 **Tatvan** Turkey
11 B4 **Tau** Norway
91 □13 **Tau i.** *American Samoa* Pac. Oc.
90 □4 **Tau i.** Tonga
142 D2 **Taua** Brazil
139 E5 **Tauariã** Brazil
145 F5 **Taubaté** Brazil
18 D4 **Tauber r.** Germany
18 D4 **Tauberbischofsheim** Germany
64 D4 **Tauchik** Kazak.
91 □10 **Tauére i.** *Fr. Poly.* Pac. Oc.
18 F4 **Taufkirchen (Vils)** Germany
90 □3 **Taula i.** Tonga
55 E4 **Taulihawa** Nepal
92 E3 **Taumarunui** N.Z.
42 A2 **Taungdwingyi** Myanmar
42 B2 **Taung-gyi** Myanmar
42 B2 **Taunglau** Myanmar
42 B4 **Taungnyo Range mt. ra.** Myanmar
42 A2 **Taungtha** Myanmar
91 □11 **Taunoa** *Fr. Poly.* Pac. Oc.
42 A3 **Taunqup** Myanmar
54 B3 **Taunsa** Pakistan
17 F6 **Taunton** U.K.
121 H4 **Taunton** U.S.A.
93 □1 **Taupeka Pt pt** *Chatham Is* N.Z.
92 F3 **Taupo** N.Z.
92 E3 **Taupo, Lake l.** N.Z.
11 F5 **Tauragė** Lithuania
92 F2 **Tauranga** N.Z.
115 J3 **Taureau, Réservoir resr** Can.
27 F6 **Taurianova** Italy
92 D1 **Tauroa Pt pt** N.Z.
25 F2 **Tauste** Spain
91 □14 **Tautama pt** *Pitcairn I.* Pac. Oc.
91 □11 **Tautira** *Fr. Poly.* Pac. Oc.
90 □1 **Tauu or Mortlock Is is** P.N.G.
60 B2 **Tavas** Turkey
21 G3 **Tavaux** France
25 F3 **Tavernes de la Valldigna** Spain
90 □6 **Taveuni i.** Fiji
21 J5 **Tavignano r.** France
24 C4 **Tavira** Portugal
17 E6 **Tavistock** U.K.
43 B4 **Tavoy** Myanmar
43 B4 **Tavoy Pt pt** Myanmar
65 H2 **Tavricheskoye** Rus. Fed.
15 E3 **Tavriys'k** Ukraine
60 B2 **Tavşanlı** Turkey
90 □8 **Tavua i.** Fiji
90 □8 **Tavua** Fiji
17 F6 **Taw r.** U.K.
93 E4 **Tawa** N.Z.
123 F3 **Tawas Bay b.** U.S.A.
123 F3 **Tawas City** U.S.A.
41 A5 **Tawau** Malaysia
41 A5 **Tawau, Telukan b.** Malaysia
41 A5 **Tawitawi i.** Phil.
42 B1 **Tawmaw** Myanmar
51 H4 **T'a-wu** Taiwan
131 F5 **Taxco** Mexico
65 J5 **Taxkorgan** China
110 C2 **Tay r.** Can.
16 F3 **Tay r.** U.K.
41 B3 **Tayabas Bay b.** Phil.
40 B1 **Tayan** Indon.
10 J1 **Taybola** Rus. Fed.
80 D4 **Tayeeglow** Somalia
48 A3 **Taygan** Mongolia
15 D3 **Tayirove** Ukraine
101 C7 **Tay, L. salt flat** Aust.
16 E3 **Tay, Loch l.** U.K.
110 E3 **Taylor** Can.
129 G4 **Taylor** U.S.A.
123 F4 **Taylor** U.S.A.
122 B6 **Taylor** U.S.A.
124 D3 **Taylor** U.S.A.
125 D6 **Taylor** U.S.A.
93 C5 **Taylor, Mt mt.** N.Z.
121 E5 **Taylors Island** U.S.A.
118 B4 **Taylorville** U.S.A.
73 G2 **Taymā'** Saudi Arabia
63 L3 **Taymura r.** Rus. Fed.
63 M2 **Taymyr, Ozero l.** Rus. Fed.
63 L2 **Taymyr, Poluostrov pen.** Rus. Fed.
43 D5 **Tây Ninh** Vietnam
16 F3 **Tayport** U.K.
41 A4 **Taytay** Phil.
41 B3 **Taytay** Phil.
41 A4 **Taytay Bay b.** Phil.
40 B3 **Tayu** Indon.
49 H2 **Tayuan** China
57 E2 **Tayyebād** Iran
61 C5 **Ṭayyib al Ism** Saudi Arabia
62 K3 **Taz r.** Rus. Fed.
74 D2 **Taza** Morocco
60 F3 **Tāza Khurmātū** Iraq
47 H4 **Tazawa-ko l.** Japan
42 A2 **Taze** Myanmar
60 F2 **Tazeh Kand** Azerbaijan
120 B6 **Tazewell** U.S.A.
120 C6 **Tazewell** U.S.A.
111 H2 **Tazin r.** Can.
111 H3 **Tazin Lake l.** Can.
72 D2 **Tāzirbū** Libya
72 D2 **Tazirbu Water Wells' Field well** Libya
28 F1 **Tazlău** Romania
62 J3 **Tazovskaya G. chan.** Rus. Fed.
75 F4 **Tazrouk** Algeria
13 H7 **T'bilisi** Georgia
13 G6 **Tbilisskaya** Rus. Fed.
78 B2 **Tchabal Mbabo mt.** Cameroon
77 E5 **Tchamba** Togo
77 E5 **Tchaourou** Benin
79 B4 **Tchibanga** Gabon
77 F3 **Tchidoutene w** Niger
72 C4 **Tchié well** Chad
77 G2 **Tchigaï, Plateau du plat.** Niger
79 B6 **Tchindjenje** Angola
77 F3 **Tchin-Tabaradene** Niger
78 B2 **Tcholliré** Cameroon
19 J1 **Tczew** Poland
130 D4 **Teacapán** Mexico
101 C5 **Teague, L. salt flat** Aust.
91 □11 **Teahupoo** *Fr. Poly.* Pac. Oc.
93 A6 **Te Anau** N.Z.
93 A6 **Te Anau, L. l.** N.Z.
131 G5 **Teapa** Mexico
92 G2 **Te Araroa** N.Z.
92 E2 **Te Aroha** N.Z.
91 □11 **Teavaro** *Fr. Poly.* Pac. Oc.
92 E3 **Te Awamutu** N.Z.
40 B1 **Tebas** Indon.
40 B1 **Tebedu** Malaysia
13 G7 **Teberda** Rus. Fed.
111 K2 **Tebesjuak Lake l.** Can.
75 F1 **Tébessa** Algeria
141 E5 **Tebicuary r.** Paraguay
43 B7 **Tebingtinggi** Indon.
27 B7 **Tébourba** Tunisia
75 F1 **Téboursouk** Tunisia
130 A1 **Tecate** Mexico
64 F1 **Techa r.** Rus. Fed.
76 D5 **Techiman** Ghana
28 G2 **Techirghiol** Romania
147 B5 **Tecka r.** Arg.
147 B5 **Tecka** Arg.
131 F4 **Tecolutla** Mexico
130 E5 **Tecomán** Mexico
128 D4 **Tecopa** U.S.A.
130 D3 **Tecoríchic** Mexico
130 C2 **Tecoripa** Mexico
131 E5 **Técpan** Mexico
28 F2 **Tecuci** Romania
123 F5 **Tecumseh** U.S.A.
80 D4 **Ted** Somalia
72 C3 **Tédogora w** Chad
57 E2 **Tedzhen r.** Iran/Turkmenistan
64 F5 **Tedzhen** Turkmenistan
57 E1 **Tedzhenstroy** Turkmenistan
129 H3 **Teec Nos Pos** U.S.A.
65 M2 **Teeli** Rus. Fed.
17 G4 **Tees r.** U.K.
139 D4 **Tefé r.** Brazil
75 F4 **Tefedest mts** Algeria
139 E4 **Tefé, Lago l.** Brazil
60 B2 **Tefenni** Turkey
40 B3 **Tegal** Indon.
77 F4 **Tegina** Nigeria
40 A3 **Tegineneng** Indon.
90 □2 **Tégua i.** Vanuatu
130 J6 **Tegucigalpa** Honduras
77 F3 **Teguidda-n-Tessoumt** Niger
25 □ **Teguise** *Canary Is* Spain
128 C4 **Tehachapi** U.S.A.
127 C5 **Tehachapi Mts mt. ra.** U.S.A.
128 C4 **Tehachapi Pass pass** U.S.A.
111 K2 **Tehek Lake l.** Can.
76 D5 **Téhini** Côte d'Ivoire
57 B2 **Tehrān div.** Iran
57 B2 **Tehrān** Iran
54 D3 **Tehri** India
131 F5 **Tehuacán** Mexico
131 G6 **Tehuantepec, Golfo de g.** Mexico
131 G5 **Tehuantepec, Istmo de isth.** Mexico
131 G5 **Tehuantepec Ridge** Pac. Oc.
131 F5 **Tehuitzingo** Mexico
25 □ **Teide, Pico del mt.** *Canary Is* Spain
17 E5 **Teifi r.** U.K.
17 F6 **Teign r.** U.K.
47 □2 **Teima** Japan
28 D1 **Teiuș** Romania
142 E2 **Teixeira** Brazil
145 J2 **Teixeira de Freitas** Brazil
145 G4 **Teixeiras** Brazil
40 C4 **Tejakula** Indon.
25 □ **Tejeda** *Canary Is* Spain
77 F4 **Tejira well** Niger
24 B3 **Tejo r.** Portugal
128 C4 **Tejon Pass pass** U.S.A.
92 D1 **Te Kao** N.Z.
93 C6 **Tekapo r.** N.Z.
93 C5 **Tekapo, L. l.** N.Z.
55 F4 **Tekari** India
92 E2 **Te Kauwhata** N.Z.
131 H4 **Tekax** Mexico
64 F3 **Tekeli** Kazak.
65 J4 **Tekeli** Kazak.
65 H2 **Teke, Oz. salt l.** Kazak.
65 K4 **Tekes r.** China
80 C2 **Tekezē Wenz r.** Africa
54 E1 **Tekiliktag mt.** China
49 K2 **Tekin** Rus. Fed.
60 A1 **Tekirdağ** Turkey
29 F4 **Tekirdağ div.** Turkey
56 D2 **Tekkali** India
55 H5 **Teknaf** Bangladesh
122 E4 **Tekonsha** U.S.A.
92 D2 **Te Kopuru** N.Z.
92 E3 **Te Kuiti** N.Z.
55 E5 **Tel r.** India
130 J6 **Tela** Honduras
75 D2 **Télagh** Algeria
77 E3 **Télataï** Mali
13 H7 **T'elavi** Georgia
61 C3 **Tel Aviv-Yafo** Israel
19 G4 **Telč** Czech Rep.
131 H4 **Telchac Puerto** Mexico
14 C3 **Tel'ch'ye** Rus. Fed.
28 E1 **Telciu** Romania
78 D3 **Tele r.** Zaire
40 C2 **Telegapulang** Indon.
14 G3 **Telegino** Rus. Fed.
110 C3 **Telegraph Creek** Can.
144 C6 **Telêmaco Borba** Brazil
11 B4 **Telemark div.** Norway
146 C4 **Telén** Arg.
40 D1 **Telen r.** Indon.
15 C3 **Telenești** Moldova
28 E2 **Teleorman r.** Romania
75 F4 **Telertheba, Djebel mt.** Algeria
128 D3 **Telescope Peak summit** U.S.A.
133 □8 **Telescope Pt pt** *Grenada* Caribbean
141 E1 **Teles Pires r.** Brazil
65 L2 **Teletskoye, Ozero l.** Rus. Fed.
17 F5 **Telford** U.K.
18 E5 **Telfs** Austria
130 J6 **Telica** Nicaragua
76 D2 **Telîg well** Mali
76 B4 **Télimélé** Guinea
72 E5 **Teljo, Jebel mt.** Sudan
60 E2 **Tel Kotchek** Syria
110 D4 **Telkwa** Can.
108 B3 **Teller** U.S.A.
60 E3 **Tell es Suwar** Syria
56 A4 **Tellicherry** India
15 D3 **Tellodar** Ukraine
64 E4 **Tel'mansk** Turkmenistan
48 A2 **Telmen Nuur salt l.** Mongolia
43 □ **Telok Blangah** Singapore
131 F5 **Teloloapán** Mexico
147 C5 **Telsen** Arg.
11 F5 **Telšiai** Lithuania
43 C6 **Teluk Anson** Malaysia
40 B2 **Telukbatang** Indon.
40 B2 **Telukpakedai** Indon.
14 C3 **Telyazh'ye** Rus. Fed.
76 E5 **Tema** Ghana
115 F3 **Temagami** Can.
115 F3 **Temagami Lake l.** Can.
40 B1 **Temaju i.** Indon.
40 B3 **Temanggung** Indon.
92 E3 **Te Mapou h.** N.Z.
131 H4 **Temax** Mexico
40 A2 **Tembilahan** Indon.
82 D4 **Tembisa** R.S.A.
79 C5 **Tembo Aluma** Angola
17 F5 **Teme r.** U.K.
128 D5 **Temecula** U.S.A.
48 A2 **Temenchula, G. mt.** Rus. Fed.
76 D3 **Téméra** Mali
28 B2 **Temerin** Yugo.
43 C7 **Temerloh** Malaysia
64 E3 **Temir** Kazak.
65 G4 **Temirlanovka** Kazak.
65 H2 **Temirtau** Kazak.
65 L2 **Temirtau** Rus. Fed.
115 F3 **Temiscaming** Can.
115 F3 **Témiscamingue, Lac l.** Can.
113 G4 **Témiscouata, L. l.** Can.
40 A1 **Temiyang i.** Indon.
14 B2 **Temkino** Rus. Fed.
97 F5 **Temma** Aust.
10 G2 **Temmes** Finland
14 F2 **Temnikov** Rus. Fed.
97 F3 **Temora** Aust.
130 D2 **Temósachic** Mexico
129 G5 **Tempe** U.S.A.
40 D3 **Tempe, D. l.** Indon.
98 C5 **Tempe Downs** Aust.
40 A2 **Tempino** Indon.
27 B5 **Tempio Pausania** Italy
122 E3 **Temple** U.S.A.
125 D6 **Temple** U.S.A.
99 E2 **Temple B. b.** Aust.
17 D5 **Templemore** Rep. of Ire.
41 A4 **Templer Bank sand bank** Phil.
98 D4 **Templeton w** Aust.
131 F4 **Tempoal** Mexico
79 C6 **Tempué** Angola
13 F6 **Temryuk** Rus. Fed.
13 F6 **Temryukskiy Zaliv b.** Rus. Fed.
147 B4 **Temuco** Chile
93 C6 **Temuka** N.Z.
138 B4 **Tena** Ecuador
128 D1 **Tenabo, Mt mt.** U.S.A.
76 D4 **Ténado** Burkina
56 C2 **Tenali** India
131 F5 **Tenancingo** Mexico
43 B4 **Tenasserim** Myanmar
43 B4 **Tenasserim div.** Myanmar
43 B4 **Tenasserim r.** Myanmar
17 E6 **Tenby** U.K.
114 D3 **Tenby Bay** Can.
21 G4 **Tence** France
80 D2 **Tendaho** Ethiopia
21 H4 **Tende** France
43 A5 **Ten Degree Channel chan.** *Andaman and Nicobar Is* India
73 F5 **Tendelti** Sudan
47 H4 **Tendō** Japan
75 D2 **Tendrara** Morocco
15 D3 **Tendrivs''ka Kosa, Ostriv spit** Ukraine
15 D3 **Tendrivs'ka Zatoka b.** Ukraine
60 E2 **Tendürük Daği mt.** Turkey
76 D4 **Ténenkou** Mali
141 E2 **Tenente Marques r.** Brazil
77 G3 **Ténéré reg.** Niger
77 G2 **Ténéré du Tafassâsset desert** Niger
25 □ **Tenerife i.** *Canary Is* Spain
75 E1 **Ténès** Algeria
28 F3 **Tenevo** Bulgaria
40 D3 **Tengah, Kep. is** Indon.
50 B3 **Tengchong** China
43 □ **Tengeh Res. resr** Singapore
40 D2 **Tenggarong** Indon.
48 C5 **Tengger Shamo desert** China
43 C6 **Tenggul i.** Malaysia
65 G2 **Tengiz, Oz. salt l.** Kazak.
76 C4 **Tengréla** Côte d'Ivoire
14 F2 **Ten'gushevo** Rus. Fed.
51 G1 **Teng Xian** China
51 E4 **Teng Xian** China
141 D4 **Teniente Enciso, Parque Nacional nat. park** Paraguay
152 B2 **Teniente Jubany Argentina Base** Ant.
152 B2 **Teniente Rodolfo Marsh Chile Base** Ant.
79 E6 **Tenke** Zaire
63 O2 **Tenkeli** Rus. Fed.
76 D4 **Tenkodogo** Burkina
26 D4 **Tenna r.** Italy
98 C3 **Tennant Creek** Aust.
119 C5 **Tennessee r.** U.S.A.
120 B6 **Tennessee div.** U.S.A.
127 F4 **Tennessee Pass pass** U.S.A.
10 E1 **Tennevoll** Norway
146 B3 **Teno r.** Chile
10 G1 **Tenojoki r.** Finland
131 H5 **Tenosique** Mexico
74 C3 **Tenouchchad w** *Western Sahara*
47 F6 **Tenryū** Japan
47 F6 **Tenryū r.** Japan
126 F2 **Ten Sleep** U.S.A.
40 E2 **Tenteno** Indon.
97 H2 **Tenterfield** Aust.
119 D7 **Ten Thousand Islands is** U.S.A.
24 C3 **Tentudia mt.** Spain
144 B5 **Teodoro Sampaio** Brazil
145 H2 **Teófilo Otôni** Brazil
15 B2 **Teofipol'** Ukraine
41 B5 **Teomabal i.** Phil.
93 □1 **Te One** *Chatham Is* N.Z.
55 E4 **Teonthar** India
131 G5 **Teopisca** Mexico
131 F5 **Teotihuacan** Mexico
90 □2 **Téouta** Pac. Oc.
39 J8 **Tepa** Indon.
127 E6 **Tepachi** Mexico
92 D1 **Te Paki** N.Z.
130 E5 **Tepalcatepec** Mexico
91 □11 **Tepati** *Fr. Poly.* Pac. Oc.
130 E4 **Tepatitlán** Mexico
130 D3 **Tepehuanes** Mexico
131 F5 **Tepeji** Mexico
29 C4 **Tepelenë** Albania
131 F5 **Tepelmemec** Mexico
40 D1 **Tepianlangsat** Indon.
130 D4 **Tepic** Mexico
93 C5 **Te Pirita** N.Z.
19 F3 **Teplice** Czech Rep.
12 K2 **Teplogorka** Rus. Fed.
49 J2 **Teploozersk** Rus. Fed.
14 H3 **Teplovka** Rus. Fed.
14 D3 **Teploye** Rus. Fed.
14 C3 **Teploye** Rus. Fed.
15 C2 **Teplyk** Ukraine
130 B2 **Tepoca, C. hd** Mexico
91 □10 **Tepoto i.** *Fr. Poly.* Pac. Oc.
92 F2 **Te Puke** N.Z.
131 G5 **Tequisistlán** Mexico
131 F4 **Tequisquiapán** Mexico
25 H1 **Ter r.** Spain
77 E4 **Téra** Niger
24 D2 **Tera r.** Spain
87 L4 **Teraina i.** Kiribati
54 D2 **Teram Kangri mt.** China/Jammu and Kashmir
26 D4 **Teramo** Italy
97 E4 **Terang** Aust.
54 B3 **Teratani r.** Pakistan
93 E4 **Terawhiti, Cape c.** N.Z.
14 D3 **Terbuny** Rus. Fed.
60 E2 **Tercan** Turkey
14 B3 **Tereben'** Rus. Fed.
15 A2 **Terebovlya** Ukraine
28 D2 **Teregova** Romania
13 H7 **Terek** Rus. Fed.
13 H7 **Terek r.** Rus. Fed.
65 L2 **Terektinskiy Khr. mt. ra.** Rus. Fed.
12 J4 **Teren'ga** Rus. Fed.
43 C6 **Terengganu div.** Malaysia
144 A4 **Terenos** Brazil
64 F3 **Terenozek** Kazak.
40 B2 **Terentang** Indon.
138 D2 **Terepaima, Parque Nacional nat. park** Venezuela
144 C6 **Teresa Cristina** Brazil
13 H4 **Tereshka r.** Rus. Fed.
142 D2 **Teresina** Brazil
145 G5 **Teresópolis** Brazil
19 L2 **Terespol** Poland
43 A5 **Teressa I. i.** *Andaman and Nicobar Is* India
91 □16 **Terevaka h.** *Easter I.* Chile
140 D3 **Terevinto** Bolivia
21 F2 **Tergnier** France
15 C1 **Termakhivka** Ukraine
60 D1 **Terme** Turkey
65 G5 **Termez** Uzbekistan
27 D7 **Termini Imerese** Italy
26 D4 **Terminillo, Monte mt.** Italy
131 H5 **Términos, Lag. de lag.** Mexico
77 G3 **Termit well** Niger
77 G3 **Termit-Kaoboul** Niger
27 E5 **Termoli** Italy
39 J6 **Ternate** Indon.
18 A3 **Terneuzen** Netherlands
26 D4 **Terni** Italy
19 H5 **Ternitz** Austria
15 G2 **Ternivka** *Dnipropetrovs'k* Ukraine
15 E3 **Ternivka** *Mykolayiv* Ukraine
15 C2 **Ternivka** *Vinnytsya* Ukraine
15 A2 **Ternopil' div.** Ukraine
15 A2 **Ternopil'** Ukraine
14 E4 **Ternovka** Rus. Fed.
15 G3 **Ternuvate** Ukraine
15 E1 **Terny** Ukraine
96 D3 **Terowie** Aust.
45 Q2 **Terpeniya, Mys** Rus. Fed.
45 Q2 **Terpeniya, Zaliv g.** Rus. Fed.
144 B5 **Terra Boa** Brazil
145 G2 **Terra Branca** Brazil
110 D4 **Terrace** Can.
114 B2 **Terrace Bay** Can.
101 C6 **Terraces, The h.** Aust.
27 D5 **Terracina** Italy
82 C4 **Terra Firma** R.S.A.
10 D2 **Terråk** Norway
27 B6 **Terralba** Italy
113 K4 **Terra Nova Nat. Pk nat. park** Can.
144 B5 **Terra Rica** Brazil
144 A6 **Terra Roxa d'Oeste** Brazil
27 D6 **Terrasini** Italy
20 E4 **Terrasson-la-Villedieu** France
152 B6 **Terre Adélie reg.** Ant.
125 F6 **Terre Bonne Bay b.** U.S.A.
133 □5 **Terre de Bas i.** *Guadeloupe* Caribbean
133 □5 **Terre de Haut i.** *Guadeloupe* Caribbean
118 C4 **Terre Haute** U.S.A.
113 K4 **Terrenceville** Can.
21 G3 **Terre Plaine plain** France
126 F2 **Terry** U.S.A.
13 G5 **Tersa r.** Rus. Fed.
65 G2 **Tersakkan r.** Kazak.
18 B2 **Terschelling i.** Netherlands
65 J4 **Terskey Ala-Too mt. ra.** Kyrgyzstan
12 F1 **Terskiy Bereg** Rus. Fed.
15 F3 **Tersyanka** Ukraine
27 B6 **Tertenia** Italy
25 F2 **Teruel** Spain
43 B6 **Terutao i.** Thailand
28 F3 **Tervel** Bulgaria
10 G2 **Tervola** Finland
26 F3 **Tešanj** Bos.-Herz.
80 C1 **Tesenay** Eritrea
14 F2 **Tesha r.** Rus. Fed.
14 F2 **Tesha** Rus. Fed.
46 K2 **Teshikaga** Japan
46 H1 **Teshio** Japan
46 J2 **Teshio-dake mt.** Japan
46 H1 **Teshio-gawa r.** Japan
46 H1 **Teshio-sanchi mt. ra.** Japan
48 A2 **Tesiyn Gol r.** Mongolia
26 F3 **Teslić** Bos.-Herz.
110 C2 **Teslin** Can.
110 C2 **Teslin r.** Can.
110 C2 **Teslin Lake l.** Can.
142 B3 **Tesouras r.** Brazil
144 B2 **Tesouro** Brazil
12 D3 **Tesovo-Netyl'skiy** Rus. Fed.
77 E2 **Tessalit** Mali
77 F4 **Tessaoua** Niger
77 F3 **Tesséroukane well** Niger
77 E2 **Tessoûnfat well** Mali
27 B7 **Testour** Tunisia
140 B4 **Tetas, Pta pt** Chile
78 D2 **Tété r.** C.A.R.
83 E2 **Tete** Mozambique
83 E2 **Tete div.** Mozambique
92 F3 **Te Teko** N.Z.
90 □1 **Tetepare i.** Solomon Is.
15 C1 **Teteriv r.** Ukraine
18 F2 **Teterow** Germany
28 E3 **Teteven** Bulgaria
91 □10 **Tetiaroa i.** *Fr. Poly.* Pac. Oc.
15 C2 **Tetiyiv** Ukraine
15 F1 **Tetkino** Rus. Fed.
126 E2 **Teton r.** U.S.A.
126 E3 **Teton Ra. mts** U.S.A.
74 C1 **Tétouan** Morocco
28 C3 **Tetovo** Macedonia
54 B5 **Tetpur** India
12 J4 **Tetyushi** Rus. Fed.
46 B8 **Teuchi** Japan
146 D1 **Teuco r.** Arg.
27 B6 **Teulada, Capo pt** Italy
46 H1 **Teuri-tō i.** Japan
11 F3 **Teuva** Finland
27 D5 **Tevere r.** Italy
61 C3 **Teverya** Israel
17 F4 **Teviot r.** U.K.
93 A7 **Te Waewae Bay b.** N.Z.
40 C2 **Tewah** Indon.
99 H5 **Tewantin** Aust.
40 C2 **Teweh r.** Indon.
92 F3 **Te Whaiti** N.Z.
93 □1 **Te Whanga Lagoon lag.** *Chatham Is* N.Z.
93 E4 **Te Wharau** N.Z.
50 C1 **Têwo** China
110 E5 **Texada I. i.** Can.
125 E5 **Texarkana** U.S.A.
99 G6 **Texas** Aust.
125 D6 **Texas div.** U.S.A.
125 E6 **Texas City** U.S.A.
18 B2 **Texel i.** Netherlands
125 C4 **Texhoma** U.S.A.
125 D5 **Texoma, Lake l.** U.S.A.
82 D4 **Teyateyaneng** Lesotho
14 E1 **Teykovo** Rus. Fed.
57 F2 **Teyvareh** Afghanistan
14 E1 **Teza r.** Rus. Fed.
131 F5 **Teziutlán** Mexico
55 H4 **Tezpur** India
55 H4 **Tezu** India
74 B3 **Tfaritiy** *Western Sahara*
111 K2 **Tha-anne r.** Can.
83 D4 **Thabana-Ntlenyana mt.** Lesotho
83 D4 **Thaba-Tseka** Lesotho
82 D3 **Thabazimbi** R.S.A.
42 B2 **Thabeikkyin** Myanmar
42 C3 **Tha Bo** Laos
82 D4 **Thabong** R.S.A.
61 C5 **Thabt, G. el mt.** Egypt
43 B4 **Thagyettaw** Myanmar
42 D2 **Thai Binh** Vietnam
54 B3 **Thai Desert desert** Pakistan
33 L8 **Thailand country** Asia
43 C5 **Thailand, Gulf of g.** Asia
42 D2 **Thai Nguyên** Vietnam
90 □6 **Thakau Matathuthu reef** Fiji
90 □6 **Thakaundrove Pen. pen.** Fiji
90 □6 **Thakau Vuthovutho reef** Fiji
55 G4 **Thakurgaon** Bangladesh
54 E5 **Thakurtola** India
54 B2 **Thal** Pakistan
75 F1 **Thala** Tunisia
43 B5 **Thalang** Thailand
43 C6 **Thale Luang lag.** Thailand
18 F5 **Thalgau** Austria
42 C3 **Tha Li** Thailand
99 G6 **Thallon** Aust.
57 F3 **Thalo** Pakistan
72 C2 **Thamad Bū Hashīshah well** Libya
82 D3 **Thamaga** Botswana
59 H6 **Thamarīt** Oman
80 E2 **Thamar, J. mt.** Yemen
92 E2 **Thames** N.Z.
17 H6 **Thames est.** U.K.
114 E5 **Thamesville** Can.
42 B3 **Thanatpin** Myanmar
42 B4 **Thanbyuzayat** Myanmar
54 C5 **Thandla** India
54 B5 **Thangadh** India
42 E4 **Thăng Binh** Vietnam
100 C3 **Thangoo** Aust.
99 G5 **Thangool** Aust.
42 D3 **Thanh Hoa** Vietnam
56 B4 **Thanjavur** India
54 A4 **Thano Bula Khan** Pakistan
82 C2 **Thaoge r.** Botswana
42 C3 **Tha Pla** Thailand
43 B5 **Thap Put** Thailand
43 B5 **Thap Sakae** Thailand
54 B4 **Tharad** India
99 E5 **Thargomindah** Aust.
54 B4 **Thar or Indian Desert desert** India
42 A3 **Tharrawaddy** Myanmar
42 A3 **Tharrawaw** Myanmar
29 E4 **Thasos i.** Greece
29 E4 **Thasos** Greece
129 H5 **Thatcher** U.S.A.
42 D2 **Thât Khê** Vietnam
42 B3 **Thaton** Myanmar
21 F5 **Thau, Bassin de lag.** France
42 A1 **Thaungdut** Myanmar
42 B3 **Thaungyin r.** Myanmar/Thailand
43 B4 **Thayetchaung** Myanmar
42 A3 **Thayetmyo** Myanmar
42 A3 **Thazi** Myanmar
42 B2 **Thazi** Myanmar
129 F5 **Theba** U.S.A.
73 F2 **Thebes** Egypt
124 C3 **Thedford** U.S.A.
43 B5 **Theinkun** Myanmar
42 B3 **Theinzeik** Myanmar
111 H2 **Thekulthili Lake l.** Can.
111 J2 **Thelon r.** Can.
111 J2 **Thelon Game Sanctuary res.** Can.
18 E3 **Themar** Germany
75 E1 **Theniet El Had** Algeria
99 G5 **Theodore** Aust.
141 D1 **Theodore Roosevelt r.** Brazil
129 G5 **Theodore Roosevelt Lake l.** U.S.A.
124 C2 **Theodore Roosevelt Nat. Park nat. park.** U.S.A.
121 F2 **Theresa** U.S.A.
99 F4 **Theresa Cr. r.** Aust.
81 □2 **Thérèse I. i.** Seychelles
29 D4 **Thermaïkos Kolpos g.** Greece
128 B2 **Thermalito** U.S.A.
29 C5 **Thermo** Greece
126 E3 **Thermopolis** U.S.A.
108 F2 **Thesiger Bay b.** Can.
29 C5 **Thessalia div.** Greece
114 D3 **Thessalon** Can.
29 D4 **Thessaloniki** Greece
17 H5 **Thetford** U.K.
115 K3 **Thetford Mines** Can.
42 D3 **Theun r.** Laos
96 C3 **Thevenard** Aust.
100 A4 **Thevenard I. i.** Aust.
125 F6 **Thibodaux** U.S.A.
111 K3 **Thicket Portage** Can.
124 D1 **Thief River Falls** U.S.A.
152 B4 **Thiel Mts mts** Ant.
21 F4 **Thiers** France
76 A4 **Thiès** Senegal
81 C5 **Thika** Kenya
53 D9 **Thiladhunmathee Atoll atoll** Maldives
55 G4 **Thimphu** Bhutan
10 L2 **Þingvallavatn l.** Iceland
90 □2 **Thio** Pac. Oc.
21 H2 **Thionville** France
29 E6 **Thira i.** Greece
29 E6 **Thirasia i.** Greece
73 F4 **3rd Cataract rapids** Sudan
17 G4 **Thirsk** U.K.
101 C7 **Thirsty, Mt h.** Aust.
11 C4 **Thisted** Denmark
10 N2 **Þistilfjörður b.** Iceland
96 D3 **Thistle I. i.** Aust.
29 D5 **Thiva** Greece
20 E4 **Thiviers** France
111 K2 **Thlewiaza r.** Can.
111 H2 **Thoa r.** Can.
42 C3 **Thoeng** Thailand
83 E3 **Thohoyandou** R.S.A.
101 B5 **Thomas r.** Aust.
120 D5 **Thomas** U.S.A.
96 D1 **Thomas, L. salt flat** Aust.
119 C5 **Thomaston** U.S.A.
121 J2 **Thomaston** U.S.A.
121 K2 **Thomaston Corner** Can.
17 D5 **Thomastown** Rep. of Ire.
119 D6 **Thomasville** U.S.A.
110 E4 **Thompson r.** Can.
111 K3 **Thompson** Can.
122 D3 **Thompson** U.S.A.
124 E3 **Thompson r.** U.S.A.
121 F4 **Thompson** U.S.A.
126 D2 **Thompson Falls** U.S.A.
93 A6 **Thompson Sound inlet** N.Z.
99 E5 **Thomson w** Aust.
119 D5 **Thomson** U.S.A.
42 D3 **Thôn Cư Lai** Vietnam
42 B3 **Thongwa** Myanmar
21 H3 **Thonon-les-Bains** France
43 E5 **Thôn Sơn Hai** Vietnam
127 E5 **Thoreau** U.S.A.
122 E4 **Thornapple r.** U.S.A.
115 F3 **Thorne** Can.
128 C2 **Thorne** U.S.A.
110 C3 **Thorne Bay** U.S.A.
17 F4 **Thornhill** U.K.
122 D5 **Thorntown** U.S.A.
122 B3 **Thorp** U.S.A.
152 D3 **Thorshavnheiane mt. ra.** Ant.
20 D3 **Thouars** France
55 H4 **Thoubal** India
100 B4 **Thouin Pt pt** Aust.
121 E2 **Thousand Islands is** Can.
129 G2 **Thousand Lake Mt mt.** U.S.A.
128 C4 **Thousand Oaks** U.S.A.
29 E4 **Thrakiko Pelagos sea** Greece
126 E2 **Three Forks** U.S.A.
110 G4 **Three Hills** Can.
97 F5 **Three Hummock I. i.** Aust.
92 D1 **Three Kings Is is** N.Z.
122 C3 **Three Lakes** U.S.A.
122 D5 **Three Oaks** U.S.A.
42 B4 **Three Pagodas Pass pass** Myanmar/Thailand
76 D6 **Three Points, Cape c.** Ghana
122 E5 **Three Rivers** U.S.A.
125 D6 **Three Rivers** U.S.A.
126 B2 **Three Sisters mt.** U.S.A.
125 D5 **Throckmorton** U.S.A.
101 D5 **Throssell, L. salt flat** Aust.
100 C4 **Throssel Ra. h.** Aust.
111 G2 **Thubun Lakes l.** Can.
43 D5 **Thu Dâu Môt** Vietnam
18 B3 **Thuin** Belgium
54 B3 **Thul** Pakistan
83 D3 **Thuli** Zimbabwe
93 C5 **Thumbs, The mt.** N.Z.
21 H3 **Thun** *Bern* Switz.
99 E5 **Thunda** Aust.
101 B6 **Thundelarra** Aust.
114 A2 **Thunder Bay b.** Can.
114 A2 **Thunder Bay** Can.
123 F3 **Thunder Bay b.** U.S.A.
132 B3 **Thunder Knoll** Caribbean
43 B5 **Thung Song** Thailand
43 B6 **Thung Wa** Thailand
18 E3 **Thüringen div.** Germany
18 E3 **Thüringer Becken reg.** Germany
18 E3 **Thüringer Wald mts** Germany
17 D5 **Thurles** Rep. of Ire.
120 E5 **Thurmont** U.S.A.
115 H4 **Thurso** Can.
16 F2 **Thurso** U.K.
16 F2 **Thurso r.** U.K.
152 A3 **Thurston I. i.** Ant.
152 A3 **Thwaites Gl. gl.** Ant.
11 C4 **Thyborøn** Denmark
99 E5 **Thylungra** Aust.
29 F6 **Thymaina i.** Greece
140 C3 **Tiahuanaco** Bolivia
133 E5 **Tía Juana** Venezuela
48 A4 **Tiancang** China
51 G1 **Tianchang** China
50 D4 **Tiandeng** China
50 D4 **Tiandong** China
50 D3 **Tian'e** China
51 G2 **Tianfanjie** China
142 D1 **Tianguá** Brazil
76 B4 **Tiânguél Bôri** Guinea
49 F5 **Tianjin div.** China
49 F5 **Tianjin** China
48 A5 **Tianjun** China
50 D3 **Tianlin** China
51 F2 **Tianmen** China
51 G2 **Tianmu Shan mt. ra.** China
49 J4 **Tianqiaoling** China
50 C2 **Tianquan** China
49 H4 **Tianshifu** China
50 D1 **Tianshui** China
54 D2 **Tianshuihai** China/Jammu and Kashmir
51 H2 **Tiantai** China
49 F4 **Tiantaiyong** China
50 D4 **Tianyang** China
51 E3 **Tianzhu** China
48 B5 **Tianzhu** China
91 □11 **Tiarel** *Fr. Poly.* Pac. Oc.
75 E1 **Tiaret** Algeria
75 G2 **Tiaret well** Tunisia
90 □2 **Tiari** Pac. Oc.
99 H5 **Tiaro** Aust.
76 D5 **Tiassalé** Côte d'Ivoire
91 □12 **Tiavea** Western Samoa
144 C6 **Tibagi r.** Brazil
144 C6 **Tibaji** Brazil
60 E3 **Tibal, Wādī w** Iraq
78 B2 **Tibati** Cameroon
54 B3 **Tibba** Pakistan
76 C5 **Tibé, Pic de summit** Guinea
61 C3 **Tiberias, L. l.** Israel
126 E1 **Tiber Res. resr** U.S.A.
72 C3 **Tibesti plat.** Chad
139 F2 **Tiboku Falls waterfall** Guyana
97 E2 **Tibooburra** Aust.
55 E3 **Tibrikot** Nepal
11 D4 **Tibro** Sweden
130 B2 **Tiburón i.** Mexico
41 B3 **Ticao i.** Phil.
115 G4 **Tichborne** Can.
74 C5 **Tîchît** Mauritania
74 B4 **Tichla** *Western Sahara*
26 B3 **Ticino r.** Italy
28 D2 **Ţicleni** Romania
121 G3 **Ticonderoga** U.S.A.
131 H4 **Ticul** Mexico
11 D4 **Tidaholm** Sweden
77 E3 **Tidarmène** Mali
42 A2 **Tiddim** Myanmar
43 A6 **Tiden** *Andaman and Nicobar Is* India
77 E3 **Tidjerouene well** Mali
74 B5 **Tidjikja** Mauritania
18 B3 **Tiel** Netherlands
76 A4 **Tiel** Senegal
49 H3 **Tieli** China
49 G4 **Tieling** China
54 D2 **Tielongtan** China/Jammu and Kashmir
65 J4 **Tien Shan mt. ra.** China/Kyrgyzstan
11 E3 **Tierp** Sweden
138 B2 **Tierra Alta** Colombia
146 B2 **Tierra Amarilla** Chile
127 F4 **Tierra Amarilla** U.S.A.
131 F5 **Tierra Blanca** Mexico
131 F5 **Tierra Colorada** Mexico
147 C7 **Tierra del Fuego div.** Arg.
147 C7 **Tierra del Fuego, Isla Grande de i.** Arg./Chile
24 C4 **Tierra Llana de Huelva plain** Spain
24 D2 **Tiétar r.** Spain
24 D2 **Tiétar, Valle de v.** Spain
144 C4 **Tietê r.** Brazil
144 E5 **Tietê** Brazil
96 C1 **Tieyon** Aust.
120 B4 **Tiffin** U.S.A.
119 D6 **Tifton** U.S.A.
90 □2 **Tiga i.** Pac. Oc.
64 D4 **Tigen** Kazak.
15 C3 **Tighina** Moldova
65 K2 **Tigiretskiy Khr. mt. ra.** Kazak./Rus. Fed.
55 F5 **Tigiria** India
78 B2 **Tignère** Cameroon
113 H4 **Tignish** *Prince Edward I.* Can.
138 C4 **Tigre r.** Ecuador/Peru
139 E2 **Tigre r.** Venezuela
60 F3 **Tigris r.** Iraq/Turkey
75 E3 **Tiguelguemine well** Algeria
74 A5 **Tiguent** Mauritania
72 C4 **Tigui** Chad
73 H4 **Tihāmah reg.** Saudi Arabia
61 B5 **Tîh, Gebel el plat.** Egypt
72 B1 **Tījī** Libya
130 A1 **Tijuana** Mexico
144 D3 **Tijuco r.** Brazil
131 H5 **Tikal** Guatemala
54 D4 **Tikamgarh** India
108 C3 **Tikchik L. l.** U.S.A.
91 □10 **Tikehau i.** *Fr. Poly.* Pac. Oc.
78 C2 **Tikem** Chad
14 D1 **Tikhmenevo** Rus. Fed.
13 G6 **Tikhoretsk** Rus. Fed.
12 E3 **Tikhvin** Rus. Fed.
12 E3 **Tikhvinskaya Gryada ridge** Rus. Fed.
92 G2 **Tikitiki** N.Z.
90 □8 **Tikituru h.** Fiji
92 F3 **Tikokino** N.Z.
86 H6 **Tikopia i.** Solomon Islands
60 E3 **Tikrīt** Iraq
10 H3 **Tiksheozero, Oz. l.** Rus. Fed.
63 O2 **Tiksi** Rus. Fed.
55 E3 **Tila r.** Nepal
61 D1 **Tilbeşar Ovasi plain** Turkey
99 F5 **Tilbooroo** Aust.
18 B3 **Tilburg** Netherlands
146 C1 **Tilcara** Arg.
77 E3 **Tilemsès** Niger
77 E3 **Tîlemsi, Vallée du w** Mali
54 D4 **Tilhar** India
42 A2 **Tilin** Myanmar
77 E4 **Tillabéri div.** Niger
77 E4 **Tillabéri** Niger
126 B2 **Tillamook** U.S.A.
43 A5 **Tillanchong I. i.** *Andaman and Nicobar Is* India
77 E3 **Tillia** Niger
114 E5 **Tillsonburg** Can.
77 E3 **Tiloa** Niger
140 C4 **Tilomonte** Chile
29 F6 **Tilos i.** Greece
97 F2 **Tilpa** Aust.
75 E2 **Tilrhemt** Algeria
14 C3 **Tim r.** Rus. Fed.
14 C4 **Tim** Rus. Fed.
73 F2 **Tima** Egypt
25 □ **Timanfaya h.** *Canary Is* Spain
62 F3 **Timanskiy Kryazh ridge** Rus. Fed.
93 C6 **Timaru** N.Z.
13 F6 **Timashevsk** Rus. Fed.
142 E2 **Timbaúba** Brazil
74 C5 **Timbedgha** Mauritania
98 B2 **Timber Creek** Aust.
128 D3 **Timber Mt mt.** U.S.A.
120 D5 **Timberville** U.S.A.
143 B6 **Timbo r.** Brazil
97 E4 **Timboon** Aust.
83 F2 **Timbué, Pta pt** Mozambique
77 D3 **Timétrine reg.** Mali
77 D3 **Timétrine** Mali
77 F3 **Timia** Niger
75 E4 **Timïaouine** Algeria
75 E3 **Timimoun** Algeria
65 G2 **Timiryazevo** Kazak.
14 F1 **Timiryazevo** Rus. Fed.
28 D2 **Timiș r.** Romania
28 C2 **Timișoara** Romania
77 F3 **Ti-m-Meghsoi w** Niger
114 E2 **Timmins** Can.
12 F3 **Timokhino** Rus. Fed.
142 D2 **Timon** Brazil
39 J8 **Timor i.** Indon.
86 D6 **Timor Sea sea** Aust./Indonesia
146 D4 **Timote** Arg.
145 G3 **Timóteo** Brazil
75 D3 **Timoudi** Algeria
11 E3 **Timrå** Sweden
61 B4 **Timsâh, L. l.** Egypt
119 C5 **Tims Ford L. l.** U.S.A.
65 G4 **Timur** Kazak.
54 D5 **Timurni Muafi** India
138 D2 **Tinaco** Venezuela
76 D3 **Ti-n-Aguelhay** Mali
25 □ **Tinajo** *Canary Is* Spain
72 B3 **Tin Alkoum** Algeria/Libya
77 E3 **Ti-n-Azabo well** Mali
74 C4 **Ti-n-Bessaïs well** Mauritania
20 D2 **Tinchebray** France
77 D2 **Ti-n-Didine well** Mali
56 B3 **Tindivanam** India
74 C3 **Tindouf** Algeria
76 D3 **Ti-n-Echeri well** Mali
21 H4 **Tinée r.** France
24 C1 **Tineo** Spain
77 E3 **Ti-n-Essako** Mali
74 C3 **Tinfouchy** Algeria
51 G3 **Ting r.** China
43 D7 **Tinggi i.** Malaysia
97 G2 **Tingha** Aust.
76 B5 **Tingi Mts mts** Sierra Leone
140 A1 **Tingo Maria** Peru
55 F3 **Tingri** China
11 D4 **Tingsryd** Sweden
146 B3 **Tinguiririca, Vol. vol** Chile
10 C3 **Tingvoll** Norway
142 E3 **Tinharé, I. de i.** Brazil
42 D3 **Tinh Gia** Vietnam
39 M4 **Tinian i.** *Northern Mariana Is* Pac. Oc.
40 A3 **Tinjil i.** Indon.
76 C4 **Tinkisso r.** Guinea
146 C2 **Tinogasta** Arg.
29 E6 **Tinos i.** Greece
29 E6 **Tinos** Greece
25 F4 **Tiñoso, Cabo hd** Spain
75 E4 **Ti-n-Rerhoh well** Algeria
75 F3 **Tinrhert, Plateau du plat.** Algeria
55 H4 **Tinsukia** India
74 B5 **Ţinţâne** Mauritania
77 E3 **Ti-n-Tékouffé well** Mali
146 D2 **Tintina** Arg.
96 E3 **Tintinara** Aust.
93 F4 **Tinui** N.Z.
77 E3 **Ti-n-Zaouâtene** Mali
120 E4 **Tioga r.** U.S.A.
43 D7 **Tioman i.** Malaysia
114 D2 **Tionaga** Can.
120 D4 **Tionesta Lake l.** U.S.A.
121 E3 **Tioughnioga r.** U.S.A.
75 E1 **Tipasa** Algeria
130 J6 **Tipitapa** Nicaragua
122 D5 **Tippecanoe r.** U.S.A.
122 E5 **Tippecanoe Lake l.** U.S.A.
17 C5 **Tipperary** Rep. of Ire.
55 F4 **Tiptala Bhanjyang pass** Nepal
122 D5 **Tipton** U.S.A.
122 B5 **Tipton** U.S.A.
129 E4 **Tipton, Mt mt.** U.S.A.
114 B2 **Tip Top Hill h.** Can.
140 C3 **Tipuani** Bolivia
138 D3 **Tiquié r.** Brazil
131 H6 **Tiquisate** Guatemala
57 B2 **Tīrān** Iran
61 C6 **Tīrān i.** Saudi Arabia
29 B4 **Tiranë** Albania
26 C2 **Tirano** Italy
15 C3 **Tiraspol** Moldova
61 A4 **Tir'at el Ismâ'ilîya canal** Egypt
92 E2 **Tirau** N.Z.
82 B4 **Tiraz Mts mts** Namibia
60 A2 **Tire** Turkey
16 D3 **Tiree i.** U.K.
75 E4 **Tirek well** Algeria
77 E2 **Tirest well** Mali
54 B1 **Tirich Mir mt.** Pakistan
74 C4 **Tiris Zemmour div.** Mauritania
56 B2 **Tirna r.** India
18 E5 **Tirol div.** Austria
145 F3 **Tiros** Brazil
78 D2 **Tiroungoulou** C.A.R.
27 C5 **Tirreno, Mare sea** Italy
27 B5 **Tirso r.** Italy
56 A3 **Tirthahalli** India
55 F5 **Tirtol** India
56 B4 **Tiruchchendur** India
56 B4 **Tiruchchirāppalli** India
56 B4 **Tiruchengodu** India
56 B4 **Tirunelveli** India
140 A1 **Tiruntán** Peru
56 B3 **Tirupati** India
56 B3 **Tiruppattur** India
56 B4 **Tiruppur** India
56 B4 **Tirutturaippundi** India
56 B3 **Tiruvannamalai** India
56 B4 **Tisaiyanvilai** India
28 F2 **Tisău** Romania
111 J4 **Tisdale** Can.
61 D3 **Ţisīyah** Syria
56 C5 **Tissamaharama** Sri Lanka
75 E1 **Tissemsilt** Algeria
55 G4 **Tista r.** India
19 K5 **Tisza r.** Europe
19 K5 **Tiszaföldvár** Hungary
19 K5 **Tiszafüred** Hungary
19 K5 **Tiszakécske** Hungary
19 K5 **Tiszántúl reg.** Hungary
19 K5 **Tiszaújváros** Hungary
19 K5 **Tiszavasvári** Hungary
75 E3 **Tit** *Adrar* Algeria
75 F4 **Tit** *Tamanrasset* Algeria
152 B4 **Titan Dome ice feature** Ant.
63 O2 **Tit-Ary** Rus. Fed.
28 C2 **Titel** Yugo.
140 C3 **Titicaca, Lago l.** Bolivia/Peru
55 E5 **Titlagarh** India
26 E3 **Titova Korenica** Croatia
26 F3 **Titov Drvar** Bos.-Herz.
14 F3 **Titovo** Rus. Fed.
28 B3 **Titovo Užice** Yugo.
98 C4 **Ti Tree** Aust.
123 E4 **Tittabawassee r.** U.S.A.
18 F4 **Tittmoning** Germany
28 E2 **Titu** Romania
119 D6 **Titusville** U.S.A.
120 D4 **Titusville** U.S.A.
54 C4 **Tivari** India
28 B3 **Tivat** Yugo.
114 E4 **Tiverton** Can.
17 F6 **Tiverton** U.K.
27 D5 **Tivoli** Italy
131 H4 **Tixkokob** Mexico
131 F5 **Tixtla** Mexico
61 D2 **Tiyās** Syria
130 E4 **Tizapán el Alto** Mexico
74 C3 **Tizi Mighert pass** Morocco
131 H4 **Tizimín** Mexico
74 C2 **Tizi-n-Test pass** Morocco
74 C2 **Tizi-n-Tichka pass** Morocco
75 E1 **Tizi Ouzou** Algeria
65 J5 **Tiznap r.** China
74 C3 **Tiznit** Morocco
130 E3 **Tizoc** Mexico
10 E2 **Tjappsåive** Sweden
16 K1 **Tjeldstø** Norway
11 B4 **Tjorhom** Norway
131 F5 **Tlacolula** Mexico
131 G5 **Tlacotalpán** Mexico
125 C7 **Tlahualilo** Mexico
131 F5 **Tlalnepantla** Mexico
131 F5 **Tlapa** Mexico
131 F5 **Tlaxcala div.** Mexico
131 F5 **Tlaxcala** Mexico
131 F5 **Tlaxiaco** Mexico
75 D2 **Tlemcen** Algeria
24 D5 **Tleta des Beni Yder Cherki** Morocco
24 D5 **Tleta Rissana** Morocco
82 D3 **Tlokweng** Botswana
15 A2 **Tlumach** Ukraine
19 K2 **Tłuszcz** Poland
13 H7 **Tlyarata** Rus. Fed.
14 B1 **T'ma r.** Rus. Fed.
72 C2 **Tmassah** Libya
74 B4 **Tmeïmîchât** Mauritania
110 D3 **Toad River** Can.
41 □1 **Toagel Mlungui chan.** Palau
83 H2 **Toamasina** Madagascar
83 H2 **Toamasina div.** Madagascar
91 □11 **Toanoano** *Fr. Poly.* Pac. Oc.
91 □10 **Toau i.** *Fr. Poly.* Pac. Oc.
73 G3 **To Awai well** Sudan
146 D4 **Toay** Arg.
50 B2 **Toba** China
47 F6 **Toba** Japan
54 A3 **Toba & Kakar Ranges mt. ra.** Pakistan
133 □2 **Tobago i.** Trin. & Tobago
25 F3 **Tobarra** Spain
39 J6 **Tobelo** Indon.
98 D4 **Tobermory** Aust.
99 E5 **Tobermory** Aust.
114 E4 **Tobermory** Can.
16 D3 **Tobermory** U.K.
46 H2 **Tōbetsu** Japan
47 □1 **Tobiishi-hana c.** Japan
109 Q2 **Tobin, Kap c.** Greenland
111 J4 **Tobin L. l.** Can.
128 D1 **Tobin, Mt mt.** U.S.A.
121 K1 **Tobique r.** Can.
47 G4 **Tobi-shima i.** Japan
40 A2 **Toboali** Indon.
62 H4 **Tobol r.** Kazak.
64 F2 **Tobol** Kazak.
65 G1 **Tobol r.** Kazak./Rus. Fed.
62 H4 **Tobol'sk** Rus. Fed.
43 E4 **Tô Bong** Vietnam
41 B4 **Toboso** Phil.
142 C2 **Tocantinópolis** Brazil
142 C1 **Tocantins r.** *Maranhão/Tocantins* Brazil
139 F5 **Tocantins r.** *Pará* Brazil
142 C3 **Tocantins div.** Brazil
142 C3 **Tocantinzinha r.** Brazil
119 D5 **Toccoa** U.S.A.
54 B2 **Tochi r.** Pakistan
47 G5 **Tochigi div.** Japan
47 G5 **Tochio** Japan
11 C4 **Töcksfors** Sweden
133 □3 **Toco** Trin. & Tobago
140 C4 **Toconao** Chile
140 B4 **Tocopilla** Chile
138 D1 **Tocuyc r.** Venezuela
98 C5 **Todd w** Aust.
39 H7 **Todeli** Indon.
26 D4 **Todi** Italy
47 J4 **Todoga-saki pt** Japan
46 H3 **Todohokke** Japan
145 H2 **Todos os Santos r.** Brazil
140 C3 **Todos Santos** Bolivia
130 C4 **Todos Santos** Mexico
128 D6 **Todos Santos, Bahía de b.** Mexico
93 B7 **Toetoes Bay b.** N.Z.
110 G4 **Tofield** Can.
110 D5 **Tofino** Can.
122 B2 **Tofte** U.S.A.
90 □5 **Tofua i.** Tonga
90 □2 **Toga i.** Vanuatu
55 E2 **Togatax** China
80 E3 **Togdheer div.** Somalia
47 F5 **Togi** Japan
39 H7 **Togian, Kepulauan is** Indon.
69 E5 **Togo country** Africa
46 C7 **Tōgō** Japan
122 A2 **Togo** U.S.A.
48 D4 **Togtoh** China
47 □2 **Toguchi** Japan
65 K1 **Toguchin** Rus. Fed.
65 L2 **Togul** Rus. Fed.
54 C3 **Tohana** India
129 H4 **Tohatchi** U.S.A.
40 C1 **Tohenbatu mt.** Malaysia
91 □11 **Tohiea mt.** *Fr. Poly.* Pac. Oc.
10 G3 **Toholampi** Finland
48 C4 **Tohom** China
48 D3 **Töhöm** Mongolia
47 G6 **Toi** Japan
43 A5 **Toibalewe** *Andaman and Nicobar Is* India
11 F3 **Toijala** Finland
46 C8 **Toi-misaki pt** Japan
11 G3 **Toivakka** Finland
128 D2 **Toiyabe Range mts** U.S.A.
40 E2 **Toja** Indon.
46 D6 **Tōjō** Japan
64 D2 **Tok r.** Rus. Fed.
108 D3 **Tok** U.S.A.
46 J2 **Tokachi-gawa r.** Japan
47 F6 **Tōkai** Japan
19 K4 **Tokaj** Hungary
47 G5 **Tōkamachi** Japan
93 B7 **Tokanui** N.Z.
73 G4 **Tokar** Sudan
45 N6 **Tokara-rettō is** Japan
14 E4 **Tokarevka** Rus. Fed.
14 E2 **Tokarevo** Rus. Fed.
60 D1 **Tokat** Turkey
49 H5 **Tŏkchoktŏ i.** S. Korea
49 H5 **Tŏkch'ŏn** N. Korea
87 K5 **Tokelau terr.** Pac. Oc.
65 J4 **Tokmak** Kyrgyzstan
15 F3 **Tokmak** Ukraine
92 G3 **Tokomaru Bay** N.Z.
47 F6 **Tokoname** Japan
92 E3 **Tokoroa** N.Z.
46 J2 **Tokoro-gawa r.** Japan
76 C5 **Tokounou** Guinea
44 E3 **Toksun** China
46 C5 **Tok-tō i.** Japan
65 H4 **Toktogul** Kyrgyzstan
65 H4 **Toktogul Suu Saktagychy resr** Kyrgyzstan
46 E7 **Tokushima div.** Japan
46 E6 **Tokushima** Japan
46 C6 **Tokuyama** Japan
47 G6 **Tōkyō div.** Japan
47 G6 **Tōkyō** Japan
47 G6 **Tōkyō-wan b.** Japan
57 F2 **Tokzār** Afghanistan
92 G3 **Tolaga Bay** N.Z.
83 H3 **Tôlañaro** Madagascar
146 C2 **Tolar, Co mt.** Arg.
14 G2 **Tolba** Rus. Fed.
64 E2 **Tolbazy** Rus. Fed.
14 E1 **Tolbukhino** Rus. Fed.
49 H1 **Tolbuzino** Rus. Fed.
130 K7 **Tolé** Panama
131 F4 **Toleant** Mexico
144 B6 **Toledo** Brazil
24 D3 **Toledo** Spain
122 A5 **Toledo** U.S.A.
120 B4 **Toledo** U.S.A.
125 E6 **Toledo Bend Res. resr** U.S.A.
26 D4 **Tolentino** Italy
146 B4 **Tolhuaca, Parque Nacional nat. park** Chile
83 G3 **Toliara div.** Madagascar
83 G3 **Toliara** Madagascar
40 E1 **Tolitoli** Indon.
40 E1 **Tolitoli, Tk b.** Indon.
62 K3 **Tol'ka** Rus. Fed.
19 J1 **Tolkmicko** Poland
18 F2 **Tollense r.** Germany
12 D3 **Tolmachevo** Rus. Fed.
26 D2 **Tolmezzo** Italy
19 J5 **Tolna** Hungary
79 C4 **Tolo** Zaire
45 □ **Tolo Channel chan.** Hong Kong
45 □ **Tolo Harbour b.** Hong Kong
25 E1 **Tolosa** Spain
49 H6 **Tolsan Do i.** S. Korea
114 D4 **Tolsmaville** Can.
138 B2 **Tolú** Colombia
131 F5 **Toluca** Mexico
10 H2 **Tolvand, Oz. l.** Rus. Fed.
12 J4 **Tol'yatti** Rus. Fed.
64 F2 **Tolybay** Kazak.
65 L2 **Tom' r.** Rus. Fed.
49 J2 **Tom' r.** Rus. Fed.
76 D4 **Toma** Burkina
122 B4 **Tomah** U.S.A.
122 C3 **Tomahawk** U.S.A.
46 H2 **Tomakomai** Japan
40 E2 **Tomali** Indon.
46 H1 **Tomamae** Japan
90 □8 **Tomanivi mt.** Fiji
139 E4 **Tomar** Brazil
24 B3 **Tomar** Portugal
46 H2 **Tomari** Japan
15 G1 **Tomarovka** Rus. Fed.
60 C2 **Tomarza** Turkey
140 C3 **Tomás Barron** Bolivia
146 E3 **Tomás Gomensoro** Uruguay
15 B1 **Tomashhorod** Ukraine
15 C2 **Tomashpil'** Ukraine
19 L3 **Tomaszów Lubelski** Poland
19 K3 **Tomaszów Mazowiecki** Poland
130 D5 **Tomatlán** Mexico
144 D5 **Tomazina** Brazil
46 D6 **Tombara** Japan
119 B6 **Tombigbee r.** U.S.A.
79 B5 **Tomboco** Angola
145 G4 **Tombos** Brazil
76 D3 **Tombouctou** Mali
76 D3 **Tombouctou div.** Mali
129 G6 **Tombstone** U.S.A.
79 B7 **Tombua** Angola
83 D3 **Tom Burke** R.S.A.
146 B4 **Tomé** Chile
11 D5 **Tomelilla** Sweden
24 E3 **Tomelloso** Spain
115 F3 **Tomiko** Can.
97 G3 **Tomingley** Aust.
76 D4 **Tominián** Mali
40 E2 **Tomini, Teluk g.** Indon.
47 H5 **Tomioka** Japan
26 F4 **Tomislavgrad** Bos.-Herz.
96 B1 **Tomkinson Ranges mt. ra.** Aust.
10 D2 **Tømmerneset** Norway
63 O4 **Tommot** Rus. Fed.
138 D2 **Tomo r.** Colombia
138 D3 **Tomo** Colombia
48 E4 **Tomortei** China
40 D2 **Tompo** Indon.
63 P3 **Tompo** Rus. Fed.
100 B4 **Tom Price** Aust.
62 K4 **Tomsk** Rus. Fed.
63 Q3 **Tomtor** Rus. Fed.
61 C1 **Tömük** Turkey
46 J2 **Tomuraushi-yama mt.** Japan
13 G6 **Tomuzlovka r.** Rus. Fed.
131 G5 **Tonalá** Mexico
129 G3 **Tonalea** U.S.A.
47 F5 **Tonami** Japan
138 D4 **Tonantins** Brazil
126 C1 **Tonasket** U.S.A.
139 G2 **Tonate** French Guiana
39 J6 **Tondano** Indon.
11 C5 **Tønder** Denmark
47 H6 **Tone-gawa r.** Japan
97 E2 **Tonga** Aust.
87 K7 **Tonga country** Pac. Oc.
83 E4 **Tongaat** R.S.A.
51 G3 **Tong'an** China
87 M5 **Tongareva atoll** *Cook Islands* Pac. Oc.
92 E3 **Tongariro mt.** N.Z.
92 E3 **Tongariro National Park nat. park** N.Z.
90 □4 **Tongatapu i.** Tonga
90 □4 **Tongatapu Group is** Tonga
150 H7 **Tonga Tr.** Pac. Oc.
51 F1 **Tongbai** China
51 F1 **Tongbai Shan mt. ra.** China
51 G2 **Tongcheng** China
51 F2 **Tongcheng** China
51 E1 **Tongchuan** China
51 E3 **Tongdao** China
50 C1 **Tongde** China
49 H5 **Tongduch'ŏn** S. Korea
18 B3 **Tongeren** Belgium
51 F2 **Tonggu** China
51 E1 **Tongguan** China
51 E5 **Tonggu Jiao** China
49 J5 **Tonghae** S. Korea
50 C3 **Tonghai** China
49 J3 **Tonghe** China
49 H4 **Tonghua** China
49 K3 **Tongjiang** China
50 D2 **Tongjiang** China
49 H3 **Tongken r.** China
50 D4 **Tongking, Gulf of g.** China/Vietnam
50 D2 **Tongliang** China
49 G4 **Tongliao** China
51 G2 **Tongling** China
51 G2 **Tongling** China
51 G2 **Tonglu** China
50 D2 **Tongnan** China
90 □2 **Tongoa i.** Vanuatu
83 G3 **Tongobory** Madagascar
41 B5 **Tongquil i.** Phil.
51 E3 **Tongren** China
50 C1 **Tongren** China
55 G4 **Tongsa r.** Bhutan
55 G4 **Tongsa** Bhutan
51 F2 **Tongshan** China
50 A1 **Tongtian r.** China
16 E2 **Tongue** U.K.
126 F2 **Tongue r.** U.S.A.
132 C1 **Tongue of the Ocean chan.** The Bahamas
50 D1 **Tongwei** China
49 F5 **Tong Xian** China
48 C5 **Tongxin** China
51 G2 **Tongyanghe** China
49 G3 **Tongyu** China
50 D2 **Tongzi** China
122 C5 **Tonica** U.S.A.
130 C2 **Tónichi** Mexico
78 E2 **Tonj w** Sudan
78 E2 **Tonj** Sudan
54 C4 **Tonk** India
57 B1 **Tonkābon** Iran
42 D2 **Tonkin reg.** Vietnam
12 H3 **Tonkino** Rus. Fed.
43 D5 **Tônle Basăk r.** Cambodia
43 C4 **Tônlé Sab l.** Cambodia
20 E4 **Tonneins** France
21 F3 **Tonnerre** France
18 D1 **Tönning** Germany
47 H4 **Tōno** Japan
128 D2 **Tonopah** U.S.A.
46 E6 **Tonoshō** Japan
130 K8 **Tonosí** Panama
11 C4 **Tønsberg** Norway
11 B4 **Tonstad** Norway
129 G5 **Tonto National Monument res.** U.S.A.
90 □5 **Tonumea i.** Tonga
42 A2 **Tonzang** Myanmar
99 G6 **Toobeah** Aust.
76 C5 **Toobli** Liberia
126 D3 **Tooele** U.S.A.
99 F5 **Toompine** Aust.
97 G2 **Tooraweenah** Aust.

42 B3 To or China Bakir r. Myanmar
99 G5 Toowoomba Aust.
80 F2 Tooxin Somalia
129 G6 Topawa U.S.A.
128 C2 Topaz U.S.A.
81 ○3 Topaze B. b. Rodrigues i. Mauritius
65 K2 Topchikha Rus. Fed.
124 E4 Topeka U.S.A.
130 D3 Topia Mexico
132 D2 Topkanovo Rus. Fed.
65 L1 Topki Rus. Fed.
110 D4 Topley Landing Can.
28 E1 Toplița Romania
146 B3 Topocalma, Pta pt Chile
129 E4 Topock U.S.A.
28 C2 Topola Yugo.
19 J4 Topoľčany Slovakia
130 C3 Topolobampo Mexico
28 G2 Topolog Romania
28 E2 Topoloveni Romania
28 F3 Topolovgrad Bulgaria
15 B1 Topory Ukraine
12 D1 Topozero, Oz. l. Rus. Fed.
126 B2 Toppenish U.S.A.
121 K2 Topsfield U.S.A.
129 F3 Toquerville U.S.A.
81 B3 Tor Ethiopia
60 A2 Torbalı Turkey
57 D2 Torbat-e Ḩeydarīyeh Iran
57 E2 Torbat-e Jām Iran
14 F2 Torbeyevo Rus. Fed.
14 F2 Torbeyevo Rus. Fed.
14 E1 Torchino Rus. Fed.
122 E3 Torch Lake l. U.S.A.
15 A1 Torchyn Ukraine
24 D2 Tordesillas Spain
25 F2 Tordesilos Spain
17 F6 Töre Sweden
25 H1 Torelló Spain
24 C1 Toreno Spain
48 C2 Torey Rus. Fed.
18 F3 Torgau Germany
19 G2 Torgelow Germany
13 H5 Torhout Belgium
20 D2 Torigni-sur-Vire France
130 ○3 Torin Mexico
26 A3 Torino Italy
86 F2 Tori-shima i. Japan
80 B4 Torit Sudan
144 B2 Torixoréu Brazil
24 D2 Tormes r. Spain
19 K4 Tornala Slovakia
16 E1 Torneälven r. Sweden
16 D1 Torneträsk l. Sweden
10 E1 Torngat Mountains mt. ra. Can.
10 G2 Tornio Finland
146 D4 Tornquist Arg.
77 F4 Toro Nigeria
24 E2 Toro Spain
146 C2 Toro, Co del mt. Chile
77 E4 Torodi Niger
72 C4 Toro Doum well Chad
46 H3 Törökszentmiklós Hungary
97 G3 Toronto Aust.
115 F5 Toronto Can.
115 F5 Toronto airport Can.
12 D3 Toropets Rus. Fed.
128 D5 Toro Pk summit U.S.A.
60 B1 Toros Dağları mt. ra. Turkey
11 J5 Torquay U.K.
128 C5 Torrance U.S.A.
24 B3 Torrão Portugal
27 E5 Torre mt. Portugal
27 E5 Torre Annunziata Italy
25 G2 Torreblanca Spain
25 G5 Torre Cavallo, Capo di pt Italy
27 E5 Torre del Greco Italy
24 C2 Torre de Moncorvo Portugal
24 E4 Torredonjimeno Spain
24 D3 Torrejón-Tajo, Emb. de resr Spain
24 E3 Torrelaguna Spain
24 D1 Torrelavega Spain
24 D4 Torremolinos Málaga Spain
99 F4 Torrens Cr. w. Aust.
99 F4 Torrens Creek Aust.
96 D2 Torrens, Lake salt flat Aust.
25 F3 Torrent Spain
130 E3 Torreón Mexico
25 E4 Torre Orsaia Italy
25 F4 Torre-Pacheco Spain
143 C6 Torres Brazil
130 C2 Torres Mexico
147 B7 Torres del Paine, Parque Nacional nat. park Chile
90 ○1 Torres Islands is Vanuatu
24 B3 Torres Novas Portugal
95 H1 Torres Strait str. Aust./P.N.G.
24 B3 Torres Vedras Portugal
25 F3 Torrevieja Spain
129 G2 Torrey U.S.A.
17 E6 Torridon, Loch inlet U.K.
26 B3 Torriglia Italy
24 D3 Torrijos Spain
121 G4 Torrington U.S.A.
124 C3 Torrington U.S.A.
25 H1 Torroella de Montgrí Spain
24 E4 Torrox Spain
55 G4 Torsa r. Bhutan
9 E3 Torsby Sweden
16 D1 Tórshavn Faeroes
119 ○3 Tortola i. Virgin Is Caribbean
146 C2 Tórtolas, Co Las mt. Chile
26 D3 Tortolì Italy
26 A4 Tortona Italy
25 G2 Tortosa Spain
130 B3 Tortugas, Bahía Mexico
60 E1 Tortum Turkey
57 D1 Torūd Iran
60 D1 Toru'l Turkey
19 J2 Toruń Poland
17 C4 Tory Island i. Rep. of Ire.
19 J3 Torysa r. Slovakia
14 E1 Torzhok Rus. Fed.
87 H6 Tosa Japan
87 H6 Tosa-shimizu Japan
87 H6 Tosa-wan b. Japan
16 D2 Tosbotn Norway
26 C3 Toscana, Arcipelago is Italy
87 H6 Tōshima-yama mt. Japan
12 D4 Tosno Rus. Fed.
48 A2 Tosontsengel Mongolia
146 D2 Tostado Arg.
18 D2 Tostedt Germany
46 C7 Tosu Japan
92 J3 Totana Spain
15 C2 Tot'ma Rus. Fed.
12 G3 Tot'ma Rus. Fed.
131 H5 Totness Surinam
131 H5 Totolapan Mexico
140 C3 Totora Bolivia
146 B3 Totoral Chile

76 C5 Totota Liberia
90 ○7 Totoya i. Fiji
152 C6 Totten Glacier gl. Ant.
97 F3 Tottenham Aust.
11 G6 Totton U.K.
46 E6 Tottori Japan
77 F2 Touârêt well Niger
76 C4 Touba Côte d'Ivoire
74 C2 Toubkal, Jbel mt. Morocco
72 B3 Touboro Cameroon
21 F3 Toucy France
74 B4 Toueirma well Mauritania
76 B2 Touerât well Mali
76 D2 Toufourine well Mali
76 A2 Tougan Burkina
75 F2 Touggourt Algeria
76 C4 Tougouri Burkina
76 B4 Tougué Guinea
90 ○2 Touho New Caledonia
74 C5 Touijinet well Mauritania
76 A4 Touli Mauritania
76 C4 Toukoto Mali
21 G2 Toul France
76 C5 Toulépleu Côte d'Ivoire
21 G5 Toulon France
21 E5 Toulouse Haute-Garonne France
77 F3 Toumbélaga well Niger
77 G2 Toummo well Niger
76 B4 Toumodi Côte d'Ivoire
77 F3 Toumfaminir well Niger
77 F5 Toungo Nigeria
42 B3 Toungoo Myanmar
21 G3 Tournus France
122 B3 Touros Brazil
20 E3 Tours France
21 F4 Toury France
76 C4 Toussiana Burkina
72 C3 Tousside, Pic mt. Chad
72 D3 Toussoro, Mt mt. C.A.R.
82 C5 Touws River R.S.A.
19 H3 Toužim Czech Rep.
48 C3 Töv div. Mongolia
138 C2 Tovar Venezuela
14 B2 Tovarkovo Rus. Fed.
14 F2 Tovarkovskiy Rus. Fed.
60 F1 Tovuz Azerbaijan
46 H3 Towada Japan
46 H3 Towada-Hachimantai National Park nat. park. Japan
46 H3 Towada-ko l. Japan
92 E1 Towak Hd i. Indon.
133 H6 Towakaima Guyana
121 E4 Towanda U.S.A.
129 H3 Towaoc U.S.A.
99 G4 Tower Aust.
61 B1 Towerhill Cr. w. Aust.
111 J5 Towner U.S.A.
128 D3 Townes Pass pass U.S.A.
97 F3 Townsend Aust.
98 C2 Townsend U.S.A.
126 E2 Townsend U.S.A.
99 G4 Townshend I. i. Aust.
17 F3 Townsville Aust.
80 B3 Towot Sudan
120 C5 Towson U.S.A.
24 C1 Toxkan r. China
46 F1 Tōya-ko l. Japan
46 H3 Toyama Japan
46 H3 Toyama-wan b. Japan
15 A1 Toykut Ukraine
46 D7 Tōyo Japan
47 H6 Toyohashi Japan
47 H6 Toyokawa Japan
46 C6 Toyooka Japan
47 H6 Toyota Japan
46 H1 Toyotomi Japan
65 G4 Toytepa Uzbekistan
75 F2 Tozeur Tunisia
13 G2 Tqibuli Georgia
13 G7 Tqvarch'eli Georgia
13 □ Trâblous Lebanon
28 C4 Trabotivište Macedonia
60 D1 Trabzon Turkey
121 G2 Tracy Can.
123 A5 Tracy U.S.A.
128 B3 Tracy U.S.A.
122 A4 Traer U.S.A.
25 F2 Trafalgar, Cabo pt Spain
25 F2 Tragacete Spain
146 B4 Traiguén Chile
110 D4 Trail Can.
10 Q2 Traill Ø i. Greenland
145 L2 Traíras r. Brazil
145 J3 Traisen r. Austria
145 J3 Trajano de Morais Brazil
11 G5 Trakai Lithuania
12 J2 Trakt Rus. Fed.
17 C5 Tralee Rep. of Ire.
139 E2 Tramán Tepuí mt. Venezuela
17 C5 Tramore Rep. of Ire.
25 H3 Tramuntana, Serra de mt. ra. Spain
11 D4 Tranås Sweden
146 C2 Trancas Arg.
11 D4 Tranemo Sweden
146 J2 Trangan i. Indon.
97 F2 Trangie Aust.
26 F4 Trani Italy
83 B3 Tranoroa Madagascar
146 B3 Tranqueras Uruguay
152 D3 Transantarctic Mountains mts Ant.
111 H4 Trans Canada Highway Can.
111 H4 Transcona Can.
26 A2 Transpi Italy
20 F2 Trappes France
74 A4 Trarza div. Mauritania
26 E4 Trasacco Italy
24 D3 Trás-os-Montes reg. Portugal
14 J3 Tratsino Rus. Fed.
43 B5 Trat Thailand
18 F3 Trautenau Germany
18 E5 Traunstein Germany
13 C5 Travellers L. l. Aust.
152 ○1 Traversay Is is S. Atlantic Ocean
122 D3 Traverse City U.S.A.
122 C3 Travers, Mt N.Z.
43 D5 Tra Vinh Vietnam
26 E2 Travis, L. l. U.S.A.
26 G2 Travnik Bos.-Herz.
26 E2 Trbovlje Slovenia

133 ○1 Treasure Beach Jamaica
90 ○1 Treasury Is is Solomon Is.
14 B3 Trebbia r. Italy
19 G3 Trebbin Germany
19 H4 Třebíč Czech Rep.
27 F6 Trebisacce Italy
19 K4 Trebišov Slovakia
26 E3 Trebnje Slovenia
19 G4 Třeboň Czech Rep.
122 B3 Trego U.S.A.
115 F2 Trégrois reg. France
99 G3 Tregosse Islets & Reefs is Coral Sea Islands Terr. Pac. Oc.
146 F3 Treinta-y-Tres Uruguay
133 ○3 Trelawney div. Jamaica
20 D1 Trélazé France
147 C5 Trelew Arg.
11 D5 Trelleborg Sweden
115 H3 Tremblant, Mt h. Can.
81 ○5 Tremblet Réunion Indian Ocean
27 F4 Tremiti, Isole is Italy
128 D3 Tremonton U.S.A.
19 G4 Třemošná Czech Rep.
25 G1 Tremp Spain
122 B3 Trempealeau r. U.S.A.
146 D4 Trenque Lauquén Arg.
17 G5 Trent r. U.K.
26 C2 Trentino Alto Adige div. Italy
26 D2 Trento Italy
115 G4 Trenton Can.
124 E3 Trenton U.S.A.
121 F4 Trenton U.S.A.
113 K4 Trepassey Can.
146 D4 Tres Arroyos Arg.
54 E3 Tres Cerros Arg.
145 E4 Três Corações Brazil
138 B3 Tres Esquinas Colombia
146 D2 Tres Isletas Arg.
14 G3 Treskavica mts Bos.-Herz.
14 C3 Treskino Rus. Fed.
144 C4 Três Lagoas Brazil
87 B6 Tres Lagos Arg.
54 B7 Tres Lagos Arg.
140 C2 Tres Mapajos Bolivia
54 B7 Trudy r. Rus. Fed.
147 B6 Três Montes, Pen. pen. Chile
131 G6 Três Picos Brazil
131 G5 Três Picos, Co mt. Arg.
127 F4 Três Piedras U.S.A.
145 F2 Três Pontas Brazil
144 D6 Tredos, Pico mt. Chile
147 C6 Tres Puntas, C. c. Arg.
144 E3 Três Rios Brazil
131 F5 Três Valles Mexico
130 B3 Três Vírgenes, Vol. Las vol Mexico
131 G5 Três Zapotes Mexico
11 C4 Tretten Norway
26 B3 Treviglio Italy
26 D3 Treviso Italy
81 ○1 Trevor Pt pt Seychelles
11 E6 Trevose Head hd U.K.
28 D3 Trgovište Yugo.
98 D2 Trial B. b. Aust.
42 B1 Triangle, The mt. ra. Myanmar
29 G6 Tria Nisia i. Greece
29 G6 Trianta Greece
29 D5 Trikora, Pk mt. Greece
54 B4 Trichur India
56 B4 Tricase Italy
144 D2 Trindade, Ilha da i. Atlantic Ocean
140 D2 Trinidad Bolivia
138 D2 Trinidad Colombia
133 □2 Trinidad Cuba
133 □2 Trinidad i. Trin. & Tobago
146 E3 Trinidad Uruguay
127 F4 Trinidad U.S.A.
104 M8 Trinidad and Tobago country Caribbean
111 K4 Trinity Bay b. Can.
133 □3 Trinity Hills h. Trinidad
128 B1 Trinity Range mts U.S.A.
81 □4 Triolet Mauritius
119 C5 Trion U.S.A.
110 Q2 Traill Ø i. Greenland
145 L2 Traisen r. Austria
72 B1 Tripolitania reg. Libya
55 G5 Tripura div. India
15 E2 Trischen i. Germany
82 A5 Tristan da Cunha i. Atlantic Ocean
54 B4 Trisul mt. India
131 G5 Triunfo r. Brazil
56 B4 Trivandrum India
26 E4 Trivento Italy
19 C6 Trnava Slovakia
82 A4 Trobriand Islands is P.N.G.
19 C5 Trofaiach Austria
29 H2 Trogir Croatia
26 E2 Troia Italy
27 E7 Troina Italy
81 C5 Trois Bassins Réunion Indian Ocean
18 C3 Troisdorf Germany
81 □3 Trois Fourches, Cap des hd Morocco
115 H3 Trois-Rivières Can.
133 □5 Trois-Rivières Guadeloupe Caribbean
111 M3 Trois-Rivières Can.
28 D2 Troitsa Rus. Fed.
65 K2 Troitskoye Rus. Fed.
11 C4 Troitskoye Rus. Fed.
64 F2 Troitsk Rus. Fed.
64 F2 Troitsk Rus. Fed.
83 □1 Troitsko-Pechorsk Rus. Fed.
11 C4 Trolla mt. Norway
72 D4 Trollhättan Sweden
149 H5 Tromelin, Île i. Indian Ocean
110 D4 Tromsø Norway
146 C2 Tromen, Volcán vol Arg.
146 C2 Tromen, Volcán vol Arg.
16 D1 Tromsø Norway
11 C4 Trondheim Norway
16 D1 Trondheimsfjorden chan. Norway
81 D4 Troodos Cyprus
29 C6 Tropaia Greece

143 C4 Tropeiros, Sa dos h. Brazil
129 F3 Tropic U.S.A.
14 B3 Trosna Rus. Fed.
18 F1 Trostberg Germany
15 F1 Trostyanets' Sumy Ukraine
15 C2 Trostyanets' Vinnytsya Ukraine
15 A1 Trostyanets' Volyn Ukraine
15 C1 Trout r. Can.
115 E2 Trout Creek Can.
110 F2 Trout Creek Can.
110 G3 Trout Lake Can.
110 E2 Trout Lake Can.
122 E2 Trout Lake l. Can.
122 C2 Trout Lake l. U.S.A.
122 E2 Trout Lake l. U.S.A.
120 E4 Trout Run U.S.A.
17 F6 Trowbridge U.K.
75 B3 Trowutta Aust.
19 C6 Troy Jamaica
60 A2 Troy Turkey
125 D5 Troy U.S.A.
121 G3 Troy U.S.A.
121 G3 Troy U.S.A.
120 E4 Troy U.S.A.
28 D3 Troyan Bulgaria
15 D2 Troyanka Ukraine
14 C3 Troyekurovo Rus. Fed.
14 C3 Troyekurovo Rus. Fed.
21 G2 Troyes France
15 C3 Troyits'ke Ukraine
15 E2 Troyits'ko-Safonove Ukraine
128 D4 Troy Lake l. U.S.A.
129 E2 Troy Peak summit U.S.A.
28 C3 Trstenik Yugo.
98 B1 Trust I. i. Aust.
14 A3 Trubchevsk Rus. Fed.
14 D3 Trubetchino Rus. Fed.
15 D1 Trubizh r. Ukraine
24 C1 Truchas Spain
57 C4 Trucial Coast U.A.E.
49 K4 Trudovoye Rus. Fed.
54 B7 Trudy r. Rus. Fed.
131 G5 Trujillo Honduras
140 A1 Trujillo Peru
24 D3 Trujillo Spain
138 C2 Trujillo Venezuela
131 G4 Trumbull U.S.A.
129 F3 Trumbull, Mt mt. U.S.A.
28 D3 Trün Bulgaria
97 F3 Trundle Aust.
43 D5 Trưng Hiệp Vietnam
42 B3 Trung Khanh Vietnam
113 H4 Truro Can.
17 E6 Truro U.K.
28 E1 Truşeşti Romania
28 E3 Trūstenik Bulgaria
28 E2 Trůstenik Bulgaria
15 B1 Trutch Ukraine
127 F5 Truth or Consequences U.S.A.
19 G3 Trutnov Czech Rep.
17 F5 Truyère r. France
15 A2 Trybukhivtsi Ukraine
11 D3 Trysil Norway
19 H2 Trzcianka Piła Poland
19 J2 Trzciel Poland
19 J3 Trzebiatów Poland
19 J3 Trzebinia Poland
19 G2 Trzemeszno Poland
19 G2 Trzcińsko-Zdrój Poland
44 E4 Tsagaannuur Bayan Ölgiy Mongolia
49 F3 Tsagaan Dornod Mongolia
48 A3 Tsagaan-Olom Mongolia
48 A3 Tsagaan Ovoo Mongolia
13 H6 Tsagan Aman Rus. Fed.
13 H6 Tsagan-Nur Rus. Fed.
54 D2 Tsaka La China
78 B4 Tsau i Congo
83 H2 Tsaratanana Madagascar
83 H1 Tsaratanana, Massif du mts Madagascar
83 H1 Tsaratanana, Réserve de res. Madagascar
14 B2 Tsarevo-Zaymishche Rus. Fed.
14 G3 Tsarevshchino Rus. Fed.
82 A5 Tsaris Mts mts Namibia
15 F1 Tsarychanka Ukraine
80 C3 Tsatsa r. Kenya
81 C5 Tsavo National Park nat. park Kenya
15 L2 Tsebrykove Ukraine
119 C5 Tselinnoye Rus. Fed.
48 B2 Tsengel Mongolia
12 H1 Tsenogora Rus. Fed.
12 J3 Tsentral'nyy Rus. Fed.
72 B1 Tsentral'nyy Rus. Fed.
145 G5 Tsépia Brazil
77 G5 Tsévié Togo
79 D5 Tshabong Botswana
79 D5 Tshane Botswana
79 D5 Tshela Zaire
79 D5 Tshibala Zaire
79 D5 Tshibwika Zaire
79 D5 Tshikapa Zaire
79 D5 Tshikapa r. Zaire
79 D5 Tshimbo Zaire
79 D5 Tshimbulu Zaire
79 D5 Tshitanzu Zaire
79 D5 Tshitanzu Zaire
79 D5 Tshofa Zaire
79 D5 Tsholotsho Zimbabwe
79 D5 Tshopo r. Zaire
78 C4 Tshuapa r. Zaire
13 H6 Tsimlyansk Rus. Fed.
13 H6 Tsimlyanskoye Vdkhr. resr Rus. Fed.
45 □1 Tsing Yi i. Hong Kong
83 E5 Tsiombe Madagascar
83 H2 Tsiroanomandidy Madagascar
81 □4 Tsitsihar see Qiqihar Madagascar
110 D4 Tsitsutl Peak summit Can.
83 H2 Tsivil'sk Rus. Fed.
13 G7 Ts'khinvali Georgia
15 C1 Tsna r. Ukraine
43 □2 Tsodilo Hill Botswana
13 H6 Tso Morari L. l. India
83 H2 Tsqaltubo Georgia
46 E7 Tsu Japan
43 C5 Tsumkwe Namibia
47 G5 Tsuchiura Japan

45 □1 Tsuen Wan Hong Kong
46 H3 Tsugarū-kaikyō chan. Japan
47 G5 Tsugawa Japan
47 H2 Tsuken-jima i. Japan
46 H2 Tsukigata Japan
47 H5 Tsukuba Japan
46 C7 Tsukumi Japan
48 C3 Tsul-Ulaan Mongolia
15 A1 Tsuman' Ukraine
82 B2 Tsumeb Namibia
82 B3 Tsumis Park Namibia
82 C2 Tsumkwe Namibia
46 C6 Tsuno-shima i. Japan
46 D7 Tsurugi-san mt. Japan
46 D7 Tsurumi-zaki pt Japan
47 G4 Tsuruoka Japan
46 H2 Tsuruta Japan
47 H5 Tsushima i. Japan
15 C2 Tsuyama Japan
15 C2 Tsvitne Ukraine
15 E2 Tsybuliv Ukraine
10 J1 Tsyp-Navolok Rus. Fed.
15 E3 Tsyurupyns'k Ukraine
92 E2 Tuakau N.Z.
39 K8 Tual Indon.
91 □10 Tuamotu, Archipel des is Fr. Poly. Pac. Oc.
90 C2 Tuân Giáo Vietnam
90 □13 Tu'anuku Tonga
21 G2 Tuas Singapore
91 □12 Tuasivi Western Samoa
93 A7 Tuatapere N.Z.
128 C3 Tuba City U.S.A.
40 C3 Tuban Indon.
143 C6 Tubarão Brazil
73 G1 Tubarjal Saudi Arabia
28 E1 Tubas r. Israel
41 A4 Tubbataha Reefs reef Phil.
18 D4 Tübingen Germany
76 B5 Tubmanburg Liberia
81 B4 Tubod Phil.
72 D1 Tubruq Libya
151 K7 Tubuai i. Fr. Poly. Pac. Oc.
151 J7 Tubuai, Îles is Fr. Poly. Pac. Oc.
130 C2 Tubutama Mexico
133 □3 Tucacas Venezuela
133 E5 Tucacas Venezuela
73 G4 Tucandaí well Sudan
146 B3 Tucapel, Pta hd Chile
74 F4 Tucavaca r. Bolivia
81 □7 Tuchitua Can.
110 D2 Tuchitua Can.
14 C2 Tuchkovo Rus. Fed.
19 H2 Tuchola Poland
15 B1 Tuchyn Ukraine
119 □1 Tucker's Town Bermuda
121 F5 Tuckerton U.S.A.
129 G5 Tucson U.S.A.
130 L7 Tucson airport U.S.A.
129 G5 Tucson Mts mts U.S.A.
146 D2 Tucuman div. Arg.
139 G2 Tucuman U.S.A.
142 C1 Tucupará Brazil
142 C1 Tucuruí Brazil
139 F2 Tucupita Venezuela
142 C1 Tucuruí Brazil
24 D2 Tudela Spain
24 D2 Tudela de Duero Spain
28 F2 Tudor Vladimirescu Romania
14 A1 Tudovka r. Rus. Fed.
14 C2 Tudu r. Rus. Fed.
55 H4 Tuem Num Hong Kong
55 H4 Tuensang India
142 B1 Tuerê r. Brazil
81 D2 Tufanovo Rus. Fed.
81 □1 Tufayḩ Saudi Arabia
90 □1 Tufi P.N.G.
41 C4 Tugela r. R.S.A.
41 C4 Tuguegarao Phil.
82 E3 Tuguegarao Phil.
83 E3 Tugwi r. Zimbabwe
49 J5 Tuhai r. China
24 B3 Tui Spain
24 B3 Tui Spain
130 L7 Tuineje Canary Is Spain
25 □ Tukangbesi, Kepulauan is Indon.
112 E2 Tukarak Island i. Can.
55 G3 Tukche Nepal
54 D2 Tukhkit India
81 C5 Tuktoyaktuk Can.
14 F4 Tukums Latvia
81 B6 Tukuyu Tanzania
81 B6 Tula American Samoa
14 C3 Tula div. Rus. Fed.
130 L7 Tula Jalisco Mexico
131 F4 Tula Tamaulipas Mexico
91 □13 Tula American Samoa
14 C3 Tula Rus. Fed.
79 D5 Tulagi Solomon Is.
55 G1 Tulagt Ar Gol r. China
55 G2 Tulancingo Mexico
131 F4 Tulancingo Mexico
131 F4 Tulare U.S.A.
128 C3 Tulare Lake Bed l. U.S.A.
127 F5 Tularosa U.S.A.
138 B3 Tulcán Ecuador
28 G1 Tulcea Romania
15 C2 Tul'chyn Ukraine
94 O2 Tula Rus. Fed.
55 G1 Tulemalu Lake l. Can.
14 C3 Tule Mod China
28 G2 Tulghes Romania
91 □ Tuliara Madagascar

61 D3 Tulul el Ashaqif reg. Jordan
131 J4 Tulum Mexico
146 C3 Tulum, Valle de v. Arg.
54 H1 Tulun Rus. Fed.
55 H4 Tulung La China
41 A4 Tulu'an i. Phil.
81 □ Tulu Welel mt. Ethiopia
15 E1 Tulyholove Ukraine
80 C4 Tuma r. Rus. Fed.
14 D2 Tuma Rus. Fed.
132 C1 Tumaco Colombia
82 D4 Tumahole R.S.A.
55 G2 Tumain China
13 J6 Tumak Rus. Fed.
57 E2 Tūmān Āqā Iran
139 F2 Tumatumari Guyana
11 E4 Tumba Sweden
79 D4 Tumba Zaire
78 C4 Tumba, Lac l. Zaire
40 C2 Tumbangsamba Indon.
40 B2 Tumbangtiti Indon.
41 C5 Tumbao Phil.
97 G3 Tumbarumba Aust.
138 A4 Tumbes Peru
110 E3 Tumbler Ridge Can.
96 D3 Tumby Bay Aust.
54 F4 Tum Yougi China
48 D4 Tümd Zuoqi China
49 J4 Tumen r. China
49 J4 Tumen r. China/North Korea
48 B5 Tumenzi China
139 E2 Tumereng Venezuela
139 E2 Tumereng Guyana
41 A5 Tumindao i. Phil.
145 H3 Tumiritinga Brazil
56 B3 Tumkur India
72 B3 Tummo, Mountains of mts Libya/Niger
41 □2 Tumon Bay b. Guam Pac. Oc.
40 B2 Tumpah Indon.
97 G3 Tumut Aust.
65 H4 Tumxuk China
43 □3 Tuna, Pta pt Puerto Rico
133 □3 Tunapuna Trin. & Tobago
60 D2 Tunceli Turkey
51 E5 Tunchang China
97 H3 Tuncurry Aust.
73 G4 Tundubai well Sudan
77 F4 Tundun-Wada Nigeria
81 C7 Tunduru Tanzania
28 F3 Tundzha r. Bulgaria
51 □ Tunel la Cumbre tun. Chile
14 C2 Tunḥovo Rus. Fed.
77 F5 Tunga Nigeria
56 B3 Tungabhadra r. India
56 B3 Tungabhadra Reservoir resr India
111 H4 Tunga pass pass China/India
80 B2 Tungaru Sudan
41 B5 Tungawan Phil.
45 □1 Tung Chung Wan b. Hong Kong
10 M2 Tungnaá r. Iceland
110 D2 Tungsten Can.
90 □5 Tungua i. Tonga
40 C1 Tungun, Bukit mt. Indon.
55 G3 Tungnath India
50 C3 Tungsha, Nizhnyaya r. Rus. Fed.
56 C2 Tuni India
54 B4 Tunis Tunisia
75 G1 Tunis, Golfe de g. Tunisia
68 E2 Tunisia country Africa
138 C2 Tunja Colombia
48 E2 Tunka r. China
110 F4 Tunkás Mexico
91 □13 Tunnsjøen i. Norway
14 E1 Tunoshna r. Rus. Fed.
10 M2 Tungnaá r. Iceland
19 J3 Tuszyn Poland
50 D3 Tütak Iran
54 E2 Tŭtak Iran
146 C4 Tunuyán r. Arg.
146 C3 Tunuyán r. Arg.
51 G1 Tuo r. China
50 D2 Tuo r. China
49 G5 Tuoji Dao i. China
43 D5 Tuôl Khpos Cambodia
13 □ Tuolumne r. U.S.A.
130 L7 Tuon r. Panama
73 G4 Tukanqbesi, Kepulauan reg. Indon.
112 E2 Tuotuo r. China
128 C3 Tuotuo r. China
91 □13 Tutuila i. American Samoa Pac. Oc.
55 G4 Tupa India
80 D3 Tupa r. Botswana
127 F5 Tupaciguara Brazil
143 B6 Tupanciretã Brazil
139 F5 Tupai i. Fr. Poly. Pac. Oc.
108 E3 Tupper Lake U.S.A.
144 D2 Tupi Paulista Brazil
139 F4 Tupinambarama, Ilha i. Brazil
144 C4 Tupiza Bolivia
140 F2 Tupungato Arg.
146 C3 Tupungato vol Arg.
40 D1 Tuquan China
138 B3 Tuquerres Colombia
130 E4 Tuxpan Jalisco Mexico
131 F4 Tuxpan Veracruz Mexico
13 H6 Tura Rus. Fed.
28 E1 Turabah Saudi Arabia
138 D1 Turabo Colombia
80 B3 Turahkarai reg. Uganda
28 G3 Turbat Pak.
28 G2 Turda Romania
28 F3 Turbe Bos.-Herz.
60 C2 Turbe Bos.-Herz.
60 C2 Turbo Colombia
73 F2 Turbo Colombia
28 D1 Turda Romania
19 □3 Türeh Iran
101 J3 Turek Poland
19 J3 Turek Poland

11 G4 Türi Estonia
25 F3 Turia r. Spain
142 C1 Turiaçu Brazil
142 C1 Turiaçu r. Brazil
64 H1 Turinsk Rus. Fed.
15 A1 Turiya r. Ukraine
15 A1 Turiya r. Ukraine
44 J1 Turka r. Rus. Fed.
19 L4 Turka Rus. Fed.
80 C4 Turkana, Lake salt l. Ethiopia/Kenya
65 G4 Turkestan Kazak.
65 G5 Turkestan Range mt. ra. Asia
32 E6 Turkey country Asia
122 B4 Turkey r. U.S.A.
100 E3 Turkey Creek Aust.
14 F4 Türi Est.
60 B2 Türkmen Daği mt. Turkey
57 E1 Türkoğlu Turkey
64 D5 Turkmenskiy Zaliv b. Turkmenistan
60 D2 Türkoğlu Turkey
104 L8 Turks and Caicos Islands terr. Caribbean
133 E2 Turks Is is Turks and Caicos Is Caribbean
133 E2 Turks and Caicos Is Caribbean
11 F3 Turku Finland
11 F3 Turku-Pori div. Finland
80 C4 Turkwel r. Kenya
128 B3 Turlock U.S.A.
128 B3 Turlock U.S.A.
145 G2 Turmalina Brazil
73 H2 Turmus, W. at w Saudi Arabia
92 F4 Turnagain, Cape c. N.Z.
129 G5 Turnbull, Mt mt. U.S.A.
100 B4 Turner r. Aust.
123 F3 Turner U.S.A.
13 G5 Türnitz Austria
111 H3 Turnor Lake l. Can.
19 G3 Turnov Czech Rep.
28 E3 Turnu Măgurele Romania
28 D2 Turochak Rus. Fed.
51 E5 Turpan China
97 H3 Turon r. Aust.
41 C4 Turón r. Aust.
132 C2 Turón r. Cuba
16 F3 Turriff U.K.
60 D3 Turtkul' Uzbekistan
64 F4 Turtle I. i. Coral Sea Islands Terr. Pac. Oc.
41 A5 Turtle Is is Phil.
76 B5 Turtle Islands is Sierra Leone
122 A2 Turtle Lake U.S.A.
110 D2 Turtkul' Uzbekistan
124 C2 Turtle Lake U.S.A.
111 H4 Turtleford Can.
12 H3 Turukhansk Rus. Fed.
64 K3 Turukhansk Rus. Fed.
13 F3 Turuntayevo Rus. Fed.
144 E2 Turvo r. Goiás Brazil
143 B6 Turvo r. Rio Grande do Sul Brazil
144 D2 Turvo r. São Paulo Brazil
144 D2 Turvo r. São Paulo Brazil
145 F2 Turvo r. São Paulo Brazil
143 G2 Turvo Brazil
129 F4 Tusayan U.S.A.
119 C5 Tuscaloosa U.S.A.
125 C5 Tuscola U.S.A.
54 C4 Tusharik Iran
21 E5 Tussey Mts h. U.S.A.
113 H2 Tunungayualok Island i. Can.
19 J3 Tuszyn Poland
50 D3 Tütak Iran
54 E2 Tūtak Iran
125 C5 Tuticorin India
142 D1 Tutóia Brazil
28 F2 Tutrakan Bulgaria
124 D2 Tuttle Creek Res. resr U.S.A.
18 D5 Tuttlingen Germany
109 P2 Tuttut Nunaat reg. Greenland
91 □13 Tutuila i. American Samoa Pac. Oc.
80 B3 Tutume Botswana
10 N3 Tutupaca, volcán Peru
42 D5 Tuy Hòa Vietnam
60 D2 Tuyükardan Aust.
93 A7 Tuwhare Head hd N.Z.
57 D2 Tuyen Iran
64 E2 Tuymazy Rus. Fed.
57 E2 Tüysärkän Iran
72 C1 Tūz, Gölü salt l. Turkey
61 E3 Tuz Gölü salt l. Turkey
60 F2 Tuzi Yugo.
73 G1 Tuz Khūrmātū Iraq
28 G3 Tuzla Bos.-Herz.
60 C1 Tuzla Turkey
60 F2 Tuzla r. Turkey
13 H6 Tuzlov r. Rus. Fed.
14 D2 Tvardita r. Moldova
11 C4 Tvedestrand Norway
14 D2 Tver' Rus. Fed.
14 D2 Tver' div. Rus. Fed.
15 D2 Tverdohlebu Moldova
11 C4 Tvøroyri Faeroes
16 K1 Tweed r. U.K.
11 B4 Tweed Heads Aust.
110 D4 Tweedsmuir Prov. Park res. Can.
129 G5 Twentynine Palms U.S.A.
113 K4 Twillingate Can.
121 G2 Twin Buttes Res. resr U.S.A.
126 D3 Twin Falls Can.
113 H3 Twin Falls U.S.A.
100 C4 Twin Heads h. Aust.
125 H2 Twin Lakes U.S.A.
126 D3 Twin Lakes U.S.A.
120 C6 Twin Oaks U.S.A.

128 B2 Twin Peak summit U.S.A.
142 C1 Twins, The Aust.
97 G4 Two Guns U.S.A.
129 G4 Two Harbors U.S.A.
122 B2 Two Hills Can.
121 G1 Two Medicine r. U.S.A.
120 D1 Two Rivers U.S.A.
122 D3 Two Rivers U.S.A.
28 D1 Tyachiv Ukraine
55 H5 Tyao r. India
15 C2 Tyasmyn r. Ukraine
19 L4 Tyatya r. Rus. Fed.
10 C3 Tygda' Norway
120 D5 Tygart Valley v. U.S.A.
49 H1 Tygda Rus. Fed.
64 E1 Tyhda r. Rus. Fed.
122 D1 Tylawa Ukraine
122 C2 Tyler U.S.A.
125 E5 Tyler U.S.A.
125 D5 Tylertown U.S.A.
15 D2 Tylihul r. Ukraine
15 E2 Tymchenky Ukraine
29 F7 Tympaki Greece
64 D3 Tynda Rus. Fed.
110 A2 Tyndall Gl. gl. U.S.A.
15 D2 Tynivka Ukraine
11 C3 Tynset Norway
19 L3 Tyrawa Ukraine
111 H2 Tyrell Lake l. Can.
49 K2 Tyrma r. Rus. Fed.
49 K2 Tyrma Rus. Fed.
63 □2 Tyrma r. Rus. Fed.
11 F3 Tyrnävä Finland
29 D5 Tyrnavos Greece
14 D2 Tyrnovo Rus. Fed.
120 D4 Tyrone U.S.A.
97 E3 Tyrrell r. Aust.
97 E3 Tyrrell, L. l. Aust.
27 C5 Tyrrhenian Sea sea Italy
128 D1 Tyrsa r. Romania/Ukraine
15 D2 Tyshkivka Ukraine
15 A2 Tysmenytsya Ukraine
16 K1 Tysse Norway
19 L3 Tyszowce Poland
110 A2 Tyub-Karagan, Mys hd Kazak.
65 H1 Tyukalinsk Rus. Fed.
64 D4 Tyulen'i, Ostrova is Rus. Fed.
64 E2 Tyul'gan Rus. Fed.
65 G1 Tyumen' Rus. Fed.
62 H4 Tyumen'-Aryk Kazak.
65 G2 Tyung r. Rus. Fed.
15 C2 Tyvriv Ukraine
64 E2 Tywi r. Aust.
83 E1 Tzaneen R.S.A.

56 A3 Udupi India
90 □6 Udu Pt pt Fiji
15 G1 Udy Ukraine
63 P4 Udyl', Ozero l. Rus. Fed.
19 F2 Uecker r. Germany
19 G2 Ueckermünde Germany
47 G5 Ueda Japan
40 E2 Uekuli Indon.
78 D3 Uele r. Zaire
78 D3 Uel'kal Rus. Fed.
108 A3 Uel'kal Rus. Fed.
18 E2 Uelzen Germany
47 F6 Ueno Japan
78 E3 Uere r. Zaire
64 E1 Ufa r. Rus. Fed.
64 E2 Ufa Rus. Fed.
80 B2 Uffat r. Sudan
18 E4 Uffenheim Germany
82 B3 Ugab r. Namibia
81 B6 Ugalla r. Tanzania
81 B6 Ugalla River Game Reserve res. Tanzania
69 H5 Uganda country Africa
48 E1 Ugdan Rus. Fed.
22 G6 Ugento Italy
16 K1 Uggdal Norway
77 F5 Ughelli Nigeria
52 G2 Uglegorsk Rus. Fed.
14 D1 Uglich Rus. Fed.
49 J2 Ugljan i. Croatia
14 E2 Uglovoye Rus. Fed.
65 K2 Uglovskoye Rus. Fed.
63 □3 Ugol'naya Zyryanka Rus. Fed.
63 T3 Ugol'nyye Kopi Rus. Fed.
14 D2 Ugra r. Rus. Fed.
14 B2 Ugra r. Rus. Fed.
19 H4 Uherské Hradiště Czech Rep.
18 F4 Uhlava r. Czech Rep.
19 L3 Uhniv Ukraine
120 C4 Uhrichsville U.S.A.
15 F1 Uhroyidy Ukraine
79 C5 Uíge Angola
79 C5 Uíge div. Angola
90 □5 Uiha i. Tonga
49 H5 Üijŏngbu S. Korea
64 E3 Uil r. Kazak.
64 E3 Uil Kazak.
13 G7 Uil Kazak.
10 H3 Uimaharju Finland
129 F3 Uinkaret Plateau plat. U.S.A.
116 D3 Uinta Mts mts U.S.A.
82 B6 Üisŏng S. Korea
82 A5 Uis Mine Namibia
49 H5 Üisŏng S. Korea
82 D5 Uitenhage R.S.A.
13 G5 Uithuizen Netherlands
64 □2 Ujivak, Cape hd Can.
19 K4 Ujfehértó Hungary
47 F6 Uji Japan
46 A8 Uji-guntō is Japan
81 A5 Ujiji Tanzania
55 G4 Ujjain India
19 H2 Ujście Poland
40 D3 Ujung Pandang Indon.
47 □2 Uka Japan
81 B5 Ukerewe I. i. Tanzania
73 H4 Ukhdūd Saudi Arabia
55 H4 Ukhrul India
12 K2 Ukhta r. Rus. Fed.
14 E1 Ukhtokhma r. Rus. Fed.
128 A2 Ukiah U.S.A.
126 C2 Ukiah U.S.A.
109 N2 Ukkusissat Greenland
5 H4 Ukraine country Europe
15 □1 Ukrayinka r. Rus. Fed.
26 E1 Ukrina r. Bos.-Herz.
19 J2 Uktym Rus. Fed.
79 B6 Uku Angola
46 B7 Uku-jima i. Japan
82 C3 Ukwi Pan salt pan Botswana
54 C2 Ula r. India
44 E4 Ulaanbaatar Mongolia
48 E1 Ulaan-Ereg Mongolia
44 F2 Ulaangom Mongolia
48 C4 Ulaanhad Mongolia
44 F2 Ulaanhudag Mongolia
15 C2 Uladivka Ukraine
48 D3 Ulaan-Uul Mongolia
97 G3 Ulan Aust.
52 J3 Ulan Kazak.
52 J3 Ulan Kazak.
13 □7 Ulanbel' Kazak.
48 C4 Ulan Buh Shamo desert China
44 F2 Ulan-Burgasy, Khr. mt. ra. Rus. Fed.
13 H6 Ulan Erge Rus. Fed.
14 B4 Ulanovo Rus. Fed.
14 D3 Ulan-Ude Rus. Fed.
48 D1 Ulan Tohoi China
15 □2 Ulanów Poland
97 G3 Ulan r. Aust.
48 D1 Ulaşlı Turkey
76 □ Ulawa i. Solomon Is.
91 □1 Ulaya Tanzania
79 C5 Ulawa i. S. Korea
42 K5 Ulaya r. Aust.
54 C2 Ul'ba Kazak.
60 D2 Ulcinj Yugo.
18 E5 Ulm Germany
47 J1 Ul'ma r. Rus. Fed.
97 H2 Ulmarra Aust.
28 D1 Ulmeni Maramureş Romania
28 E2 Ulmeni Călărasi Romania
28 G4 Ulog Bos.-Herz.
54 D4 Uloowaranie, L. salt flat Aust.
49 J6 Ulsan S. Korea
10 C3 Ulsberg Norway
17 D3 Ulster reg. Rep. of Ire./U.K.
97 G3 Ulubat Gölü l. Turkey
29 M4 Ulubat Gölü l. Turkey
60 B1 Uluborlu Turkey
60 B1 Uludağ mt. Turkey
43 C6 Ulu Kali, Gunung mt. Malaysia
60 C2 Ulukışla Turkey
64 K3 Ulukhaktok Can.
57 D1 Ulun China
42 □ Ulu Pandan Singapore
98 B5 Uluru Nat. Park nat. park Aust.
13 E7 Ulus r. Turkey
97 H4 Ulverstone Aust.
11 D3 Ulvsjön Sweden

U

14 C1 Ul'yanikha Rus. Fed.
12 H4 Ul'yankovo Rus. Fed.
15 D2 Ul'yanovka Ukraine
14 B3 Ul'yanovo Rus. Fed.
12 J4 Ul'yanovsk Rus. Fed.
14 H3 Ul'yanovsk div. Rus. Fed.
65 H2 Ul'yanovskiy Kazak.
49 F2 Ulyetuy Rus. Fed.
125 C4 Ulysses U.S.A.
65 G3 Ulytau Kazak.
65 G3 Uyzhilanshik r. Kazak.
49 G1 Uma Rus. Fed.
131 H4 Umán Mexico
15 D2 Uman' Ukraine
146 C2 Umango, Co. mt. Arg.
54 A3 Umarao Pakistan
54 C4 Umaria India
54 B4 Umarkhed India
56 C2 Umarkot India
54 B4 Umarkot Pakistan
41 □2 Umatac Guam Pac. Oc.
126 C2 Umatilla U.S.A.
121 H2 Umba Rus. Fed.
121 H2 Umba Lake l. U.S.A.
78 D2 Umbelasha w Sudan
26 D4 Umbertide Italy
90 □1 Umboi i. P.N.G.
93 B6 Umbrella Mts mts N.Z.
133 □1 Umbrella Pt pt Jamaica
26 D4 Umbria div. Italy
83 D2 Umbu r. Zimbabwe
10 F3 Umeå Sweden
10 D2 Umeälven r. Sweden
61 □3 Um ed Daraj, J. mt. Jordan
14 F3 Umet Rus. Fed.
14 F2 Umet Rus. Fed.
108 H3 Umingmaktok Can.
112 E2 Umiujaq Can.
83 E4 Umlazi R.S.A.
73 G3 Umm al Birak Saudi Arabia
57 C4 Umm al Qaywayn U.A.E.
73 H2 Umm al Qalbān Saudi Arabia
57 B4 Umm Bâb Qatar
73 E5 Umm Bel Sudan
61 B5 Umm Bugma Egypt
72 C2 Umm Farud Libya
73 F3 Umm Gerifat waterhole Sudan
73 E5 Umm Keddada Sudan
73 G2 Umm Lajj Saudi Arabia
61 C5 Umm Mafrûd, G. mt. Egypt
61 C5 Umm Nukhaylah well Saudi Arabia
60 F4 Umm Qasr Iraq
73 E4 Umm Qurein well Sudan
73 F5 Umm Rimtha well Sudan
73 F5 Umm Ruwaba Sudan
72 E1 Umm Sa'ad Libya
73 F5 Umm Saiyala Sudan
61 D5 Umm Shajtiya waterhole Egypt
61 B5 Umm Shomar, G. mt. Egypt
73 E4 Umm Sunaita well Sudan
61 B5 Umm Tinâṣṣib, G. mt. Egypt
73 G2 Umm Urûmah i. Saudi Arabia
61 B5 Umm Zanatir mt. Egypt
104 B4 Umnak I. i. U.S.A.
126 A3 Umpqua r. U.S.A.
79 C6 Umpulo Angola
54 D5 Umred India
56 A1 Umreth India
73 ■ Umtata R.S.A.
77 F5 Umuahia Nigeria
144 B5 Umuarama Brazil
90 □3 Umuna i. Tonga
29 F4 Umurbey Turkey
83 E5 Umzinto R.S.A.
145 J1 Una Brazil
61 D4 'Unāb, W. al w Jordan
145 E2 Unaí Brazil
57 G2 Unai P. pass Afghanistan
108 B3 Unalakleet U.S.A.
108 B4 Unalaska U.S.A.
81 C7 Unango Mozambique
60 C4 'Unayzah Jordan
73 H2 'Unayzah Saudi Arabia
54 C4 Unchahra India
140 C3 Uncia Bolivia
127 E4 Uncompahgre Plateau plat. U.S.A.
49 F2 Unda r. Rus. Fed.
49 F2 Unda Rus. Fed.
96 E3 Underbool Aust.
12 C2 Underwood U.S.A.
40 C4 Undu, Tg pt Indon.
49 E1 Unecha Rus. Fed.
14 H2 Unga r. Rus. Fed.
108 B4 Unga I. i. U.S.A.
97 J5 Ungarie Aust.
113 G2 Ungava Bay b. Can.
112 F1 Ungava, Péninsule d' pen. Can.
49 J4 Unggi N. Korea
15 B3 Ungheni Moldova
81 C5 Ungwana Bay b. Kenya
12 J3 Uni Rus. Fed.
142 D1 União Brazil
143 H6 União da Vitória Brazil
142 E2 União dos Palmares Brazil
54 D4 Uniara India
19 J3 Uniejów Poland
108 B4 Unimak I. i. U.S.A.
139 E4 Unini r. Brazil
141 G4 Unini Peru
133 □5 Unini St. Vincent
121 J2 Union U.S.A.
119 D5 Union U.S.A.
120 C6 Union U.S.A.
120 A4 Union City U.S.A.
120 C4 Union City U.S.A.
119 B4 Union City U.S.A.
129 H4 Union City U.S.A.
119 C5 Union Springs U.S.A.
120 D5 Uniontown U.S.A.
133 □3 Union Vale Mauritius
123 F4 Unionville U.S.A.
57 G5 United Arab Emirates country Asia
4 E3 United Kingdom country Europe
106 H4 United States of America country N. America
111 H4 Unity Can.
121 J2 Unity U.S.A.
126 C2 Unity U.S.A.
82 A3 Unjab w Namibia
54 D3 Unnao India
49 H5 Ûn'ŏn'ga N. Korea
49 H5 Ûnsan N. Korea
16 G1 Unst i. U.K.
47 □2 Unten Japan
46 C7 Unten-dake vol Japan
46 C7 Unzen-dake vol Japan
47 H5 Uozu Japan
14 C2 Upa r. Rus. Fed.
55 F5 Upar Ghat India
139 E2 Upata Venezuela
79 E5 Upemba, Lac l. Zaire
79 E5 Upemba, Parc National de l' nat. park Zaire
109 N2 Upernavik Greenland
109 N2 Upernavik Kujalleq Greenland
41 C5 Upía Phil.
138 C3 Upía r. Colombia
82 C4 Upington R.S.A.
54 B5 Upleta India
37 □ Upoloksha r. Rus. Fed.
90 □1 Upolu i. Western Samoa
126 C1 Upper Arlington U.S.A.
110 F4 Upper Arrow L. l. Can.

76 D4 Upper East div. Ghana
93 E4 Upper Hutt N.Z.
122 B4 Upper Iowa r. U.S.A.
121 K1 Upper Kent Can.
126 B3 Upper Klamath L. l. U.S.A.
126 B3 Upper L. l. U.S.A.
128 A2 Upper Lake U.S.A.
110 D2 Upper Liard Can.
17 D4 Upper Lough Erne l. U.K.
133 □3 Upper Manzanilla Trin. & Tobago
120 E5 Upper Marlboro U.S.A.
80 B3 Upper Nile div. Sudan
43 □ Upper Peirce Res. resr Singapore
113 J4 Upper Salmon Reservoir resr Can.
120 B4 Upper Sandusky U.S.A.
121 F2 Upper Saranac Lake l. U.S.A.
76 D4 Upper Takoru N.Z.
76 D4 Upper West div. Ghana
10 F3 Uppsala div. Sweden
11 F4 Uppsala Sweden
112 B4 Upsala Can.
11 G3 Upshi India
99 F3 Upstart B. b. Aust.
99 F3 Upstart, C. hd Aust.
13 G6 Upton U.S.A.
27 D6 Upton U.S.A.
91 □4 Upua N.Z.
61 D2 'Uqayribât Syria
61 C4 'Uqeiqa, W. w Jordan
60 F4 Uqlat al 'Udhaybah well Iraq
73 H2 'Uqlat aṣ Ṣuqûr Saudi Arabia
138 B2 Urabá, Golfo de b. Colombia
48 D4 Urad Qianqi China
48 D4 Urad Zhonghou Lianheqi China
57 D3 Ûrâf Iran
48 D5 Uraga-suid ŏ chan. Japan
47 G5 Uragawara Japan
51 □ Urai Brazil
32 J2 Urakawa Japan
97 F3 Ural h. Aust.
64 D2 Ural r. Kazak./Rus. Fed.
97 G2 Uralla Aust.
49 G1 Ust'-Lubiya Rus. Fed.
64 D2 Ural'sk Kazak.
64 C4 Ural'skiy Khrebet mt. ra. Rus. Fed.
81 D5 Urambo Tanzania
97 F3 Urana Aust.
97 F3 Urana, L. l. Aust.
97 J2 Urandangi Aust.
145 H1 Urandi Brazil
111 H3 Uranium City Can.
139 E4 Uraricoera r. Brazil
139 E3 Uraricuera r. Brazil
139 E4 Urase Japan
129 H2 Urasoe Japan
122 C5 Urbana U.S.A.
120 A5 Urbana U.S.A.
26 D3 Urbino Italy
142 D1 Urbano Santos Brazil
26 D4 Urbino Italy
26 D4 Urcos Peru
13 H5 Urda Spain
14 G2 Urdoma Rus. Fed.
12 J2 Urdoma Rus. Fed.
12 F4 Ure r. U.K.
12 H2 Urdoma r. Rus. Fed.
14 H2 Ureno-Karlinskoye Rus. Fed.
93 E3 Urenui N.Z.
90 □2 Ureparapara i. Vanuatu
15 E3 Urewera National Park nat. park N.Z.
61 B6 'Urf, G. el mt. Egypt
80 E4 Urga r. Rus. Fed.
80 E2 Urgal r. Rus. Fed.
65 H5 Urgench Uzbekistan
60 D2 Ürgüp Turkey
65 G5 Urho China
15 D3 Urho Kekkonen kansal- lispuisto nat. park Finland
93 C5 Uriah, Mt mt. N.Z.
138 C1 Uribia Colombia
65 G2 Urisino Aust.
46 E2 Uritskiy Kazak.
73 J1 Urk Netherlands
18 E2 Urla Turkey
28 F2 Urlați Romania
48 C2 Urluk Rus. Fed.
79 E6 Urmston Road chan. Hong Kong
77 F5 Uromi Nigeria
28 B3 Uroševac Yugo.
90 □2 Urevera National Park nat. park N.Z.
19 J3 Urszulin Poland
144 E2 Uru r. Brazil
144 D2 Uruana Brazil
140 B2 Uruapan Mexico
141 E4 Urubamba r. Peru
144 C4 Urubupungá, Salto do waterfall Brazil
139 F4 Urucará Brazil
47 G5 Uruch'ye Rus. Fed.
11 E4 Urucu r. Brazil
145 J1 Uruçuca Brazil
142 C2 Uruçuí Brazil
142 C2 Uruçuí Prêto r. Brazil
144 D1 Urucuia Brazil
142 C2 Urucuia r. Brazil
142 C2 Urucurituba Brazil
147 G1 Uruguaiana Brazil
147 F1 Uruguay r. Arg./Uruguay
147 F2 Uruguay country S. America
49 H2 Urulga Rus. Fed.
48 B4 Urt Mongolia
144 D3 Uruaçu r. Brazil
144 D1 Uruana Brazil
141 G6 Uru-Uru, L. l. Bolivia
44 C2 Ürümqi China
97 H2 Urunga Aust.
65 J3 Urup r. Rus. Fed.
31 H7 Urup Rus. Fed.
32 E4 Urus-Martan Rus. Fed.
54 D3 Urusovo Rus. Fed.
12 J3 Urussu Rus. Fed.
142 E2 Uruti N.Z.
46 H2 Uryl' Kazak.
14 F2 Urzhum Rus. Fed.
28 F2 Urziceni Romania
60 B1 Uşak Turkey
82 B2 Usakos Namibia
147 E7 Usborne, Mt h. Falkland Is
51 □ Uşe Tuçh
19 F2 Usedom Germany
31 □1 Usedom i. Germany
101 A5 Useless Loop Aust.
80 C2 Ushashi Tanzania
92 E3 Urenui N.Z.
92 □2 Ûreparapara i. Vanuatu
101 J2 Urewera National Park nat. park N.Z.
19 J3 Urt' Mongolia
15 D3 Urshel'sky Rus. Fed.
19 J3 Urszulin Poland
144 E2 Urubu r. Brazil
144 C2 Urubu r. Brazil
141 E2 Uruapan Mexico
131 E5 Uruapan Mexico
48 F2 Urluk Rus. Fed.
65 L3 Urgench Uzbekistan
46 H2 'Ushâmnlyah Syria
46 H2 Urluk Can.
77 D5 Urumston Road chan. Hong Kong
28 A3 Uroševac Yugo.
55 F3 Urmston Road chan. Hong Kong
54 A4 Urthal Pakistan
61 D2 'Uthmâniyah Syria
63 A3 U Thong Thailand
115 G2 Utiariti Brazil
121 J3 Utica U.S.A.
13 H4 Utiel Spain
110 H3 Utikuma Lake l. Can.
144 D3 Utinga r. Brazil
15 D1 Utlyuks'ky Lyman est. Ukraine
46 D7 Uto Japan
11 G4 Utraula India
18 E2 Utrecht Netherlands
18 D2 Utrecht div. Netherlands
18 D3 Utrera Spain
16 H2 Utsira i. Norway
47 G5 Utsjoki Finland
47 G5 Utsunomiya Japan
13 L5 Utta Rus. Fed.
62 C2 Uttaradit Thailand
54 D3 Uttarkashi India
54 D3 Uttar Pradesh India
133 □3 Utuado Puerto Rico
91 □4 Utuloa Fr. Poly. Pac. Oc.
91 □3 Utuofai Fr. Poly. Pac. Oc.
12 C4 Utura r. U.K.
25 G3 Utrera Spain
17 B6 Utukok r. U.S.A.
110 D3 Utupua i. Solomon Is.
114 A2 Uvá r. Colombia
81 B4 Uvá r. Colombia
80 C4 Uvinza Tanzania
80 C4 Uvira Zaire
55 E4 Uvod' r. Rus. Fed.
46 E2 Uwa Japan
72 B2 'Uwaynât Wannîn Libya
73 E2 'Uwaynat, Jebel mt. Sudan
40 C2 Uwi i. Indon.
29 G5 Uşak div. Turkey
82 B3 Usakos Namibia
82 B3 Usarp Mts mt. N.Z.
19 F2 Usborne, Mt h. Falkland Is.
11 G4 Uxbridge Can.
45 D3 Uxin Ju China
48 D5 Uxin Qi China
11 B6 Uxmal Mexico
131 H4 Uyaly Kazak.
48 B3 Uydzin Mongolia
41 B3 Uyega Rus. Fed.
77 F5 Uyo Nigeria
46 E2 Uyu Chaung r. Myanmar
62 J1 Uyuk r. Kazak.
61 B5 'Uyûn Mûsa spring Egypt
71 B4 Uza r. Rus. Fed.
14 E3 Uza r. Rus. Fed.
26 A3 Uzel France
25 G3 Uzdin Yugo.
115 J2 Val-Jalbert Can.
11 G4 Uzerche France
21 G4 Uzès France

65 J3 Ushtobe Kazak.
147 C7 Ushuaia Arg.
49 H1 Ushumun Rus. Fed.
55 E4 Uska India
61 D4 Usman' r. Rus. Fed.
60 B2 Usman' r. Turkey
12 J2 Usogorsk Rus. Fed.
15 D2 Usol'ye-Sibirskoye Rus. Fed.
64 F4 Uznkair Kazak.

V

78 D2 Vaal r. C.A.R.
82 C4 Vaal r. R.S.A.
10 G2 Vaala Finland
83 D4 Vaal Dam dam R.S.A.
10 F3 Vaasa Finland
10 G3 Vaasa div. Finland
14 A3 Vablya r. Rus. Fed.
45 J1 Vác Hungary
145 F4 Vacaré r. Brazil
28 B2 Vacaria Brazil
49 F1 Vacaria r. Brazil
13 G6 Vacaville Brazil
27 D6 Vacaria, Serra h. Brazil
144 H1 Vacaria r. Brazil
143 B5 Vacaria, Serra h. Brazil
128 B2 Vacaville U.S.A.
26 D5 Vacha Rus. Fed.
21 G4 Vacoas Mauritius
81 □4 Vacoas Mauritius
14 G2 Vad r. Rus. Fed.
56 A2 Vada India
28 F2 Vădeni Romania
14 F3 Vadinsk Rus. Fed.
10 D3 Vadla Norway
56 A2 Vadodara India
10 H1 Vadsø Norway
18 D5 Vaduz Liechtenstein
10 E1 Værøy i. Norway
10 G2 Vaga r. Rus. Fed.
10 D3 Vågåmo Norway
26 E3 Vaganski Vrh mt. Croatia
16 D1 Vágar i. Faeroes
13 J5 Vågsli Norway
19 H4 Váh r. Slovakia
19 H4 Váhárvi r. Slovakia
91 □1 Vaiau, Pte pt Fr. Poly. Pac. Oc.
11 G4 Vaida India
56 B4 Vaigai r. India
91 □10 Vaihu i. Easter I. Chile
129 G5 Vail U.S.A.
90 □10 Vairao Fr. Poly. Pac. Oc.
90 □4 Vanna Tonga
91 □11 Vairao Fr. Poly. Pac. Oc.
91 □3 Vaison-la-Romaine France
91 □11 Vaitape i. Fr. Poly. Pac. Oc.
150 G6 Vaitupu i. Tuvalu
90 □1 Vaiusu Western Samoa
90 □3 Vaka'eitu i. Tonga
90 □2 Vakaga div. C.A.R.
64 E2 Vakh r. Rus. Fed.
65 G5 Vakhsh Tajikistan
57 D3 Vakīlābād Iran
56 B4 Valachchenai Sri Lanka
142 E2 Valamaz Rus. Fed.
29 D4 Valandovo Macedonia
19 J4 Valašské Klobouky Czech Rep.
19 H4 Valašské Meziříčí Czech Rep.
29 C5 Valaxa i. Greece
115 H3 Val-Barrette Can.
147 C5 Valcheta Arg.
114 C2 Val-Côté r. Can.
26 C3 Valdagno Italy
21 H3 Valdahon France
21 J3 Valdaíra r. Spain
12 D3 Valday Rus. Fed.
14 A1 Valdayskaya Vozvyshennost' h. Rus. Fed.
24 D3 Valdecañas, Embalse de resr Spain
11 F4 Valdemārpils Latvia
11 F4 Valdemarsvik Sweden
24 E2 Valdemoro Spain
21 G2 Valdepeñas Spain
24 E3 Valderaduey r. Spain
13 H4 Valderas Spain
115 H4 Val-de-Reuil France
147 H5 Valdés, Península pen. Arg.
138 B3 Valdez Ecuador
108 D3 Valdez U.S.A.
21 G4 Val-d'Isère France
147 B4 Valdivia Chile
26 B2 Valdobbiadene Italy
115 G2 Val-d'Or Can.
119 C6 Valdosta U.S.A.
13 J5 Valdres r. Norway
126 C2 Vale U.S.A.
21 J4 Vale Georgia
114 F4 Valea lui Mihai Romania
110 F4 Valemount Can.
145 H3 Valença Brazil
142 E2 Valença Brazil
142 D2 Valença do Piauí Brazil
21 G3 Valençay France
21 H4 Valence Rhône-Alpes France
25 F3 Valencia Spain
25 F3 Valencia div. Spain
133 □3 Valencia Trin. & Tobago
138 D1 Valencia Venezuela
24 D3 Valencia de Alcántara Spain
24 E2 Valencia de Don Juan Spain
25 G3 Valencia, Golfo de g. Spain
17 B6 Valencia Island i. Rep. of Ire.
133 □3 Valencia, L. de l. Venezuela
21 F1 Valenciennes France
115 J2 Vălenii de Munte Romania
21 H5 Valensole, Plateau de plat. France
129 F4 Valentine U.S.A.
11 G4 Valentine U.S.A.
26 D3 Valentine U.S.A.
126 B3 Valenza Italy
11 F4 Valenzuela Phil.
138 C2 Valera Venezuela
21 G4 Valera r. Macedonia
28 D4 Valeni r. Macedonia
26 C3 Valença Macedonia
11 F4 Valga Latvia
11 G4 Valga Estonia
11 F4 Valkeakoski Finland
18 B3 Valkenswaard Netherlands
21 H5 Valkö Estonia
26 F2 Varaždin Croatia
26 A3 Varazze Italy
11 D4 Varberg Sweden
13 H4 Varbech r. Spain
152 C4 Valkyriedomen ice feature Ant.
24 D3 Valladolid Mexico
131 H4 Valladolid Spain
24 D2 Valladolid Spain
131 E4 Vallarta, Pto Mexico
21 H5 Valldemossa Spain
25 F3 Valle Norway
26 A3 Valle d'Aosta div. Italy
138 C2 Valle de la Pascua Venezuela
138 C2 Valledupar Colombia
115 K3 Vallée-Jonction Can.

15 C1 Uzh r. Ukraine
13 B5 Uzhhorod Ukraine
14 G2 Uzhovka Rus. Fed.
14 D3 Uzlovaya Rus. Fed.
14 F1 Uzola r. Rus. Fed.
60 B2 Üzümlü Turkey
12 J3 Uzunagach Kazak.
60 A1 Uzunköprü Turkey
15 D2 Uzyn Ukraine
64 F4 Uzynkair Kazak.

146 C3 Valle Fértil, Sa de mt. ra. Arg.
140 D3 Valle Grande Bolivia
147 C6 Valle Hermosa Arg.
131 F3 Valle Hermoso Mexico
25 □ Vallehermoso Canary Is
128 A2 Vallejo U.S.A.
27 D7 Vallelunga Pratameno Italy
131 F5 Valle Nacional Mexico
146 B2 Vallenar Chile
27 E7 Valletta Malta
124 D2 Valley City U.S.A.
126 B3 Valley Falls U.S.A.
41 B2 Valley Head pt Phil.
120 C5 Valley Head U.S.A.
73 F2 Valley of The Kings Egypt
133 G3 Valley, The Anguilla Caribbean
60 E2 Valleyview Can.
55 E4 Valls Spain
25 G2 Valls Spain
110 G4 Valmiera Latvia
20 C4 Valognes France
24 C2 Valpaços Portugal
115 F2 Val-Paradis Can.
144 C4 Valparaíso Brazil
147 B4 Valparaíso div. Chile
146 B3 Valparaíso Chile
122 D5 Valparaiso U.S.A.
26 D3 Valpovo Croatia
21 G4 Valréas France
26 B2 Valsan r. Italy
82 C4 Valspan R.S.A.
45 J1 Vals, Tg c. Indon.
12 H1 Val'tevo r. Rus. Fed.
28 D1 Vaşcău Romania
12 H2 Valtimo Finland
28 D1 Valton Mauritius
29 C5 Valtou mt. ra. Greece
26 C3 Valtournenche Italy
90 □8 Valukoula Fiji
14 B1 Valuyevka Rus. Fed.
13 F5 Valuyki Rus. Fed.
24 C4 Valverde del Camino Spain
19 H3 Vamberk Czech Rep.
43 D5 Vam Co Tay r. Vietnam
123 F4 Vamizi, Ilha i. Mozambique
11 F3 Vammala Finland
72 B2 Vamsadhara r. India
60 E2 Van Turkey
139 G2 Vanavara r. Rus. Fed.
11 H3 Vanatori r. Romania
10 D3 Vanajavesi l. Finland
21 H3 Vanavana i. Fr. Poly. Pac. Oc.
10 F2 Van Buren U.S.A.
121 K1 Van Buren U.S.A.
43 E4 Van Canh Vietnam
120 C6 Vanceburg U.S.A.
110 E5 Vancouver Can.
110 E5 Vancouver, C. c. Aust.
110 D5 Vancouver Island i. Can.
110 D5 Vancouver, Mt mt. U.S.A.
92 □2 Vancouver Rock i. Snares Is N.Z.
118 B4 Vandalia U.S.A.
120 A5 Vandalia U.S.A.
82 D4 Vanderbijlpark R.S.A.
123 C4 Vanderhoof Can.
120 D4 Vandergrift U.S.A.
110 E4 Vanderhoof Can.
98 C2 Vanderlin I. i. Aust.
146 B2 Van Diemen G. g. Aust.
98 D1 Van Diemen, C. c. Aust.
98 C1 Van Diemen Gulf b. Aust.
11 G4 Vändra Estonia
21 H4 Vandry France
10 E2 Vänern l. Sweden
10 E3 Vänersborg Sweden
81 E6 Vangaindrano Madagascar
60 E2 Van Gölü salt l. Turkey
99 H3 Vanguard, I. Solomon Is.
125 C6 Van Horn U.S.A.
115 H4 Vanier Can.
45 J2 Vanimo P.N.G.
81 E6 Vanino Rus. Fed.
56 B3 Vaniyambadi India
140 B3 Vanju Mare Romania
108 H3 Vankarem Rus. Fed.
10 E2 Vankleek Hill Can.
11 D4 Vännäs Norway
21 E3 Vannes France
65 H5 Vannovka Kazak.
14 B1 Vanoise, Massif de la mts France
82 B4 Vanrhynsdorp R.S.A.
99 E3 Vanrook Aust.
98 D3 Vanrook Cr. r. Aust.
28 B2 Vansbro Sweden
100 D2 Vansittart B. b. Aust.
99 F1 Vansittart I. i. Can.
108 H2 Vanthli India
43 E4 Van Tri Vietnam
90 □7 Vanua Balavu i. Fiji
90 □3 Vanua Lava i. Vanuatu
90 □8 Vanua Levu i. Fiji
90 □8 Vanua Levu Barrier Reef reef Fiji
86 H6 Vanuatu country Pac. Oc.
120 A4 Van Wert U.S.A.
21 □2 Vanwyksvlei l. R.S.A.
82 C5 Vanwyksvlei R.S.A.
43 D4 Van Yên Vietnam
82 C4 Vanzylsrus R.S.A.
56 A2 Vapi India
15 C2 Vapnyarka Ukraine
119 E4 Var r. France
21 H4 Var r. France
56 A3 Varada r. India
25 G3 Varades France
11 G4 Varāfjāll mt. Iceland
28 C2 Varakļāni Latvia
28 C2 Varaklani Latvia
26 C3 Varallo Italy
57 C1 Varāmin Iran
54 E4 Varanasi India
28 C2 Varangerfjorden chan. Norway
21 G4 Varangerhalvøya pen. Norway
10 H1 Varanger-halvøya pen. Norway
26 F2 Varaždin Croatia
26 A3 Varazze Italy
11 D4 Varberg Sweden
13 H4 Varbech r. Spain
28 B3 Vardar r. Macedonia
11 C4 Varde Denmark
10 H1 Vardø Norway
11 G4 Varēna Lithuania
28 D1 Vărẽu Romania
21 D2 Varennes-sur-Allier France
26 F3 Vareš Bos.-Herz.
26 C3 Varese Italy
145 F4 Vargem r. Brazil
144 B4 Vargem r. Brazil
145 F4 Vargem r. Brazil
144 B2 Vargem r. Brazil
145 F4 Vargem Grande do Sul Brazil
142 E2 Vargem r. Brazil

145 E4 Vargem Grande do Sul Brazil
15 A2 Varginha Brazil
28 C3 Varillas Chile
10 H3 Varkaus Finland
11 D4 Värmland div. Sweden
11 D4 Värmland div. Sweden
10 G1 Varna Bulgaria
64 F2 Varna Rus. Fed.
11 D3 Värnamo Sweden
14 G1 Varnavino Rus. Fed.
61 B2 Varosha Cyprus
26 C3 Varoška Rijeka Bos.-Herz.
10 G3 Varpaisjärvi Finland
19 J5 Várpalota Hungary
57 G1 Varsaj Afghanistan
60 E2 Varto Turkey
55 H4 Vártop Romania
55 B4 Varuna r. India
15 E1 Varva Ukraine
28 C3 Varvarin Yugo.
76 A3 Varvarivka Ukraine
77 G3 Varvarivka Kharkiv Ukraine
15 F1 Varvarivka Ukraine
14 C1 Varzaneh Rus. Fed.
143 D6 Varzea r. Paraná Brazil
14 E1 Várzea r. Rio Grande do Sul Brazil
142 C2 Várzea da Palma Brazil
145 F1 Varzelândia Brazil
26 B2 Varzo Italy
14 F2 Varzuga Rus. Fed.
142 E3 Vasa Barris r. Brazil
39 M4 Vásárosnamény Hungary
28 D1 Vaşcău Romania
12 F2 Vashka r. Rus. Fed.
14 C2 Vashkivtsi Ukraine
14 A1 Vasil'yevskiy Mokh Rus. Fed.
14 G1 Vasil'yevskoye Rus. Fed.
14 G3 Vasil'yevo Rus. Fed.
25 □ Vasknarva Estonia
15 C1 Vas'kovychi Ukraine
15 F2 Vasshere r. Rus. Fed.
11 G3 Vaslui Romania
123 F4 Vassar U.S.A.
144 D3 Vassouras Brazil
28 D6 Västerås Sweden
11 E4 Västerbotten div. Sweden
11 D3 Västerbotten div. Sweden
11 D3 Västerdalälven r. Sweden
10 E2 Västerfjäll Sweden
11 E4 Västerhaninge Sweden
10 E3 Västernorrland div. Sweden
11 F4 Västervik Sweden
11 E3 Västmanland div. Sweden
27 E6 Vasto Italy
27 D7 Vasyl'kivka Ukraine
19 H5 Vasvár Hungary
15 A1 Vasyl'kiv Kirovohrad Ukraine
15 C1 Vasyl'kiv Kyiv Ukraine
15 F1 Vasylivka Sumy Ukraine
15 E2 Vasylivka Zaporizhzhya Ukraine
15 C2 Vasyl'kiv Ukraine
15 G2 Vasyutyntsi Ukraine
15 C2 Vasyl'kiv Ukraine
15 G1 Vatan France
56 A2 Vathar India
27 B7 Vatican City country Europe
98 D2 Vatican City country Europe
10 ■1 Vatnajökull ice cap Iceland
83 □1 Vato Loha mt. Madagascar
81 E5 Vatomandry Madagascar
28 E1 Vatra Dornei Romania
28 E1 Vatra Moldovei Romania
11 E4 Vättern l. Sweden
90 □8 Vatu-i-Ra Channel chan. Fiji
90 □9 Vatulele i. Fiji
90 □10 Vatu Vara i. Fiji
90 □8 Vatu Vara i. Fiji
90 □7 Vatutinski Ukraine
90 □1 Vatu-i-Thake i. Fiji
90 □9 Vatulele i. Fiji
90 □6 Vatu Vara i. Fiji
90 □5 Vatu Vara i. Fiji
21 G5 Vaucluse, Monts de mts France
20 D2 Vaucouleurs France
21 G3 Vaugneray France
21 G2 Vaulx-en-Velin France
25 □ Vaupés r. Colombia
110 H5 Vauxhall Can.
81 □4 Vavatenina Madagascar
90 □7 Vava'u Group is Tonga
81 B4 Vavoua Côte d'Ivoire
56 B4 Vavuniya Sri Lanka
11 J4 Vawkavysk Belarus
11 F4 Växjö Sweden
26 D2 Vaygach Rus. Fed.
64 D2 Vaygach, O. i. Rus. Fed.
145 G2 Vazante Brazil
14 F3 Vazuza r. Rus. Fed.
14 A2 Vazuzskoye Vdkhr. resr Rus. Fed.
91 □10 Veal Vêng Cambodia
11 □3 Vechta Germany
79 □7 Vechte r. Germany
11 D4 Vedaranniyam India
13 H4 Veddige Sweden
11 C4 Vedea r. Romania
28 E3 Vedea r. Romania
32 E2 Vedea r. Romania
13 H4 Vedi Armenia
14 G2 Vedlozero Rus. Fed.
25 □ Vedra, Isla del i. Spain
110 H4 Vegreville Can.
125 C5 Vega U.S.A.
24 E2 Vega Baja Puerto Rico
24 C1 Vegadeo Spain
110 H4 Vegreville Can.

12 E2 Velikaya Guba Rus. Fed.
15 A2 Veliki Birky Ukraine
28 C3 Veliki Jastrebac mts Yugo.
15 D2 Velikiy Luki Rus. Fed.
11 D4 Värmland div. Sweden
15 D1 Velikiy Lystven Ukraine
28 C2 Velikiy Ustyug Rus. Fed.
64 F2 Varna Rus. Fed.
15 B2 Velikiy Zhvanchyk Ukraine
121 G2 Vergennes U.S.A.
14 D1 Verigino Rus. Fed.
14 C1 Veliki Novoselka Ukraine
28 C2 Veliki Gradište Yugo.
26 D2 Velikonda Range mt. ra. India
14 A1 Velikooktyabr'skiy Rus. Fed.
28 E2 Veliko Tŭrnovo Bulgaria
14 C1 Velikiye Luki Rus. Fed.
14 C1 Velikoye, Oz. l. Rus. Fed.
15 F1 Velikaya Novosilka Ukraine
13 J5 Velikyy Burluk Ukraine
11 J3 Velingara Kolda Senegal
76 A3 Vélingara Louga Senegal
27 D4 Velino, Monte mt. Italy
10 H1 Velizh Rus. Fed.
14 A2 Velichky Krtiš Slovakia
15 H5 Velký Meder Slovakia
15 F1 Vel'ky Shergol'dzhin Rus. Fed.
65 F1 Vel'sk Rus. Fed.
28 B1 Veluwe reg. Netherlands
18 E2 Velten Germany
14 F1 Velva U.S.A.
14 C2 Vel'yaminovo Rus. Fed.
15 F2 Velyka Bahachka Ukraine
15 E2 Velyka Bilozerka Ukraine
15 E2 Velyka Burimka Ukraine
15 D3 Velyka Korenykha Ukraine
15 C1 Velyka Lepetykha Ukraine
48 D2 Verkhniy Ul'khun Rus. Fed.
12 E1 Velyka Mykhaylivka Ukraine
15 D2 Velyka Oleksandrivka Ukraine
14 C4 Velyka Pysarivka Ukraine
15 E2 Velyka Rublivka Ukraine
15 B1 Velyka Tsvilya Ukraine
15 C2 Velyka Vys' r. Ukraine
15 C2 Velyka Vyska Ukraine
15 G2 Velyki Korovyntsi Ukraine
19 H5 Velký Krtíš Slovakia
15 A1 Velyki Mosty Ukraine
15 E1 Velyki Sorochyntsi Ukraine
15 D2 Velykyy Khutir Ukraine
15 E2 Velykodolyns'ke Ukraine
15 C2 Velykomykhaylivka Ukraine
11 G2 Velykyy Burluk Ukraine
15 E1 Velykyy Bychkiv Ukraine
148 G5 Vema Fracture feature Atlantic Ocean
122 E2 Vemba R.S.A.
149 J4 Vema Trough Indian Ocean
56 A4 Vembanad L. l. India
49 E1 Vembanad L. l. Rus. Fed.
146 B2 Venado Tuerto Arg.
83 H2 Vanga India
144 C5 Venâncio Aires Brazil
142 C2 Venda Nova Brazil
145 H4 Venda Nova Brazil
144 C2 Vendinha r. Brazil
142 C2 Vendinha r. Brazil
21 E2 Vendôme France
18 E2 Vendôme Ukraine
56 A2 Veneta, Laguna lag. Italy
26 D3 Veneto div. Italy
12 F4 Venev Rus. Fed.
26 D3 Venezia Italy
26 D3 Venezia, Golfo di g. Italy
25 □ Venezuela, Golfo de g. Venezuela
138 C2 Venezuela country S. America
21 G5 Vengurla India
56 A3 Vengurla India
21 F4 Venice U.S.A.
128 □ Venice, La. lag. Italy
119 D7 Venice U.S.A.
121 E4 Venkatagiri India
110 H4 Vennachar Junction Can.
10 D3 Vennesla Norway
18 E3 Venlo Netherlands
10 D3 Venray Netherlands
18 E3 Venta de Baños Spain
24 E2 Venta de Baños Spain
147 H4 Venta, Serra de la h. Arg.
28 E2 Ventenac Romania
147 H4 Vedische Germany
65 K1 Vodovino Rus. Fed.
147 H3 Vinşanţţ I. i. Can.
90 □7 Vanua Balavu i. Fiji
91 □3 Vent, Îles du is Fr. Poly. Pac. Oc.
14 C1 Ventimiglia Italy
90 □1 Vent, Îles sous le is Fr. Poly. Pac. Oc.
26 A3 Ventimiglia Italy
11 F4 Ventspils Latvia
139 E3 Ventuari r. Venezuela
128 C4 Ventura U.S.A.
14 C2 Venus B. b. Aust.
97 E4 Venus B. b. Aust.
11 G4 Venus B. b. Aust.
131 E4 Venustiano Carranza Mexico
10 D3 Venzone Italy
141 D5 Vera Arg.
146 D2 Vera Arg.
140 A2 Vera Spain
25 F4 Vera Spain
25 G2 Verberie France
140 C1 Veracruz div. Mexico
131 F5 Veracruz Mexico
131 F5 Veracruz Mexico
119 D5 Veraguas div. Panama
56 A2 Veraval India
24 C2 Verbania Italy
26 B3 Vercelli Italy
21 H4 Vercors reg. France
10 D2 Verdal r. Norway
142 C3 Verde r. Bahia Brazil
145 G1 Verde r. Goiás Brazil
144 B3 Verde r. Goiás/Minas Gerais Brazil
144 B2 Verde r. Mato Grosso do Sul Brazil
144 B2 Verde r. Mato Grosso do Sul Brazil
145 E3 Verde r. Minas Gerais Brazil
144 B4 Verde r. Minas Gerais Brazil
142 D2 Verde r. Minas Gerais Brazil
144 B2 Verde r. Mato Grosso Brazil
142 A2 Verde r. Goiás Brazil
131 F5 Verde r. Oaxaca Mexico
129 G5 Verde r. U.S.A.
125 D5 Verde r. U.S.A.
26 E3 Verde, Cabo de pt Colombia
19 J3 Verde, Pen. pt Arg.
147 H5 Verde, Pen. pt Arg.
144 B3 Verde Pequeno r. Brazil
140 A3 Verdigris r. U.S.A.
91 □6 Verdun, Îles du is Fr. Poly.
21 G3 Verdun France

12 E2 Velikaya Guba Rus. Fed.
20 E5 Verdun-sur-Garonne France
83 D4 Vereeniging R.S.A.
15 E2 Veremiyivka Ukraine
115 G3 Vérendrye, Réserve fau- nique La res. Can.
21 □2 Vereya r. Uruguay
146 F3 Vergara Uruguay
99 □4 Vergemont Cr. w Aust.
121 G2 Vergennes U.S.A.
14 D1 Verigino Rus. Fed.
15 D1 Verín Spain
19 □3 Verín Spain
15 E2 Verkhivtseve Ukraine
64 E2 Verkhne-Avzyan Rus. Fed.
14 A2 Verkhnedneprovskiy Rus. Fed.
62 K3 Verkhneimbatskoye Rus. Fed.
12 H3 Verkhnespasskoye Rus. Fed.
10 H1 Verkhnetulomskiy Rus. Fed.
14 F3 Verkhneturovo Rus. Fed.
64 E1 Verkhneural'sk Rus. Fed.
63 D3 Verkhnevilyuysk Rus. Fed.
19 H4 Verkhnevolzhskoye Rus. Fed.
15 G2 Verkhneye Talyzino Rus. Fed.
15 H5 Verkhnyeye Talyzino Rus. Fed.
14 C1 Verkhniy Baskunchak Rus. Fed.
13 J5 Verkhniy Byshkyn Ukraine
56 B4 Verkhniy Kushum Rus. Fed.
48 D2 Verkhniy Landekh Rus. Fed.
14 F3 Verkhniy Lomov Rus. Fed.
12 E1 Verkhniy Rohachyk Ukraine
48 D2 Verkhniy Ul'khun Rus. Fed.
12 E1 Verkhniy Vyalozerskiy Rus. Fed.
14 C1 Verkhnyaya Grayvoronka Rus. Fed.
65 K2 Verkhnyaya Irmen' Rus. Fed.
14 F3 Verkhnyaya Khava Rus. Fed.
15 F2 Verkhnyaya Khila Rus. Fed.
12 F2 Verkhnyaya Pirenga, Oz. l. Rus. Fed.
12 E2 Verkhnyaya Toyma Rus. Fed.
14 C1 Verkhnyaya Troitsa Rus. Fed.
12 J3 Verkhoshizhem'ye Rus. Fed.
12 G2 Verkhov'ye Rus. Fed.
14 C1 Verkhovazh'ye Rus. Fed.
63 P3 Verkhoyansk Rus. Fed.
63 O2 Verkhoyanskiy Khrebet mt. ra. Rus. Fed.
12 H3 Verkhozim Rus. Fed.
49 E1 Verkh-Usugli Rus. Fed.
12 E1 Verkhne Kuyto, Oz. l. Rus. Fed.
142 C2 Vermelho r. Brazil
142 D2 Vermelho r. Brazil
142 C2 Vermelho r. Brazil
111 L5 Vermilion Can.
123 F4 Vermilion U.S.A.
122 A1 Vermilion L. l. U.S.A.
110 D3 Vermilion Range h. U.S.A.
122 A2 Vermilion Bay Can.
121 G3 Vermont div. U.S.A.
111 K3 Vernadovka Rus. Fed.
20 E2 Vermoulen r. U.S.A.
126 E3 Vernal U.S.A.
111 K5 Verneuil-sur-Avre France
114 C2 Vernon r. Can.
146 C4 Vernon Can.
122 A1 Vernon U.S.A.
125 D5 Vernon U.S.A.
128 □2 Vernon U.S.A.
119 D6 Vero Beach U.S.A.
29 D4 Verona div. Italy
26 D3 Verona Italy
22 D2 Versailles France
20 E2 Versailles France
21 G2 Versailles France
21 F3 Vienne France
21 G3 Vienne France
20 D3 Vienne r. France
147 H3 Vertientes Cuba
142 E2 Vertentes Brazil
76 A3 Vertou France
20 C3 Vertou France
21 G2 Vertus France
147 D5 Verviers Belgium
18 D3 Verviers Belgium
21 F1 Vervins France
15 D2 Verkhivtseve Ukraine
19 H5 Veszprém Hungary
11 E4 Vetlanda Sweden
12 H3 Vetluga r. Rus. Fed.
14 G1 Vetluga Rus. Fed.
14 G1 Vetluzhskiy Rus. Fed.
14 G1 Vetluzhskiy Rus. Fed.
28 E3 Vetren Bulgaria
29 F4 Vetren Bulgaria

79 B5 Viana Angola
145 H4 Viana Espírito Santo Brazil
142 D1 Viana Maranhão Brazil
24 C3 Viana do Alentejo Portugal
24 B2 Viana do Castelo Portugal
24 B2 Viana do Castelo div. Portugal
43 D4 Viangchan Laos
42 C2 Viangphoukha Laos
24 C4 Viar r. Spain
26 C4 Viareggio Italy
11 C4 Viborg Denmark
27 F6 Vibo Valentia Italy
25 G3 Vic Spain
152 B2 Vicecomodoro Marambio Argentina Base Ant.
20 E5 Vic-en-Bigorre France
130 A2 Vicente Guerrero Mexico
128 C3 Vicente, Pt pt U.S.A.
26 D3 Vicenza Italy
138 D3 Vichada r. Colombia
146 C2 Vichina r. Chile
21 F3 Vichy France
125 F5 Vicksburg U.S.A.
21 F4 Vic-le-Comte France
44 B2 Viçosa Brazil
11 C4 Victor Harbour Aust.
27 F6 Vibo Valentia Italy
152 E2 Victoria Grenada Caribbean
133 □8 Victoria Grenada Caribbean
146 B4 Victoria Chile
133 J5 Victoria Honduras
27 F7 Victoria Malta
133 □8 Victoria Brăila Romania
28 E2 Victoria Braşov Romania
81 □1 Victoria Seychelles
133 □3 Victoria div. Trinidad Trin. & Tobago
132 C2 Victoria de las Tunas Cuba
79 E7 Victoria Falls waterfall Zambia/Zimbabwe
82 D2 Victoria Falls Zimbabwe
109 O3 Victoria Fjord inlet Greenland
45 □ Victoria Harbour chan. Hong Kong
132 D2 Victoria Hill The Bahamas
147 B6 Victoria, Isla i. Chile
108 H2 Victoria Island i. Africa
76 C5 Victoria, Lake l. Africa
108 H2 Victoria, Lake l. Can.
42 A2 Victoria, Mt mt. Myanmar
93 B4 Victoria, Mt mt. N.Z.
90 □1 Victoria, Mt mt. P.N.G.
81 B4 Victoria Nile r. Sudan/Uganda
94 □1 Victoria Pt pt Macquarie I. Pac. Oc.
93 B5 Victoria Range mt. ra. N.Z.
98 B2 Victoria River Downs Aust.
115 F4 Victoria, Sa de la h. Arg.
82 C5 Victoriaville R.S.A.
82 C5 Victorica R.S.A.
128 D4 Victorville U.S.A.
140 A2 Victor, Mt mt. Ant.
129 □1 Victorville U.S.A.
129 F4 Vidal Junction U.S.A.
142 □2 Videle Romania
28 C3 Vidin Bulgaria
54 D4 Vidisha India
25 G1 Viditsa Italy
10 ■2 Vidnoye Rus. Fed.
12 J3 Vidsel Sweden
47 □ Vidzy Belarus
147 B6 Viedma Arg.
147 B6 Viedma, L. l. Arg.
19 H4 Viechtach Germany
24 B1 Viella Spain
30 G1 Vielha Spain
18 E3 Vielsalm Belgium
19 F4 Vienenburg Germany
18 D3 Vienna Austria
120 C5 Vienna U.S.A.
21 F3 Vienne France
21 G3 Vienne France
20 D3 Vienne r. France
133 □8 Vieques Puerto Rico
133 □8 Vieques i. Puerto Rico
11 G3 Vieremä Finland
18 D4 Vierwaldstätter See l. Switz.
21 G2 Vierzon France
11 F4 Viesite Latvia
27 F6 Vieste Italy
42 D1 Viêt Tri Vietnam
42 M8 Vietnam country Asia
42 D1 Viêt Tri Vietnam
133 □3 Vieux Bourg Guadeloupe Caribbean
133 □ Vieux Fort St Lucia
133 □3 Vieux Fort, Pte du pt Guadeloupe Caribbean
133 □3 Vieux Habitants Guadeloupe Caribbean
41 B3 Vigan Phil.
83 □2 Vigan Phil.
26 A3 Vigevano Italy
142 □ Vigia Brazil
131 G4 Vigía Chico Mexico
24 B2 Vignola Italy
24 B2 Vigo Spain

79 B5 Viana Angola
145 H4 Viana Espírito Santo Brazil
142 D1 Viana Maranhão Brazil
24 C3 Viana do Alentejo Portugal

(various)

Column 1

24 B3 Vila Franca de Xira Portugal
24 B1 Vilagarcía de Arousa Spain
83 E3 Vila Gomes da Costa Mozambique
20 C3 Vilaine r. France
24 C1 Vilalba Spain
83 G2 Vilanandro, Tanjona c. Madagascar
83 F3 Vilanculos Mozambique
142 A1 Vila Nova Brazil
24 C2 Vila Nova de Foz Coa Portugal
24 B3 Vila Nova de Ourém Portugal
25 G2 Vilanova i la Geltrú Spain
76 □ Vila Nova Sintra Cape Verde
24 C2 Vila Real Portugal
24 C2 Vila Real div. Portugal
25 F3 Vila-real de los Infantes Spain
24 C2 Vilar Formoso Portugal
56 B4 Vilavankod India
139 G3 Vila Velha Amapá Brazil
145 H4 Vila Velha Espírito Santo Brazil
24 B2 Vila Verde Viseu Portugal
140 B2 Vilcabamba, Cordillera mt. ra. Peru
15 C1 Vil'cha Ukraine
12 J2 Vilfport Rus. Fed.
10 E2 Vilhelmina Sweden
141 D2 Vilhena Brazil
11 G4 Viljandi Estonia
11 F5 Vilkaviskis Lithuania
11 F5 Vilkija Lithuania
62 J2 Vil'kitskogo, O. i. Rus. Fed.
63 L2 Vil'kitskogo, Proliv str. Rus. Fed.
140 C4 Villa Abecia Bolivia
130 D2 Villa Ahumada Mexico
131 F5 Villa Alta Mexico
146 D2 Villa Angela Arg.
140 C2 Villa Bella Bolivia
146 D2 Villa Berthet Arg.
27 B6 Villablino Spain
146 E3 Villa Cañás Arg.
24 E3 Villacañas Spain
24 E3 Villacarrillo Spain
19 F5 Villach Austria
146 E3 Villa Constitución Arg.
130 C3 Villa Constitución Mexico
130 E5 Villa de Alvarez Mexico
130 E4 Villa de Cos Mexico
137 E3 Villa de Cura Venezuela
146 D3 Villa del Rosario Arg.
24 D1 Villadiego Spain
146 E3 Villa Dolores Arg.
146 E3 Villa Federal Arg.
131 G5 Villa Flores Mexico
141 E5 Villa Florida Paraguay
25 F2 Villafranca del Cid Spain
24 C3 Villafranca de los Barros Spain
26 C3 Villafranca di Verona Italy
125 F5 Village, Lake U.S.A.
146 E4 Villa Gesell Arg.
131 F3 Villagrán Mexico
146 E3 Villaguay Arg.
25 F2 Villa Hayes Paraguay
131 G5 Villahermosa Mexico
146 D3 Villa Huidobro Arg.
20 D2 Villaines-la-Juhel France
146 D4 Villa Iris Arg.
122 A2 Villajoyosa Spain
131 F3 Villaldama Mexico
147 D4 Villalonga Arg.
147 D4 Villalonga Arg.
146 D3 Villa María Córdoba Arg.
146 E3 Villa María Grande Arg.
140 C4 Villa Martín Bolivia
138 □ Villamil Galápagos Is Ecuador
140 D4 Villa Montes Bolivia
138 B4 Villano Ecuador
138 C1 Villanueva Colombia
25 E2 Villanueva de Alcorón Spain
24 D3 Villanueva de Córdoba Spain
24 D3 Villanueva de la Serena Spain
24 C4 Villanueva de los Castillejos Spain
146 E2 Villa Ocampo Arg.
130 D3 Villa Ocampo Mexico
125 B7 Villa O. Pereyra Mexico
140 C3 Villa Oropeza Bolivia
27 B6 Villaputzu Italy
140 D3 Villar Bolivia
25 F3 Villar del Humo Spain
24 C3 Villar del Rey Spain
147 C4 Villa Regina Arg.
147 B4 Villarrica Chile
141 E5 Villarrica Paraguay
147 B4 Villarrica, L. l. Chile
147 B4 Villarrica, Parque Nacional nat. park Arg./Chile
147 B4 Villarrica, Volcán vol Chile
25 E3 Villarrobledo Spain
25 E3 Villarrubia de los Ojos Spain
24 E1 Villasana de Mena Spain
27 E6 Villa San Giovanni Italy
146 E3 Villa San José Arg.
146 E3 Villa San Martín Arg.
27 E5 Villa Santa María Italy
25 F3 Villa Santa Rita de Catuna Arg.
146 C2 Villa Unión Arg.
131 E2 Villa Unión Coahuila Mexico
130 D4 Villa Unión Durango Mexico
130 D4 Villa Unión Sinaloa Mexico
146 D3 Villa Valeria Arg.
138 C3 Villavicencio Colombia
24 D1 Villaviciosa de Asturias Spain
24 D3 Villaviciosa de Córdoba Spain
140 C4 Villa Viscarra Bolivia
140 D2 Villazon Bolivia
20 D2 Villedieu-les-Poêles France
20 E5 Villefranche-de-Lauragais France
21 F4 Villefranche-de-Rouergue France
21 G4 Villefranche-sur-Saône France
24 G2 Villel Spain
115 F3 Ville-Marie Can.
25 F3 Villemontel Can.
21 G5 Villeneuve Provence-Alpes-Côte-d'Azur France
20 D5 Villeneuve-de-Marsan France
20 E4 Villeneuve-sur-Lot France
21 F2 Villeneuve-sur-Yonne France
125 E6 Ville Platte U.S.A.
20 D2 Villers-Bocage Basse-Normandie France
21 F2 Villers-Cotterêts France
21 G4 Villers-sur-Mer France
21 G4 Villeurbanne Rhône France
18 D4 Villingen Germany
11 G4 Vilnia r. Lithuania
11 G5 Vilnius Lithuania

Column 2

15 F2 Vil'nohirs'k Ukraine
15 F3 Vil'nyans'k Ukraine
11 G3 Vilppula Finland
18 F4 Vils r. Bayern Germany
15 D2 Vil'shana Cherkasy Ukraine
15 E1 Vil'shana Chernihiv Ukraine
15 D2 Vil'shana Kharkiv Ukraine
15 D2 Vil'shanka Ukraine
56 A2 Viluppuram India
18 B3 Vilvoorde Belgium
12 F2 Vilya r. Rus. Fed.
12 C4 Vileyka Belarus
63 M3 Vilyuy r. Rus. Fed.
63 M3 Vilyuyskoye Vdkhr. resr Rus. Fed.
26 B3 Vimercate Italy
11 D4 Vimmerby Sweden
20 C2 Vimoutiers France
19 F4 Vimperk Czech Rep.
128 A2 Vina r. U.S.A.
146 B3 Viña del Mar Chile
121 J2 Vinalhaven U.S.A.
83 H2 Vinanivao Madagascar
25 G2 Vinaros Spain
81 □ Vincendo Réunion Indian Ocean
118 C4 Vincennes U.S.A.
152 C6 Vincennes Bay b. Ant.
95 □ Vincent, Pt pt Norfolk I. Pac. Oc.
10 E2 Vindelälven r. Sweden
10 E2 Vindeln Sweden
54 C5 Vindhya Range India
14 F2 Vinderup Denmark
121 F5 Vineland U.S.A.
121 H4 Vineyard Haven U.S.A.
42 D3 Vinh Vietnam
83 B3 Vinh Linh Vietnam
43 D5 Vinh Long Vietnam
43 D5 Vinh Rach Gia b. Vietnam
42 D2 Vinh Yên Vietnam
28 D4 Vinica Macedonia
125 E4 Vinita U.S.A.
15 E1 Vin'kivtsi Ukraine
26 G3 Vinkovci Croatia
15 C2 Vinnytsya div. Ukraine
15 C2 Vinnytsya Ukraine
152 B3 Vinson Massif mt. Ant.
122 A4 Vinton U.S.A.
18 E5 Vinukonda India
79 B4 Vinza Congo
63 □ Vinzili Rus. Fed.
100 D3 Violet Valley Abor. Reserve Res. res. Aust.
81 B7 Viphya Mountains mts Malawi
26 C2 Vipiteno Italy
26 E3 Vir i. Croatia
41 C3 Virac Phil.
54 B4 Viramgam India
60 D2 Viranşehir Turkey
54 B4 Virawah Pakistan
111 J5 Virden Can.
20 D2 Vire France
20 D2 Vire r. France
79 B7 Virei Angola
19 F4 Vírful Highiş h. Romania
145 G2 Virgem da Lapa Brazil
25 F2 Virgen, Sierra de la mt. ra. Spain
115 F2 Virginatown Can.
119 □ Virgin Gorda i. Virgin Is Caribbean
82 D4 Virginia R.S.A.
122 A2 Virginia U.S.A.
120 D6 Virginia div. U.S.A.
121 E6 Virginia Beach U.S.A.
128 C2 Virginia City U.S.A.
104 M8 Virgin Islands (U.K.) terr. Caribbean
104 M8 Virgin Islands (U.S.A.) terr. Caribbean
129 F3 Virgin Mts mts U.S.A.
145 G3 Virginópolis Brazil
119 □ Virgin Passage chan. Caribbean
11 J4 Virkkala Finland
43 D4 Virôchey Cambodia
26 F3 Virovitica Croatia
19 K3 Virrat Finland
18 B4 Virton Belgium
140 A1 Virú Peru
56 B4 Virudunagar India
78 E4 Virunga, Parc National des nat. park Zaire
26 E4 Vis Croatia
11 C5 Visaginas Lithuania
54 B5 Visakhapatnam India
54 B5 Visavadar India
24 E3 Visayan Sea sea Phil.
11 E4 Visby Sweden
145 G4 Visconde do Rio Branco Brazil
108 G2 Viscount Melville Sound str. Can.
26 E4 Višegrad Bos.-Herz.
62 J2 Vise, O. i. Rus. Fed.
24 C2 Viseu Portugal
24 C2 Viseu div. Portugal
28 E1 Viseu de Sus Romania
29 C5 Vistheni India
54 C4 Visnagar India
26 A3 Viso, Monte mt. Italy
26 G4 Visoko Bos.-Herz.
143 A4 Vista Alegre Brazil
31 J4 Visun' r. Ukraine
54 B3 Vitakri Pakistan
27 D4 Viterbo Italy
26 E3 Vitez Bos.-Herz.
140 C4 Vitichi Bolivia
93 J4 Viti Levu i. Fiji
63 N3 Vitim r. Rus. Fed.
45 K1 Vitimskoye Ploskogor'ye plat. Rus. Fed.
29 C4 Vitolište Macedonia
145 H4 Vitória Espírito Santo Brazil
142 E1 Vitória Pará Brazil
145 H1 Vitória da Conquista Brazil
142 □ Vitória de Mearim Brazil
24 E1 Vitoria-Gasteiz Spain
21 D5 Vitré France
21 G5 Vitry-le-François France
12 D4 Vitsyebsk Belarus
21 G2 Vittangi Sweden
27 D7 Vittoria Italy
26 D3 Vittorio Veneto Italy
150 D3 Vityaz Depth depth Pac. Oc.
26 B3 Vivaro, Monts du mt. ra. France
25 F3 Viveiro Spain
96 D4 Vivonne B. b. Aust.
15 F3 Viwa i. Fiji
130 B3 Vizcaíno, Desierto de desert Mexico

Column 3

60 A1 Vize Turkey
12 J1 Vizhas r. Rus. Fed.
12 J1 Vizhas Rus. Fed.
56 C2 Vizianagaram India
15 D2 Vizinga r. Rus. Fed.
12 J2 Vizinga Rus. Fed.
18 B3 Vlaardingen Netherlands
28 E1 Vlădeni Romania
28 C3 Vlădicin Han Yugo.
13 H7 Vladikavkaz Rus. Fed.
14 E1 Vladimir Rus. Fed.
12 G4 Vladimir div. Rus. Fed.
14 A2 Vladimirsky Tupik Rus. Fed.
12 G4 Vladimirskoye Rus. Fed.
49 J4 Vladivostok Rus. Fed.
15 G1 Vladyslavivka Ukraine
15 D2 Vladychnoye Rus. Fed.
28 C2 Vlăhița Romania
26 G3 Vlasenica Bos.-Herz.
28 B2 Vlašić Planina mts Yugo.
19 F4 Vlašim Czech Rep.
15 E2 Vlasivka Ukraine
14 D1 Vlasovo Rus. Fed.
18 D2 Vlieland i. Netherlands
18 C3 Vlissingen Netherlands
29 B4 Vlorë Albania
19 G4 Vltava r. Czech Rep.
26 E4 Vöcklabruck Austria
26 E4 Vodice Croatia
12 F2 Vodlozero, Ozero l. Rus. Fed.
14 F2 Vodňany Czech Rep.
19 G4 Vodní nádrž Lipno l. Czech Rep.
21 H2 Vôge, la reg. France
26 B3 Voghera Italy
90 □ Voh Pac. Oc.
83 H3 Vohilava Madagascar
83 H3 Vohimena, Tanjona c. Madagascar
83 H3 Vohipeno Madagascar
83 H3 Vohitrandriana Madagascar
11 G4 Võhma Estonia
15 E2 Voi r. Kenya
79 D5 Voi Kenya
76 C5 Voinjama Liberia
21 G4 Voiron France
11 D5 Vojens Denmark
26 F3 Vojnik mt. Slovenia
82 B2 Voko Cameroon
12 F3 Vokhtoga Rus. Fed.
81 A5 Volcanoes National Park nat. park Uganda
65 H5 Volchikha Rus. Fed.
12 H5 Volda Norway
12 H5 Volga r. Rus. Fed.
12 H5 Volga r. U.S.A.
13 G6 Vol'ginskiy Rus. Fed.
13 G5 Volgodonsk Rus. Fed.
13 H5 Volgograd Rus. Fed.
13 H5 Volgograd. Rus. Fed.
15 D1 Volintiri Moldova
27 B5 Völkermarkt Austria
12 D3 Völklingen Germany
12 E3 Volkhov r. Rus. Fed.
82 B5 Vredendal R.S.A.
12 E3 Volkhov Rus. Fed.
86 B2 Völklingen Germany
49 J4 Vol'no-Nadezhdinskoye Rus. Fed.
63 L2 Volochanka Rus. Fed.
15 C2 Volochys'k Ukraine
15 D2 Volodarka Ukraine
15 E2 Volodars'ke Ukraine
15 J6 Volodars'koye Kazak.
15 C1 Volodars'k-Volyns'kyy Ukraine
15 E1 Volodymyrets' Ukraine
15 B1 Volodymyr-Volyns'kyy Ukraine
12 F2 Vologda div. Rus. Fed.
12 F3 Vologda Rus. Fed.
28 E1 Voloka Ukraine
14 E3 Volokolamsk Rus. Fed.
15 E1 Volokonovka Rus. Fed.
29 D5 Volos Greece
12 D2 Volosovo Rus. Fed.
14 D4 Volot Rus. Fed.
14 F3 Volovo Rus. Fed.
13 J6 Vol'sk Rus. Fed.
76 D4 Volta r. Ghana
76 D5 Volta r. Ghana
122 E4 Volta, Lake l. Ghana
76 D4 Volta Redonda Brazil
145 H5 Volta Redonda Brazil
27 D6 Volterra Italy
27 E6 Volturno r. Italy
29 D4 Voluntari Romania
29 D4 Volvi, L. l. Greece
81 B6 Vowa Tanzania
15 D1 Volyn' div. Ukraine
15 F1 Volynka Ukraine
13 G5 Volzhskiy Rus. Fed.
15 F2 Volytsya Ukraine
12 H4 Volzhsk Rus. Fed.
83 H3 Vomo Madagascar
65 B5 Vondrozo Madagascar
29 D5 Vonitsa Greece
10 □ Vop' r. Rus. Fed.
10 M2 Vopnafjördur Iceland
10 M2 Vopnafjördur b. Iceland
11 H3 Võra Finland
12 □ Voranava Belarus
12 J2 Vorchegda r. Rus. Fed.
29 C5 Voreioi Sporades is Greece
12 C4 Voreiоs Evvoïkos Kolpos chan. Greece
14 G3 Vorga Rus. Fed.
11 F4 Vormsi i. Estonia
19 L4 Vorob'yevka Rus. Fed.
14 F4 Vorona r. Rus. Fed.
14 F4 Voronezh r. Rus. Fed.
13 F5 Voronezh Rus. Fed.
15 D2 Voronizh Ukraine
12 J2 Voronov, Mys pt Rus. Fed.
14 F3 Voronovo Rus. Fed.
12 D4 Voronovytsya Ukraine
14 D2 Vorot'kovo Rus. Fed.
14 F4 Vorozhba Ukraine
14 □ Vorskla r. Ukraine
14 E4 Vorsma Rus. Fed.
11 G4 Vörtsjärv l. Estonia
11 G4 Võru Estonia
65 H5 Vorya r. Rus. Fed.
65 G5 Vose Tajikistan

Column 4 / W

64 E4 Vostochnyy Chink Ustyurta escarpment Uzbekistan
44 G1 Vostochnyy Sayan mt. Kazak.
87 M6 Vostok Island i. Kiribati
19 G4 Votice Czech Rep.
93 □ Voti Voti Pt pt Fiji
62 G4 Votkinsk Rus. Fed.
14 A2 Votrya r. Rus. Fed.
90 □ Vot Tandé i. Vanuatu
144 D4 Votuporanga Brazil
24 B2 Vouga r. Portugal
20 E3 Vouillé Poitou-Charentes France
21 G2 Vouziers France
21 G1 Voves France
15 G1 Vovcha r. Ukraine
15 G1 Vovchans'k Ukraine
20 E2 Voves France
15 D2 Vovkovyntsi Ukraine
118 A1 Voyageur's Nat. Park nat. park U.S.A.
10 H2 Voynitsa Rus. Fed.
12 H2 Voyvozh Rus. Fed.
12 J3 Vozhayel' Rus. Fed.
12 J3 Vozhega Rus. Fed.
12 J1 Vozhgaly Rus. Fed.
12 J1 Vozhgory Rus. Fed.
15 D3 Voznesens'k Ukraine
15 D3 Voznesens'ke Ukraine
14 F2 Voznesenskoye Rus. Fed.
15 E2 Voznsen'ye Rus. Fed.
12 E2 Voznsen'ye Rus. Fed.
73 E5 Vozrozdeniye Uzbekistan
64 E4 Vozrozhdeniya, O. i. Uzbekistan
64 F5 Vozvyshennost' Karabil' h. Turkmenistan
14 G2 Vozvyshennost' Mezhdyan'ye h. Rus. Fed.
49 J2 Vozzhayevka Rus. Fed.
28 C3 Vranica mt. Bos.-Herz.
28 D3 Vranje Yugo.
19 K4 Vranov nad Toplou Slovakia
28 D3 Vrapčiste Macedonia
28 F2 Vratsa Bulgaria
26 F3 Vrbanja r. Bos.-Herz.
26 F3 Vrbas r. Bos.-Herz.
28 B2 Vrbas Yugo.
26 F3 Vrbovsko Croatia
19 H3 Vrchlabí Czech Rep.
82 B5 Vredefort R.S.A.
82 B5 Vredenburg R.S.A.
82 B5 Vredendal R.S.A.
18 E4 Vresse Belgium
56 B4 Vriddhachalam India
11 D4 Vrigstad Sweden
26 F4 Vrnjačka Banja Yugo.
18 D3 Vroomshoop Netherlands
82 C4 Vryburg R.S.A.
83 E4 Vryheid R.S.A.
19 H4 Vsetín Czech Rep.
14 D2 Vsevolozhsk Rus. Fed.
63 S3 Vstrechnyy Rus. Fed.
61 D4 Vtoraya Levyye Lamki Rus. Fed.
93 □ Vuagava i. Fiji
28 C3 Vučitrn Yugo.
28 D3 Vuhledar Ukraine
29 G4 Vukovar Croatia
28 D2 Vulcan Romania
27 E5 Vulcano, Isola i. Italy
28 D3 Vulchedrūm Bulgaria
129 F5 Vulture Mts mts U.S.A.
90 □ Vuna Pt pt Fiji
43 D5 Vung Tau Vietnam
82 D3 Vungu r. Zimbabwe
90 □ Vunidawa Fiji
15 D1 Vunisea Fiji
15 D2 Vuohijärvi Finland
10 G2 Vuojoki Finland
90 □ Vuollerim Sweden
10 G2 Vuostimo Finland
14 F2 Vurnary Rus. Fed.
28 F1 Vurzeni Romania
15 D2 Vuzlove L'viv Ukraine
15 F1 Vvedenno'ye Rus. Fed.
10 □ Vwawa Tanzania
81 B6 Vwawa Tanzania
12 □ Vyatka r. Rus. Fed.
12 □ Vyatskiye Polyany Rus. Fed.
49 □ Vyazemskiy Rus. Fed.
14 F3 Vyaz'ma Rus. Fed.
14 F2 Vyazniki Rus. Fed.
14 F4 Vyazovka Rus. Fed.
14 F2 Vyazyma Rus. Fed.
14 D2 Vyborg Rus. Fed.
12 J2 Vychegda r. Rus. Fed.
12 J2 Vychegodskiy Rus. Fed.
19 J4 Východočeský div. Czech Rep.
14 D3 Vydrino Rus. Fed.
12 C4 Vyerkhnyadzvinsk Belarus
14 B3 Vygonichi Rus. Fed.
12 □ Vygozero, Ozero l. Rus. Fed.
14 F2 Vyksa Rus. Fed.
14 E1 Vyl'gort Rus. Fed.
14 □ Vym' r. Rus. Fed.
12 F2 Vynnytsi Ukraine
15 D2 Vynohradiv Ukraine
15 C2 Vynohradove Ukraine
15 F2 Vypolzovo Rus. Fed.
12 E3 Vyritsa Rus. Fed.
14 D2 Vyselki Rus. Fed.
14 □ Vysha r. Rus. Fed.
14 □ Vyshcha Dubechnya Ukraine
15 □ Vyshhorod Ukraine
15 □ Vyshkovo Rus. Fed.
14 □ Vyshneve Dnipropetrovs'k Ukraine
127 □ Vyshnevolots'ka Gryada ridge Rus. Fed.
14 E2 Vyshniy-Ol'shanoye Rus. Fed.
14 E2 Vyshniy Volochek Rus. Fed.
19 H4 Vyškov Czech Rep.
15 □ Vysoka Pich Ukraine
19 H4 Vysoké Mýto Czech Rep.
14 G5 Vysokovsk Rus. Fed.
139 F2 Vysokoye Rus. Fed.
90 □ Vysoye Rus. Fed.
15 B1 Vystavka Rus. Fed.
63 F2 Vytegra Rus. Fed.
63 □ Vyzhnytsya Ukraine

W

76 D4 Wa Ghana
80 D4 Waajid Somalia
80 B3 Waat Sudan
114 B1 Wababimiga Lake l. Can.
112 B3 Wabakimi L. l. Can.
112 B2 Wabasca r. Can.
118 A1 Wabasca Can.
110 D3 Wabasca r. Can.
118 C4 Wabash r. U.S.A.
122 E5 Wabash U.S.A.
122 A3 Wabasha U.S.A.
114 C2 Wabatongushi Lake l. Can.
80 D4 Wabē Gestro r. Ethiopia
80 D3 Wabē Shebelê Wenz r. Ethiopia
111 K4 Wabowden Can.
114 C2 Wabuk Pt pt Can.
112 C2 Wabush r. Can.
113 G3 Wabush Can.
113 G3 Wabush L. l. Can.
128 C2 Wabuska U.S.A.
119 D6 Waccasassa Bay b. U.S.A.
125 D6 Waco U.S.A.
54 A4 Wad Pakistan
73 E5 Wad Banda Sudan
72 C2 Waddān Libya
72 C2 Waddān, Jabal al h. Libya
18 B2 Waddenzee chan. Netherlands
110 D4 Waddington, Mt mt. Can.
17 E6 Wadebridge U.K.
11 J4 Wadena Can.
124 E2 Wadena U.S.A.
61 D4 Wad en Nail Sudan
56 A2 Wadgaon India
73 F4 Wad Hamid Sudan
72 D5 Wādī Abū Hamra w Sudan
54 C1 Wādī al Bāṭin w Asia
72 D1 Wādī al Fārigh w Libya
73 D1 Wādī al Ḥamīm w Libya
73 E4 Wādī 'Amur w Sudan
72 B2 Wādī 'Araba w Jordan
72 C2 Wādī al Ghalla w Sudan
72 B2 Wādī el Ku w Sudan
72 A2 Wādī el Milk w Sudan
61 D4 Wādī el Rīl w Sudan
72 B2 Wādī Feirān Egypt
78 D1 Wādī Gandi w Sudan
61 D4 Wādī Hadraj w Saudi Arabia
73 F4 Wādī Hodein w Egypt
73 F4 Wādī Ibra w Sudan
73 F4 Wādī Magrur w Sudan
73 F4 Wādī Mugarih w Sudan
73 F4 Wādī Muheit w Sudan
78 D1 Wādī Mūsā w Sudan
78 D1 Wadi Oko w Sudan
72 E5 Wadi Shaqq el Giefer w Sudan
73 F4 Wadi Umm Saggat w Sudan
72 E5 Wādī Zamzam w Libya
72 D2 Wād Medani Sudan
90 □ Wadjana Aust.
127 □ Wadsworth U.S.A.
78 □ Wafra Kuwait
47 H4 Waga-gawa r. Japan
93 □ Wagait Abor. Land res. Aust.
101 F4 Wagin Aust.
98 □ Wagner U.S.A.
97 B3 Wagga Wagga Aust.
101 A7 Wagin Aust.
11 □ Wägrowiec Poland
80 □ Wah Pakistan
127 B7 Wahiawa U.S.A.
127 □ Wahoo U.S.A.
124 D2 Wahpeton U.S.A.
56 A2 Wai India
127 B7 Waialee U.S.A.
127 B7 Waialua U.S.A.
127 □ Waialua Bay b. U.S.A.
127 □ Waianae Ra. mt. ra. U.S.A.
93 □ Waiau r. N.Z.
93 B6 Waiau r. N.Z.
93 D5 Waiau N.Z.
92 E3 Waiau r. N.Z.
93 A6 Waiau r. N.Z.
92 E3 Waihi N.Z.
92 F4 Waikanae N.Z.
92 E2 Waikare, L. l. N.Z.
92 E1 Waikaremoana, L. l. N.Z.
92 E2 Waikato div. N.Z.
92 E2 Waikato r. N.Z.
97 F2 Waikawa Pt pt N.Z.
127 □ Waikiki Beach beach U.S.A.
90 □ Waikouaiti N.Z.
93 □ Wailagi Lala i. Fiji
91 □ Wailuku U.S.A.
127 □ Waimakariri r. N.Z.
96 B2 Waimana N.Z.
92 F3 Waimangaroa N.Z.
40 □ Waimanguar i. Indon.
92 E3 Waimarama N.Z.
92 C7 Waimate N.Z.
127 □ Waimea U.S.A.
92 F3 Waimea N.Z.
54 □ Wainganga r. India
92 E1 Waingapu Indon.
127 □ Wainunu B. b. Fiji
108 C2 Wainwright U.S.A.

15 C1 Vystupovychi Ukraine
12 F2 Vytegra Rus. Fed.
63 S3 Vyvenka Rus. Fed.
14 F2 Vyyezdnoye Rus. Fed.
15 A2 Vyzhnytsya Ukraine
127 B7 Waipahu U.S.A.
92 E1 Waipaoa r. N.Z.
93 B7 Waipapa Pt pt N.Z.
92 D5 Waipara r. N.Z.
92 E3 Waipawa N.Z.
92 E1 Waipu N.Z.
92 E3 Waipukurau N.Z.
92 E3 Wairakei N.Z.
93 D4 Wairau r. N.Z.
92 F3 Wairoa r. N.Z.
92 E1 Wairoa r. N.Z.
92 F3 Wairoa N.Z.
92 E3 Waitahanui N.Z.
93 B6 Waitahuna N.Z.
92 E3 Waitakaruru N.Z.
92 C6 Waitaki r. N.Z.
92 E3 Waitara N.Z.
93 D1 Waitangi Chatham Is N.Z.
93 □ Waitara N.Z.
92 E2 Waitotara N.Z.
92 E2 Waiuku N.Z.
46 E7 Wajiki Japan
47 F5 Wajima Japan
80 D3 Wajir Kenya
78 D3 Wakasa Équateur Zaire
78 D3 Wakasa Japan
47 E6 Wakasa Japan
47 E6 Wakasa-wan b. Japan
93 B6 Wakatipu, Lake l. N.Z.
111 H4 Wakaw Can.
47 E6 Wakayama div. Japan
47 E6 Wakayama Japan
124 D4 Wa Keeney U.S.A.
115 H4 Wakefield Can.
93 C4 Wakefield Jamaica
124 E2 Wakefield U.S.A.
17 G5 Wakefield U.K.
122 C5 Wakefield U.S.A.
89 □ Wake Island i. Pac. Oc.
46 H3 Wakkanai Japan
83 E4 Wakkerstroom R.S.A.
97 F3 Wakool r. Aust.
97 F3 Wakool Aust.
113 G3 Wakuach, Lac l. Can.
79 C6 Waku-Kungo Angola
81 B6 Wala r. Tanzania
92 H2 Walbrzych Poland
111 H4 Walcz Poland
18 B3 Walcheren reg. Neth.
121 K1 Waldboro U.S.A.
121 G3 Walden U.S.A.
121 F4 Walden Montgomery U.S.A.
18 F3 Waldkraiburg Germany
18 E5 Waldorf U.S.A.
18 D5 Waldshut Germany
18 D5 Walenstadt Switz.
54 B3 Walgett Aust.
152 A3 Walgreen Coast Ant.
78 D3 Walikale Zaire
124 E2 Walker r. U.S.A.
126 C2 Walker r. U.S.A.
119 □ Walker Cay i. Bahamas
152 A3 Walker Mts mt. ra. Ant.
124 E2 Walker Pass pass U.S.A.
114 C2 Walkerton Can.
120 □ Wall U.S.A.
92 E2 Wallaby I. i. Aust.
99 □ Wallabi Group is Aust.
99 □ Wallangarra Aust.
99 □ Wallaroo Aust.
96 D3 Walla Walla Aust.
97 □ Walla Walla U.S.A.
128 C2 Wallaroo Aust.
18 E5 Walldorf Germany
109 M1 Wallingford U.S.A.
121 G4 Wallis and Futuna terr. Pac. Oc.
97 □ Wallis, Îles is Wallis & Futuna Pac. Oc.
97 □ Wallis L. l. Aust.
126 C2 Wallowa Mts mt. ra. U.S.A.
111 □ Walmsley Lake l. Can.
17 F5 Walney, Isle of i. U.K.
80 □ Walnut Canyon National Monument res. U.S.A.
101 □ Walnut Ridge U.S.A.
19 J3 Wałcz Poland
101 □ Walpole i. Pac. Oc.
101 □ Walpole-Nornalup Nat. Park nat. park Aust.
18 □ Walsenburg U.S.A.
99 □ Walsh r. Aust.
99 □ Walsh Aust.
18 □ Walsrode Germany
80 D4 Waltair India
93 □ Waltham U.S.A.
99 □ Waltham's Ra. h. Aust.
54 □ Waltham U.S.A.
121 □ Waltman U.S.A.
17 □ Walton-on-Thames U.K.
82 B3 Walvis Bay Namibia
84 □ Walvis Ridge Atlantic Ocean
81 B4 Wamala, L. l. Uganda
78 □ Wamba Équateur Zaire
78 □ Wamba Haute-Zaïre Zaire
79 □ Wamba r. Zaire
78 C4 Wamba Nigeria
124 □ Wamego U.S.A.
40 □ Wamena Indon.
40 □ Wamulan Indon.
92 □ Wan'an China
132 □ Wanaaring Aust.
93 □ Wanaka N.Z.
92 □ Wanaka, L. l. N.Z.
114 □ Wanapitei Lake l. Can.
121 □ Wanaque Reservoir resr U.S.A.
96 □ Wanbi Aust.
121 □ Wanbrow, Cape c. N.Z.
49 □ Wanda Shan mt. ra. China
40 □ Wandel S. sea Greenland
18 □ Wanderer Germany
18 □ Wandlitz Germany
80 □ Wando S. Korea
40 □ Wandoan Aust.
111 □ Wanganui N.Z.
92 □ Wanganui r. N.Z.
92 □ Wangaratta Aust.
49 □ Wangcang China
50 □ Wangdu China
55 □ Wangdu-Phodrang Bhutan
18 □ Wangerooge i. Germany
18 □ Wangerooge Germany

40 E4 Wanggamet, G. mt. Indon.
51 G4 Wanghai Shan h. China
51 G2 Wangjiang China
49 H3 Wangkui China
52 D1 Wangmao China
50 D3 Wangmo China
49 J4 Wangqing China
52 D1 Wangziguan China
78 E3 Wanie-Rukula Zaire
54 B5 Wankaner India
80 □ Wanlaweyn Somalia
101 A6 Wanneroo Aust.
49 E4 Wanning China
51 G2 Wannian China
49 E4 Wanquan China
133 □ Wanstead Trin.& Tobago
114 C3 Wanstead China
52 B4 Wan Xian China
52 D1 Wanxian China
92 E1 Wanyuan China
51 F2 Wanzai China
80 D4 Wapakoneta U.S.A.
112 C3 Wapello U.S.A.
110 C4 Wapiti r. Can.
122 E5 Wappapello, L. l. U.S.A.
122 A5 Wappingers Falls U.S.A.
50 C1 Waqên China
80 D4 Warabeye Somalia
80 D3 Warandab Ethiopia
56 B2 Warangal India
97 F4 Waranga Reservoir resr Aust.
54 E5 Warasaoni India
111 A6 Waratah Aust.
18 B3 Warburg Germany
96 D1 Warburton r. Aust.
96 □ Warburton Aust.
101 J2 Warburton Aust.
81 D4 Wardeglo waterhole Kenya
56 B1 Wardha r. India
56 B1 Wardha India
93 D5 Ward, Mt mt. N.Z.
114 E3 Ware Can.
121 G3 Ware U.S.A.
18 F2 Waren Germany
18 F2 Warendorf Germany
121 H3 Warminster U.S.A.
98 B3 Wave Hill Aust.
81 □ Warmbad Namibia
18 F2 Warminster U.K.
121 F4 Warminster U.S.A.
121 K1 Warner Springs U.S.A.
126 B3 Warner Robins U.S.A.
141 D3 Warnes Bolivia
101 □ Warning, Mt mt. Aust.
18 □ Warnemünde Germany
92 E3 Waroona Aust.
101 A5 Warora India
114 C2 Warracknabeal Aust.
111 J4 Warragul Aust.
98 D1 Warrandirrnna, L. salt flat Aust.
100 C4 Warrawagine Aust.
97 F2 Warrego r. Aust.
119 □ Warren Bolivia
121 K1 Warren U.S.A.
120 □ Warren Ohio U.S.A.
121 □ Warren Pennsylvania U.S.A.
17 □ Warrenpoint U.K.
122 □ Warrensburg U.S.A.
82 C4 Warrenton R.S.A.
120 □ Warrenton U.S.A.
76 D5 Warri Nigeria
101 □ Warrnambool Aust.
99 □ Warroad U.S.A.
17 □ Warrnambool Aust.
121 □ Warsaw U.S.A.
19 □ Warsaw Poland
19 □ Warszawa Poland
19 □ Warta r. Poland
19 □ Warthe r. Poland
18 □ Warud India
121 □ Warwick U.S.A.
17 □ Warwick U.K.
99 □ Warwick Aust.
122 □ Warwick U.S.A.
93 □ Wasatch Range mt. ra. U.S.A.
54 □ Wasbank R.S.A.
128 C2 Washap Pakistan
127 B7 Washburn U.S.A.
54 □ Washburn U.S.A.
54 C5 Washim India
120 □ Washington U.S.A.
121 □ Washington U.S.A.
119 □ Washington Island i. U.S.A.
40 □ Washington Court House U.S.A.
96 □ Waspán Nicaragua

128 C2 Wassuk Range mts U.S.A.
115 H2 Waswanipi Can.
115 G2 Waswanipi, Lac l. Can.
40 D3 Watampone Indon.
40 D3 Watansoppeng Indon.
121 H2 Waterbury U.S.A.
112 C2 Waterbury Lake l. Can.
117 D5 Waterford Rep. of Ire.
120 D4 Waterford U.S.A.
111 H4 Waterhen r. Can.
98 B3 Waterhouse Ra. Aust.
113 J4 Waterloo Can.
115 G2 Waterloo Can.
54 B5 Waterloo Sierra Leone
49 E4 Waterloo U.S.A.
133 □ Waterloo Trin.& Tobago
121 H3 Waterloo U.S.A.
121 □ Waterton Lakes Nat. Park nat. park U.S.A.
124 C4 Watertown U.S.A.
121 □ Watertown U.S.A.
121 □ Watertown U.S.A.
114 □ Watervale Aust.
121 J2 Waterville U.S.A.
124 □ Watford City U.S.A.
101 □ Watheroo Aust.
61 □ Watir, W. w Egypt
115 □ Watrous Can.
80 □ Watsa Zaire
122 D4 Watsi Kengo Zaire
18 □ Watsonville U.S.A.
110 □ Watson Lake Can.
128 □ Watsonville U.S.A.
111 □ Watson Lake l. Can.
90 □ Watt, Mt h. Can.
73 □ Watubela, Kepulauan is Indon.
90 □ Wau P.N.G.
78 □ Wau Sudan
110 □ Wauchope Aust.
97 □ Wauchope N.Z.
40 □ Waukara, G. mt. Indon.
100 C4 Waukarlycarly, L. salt flat Aust.
124 □ Waukegan U.S.A.
122 □ Waukesha U.S.A.
76 □ Waunch Shet' r. Ethiopia
80 □ Waupaca U.S.A.
125 □ Waupun U.S.A.
122 □ Wausau U.S.A.
80 □ Wautoma U.S.A.
122 □ Wauwatosa U.S.A.
114 □ Waveney r. U.K.
98 □ Waverley N.Z.
121 □ Waverly U.S.A.
119 □ Waverly U.S.A.
122 □ Wawa Can.
72 □ Wâw an Nāmūs crater Libya
72 □ Wāwa Nigeria
128 □ Waxahachie U.S.A.
90 □ Waya i. Fiji
98 □ Waya Lailai i. Fiji
119 □ Waycross U.S.A.
124 □ Wayland U.S.A.
122 □ Wayne U.S.A.
124 □ Waynesboro U.S.A.
120 □ Waynesboro U.S.A.
120 □ Waynesboro U.S.A.
120 □ Waynesville U.S.A.
124 □ Waynesville U.S.A.
124 □ Waynoka U.S.A.
54 □ Wazirabad Pakistan
77 □ W du Niger, Parcs Nationaux du nat. park Niger
74 □ Waza Cameroon
78 □ Waza Zaire
121 □ Wazzan Morocco
57 □ Wazi Khwa Afghanistan
115 □ Weslemkoon Lake l. Can.
113 □ Wesley U.S.A.
113 □ Wessel, C. c. Aust.
98 □ Wessel Is is Aust.

19 J1 Wejherowo Poland
111 K4 Wekusko Can.
111 K4 Wekusko Lake l. Can.
42 B1 Welatam Myanmar
96 C1 Welbourn Hill Aust.
120 C6 Welch U.S.A.
121 H2 Weld U.S.A.
80 C2 Weldiya Ethiopia
128 C4 Weldon U.S.A.
82 D4 Welkom R.S.A.
114 □ Welk'īt'ē Ethiopia
115 □ Welland Can.
114 □ Welland Canal Can.
115 □ Welland U.S.A.
56 □ Wellawaya Sri Lanka
114 □ Wellesley Is is Aust.
121 □ Wellfleet U.S.A.
147 B6 Wellington, Isla i. Chile
114 □ Wellington, L. l. Aust.
122 □ Wellman U.S.A.
10 E4 Wells U.K.
17 F6 Wells U.K.
116 □ Wells U.S.A.
128 □ Wells U.S.A.
124 □ Wellsboro U.S.A.
129 □ Wells Gray Prov. Park res. Can.
101 □ Wells, L. salt flat Aust.
129 □ Wells-next-the-Sea U.K.
128 □ Wellton U.S.A.
19 G4 Welse r. Germany
111 □ Welshpool Can.
17 □ Welshpool U.K.
78 □ Wema Zaire
81 □ Wembere r. Tanzania
78 □ Wembley Can.
101 □ Wemel Shet' r. Ethiopia
112 □ Wemindji Can.
119 □ Wemyss Bight The Bahamas
51 □ Weng'an China
51 □ Wengyuan China
51 □ Wenlin China
51 □ Wenling China
138 □ Wenman, I. i. Galápagos Is Ecuador
122 □ Wenona U.S.A.
50 □ Wenquan China
51 □ Wenquanzhen China
51 □ Wenshan China
48 □ Wenshui China
122 □ Wensu China
21 □ Wentworth U.S.A.
121 □ Wentworth Aust.
121 □ Wentworth U.S.A.
121 □ Wenxi China
50 □ Wen Xian China
48 □ Wenyu r. China
51 □ Wenzhou China
51 □ Wenzhou China
80 □ Werda Botswana
80 □ Werdër Ethiopia
18 □ Wernberg-Köblitz Germany
110 □ Wernecke Mountains Can.
40 □ Werota Ethiopia
18 □ Werribee Aust.
18 □ Werrikee Aust.
101 □ Werris Creek Aust.
18 □ Wertheim Germany
18 □ Wesendorf Germany
18 □ Weser r. Germany
18 □ Wessegberge h. Germany
115 □ Weslemkoon Lake l. Can.
113 □ Wesley U.S.A.
113 □ Wessel, C. c. Aust.

19 J1 Wejherowo Poland
111 K4 Wekusko Can.
96 C1 Welbourn Hill Aust.
120 C6 Welch U.S.A.
121 H2 Weld U.S.A.
80 C2 Weldiya Ethiopia
82 D4 Welkom R.S.A.
55 □ Wellawaya Sri Lanka
114 □ Wellesley Is is Aust.
121 H4 Wellfleet U.S.A.
19 J1 Wellingborough U.K.
93 E4 Wellington div. N.Z.
82 B5 Wellington R.S.A.
17 F6 Wellington U.K.
128 □ Wellington U.S.A.
124 □ Wellington U.S.A.
122 □ Wellington U.S.A.
121 J1 Wellsville U.S.A.
147 B6 Wellington, Isla i. Chile
114 □ Wellington, L. l. Aust.
122 □ Wellman U.S.A.
10 E4 Wells U.K.
17 F6 Wells U.K.
116 □ Wells U.S.A.
128 □ Wells U.S.A.
124 □ Wellsboro U.S.A.
129 □ Wells Gray Prov. Park res. Can.
101 □ Wells, L. salt flat Aust.
129 □ Wells-next-the-Sea U.K.
128 □ Wellton U.S.A.
19 G4 Welse r. Germany
111 □ Welshpool Can.
17 □ Welshpool U.K.
78 □ Wema Zaire
81 □ Wembere r. Tanzania
78 □ Wembley Can.
80 □ Wemel Shet' r. Ethiopia
112 □ Wemindji Can.
119 □ Wemyss Bight The Bahamas
51 G1 Weng'an China
51 □ Wengyuan China
76 B4 Wéndou Mbôrou Guinea
51 □ Wenling China
81 B5 Wembere r. Tanzania
78 □ Wembley Can.
138 □ Wenman, I. i. Galápagos Is Ecuador
122 A6 Wenona U.S.A.
50 □ Wenquan China
51 □ Wenquanzhen China
51 □ Wenshan China
48 □ Wenshui China
122 □ Wensu China
48 D5 Wenyu r. China
51 □ Wenzhou China
80 □ Werda Botswana
80 □ Werdër Ethiopia
18 □ Wernberg-Köblitz Germany
110 □ Wernecke Mountains Can.
18 □ Werribee Aust.
101 □ Werris Creek Aust.
18 □ Wertheim Germany
18 □ Wesendorf Germany
18 □ Weser r. Germany
149 L5 West Australian Basin Indian Ocean
149 L6 West Australian Ridge Indian Ocean
98 □ West Baines r. Aust.
74 □ West Banas r. Asia
113 J3 West Bay U.S.A.
125 □ West Bay b. U.S.A.
125 □ West Bend U.S.A.
55 □ West Bengal India
123 □ West Branch U.S.A.
17 G5 West Bromwich U.K.
123 □ West Branch Susquehanna r. U.S.A.
120 □ Westbrook U.S.A.
121 □ Westby U.S.A.
99 □ West C. c. N.Z.
93 □ West Cape Howe c. Aust.
101 □ West Chester U.S.A.
18 □ West Coast div. N.Z.
93 □ West End Grand Bahama I. The Bahamas
119 □ West End pt The Bahamas
133 □ Westerhall Grenada Caribbean
18 □ Westerland Germany
121 □ Western div. Aust.
91 □ Western div. P.N.G.
76 □ Western r. Aust.
71 □ Western div. Zambia
82 □ Western Australia div. Aust.
101 □ Western Cape div. R.S.A.
51 □ Western Chain is Snares Is N.Z.
73 □ Western Desert desert Egypt
54 □ Western Ghats mt. ra. India
93 □ Western Group is Bounty Is N.Z.
51 □ Western Port b. Aust.
68 □ Western Reef reef Africa
149 □ Western Samoa country Pac. Oc.
18 □ Westerstede Germany

18 C3 **Westerwald reg.** Germany
147 D7 **West Falkland i.** Falkland Is.
124 D2 **West Fargo** U.S.A.
122 D5 **Westfield** U.S.A.
121 K1 **Westfield** U.S.A.
121 G3 **Westfield** U.S.A.
120 D3 **Westfield** U.S.A.
99 F5 **Westgate** Aust.
121 K2 **West Grand Lake l.** U.S.A.
16 F3 **Westhill** U.K.
124 C1 **Westhope** U.S.A.
98 D2 **West I. i.** Aust.
94 □1 **West I. i.** *Cocos Is* Indian Ocean
152 D5 **West Ice Shelf ice feature** Ant.
45 □ **West Lamma Chan. chan.** Hong Kong
120 B5 **West Lancaster** U.S.A.
99 E4 **Westland** Aust.
93 C5 **Westland National Park nat. park** N.Z.
128 B3 **Westley** U.S.A.
120 B6 **West Liberty** U.S.A.
120 B4 **West Liberty** U.S.A.
110 G4 **Westlock** Can.
114 E5 **West Lorne** Can.
79 D6 **West Lunga r.** Zambia
79 D6 **West Lunga National Park nat. park** Zambia
125 F5 **West Memphis** U.S.A.
120 E5 **Westminster** U.S.A.
119 D5 **Westminster** U.S.A.
98 D3 **Westmoreland** Aust.
133 □1 **Westmorland div.** Jamaica
83 D3 **West Nicholson** Zimbabwe
120 C5 **Weston** U.S.A.
17 F6 **Weston-super-Mare** U.K.
121 F5 **Westover** U.S.A.
119 D7 **West Palm Beach** U.S.A.
125 F4 **West Plains** U.S.A.
96 C3 **West Point pt** Aust.
97 F5 **West Point pt** Aust.
125 F5 **West Point** U.S.A.
121 F4 **West Point** U.S.A.
115 G4 **Westport** Can.
93 C4 **Westport** N.Z.
17 C5 **Westport** Rep. of Ire.
128 A2 **Westport** U.S.A.
132 □2 **Westpunt** *Curaçao* Netherlands Ant.
111 J4 **Westray** Can.
16 F2 **Westray i.** U.K.
114 E3 **Westree** Can.
110 E4 **West Road r.** Can.
97 F4 **West Sister I. i.** Aust.
121 H2 **West Stewartstown** U.S.A.
18 B2 **West-Terschelling** Netherlands
121 H4 **West Tisbury** U.S.A.
122 D2 **West Topsham** U.S.A.
121 G2 **West Townshend** U.S.A.
122 B4 **West Union** U.S.A.
120 B5 **West Union** U.S.A.
120 D5 **West Union** U.S.A.
122 D5 **Westville** U.S.A.
120 C5 **West Virginia div.** U.S.A.
18 A3 **West-Vlaanderen div.** Belgium
128 C2 **West Walker r.** U.S.A.
99 G4 **Westwood** Aust.
128 B1 **Westwood** U.S.A.
97 F3 **West Wyalong** Aust.
126 E2 **West Yellowstone** U.S.A.
39 J8 **Wetar i.** Indon.
110 G4 **Wetaskiwin** Can.
81 C6 **Wete** Tanzania
122 D2 **Wetmore** U.S.A.
18 D3 **Wetzlar** Germany
90 □1 **Wewak** P.N.G.
17 D5 **Wexford** Rep. of Ire.
111 H4 **Weyakwin** Can.
122 C3 **Weyauwega** U.S.A.
111 J5 **Weyburn** Can.
19 G5 **Weyer Markt** Austria
18 D2 **Weyhe** Germany
17 F6 **Weymouth** U.K.
121 H3 **Weymouth** U.S.A.
92 F3 **Whakatane r.** N.Z.
92 F2 **Whakatane** N.Z.
43 B5 **Whale B. b.** Myanmar
110 B3 **Whale B. b.** U.S.A.
132 C1 **Whale Cay i.** The Bahamas
111 L2 **Whale Cove** Can.
97 G2 **Whallan Cr. r.** Aust.
16 G1 **Whalsay i.** U.K.
92 E3 **Whangaehu r.** N.Z.
92 E2 **Whangamata** N.Z.
92 E3 **Whangamomona** N.Z.
92 E2 **Whangaparaoa** N.Z.
92 G3 **Whangara** N.Z.
92 E1 **Whangarei** N.Z.
92 E1 **Whangaruru Harbour b.** N.Z.
112 E2 **Whapmagoostui** Can.
17 G5 **Wharfe r.** U.K.
114 D3 **Wharncliffe** Can.
111 J2 **Wharton Lake l.** Can.
93 C5 **Whataroa** N.Z.
122 A5 **What Cheer** U.S.A.
126 F3 **Wheatland** U.S.A.
122 C5 **Wheaton** U.S.A.
94 □4 **Wheatsheaf I. i.** *Lord Howe I.* Pac. Oc.
129 E2 **Wheeler Peak summit** U.S.A.
127 F4 **Wheeler Peak summit** U.S.A.
120 C4 **Wheeling** U.S.A.
17 F4 **Whernside h.** U.K.
96 C3 **Whidbey Pt pt** Aust.
96 B1 **Whitham, Mt mt.** Aust.
126 B3 **Whiskeytown-Shasta-Trinity Nat. Recreation Area res.** U.S.A.
115 F5 **Whitby** Can.
17 G4 **Whitby** U.K.
93 C5 **Whitcombe, Mt mt.** N.Z.
114 C2 **White r.** Can.
110 A2 **White r.** Can./U.S.A.
133 □1 **White r.** Jamaica
129 G5 **White r.** U.S.A.
125 E4 **White r.** U.S.A.
126 E3 **White r.** U.S.A.
118 C4 **White r.** U.S.A.
122 D4 **White r.** U.S.A.
129 E2 **White r.** U.S.A.
124 C3 **White r.** U.S.A.
122 B2 **White r.** U.S.A.
99 E4 **White, L. salt flat** Aust.
113 J3 **White Bay b.** Can.
124 C2 **White Butte mt.** U.S.A.
97 E2 **White Cliffs** Aust.
126 E2 **White Cloud** U.S.A.
110 F4 **Whitecourt** Can.
122 A2 **Whiteface Lake l.** U.S.A.
115 H4 **Whiteface Mt mt.** U.S.A.
121 H2 **Whitefield** U.S.A.
114 E3 **Whitefish** Can.
122 D3 **Whitefish r.** U.S.A.
126 D1 **Whitefish** U.S.A.
111 H2 **Whitefish Lake l.** Can.
112 C2 **Whitefish Pt pt** U.S.A.
121 G3 **Whitehall** U.S.A.
122 B3 **Whitehall** U.S.A.
17 F4 **Whitehaven** U.K.
110 B2 **Whitehorse** Can.
129 E1 **White Horse Pass pass** U.S.A.
133 □1 **White Horses** Jamaica
152 D4 **White I. i.** Ant.
92 F2 **White I. i.** N.Z.
98 B4 **White, L. salt flat** Aust.
125 E6 **White L. l.** U.S.A.
122 D4 **White L. l.** U.S.A.
114 C2 **White Lake l.** Can.
97 G5 **Whitemark** Aust.
121 H2 **White Mountains mt. ra.** U.S.A.
128 C3 **White Mt Peak summit** U.S.A.
73 F4 **White Nile Dam dam** Sudan
82 B3 **White Nossob w** Namibia
129 E2 **White Pine Range mts** U.S.A.
121 G4 **White Plains** U.S.A.
114 C2 **White River** Can.
129 H5 **Whiteriver** U.S.A.
121 G2 **White River Junction** U.S.A.
118 F3 **White River Junction** U.S.A.
129 E2 **White River Valley v.** U.S.A.
99 F3 **White Rock** Aust.
129 E2 **White Rock Peak summit** U.S.A.
127 F5 **White Sands Nat. Mon. res.** U.S.A.
120 B6 **Whitesburg** U.S.A.
111 K4 **Whiteshell Prov. Park res.** Can.
126 E2 **White Sulphur Springs** U.S.A.
120 C6 **White Sulphur Springs** U.S.A.
119 E5 **Whiteville** U.S.A.
76 D5 **White Volta r.** Ghana
122 C4 **Whitewater** U.S.A.
112 C3 **Whitewater L. l.** Can.
99 E4 **Whitewood** Aust.
111 J4 **Whitewood** Can.
17 E4 **Whithorn** U.K.
92 E2 **Whitianga** N.Z.
121 K2 **Whiting** U.S.A.
119 D5 **Whitmire** U.S.A.
115 F4 **Whitney** Can.
128 C3 **Whitney, Mt mt.** U.S.A.
121 K2 **Whitneyville** U.S.A.
99 G4 **Whitsunday I. i.** Aust.
99 G4 **Whitsundays, The is** Aust.
97 F3 **Whitton** Aust.
99 E5 **Whitula w** Aust.
111 H2 **Wholdaia Lake l.** Can.
129 F5 **Why** U.S.A.
96 D3 **Whyalla** Aust.
42 B2 **Wiang Phran** Thailand
42 C3 **Wiang Sa** Thailand
114 E4 **Wiarton** Can.
76 D4 **Wiasi** Ghana
76 D5 **Wiawso** Ghana
125 D4 **Wichita** U.S.A.
125 D5 **Wichita Falls** U.S.A.
125 D5 **Wichita Mts mts** U.S.A.
16 F2 **Wick** U.K.
129 F5 **Wickenburg** U.S.A.
101 B7 **Wickepin** Aust.
98 B3 **Wickham r.** Aust.
97 E4 **Wickham, C. c.** Aust.
98 B3 **Wickham, Mt h.** Aust.
17 D5 **Wicklow** Rep. of Ire.
17 E5 **Wicklow Head hd** Rep. of Ire.
17 D5 **Wicklow Mountains mts** Rep. of Ire.
19 J3 **Widawka r.** Poland
99 H5 **Wide B. b.** Aust.
99 F6 **Widgeegoara w** Aust.
101 C6 **Widgiemooltha** Aust.
49 H6 **Wi Do i.** S. Korea
19 H2 **Więcbork** Poland
18 C3 **Wiehl** Germany
19 H3 **Wielka Sowa mt.** Poland
19 J3 **Wieluń** Poland
19 H4 **Wien** Austria
19 H5 **Wiener Neustadt** Austria
19 L3 **Wieprz r.** Poland
18 B2 **Wieringermeer Polder reclaimed land** Netherlands
19 J3 **Wieruszów** Poland
18 D3 **Wiesbaden** Germany
18 D4 **Wiesloch** Germany
17 F5 **Wigan** U.K.
125 F6 **Wiggins** U.S.A.
17 G6 **Wight, Isle of i.** U.K.
111 H2 **Wignes Lake l.** Can.
17 E4 **Wigtown** U.K.
18 B3 **Wijchen** Netherlands
129 F4 **Wikieup** U.S.A.
80 C2 **Wik'ro** Ethiopia
114 E4 **Wikwemikong** Can.
19 J3 **Wil** Switz.
126 C2 **Wilbur** U.S.A.
97 E2 **Wilcannia** Aust.
111 J4 **Wildcat Hill Wilderness Area res.** Can.
128 D2 **Wildcat Peak summit** U.S.A.
83 D5 **Wild Coast** R.S.A.
114 A2 **Wild Goose** Can.
110 F4 **Wildhay r.** Can.
21 H3 **Wildhorn mt.** Switz.
19 G5 **Wildon** Austria
122 A2 **Wild Rice Lake l.** U.S.A.
97 F5 **Wild Rivers Nat. Park nat. park** Aust.
119 D6 **Wildwood** U.S.A.
121 F5 **Wildwood** U.S.A.
83 D4 **Wilge r.** R.S.A.
152 C5 **Wilhelm II Land reg.** Ant.
120 C4 **Wilhelm, Lake l.** U.S.A.
90 □1 **Wilhelm, Mt mt.** P.N.G.
18 D2 **Wilhelmshaven** Germany
133 □1 **Williamsfield** Jamaica
121 F4 **Wilkes-Barre** U.S.A.
152 B6 **Wilkes Coast** Ant.
152 B6 **Wilkes Land reg.** Ant.
111 H4 **Wilkie** Can.
152 B2 **Wilkins Coast** Ant.
152 B2 **Wilkins Ice Shelf ice feature** Ant.
96 C2 **Wilkinson Lakes salt flat** Aust.
126 B2 **Willamette r.** U.S.A.
97 F3 **Willandra Billabong w** Aust.
126 B1 **Willapa B. b.** U.S.A.
120 B4 **Willard** U.S.A.
127 F5 **Willards** U.S.A.
129 H5 **Willcox** U.S.A.
132 □2 **Willemstad** *Curaçao* Netherlands Ant.
98 B2 **Willeroo** Aust.
111 H3 **William r.** Can.
96 D2 **William Cr.** Aust.
97 E4 **William, Mt mt.** Aust.
99 E4 **Williams r.** Aust.
101 B7 **Williams** Aust.
129 F4 **Williams** U.S.A.
128 A2 **Williams** U.S.A.
122 A5 **Williamsburg** U.S.A.
120 A6 **Williamsburg** U.S.A.
122 E3 **Williamsburg** U.S.A.
120 E6 **Williamsburg** U.S.A.
132 C1 **Williams I. i.** The Bahamas
110 E4 **Williams Lake** Can.
113 H1 **William Smith, Cap c.** Can.
120 E3 **Williamson** U.S.A.
120 B6 **Williamson** U.S.A.
122 D5 **Williamsport** U.S.A.
120 E4 **Williamsport** U.S.A.
119 E5 **Williamston** U.S.A.
120 A5 **Williamstown** U.S.A.
121 G3 **Williamstown** U.S.A.
121 F3 **Williamstown** U.S.A.
120 C5 **Williamstown** U.S.A.
133 □7 **Willikie's** *Antigua* Caribbean
121 G4 **Willimantic** U.S.A.
93 □ **Willis Group atolls** *Coral Sea Islands Terr.* Pac. Oc.
82 C5 **Williston** R.S.A.
119 D6 **Williston** U.S.A.
124 C1 **Williston** U.S.A.
110 E3 **Williston Lake l.** Can.
128 A2 **Willits** U.S.A.
124 E2 **Willmar** U.S.A.
110 F4 **Willmore Wilderness Prov. Park res.** Can.
110 D3 **Will, Mt mt.** Can.
96 D2 **Willochra w** Aust.
110 E4 **Willow r.** Can.
111 H5 **Willow Bunch** Can.
120 E4 **Willow Hill** U.S.A.
110 F2 **Willow Lake l.** Can.
82 C5 **Willowmore** R.S.A.
98 C4 **Willowra** Aust.
98 C4 **Willowra Aboriginal Land Trust res.** Aust.
122 C3 **Willow Reservoir resr** U.S.A.
122 A2 **Willows** U.S.A.
125 F4 **Willow Springs** U.S.A.
121 G2 **Willsboro** U.S.A.
98 D4 **Wills Cr. w** Aust.
100 E4 **Wills, L. salt flat** Aust.
96 D3 **Wilmington** Aust.
96 D3 **Wilmington** Aust.
121 F5 **Wilmington** U.S.A.
119 E5 **Wilmington** U.S.A.
120 B5 **Wilmington** U.S.A.
121 G3 **Wilmington** U.S.A.
96 D2 **Wilpena w** Aust.
100 D3 **Wilson r.** Aust.
114 E4 **Wilson** U.S.A.
119 E5 **Wilson** U.S.A.
152 B5 **Wilson Hills h.** Ant.
127 F4 **Wilson, Mt mt.** U.S.A.
129 E2 **Wilson, Mt mt.** U.S.A.
124 D4 **Wilson Res. resr** U.S.A.
121 H2 **Wilsons Mills** U.S.A.
97 F4 **Wilson's Promontory pen.** Aust.
98 C2 **Wilton r.** Aust.
122 B5 **Wilton** U.S.A.
121 H2 **Wilton** U.S.A.
18 B4 **Wiltz** Luxembourg
101 C5 **Wiluna** Aust.
20 E1 **Wimereux** France
122 D5 **Winamac** U.S.A.
81 B5 **Winam G. b.** Kenya
17 F6 **Wincanton** U.K.
121 G3 **Winchendon** U.S.A.
115 H4 **Winchester** Can.
93 C6 **Winchester** N.Z.
17 G6 **Winchester** U.K.
122 B6 **Winchester** U.S.A.
122 E5 **Winchester** U.S.A.
120 A6 **Winchester** U.S.A.
121 G3 **Winchester** U.S.A.
119 C5 **Winchester** U.S.A.
120 D5 **Winchester** U.S.A.
126 E3 **Wind r.** U.S.A.
96 D2 **Windabout, L. salt flat** Aust.
124 C3 **Wind Cave Nat. Park nat. park.** U.S.A.
17 F4 **Windermere** U.K.
17 F4 **Windermere l.** U.K.
82 B3 **Windhoek** Namibia
19 G5 **Windischgarsten** Austria
124 E3 **Windom** U.S.A.
99 E5 **Windorah** Aust.
129 H4 **Window Rock** U.S.A.
122 D4 **Wind Pt pt** U.S.A.
126 E3 **Wind River Range mt. ra.** U.S.A.
97 G3 **Windsor** Aust.
113 J4 **Windsor** Can.
113 H5 **Windsor** Can.
114 D5 **Windsor** Can.
115 J4 **Windsor** Can.
17 G6 **Windsor** U.K.
121 G4 **Windsor** U.S.A.
119 E5 **Windsor** U.S.A.
121 F3 **Windsor** U.S.A.
121 G3 **Windsor** U.S.A.
120 E6 **Windsor** U.S.A.
132 D2 **Windsor, Lake l.** The Bahamas
121 G4 **Windsor Locks** U.S.A.
93 □3 **Windward Is is** *Antipodes Is* N.Z.
133 G4 **Windward Islands is** Caribbean
132 D3 **Windward Passage chan.** Cuba/Haiti
119 C5 **Winfield** U.S.A.
122 B5 **Winfield** U.S.A.
125 D4 **Winfield** U.S.A.
98 B2 **Wingate Mts h.** Aust.
97 G2 **Wingen** Aust.
97 H2 **Wingham** Aust.
114 E5 **Wingham** Can.
100 C4 **Winifred, L. salt flat** Aust.
112 C3 **Winisk** Can.
112 C2 **Winisk r.** Can.
112 C3 **Winisk L. l.** Can.
112 C3 **Winisk River Provincial Park res.** Can.
42 B4 **Winkana** Myanmar
111 K5 **Winkler** Can.
121 J2 **Winn** U.S.A.
76 D5 **Winneba** Ghana
122 C3 **Winnebago, Lake l.** U.S.A.
98 B3 **Winnecke Cr. w** Aust.
122 C3 **Winneconne** U.S.A.
126 C3 **Winnemucca** U.S.A.
128 C1 **Winnemucca Lake l.** U.S.A.
18 D4 **Winnenden** Germany
124 D3 **Winner** U.S.A.
125 E6 **Winnfield** U.S.A.
124 E2 **Winnibigoshish L. l.** U.S.A.
101 A4 **Winning** Aust.
111 K5 **Winnipeg** Can.
111 K4 **Winnipeg r.** Can.
111 K4 **Winnipeg, Lake l.** Can.
111 J4 **Winnipegosis** Can.
111 J4 **Winnipegosis, Lake l.** Can.
121 H3 **Winnipesaukee, L. l.** U.S.A.
125 F5 **Winnsboro** U.S.A.
129 G4 **Winona** U.S.A.
125 F5 **Winona** U.S.A.
122 B3 **Winona** U.S.A.
121 G2 **Winooski** U.S.A.
121 G2 **Winooski r.** U.S.A.
18 D2 **Winsen (Aller)** Germany
18 E2 **Winsen (Luhe)** Germany
129 G4 **Winslow** U.S.A.
121 G4 **Winsted** U.S.A.
119 D4 **Winston-Salem** U.S.A.
18 D3 **Winterberg** Germany
119 D6 **Winter Haven** U.S.A.
121 J2 **Winterport** U.S.A.
128 B2 **Winters** U.S.A.
18 C3 **Winterswijk** Netherlands
21 J3 **Winterthur** Switz.
121 J1 **Winterville** U.S.A.
121 H2 **Winthrop** U.S.A.
99 E4 **Winton** Aust.
93 B7 **Winton** N.Z.
119 □2 **Winton** The Bahamas
40 A2 **Wiralaga** Indon.
96 D3 **Wirrabara** Aust.
17 F5 **Wirral pen.** U.K.
96 C2 **Wirraminna** Aust.
96 C2 **Wirrulla** Aust.
17 H5 **Wisbech** U.K.
121 J2 **Wiscasset** U.S.A.
122 B4 **Wisconsin r.** U.S.A.
122 C3 **Wisconsin div.** U.S.A.
122 C4 **Wisconsin Dells** U.S.A.
122 C3 **Wisconsin, Lake l.** U.S.A.
122 C3 **Wisconsin Rapids** U.S.A.
120 B6 **Wise** U.S.A.
80 E3 **Wisil Dabarow** Somalia
19 K3 **Wisła r.** Poland
19 K3 **Wisłoka r.** Poland
18 E2 **Wismar** Germany
122 B3 **Wissota L. l.** U.S.A.
110 D4 **Wistaria** Can.
19 L3 **Wisznice** Poland
83 D4 **Witbank** R.S.A.
17 G5 **Witham r.** U.K.
121 G2 **Witherbee** U.S.A.
17 H5 **Withernsea** U.K.
96 C1 **Witjira Nat. Park nat. park** Aust.
19 H2 **Witkowo** *Konin* Poland
17 G6 **Witney** U.K.
19 G2 **Witnica** *Gorzów* Poland
21 G2 **Witry-lès-Reims** France
122 C3 **Wittenberg** U.S.A.
18 E2 **Wittenberge** Germany
18 E2 **Wittenburg** Germany
21 H3 **Wittenheim** France
100 B4 **Wittenoom** Aust.
132 □3 **Witte Pan salt pan** *Bonaire* Netherlands Ant.
18 E2 **Wittingen** Germany
18 C4 **Wittlich** Germany
18 C2 **Wittmund** Germany
18 F2 **Wittow pen.** Germany
18 F2 **Wittstock** Germany
90 □1 **Witu Is is** P.N.G.
82 B3 **Witvlei** Namibia
18 D3 **Witzenhausen** Germany
99 H5 **Wivenhoe, Lake l.** Aust.
114 C5 **Wixom Lake l.** U.S.A.
19 L2 **Wizna** Poland
19 K2 **Wkra r.** Poland
19 J2 **Władysławowo** Poland
19 J2 **Włocławek** Poland
19 L3 **Włodawa** Poland
19 J3 **Włoszczowa** Poland
121 H2 **Woburn** Can.
97 F4 **Wodonga** Aust.
19 J3 **Wodzisław Śląski** Poland
19 L3 **Wojsławice** Poland
39 K8 **Wokam i.** Indon.
35 H4 **Woken r.** China
55 H4 **Wokha** India
17 G6 **Woking** U.K.
99 E4 **Wokingham w** Aust.
122 D5 **Wolcott** U.S.A.
120 E3 **Wolcott** U.S.A.
19 H3 **Wołczyn** Poland
49 G6 **Woldegk** Germany
76 B4 **Woleu-Ntem div.** Gabon
110 C2 **Wolf r.** Can.
122 C3 **Wolf r.** U.S.A.
126 D2 **Wolf Creek** U.S.A.
127 F4 **Wolf Creek Pass pass** U.S.A.
121 H3 **Wolfeboro** U.S.A.
115 G4 **Wolfe I. i.** Can.
18 F3 **Wolfen** Germany
18 E2 **Wolfenbüttel** Germany
110 C2 **Wolf Lake l.** Can.
126 F1 **Wolf Point** U.S.A.
19 G5 **Wolfsberg** Austria
18 E2 **Wolfsburg** Germany
18 C4 **Wolfstein** Germany
113 H4 **Wolfville** Can.
138 □ **Wolf, Vol. vol** *Galapagos Is* Ecuador
19 F1 **Wolgast** Germany
19 G2 **Wolin i.** Poland
19 G2 **Wolin** Poland
147 C7 **Wollaston, Islas is** Chile
111 J3 **Wollaston Lake** Can.
111 J3 **Wollaston Lake l.** Can.
97 G3 **Wollongong** Aust.
18 E2 **Wolmirstedt** Germany
76 C5 **Wologizi Mts mts** Liberia
19 K2 **Wołomin** Poland
19 H3 **Wołów** Poland
96 E4 **Wolseley** Aust.
19 H2 **Wolsztyn** Poland
18 C2 **Wolvega** Netherlands
17 F5 **Wolverhampton** U.K.
114 C3 **Wolverine** U.S.A.
97 F3 **Wondai** Aust.
101 B6 **Wongan Hills** Aust.
78 A4 **Wonga Wongué, Réserve de res.** Gabon
45 □ **Wong Chuk Hang** Hong Kong
49 H5 **Wŏnju** S. Korea
97 E2 **Wonominta w** Aust.
40 B3 **Wonosari** Indon.
40 B3 **Wonosobo** Indon.
49 H5 **Wŏnsan** N. Korea
97 F4 **Wonthaggi** Aust.
96 C2 **Woocalla** Aust.
98 D2 **Woodah I. i.** Aust.
122 E5 **Woodbridge** U.S.A.
110 G3 **Wood Buffalo National Park nat. park** Can.
97 H2 **Woodburn** Aust.
126 B2 **Woodburn** U.S.A.
122 E4 **Woodbury** U.S.A.
121 F5 **Woodbury** U.S.A.
97 E4 **Woodcock, Mt h.** Aust.
120 A6 **Wood Creek Lake l.** U.S.A.
97 H2 **Woodenbong** Aust.
133 □8 **Woodford** *Grenada* Caribbean
128 C2 **Woodfords** U.S.A.
128 C3 **Woodlake** U.S.A.
128 B2 **Woodland** U.S.A.
127 F4 **Woodland Park** U.S.A.
43 □ **Woodlands** Singapore
90 □1 **Woodlark I. i.** P.N.G.
98 D4 **Woodroffe w** Aust.
96 B1 **Woodroffe, Mt mt.** Aust.
122 D3 **Woodruff** U.S.A.
120 C5 **Woodsfield** U.S.A.
98 C3 **Woods, L. salt flat** Aust.
111 B4 **Woods, Lake of the l.** Can./U.S.A.
97 F4 **Woods Pt** Aust.
113 G4 **Woodstock** Can.
114 E5 **Woodstock** Can.
122 C4 **Woodstock** U.S.A.
120 D5 **Woodstock** U.S.A.
121 G3 **Woodstown** U.S.A.
121 G2 **Woodsville** U.S.A.
92 E4 **Woodville** N.Z.
120 E3 **Woodville** U.S.A.
125 E6 **Woodville** U.S.A.
125 D4 **Woodward** U.S.A.
97 F4 **Woolber** U.K.
97 G2 **Woolgoolga** Aust.
96 D2 **Wooltana** Aust.
98 C2 **Woolwonga Abor. Land res.** Aust.
96 C2 **Woomera** Aust.
96 C2 **Woomera Prohibited Area res.** Aust.
121 H4 **Woonsocket** U.S.A.
99 G5 **Woorabinda** Aust.
101 A5 **Wooramel r.** Aust.
120 C4 **Wooster** U.S.A.
80 D2 **Wooqoyi Galbeed div.** Somalia
21 H3 **Worb** Switz.
99 E2 **Worbody Pt pt** Aust.
82 B5 **Worcester** R.S.A.
17 F5 **Worcester** U.K.
121 H3 **Worcester** U.S.A.
19 F5 **Wörgl** Austria
17 F4 **Workington** U.K.
126 F2 **Worland** U.S.A.
18 D4 **Worms** Germany
17 C6 **Worms Head hd** U.K.
76 D4 **Worofla** Côte d'Ivoire
18 D4 **Wörth am Rhein** Germany
133 □9 **Worthing** *Barbados* Caribbean
17 G6 **Worthing** U.K.
124 E3 **Worthington** U.S.A.
40 E2 **Wotu** Indon.
124 C3 **Wounded Knee** U.S.A.
39 H7 **Wowoni i.** Indon.
110 C3 **Wrangell** U.S.A.
110 C3 **Wrangell I. i.** U.S.A.
108 D3 **Wrangell Mountains mt. ra.** Can./U.S.A.
16 E2 **Wrath, Cape c.** U.K.
124 C3 **Wray** U.S.A.
82 B4 **Wreck Point pt** R.S.A.
17 F5 **Wrexham** U.K.
19 G2 **Wriezen** Germany
41 C4 **Wright** Phil.
126 F3 **Wright** U.S.A.
55 H3 **Wrightmyo** *Andaman and Nicobar Is* India
125 E5 **Wright Patman L. l.** U.S.A.
129 G6 **Wrightson, Mt mt.** U.S.A.
110 E2 **Wrigley** Can.
19 H3 **Wrocław** Poland
19 H2 **Wronki** Poland
19 H2 **Września** Poland
19 H3 **Wschowa** Poland
50 E2 **Wu r.** China
48 E5 **Wu'an** China
101 B6 **Wubin** Aust.
48 D5 **Wubu** China
49 G3 **Wuchagou** China
49 H3 **Wuchang** China
51 F2 **Wuchang** China
51 E4 **Wuchuan** China
48 D4 **Wuchuan** China
50 D2 **Wuchuan** China
48 C5 **Wuda** China
51 E1 **Wudang Shan mt. ra.** China
51 E1 **Wudang Shan mt.** China
49 G5 **Wudao** China
55 H2 **Wudaoliang** China
49 F5 **Wudi** China
77 F4 **Wudil** Nigeria
50 C3 **Wuding** China
48 D5 **Wuding r.** China
96 C3 **Wudinna** Aust.
50 D1 **Wudu** China
49 E2 **Wufeng** China
51 E3 **Wugang** China
51 D2 **Wugong** China
50 E1 **Wugong** China
48 C5 **Wuhai** China
51 F2 **Wuhan** China
51 G1 **Wuhe** China
51 G1 **Wuhu** China
51 F4 **Wuhua** China
54 D2 **Wüjang** China
51 E4 **Wujia** China
77 F5 **Wukari** Nigeria
50 A2 **Wulang** China
54 C2 **Wular L. l.** India
49 F3 **Wuleidao Wan l.** China
49 F6 **Wulian** China
50 C2 **Wulian Feng mt. ra.** China
50 C3 **Wuliang Shan mt. ra.** China
39 K8 **Wuliaru i.** Indon.
51 E2 **Wuling Shan mt. ra.** China
78 B2 **Wum** Cameroon
50 C3 **Wumeng Shan mt. ra.** China
50 E4 **Wuming** China
50 C3 **Wungda** China
51 F2 **Wuning** China
78 F2 **Wun Rog** Sudan
78 E2 **Wun Shwai** Sudan
18 F3 **Wunsiedel** Germany
42 A2 **Wuntho** Myanmar
129 G4 **Wupatki National Monument res.** U.S.A.
51 G3 **Wuping** China
18 C3 **Wuppertal** Germany
48 D5 **Wuqi** China
49 F5 **Wuqiao** China
77 F4 **Wurno** Nigeria
18 D4 **Würzburg** Germany
18 F3 **Wurzen** Germany
50 D1 **Wushan** China
51 D2 **Wushan** China
50 D2 **Wushan** China
51 F2 **Wusheng Guan pass** China
51 E4 **Wushi** China
65 J4 **Wushi** China
18 D3 **Wüstegarten h.** Germany
49 K3 **Wusuli r.** China/Rus. Fed.
48 E5 **Wutai** China
48 E5 **Wutai Shan mt.** China
39 M7 **Wuvulu I. i.** P.N.G.
51 G2 **Wuwei** China
48 B5 **Wuwei** China
51 E2 **Wuxi** China
51 H2 **Wuxi** China
54 D2 **Wuxu** China
51 E4 **Wuxuan** China
51 E4 **Wuyang** China
49 F2 **Wuyi** China
49 F2 **Wuyiling** China
51 G3 **Wuyi Shan mt. ra.** China
48 D4 **Wuyuan** China
51 G2 **Wuyuan** China
51 E2 **Wuzhai** China
48 E5 **Wuzhi Shan mt.** China
51 D2 **Wuzhong** China
51 E4 **Wuzhou** China
99 E3 **Wyaaba Cr. r.** Aust.
122 B5 **Wyaconda r.** U.S.A.
101 B6 **Wyalkatchem** Aust.
123 F4 **Wyandotte** U.S.A.
122 C5 **Wyanet** U.S.A.
19 L2 **Wydminy** Poland
17 F5 **Wye r.** U.K.
101 B6 **Wyemandoo h.** Aust.
18 D1 **Wyk auf Föhr** Germany
19 L2 **Wyloo** Aust.
17 H5 **Wymondham** U.K.
100 E2 **Wyndham** Aust.
125 F5 **Wynne** U.S.A.
97 F5 **Wynyard** Aust.
111 J4 **Wynyard** Can.
96 B2 **Wyola L. salt flat** Aust.
122 C5 **Wyoming** U.S.A.
122 E4 **Wyoming** U.S.A.
126 E3 **Wyoming div.** U.S.A.
126 E3 **Wyoming Peak summit** U.S.A.
97 G3 **Wyong** Aust.
96 E3 **Wyperfeld Nat. Park nat. park** Aust.
19 H2 **Wysoka** *Piła* Poland
19 L2 **Wysokie Mazowieckie** Poland
121 E4 **Wysox** U.S.A.
19 K2 **Wyszków** Poland
120 C6 **Wytheville** U.S.A.
115 F4 **Wytopitlock** U.S.A.
152 □ **Wyville-Thomson, Mt h.** *Kerguelen* Indian Ocean
19 L3 **Wyżyna Lubelska reg.** Poland

X

80 F2 **Xaafuun** Somalia
60 G1 **Xaçmaz** Azerbaijan
55 H3 **Xagquka** China
54 D1 **Xaidulla** China
55 G3 **Xainza** China
83 E3 **Xai Xai** Mozambique
131 H4 **Xal, Co de h.** Mexico
142 C2 **Xambioa** Brazil
144 B5 **Xambrê r.** Brazil
144 B5 **Xambrê** Brazil
42 D2 **Xam Hua** Laos
79 C5 **Xá-Muteba** Angola
42 C3 **Xan r.** Laos
82 C3 **Xanagas** Botswana
55 H2 **Xangd** China
48 D4 **Xangdin Hural** China
79 B7 **Xangongo** Angola
60 G3 **Xankändi** Azerbaijan
13 H7 **Xanlar** Azerbaijan
29 E4 **Xanthi** Greece
143 B6 **Xanxerê** Brazil
140 C2 **Xapuri r.** Brazil
140 C2 **Xapuri** Brazil
43 D4 **Xaqung** China
81 E2 **Xarardheere** Somalia
60 G2 **Xärä Zirä Adasi is** Azerbaijan
55 F3 **Xarba La** China
64 C5 **Xaraba Sähär Sayı i.** Azerbaijan
48 C4 **Xar Burd** China
48 E3 **Xar Hudag** China
48 E4 **Xar Moron r.** *Inner Mongolia* China
49 F4 **Xar Moron r.** *Inner Mongolia* China
29 C5 **Xarrë** Albania
25 F3 **Xátiva** Spain
82 C2 **Xaudum w** Botswana/Namibia
82 C3 **Xau, Lake l.** Botswana
144 B4 **Xavantina** Brazil
43 D5 **Xa Vo Đat** Vietnam
65 K4 **Xayar** China
65 L3 **Xazgat** China
42 D3 **Xé Bangfai r.** Laos
42 C3 **Xé Banghiang r.** Laos
42 D4 **Xé Don r.** Laos
42 D4 **Xé Kong r.** Laos
120 B5 **Xenia** U.S.A.
42 D3 **Xé Noy r.** Laos
43 D4 **Xé Xan r.** Vietnam
82 C3 **Xhorodomo Pan salt pan** Botswana
82 C3 **Xhumo** Botswana
51 F4 **Xi r.** *Guangdong* China
48 B4 **Xi r.** *Inner Mongolia* China
49 G4 **Xi r.** *Liaoning* China
49 H2 **Xiabole Shan mt.** China
51 F4 **Xiachuan Dao** China
50 C1 **Xiahe** China
51 F3 **Xiajiang** China
49 F5 **Xiajin** China
51 G3 **Xiamen** China
48 D6 **Xi'an** China
51 F1 **Xiancheng** China
48 C5 **Xianfeng** China
51 E2 **Xianfeng** China
51 F3 **Xiang r.** China
50 B2 **Xiangcheng** China
51 E1 **Xiangcheng** China
51 F1 **Xiangfan** China
48 D6 **Xiangfen** China
48 E4 **Xianghuang Qi** China
42 C3 **Xiangkhoang** Laos
48 D6 **Xiangning** China
54 E3 **Xiangquan r.** China
51 H2 **Xiangshan** China
51 E3 **Xiangtan** China
51 F3 **Xiangxiang** China
51 F3 **Xiangyin** China
48 E5 **Xiangyuan** China
50 C3 **Xiangyun** China
51 E2 **Xianju** China
51 F2 **Xianning** China
50 C2 **Xianshui r.** China
51 G3 **Xianxia Ling mt. ra.** China
49 F5 **Xian Xian** China
48 C5 **Xianyang** China
51 G3 **Xianyou** China
50 E4 **Xiaodong** China
49 G2 **Xiao'ergou** China
51 F2 **Xiaogan** China
49 H2 **Xiao Hinggan Ling mt. ra.** China
50 C2 **Xiaojin** China
51 G2 **Xiaomei** China
55 H2 **Xiaonanchuan** China
51 H2 **Xiaoshan** China
50 C2 **Xiao Surmang** China
51 G2 **Xiaotao** China
49 E5 **Xiaowutai Shan mt.** China
51 G1 **Xiao Xian** China
50 B2 **Xiaoxiang Ling mt. ra.** China
48 D5 **Xiaoyi** China
51 H3 **Xiapu** China
48 D6 **Xiayukou** China
50 C3 **Xichang** China
51 E4 **Xichang** China
50 D2 **Xichong** China
50 D4 **Xichou** China
51 E1 **Xichuan** China
50 C2 **Xide** China
51 E4 **Xieyang Dao** China
51 G1 **Xifei r.** China
49 H4 **Xifeng** China
51 E3 **Xifeng** China
48 C6 **Xifengzhen** China
55 G3 **Xigazê** China
50 D1 **Xihan Shui r.** China
50 D1 **Xihe** China
51 F1 **Xihua** China
48 C6 **Xiji** China
55 G2 **Xijir** China
55 G2 **Xijir Ulan Hu salt l.** China
48 B5 **Xijishui** China
49 G1 **Xikouzi** Rus. Fed.
48 C4 **Xil** China
49 G3 **Xilaotou Shan mt.** China
49 G4 **Xiliao r.** China
50 D3 **Xilin** China
51 E2 **Xiling Xia r.** China
49 F4 **Xilinhot** China
48 C3 **Xilin Qagan Obo** China
48 B4 **Ximiao** China
51 G2 **Xin'an** China
51 G2 **Xin'anjiang Sk. resr** China
49 F2 **Xin Barag Youqi** China
49 F2 **Xin Barag Zuoqi** China
49 F4 **Xinbin** China
49 G2 **Xin Bulag Dong** China
51 F1 **Xincai** China
51 F3 **Xincheng** China
50 C2 **Xincheng** China
48 D5 **Xinchengbu** China
51 E5 **Xincun** China
49 F3 **Xindian** China
51 H3 **Xindu** China
51 E4 **Xindu** China
51 F3 **Xinfeng** China
51 F3 **Xinfeng** China
51 F4 **Xinfengjiang Sk. resr** China
51 F3 **Xingan** China
51 E3 **Xing'an** China
49 G4 **Xingcheng** China
51 F3 **Xingguo** China
48 A6 **Xinghai** China
48 E4 **Xinghe** China
51 G1 **Xinghua** China
51 G1 **Xinghua Wan b.** China
49 K3 **Xingkai** China
49 K3 **Xingkai Hu l.** China/Rus. Fed.
49 H2 **Xinglong** China
49 F4 **Xinglong** China
49 F4 **Xinglongzhen** China
51 F3 **Xingning** China
51 F2 **Xingou** China
50 E1 **Xingping** China
50 D3 **Xingren** China
50 C1 **Xingsagoinba** China
51 E2 **Xingshan** China
48 E5 **Xingtai** China
48 E5 **Xingtang** China
142 B1 **Xingu r.** Brazil
142 B3 **Xingu, Parque Indigena do nat. park** Brazil
50 D2 **Xingwen** China
50 D2 **Xing Xian** China
51 F3 **Xingyang** China
50 D3 **Xingyi** China
51 E2 **Xinhua** China
49 E5 **Xinhe** China
65 K4 **Xinhe** China
48 E3 **Xinhua** China
48 B5 **Xinhuacun** China
51 E3 **Xinhuang** China
51 F4 **Xinhui** China
48 B5 **Xining** China
51 G1 **Xinji** China
48 E5 **Xinji** China
50 D4 **Xinjiang** China
48 D6 **Xinjiang** China
65 J4 **Xinjiang Uygur Zizhiqu div.** China
50 B3 **Xinjie** China
50 D3 **Xinjie** China
49 G5 **Xinjin** China
49 G3 **Xinkai r.** China
49 G2 **Xinlitun** China
50 C1 **Xinlong** China
49 G4 **Xinmin** China
51 E3 **Xinning** China
50 C3 **Xinping** China
49 J2 **Xinqing** China
50 G5 **Xinquan** China
49 F6 **Xintai** China
51 F3 **Xintian** China
51 F2 **Xin Xian** China
48 E5 **Xin Xian** China
51 F1 **Xinxiang** China
51 E4 **Xinxing** China
51 F1 **Xinyang** China
51 F1 **Xinyang** China
51 H1 **Xinyang Gang r.** China
51 F1 **Xinye** China
51 F1 **Xinye r.** China
51 G1 **Xinyi** China
51 E4 **Xinyi** China
51 E5 **Xinying** China
51 F3 **Xinyu** China
65 K4 **Xinyuan** China
48 E5 **Xinzhou** China
24 C1 **Xinzo de Limia** Spain
49 G4 **Xiongyuecheng** China
51 G2 **Xiping** China
51 F1 **Xiping** China
50 C1 **Xiqing Shan mt. ra.** China
142 D3 **Xique Xique** Brazil
50 D2 **Xishui** China
51 F2 **Xishui** China
76 B4 **Xitole** Guinea-Bissau
49 F3 **Xi Ujimqin Qi** China
51 G2 **Xiuning** China
51 E2 **Xiushan** China
51 F2 **Xiushui** China
51 F2 **Xiu Shui r.** China
50 D3 **Xiuwen** China
51 F1 **Xiuwu** China
49 G4 **Xiuyan** China
51 E5 **Xiuying** China
50 B1 **Xiwu** China
55 F3 **Xixabangma Feng mt.** China
51 E1 **Xixia** China
51 F1 **Xi Xian** China
48 D5 **Xi Xian** China
50 D1 **Xi Xiang** China
50 E4 **Xiyang r.** China
51 H3 **Xiyang Dao i.** China
55 F2 **Xizang Gaoyuan plat.** China
55 F3 **Xizang Zizhiqu div.** China
49 G5 **Xizhong Dao i.** China
80 E2 **Xjis** Somalia
55 H3 **Xoka** China
43 D5 **Xom An Lôc** Vietnam
43 D5 **Xom Duc Hanh** Vietnam
51 G2 **Xuancheng** China
51 E2 **Xuan'en** China
50 C2 **Xuanhan** China
51 G5 **Xuanhepu** China
48 E4 **Xuanhua** China
43 D5 **Xuân Lôc** Vietnam
50 D3 **Xuanwei** China
51 F1 **Xuchang** China
60 G1 **Xudat** Azerbaijan
80 D4 **Xuddur** Somalia
80 E3 **Xudun** Somalia
51 E3 **Xuefeng Shan mt. ra.** China
55 H2 **Xugui** China
50 B1 **Xümatang** China
51 E1 **Xun r.** China
51 E4 **Xun r.** China
49 J2 **Xun r.** China
50 C3 **Xundian** China
55 E2 **Xungba** China
55 F3 **Xungru** China
49 H2 **Xunhe** China
49 J2 **Xunke** Rus. Fed.
51 F3 **Xunwu** China
48 E6 **Xun Xian** China
51 F3 **Xunyang** China
50 E1 **Xunyi** China
51 E3 **Xupu** China
55 F3 **Xuru Co l.** China
49 E5 **Xushui** China
51 E4 **Xuwen** China
51 G1 **Xuyi** China
50 D2 **Xuyong** China
51 G1 **Xuzhou** China
29 D5 **Xylokastro** Greece

Y

50 C2 **Ya'an** China
97 E3 **Yaapeet** Aust.
78 A3 **Yabassi** Cameroon
80 C4 **Yabēlo** Ethiopia
80 C4 **Yabēlo Wildlife Sanctuary res.** Ethiopia
28 E3 **Yablanitsa** Bulgaria
28 F3 **Yablanovo** Bulgaria
14 E3 **Yablonovets** Rus. Fed.
36 D2 **Yablonovyy Khrebet mt. ra.** Rus. Fed.
15 A2 **Yabluniv** Ukraine
77 F4 **Yabo** Nigeria
48 B5 **Yabrai Shan mt. ra.** China
48 B5 **Yabrai Yanchang** China
61 D3 **Yabrūd** Syria
119 □3 **Yabucoa** Puerto Rico
49 J3 **Yabuli** China
15 C1 **Yabunets'** Ukraine
138 D2 **Yacambu, Parque Nacional nat. park** Venezuela
90 □6 **Yacata i.** Fiji
51 E5 **Yacheng** China
97 F4 **Yackandandah** Aust.
140 C2 **Yacuma r.** Bolivia
78 C2 **Yadé, Massif du mts** C.A.R.
56 B2 **Yadgir** India
55 G4 **Yadong** China
14 H2 **Yadrin** Rus. Fed.
90 □6 **Yadua i.** Fiji
61 F5 **Yafran** Libya
76 D4 **Yagaba** Ghana
47 □2 **Yagaji-jima i.** Japan
62 J3 **Yagel'naya** Rus. Fed.
46 H1 **Yagishiri-tō i.** Japan
63 Q3 **Yagodnoye** Rus. Fed.
63 Q3 **Yagodnoye** Rus. Fed.
78 C1 **Yagoua** Cameroon
55 E3 **Yagra** China
50 A1 **Yagradagzê Shan mt.** China
43 C6 **Yaha** Thailand
47 F6 **Yahagi-gawa r.** Japan
78 D3 **Yahuma** Zaire
60 C2 **Yahyalı** Turkey
57 G3 **Yahya Wana** Afghanistan
47 G5 **Yaita** Japan
25 □ **Yaiza** *Canary Is* Spain
47 G6 **Yaizu** Japan
50 C2 **Yajiang** China
78 C3 **Yaka** C.A.R.
49 G2 **Yakeshi** China
57 F3 **Yakhehal** Afghanistan
14 C1 **Yakhroma** Rus. Fed.
126 B2 **Yakima** U.S.A.
126 B2 **Yakima r.** U.S.A.
57 E4 **Yakinish** Iran
57 G3 **Yakmach** Pakistan
76 D4 **Yako** Burkina
78 C3 **Yakoma** Zaire
28 D4 **Yakoruda** Bulgaria
14 H3 **Yakovlevka** Rus. Fed.
15 G1 **Yakovlevo** Rus. Fed.
46 H2 **Yakumo** Japan
46 □ **Yaku-shima i.** Japan
110 B3 **Yakutat** U.S.A.
108 D4 **Yakutat Bay b.** U.S.A.
63 O3 **Yakutsk** Rus. Fed.
15 F3 **Yakymivka** Ukraine
43 C6 **Yala** Thailand
82 A5 **Yalata Abor. Reserve res.** Aust.
123 F4 **Yale** U.S.A.
78 D3 **Yaleko** Zaire
90 □7 **Yalewa Kalou i.** Fiji
50 B2 **Yalga** Rus. Fed.
101 B6 **Yalgoo** Aust.
29 F6 **Yalıkavak** Turkey
78 D2 **Yalinga** C.A.R.
131 H4 **Yalkubul, Pta pt** Mexico
133 □1 **Yallahs** Jamaica
99 F5 **Yalleroi** Aust.
78 C2 **Yaloké** C.A.R.
50 C3 **Yalong r.** China
78 D3 **Yalongwe** Zaire
60 B1 **Yalova** Turkey
15 G3 **Yalta** *Donets'k* Ukraine
13 E6 **Yalta** *Krym* Ukraine
18 B2 **Yaltushkiv** Ukraine
49 G3 **Yalu r.** China
49 G3 **Yalu r.** China/North Korea
49 H5 **Yalujiang Kou river mouth** N. Korea
65 G1 **Yalutorovsk** Rus. Fed.
60 B2 **Yalvaç** Turkey
47 G4 **Yamada** Japan
47 G4 **Yamagata div.** Japan
47 H4 **Yamagata** Japan
46 C8 **Yamagawa** Japan
46 C6 **Yamaguchi div.** Japan
46 C6 **Yamaguchi** Japan
62 H2 **Yamal, Poluostrov pen.** Rus. Fed.
47 G6 **Yamanashi div.** Japan
48 D2 **Yamarovka** Rus. Fed.
47 H5 **Yamatsuri** Japan
97 H2 **Yamba** Aust.
97 E4 **Yambacoona** Aust.
111 G2 **Yamba Lake l.** Can.
78 E3 **Yambio** Sudan
14 F2 **Yambirno** Rus. Fed.
28 F3 **Yambol** Bulgaria
138 B5 **Yambrasbamba** Peru
62 J3 **Yamburg** Rus. Fed.
55 E3 **Yamdena i.** Indon.
62 D7 **Yame** Japan
48 B5 **Yamenzhuang** China
42 B2 **Yamethin** Myanmar
41 B1 **Y'ami i.** Phil.
47 G5 **Yamizo-san mt.** Japan
11 H4 **Yamm** Rus. Fed.
99 E5 **Yamma Yamma, L. salt flat** Aust.
76 C5 **Yamoussoukro** Côte d'Ivoire
126 E3 **Yampa r.** U.S.A.
15 B2 **Yampil'** *Khmel'nyts'kyy* Ukraine
14 A4 **Yampil'** *Sumy* Ukraine
15 C2 **Yampil'** *Vinnytsya* Ukraine
54 E3 **Yamuna r.** India
54 D3 **Yamunanagar** India
65 J2 **Yamyshevo** Kazak.
55 G3 **Yamzho Yumco l.** China
51 G1 **Yan r.** China
63 P3 **Yana r.** Rus. Fed.
76 B5 **Yana** Sierra Leone
96 E4 **Yanac** Aust.
140 A2 **Yanachaga-Chemillen, Parque Nacional nat. park** Peru
47 □2 **Yanaha-jima i.** Japan
46 D7 **Yanai** Japan
48 C5 **Yanam** India
48 C5 **Yan'an** China
140 B2 **Yanaoca** Peru
64 E1 **Yanaul** Rus. Fed.
50 C2 **Yanbian** China
73 G3 **Yanbu' al Bahr** Saudi Arabia
73 G3 **Yanbu' an Nakhl reg.** Saudi Arabia
51 H1 **Yancheng** China
101 A6 **Yanchep** Aust.
48 C5 **Yanchi** China
48 D5 **Yanchuan** China
97 F2 **Yanda w** Aust.
96 E2 **Yandama Cr. w** Aust.
90 □1 **Yandina** Solomon Is.
78 C4 **Yandja** Zaire
42 A3 **Yandoon** Myanmar
76 C4 **Yanfolila** Mali
49 E4 **Yang r.** China
78 D2 **Yangalia** C.A.R.
78 D3 **Yangambi** Zaire
55 H3 **Ya'ngamdo** China
76 C4 **Yangasso** Mali
55 G3 **Yangbajain** China
55 F3 **Yangbi** China
51 F4 **Yangcheng** China
42 H5 **Yangchun** China
48 E4 **Yangdok** N. Korea
51 G2 **Yanggao** China
49 J2 **Yanggu** China
54 D2 **Yangi Davan pass** China
57 B1 **Yangi Kand** Iran
65 G4 **Yangirabad** Uzbekistan
65 G4 **Yangiyul'** Uzbekistan
48 E4 **Yangjiang** China
42 B3 **Yangon div.** Myanmar
42 B3 **Yangon** Myanmar
51 E2 **Yangping** China
48 E5 **Yangquan** China
51 E3 **Yangshan** China
50 C3 **Yangshuo** China
51 E3 **Yangtouyan** China
80 D2 **Yangudi Rassa National Park nat. park** Ethiopia
50 D1 **Yang Xian** China
48 E4 **Yangyuan** China
51 G1 **Yangzhou** China
50 E2 **Yanhe** China
55 E2 **Yanhuqu** China
11 H3 **Yanis'yarvi, Ozero l.** Finland
49 J4 **Yanji** China
50 B2 **Yanjin** China
50 D2 **Yanjing** China
97 F3 **Yankara Nat. Park nat. park** Nigeria
124 D3 **Yankton** U.S.A.
63 Q2 **Yano-Indigirskaya Nizmennost' lowland** Rus. Fed.
14 A2 **Yanovo** Rus. Fed.
62 K3 **Yanov Stan** Rus. Fed.
56 C5 **Yan Oya r.** Sri Lanka
44 E3 **Yanqi** China
49 E4 **Yanqing** China
49 F5 **Yanshan** China
51 G2 **Yanshan** China
50 D4 **Yanshan** China
49 F4 **Yan Shan mt. ra.** China
55 H2 **Yanshiping** China
49 J3 **Yanshou** China
63 P2 **Yanskiy Zaliv g.** Rus. Fed.
97 F2 **Yantabulla** Aust.
49 G5 **Yantai** China
11 E4 **Yantarnyy** Rus. Fed.
51 G3 **Yantongshan** China
18 E3 **Yantra r.** Bulgaria
90 □8 **Yanuca i.** Fiji
90 □6 **Yanuca reef** Fiji
73 H3 **Yanūfi, J. al h.** Saudi Arabia
90 □8 **Yanuya i.** Fiji
51 E2 **Yanwa** China
65 G4 **Yany-Kurgan** Kazak.
50 C4 **Yanyuan** China
51 G1 **Yanzhou** China
55 H4 **Yao'an** China
78 B3 **Yaoundé** Cameroon
51 E1 **Yao Xian** China
49 H2 **Yaoxiaoling** China
15 J5 **Yap i.** Fed. States of Micronesia
39 L7 **Yapen i.** Indon.
99 E3 **Yappar r.** Aust.
150 E5 **Yap Tr.** Pac. Oc.
139 F3 **Yapukarri** Guyana
90 □6 **Yaqaga i.** Fiji
90 □8 **Yaqeta i.** Fiji
130 C2 **Yaqui r.** Mexico
14 G1 **Yar** Rus. Fed.
99 E5 **Yaraka** Aust.
14 H1 **Yaransk** Rus. Fed.
96 C3 **Yardea** Aust.
60 B2 **Yardımcı Burnu pt** Turkey
60 G2 **Yardımlı** Azerbaijan
17 H5 **Yare r.** U.K.
12 K2 **Yarega** Rus. Fed.
62 G3 **Yaremcha** Ukraine
12 K2 **Yarensk** Rus. Fed.
138 C3 **Yarí r.** Colombia
47 F5 **Yariga-take mt.** Japan
80 D2 **Yarīm** Yemen
139 G3 **Yaripo** Brazil
138 D1 **Yaritagua** Venezuela
65 J5 **Yarkant r.** China
115 G4 **Yarker** Can.
54 C1 **Yarkhun r.** Pakistan
55 H3 **Yarlung Zangbo r.** China
15 B2 **Yarmolyntsi** Ukraine
113 G5 **Yarmouth** Can.
121 H4 **Yarmouth Port** U.S.A.
129 F4 **Yarnell** U.S.A.
14 E1 **Yarok** Rus. Fed.
15 E1 **Yaroslavets'** Ukraine
14 D1 **Yaroslavl' div.** Rus. Fed.
14 D1 **Yaroslavl'** Rus. Fed.
97 F4 **Yarram** Aust.
99 G5 **Yarraman** Aust.
101 A6 **Yarra Yarra Lakes salt flat** Aust.
99 F5 **Yarronvale** Aust.
97 F4 **Yarrowmere** Aust.
55 H3 **Yartö Tra La** China
14 A2 **Yartsevo** Rus. Fed.
138 B2 **Yarumal** Colombia
50 B2 **Yarzhong** China
79 C4 **Yasa** Zaire
90 □7 **Yasawa i.** Fiji
90 □8 **Yasawa Group is** Fiji
28 F3 **Yasenkovo** Bulgaria
77 F4 **Yashi** Nigeria
77 E5 **Yashikera** Nigeria
65 H5 **Yashilkŭl l.** Tajikistan
46 D7 **Ya-shima i.** Japan
47 H4 **Yashima** Japan
46 D7 **Yashiro-jima i.** Japan
13 H6 **Yashkul'** Rus. Fed.
28 F3 **Yasna Polyana** Bulgaria
49 E2 **Yasnogorsk** Rus. Fed.
14 C2 **Yasnogorsk** Rus. Fed.
15 D1 **Yasnohorodka** Ukraine
64 E2 **Yasnyy** Rus. Fed.
97 G3 **Yass** Aust.
46 D6 **Yasugi** Japan
57 B3 **Yāsūj** Iran
15 G2 **Yasynuvata** Ukraine
77 G2 **Yat well** Niger
78 D2 **Yata r.** C.A.R.
60 B2 **Yatağan** Turkey
81 C5 **Yata Plateau plat.** Kenya
90 □2 **Yaté** Pac. Oc.
125 E4 **Yates Center** U.S.A.
93 A6 **Yates Pt pt** N.Z.
111 K2 **Yathkyed Lake l.** Can.
78 D3 **Yatolema** Zaire
47 G6 **Yatsuga-take vol** Japan
46 C7 **Yatsushiro** Japan
46 C7 **Yatsushiro-kai b.** Japan
61 C4 **Yatta** Israel
119 □3 **Yauco** Puerto Rico
140 A2 **Yauli** Peru
138 C4 **Yauna Maloca** Colombia
140 B2 **Yauri** Peru
45 □ **Yau Tong** Hong Kong
140 A2 **Yauyos** Peru
138 C4 **Yavari r.** Brazil
130 C3 **Yavaros** Mexico
14 F2 **Yavas r.** Rus. Fed.
14 F2 **Yavas** Rus. Fed.
54 D5 **Yavatmāl** India
139 D2 **Yavi, Co mt.** Venezuela
15 E3 **Yavkyne** Ukraine
15 A2 **Yavoriv** *Ivano-Frankivs'k* Ukraine
13 B5 **Yavoriv** *L'viv* Ukraine
47 D7 **Yawatahama** Japan
65 K5 **Yawatongguz r.** China
65 K5 **Yawatongguzlangar** China
50 B4 **Yawng-hwe** Myanmar
76 B5 **Yawri Bay b.** Sierra Leone
131 H5 **Yaxchilan** Guatemala
61 G2 **Yayladağı** Turkey
14 G2 **Yaz** Rus. Fed.
42 A2 **Yazagyo** Myanmar
57 C3 **Yazd div.** Iran
57 C3 **Yazd** Iran
57 C2 **Yazdān** Iran
57 C3 **Yazd-e Khvāst** Iran
125 F5 **Yazoo r.** U.S.A.
125 F5 **Yazoo City** U.S.A.
14 H2 **Yazykovo** Rus. Fed.
14 H2 **Yazykovo** Rus. Fed.
19 G5 **Ybbs r.** Austria
19 G4 **Ybbs an der Donau** Austria
29 D6 **Ydra** Greece
29 D6 **Ydra i.** Greece
42 B4 **Ye** Myanmar
42 B4 **Ye r.** Myanmar
97 F4 **Yea** Aust.
72 C3 **Yebbi-Bou** Chad
72 C3 **Yebbi-Souma** Chad
65 J5 **Yecheng** China
25 F3 **Yecla** Spain
130 C2 **Yécora** Mexico
42 B3 **Yedashe** Myanmar
14 H2 **Yedoma** Rus. Fed.
72 C3 **Yedri well** Chad
101 D7 **Yeehaw Junction** U.S.A.
96 C3 **Yeelanna** Aust.
14 F2 **Yefanovo** Rus. Fed.
14 E3 **Yefremovskiy** Rus. Fed.
14 F2 **Yefremov** Rus. Fed.
77 G3 **Yegguebe well** Niger
60 F2 **Yeghegnadzor** Armenia
65 J2 **Yegindybulak** Kazak.
13 G6 **Yegorlykskaya** Rus. Fed.
14 E2 **Yegor'ye** Rus. Fed.
14 F2 **Yegor'yevsk** Rus. Fed.
77 E5 **Yégué** Togo
78 F2 **Yei r.** Sudan
80 B4 **Yei** Sudan
76 D5 **Yeji** Ghana
51 F1 **Yejiaji** China
64 F1 **Yekaterinburg** Rus. Fed.
49 J2 **Yekaterinoslavka** Rus. Fed.
14 G3 **Yekaterinovka** Rus. Fed.
13 H5 **Yekaterinovka** Rus. Fed.
14 C4 **Yékia well** Chad
15 C4 **Yekimovichi** Rus. Fed.
42 A3 **Ye Kyun i.** Myanmar
13 G5 **Yelan'** Rus. Fed.
14 F4 **Yelan'-r.** Rus. Fed.
15 D3 **Yelanets'** Ukraine
99 G6 **Yelarbon** Aust.
14 H1 **Yelasy** Rus. Fed.
14 E2 **Yelat'ma** Rus. Fed.
64 F5 **Yelbarsli** Turkmenistan
14 F2 **Yelenskiy** Rus. Fed.
14 E5 **Yelets** Rus. Fed.
76 B3 **Yélimané** Mali
16 F1 **Yell i.** U.K.
56 C2 **Yellandu** India
56 A3 **Yellapur** India
110 G2 **Yellow r.** U.S.A.
120 D4 **Yellow Creek** U.S.A.
108 G3 **Yellowknife** Can.
97 F3 **Yellow Mt h.** Aust.
49 G6 **Yellow Sea sea** Asia
126 F2 **Yellowstone r.** U.S.A.
126 E2 **Yellowstone L. l.** U.S.A.
126 E2 **Yellowstone Nat. Park nat. park.** U.S.A.
126 E2 **Yellowtail Res. resr** U.S.A.
16 G1 **Yell Sound chan.** U.K.
12 G2 **Yel'niki** Rus. Fed.
14 A2 **Yel'nya** Rus. Fed.
15 G1 **Yeloshnoye** Rus. Fed.
64 F5 **Yeloten** Turkmenistan
15 C2 **Yel'sk** Belarus
15 E1 **Yel'tsovka** Rus. Fed.
15 E3 **Yelyseyivka** Ukraine
15 E2 **Yelyzavethradka** Ukraine
64 F2 **Yemanzhelinsk** Rus. Fed.
32 F8 **Yemen country** Asia
65 G1 **Yemets r.** Rus. Fed.
12 G2 **Yemetsk** Rus. Fed.
12 G2 **Yemil'chyne** Ukraine
12 G2 **Yemtsa** Rus. Fed.
12 J2 **Yemva** Rus. Fed.
10 H2 **Yena** Rus. Fed.
77 F6 **Yenagoa** Nigeria
13 F5 **Yenakiyeve** Ukraine
42 A2 **Yenangyat** Myanmar
42 A2 **Yenangyaung** Myanmar

Column 1

42 A3 Yenanma Myanmar
42 D2 Yên Bai Vietnam
76 D5 Yendi Ghana
79 B4 Yénéganou Congo
42 B2 Yengan Myanmar
57 A1 Yengejeh Iran
76 B5 Yengema Sierra Leone
65 J5 Yengisar China
78 C3 Yengo Congo
48 D2 Yengorboy Rus. Fed.
29 F5 Yenice Çanakkale Turkey
61 C1 Yenice İçel Turkey
60 C2 Yeniceoba Turkey
29 F6 Yenihisar Turkey
29 G5 Yeniköy Turkey
29 G6 Yenipazar Turkey
29 F5 Yenişakran Turkey
44 F1 Yenisey r. Rus. Fed.
62 L4 Yeniseysk Rus. Fed.
63 L4 Yeniseyskiy Kryazh h. Rus. Fed.
62 J2 Yeniseyskiy Zaliv b. Rus. Fed.
50 B1 Yeniugou China
42 D2 Yên Minh Vietnam
13 H6 Yenotayevka Rus. Fed.
101 D5 Yeo L. salt flat Aust.
54 C5 Yeola India
97 G3 Yeoval Aust.
17 F6 Yeovil U.K.
130 C2 Yepachic Mexico
14 D3 Yepifan' Rus. Fed.
99 G4 Yeppoon Aust.
128 C2 Yerakhtur Rus. Fed.
64 D4 Yeraliyev Kazak.
60 F1 Yerevan Armenia
13 H6 Yergeni h. Rus. Fed.
101 C6 Yerilla Aust.
128 C2 Yerington U.S.A.
60 C2 Yerköy Turkey
56 A2 Yerla r. India
65 J2 Yermak China
49 H1 Yermakovo Rus. Fed.
48 E2 Yermentau Kazak.
14 F2 Yermish' Rus. Fed.
125 B7 Yermo Mexico
128 D4 Yermo U.S.A.
14 C1 Yermolino Rus. Fed.
14 C2 Yermolino Rus. Fed.
51 M1 Yerofey-Pavlovich Rus. Fed.
61 C4 Yeroham Israel
14 B2 Yershi Rus. Fed.
49 H3 Yershichi Rus. Fed.
13 J5 Yershov Rus. Fed.
12 G2 Yertsevo Rus. Fed.
140 A2 Yerupaja mt. Peru
13 H5 Yeruslan r. Rus. Fed.
42 A2 Yesagyo Myanmar
49 H5 Yesan S. Korea
51 C2 Yesenovichi Rus. Fed.
65 G2 Yesil' Kazak.
61 B1 Yeşildere Turkey
60 C2 Yeşilhisar Turkey
29 D1 Yeşilırmak r. Turkey
61 B2 Yeşilova Turkey
13 G6 Yessentuki Rus. Fed.
63 K3 Yessey Rus. Fed.
97 G2 Yetman Aust.
42 A2 Yeu Myanmar
20 C3 Yeu, Île d'i France
49 H4 Yevgashchino Rus. Fed.
13 E6 Yevlax Azerbaijan
60 F1 Yevlax Azerbaijan
13 E6 Yevpatoriya Ukraine
49 J2 Yevreyskaya Avtonomnaya Oblast' div. Rus. Fed.

49 F5 Ye Xian China
51 F1 Ye Xian China
13 H6 Yeya r. Rus. Fed.
55 E1 Yeyik China
51 F5 Yeysk Rus. Fed.
65 L4 Yeyungou China
12 H1 Yezhuga r. Rus. Fed.
12 D4 Yezyaryshcha Belarus
144 A6 Yguazú r. Paraguay
51 F1 Yi r. Henan China
51 F1 Yi r. Shandong China
61 B4 Yi'allaq, G. mt. Egypt
49 H3 Yi'an China
73 H4 Yibā, W. w Saudi Arabia
50 D2 Yibin China
55 F2 Yibug Caka salt l. China
51 E2 Yichang China
51 E3 Yicheng China
48 D6 Yichun China
51 E3 Yichun China
51 F2 Yidu China
49 F5 Yidun China
51 F2 Yifeng China
51 F2 Yigo Guam Pac. Oc.
51 E1 Yijun China
49 H2 Yilaha China
49 J3 Yilan China
51 F2 Yildiz Dağları mt. ra. Turkey
128 C2 Yildizeli Turkey
41 J5 Yildiz D. mt. Turkey
49 J2 Yilehuli Shan mt. ra. China
50 C3 Yiliang China
120 E5 Yiliang China
119 D5 Yilong China
99 E1 Yilong Hu l. China
51 F3 Yimianpo China
51 F3 Yimin r. China
49 F6 Yinan China
101 C6 Yindarlgooda, L. salt flat Aust.
51 F1 Ying r. China
51 F1 Yingcheng China
49 H4 Yingchengzi China
51 F3 Yingde China
50 B3 Yingjiang China
49 G4 Yingjing China
49 G4 Yingkou China
50 D2 Yingpanshui China
51 E2 Yingshan China
51 E2 Yingshan China
51 F1 Yingtan China
51 G2 Yingtan China
54 E1 Yining China
65 K4 Yining China
49 H3 Yinjiang China
49 H3 Yinma r. China
42 A2 Yinmabin Myanmar

Column 2

48 D4 Yin Shan mt. ra. China
50 A2 Yi'ong Zangbo r. China
50 C3 Yipinglang China
145 F5 Yira Chapeu, Monte mt. Brazil
80 C3 Yirga Alem Ethiopia
80 C3 Yirga Ch'efē Ethiopia
55 G2 Yirna Tso salt l. China
80 B3 Yirol Sudan
49 F3 Yirshi China
49 F5 Yi Shan mt. ra. China
50 E3 Yishan China
49 F6 Yishui China
43 Yishun Singapore
49 H4 Yitong China
50 C3 Yitulihe China
44 F3 Yiwu China
50 C4 Yiwu China
51 G3 Yi Xian China
49 G4 Yi Xian China
51 E3 Yixing China
51 F2 Yiyang China
51 F2 Yiyang China
49 F5 Yiyuan China
49 H3 Yizhang China
11 F3 Ylihärmä Finland
10 G2 Yli-Ii Finland
10 G2 Yli-Kärppä Finland
10 G2 Ylikiiminki Finland
10 G2 Yli-Kitka l. Finland
10 F3 Ylistaro Finland
11 F3 Ylitornio Finland
16 F3 Ythan r. U.K.
11 F3 Ytyk-Kyuyel' Rus. Fed.
51 H4 Yuxi China
50 C3 Yuanan China
51 E2 Yuan r. Hunan China
50 C4 Yuan r. Yunnan China
51 E3 Yuan'an China
51 E3 Yuanbao Shan mt. China
51 J2 Yuanjiang China
51 F2 Yuanjiang China
51 H3 Yuanli Taiwan
50 D3 Yuanling China
50 D2 Yuanmou China
50 C3 Yuanping China
47 E6 Yuanshan China
47 E6 Yuanshanzi China
50 D1 Yuanyang China
14 F1 Yuasa Japan
128 B2 Yuba r. U.S.A.
128 B2 Yuba City U.S.A.
46 J2 Yūbari r. Japan
46 J2 Yūbari-sanchi mt. ra. Japan
46 J1 Yūbetsu Japan
46 J1 Yūbetsu-gawa r. Japan
130 C3 Yucatán div. Mexico
131 H6 Yucatán pen. Mexico
132 A2 Yucatan Channel str. Cuba/Mexico
129 E4 Yucca U.S.A.
128 D4 Yucca Valley U.S.A.
51 F1 Yucheng China
14 C1 Yudino Rus. Fed.
14 C1 Yudi Shan mt. China
50 D2 Yuechi China
42 B3 Yueliang Pao l. China
98 B4 Yuendumu Aust.
98 B4 Yuendumu Abor. Reserve res. Aust.

49 Yuen Long Hong Kong
51 H2 Yuexi China
51 F2 Yuexi China
51 F2 Yueyang China
50 D3 Yugan China
5 H4 Yugoslavia country Europe
63 R3 Yugo-Tala Rus. Fed.
51 F2 Yuhuan China
63 R3 Yukagirskoye Ploskogor'ye plat. Rus. Fed.
14 D2 Yukhnov Rus. Fed.
79 C4 Yuki Yaire
110 B2 Yukon r. Can./U.S.A.
110 F2 Yukon Territory div. Can.
57 F2 Yüksekova Turkey
46 C7 Yukuhashi Japan
64 E2 Yuldybayevo Rus. Fed.
51 H3 Yule r. Aust.
119 D6 Yule r. U.S.A.
51 H3 Yulin Taiwan
48 E5 Yulin China
51 F3 Yulin China
50 D3 Yulongxue Shan mt. China

51 G3 Yunhe China
129 E5 Yuma Desert desert U.S.A.
78 B4 Yumbi Bandundu Zaire
78 B3 Yumbi Kivu Zaire
50 C3 Yumen China
61 C1 Yumurtalik Turkey
49 H4 Yuna Dom. Rep.
15 F1 Yunakivka Ukraine
50 D3 Yunan China
51 G3 Yuncheng China
51 G3 Yunfu China
75 G3 Yungas reg. Bolivia
142 B4 Yungay Antofagasta Chile
50 B3 Yungay Perú
50 C3 Yun Gui Gaoyuan plat. China
51 E3 Yunhe China
51 H2 Yunjinghou China
50 D3 Yunkai Dashan mt. ra. China
50 D3 Yun Ling mt. ra. China
50 D3 Yunnan div. China
46 C7 Yunomae Japan
47 G6 Yunoshima Japan
46 E7 Yunomae Japan
46 G5 Yunoshima Japan
96 D3 Yunta Aust.
51 F2 Yunxi China
50 D3 Yun Xian China
51 G4 Yunxiao China

Column 3

17 D6 Youghal Rep. of Ire.
120 D5 Youghiogheny River Lake l. U.S.A.
76 B4 Youkounkoun Guinea
97 G3 Young Aust.
146 E3 Young Uruguay
95 ^1 Young, C. c. Chatham Is N.Z.
96 D2 Younghusband, L. salt flat Aust.
96 D3 Younghusband Pen. pen. Aust.
152 A6 Young I. i. Ant.
91 ^14 Young's Rock rock Pitcairn I. Pac. Oc.
120 C4 Youngstown U.S.A.
74 C2 Youssoufia Morocco
76 D3 Youvarou Mali
50 D3 Youxi China
76 D3 You Xian China
50 E2 Youyang China
65 L3 Youyi Feng mt. China/Rus. Fed.
51 H3 Youyu China
15 G3 Yovon Tajikistan
60 C2 Yozgat Turkey
141 E4 Ypané r. Paraguay
141 E4 Ypé-Jhú Paraguay
126 B3 Yreka U.S.A.
77 G4 Ysdseram w Nigeria
11 D5 Ystad Sweden
65 J4 Ysyk-Köl salt l. Kyrgyzstan
16 F3 Ythan r. U.K.
65 J4 Ysyk-Köl Kyrgyzstan
11 F3 Ytyk-Kyuyel' Rus. Fed.
51 H4 Yuxi China
46 C7 Yūbetsu Japan

96 J1 Yūbetsu Japan
46 J2 Yūbetsu-gawa r. Japan
130 C3 Yucatán div. Mexico
131 H6 Yucatán pen. Mexico
132 A2 Yucatan Channel str. Cuba/Mexico
129 E4 Yucca U.S.A.
128 D4 Yucca Valley U.S.A.
51 F1 Yucheng China
14 C1 Yudino Rus. Fed.
21 H3 Yverdon Switz.
42 A2 Ywamun Myanmar
42 B3 Ywathit Myanmar

Z

18 B2 Zaandam Netherlands
23 Zabaykal'sk China
60 F2 Zab-e Kuchek r. Iran
78 E3 Zabia Zaire
80 D2 Zabid Yemen
80 D2 Zabid, W. w Yemen
19 L2 Ząbkowice Śląskie Poland
19 L2 Żabludów Poland
19 J2 Żabno Poland
26 E2 Zabok Croatia
57 E4 Zābol Iran
57 D4 Zāboli Iran
15 A1 Zabolottya Ukraine
76 D4 Zabré Burkina
64 E2 Zabrykan Rus. Fed.
19 H2 Zabrze Poland
77 E5 Zabzugu Ghana
131 H6 Zacapa Guatemala
142 B3 Zacapu Mexico
130 E5 Zacatecas div. Mexico
130 E4 Zacatecas Mexico
29 C6 Zacharo Greece
15 G3 Zachepylivka Ukraine
19 H2 Zadar Croatia
43 B5 Zadetkale Kyun i. Myanmar
43 B5 Zadetkyi Kyun i. Myanmar
14 D1 Zadoi China
15 E3 Zadonsk Rus. Fed.
74 C2 Z'afarāna Egypt
29 F6 Zafora i. Greece
24 C3 Zafra Spain
19 J4 Zag Morocco
54 B4 Zagań Poland
61 C5 Zaghdeh well Iran
57 D2 Zaghdeh-ye-Bālā Iran
15 D3 Zaghouan Tunisia
74 C3 Zagora Morocco
26 E2 Zagorá Greece
19 L2 Zagórz Poland
14 D3 Zagoskino Rus. Fed.
26 E2 Zagreb Croatia
57 D2 Zagros Mountains mt. ra. Iran
72 D2 Zaqqui Libya
57 D3 Za Qu r. China
60 E2 Zara Turkey
15 F4 Zaragoza Colombia
138 C2 Zaragoza Coahuila Mexico
130 E3 Zaragoza Coahuila Mexico
131 E2 Zaragoza Nuevo León Mexico
25 F2 Zaragoza Spain
57 C2 Zarand Iran
57 D3 Zarand Iran
57 D3 Zaranj Afghanistan
11 F5 Zarasai Lithuania
146 E3 Zárate Arg.
25 E1 Zarautz Spain

Column 4

50 E2 Yunyang China
51 F1 Yunyang China
51 F3 Yuping China
28 D3 Zaječar Yugo.
140 C4 Yura Bolivia
47 E6 Yura-gawa r. Japan
65 K1 Yurga Rus. Fed.
138 B5 Yurimaguas Peru
14 H1 Yurino Rus. Fed.
12 H1 Yuroma r. Rus. Fed.
14 F1 Yuronga r. Rus. Fed.
14 F1 Yurovo Rus. Fed.
138 D1 Yurubí, Parque Nacional nat. park Venezuela
14 G2 Yur'ya Rus. Fed.
14 F1 Yur'yevets Rus. Fed.
51 F3 Yur'yevets Rus. Fed.
14 D1 Yur'yevo Opol'ye reg. Rus. Fed.
15 G2 Yur'yev-Pol'skiy Rus. Fed.
15 G2 Yur'yivka Ukraine
15 G3 Yur'yivka Zaporizhzhya Ukraine
64 F1 Yuryuzan' r. Rus. Fed.
130 J6 Yuscarán Honduras
51 H4 Yu Shan mt. Taiwan
51 H2 Yushan Liedao is China
63 R3 Yushe China
12 E1 Yushkozero Rus. Fed.
50 B1 Yushu China
13 H6 Yusta Rus. Fed.
46 D7 Yusufeli Turkey
46 E7 Yusuhara Japan
57 C2 Yutai China
14 D3 Yuti Bolivia
51 F2 Yutian China
141 D3 Yuty Paraguay
48 C5 Yuwang China
51 G4 Yuxi China
51 E2 Yuxiakou China
51 F1 Yu Xian China
51 H2 Yu Xian China
14 H2 Yuyao China
14 F1 Yuzha Rus. Fed.
15 D3 Yuzhne Ukraine
65 G4 Yuzhno-Kazakhstan div. Kazak.
45 Q2 Yuzhno-Sakhalinsk Rus. Fed.
13 H6 Yuzhno-Sukhokumsk Rus. Fed.
64 F2 Yuzhnoural'sk Rus. Fed.
65 K2 Yuzhnoye Rus. Fed.
65 K2 Yuzhnyy Rus. Fed.
48 C6 Yuzhong China
59 D5 Yūzidar Iran
21 H3 Yverdon Switz.
42 A2 Ywamun Myanmar

Column 5

79 B5 Zaire div. Angola
78 B4 Zaire r. Congo/Zaire
28 D3 Zaječar Yugo.
83 E3 Zaka Zimbabwe
48 B2 Zakamensk Rus. Fed.
15 A2 Zakhidnyy Buh r. Ukraine
57 G2 Zakhmet Turkmenistan
60 E2 Zākhō Iraq
15 B2 Zaklików Poland
19 J4 Zakopane Poland
78 C1 Zakouma Chad
78 C1 Zakouma, Parc National nat. park Chad
15 B2 Zakupne Ukraine
29 C6 Zakynthos i. Greece
29 C6 Zakynthos Greece
19 H5 Zalaegerszeg Hungary
19 H5 Zalai-domsag h. Hungary
19 H5 Zalakomár Hungary
24 D3 Zalamea de la Serena Spain
77 G4 Zalanga Nigeria
49 F3 Zalantun China
19 J4 Zalaszentgrót Hungary
19 L7 Zalău Romania
27 C5 Zalec Slovenia
21 H2 Zalegoshch' Rus. Fed.
65 G2 Zalesovo Rus. Fed.
19 L2 Zalew Szczeciński b. Poland
73 H3 Zalim Saudi Arabia
72 D5 Zalingei Sudan
15 A2 Zalishchyky Ukraine
15 A2 Zalissya Ukraine
15 B1 Zalizci Ukraine
15 B2 Zalizniy Port Ukraine
15 B1 Zaliztsi Ukraine
13 H6 Zaliznyy Rus. Fed.
83 E3 Zama Zambia
41 B3 Zambales Mts mt. ra. Phil.
79 D6 Zambeze r. Angola
82 E2 Zambeze r. Mozambique
79 D7 Zambezi r. Zambia
19 D6 Zambezi Zambia
83 F2 Zambézia div. Mozambique
83 D4 Zambia country Africa
41 B5 Zamboanga Phil.
41 B5 Zamboanga Peninsula pen. Phil.
83 E4 Zambue Mozambique
77 F4 Zamfara r. Nigeria
138 B4 Zamora r. Ecuador
138 B4 Zamora Ecuador
130 E5 Zamora de Hidalgo Mexico
15 C2 Zamość Poland
47 ^2 Zampa-misaki b. Japan
15 C1 Zamtang China
138 D1 Zamuro, Pta pt Venezuela
79 B4 Zanaga Congo
54 D3 Zanda China
65 K3 Zanesville U.S.A.
60 F2 Zangguy China
65 J5 Zangla China
15 D2 Zanjān div. Iran
27 D5 Zannone, Isola i. Italy
83 B2 Zanzibar Tanzania
81 C6 Zanzibar Channel chan. Tanzania
81 C6 Zanzibar I. i. Tanzania
75 F3 Zaori Algeria
23 F4 Zaouatallaz Algeria
73 G3 Zaouiet l. l. Egypt
47 H4 Zao-san vol Japan
75 E3 Zaozer'ye Rus. Fed.
60 F2 Zap r. Turkey
12 D3 Zapadna Dvina r. Rus. Fed.
12 D3 Zapadnaya Dvina Rus. Fed.
28 D4 Zapadni Rodopi mt. ra. Bulgaria
64 D3 Zapadno-Kazakhstan div. Kazak.
62 J4 Zapadno-Sibirskaya Ravnina plain Rus. Fed.
64 D4 Zapadnyy Chink Ustyurta escarpment Kazak.
10 J1 Zapadnyy Kil'din Rus. Fed.
45 H1 Zapadnyy Sayan mt. ra. Rus. Fed.
15 B2 Zapadyntsi Ukraine
147 B4 Zapala Arg.
142 C4 Zapaleri, Co mt. Chile
138 B3 Zapata, Pen. de pen. Cuba
138 C2 Zapatoca Colombia
19 C2 Zapiga Chile
131 E2 Zapolyarnyy Rus. Fed.
12 F1 Zapol'ye Rus. Fed.
15 G3 Zaporizhzhya div. Ukraine
15 G3 Zaporizhzhya Ukraine
14 D4 Zapotal Ecuador
13 G3 Zaprudnya Rus. Fed.
15 B1 Zapytiv Ukraine
57 B2 Zaqatala Azerbaijan
57 C1 Zäqän Iran
83 D2 Zaqqui Libya
57 E2 Zarand Iran

Column 6

14 D2 Zaraysk Rus. Fed.
139 D2 Zaraza Venezuela
15 H5 Zardaly Kyrgyzstan
57 B2 Zāreh Iran
57 C2 Zarembo I. i. U.S.A.
60 E2 Zārch Iran
19 J4 Zargün Shahr Afghanistan
57 B2 Zargün mt. Afghanistan
77 F4 Zaria Nigeria
15 B1 Zarichne Ukraine
15 E2 Zarinsk Rus. Fed.
57 C3 Zarmardan Afghanistan
60 D3 Zarqā' Jordan
57 C2 Zarqā' r. Jordan
57 C2 Zarqān Iran
57 C2 Zarrīn Iran
138 A4 Zarumilla Peru
54 C2 Zary Poland
64 E3 Zarya Oktyabrya Kazak.
75 F3 Zarzaïtine Algeria
13 G3 Zasechnoye Rus. Fed.
65 H3 Zaskar r. India
54 D2 Zaskar Mts mt. ra. India
12 C4 Zaslawye Belarus
15 A2 Zastavna Ukraine
14 H1 Zasur'ye Rus. Fed.
61 D3 Zatara w Jordan
64 F2 Zatobol'sk Kazak.
19 J4 Zhanakentkala salt l. Kazak.
19 G1 Zatoka Pomorska b. Poland
15 G3 Zatoka Syvash b. Ukraine
15 A3 Zaturtsi Ukraine
15 E2 Zatyshshya Ukraine
64 E4 Zaunguzskiye Karakumy desert Turkmenistan
57 D2 Zavallya Ukraine
57 C2 Zavareh Iran
26 E3 Zavidovići Bos.-Herz.
14 F2 Zavitinsk Rus. Fed.
65 G1 Zavodoukovsk Rus. Fed.
15 A2 Zavods'ke Ukraine
14 F1 Zavolzh'ye Rus. Fed.
15 A2 Zavolzh'ye Rus. Fed.
43 F2 Zawa China
19 J3 Zawiercie Poland
72 C2 Zāwīyah, J. az h. Syria
72 D1 Zāwiyat Masūs Libya
80 D1 Zaydī, Wādī az r. Syria
65 K3 Zaysan, Oz. l. Kazak.
65 K3 Zaysan, Oz. l. Kazak.
65 K3 Zayü Tibet China
65 K3 Zayü China
19 G4 Zbąszynek Poland
15 A1 Zboriv Ukraine
15 A1 Zbruch r. Ukraine
19 G4 Żdar nad Sázavou Czech Rep.
15 B1 Zdolbuniv Ukraine
19 J3 Zduńska Wola Poland
19 L2 Zdvyzh r. Ukraine
11 C5 Zealand i. Denmark
57 D2 Zēbāk Afghanistan
60 F2 Zēbār Iraq
73 G3 Zebirget I. i. Egypt
74 D4 Zebrak Czech Rep.
14 K3 Zborovsky Rus. Fed.
97 F5 Zeehan Aust.
18 C2 Zeeland div. Netherlands
19 L2 Zefat Israel
18 E3 Żednieck Germany
61 B6 Zeit, G. el h. Egypt
18 D2 Zeitz Germany
15 D3 Żekog China
15 E3 Zelechów Poland
19 H5 Żelena Croatia
15 E3 Zelena Ukraine
14 H2 Zelenchuk, B. r. Rus. Fed.
65 E2 Zelenchuk, B. r. Rus. Fed.
10 J2 Zelenoborskiy Rus. Fed.
14 H1 Zelenodol'sk Rus. Fed.
15 F1 Zelenogorsk Ukraine
11 E6 Zelenogradsk Rus. Fed.
13 G6 Zelenokumsk Rus. Fed.
15 E3 Zelenyy Gay r. Ukraine
75 E2 Zelfana Algeria
19 J4 Żeliezovce Slovakia
26 D2 Żelina Croatia
54 E3 Zēmag China
58 D2 Zémdasam China
57 B2 Zemetchino Rus. Fed.
78 E2 Zémio C.A.R.
40 C3 Zenhai China
42 C3 Zenica Bos.-Herz.
26 E3 Zenipa China
58 B5 Zen'kov Ukraine
57 G4 Zerafshon r. Uzbekistan

Column 7

14 D2 Zaraysk Rus. Fed.
18 D2 Zeven Germany
10 H2 Zhireken Rus. Fed.
13 H5 Zhirnovsk Rus. Fed.
49 N1 Zeya r. Rus. Fed.
48 J2 Zeya r. Rus. Fed.
57 E4 Zeyarat-e Shamil Iran
57 C4 Zeydābād Iran
60 F3 Zēydar Iran
57 D3 Zeynalābād Iran
49 J2 Zeysko-Bureinskaya Vpadina depression Rus. Fed.
63 O4 Zeyskoye Vdkhr. resr Rus. Fed.
29 G5 Zeytindağ Turkey
24 B3 Zêzere r. Portugal
61 C2 Zgharta Lebanon
19 J3 Zgierz Poland
15 B2 Zguritsa Moldova
15 A2 Zhabinka Belarus
65 G2 Zhaksykon r. Kazak.
65 H3 Zhaksy Sarysu w Kazak.
65 G2 Zhaltyr Kazak.
65 G2 Zhaltyr, Oz. l. Kazak.
64 F3 Zhamanakkol', Oz. salt l. Kazak.
64 D3 Zhamansor Kazak.
14 H1 Zhanar'yk r. Kazak.
61 D3 Zhanatobe Kazak.
64 F2 Zhanabas Kazak.
65 G3 Zhananpa Kazak.
65 G3 Zhanang China
15 A3 Zhanaortalyk Kazak.
14 H2 Zhanaozen Kazak.
54 D3 Zhanbay Kazak.
19 J2 Zhangbei China
49 J2 Zhangguangcai Ling mt. ra. China
51 E4 Zhanghuang China
53 J2 Zhangjiakou China
49 H6 Zhangjiajing China
54 E2 Zhangling China
51 E3 Zhangping China
51 E2 Zhangpu China
51 H4 Zhuji China
51 F2 Zhangqiangzhen China
49 F5 Zhangwei Xinhe r. China
49 G1 Zhangwu China
51 E2 Zhang Xian China
42 B2 Zhangye China
19 J3 Zhangzhou China
51 F3 Zhanhua China
50 E4 Zhanjiang China
65 K2 Zhanterek r. Kazak.
51 H2 Zhanyi China
51 F4 Zhao'an China
48 A5 Zhaojiao China
48 A5 Zhaojue China
51 F2 Zhaoping China
51 E4 Zhaoqing China
65 K3 Zhaosu China
51 D2 Zhaotong China
49 G1 Zhao Xian China
51 F2 Zhaoyang Hu l. China
50 D4 Zhapo China
64 F3 Zharkamys Kazak.
65 K3 Zharkovskiy Rus. Fed.
14 B3 Zharma Kazak.
65 K3 Zhaxi Co salt l. China
131 E5 Zhaxigang China
50 D2 Zhaxizê China
49 J2 Zhayrem Kazak.
29 E3 Zhdanov Rus. Fed.
15 G6 Zhdanovka Rus. Fed.
14 B3 Zheltorangy Kazak.
15 G3 Zheltoragys Kazak.
75 E3 Zelfana Algeria
14 C3 Zhdanovka Ukraine
29 E3 Zhdelaniya, M. c. Rus. Fed.
15 E1 Zheleznodorozhnyy Rus. Fed.
15 K1 Zheleznodorozhnyy Rus. Fed.
13 G6 Zheleznogorsk Rus. Fed.
49 H2 Zhenai China
51 F4 Zheng'an China
54 E1 Zhengding China
49 G4 Zhenghe China
46 H3 Zhengxiangbai Qi China
58 F4 Zhengyang China
51 F1 Zhengzhou China
57 G4 Zhenhai China
19 H2 Zhenjiang China
58 F4 Zhenlai China
49 J2 Zhenlai China
50 D3 Zhenning China
15 H4 Zhenping China
58 C2 Zhenxi China
50 D3 Zhenxiong China
50 D3 Zhenyuan China
12 J4 Zhenzhou China
128 A3 Zenia U.S.A.
46 D7 Zentsūji Japan
51 H4 Zenza China
19 H5 Zercsard China

Column 8

14 C3 Zhilino Rus. Fed.
49 F1 Zhiren China
13 H5 Zhirnovsk Rus. Fed.
14 H3 Zhiryatino Rus. Fed.
14 B3 Zhizdra r. Rus. Fed.
13 D4 Zhlobin Belarus
15 D4 Zhmerynka Ukraine
63 R2 Zhokhova, O. i. Rus. Fed.
63 R2 Zhokhova, O. i. Rus. Fed.
58 B3 Zhob Pakistan
54 B3 Zhob r. Pakistan
48 C5 Zhob r. Pakistan
55 B3 Zhongba China
50 B3 Zhongdian China
48 C5 Zhongning China
51 E2 Zhongshan China
51 F3 Zhongshan China
49 H2 Zhoujiajing China
55 H3 Zhouning China
51 H2 Zhoukou China
51 G3 Zhouming China
51 H2 Zhoushan Dao i. China
51 H2 Zhoushan Qundao is China
48 E4 Zhouzi China
50 D3 Zhovti Vody Ukraine
15 D2 Zhovten' Ukraine
15 F2 Zhovtneve Ukraine
15 F2 Zhovtnevo Poltava Ukraine
51 E4 Zhuanghe China
49 H2 Zhangjiazhen China
50 D1 Zhucheng China
51 E4 Zhugqu China
51 F4 Zhuhai China
51 H4 Zhuji China
65 J2 Zhukovka Rus. Fed.
14 A3 Zhukovka Rus. Fed.
14 C2 Zhukovskiy Rus. Fed.
15 D1 Zhukyn r. Ukraine
51 H2 Zhumadian China
50 D1 Zhuo Xian China
49 F4 Zhuozhou China
48 E4 Zhurbin Rus. Fed.
13 G6 Zhurivka Ukraine
15 D1 Zhurivka Ukraine
51 F3 Zhuzhou China
15 C1 Zhydachiv Ukraine
13 C4 Zhyttkavichy Belarus
15 E1 Zhytomyr div. Ukraine
15 C1 Zhytomyr Ukraine
19 J3 Zhznaky China
50 D2 Ziang China
54 A3 Zhob Pakistan
19 L3 Ziar nad Hronom Slovakia
54 A3 Ziarat Pakistan
72 C2 Zibo China
50 D3 Zichang China
146 A4 Zielona Góra Poland
98 C4 Ziel, Mt mt. Aust.
19 G3 Zielona Góra Poland
64 F3 Zharkamys Kazak.
42 A2 Ziganqi China
72 D2 Zighan Libya
29 D3 Zigong China
72 C2 Ziguey China
76 A4 Ziguinchor Senegal
15 G6 Zila China
131 E5 Zihuatanejo Mexico
18 D3 Zijin China
15 E3 Zikeyevo Rus. Fed.
61 C3 Zikhron Ya'aqov Israel
60 C1 Zile Turkey
19 L4 Žilina Slovakia
72 C2 Zillah Libya
131 F5 Zimatlán Mexico
83 D2 Zimba Zambia
83 E3 Zimbabwe country Africa
83 E3 Zimbabwe Zimbabwe
76 B4 Zimmi Sierra Leone
28 F3 Zimnicea Romania
19 J3 Zimniy Bereg Rus. Fed.
13 F5 Zimovniki Rus. Fed.
57 F2 Zindajan Afghanistan
77 F4 Zinder div. Niger
80 D2 Zinjibār Yemen
15 D1 Zin'kiv Ukraine
72 B1 Zinovo China
72 B1 Zīnti Libya
133 ^3 Zion St Kitts-Nevis
129 F3 Zion Nat. Park nat. park U.S.A.
138 D2 Zipaquirá Colombia
138 C2 Zipaquirá Colombia
25 J2 Żirǵe China
14 C2 Zirc Hungary
26 E2 Ziri Slovenia
128 E4 Ziro India
19 H5 Zistersdorf Austria
14 D2 Zitsa Greece
142 E1 Zitua r. Brazil

Column 9

50 E1 Ziyang China
51 E3 Ziyuan China
50 D3 Ziyun China
48 D5 Zizhou China
28 B3 Zlatar mts Yugo.
Slovakia
28 D1 Zlatibor mts Yugo.
28 D1 Zlatica r. Yugo.
28 D1 Zlatna Romania
64 F1 Zlatoust Bulgaria
29 E4 Zlatoust Rus. Fed.
19 H4 Zlín Czech Rep.
72 B1 Zlïtan Libya
19 H2 Złocieniec Poland
19 J3 Złoczew Poland
19 G3 Złotoryja Poland
15 D2 Złotów Poland
65 K2 Zmeinogorsk Rus. Fed.
19 H3 Żmigród Poland
15 G2 Zmiyiv Ukraine
14 B3 Znamenka Kazak.
14 J2 Znamenka Rus. Fed.
14 B3 Znamenka Rus. Fed.
14 H1 Znamensk Rus. Fed.
14 B3 Znamenskoye Rus. Fed.
15 E2 Znam''yanka Druha Ukraine
19 H3 Znin Poland
14 A3 Znob Novhorods'ke Ukraine
19 J4 Znojmo Czech Rep.
78 B3 Zoetelé Cameroon
50 B2 Zogang China
15 D2 Zoïğé China
14 F1 Zoji La pass India
15 F1 Zolochiv Kharkiv Ukraine
15 A2 Zolochiv L'viv Ukraine
63 O4 Zolotarevka Rus. Fed.
51 E2 Zolotkovo Rus. Fed.
51 H3 Zolotonosha Ukraine
14 A3 Zolotyy Potik Ukraine
15 L3 Żołynia Poland
83 F2 Zomba Malawi
79 B5 Zongo Zaire
21 J6 Zonza France
77 G3 Zoo Baba well Niger
79 D4 Zongo Burkina
54 C1 Zorkūl l. Afghanistan/Tajikistan
28 F1 Zorleni Romania
19 J3 Zornitsa Bulgaria
138 A4 Zorritos Peru
19 L3 Zory Poland
19 L3 Zouar Chad
74 B4 Zouérat Mauritania
51 E4 Zouping China
48 E5 Zouyun China
19 K5 Zrenjanin Yugo.
19 H5 Zrmanja r. Croatia
19 J3 Zsadány Hungary
57 D2 Zu Algâagoum China
146 D4 Zubillaga Arg.
14 F2 Zubova Polyana Rus. Fed.
14 B2 Zubtsov Rus. Fed.
79 D4 Zucanina Spain
76 B5 Zuénoula Côte d'Ivoire
21 G2 Zug Switz.
13 G7 Zugdidi Georgia
18 E5 Zugspitze mt. Austria/Germany
77 F4 Zungeru Nigeria
18 C2 Zuider Zee inlet Netherlands
18 B3 Zuid-Holland div. Netherlands
24 D3 Zújar r. Spain
19 J3 Zukowo Poland
19 H2 Zülpich Germany
83 E2 Zumbo Mozambique
122 A3 Zumbro r. U.S.A.
131 F5 Zumpango Mexico
77 F5 Zungeru Nigeria
52 H4 Zunhua China
129 H4 Zuni Mts mt. ra. U.S.A.
50 D3 Zunyi China
19 H5 Zupanja Croatia
19 J2 Żuromin Poland
21 J3 Zürich Switz.
57 G2 Zurmat reg. Afghanistan
77 F4 Zurmi Nigeria
80 B3 Zvai China
72 B1 Zuwārah Libya
72 B1 Zuwayzā Libya

Column 10 (rightmost partial)

28 B3 Zlatibor mts Yugo.
72 H4 Zliten Libya
19 H2 Zloczew Poland
19 J3 Złotoryja Poland
15 G3 Zlynka Ukraine
65 K2 Zmeinogorsk Rus. Fed.
19 H4 Żmigród Poland
15 G2 Zmiyiv Ukraine
14 J2 Znamenka Kazak.
14 B3 Znamenka Rus. Fed.
14 H1 Znamensk Rus. Fed.
14 B3 Znamenskoye Rus. Fed.
19 J4 Znojmo Czech Rep.
50 C1 Zogang China
15 F1 Zoïğé China
15 F1 Zoloche Ukraine
63 O4 Zolotnyky Ukraine
19 L3 Żołynia Poland
83 F2 Zomba Malawi
21 J6 Zonza France
77 G3 Zoo Baba well Niger
54 C1 Zorkūl l. Afghanistan/Tajikistan
82 D5 Zwelitsha R.S.A.
14 F3 Zwettl Austria
18 D3 Zwickau Germany
18 D3 Zwolle Netherlands
15 C1 Zydachiv Ukraine
18 D1 Zyrardów Poland
80 K3 Zyryan Haykk'l. Ethiopia
52 D3 Zixi China
13 J5 Zyrzyn Poland
19 L1 Zyryanka Rus. Fed.
49 L1 Zyul'zya Rus. Fed.
19 J4 Żywiec Poland

GLOSSARY of alternative name forms

Abergwaun see Fishguard
Abertawe see Swansea
Abkhazskaya Respublika see Abkhazia
Abqaiq see Buqayq
Abu Dhabi see Abū Ẓabī
Acre see 'Akko
A.C.T. div. see Australian Capital Territory
Adalia see Antalya
Aden see 'Adan
Adzharia see Ajaria
Adzharskaya Respublika see Ajaria
Afal w see 'Ifāl, W.
Agdash see Agdaş
Agdzhabedi see Ağcabädi
Aguapei r. see Feio ou Aguapei
Ahwāz see Ahvāz
Ajanta Range h. see Sahyadriparvat
a-Jiddét gravel area see Jiddat al Ḥarāsīs
Akhsu see Ağsu
Akyab see Sittwe
Alagez mt. see Aragats Lerr
Alappuzha see Alleppey
Alataw Shankou pass see Dzungarian Gate
Aleppo see Ḥalab
Alevisik see Samandağı
Alexandretta see İskenderun
Algiers see Alger
Alma-Ata see Almaty
Amazon r. see Amazonas
Amboina see Ambon
Amherst see Kyaikkami
Amirabad see Fūlād Maïalleh
Amne Machin Range mt. ra. see A'nyêmaqên Shan
Amoy see Xiamen
Anadyrskiy Khrebet mt. ra. see Chukotskiy Khrebet
Anaypazari see Gülnar
An Cóbh see Cóbh
Anda see Daqing
Angmagssalik see Tasiilaq
Anhwei see Anhui
Anjouan i. see Nzwani
An Muileann gCearr see Mullingar
An Nás see Naas
An Tairbeart see Tarbert
Antakya see Hatay
An tAonach see Nenagh
Anti-Lebanon mt. ra. see Sharqi, Jebel esh
An tInbhear Mór see Arklow
Antioch see Hatay
Antwerp see Antwerpen
An Uaimh see Navan
Anvers see Antwerpen
Aoraki, Mt mt. see Cook, Mt
Araks r. see Araz
Araks r. see Aras
Aral'skoye More salt l. see Aral Sea
Ararat, Mt mt. see Büyük Ağri
Archangel see Arkhangel'sk
Armageddon see Megiddo
Armavir see Hoktemberyan
Ashkhabad see Ashgabat
Ash Shurayf see Khaybar
Astalu I. i. see Astola I.
Asterabad see Gorgān
Astin Tagh mt. ra. see Altun Shan
Astipalaia i. see Astypalaia
Astrakhan' Bazar see Cäilabad
Atas I. i. see South Island
Athens see Athina
Attalea see Antalya
Azbine mts see Aïr, Massif de l'
Badaojiang see Hunjiang
Bago see Pegu
Bagrax Hu l. see Bosten Hu
Bahāmabād see Rafsanjān
Baikal, Lake l. see Baykal, Ozero
Baile Átha Cliath see Dublin
Baile Átha Luain see Athlone
Baku see Bakı
Baky see Bakı
Balearic Islands see Baleares, Islas
Balkan Mts mts see Stara Planina
Balmer see Barmer
Balykchy see Ysyk-Köl
Bandar see Machilipatnam
Bandar-e Pahlavi see Bandar-e Anzalī
Bandar-e Shāhpūr see Bandar Khomeynī
Ban Don see Surat Thani
Banow see Andarāb
Ban Pla Soi see Chon Buri
Ba'oan see Shenzhen
Barak see Kargamiş
Barcoo Creek w see Cooper Cr.
Baroda see Vadodara
Basle see Basel
Basra see Al Başrah
Basuo see Dongfang
Batum see Bat'umi
Bay see Baicheng
Béal an Átha see Ballina
Béal Átha na Sluaighe see Ballinasloe
Beersheba see Be'ér Sheva'
Beinn na Faoghla i. see Benbecula
Belgrade see Beograd
Bellin see Kangirsuk
Beyrouth see Beirut
Bezwada see Vijayawada
Bhādrachalam Road Sta. see Kottagudem
Bhatnair see Hanumangarh
Biblos see Jbail
Bideford Bay b. see Barnstaple Bay
Billabong r. see Moulamein
Bi'r Ibn Hirmās see Al Bi'r
Bishbek see Bishkek
Black Pagoda see Konārka
Black River r. see Sông Đa
Black Rock h. see El 'Ināb
Black Volta r. see Mouhoun
Blue Nile r. see Bahr el Azraq
Bokombayevskoye see Bökönbaev
Bol'shoy Kavkaz mt. ra. see Caucasus
Bonin Is is see Ogasawara-shotō
Bortala see Bole
Borzhomi see Borjomi
Bosporus str. see İstanbul Boğazı
Bowo see Bomi
Bozyaka see Beskonak
Bré see Bray
Brewster, Kap c. see Kangikajik
Brezhnev see Naberezhnyye Chelny
Brittany div. see Bretagne
Brothers, The is see Al Ikhwān
Bruges see Brugge
Brussel see Bruxelles
Brussels see Bruxelles
Bucharest see Bucureşti
Buckner Bay b. see Nakagusuku-wan
Bügür see Luntai
Burgundy div. see Bourgogne
Burma see Myanmar
Bûr Sa'îd see Port Said
Būr Sudan see Port Sudan
Burultokay see Fuhai
Bushire see Būshehr
Cabora Bassa Dam dam see Cahora Bassa, Barragem de
Caerdydd see Cardiff
Caerfyrddin see Carmarthen
Caergybi see Holyhead
Caisléan an Bharraigh see Castlebar
Çamalan see Gülek
Cambay see Khambhat
Cambay, Gulf of b. see Khambhat, Gulf of
Canary Islands is see Canarias, Islas
Cantabrian Mountains mt. ra. see Cantábrica, Cordillera
Canton see Guangzhou
Carraig na Siuire see Carrick-on-Suir
Casnewydd see Newport
Castell-y-Nedd see Neath
Ceanannus Mór see Kells
Ceatharlach see Carlow
Celebes i. see Sulawesi
Cephalonia i. see Kefallonia
Chanda see Chandrapur
Charleville see Rathluirc
Charlotte Town see Gouyave
Chayek see Chaek
Chechenia div. see Chechnya
Chefoo see Yantai
Chekiang see Zhejiang
Chengchow see Zhengzhou
Chengtu see Chengdu
Chernobyl see Chornobyl'
Chicacole see Srikakulam
Chihli, Gulf of g. see Bo Hai
Chonggye see Qonggyai
Christianshåb see Qasigiannguit
Christmas Island i. see Kiritimati
Chudskoye Ozero l. see Peipus, Lake
Chungking see Chongqing
Churubay Nura see Abay
Cill Airne see Killarney
Cill Chainnigh see Kilkenny
Cill Mhantáin see Wicklow
Cluain Meala see Clonmel
Cocanada see Kākināda
Colair L. l. see Kolleru L.
Cologne see Köln
Coney I. i. see Serangoon, P.
Coondapoor see Kundāpura
Copenhagen see København
Coracesium see Alanya
Corcaigh see Cork
Cordova see Córdoba
Corfu i. see Kerkyra
Corn Is i. see Maíz, Is del
Correntina r. see Éguas
Corsica i. see Corse
Cort Adelaer, Kap hd see Kangeq
Crete i. see Kriti
Crete div. see Kriti
Crimea pen. see Krym'
Cristalino r. see Mariembero
Cumberland, Cape c. see Nahoï, Cap
Cuzco see Cusco
Cyclades is see Kyklades
Dabba see Daocheng
Dagxoi see Yidun
Dairen see Dalian
Dalmatia reg. see Dalmacija
Damascus see Dimashq
Damietta see Dumyât
Dammam see Ad Dammām
Damqoq Kanbab r. see Maquan
Dangla mt. ra. see Tanggula Shan
Dannebrogsø i. see Qillak
Dantu see Zhenjiang
Danube r. see Donau
Danube r. see Dunav
Danube r. see Dunaj
Dardanelles str. see Çanakkale Boğazı
Dardo see Kangding
Dashkesan see Daşkäsän
Daulatabad see Malāyer
Dawei see Tavoy
Dawukou see Shizuishan
Deh Barez see Rudan
Deir-ez-Zor see Dayr az Zawr
Den Haag see 's-Gravenhage
Derry see Londonderry
Dhahran see Az̧ Z̧ahrān
Dilizhan see Dilijan
Disappointment Is is see Désappointement, Îles de
Disko i. see Qeqertarsuatsiaq
Disko Bugt b. see Qeqertarsuup Tunua
Divichi see Däväci
Dizak see Dāvar Panāh
Dnieper r. see Dnyapro
Dnieper r. see Dnepr
Dnieper r. see Dnipro
Dniester r. see Dnister
Dodecanese is see Dodekanisos
Doha see Ad Dawḩah
Dohad see Dāhod
Dolonnur see Duolon
Domel I. i. see Letsok-aw Kyun
Dorbiljin see Emin
Dorbod Qi see Siziwang Qi
Droichead Átha see Drogheda
Dubai see Dubayy
Duke of Gloucester Is is see Duc de Gloucester, Îles
Dundas see Uummannaq
Dún Dealgan see Dundalk
Dún Garbhán see Dungarvan
Dunkirk see Dunkerque
Dura Europos see Qal'at as Sālihīyah
Durlas see Thurles
Duzdab see Zāhedān
Dzhalalabad see Cäilabad
Dzhalal-Abad see Jalal-Abad
Dzhul'fa see Culfa
Dzungarian Basin basin see Junggar Pendi
East Cape c. see Dezhneva, Mys
Eastern Group is see Lau Group
East Retford see Retford
East Siberian Sea sea see Vostochno-Sibirskoye More
Echmiadzin see Ejmiadzin
Edwardesabad see Banmi
Eilat see Elat
Eilean Barraigh i. see Barra
Eilean Leodhais i. see Lewis
Eksere see Gündoğmuş
El Iskandarîya see Alexandria
El Khartum see Khartoum
El Qâhira see Cairo
El Suweis see Suez
El Uqşur see Luxor
Elvanlı see Tömük
Engaños, R. de los r. see Yari
Eochaill see Youghal
Epirus div. see Ipeiros
Erevan see Yerevan
Ergun r. see Argun'
Erronan i. see Futuna
Euboea i. see Evvoia
Eynihal see Kale
Færingehavn see Kangerluarsoruseq
Falcon i. see Fonuafo'ou
Famagusta see Ammochostos
Farrukhabad see Fatehgarh
Farvel, Kap c. see Uummannarsuaq
Fener Burun c. see Karataş Burun
Fergana Range mt. ra. see Fergana Too Tizmegi
Fez see Fès
Finisterre, Cape c. see Fisterra, Cabo
Firuzabad see Räsk
Fiskenæsset see Qeqertarsuatsiaat
Florence see Firenze
Foochow see Fuzhou
Formosa see Taiwan
Føroyar is see Faeroes
Fort-Chimo see Kuujjuaq
Fort Hertz see Putao
Fort Sandeman see Zhob
Franz Josef Land is see Zemlya Frantsa-Iosifa
Frederikshåb see Paamiut
Frunze see Bishkek
Fujairah see Al Fujayrah
Fukien see Fujian
Fuxian see Wafangdian
Gaillimh see Galway
Galilee, Sea of l. see Tiberias, L.
Gand see Gent
Gandzha see Gäncä
Ganges r. see Ganga
Gaoxiong see Kao-hsiung
Gargunsa see Gar
Gartar see Qianning
Gartok see Garyarsa
Gascuña, Golfo de g. see Gascogne, Golfe de
Geneva see Genève
Geneva, Lake l. see Léman, Lac
Genoa see Genova
Gey see Nikshahr
Ghent see Gent
Gılındire see Aydıncık
Godthåb see Nuuk
Godwin-Austen, Mt mt. see K2
Gogra r. see Ghaghara
Gomel' see Homyel'
Gonabad see Jüymand
Goradiz see Horadiz
Gor'kiy see Nizhniy Novgorod
Graham Bell I. i. see Greem Bell,O.
Grande Comore i. see Njazidja
Grodno see Hrodna
Guanghua see Laohekou
Guanyinqiao see Chuosijia
Gulja see Yining
Güma see Pishan
Gurdzhaani see Gurjaani
Gyaisi see Jiulong
Gyandzha see Gäncä
Gyangtse see Gyangzê
Hague, The see 's-Gravenhage
Haifa see Ḥefa
Hainan Strait see Qiongzhou Haixia
Hakha see Haka
Hangchow see Hangzhou
Hanjiang see Yangzhou
Hanoi see Ha Nôi
Hardy, Mt mt. see Rangipoua
Havana see Habana
Heihe see Aihui
Hengnan see Hengyang
Herlen Gol r. see Kerulen
Hermon, Mt mt. see Shaykh, Jabal esh
High Atlas mt. ra. see Haut Atlas
Hingol r. see Girdar Dhor
Hobot Xar Qi see Xianghuang Qi
Hodeida see Al Hudaydah
Hofuf see Al Hufuf
Hokang see Hegang
Holsteinsborg see Sisimiut
Homs see Ḥimş
Horn, C. c. see Hornos, Cabo de
Hpa-an see Pa-an
Huang Hai sea see Yellow Sea
Huhehot see Hohhot
Huiyang see Huizhou
Hulun see Hailar
Hupeh div. see Hubei
Hwlffordd see Haverfordwest
Ibiza i. see Eivissa
Ibiza see Eivissa
Iguaçu Falls rapids see Iguazú, Cataratas del
Il'ichevsk see Şärur
imeni 26 Bakinskikh Komissarov see Bakı Komissarı, 26
Imishli see İmişli
Indur see Nizamabad
Inguri r. see Enguri
Inis see Ennis
Inis Córthaidh see Enniscorthy
Inland Sea see Seto-naikai
Inner Mongolian Aut. Region div. see Nei Monggol Zizhiqu
Ionian Islands div. see Ionioi Nisoi
Iraklion see Irakleio
Iranshahr see Fahraj
Isfahan see Eşfahan
Isfandaqeh see Gāv Koshī
Ismailly see İsmayıllı
Issyk-Kul', Ozero salt l. see Ysyk-Köl
Istria pen. see Istra
Ithaca see Ithaki
Iwo Jima i. see Iō-Jima
Jacobshavn see Ilulissat
Jaffa see Tel Aviv-Yafo
Jagok Tso salt l. see Urru Co
Japan Alps Nat. Park see Chibu-Sangaku Nat. Park
Java i. see Jawa
Javaés r. see Formoso
Jedda see Jiddah
Jethro see Maghā'ir Shu'ayb
Jiaji see Qionghai
Jiayi see Chia-i
Jilong see Chi-lung
Jing see Jinghe
Jogjakarta see Yogyakarta
Kaba see Habahe
Kadzhi-Say see Kajy-Say
Kahnu see Kahnūj
Kailas mt. see Kangrinboqê Feng
Kailas Range mt. ra. see Gangdisê Shan
Kakhi see Qax
Kalaallit Nunaat terr. see Greenland
Kalāt see Kabūd Gonbad
Kalgan see Zhangjiakou
Kalinino see Tashir
Kâmpóng Saôm see Sihanoukville
Kampuchea country see Cambodia
Kang-ma see Kangmar
Kanniya Kumari c. see Comorin, Cape
Kannur see Cannanore
Kansu div. see Gansu
Kara Deniz sea see Black Sea
Karaklis see Vanadzor
Kara Sea sea see Karskoye More
Karaxahar r. see Kaidu
Karghalik see Yecheng
Karl-Marx-Stadt see Chemnitz
Karpaty mt. ra. see Carpathian Mts
Kashgar see Kashi
Kashmir terr. see Jammu and Kashmir
Kaspiyskoye More sea see Caspian Sea
Kazakh see Qazax
Kazi Magomed see Qazımämmäd
Kéamu i. see Anatom
Keferdiz see Sakçagöze
Keriya see Yutian
Kerulen r. see Herlen
Khabis see Shahdāb
Khachmas see Xaçmaz
Khankendi see Xankändi
Khan Tengri mt. see Hantengri Feng
Kharari see Abu Road
Khar'kov see Kharkiv
Khudat see Xudat
Kiangsu see Jiangsu
Kiev see Kyyiv
Kilyazi see Gilazi
King I. i. see Kadan Kyun
Kingisseppa see Kuressaare
Kirgizskiy Khrebet mt. ra. see Kirghiz Range
Kirobasi see Mağara
Kirovabad see Gäncä
Kirovakan see Vanadzor
Kishinev see Chişinău
Kisseraing I. i. see Kanmaw Kyun
Kistna r. see Krishna
Koartac see Quaqtaq
Kochi see Cochin
Koktokay see Fuyun
Kolab r. see Sābari
Kola Peninsula pen. see Kol'skiy Poluostrov
Kollam see Quilon
Korat see Nakhon Ratchasima
Kozhikode see Calicut
Krivoy Rog see Kryvyy Rih
Krungkao see Ayutthaya
Krung Thep see Bangkok
Kuba see Quba
Kumayri see Gyumri
Künes see Xinyuan
Kura r. see Kür
Kuril Is is see Kuril'skiye Ostrova
Kurinskaya Kosa pen. see Kür Dili
Kurskiy Zaliv lag. see Courland Lagoon
Kusary see Qusar
Kut-al-Imara see Al Kūt
Kuujjuarapik see Poste-de-la-Baleine
Kuwaé i. see Tongoa
Kuwait see Al Kuwayt
Kuybyshev see Samara
Kvareli see Qvareli
Kwangsi div. see Guangxi
Kwangtung div. see Guangdong
Kweichow see Guizhou
Kweiyang see Guiyang
Kyurdamir see Kürdämir
Ladoga, Lake l. see Ladozhskoye Ozero
Lanchow see Lanzhou
Langmusi see Dagcanglhamo
Languiaru r. see Iquê
Laowohi see Khardung La
Laptev Sea sea see Laptevykh, More
Laranda see Karaman
Latakia see Al Lādhiqīyah
Leghorn see Livorno
Leizhou see Haikang
Leninakan see Gyumri
Leningrad see Sankt-Peterburg
Lesbos i. see Lesvos
Lesser Caucasus mt. ra. see Malyy Kavkaz
Lianzhou see Hepu
Lima Is is see Wanshan Qundao
Limassol see Lemesos
Lindisfarne i. see Holy Island
Lisbon see Lisboa
Loch Garman see Wexford
Lohil r. see Zavü Qu
Lower California pen. see Baja California
Loyalty Is is see Loyauté, Îs
Loyang see Luoyang
Luar I. i. see Horsburgh I.
Lucerne see Luzern
Lüda see Dalian
Luik see Liège
Luimneach see Limerick
Lyallpur see Faisalabad
Macar see Gebiz
Macintyre r. see Barwon
Mackillop, L. salt flat see Yamma Yamma, L.
Magas see Zābolī
Magway see Magwe
Mahabalipuram see Māmallapuram
Makharadze see Ozurget'i
Makran Coast Range mt. ra. see Talar-i-Band
Mala see Mallow
Malawi, Lake l. see Nyasa, Lake
Malvinas, Islas is see Falkland Islands
Mamisonskiy Pereval pass see Mamisonis Ugheltekhili
Manche, La str. see English Channel
Mangshi see Luxi
Manikgarh see Rajura
Manipur see Imphal
Mar Cantábrico see Biscay, Bay of
Marjan see Wazi Khwa
Marmara, Sea of sea see Marmara Denizi
Marquesas Islands is see Marquises, Îles
Marrakesh see Marrakech
Mashtagi see Maştağa
Masulipatam see Machilipatnam
Matapan, Cape pt see Akra Tainaro
Matturai see Matara
Matun see Khowst
Mawlamyine see Moulmein
Mecca see Makkah
Medina see Al Madīnah
Medu Kongkar see Maizhokunggar
Meilü see Wuchuan
Mei Xian see Meizhou
Mekong r. see Mènam Khong
Mersin see İçel
Merv see Mary
Meshed see Mashhad
Midway see Thamarīt
Milan see Milano
Mindzhivan see Mincivan
Mingechaur see Mingäçevir
Mingechaurskoye Vdkhr. l. see Mingäçevir Su Anbarı
Min-Kush see Ming-Kush
Minya Konka mt. see Gongga Shan
Mobutu, Lake l. see Albert, Lake
Mocha see Al Mukhā
Mogadishu see Muqdisho
Moḩammadābād see Darreh Gaz
Moheli i. see Mwali
Moluccas is see Maluku
Môn i. see Anglesey
Monggolküre see Zhaosu
Monze, C. c. see Mauri, Ras
Mortes r. see Rio Manso
Morvi see Morbi
Mosul see Al Mawşil
Mughalbhin see Jati
Muineachán see Monaghan
Mukden see Shenyang
Mumbai see Bombay
Munich see München
Muscat see Masqaţ
Nada see Dan Xian
Nagorno-Karabakh div. see Qarabağ
Nagornyy Karabakh div. see Qarabağ
Nai-tung see Nêdong
Nakhichevan' see Naxçıvan
Nam Mao r. see Shweli
Nandi see Nadi
Nanking see Nanjing
Naples see Napoli
Narbada r. see Narmada
Nasirabad see Mymensingh
Nasosnyy see Hacı Zeynalabdin
Nasratabad see Zābol
Neftechala see Neftçala
New Siberia Islands is see Novosibirskiye Ostrova
Ngawa see Aba
Niassa, L. l. see Nyasa, Lake
Nicosia see Lefkosia
Nimbhera see Nimbahera
Ningsia div. see Ningxia
Nippon Hai sea see Japan, Sea of
Nîshāpūr see Neyshābūr
Niya see Minfeng
Nonni r. see Nen
Normandes, Îles is see Channel Islands
Northern Sporades is see Voreioi Sporades
Nouveau-Comptoir see Wemindji
Nouvelle Calédonie terr. see New Caledonia
Nowgong see Nagaon
Nyagquka see Yajiang
Nyagrong see Xinlong
Nyenchen Tanglha Range mt. ra. see Nyainqêntanglha Shan
Oder r. see Odra
Odessa see Odesa
Okhotsk, Sea of sea see Okhotskoye More
Oktemberyan see Hoktemberyan
Omba i. see Aoba
Onega, Lake l. see Onezhskoye Ozero
Oporto see Porto
Oranje r. see Orange
Ordu see Yayladaği
Ordzhonikidze see Vladikavkaz
Orontes r. see Asi
Ostend see Oostende
Padua see Padova
Paknampho see Muang Nakhon Sawan
Palakkat see Palghat
Palmyra see Tadmur
Panama City see Panamá
Panjang I. i. see West I.
Panjim see Panaji
Papagaio r. see Sauêruiná
Paphos see Pafos
Pascua, Isla de i. see Easter I.
Pas de Calais str. see Dover, Strait of
Patan see Somnath
Pathein see Bassein
Patteson Pass. chan. see Lolvavana, Pass.
Pechora Sea sea see Pechorskoye More
Peipsi Järve l. see Peipus, Lake
Peking see Beijing
Pelusium, B. of b. see Khalîg el Tîna
Pentecôte, Î. i. see Pentecost I.
Pereval Bedel pass see Bedel Pass
Pereval Torugart pass see Turugart Pass
Persia see Iran
Persian Gulf g. see Gulf, The
Pescadores is see P'eng-hu Lieh-tao
Phnom Penh see Phnum Penh
Pindu Pass pass see Pedo La
Pindus Mountains mt. ra. see Pindos
Pingdong see P'ing-tun
Piraeus see Peiraias
Pishpek see Bishkek
Pomo Tso l. see Puma Yumco
Poona see Pune
Port Arthur see Lüshun
Port Harrison see Inukjuak
Port Klang see Pelabuhan Kelang
Port Láirgé see Waterford
Port-Nouveau-Québec see Kangiqsualujjuaq
Porto Novo see Parangipettai
Port Taufiq see Bûr Taufiq
Prague see Praha
Pripet r. see Prypyats'
Pripet r. see Pryp''yat'
Prome see Pyè
Prøven see Kangersuatsiaq
Przheval'sk see Karakol
Pudai w see Dor
Puduchcheri see Pondicherry
Pushkino see Biläsuvar
Qagchêng see Xiangcheng
Qarkilik see Ruoqiang
Qarqan see Qiemo
Qogir Feng mt. see K2
Qomolangma Feng mt. see Everest, Mt
Qoqek see Tacheng
Queen Maud Land reg. see Dronning Maud Land
Quelpart I. i. see Cheju Do
Quemoy see Chinmen
Quqên see Jinchuan
Qurlurtuuq see Coppermine
Qu Xian see Quzhou
Qyteti Stalin see Kuçovë
Rabkob see Dharmjaygarh
Rahaeng see Tak
Raibu i. see Air
Ramnad see Ramanathapuram
Rampur Boalia see Rajshahi
Rangoon see Yangon
Razdan see Hrazdan
Rebiana Sand Sea desert see Ramlat Rabyānah
Red River r. see Hông, S.
Red Volta r. see Nazinon
Reef Islands is see Rowa
Renland reg. see Tuttut Nunaat
Rhine r. see Rhein
Rhodes i. see Rodos
Rhum i. see Rum
Rīgas Jūras Līcis b. see Riga, Gulf of
Riia Laht g. see Riga, Gulf of
Riyadh see Ar Riyāḑ
Rome see Roma
Rongzhag see Danba
Rosetta see Rashîd
Ross Island i. see Daung Kyun
Roti i. see Rote
Routh Bank sand bank see Seahorse Bank
Rubha Robhanais hd see Butt of Lewis
Rybach'ye see Ysyk-Köl
Saatly see Saatli
Sabzawar see Shindand
Sabzvārān see Jīroft
Saddle I. i. see Mota Lava
Safad see Z̲efat
Sagaredzho see Sagarejo
Saharan Atlas mt. ra. see Atlas Saharien
Sahyadri mt. ra. see Western Ghats
Saigon see Hô Chi Minh
Saīn Qal'eh see Sa'īndezh
St Christopher i. see St Kitts
St Christopher see Fig Tree
St Luke's i. see Zadetkale Kyun
St Matthew's I. i. see Zadetkyi Kyun
St Petersburg see Sankt-Peterburg
St Vincent, Cape c. see São Vicente, Cabo de
Sal'yany see Salyan
Samirum see Yazd-e Khvāst
Sangachaly see Sanqaçal
Santorini i. see Thira
Sardinia i. see Sardegna
Sar Eskandar see Āzarān
Sarıoğlan see Belören
Sāūjbolāgh see Mahābād
Savanat see Eşţahbānāt
Sawu i. see Savu
Scarpanto i. see Karpathos
Scheldt r. see Schelde
Scoresbysund see Ittoqqortoormiit
Seleucia see Silifke
Seleucia Pieria see Samandağı
Sellore I. i. see Saganthit Kyun
Seoul see Sŏul
Serbia div. see Srbija
Sevan, Ozero l. see Sevana Lich
Seven Pagodas see Māmallapuram
Seville see Sevilla
Seyhan see Adana
Shāhpūr see Salmās
Shahrezā see Qomishēh
Shakhagach see Şahağac
Shakhbuz see Şahbuz
Shamkhor see Şämkir
Shangxian see Shangzhou
Shantung div. see Shandong
Shan Xian see Sanmenxia
Sharjah see Ash Shāriqah
Sharur see Şärur
Sheikh Othman see Ash Shaykh 'Uthman
Sheki see Şäki
Shemakha see Şamaxı
Shensi div. see Shaanxi
Shiliu see Changjiang
Shiquanhe see Ali
Shohi Pass pass see Tal Pass
Shuicheng see Liupanshui
Shusha see Şuşa
Sian see Xi'an
Siazan' see Siyäzän
Sicily i. see Sicilia
Side see Selimiye
Sidon see Saïda
Silistat see Bozkır
Simbirsk see Ul'yanovsk
Simbor i. see Pānikoita
Sinai, Mount mt. see Katherîna,G.
Sind see Thul
Singora see Songkhla
Sinkiang Uighur Aut. Region div. see Xinjiang Uygur Zizhiqu
Sinneh see Sanandaj
Sirjan see Sa'īdābād
Sirte see Surt
Sirte, Gulf of g. see Khalīj Surt
Sis see Kozan
Sligeach see Sligo
Society Islands is see Société, Archipel de la
Socotra i. see Suquţrā
Sofia see Sofiya
Soochow see Suzhou
South Cape c. see Ka Lae
Stalingrad see Volgograd
Stampalia i. see Astypalaia
Stepanakert see Xankändi
Sui Xian see Suizhou
Sukhumi see Sokhumi
Sukkertoppen see Maniitsoq
Sulaymaniyah see As Sulaymānīyah
Sullivan I. i. see Lanbi Kyun
Sultanabad see Arāk
Sumatra i. see Sumatera
Sumgait see Sumqayıt
Sungari r. see Songhua
Sungqu see Songpan
Su Xian see Suzhou
Sverdlovsk see Yekaterinburg
Syracuse see Siracusa
Syrian Desert desert see Bādiyat ash Shām
Szechwan div. see Sichuan
Taganrogskiy Zaliv g. see Taganrog, Gulf of
Tagus r. see Tejo
Taibei see T'ai-pei
Taiwan Haixia str. see Taiwan Strait
Taizhong see T'ai-chung
Taklimakan Desert desert see Taklimakan Shamo
Talas Range mt. ra. see Talas Ala-Too
Taldysu see Taldy-Suu
Talyshskiye Gory mts see Talıs Dağları
Tangdan see Dongchuan
Tangier see Tanger
Tanintharyi see Tenasserim
Tanjore see Thanjavur
Taranaki, Mt vol see Egmont, Mt
Tarim Basin basin see Tarim Pendi
Tashi Chho see Thimphu
Tāshqurghān see Kholm
Tauriuiná r. see Verde
Tauz see Tovuz
Tavoy I. i. see Mali Kyun
Teheran see Tehrān
Tehri see Tikamgarh
Terter r. see Tärtär
Tetuán see Tétouan
Tha Hin see Lop Buri
Thalassery see Tellicherry
Thanlwin r. see Salween
Thiruvananthapuram see Trivandrum
Thrissur see Trichur
Thule see Qaanaaq
Tian Shan mt. ra. see Tien Shan
Tiber r. see Tevere
Tiberias see Teverya
Tibet Aut. Region see Xizang Zizhiqu
Tibet, Plateau of plat. see Xizang Gaoyuan
Tientsin see Tianjin
Tiflis see T'bilisi
Tirana see Tiranë
Tkibuli see Tqibuli
Tkvarcheli see Tqvarch'eli
Tokkuztara see Gongliu
Toksu see Xinhe
Toling see Zanda
Tomur Feng mt. see Pobedy, Pik
Tongshan see Xuzhou
Trá Lí see Tralee
Trá Mhór see Tramore
Transylvanian Alps mts see Carpaţii Meridionali
Trefaldwyn see Montgomery
Tripoli see Ţarābulus
Truk is see Chuuk
Tsinan see Jinan
Tsinghai div. see Qinghai
Tsingtao see Qingdao
Tsiteli Tskaro see Dedoplis Tsqaro
Tsitsihar see Qiqihar
Tskhaltubo see Tsqaltubo
Tsona see Cona
Tsushima-kaikyō str. see Korea Strait
Tulach Mhór see Tullamore
Tunxi see Huangshan
Tupai i. see Motu Iti
Turfan see Turpan
Turin see Torino
Tuva div. see Tyva
Tuz, L. salt l. see Tuz Gölü
Tyre see Soûr
Tyuratam see Leninsk
Udzhary see Ucar
Uibhist a' Deas i. see South Uist
Uibhist a' Tuath i. see North Uist
Ulan Bator see Ulaanbaatar
Ulanhad see Chifeng
Ulanhot see Horqin Youyi Qianqi
Uluru h. see Ayers Rock
Ulvéah i. see Lopévi
Upper Chindwin see Mawlaik
Uqturpan see Wushi
Uracas i. see Farallon de Pajaros
Ural Mountains mt. ra. see Ural'skiy Khrebet
Urmia see Orūmīyeh
Urmia, L. salt l. see Daryācheh-ye Orūmīyeh
Uruk see Erech
Urumchi see Ürümqi
Ussuri r. see Wusuli
Ustinov see Izhevsk
Utu see Miao'ergou
Van, L. salt l. see Van Gölü
Vartashen see Oğuz
Vasht see Khāsh
Vaté i. see Éfaté
Venice see Venezia
Vesuvius vol see Vesuvio
Victoria, Mt mt. see Tomanivi
Vienna see Wien
Vientiane see Viangchan
Vistula r. see Wisła
Vizagapatam see Vishakhapatnam
Volcano Bay b. see Uchiura-wan
Volcano Is. is see Kazan-rettō
Volta Blanche w see Nakambé
Volta Rouge r. see Nazinon
Voroshilovgrad see Luhans'k
Wakeham see Kangiqsujuaq
Wang Mai Khon see Sawankhalok
Warsaw see Warszawa
Western Dvina r. see Zapadnaya Dvina
White Sea g. see Beloye More
White Volta w see Nakambé
Wrangel I. i. see Vrangelya, O.
Wrecsam see Wrexham
Wujin see Changzhou
Wuxing see Huzhou
Xangdoring see Xungba
Xianguan see Dali
Xiangyang see Xiangfan
Xiaoshi see Benxi
Xinzhu see Hsin-chu
Xulun Hobot Qagan Qi see Zhengxiangbai Qi
Xulun Hoh Qi see Zhenglan Qi
Yacha see Baisha
Yangtse, Mouth of the river mouth see Changjiang Kou
Yangtze r. see Jinsha
Yangtze r. see Chang
Yardymly see Yardımlı
Yarkant see Shache
Yaxian see Sanya
Yekhegnadzor see Yeghegnadzor
Yeotmal see Yavatmāl
Yeo Yeo r. see Bland
Yerushalayim see Jerusalem
Yevlakh see Yevlax
Y-Fenni see Abergavenny
Yin Xian see Ningbo
Yr Wyddfa mt. see Snowdon
Yugo-Osetinskaya Avtonomnaya Oblast' see South Ossetia
Yushuwan see Huaihua
Zainlha see Xiaojin
Zakataly see Zaqatala
Zante i. see Zakynthos
Zestafoni see Zestap'oni
Zhaggo see Luhuo
Zhangde see Anyang
Zhanghua see Chang-hua
Zhi Qu r. see Tongtian
Zhiziluo see Bijiang
Zhuji see Shangqiu
Zogainrawar see Huashixia
Zongga see Gyirong